PROFESSIONAL BOOKS
LAW REFERENCE LIBRARY
VOLUME ONE

LAWYERS' LAW BOOKS

This book is dedicated to
Fleur and Mark

PROFESSIONAL BOOKS
LAW REFERENCE LIBRARY
VOLUME ONE

LAWYERS' LAW BOOKS

A Practical Index to
Legal Literature

by
DONALD RAISTRICK
Chief Librarian, The Lord Chancellor's Department

SECOND EDITION

with a Foreword by
The Rt. Hon. LORD SCARMAN
A Lord of Appeal in Ordinary

PROFESSIONAL BOOKS
1985

First Edition 1977
Second Edition 1985
Published in 1985 by Professional Books Limited,
Milton Trading Estate, Abingdon, Oxon.
Typeset by Oxford Publishing Services, Oxford, and
printed and bound by Billing & Sons Limited, Worcester.

ISBN 0 86205 072 3

All rights reserved. No part of this publication may be reproduced or transmitted in any form or by any means, electronic, mechanical, photocopying, recording or otherwise, or stored in any retrieval system of any nature, without the written permission of the publishers.

© 1985 Professional Books Ltd.

CONTENTS

	PAGE
Foreword	vii
Introduction	ix
Subject Headings and Cross-References	xi
A PRACTICAL INDEX TO LEGAL LITERATURE	1
Regnal Years of English Sovereigns	493
Law Reports: United Kingdom and Ireland	497
Author and Short Title Index	517

FOREWORD

It is a tribute to the value of Mr. Raistrick's compilation that a second edition is now being published. The first edition has proved its worth to libraries, lawyers, scholars and (I suspect) to very many members of the public. The place of law in society is one of the controversial issues of our times. It is not, however, a topic which can be discussed intelligently without some knowledge of the literature of the law.

LAWYERS' LAW BOOK is a work which helps all who are interested while at the same time being an indispensable tool of the lawyer's trade. I have no doubt that it is to be found in every law library. I would hope that it is to be found in barristers' chambers and solicitors' offices. And I think it merits a place in those public libraries which aim to provide a general service.

I particularly commend one feature of the work. It is not confined to the lawyer's traditional "sources" (law reports, collections of statute law and textbooks), but gathers into its index other works having an important bearing either generally or in a specific field upon the law.

I confidently hope that the work will be updated by the publication of further editions as and when required.

Scarman
28th February 1985

INTRODUCTION

This second edition of Lawyers' Law Books (LLB) follows the pattern established seven years ago by the first edition. In addition, however, to the main listings by subject and its companion subject and author indexes, this volume includes an alphabetical list of United Kingdom and Irish Law Reports and a table of regnal years. The list of subjects has been slightly altered. In attempting to achieve a balanced and comprehensive coverage as possible, a few new topics have been added, including China, Cohabitation, Plea Bargaining, Soviet Law and Statutory Sick Pay. Some minor topics, such as Abstract of Title, Bill Posting, Land Compensation and Joint Tenure have been absorbed by broader headings and some almost synonymous headings have been merged; as examples, Business Law has been subsumed under Commercial Law, and Hire Purchase under Consumer Credit.

As before, although primarily a bibliography of UK legal literature, LLB includes references to allied subjects and to related legal systems, whether that relation be a European one through membership of the EEC, or an historical one through the shared common law tradition.

The first part of the book is an index of subject headings, those used in the main subject listings, referring to the page on which that subject commences. Included in this index are cross-references not used. The main part of the work, the bibliographical listing by subject, has been improved in its layout but retains the same basic ingredients as before. Each subject heading is followed, where appropriate, by *"see also"* references to related topics. The entries under the headings are divided into two categories: Encyclopaedias and Periodicals, and Texts. No reference has been made to the *Law Reports, Weekly Law Reports* or *All England Law Reports,* since their reporting covers the whole spectrum of law. Similarly, constant reference to the five main general law periodicals has been avoided. These publications, the *Cambridge Law Journal, Law Quarterly Review, Modern Law Review, New Law Journal* and *Solicitors Journal* are so general in their coverage that they are worth checking for almost any topic. Most texts listed are of recent origin, but older and still useful titles are also included. Many texts will be found under more than one subject heading. With certain jurisdictions I felt that it would be useful to list titles of specific topics under the country as well as under their subject heading, but most usually the entries to be found under particular country headings are limited to the more general topics, such as constitution and legal systems. Some subjects which have an extensive literature, see especially European Community and International Law, have been sub-divided to simplify the search process. Publishers' names as well as dates of publication are now given for each text entry. Following the subject listing is an alphabetical guide to the Law Reports of the UK and Ireland. For the sake of conciseness full bibliographical titles have been avoided, and only the minimum information necessary to identify a particular report has been given. The number of volumes in each series have been noted for non-current reports, and where appropriate for identity, the series or court is shown. The final column indicates the dates covered. The fourth part is a one page table indicating the regnal years of the English monarchs and the final section comprises an Author Index to the texts that are listed under the subject headings. To aid identification, a short title, or some catchword for the title, follows each author's name.

The differences in layout will be immediately apparent to the reader familiar with the first edition. Gone are the reference numbers attached to each subject heading; the references in both subject and author indexes are now to page numbers. The use of subject numbers facilitated immediate compilation of the author and subject indexes, but discouraged the insertion of new topics or deletion of redundant ones. The new layout is therefore more flexible, as well as neater in appearance. This is the first publication that I have submitted almost entirely on computer disk rather than in manuscript form. The flexibility of this method of compilation is an enormous advantage with a publication of this nature, but for the second edition being merely "a scissors and paste job" the whole work has had to be re-assessed, in many areas restructured and thereby, I hope, improved. Of course, I now have the perfect excuse for any errors that may be found — it was the computer's fault.

With this work, more than with any other attributed to me, it is necessary that I record my gratitude for assistance so unstintingly given and so unashamedly taken. Two in particular, without whom this book would still be months away from publication, deserve special mention. Firstly, to my wife Fleurette, who typed all this publication, including the necessary modifications and amendments, I offer my sincere thanks for the many, many hours she has spent at the keyboard. But it is for more than just that long slog that I thank her, because there is also the patience and understanding that Fleur has shown so often in difficult circumstances. This book is dedicated to her and our son Mark. I acknowledge my failings and apologise for the chaos. Secondly, to Stuart Cole, friend and colleague, my deep appreciation for the considerable amount of time spent on my behalf during his evenings and weekends in checking and verifying important and necessary details; so much help, so readily offered. To Mary Cole, Stuart's wife, a big thank you, not only for the assistance that she too gave, but for her understanding over the interruptions to many of their evenings and weekends. I greatly appreciate, also, assistance in filing and sorting from my father Roland Raistrick, and from Esther Braybrook, and to many friends for help and advice. Once again, I am very grateful to Lord Scarman for writing a new Foreword to this edition and for his continued interest. The publishers have had to put up with more than the usual number of problems this time. I am thankful for their patience and for that of Oxford Publishing Services who had to grapple with my disks and manuscript.

Donald Raistrick
February 1985

SUBJECT HEADINGS
AND
CROSS-REFERENCES

SUBJECT HEADINGS AND CROSS-REFERENCE

ABBREVIATIONS 3
see also Dictionaries.
ABORTION 3
see also Criminal Law; Medical Jurisprudence.
ABSTRACT OF TITLE —
see Title.
ACCIDENTS 5
see also Aviation; Employer's Liability; Industrial Injuries; Negligence; Personal Injuries; Road Traffic; Tort; Workmen's Compensation.
ACCOMMODATION AGENCIES—
see Estate Agents.
ACCOUNTS & ACCOUNTING. 5
see also Banks & Banking; Solicitors; Trusts & Trustees.
ACQUISITION OF LAND—
see Compulsory Purchase & Compensation.
ACT OF STATE 6
see also Constitutional Law; International Law.
ACTS OF PARLIAMENT—
see Statutes.
ADMINISTRATION OF ESTATES
see Probate.
ADMINISTRATION OF JUSTICE 7
see also Civil Rights & Liberties; Contempt; Courts; Judicial Review; Prosecution.
ADMINISTRATIVE LAW 7
see also Civil Service; Constitutional Law; Crown; Delegated Legislation; Government; Judicial Review; Legislation; Ombudsman; Parliament; Public Administration; Tribunals & Inquires.
ADMINISTRATIVE TRIBUNALS—
see Tribunal & Inquiries.
ADMIRALTY 10
see also Shipping.
ADOPTION 11
see also Children & Young Persons; Family Law.
ADVERTISING 12
see also Contract; Copyright; Libel & Slander; Press Law; Printers & Publishers; Town & Country Planning; Trade Descriptions.
ADVOCATES & ADVOCACY 13
see also Bar & Barristers; Legal Profession.
AERIAL PIRACY —
see Hijacking.

AFFILIATION —
see Legitimacy & Illegitimacy.
AFFIRMATIONS —
see Oaths & Affirmations.
AFRICA 14
see also Countries by name.
AGENCY 15
see also Commercial Law; Contract; Estate Agents; Partnership; Powers of Attorney.
AGRICULTURE 16
see also Animals.
AIR FORCE 17
see also Court Martial; Military Law.
AIR LAW —
see Aviation.
AIR POLLUTION —
see Pollution.
ALCOHOL/ALCOHOLISM 17
see also Drinking & Driving; Vagrancy.
ALIENS 18
see also Asylum; Extradition; Human Rights; Immigration; International Law; Nationality & Citizenship.
ALIMONY —
see Maintenance.
ALLOTMENTS 19
AMERICA —
see United States of America.
ANAESTHETICS 19
see also Dentists; Doctors; Medical Jurisprudence.
ANATOMY 19
see also Forensic Science.
ANGLING 20
see also Fishing & Fisheries; Game Laws; Waters & Watercourses.
ANIMALS 20
see also Criminal Law; Public Health; Tort; Vivisection.
ANNUITIES 21
see also Insurance.
ANTENATAL INJURIES —
see Prenatal Injuries.
ANTI-TRUST —
see Competition
APPEALS 22
see also Court Martial; Criminal Law; Practice & Procedure; Privy Council.
APPORTIONMENT 23
see also Trusts & Trustees; Wills.
APPROVED SCHOOL 23
see also Borstal; Detention Centres; Prisons; Punishment.
ARBITRATION 24
see also Trade Unions.
ARCHITECTS & SURVEYORS ... 25
see also Building & Engineering Law.

SUBJECT HEADINGS AND CROSS-REFERENCES

ARCTIC & ANTARCTIC............ 26
  see also Sea, Law of.
ARMY.. 26
  see also Court Martial; Military Law.
ARREST... 27
  see also Admiralty; Police.
ART... 27
ARTIFICIAL INSEMINATION 28
  see also Human Transplants.
ASSIGNMENT................................. 28
  see also Landlord & Tenant.
ASSIZES... 29
  see also Crown Court.
ASSOCIATIONS............................. 29
  see also Clubs; Conspiracy;
  Corporations.
ASSUMPSIT —
  see Contract.
ASSURANCE —
  see Insurance.
ASYLUM... 29
ATOMIC ENERGY —
  see Nuclear Energy.
ATTACHMENT OF EARNINGS 30
  see also Debts & Debtors;
  Maintenance
ATTORNEY-GENERAL —
  see Law Officers.
AUCTIONS & AUCTIONEERS 30
  see also Estate Agents; Sale of Goods.
AUSTRALIA..................................... 31
AUTHOR... 33
  see also Copyright; Press Law.
AUTREFOIS —
  see Double Jeopardy.
AVIATION.. 33
  see also Transport.

BACK DUTY.................................... 35
  see also Revenue Law.
BAIL... 35
  see also Admiralty; Remand.
BAILIFFS... 36
  see also Execution; Sheriffs.
BAILMENT....................................... 36
  see also Carriers/Carriage of Goods;
  Contract; Liens; Pawnbrokers; Tort.
BALLOT —
  see Elections.
BANGLADESH............................... 36
BANKRUPTCY............................... 37
  see also Debts & Debtors; Deeds of
  Arrangement; Liquidators;
  Receivers.
BANKS & BANKING.................. 38
  see also Bills of Exchange; Money;
  Negotiable Instruments.

BAR & BARRISTERS................... 40
  see also Advocates & Advocacy; Inns
  of Court; Legal Education; Legal
  Profession; Notaries; Solicitors.
BASTARDY —
  see Legitimacy & Illegitimacy.
BATTERED CHILDREN —
  see Child Abuse.
BATTERED WOMEN —
  see Domestic Violence.
BEGGARS & BEGGING —
  see Vagrancy.
BENEFICES —
  see Ecclesiastical Law.
BETTING & GAMING................ 41
  see also Clubs.
BIBLE... 41
BIBLIOGRAPHIES....................... 42
BIGAMY —
  see Marriage
BILL OF RIGHTS.......................... 45
  see also Civil Rights & Liberties;
  Constitutional Law; Human Rights.
BILL POSTING —
  see Advertising.
BILLS —
  see Parliament.
BILLS OF EXCHANGE................ 46
  see also Banks & Banking; Negotiable
  Instruments.
BILLS OF LADING....................... 47
  see also Carriers/Carriage of Goods;
  Shipping.
BILLS OF SALE.............................. 47
  see also Sale of Goods.
BIOGRAPHIES............................... 47
BIRCHING —
  see Corporal Punishment.
BIRDS —
  see Animals.
BIRTH CONTROL........................ 48
BIRTHS, MARRIAGES &
  DEATHS.. 48
BLACKMAIL................................... 49
  see also Criminal Law.
BLASPHEMY................................... 49
  see also Criminal Law; Ecclesiastical Law.
BLASTING —
  see Mines & Quarries.
BLIND PERSONS......................... 49
BLOCKADE...................................... 50
  see also International Law; Prize Law;
  War.
BLOOD TESTS............................... 50
  see also Drinking & Driving;
  Legitimacy & Illegitimacy.
BOATS.. 51
  see also Shipping.

SUBJECT HEADINGS AND CROSS-REFERENCE

BONA VACANTIA 51
see also Wills.
BOOK-KEEPING —
see Accounts & Accounting.
BOROUGHS —
see Local Government.
BORSTAL... 51
see also Delinquency; Detention Centres; Punishment.
BOTTOMRY 52
see also Shipping; Insurance.
BOUNDARIES —
see International Law.
BOUNDARIES & FENCES 53
see also Animals; Occupiers' Liability; Party Walls; Rights of Way; Trespass.
BREACH OF CONTRACT —
see Contract.
BREACH OF PROMISE —
see Marriage.
BREAKING & ENTERING —
see Criminal Law.
BREATHALYSER —
see Drinking & Driving.
BRIBERY & CORRUPTION 53
see also Agency; Criminal Law; Elections.
BRIDGES —
see Highways & Bridges.
BROADCASTING —
see Radio & Television.
BROKERS —
see Agency; Stock Exchange.
BROTHELS —
see Criminal Law; Prostitution.
BUILDING & ENGINEERING CONTRACTS 54
see also Contract.
BUILDING & ENGINEERING LAW 55
see also Architects & Surveyors.
BUILDING SOCIETIES 56
see also Mortgages.
BURDEN OF PROOF —
see Evidence.
BURGLARY —
see Criminal Law; Theft.
BURIALS & CREMATION 57
see also Ecclesiastical Law; Public Health.
BUSINESS LAW —
see Commercial Law.
BUSINESS NAMES 58
see also Trade Marks.
BUSINESS TENANCIES 58
see also Landlord & Tenant.

BY-LAWS.. 58
see also Delegated Legislation; Local Government.

C.I.F. & F.O.B. CONTRACTS 59
see also Charterparties; Commercial Law; Laytime.
C.M.R. —
see Carriers/Carriage of Goods.
CABINET... 59
see also Constitutional Law; Government; Parliament; Privy Council.
CABS —
see Taxicabs.
CAMBRIDGE UNIVERSITY 60
CANADA 60
see also Commonwealth.
CANALS 62
see also Waters & Watercourses.
CANON LAW —
see Ecclesiastical Law.
CAPITAL GAINS TAX 62
see also Revenue Law.
CAPITAL PUNISHMENT 63
see also Corporal Punishment; Criminal Law; Punishment.
CAPITAL TRANSFER TAX 64
see also Estate Duty; Executors & Administrators; Probate; Revenue Law.
CAPTURE —
see Prize Law; War.
CAR PARKS 65
CARAVANS & CAMP SITES 65
see also Gipsies; Public Health.
CARE & PROTECTION —
see Children & Young Persons.
CARGO —
see Commercial Law; Shipping; Transport.
CARRIERS/CARRIAGE OF GOODS 66
see also Aviation; Commercial Law; Railways; Shipping.
CARTEL —
see Monopolies & Restrictive Trade Practices.
CATERING —
see Inns & Innkeepers
CATTLE —
see Agriculture; Animals.
CAUSATION —
see Tort.
CELTIC LAW —
see Wales.
CEMETERIES —
see Burials & Cremation; Public Health.

SUBJECT HEADINGS AND CROSS-REFERENCES

CENSORSHIP............................... 67
see also 'D' Notice; Films; Obscenity;
Press Law; Theatres.
CERTIORARI............................... 68
see also Habeas Corpus; Mandamus;
Prerogative Orders; Prohibition.
CEYLON —
see Sri Lanka.
CHANCERY PRACTICE.............. 68
see also Equity.
CHANGE OF NAME —
see Names.
CHANNEL ISLANDS.................... 68
see also Isle of Man.
CHARITIES................................... 69
see also Cy-Pres Doctrine; Equity;
Law Officers; Mortmain; Trusts &
Trustees.
CHARTERPARTIES...................... 70
see also C.I.F. & F.O.B. Contracts;
Carriers/Carriage of Goods;
Commercial Law; Laytime;
Shipping.
CHATTELS —
see Personal Property.
CHEQUES —
see Banks & Banking.
CHIEF JUSTICE —
see Judges.
CHILD ABUSE.............................. 71
see also Domestic Violence.
CHILDREN & YOUNG
PERSONS..................................... 72
see also Adoption; Delinquency;
Family Law; Juvenile Courts;
Legitimacy & Illegitimacy.
CHINA... 74
CHIVALRY, COURT OF.............. 74
see also History.
CHRISTIAN NAME —
see Names.
CHURCH —
see Ecclesiastical Law; Parish
Church.
CINEMA —
see Films.
CIRCUMSTANTIAL EVIDENCE —
see Evidence.
CITATIONS —
see Abbreviations.
CITIZENSHIP —
see Nationality & Citizenship.
CIVIL ACTIONS —
see Practice & Procedure.
CIVIL AVIATION —
see Aviation.
CIVIL DISORDER —
see Public Order.

CIVIL EVIDENCE —
see Evidence.
CIVIL LAW.................................... 75
see also Roman Law; Scotland; South
Africa.
CIVIL LIBERTIES —
see Civil Rights & Liberties.
CIVIL PROCEDURE —
see Practice & Procedure.
CIVIL RIGHTS & LIBERTIES..... 75
see also Administration of Justice;
Human Rights.
CIVIL SERVICE............................ 77
see also Administrative Law;
Constitutional Law; Government
Departments.
CIVIL STATISTICS —
see Statistics.
CLERGY —
see Ecclesiastical Law.
CLUBS... 78
see also Associations; Betting &
Gaming; Friendly Societies.
COAL MINES —
see Mines & Quarries.
CODIFICATION OF LAW............ 78
COHABITATION.......................... 79
see also Family Law; Marriage; Social
Security.
COINAGE —
see Money.
COLLIERIES —
see Mines & Quarries.
COLLISIONS AT SEA................... 79
see also Shipping.
COLLISIONS ON LAND —
see Road Traffic.
COLONIAL LAW —
see Commonwealth.
COMMERCIAL CREDITS............ 80
see also Banks & Banking.
COMMERCIAL LAW.................... 80
see also Carriers/Carriage of Goods;
Contract; Export Trade; Sale of
Goods.
COMMITTAL PROCEEDINGS —
see Magistrates.
COMMITTEES —
see Meetings.
COMMON LAW............................ 84
COMMON MARKET —
see European Communities.
COMMONS & INCLOSURES...... 85
see also Footpaths; National Parks;
Rights of Way.
COMMONWEALTH LAW........... 86
see also Constitutional Law.
COMMUNITY LAND................... 87

SUBJECT HEADINGS AND CROSS-REFERENCE

COMMUNITY SERVICE................ 87
COMPANIES 88
see also Commercial Law;
Corporations; Liquidators;
Partnership.
COMPARATIVE LAW 92
see also Conflict of Laws;
International Law.
COMPENSATION —
see Compulsory Purchase &
Compensation; Criminal Injuries;
Restitution.
COMPETITION 94
COMPULSORY PURCHASE &
COMPENSATION 96
see also Community Land; Town &
Country Planning.
COMPUTERS 97
see also Privacy.
CONFESSIONS 99
see also Criminal Law; Evidence.
CONFLICT OF LAWS 99
see also Comparative Law;
International Law; Nationality &
Citizenship.
CONJUGAL RIGHTS —
see Matrimonial Proceedings; Family
Law.
CONSERVATION —
see Environment Law.
CONSIDERATION —
see Contract.
CONSISTORY COURT —
see Ecclesiastical Law.
CONSPIRACY 101
see also Criminal Law; Fraud.
CONSTABLE —
see Police.
CONSTITUTIONAL LAW 102
see also Act of State; Administrative
Law; Bill of Rights; Cabinet; Civil
Rights & Liberties; Civil Service;
Commonwealth; Crown;
Government; Parliament;
Prerogative Orders; Privy Council.
CONSTITUTIONAL RIGHTS —
see Civil Rights & Liberties.
CONSTRUCTION OF DEEDS —
see Deeds.
CONSULAR LAW —
see Diplomatic Law & Practice.
CONSUMER CREDIT 105
see also Banks & Banking.
CONSUMER PROTECTION 107
see also Fair Trading.
CONTEMPT 108
see also Administration of Justice;
Criminal Law; Parliament.

CONTINENTAL SHELF 109
see also International Law; Sea, Law
of; Territorial Waters.
CONTINGENT REMAINDERS —
see Wills.
CONTRACEPTION —
see Birth Control.
CONTRACT 110
see also Advertising; Building &
Engineering Contracts; C.I.F. &
F.O.B. Contracts; Commercial Law;
Consumer Credit; Employment
Law; Mortgages; Specific
Performance.
CONTRIBUTORY NEGLIGENCE
see Negligence.
CONVENTIONS —
see Cabinet; Constitutional Law;
Treaties.
CONVERSION OF GOODS —
see Theft.
CONVEYANCING.......................... 115
see also Contract; Copyhold;
Gazumping; Land; Land Charges;
Land Registration; Mortgages; title;
Torrens Title; Vendor & Purchaser.
CONVICTIONS —
see Criminal Law; Rehabilitation of
Offenders.
CO-OWNERSHIP —
see Housing Associations;
Matrimonial Property.
COPYHOLD.................................... 116
see also Conveyancing; Gavelkind;
Real Property.
COPYRIGHT 117
see also Advertising; Author; Patents;
Press Law; Printers & Publishers;
Trade Marks.
CORONER 119
see also Forensic Science; Treasure
Trove.
CORPORAL PUNISHMENT 120
see also Punishment.
CORPORATION TAX.................... 120
see also Revenue Law.
CORPORATIONS.......................... 121
see also Companies; Local
Government; Public Authorities;
Ultra Vires.
CORRUPTION —
see Bribery & Corruption; Election
Law.
COSTS 122
see also Practice & Procedure.
COUNCIL OF EUROPE................ 123
COUNCILS —
see Local Government.

COUNTY COURT 123
COUNTY PALATINE.................... 124
COURT FORMS —
see Forms & Precedents; Practice & Procedure.
COURT HAND 124
COURT MARTIAL 125
see also Air Force; Army; Military Law; Navy.
COURT OF PROTECTION 125
see also Mental Health.
COURTS 126
see also Individual Courts by Name; Administration of Justice; Appeals; History; Practice & Procedure.
CREDITORS —
see Bankruptcy.
CREMATION —
see Burials & Cremation.
CRIME PREVENTION 127
CRIMINAL APPEALS 127
see also Appeals.
CRIMINAL INJURIES 128
CRIMINAL INVESTIGATION 128
see also Forensic Science; Police.
CRIMINAL JUSTICE.................... 129
see also Administration of Justice.
CRIMINAL LAW 131
see also Animals; Bribery & Corruption; Confessions; Conspiracy; Corporations; Criminology; Evidence; Homicide; Juries; Obscenity; Perjury; Plea Bargaining; Prostitutioin; Rape; Theft; Treason.
CRIMINAL STATISTICS —
see Statistics.
CRIMINOLOGY............................ 136
see also Criminal Law; Punishment.
CROSS EXAMINATION —
see Advocates & Advocacy; Evidence.
CROWN 139
see also Administrative Law; Petition of Right.
CROWN COURT 139
see also Assizes.
CROWN OFFICE 140
CROWN PRIVILEGE —
see Privilege.
CURRENCY —
see Money.
CUSTOM —
see Common Law; International Law.
CUSTOMS & EXCISE 140
see also Civil Service; Inland Revenue; Revenue Law; Value Added Tax.

CY-PRES DOCTRINE................... 141
see also Charities.

'D' NOTICE.................................. 141
see also Censorship.
DAIRIES —
see Food & Drugs; Public Health.
DAMAGES.................................... 141
see also Industrial Injuries; Negligence; Personal Injuries.
DANCING —
see Entertainment; Licencing.
DANGEROUS DRIVING —
see Motor Vehicles; Road Traffic.
DANGEROUS THINGS —
see Negligence; Occupiers' Liability; Tort.
DEATH DUTIES —
see also Estate Duty.
DEATH PENALTY —
see Capital Punishment.
DEATH REGISTRATION —
see Births, Marriages & Deaths.
DEBENTURES —
see Companies; Stock Exchange.
DEBTS & DEBTORS..................... 142
see also Attachment of Earnings; Bankruptcy; Liens; Receivers.
DECLARATIONS —
see Evidence; Pleading.
DECLARATORY JUDGMENT 143
see also Administrative Law; Judicial Review.
DECREES —
see Divorce; Government; Marriage.
DEEDS 143
see also Conveyancing; Mortgages; Real Property; Vendor & Purchaser.
DEEDS OF ARRANGEMENT...... 144
see also Bankruptcy; Receivers.
DEFAMATION —
see Libel & Slander.
DEFINITIONS —
see Dictionaries; Encyclopaedias.
DELEGATED LEGISLATION..... 144
see also Administrative Law; By-Laws; Local Government; Public Authorities.
DELICT 145
see also Tort
DELINQUENCY........................... 145
see also Criminology.
DEMURRAGE 147
see also Shipping.
DENTISTS 147
see also Anaesthetics; Doctors; Medical Jurisprudence; National Health.

SUBJECT HEADINGS AND CROSS-REFERENCE

DESCENT —
see Inheritance.
DESERTION —
see Divorce; Family Law.
DESIGNS —
see Patents.
DETENTION CENTRES 148
see also Borstal; Prisons.
DETINUE —
see Sale of Goods; Tort.
DEVELOPMENT —
see Town & Country Planning.
DEVELOPMENT TAX 148
see also Revenue Law.
DEVOLUTION 149
see also Constitutional Law.
DICTIONARIES 149
see also Encyclopaedias; Legal Maxims.
DIGESTS 152
DILAPIDATIONS 153
see also Ecclesiastical Law; Fixtures; Landlord & Tenant.
DIMINISHED RESPONSIBILITY —
see Criminal Law; Homicide; Insanity.
DIPLOMATIC LAW & PRACTICE 153
DIRECTORIES 154
DIRECTORS — see Companies.
DISCOVERY 154
DISCRIMINATION —
see Equal Opportunities / Equal Pay.
DISEASES —
see Animals; Hospitals; Public Health.
DISTRICT COUNCILS —
see Local Government.
DIVORCE 155
see also Family Law; Marriage; Matrimonial Proceedings.
DOCKS & HARBOURS 157
see also Shipping; Waters & Watercourses.
DOCTORS 157
see also Anaesthetics; Dentists; Hospitals; Medical Jurisprudence; National Health.
DOGS —
see Animals.
DOMESTIC RELATIONS —
see Family Law.
DOMESTIC VIOLENCE 158
see also Child Abuse.
DOMICILE 158
see also Conflict of Laws; Divorce.
DOUBLE JEOPARDY 159
DOUBLE TAXATION 159
see also Revenue Law.

DRAFTING 160
see also Conveyancing; Forms & Precedents; Statutes.
DRAINS & SEWERS 161
see also Local Government; Public Health.
DRAMA —
see Theatres.
DRAMATIC COPYRIGHT —
see Copyright.
DRINKING & DRIVING 161
see also Blood Tests; Road Traffic.
DRUGS 162
see also Food & Drugs.
DRUNKENNESS —
see Alcohol/Alcoholism; Drinking & Driving.
DURESS —
see Contract; Criminal Law.
DUTY —
see Customs & Excise; Revenue Law.

EARLY CLOSING —
see Shops & Offices.
EASEMENTS 163
see also Light & Air; Party Walls; Rights of Way.
ECCLESIASTICAL LAW 163
see also Blasphemy; Burials & Cremation; Dilapidations; Parish Church; Religion.
EDUCATION 165
see also Legal Education.
EIRE —
see Ireland.
ELECTIONS 165
see also Bribery & Corruption; Parliament.
ELECTRICITY 166
see also Gas.
EMBARGO —
see Blockade; International Law.
EMBEZZLEMENT —
see Criminal Law; Theft.
EMPLOYER'S LIABILITY 167
see also Employment Law; Factories; Negligence; Occupational Diseases; Personal Injuries; Shops & Offices; Statutory Sick Pay; Strict Liability; Tort.
EMPLOYMENT LAW 168
see also Children & Young Persons; Contract; Employer's Liability; Factories; Industrial Law; Industrial Relations; Redundancy; Shops & Offices; Statutory Sick Pay; Trade Unions; Workmen's Compensation.

EMPLOYMENT PROTECTION 171
see also Unfair Dismissal.
ENCLOSURES —
see Commons & Inclosures.
ENCYCLOPAEDIAS.................... 172
ENFRANCHISEMENT —
see Copyhold; Elections.
ENGINEERING CONTRACTS —
see Building & Engineering
Contracts.
ENGINEERING LAW —
see Architects & Surveyors; Building
& Engineering Law.
ENGLISH LEGAL SYSTEM......... 172
see also Constitutional Law; Courts;
Jurisprudence & Legal Philosophy.
ENTAIL —
see Real Property.
ENTERTAINMENT....................... 173
see also Theatres.
ENVIRONMENT LAW.................. 174
see also Pollution; Town & Country
Planning.
EQUAL OPPORTUNITIES/PAY 175
EQUITY... 176
see also Chancery Practice; Charities;
Gifts; Injunctions.
ESTATE AGENTS.......................... 177
see also Agency; Auctions &
Auctioneers.
ESTATE DUTY................................ 178
see also Capital Transfer Tax;
Probate; Revenue Law.
ESTOPPEL.. 178
see also Equity; Judgments; Res
Judicata.
EUROPEAN COMMUNITIES..... 179
EUROPEAN FREE TRADE
ASSOCIATION........................... 185
EUTHANASIA................................ 185
see also Homicide.
EVIDENCE....................................... 186
see also Confessions; Criminal Law;
Estoppel; Oaths & Affirmations;
Witnesses.
EXCESS PROFITS —
see Companies.
EXCHANGE CONTROL —
see Banks & Banking.
EXCISE —
see Customs & Excise.
EXCOMMUNICATION —
see Ecclesiastical Law.
EXECUTION................................... 188
see also Sheriffs.
EXECUTORS &
ADMINISTRATORS................. 189
see also Capital Transfer Tax; Estate

Duty; Probate; Succession; Trusts &
Trustees; Wills.
EXEMPTION CLAUSES —
see Contract.
EXPLOSIVES................................... 190
see also Firearms; Mines & Quarries.
EXPORT TRADE............................ 190
see also Commercial Law.
EXPROPRIATION —
see Compulsory Purchase &
Compensation; International Law.
EXTORTION —
see Criminal Law.
EXTRADITION................................ 191
see also Aliens; Asylum; International
Law.
EXTRATERRITORIAL
JURISDICTION —
see International Law.

F.O.B. CONTRACTS —
see C.I.F. & F.O.B. Contracts.
FACTORIES..................................... 191
see also Employer's Liability;
Employment Law; Industrial Law;
Shops & Offices; Trade Unions.
FACTORS —
see Agency; Commercial Law;
Contract; Sale of Goods.
FAIR TRADING.............................. 192
see also Consumer Protection;
Product Liability.
FAIRS —
see Markets & Fairs.
FALSE IMPRISONMENT —
see Habeas Corpus; Tort.
FAMILY ALLOWANCES —
see Social Security.
FAMILY LAW................................. 192
see also Adoption; Children & Young
Persons; Cohabitation; Divorce;
Maintenance; Marriage;
Matrimonial Proceedings.
FAMILY PROVISION..................... 196
see also Inheritance.
FARMS —
see Agriculture.
FATAL ACCIDENTS —
see Damages.
FEES —
see Costs.
FELONY —
see Criminal Law.
FENCES —
see Boundaries & Fences.
FERRIES —
see Shipping.

SUBJECT HEADINGS AND CROSS-REFERENCE

FIDUCIARY RELATIONSHIP —
see Trusts & Trustees.
FILMS 197
see also Censorship; Obscenity.
FINGERPRINTS —
see Criminal Investigation.
FIRE INSURANCE —
see Insurance.
FIRE LAW 198
FIREARMS 198
see also Criminal Law.
FISHING & FISHERIES 199
see also Angling; Sea, Law of; Waters & Watercourses.
FIXTURES 200
see also Dilapidations; Landlord & Tenant; Personal Property.
FLATS 200
see also Landlord & Tenant; Rent.
FOOD & DRUGS 200
see also Drugs; Public Health.
FOOTPATHS 201
see also Commons & Inclosures; Rights of Way.
FORCIBLE ENTRY —
see Criminal Law; Trespass.
FOREIGN JUDGMENTS 201
see also Judgments.
FORENSIC SCIENCE 202
see also Coroner; Criminal Investigation.
FORESHORE —
see Seashore.
FORESTS 203
see also Agriculture.
FORGERY —
see Criminal Law; Fraud.
FORMS & PRECEDENTS 203
see also Drafting; Pleading.
FOSTERING —
see Adoption.
FRANCE 204
see also European Communities.
FRAUD 205
see also Conspiracy; Criminal Law; Mistake.
FREIGHT —
see Carriers/Carriage of Goods; Shipping; Transport.
FRIENDLY SOCIETIES 206
see also Clubs.
FUNERALS —
see Burials & Cremation.
FURNISHED LETTINGS —
see Flats; Landlord & Tenant.
G.A.T.T. —
see General Agreement on Tariffs & Trade.

GAMBLING —
see Betting & Gaming.
GAME LAWS 206
see also Angling; Criminal Law.
GAOLS —
see Prisons.
GAS 206
see also Electricity; Oil; Public Health.
GAVELKIND 207
see also Copyhold.
GAZUMPING 207
GENERAL AGREEMENT ON TARIFFS & TRADE 208
GENOCIDE 208
see also War Crimes.
GENTOO LAW —
see Hindu Law.
GERMANY 209
see also European Communities.
GHANA 210
see also Africa.
GIBRALTAR 210
GIFTS 211
see also Equity; Wills.
GIPSIES 211
see also Caravans & Camp Sites.
GLEBE LANDS —
see Ecclesiastical Law.
GOLD CLAUSE 211
GOODS, SALE OF —
see Sale of Goods.
GOVERNMENT 212
see also Administrative Law; Cabinet; Constitutional Law; Legislation; Parliament; Privy Council; Sovereignty.
GOVERNMENT DEPARTMENTS 213
see also Departments by name; Civil Service.
GOVERNMENT LIABILITY 215
see also Crown.
GRAVES —
see Burials & Cremation; Public Health.
GRAY'S INN —
see Inns of Court.
GUARANTEE INSURANCE —
see Insurance.
GUARANTEES 215
see also Contract; Mortgages.
GUARDIAN & WARD —
see Adoption; Children & Young Persons; Family Law; Mental Health.
GYPSIES —
see Gipsies.

SUBJECT HEADINGS AND CROSS-REFERENCES

HABEAS CORPUS 215
  see also Certiorari; Constitutional
  Law; Prerogative Orders.
HACKNEY CARRIAGES —
  see Taxicabs.
HAGUE RULES —
  see Carriers / Carriage of Goods.
HALL MARKING 216
HANGING —
  see Capital Punishment.
HARBOURS —
  see Docks & Harbours.
HEARSAY EVIDENCE —
  see Evidence.
HEBREW LAW —
  see Jewish Law.
HEIRS —
  see Inheritance; Succession.
HERIOTS —
  see Copyhold.
HIGH SHERIFF —
  see Sheriffs.
HIGHWAYS & BRIDGES 216
HIJACKING 217
  see also Aviation Law; Piracy.
HINDU LAW 218
HIRE PURCHASE —
  see Consumer Credit.
HISTORY 218
  see also Primitive Law.
HOMICIDE 222
  see also Criminal Law.
HOMOSEXUALITY 223
  see also Sexual Offences.
HONG KONG 224
HORSES —
  see Animals.
HOSPITALS 224
  see also Doctors; Medical
  Jurisprudence; National Health;
  National Insurance; Nursing.
HOTELS & CATERING —
  see Inns & Innkeepers.
HOUSE AGENTS —
  see Estate Agents.
HOUSE OF COMMONS —
  see Parliament.
HOUSE OF LORDS —
  see Parliament.
HOUSEBREAKING —
  see Criminal Law; Theft.
HOUSING 225
  see also Building & Engineering Law;
  Flats; Landlord & Tenant; Rent;
  Town & Country Planning.
HOUSING ASSOCIATIONS 226
HOVERCRAFT 227
  see also Aviation; Shipping.

HUMAN RIGHTS 227
  see also Bill of Rights; Civil Rights &
  Liberties.
HUMAN TRANSPLANTS 230
  see also Medical Jurisprudence.
HUNTING —
  see Game Law.
HUSBAND & WIFE —
  see Family Law.
HYGIENE —
  see Public Health.

I.M.F. —
  see International Law.
IDENTIFICATION 230
  see also Evidence.
IDIOTS —
  see Mental Health.
ILLEGITIMACY —
  see Legitimacy & Illegitimacy.
IMMIGRATION 231
  see also Race Relations.
IMPEACHMENT 232
  see also Trials.
IMPORT DUTIES —
  see Customs & Excise; Revenue Law.
IMPRISONMENT —
  see Prisons.
INCEST 232
  see also Sexual Offences.
INCHOATE OFFENCES —
  see Conspiracy; Criminal Law.
INCITEMENT —
  see Criminal Law.
INCLOSURES —
  see Common & Inclosures.
INCOME TAX 232
  see also Revenue Law; Tax Havens;
  Tax Planning.
INCORPORATED COMPANIES —
  see Companies.
INDECENCY —
  see Criminal Law; Sexual Offences.
INDECENT ASSAULT —
  see Criminal Law; Sexual Offences.
INDIA 234
INDICTMENTS 235
  see also Magistrates; Prosecutions.
INDUSTRIAL & PROVIDENT
  SOCIETIES 235
  see also Insurance.
INDUSTRIAL ARBITRATION —
  see Arbitration.
INDUSTRIAL DESIGNS —
  see Copyright; Patents.
INDUSTRIAL DISEASES —
  see Industrial Injuries; Occupational
  Diseases.

SUBJECT HEADINGS AND CROSS-REFERENCE

INDUSTRIAL INJURIES 236
 see also Damages; Employer's Liability; National Insurance; Workmen's Compensation.
INDUSTRIAL LAW 237
 see also Employment Law; Factories; Trade Unions.
INDUSTRIAL PROPERTY —
 see Copyright; Patents.
INDUSTRIAL RELATIONS 238
 see also Employment Law; Trade Unions.
INDUSTRIAL TRIBUNALS 239
 see also Tribunals & Inquiries.
INEBRIATES —
 see Alcohol/Alcoholism.
INFANTICIDE —
 see Criminal Law; Homicide.
INFANTS —
 see Children & Young Persons.
INFECTIOUS DISEASES —
 see Animals; Public Health.
INFORMATIONS 240
 see also Indictments;Magistrates; Prosecutions.
INHERITANCE —
 see Family Provision; Probate; Wills.
INJUNCTIONS 240
 see also Equity; Prerogative Orders; Ultra Vires.
INJURIES —
 see Industrial Injuries; Personal Injuries; Prenatal Injuries.
INLAND REVENUE 241
 see also Civil Service; Customs & Excise; Revenue Law.
INLAND TRANSPORT —
 see Transport.
INLAND WATERWAYS —
 see Waters & Watercourses.
INNER TEMPLE —
 see Inns of Court.
INNS & INNKEEPERS 241
 see also Bailment.
INNS OF COURT 242
INQUIRIES —
 see Tribunals & Inquiries.
INSANITY 244
 see also Criminal Law; Mental|Health.
INSOLVENCY —
 see Bankruptcy.
INSTALMENT CREDIT —
 Consumer Credit.
INSURANCE 245
 see also Industrial & Provident Societies; National Insurance.
INTELLECTUAL PROPERTY —
 see Copyright.

INTERNATIONAL ARBITRATION
 see Arbitration; International Law.
INTERNATIONAL LAW 248
 see also Act of State; Comparative Law; Conflict of Laws; Extradition; General Agreement on Tariffs & Trade; Peace; Prize Law; Treaties; United Nations; War.
INTERNATIONAL LAW, PRIVATE —
 see Conflict of Laws.
INTERNATIONAL MONETARY FUND —
 see International Law.
INTERPRETATION 257
 see also Drafting; Legislation; Statutes.
INTESTACY —
 see Executors & Administrators.
INVENTIONS —
 see Patents.
INVESTMENT 258
 see also Banks & Banking.
IRELAND 259
 see also Northern Ireland.
IRON & STEEL 260
 see also European Communities.
ISLAMIC LAW 260
ISLE OF MAN 261
 see also Channel Islands.
ITALY 262
 see also European Communities.

JAILS —
 see Prisons.
JAMAICA 263
JERSEY —
 see Channel Islands.
JEWISH LAW 263
JOINT TENANCY —
 see Landlord & Tenant.
JOINT TORTFEASORS —
 see Tort.
JOURNALISTS & JOURNALISM —
 see Press Law.
JUDGES 264
 see also Administration of Justice; Magistrates.
JUDGMENT SUMMONS —
 see Debts & Debtors.
JUDGMENTS 265
 see also Estoppel; Foreign Judgments.
JUDICIAL DICTIONARIES —
 see Dictionaries.
JUDICIAL PRECEDENT 266
JUDICIAL REVIEW 266
 see also Declaratory Judgment.

JUDICIAL STATISTICS —
see Statistics.
JURIES 267
see also Constitutional Law; Criminal Law.
JURISDICTION —
see Certiorari; Judgments; Locus Standi; Prohibition.
JURISPRUDENCE & LEGAL PHILOSOPHY 268
see also English Legal System.
JUSTICE OF THE PEACE —
see Magistrates.
JUVENILE COURTS 272
see also Children & Young Persons; Magistrates.
JUVENILE DELINQUENCY —
see Delinquency.

KENYA 273
see also Africa
KIDNAPPING —
see Criminal Law; Diplomatic Law & Practice.
KING'S REMEMBRANCER 274

LABORATORIES 274
see also Hospitals.
LABOUR LAW —
see Employment Law.
LABOUR RELATIONS —
see Industrial Relations.
LACHES —
see Equity; Estoppel; Limitation of Actions; Trusts & Trustees.
LADING, BILLS OF —
see Bills of Lading.
LANCASTER —
see County Palatine.
LAND 274
see also Conveyancing; Crown; Drains & Sewers; Real Property.
LAND CHARGES 276
LAND COMPENSATION —
see Compulsory Purchase & Compensation.
LAND REGISTRATION 277
see also Conveyancing; Real Property; Title.
LAND TENURE 278
see also Conveyancing; Copyhold; Landlord & Tenant; Leases; Mortmain; Real Property; Title.
LAND TRANSFER 278
see also Land Registration; Real Property; Stamp Duties.
LAND VALUATION —
see Rating & Valuation.

LAND VALUE TAX —
see Landlord & Tenant.
LANDLORD & TENANT 279
see also Dilapidations; Fixtures; Flats; Housing; Land Tenure; Leases; Light & Air; Party Walls; Real Property; Rent.
LANDS TRIBUNAL 280
LANGUAGE, LEGAL —
see Legal Language.
LARCENY —
see Theft.
LATIN —
see Dictionaries; Legal Maxims.
LAUNDRIES —
see Factories; Public Health.
LAW & ORDER —
see Police; Public Order.
LAW COMMISSION 281
see also Law Reform; Scottish Law Commission.
LAW COURTS —
see Courts.
LAW DICTIONARIES —
see Dictionaries.
LAW EXAMINATIONS —
see Legal Education.
LAW LEXICONS —
see Dictionaries.
LAW LIBRARIES —
see Libraries.
LAW MERCHANT 281
see also Commercial Law.
LAW OF NATIONS —
see International Law.
LAW OF THE SEA —
see Sea, Law of.
LAW OFFICERS 282
LAW REFORM 282
see also Law Commission; Scottish Law Commission.
LAW REPORTERS & REPORTING 283
LAW REVISION —
see Law Reform.
LAW SCHOOLS —
see Legal Education.
LAYTIME 284
see also C.I.F. & F.O.B. Contracts; Carriers/Carriage of Goods; Charterparties; Demurrage; Shipping.
LEAGUE OF NATIONS 284
see also International Law; United Nations.
LEASES 285
see also Conveyancing; Land Tenure; Landlord & Tenant; Real Property; Title.

SUBJECT HEADINGS AND CROSS-REFERENCE

LEGACIES —
see Executors & Administrators; Probate; Succession; Wills.
LEGAL AID & ADVICE 286
see also Solicitors; Welfare Law.
LEGAL BIBLIOGRAPHY —
see Bibliographies.
LEGAL BIOGRAPHY —
see Biographies.
LEGAL COSTS —
see Costs; Legal Aid & Advice.
LEGAL DRESS 287
LEGAL EDUCATION 287
see also Education.
LEGAL ENCYCLOPAEDIAS —
see Encyclopaedias.
LEGAL ESTATE —
see Probate; Real Property.
LEGAL EXECUTIVES 288
see also Legal Profession.
LEGAL HISTORY —
see English Legal System; History.
LEGAL MAXIMS 288
see also Dictionaries.
LEGAL PHILOSOPHY —
see Jurisprudence & Legal Philosophy.
LEGAL PROFESSION 289
see also Advocates & Advocacy; Bar & Barristers; Legal Executives; Notaries; Solicitors.
LEGISLATION 290
see also Administrative Law; Delegated Legislation; Drafting; Government; Interpretation; Parliament; Statutes.
LEGISLATION, DELEGATED —
see Delegated Legislation.
LEGISLATURE —
see Parliament.
LEGITIMACY & ILLEGITIMACY 291
see also Children & Young Persons; Marriage.
LESOTHO 292
see also Africa.
LETTERS OF ADMINISTRATION
see Executors & Administrators; Probate.
LETTERS OF CREDIT 292
see also Banks & Banking; Commercial Credits; Negotiable Instruments.
LEXICONS —
see Dictionaries.
LIABILITY —
see Criminal Law; Government Liability; Partnership; Strict Liability; Tort; Vicarious Liability.

LIABILITY INSURANCE —
see Insurance.
LIBEL & SLANDER 293
see also Criminal Law; Press Law; Printers & Publishers; Tort.
LIBERTY —
see Bill of Rights; Civil Rights & Liberties.
LIBERTY OF THE PRESS —
see Censorship; 'D' Notice; Libel & Slander; Press Law.
LIBRARIES 294
see also Museums.
LICENSING 295
see also Magistrates.
LIENS 296
see also Bailment; Debts & Debtors; Mortgages; Personal Property; Shipping.
LIFE INSURANCE —
see Insurance.
LIGHT & AIR 297
see also Easements; Landlord & Tenant.
LIMITATION OF ACTIONS 297
see also Prescription.
LIMITATIONS —
see Limitation of Actions; Perpetuities; Real Property.
LINCOLN'S INN —
see Inns of Court.
LIQUIDATORS 298
see also Bankruptcy; Companies; Receivers.
LITERARY PROPERTY —
see Copyright.
LITIGANTS IN PERSON 299
LIVERPOOL COURT OF PASSAGE 299
see also Courts; History.
LIVINGS —
see Ecclesiastical Law.
LOCAL GOVERNMENT 300
see also By-Laws; Delegated Legislation; Drains & Sewers; Public Health; Rating & Valuation.
LOCAL TAXATION —
see Rating & Valuation.
LOCKS —
see Waters & Watercourses.
LOCUS STANDI 302
see also Courts; Practice & Procedure.
LODGERS —
see Landlord & Tenant.
LONDON 303
see also Mayor's Court.
LORD CHANCELLOR 304
see also Biographies.

SUBJECT HEADINGS AND CROSS-REFERENCES

LOTTERIES —
see Betting & Gaming.
LUNACY —
see Insanity; Mental Health.

MADNESS —
see Insanity.
MAGISTRATES 304
see also Licensing; Remand.
MAGNA CARTA —
see Bill of Rights; Constitutioinal Law; History.
MAHOMEDAN LAW —
see Islamic Law.
MAIL SERVICE —
see Postal Services.
MAINTENANCE & CHAMPERTY 307
MAINTENANCE OF DEPENDANTS 307
see also Divorce; Family Law; Family Provision.
MALAWI 308
see also Africa.
MALAYA/MALAYSIA 308
MALICIOUS DAMAGE —
see Criminal Law.
MAN, ISLE OF —
see Isle of Man.
MANDAMUS 309
see also Certiorari; Prerogative Orders; Prohibition.
MANDATES —
see International Law.
MANSLAUGHTER —
see Homicide.
MARINE INSURANCE —
see Insurance.
MARITIME COLLISIONS —
see Collisions at Sea.
MARITIME LAW —
see Shipping.
MARKETS & FAIRS 310
MARRIAGE 310
see also Cohabitation; Divorce; Ecclesiastical Law; Family Law; Legitimacy & Illegitimacy; Matrimonial Proceedings; Women.
MARRRIAGE REGISTRATION —
see Births, Deaths & Marriages.
MARTIAL LAW —
see Court Martial; Military Law.
MASTER & SERVANT —
see Employment Law.
MATRIMONIAL CAUSES —
see Divorce; Matrimonial Proceedings.

MATRIMONIAL PROCEEDINGS 312
see also Divorce; Family Law; Marriage.
MATRIMONIAL PROPERTY —
see Family Provision.
MAXIMS —
see Legal Maxims.
MAYOR'S COURT 313
MEASURES —
see Weights & Measures.
MEDIA LAW —
see Press Law; Radio & Television.
MEDICAL EVIDENCE 314
see also Evidence.
MEDICAL JURISPRUDENCE 314
see also Anaesthetics; Dentists; Doctors; Drugs; Forensic Science; Hospitals; Human Transplants; Nursing; Personal Injuries.
MEDICAL NEGLIGENCE 315
see also Negligence; Tort.
MEDIEVAL LAW —
see History.
MEETINGS 316
see also Companies.
MENS REA —
see Criminal Law; Strict Liability.
MENTAL DEFICIENCY —
see Insanity; Mental Health.
MENTAL HEALTH 317
see also Court of Protection; Insanity.
MERCANTILE LAW —
see Commercial Law.
MERCHANDISE MARKS —
see Trade Marks.
MERCHANT SHIPPING —
see Shipping.
MERGERS —
see Take-overs & Mergers.
MIDDLE TEMPLE —
see Inns of Court.
MIDWIVES 318
see also Nursing; Public Health.
MILITARY LAW 318
see also Air Force; Army; Court Martial; Navy; Public Order; War.
MILK —
see Food & Drugs; Public Health.
MINERALS 319
see also Mines & Quarries; Oil.
MINES & QUARRIES 319
see also Explosives; Minerals; Stannaries.
MINORITIES —
see Race Relations; International Law.
MINORS —
see Children & Young Persons.

SUBJECT HEADINGS AND CROSS-REFERENCE

MISPRISION —
see Criminal Law.
MISREPRESENTATION —
see Companies; Fraud; Tort.
MISTAKE 320
see also Fraud.
MOBILE HOMES —
see Caravans & Camp Sites.
MOHAMMEDAN LAW —
see Islamic Law.
MONARCHY —
see Crown.
MONEY 320
see also Banks & Banking; Bills of Exchange; Criminal Law.
MONEY LENDERS 321
see also Pawnbrokers.
MONOPOLIES & RESTRICTIVE TRADE PRACTICES 321
see also Companies; Competition.
MORTGAGES 323
see also Building Societies; Contract; Conveyancing; Deeds; Guarantees; Liens; Title.
MORTMAIN 323
see also Charities; Land Tenure.
MORTUARIES — *see* Burials & Cremation; Hospitals.
MOTOR INSURANCE —
see Insurance.
MOTOR VEHICLES 324
see also Road Traffic.
MUHAMMADAN LAW —
see Islamic Law.
MUNICIPAL CORPORATIONS —
see Local Government.
MUNICIPAL ELECTIONS —
see Election Law.
MURDER —
see Criminal Law; Homicide.
MUSEUMS 325
see also Libraries.
MUSIC —
see Copyright; Entertainment.
MUSLIM LAW —
see Islamic Law.
MUTINY —
see Military Law; Naval Law.

NAMES 325
see also Trade Marks.
NARCOTICS —
see Drugs.
NATIONAL ASSISTANCE —
see Social Security.
NATIONAL HEALTH 326
see also Dentists; Doctors; Hospitals; Nursing; Public Health.

NATIONAL INSURANCE 327
see also Hospitals; Industrial Injuries; Insurance; Pensions; Social Security.
NATIONAL PARKS 328
see also Commons & Inclosures.
NATIONALISED INDUSTRIES —
see Public Authorities.
NATIONALITY & CITIZENSHIP 328
see also Aliens; Conflict of Laws.
NAVY 329
see also Court Martial; Military Law; Prize Law; Shipping; War.
NAVIGATION —
see Aviation; Sea, Law of; Shipping; Waters & Watercourses.
NEGLIGENCE 330
see also Accidents; Damages; Employer's Liability; Medical Negligence; Roman Law; Tort.
NEGOTIABLE INSTRUMENTS ... 330
see also Banks & Banking; Bills of Exchange; Letters of Credit.
NEUTRALITY —
see War.
NEW ZEALAND 331
NEWSPAPERS —
see Press Law.
NIGERIA 332
see also Africa.
NISI PRIUS 334
see also Juries.
NOBILITY —
see Peerage Law.
NOISE 335
see also Nuisance; Public Health.
NOLLE PROSEQUI —
see Criminal Law; Law Officers.
NORTH ATLANTIC TREATY ORGANISATION 336
see also International Law; Treaties.
NORTHERN IRELAND 336
see also Constitutional Law; Ireland.
NOTARIES 337
see also Legal Profession; Solicitors.
NOVATION —
see Contract.
NUCLEAR ENERGY 337
NUCLEAR WARFARE & WEAPONS 339
NUISANCE 339
see also Noise; Public Health; Tort.
NULLITY OF MARRIAGE —
see Marriage.
NURSERIES —
see Children & Young Persons.

SUBJECT HEADINGS AND CROSS-REFERENCES

NURSING 340
  see also Hospitals; Medical Jurisprudence; National Health.

OATHS & AFFIRMATIONS 341
  see also Evidence; Perjury.
OBLIGATION —
  see Contract; Roman Law.
OBSCENITY 341
  see also Censorship; Criminal Law; Films; Press Law; Printers & Publishers; Theatres.
OCCUPATIONAL DISEASES 342
  see also Employer's Liability; Industrial Injuries; Workmen's Compensation.
OCCUPIERS' LIABILITY 343
  see also Tort.
OFFICES —
  see Shops & Offices.
OFFICIAL SECRETS 343
  see also 'D' Notice; Press Law.
OIL 344
  see also Gas; Pollution.
OMBUDSMAN 345
  see also Administrative Law; Parliament.
OPEN SPACES —
  see Commons & Inclosures; National Parks.
ORIGINATING SUMMONS —
  see Practice & Procedure.
OUTER SPACE —
  see Space Law.
OXFORD UNIVERSITY 346

PACKAGING 347
PAINTINGS —
  see Art.
PAKISTAN 347
PALEOGRAPHY —
  see Court Hand.
PAPUA NEW GUINEA 348
PARENT & CHILD —
  see Children & Young Persons.
PARISH CHURCH 348
  see also Ecclesiastical Law.
PARISH COUNCILS 349
  see also Local Government.
PARKING —
  see Car Parks.
PARKS & GARDENS 349
  see also National Parks.
PARLIAMENT 350
  see also Administrative Law; Cabinet; Constitutional Law; Elections; Government; Legislation; Privilege.

PARLIAMENTARY COMMISSIONER FOR ADMINISTRATION —
  see Ombudsman.
PARLIAMENTARY DRAFTING —
  see Drafting.
PARLIAMENTARY ELECTIONS —
  see Elections.
PAROL CONTRACTS —
  see Contract.
PAROL EVIDENCE —
  see Evidence.
PAROLE 352
  see also Probation.
PARTNERSHIP 353
  see also Agency; Companies.
PARTY WALLS 354
  see also Boundaries & Fences; Easements; Landlord & Tenant.
PASSING OFF 355
  see also Copyright; Tort; Trade Marks.
PASSPORTS 355
PATENTS 355
  see also Copyright; Trade Marks.
PAWNBROKERS 358
  see also Bailment; Money Lenders.
PAY/PRICE CONTROL 358
PEACE 359
  see also International Law; War.
PEERAGE LAW 359
  see also Law Officers; Parliament.
PENAL LAW —
  see Criminal Law.
PENAL REFORM —
  see Prisons.
PENOLOGY —
  see Punishment.
PENSIONS 360
  see also Employment Law; National Insurance; Social Security.
PERFORMING RIGHTS —
  see Copyright.
PERJURY 360
  see also Criminal Law; Oaths & Affirmations.
PERPETUITIES 361
  see also Cy-Pres Doctrine; Real Property; Trusts & Trustees.
PERSONAL INJURIES 361
  see also Accidents; Criminal Injuries; Damages; Employer's Liability; Tort; Workmen's Compensation.
PERSONAL PROPERTY 363
  see also Bailment; Fixtures; Liens; Possession; Real Property.
PERSONAL REPRESENTATIVES —
  see Executors & Administrators; Probate.

SUBJECT HEADINGS AND CROSS-REFERENCE

PETITION —
see Bankruptcy; Chancery Practice; Companies.
PETITION OF RIGHT 364
see also Crown.
PETROLEUM —
see Oil.
PEWS —
see Parish Church.
PHARMACY —
see Drugs; Food & Drugs; Medical Jurisprudence.
PICKETING —
see Employment Law; Industrial Law; Industrial Relations; Trade Unions.
PILOTAGE —
see Docks & Harbours; Shipping; Waters & Watercourses.
PIRACY 364
see also Criminal Law; Hijacking; Prize Law; Shipping.
PLANNING —
see Town and Country Planning.
PLEA BARGAINING 364
see also Criminal Law.
PLEADING 365
see also Criminal Law; Forms & Precedents; Practice & Procedure.
PLEBISCITES —
see Elections; International Law.
PLEDGES —
see Bailment; Liens; Mortgages; Pawnbrokers.
POISONING —
see Criminal Law; Homicide.
POISONS —
see Food & Drugs; Forensic Science.
POLICE 365
see also Arrest; Bail; Civil Rights & Liberties; Criminal Investigation; Forensic Science; Public Order.
POLICE COURTS —
see Magistrates.
POLLUTION 368
see also Environment Law; Oil; Public Health; Waters & Watercourses.
POLYGAMY —
see Marriage.
POOR LAW 371
see also Social Security; Welfare Law.
POOR PERSONS 372
see also Legal Aid & Advice.
PORNOGRAPHY —
see Obscenity.
PORTS —
see Docks & Harbours.

POSSESSION 373
see also Bailment; Personal Property; Real Property.
POST MORTEM —
see Coroner; Forensic Science; Medical Jurisprudence.
POSTAL SERVICES 373
see also Telecommunications.
POWERS 374
see also Personal Property; Real Property; Trusts & Trustees; Ultra Vires.
POWERS OF ATTORNEY 374
see also Agency; Solicitors.
PRACTICE & PROCEDURE 375
see also Pleading.
PRECEDENTS —
see Forms & Precedents; Judicial Precedent.
PRENATAL INJURIES 377
PREROGATIVE 377
see also Constitutional Law; Crown.
PREROGATIVE ORDERS 377
see also Certiorari; Habeas Corpus; Mandamus; Prohibition.
PRESCRIPTION 378
see also Limitation of Actions; Title.
PRESS LAW 378
see also Advertising; Censorship; Copyright; 'D' Notice; Libel & Slander; Obscenity; Official Secrets; Printers & Publishers; Privacy.
PRESUMPTION —
see Evidence.
PRESUMPTION OF DEATH —
see Probate.
PREVENTION OF CRIME —
see Crime Prevention.
PREVENTIVE DETENTION —
see Prisons; Remand.
PRICE MAINTENANCE —
see Monopolies & Restrictive Trade Practices.
PRIMITIVE LAW 380
PRINCIPAL & AGENT —
see Agency.
PRINCIPAL & SURETY —
see Commercial Law; Contract; Guarantees; Mortgages.
PRINTERS & PUBLISHERS 380
see also Advertising; Copyright; Libel & Slander; Press Law.
PRISONS 381
see also Detention Centres.
PRIVACY 382
see also Computers; Press Law.
PRIVATE ACTS 384
see also Statutes.

PRIVATE ARRANGEMENT —
see Bankruptcy.
PRIVATE COMPANIES —
see Companies.
PRIVATE INTERNATIONAL LAW
see Conflict of Laws.
PRIVILEGE 384
see also Libel & Slander; Parliament.
PRIVY COUNCIL 384
see also Constitutional Law;
Government.
PRIZE LAW 385
see also International Law; Navy; Sea,
Law of; Shipping; War.
PROBATE 386
see also Capital Transfer Tax; Estate
Duty; Executors & Administrators;
Revenue Law; Succession; Wills.
PROBATION 387
see also Delinquency; Magistrates;
Parole; Rehabilitation of Offenders.
PROCEDURE —
see Practice & Procedure.
PROCESSIONS —
see Meetings; Public Order.
PRODUCT LIABILITY 388
see also Contract; Fair Trading; Sale
of Goods; Tort.
PROFANITY —
see Blasphemy.
PROFITS TAX —
see Revenue Law.
PROHIBITION 389
see also Prerogative Orders.
PROMISSORY NOTES —
see Bills of Exchange.
PROOF —
see Evidence.
PROPERTY —
see Matrimonial Property; Personal
Property; Real Property; Roman
Law.
PROPORTIONAL
REPRESENTATION —
see Elections.
PROSECUTIONS 389
see also Administration of Justice;
Double Jeopardy; Indictments;
Informations; Law Officers; Police.
PROSPECTUSES —
see Companies.
PROSTITUTION 390
see also Criminal Law; Sexual
Offences.
PROTECTION, COURT OF —
see Court of Protection.
PROTECTORATES —
see International Law.

PROVIDENT SOCIETIES —
see Industrial & Provident Societies.
PUBLIC ADMINISTRATION 391
see also Administrative Law; Civil
Service.
PUBLIC ASSISTANCE —
see Social Security.
PUBLIC AUTHORITIES 391
see also By-Laws; Delegated
Legislation.
PUBLIC ENTERTAINMENT —
see Entertainment.
PUBLIC HEALTH 392
see also Burials & Cremation; Drains
& Sewers; Food & Drugs; Gas;
Housing; Local Government;
Midwives; Nuisance; Pollution;
Waters & Watercourses.
PUBLIC HOUSES —
see Inns & Innkeepers; Licensing.
PUBLIC LENDING RIGHT 393
see also Libraries.
PUBLIC LIBRARIES —
see Libraries.
PUBLIC MEETINGS —
see Meetings; Public Order.
PUBLIC ORDER 394
see also Civil Rights & Liberties;
Constitutional Law; Police.
PUBLIC PROSECUTOR —
see also Prosecutions.
PUBLIC RECORDS 395
PUBLIC WORSHIP —
see Ecclesiastical Law.
PUBLISHERS —
see Printers & Publishers.
PUNISHMENT 395
see also Capital Punishment;
Corporal Punishment; Criminal
Law; Parole; Prisons; Probation.
PURCHASE TAX —
see Revenue Law; Value Added Tax.

QUANTUM OF DAMAGES —
see Damages.
QUARRIES —
see Mines & Quarries.
QUASI CONTRACT —
see Contract.
QUAYS —
see Docks & Harbours.
QUEEN'S BENCH 397
see also Courts.
QUEEN'S REGULATIONS —
see Air Force; Army; Navy.

RACE RELATIONS 398
see also Immigration.

SUBJECT HEADINGS AND CROSS-REFERENCE

RADIATION —
  see Nuclear Energy.
RADIO & TELEVISION 399
  see also Telecommunications.
RAILWAYS 400
  see also Carriers/Carriage of Goods; Transport.
RAPE 400
  see also Criminal Law; Sexual Offences.
RATING & VALUATION 401
  see also Local Government.
REAL PROPERTY 402
  see also Conveyancing; Copyhold; Deeds; Land; Land Registration; Land Tenure; Landlord & Tenant; Leases; Mortgages; Personal Property; Possession; Powers; Restrictive Covenants; Succession; Title; Vendor & Purchaser.
REBELLION —
  see Public Order; Revolution.
RECEIVERS 404
  see also Bankruptcy; Banks & Banking; Debts & Debtors; Liquidators.
RECEIVING —
  see Criminal Law; Theft.
RECOGNISANCES —
  see Bail; Magistrates; Remand.
RECOGNITION —
  see International Law.
RECORDS —
  see Public Records
REDUNDANCY 404
  see also Employment Law.
REFUGEES 405
  see also International Law.
REGISTERED CONVEYANCING —
  see Conveyancing; Land Registration.
REGISTRATION OF BIRTHS, MARRIAGES & DEATHS —
  see Births, Marriages & Deaths.
REGISTRATION OF LAND —
  see Land Registration.
REHABILITATION OF OFFENDERS 406
  see also Parole; Probation
RELIGION 407
  see also Ecclesiastical Law; Hindu Law; Islamic Law.
REMAND 407
  see also Magistrates.
REMEDIES 407
  see also Prerogative Orders.
REMINISCENCES 408
RENT 408
  see also Landlord & Tenant.

RENTCHARGES 409
  see also Conveyancing.
REPORT WRITING —
  see Law Reporters & Reporting.
RES JUDICATA 410
  see also Estoppel; Judgments.
RESALE PRICE MAINTENANCE
  see Monopolies & Restrictive Trade Practices.
RESCISSION OF CONTRACTS —
  see Contract.
RESIDENCE —
  see Domicile.
RESTITUTION 410
  see also Criminal Injuries.
RESTRICTIVE COVENANTS 411
  see also Land Charges; Landlord & Tenant; Real Property.
RESTRICTIVE TRADE PRACTICES
  see Monopolies & Restrictive Trade Practices.
REVENUE LAW 411
  see also Back Duty; Capital Gains Tax; Capital Transfer Tax; Corporation Tax; Customs & Excise; Double Taxation; Estate Duty; Income Tax; Inland Revenue; Probate; Stamp Duties; Tax Planning; Value Added Tax.
REVERSIONS 414
  see also Conveyancing.
REVOLUTION 415
  see also Public Order.
RIBBON DEVELOPMENT —
  see Town & Country Planning.
RIGHTS, BILL OF —
  see Bill of Rights.
RIGHTS OF COMMON —
  see Commons & Inclosures.
RIGHTS OF ENTRY —
  see Police; Trespass.
RIGHTS OF WAY 415
  see also Boundaries & Fences; Commons & Inclosures; Footpaths.
RIOT —
  see Criminal Law; Magistrates; Public Order.
RIVERS —
  see Waters & Watercourses.
ROAD ACCIDENTS —
  see Accidents; Road Traffic.
ROAD TRAFFIC 416
  see also Drinking & Driving; Police; Transport.
ROADS —
  see Highways & Bridges.
ROBBERY —
  see Criminal Law; Theft.

ROMAN DUTCH LAW 417
  see also Roman Law.
ROMAN LAW 418
RULE OF LAW —
  see Constitutional Law.
RUSSIAN LAW —
  see Soviet Law.

SALE OF GOODS 419
  see also Auctions & Auctioneers;
  Commercial Law; Consumer Credit;
  Consumer Protection; Product
  Liability; Trade Descriptions.
SALE OF LAND —
  see Conveyancing; Land; Real
  Property.
SALVAGE 420
  see also Collisions at Sea; Shipping.
SANCTIONS —
  see Blockade; International Law.
SANITARY LAW —
  see Public Health.
SAUDI ARABIA 421
SAVINGS BANKS —
  see Banks & Banking.
SCHOOLS —
  see Education.
SCOTLAND 421
  see also Devolution.
SCOTTISH LAW COMMISSION 423
  see also Law Commission; Law Reform.
SEA, LAW OF 423
  see also Fishing & Fisheries;
  International Law; Shipping;
  Territorial Waters.
SEARCHES —
  see Conveyancing; Land
  Registration; Title.
SEASHORE 426
  see also Waters & Watercourses.
SECRETS, OFFICIAL —
  see Official Secrets.
SECRETS, TRADE —
  see Trade Secrets.
SECURITIES —
  see Banks & Banking; Commercial
  Law; Investment; Money Lenders;
  Pawnbrokers; Stock Exchange.
SECURITY OF TENURE —
  see Landlord & Tenant.
SEDITION 426
  see also Criminal Law.
SELECTIVE EMPLOYMENT TAX
  see Revenue Law.
SENTENCING 427
  see also Punishment.
SEPARATION —
  see Divorce; Family Law.

SERVITUDES —
  see Easements; Light & Air; Party
  Walls; Rights of Way.
SETTLED LAND —
  see Conveyancing; Real Property.
SETTLEMENTS —
  see Marriage.
SEWERS —
  see Drains & Sewers.
SEX DISCRIMINATION —
  see Equal Opportunities/Pay.
SEXUAL OFFENCES 429
  see also Homosexuality; Incest;
  Prostitution; Rape.
SHARES —
  see Stock Exchange.
SHERIFFS 429
  see also Execution.
SHIPPING 430
  see also Admiralty; Bottomry;
  Carriers/Carriage of Goods;
  Charterparties; Collisions at Sea;
  Demurrage; Laytime; Prize Law;
  Sea, Law of; Transport.
SHOPS & OFFICES 433
  see also Employer's Liability;
  Employment Law; Factories; Trade
  Unions.
SINGAPORE 434
  see also Malaya/Malaysia.
SHORE —
  see Seashore.
SLANDER —
  see Libel & Slander.
SLUM CLEARANCE —
  see Housing; Town & Country
  Planning.
SMOKE —
  see Nuisance; Pollution.
SOCIAL SECURITY 434
  see also National Insurance;
  Pensions; Poor Law; Welfare Law.
SOCIAL WORKERS 436
SOLICITORS 437
  see also Advocates & Advocacy; Bar &
  Barristers; Legal Aid & Advice;
  Legal Executives; Legal Profession;
  Notaries.
SOUTH AFRICA 439
SOVEREIGNTY 440
  see also Crown; Jurisprudence and
  Legal Theory.
SOVIET LAW 441
SPACE LAW 442
  see also Aviation Law; International
  Law.
SPECIFIC PERFORMANCE 443
  see also Contract; Equity.

SUBJECT HEADINGS AND CROSS-REFERENCE　　　　xxxiii

SPORTING RIGHTS —
　see Game Laws.
SQUATTING 443
　see also Trespass.
SRI LANKA 444
STAMP DUTIES.............................. 444
　see also Revenue Law.
STANDING ORDERS —
　see Parliament.
STANNARIES................................. 445
　see also Mines & Quarries.
STARE DECISIS —
　see Judicial Precedent.
STATELESSNESS —
　see Aliens; International Law;
　Nationality & Citizenship.
STATISTICS 445
STATUTE OF FRAUDS —
　see Frauds.
STATUTE OF LIMITATIONS —
　see Limitation of Actions.
STATUTE OF WESTMINSTER 446
　see also Commonwealth Law;
　Constitutitional Law.
STATUTES 446
　see also Drafting; Interpretation;
　Legislation.
STATUTORY INSTRUMENTS 447
　see also Delegated Legislation.
STATUTORY SICK PAY 447
　see also Employment Law.
STEALING —
　see Criminal Law; Theft.
STOCK EXCHANGE...................... 448
STOCKS & SHARES —
　see Banks & Banking; Investment;
　Stock Exchange.
STOWAGE —
　see Shipping.
STREET TRADING —
　see Markets & Fairs.
STREETS —
　see Highways & Bridges.
STRICT LIABILITY 448
　see also Tort.
STRIKES —
　see Employment Law; Industrial
　Law; Industrial Relations; Trade|Unions.
SUBSIDENCE & SUPPORT —
　see Mines & Quarries; Party Walls.
SUCCESSION.................................. 448
　see also Executors & Administrators;
　Probate; Real Property; Wills.
SUMMARY JUDGMENT —
　see Magistrates.
SUMMONS —
　see Criminal Law; Practice &
　Procedure.

SUPERANNUATION —
　see Pensions.
SUPPLEMENTARY BENEFITS —
　see Social Security.
SUPREME COURT —
　see Practice & Procedure.
SURNAMES —
　see Names.
SURTAX —
　see Income Tax; Revenue Law; Tax
　Planning.
SURVEYORS —
　see Architects & Surveyors.

TAKE-OVERS & MERGERS........ 449
　see also Companies.
TANZANIA....................................... 450
　see also Africa.
TAX LAW —
　see Revenue Law.
TAX HAVENS 450
　see also Income Tax; Revenue Law;
　Tax Planning.
TAX PLANNING............................. 451
　see also Income Tax; Revenue Law;
　Tax Havens.
TAXATION OF COSTS —
　see Costs.
TAXICABS 452
TEACHERS —
　see Education.
TELECOMMUNICATIONS......... 452
　see also Postal Services; Radio &
　Television
TELEVISION —
　see Radio & Television.
TENANCY —
　see Agricultural Holdings; Joint
　Tenancy; Landlord & Tenant.
TENURES —
　see Land Tenure.
TERRITORIAL WATERS 453
　see also Continental Shelf;
　International Law; Sea, Law of.
THEATRES 454
　see also Censorship; Entertainment.
THEFT 454
　see also Criminal Law.
THEORY OF LAW —
　see Jurisprudence & Legal
　Philosophy.
TIME —
　see Limitation of Actions.
TITHES —
　see Ecclesiastical Law.
TITLE.. 455
　see also Conveyancing; Land
　Registration; Land Tenure; Leases;

Mortgages; Prescription; Real
Property; Vendor & Purchaser.
TOLLS —
see Highways & Bridges.
TORRENS TITLE 455
see also Land Registration.
TORT 456
see also Accidents; Delict; Employer's
Liability; Libel & Slander;
Negligence; Nuisance; Occupiers'
Liability; Passing Off; Personal
Injuries; Prenatal Injuries; Strict
Liability; Trespass; Vicarious
Liability.
**TOWN & COUNTRY
PLANNING** 458
see also Environment Law; Housing.
TOXICOLOGY —
see Forensic Science; Medical
Jurisprudence.
TRADE —
see Commercial Law.
TRADE DESCRIPTIONS 460
see also Passing Off; Sale of Goods.
TRADE DISPUTES —
see Industrial Relations; Trade
Unions.
TRADE MARKS 461
see also Business Names; Copyright;
Passing Off; Patents.
TRADE RESTRAINT —
see Monopolies & Restrictive Trade
Practices.
TRADE SECRETS 462
see also Competition; Patents.
TRADE UNIONS 462
see also Arbitration; Employment
Law; Factories; Industrial Law;
Industrial Relations; Shops &
Offices.
TRADING WITH THE ENEMY —
see War & Contract.
TRAFFIC —
see Road Traffic.
TRAFFIC ACCIDENTS —
Accidents; Road Traffic.
TRANSFER OF LAND —
see Conveyancing; Land
Registration.
TRANSPORT 463
see also Aviation; Carriers/Carriage
of Goods; Railways; Shipping.
TREASON 464
see also Criminal Law; Revolution.
TREASURE TROVE 465
see also Coroner.
TREATIES 465
see also International Law.

TRESPASS 466
see also Boundaries & Fences;
Criminal Law; Rights of Way;
Squatting; Tort.
TRIALS 467
see also Court Martial; Impeachment.
TRIBUNALS & INQUIRIES 467
see also Industrial Tribunals.
TRUSTEE SAVINGS BANK —
see Banks & Banking.
TRUSTS & TRUSTEES 468
see also Charities; Executors &
Administrators; Perpetuities;
Powers.
TUG & TOW 470
see also Shipping.

ULSTER —
see Northern Ireland.
ULTRA VIRES 470
see also Companies; Injunctions;
Judicial Review.
UNDUE INFLUENCE —
see Bribery & Corruption; Contract;
Fraud.
UNEMPLOYMENT INSURANCE —
see National Insurance; Redundancy;
Social Security.
UNFAIR DISMISSAL 471
see also Employment Law;
Employment Protection; Industrial
Law; Industrial Relations.
UNITED NATIONS 474
see also International Law; League of
Nations.
UNIVERSITIES —
see Cambridge University;
Education; Oxford University.
USES —
see Charities; Powers; Trusts & Trustees.
USURY —
see Money Lenders.

VAGRANCY 475
see also Poor Law.
VALUATION —
see Rating & Valuation.
VALUE ADDED TAX 475
see also Customs & Excise; Revenue
Law.
VANDALISM —
see Criminal Law; Criminology.
VENDOR & PURCHASER 476
see also Contract; Conveyancing;
Deeds; Real Property; Sale of
Goods; Title.
VETERINARY LAW 477

SUBJECT HEADINGS AND CROSS-REFERENCE

VEXATIOUS ACTION —
see Tort.
VICARIOUS LIABILITY 477
see also Criminal Law; Employment Law; Tort.
VICTIMS OF CRIME —
see Criminal Injuries; Restitution.
VILLAGE HALLS 478
VIOLENCE 478
see also Child Abuse; Criminal Law; Criminology; Domestic Violence.
VIVISECTION 479
VOLUNTARY LIQUIDATION —
see Companies.
VOTERS & VOTING —
see Elections.

WALES 479
see also Devolution.
WALLS —
see Boundaries & Fences.
WAR 480
see also Air Force; Army; International Law; Military Law; Navy; Peace; Prize Law; United Nations.
WAR & CONTRACT 482
WAR COMPENSATION 482
WAR CRIMES 483
WAR PENSIONS —
see Pensions.
WARDS —
see Children & Young Persons.
WATERS & WATERCOURSES 484
see also Angling; Canals; Pollution; Public Health.
WEIGHTS & MEASURES 485
see also Food & Drugs.
WELFARE LAW 485
see also Legal Aid & Advice; Social Security.

WEST AFRICA —
see Africa.
WHALING —
see Fishing & Fisheries.
WILLS 486
see also Executors & Administrators; Perpetuities; Probate; Succession.
WINDING-UP —
see Bankruptcy; Companies; Receivers.
WITNESSES 488
see also Evidence; Perjury.
WOMEN 488
see also Domestic Violence; Equal Opportunities/Pay; Marriage.
WORKMEN'S COMPENSATION 489
see also Accidents; Employer's Liability; Industrial Injuries; Occupational Diseases; Personal Injuries.
WORLD BANK 490
WRECKS —
see Salvage.
WRONGS —
see Tort.

X-RAY 490
see also Medical Jurisprudence.

YACHTS —
see Boats.
YEAR BOOKS 490
see also History.
YORK ANTWERP RULES 491
see also Shipping.
YOUNG PERSONS —
see Children & Young Persons.

ZAMBIA 491
see also Africa.

A PRACTICAL INDEX TO LEGAL LITERATURE

ABBREVIATIONS

See also Dictionaries

Texts

BIEBER, D.M.
Current American legal citations with 2100 examples. Hein, 1983(USA).

BIEBER, D.M.
Dictionary of legal abbreviations used in American law books. Hein, 1979(USA).

BRANCH, A.E. (ed.)
Dictionary of shipping: international trade terms and abbreviations. 2ed. Witherby, 1982.

BROWN, R.H.
Marine reinsurance terms and abbreviations. Witherby, 1981.

BUTTRESS, F.A.
World guide to abbreviations of organisations. 6ed. L.Hill, 1980.

The DIGEST. Butterworths. Vol. 1 and current noter-up.

EUROPEAN COMMUNITIES COUNCIL
Multilingual glossary of abbreviations. E.C., 1983.

INSTITUTE OF ADVANCED LEGAL STUDIES
A manual of legal citations. Pt. 1: British Isles. 1959. Pt. 2: The Commonwealth. I.A.L.S., 1960.

OSBORN, P.G.
Concise law dictionary. 7ed. Sweet & Maxwell, 1983.

PRICE, M.O.
Practical manual of standard legal citations. Oceana, 1958(USA).

RAISTRICK, D.
Index to legal citations and abbreviations. Professional Books, 1981.

SPRUDZ, A.
Benelux abbreviations & symbols: law and related subjects. Oceana, 1971.

SPRUDZ, A.
Foreign law abbreviations: French. Oceana, 1968.

SPRUDZ, A.
Italian abbreviations and symbols: law and related subjects. Oceana, 1969.

SWEET & MAXWELL
Guide to law reports & statutes. 4ed. 1962.

ABORTION

See also Criminal Law; Medical Jurisprudence.

Encyclopaedias and periodicals

Halsbury's Laws of England. 4ed. vols 8, ll.
Halsbury's Statutes of England. 3ed. vols 8, 2l.

Breaking Chains: the Newspaper of the Abortion Law Reform Association. 1977–
British Journal of Criminology. 1960– (as

British Journal of Delinquency. 1950–59).
British Medical Journal. 1857–
Criminal Law Review. 1954–
The Lancet. 1823–
Public Health. 1888–

Texts

ABORTION LAW REFORM ASSOCIATION
The Abortion Act inquiry: summary of conclusions. 1974.

ANDERSON, N.
Issues of life and death. Norfolk P., 1976.

COMMONWEALTH SECRETARIAT
Emerging issues in Commonwealth abortion laws, 1982. 1983.

COOK, R.J. & SENANAYAKE, P.
Human problem of abortion: medical and legal dimensions. International Planned Parenthood Federation, 1979.

FELDMAN, D.M.
Birth control in Jewish law: marital relations, contraception and abortion as set forth in the classic texts of Jewish law. New ed. Greenwood P., 1980.

FROHOCK, F.M.
Abortion: a case study in law and morals. Greenwood P., 1983.

GARDNER, R.F.R.
Abortion: the personal dilemma. Paternoster P., 1972.

GREENWOOD, V. & YOUNG, J.
Abortion in demand. Pluto P., 1976.

HALL, R.E. (ed.)
Abortion in a changing world. Columbia U.P., 1970. 2 vols.

HEALTH AND SOCIAL SECURITY, DEPARTMENT OF
Report of the Committee on the working of the Abortion Act (Lane). HMSO, 1974 (Cmnd. 5579–I; 5579–II).

HINDELL, K. & SIMMS, M.
Abortion law reformed. P.Owen, 1971.

HORDERN, A.
Legal abortion: the English experience. Pergamon, 1971.

KOHL, M.
The morality of killing: sanctity of life, abortion and euthanasia. P.Owen, 1974.

LADER, L.
Abortion. Bobbs-Merrill, 1966(USA).

LADER, L.
Abortion II: making the revolution. Beacon P., 1973(USA).

LITCHFIELD, M. & KENTISH, S.
Babies for burning. Serpentine P., 1974.

MEDICAL PRACTITIONERS SOCIETY & ROYAL COLLEGE OF GENERAL PRACTITIONERS
Abortion Act 1967: proceedings of a symposium. Pitman Medical, 1969.

NOONAN, J.T.
Morality of abortion: legal and historical perspectives. New ed. Harvard U.P., 1973.

O'NEILL, J.
Fetus-in-law. Independent Pub. Co., 1976(New Zealand).

POTTS, M.
A guide to the Abortion Act 1967. Abortion Law Reform Association, 1968.

SARVIS, B. & RODMAN, H.
The abortion controversy. 2ed. Columbia U.P., 1974.

SMITH, D.T. (ed.)
Abortion and the law: essays. Case Western Reserve U.P., 1967(USA).

SOCIETY FOR THE PROTECTION OF UNBORN CHILDREN
Comments on the Lane Committee on the Working of the Abortion Act. 1974.

STIRRAT, G.M.
Legalised abortion: the continuing dilemma. Christian Medical Fellowship, 1979.

TATALOVICH, R. & DAYNES, B.W.
Politics of abortion: study of community conflict in public policymaking. Praeger, 1982.

WALBERT, D.F. & BUTLER, J.D.
Abortion, society and the law. Case Western Reserve U.P., 1973(USA).

WARDLE, L.D. & WOOD, M.A.
Lawyer looks at abortion. Brigham Young U.P.: Eurospan, 1982 (USA).

WILLIAMS, G.
The sanctity of life and the criminal law. Faber, 1958.

WILSON, P.
The sexual dilemma: abortion, homosexuality, prostitution and the criminal threshold. Queensland U.P., 1971(Australia).

WOJCICHOWSKY, S.
Ethical-social-legal annotated bibliography of English language studies on abortion 1967–1972. Toronto Inst. Public Communications, 1973.

WORLD HEALTH ORGANISATION
Abortion laws: a survey of current world legislation. 1971.

WORLD HEALTH ORGANISATION
Abortion laws in Commonwealth countries. 1980.

ACCIDENTS

See also Aviation; Employer's Liability; Industrial Injuries; Negligence; Personal Injuries; Road Traffic; Tort; Workmen's Compensation.

Encyclopaedias and periodicals

Halsbury's Laws of England. 4ed. see index vols.
Halsbury's Statutes of England. 3ed. vol 26. Railway Accidents; vol. 42. Road Traffic.

Texts

ALLEN, D.K., BOURN, C.J. & HOLYOAK, J.H.
Accident compensation after Pearson. Sweet & Maxwell, 1979.

ATIYAH, P.S.
Accidents, compensation and the law. 3ed. Weidenfeld & N., 1980.

CALABRESI, G.
The costs of accidents: a legal and economic analysis. Yale U.P., 1970 (USA).

ELLIOT, D.W. & STREET, H.
Road accidents. Allen Lane, 1968.

INSURANCE INSTITUTE OF LONDON
Advantages and disadvantages of the tort system and alternative methods of accident compensation. Insurance Inst., 1978.

ISON, T.G.
Accident compensation: a commentary on the New Zealand system. Croom Helm, 1980.

JUSTICE
No fault on the roads. Stevens, 1974.

JUSTICE
Trial of motor accident cases. Stevens, 1966.

KEMP, D. & KEMP, M.
Quantum of damages. Sweet & Maxwell, 1975. 2 vols.

OGUS, A.I.
Damages. Butterworths, 1973.

SHAW, L. & SICHEL, H.
Accident proneness research in the occurrence, causation and prevention of road accidents. Pergamon, 1971.

SRIVASTAVA, V.P.
Accidents, compensation, and the law. Eastern Book Co., 1978 (India).

VANDYK, N.D.
Accidents and the law. 2ed. Oyez, 1979 (It's your law series no. 6).

ACCOUNTS AND ACCOUNTING

See also Banks and Banking; Solicitors; Trusts and Trustees.

Encyclopaedias and periodicals

Halsbury's Laws of England. 3 & 4eds. vols. 6, 16, 26, 28.
Halsbury's Statutes of England. 3ed. see under name of appropriate subject or name of body or authority.
Encyclopaedia of Court Forms in Civil Proceedings (Atkin), 2ed. vol. 1, 41; see also index under Account.
Encyclopaedia of Forms and Precedents. 4ed. vols. 1, 5, 6, 16, 22.

Accountancy. 1928–
Accountancy Ireland. 1969–
Accountants Weekly. 1970–
Company Accountant. 1931–
Income Tax Digest & Accountants Review. 1940–
Management Accounting. 1965–
Transactions of Faculty of Actuaries in Scotland. 1901–

Texts

BAILEY, F.
Current practice in company accounts. Haymarket P., 1973.

BAKKER, P.
Inflation and profit control: how to account for inflation in business. Methuen, 1975..

BULL, R.J.
Accounting in business. 4ed. Butterworths, 1980.

CARR, J.G.
Accountancy law and practice manual. Gower P., 1978.

CLIFT, R.C.
Accounting: communication and control. 2ed. Butterworths (Australia), 1982.

COWAN, T.K.
The cost accounting function. Sweet & Maxwell, 1965.

DICKERSON, R.W.V.
Accountants and the law of negligence. Canadian Inst. Chartered Accountants, 1966 (Canada).

HALBERSTADT, R.
Basic bookkeeping for solicitors. 2ed. Sweet & Maxwell, 1982.

HOPKINS, L. and others
Accountancy and the law. 7ed. VNU Business Pubns., 1980.

HUGHES-ONSLOW, H.
Lawyer's manual of book-keeping. 3ed. 1935.

JOHNSTON, T.R. & EDGAR, G.C.
Law and practice of company accounting in New Zealand. 5ed. Butterworths (Australia), 1978.

JOHNSTON, T.R., JAGER, M.O. & TAYLOR, R.B.
Law & practice of company accounting. 5ed. Butterworths (Australia), 1983.

JONES, F.H.
Accounting requirements for companies. 12ed. Barkeley Book Co., 1980.

JONES, F.H.
Guide to company balance sheets, and profit & loss accounts. 8ed. Barkeley Book Co., 1977.

LAWSON, E.
Accountancy for solicitors. Butterworths, 1975.

POCKSON, J.R.H.H.
Accountants' professional negligence: development in legal liability. Macmillan, 1982.

REID, W. & MYDDLETON, D.R.
Meaning of company accounts. 3ed. Gower Pub. Co., 1981.

ROCKLEY, L.E.
Public & local authority accounts. Heinemann, 1975.

SOLOMONS, D.
Studies in cost analysis. 2ed. Sweet & Maxwell, 1968.

SPICER, E.E. & PEGLER, E.C.
Bookkeeping and accounts. 18ed. H.F.L., 1980.

STAMP, E. & MARLEY, C.
Accounting principles and the City code: the case for reform. Butterworths, 1970.

TOUCHE, A.G.
Accounting requirements of the Companies Acts. 2ed. Butterworths, 1979.

VICKERY, B.F.
Law and accounts of executors, administrators and trustees. 20ed. Cassell, 1980.

WILLIAMS, D.B. & STEIN, M.A.
Solicitors introduction to accounts. Sweet & Maxwell, 1975.

WILLOTT, R.
Current accounting law and practice. Quinta Pub., annual.

ACT OF STATE

See also Constitutional Law; International Law.

Encyclopaedias

Halsbury's Laws of England. 4ed. vols. 1, 8.
Halsbury's Statutes of England. 3ed. vol. 12.

Texts

MOORE, W.H.
Acts of State. Murray, 1906.

ADMINISTRATION OF JUSTICE

See also Civil Rights and Liberties; Contempt; Courts; Judicial Review; Prosecutions.

Periodicals

Cambridge Law Journal. 1921–
Civil Justice Quarterly. 1982–
Journal of the Society of Public Teachers of Law. 1934–
Law Quarterly Review. 1885–
Legal Action 1973–
Modern Law Review. 1937–
New Law Journal. 1965–
Public Law. 1956–
Solicitors' Journal, 1857–

Texts

ATKINSON, J.M. & DREW, P.
Order in court: the organisation of verbal interaction in judicial settings. Macmillan, 1979.

DELANEY, V.T.H.
Administration of justice in Ireland. 4ed. Inst. of Public Admin., 1975.

DENNING, A.T. Lord
Freedom under the law. Stevens, 1949.

DENNING, A.T. Lord
Road to justice. Sweet & Maxwell, 1968.

DOWRICK, F.E.
Justice according to the English common lawyers. Butterworths, 1961.

GRILLIOT, H.J.
Introduction to law and the legal system. 2ed. Houghton Mifflin, 1979 (USA).

JACKSON, R.M.
Machinery of justice in England. 7ed. Cambridge U.P., 1977.

JUSTICE
The citizen and the administration: the redress of grievances. Stevens, 1961.

LAW COMMISSION
Criminal law: offences relating to interference with the course of justice. HMSO, 1979 (Law Com. No. 96).

LAW COMMISSION
Offences relating to the administration of justice. 1975 (Working Paper No 62).

LEWIS, D.
Just how just? Secker & Warburg, 1975.

LUCAS, J.R.
On justice. Oxford U.P., 1980.

MARK, R.
Minority verdict. BBC, 1974 (1973 Dimbleby lecture).

MORE, H.W. (ed.)
Principles & procedures in the administration of justice. Wiley, 1975 (USA).

NAUNTON, B.
Tree of law and order. Justice of the Peace, 1970.

RENDEL, M.
The administrative functions of the French Conseil d'Etat. Weidenfeld & N., 1970.

SMITH, T.B.
British justice: the Scottish contribution. Stevens, 1961 (Hamlyn lecture).

STREET, H.
Justice in the welfare state. Stevens, 1975.

VICK, R.W. & SCHOOLBRED, C. F.
Administration of civil justices in England & Wales. Pergamon, 1968.

ADMINISTRATIVE LAW

See also Civil Service; Constitutional Law; Crown; Delegated Legislation; Government; Judicial Review; Legislation; Ombudsman; Parliament; Public Administration; Tribunals and Inquiries.

Encyclopaedias and periodicals

Halsbury's Laws of England. 4ed. vol. 1.

Cambridge Law Journal. 1920–

Common Market Law Review. 1963–
Law Quarterly Reivew. 1885–
Law Reports in the Commonwealth:
Constitutional and Administrative Law.
1985–
Legal Action Group Bulletin. 1973–

Local Government Review. 1971–
Modern Law Review. 1937–
New Law Journal. 1965–
Public Administration. 1923–
Public Law. 1956– (as British Journal of Administrative Law. 1954).

Texts

ADLER, M. & BRADLEY, A.
Justice, discretion and poverty. Professional Books, 1975.

ALLEN, C.K.
Administrative jurisprudence. Stevens, 1956.

ALLEN, C.K.
Aspects of justice. Sweet & Maxwell, 1958.

ALLEN, C.K.
Law and orders: an inquiry into the nature and scope of delegated legislation and executive powers in English law. 3ed. Sweet & Maxwell, 1965.

ALLEN, C.K.
Law in the making. 7ed. Oxford U.P., 1964.

ANDREWS, J.A.
Welsh studies in public law. Univ. of Wales P., 1970.

BAILEY, S.H. and others
Cases and materials in administrative law. Sweet & Maxwell, 1977.

BEATSON, J. & MATTHEWS, M.H.
Administrative law: cases and materials. Oxford U.P., 1983.

BORRIE, G.J.
Public law. 2ed. Sweet & Maxwell, 1970 (Concise college texts).

BOYLE, K., HADDEN, T. & HILLYARD, P.
Law and state: the case of Northern Ireland. Robertson, 1975.

BRETT, P. & HOGG, P.W.
Cases and materials on administrative law. 2ed. Butterworths (Australia), 1972.

BROWN, L.N. & GARNER, J.F.
French administrative law. 3ed. Butterworths, 1983.

BRUNTON, J.D.
Law and the individual. Macmillan, 1979.

CARR, C.T.
Concerning English administrative law. 1941 repr. AMS, 1972.

CARTWRIGHT, T.J.
Royal Commissions & Departmental Committees in Britain. Hodder, 1975.

CLARKE, H.W.
Cases and statutes on constitutional and administrative law. Sweet & Maxwell, 1973 (Concise college texts).

CLARKE, H.W.
Constitutional and administrative law. Sweet & Maxwell, 1971 (Concise college texts).

COMMITTEE ON MINISTER'S POWERS
Report (Donoughmore). HMSO, 1932 (Cmd. 4060).

DAVIS, K.C.
Basic text on administrative law. 3ed. West, 1972 (USA).

DENNING, A.T. Lord
The changing law. Stevens, 1953.

DENNING, A.T. Lord
Freedom under the law. Sweet & Maxwell, 1968 (Hamlyn lectures, no. 1).

DE SMITH, S.A.
Constitutional & administrative law. Penguin, 1981.

DE SMITH, S.A.
Judicial review of administrative action. 4ed. Sweet & Maxwell, 1980.

DREWRY, G.
Law, justice & politics. 2ed. Longman, 1982.

ELCOCK, H.J.
Administrative justice. Longman, 1969.

FOULKES, D.
Introduction to administrative law. 5ed. Butterworths, 1982.

FREEDMAN, J.
Crisis and legitimacy: administrative process and American government. Cambridge U.P., 1979.

ADMINISTRATIVE LAW

FRIEDMANN, W.G.
Transnational law in a changing society: essays in honour of Philip C. Jessup. Columbia U.P., 1972.

GALBRAITH, V.H.
Domesday book: its place in administrative history. Oxford U.P., 1975.

GANZ, G.
Administrative procedures. Sweet & Maxwell, 1974.

GARNER, J.F.
Administrative law. 5ed. Butterworths, 1979.

GRIFFITH, J.A.G.
Central departments and local authorities. Allen & Unwin, 1966.

GRIFFITH, J.A.G.
From policy to administration: essays in honour of William A. Robson. Allen & Unwin, 1976.

GRIFFITH, J.A.G
Local authorities and central control. B.Rose, 1974.

GRIFFITH, J.A.G. & STREET, H.
Casebook of administrative law. Pitman, 1964.

GRIFFITH, J.A.G. & STREET, H.
Principles of administrative law. 5ed. Pitman, 1973.

HARLOW, C. & RAWLINGS, R.
Law and administration. Weidenfeld & Nicholson, 1984.

HAWKE, N.
Introduction to administrative law. E.S.C., 1984.

HAYEK, F.A.
Law, legislation and liberty: a new statement of the liberal principles of justice and political economy. Vol. 1: rules and orders. Routledge, 1973.

HENDERSON, E.G.
Foundations of English administrative law: certiorari and mandamus in the seventeenth century. 1963 repr. Kelley, 1978 (USA).

HIGGINS, A.P.
New province for law and order. Constable, 1922 repr. 1968.

HOLLAND, R.H.C. & SCHWARZENBERGER, G. (eds.)
Law, justice and equity. Pitman, 1967.

JACKSON, P.
Natural justice. 2ed. Sweet & Maxwell, 1979.

JACKSON, R.M.
Machinery of justice in England. 7ed. Cambridge U.P., 1977.

JUSTICE
Administration under law. Stevens, 1961.

JUSTICE
The citizen and the administration. Stevens, 1961.

LAUWAARS, R.H.
Lawfulness and legal force of community decisions. Sijthoff, 1973.

LAW COMMISSION
Administrative law. HMSO, 1969 (Law Com. no. 20, Cmnd. 4059).

LAW COMMISSION
Exploratory working paper on administrative law. 1967 repr. 1977 (Working paper no. 13).

LAW COMMISSION
Remedies in administrative law. 1971 (Working paper no. 40).

LAW COMMISSION
Report on remedies in administrative law. HMSO, 1976 (Law Com. no. 73).

NEDJATI, Z.M. & TRICE, J.E.
English and continental systems of administrative law. North Holland Pub. Co., 1978.

PEARCE, D.C.
The Australian administrative law service. Butterworths (Australia), 1979. Looseleaf.

PHILLIPS, O.H.
Constitutional and administrative law. 6ed. Sweet & Maxwell, 1978.

PHILLIPS, O.H. & JACKSON, P.
Leading cases in constitutional and administrative law. 5ed. Sweet & Maxwell, 1979.

POUND, R.
Justice according to law. 1951 repr. Kennikat, 1973.

ROBSON, W.A.
Justice and administrative law: a study of the British constitution. 3ed. 1951 repr. Greenwood, 1970.

SAMPSON, A.
Changing anatomy of Britain. Hodder & S., 1982.

SAWER, G.
Law in society. Oxford U.P., 1965.

SCHWARTZ, B. & WADE, H.W.R.
Legal control of government: administrative law in Britain and the United States. Oxford U.P., 1972.

SCOTTISH LAW COMMISSION
Remedies in administrative law. 1971 (Memorandum no. 14).

STREET, H.
Freedom, the individual and the law. Penguin, 1972.

SYKES, E.I. & TRACEY, R.R.S.
Cases and materials on administrative law. 4ed. Butterworths (Australia), 1982.

SYKES, E.I., LANHAM, D.J. & TRACEY, R.R.S.
General principles of administrative law. 2ed. Butterworths (Australia), 1983.

TWINING, W. & MIERS, D.
How to do things with rules. 2ed. Weidenfeld & N., 1982.

WADE, E.C.S. & PHILLIPS, G.G.
Constitutional and administrative law. 9ed. Longman, 1977.

WADE, H.W.R.
Administrative law. 5ed. Oxford U.P., 1982.

WHEARE, K.C.
Maladministration and its remedies. Stevens, 1973 (Hamlyn lectures).

WILLIAMS, D.W.
Maladministration: remedies for injustice. A guide to the powers and practice of the British Ombudsmen and similar bodies. Oyez, 1977.

WILSON, G.P.
Cases and materials on constitutional and administrative law. 2ed. Cambridge U.P., 1976.

WRAITH, R.E. & HUTCHESSON, P.G.
Administrative tribunals. Allen & Unwin, 1973.

WYNES, W.A.
Legislative, executive and judicial powers in Australia. 5ed. Sweet & Maxwell (Australia), 1976.

YARDLEY, D.C.M.
Source book of English administrative law. 2ed. Butterworths, 1970.

ZANDER, M.
The lawmaking process. Weidenfeld & N., 1980.

ADMIRALTY

See also Shipping.

Encyclopaedias and periodicals

Halsbury's Laws of England. 4ed. vol. 1.
Halsbury's Statutes of England. 3ed. vols. 1, 41.
The Digest. vol. 1.
Encyclopaedia of Court Forms in Civil Proceedings (Atkin). 2ed. vol. 3.

Encyclopaedia of Forms and Precedents. 4ed. vol. 21.

Lloyd's Law Reports. 1919–
Lloyd's Maritime and Commercial Law Quarterly. 1974–
Lloyd's Maritime Law Newsletter.

Texts

BENEDICT, E. & KNAUTH, A.D.
Law of American admiralty, its jurisdiction and practice. rev. ed. Bender, 1973. 16 vols. looseleaf.

BROWNE, A.
Compendious view of the civil law and the law of admiralty. 2ed. Butterworths, 1802. 2 vols.

BROWNE, R.G.M.
Admiralty procedure against merchant ships and cargoes. Norie & Wilson, 1887.

COKE, E.
The fourth part of the institutes of the laws of England, concerning the jurisdiction of courts. Brooke, 1797.

COLOMBOS, C.J.
International law of the sea. 6ed. Longman, 1967.

CONKLING, A.
Admiralty jurisdiction, law and practice. W.C.Little, 1848 (USA).

COOTE, H.C.
Admiralty practice. 2ed. Butterworths, 1868.

GILMORE, G. & BLACK, C.L.
The law of admiralty. 2ed. Foundation P., 1975 (USA).

McGUFFIE, K.C.
Admiralty practice. 2ed. Sweet & Maxwell, 1981.

McGUFFIE, K.C.
Notes on four Admiralty registry letter books. McGuffie, 1964.

PARSONS, T.
A treatise on maritime law, including the law of shipping...and the law and practice of admiralty. Little, Brown & Co., 1869 (USA). 2 vols.

PRICE, G.
Law of maritime liens. Sweet & Maxwell, 1940.

PRITCHARD, W.T. & HANNEN, J.C.
Digest of law & practice of the Court of Admiralty. 3ed. Benning, 1887. 2 vols.

ROBERTS, D.
A treatise on admiralty and prize. Hurd & Houghton, 1869 (USA).

ROSCOE, E.S.
The High Court of Admiralty: the last phase. Stevens, 1927.

ROSCOE, E.S.
History of the Admiralty Court and Prize Court. 2ed. Stevens, 1932.

ROSCOE, E.S.
Jurisdiction and practice of the Court of Admiralty. 5ed. Stevens, 1931 repr. Professional Books.

SAINTY, J.C. (ed.)
Admiralty officials 1660–1870. Univ. of London Inst. of Hist. Res., 1975.

SENIOR, W.
Doctors' Commons and the old Court of Admiralty. Longmans, Green, 1922.

SMITH, T.E.
Law and practice in admiralty. 4ed. Stevens, 1892.

THOMPSON, G.H.M.
Admiralty Registrars. McGuffie, 1958.

TWISS, T.
Black book of the admiralty. Butterworths, 1871–76. 4 vols.

WILLIAMS, R.G. & BRUCE, G.
Jurisdiction and practice of the English Courts in Admiralty actions and appeals. 3ed. Sweet & Maxwell, 1902.

WISWALL, F.L.
The development of Admiralty jurisdiction and practice since 1800. Cambridge U.P., 1970.

ZOUCHE, R.
The jursidiction of the Admiralty. Tyton & Dring, 1663.

ADOPTION

See also Children and Young Persons; Family Law.

Encyclopaedias and periodicals

Statutes in Force. Group: Family Law.
Halsbury's Laws of England. 4ed. vol. 8 also vol. 1.
Halsbury's Statutes of England. 3ed. vol. 45.
The Digest. vol. 28 (2).
Encyclopaedia of Court Forms in Civil Proceedings (Atkin). 2ed. vol. 21.
Encyclopaedia of Forms and Precedents. 4ed. generally vol. 10.

Adoption & Fostering. 1976–
Family Law. 1971–
Family Law Reports.

Texts

ABRAMSON, H.J.
Issues in adoption in Ireland. Economic & Social Res. Inst., 1984.

BEVAN, H.K.
Law relating to children. 2ed. Butterworths, 1983.

BEVAN, H.K & PARRY, M.L.
The Children Act 1975. Butterworths, 1979.

BOURKE, J.P. & FOGARTY, J.F.
Maintenance, custody and adoption law – Victoria. 3ed. Butterworths (Australia), 1972.

CRETNEY, S.M.
Adoption: the new law and practice.
Butterworths, 1977.

DELUPIS, I.
International adoptions and the conflict of laws. Almqvist, 1976.

FITZGERALD, J.
Building new families: through adoption and fostering. Blackwell, 1982.

FREEMAN, M.D.A.
The Child Care and Foster Children Acts 1980. Sweet & Maxwell, 1980.

FREEMAN, M.D.A.
The Children Act 1975. Sweet & Maxwell, 1976.

GRANT, D.W. & COOK, H.S.
Adoption proceedings in juvenile courts. B.Rose, 1973.

HARRIS, B.
Guide to the new law of family proceedings in magistrates' courts including adoption. B.Rose, 1979.

HEALTH AND SOCIAL SECURITY, DEPARTMENT OF
Mine, yours or ours? Study of step-parent adoption. HMSO, 1983.

HEIM, A.W.
Thicker than water? Adoption: its loyalties, pitfalls and joys. Secker & Warburg, 1983.

HOME OFFICE
Report of the Departmental Committee on the Adoption of Children (Stockdale & Houghton). 1972 (Cmnd. 5107).

JACKA, A.A.
Adoption in brief; research and other literature in the US, Canada and GB 1966–72. NFER Pub. Co., 1973.

JOSLING, J.F.
Adoption of children. 9ed. Oyez, 1981 (Oyez practice notes No 3).

KORNITZER, M.
Adoption. 5ed. Putnam, 1976.

KORNITZER, M.
Adoption and family life. Putnam, 1968.

McNEILL, P.G.B.
Adoption of children in Scotland. Green, 1982.

RAYNOR, L.
Adoption of non-white children: experience of the British adoption policy. Allen & Unwin, 1971.

RUDINGER, A. (ed.)
How to adopt. Consumers' Association, 1973.

SMITH, C.R.
Adoption and fostering. Macmillan, 1984

ADVERTISING

See also Contract; Copyright; Libel & Slander; Press Law; Printers and Publishers; Town and Country Planning; Trade Descriptions.

Encyclopaedias and periodicals

Halsbury's Laws of England. 4ed. index vol. Advertisement.
Halsbury's Statutes of England. 3ed. index vol. Advertisement.
Encyclopaedia of Forms and Precedents. 4ed. vol. 1.

Journal of Planning & Environment Law. 1975– (as Journal of Planning Law. 1948–1974).

Texts

BRAUN, J.
Advertisements in court. Fanning, 1965.

BUREAU EUROPEEN DES UNIONS DE CONSOMMATEURS
A study of advertising in the U.K. and Germany. 1974.

CODE OF ADVERTISING PRACTICE COMMITTEE
British code of advertising practice. 5ed. 1974.

EGAN, B.
Trade descriptions: the new law. LRS Pubns., 1968.

EGAN, B.
Trade descriptions: prosecutions, enforcement and complaints. LRS Pubns., 1970.

EUROPEAN ASSOCIATION OF ADVERTISING AGENCIES
Laws and regulations governing advertising in European countries. 1972.

INDEPENDENT BROADCASTING AUTHORITY
Code of advertising standards and practice. 1972.

INSTITUTE OF PRACTITIONERS IN ADVERTISING
Advertising conditions in France. 1974.

INSTITUTE OF PRACTITIONERS IN ADVERTISING
Advertising conditions in the Netherlands. 1972.

INSTITUTE OF PRACTITIONERS IN ADVERTISING
Advertising conditions in the U.K. 1973.

INSTITUTE OF PRACTITIONERS IN ADVERTISING
Is it legal? a guide to the laws affecting the design and content of food labels and advertisements. 3ed. 1979.

LAWSON, R.G.
Advertising and labelling laws in the Common Market. 3ed. Jordan, 1982. Looseleaf.

LEAPER, W.J.
The law of advertising. 2ed. Butterworths, 1961.

ROSDEN, G. & ROSDEN, P.
Law of advertising. Bender, 1974 (USA). 3 vols.

WOOLLEY, D.
Advertising law handbook. 2ed. Business Books, 1976.

ADVOCATES AND ADVOCACY

See also Bar and Barristers; Legal Profession.

Encyclopaedias

Halsbury's Laws of England. 4ed. vol. 3.
The Digest. vol. 3 and see index vol.

Texts

ATKINSON, J.M. & DREW, P.
Order in court: the organisation of verbal interaction in judicial settings. Macmillan, 1979.

BOULTON, W.W.
Guide to conduct and etiquette at the Bar of England & Wales. 6ed. Butterworths, 1975 supp. 1978.

CLITHEROE, J.
Guide to conducting a criminal defence. Oyez, 1980.

CODDINGTON, F.J.O.
Advice on advocacy in lower courts. Justice of the Peace, 1954.

DONOVAN, J.W.
Tact in court. Sweet & Maxwell, 1956.

DU CANN, R.
The art of the advocate. Penguin, 1964.

EVANS, K.
Advocacy at the bar. Financial Training Pubns, 1983.

FORSYTH, W.
Hortensius: historical essay on the duties of an advocate. Murray, 1879.

HARRIS, R.
Hints on advocacy. Stevens, 1943.

HARRIS, R.
Illustrations in advocacy. Stevens & Haynes, 1915.

HARVEY, C.P.
The advocate's devil. Sweet & Maxwell, 1958.

HILBERY, M.
Duty and art in advocacy. Stevens, 1946.

JUTA, H.
The conduct of trial cases. Juta, 1919 (S.Africa).

MACPHERSON, J. (ed.)
The minutes of the Faculty of Advocates. Vol.1. 1661–1712 (Stair Society No 29). 1976.

MONOPOLIES & MERGERS COMMISSION
Advocates' services: a report on the supply of advocates' services in relation to restriction on advertising. HMSO, 1976 (1975–76 H.C. 560).

MORTON, J.
Defending: the solicitor's practical guide. D.Beattie. 1982.

MUNKMAN, J.H.
The technique of advocacy. Stevens, 1951.

NAPLEY, D.
The technique of persuasion. 3ed. Sweet & Maxwell, 1983.

O'BARR, W.M.
Linguistic evidence: language, power and strategy in the courtroom. Academic Press, 1982.

PAGE, L.
First steps in advocacy. Faber, 1943.

SINGLETON, J.E.
Conduct at the Bar and problems of advocacy. Sweet & Maxwell, 1933.

WROTTESLY, F.T.
Examination of witnesses in court. 3ed. Sweet & Maxwell, 1961.

AFRICA

See also Ghana; Kenya; Nigeria; South Africa; Tanzania; Zambia.

Periodicals

Africa. 1928–
African Law Studies (USA). 1969–
Annual Survey of African Law. 1967–
Annual Survey of Commonwealth Law. 1965–
Commonwealth. 1961– .(Published as United Empire, 1910; Journal of the Royal Commonwealth Society, 1958).

Commonwealth Law Bulletin. 1974–
East African Law Journal. 1965–
East African Law Review. 1968–
Journal of Administration Overseas. 1962– .(As Journal of African Administration, 1949–61)
Journal of African Law. 1957–
Journal of Modern African Studies. 1963–

Texts

AKINTAN, S.A.
Law of international economic institutions in Africa. Sijthoff, 1977 (Netherlands).

ALLOT, A.N.
Essays in African law with special reference to the law of Ghana. 1960 repr. Greenwood P., 1974.

ALLOT, A.N.
Judicial and legal systems in Africa. 2ed. Butterworths, 1970.

ALLOT, A.N.
New essays in African law. Butterworths, 1970.

BAADE, H.W. & EVERETT, R.O.
African law. Oceana, 1963 (USA).

BAINBRIDGE, J.S.
Study and teaching of law in Africa. Rothman, 1972.

BENTSI-ENCHILL, K.
Choice of law in ex-British Africa. Sweet & Maxwell, 1970.

BRETT, E.A.
Colonialism and underdevelopment in East Africa. Heinemann, 1978.

BROWNLIE, I.
African boundaries: a legal and diplomatic encyclopaedia. C.Hurst, 1979.

BYAMUGISHA, J.B.
Insurance law in East Africa. H.Zell, 1977.

COTRAN, E & RUBIN, N.N.
Readings in African law. F.Cass, 1970. 2 vols.

DANIELS, W.C.E.
The common law in West Africa. Butterworths (S.Africa), 1964.

ELIAS, T.O.
Africa and the development of international law. Sijthoff, 1972.

ELIAS, T.O.
The nature of African customary law. Manchester U.P., 1962.

GLUCKMAN, M.
African traditional laws in historical perspective. Oxford U.P., 1975.

GLUCKMAN, M.
Custom and conflict in Africa. Blackwell, 1955.

GLUCKMAN, M.
Ideas and procedures in African customary law. Oxford U.P., 1969.

GOWER, L.C.
Independent Africa: the challenge to the legal profession. Harvard U.P., 1968.

HARVEY, W.B.
Introduction to the legal system in East Africa. H.Zell, 1977.

HIGGINS, R.
United Nations peacekeeping, 1946–1967. 3: Africa. Oxford U.P., 1980.

HODGIN, R.W.
Law of contract in East Africa. H.Zell, 1977.

HOLLEMAN, J.F.
Issues in African law. Moulton, 1974.

JACKSON, T.
Guide to the legal profession in East Africa. Sweet & Maxwell, 1970.

KATENDE, J.W. and others
Law of business organizations in East and Central Africa. H.Zell, 1977.

KIAPI, A.
Civil service laws in East Africa. H.Zell, 1977.

MEEK, C.K.
Colonial law: a bibliography with special reference to native African systems of law and land tenure. repr. Greenwood P., 1979.

MORRIS, H.F. & READ, J.S.
Indirect rule and the search for justice: essays in the East African legal system. Oxford U.P., 1972.

NWABUEZE, B.O.
Constitutionalism in the Emergent States. C.Hurst, 1978.

NWABUEZE, B.O.
Judicialism in Commonwealth Africa. C.Hurst, 1977.

NWABUEZE, B.O.
Presidentialism in Commonwealth Africa. C.Hurst, 1978.

OKOYE, F.C.
International law and the new African states. Sweet & Maxwell, 1972.

OLUYEDE, P.A.
Administraive law in East Africa. H.Zell, 1977.

PHILLIPS, A. & MORRIS, H.F.
Marriage laws in Africa. Oxford U.P., 1971.

SANDERS, A.J.G.M.
International law in African context. Butterworths (S.Africa), 1978.

VANDERLINDEN, J.
Bibliographe de droit Africain. 1947–1966. Haile Sellassie I Univ., 1972.

WRAITH, R.E.
Local administration in West Africa. Allen & Unwin, 1972.

AGENCY

See also Commercial Law; Contract; Estate Agents; Partnership; Powers of Attorney.

Encyclopaedias and periodicals

Statutes in Force. Group: Agency.
Halsbury's Laws of England,. 4ed. vol. l.
The Digest, vol. l.
Encyclopaedia of Court forms in Civil Proceedings (Atkin). 2ed. vol. 4.
Encyclopaedia of Forms and Precedents. 4ed. vol. l.

Journal of Business Law. 1957–
Modern Law Review. 1937–
Law Quarterly Review. 1885–
New Law Journal. 1965–

Texts

BOWSTEAD, W.
Law of agency. l4ed. Sweet & Maxwell, 1976.

CAWTHRA, B.
Restrictive agreements in the EEC: the need to notify. Butterworths, 1972.

CONRICK, V.M. & THOMPSON, D.C.
Sale of real property and law of agency in
New South Wales. 2ed. Butterworths
(Australia), 1973.

FRIDMAN, G.H.L.
Law of agency. 5ed. Butterworths, 1983.

GUYENOT, J.
French agency agreements. Oyez, 1977.

HANBURY, H.G.
Principles of agency. 2ed. Stevens, 1960.

IVAMY, E.R.H.
Casebook on agency. 2ed. Lloyd's, 1980.

JOSKE, P.E.
Commission agency. Butterworths
(Australia), 1974.

KERR, A.J.
Law of agency. Butterworths (S.Africa),
1972.

LA VILLA, G. & CARTELLA, M.
The Italian law of agency and
distributorship agreements. Oyez, 1977.

LAW COMMISSION
Law of contract: report on the proposed
EEC Directive on the law relating to
commercial agents. HMSO, 1977 (Law
Com. no. 84).

MARKESINIS, B.S. & MUNDAY, R.J.C.
Outline of the law of agency. Butterworths,
1979.

MARSHALL, E.A.
Scottish cases on agency. Green, 1980.

POWELL, R.
Law of agency. 2ed. Pitman, 1961.

STAUBACH, F.
The German law of agency and
distributorship agreements. Oyez, 1977.

STOLJAR, S.J.
Law of agency. Sweet & Maxwell, 1961.

AGRICULTURE

See also Animals

Encyclopaedias and periodicals

Statutes in Force. Group: Agriculture.
Halsbury's Laws of England. 4ed. vol. 1.
Halsbury's Statutes of England. 3ed. vol. 1.
The Digest. vol. 2.
Encyclopaedia of Court Forms in Civil
Proceedings (Atkins). 2ed. vol. 4.

Encyclopaedia of Forms and Precedents.
4ed. vol. 1; see also vols. 17. 20.

Farmers Weekly 1934–
Farmland Market. 1974–
Rating & Valuation Reporter. 1961–

Texts

COLLEGE OF LAW
The farmer, the landowner and the law.
1978.

COLLEGE OF LAW
Residential tenancies (including the Rent
(Agriculture) Act 1976 and the Rent Act
1977). 1977.

FORDHAM, C.M.
The valuation of agricultural holdings for
rent, rev. ed. R.I.C.S., 1974.

GILL, R.
Law of agricultural holdings in Scotland.
Green, 1982.

GREGORY, M. & PARRISH, M.
Essential law for landowners and farmers.
Granada, 1980.

HAMILTON, R.N.D.
Compensation for compulsory acquisition
of agricultural land and of rights in and over
land. 3ed. R.I.C.S., 1980.

HEALTH AND SAFETY EXECUTIVE
Guide to agricultural legislation. HMSO,
1979.

JENKINS, P.H.D.
The letting of agricultural holdings by
tender. R.I.C.S., 1974.

MOLLER, N.H.
Manual of farm law. Sweet & Maxwell,
1938.

MUSTOE, N.E.
Agricultural law and tenant right. 4ed.
Estates Gazette, 1950.

POLLARD, R.S.W.
Trees and the law. 2ed. Arboricultural Assn., 1976.

RAY, P.K.
Agricultural insurance. Pergamon, 1967.

ROSSI, H.
Guide to the Rent (Agriculture) Act 1976. Shaw, 1977.

ROYAL INSTITUTION OF CHARTERED SURVEYORS
Agricultural holdings legislation: report. 1978.

SCAMMELL, W.S. & DENSHAM, H.A.C.
Law of agricultural holdings. 6ed. Butterworths, 1978 supp. 1980.

STANLEY, O.
Taxation of farmers and landowners. 2ed. Butterworths, 1984.

STEPHENSON, I.S.
Law relating to agriculture. Gower, 1975.

WALMSLEY, R.C.
Agricultural arbitrations: a handbook of procedure and practice under the Agricultural Arbitration Code in England & Wales. 3ed. Estates Gazette, 1970.

WATT, J.M.
Agricultural holdings. 12ed. Sweet & Maxwell, 1967 supp. 1979.

AIR FORCE

See also Court Martial; Military Law.

Encyclopaedias

Statutes in Force. Group: Armed Forces.
Halsbury's Laws of England. 4ed. vol. 8.
Halsbury's Statutes of England. 3ed. vol. 29.

Texts

AIR FORCE DEPARTMENT
Regulations for civilian industrial employees at Ministry of Defence (Air Force Dept) establishments. 7ed. HMSO, 1965.

MANUAL of Air Force law.
Vol. 1. parts 1-3. 6ed. HMSO, 1983. Looseleaf.
Vol .2. Parts 4-8. 5ed. HMSO, 1971. Looseleaf.
Vol. 3 Civilian. HMSO, 1977. Looseleaf.

QUEEN's regulations for the Royal Air Force 1964. 4ed. HMSO, 1971.
Consolidated ed. incorporating amndts. 1-55; amendts. 56-106. HMSO, 1971-1983.

ALCOHOL/ALCOHOLISM

See also Drinking and Driving; Vagrancy.

Encyclopaedias and periodicals

Statutes in Force. Group:Intoxicating Liquor.

Addictive Behaviours. 1975-
British Journal of Addiction. 1947.
British Journal of Criminology. 1960- (as British journal of delinquency. 1950-1959)
Medicine Science & the Law. 1960-
Medico-Legal Journal. 1901-

Texts

BRITISH MEDICAL ASSOCIATION
Report of a working party on alcohol, drugs & driving. 1974.

CARUANA, S.
Alcohol and alcoholism. B.Edsall, 1979. (Health visitors handbook No.1)

COOK, T.
Vagrant alcoholics. Routledge, 1975.

EDWARDS, G. (ed.)
Alcohol dependence and smoking behaviour. Saxon House, 1976.

FARRIER, D.
Drugs and intoxication. Sweet & Maxwell, 1980.

HOME OFFICE
Report of the Working Party on Habitual Drunken Offenders (Weiler). HMSO, 1971.

INTERNATIONAL COUNCIL ON ALCOHOL & ADDICTION
International symposium on the drunkeness offence. 1968.

MEYER, M.-L.
Counselling families of alcoholics: a guideline for the helping profession. London Council on Alcoholism, 1978.

TUCK, M.
Alcoholism and social policy: are we on the right lines. HMSO, 1981 (Home Office Research Studies, No.65).

TURNER, A.J. & COOPER, M.
Points and excess alcohol provisions of the Transport Act, 1981. B.Rose, 1983.

ALIENS

See also Asylum; Extradition; Human Rights; Immigration; International Law; Nationality and Citizenship

Encyclopaedias and periodicals

Statutes in Force. Groups: Immigration; Nationality.
Halsbury's Laws of England. 4ed. vol. 4
Halsbury's Statutes of England. 3ed. vol. 1
The Digest. vol. 2.

Human Rights Review. 1976–
International & Comparative Law Quarterly. 1952–
Public Law. 1956–

Texts

BOHNING, W.R.
Migration of works in the UK and the European Community. Oxford U.P., 1972.

DAVIES, W.A.
Law relating to aliens. Stevens, 1931.

DAWSON, F.G. & HEAD, I.L.
International law, national tribunals and the rights of aliens. Syracuse, 1971 (USA).

FOIGHEL, I.
Nationalization: study in the protection of alien property in international law. Greenwood, 1982.

FRADER, C.F.
Control of aliens in the British Commonwealth of Nations. 1940.

JOHNSON, K.W. & WILLIAMS, M.W.
Illegal aliens in the western hemisphere. Praeger, 1980.

MACKENZIE, N.A.M.
Legal status of aliens in Pacific countries. Kraus Thomson, 1975 repr. of 1937 ed.

MUTHARIKA, A.P.
The alien under American law: text, materials, cases. Oceana, 1980. Looseleaf.

MUTHARIKA, A.P.
Regulation of statelessness under national and international law: text and documents. Oceana, 1977. 2 vols. looseleaf.

PARRY, C.
British nationality, including citizenship of the United Kingdom and colonies and the status of aliens. Stevens, 1951.

PLENDER, R.
International migration law. Sijthoff, 1972.

ROTH, A.H.
The minimum standard of international law applied to aliens. Sijthoff, 1949.

SAMPAT-MEHTA, R.
International barriers: aliens, immigration and citizenship in Canada. Canada Res. Bureau, 1973.

SUNDBERG-WEITMAN, B.
Discrimination on grounds of nationality. North-Holland Pub. Co., 1977.

VERZUL, J.H.W.
International law in historical perspectives. Vol. 5. Nationality and other matters relating to individuals. Sijthoff, 1972.

ALLOTMENTS

Encyclopaedias

Statutes in Force. Group: Agriculture: Sub-Group 5, 6.
Halsbury's Laws of England. 4ed. vol. 2.
Halsbury's Statutes of England. 3ed. vol. 2.

Encyclopaedia of Court Forms in Civil Proceedings (Atkins). 2ed. vol. 4.
Encyclopaedia of Forms and Precedents. 4ed. vol. 1.

Texts

EVANS, W.
The law for gardens and small estates. David & Charles, 1975.

GARNER, J.F.
Law of allotments. 4ed. Shaw, 1984.

SPENCER, A.J.
The Small Holdings Act. 4ed. Stevens, 1927.

ANAESTHETICS

See also Dentists; Doctors; Medical Jurisprudence.

Encyclopaedias and periodicals

Halsbury's Laws of England. 4ed. see index vol.
Halsbury's Statutes of England. 3ed. see index vol.

Anaesthesia. 1946.
British Journal of Anaesthesia. 1923–
Medicine, Science and the Law. 1960–
Medico-Legal Journal. 1901–

Texts

DORNETTE, W.H.L.(ed.)
Legal aspects of anaesthesia. F.A.Davis, 1970 (USA).

FORBES G. & WATSON A.A.
Legal aspects of dental practice. J.Wright, 1975.

GRAY, T.C. & NUNN, J.F.
General anaesthesia. Butterworths, 1971. 2 vols.

KNIGHT, B.
Legal aspects of medical practice. 2ed. Churchill Livingstone, 1976.

MANNINO, M.J.
Nursing anaesthetist and the law. Grune, 1982.

ANATOMY

See also Forensic Science

Encyclopaedias

Halsbury's Laws of England. 4ed. vol. 10.
Halsbury's Statutes of England. 3ed. vol. 21.

Texts

ARMSTRONG, K.F.
Anatomy and physiology. 9ed. Bailliere, 1979.

FABER
Faber's anatomical atlas for nurses and students. Faber, 1962.

GRAY, H.
Anatomy. 35ed. Longman, 1973.

ANGLING

See also Fishing and Fisheries; Game Laws; Waters and Watercourses.

Encyclopaedias

Halsbury's Laws of England. 4ed. vols. 6, 8
Halsbury's Statutes of England. 3ed. vols. 24, 39
The Digest. vol. 25.

Encyclopaedia of Court Forms in Civil Proceedings (Atkin). 2ed. vols. 9, 17
Encyclopaedia of Forms and Precedents. 4ed. vol. 12.

Texts

COULSON, H.J.W. & FORBES, U.A.
The law of waters, sea, tidal and inland. 6ed. Sweet & Maxwell, 1952.

GREGORY, M.
Angling and the law. 2ed. Charles Knight, 1974.

JAUNCEY, Lord
Fishing in Scotland: law for the angler. 2ed. Green, 1984.

LITTLER, P.
Water rights including fishing rights. 2ed. Oyez, 1981.

OKE, G.C.
Fishery laws. 4ed. Butterworths, 1924.

WISDOM, A.S.
Aspects of water law. B.Rose, 1982.

WISDOM, A.S.
Water rights including fishing rights. Oyez, 1969 (Practice notes no. 61).

WOOLRYCH, H.W.
Law of waters including rights in the sea, rivers, canals etc. 2ed. Butterworths, 1851.

WOOSNAM, C.R.
Letting of fishing rights in England and Wales. R.I.C.S., 1979.

ANIMALS

See also Criminal Law; Public Health;, Tort; Vivisection.

Encyclopaedia and periodicals

Statutes in Force. Group: Animals.
Halsbury's Laws of England. 4ed. vol. 2.
Halsbury's Statutes of England. 3ed. vol. 2. Animals; vol. 43. Breeding of Dogs.
The Digest. vol. 2.
Encyclopaedia of Court Forms in Civil Proceedings (Atkin). 2ed. vol. 4
Encyclopaedia of Forms and Precedents. 4ed. vol. 1.

Stone's Justices' Manual. Annual.

Animals' Defender & Anti-Vivisection News. 1881–
Law Quarterly Review. 1885–
Modern Law Review. 1937–

Texts

AGRICULTURE, FISHERIES & FOOD, MINISTRY OF
Disease of animals. 1951. Handbook of orders in force, 31 Dec 1971. 3ed. HMSO, 1973.

BRITISH VETERINARY ASSOCIATION
The Animal Boarding Establishment Act 1963: a guide for district authorities and their veterinary inspectors. 1975.

BRITISH VETERINARY ASSOCIATION
The Pet Animals Act 1951: a guide for local authorities. 1976.

BRITISH VETERINARY ASSOCIATION
The Riding Establishments Acts 1964 and 1970: a guide for local authorities and their inspectors. 1976.

DAVIS, R.P.
The protection of wild birds. B.Rose, 1979.

EMANUEL, M.R.
The law relating to dogs. Stevens, 1908.

FAVRE, D.S.
Animal law. Quorum Books:Greenwood Press, 1983 (USA).

INGHAM, J.H.
The law of animals: a treatise on property in animals, wild and domestic, and the rights and responsibilities arising therefrom. Johnson & Co., 1900 (USA).

LAW COMMISSION
Civil liability for animals. HMSO, 1967 (Law Com. No.13).

LAW REFORM COMMITTEE FOR SCOTLAND
Twelfth report: the law relating to civil liability for loss, injury and damage caused by animals. HMSO, 1963 (Cmnd. 2185).

LUND, T.A.
American wild life law. Univ. California P., 1980.

MORGAN, E.D.
Law of animals. Butterworths (New Zealand), 1967.

NORTH,, P.M.
Modern law of animals. Butterworths, 1972.

OLIPHANT, G.H.H.
Law of horses. Sweet, 1908.

PANNAM, C.
The horse and the law. Law Book Co., 1979 (Australia).

ROBSON, W.N.
Principles of legal liability for trespasses and injuries by animals. Cambridge U.P., 1915.

SANDYS-WINSCH, G.
Animal law. 2ed. Shaw, 1984.

SOPHIAN, T.J.
Horses and the law. Allen & Unwin, 1972.

THOMAS, J.L.
Diseases of animals law. Police Review Pub., 1975.

UNIVERSITIES FEDERATION FOR ANIMAL WELFARE
Animals and the law: symposium. 1974.

UNIVERSITIES FEDERATION FOR ANIMAL WELFARE
Welfare of laboratory animals: legal, scientific and humane requirements. Churchill Livingstone, 1977.

WEATHERILL, J.
Horses and the law. Pelham, 1979.

WILLIAMS, G.L.
Liability for animals. Cambridge U.P., 1939.

ANNUITIES

See also Insurance

Encyclopaedias and periodicals

Halsbury's Laws of England. 4ed. vol. 39.
Halsbury's Statutes of England. 3ed. see index vol.
Encyclopaedia of Court Forms in Civil Proceedings (Atkin). 2ed. vol. 33.
Encyclopaedia of Forms and Precedents. 4ed. vol. 2.

Stone & Cox Unity Linked Assurance & Annuity Tables. 1970–

Texts

ARCHER, J.A.
Compound interest and annuity tables. 11ed. Shaw, 1974. 3 vols.

BOWLES, M.
Testamentary annuities considered from the point of view of executors and trustees. Stevens, 1931.

DONALD, D.W.A.
Compound interest and annuities certain. Heinemann, 1975.

INSURANCE INSTITUTE OF LONDON
History of individual annuity contracts. 1969.

KNICKERBOCKER, D.C. &
SILVERSTEIN, L.L.
Annuities. Tax Management, 1973.
Looseleaf.

WATT, J.Y.
Law of savings banks, government annuities and national savings certificates. 3ed. 1948. 2 vols. supp. 1949.

APPEALS

See also Court Martial; Criminal Law; Practice and Procedure; Privy Council.

Encyclopaedias

Statutes in Force. Group: Courts, House of Lords and Privy Council.
Halsbury's Laws of England. 3ed. & 4ed, see index vol. under name of court or subject matter.

Encyclopaedia of Court Forms in Civil Proceedings (Atkin). 2ed. vol. 5.
Encyclopaedia of Forms and Precedents. 4ed. vol. 10.

Texts

ARCHBOLD, J.F.
Pleading evidence and practice in criminal cases. 41ed. Sweet & Maxwell, 1982.

BLOM-COOPER, L.J. & DREWRY, G.
Final appeal: a study of the House of Lords in its judicial capacity. Oxford U.P., 1972.

COMMONWEALTH SECRETARIAT
Appeals by the prosecution against sentences and acquittals. 1982.

DENISON, C.M. & SCOTT, C.H.
Procedure and practice relative to English, Scotch & Irish appeals. Butterworths, 1879.

ENVIRONMENT, DEPARTMENT OF THE
Planning appeals: a guide to procedure. 6ed. HMSO, 1974.

EVERSHED, F.R.
The court of appeal in England. Athlone P., 1950.

GORDON, J.W.
Appellate jurisdiction of the House of Lords and of the full Parliament. Sweet, 1905.

HOME OFFICE
Report of the Departmental Committee on New Trials in Criminal Cases (Tucker). HMSO, 1954 (Cmd. 9150).

HOME OFFICE
Report of the Interdepartmental Committee on the Court of Criminal Appeal (Donovan). HMSO, 1965 (Cmnd. 2755).

HOUSE OF LORDS
Form of appeal: directions as to procedure, and standing orders applicable to, civil appeals. Judicial Office, 1979.

HOUSE OF LORDS
Form of appeal: directions as to procedure applicable to criminal appeals from England, Wales & Northern Ireland. Judicial Office, 1982.

JUSTICE
Criminal appeals. Stevens, 1964.

KARLEN, D.
Appellate courts in the United States and England. New ed. Greenwood Press, 1984.

KNIGHT, M.
Criminal appeals: a study of the powers of the Court of Appeal, Criminal Division. Stevens, 1970 supp. 1975.

LAW COMMISSION
Report on the powers of appeal courts to sit in private and the restrictions upon publicity in domestic proceedings. HMSO, 1966 (Law Com. no. 8).

McLEAN, I.
Criminal appeals: a practical guide to appeals to and from the Crown Court. Sweet & Maxwell, 1980.

MEADOR, D.J.
Criminal appeals: English practices and American reforms. Virginia U.P., 1973.

MORRISH, P. & McLEAN, I.
A practical guide to appeals in criminal courts. Sweet & Maxwell, 1971.

PATERSON, A.
The Law Lords. Macmillan, 1983.

PENSION APPEAL TRIBUNAL
Assessment appeal – notes for the guidance of appellants. HMSO, 1963.

PLUNKETT, H.G.S. & CHAPMAN, P.F.A.
Taxation appeals. 3ed. Oyez, 1975.

PRICE, D.
Appeals. Fourmat Pub., 1982.

SAMUELS, H.
Appeals from the decisions of local authorities. Pitman, 1935.

STEVENS, R.
Law and politics: the House of Lords as a judicial body, 1800–1976. Weidenfeld & N., 1979.

SUPREME Court practice 1985. Sweet & Maxwell, 1984. 2 vols.

THOMPSON, D.R. & WOLLASTON, H.W.
Court of Appeal, Criminal Division. Charles Knight, 1969.

WHEELER, G.
Privy Council law: appeals from 1876–1891. Butterworths, 1893.

APPORTIONMENT

See also Trusts and Trustees; Wills.

Encyclopaedias

Halsbury's Laws of England. 4ed. vol. 6.
Halsbury's Statutes of England. 3ed. vol. 18
Encyclopaedia of Forms and Precedents. 4ed. vol. 2.

Texts

BAIN, A. & INGLIS R.M.G.
Apportioning tables. Gall & I., 1970.

BOLTON, H.
Apportionment tables. Stevens, 1970.

GROVER, L.G.E.
An aid to apportionment. Oyez, 1971.

JOSLING, J.F.
Apportionment for executors and trustees. 4ed. Oyez, 1976 (Practice notes no.5)

MEGARRY, R.E.
The Rent Acts. 10ed. Sweet & Maxwell, 1967–70. 3 vols.

WOODFALL, W.
The law of landlord and tenant. 28ed. Sweet & Maxwell, 1978. 3 vols. looseleaf.

APPROVED SCHOOL

See also Borstals; Detention Centres; Prisons; Punishment.

Encyclopaedias and periodicals

Halsbury's Laws of England. 4ed. see index vol.
Halsbury's Statutes of England. 3ed. vol. 17.
Encyclopaedia of Court Forms in Civil Proceedings (Atkin). 2ed. vol. 21.
Encyclopaedia of Forms and Precedents. 4ed. vol. 8.

British Journal of Criminology. 1960–
Crime & Delinquency (USA). 1955–
Criminal Law Review. 1954–
International Journal of Criminology & Penology. 1973–
Prison Service Journal. 1960–

Texts

CARLEBACH, J.
Caring for children in trouble. Routledge, 1970.

CLARKE, R.V.G. & MARTIN, D.N.
Absconding from approved schools. HMSO, 1971 (Home Office research unit report no. 12).

COUNCIL OF EUROPE
Short term methods of treatment for young offenders. Council, 1967.

DUNLOP, A.B.
Approved school experience. HMSO, 1974 (Home Office research unit report no.25).

FIELD, E., HAMMOND, W.H. & TIZARD, J.
Thirteen-year-old approved school boys in 1962. HMSO, 1971 (Home Office research unit report no.11).

GILL, O.
Whitegate, an approved school in transition. Liverpool U.P., 1974

MILLHAM, S. and others
After grace, teeth: comparative study of the residential experience of boys in approved shools. Human Context Books, 1975.

RICHARDSON, H.J.
Adolescent girls in approved schools. Routledge, 1969.

ROSE, G.
Schools for young offenders. Tavistock Pubns., 1967.

WILLS, W.D.
Spare the child: the story of an experimental approved school. Penguin, 1971.

YOUNGER, K.
Advisory Council on the penal system: young adult offenders. HMSO, 1974.

ARBITRATION

See also Trade Unions

Encyclopaedias and periodicals

Statutes in Force. Group: Arbitration.
Halsbury's Laws of England. 4ed. vol. 2.
Halsbury's Statutes of England. 3ed. vol.2, 45.
Encyclopaedia of Court Forms in Civil Proceedings (Atkin). 2ed. vol. 6.
Encyclopaedia of Forms and Precedents. 4ed. vol. 2.

Arbitration. 1915– (as Journal of Institute of Arbitrators 1915–1954)
Arbitration Journal (USA). 1937–
Journal of Business Law. 1957–
Journal of World Trade Law. 1967–
Lloyd's Maritime & Commercial Law Quarterly. 1974–
Yearbook of Commercial Arbitration. 1976–

Texts

BLEGVAD, B.M. and others
Arbitration as a means of solving conflicts. New Social Science Monographs, 1973 (USA).

CHERIAN, J.
Investment contracts & arbitration the World Bank Convention on the settlement of investment disputes. Sijthoff, 1975.

COHN, E.J., DOMKE, M. & EISEMAN, F. (eds.)
Institutional arbitration in international trade – rules, facts and figures. North-Holland Pub. Co., 1977.

COMMERCIAL COURT COMMITTEE
Report on arbitration (Donaldson). HMSO, 1978 (Cmnd. 7284).

DOMKE, M.
International trade arbitration, a road to world wide cooperation. 1958 repr. Greenwood, 1975 (USA).

FAY, E.
Official Referee's business. Sweet & Maxwell, 1983.

FOSKETT, D.
Law and practice of compromise. Sweet & Maxwell, 1980.

GILL, W.H.
Law of arbitration. 3ed. Sweet & Maxwell, 1975 (Concise college texts).

GINNINGS, A.T.
Arbitration: a practical guide. Gower Pub. Co., 1984.

HEALEY, B.
Federal arbitration in Australia: an historical outline. Georgian P., 1972.

INTERNATIONAL LABOUR OFFICE
Conciliation and arbitration procedures in labour disputes: a comparative study. 1980.

JACOBS, M.S.
The law of arbitration in South Africa. Juta, 1977.

KOS-RABCEWICZ-ZUBKOWSKI, L.
East European rules on the validity of international commercial arbitration agreements. Oceana, 1970.

LOCKYER, J.
Industrial arbitration in Great Britain. Inst. of Personnel Management, 1980.

MUSTILL, Sir M.J. & BOYD, S.
Commercial arbitration. Butterworths, 1982.

PALMER, E.E.
Collective agreement arbitration. Butterworths (Canada), 1978.

PARKER, Lord Chief Justice
The history and development of commercial arbitration: recent developments in the supervisory powers of the courts over inferior tribunals. Oxford U.P., 1959.

PARRIS, J.
Arbitration: principles and practice. Granada, 1983.

PARRIS, J.
Casebook of arbitration law. Godwin, 1977.

RANDOLPH, L.L.
Third party settlement of disputes in theory and practice. Oceana, 1973.

RANKING, D.F.deH.
Mercantile law incorporating partnership law and the law of arbitration and awards. 14ed. HFL, 1975.

RUSSELL, F.
Law of arbitration. 20ed. Sweet & Maxwell, 1982.

SCHMITTHOFF, C.M.
International commercial arbitration. Oceana, 1974. Looseleaf.

SEIDE, K.
Dictionary of arbitration and its terms. Oceana, 1970 (USA).

SLABOTZKY, A.
Grain contracts and arbitration. Lloyd's, 1984.

STEPHENSON, D.A.
Arbitration for contractors. Northwood Pubns., 1982.

STUYT, A.M.
Survey of international arbitrations, 1794–1970. Oceana, 1972 (USA).

WALMSLEY, R.C.
Agricultural arbitrations. 3ed. Estates Gazette, 1970.

ARCHITECTS AND SURVEYORS

See also Building and Engineering Law

Encyclopaedias and periodicals

Statutes in Force. Group: Architects.
Halsbury's Laws of England. 4ed. see index vol.
Halsbury's Statutes of England. 3ed. vol. 2.
Encyclopaedia of Court Forms in Civil Proceedings (Atkin). 2ed. vol. 8
Encyclopaedia of Forms and Precedents. 4ed. vol. 2 Architects. vols. 2, 11, 14, Surveyors.

Architect & Surveyor. 1965–
Architects' Journal. 1895–
Building Law Reports. 1976–
Estates Gazette. 1858–
Journal of Planning & Environment Law. 1936–
Property & Compensation Reports. 1950–

Texts

ARCHITECTS' JOURNAL
Legal handbook. 3ed. Architectural P., 1982.

BEATON, R.
The architect and the law. Butterworths (Australia), 1980.

BRICE, A.M.
Legal liabilities of the architect. Stevens, 1908.

BRICE, A.M.
Law relating to architects. Stevens, 1925.

ELDER, A.J.
Guide to the Building Regulations, 1976. rev.ed. Architectural P., 1981 supp. 1983.

GREENSTREET, B.
Legal and contractual procedures for architects. 2ed. Architectural P., 1984.

HUDSON, A.A.
Building and engineering contracts: including the duties & laibilities of architects, engineers & surveyors. 10ed. Sweet & Maxwell, 1970 supp. 1979.

KEATING, D.
Law & practice of building contracts: including the law relating to architects & surveyors. 4ed. Sweet & Maxwell, 1978 supp. 1982.

KEMELFIELD, R.L.
Law for architects, builders and engineers: an introduction. 2ed. Butterworths (Australia), 1983.

RIMMER, E.J.
Law relating to the architect. 2ed. Stevens, 1964.

TOMSON, B. & COPLAN, N.
Architectural and engineering law. 2ed. Book Centre Ltd., 1968.

WALKER, N.
Legal pitfalls in architecture, engineering and building construction. 2ed. McGraw-Hill, 1979.

WOOD, R.D.
Building & civil engineering claims. Estates Gazette, 1971.

ARCTIC/ANTARCTIC

See also Sea, Law of

Encyclopaedias

Halsbury's Laws of England. 4ed. vol. 2.
Halsbury's Statutes of England. 3ed. vol. 2.

Texts

AUBURN, F.M.
Antarctic law and politics. C.Hurst, 1982.

AUBURN, F.M.
The Ross dependency. Nijhoff, 1972.

MACDONALD, R.St.J.(ed.)
The Arctic frontier. Toronto U.P., 1966.

PHARAND, D.
Law of the sea of the Arctic, with special reference to Canada. Ottawa U.P., 1973.

THEUTENBERG, B.J.
Evolution of the law of the sea, with special regard to the polar areas: a study of resources and strategy. Tycooly International, 1984.

ARMY

See also Court Martial; Military Law.

Encyclopaedias

Statutes in Force. Group: Armed Forces.
Halsbury's Laws of England. 4ed. vol. 8.
Halsbury's Statutes of England. 3ed. vol. 29.

The Digest. vol. 39.
Encyclopaedia of Court Forms in Civil Proceedings (Atkin). 2ed. vol. 14.

Texts

ARMY DEPARTMENT
Cadet force regulations. HMSO, 1973.

ARMY DEPARTMENT
Queen's regulations for the army. HMSO, 1975. Looseleaf.

ARMY DEPARTMENT
Regulations for the TAVR. HMSO, 1978. Looseleaf.

KARSTEN, P.
Law, soldiers and combat. Greenwood P., 1978 (USA).

MANUAL of military law. HMSO.
Part 1. 12ed. 1977. Looseleaf.
Part 2. 9ed. 1969. Looseleaf.
  S.IIIa Enlistment. 1965.
  S.IIIb Regular army enlistment and service regulations. 1968.
  S IVa The courts of law in relation to officers and courts' martial. 1969.
  S.IVb Relation of officers and soldiers to civil life. 1968.
  S.V. Employment of troops in aid of the civil power. 1968.
  S.VI Reserve forces. 9ed. 1969.
  S.VII The women's services. 1965.
  S.X. Official Secrets Act.
  S.XI Regimental debts. 1967.
  S.XII Visiting forces.
Part 3. The law of war on land. 1969.

ULSTER DEFENCE REGIMENT
Regulations for the Ulster Defence Regiment. HMSO, 1969. Looseleaf.

WILLIAMS, W.L.
Intergovernmental military forces and world public order. Sijthoff, 1971.

YOUNG, T. & KETTLE, M.
Incitement to disaffection. Cobden Trust, 1976.

ARREST

See also Admiralty; Police.

Encyclopaedias and periodicals

Halsbury's Laws of England. 4ed. vols. 7, 8, 9, 11
Halsbury's Statutes of England. 3ed. mainly vol. 8.
Encyclopaedia of Court Forms in Civil Proceedings (Atkin). 2ed. mainly vol. 4.

Criminal Law Review. 1954–
Justice of the Peace. 1837–
Magistrate. 1922–
Police Review. 1893–

Texts

ADVISORY COMMITTEE ON DRUG DEPENDENCE
Powers of arrest and search in relation to drug offences. HMSO, 1970.

ARREST of ships: law and practice. Lloyd's, 1984.

CALVERT, F.
The constable's pocket guide to powers of arrest & charges. 7ed. Butterworths, 1982.

GARDNER, T.J. & MANIAN, V.
Principles and cases of the law of arrest, search and seizure. McGraw-Hill, 1974 (USA).

HAGBERG, L. (ed.)
Maritime law. Vol. 1: arrest of vessels. Kluwer, 1976.

HOME OFFICE
Race, crime and arrests. HMSO, 1979 (Research studies).

LEIGH, L.H.
Police powers in England and Wales. Butterworths, 1975.

MATHER, P.E.
Sheriff and execution law. 3ed. Stevens, 1935.

POWELL, C.M.
Arrest and bail in Canada. 2ed. Butterworths, 1976.

STONE's Justices' manual. 3 vols. Annual.

WADDINTON, L.C.
Arrest, search and seizure. Glencoe P., 1974 (USA).

ART

Encyclopaedias

Halsbury's Laws of England. 4ed. vol. 5 and see index vol.

Encyclopaedia of Court Forms in Civil Proceedings (Atkin). 2ed. vol. 12.

ART

Texts

ARNOLD-BAKER, C.
Practical law for art administrators. J.Offord Pubns., 1983.

BATOR, P.M.
International trade in art. University of Chicago Press, 1983.

DUBOFF, L.D. (ed.)
Art law, domestic and international. Rothman, 1975 (USA).

DUBOFF, L.D. (ed.)
The deskbook of art law. Federal Pubns., 1977 (USA).

DUFFY, R.E.
Art law: representing artists, dealers and collectors. Practising Law Inst., 1977 (USA).

GIBBS-SMITH C.H.
Copyright law concerning works of art, photographs and the written and spoken word. Museums Association, 1976.

HODES, S.
The law of art and antiques: a primer for artists and collectors. Oceana, 1966 (USA).

HOLLANDER, B.
International law of art for lawyers, collectors and artists. Bowes & Bowes, 1959.

ARTIFICIAL INSEMINATION

See also Human Transplants.

Encyclopaedias

Halsbury's Laws of England. 4ed. vol. 1
Halsbury's Statutes of England. 3ed. vol. 2.

Texts

CATHOLIC BODY IN ENGLAND & WALES
Artificial insemination: evidence to the Departmental Committee on Artificial Insemination. 1960.

FINEGOLD, W.J.
Artificial insemination. C.C.Thomas, 1976 (USA).

HARING, B.
Medical ethics. St Paul Pubns., 1972.

HOME OFFICE & SCOTTISH HOME DEPARTMENT
Departmental Committee on Human Artificial Insemination (Feversham Committee). HMSO, 1960 (Cmnd. 1105).

SCHELLEN, A.M.C.M.
Artificial insemination in the human. Cleaver-Hume, 1957.

SYMPOSIUM on legal and other aspects of AID and embryo transfer. Elsevier, 1973 (Ciba Foundation Symposium, No. 17).

ASSIGNMENT

See also Landlord and Tenant

Texts

BISCOE, P.M.
Law and practice of credit factoring. Butterworths, 1975.

COOTE, R.H.
Law of mortgage. 9ed. Stevens, 1927.

MARSHALL, O.R.
The assignment of choses in action. Pitman, 1950.

MESTON, M.
Law relating to moneylenders. 5ed. Oyez, 1968.

STARKE, J.G.
Assignments of choses in action in Australia. Butterworths (Australia), 1972.

ASSIZES

See also Crown Court

Encyclopaedias

Halsbury's Statutes of England. 3ed. vol. 41.

Texts

COCKBURN, J.S.
History of English assizes, 1558—1714. Cambridge U.P., 1972.

LONDON RECORD SOCIETY
London assize of nuisances 1301–1431: a calendar. 1973.

NIELD, B.
Farewell to the assizes: the sixty-one towns. Garnstone P., 1973.

PRITCHARD, F.E.
The common calender. Butterworths, 1958.

ROYAL COMMISSION ON ASSIZES & QUARTER SESSIONS
Report (Beeching). HMSO, 1969 (Cmnd. 4153).

SUTHERLAND, D.W.
Assize of novel disseisin. Oxford U.P., 1973.

ASSOCIATIONS

See also Clubs; Conspiracy; Corporations

Encyclopaedias

Halsbury's Laws of England. 4ed. vols. 5, 7, 8.

Texts

AFTERMAN, A.B. & BAXT, R.
Cases and materials on corporations and associations. 4ed. Butterworths (Australia), 1984.

FORD, H.A.J.
Unincorporated non-profit associations. Oxford U.P., 1959.

HORSLEY, M.G.
The law and administration of associations in Australia. Butterworths (Australia), 1976.

JOSLING, J.F. & ALEXANDER, I.
The law of clubs, with a note on unincorporated associations. 4ed. Oyez, 1981.

LLOYD, D.
The law relating to unincorporated associations. Sweet & Maxwell, 1938.

SMITH, H.A.
The law of associations, corporate and unincorporate. Oxford U.P., 1914.

ASYLUM

Periodicals

Bulletin of the International Commission of Jurists for the Rule of Law. 1954–
International and Comparative Law Quarterly. 1952–
Journal of the International Commission of Jurists. 1957–

Texts

GRAHL-MADSEN, A.
The status of refugees in international law.
Vol. II Asylum, entry and sojourn. Sijthoff,
1972.

RONNING, C.N.
Diplomatic asylum: legal norms and
political reality in Latin American relations.
Nijhoff, 1965.

SINHA, S.P.
Asylum and international law. Sijthoff,
1971.

ATTACHMENT OF EARNINGS

See also Debts and Debtors; Maintenance

Encyclopaedias

Halsbury's Laws of England. 4ed. vol. 10.
Halsbury's Statutes of England. 3ed. vol. 41.
Encyclopaedia of Court Forms in Civil Proceedings (Atkin). 2ed. vol. 19.

Texts

FREEDLAND, M.R.
Attachment of earnings: a guide to the
Attachment of Earnings Act 1971. Jordan,
1971.

HOME OFFICE
The Attachment of Earnings Act 1971,
explanatory booklet for employees. HMSO,
1971.

AUCTIONS AND AUCTIONEERS

See also Estate Agents; Sale of Goods

Encyclopaedias and periodicals

Statutes in Force. Group: Sale of Goods, sub-group 2.
Halsbury's Laws of England. 4ed. vol. 2.
Halsbury's Statutes of England. 3ed. vols. 2, 30.
The Digest. vol. 3.
Encyclopaedia of Court Forms in Civil Proceedings (Atkin). 2ed. vol. 6.

Encyclopaedia of Forms & Precedents. 4ed. vols. 1, 2; see also 17, 18.

Estates Gazette, 1858–
Property and Compensation Reports. 1950–
Property and Investment Review. 1970–

Texts

BATEMAN, J
Law of auctions. 11ed. 1953.

GRATTAN-DOYLE, H.N.
Law of auctioneers' and estate agents' commission. 2ed. 1957.

MacINTYRE, D.
Law relating to auctioneers and estate agents. 1957.

MURDOCH, J.R.
Law of estate agency and auctions. 2ed.
Estates Gazette, 1984.

NOKES, G.D.
Law relating to sales by auction. Sweet & Maxwell, 1926.

AUSTRALIA

Encyclopaedias and periodicals

Halsbury's Laws of England. 4ed. vol. 6.
Halsbury's Statutes of England. 3ed. vol. 4.
The Digest. vol. 8(2)
Encyclopaedia of Court Forms in Civil Proceedings (Atkin). 2ed. vol. 5, 35.
Adelaide Law Review. 1960–
Annual Survey of Commonwealth Law. 1965–
Australian Digest. 2ed. 1963–
Australian Law Journal. 1927–
Australian Lawyer. 1960–
Australian Yearbook of International Law. 1965–

Commonwealth Law Reports. 1903–
International and Comparative Law Quarterly. 1952–
Melbourne University Law Review. 1957–
Monash University Law Review. 1974–
New South Wales Law Reports. 1971– (as State Reports N.S.W. 1901).
Sydney Law Review. 1953–
University of Western Australia Law Review. 1948–
Victorian Reports. 1957– (as Victorian Law Reports. 1851).

Texts

ATKINS, R. & GRAYCAR, A.
Governing Australia. Wiley, 1972

BAALMAN, J. & FLICK
Outline of law in Australia. 4ed. Law Book Co., 1979.

BARWICK, G.
Precedent in the Southern Hemisphere. Oxford U.P., 1970.

BENNETT, J.M. (ed.)
A history of the New South Wales Bar. Law Book Co., 1969.

BENNETT, J.M.
A history of the Supreme Court of New South Wales. Law Book Co.,1974.

CAMILLERI, B.J.
Practice and procedure of the High Court and Federal Court of Australia. Butterworths (Australia), 1978. Looseleaf.

CASTLES, A.C.
Australian legal history. Law Book Co., 1982.

CHAPPEL, D. & WILSON, P.
Australian criminal justice system. 2ed. Butterworths (Australia), 1977.

CHISOLM, R.
Understanding law: an introduction to Australia's legal system. Butterworths (Australia), 1974.

COWEN, Z. & ZINES, L.
Federal jurisdiction in Australia. 2ed. Oxford U.P., 1980.

CRAWFORD, J.
Australian courts of law. Oxford U.P.(Australia), 1983.

DERHAM, D.P.
Introduction to law. 4ed. Law Book Co., 1983.

DOUGLAS, R.N.
Social aspects of law: an Australian perspective. Heinemann, 1973.

ELSE-MITCHELL, R. (ed.)
Essays on the Australian constitution. 2ed. Law Book Co., 1961.

ENCEL, S.
Cabinet government in Australia. Melbourne U.P., 1975.

ENRIGHT, C.
Constitutional law. Law Book Co., 1977.

FAJGENBAUM, J. & HANKS, P.
Australian constitutional law: cases, materials and text. 2ed. Butterworths (Australia), 1980.

HOLDER, W.E. & BRENNAN, G.A.
The international legal system: cases and materials with emphasis on the Australian perspective. Butterworths (Australia), 1972.

HOWARD, C.
Australian Federal constitutional law. 2ed. Law Book Co., 1972.

JOSKE, P.E.
Australian federal government. 3ed. Butterworths (Australia), 1977.

KIRBY, M.
Reform the law: essays on the renewal of the Australian legal system. Oxford U.P. (Australia), 1984.

LANE, P.H.
The Australian federal system with U.S. analogues. 2ed. Law Book Co., 1972.

LANE, P.H.
A digest of Australian constitutional cases. 2ed. Law Book Co., 1982.

LANE, P.H.
An introduction to the Australian constitution. 3ed. Law Book Co., 1984.

LANE, P.H.
A students' manual of Australian constitutional law. 2ed. Law Book Co., 1980.

LUMB, R.D.
Australian constitutionalism. Butterworths (Australia), 1983.

LUMB, R.D.
Constitutions of the Australian states. 3ed. Queensland U.P., 1972.

LUMB, R.D. & RYAN, K.W.
The constitution of the Commonwealth of Australia. 3ed. Butterworths (Australia), 1981.

MACKEN, J.J.
Australian industrial law: the constitutional basis. 2ed. Law Book Co., 1980.

McMINN, W.G.
A constitutional history of Australia. Oxford U.P., 1979.

MAHER, F.K.H., WALLER, P.L. & DERHAM, D.P.
Cases and materials on the legal process. 4ed. Law Book Co., 1984.

MARTIN, A.W.
Essays in Australian federation. Melbourne U.P., 1969.

NASH, G.
Civil procedure: cases and text. Law Book Co., 1976.

O'KEEFE, P.J. & TEDESCHI, M.A.G.
The law of international business in Australia. Butterworths (Australia), 1980.

PEARCE, D.C.
Delegated legislation in Australia and New Zealand. Butterworths (Australia), 1977.

QUICK, J. & GARRAN, R.R.
The annotated constitution of the Australian Commonwealth. Angus & Robertson, 1901 repr. 1976.

RICHARDSON, J.E.
Patterns of Australian federalism. Australian National University P., 1973.

RYAN, K.W.
Introduction to the civil law. Law Book Co., 1962.

SAWER, G.
Australian and the law. 2ed. Penguin, 1972.

SAWER, G.
Australian constitutional cases. 4ed. Law Book Co., 1982.

SAWER, G.
Australian federalism in the courts. Melbourne U.P., 1968.

TAY, A.E.-S. & KAMENKA, E.
Law-making in Australia. Law Book Co., 1980.

TAYLOR, G.D.S. & BRENNER, P.J.
The Australian legal process: an introduction. Butterworths (Australia), 1975.

TEECE, R.C.
The law and conduct of the legal profession in New South Wales. 2ed. Law Book Co., 1963.

TOMASIC, R.
Legislation and society in Australia. Allen & Unwin, 1980.

WALKER, R.E.
Practice of the Supreme Court of New South Wales. 5ed. Law Book Co., 1971.

WHITFIELD, L.A.
Founders of the law in Australia. Butterworths (Australia), 1971.

WYNES, W.A.
Legislative, executive and judicial powers in Australia. 5ed. Law Book Co., 1976.

ZINES, L.
Commentaries on the Australian constitution: a tribute to Geoffrey Sawer. Butterworths (Australia), 1977.

ZINES, L.
The High Court and the constitution. Butterworths (Australia), 1981.

AUTHOR

See also Copyright; Press Law.

Periodicals

The Author. 1891–
The Writers' and Artists' Year Book. 1902–

Texts

BARNES, J.J.
Authors, publishers and politicians: the quest for an Anglo-American copyright agreement, 1815–1854. Routledge, 1974.

BRITISH COPYRIGHT COUNCIL
Photocopying and the law: a guide to librarians and teachers and other suppliers and users of photocopies of copyright works. 1970.

CAVENDISH, J.M.
A handbook of copyright in British publishing practice. Cassell, 1974.

CLOUTMAN, B.M.
Law relating to authors and publishers. J.Bale, 1927.

JONES, M.
Justice and journalism. B.Rose, 1974.

NICHOLSON, M.
A manual of copyright practice for writers, publishers and agents. 2ed. Oxford U.P., 1970.

PUBLISHERS ASSOCIATION
A guide to royalty agreements. 5ed. 1971.

PUBLISHERS ASSOCIATION
Memorandum on publishers' practice. 1971.

SARNA, L.
Authors and publishers: agreements and legal aspects of publishing. Carswell, 1980 (Canada).

SOCIETY OF AUTHORS
Publishing contracts. 1974.

AVIATION

See also Hijacking; Transport

Encyclopaedias and periodicals

Statutes in Force. Group: Aviation.
Halsbury's Laws of England. 4ed. vol. 2.
Halsbury's Statutes of England. 3ed. vols. 2, 9, 41, 43, 44.
The Digest. vol. 8 (2).
Encyclopaedia of Court Forms in Civil Proceedings (Atkin). 2ed. vols. 3, 8, 9.
Encyclopaedia of Forms & Precedents. 4ed. vols. 4, 13.

Air Law Review (USA). 1930–1941.
Annals of Air and Space Law. Annual (Canada). 1976–
International & Comparative Law Quarterly. 1952–
Journal of Air Law and Commerce (USA). 1930–
Yearbook of Air and Space Law (Canada). 1965–1975.

Texts

AIR navigation orders and regulations. Consolidated ed. HMSO, 1975. Looseleaf.

AVIATION, MINISTRY OF
Report of the Committee on Civil Aviation Accident Investigation and Licence Control (Cairns). HMSO, 1961.

BRANCKER, J.W.S.
I.A.T.A. and what it does. Sijthoff, 1977.

BUERGENTHAL, T.
Law making in the international civil aviation organization. Syracuse U.P., 1969 (USA).

CHENG, B.
The law of international air transport. Stevens, 1962 repr. 1977.

CHUANG, R.Y.
The international air transport association: a case study of quasi-governmental organization. Sijthoff, 1972.

CIVIL AVIATION AUTHORITY
Aviation law for applicants for the private pilot's licence. 5ed. 1979.

COMMONWEALTH SECRETARIAT
Three international conventions on hijacking and offences on board aircraft. 1982.

DRION, H.
Limitations of liabilities in international air law. Nijhoff, 1954.

FREEMAN, W.M.
Air and aviation law. Pitman, 1931.

GOEDHUIS, D.
National air legislations and the Warsaw Conventions. Nijhoff, 1937.

HAANAPPEL, P.P.C.
Pricing and capacity determination in international air transport: a legal analysis. Kluwer, 1984.

HAANAPPEL, P.P.C.
Ratemaking in international air transport. Kluwer, 1977.

HEERE, W.P.
International bibliography of air law, 1900–1971. Sijthoff:Oceana. Supps. 1972–1976, 1977–1980.

HONIG, J.P.
The legal status of aircraft. Nijhoff, 1956.

INSTITUTE OF ADVANCED LEGAL STUDIES
Union list of air and space law literature. 2ed. 1975.

JOHNSON, D.
Rights in air space. Oceana, 1965.

JOYNER, N.D.
Aerial hijacking as an international crime. Oceana, 1974.

LOWENFELD, A.
Aviation law: cases and materials. Bender, 1972. Looseleaf.

LUPTON, G.W.
Civil aviation law. Callaghan, 1935 (USA).

McNAIR, A.D.
The law of the air. 3ed. Stevens, 1964.

McWHINNEY, E. & BRADLEY, M.A.
The freedom of the air. Sijthoff:Oceana, 1968.

MANCE, H.O.
International air transport. Oxford U.P., 1943.

MASON, J.K.
Aviation accident pathology. Butterworths, 1962.

MARGO, R.D.
Aviation insurance: the law and practice of aviation insurance including hovercraft and satellite insurance. Butterworths, 1980.

MATTERN, T.
Manual of civil aviation law. Oceana, 1952 (USA).

MOLLER, N.H.
The law of civil aviation. Sweet & Maxwell, 1936.

NOKES, G.D. & BRIDGES, H.P.
The law of aviation. Chapman & Hall, 1930.

PRICE, N.
Essential law for pilots and their crews. Oyez, 1980.

SEABROOKE, G.A.
Air law. Univ. of London P., 1964.

SHAWCROSS, C.N. & BEAUMONT, K.M.
Air law. 4ed. Butterworths, 1977. 2 vols.

SHUBBER, S.
Jurisdiction over crimes on board aircraft. Nijhoff, 1973.

SPEISER, S.M.
Lawyers' aviation handbook: guide to cases, statutes, forms, regulations, law reviews, tables. Lawyers Co-operative Pub. Co., 1964 (USA).

STEVENS, P.J.
Fatal civil aircraft accidents; their medical & pathological investigation. J.Wright, 1970.

TAYLOR, S.E.T. & PARMAR, H.A.
Aviation law for pilots. 4ed. Granada, 1983.

WAGNER, W.J.
International air transportation as affected by state sovereignty. Brussels, Bruylant, 1970.

WASSENBERGH, H.A.
Aspects of air law and civil air policy in the seventies. Kluwer, 1970.

WASSENBERGH, H.A.
Public international air transportation law in a new era. Kluwer, 1977.

WHEATCROFT, S.
The economics of European air transport. Harvard U.P., 1956.

BACK DUTY
See also Revenue Law.

Periodicals
British Tax Review. 1956–
Taxation. 1927–

Texts
PRITCHARD, W.E. & JONES, I.J.
Back duty. Butterworths, 1976.

SIMON, S.I.
Back duty law and practice. Oyez, 1970.

BAIL
See also Admiralty; Remand

Encyclopaedias and periodicals
Statutes in Force. Group: Criminal Law.
Halsbury's Laws of England. 4ed. vol. 1 Admiralty; vol. 11 Criminal law.
Halsbury's Statutes of England. 3ed. vols. 8, 21, 43 Bail Hostels.
Encyclopaedia of Court Forms in Civil Proceedings (Atkin). 2ed. vols. 3, 5, 14, 22.

Court. 1976–
Criminal Law Review. 1954–
Journal of Criminal Law. 1973–
Justice of the Peace. 1837–
Magistrate. 1922–
Police Review. 1893–
Stone's Justices Manual. Annual.

Texts
ARCHBOLD, J.F.
Pleading evidence & practice in criminal cases. 41ed. Sweet & Maxwell, 1982.

ANTHONY, E. & BERRYMAN, J.D.
Magistrates court guide. Butterworths, annual.

BOWDEN, J.
Binding over in the magistrates' court. Rose, 1976.

BRADLEY, E.L. & SENIOR, J.J.
Bail in magistrates' courts. B.Rose, 1977.

GORDON, G.H.
Criminal law of Scotland. 2ed. Green, 1978.

HARRIS, B.
New law of bail. B.Rose, 1978.

HOME OFFICE
Bail procedures in magistrates' courts. HMSO, 1974.

HOWARD LEAGUE FOR PENAL REFORM
Granting bail in magistrates' courts: proposals for reform. 1972.

KING, M.
Bail or custody? 2ed. Cobden Trust, 1973.

POWELL, C.M.
Arrest and bail in Canada. Butterworths (Canada), 1976.

RAYMOND, B.
Bail: a practical guide. Oyez, 1979.

RENTON, R.W. & BROWN, R.H.
Criminal procedure according to the law of Scotland. 5ed. Green, 1983.

RUSSELL, W.O.
Crime: a treatise. 12ed. Stevens, 1964. 2 vols.

SIMON, F. & WILSON, S.
Field Wing Bail Hostel: the first nine months. HMSO, 1975 (Home Office research unit report No. 30).

STEPHEN, H.J.
Commentaries on the laws of England. 21ed. Butterworths, 1950. 4 vols.

BAILIFFS

See also Execution; Sheriffs

Encyclopaedias

Halsbury's Laws of England. 3ed. & 4ed. see index vols.
Halsbury's Statutes of England. 3ed. see index vols.
Encyclopaedia of Court Forms in Civil Proceedings (Atkin). 2ed. see index vol.
County Court Practice. Annual.

Texts

ANDERSON, T.K.
Law of execution, including the powers, duties and liabilities (of) executive officers. Butterworths, 1889.

BLACK, A.
Execution of a judgment, including other methods of enforcement. 6ed. Oyez, 1979.

MATHER, P.E.
Sheriff and execution law. 3ed. Stevens, 1935.

BAILMENT

See also Carriers/Carriage of Goods; Contract; Liens; Pawnbrokers; Tort.

Encyclopaedias

Halsbury's Laws of England. 4ed. vol. 2.
Halsbury's Statutes of England. 3ed. vol. 2
The Digest. vol. 3.
Encyclopaedia of Court Forms in Civil Proceedings (Atkin). 2ed. vol. 6.
Encyclopaedia of Forms & Precedents. 4ed. vol. 20.

Texts

BEAL, E.
Law of bailments. Stevens, 1900.

GOODEVE, L.A.
Modern law of personal property. 9ed. Sweet & Maxwell, 1949.

HALL, L.E.
Possessory liens in English law. Sweet & Maxwell, 1917.

JONES, W.
An essay on the law of bailments. 4ed. Sweet & Maxwell, 1833.

PALMER, N.E.
Palmer on bailment. Law Book Co., 1979.

PATON, G.W.
Bailment in the common law. Stevens, 1952.

SAUVERPLANNE, J.G.
Security over corporeal movables. Kluwer, 1974.

STORY, J.
Commentaries on the law of bailments. 9ed. Little, Brown, 1878 (USA).

VAINES, J.C.
Personal property. 5ed. Butterworths, 1973.

WILKINSON, H.W.
Personal property. Sweet & Maxwell, 1971.

BANGLADESH

Encyclopaedias

Halsbury's Laws of England. 4ed. vol. 6.
Halsbury's Statutes of England. 3ed. vol. 43.

Texts

CHOWDHURRY, S.R.
The genesis of Bangladesh. 1972.

PEARL, D.
Interpersonal conflict of laws in India, Pakistan and Bangladesh. Sweet & Maxwell, 1981.

BANKRUPTCY

See also Debts and Debtors; Deeds of Arrangement; Liquidators; Receivers

Encyclopaedias and periodicals

Statutes in Force, Group: Bankruptcy and Deeds of Arrangement.
Halsbury's Laws of England. 4ed. vol. 3.
Halsbury's Statutes of England. 3ed. vol. 3.
The Digest. vols. 4, 5.
Encyclopaedia of Court Forms in Civil Proceedings (Atkin). 2ed. vol. 7.

Encyclopaedia of Forms & Precdents. 4ed. see index vol.

Insolvency Administration Newsletter. 1977–

Texts

ADAMS, J.E.
Insolvency. The Law Society, 1979.

BALL, W.V.
Bankruptcy, deeds of arrangement and bills of sale. 5ed. Pitman, 1934.

BERRY, S. & OLSEN, T.
Liquidation and bankruptcy aspects of conveyancing. Gower Pub. Co., 1982.

BERTRAM, D.
Tax consequences of receiverships. Butterworths, 1982.

CORK, K.
European insolvency practitioners handbook. Macmillan, 1984.

CRUCHLEY, I.
Handbook on bankruptcy law and practice. 3ed. Oyez, 1978.

CRYSTAL, M. & NICHOLSON, B.
A handbook on bankruptcy and deeds of arrangement law and practice. 3ed. Oyez, 1978.

DALHUISEN, J.
International insolvency and bankruptcy. Bender, looseleaf.

EALES, P.G. & DE VOS, P.A.F.
A guide to bankruptcy. Professional Books, 1978.

FAIRBURN, W.J.G.
Handbook for trustees and liquidators. 4ed. Juta, 1980 (S.Africa).

FARRAR, J.
Company insolvency. Sweet & Maxwell, 1979.

FLETCHER, I.F.
Law of bankruptcy. Macdonald & Evans, 1978.

FRIDMAN, G.H.L.
Bankruptcy law and practice. Butterworths, 1970.

GOUDY, H.
A treatise on the law of bankruptcy in Scotland. 4ed. T.& T.Clark, 1914.

HOUGHTON, A.R. & COOPER, N.H.
European insolvency guide. Tolley, 1984.

HOULDEN, L.W. & MORAWETZ, C.H.
Bankruptcy law of Canada. Carswell, 1960. Looseleaf.

HUNTER, J.M.
Northern Ireland bankruptcy law and practice. SLS Legal Pubns.(NI), 1984.

INSOLVENCY LAW REVIEW COMMITTEE
Insolvency law and practice: final report (Cork). HMSO, 1982 (Cmnd. 8558).

JUSTICE
Report on the committee on bankruptcy. Stevens, 1975.

LEWIS, A.N.
Australian bankruptcy law. 8ed. Law Book Co., 1984.

LIVIDAS, C.
Winding up of insolvent companies in England and France. Kluwer, 1983.

McDONALD, E.F., DARVALL, C. & FERNON, N.T.F.
Australian bankruptcy law and practice. 5ed. Law Book Co., 1977 (Australia).

MACNEIL, I.R.
Bankruptcy law in East Africa. Oceana, 1965.

MARSHALL, E.
Rights in security over moveables, cautionary obligations and bankruptcy. Green, 1983.

MULLA, D.F. & CHOPPA, D.S.
Law of insolvency. 2ed. Tripathi, 1977 (India).

ROSS, I.A.
European bankruptcy law. A.B.A., 1974 (USA).

SALES, C.A.
Law relating to bankruptcy, liquidations and receiverships. 6ed. Macdonald & Evans, 1977

SAMUELS, A.
Insolvency. Butterworths, 1977.

SCHNEPPER, J.A.
New bankruptcy law: a professional handbook. Addison-Wesley, 1981.

SHERIDAN, L.A.
Rights in security. Macdonald & Evans, 1975.

SMITH, C.H.
Law of insolvency. Butterworths (S.Africa), 1973.

SPRATT, F.C. & McKENZIE, P.D.
Law and practice of insolvency. 2ed. Butterworths (New Zealand), 1972.

THOMPSON, J.H.
The principles of bankruptcy law. H.F.L., 1967.

TRADE, DEPARTMENT OF
Bankruptcy: a consultative document. HMSO, 1980 (Cmnd. 7967).

TRADE, DEPARTMENT OF
Bankruptcy Law and Deeds of Arrangement Law Amendment Committee report (Blagden). HMSO, 1957 (Cmnd. 221).

TRADE & INDUSTRY, DEPARTMENT OF
A revised framework for insolvency law. HMSO, 1984 (Cmnd. 9175).

WATERS, D.F.
The law of insolvency in South Africa. 7ed. Juta, 1980.

WEAVING, J.F.
Notes on bankruptcy practice and procedure in county courts. 7ed. Oyez, 1978 (Practice notes).

WILLIAMS, Sir R.V.
The law and practice in bankruptcy. 19ed. Sweet & Maxwell, 1979.

BANKS AND BANKING

See also Bills of Exchange; Money; Negotiable Instruments

Encyclopaedias and periodicals

Statutes in Force. Group: Banking and Currency.
Halsbury's Laws of England. 4ed. vol. 3.
Halsbury's Statutes of England. 3ed. vol. 3.
The Digest. vol. 3.
Encyclopaedia of Court Forms in Civil Proceedings (Atkin). 2ed. vol. 6.

Texts

ALLAN, D.E.
Credit & security: legal problems of development financing. Univ. of Queensland P., 1975 (Australia).

BAXTER, I.
Law of banking and the Canadian Bank Act. 3ed. Carswell, 1981.

Encyclopaedia of Forms & Precedents. 4ed. vol. 2.

The Banker. 1926–
Banker's Magazine. 1844–
Journal of the Institute of Bankers. 1879–
Legal Decisions affecting Bankers. 1900–

BURNS, C.B.
Law of banking in Scotland. 2ed. W.Hodge, 1983.

CHORLEY, R.S.T.
Law of banking. 6ed. Sweet & Maxwell, 1974.

BANKS AND BANKING

CHORLEY, R.S.T. & SMART, P.E.
Leading cases in the law of banking. 5ed.
Sweet & Maxwell, 1983.

CLEMENS, J.H.
Balance sheets and the lending banker. 5ed.
Europa, 1979.

CRESSWELL, P.
Encyclopaedia of banking law.
Butterworths, 1981. Looseleaf.

DOYLE, E.P.
Banking law for TSBs. Savings Banks Inst., 1977.

DROVER, C.B. & BOSLEY, R.W..B.
Practice and law of banking. 10ed.
Macdonald & Evans, 1972.

EFFROS, R.C. (ed.)
Emerging financial centres: legal and institutional framework. I.M.F., 1982.

GHEERBRANT, P.A. & PALFREMAN, D.
Cases in banking law. 3ed. Macdonald & Evans, 1983.

GRANT, J.
Law relating to bankers and banking companies. 7ed. Butterworths, 1923.

GREGORY, T. (ed.)
Select statutes, documents and reports relating to British banking, 1832–1928.
Cass, 1964. 2 vols.

GUTTERIDGE, H.C. & MEGRAH, M.
The law of bankers' commercial credit. 6ed.
Europa, 1979.

HART, H.L.
Law of banking and stock exchange transactions. 4ed. Stevens, 1931. 2 vols.

HENNESSY, J.M.
TSB legislation and management. Savings Banks Inst., 1977.

HOLDEN, J.M.
Law and practice of banking. Vol. 1: Banker and customer. 3ed. Pitman, 1982. Vol. 2: Securities for banker's advances. 6ed.
Pitman, 1980.

ISAACS, S.A.
EEC banking law. Lloyd's, 1984.

JOHNSTON, D.L.
Canadian securities regulation.
Butterworths (Canada), 1977.

KARAM, N.H.
Banking laws of Kuwait. Graham & Trotman, trans. 1979.

KELLY, J.E. & PERRY, F.E.
Banking points from case and statute law, 1976–81. Waterlow, 1982.

KING, D. & THOMAS, P.
Legal nature of travellers' cheques in Canada. Manitoba Legal Res.Inst., 1973.

LEES, F.
International banking and financing.
Macmillan, 1974 (USA).

MANN, F.A.
Legal aspects of money. 4ed. Oxford U.P., 1982.

MATHER, L.C.
Securities acceptable to the lending banker.
4ed. Waterlow, 1979.

MEZNERICS, I.
Law of banking in East-West trade.
Sijthoff:Oceana, 1973.

MILNER, A. & ABRAHAMS, S.
Modern African banking cases. Trinity College, Oxford, 1974.

MORISON, I.C., TILLETT, J.P.K. & WELCH, M.J.C.
The Banking Act 1979. Butterworths, 1980.

PAGET, J.
Law of banking. 9ed. Butterworths, 1982.

PENNINGTON, R.R., HUDSON, A.H. & MANN, J.E.
Commercial banking law. Macdonald & Evans, 1978.

PERRY, F.E.
Dictionary of banking. 2ed. Macdonald & Evans, 1983.

PERRY, F.E.
The elements of banking. 3ed. Methuen, 1981.

PERRY, F.E.
Law and practice relating to banking. 2ed.
Methuen, 1983.

REEDAY, T.G.
Law relating to banking. 4ed. Butterworths, 1980.

ROBINSON, J.M.
Comparative survey of securities laws: a review of the securities and related laws of fourteen nations. Kluwer, 1980.

RYDER, F.R.
Banking Act, 1979. Sweet & Maxwell, 1979.

SHELDON, H.P.
Practice and law of banking. 11ed.
Macdonald & Evans, 1982.

SHERIDAN, L.A.
Rights in security. Macdonald & Evans, 1974.

SMART, P.E.
Cases in the law of banking, 1977–1980.
Sweet & Maxwell, 1981.

SYZ, J.
International development banks.
Sijthoff:Oceana, 1974.

THOMSON, W.
Dictionary of banking. 12ed. Pitman, 1974.

TRITTEN, K.
European banks. 7ed. Macdonald & Evans, 1981.

VENTRIS, F.M.
Bankers' documentary credits. 2ed. Lloyd's, 1983.

WEERASOORIA, W.L.S. & COOPS, F.C.
Banking law and practice in Australia.
Butterworths (Australia), 1976.

WADSWORTH, F.E.
Banks and the monetary system in the United Kingdom, 1959–1971. Methuen, 1973.

WOOD, P.
International banking set-off. Sweet & Maxwell, 1984.

BAR AND BARRISTERS

See also Advocates and Advocacy; Inns of Court; Legal Education; Legal Profession; Notaries; Solicitors

Encyclopaedias

Statutes in Force. Group: Lawyers and Notaries.
Halsbury's Laws of England. 4ed. vol.3.
The Digest. vol. 3.
Encyclopaedia of Court Forms in Civil Proceedings (Atkin). 2ed. vols. 5, 18, 25, 40.
Encyclopaedia of Forms and Precedents. 4ed. vols. 2, 7, 23

Texts

BOULTON, W.W.
A guide to conduct and etiquette at the Bar of England & Wales. 6ed. Butterworths, 1975 supp. 1978.

CECIL, H.
Brief to counsel. 3ed. B.Rose, 1982.

CLITHEROE, J.
Guide to conducting a criminal defence.
Oyez, 1980.

COCKS, R.
Foundations of the modern Bar. Sweet & Maxwell, 1983.

COHEN, H.J.
A history of the English bar and attornatus to 1450. Sweet & Maxwell, 1929 repr. Wildy, 1967.

COLTON, M.
State of the Bar: a study in professional disorganisation. Bow Pubns., 1977.

COOPER, J.
Public legal services: comparative study.
Sweet & Maxwell, 1983.

DUMAN, D.
English and colonial bars in the nineteenth century. Croom Helm, 1982.

FLOOD, J.A.
Barristers' clerks: the law's middlemen.
Manchester U.P., 1983.

HAZELL, R.
The Bar on trial. Quartet, 1979.

INTERNATIONAL BAR ASSOCIATION
Responsibilities and liabilities of lawyers as directors. I.B.A., 1979.

MEGARRY, R.E.
Lawyer & litigant in England. Stevens, 1962 (Hamlyn lecture no. 14).

MONOPOLIES AND MERGERS COMMISSION
Barristers' services: a report on the supply of barristers' services in relation to restrictions on advertising. HMSO, 1976 (1975–76 HC. 559).

ROYAL COMMISSION ON LEGAL SERVICES
Final report (Benson). HMSO, 1979 (Cmnd. 7648).

ROYAL COMMISSION ON LEGAL SERVICES IN SCOTLAND
Report (Hughes). HMSO, 1980 (Cmnd. 7846).

ZANDER, M.
Lawyers and the public intrest. Weidenfeld & N., 1968.

ZANDER, M.
The state of knowledge about the English legal profession. B.Rose, 1980.

BETTING AND GAMING

See also Clubs

Encyclopaedias

Statutes in Force. Group: Betting, Gaming and Lotteries.
Halsbury's Laws of England. 4ed. see index vol.
Halsbury's Statutes of England. 3ed. vols. 14, 42.

Encyclopaedia of Court Forms in Civil Proceedings (Atkin). 2ed. vol. 20
Encyclopaedia of Forms and Precedents. 4ed. vols. 9, 12.

Texts

CHENERY, T.T.
The law and practice of bookmaking, betting, gaming and lotteries. 2ed. Sweet & Maxwell, 1963.

CORNISH, D.B.
Gambling: a review of the literature and its implication for policy and research. HMSO, 1978 (Home Office research studies).

EDDY, J.P. & LOEWE, L.L.
The new law of gaming. Butterworths, 1969. supp. 1970.

FINNEY, J.
Gaming, lotteries, fundraising and the law. Sweet & Maxwell, 1982.

HOME OFFICE
Report of the Interdepartmental Working Party on Lotteries (Witney). HMSO, 1973 (Cmnd. 5506).

LIECK, A.
Betting and lotteries. Butterworths, 1935.

MESTON, Lord
Guide to the law of betting and lotteries. 4ed. B.Rose, 1970.

NATIONAL COUNCIL OF SOCIAL SERVICE
Lotteries and gaming: voluntary organisations and the law. 3ed. Bedford Square P., 1981.

ROYAL COMMISSION ON GAMBLING
Final report (Rothschild). HMSO, 1978 (Cmnd. 7200). 2 vols.

SHOOLBRED, C.F.
The law of gaming and betting. 2ed. Pitman, 1935.

STREET, H.A.
Law of gaming. Sweet & Maxwell, 1937.

UNDERHILL, M.
The licensing of gaming clubs and the control of gaming machines. Oyez, 1969.

BIBLE

Encyclopaedias

Halsbury's Laws of England. 4ed. vols. 5, 9.
Halsbury's Statutes of England. 3ed. vol. 10.

Encyclopaedia of Court Forms in Civil Proceedings (Atkin). 2ed. vol. 2.

Texts

DAUBE, D.
Studies in Biblical law. Cambridge U.P., 1947.

EHRLICH, J.W.
The Holy Bible and the law. Oceana, 1962.

MARCUS, R.
Law in the Apocrypha. 1927 repr. AMS Press, 1966 (USA).

RAND, H.B.
Digest of the divine law. Destiny Publishers, 1943.

WHITE, E.J.
Law in the scriptures. Thomas Law, 1935 (USA).

ZIMMERLI, W.
Law and the prophets: a study of the meaning of the Old Testament. Blackwell, 1965.

BIBLIOGRAPHIES

Periodicals

Annual Legal Bibliography. 1960–1979.
Index to Foreign Legal Periodicals.
Index to Legal Periodicals. 1908–
Index to Periodical Articles related to Law. 1959–
Law Books in Print. Annual.

Legal

ADAMIAK, R. (ed.)
Law book price guide. Adamiak (USA):Sweet & Maxwell, 1983.

ADAMS, J.N. & AVEBURY, G. (ed.)
Bibliography of eighteenth century legal literature: a subject and author catalogue of law treatises and all law-related literature held in the main legal collections in England (microfiche). Avero Pubns., 1982.

BEALE, J.H.
A bibliography of early English law books. Harvard U.P., 1926 supp. 1943 repr. Professional Books.

BENNETT, G.F. & BENNETT, J.C.
Environmental literature: a bibliography. Noyes, 1974 (USA).

BERELSON, P. & SWANSON, L.G.
Law book guide. G.K.Hall, 1973 (USA).

BESTERMAN, T.
Law and international law: a bibliography of bibliographies. Rowman & Littlefield, 1971 (USA).

BOULT, R.
Bibliography of Canadian law. Canadian Law Information Council, 1977.

BRIDGMAN, R.W.
Short view of legal bibliography. W.Reed, 1807.

BRITISH & IRISH ASSOCIATION OF LAW LIBRARIANS
Community law: a selection of publications. 1973.

BRITISH & IRISH ASSOCIATION OF LAW LIBRARIANS
Recommended holdings for law libraries: appendixes VI-XI of the Standards for Law Libraries. Published as a special issue of The Law Librarian, January 1983. Sweet & Maxwell, 1983.

BRITISH INSTITUTE OF INTERNATIONAL & COMPARATIVE LAW
Where to find your community law. 2ed. 1973.

BROCKWELL, C.J. (ed.)
Aborigines and the law: a bibliography. Australian National University:Eurospan, 1982.

CAMPBELL, D.J.
Annotated bibliography on the legal profession and legal services, 1960–78. Univ. Coll. of Cardiff P., 1980.

CHLOROS, A.G.
Bibliographical guide to the law of the United Kingdom, the Channel Islands and the Isle of Man. 2ed. I.A.L.S., 1973.

BIBLIOGRAPHIES

COHEN, M.L.
Law and science: a selected bibliography. 2ed. M.I.T.P., 1980.

COLLECTION of bibliographic and research sources: international law bibliography. Oceana, 1983–4. 2 vols. looseleaf.

COMMONWEALTH SECRETARIAT
Legal literature in small jurisdictions. 1981.

COWLEY, J.D.
A bibliography of abridgements, digests, dictionaries and indexes of English law to the year 1800. Selden Society, 1932 repr. Professional Books, 1980.

DAU, H.
Bibliography of legal Festschriften titles and contents: Germany – Switzerland – Austria, 1967–1974. Kurt Runge, 1977.

DEIGHTON, S. (ed.)
New criminals: bibliography of computer related crime. Inst. Elec. Engineers, 1978.

DELUPIS, L.
Bibliography of international law. Bowker, 1975.

DIAS, R.W.M.
A bibliography of jurisprudence. 3ed. Butterworths, 1979.

DYKSTRA, G.
Bibliography of Canadian legal materials. Butterworths (Canada), 1977.

ELZAKI, A.
Papua New Guinea legal materials: a bibliographic guide. Univ. of Papua New Guinea, 1979.

FARRAR, J.H.
Introduction to legal method. Sweet & Maxwell, 1977.

FRIEND, W.L.
Anglo American legal bibliographies. 1944 repr. Rothman, 1966.

GRAULICH, P.
Guide to foreign legal materials: Belgium, Luxembourg, Netherlands. Oceana, 1968.

GREEN, A.W.
Bibliography on British legal education. West Chester State College, 1973 (USA).

GRISOLI, A.
Guide to foreign legal materials: Italian. Oceana, 1965.

HARLOW, P.A.
Contractual claims: an annotated bibliography. 3ed. Inst. of Building, 1979.

HEPPLE, B.A. & O'HIGGINS, P.
A bibliography of the literature on British and Irish labour law to 1978. Sweet & Maxwell, 1981.

HOLDSWORTH, W.S.
Sources and literature of English law. Clarendon P., 1925.

INDEX to Canadian legal literature. Carswell, 1981. 3 vols.

INSTITUTE OF ADVANCED LEGAL STUDIES
Union list of air and space law literature in the libraries of Oxford and London. 2ed. 1975.

INSTITUTE OF ADVANCED LEGAL STUDIES
Union list of Commonwealth and South African law. 1963.

INSTITUTE OF ADVANCED LEGAL STUDIES
Union list of legal periodicals: a location guide to holdings of legal periodicals in libraries in the United Kingdom. 4ed. 1978.

INSTITUTE OF ADVANCED LEGAL STUDIES
Union list of United States law literature. 2ed. 1967.

INSTITUTE OF ADVANCED LEGAL STUDIES
Union list of West European legal literature. 1966.

JEGEDE, O.
Nigerian legal bibliography: a classified list of materials related to Nigeria. 2ed. Oceana, 1983.

JOBLING, M.
The abused child: an annotated bibliography. National Children's Bureau, 1976.

KEMMER, E.J.
Rape and rape-related issues: an annotated bibliography. Garland Pub., 1977 (USA).

KUO LEE LI
Worldwide space law bibliography. McGill Univ., 1978.

LANSKY, R.
Books in English on the law of the Federal Republic of Germany. Arbeitsgemeinschaft fur juristisches Bibliothek und Dokumentationswesen, 1979.

LANSKY, R.
Handbook of bibliographies on the laws of developing countries. Ubersee-Dokumentation, 1977.

LAW books 1876–1981: books and serials on law and its related subjects. Bowker, 1981 (USA). 4 vols.

MEEK, C.K.
Colonial law: a bibliography with special reference to native African systems of law and land tenure. repr. Greenwood, 1979.

MERRILLS, J.G. (ed.)
Current bibliography of international law. Butterworths, 1978.

MERSKY, R.M. and others
Manual on medical literature for law librarians: a handbook and annotated bibliography. Glanville, 1974 (USA).

MORRIS, L.C.
Bibliography of air and space law. Monash Univ., 1978.

NEUMANN, I.S. & ROSENBAUM, R.A. (eds.)
European war crimes trials: bibliography. Greenwood, 1978.

NORTHEY, J.F.
Index to New Zealand legal writing. Legal Research Foundation Inc., 1977.

O'HIGGINS, P. (ed.)
Bibliography of Irish trials and other legal proceedings. Professional Books, 1985.

O'HIGGINS, P.
A bibliography of periodical literature relating to Irish law. SLS Legal Pubns.(NI), 1966. 1st supp. 1966–1972. 1973; 2nd supp. 1974–1981. 1983.

PALMER, D.M.
Sources of information on the European Communities. Mansell, 1979.

PIMSLEUR, M.G.
Checklist of basic American legal publications. Rothman. 2 vols. Looseleaf.

PLUCKNETT, T.F.T.
Early English legal literature. Cambridge U.P., 1958 repr. Seer Books, 1980.

RADZINOWICZ, Sir L. & HOOD, R.
Criminology and the administration of criminal justice: a bibliography. Mansell, 1976.

REYNOLDS, T.H.
Rare books for law libraries. Glanville, 1983 (USA)

ROBERTS, L.M.
A bibliography of legal Festschriften. Nijhoff, 1972.

SOCIETY OF COMPUTERS AND LAW
Applications of computer technology to law: a selected bibliography for British lawyers, 1969–81. 1982.

SQUIRE LAW LIBRARY
Law catalogue. Oceana, 1974.

STAIR SOCIETY
An introductory survey of the sources and literature of Scots law. 1936 (S.S.,vol. 1).

SWEET & MAXWELL
A legal bibliography of the British Commonwealth of Nations. 1955–1964. 7 vols.

SZLADITS, C.A.
Bibliography on foreign & comparative law. Oceana, 1962 + supps.

SZLADITS, C.A.
Guide to foreign legal materials: French, German, Swiss. Oceana, 1959.

TAYLOR, B.W. & MUNRO, R.J.
American law publishing 1860–1900: readings and bibliography. Glanville, 1982. 3 vols.

TEARLE, B. (ed.)
Index to legal essays. Mansell, 1983.

UNITED NATIONS
The sea: a select bibliography on the legal, political, economic and technological aspects. 1976–78. 1978.

WIKTOR, C.L.
Canadian bibliography of international law. Univ. of Toronto P., 1983.

WINFIELD, P.H.
Chief sources of English legal history. Harvard U.P., 1925.

WING, D.
Short title catalogue of books printed in England, Scotland, Ireland and Wales and British America and of English books printed in other countries, 1641–1700. 2.ed. Modern Language Assoc., 1972–3.

WRIGHT, M. (ed.)
Use of criminology literature. Butterworths, 1974.

Official publications

BUTCHER, D.
Official publications in Britain. Bingley, 1983.

FORD, P.
Select list of British Parliamentary papers, 1955–1964. Irish U.P., 1970.

FORD, P. & FORD, G.
A breviate of parliamentary papers, 1900–1954. Irish U.P., 1961.

FORD, P. & FORD, G.
Select list of British parliamentary papers, 1833–1899. Irish U.P., 1969.

FORD, P. & FORD, G.
A guide to parliamentary papers: what they are, how to find them, how to use them. Irish U.P., 1956.

JEFFRIES, J.
A guide to the official publications of the European Communities. 2ed. Mansell, 1980.

JOHANSSON, E. (ed.)
Official publications of Western Europe. Vol. 1: Denmark, Finland, France, Ireland, Italy, Luxembourg, Netherlands, Spain, Turkey. Mansell, 1984.

MALBY, A. & McKENNA, B.
Irish official publications: a guide to Republic of Ireland papers, with a breviate of reports, 1922–77. Pergamon, 1981.

MORGAN, A.M.
British government publications: an index to chairmen and authors, 1941–1966. Library Association, 1967.

OLLE, J.G.
An introduction to British government publications. 2ed. Assoc. of Assistant Librarians, 1973.

PEMBERTON, J.E.
British official publications. 2ed. Pergamon, 1973.

RICHARDS, S.
Directory of British official publications: a guide to sources. Mansell, 1981.

RODGERS, F.
A guide to British government publications. H.W.Wilson, 1980 (USA).

BILL OF RIGHTS

See also Civil Rights and Liberties; Constitutional Law; Human Rights.

Encyclopaedias and periodicals

Halsbury's Laws of England. 4ed. vol. 8.

Human Rights Review. 1976–

Modern Law Review. 1937–

New Law Journal. 1965–

New Society. 1962–

Rights. (formerly Civil Liberties) 1976–

Texts

CAMPBELL, C.M.
Do we need a Bill of Rights? M.T.Smith, 1980.

HALPERN, S.
Future of our liberties: perspectives on the Bill of Rights. Greenwood Press, 1982 (Contributions in legal studies).

HOOSON, E.
Case for a Bill of Rights. Liberal Pub. Dept., 1978.

JACONELLI, J.
Enacting a Bill of Rights: the legal problems. Oxford U.P., 1980.

MACDONALD, J.
Bill of Rights. Liberal Research Dept., 1969.

NATIONAL ASSOCIATION FOR FREEDOM
Charter of rights and liberties. 1976.

NORTHERN IRELAND CIVIL
RIGHTS ASSOCIATION
Bill of Rights (Northern Ireland) Act. 1975.

PALLISTER, A.
Magna Carta: the heritage of liberty.
Clarendon P., 1971.

RUTLAND, R..A.
The birth of the Bill of Rights. Collier
Macmillan, 1955.

SCARMAN, L.
English law: the new dimension. Sweet &
Maxwell, 1974.

SCHWARTZ, B.
Bill of Rights: a documentary history.
McGraw-Hill, 1971 (USA). 2 vols.

SCHWARTZ, B.
The great rights of mankind: a history of the
American Bill of Rights. McGraw-Hill,
1977.

SOCIETY OF CONSERVATIVE
LAWYERS
Another Bill of Rights? 1976.

STACY, F.
A new Bill of Rights for Britain. David &
Charles, 1973.

TARNOPOLSKY, W.S.
The Canadian Bill of Rights. 2ed. Carswell,
1976.

ZANDER, M.
A Bill of Rights? 2ed. B.Rose, 1980.

ZELLICK, G.
A policy for liberty. Cobden Trust, 1971.

BILLS OF EXCHANGE

See also Banks and Banking; Negotiable Instruments

Encyclopaedias

Statutes in Force Group: Bills of Exchange
and Promissory Notes.
Halsbury's Laws of England. 4ed. vol. 4.
The Digest. vol. 6.

Encyclopaedia of Court Forms in Civil
Proceedings (Atkin). 2ed. vol. 8.
Encyclopaedia of Forms & Precedents. 4ed.
vol. 3.

Texts

BYLES, J.B.
The laws of bills of exchange. 25ed. Sweet
& Maxwell, 1983.

CHALMERS, M.D.
Bills of exchange. 13ed. Sweet & Maxwell,
1964.

ACTIONS AND BILLS OF
EXCHANGE
ACTIONS & BILLS OF EXCHANGE
Report (McNair). HMSO, 1945 (Cmd.
6591).

JACOBS, B.
A short treatise on the law of bills of
exchange, cheques, promissory notes and
negotiable instruments. 4ed. Sweet &
Maxwell, 1944.

MEGRAH, M.H.
Law of bills of exchange. 23ed. Sweet &
Maxwell, 1972.

NISHIMURA, S.
Decline of inland bills of exchange in the
inland London money market. 1855–1913.
Cambridge U.P., 1971.

RICHARDSON, D.
Guide to negotiable instruments & the Bills
of Exchange Acts. 7ed. Butterworths, 1983.

BILLS OF LADING

See also Carriers/Carriage of Goods; Shipping

Encyclopaedias and periodicals

Halsbury's Laws of England. 4ed. see index vol.

Halsbury's Statutes of England. 3ed. vol. 31.

Encyclopaedia of Court Forms in Civil Proceedings (Atkin). 2ed. vol. 8.

Encyclopaedia of Forms and Precedents. 4ed. vol. 21.

Lloyd's Maritime & Commercial Law Quarterly. 1976–

Lloyd's Maritime Law Newsletter. 1979–

Texts

ASTLE, W.E.
Bills of lading law. Fairplay Pubns., 1982.

CARVER, T.G.
Carriage by sea. 13ed. Sweet & Maxwell, 1982. 2 vols.

CLARKE, M.A.
Aspects of the Hague Rules: a comparative study in English and French law. Nijhoff, 1976.

GANDHI, A.B.
Carriage of goods by sea and bills of lading. Milan, 1973 (India).

POOR, W.
American law of charterparties and ocean bills of lading. 5ed. Bender, 1968 (USA).

POWERS, C.F.
A practical guide to bills of lading. Oceana, 1966 (USA).

SCRUTTON, T.E.
Charterparties and bills of lading. 19ed. Sweet & Maxwell, 1984.

BILLS OF SALE

See also Sale of Goods

Encyclopaedias

Statutes in Force, Group: Bills of Sale, England and Wales.

Halsbury's Laws of England. 4ed. vol. 4.

Halsbury's Statutes of England. 3ed. vol. 3.

The Digest. vol. 7.

Encyclopaedia of Court Forms in Civil Proceedings (Atkin). 2ed. vol. 8.

Encyclopaedia of Forms and Precedents. 4ed. vol. 3.

Texts

BALDWIN, E.T.
The law of bankruptcy and bills of sale. 11ed. Stevens & Haynes, 1915.

BALL, W.V.
Bankruptcy, deeds of arrangement and bills of sale. 5ed. Pitman, 1934.

EAGLESON, J.G.
The law relating to bills of sale, contracts of sale, liens on crops and wool and stock mortgages. Sweet & Maxwell, 1911.

REED, H.P.
Bills of Sale Acts. 14ed. Waterlow, 1926.

BIOGRAPHIES

Texts

ATLAY, J.B.
Lives of the Victorian Chancellors. 1906 repr. Wildy, 1972.

CAMPBELL, J.
Lives of the Lord Chancellors. Murray, 1868 repr. AMS, 1973. 10 vols.

CAMPBELL, J.
Lives of the Chief Justices. Murray, 1874. 4 vols.

DICTIONARY of national biography from the earliest times to 1900. 1908. 22 vols.
supps. 1901–11; 1912–21; 1922–30; 1931–40; 1941–50; 1951–60; 1961–70. Compact edition with 20th century supplement. Oxford U.P., 1975. 2 vols.

FOSS, E.
Biographia juridica: biographical dictionary of the judges of England, 1066–1870. Murray, 1870.

FOSS, E.
Judges of England, 1066–1864. Murray, 1846–64. 9 vols.

HEUSTON, R.F.V.
Lives of the Lord Chancellors, 1885–1940. 1940 repr. Wildy 1976.

O'FLANAGAN, J.R.
Lives of the Lord Chancellors and Keepers of the Great Seal of Ireland. 1870 repr. Rothman, 1971. 2 vols.

SIMPSON, A.W.B.
Biographical dictionary of the common law. Butterworths, 1984.

WHO was who
Vol. 1: 1897–1915; vol. 2: 1916–28; vol. 3: 1929–40; vol. 4: 1941–50; vol. 5: 1951–60; vol. 6: 1961–70; vol. 7: 1971–80. Black.

WHO's who : an annual biographical dictionary. Black.

WHO's who in American law. 3ed. Marquis Pubns., 1983 (USA).

BIRTH CONTROL

Texts

CALLAHAN, D.
Catholic case for contraception. Macmillan, 1969.

DIENES, C.T.
Law, politics and birth control. Univ. of Illinois P., 1972.

FELDMAN, D.M.
Birth control in Jewish law: marital relations, contraception and abortion as set forth in the classical texts of Jewish law. New ed. Greenwood P., 1980.

LEE, L.T. & PAXMAN, J.M.
Legal aspects of menstrual regulation. Fletcher School of Law & Diplomacy, 1974 (USA).

PAXMAN, J.M.
Law and planned parenthood. Int. Planned Parenthood Fed., 1980.

ST JOHN-STEVAS, N.
Agonizing choice: birth control, religion and the law. Eyre & Spottiswoode, 1971.

STEPAN, J. & KELLOGG, E.H.
Comparative study of law on contraceptives. Smithsonian Inst., 1974.

STEPAN, J. & KELLOGG, E.H.
The world's laws on contraceptives. Fletcher School of Law & Diplomacy, 1974 (USA).

WEINBERG, R.D.
Family planning and the law. 2ed. Oceana, 1978 (USA).

WORLD HEALTH ORGANISATION
Family planning legislation: report on a survey. 1984.

BIRTHS, MARRIAGES AND DEATHS

Encyclopaedias

Statutes in Force, Group: Registration of Births, Deaths and Marriages.
Halsbury's Laws of England. 4ed. see index vol.

Halsbury's Statutes of England. 3ed. vol. 27
Encyclopaedia of Forms and Precedents. 4ed. vol. 15.

Texts

BURN, J.S.
Marriage and Registration Acts. Stevens, 1837.

DAVEY, H.
Statutes relating to registration of births, deaths and marriages. Hadden, Best, 1899.

GLEN, W.C. & GLEN, A.
Law of registration of births, deaths and marriages. 2ed. Butterworths, 1875.

STONE's Justices' manual. Butterworths. 3 vols. annual.

BLACKMAIL

See also Criminal Law

Encyclopaedias

Halsbury's Laws of England. 4ed. vol. 11.
Halsbury's Statutes of England. 3ed. vol. 8.

Texts

HEPWORTH, M.
Blackmail: publicity and secrecy in everyday life. Routledge, 1975.

BLASPHEMY

See also Criminal Law; Ecclesiastical Law

Encyclopaedias

Statutes in Force. Group: Church of England.
Halsbury's Laws of England. 4ed. vols. 9, 11.

Halsbury's Statutes of England. 3ed. vol. 19.
Encyclopaedia of Court Forms in Civil Proceedings (Atkin). 2ed. vol. 32.

Texts

ASPLAND, L.M.
Law of blasphemy. Stevens & Haynes, 1884.

LAW COMMISSION
Offences against religion and public worship. HMSO, 1981 (Working paper no. 79).

LEVY, L.
Treason against God: a history of the offence of blasphemy. Schocken Books, 1980.

NOKES, G.D.
History of the crime of blasphemy. Sweet & Maxwell, 1928.

POLLARD, R.S.W.
Abolish the blasphemy laws. Soc. for the Abolition of the Blasphemy Laws, 1957.

WALTER, N.
Blasphemy in Britain: the practice and punishment of blasphemy, and the trial of 'Gay News'. Rationalist Press Ass., 1977.

BLIND PERSONS

Encyclopaedias

Halsbury's Laws of England. 4ed. see index vol.
Halsbury's Statutes of England. 3ed. see index vol.

Encyclopaedia of Court Forms in Civil Proceedings (Atkin). 2ed. vol. 28
Encyclopaedia of Forms and Precedents. 4ed. vols. 4, 22.

Texts

LOWRY, D.R.
Blind rights: an examination of the law relating to the blind in Canada; with particular reference to Nova Scotia. Blind Rights Action Movement, St Mary's Univ., 1972.

SKOTTOWE, P.F.
Law relating to the blind. 2ed. Butterworths, 1967.

BLOCKADE

See also International Law; Prize Law; War.

Encyclopaedias and periodicals

Halsbury's Laws of England. 4ed. see index vol.

American Journal of International Law. 1907–

Texts

DEANE, H.B.
Law of blockade. Layrians Green, 1870 repr. Hein, 1972.

HOGAN, A.E.
Pacific blockade. Oxford U.P., 1908.

LAWYERS COMMITTEE ON BLOCKADES
The United Nations and the Egyptian blockade of the Suez Canal. The Committee, 1953 (USA).

MACQUEEN, J.F.
Laws of war and neutrality, search and blockade. Chambers, 1862.

BLOOD TESTS

See also Drinking and Driving; Legitimacy and Illegitimacy.

Encyclopaedias

Halsbury's Laws of England. 4ed. vol. 1.
Halsbury's Statutes of England. 3ed. vol. 40:Paternity; vol. 42:Drinking and driving.

Encyclopaedia of Court Forms in Civil Proceedings (Atkin). 2ed. vol. 16.

Texts

HARRIS, B. (ed.)
The use of blood tests in determining paternity: a handbook for solicitors, doctors and court officials. B.Rose, 1973.

LAW COMMISSION
Blood tests and the proof of paternity in civil proceedings. HMSO, 1968 (Law Com. no. 16).

SUSSMAN, L.N.
Paternity testing by blood grouping. 2ed. Thomas, 1976 (USA).

BOATS
See also Shipping.

Encyclopaedias
Encyclopaedia of Court Forms in Civil Proceedings (Atkin). 2ed. vol. 32.
Encyclopaedia of Forms and Precedents. 4ed. vols. 9, 12.

Texts
PHELAN, A.
The law for small boats. 2ed. Charles Knight, 1970.

PAINTER, A.A.
Consumer protection for boat users. Nautical Pub. Co., 1979.

BONA VACANTIA
See also Wills.

Encyclopaedias
Halsbury's Laws of England. 4ed. see index vol.
Halsbury's Statutes of England. 3ed. vols. 5, 13, 27.

Encyclopaedia of Court Forms in Civil Proceedings (Atkin). 2ed. vols. 1, 14.
Encyclopaedia of Forms and Precedents. 4ed. vols. 6, 8, 18.

Texts
ENEVER, F.A.
Bona vacantia under the law of England. HMSO, 1927.

ING, N.D.
Bona vacantia. Butterworths, 1971.

MACMILLAN, A.R.G.
Law of bona vacantia. Green, 1936 (Scotland).

BORSTAL
See also Delinquency; Detention Centres; Punishment.

Encyclopaedias and periodicals
Halsbury's Laws of England. 4ed. see index vol.
Halsbury's Statutes of England. 3ed. vols. 8, 25, 43.

British Journal of Criminology, Deliquency and Deviant Social Behaviour. 1960–
British Journal of Delinquency. 1950–1960.
Court. 1976–
Crime and Delinquency (USA). 1955–
Criminal Law Review. 1954–
Howard Journal of Penology and Crime

Prevention. 1921–
New Society. 1962–
Prison Service Journal. 1960–
Probation Journal. 1936–
Report on the Work of the Prison Department. Annual.
Report on the Work of the Probation and After Care Department. Triennial.
Statistics relating to Approved Schools, Remand Homes and Attendance Centres in England and Wales. Annual.

Texts

ANTHONY, H.S.
Depression, psychopathic personality and attempted suicide in a borstal sample. HMSO, 1973 (Home Office research study no. 19).

BOTTOMS, A.E. & McCLINTOCK, F.H.
Criminals coming of age. Heinemann, 1973.

BURNETT, M.
The delinquent's challenge. B.Rose, 1978.

CORNISH, D.B. & CLARKE, R.V.G.
Residential treatment and its effects on delinquency. HMSO, 1975 (Home Office research study no. 32).

GIBBENS, T.C.N.
Psychiatric studies of borstal lads. Oxford U.P., 1963.

HANNEN, J.R.
Review of borstal policy in New Zealand. Govt. Printer, 1969.

HOME OFFICE
Young adult offenders: report of the Advisory Council on the Penal System (Younger). HMSO, 1974.

HOME OFFICE
Youth custody and supervision: a new sentence. HMSO, 1978 (Cmnd. 7406).

HOOD, R.
Borstal re-assessed. Heinemann, 1965.

HOOD, R.
Homeless borstal boys. Bell, 1966.

LAYCOCK, G.K.
Absconding from borstals. HMSO, 1977 (Home Office research studies).

LOWSON, D.M.
City lads in borstal. Liverpool U.P., 1970.

MANNHEIM, H. & WILKINS, L.T.
Prediction methods in relation to borstal training. HMSO, 1955 (Home Office studies in the causes of delinquency No. 1).

OSBOROUGH, N.
Borstal in Ireland: custodial provision for the young adult offender, 1906–1974. Inst. for Public Admin., 1975.

STRATTA, E.
The education of borstal boys: a study of their educational experiences prior to, and during, borstal training. Routledge & Kegan Paul, 1970.

WALTER, J.A.
Sent away: study of young offenders in care. Saxon House, 1978.

WEST, D.J.
The young offender. Duckworth, 1967.

BOTTOMRY

See also Insurance; Shipping.

Encyclopaedias

Halsbury's Laws of England. 4ed. vol. 1.
Halsbury's Statutes of England. 3ed. vols. 1, 17.
Encyclopaedia of Court Forms in Civil Proceedings (Atkin). 2ed. vols. 3, 22.
Encyclopaedia of Forms and Precedents. 4ed. vol. 21.

Texts

ARNOULD, J.
The law of marine insurance and average. 16ed. Stevens, 1981.

TRENERRY, C.F.
The origin and early history of insurance including the contract of bottomry. Stevens, 1926.

BOUNDARIES AND FENCES

See also Animals; Occupiers' Liability; Party Walls; Rights of Way; Trespass.

Encyclopaedias and periodicals

Halsbury's Laws of England. 4ed. vol. 4.
Halsbury's Statutes of England. 3ed. see index vol.
The Digest. vol. 7.
Encyclopaedia of Forms and Precedents. 4ed. vol. 16.

Conveyancer and Property Lawyer. 1936–
Estates Gazette. 1858–

Texts

ALDRIDGE, T.M.
Boundaries, walls and fences. 5ed. Oyez Longman, 1982.

HUNT, A.J.
Law of boundaries and fences. 6ed. Butterworths, 1912.

POWELL-SMITH, V.
Boundaries and fences. 2ed. Butterworths, 1975.

SANDYS-WINSCH, G.
Garden law. Shaw, 1982.

WOOLRYCH, H.W.
Law of party walls and fences. Butterworths, 1845.

Boundaries in international law

BLOOMFIELD, L.M.
British Honduras – Guatemala dispute. Carswell, 1953.

BLOOMFIELD, L.M. & FITZGERALD, G.F.
Boundary waters problems of Canada and the United States. Carswell, 1958.

BROWN, C.M.
Boundary control and legal principles. 2ed. Wiley, 1968.

BROWNLIE, I.
African boundaries: a legal and diplomatic encyclopaedia. Oxford U.P., 1979.

CUKWURAH, I.O.
Settlement of boundary disputes in international law. Manchester U.P., 1967.

JONES, S.B.
Boundary making, a handbook for statesmen, treaty editors and boundary commissioners. Carnegie Enndowment for International Peace, 1945 (USA).

McEWAN, A.C.
International boundaries of East Africa. Clarendon P., 1971.

PRESCOTT, J.R.V.
Boundaries and frontiers. Croom Helm, 1978.

SAVELLE, M.
Diplomatic history of the Canadian boundary, 1749–1763. Russell & Russell, 1940 repr. 1968.

BRIBERY AND CORRUPTION

See also Agency; Criminal Law; Elections.

Encyclopaedias and periodicals

Halsbury's Laws of England. 4ed. vols. 1, 11.
Halsbury's Statutes of England. 3ed. vol. 8, see also index vol.
Criminal Law Review. 1954–

Texts

CREW, A.
Secret commissions and bribes. 2ed. Pitman, 1920.

GHOSH, S.K.
Law relating to bribery and corruption in India. Eastern Book Co., 1971.

HURSTFIELD, J.
Freedom, corruption and government in Elizabethan England. Harvard U.P., 1973.

SIKES, E.A.
State and federal corrupt practices legislation. 1928 repr. AMS Press, 1974 (USA).

BUILDING AND ENGINEERING CONTRACTS

Encyclopaedias and periodicals

Halsbury's Laws of England. 4ed. vol. 4.
Halsbury's Statutes of England. 3ed. vols. 3, 16.
The Digest. vol. 7.
Encyclopaedia of Court Forms in Civil Proceedings (Atkin). 2ed. vol. 8.
Encyclopaedia of Forms and Precedents. 4ed. vol. 3.

Building and Contract Journal. 1966–
Building Law Reports. 1975–
Conveyancer and Property Lawyer. 1936–
Estates Gazette. 1858–
Journal of Planning and Environment Law. 1948–

Texts

ABRAHAMSON, M.W.
Engineering law and the I.C.E. contracts. 4ed. Applied Science Pubs., 1979.

ARMSTRONG, W.E.I.
Contractual claims under the Institution of Civil Engineers' conditions of contract. 2ed. Inst. of Building, 1979.

BARBER, M.P.
Building and civil engineering contracts and law. Estates Gazette, 1970.

BENNETT, D.M.
Brooking on building contracts. 2ed. Butterworths (Australia), 1980.

BROOKING, R.
Building contracts: the law and practice relating to building and engineering agreements. Butterworths (Australia), 1974.

BURKE, H.T.
Claims and the standard form of building contract. Inst. of Building, 1976.

ELLIOTT, R.F.
Building contract litigation. Oyez, 1981.

EMDEN, A.
Building contracts and practice. 8ed. Butterworths, 1980. Looseleaf.

FELLOWS, R.F.
J.C.T. standard form of building contract, 1980. Macmillan, 1981.

FLETCHER, L.
Construction contract dictionary. College of Estate Management, 1981.

GOLDSMITH, I.
Canadian building contracts. 3ed. Carswell, 1983.

GREENSTREET, B.
Legal and contractual procedures for architects. Architectural P., 1981.

HORGAN, M.O. & ROULSTON, F.R.
Elements of engineering contracts. Sweet & Maxwell, 1980.

HUDSON, A.A.
Building and engineering contracts including the duties and liabilities of architects, engineers and surveyors. 10ed. Sweet & Maxwell, 1970 supp. 1979.

JOHNSTON, K.F.A.
Electrical and mechanical engineering contracts. Gower, 1972.

JONES, G.P.
International civil engineering contract. Construction Press, 1979.

JONES, G.P.
A new approach to the international civil engineering conditions of contract. Construction Press, 1976. 2 vols.

JONES, G.P.
Standard form of building contract.
Construction Press, 1980.

KEATING, D.
Law and practice of building contracts including law relating to architects and surveyors. 4ed. Sweet & Maxwell, 1978 supp. 1982.

McKENZIE, H.S.
Law of building contracts and arbitration in South Africa. 3ed. Juta, 1977.

MARSH, P.
Contracting for engineers and contractors projects. 2ed. Gower, 1981.

PARRIS, J.
Standard form of building contract. Granada, 1982.

PIKE, A.
Engineering tenders, sales and contracts. Spon, 1982.

PIKE, A.
I.Mech.E./I.E.E. conditions of contract. Spon, 1984.

PORTER, R.
Guide to building contract conditions. Rev. ed. Godwin, 1980.

POWELL-SMITH, V. & FURMSTON, M.
Building contract casebook. Granada, 1984.

TURNER, D.F.
Building contracts – practical guide. 4ed. Godwin, 1983.

WALLACE, I.N.D.
Building and civil engineering standard forms. Sweet & Maxwell, 1969 supps. 1970 & 1973.

WALLACE, I.N.D.
Commentary on the fifth edition of I.C.E. Conditions of Contract. Sweet & Maxwell, 1979.

WALLACE, I.N.D.
Further building and engineering standard forms. Sweet & Maxwell, 1973.

WALLACE, I.N.D.
International civil engineering conditions of contract. 5ed. Sweet & Maxwell, 1979.

WALLACE, I.N.D.
The international civil engineering contract. Sweet & Maxwell, 1974 supp. 1980.

BUILDING AND ENGINEERING LAW

See also Architects and Surveyors.

Encyclopaedias

Statutes in Force. Group: Building.
Halsbury's Laws of England. 4ed. vol. 4.
Halsbury's Statutes of England. 3ed. vols. 26, 44.

Building Law Reports. 1975–
Construction Law Journal. 1984–
International Construction Law Review. 1983–

Texts

ARCHITECTS' JOURNAL
Legal handbook. 3ed. 1982

BAILEY, I.
Construction law in Australia. Law Book Co., 1981.

BINNS, G.D. & others
Building regulations. 2ed. C.Knight, 1973. Looseleaf.

CLAIBORNE, G.R.
Administration of building regulations: methods and procedures for enforcement. Bldg.Off. & Code Admin.Inst., 1973 (USA).

COLBY, E.
Practical legal advice for builders and contractors. Prentice, 1973 (USA).

CUTMORE, W.H.
Commentary on the building regulations, 1976. Shaw, 1977.

ECONOMIC COMMISSION FOR EUROPE
Building regulations in seven countries. 1975.

ELDER, A.J.
The guide to the building regulations 1976. Rev. ed. Architectural P., 1981 supp. 1982.

FUTURE for old buildings? Listed buildings: the law and practice. Sweet & Maxwell, 1977.

KEMELFIELD, R.L.
Law for architects, builders and engineers: an introduction. 2ed. Butterworths (Australia), 1983.

KNOWLES, C.C. & PITT, P.H.
History of building regulations in London, 1189–1972. Architectural P., 1973.

LEWIS, J.R.
Administrative law for the construction industry. Macmillan, 1976.

LORD-SMITH, P.
Arbitration for builders. Northwood, 1980.

MANSON, K.
Building law for students. 2ed. Cassell, 1974.

O'KEEFE, P. & PARLETT, D.S.
Building regulations checklists and index, England and Wales. 3ed. House Inf. Services Ltd., 1976.

PARTY wall legislation and procedure. Surveyors Pubns., 1983.

PITT, P.H. & DUFTON, J.
Building in inner London: a practical guide to building law. New ed. Architectural P., 1983.

STEED, A.N. & DALY, E.J.
The regulation of building standards in New South Wales. Butterworths (Australia), 1978. Looseleaf.

STEPHENSON, D.A.
Arbitration for contractors. Northwood Pubns., 1982.

STEPHENSON, J.
Building regulations 1976. Northwood Pubns., 1978.

STOKES, M.
Construction law in contractors language. McGraw-Hill, 1977.

SUDDARDS, R.W.
Listed buildings: the law and practice. Sweet & Maxwell, 1982.

TESCH, C.
Construction law and duties. Butterworths (Australia), 1977.

UFF, J.
Construction law. 3ed. Sweet & Maxwell, 1981 (Concise college texts).

WALKER, N.
Legal pitfalls in architecture, engineering and building construction. 2ed. McGraw-Hill, 1979.

WHYTE, W.S. & POWELL-SMITH, V.
Building regulations explained and illustrated. 6ed. Granada, 1982.

WOOD, R.D.
Building and civil engineering claims. 2ed. Estates Gazette, 1978 supp. 1981.

WOOD, R.D.
J.C.T. agreement for minor building works. Estates Gazette, 1983.

WOOD, R.D.
Principles of estimating. 6ed. Estates Gazette, 1982.

WRIGHT, J.H.G.
Building control by legislation: the U.K. experience. Wiley, 1983.

BUILDING SOCIETIES

See also Mortgages

Encyclopaedias and periodicals

Statutes in Force. Group: Building Societies.
Halsbury's Laws of England. 4ed. vol. 4.
Halsbury's Statutes of England. 3ed. vol. 3.
The Digest. vol. 7.
Encyclopaedia of Court Forms in Civil Proceedings (Atkin). 2ed. vol. 8.
Encyclopaedia of Forms and Precedents. 4ed. vol. 3.

Building Societies' Gazette. 1869–
Building Societies' Institute Quarterly. 1947–
Estates Gazette. 1858–

Texts

BODDY, M.
The building societies. Macmillan, 1980.

BUILDING SOCIETIES GAZETTE
Judicial decisions affecting building societies: reprinted from the Gazette. 1893–1909. 8 vols.

BYROM, R.
The building society valuer. Estates Gazette, 1979.

FAIREST, P.
Mortgages. 2ed. Sweet & Maxwell, 1980.

FISHER, W.R. & LIGHTWOOD, J.M.
The law of mortgage. 9ed. Butterworths, 1977.

FULLER, F.B. (ed.)
The Building Society Acts, 1874–1960. 5ed. Franey, 1961.

MILLS, J.
The Building Societies Act, 1960. Sweet & Maxwell, 1961.

NOKES, G.D.
An outline of the law of mortgages. 4ed. Estates Gazette, 1967.

RIGGE, M. & YOUNG, M.
Building societies and the consumer. National Consumer Council, 1981.

THORNTON, C.E.I. & McBRIEN, J.P.
Building society law: cases and materials. 2ed. Sweet & Maxwell, 1975.

WURTZBURG, E.A. & MILLS, J.
Building Society Law. 14ed. Sweet & Maxwell, 1976.

BURIALS AND CREMATION

See also Ecclesiastical Law; Public Health.

Encyclopaedias

Statutes in Force. Group: Burial and Cremation.
Halsbury's Laws of England. 4ed. vol. 10.
Halsbury's Statutes of England. 3ed. vol. 3.
The Digest. vol. 7.

Encyclopaedia of Court Forms in Civil Proceedings (Atkin). 2ed. see index vol.
Encyclopaedia of Forms and Precedents. 4ed. vol. 4.

Texts

BAKER, T.
Laws relating to burials. 6ed. Maxwell, 1898 supp. 1901.

BERNARD, H.
Law of death and disposal of the dead. Oceana, 1966 (USA).

FELLOWS, A.
Law of burial. 2ed. Hadden, Best, 1952.

GLEN, W.C.
Law relating to burial of the dead...4ed. Shaw, 1881.

LITTLE, J.B.
Law of burials. 3ed. Shaw, 1902.

POLSON, C.J., BRITTAIN, R.P. & MARSHALL, T.K.
The disposal of the dead. Pergamon, 1953.

RUSSEL-DAVIES, M.
Law of burials, cremation and exhumation. 5ed. Shaw, 1982.

STRUTT, Sir A.
Cremation legislation. 1976.

WATKINS, E.S.
Law of burials and burial grounds. 1948.

BUSINESS NAMES

See also Trade Marks.

Encyclopaedias

Statutes in Force. Group: Partnerships and Business Names.
Halsbury's Laws of England. 4ed. see index vol.
Halsbury's Statutes of England. 3ed. vol. 37.
Encyclopaedia of Court Forms in Civil Proceedings (Atkin). 2ed. vols. 30,38.
Encyclopaedia of Forms and Precedents. 4ed. vol. 5.

Texts

CHOWLES, V.G., WEBSTER, G.C. & PAGE, N.S.
South African law of trademarks, company names and trading styles. 2ed. Butterworths (S.Africa), 1973.

JOSLING, J.F.
Registration of business names. 3ed. Oyez, 1955 (Practice notes no.2).

KERLY, Sir D.M.
The law of trade marks and trade names. 11ed. Sweet & Maxwell, 1983.

STONE's Justices' manual. Butterworths. 3 vols. Annual.

BUSINESS TENANCIES

See also Landlord and Tenant.

Encyclopaedias and periodicals

Statutes in Force. Group: Landlord and Tenant.
Halsbury's Laws of England. 4ed. vol. 27.
Halsbury's Statutes of England. 3ed. vol. 18.
Encyclopaedia of Court Forms in Civil Proceedings (Atkin). 2ed. vol. 24.
Encyclopaedia of Forms and Precedents. 4ed. vol. 11.

Estates Gazette. 1858–

Texts

ALDRIDGE, T.M.
Letting business premises. 4ed. Oyez, 1981.

ALDRIDGE, T.M. & JOHNSON, T.A.
Managing business property: a legal handbook. Oyez, 1978.

ENVIRONMENT, DEPARTMENT OF THE
Security of tenure of business premises: how landlord and tenant are affected. 5ed. HMSO, 1977.

FOX-ANDREWS, J.
Business tenancies. 3ed. Estates Gazette, 1978.

MAGNUS, S.W.
Business tenancies. Butterworths, 1970.

RUSSELL-DAVIES, M.
Letting and managing residential or business premises: a legal and practical outline. R.I.C.S., 1978.

BY-LAWS

See also Delegated Legislation; Local Government.

Encyclopaedias

Halsbury's Laws of England. 4ed. see index vol. 4ed.
Encyclopaedia of Forms and Precedents. 4ed. see index vol.

Texts

AULT, W.O.
Open-field farming in Medieval England: a study of village by-laws. Allen, 1972.

KNIGHT, C.
Annotated model byelaws. 11ed. Knight, 1953. 2 vols.

NATIONAL WATER COUNCIL
A guide to the model water byelaws. 1977.

SCHOFIELD, A.N.
Byelaws of local authorities. Shaw, 1939.

WELSH WATER AUTHORITY
Water byelaws. 1978.

WISDOM, A.S.
Local authorities' byelaws. 5ed. B.Rose, 1978.

C.I.F. AND F.O.B. CONTRACTS

See also Charter Parties; Commercial Law; Lay-Time

Encyclopaedias

Halsbury's Laws of England. 4ed. vol. 3.
Encyclopaedia of Court Forms in Civil Proceedings (Atkin). 2ed. vol. 34.

Texts

SASSOON, D.
C.I.F. & F.O.B. contracts. 3ed. Stevens, 1984.

CABINET

See also Constitutional Law; Parliament; Privy Council.

Encyclopaedias and periodicals

Statutes in Force. Group: Parliament.
Halsbury's Laws of England. 4ed. vol. 8.
Halsbury's Statutes of England. 3ed. vol. 6.
Minster of the Crown and under name of Ministry.
The Digest. see Ministry of (by name)

Cambridge Law Journal. 1920–
Law Quarterly Review. 1885–
Modern Law Review. 1937–
Public Administration. 1923–
Public Law. 1956–

Texts

CHUBB, B.
Cabinet government in Ireland. Inst. of Public Admin., 1974.

CROSSMAN, R.H.S.
Diaries of a cabinet minister. Hamish Hamilton, 1975–1977.

CROSSMAN, R.H.S.
Myths of cabinet government. Harvard U.P., 1972 (Godkin lecture).

ENCEL, S.
Cabinet government in Australia. 2ed. Melbourne U.P., 1975.

HEADLEY, B.W.
British cabinet ministers: the roles of politicians in executive office. Allen & Unwin, 1974.

JENKS, E.
Parliamentary England: the evolution of the cabinet system. Putnam, 1903.

JENNINGS, W.I.
Cabinet government. 3ed. Cambridge U.P., 1965.

KEITH, A.B.
The British cabinet system. 2ed. Stevens, 1952.

KORNBERG, A.
Influence in Parliament: Canada. Duke Univ. P., 1976.

LOEWENSTEIN, K.
British cabinet government. Trans. from the German. Oxford U.P., 1968.

MACKINTOSH, J.P.
The British cabinet. 3ed. Sweet & Maxwell, 1977.

MOSLEY, R.K.
Story of the Cabinet Office. Routledge, 1969.

WALKER, P.G.
The cabinet. Heinemann, 1972.

WHEARE, K.C.
Government by committee. Greenwood P., 1955.

WILSON, H.
The governance of Britain. Weidenfeld & Nicolson, 1976.

CAMBRIDGE UNIVERSITY

Encyclopaedias

Statutes in Force. Group: Education – Universities, England & Wales.
Halsbury's Laws of England. 4ed. vols. 5, 9, 10.
Halsbury's Statutes of England. 3ed. vol. 11.
Encyclopaedia of Court Forms in Civil Proceedings (Atkin). 2ed. vol. 41.
Encyclopaedia of Forms and Precedents. 4ed. vol. 11.

Texts

HACKETT, M.B.
Original statutes of Cambridge University. Cambridge U.P., 1970.

SHADWELL, L.L.
Enactments in Parliament concerning Universities of Oxford & Cambridge, & the Colleges of Winchester, Eton & Westminster. Oxford U.P., 1911–12. 4 vols.

SKENE, W.B.
Acts relating to the Universities of Oxford & Cambridge. 2ed. Oxford U.P., 1898.

UNIVERSITY OF CAMBRIDGE
Statutes and ordinances. Cambridge U.P., index and supp. 1978.

WILLIAMS, J.
The law of the universities. Butterworths, 1910.

CANADA

See also Commonwealth Law

Encyclopaedias and periodicals

The Canadian Abridgement. 2ed.
Statutes in Force. Group: Commonwealth & Other Territories – Canada.
Halsbury's Laws of England. 4ed. vol. 6 (and Canadian convertors).
Halsbury's Statutes of England. 3ed. vol. 4.

Canadian Bar Journal. 1958–
Canadian Bar Review. 1923–
Canadian Yearbook of International Law. 1963–
Index to Canadian Legal Periodical Literature. 1961–
Manitoba Law Review. 1962–
Saskatchewan Law Reveiw. 1936–
Western Ontario Law Review. 1961–

CANADA

Texts

BOULT, R.
Bibliography of Canadian law. Canadian Law Information Council, 1977.

BOURINOT, J.G.
Federal Government in Canada. 1889 repr. Johnson Reprint, 1973.

BOURINOT, J.G.
Parliamentary procedure and practice in the Dominion of Canada. 1884 repr. Irish U.P., 1971.

CANADIAN GOVERNMENT PUBLISHING OFFICE
Constitution, 1982. In English and French. 1983.

CASTEL, J.G.
Civil law system of the Province of Quebec. Notes, cases and materials. Butterworths (Canada), 1962.

CHAPMAN, F.A.R.
Fundamentals of Canadian law. 2ed. McGraw-Hill, 1974.

COHEN, S.
Due process of law. Carswell, 1977.

DYKSTRA, G.
Bibliography of Canadian legal materials. Butterworths (Canada), 1977.

FLAHERTY, D.H. (ed.)
Essays in the history of Canadian law. Vol. 2. Univ. of Toronto Press, 1983.

FRANKLIN, M.
Introduction to Quebec law. Pitman (Canada), 1972.

GALL, G.L.
Canadian legal system. 2ed. Carswell, 1983.

GOTLIEB, A.E.
Canadian treaty making. Butterworths (Canada), 1968.

HOGG, P.W.
Canada Act 1982. Carswell, 1982

HOGG, P.W.
Constitutional law of Canada. Carswell, 1977.

JENNINGS, W.H. & ZUBER, T.G.
Canadian law. 2ed. McGraw-Hill, 1972.

LASKIN, B.
British tradition in Canadian law. Stevens, 1969 (Hamlyn lecture no. 21).

LASKIN, B.
Canadian constitutional law. 4ed. Carswell, 1975.

LEACH, R.H. (ed.)
Canada's new constitution. Duke Univ. Press, 1983.

McWHINNEY, E. (Ed.)
Canadian jurisprudence: the civil law and common law in Canada. Carswell, 1958.

MAGNET, J.
Constitutional law of Canada cases. Carswell, 1983.

ROWAT, D.C.
Government of federal capitals. Toronto U.P., 1972.

SAVELLE, M.
Diplomatic history of the Canadian boundary, 1749–1763. Russell & Russell, 1940 repr. 1968.

SCOTT, F.R.
Essays on the constitution: aspects of Canadian law and politics. Univ. of Toronto P., 1978.

SHEPPARD, C.A.
Law of languages in Canada. Information Canada, 1971.

SPETZ, S.N.
Legal jams: aspects of Canadian civil law. Pitman, 1972.

STEWART, J.B.
Canadian House of Commons: procedure and reform. McGill U.P., 1977.

VASAN, R.S.
Canadian law dictionary. Law & Business, 1981.

WADDAMS, S.
Introduction to the study of law. 2ed. Carswell, 1983.

WATSON, G.D., BORINS, S. & WILLIAMS, N.J.
Canadian civil procedure: cases and materials. 2ed. Butterworths (Canada), 1977.

WHYTE, J.D. & LEDERMAN, W.R.
Canadian constitutional law: cases, notes and materials. 2ed. Butterworths (Canada), 1977.

WIKTOR, C.L. & TANGUAY, G.
Constitutions of Canada: federal and provincial sources. Oceana, 1978 (USA). 4 vols. looseleaf.

CANALS

See also Waters and Watercourses

Encyclopaedias

Statutes in Force. Group: Railways, Canals and Pipelines.
Halsbury's Laws of England. 3ed. vol. 31.
Halsbury's Statutes of England. 3ed. vol. 26.
Encyclopaedia of Court Forms in Civil Proceedings (Atkin). 2ed. see index vol.
Encyclopaedia of Forms and Precedents. 4ed. vol. 16.

Texts

BAXTER, R.R.
Law of international waterways, with particular regard to interoceanic canals. Harvard U.P., 1964 (USA).

BAXTER, R.R., CARROLL, D. & TONDEL, L.M.
Panama Canal. Oceana, 1965 (USA).

BRITISH WATERWAYS BOARD
General canal byelaws.

CARTWRIGHT, D.P.
Canals and the local authority. Inst. of Municipal Engineers, 1972.

LAUTERPACHT, E. (ed.)
The Suez Canal settlement. Stevens, 1960.

LLOYD'S REGISTER
Rules for inland waterways vessels.

OBIETA, J.A.
The international status of the Suez Canal. 2ed. Nijhoff, 1970.

WOOLRYCH, H.W.
Laws of waters: including rights in the sea, rivers, canals etc. 2ed. 1851.

CAPITALS GAINS TAX

See also Revenue Law.

Encyclopaedias and periodicals

Statutes in Force. Group: Income, Corporation and Capital Gains Tax; sub-group 2.
Halsbury's Laws of England. 4ed. vol. 5.
Halsbury's Statutes of England. 3ed. see index vol.
Encyclopaedia of Court Forms in Civil Proceedings (Atkin). 2ed. vol. 31.
Encyclopaedia of Forms and Precedents. 4ed. see index vol.

Annotated Tax Cases. 1922–1975.
British Tax Review. 1956–
Capital Taxes: a Quarterly Commentary. 1984–
Money "Which". 1957–
Rating & Valuation Reporter. 1961–
Reports of Tax Cases. 1875–
Simon's Tax Intelligence. 1973–
Simon's Tax Cases. 1973–
Taxation. 1927–
Taxation Reports. 1940–

Texts

AGYEI, A.K.
Capital gains tax in Nigeria. G.Burn, 1984.

BEATTIE, C.N.
Elements of the law of income and capital gains taxation. 9ed. Stevens, 1970.

BIDDLE, L.A. & MEW, R.L.
Impact of capital gains tax on executors and trustees. Law Society, 1970.

BRITISH tax encyclopaedia. Sweet & Maxwell. 5 vols. Looseleaf.

BUTTERWORTHS
Handbook on the Capital Gains Tax Act 1979. 1979.

BUTTERWORTHS
Yellow tax handbook: income tax, corporation tax and capital gains tax. Annual.

CARMICHAEL, K.S.
Capital gains tax. 2ed. H.F.L., 1975 supp. 1978.

CAPITAL PUNISHMENT 63

COX, C. & ROSS, H.J.
Capital gains tax on businesses. Sweet & Maxwell, 1982 supp. 1983.

CRETTON, C.
Practical capital gains tax. 2ed. Butterworths, 1982.

DI PALMA, V.
Capital gains tax. 5ed. Macdonald & Evans, 1981.

FOSTER, Sir J. etc.
Capital taxes encyclopaedia. Butterworths, 1976. 3 vols. looseleaf.

HAMBRO's tax guide. Annual.

HARPER, A.C.
Stamp duty and capital duty. Inst. of Chartered Accountants, 1979.

INLAND REVENUE
The Taxes Acts. HMSO. 5 vols. annual.

MORCOM, J.B.
Estate duty saving and capital gains tax. 4ed. Butterworths, 1969.

PINSON, B.
Revenue law. 15ed. Sweet & Maxwell, 1982 supp. 1983.

PRITCHARD, W.E.
Capital gains tax. 6ed. Polytech, 1982.

SIMON's taxes. 3ed. Butterworths. 9 vols. Looseleaf.

SOPHIAN, T.J.
The taxation of capital gains. 2ed. Butterworths, 1967.

STORZ, M.
Capital gains and short term gains. Oyez, 1970.

SUMPTION, A.
Capital gains tax. Butterworths, 1981. Looseleaf.

TOLLEY's capital gains tax. Annual.

WHEATCROFT, G.S.A. & HEWSON, G.D.
Encyclopaedia of capital taxation. Sweet & Maxwell, 1977. Looseleaf.

WHITEMAN, P.G. & WHEATCROFT, G.S.A.
Capital gains tax. 3ed. Sweet & Maxwell, 1980 supp. 1984.

CAPITAL PUNISHMENT

See also Corporal Punishment; Criminal Law.

Encyclopaedias

Halsbury's Laws of England. 4ed. see index vol.
Halsbury's Statutes of England. 3ed. vol. 8.

Texts

AMNESTY INTERNATIONAL
Amnesty International and the death penalty. 1979.

ANDERSON, F.W.
Hanging in Canada. Frontier P., 1973.

BEDAU, A.(ed.)
The death penalty in America. 3ed. Oxford U.P., 1982.

CHANDLER, D.B.
Capital punishment in Canada. McClelland & Stewart, 1976.

CHRISTOPH, J.B.
Capital punishment and British politics. Univ. of Chicago P., 1962.

COOPER, D.D.
The lesson of the scaffold. Ohio U.P., 1974.

FATTAH, E.A.
Study of the deterrent effect of capital punishment with special reference to the Canadian situation. Solicitor General (Canada), 1972.

JAYEWARDENE, C.H.S.
Penalty of death: the Canadian experiment. Lexington, 1978 (USA).

JOYCE, J.A.
The right to life: a world view of capital punishment. Gollancz, 1962.

KOESTLER, A.
Refelections on hanging. Gollancz, 1956

MELTSNER, M.
Cruel and unusual: the Supreme Court and capital punishment. W.Morrow, 1974 (USA).

NATIONAL CAMPAIGN FOR THE ABOLITION OF CAPITAL PUNISHMENT
Murder and capital punishment in England & Wales. 1974.

PANNICK, D.
Judicial review of the death penalty. Duckworth, 1982.

ROYAL COMMISSION ON CAPITAL PUNISHMENT
Report. HMSO, 1953 (Cmd. 8932).

SCOTT, G.R.
The history of capital punishment. Torchstream Books, 1950.

CAPITAL TRANSFER TAX

See also Estate Duty; Executors and Administrators; Probate; Revenue Law.

Encyclopaedias and periodicals

Statutes in Force. Group: Capital Transfer Tax.
Halsbury's Statutes of England. 3ed. vol. 45.
Encyclopaedia of Forms and Precedents. 4ed. see index vol.

For journals and reports see Capital Gains Tax above.
CTT News. 1979–

Texts

BRITISH tax encyclopaedia. Sweet & Maxwell, 1962. 5 vols. Looseleaf.

BUTTERWORTH'S
Capital transfer tax tables. 3ed. 1978.

BUTTERWORTH'S
Orange tax handbook: capital transfer tax. Annual.

CHAPMAN, A.L.
Capital transfer tax. 5ed. Tolley, 1982.

CHOWN, J.
A guide to capital transfer tax. Kogan Page, 1975.

COLLEGE OF LAW
Capital transfer tax and development land tax. 2ed. Law Notes, 1977.

CONFEDERATION OF BRITISH INDUSTRY
Capital transfer tax: consequences for private limited companies. 1975.

COOMBES, J.
Capital transfer tax. Professional Books, 1977.

DAILY TELEGRAPH
Capital transfer tax and you. 1975.

DAVIES, D.T.
Will precedents and capital transfer tax. 2ed Butterworths, 1984.

DYMOND, R.
Capital transfer tax. 2ed.Oyez, 1983.

EASTAWAY, N.
Guide to the Taxes Acts and capital transfer tax. Butterworths, 1978.

EASTAWAY, N.
Principles of capital transfer tax. H.F.L., 1979.

FOSTER, Sir J., etc.
Capital taxes encyclopaedia. Butterworths, 1976. Looseleaf.

GOODMAN, W.D.
International double taxation of estates and inheritances. Butterworths, 1978.

HALLETT, V.G.H. & WARREN, N.
Settlements, wills and capital transfer tax. Sweet & Maxwell, 1979.

HAMBRO's tax guide. Annual.

HAYTON, D.J. & TILEY, J.
Capital transfer tax. 2ed. Butterworths, 1978.

HEPKER, M.Z. & WHITEHOUSE, C.J.
Capital transfer tax. Heinemann, 1975.

IND, R.C.
Capital transfer tax. 2ed. Macdonald & Evans, 1981.

INLAND REVENUE
The Taxes Acts. HMSO. 5 vols. Annual.

McCUTCHEON, B.
Capital transfer tax. 2ed. Sweet & Maxwell, 1984. 2 vols.

MELLOWS, A.R.
Taxation for executors and trustees. 5ed. Butterworths, 1980.

MORCOM, J.B. & PARRY, D.J.T.
Capital transfer tax. 2ed. Woodhead-Faulkner, 1978.

MUNKMAN, J.
Capital transfer tax. Jordan, 1975.

NEWMAN, G. & GODFREY, R.
Revised planning for capital transfer tax. Guild P., 1982.

NOCK, R.S. & SHERRINS, T.
Capital transfer tax. Sweet & Maxwell, 1975.

PINSON, B.
Revenue law. 15ed. Sweet & Maxwell, 1982 supp. 1983.

RAY, R.P.
Capital transfer tax planning. 2ed. Butterworths, 1982.

SHERRING, T.
Capital transfer tax: discretionary trusts after the Finance Act, 1982. Tolley, 1982.

SIMON's taxes. 3ed. Butterworths. 9 vols. Looseleaf.

TINGLEY, K.R. & HUGHES, P.F. (eds.)
Key to capital transfer tax. Taxation Pub. Co., 1975.

TOLLEY's capital transfer tax. Annual.

WALTERS, R.
Capital transfer tax. 5ed. Polytech, 1982.

WHEATCROFT, G.S.A. & HEWSON, G.D.
Encyclopaedia of capital taxation. Sweet & Maxwell, 1977. Looseleaf.

WHEATCROFT, G.S.A. & HEWSON, G.D.
Introduction to capital transfer tax. Sweet & Maxwell, 1977.

WILSON, H.
A practical guide to capital transfer tax. Oyez, 1975.

WRIGHT, E.K. & PENNEY, M.O.
Capital transfer tax planning. 4ed. Inst. of Chartered Accountants, 1983.

CAR PARKS

Encyclopaedias

Halsbury's Statutes of England. 3ed. vol. 28.

Encyclopaedia of Forms and Precedents. 4ed. vol. 12.

Texts

BRANDRETH, C.
Parking Law. David & Charles, 1977.

POTTER, D.C.L.
The law relating to garages and car parks. 1939.

CARAVANS AND CAMP SITES

See also Gipsies; Public Health.

Encyclopaedias and periodicals

Statutes in Force. Group: Environment-Caravan Sites.

Halsbury's Laws of England. 4ed. see index vol.

Encyclopaedia of Court Forms in Civil

Proceedings (Atkin), 2ed. vols. 9, 32, 38.

Encyclopaedia of Forms and Precedents. 4ed. vol. 4.

Caravan Industry & Park Operator. 1969–

Local Government Review. 1971–

Texts

ENVIRONMENT, DEPARTMENT OF THE
Mobile home residents: a guide to the provisions of the Caravan Sites Act 1968 and the Mobile Homes Act 1975 etc. HMSO, 1975.

ENVIRONMENT, DEPARTMENT OF THE
Report of the mobile homes review. HMSO, 1977.

GORDON, R.J.F.
Caravans and the law. Shaw, 1978.

RODDIS, R.J.
The law relating to caravans. Shaw, 1960.

CARRIERS/CARRIAGE OF GOODS

See also Aviation; Commercial Law; Railways; Shipping.

Encyclopaedias and periodicals

Statutes in Force. Group: Transport.
Halsbury's Laws of England. 4ed. vols. 2, 5.
Halsbury's Statutes of England. 3ed. see index vol.
The Digest. vol. 8(1).
Encyclopaedia of Court Forms and Civil Proceedings (Atkin). 2ed. vol. 8.

Encyclopaedia of Forms and Precedents. 4ed. vol. 4.

Lloyd's Maritime & Commercial Law Quarterly. 1974–
Lloyd's Maritime Law Newsletter.

Texts

ASTLE, W.
International cargo carriers' liabilities. 1983.

BAMFORD, B.R.
Law of shipping and carriage in South Africa. 2ed. Juta, 1973.

BES, J.
Bulk carriers: a practical guide to the subject for all connected with the shipping business. 2ed. Barker & Howard, 1972.

CARVER, T.
Carriage by sea. 13ed. Stevens, 1982. 2 vols. (British shipping laws vols. 2 & 3).

CLARKE, M.
International carriage of goods by road – C.M.R. Sweet & Maxwell, 1982.

CONRADIE, A.M.
Law of carriage of goods by railway in South Africa. Butterworths (S.A.), 1964.

DONALD, A.E.
C.M.R.: Convention on the Contract for the International Carriage of Goods by Road. Beattie, 1981.

HILL, D.J.
Freight forwarders. Sweet & Maxwell, 1972.

INTERNATIONAL ATOMIC ENERGY AGENCY
Maritime carriage of nuclear fuels. 1973.

IVAMY, E.R.H.
Casebook on carriage by sea. 5ed. Lloyd's, 1983.

JOHNSON, J.C.
Trucking mergers: a regulatory viewpoint. Lexington, 1973 (USA).

LONGLEY, H.L.
Common carriage of cargo. Bender, 1967. Looseleaf (USA).

MANKABADY, S.
Hamburg Rules on Carriage of Goods by Sea. Kluwer, 1978.

MESSENT, A.
C.M.R.: contracts for the international carriage of goods by road. Lloyd's, 1984.

PAYNE, W. & IVAMY, E.R.H.
Carriage of goods by sea. 11ed. Butterworths, 1979.

PUGH, J.
Law relating to heavy goods vehicles. B.Rose, 1980.

RIDLEY, J.
The law of the carriage of goods by land, sea and air. 6ed. Shaw, 1982.

SUMMERSKILL, M.B.
Laytime. 3ed. Sweet & Maxwell, 1982.

TETLEY, W.
Marine cargo claims. 2ed. Sweet & Maxwell, 1978.

TIBERG, H.
The law of demurrage. 3ed. Sweet & Maxwell, 1979.

TRADE, DEPARTMENT OF
Carriage of dangerous goods in ships. HMSO, 1978. Looseleaf.

TRANSPORT, DEPARTMENT OF
European Agreement concerning the International Carriage of Dangerous Goods by Road (ADR). 4ed. HMSO, 1978.

TRANSPORT, DEPARTMENT OF
International Regulations concerning the Carriage of Dangerous Goods by Rail (RID). 7ed. HMSO, 1978.

CENSORSHIP

See also 'D'Notice; Films; Obscenity; Press Law; Theatres.

Encyclopaedias and periodicals

Statutes in Force. Group: Entertainment.
Halsbury's Laws of England. 4ed. vol. 8.
Encyclopaedia of Forms and Precedents. 4ed. vol. 22.

Index on Censorship. 1972–
Kinematograph Weekly.

Texts

ADAMS, M.
Ceensorship: the Irish experience. Scepter Books (Dublin), 1968.

ANDERSON, A.J.
Problems in intellectual freedom and censorship. Bowker, 1974 (USA).

BRODY, S.
Screen violence and censorship. HMSO, 1977 (Home Office research studies).

CARMEN, I.H.
Movies, censorship and the law. Univ. of Michigan P., 1966.

CLOR, H.M.
Censorship and freedom of expression: Essays on obscenity and the law. Rand McNally, 1971 (USA).

DHAVAN, R. & DAVIES, C.
Censorship and obscenity. Martin Robertson, 1978.

GRIFFITHS, R.
Censorship and the arts. Grove Books, 1976.

HOME OFFICE
Report of the Committee on Obscenity and Film Censorship (Williams). HMSO, 1979 (Cmnd. 7772).

HUNNINGS, N.M.
Film censors and the law. Allen & Unwin, 1967.

MACMILLAN, P.R.
Censorship and public morality. Gower Pub. Co., 1983.

MUNRO, C.R.
Television censorship and the law. Gower, 1979.

O'HIGGINS, P.
Censorship in Britain. Nelson, 1972.

PATERSON, J.
The Licensing Acts. Butterworths. Annual.

ROBERTSON, G.
Obscenity: an account of censorship laws and their enforcement in England and Wales. Weidenfeld & Nicolson, 1979.

SPIGELMAN, J.J.
Secrecy: political censorship in Australia. Angus & Robertson, 1972.

TRIBE, D.H.
Questions of censorship. Allen & Unwin, 1974.

VAN DER VYVER, J.D.
The South African law of censorship. Butterworths (S.Africa), 1978.

CERTIORARI

See also Habeas Corpus; Mandamus; Prerogative Orders; Prohibition.

Encyclopaedias

Statutes in Force. Group: Courts:Supreme Court, England & Wales.
Halsbury's Laws of England. 4ed. see index vol.
Halsbury's Statutes of England. 3ed. see index vol.
Encyclopaedia of Court Forms in Civil Procedings (Atkin). 2ed. vol. 14.

Texts

BOOTE, R.
Solicitor's practice in the High Court of Chancery ....(with) the method of proceeding on Certiorari Bills etc. 6ed. 1791.

HARRIS, G.E.
A treatise on the law of certiorari at common law and under the statutes. Lawyer's Co-operative, 1893 (USA).

HENDERSON, E.G.
Foundations of English administrative law: certiorari and mandamus in the seventeenth century. Kelley, 1978 (USA).

SUPREME Court practice 1985. Sweet & Maxwell, 1984. 2 vols.

CHANCERY PRACTICE

See also Equity.

Encyclopaedias

Halsbury's Laws of England. 3ed. vol. 30. 4 ed. vol. 10.
Encyclopaedia of Court Forms in Civil Proceedings (Atkin). 2ed. see index vol.
Encyclopaedia of Forms and Precedents. 4ed. vol. 2.

Texts

BLACKFORD, R. & JAQUE, C.
Chancery practice handbook. Oyez Longman, 1983.

CHANCERY MASTERS'
Practice forms. 2ed. 1972.

CHANCERY OF LANCASTER
Rules revised to 1961. 1961.

DANIELL, E.R.
Forms and precedents in Chancery. 7ed. Stevens, 1932.

DANIELL, E.R.
Practice of the High Court of Chancery. 8ed. Stevens, 1914.

HEWARD, E.
Chancery practice. Butterworths, 1983.

LORD CHANCELLOR'S DEPARTMENT
Report of the Review Body on the Chancery Division of the High Court (Oliver). HMSO 1981 (Cmnd. 8205).

SETON, H.W.
Forms of decrees, judgements and orders in equity. 7ed. Stevens, 1912. 3 vols.

SUPREME Court practice 1985. Sweet & Maxwell, 1984. 2 vols.

CHANNEL ISLANDS

See also Isle of Man.

Encyclopaedias

Statutes in Force. Group: Constitutional Law- Isle of Man and Channel Islands.
Halsbury's Laws of England, see index vols.
Halsbury's Statutes of England. 3ed. see index vol.
Encyclopaedia of Court Forms in Civil Proceedings (Atkin). 2ed. vols. 5, 35.
Encyclopaedia of Forms and Precedents. 4ed. vol. 15.

Texts

BARNETT, A.J.
The constitution of Sark. Guernsey P., 1977.

DUNCAN, J.
The history of Guernsey; with occasional notices of Jersey, Alderney and Sark. Longman, 1841.

EHMANN, D. & MARSHALL, M.
The constitution of Guernsey. Toucan P., 1976.

HOME OFFICE
Relationships between the United Kingdom and the Channel Islands and Isle of Man. HMSO, 1973.

JEREMIE, P.
An essay on the laws of real property in Guernsey. Redstone, 1841.

KEETON, G.W. & LLOYD, D.
"The Channel Islands" in: The United Kingdom: the development of its laws and constitutions. Stevens, 1955.

LE GEYT, P.
Privileges loix et coutumes de l'isle de Jersey. J.T.Bigwood, 1953.

LE GRAS, A.J.
The laws, customs and privileges, and their administration in the island of Jersey; with notices of Guernsey. Longman, 1839.

LE GROS, C.S.
Traite du droit coutumier de l'ile de Jersey. Les Chroniques de Jersey, 1943.

LE HERISSIER, R.G.
The development of the government of Jersey, 1771–1972. States of Jersey, 1972.

LE PATOUREL, J.H.
The medieval administration of the Channel Islands, 1199–1399. Oxford U.P., 1932.

LE QUESNE, C.
A constitutional history of Jersey. Longman, 1856.

LOVERIDGE, Sir J.
The constitution and law of Guernsey. Guille-Alles Lib., 1975.

POINGDESTRE, J.
Les lois et coutumes de l'isle de Jersey. J.T.Bigwood, 1928.

SOLLY, M.
Jersey: a low-tax area. Tolley, 1982.

TAXATION in the Channel Islands and the Isle of Man. Tolley. Annual.

CHARITIES

See also Cy-Pres Doctrine; Equity; Law Officers; Mortmain; Trusts and Trustees.

Encyclopaedias and periodicals

Statutes in Force. Group: Charities.
Halsbury's Laws of England. 4ed. vol. 5.
Halsbury's Statutes of England. 3ed. vol. 3.
Encyclopaedia of Court Forms in Civil Proceedings (Atkin). 2ed. vol. 9.

Encyclopaedia of Forms and Precedents. 4ed. vol. 4.

Charities Digest. Annual.

Texts

BRADSHAW, F.M.
The law of charitable trusts. Butterworths (Australia), 1982.

CHESTERMAN, M.R.
Charities, trusts and social welfare. Weidenfeld & N., 1979.

CRACKNELL, D.G.
Law relating to charities. 2ed. Oyez Longman, 1983.

DELANY, V.T.H.
Law relating to charities in Ireland. rev. ed. Thom, 1961.

FISCH, E.L., FREED, D.J. & SCHACHTER, E.R.
Charities and charitable foundations. Univ. of London, 1974.

FUTURE of voluntary organizations: report of the Wolfenden Committee. Croom Helm, 1977.

GOODMAN, Lord
Charity law and voluntary organisations: report of the committee. Bedford Square P., 1976.

HILL, C.P.A.
A guide for charity trustees. 2ed. Faber, 1974.

HOPKINS, B.R.
Charitable giving and tax exempt organizations: impact of the 1981 Tax Act. Wiley, 1982.

JONES, G.
History of the law of charity 1532–1827. Cambridge U.P., 1969.

KEETON, G.W. & SHERIDAN, L.A.
Modern law of charities. 3ed. Univ. College Cardiff, 1983.

LAW and practice relating to charitable trusts: report (Nathan). HMSO, 1952 (Cmd. 8710).

LONGLEY, A.R.
Charity trustee's guide. 2ed. Bedford Sq. P., 1982.

NIGHTINGALE, B.
Charities. A.Lane, 1973.

NORTON, M.
Covenants: a guide to the tax advantages of giving for charities. Directory of Social Change, 1980.

PHILLIPS, A. & SMITH, K.
Charitable status: a practical handbook. 2ed. Inter-Action Imprint, 1982.

PICARDA, H.
The law and practice relating to charities. Butterworths, 1977.

PRESCOTT, D.J. and others
The administration of charities. ICSA Pub., 1985.

TUDOR, O.D.
Law of charities. 7ed. Sweet & Maxwell, 1984.

TYSSEN, A.D.
The law of charitable bequests. 2ed. Clowes, 1921.

WITHERS, A.H.
Law of mixed charities. Solicitors' Law Stat. Soc., 1926.

CHARTER PARTIES

See also C.I.F. and F.O.B. Contracts; Carriers/Carriage of Goods; Commercial Law; Laytime; Shipping.

Encyclopaedias and periodicals

Statutes in Force. Group: Shipping.
Halsbury's Laws of England. 4ed. see index vol.
Halsbury's Statutes of England. 3ed. vol. 32.
Encyclopaedia of Court Forms in Civil Proceedings (Atkin). 2ed. vol. 8.

Encyclopaedia of Forms and Precedents. 4ed. vol. 21.

Lloyd's Maritime & Commercial Law Quarterly. 1974–

Lloyd's Maritime Law Newsletter. 1979–

Texts

COLE, S.D.
Law of charters and bills of lading. Pitman, 1925.

CUFLEY, C.F.H.
Ocean freights and chartering. Crosby Lockwood, 1964.

GORTON, L.
Hybrid charter agreements. Lloyd's, 1984.

GRAM, P.
Chartering documents. Lloyd's, 1982.

IHRE, R., GORTON, L. & SANDEVARN, A.
Shipbroking and chartering practice. 2ed. Lloyd's, 1984.

INSTITUTE OF CHARTERED SHIPBROKERS
Shipbrokers manual. Vol. 1. Lloyd's, 1983.

POOR, W.
American law of charterparties and ocean bills of lading. Bender. Looseleaf.

SCRUTTON, T.W.
Charterparties. 19ed. Sweet & Maxwell, 1984.

WARING,
Charterparties. Juta, 1983.

WILFORD, M., COGHLIN, T. & HEALY, N.J.
Time charters. 2ed. Lloyd's, 1982.

CHILD ABUSE

See also Domestic Violence.

Periodicals

Child Abuse and Neglect: the International Journal. 1977–
Criminal Law Review. 1954–
Family Law. 1971–

Legal Action (formerly L.A.G. Bulletin). 1973–
The Magistrate. 1922–

Texts

BORLAND, M.
Violence in the family. Manchester U.P., 1976.

BOURNE, R. & NEWBERGER, E.H.
Critical perspectives on child abuse. Lexington Books, 1979 (USA).

COUNCIL OF EUROPE
Causes and prevention of child abuse. 1979.

CREIGHTON, S.
Trends in child abuse. NSPCC, 1984.

EBELING, N.B. & HILL, D.A. (eds.)
Child abuse: intervention and treatment. Publishing Sciences Group, 1975.

FALLER, K.
Social work with abused and neglected children. Collier-Macmillan, 1982.

FRANKLIN, A.W. (ed.)
Challenge of child abuse. Academic Press, 1977.

FRANKLIN, A.W. (ed.)
Concerning child abuse. Academic Press, 1974.

GIOVANNONO, J.M.
Defining child abuse. Collier-Macmillan, 1980.

HALL, J.G. & MITCHELL, B.H.
Child abuse: procedure and evidence in juvenile courts. B.Rose, 1978.

HALLETT, C. & STEVENSON, O.
Child abuse. Allen & Unwin, 1980.

HEALTH & SOCIAL SECURITY, DEPARTMENT OF
Child abuse reports: a study of inquiry, 1973–81. HMSO, 1982.

HEALTH & SOCIAL SECURITY, DEPARTMENT OF
Maria Colwell: report of the inquiry into the care and supervision provided in relation to Maria Colwell (Field-Fisher). HMSO, 1974.

HELFER, R.E. & KEMPE, C.
Battered child. 2ed. Chicago U.P., 1973.

HOUSE OF COMMONS. SELECT COMMITTEE ON VIOLENCE IN THE FAMILY
Report 1: Violence to children. HMSO, 1977. 3 vols.

JOBLING, M.
The abused child: an annotated bibliography. National Children's Bureau, 1976.

KORBIN, J.E.
Child abuse and neglect. Univ. of California P., 1982.

OATES, R.K.
Child abuse: a community concern. Butterworths (Australia), 1982.

RENVOIZE, J.
Children in danger: causes and prevention of baby battering. Routledge, 1975.

SMITH, S.M.
The battered child syndrome. Butterworths, 1975.

SUSSMAN, A. & COHEN, S.J.
Reporting child abuse and neglect: guidelines for legislation. Ballinger:Wiley, 1975.

VAN STOLK, M.
Battered child in Canada. McClelland, 1972.

WASZ-HOCKERT, O.
Seminar on children at risk. Manger P., 1979.

WELLS, D.P.
Child abuse: an annotated bibliography. Scarecrow P., 1980 (USA).

CHILDREN AND YOUNG PERSONS

See also Adoption; Family Law; Legitimacy and Illegitimacy.

Encyclopaedias and periodicals

Statutes in Force. Groups: Children and Young Persons; Family Law.
Halsbury's Laws of England. 4ed. vol. 21.
Halsbury's Statutes of England. 3ed. see index vol.
Encyclopaedia of Court Forms in Civil Proceedings (Atkin). 2ed. see index vol.
Encyclopaedia of Forms & Precedents. 4ed. vol. 10.

Family Law. 1971–
Family Law Reports. 1980–

Texts

ACKLAND, J.W.d
Girls in care: case study of residential treatment. Gower Pub. Co., 1982.

ALLISON, C.E.
Care proceedings. B.Rose, 1979.

ASQUITH, S.
Children and justice: decision making in children's hearings and juvenile courts. Edinburgh U.P., 1983.

BAXTER, I.F.G. & EBERTS, M.A.
Child and the courts. Carswell, 1978 (Canada).

BERLINS, M.A & WANSELL, G.
Caught in the act: children, society and the law. Penguin, 1974.

BEVAN, H.K.
Child protection and the law. Univ. of Hull, 1970.

BEVAN, H.K.
The law relating to children. 2ed. Butterworths, 1984.

BEVAN, H.K. & PARRY, M.L.
The Children Act 1975. Butterworths, 1980.

CARE OF CHILDREN COMMITTEE
Training in child care (Curtis). HMSO, 1946 (Cmd. 6760, 6922).

CARLEBACH, J.
Caring for children in trouble. Routledge & Kegan Paul, 1970.

CARLEN, P.
Magistrates' justice. Martin Robertson, 1976.

CLARKE HALL, W. & MORRISON, A.C.L.
Law relating to children and young persons. 9ed. Butterworths, 1977 supp. 1981.

COMMONWEALTH SECRETARIAT
Hague Convention on the Civil Aspects of International Child Abduction. 1981.

DINGWALL, R.
Protection of children: state intervention and family law. Blackwell, 1983.

DINGWALL, R. & EEKELAAR, J.
Care proceedings: practical guide for social workers, health visitors and others. Blackwell, 1982.

FELDMAN, L.
Care proceedings. 2ed. Oyez, 1984.

FRASER, P.
A treatise on the law of Scotland relative to parent and child and guardian and ward. 3ed. 1906.

FREEMAN, M.D.A.
The Child Care and Foster Children Acts 1980. Sweet & Maxwell, 1980.

FREEMAN, M.D.A.
Children Act, 1975: text with concise commentary. Sweet & Maxwell, 1976.

CHILDREN AND YOUNG PERSONS

FREEMAN, M.D.A.
Rights of children. New ed. F.Pinter, 1983.

GERLIS, S.
Summary matrimonial and guardianship orders. 6ed. Oyez, 1981.

GWYNNE, D. & BROWN, J.
Children under supervision: intermediate treatment requirements. Manchester Social Services Dept., 1974.

HARLAND, D.J.
The law of minors in relation to contracts and property. Butterworths (Australia), 1974.

HEALTH AND SOCIAL SECURITY, DEPARTMENT OF
Access to children in care: code of practice. HMSO, 1983.

HEALTH & SOCIAL SECURITY, DEPARTMENT OF
Children in care in England & Wales. HMSO. Annual.

HEALTH & SOCIAL SECURITY, DEPARTMENT OF
Social workers and solicitors in child care cases. HMSO, 1981.

HEALTH AND SOCIAL SECURITY FOR NORTHERN IRELAND, DEPARTMENT OF
Legislation and services for children and young persons in Northern Ireland: report of the Children and Young Persons Review Group (Black). HMSO, 1979.

HEYWOOD, J.S.
Children in care. 3ed. Routledge & Kegan Paul, 1977.

HOGGETT, B.
Parents and children. 2ed. Sweet & Maxwell, 1981.

HOLDEN, D.A.
Child legislation. Butterworths, 1970.

HOME OFFICE
Report of the Committee on Children and Young Persons (Ingelby). HMSO, 1960 (Cmnd. 1191).

HOWARD LEAGUE FOR PENAL REFORM
Between probation and custody: young adult offenders. 1975.

INSTITUTE FOR STUDY & TREATMENT OF DELINQUENCY
Children still in trouble? 1973.

KING, L. & WILSON, J.
Children and the law. Butterworths (Canada), 1978.

LAW COMMISSION & SCOTTISH LAW COMMISSION
Custody of children: jurisdiction and enforcement within the U.K. 1976 (Working Paper No.68; Memorandum No.23).

LEEDING, A.E.
Child care manual for social workers. 4ed. Butterworths, 1980 supp. 1982.

LEVY, A.
Custody and access to children. Oyez, 1983.

LORD CHANCELLOR'S OFFICE
Report of the Committee on the Age of Majority (Latey). HMSO, 1967 (Cmnd. 3342).

LOWE, N.V. & WHITE, R.A.H.
Wards of court. Butterworths, 1979.

MARTIN, F.M.
Children out of court. Scottish Academic Press, 1981.

MAYS, J.B. (ed.)
Juvenile delinquency, the family and the social group. Longman, 1972.

MAYS, J.B. (ed.)
The social treatment of young offenders. Longman, 1975.

MIND
Act on Trial: non-implementation of the Children and Young Persons Act. 1975.

MORRIS, A.
Justice for children. Macmillan, 1980.

MUMFORD, G.F. & SELWOOD, T.J.
Guide to the Children Act 1975. Shaw, 1976.

NATIONAL ASSOCIATION FOR THE CARE AND RESETTLEMENT OF OFFENDERS
Children and young persons in custody. B.Rose, 1977.

NATIONAL COUNCIL FOR CIVIL LIBERTIES
Children's Ombudsman. 1975.

NATIONAL COUNCIL FOR CIVIL LIBERTIES
Rights of children: report of the First National Conference on children's rights. 1972.

NATIONAL COUNCIL FOR ONE-PARENT FAMILIES
Tax law and child care: the case for reform. 1980.

PARSCOE, P.
Juvenile justice in Britain and the United States. Routledge, 1978.

PRIESTLEY, P. and others
Justice for juveniles: the 1969 Children and Young Persons Act – a case for reform? Routledge & Kegan Paul, 1977.

RAE, M.
First rights: guide to legal rights for young people. 2ed. NCCL, 1981.

RUSHFORTH, M.
Committal to residential care: a case study in juvenile justice. HMSO, 1978 (Scottish Office social research studies).

SLOMNICKA, B.I.
Law of child care. Macdonald & Evans, 1982.

SMITH, R.J.
Children and the courts. Sweet & Maxwell, 1979.

STONE, O.
The child's voice in a court of law. Butterworths, 1983.

SUNDAY TIMES
Thalidomide children and the law: a report by the Sunday Times. 1974.

TAYLOR, L.
In whose best interests? Unjust treatment of children in courts and institutions. Cobden Trust, 1980.

TERRY, J.
A guide to the Children Act 1975 (as amended). 2ed. Sweet & Maxwell, 1979.

WALTER, J.A.
Sent away: study of young offenders in court. Saxon House, 1978.

WASZ-HOCKERT, O.
Seminar on children at risk. Karger, 1979.

WATSON, J.A.F.
The child and the magistrate. Allen & Unwin, 1965.

WHITE, P.
Children in tax planning. Oyez, 1980.

WILKINSON, G.S.
Summary matrimonial and guardianship orders. 5ed. Oyez, 1977.

WILKINSON, M.
Children and divorce. Blackwell, 1981.

CHINA

Texts

BAUW, F.de & WIT, B.de
China trade law. Kluwer, 1983.

BLAUSTEIN, A.P.
Fundamental legal documents of communist China, Rothman, 1962.

BUTLER, W.E. (ed.)
The legal system of the Chinese Soviet Republic, 1931–34. Transnational, 1983 (USA).

CRIMINAL code of the People's Republic of China. Trans. from Chinese. Sweet & Maxwell, 1982.

LENG, S.C. & CHIU, H.
Justice in Communist China: a survey of the judicial system of the Chinese People's Republic. Oceana, 1967.

SIT, J.F.
Commercial laws and business regulations of the People's Republic of China. Macmillan, 1983.

CHIVALRY, COURT OF

See also History.

Encyclopaedias

Halsbury's Laws of England. 4ed. see index vol.
Encyclopaedia of Court Forms in Civil Proceedings (Atkin). 2ed. vol. 31.

Texts

SQUIBB, G.D
High Court of Chivalry: a study of the civil law in England. Oxford U.P., 1959.

CIVIL LAW

See also Roman Law; Scotland; South Africa.

Encyclopaedias

Halsbury's Laws of England. 4ed. see index vol.
Encyclopaedia of Court Forms in Civil Proceedings (Atkin). 3ed. vol. 31.

Texts

BOWYER, G.
Commentaries on the modern civil law. Stevens & Norton, 1848.

FEENSTRA, R. & WAAL, C.J.D.
Seventeenth century Leyden law professors and their influence on the development of civil law: a study of Bronchorst, Vinnius and Voet. North-Holland, 1975.

JENKS, E.
English civil law. 4ed. Butterworths, 1947. 2 vols.

MERRYMAN, J.H.
The civil law tradition: an introduction to the legal system of Western Europe and Latin America. Stanford U.P., 1969.

RYAN, K.W.
An introduction to the civil law. Law Book Co., 1962.

SPETZ, S.N.
Legal jams: aspects of Canadian civil law. Pitman, 1972.

WATSON, A.
Legal transplants: an approach to comparative law. Virginia U.P., 1974.

WATSON, A.
The making of the civil law. Harvard U.P., 1981.

YIANNOPOULOS, A.
Civil law in the modern world. Louisiana U.P., 1965.

CIVIL RIGHTS AND LIBERTIES

See also Adminstration of Justice; Human Rights.

Encyclopaedias and periodicals

Statutes in Force. Group: Rights of the Subject.

Cambridge Law Journal. 1921–
Human Rights Review. 1976–
Law Quarterly Review. 1885–

Legal Action (formerly L.A.G. Bulletin). 1973–
Modern Law Review. 1937–
New Law Journal. 1965–
Rights (formerly Civil Liberty). 1976–

Texts

ABERNATHY, M.G.
Civil liberties under the constitution: cases and materials on civil rights. 3ed. West, 1980 (USA).

ABRAHAM, H.J.
Freedom and the court: civil rights and liberties in the United States. 4ed. Oxford U.P.(New York), 1982.

ANDERSON, Sir N.
Liberty, law and justice. Stevens, 1978 (Hamlyn lectures).

BAILEY, S.H., HARRIS, D. & JONES, B.
Civil liberties: cases and materials. Butterworths, 1980.

BOLTON, P.M.
Civil rights in Canada. Self-Counsel, 1972.

BRIDGE, J.W. (ed.)
Fundamental rights: a volume of essays to commemmorate the 50th anniversay of the founding of the law school in Exeter. Sweet & Maxwell, 1973.

BRITISH INSTITUTE OF HUMAN RIGHTS
Report of a symposium on guarantees for human rights in the U.K. 1976.

BROOKES, E.M. & MACCAULAY, J.B.
Civil liberty in South Africa. Greenwood Press, 1973.

CAMPBELL, C.M.
Do we need a Bill of Rights? M.T.Smith, 1980.

COMMISSION OF THE EUROPEAN COMMUNITIES
The protection of fundamental rights in the European community. 1976.

COOTE, A. & GRANT, L.
Civil liberty: the N.C.C.L. guide. 2ed. Penguin, 1973.

COX, R.
Civil liberties in Britain. Penguin, 1975.

DENNING, A.
Freedom under the law. Stevens, 1968 (Hamlyn lecture No 1).

DWORKIN, R.
Taking rights seriously. Duckworth, 1974.

EWING, K.D. & FINNIE, W.
Civil liberties in Scotland: cases and materials. Green, 1982.

FINNIS, J.M.
Natural law and natural rights. Oxford U.P., 1980.

FLICK, G.
Civil liberties in Australia. Law Book Co., 1982.

FREEMAN, M.D.A.
Rights of children. New ed. F.Pinter, 1983.

GORDON, P.
Your rights: Scottish Council for Civil Liberties guide to civil liberties in Scotland. SCCL, 1980.

HEWITT, P.
Abuse of power: civil liberties in the United Kingdom. Martin Robertson, 1981.

HOME OFFICE
Legislation on human rights with particular reference to the European conventions: a discussions document. HMSO, 1976.

KADISH, M.R. & KADISH, S.R.
Discretion to disobey. Stanford U.P., 1973 (USA).

KELLY, J.M.
Fundamental rights in the Irish law and constitution. 2ed. Oceana, 1968.

KRAMER, D.C.
Comparative civil rights and liberties. Univ. Press of America, 1983.

McBRIDE, T.
New Zealand handbook of civil liberties. Price Milburn, 1973.

MacCORMICK, N.
Civil liberties and the law. Heriot-Watt Univ. P., 1977.

MacCORMICK, N.
Legal right and social democracy: essays in legal and political philosophy. Oxford U.P., 1982.

MACDERMOTT, J.C.
Protection from power under English law. Stevens, 1957.

MARTIN, R.
Personal freedom and the law in Tanzania. Oxford U.P., 1973.

MATHEWS, A.S.
Law, order and liberty in South Africa. California U.P., 1972

MEHTA, R.S.
Minority rights and obligations. Canada Res. Bur., 1973.

NARDECCHIA, N.
Citizens rights working paper. NCCL, 1970.

NATIONAL CONSUMER COUNCIL
Patients' rights: a guide for NHS patients and doctors. HMSO, 1983.

O'HIGGINS, P.
Cases and materials on civil liberties. Sweet & Maxwell, 1980.

PALLISTER, A.
Magna Carta: the heritage of liberty.
Oxford U.P., 1971.

POLYVIOU, P.
Equal protection of the laws. Duckworth, 1980.

POLYVIOU, P.
Search and seizure. Duckworth, 1982.

RAE, M.
First rights: guide to legal rights for young people. 2ed. NCCL, 1981.

SCARMAN, Sir L.
English law: the new dimension. Stevens, 1974 (Hamlyn lecture).

SCHMEISER, D.A.
Civil liberties in Canada. Oxford U.P., 1964.

STACEY, F.
A new Bill of Rights for Britain. David & Charles, 1973.

STEVENS, I.N. & YARDLEY, D.C.M.
Protection of liberty. Blackwell, 1982.

STONE, C.D.
Should trees have standing? Towards legal rights for natural objects.
W.Kaufmann:W.H.Freeman, 1981 (USA).

STONE, R.
Entry, search and seizure. Sweet & Maxwell, 1984.

STONE, V.J. (ed.)
Civil liberties and civil rights: David C. Baun Memorial Lectures. Univ. of Illinois P., 1978 (USA). .

STRACHAN, B.
Natural justice – principle & practice. Shaw, 1977.

STREET, H.
Freedom, the individual and the law. 3ed. Penguin, 1982.

TRIPATHI, P.K.
Some insights into fundamental rights. Tripathi, 1972 (India).

VIEIRA, N.
Civil rights in a nutshell. West, 1978 (USA).

YBEMA, S.B.
Constitutionalism and ciivil liberties. Leiden, 1973.

ZANDER, M.
A Bill of Rights? 2ed. B.Rose, 1980.

CIVIL SERVICE

See also Administrative Law; Constitutional Law; Government Departments.

Encyclopaedias and periodicals

Statutes in Force. Groups: Government Departments and Public Offices; Public Service Pensions.
Halsbury's Laws of England. 4ed. vol. 8.
Halsbury's Statutes of England. 3ed. see index vol.
Encyclopaedia of Court Forms in Civil Proceedings (Atkin) 2ed. vol. 14.

Cambridge Law Journal. 1921–
Law Quarterly Review. 1885–
Local Government Review. 1971–
Modern Law Review. 1937–
New Law Journal. 1965–
Public Administration. 1923–
Public Affairss. 1965–
Public Law. 1956–

Texts

AYLMER, G.E.
State's servants: the civil service of the English Repubic. 1649–1660. Routledge, 1973.

CAMPBELL, G.A.
The civil service in Britain. 2ed. Duckworth, 1965.

CARSWELL, J.
The civil servant and his world. Gollancz, 1966.

CHAPMAN, R.A.
Higher civil service in Britain. Constable, 1970.

CIVIL SERVICE DEPARTMENT
Disclosure of offical information: report on overseas practice. HMSO, 1979.

COHEN, E.
The growth of the British civil service, 1780–1939. F.Cass, 1965.

COMMITTEE ON POLITICAL
ACTIVITIES OF CIVIL SERVANTS
Report (Armitage). HMSO, 1977 (Cmnd.
7057).

COMMITTEE ON THE POLITICAL
ACTIVITY OF CIVIL SERVANTS
Report (Masterman). HMSO, 1949 (Cmd.
7718).

DALE, H.E.
The higher civil service of Great Britain.
Oxford U.P., 1941.

EMDEN, C.S.
The civil servant in the law and the
constitution. Stevens, 1923.

KIAPI, A.
Civil service laws in East Africa. H.Zell,
1977.

MUSTOE, N.E.
Law and organisation of the British civil
service. Pitman, 1932.

ROBSON, W.A.
The civil service in Britain and France.
1956 repr. Greenwood, 1975.

SAMPSON, A.
Changing anatomy of Britain. Hodder,
1982.

THOMAS, H.
Crisis in the civil service. Blond, 1968.

TREASURY
Report of the Committee on the civil
service, 1966–68 (Fulton). HMSO, 1968
(Cmnd. 3638).

CLUBS

See also Betting and Gaming; Friendly Societies.

Encyclopaedias

Statutes in Force. Groups: Betting, Gaming
and Lotteries; Friendly and Other
Societies.
Halsbury's Laws of England. 4ed. vol. 6.

Halsbury's Statutes of England. 3ed. vol.
17.
Encyclopaedia of Court Forms in Civil
Proceedings (Atkin). 2ed. vol. 9.

Texts

DALY, D.
Club law and law of unregistered Friendly
Societies. 7ed. Butterworths, 1979.

FIELD, D.
Practical club law. Sweet & Maxwell, 1979.

JOSLING, J.F. & ALEXANDER, L.
The law of clubs. 5ed. Oyez, 1984.

McDONALD, B.J.
Law of registered clubs, New South Wales.
2ed. Butterworths (Australia), 1980.

PATERSON, J.
Licensing Acts. Butterworths. Annual.

CODIFICATION OF LAW

Texts

AMOS, S.
An English code: its difficulties and the
modes of overcoming them. 1873.

BENTHAM, J.
Constitutional code. 1830.

CHLOROS, A.G.
Codification in a mixed jurisdiction. North-
Holland, 1977.

DHOKALIA, R.P.
The codification of public international law.
Manchester Univ. P., 1971.

HAMMOND, A.
The criminal code. Eyre & Strahon, 1825–
29. 7 vols.

LAW COMMISSION
First programme of the Law Commission.
HMSO, 1965 (Law Com.No.1).

LAW COMMISSION
Second programme of Law Reform.
HMSO, 1968 (Law Com. No.14)

For details of the Law Commission's proposals regarding codifiction see under the appropriate subject.

COHABITATION

See also Family Law; Marriage

Texts

BOTTOMLEY, A.
The cohabitation handbook. 2ed. Pluto P., 1984.

CLAYTON, P.
Cohabitation guide. Wildy, 1981.

COUNCIL OF EUROPE
Legal problems concerning unmarried couples. HMSO, 1983.

EEKELAAR, J.
Marriage and cohabitation in contemporary society. Butterworths, 1980.

FREEMAN, M.D.A. & LYON, C.M.
Cohabitation without marriage. Gower Pub. Co., 1983.

HOLLAND, W.
Unmarried couples: legal aspects. Carswell, 1982.

KENNY, P. (ed.)
Cohabitation in land law. Sweet & Maxwell, 1984 (Law file).

LISTER, R.
As man and wife? A study of the cohabitation rule. CPAG, 1973.

PARKER, S.
Cohabitees. Rose, 1981.

PARRY, M.
Cohabitation. Sweet & Maxwell, 1981.

SUPPLEMENTARY BENEFITS COMMISSION
Cohabitation. 2ed. HMSO, 1976.

COLLISIONS AT SEA

See also Shipping

Encyclopaedias and periodicals

Statutes in Force. Group: Shipping.
Halsbury's Laws of England. 3ed. vol. 35. 4ed. vol. 1.
Halsbury's Statutes of England. 3ed. vol. 31.
Encyclopaedia of Court Forms in Civil Proceedings (Atkin). 4ed. vol. 3.
Lloyd's Law Reports. 1919–
Lloyd's Maritime & Commercial Law Quarterly. 1974–
Lloyd's Maritime Law Newsletter. 1979–

Texts

BUZEK, F.J.
Diagrams of collisions cases. Lloyd's, 1984.

HOLDERT, H.M.C. & BUZEK, F.J.
Collision cases: judgments and diagrams. Lloyd's, 1984.

MANKABADY, S.
Collision at sea: a guide to legal consequences. North-Holland, 1978.

MARSDEN, R.G.
Law relating to collisions at sea. 11ed. Stevens, 1961 supp. 1973 (12ed. in prep.).

PINEUS, K. & ROHREKE, H.G.
Limited liability in collision cases. Lloyd's, 1984.

STURT, R.F.B.
Collision regulations. 2ed. Lloyd's, 1984.

COMMERCIAL CREDITS

See also Banks and Banking.

Encyclopaedias and periodicals

Statutes in Force. Group: Banking and Currency.

Banker, The. 1926–
Bankers' Magazine. 1844–
Bankers' Almanac and Year Book. Annual.

Texts

DAVIS, A.G.
The law relating to banker's commercial letters of credit. Butterworths, 1954.

ELLINGER, E.P.
Documentary letters of credit. Singapore U.P., 1973.

GUTTERIDGE, H.C. & MEGRAH, M.
The law of bankers' commercial credits. 6ed. Europa, 1979.

MITRA, B.C.
The law relating to bankers' letters of credits. Eastern P., 1964 (India).

HARFIELD, H.
Letters of credit. A.L.I./A.B.A., 1980.

ROOY, F.P.de
Documentary credits. Kluwer, 1983.

VENTRIS, F.M.
Bankers' documentary credits. 2ed. Lloyd's, 1984.

COMMERCIAL LAW

See also Carriers/Carriage of Goods; Contract; Export Trade; Sale of Goods.

Encyclopaedias and periodicals

Statutes in Force. Group: Trade.
Encyclopaedia of Court Forms in Civil Proceedings (Atkin). 2ed. vol. 9.

Business Law Review. 1980–
Commerce International. 1882–
Commercial Law Reports. 1981–
Commercial Laws of Europe. 1987–
The Company Lawyer. 1980–
Current Legal Problems. 1948–

Eurolaw Commercial Intelligence. 1972–
European Commercial Cases. 1978–
Journal of Business Law. 1957–
Journal of World Trade Law. 1967–
Law Reports of the Commonwealth: Commercial Law Reports. 1985–
Lloyd's Maritime and Commercial Law Quarterly. 1974–
Lloyd's Maritime Law Newsletter. 1979–

Texts

ADESANYA, M.O. & OLOYEDE, E.O.
Business law in Nigeria. Holmes, 1972.

AFFLEY, G.
Business law. Macdonald & Evans, 1982.

ANGER, W.K., ANDER, H.D. & HUME, F.R.
Summary of Canadian commercial law. rev. ed. Pitman, 1974.

ARDRA, A.
Practical business law. Macdonald & Evans, 1983.

BAILEY, H.J.
Encyclopaedia of commercial law. Warren, Gorham & Lamont, 1964. Looseleaf (USA).

BALL, B. & ROSE, F.
Principles of business law. Sweet & Maxwell, 1979.

BATES, J. & HALLY, D.
The financing of small business. 3ed. Sweet & Maxwell, 1982.

COMMERCIAL LAW

BAUW, F.de & WIT, B.de
China trade law. Kluwer, 1983.

BAXT, R. and others
An introduction to the securities industry codes. Butterworths (Australia), 1982.

BISCOE, P.M.
Credit factoring. Butterworths, 1975.

BLACKSHAW, I.
Doing business in Spain. Oyez, 1980.

BORRIE, G.J.
Commercial law. 5ed. Butterworths, 1980.

BORRIE, G.J. & GREIG, D.W.
Commercial law. 2ed. Butterworths (Australia), 1978.

BOULTON, A.H.
The making of business contracts. Sweet & Maxwell, 1972.

BRADBURY, P.L.
Law relating to business. Butterworths, 1971.

BRADBURY, P.L. & DOBSON, A.P.
Cases and statutes on commercial law. 2ed. Sweet & Maxwell, 1980.

BURN, C.R. & QUAR, J.N.
Commercial law of Scotland. 2ed. Hodge, 1973.

BUSINESS laws of Iraq, 1983. Tr. from Arabic. Graham & Trotman, 1983. 2 vols.

BUSINESS laws of Kuwait, 1983. Tr. from Arabic. Graham & Trotman, 1983. 2 vols.

BUSINESS laws of Saudi Arabia, 1983. Tr. from Arabic. Graham & Trotman, 1983. 2 vols.

BUSINESS laws of the United Arab Emirates. Tr. from Arabic. Graham & Trotman, 1983. 2 vols.

BUSINESS transactions in Germany. Bender. 4 vols. loosleaf.

CHANCE, E.W.
Principles of mercantile law. 22ed. Cassell, 1980.

CHARLESWORTH, J.
Mercantile law. 14ed. Stevens, 1984.

CHESTERMAN, M.
Small businesses. 2ed. Sweet & Maxwell, 1982.

CHRISTIE, R.
Rhodesian commercial law. Juta, 1961.

CLARKSON, K.W.
Business law: texts and cases. 2ed. West, 1984 (USA).

CLAYTON, P.
Law for the small business. 4ed. Kogan Page, 1984.

COLMAN, A.
The practice and procedure of the commercial court. Lloyd's, 1983.

COPER, M.
Freedom of interstate trade. Butterworths (Australia), 1983.

CORLEY, R.N. & HOLMES, E.M.
Fundamentals of business law. 3ed. Prentice-Hall, 1982 (USA).

CORLEY, R.N. and others
Principles of business law. 12ed. Prentice-Hall, 1983 (USA).

COUNCIL OF EUROPE
Practical guide to the recognition and enforcement of foreign judicial division in civil and commercial matters. 1975.

DALE, R.
Anti-dumping law in a liberal trade order. Macmillan, 1980.

DIXON, A.
Introduction to mercantile and commercial law. Heinemann, 1969.

FOWLSTON, B.
Understanding commercial and industrial licensing. Waterlow, 1984.

FRANK, W.F.
Legal aspects of industry and commerce. 6ed. Harrap, 1972.

FRIDMAN, G.H.L.
Studies in Canadian business law. Carswell, 1971.

FRIEDMANN, W.G.
Public and private enterprises in mixed economies. Stevens, 1974.

GARTSIDE, L.
Commerce. Macdonald & Evans, 1977.

GILES, O.C.
Uniform commercial law. Sijthoff, 1970.

GLICK, L.A.
Trading with Saudi Arabia: a guide to the shipping trade, investment and tax laws of Saudi Arabia. Croom Helm, 1980.

GOLDMAN, B. and others
European commercial law. Stevens, 1973.

GOLDRING, J., GOLDWORTHY, P.G. & LEVINE, J.R.
Cases and materials on commercial transactions. Law Book Co., 1978 (Australia). 4 vols.

GOODE, R.M.
Commercial law. A.Lane, 1982.

GOODE, R.M.
Commercial law statutes. Sweet & Maxwell, 1979.

GOW, J.J.
Mercantile and industrial law of Scotland. Green, 1964.

GRAVESON, R.H.
The Uniform Laws on International Sales Act, 1967. Butterworths, 1968.

HAGEN, W.W. & JOHNSTON, G.H.
Digest of business law. Hunt Pub. Co., 1974 (USA).

HARRIS, J.
Your business and the law. Oyez. 1975.

HERMANN, A.H.
Judges, law and businessmen. Kluwer, 1983.

HODGIN, R.W.
Cases and materials on East African mercantile law. Sweet & Maxwell, 1972.

HOOPER, G.
The law of international trade. Sweet & Maxwell, 1970.

HOPKINS, F.N.
Business and law for the shipmaster. 6ed. 1982.

HORN, N. & SCHMITTHOFF, C.M.
Transnational law of international commercial transactions. Vol. 2. Kluwer, 1983.

HOYLE, M.S.W.
Cases and materials on the law of international trade. 2ed. Van Nostrand Reinhold, 1983 (USA).

HUDSON, A.
Dictionary of commercial law.. Butterworths, 1983.

INTERNATIONAL CARGO HANDLING CO-ORDINATION ASSOCIATION
Multilingual glossary of cargo handling terms. 1982.

IVAMY, E.R.H.
Casebook on commercial law. 3ed. Butterworths, 1979 (also with Australian consumer protection supplement).

JEREMY, D. (ed.)
Dictionary of business biography: vol. 1 A-C, Butterworths, 1984.

JOLOWICZ, J.A. & JONES, G.
Judicial protection of fundamental rights under English law: infiltration of equity into English commercial law. Kluwer, 1980.

JUNG, H. & GRESS, J.
Starting business operations in Germany. Kluwer, 1984.

KITAGAWA, Z.
Doing business in Japan. Bender. 9 vols. looseleaf.

KOHLIK, G.
Digest of commercial laws of the world. Oceana, 1966– . 5 vols. Looseleaf (USA).

KOUL, A.K.
Legal framework of UNCTAD in world trade. Sijthoff, 1977.

LANGEN, E.
Transnational commercial law. Sijthoff, 1973.

LEWIS, J.R.
Law for the retailer and distributor. 3ed. Jordan, 1979.

LEWISON, K.
Drafting business leases. Oyez, 1980.

LEYS, W.C.S. & NORTHEY, J.F.
Commercial law in New Zealand. 6ed. Butterworths, 1977.

LILLIE, J.A
Mercantile law of Scotland. 6ed. Green, 1965.

LONG, M.J. & SPARROW, D.T.
Some aspects of family business. Law Society, 1979.

LOWE, R.
Commercial law. 6ed. Sweet & Maxwell, 1983.

MARSH, S.B. & SOULSBUY, J.R.
Business law. 2ed. McGraw-Hill, 1981.

MARSHALL, E.
Scots mercantile law. Green, 1983.

MASON, H.H., PRIDDLE, L.G. & FLETCHER, K.L.
Cases on commercial law. Law Book Co., 1978 (Australia).

COMMERCIAL LAW

MEINERS, R.E.
Legal environment of business. West, 1982 (USA).

MENDELSOHN, M.
Guide to franchising. 3ed. Pergamon, 1982.

MIAN, Q.J. & LERRICK, A.
Saudi business and labour law: its interpretation and application. Graham & Trotman, 1982.

MOON, R.W.
Business mergers and takeover bids. 4ed. Gee & Co. 1971.

MOYE, J.E.
Law of business organization. 2ed. West, 1982 (USA).

MUELLER, R.
Doing business in Germany. 8ed. Macdonald & Evans, 1978.

MURRAY, J.
Commercial law problems and materials. West, 1975 (USA).

OLAWOYIN, G.A. & OLAFARE, A.
Commercial law of Nigeria. Woodhead-Faulkner, 1985.

O'MALLEY, L.
Business law. Sweet & Maxwell, 1982 (Irish law texts).

O'MALLEY, L.
Commercial law. Sweet & Maxwell, 1981 (Irish law texts).

PINHEIRONETO, J.
Doing business n Brazil. Bender. Looseleaf.

POLLARD, D.E.
Law and policy of producers' associations. Oxford U.P., 1984.

PURVER, J.
Business law: text and cases. Harcourt Brace, 1983.

RANKING, D.F.
Ranking, Spicers & Pegler's mercantile law: incorporating partnership law and the law of arbitration and awards. 14ed. Cape, 1975 supp. 1978.

REDMOND, P.W.D.
Mercantile law. 5ed. Macdonald & Evans, 1979.

ROBINSON, J.M.
Comparative survey of securities laws: a review of the securities and related laws of fourteen nations. Kluwer, 1980.

ROSS, J.
Commercial leases. Butterworths, 1980.

RUSTER, B.
Business transaction in Germany. Bender. 4 vols. looseleaf.

SAUNDERS, M.R.
Tax planning for business in Europe. 2ed. Butterworths, 1984.

SCHMITTHOFF, C.M.
Commercial law in changing economic climate. 2ed. Sweet & Maxwell, 1981.

SCHMITTHOFF, C.M.
The export trade: the law and practice of international trade. 7ed. Sweet & Maxwell, 1980.

SCHMITTHOFF, C.M. (ed.)
The sources of the law of international trade, with special reference to East-West trade. Stevens, 1964.

SCHUIT, S.R.
Dutch business law. Kluwer, 1983.

SHEARS, P.
Nigerian business law. Hulton Educational, 1983.

SHERIDAN, L.A.
Rights in security. Macdonald & Evans, 1975.

SINGH, N.
Commercial law of India. Sijthoff, 1975.

SIT, J.F.
Commercial laws and business regulations of the People's Republic of China. Macmillan, 1983.

SLATER, J.A.
Mercantile law. 17ed. Pitman, 1978.

SMITH, K. & KEENAN, D.J.
Essentials of mercantile law. 5ed. Pitman, 1982.

SMITH, L.Y.
Business law: Uniform Commercial Code. 5ed. West Pub. Co. 1982 (USA).

SNOW, R.F.
The impact of EEC law on commercial dealings. College of Law, 1978.

SPIRES, J.J.
Doing business in the United States. Bender, 1978 (USA). 6 vols. looseleaf.

STANBROOK, C.
Dumping: a manual on the E.E.C. anti-dumping law and procedure. European Business Pubns., 1980.

STARR, R. (ed.)
East-West business transactions. Praeger, 1974.

STEVENS, T.M. & BORRIE, G.J.
Mercantile law. 17ed. Butterworths, 1978.

SWEET & MAXWELL
Commercial law statutes. 1979.

TAPERELL, G.G., VERMEESCH, R.B. & HARLAND, D.J.
Trade practices and consumer protection. 3ed. Butterworths (Australia), 1983.

TOLLEY's expansion kit for business. Tolley, 1983.

TOLLEY's survival kit for small business. 2ed. Tolley, 1983.

UNITED NATIONS COMMISSION ON INTERNATIONAL TRADE LAW
UNCITRAL arbitration rules. 1977.

VERCHERE, B.
Business operations in Canada. Tax Management, 1972.

VERMEESCH, R.B. & LINDGREN, K.E.
Business law of Australia. 4ed. Butterworths (Australia), 1983.

VOSKUIL, C.C.A. & WADE, J.A. (eds.)
On the law of international trade. Nijhoff, 1983.

WALLACE, C.D.
Legal control of ther multinational enterprise: national regulatory techniques and the prospects for international controls. Nijhoff, 1982.

WALLACH, F.
Intorduction to European commercial law. Oceana, 1973 (USA).

WOODCOCK, C.
The Guardian guide to running a small business. 3ed. Kogan Page, 1983.

YORSTON, K.
Australian commercial dictionary. 5ed. Law Book Co., 1972.

YORSTON, K. & FORTESCUE, E.E.
Australian mercantile law. 16ed. Law Book Co., 1981.

ZAPHIRIOU, G.A.
European business law. Sweet & Maxwell, 1970.

ZIEGEL, J.S. & FOSTER, W.F.
Aspects of comparative commercial law. Oceana, 1969 (USA).

ZWEIGERT, K. & KROPHOLLER, J.
Sources of international uniform law. vol. 1. Private and commercial law. Sijthoff, 1977.

COMMON LAW

Encyclopaedias and periodicals

Halsbury's Laws of England. 4ed. see index vol.

Cambridge Law Journal. 1921–
Law Quarterly Review. 1885–

Modern Law Review. 1937–
New Law Journal (formerly Law Journal). 1866–

Texts

ARNOLD, M.S. (ed.)
On the laws and customs of England: essays in honour of Samuel E. Thorne. Univ. of N. Carolina P., 1982.

BLACKSTONE, Sir W.
Commentaries on the laws of England. 1ed. 1765–1769; new ed. R.M. Kerr. 1876 repr. Univ. of Chicago P., 1979.

BUCKLAND, W.W., McNAIR, A.D. & LAWSON, F.H.
Roman law and common law: a comparison in outline. 2ed. Cambridge U.P., 1965 repr. 1974.

CALABRESI, G.
Common law for the age of statutes. Harvard U.P., 1982.

DANIELS, W.C.E.
Common law in West Africa. Butterworths (S.Africa), 1964.

FARRAR, J.H.
Introduction to legal method. 2ed. Sweet & Maxwell, 1984.

FIFOOT, C.H.S.
History and sources of the commons law: contract and tort. 1949 repr. Greenwood, 1970.

GRAVESON, R.H.
Status in the common law. Athlone P., 1953.

HALE, M.
History of the common law of England, various eds. 1713–1820 repr. Chicago U.P., 1971.

HOGUE, A.
Origins of the common law. 1966 repr. Archon, 1974.

HOLMES, O.W.
Common law. Macmillan, 1974.

KEETON, G.W.
Norman Conquest and the common law. Benn, 1966.

LLEWELLYN, K.N.
Common law tradition. Little, Brown, 1960 (USA).

MAITLAND, F.W.
Forms of action at common law. 2ed. Cambridge U.P., 1936 repr. 1962.

MILSOM, S.F.C.
Historical foundations of the common law. 2ed. Butterworths, 1981.

OGILVIE, Sir C.
King's government and the common law, 1471–1641. Greenwood P., 1978.

O'SULLIVAN, R.
The spirit of the common law. Fowler Wright, 1965.

PLUCKNETT, T.F.T.
Concise history of common law. 5ed. Butterworths, 1956.

POLLOCK, F.
Expansion of the common law. 1904 repr. Rothman, 1974.

POUND, R.
History and system of the common law. 1939 repr. Hein, 1980.

REINSCH, P.S.
English common law in the early American colonies. 1899 repr. Da Capo, 1970.

SIMPSON, A.W.B.
Cannibalism in the common law. Univ. of Chicago P., 1984.

STEPHEN, H.J.
Commentaries on the laws of England. 21ed. Butterworths, 1950. 4 vols.

VAN CAENEGEM, R.C.
Birth of the English common law. Cambridge U.P., 1973.

COMMONS AND ENCLOSURES

See also Footpaths; National Parks; Rights of Way.

Encyclopaedias and periodicals

Statutes in Force. Group: Commons, England and Wales.
Halsbury's Laws of England. 4ed. vol. 6.
Halsbury's Statutes of England. 3ed. vol. 3.
The Digest. vol. 11
Encyclopaedia of Court Forms in Civil Proceedings (Atkin). 2ed. vol. 9.

Encyclopaedia of Forms and Precedents. 4ed. vol. 7.

Journal of Commons, Open Spaces and Footpaths Preservation Society. 1927–
New Law Journal. 1965–

Texts

CAMPBELL, I. (ed.)
Decisions of the Commons Commissioners. Commons, Open Spaces & Footpaths Preservation Society, 1972.

CAMPBELL, I. & CLAYDEN, P.
A guide to the law of commons. 3ed. Commons, Open Spaces and Footpaths Preservation Soc., 1980.

COOKE, G.W.
Acts for facilitating the enclosure of commons in England and Wales. 4ed. Stevens & Haynes, 1864.

ELTON, C.I.
Treatise on common and waste lands. 1868 repr. Wildy.

HARRIS, B. & RYAN, G.
An outline of the law relating to common land and public access to the countryside. Sweet & Maxwell, 1967.

LANGDON-DAVIES, P.G.
Common registration. Butterworths, 1967.

PRATT, J.T.
Law for facilitating the enclosure of open and arable fields in England and Wales. Butterworths, 1937.

RYAN, G. & CAMERON, S.
The law relating to open spaces, commons and footpaths. Sweet & Maxwell, 1984.

SCRUTTON, T.E
Commons and common fields. Cambridge U.P., 1887.

WILLIAMS, J.
Rights of common and other prescriptive rights. Sweet, 1880.

WOOLRYCH, H.W.
Law of the rights of common. 2ed. Butterworths, 1850.

COMMONWEALTH LAW

See also Constitutional law.

Encyclopaedias and periodicals

Statutes in Force. Group: Commonwealth and Other Territories.
Halsbury's Laws of England. 4ed. vol. 6.
Halsbury's Statutes of England. 3ed. see index vol.
The Digest. vol. 8(2).
Annual Survey of Commonwealth Law. 1965–

Cambridge Law Journal. 1921–
Commonwealth. 1961–
Commonwealth Law Bulletin. 1975–
Journal of Commonwealth Political Studies. 1961–
Law Reports of the Commonwealth. 1985–

Texts

COMMONWEALTH SECRETARIAT
Delay in the administration of criminal justice: Commonwealth development and experience. 1980.

DALE, Sir W.
The modern Commonwealth. Butterworths, 1983.

DE SMITH, S.A.
The new Commonwealth and its constitutions. Sweet & Maxwell, 1964.

FAWCETT, J.E.S
The British Commonwealth in international law. Stevens, 1963.

GRICE, S. (ed.)
Commonwealth organizations: handbook of official and unofficial organizations active in the Commonwealth. Commonwealth Secretariat, 1977.

JENNINGS, Sir W.I.
The British Commonwealth of Nations. Hutchinson, 1948.

JENNINGS, Sir W.I.
Constitutional laws of Commonwealth. 3ed. Oxford U.P., 1957.

KEETON, G.W. (ed.)
The British Commonwealth: the development of its law and constitutions. Stevens, 1952–1967.

KEITH, A.B.
Constitutional law of the British Dominions. Macmillan, 1933.

KEITH, A.B.
The Dominion as Sovereign States; their constitutions and governments. Macmillan, 1938.

KEITH, A.B.
Dominion autonomy in practice. Oxford U.P., 1930.

KEITH, A.B.
Responsible government in the Dominions. 2ed. Oxford U.P., 1928. 2 vols.

KEITH, A.B.
Sovereignty of the British Dominion. Macmillan, 1929.

KEITH, A.B.
Speeches and documents on the British Dominion. 1918–1931: from self-government to national sovereignty. Oxford U.P., 1932 repr. 1977.

PHILLIPS, Sir F.
The evolving legal profession in the Commonwealth. Oceana, 1978 (USA).

ROBERTS-WRAY, K.
Commonwealth and colonial law. Stevens, 1966.

WHEARE, K.C.
The constitutional structure of the Commonwealth. Greenwood P.,1960 repr. 1982.

COMMUNITY LAND

Encyclopaedias and periodicals

Statutes in Force. Group: Town and Country Planning.
Halsbury's Statutes of England. 3ed. vol. 45.

New Law Journal. 1965–
Solicitors' Journal. 1857–

Texts

COLLEGE OF LAW
Development land tax and the Community Land Act 1975. 1976.

CORFIELD, F.
A guide to the Community Land Act. Butterworths, 1976.

CROSS, C.
Community Land Act, 1975. Butterworths, 1976.

DAVIES, R.V.
The nationalization of land: a description of the Community Land Act, 1975. B.Rose, 1976.

HEAP, D.
Community Land Act, 1975. Sweet & Maxwell, 1976.

JOSEPH, C. & EDWARDS, R.G.
The R.I.C.S. handbook of community land and development taxation. R.I.C.S., 1976. Looseleaf.

JOSEPH, C. & SKINNER, B.
Land development land tax and Community Land Act. 2ed. Oyez, 1976.

MOORE, V.W.E.
Community land: the new Act. Sweet & Maxwell, 1976.

NUTLEY, W.G. & BEAUMONT, C.H.
The Community Land Act, 1975. Estates Gazette, 1977.

ROYAL INSTITUTION OF CHARTERED SURVEYORS
Community Land Act 1975: the tasks facing local authorities: guidance notes. 1976.

ROSSI, H.
Shaw's guide to the Community Land Act, 1975. Shaw, 1976.

COMMUNITY SERVICE

Encyclopaedias and periodicals

Halsbury's Statutes of England. 3ed. vol. 43.

British Journal of Criminology. 1960–

Home Office Research Unit Bulletin.
Probation Journal. 1913–

Texts

INNER LONDON PROBATION &
AFTER-CARE SERVICE
Community service by offenders: a progress report on the first five years. 1975.

PEASE, K. and others
Community service assessed in 1976.
HMSO, 1976 (Home Office Research Unit report no 39).

PEASE, K. and others
Community service orders. HMSO, 1975
(Home Office Research Unit report no.29).

SUSSEX, J.
Community service by offenders: year one in Kent. Rose, 1974.

YOUNG, W.
Community service orders: the development and use of a new penal measure. Heinemann, 1979.

COMPANIES

See also Commercial Law; Corporations; Liquidators; Partnership.

Encyclopaedias and periodicals

Statutes in Force. Group: Companies.
Halsbury's Laws of England. 4ed. vol. 7.
Halsbury's Statutes of England. 3ed. vol. 6.
The Digest. vols. 9 & 10.
Encyclopaedia of Court Forms in Civil Proceedings (Atkin). 2ed. vols. 10 & 11.
Encyclopaedia of Forms and Precedents. 4ed. vols. 5. & 6.

Australian Company Law Reports. 1974–
Business Law Review. 1980–
Common Market Law Review. 1963–
Company Law Cases. 1983–
The Company Lawyer. 1980–
The Corporate Legal Letter. 1978–
Journal of Business Law. 1957–
Journal of World Trade Law. 1967–
Law Society's Gazette. 1903–
New Law Journal. 1965–

Texts

ADAMSON, A.V. & ADAMSON, M.S.
The valuation of company shares and business. 6ed. Law Book Co., 1980 (Australia).

ANDERSON, A.
Guide to the Companies Act, 1981.
Graham & Trotman, 1982.

ARDEN, M. & ECCLES, G.
Tolley's Companies Act, 1980. Tolley, 1980.

ASHE, T.M.
Insider trading. Company Communications Centre, 1980.

BAXT, R.
Introduction to company law. 2ed Law Book Co., 1982 (Australia).

BAXT, R. & AFTERMAN, A.B.
Cases and casebook on companies and securities. Butterworths (Australia), 1976.

BERKOWITZ, L. & COCKAIN, G.D.M.
Companies limited by guarantee and unlimited companies. 3ed. Oyez, 1977.

BOULTON, A.H.
Handbook on company administration. 4ed.
Jordan, 1981.

BOYLE, A. & BIRDS, J.
Company law. Jordan, 1983.

BRAMWELL, R. & DICK, J.
Taxation of companies. 2ed. Sweet & Maxwell, 1979 supp. 1983.

BROWN, S.
Company resolutions. 4ed. Law Book Co., 1982 (Australia).

BROWN, W.
Cases and statutes on company law. Sweet & Maxwell, 1976.

BRUCE, R., McKERN, B. & POLLARD, I.
Handbook of Australian corporate finance.
Butterworths (Australia), 1983.

BUCKLEY, H.B.
Companies Acts. 14ed. Butterworths, 1981.
3 vols. (1 vol. looseleaf.)

COMPANIES

BUTTERWORTHS
Companies Act 1981: regulations and related legislation. Butterworths (Australia), 1982.

BUTTERWORTHS company law handbook. 3ed. 1983.

BUTTERWORTHS company law service. Looseleaf.

CHARLESWORTH, J.
Company law. 12ed. Sweet & Maxwell, 1983.

CHESTER, M.G. & VOGELAAIR, F.O.W.
English Dutch company law: a review for lawyers and business in the light of E.E.C. requirements. Kluwer, 1973.

CHOWN, J. & EDWARDS-KER, M.
Acquisition of assets: companies and real estate in Belgium, France, Germany, Netherlands and U.K.|Int. Bur. Fiscal Document., 1974.

CILLIERS, H.S., BENADE, M.L. & DE VILLIERS, S.W.L.
Company law. 3ed. Butterworths (S.Africa), 1977.

CRAZE, J.
The Companies Act 1980. Jordan, 1980.

DALGLISH, D.J.
Company law in New Zealand. 4ed. Whitcombe, 1966.

DAVIES, P.L.
The regulation of takeovers and mergers. Sweet & Maxwell, 1976.

DEHOGHTON, C.
Company law, structure and reform in eleven countries. Free P., 1969.

ECCLES, G. & COX, J.
Companies Act, 1981. Tolley, 1982.

FARRANDS, W.L.
Company law in New Zealand. Butterworths (New Zealand), 1971.

FARRAR, J.
Company insolvency. Sweet & Maxwell, 1979.

FORD, H.A.J.
Principles of company law. 3ed. Butterworths (Australia), 1982.

FORMOY, R.R.
The historical foundations of modern company law. 1923.

FRANKS, J.A.
The company director and the law. 2ed. Oyez, 1978.

FROMMEL, S.N. & THOMPSON, J.H.
Company law in Europe. Kluwer-Harrap, 1976.

GORE-BROWNE, F.
Companies. 43ed. Jordan. Looseleaf.

GOUGH, W.J.
Company charges. Butterworths, 1978. Australian supplement. Butterworths (Australia), 1983.

GOWER, L.C.B.
The principles of modern company law. 4ed. Sweet & Maxwell, 1979 supp. 1981.

GUIDEBOOK to British company law. C.C.H., 1983.

HADDEN, T.
Company law and capitalism. 2ed. Weidenfeld & N., 1977.

HAHLO, H.R. & TREBILCOCK, M.J.
Casebook on company law. 2ed. Sweet & Maxwell, 1977.

HALL, M.J. (ed.)
Commercial companies law of the United Arab Emirates. Graham & Trotman, 1984.

HORN, N.
Legal problems of codes of conduct for multinational enterprises. Kluwer, 1980.

HORNBY, J.
An intorduction to company law. 6ed. Hutchinson, 1975.

HRIBAR, Z.
A guide to company law. 2ed. Law Book Co., 1982.

INTERNATIONAL BAR ASSOCIATION
Codes of conduct for transnational corporations. Sweet & Maxwell, 1981.

ISSUING HOUSES ASSOCIATION
The city code on takeovers and mergers. rev. ed. 1975 & supp.

IVAMY, E.R.H.
A dictionary of company law. Butterworths, 1983.

JAGER, M.O., TAYLOR, R.B. & CRAIG, R.J.
Company financial statements: form and content. Butterworths (Australia), 1975. Looseleaf.

JOFFE, V.
Companies Act 1980: a practical guide.
Oyez, 1980.

JUST, A.
How to form a private company. 29ed.
Jordan, 1980.

KAY, M.
Companies Acts. New ed. Sweet &
Maxwell, 1980.

KNIGHT, W.J.L.
Acquisition of private companies. 2ed.
Oyez, 1979.

KUUSI, J.
Host state and the transnational
corporations: analysis of legal relationships.
Saxon House, 1979.

LOOSE, P.
The company director: his functions,
powers and duties. 5ed. Jordan, 1975 supp.
1982.

McMONNIES, P.
Companies Act 1981 – a practical guide.
Oyez, 1981.

MAGNUS, S.W. & ESTRIN, M.
Companies: law and practice. 5ed.
Butterworths, 1978 supp. 1981.

MARSHALL, E.A.
Scottish cases on partnerships and
companies (excluding winding up and
reconstruction). Green, 1980.

MASON, H.H.
Casebook on Australian company law. 3ed.
Butterworths (Australia), 1980.

MAYO, J.W.
Companies limited by guarantee and
unlimited companies. 2ed. Oyez, 1968
(Practice notes no. 28).

MAYSON, S.W. & FRENCH, D.
Practical approach to company law.
Financial Training Pubns., 1982.

MEINHARDT, P.
Company law in Europe. 2ed. Gower, 1978.
Looseleaf.

MEINHARDT, P.
Company law in Great Britain. Gower,
1982.

MITCHELL, E.
The director's lawyer and company
secretary's legal guide. 4ed. Business
Books, 1978.

MORSE, G.
Company structure. Sweet & Maxwell,
1979.

MORSE, G. and others
Companies Act 1981. Sweet & Maxwell,
1982.

MOULLIN, M. & SARGENT, J.
Guide to the taxation of companies.
McGraw-Hill, 1982.

NICHOLLS, W.J. & CARR, J.G.
Company law and practice. Longman,
1976.

NORTHEY, J.F.
Introduction to company law. 8ed.
Butterworths (New Zealand), 1976.

NORTHEY, J.F. & LEIGH, L.V.
Introduction to company law. 3ed. Sweet &
Maxwell, 1981.

NUNN, E.W.
The secretarial handbook: a practical guide
to a secretary's duties under the Companies
Acts 1948 to 1976. 7ed. Oyez, 1977.

OLIVER, M.C.
Cases in company law. 3ed. Macdonald &
Evans, 1982.

OLIVER, M.C.
Company law. 9ed. Macdonald & Evans,
1982 (M & E handbook series).

OLIVER, M.C.
The private company in Germany.
Macdonald & Evans, 1977.

OROJO, J.O.
Company law and practice in Nigeria. 2ed.
Sweet & Maxwell, 1984. 2 vols.

PALMER, F.B.
Company law. 22ed. Sweet & Maxwell,
1976. 3 vols. (2 looseleaf).

PALMER, F.B.
Company precedents. 17ed. Sweet &
Maxwell, 1956–60.

PATERSON, W.E., EDNIE, H.H. &
FORD, H.A.J.
Australian company law. Butterworths
(Australia), 1982. Looseleaf.

PATERSON, W.E., EDNIE, H.H. &
FORD, H.A.J.
A guide to the national scheme and revised
Companies Bill 1980. Butterworths
(Australia), 1980.

PENNINGTON, R.R.
The Companies Acts 1980 and 1981: a
practitioners manual. Lloyd's, 1983.

COMPANIES

PENNINGTON, R.R.
Dutch company law. Oyez, 1977.

PENNINGTON, R.R.
Principles of company law. 4ed. Butterworths, 1979.

POWELL-SMITH, V.
Law and practice relating to company directors. Butterworths, 1969.

POWER, B.J.
Irish company law, 1973–83. Gill & Macmillan, 1984.

PRENTICE, D.
The Companies Act 1980. Butterworths, 1981.

PURVIS, R.N.
Proprietary companies. Butterworths (Australia), 1973.

RANKING, D.F. & SPICER, E.E.
Company law. 12ed. HFL, 1981 supp. 1982.

RIDER, B.A.K.
The regulation of insider trading. Jordan, 1983.

RYAN, F.J.O. & COOKE, J.C.
Australian company practice. 2ed. Butterworths (Australia), 1982. Looseleaf.

SANDISON, F.G.
Profit sharing and other share acquisition schemes. Tolley, 1979 supp. 1980..

SAVAGE, N.
Companies Act, 1980: a new business code. McGraw-Hill, 1980.

SCHMITTHOFF, C.M.
European company law texts. Stevens, 1974.

SCHMITTHOFF, C.M. (ed.)
The harmonisation of European company law. B.I.I.C.L., 1973.

SCOTTISH LAW COMMISSION
Examination of the Companies (Floating Charges) (Scotland) Act 1961. 1969 (Memorandum no. 10).

SCOTTISH LAW COMMISION
Report on the Companies (Floating Charges) (Scotland) Act 1961. HMSO, 1970 (Scot. Law Com. no. 14).

SCOTTISH LAW COMMISSION
Law of rights in security: company law: registration of charges: Scotland. 1976 (Memorandum no. 33).

SEALY, L.S.
Cases and materials in company law. 2ed. Butterworths, 1978.

SMITH, K. & KEENAN, D.J.
Company law. 5ed. Pitman, 1983.

SMITH, P.
Family business: company or partnership? Sweet & Maxwell, 1980.

SPRINGFIELD, D.
The company executive and the law. 2ed. Felton Press, 1977.

STAFFORD, J.
Index to companies legislation. Tolley, 1982.

SWEET & MAXWELL
Companies Acts. 1980.

TOLLEY's company law. Tolley, 1983.

TOPHAM, A.F. & IVAMY, E.R.
Principles of company law. l6ed. Butterworths, 1978.

TOPHAM, A.F. & IVAMY, E.R.
Company law, Scottish supplement (Walker, D.M.) 1974.

TOPP, A.G., TALBOT, A.E. & ROBSON, R.McK.
Guide to company law. 2ed. Butterworths (Australia), 1975 supp. 1980.

TRADE, BOARD OF
Report of the Company Law Committee (Jenkins). HMSO, 1962 (Cmnd. 1749).

TRADE, DEPARTMENT OF
Changes in company law. HMSO, 1978 (Cmnd. 7291).

TRADE, DEPARTMENT OF
The conduct of company directors. HMSO, 1977 (Cmnd. 7037).

TRADE, DEPARTMENT OF
Handbook of the companies inspection system: inspections and departmental enquiries under the Companies Acts. HMSO, 1980.

TRADE, DEPARTMENT OF
A new form of incorporation for small firms: a consultative document. HMSO, 1981 (Cmnd. 8171).

TRADE, DEPARTMENT OF
The purchase by a company of its own shares: a consultative document. HMSO, 1980 (Cmnd. 7944).

TRADE, DEPARTMENT OF
Report of the Committee of Inquiry on Industrial Democracy (Bullock). HMSO, 1977 (Cmnd. 6706).

USSHER, P.
Company law. Sweet & Maxwell, 1984 (Irish law texts).

VAN HOORN, J. (ed.)
Taxation of companies in Europe. Int. Bur. Fiscal Document. 1972. 2 vols.

VERRUCOLI, A.
Italian company law. Oyez, 1977.

VOGELAAR, F.O.W. & CHESTER, M.G.
Dutch/English company law; comparative review. Kluwer, 1973.

WALMSLEY, K.
A handbook on company administration. 4ed. Jordan, 1981.

WASSERSTEIN, B.
Corporate finance law. McGraw-Hill, 1978 (USA).

WEGENAST, F.
Law of Canadian companies. Carswell, 1931 repr. 1980.

WEINBERG, M.A., BLANK, M.V. & GREYSTOKE, A.L.
Weinberg on take-overs and mergers. 4ed. Sweet & Maxwell, 1979.

WINE, H.M.
Buying and selling private limited companies and business. 2ed. Butterworths, 1983.

WOLSTENHOLME, P.H. & WILLOTT, R.
Purchase or redemption by a company of its own shares. Tolley, 1982.

WOOLDRIDGE, F.
Groups of companies: the law and practice in Britain, France and Germany. I.A.L.S., 1981.

WURDINGER, H.
German company law. Oyez, 1975.

WYATT, M.C.
Company acquisition of own shares. Oyez, 1983.

COMPARATIVE LAW

See also Conflict of Laws; International Law.

Encyclopaedias and periodicals

International Encyclopaedia of Comparative Law. 1971–

American Journal of Comparative Law. 1952–

Comparative Law Yearbook.

Current Legal Problems. 1948–

Harvard International Law Journal. 1959–

Harvard Law Review. 1887–

International and Comparative Law Quarterly. 1952–

Journal of Comparative Legislation and International Law. 1896–1951.

Texts

ABRAHAM, H.J.
Judicial process: an introductory analysis of the courts of the United States, England and France. 4ed. Oxford U.P., 1980.

ANDERSON, J.N.D. (ed.)
Changing law in developing countries. Allen & Unwin, 1963.

BUTLER, W.E.
International law in comparative perspective. Kluwer, 1980.

CALLUND, D.
Employee benefits in Europe: international survey of state and private schemes in 16 countries. 3ed. Callund & Co., 1979.

DAVID, R.
English law and French law. Stevens, 1980.

DAVID, R. & BRIERLEY, J.E.C.
Major legal systems in the world today: an introduction to the comparative study of law. 2ed. Stevens, 1978.

COMPARATIVE LAW

DAWSON, J.P.
Gifts and promises: continental and American law compared. Yale U.P., 1980 (USA).

EHRMANN, H.W.
Comparative legal cultures. Prentice-Hall, 1976 (USA).

ESSAYS on international and comparative law: in honour of Judge Erades. Nijhoff, 1983.

FINER, S.E. (ed.)
Five constitutions: contrasts and comparisons. Harvester P., 1979.

GROVES, H.E.
Comparative constitutional law. Oceana, 1963.

GRUMM, J.G.
Paradigm for the comparative analysis of legislative systems. Sage, 1973.

GUPTA, B.B.
Comparative study of six living constitutions: India, U.K., U.S.S.R., Switzerland, France, U.S.A. Tripathi, 1978 (India).

GUTTERIDGE, H.C.
Comparative law: an introduction to the comparative method of legal study and research. 2ed. Cambridge U.P., 1949 repr. 1971.

HALL, J.
Comparative law and social theory. Louisiana U.P., 1963 (USA).

HAZARD, J.N. & HOYA, T.E.
Soviet law and Western legal systems: a manual for comparison. 2ed. Columbia U.P., 1970.

INGRAHAM, B.
Political crime in Europe: a comparative study of France, Germany and England. Univ. of California P., 1979.

JAFFE, L.L.
English and American judges as lawmakers. Oxford U.P., 1969.

KEETON, G.W. & SHERIDAN, L.A.
The comparative law of trusts in the Commonwealth and the Irish Republic. B.Rose, 1977 supp. 1981.

KIRALFY, A.K.R.
Comparative law of matrimonial property. Kluwer, 1972.

KITTRIE, N.N.
Comparative law of Israel and the Middle East. Lerner, 1971.

LAWSON, F.H. & MARKESINIS, B.S.
Tortious liability for unintentional harm in the common law and the civil law. Cambridge U.P., 1982. 2 vols.

MARKESINIS, B.S.
Theory and practice of dissolution of parliament: a comparative study with special reference to the United Kingdom and Greek experience. Cambridge U.P., 1972.

MEADOR, D.J.
Criminal appeals: English practices and American reforms. Virginia U.P., 1973.

MERRYMAN, J.H.
Civil law tradition: an introduction to the legal systems of Western Europe and Latin America. Stanford U.P., 1969.

MURPHY, W.F.
Comparative constitutional law: cases and commentaries. Macmillan, 1977.

NEDJATI, Z.M. & TRICE, J.E.
English and continental systems of administrative law. North-Holland, 1978.

NEWMAN, R.A.
Equity in the world's legal systems: a comparative study. Hein, 1974.

PALSSON, L.
Marriage and divorce in comparative conflict of laws. Sijthoff, 1974.

REICH, N. & MICKLITZ, H.W.
Consumer legislation in the European Community countries: a comparative analysis. Van Nostrand Reinhold, 1980.

ROBINSON, J.M.
Comparative survey of securities laws: a review of the securities and related laws of fourteen nations. Kluwer, 1980.

ROTONDI, M.
Comparative law: tasks and methods. Oceana, 1973 (USA).

SCHLESINGER, R.B.
Comparative law: cases, text, materials. 3ed. Foundation P., 1972.

SCHMIDT, F. (ed.)
Discrimination in employment: a study of six countries by the Comparative Labour Law Group. Almqvist, 1978.

SCHUBERT, G. & DANELSKI, D.J.
Comparative judicial behaviour: cross-cultural studies of political decision-making in the East and West. Oxford U.P., 1969.

SCHULTZ, J.S.
Comparative statutory sources. Hein, 1973 (USA).

SIFFIN, W.J.
Toward the comparative study of public administration. Greenwood, 1973.

SZABO, I. & PETERI, Z. (eds.)
A socialist approach to comparative law. Sijthoff, 1977.

WATSON, A.
Legal transplants: an approach to comparative law. Virginia U.P., 1970.

ZWEIGERT, K. & KOTZ, H.
Introduction to comparative law. Kluwer, 1977. 2 vols.

COMPETITION

Encyclopaedias and periodicals

Statutes in Force. Group: Trade, 1: General.
Halsbury's Laws of England. 4ed. see index vol.
Encyclopaedia of Forms and Precedents. 4ed. see index vol.
Antitrust Bulletin (USA). 1955–
Antitrust Law and Economics Review (USA). 1967–

Antitrust Law Journal (USA). 1968–
Antitrust Law Symposium (USA).
Commercial Law Journal (USA). 1888–
Common Market Law Review. 1964–
European Competition Law Review. 1980–
Journal of Business Law. 1957–
Journal of Law and Economics (USA). 1958–
Journal of World Trade Law. 1967–

Texts

ALEXANDER, W.
The EEC rules of competition. Kluwer-Harrap, 1973.

ALHADEFF, D.A.
Competition and controls in banking: study of the regulations of banks' competition in Italy, France and England. Univ. of California P., 1969.

AXINN, S.M.
Acquisition under the Hart-Scott-Rodino Antitrust Improvement Act. Graham & Trotman, 1980 (USA).

BAROUNOS, D., HALL, D.F. & JAMES, J.R.
EEC anti-trust law: principles and practice. Butterworths, 1975.

BECKERLEY, G.B. (ed.)
European Economic Community competition law: an analysis of recent decisions and developments. ESC Pub., 1978.

BELLAMY, C. & CHILD G.
Common market law of competition. 2ed. Sweet & Maxwell, 1978.

BREIT, W. & ELZINGA, K.G.
Landmark antitrust cases. Holt, R. & W., 1982.

BRITISH INSTITUTE OF INTERNATIONAL AND COMPARATIVE LAW
Unfair competition: some comparatie aspects of the laws of the US, Germany, France and the UK. 1966.

CAWTHRA, B.
Restrictive agreements in the EEC: the need to notify. Butterworths, 1972.

CROTTI, A.D.
Trading under E.E.C. and U.S. antitrust laws. Butterworths, 1977.

CUNNINGHAM, J.P
Copmpetition law of the EEC. Kogan Page, 1973 supp. 1975.

CUNNINGHAM, J.P.
Competition policy and the control of restrictive practices. Industrial Educational & Research Foundn., 1972.

CUNNINGHAM, J.P.
Restrictive practices and monopolies in EEC law. Kogan Page, 1973.

CUNNINGHAM, J.P. & TINNION, J.
Competition Act, 1980. Kogan Page, 1980.

COMPETITION

DERINGER, A.
Competition law of the E.E.C.: a commentary on articles 85–90. CCH, 1968 (USA).

ELZINGA, K.G.
The antitrust penalties: a study in law and economics. Yale U.P., 1976.

ERICKSON, M.L.
Antitrust and trade regulations: cases and materials. Grid Pub., U.S.: Wiley, 1982.

EUROPA INSTITUTE (LEYDEN)
European competition policy. Kluwer, 1973.

EVERTON, A.R.
Trade winds: introduction to the U.K.'s law of competition. Osborne, 1978.

FOLSOM, R.H.
Corporate competition law in the European Communities. Lexington, 1978 (USA).

FUGATE, W.L.
Foreign commerce and the antitrust laws. Little, Brown, 1973 (USA).

GELLHORN, E.
Antitrust law and economics. 2ed. West, 1981.

GEORGE, K.D. & JOLL, C. (eds.)
Competition policy in the UK and EEC. Cambridge U.P., 1975.

GIJLSTRA, D. & MURPHY, F. (eds.)
Competition law in Western Europe and the USA. Kluwer, 1976 Looseleaf. 2 vols.

GIJLSTRA, D.J. & MURPHY, D.F.
Leading cases and materials on the competition law of the EEC. Kluwer, 1976.

GOSSE, R.
Law of competition in Canada. Carswell, 1962.

GRAUPNER, R.
The rules of competition in the European Economic Community. Nijhoff, 1965.

HAVENGA, J.D.
Retailing: competition and trade practices. Sijthoff, 1973.

HOFFMANN, D. & SCHAUB, S.
German competition law: legislation and commentary. Kluwer, 1984.

HUNTER, A.
Competition and the law. Allen & Unwin, 1966.

JOLIET, R.
The rule of reason in anti-trust law: American, German and Common Market laws in comparative perspective. Nijhoff, 1967.

KALINOWSKI, J.
World law of competition. Bender. Looseleaf.

KERSE, C.S.
European Economic Community antitrust procedure. European Law Centre, 1981.

KORAH, V.
Competition law of Britain and the Common Market. Elek, 1975.

McLACHLAN, D.L. & SWANN, D.
Competition policy in the European Community. Oxford U.P., 1967.

MAGWOOD, J.
Competition law of Canada. Carswell, 1981.

MERKIN, R. & WILLIAMS, K.
Competition law: antitrust policy in the United Kingdom and EEC. Sweet & Maxwell, 1984.

MUELLER, R. & SCHNEIDER, R.
The German law against restraints of competition. Macdonald & Evans, , 1975.

NEALE, A.D.
Antitrust laws of the U.S.A.: a study of competition enforced by law. 3ed. Nat.Inst. of Econ. & Soc. Research, 1981.

OBERDORFER, C.W. and others
Common Market cartel law. 2ed. CCH, 1971.

PINNER, H.L.
World unfair competition law: an encyclopedia. Rev. ed. Kluwer, 1979–80. 4 vols. looseleaf.

ROBERTS, R.J.
Anticombines and antitrust: the competition law of Canada and the antitrust law of the United States. Butterworths (Canada), 1980.

ROBERTS, R.J.
The antitrust law of Canada. Butterworths (Canada), 1978.

SULLIVAN, L.
Hornbook on the law of antitrust. West, 1977 (USA).

SUNDSTROM, G.O.Z.
Contributions to Community competition law. Almqvist, 1978.

SWANN, D.
Competition in British industry; restrictive practice legislation in theory and practice. Allen & Unwin, 1974.

SWANN, D. & LESS, D.
Antitrust policy in Europe. Finan.Times, 1972.

TOEPKE, U.P.
European Economic Community competition law: business issues and legal principles in Common Market antitrust cases. Wiley, 1982.

TOWNSEND, J.B.
Extraterritorial antitrust. Westview, 1980 (USA).

WALSH, A.E. & PAXTON, J.
Competition policy: European and international trends and practices. Macmillan, 1975.

ZWEIGERT, K. & KROPHOLLER, J.
Law of copyright, competition policy and industrial property. Sijthoff, 1973.

COMPULSORY PURCHASE AND COMPENSATION

See also Community Land; Town and Country Planning

Encyclopaedias and periodicals

Statutes in Force, Group: Compulsory Acquisition
Halsbury's Laws of England. 4ed. vol. 8.
Halsbury's Statutes of England. 3ed. vol. 6.
The Digest. vol. 11.
Encyclopaedia of Court Forms in Civil Proceedings (Atkin). 2ed. vol. 12.
Encyclopaedia of Forms and Precedents. 4ed. vol. 7.

Conveyancer and Property Lawyer. 1936–
Estates Gazette. 1858–
Journal of Planning and Environment Law. 1948–
Land Tribunal Cases. 1973–
Law Society's Gazette. 1903–
Property and Compensation Reports. 1950–

Texts

AGARWALA, O.
Compulsory acquisition of land in India. 4ed. University Books, 1973. 2 vols.

BOYNTON, J.K.
Compulsory purchase and compensation. 4ed. Oyez, 1977 (Practice note no.53).

BRENNAN, J.P.
Digest of cases on compensation for the resumption of land. Butterworths (Australia), 1977.

BROWN, D.
Land acquisition. Butterworths (Australia), 1983.

BROWN, H.J.J. (ed.)
Encyclopaedia of the law of compulsory purchase and compensation. Sweet & Maxwell, 1960. Looseleaf. 2 vols.

BROWN, H.J.J.
The Land Compensation Act, 1973. Sweet & Maxwell, 1973.

CORFIELD, Sir F. & CARNWATH, R.J.A.
Compulsory acquisition and compensation. Butterworths, 1978.

CRIPPS, C.A.
On compulsory acuisition of land: powers, procedure and compensation. 11ed. Stevens, 1962.

DAVIES, K.
Law of compulsory purchase and compensation. 4ed. Butterworths, 1984.

DENYER-GREEN, B.
Compulsory purchase and compensation. Estates Gazette, 1980.

FRICKE, G.
Compulsory acquisition of land in Australia. 2ed. Law Book Co., 1982.

GARNER, J.F. (ed.)
Compensation for compulsory purchase: a comparative study. Oyez, 1975.

GARNER, J.F.
Slum clearance and compensation 4ed.
Oyez, 1975 (Practice notes no.45).

GORDON, R.A.
A handbook on compulsory acquisition of land and compensation. 2ed. Stevens, 1936.

HAMILTON, R.N.D.
Compensation for compulsory acquisition of agricultural land and of rights in and over such land. 3ed. R.I.C.S., 1980.

JOURNAL OF PLANNING AND ENVIRONMENT LAW
Compensation for compulsory purchase: occasional papers. 1975.

JUSTICE
Compensation for compulsory acquisition and remedies for planning restrictions. 2ed. Stevens, 1973.

LAWRANCE, D.M.
Compulsory purchase and compensation. 5ed. Estates Gazette, 1972.

LEACH, W.A.
Disturbance on compulsory purchase. 3ed. Estates Gazette, 1975 supp. 1976.

LOMNICKI, A.J.
Summary of town and country planning law and the law of compulsory purchase and compensation. Batsford, 1973.

NUTLEY, W.G. & BEAUMONT, C.H.
Land Compensation Act 1973. Butterworths, 1974.

O'SULLIVAN, P.
Irish planning and acquisition law. Inst. of Public Admin., 1978.

ROYAL INSTITUTION OF CHARTERED SURVEYORS
Appeal cases, includes cases on compulsory purchase valuation. 1968.

STEWART-BROWN, R.D.
A guide to compulsory purchase and compensation. 5ed. Sweet & Maxwell, 1962.

UMEH, J.A.
Compulsory acquisition of land in Nigeria. Sweet & Maxwell, 1973.

WISDOM, A.S.
Appropriation of land by local authorities. 3ed. B.Rose, 1978.

WISDOM, A.S.
Local authorities' powers of purchase: a summary. 7ed. B.Rose, 1978.

COMPUTERS

See also Privacy

Encyclopaedias and periodicals

Halsbury's Statutes of England. 3ed. see index vol.

Encyclopaedia of Court Forms in Civil Procedings. 2ed. vol. 18.

Encyclopaedia of Forms and Precedents. 4ed. vol. 16.

Computer Law and Practice. 1984–

Computers and the Law. 1974–

Texts

BELLORD, N.
Computers for lawyers. Sinclair Browne:Wiley, 1983.

BENDER, D.
Computer law: evidence and procedure. Bender. Looseleaf.

BEQUAI, A.
Computer crime. Lexington Books, 1978 (USA).

BEQUAI, A.
How to prevent computer crime: guide for managers. Wiley, 1983.

BERNACCHI, R.L. & LARSEN, G.H.
Date processing contracts and the law. Little, Brown, 1974 (USA).

BING, J. & HARVOLD, T.
Legal decisions and information systems. Universitetsforlaget, 1977.

BING, J. & SELMER, K.S. (eds.)
A decade of computers and law. Universitetsforlaget, 1980.

BURRIS, R.W.
Teaching law with computers. Westview P., 1980 (USA).

CAMPBELL, C.
Data processing and the law. Sweet & Maxwell, 1984.

COMMITTEE ON DATA PROTECTION
Report (Lindop). HMSO, 1978 (Cmnd. 7341).

COUNCIL OF EUROPE
Common standards for legal retrieval systems: important features of a common command language within a network of legal information systems. HMSO, 1984.

DEIGHTON, S. (Ed.)
New criminals: bibliography of computer related crime. Inst. of Elect. Engineers, 1978.

DUGGAN, M.
Law and the computer: a KWIC bibliography. Collier-Macmillan, 1973.

EDGE, C.T.
Microcomputers for solicitors. Gower, 1982.

EDGE, C.T.
Small computer systems for solicitors. Gower, 1983.

EDWARDS, M.
Understanding computer contracts. Pergamon, 1983.

EUROPEAN COMMITTEE ON CRIME PROBLEMS
Protection of users of legal data processing systems: symposium proceedings, 1979. Council of Europe, 1980.

EUROPEAN COMMITTEE ON LEGAL CO-OPERATION
The protection of users of computerised legal information services. Recommendation no. R(83)3. Council of Europe, 1983.

FLAHERTY, D.H.
Privacy and government data banks: an international perspective. Mansell, 1979.

GIANNANTONIO, E.
Italian legal information retrieval. Sweet & Maxwell, 1984.

HEWITT, P.
Computers, records and the right to privacy. Input Two-Nine, 1979.

HOME OFFICE
Data protection: the government's proposals for legislation. HMSO, 1982 (Cmnd. 8539).

HONDIUS, F.W.
The computer and international law. Nijhoff, 1981.

HONDIUS, F.W.
Emerging data protection in Europe. North-Holland, 1975.

KELMAN, A. & SIZER, R.
Computer in court. Gower, 1982.

KIRKWOOD, J.S.
Information technology and land administration. Estates Gazette, 1984.

KOZAK, E.
Applications of computer technology to law, 1969–1978: a selected bibliography. Canadian Law Information Council, 1980.

KRAUSS, L.I.
Computer fraud and countermeasures. Prentice-Hall, 1979.

LAHORE, J.
Information technology: the challenge to copyright. Sweet & Maxwell, 1984.

McKNIGHT, G.
Computer crime. Joseph, 1973.

MORGAN, R.
Computer contracts. 2ed. Oyez, 1984.

NIBLETT, B. (ed.)
Computer science and law – an advanced course. Cambridge U.P., 1980.

NIBLETT, B.
Legal protection of computer programs. Oyez, 1980.

NORMAN, A.
Computer insecurity. Chapman & Hall, 1983.

ONLINE INFORMATION CENTRE
Law data bases, 1983. O.I.C., 1984.

ORGANISATION FOR ECONOMIC CO-OPERATION AND DEVELOPMENT
Exploration of legal issues in information and communication technologies. OECD:HMSO, 1984.

REMER, D.
Legal care for your software: a step-by-step guide for computer software writers. Gower, 1984.

RENNIE, M.T.M.
Computer contracts handbook. Sweet & Maxwell, 1984.

CONFLICT OF LAWS

ROSENBURG, J.W.L.
Effects of manual versus computerised methods of information retrieval on legal research. University Microfilms, 1973.

RUOFF, T.B.F.
The solicitor and the automated office. Sweet & Maxwell, 1984.

RUOFF, T.B.F.
The solicitor and the silicon chip. Oyez, 1981.

SELMER, K.S. (ed.)
Swansea debriefing: workshop on computer science on law. Norwegian Research Centre for Computers & Law, 1980.

SIEGHART, P.
Privacy and computers. Latimer New Dimensions, 1976.

SOCIETY FOR COMPUTERS AND LAW
Applications of computer technology to law: a select bibliography (1969–1981) for British Lawyers. S.C.L., 1982.

SOCIETY FOR COMPUTERS AND LAW
Communications: guide to the electronic office for practising lawyers. S.C.L., 1983.

SOCIETY FOR COMPUTERS AND LAW
Lawyers in the eighties: conference proceedings. S.C.L., 1980.

SOCIETY FOR COMPUTERS AND LAW
Tomorrow's lawyers: computers and legal training. S.C.L., 1981.

TAPPER, C.
Computer law. 3ed. Longman, 1982.

CONFESSIONS

See also Criminal Law; Evidence

Encyclopaedias and periodicals

Encyclopaedia of Court Forms in Civil Proceedings (Atkin). 2ed. vol. 32 and 38.

Criminal Law Review. 1954–
Journal of Criminal Law. 1937–

Texts

ARCHBOLD, J.F.
Pleading, evidence and practice in criminal cases. 41ed. Sweet & Maxwell, 1982.

CROSS, R.
On evidence. 5ed. Butterworths, 1979.

KAUFMAN, K.
Admissibility of confessions in criminal matters. 3ed. Carswell, 1980 (Canada).

REIK, T.
Compulsion to confess: on the psychoanalysis of crime and pubishment. 1959 repr. Books for Libraries, 1972.

ROGGE, O.J.
Why men confess. 1959 repr. Da Capo P., 1971.

SCHAFER, W.J.
Confessions and statements. C.C.Thomas, 1968 (USA).

STEPHENS, O.H.
The Supreme Court and confessions of guilt. Univ. of Tennessee P., 1973.

CONFLICT OF LAWS

See also Comparative Law; International Law; Nationality and Citizenship.

Encyclopaedias and periodicals

Halsbury's Laws of England. 4ed. vol. 8.
The Digest. vol. 11
Encyclopaedia of Forms and Precedents. 4ed. vol. 13.

Australian Law Journal. 1927–
British Yearbook of International Law. 1920–
Cambridge Law Journal. 1954–

Current Legal Problems. 1948–
Harvard International Law Review. 1959–
International and Comparative Law
Quarterly. 1952–

International Law Reports. 1950–
Journal of World Trade Law. 1967–
Juridical Review. 1889–
Public Law. 1956–

Texts

AMERICAN LAW INSTITUTE
Restatement of the law: conflict of laws.
2ed. 1971. 3 vols.

ANTON, A.E.
Private international law, a treatise from the standpoint of Scots Law. Green, 1967.

BEALE, J.H.
A treatise on the conflict of laws. Baker, Voorhis, 1935 (USA).

CASTEL, J.G.
Canadian conflicts of laws. Butterworths (Canada). Vol. 1. 1975 supp. 1977; Vol. 2: Choice of law. 1977.

CASTEL, J.G.
Conflict of laws: cases, notes and materials. 4ed. Butterworths (Canada), 1978.

CHESHIRE, G.C. & NORTH, P.M.
Private international law. 10ed. Butterworths, 1979.

COWEN, Z.
American-Australian private international law. Oceana, 1957.

DAVIS, J.L.R.
Casebook on conflict of laws. Butterworths (Australia), 1972.

DICEY, A.V. & MORRIS, J.H.C.
The conflict of laws. 10ed. Sweet & Maxwell, 1980 supp. 1984.

DIWAN, P.
Indian and English private international law. Tripathi, 1977.

DROBNIG, U.
American-German private international law. rev. ed. Oceana, 1972.

EHRENZWEIG, A.A.
Conflicts. 3ed. West, 1974 (USA).

FALCONBRIDGE, J.D.
Essays on the conflict of laws. 2ed. Canada Law Book Co., 1954.

FLETCHER, I.F.
Conflict of laws and European Community law: with special reference to the Community conventions on private international law. North-Holland, 1982.

GRAVESON, R.H.
Conflict of laws; private international law. 7ed. Sweet & Maxwell, 1974.

GRAVESON, R.H.
Selected essays:
Vol. 1 Comparative conflict of laws;
Vol. 2 One law: jurisprudence and the unification of law. North-Holland, 1976.

GUTTERIDGE, H.C.
Codification of private international law. Jackson, 1951.

GUTTERIDGE, H.C.
Comparative law and conflict of laws. 2ed. Grotius Society, 1949.

HERTZ, M.
Introduction to the conflict of laws. Carswell, 1978.

HOYLE, M. (ed.)
Private international law: cases and materials. Laureate Press, 1982.

JACKSON, D.C.
The "conflicts" process: jurisdiction and choice in private international law. Oceana, 1975.

KAHN-FREUND, O.
General problems of private international laws. Sijthoff, 1976.

KOLLEWIJN, R.D.
American-Dutch private international law. 2ed. Oceana, 1962 (USA).

KUHN, A.K.
Comparative commentaries on private international law. Macmillan, 1937 (USA).

LAW COMMISSION
Classification of limitation in private international law. HMSO, 1980 (Working paper no. 75).

LAW COMMISSION & SCOTTISH LAW COMMISSION
Private international law: report on the choice of law rules in the draft Non-Life Insurance Services Directive. 1979.

LEVONTIN, A.V.
Choice of law and conflicts of laws. Sijthoff, 1976.

LIPSTEIN, K. (ed.)
Harmonisation of private international law by the E.E.C. I.A.L.S., 1978.

LIPSTEIN, K.
Principles of the conflict of laws. Nijhoff, 1981.

McLEOD, J.
Conflict of laws. Carswell, 1983.

MORRIS, J.H.C.
Cases on private international law. 4ed. Oxford U.P., 1968.

MORRIS, J.H.C.
Conflict of laws. 3ed. Stevens, 1984.

MORSE, C.G.J.
Torts in private international law. North-Holland, 1979.

NORTH, P.M.
Contract conflicts: the EEC Convention on the Law Applicable to Contractual Obligations – a comparative study. North-Holland, 1982.

NORTH, P.M.
The private international law of matrimonial causes in the British Isles and the Republic of Ireland. North-Holland, 1978.

NUSSBAUM, A.
Principles of private international law. Oxford U.P., 1943.

NYGH, P.E.
Conflict of laws in Australia. 3ed. Butterworths (Australia), 1976.

PEARL, D.
Interpersonal conflict of laws in India, Pakistan and Bangladesh. Sweet & Maxwell, 1981.

PHILLIP, A.
American-Danish private international law. Oceana, 1957.

PRYLES, M.C. & HANKS, P.
Federal conflict of laws. Butterworths (Australia), 1974.

SCOTT, A.W.
Private international law: conflict of laws. 2ed. Macdonald & Evans, 1979.

SIEGEL, D.
Conflicts. West, 1982 (USA).

SPIRO, E.
General principles of the conflict of laws. Juta, 1982 (South Africa).

SYKES, E.I. & PRYLES, M.C.
Australian private international law. Law Book Co., 1979.

SYKES, E.I. & PRYLES, M.C.
International and interstate conflict of laws: cases and materials. 2ed. Butterworths (Australia), 1981.

SZASZY, I.
Conflict of laws in the Western socialist and developing countries: a comparative study. Sijthoff, 1974.

SZASZY, I.
Private international law in the European people's democracies. Akademiai Kiado, 1964.

VAN HECKE, G.A.
American-Belgian private international law. Oceana, 1968.

VERNON, D.H.
Conflict of laws: cases, problems and essays. Bender, 1973 (USA) Looseleaf.

WOLFF, M.
Private international law. repr. Scientia, 1977 (USA).

CONSPIRACY

See also Criminal law; Fraud

Encyclopaedias and periodicals

Statutes in Force. Group: Criminal Law.
Halsbury's Laws of England. 4ed. vol. 11.
Halsbury's Statutes of England. 3ed. vol. 8.
Encyclopaedia of Court Forms in Civil Proceedings (Atkin). 2ed. vol. 38.
Encyclopaedia of Forms and Precedents. 4ed. vol. 22.

Cambridge Law Journal. 1921–
Criminal Law Review. 1954–
Law Quarterly Review. 1885–
Modern Law Review. 1937–

Texts

BRYAN, J.W.
Development of the English law of conspiracy. 1909 repr. Johns Hopkins P., 1973.

GILLIES, P.
The law of criminal conspiracy. Law Book Co., 1981.

GOODE, M.R.
Criminal conspiracy in Canada. Carswell, 1975.

HAZELL, R.
Conspiracy and civil liberties (memo submitted to the Law Commission). NCCL, 1974.

LAW COMMISSION
Codification of the criminal law; inchoate offences, conspiracy, attempt and incitment. HMSO, 1973 (Working paper no. 50).

LAW COMMISSION
Criminal law: attempt, and impossibility in relation to attempt, conspiracy and incitement. HMSO, 1980 (Law Com. no. 102).

LAW COMMISSION
Criminal law: report on conspiracy and criminal law reform. HMSO, 1976 (Law Com. no. 76).

ROBERTSON, G.
Whose conspiracy? N.C.C.L., 1974.

WINFIELD, P.H.
History of conspiracy and abuse of legal procedure. Cambridge U.P., 1921.

WRIGHT, R.S.
Law of criminal conspiracies and agreements. Butterworths, 1873 repr. Wildy, 1980.

CONSTITUTIONAL LAW

See also Act of State; Administrative Law; Bill of Rights; Cabinet; Civil Rights and Liberties; Civil Service; Commonwealth Law; Crown; Government; Parliament; Prerogative Orders; Privy Council; and under the names of individual countries.

Encyclopaedias and periodicals

Statutes in Force. Group: Constitutional Law.
Halsbury's Laws of England. 4ed. vol. 8.
The Digest. vol. 11.

Anglo-American Law Review. 1972.
Cambridge Law Journal, 1921–
Journal of the Society of Public Teachers of Law. 1924–1980.

Jurist. 1827–1833; 1837–1867.
Juridical Review. 1889–
Law Reports of the Commonwealth: Constitutional and Administrative. 1985–
Legal Studies. 1981–
Modern Law Review. 1937–
Law Quarterly Review. 1885–

General texts

AMERY, L.C.M.S.
Thoughts on the constitution. 2ed. Oxford U.P., 1953.

AMOS, M.S.
The English constitution. Longmans, Green, 1930.

ANSON, W.R.
The law and customs of the constitution:
Vol. 1 Parliament. 5ed. Oxford U.P., 1922
Vol. 2 The Crown. 4ed. Oxford U.P., 1935.
2 vols.

BAGEHOT, W.
The English constitution. 1969 repr. Fontana, 1983..

BLAUSTEIN, A.P. & FLANZ, G.H. (eds.)
Constitutions of the countries of the world. Oceana, 1966–1971. 13 vols. Looseleaf.

BROOM, H.
Constitutional law, viewed in relation to common law and exemplified by cases. 2ed. Maxwell, 1885.

CALVERT, H.G.
Constitutional law in Northern Ireland. Sweet & Maxwell, 1968.

CASEY, J.
Constitutional law. Sweet & Maxwell, 1984 (Irish law texts).

CHUBB, B.
The constitution and constitutional change in Ireland. 3ed. Inst. of Public Admin., 1978.

CREASY, E.S.
Rise and progress of the English constituion. 17ed. Macmillan, 1907.

DALTON, P.J. & DEXTER R.S.
Constitutional law. Oyez, 1976.

DE SMITH, S.A.
Constitutional and administrative law. 4ed. Penguin, 1981.

DE SMITH, S.A.
The new Commonwealth and its constitutions. Sweet & Maxwell, 1964.

DICEY, A.C.
Introduction to the study of the constituion. 10ed. Macmillan, 1961.

DOOLAN, B.
Constitutional law and constitutional rights in Ireland. Gill & Macmillan, 1984.

EMDEN, C.S.
Principles of British constitutional law. Methuen, 1925.

FINER, S.E. (ed.)
Five constitutions: contrasts and comparisons. Harvester Press, 1979.

FRASER OF TULLYBELTON, W.I.R. Lord
Outline of constitutional law of Scotland. 2ed. Hodge, 1948.

GUPTA, B.B.
Comparative study of six living constitutions: India, U.K., U.S.S.R., Switzerland, France, U.S.A. Tripathi, 1978 (India).

HEUSTON, R.F.V.
Essays in constitutional law. 2ed. Sweet & Maxwell, 1964.

HOME OFFICE
Relationship between the United Kingdom and the Channel Islands and the Isle of Man. HMSO, 1973.

JENNINGS, I.
The British constitution. 5ed. Cambridge U.P., 1966.

JOHNSON, N.
In search of the constitution: reflections on state and society in Britain. Pergamon, 1977.

KEITH, A.R.
Theory of state succession. Waterlow, 1907.

KELLY, J.M.
The Irish constitution. 2ed. Jurist Pub. Co., 1984.

KENNEDY, W.P.M.
Essays in constitutional law. Oxford U.P., 1934.

LASKI, H.J.
Reflections on the constitution. Manchester U.P., 1951.

LASKI, H.J.
The state in theory and practice. Allen & Unwin, 1949.

LAWSON, F.H. & BENTLEY, D.J.
Constitutional and administrative law. Butterworths, 1961.

LOLME, J.L.de
The constitution of England. Bohn, 1853.

MARSHALL, G.
Constitutional conventions: the forms of political accountability. Oxford U.P., 1984.

MARSHALL, G.
Constitutional theory. Oxford U.P., 1980.

MARSHALL, G. & MOODIE, G.C.
Some problems of the constitution. 4ed. Hutchinson, 1967.

MITCHELL, J.
Constitutional law. 2ed. Green, 1968.

NWABUEZE, B.O.
Constitutionalism in the emergent states. C.Hurst, 1978.

PALLEY, C.
Constitutional law and minorities. Minority Rights Group, 1980.

PHILLIPS, O.H.
Constitutional and administrative law. 6ed. Sweet & Maxwell, 1978.

QUEKETT, A.S.
Constitution of Northern Ireland. HMSO, 1928-1946. 3 vols.

ROBSON, P. & WATCHMAN, P.
Justice, Lord Denning and the constitution. Gower, 1981.

ROBSON, W.A.
Justice and administrative law: a study of the British constitution. 3ed. Greenwood, 1970.

ROSEN, F.
Jeremy Bentham and representative democracy: a study of the constitutional code. Oxford U.P., 1983.

ROYAL COMMISSION ON THE CONSTITUTION 1968–1973
Report (Kilbrandon). HMSO, 1973(Cmnd. 5460).
Memorandum of Dissent (Crowther-Hunt & Peacock). HMSO, 1973 (Cmnd. 5460-1).

SCHWARZENBERGER, G.
International constitutional law. Sweet & Maxwell, 1976 (Vol 3 of International law as applied by international courts).

STEPHEN, H.J.
Commentaries on the laws of England. 21ed. Butterworths, 1950 4 vols.

STEVENS, I.
Constitutional and administrative law. Macdonald & Evans, 1982.

WADE, E.C.S. & PHILLIPS, G.G.
Constitutional and administrative law. 9ed. Longman, 1977.

WADE, H.W.R.
Constitutional fundamentals. Sweet & Maxwell, 1980.

WHEARE, K.C.
Government by committee: essay on the British constitution. Greenwood P., 1979.

YARDLEY, D.C.M.
Introduction to British constitutional law. 6ed. Cambridge U.P., 1984.

History

ADAMS, G.B.
Constitutional history of England. 2ed. Cape, 1935.

CHRIMES, S.B.
English constitutional history. 4ed. Oxford U.P., 1967.

CHRIMES, S.B.
English constitutional history: a select bibliography. Historical Association, 1958.

CHRIMES, S.B.
English constitutional idea in the 15th centry. Oxford U.P.,1936.

CHRIMES, S.B.
Introduction to the administrative history of medieval England. 3ed. 1952 repr. Blackwell, 1980.

GOUGH, J.W.
Fundamental law in English constitutional history. Oxford U.P., 1955.

HALLAM, H.
The constitutional history of England from the accession of Henry VII to the death of George II. 1827 repr. Garland P., 1978.

HOLDSWORTH, W.S.
History of English law. 7ed. Sweet & Maxwell, 1956. 17 vols.

HOYT, R.S.
Royal demesne in English constitutional history, 1066–1272. 1950 repr. Cornell U.P., 1963.

JOLIFFE, J.A.
The constitutional history of medieval England from the English settlement to 1485. 4ed. Blackwell, 1961.

KEIR, D.L.
Constitutional history of modern Britain since 1485. 9ed. Blackwell, 1969.

LAPSLEY, G.T.
Crown, community and parliament in the later Middle Ages. Blackwell, 1951.

LOVELL, C.R.
English constitutional and legal history – a survey. Oxford U.P., 1962.

MAITLAND, F.W.
Constitutional history of England. Cambridge U.P., 1908.

MARCHAM, F.G.
Constitutional history of modern England, 1485 to the present. Hamilton, 1960.

MAY, T.E.
Constitutional history of England since the accession of George III. 2ed. Longman, 1892.

MEDLEY, D.J.
Original illustrations of English constitutional history. 2ed. Methuen, 1926.

PICKTHORN, K.
Some historical principles of the constitution. Allan, 1925.

SCHWARTZ, B.
Roots of freedom: a constitutional history of England. Chatto & Windus, 1967.

STUBBS, W.
Constitutional history of England in its origins and development: selections. Univ. of Chicago P., 1979.

TANNER, J.R.
English constitutional conflicts of the seventeenth century, 1603–89. Greenwood Press, 1983.

TASWELL-LANGMEAD, T.P.
English constitutional history. 11ed. Sweet & Maxwell, 1960.

Sources – cases and documents

BICKNELL, B.A.
Cases on the law of the constitution. Oxford U.P., 1926.

COSTIN, W.C. & WATSON, J.S.
The law and working of the constitution: documents 1660–1914 2ed. Blackwell, 1964. 2 vols.

ELTON, G.R.
Tudor constitution: documents and commentary. 2ed. Cambridge U.P., 1982.

GARDINER, S.R.
The constitutional documents of the Puritan revoluation, 1625–1660. 3ed. Oxford U.P., 1906.

HANHAM, H.J.
The nineteenth century constitution: 1815–1914. Documents and commentary. Cambridge U.P., 1969.

KEIR, Sir D.L. & LAWSON, F.H.
Cases in constitutional law. 6ed. Oxford U.P., 1979.

LODGE, E.C. & THORNTON, G.A.
English constitutional documents, 1307–1453. Cambridge U.P., 1935 repr. 1972.

MURPHY, W.F.
Comparative constitutional law: cases and commentaries. Macmillan, 1977.

WILKINSON, B.
Constitutional history of medieval England, 1216–1399. Green, 1948–1958.

WILKINSON, B.
Studies in the constitutional history of the 13th and 14th centuries. Manchester U.P., 1952.

PHILLIPS, O.H. & JACKSON, P.
Leading cases in constitutional and administrative law. 5ed. Sweet & Maxwell, 1979.

PROTHERO, G.W.
Select statutes and constitutional documents illustrative of the reigns of Elizabeth and James I. 4ed. Oxford U.P., 1913.

STEPHENSON, C. & MARCHAM, F.G.
Sources of English constitutional history: a selection of documents from AD 600 to the present. rev. ed. Harper & Row, 1972.

STUBBS, W.
Select charters and other illustrations of English constitutional history. 9ed. Oxford U.P., 1913.

TANNER, J.R.
Constitutional documents of the reign of James I, 1603–1625. Cambridge U.P., 1930.

TANNER, J.R.
Tudor constitutional documents, 1485–1603. 2ed. Cambridge U.P., 1951.

WILSON, G.P.
Cases and materials on constitutional and administrative law. 2ed. Cambridge U.P., 1976.

CONSUMER CREDIT

See also Banks and Banking.

Encyclopaedias and periodicals

Statutes in Force. Group: Hire Purchase and Consumer Credit.
Halsbury's Laws of England. 4ed. see index vol.
Halsbury's Statutes of England. 3ed. vols. 30, 44.
The Digest. mainly vol. 26.
Encyclopaedia of Court Forms in Civil Proceedings (Atkin). 2ed. vol. 20.

Encyclopaedia of Forms and Precedents. 4ed. vol. 10.

Cambridge Law Journal. 1921–
Journal of Business Law. 1957–
Law Quarterly Review. 1885–
Modern Law Review. 1937–
New Law Journal. 1965–
Solicitors Journal. 1857–

Texts

ATIYAH, S.
The sale of goods. 6ed. Pitman, 1980.

BENNION, F.A.R.
Consumer Credit Act manual. 2ed. Oyez, 1981.

BENNION, F.A.R.
Consumer credit control. Oyez, 1976. Looseleaf.

CHARLESWORTH, J.
Mercantile law. 14ed. Stevens, 1984.

DIAMOND, A.L.
Commercial and consumer credit – an introduction. Butterworths, 1982.

DIAMOND, A.L. (ed.)
Instalment credit. Sweet & Maxwell, 1970.

DOBSON, A.P.
Sale of goods and consumer credit. 3ed. Butterworths, 1984.

DUGDALE, D.F.
New Zealand hire purchase law. 3ed. Butterworths (New Zealand), 1977.

GOODE, R.M. (ed.)
Consumer Credit Act: a student's guide. Butterworths, 1979.

GOODE, R.M.
Consumer Credit Act 1974. Butterworths, 1974.

GOODE, R.M.
Consumer credit legislation. Butterworths, 1977. Looseleaf.

GOODE, R.M.
Hire purchase law and practice. 2ed. Butterworths, 1970 + supp.

GOODE, R.M.
Legal problems of credit and security. Sweet & Maxwell, 1982.

GOODE, R.M. & ZIEGEL, J.S.
Hire-purchase and conditional sale: a comparative survey of Commonwealth and American law. B.I.I.C.L., 1965.

GOW, J.J.
Law of hire purchase in Scotland. Green, 1968.

GUEST, A.G. (ed.)
Encyclopaedia of consumer credit law. Sweet & Maxwell, 1975. Looseleaf.

GUEST, A.G.
The law of hire-purchase. Sweet & Maxwell, 1966.

GUEST, A.G. & LOMNICKA, E.
Introduction to the law of credit and security. Sweet & Maxwell, 1978.

LOWE, R. & WOODROFFE, G.
Consumer law and practice. Sweet & Maxwell, 1980.

MACLEOD, J.K.
Sale and hire-purchase. Butterworths, 1971.

MESTON, Lord
Guide to the Consumer Credit Act, 1974. B.Rose, 1982.

NATIONAL CONSUMER COUNCIL
Consumers and credit. 1980.

PARK, W.D.
Hire-purchase and other credit transactions. 5ed. Oyez, 1969.

PHILLIPS, J.D.
Sale of goods, hire-purchase and agency. Sweet & Maxwell, 1969.

PRICES AND CONSUMER PROTECTION, DEPARTMENT OF
Reform of the law on consumer credit. HMSO, 1973 (Cmnd. 5427).

SAMUEL, G.
Cases in consumer law. Macdonald & Evans, 1979.

TRADE, BOARD OF
Final report of the Committee on Consumer Credit (Maloney). HMSO, 1962 (Cmnd. 1781).

TRADE & INDUSTRY, DEPARTMENT OF
Report of the committee on consumer credit (Crowther). HMSO, 1971 (Cmnd. 4596). 2 vols.

CONSUMER PROTECTION

See also Fair Trading

Encyclopaedias and periodicals

Statutes in Force. Groups: Contract; Hire-Purchase and Consumer Credit.
Halsbury's Statutes of England. 3ed. vols. 30 & 43.

Consumer Law Today. 1977–
Journal of Business Law. 1957–
New Law Journal. 1965–

Texts

ARONSTAM, P.
Consumer protection, freedom of contract. Juta, 1974 (South Africa).

BORRIE, G.J.
Development of consumer law and policy: bold spirits and timorous souls. Stevens, 1984 (Hamlyn lecture).

BORRIE, G.J. & DIAMOND, A.L.
Consumer, society and the law. 4ed. Penguin, 1981.

CAPLOVITZ, D.
Consumers in trouble. Appleton, 1973 (USA).

CLAYTON, P.
Consumer law for the small business. 3ed. Kogan Page, 1983.

CONSUMER PROTECTION ADVISORY COMMITTEE
Disguised business sales: a report on the practice of seeking to sell goods without revealing that they are being sold in the course of a business. HMSO, 1975–76 (H.C. 355)

CONSUMER PROTECTION ADVISORY COMMITTEE
Rights of consumers: a report on practices relating to the purported exclusion of inalienable rights of consumers and failure to explain their existence. HMSO, 1974–75. (H.C. 6).

COUNCIL OF EUROPE
Role of criminal law in consumer protection. HMSO, 1983.

COUNCIL OF EUROPE. COMMITTEE OF EXPERTS ON THE LEGAL PROTECTION OF CONSUMERS
Unfair terms in consumers' contracts and an appropriate method of control. Resolution (76)47. 1977.

CRANSTON, R.
Consumers and the law. 2ed. Weidenfeld & N., 1984.

CRANSTON, R.
Regulating business: law and consumer agencies. Macmillan, 1979.

CUNNINGHAM, J.P.
The Fair Trading Act 1973: consumer protection and competition law. Sweet & Maxwell, 1974 supp. 1978.

DUGGAN, A.J. & DARVALL, L.W.
Consumer protection law and theory. Law Book Co., 1980 (Australia).

ENCYCLOPAEDIA of consumer law. Sweet & Maxwell, 1980– . Looseleaf.

FELDMAN, L.P.
Consumer protection: problems and prospects. 2ed. West, 1980 (USA).

FONTAINE, M. & BOURGOINE, T.
Consumer legislation in Belgium and Luxembourg. Van Nostrand Reinhold, 1982.

GOLDRING, J. & MAHER, L.W.
Consumer protection law in Australia. 2ed. Butterworths (Australia), 1983.

HARRIES, J.V.
Consumers, know your rights. 3ed. Oyez, 1983.

HARVEY, B.W.
Law of consumer protection and fair trading. 2ed. Butterworths, 1982.

HONDIUS, E.H.
Consumer legislation in the Netherlands. Van Nostrand Reinhold, 1980.

IRVING, R.
Outline of the law of product liability and consumer protection. B.Rose, 1980.

LEDER, M.
Consumer law. Macdonald & Evans, 1980.

LOWE, R. & WOODROFFE, G.
Consumer law and practice. Sweet & Maxwell, 1980.

McCALL, J.
Cases on consumer protection. West, 1977 (USA).

MICKLEBURGH, J.
Consumer protection. Professional Books, 1979.

NATIONAL FEDERATION OF CONSUMER GROUPS
Handbook of consumer law. Hodder, 1982.

OFFICE OF FAIR TRADING
Fair deal: a shopper's guide. HMSO.

OFFICE OF FAIR TRADING
Review of the Trade Descriptions Act 1968. HMSO, 1976.

PAINTER, A.A.
Consumer protection for boat users. Nautical Pub. Co., 1979.

PAINTER, A.A.
Guide to consumer protection law. B.Rose, 1978.

REAMS, B.D. & FERGUSON, J.R.
Consumer protection: basic documents and laws, federal and state. Oceana, 1978 (USA). 6 looseleaf vols.

REICH, N. & MICKLITZ, H.W.
Consumer legislation in the European Community countries: a comparative analysis. Van Nostrand Reinhold, 1980.

SAMUEL, G.
Cases in consumer law. Macdonald & Evans, 1979.

SMITH, P. & SWANN, D.
Protecting the consumer. Martin Robertson, 1979.

STEPHENSON, G.
Criminal law and consumer protection. B.Rose, 1983.

TAPERELL, G.G., VERMEESCH, R.B. & HARLAND, D.J.
Trade practices and consumer protection. 3ed. Butterworths (Australia), 1983.

WHINCUP, M.H.
Consumer legislation in the United Kingdom and the Republic of Ireland: a study prepared for the E.C. Commission. Van Nostrand Reinhold, 1980.

WHINCUP, M.H.
Consumer protection law in America, Canada and Europe. Stationery Office, Dublin, 1973.

WOODROFFE, G.
Consumer law in the E.E.C. Sweet & Maxwell, 1984.

WORDSALL, A.
Consumer law for the motor trade. Butterworths, 1981.

CONTEMPT

See also Administration of Justice; Criminal Law; Parliament.

Encyclopaedias and periodicals

Statutes in Force. Group: Courts, Supreme Court, England and Wales.
Halsbury's Laws of England. 4ed. vol. 9.
Halsbury's Statutes of England. 3ed. vol. 7.
The Digest. vol. 16.
Encyclopaedia of Court Forms in Civil Proceedings (Atkin). 2ed. vol. 7.

Criminal Law Review. 1954–
Law Quarterly Review. 1885–
Modern Law Review. 1937–
New Law Journal. 1965–

Texts

BORRIE, G.J. & LOWE, N.V.
The law of contempt. 2ed. Butterworths, 1983.

FOX, J.C.
The history of contempt of court. Oxford U.P., 1927 repr. Professional Books, 1974.

GOLDFARB, R.L.
The contempt power. Columbia U.P., 1963 (USA).

JUSTICE
Contempt of court. Stevens, 1959.

LAW COMMISSION
Offences relating to the administration of justice (Working paper no. 62). HMSO, 1975.

LORD CHANCELLOR'S OFFICE
Contempt of court: a discussion paper. HMSO, 1978 (Cmnd. 7145).

LORD CHANCELLOR'S OFFICE
Report of the Committee on Contempt of Court (Phillimore). HMSO, 1974 (Cmnd. 5794).

LORD CHANCELLOR'S OFFICE
Report on the Interdepartmental Committee on the Law of Contempt as it affects Tribunals of Inquiry (Salmon). HMSO, 1969 (Cmnd. 4078).

MILLER, C.J.
Contempt of court. Elek, 1976.

NICOL, A. & ROGERS, H.
Changing contempt of court. N.C.C.L., 1981.

OSWALD, J.F.
Contempt of court. 3ed. Butterworths, 1910.

ROSSI, M.G.
Il contempt of court e la specific performance nel diritto inglese. Vittorio Ferri, 1934 (Italy).

STARKIE, T.
Law of slander & libel .... contempts of court etc. Butterworths, 1908.

SUPREME Court practice 1985. Sweet & Maxwell, 1984. 2 vols.

VARMA, B.R.
Law of contempt in India. Tripathi, 1974.

CONTINENTAL SHELF

See also International Law; Sea, Law of; Territorial Waters.

Encyclopaedias

Statutes in Force. Group: Mines and Minerals.
Halsbury's Statutes of England. 3ed. vol. 22 & 43.
Encyclopaedia of Forms and Precedents. 4ed. vol. 13.

Texts

AMIN, S.H.
Customary rules of delimitation of the continental shelf. Royston, 1984.

ANDRASSY, J.
International law and the resources of the sea. Columbia U.P., 1970.

AUGUSTE, B.L.
The continental shelf: the practice and policy of the Latin American States. Dros:Lounz, 1961 (USA).

JUDA, L.
Ocean space rights: developing U.S. policy. Praeger, 1975.

MARSTON, G.
Marginal seabed: United Kingdom legal practice. Oxford U.P., 1981.

MOUTON, M.W.
The continental shelf. Nijhoff, 1952 repr. 1969.

PARK, C.
Continental shelf issues in the Yellow Sea and the East China Sea. Law of the Sea Inst., 1972.

WILLIAMS, W.W.
Coastal changes. 1960 repr. Greenwood, 1975.

CONTRACT

See also Advertising; Building and Engineering Contracts; C.I.F. and F.O.B. Contracts; Commercial Law; Consumer Credit; Employment Law; Mortgages; Specific Performance.

Encyclopaedias and periodicals

Statutes in Force. Group: Contract.
Halsbury's Laws of England. 4ed. vol. 9.
Halsbury's Statutes of England. 3ed. vol. 7.
The Digest. vol. 12.
Encyclopaedia of Court Forms in Civil Proceedings (Atkin). 2ed. see index vol.
Encyclopaedia of Forms and Precedents. 4ed. see index vol.

Australian Law Journal. 1927–
Banking Law Journal (USA) 1889–
Cambridge Law Journal. 1921–
Common Market Law Review. 1963–
Contract Journal. 1879–
Current Legal Problems. 1948=
Current Law. 1947–

European Law Review. 1975–
Harvard Law Review. 1887–
Irish Law Times. 1867–
Judicial Review. 1889–
Law Quarterly Review. 1885–
Law Society's Gazette. 1903–
Lloyd's Maritime & Commercial Law Quarterly. 1974–
Modern Law Review. 1937–
New Zealand Law Journal. 1925–
New Law Journal. 1966–
Scots Law Times. 1948–
Solicitors' Journal. 1857–
South African Law Journal. 1884–

General texts

ACHIKE, O.
Nigerian law of contract. Nwamife, 1972.

ADDISON, C.G.
A treatise on the law of contracts. 11ed. Stevens, 1911.

ALLAN, D.E. (ed.)
Asian contract law. Melbourne U.P., 1969.

AMERICAN LAW INSTITUTE
Restatement of the law. 2ed. Contracts. 1973.

ANDERSON, R. & SIMON, M.
English-French glossary of terms in English law of contract. Sweet & Maxwell, 1975.

ANSON, W.R.
Principles of the English law of contract. 25ed. Oxford U.P., 1979.

ATIYAH, L.R.
Introduction to the law of contract. 3ed. Oxford U.P., 1981.

ATIYAH, P.S.
Rise and fall of freedom of contract. Oxford U.P., 1979.

BOWDEN, G.F. & MORRIS, A.S.
Introduction to the law of contract and tort. Estates Gazette, 1978.

BOYLE, C.L.M. & PERCY, D.R.
Contracts: cases and commentaries. 2ed. Carswell, 1981.

BRAZIER, R.
Cases and statutes on contract law. 3ed. Sweet & Maxwell, 1979.

CANEY, L.R.
A treatise on the law of novation in South Africa. 2ed. Juta, 1973.

CHESHIRE, G.C.
International contracts. Jackson, 1948.

CHESHIRE, G.C. & FIFOOT, C.H.S.
Cases on the law of contract. 7ed. Butterworths, 1977.

CHESHIRE, G.C. & FIFOOT, C.H.S.
The law of contract. 10ed. Butterworths, 1981.

CHESHIRE, G.C. & FIFOOT, C.H.S.
The law of contract. 4ed. Butterworths (Australia), 1981.

CHESHIRE, G.C. & FIFOOT, C.H.S.
The law of contract. 4ed. Butterworths (New Zealand), 1974.

CHITTY, J.
Law of contracts. 24ed. Sweet & Maxwell, 1977. 2 vols & supp. 1979.

CHITTY, J.
Practical treatise on the law of contracts not under seal. 1826 repr. Garland P., 1979.

CORBIN, A.
Textbook on contracts. West, 1952 (USA).

COULSON, N.J.
Contract law in Saudi Arabia and the Gulf States. Graham & Trotman, 1980.

DAVIES, F.R.
Contract. 4ed. Sweet & Maxwell, 1981.

DEUTCH, S.
Unfair contracts: doctrine of unconscionability. Lexington, 1977 (USA).

EUROPEAN COMMITTEE ON CRIME PROBLEMS
Standard terms in contracts: colloquy proceedings. Council of Europe, 1980.

FESSLER, D.
Cases and materials on contracts. West, 1982 (USA).

FIFOOT, C.H.S.
History and sources of the common law, tort and contract. Stevens, 1949.

FREEDMAN, M.
Cases and materials on contracts. West, 1973 (USA).

FRIDMAN, G.
The law of contracts. Carswell, 1976 supp. 1980.

GILMORE, G.
The death of contracts. Ohio State U.P., 1974 (USA).

HARLAND, D.J.
The law of minors in relation to contracts and property. Butterworths (Australia), 1974.

HARLOW, P.A. (Ed.)
Contractual claims: an annotated bibliography. 3ed. Inst. of Building, 1979.

JACKSON, R.M.
The history of quasi-contract in English law. Cambridge U.P., 1936.

KEENER, W.A.
A treatise on the law of quasi-contracts. Baker, Voorhis, 1893 (USA).

KERR, A.J.
The principles of the law of contract. 2ed. Butterworths (S.Africa), 1975.

KNIPE, J.C.
Law of contract: general rules and their exceptions. 2ed. Lang, 1980.

LAW COMMISSION
Contribution. HMSO, 1975 repr. 1977 (Working paper no. 59).

LAW COMMISSION
Law of contract.: report on contribution. HMSO, 1977 (Law Com. no. 79).

LAW COMMISSION
Law of contract: report on interest. HMSO, 1978 (Law Com. no. 88).

LAW COMMISSION
Law of contract: report on the proposed EEC Directive on the law relating to commercial agents. HMSO, 1977 (Law Com. no. 84).

LAW COMMISSION
Law of contract: the parol evidence rule. HMSO, 1976 (Working paper no. 70).

LAW COMMISSION & SCOTTISH LAW COMMISSION
Provisional proposals relating to amendments to section 12–15 of the Sales of Goods Act 1893 and contracting out of the conditions and warranties implied by those sections. HMSO, 1968 repr. 1977 (Working paper no. 18; Memorandum no.7).

LAW REFORM COMMITTEE
Eighth report: sealing of contracts by bodies corporate. HMSO, 1958 (Cmnd. 622).

LEAKE, S.M.
Principles of the law of contracts. 8ed. Stevens, 1931.

LINDGREN, K.E.
Time in the performance of contracts. 2ed. Butterworths (Australia), 1982.

MAJOR, W.T.
Cases in contract law. 4ed. Macdonald & Evans, 1983.

MAJOR, W.T.
The law of contract. 6ed. Macdonald & Evans, 1983.

MARSH, P.D.V.
Contract negotiation handbook. 2ed. Gower, 1984.

MARSHALL, E.A.
Scottish cases on contract. Green, 1978.

MARSHALL, O.R.
The assignment of choses in action. Pitman, 1950.

MILNER, J.B.
Cases and materials on contracts. 3ed. Univ. of Toronto P., 1977 (Canada).

NICHOLAS, B.
French law of contract. Butterworths, 1982.

NORTH, P.M.
Contract conflicts: the EEC Convention on the Law Applicable to Contractual Obligations – a comparative study. North-Holland, 1982.

PANNAM, C.
Cases and materials on contract. 4ed. Law Book Co., 1979.

PEDEN, J.R.
Law of unjust contracts. Butterworths (Australia), 1982.

POLLOCK, F.
Principles of contract. 13ed. Stevens, 1950.

POWELL-SMITH, V.
Contract. 6ed. Butterworths, 1982.

ROEBUCK, D.
Law of contract – text and materials. Sweet & Maxwell, 1974 (Australia).

ROGERS, W.V.H. & CLARKE, M.G. (eds.)
Unfair Contract Terms Act, 1977. Sweet & Maxwell, 1978.

ROWLATT, Sir A.T.
Principal and surety. 4ed. Sweet & Maxwell, 1982.

SAGAY, I.E.
Casebook on the Nigerian law of contract. Professional Books, 1983.

SCHLESINGER, R.B.
Formation of contracts: a study of the common core of legal systems. Oceana, 1968. 2 vols.

SIMPSON. A.W.B.
History of the common law of contract: the rise of the action of assumpsit. Oxford U.P., 1975.

SIMPSON, L.
Hornbook on contracts. 2ed. West, 1965.

SINNADURAI, V.
The law of contract in Malaysia and Singapore: cases and commentary. Oxford U.P., 1979.

SMITH, J.C. & THOMAS, J.A.C.
Casebook on contract. 7ed. Sweet & Maxwell, 1982.

SPENCER BOWER, G. & TURNER, A.K.
Estoppel by misrepresentation. 3ed. Butterworths, 1977.

STARKE, J.G., HIGGINS, P.F.P. & SWANTON, J.
Casebook on the law of contract. Butterworths (Australia), 1975.

STOLJAR, S.J.
A history of contract at common law. Australian National Univ. P., 1975.

STOLJAR, S.J.
The law of quasi-contract. Law Book Co., 1964 (Australia).

SUTTON, R. & SHANNON, N.P.
On contracts. 7ed. Butterworths, 1970.

THOMPSON, P.K.J.
Unfair Contract Terms Act, 1977. Butterworths, 1978.

TREITEL, G.H.
The law of contract. 6ed. Stevens, 1983.

TREITEL, G.H.
An outline of the law of contract. 3ed. Butterworths, 1984.

WALDRON, J.K.
Guidelines on the law of contract and agency. Waldron, 1972.

WALKER, D.M.
Law of contracts and related obligations in Scotland. Butterworths, 1979.

WILLIAMS, G.L.
Joint obligations. Butterworths, 1949.

WINFIELD, P.H.
The law of quasi-contracts. Sweet & Maxwell, 1952.

WOODWARD, F.C.
The law of quasi-contracts. Little, Brown & Co., 1913 (USA).

ZIMAN, L.D.
Law and practice of commercial contract. Butterworths, 1980.

Particular contracts

BLACKBURN, Lord
A treatise on the effect of the contract of sale. 3ed Stevens, 1910.

CLARKE, M. (ed.)
Shipbuilding contracts. Lloyd's, 1982.

CONTRACT

CONFEDERATION OF BRITISH INDUSTRY
A guide to government contracts for stores and services: a survey of procedures and practices of government purchasing departments. C.B.I., 1975.

DIX, D. & CRUMP, D.W.
Contracts of employment. 6ed. Butterworths, 1980.

FARRAND, J.T.
Contract and conveyance. 2ed. Oyez, 1973.

FREEDLAND, M.R.
Contract of employment. Oxford U.P., 1976.

GORTON, L. & IHRE, R.
Contracts of affreightment. Lloyd's, 1985.

GREENSTREET, B.
Legal and contractual procedures for architects. 2ed. Architectural P., 1984.

HEYDON, J.D.
The restraint of trade doctrine. Butterworths, 1971.

HUDSON, A.A.
Building and engineering contracts. 10ed. Sweet & Maxwell, 1970 supp. 1979.

KEATING, D.
Law and practice of building contracts. 4ed. Sweet & Maxwell, 1978 supp. 1982.

KEYES, W.
Government contracts. West, 1979 (USA).

LAW COMMISSION
Loss of services. 1968 repr. 1977 (Working Paper No.19).

MORGAN, R.
Computer contracts. Oyez, 1979.

RENNIE, M.T.M.
Computer contracts handbook. Sweet & Maxwell, 1984.

SLABOTZKY, A.
Grain contracts and arbitration. Lloyd's, 1984.

TURPIN, C.
Government contracts. Penguin, 1972.

WALLACE, I.N.D.
International form of contract. Sweet & Maxwell, 1974.

WALLACE, I.N.D.
The international civil engineering contract. Sweet & Maxwell, 1974 supp. 1980.

WILFORD, M., COGHLIN, T. & HEALY, N.J.
Time charters. 2ed. Lloyd's, 1982.

Elements – consideration, etc.

ATIYAH, P.S.
Consideration in contracts: a fundamental restatement. Australian National Univ. P., 1971.

JENKS, E.
History of the doctrine of consideration in English law. Clay, 1892 repr. 1969.

LAW COMMISSION
Firm offers. HMSO, 1975 repr. 1977 (Working paper no. 60).

LAW COMMISSION
Law of contract: implied terms in contracts for the supply of goods. HMSO, 1977 (Working paper no. 77).

LAW REVISION COMMITTEE
Statute of frauds and the doctrine of consideration. 6th interim report. HMSO, 1937 (Cmd. 5449).

SUTTON, K.C.T.
Consideration reconsidered: studies on the doctrine of consideration of the law of contract. Univ. of Queensland P., 1974.

TREITEL, G.H.
Doctrine and discretion in the law of contract. Oxford U.P., 1981.

Vitiating elements

CHAMPNESS, R.
Mistake in the law of contract. Stevens, 1933.

COOTE, B.
Exception clauses. Sweet & Maxwell, 1964.

GOODE, R.M. & GRABINER, A.S.
Exemption clauses. Law Society, 1979.

KERR, W.
The law of fraud and mistake. 7ed. Sweet & Maxwell, 1952.

LAW COMMISSION & SCOTTISH
LAW COMMISSION
Exemption clauses in contracts: first report.
HMSO, 1969 (Law Com. no. 24; Scot.
Law Com. no. 12).

LAW COMMISSION & SCOTTISH
LAW COMMISSION
Exemption clauses: second report. HMSO,
1975 (Law Com. no. 69; Scot. Law Com.
no. 39).

LAW COMMISSION & SCOTTISH
LAW COMMISSION
Exemption clauses in contracts for services.
HMSO, 1971 repr. 1977 (Working paper
no. 39; Memorandum no. 15).

LAW COMMISSION
Implied terms in contracts for the supply of
goods. HMSO, 1979 (Law Com. no. 95).

LAW COMMISSION
Penalty clauses and forfeiture of monies
paid. HMSO, 1975 repr. 1977 (Working
paper no. 61).

LAW REFORM COMMITTEE
Tenth report: innocent misrepresentation.
HMSO, 1962 (Cmnd. 1782).

LAWSON, R.
Exclusion clauses: after the Unfair Contract
Terms Act. 2ed. Oyez, 1983.

LINDGREN, K.E.
Time in the performance of contracts
especially contracts for the sale of property.
2ed. Butterworths (Australia), 1982.

McELROY, R.G.
Impossibility of performance. Cambridge
U.P., 1941.

SPENCER BOWER, G. & TGURNER,
A.K.
The law of actionable misrepresentation.
3ed. Butterworths, 1974.

STEIN, P.
Fault in the formation of contract in Roman
law and Scots law. Oliver & Boyd, 1958.

STOLJAR, S.J.
Mistake and misrepresentation. Sweet &
Maxwell, 1968.

YATES, D.
Exclusion clauses in contracts. 2ed. Sweet
& Maxwell, 1982.

Remedies

BEALE, H.
Remedies for breach of contract. Sweet &
Maxwell, 1980.

CARTER, J.
Breach of contract. Sweet & Maxwell, 1984.

DOBBS, D.
Hornbook on remedies. West, 1973 (USA).

DOBBS, D.
Problems in remedies. West, 1974 (USA).

FRIDMAN, G.
Restitution. Carswell, 1982 (Canada).

FRIEDMAN, J.
Contract remedies. West, 1981 (USA).

FRY, E.
A treatise on the specific performance of
contracts. 6ed. Stevens, 1921.

GOFF, Sir F. & JONES, G.
The law of restitution. 2ed. Sweet &
Maxwell, 1978.

LAW COMMISSION
Pecuniary restitution on breach of contract.
HMSO, 1975 (Working paper no. 65).

O'CONNELL, J.
Remedies. West, 1977 (USA).

SPRY, J.C.F.
Equitable remedies, injunctions and
specific performance. 2ed. Sweet &
Maxwell, 1980.

CONVEYANCING

See also Contract; Copyhold; Gazumping; Land; Land Charges; Land Registration; Mortgages; Title; Torrens Title; Vendor and Purchaser.

Encyclopaedias and periodicals

Statutes in Force. Groups: Property, England & Wales, Sub-groups 1, 2, Conveyancing and Registration of Writs, Scotland.
Halsbury's Statutes of England. 3ed. see index vol.
Encyclopaedia of Court Forms in Civil Proceedings (Atkin). 2ed. see index vol.
Encyclopaedia of Forms and Precedents. 4ed. see index vol.

Conveyancer. 1915–1936.
Conveyancer and Property Lawyer. 1936–
Estates Gazette. 1858–
Journal of the Law Society for Scotland. 1956–
Law Society's Gazette. 1903–

Texts

ADAMS, E.C.
The Land Transfer Act 1952. 2ed. Butterworths, 1971 (New Zealand).

ADAMS, J.E. (ed.)
Precedents for the conveyancer. Sweet & Maxwell, 1978. 2 vols. looseleaf.

AHERN, J.
Victorian conveyancing costs. 2ed. Butterworths (Australia), 1976 supp. 1978.

ALDRIDGE, T.M.
Guide to enquiries before contract. Oyez, 1978.

ALDRIDGE, T.M.
Guide to enquiries of local authorities. Oyez, 1978.

ALDRIDGE, T.M.
Guide to National Conditions of Sale. 19ed. Oyez, 1979.

ALDRIDGE, T.M.
Guide to the Law Society's Conditions of Sale. Oyez, 1981.

ALDRIDGE, T.M.
Practical conveyancing precedents. Oyez Longman, 1984. Looseleaf.

ANNAND, R. & CAIN, B.
Modern conveyancing. Sweet & Maxwell, 1984.

BARNSLEY, D.G.
Conveyancing law and practice. 2ed. Butterworths, 1982.

BURKE, D.B.
American conveyancing patterns: past improvements and current debates. Lexington Books, 1978 (USA).

BURNETT, J.F.R.
Elements of conveyancing. 8ed. Sweet & Maxwell, 1952.

BUTTERWORTH's conveyancing costs (NSW). 2ed. Butterworths (Australia), 1977 supp. 1980.

CHARLEBOIS, L.H., FRANCIS, E.A. 7 YOUNG, P.W.
Conveyancing service (NSW). Butterworths (Australia), 1981. Looseleaf.

CHAVASSE, C.P.G.
Conveyancing and other non-contentions costs. 7ed. Oyez, 1980 (Practice notes, no.20).

CONSUMERS' ASSOCIATION
The legal side of buying a house. Rev. ed. Hodder, 1983.

CONVEYANCER & PROPERTY LAWYER
Precedents for the conveyancer. Sweet & Maxwell. Looseleaf.

EMMET, L.E.
Notes on perusing titles and on practical conveyancing. 18ed. Oyez, 1983 supp. 1984.

FARRAND, J.T.
Contract and conveyance. 4ed. Oyez, 1983.

GALE, C.J.
The law of easements. 14ed. Sweet & Maxwell, 1972.

GEORGE, E.F. & GEORGE, A.
The sale of flats. 5ed. Sweet & Maxwell, 1984.

GIBSON, A.
Conveyancing. 21ed. Law Notes, 1980 supp. 1982.

HALLIDAY, J.M.
The Conveyancing and Feudal Reform (Scotland) Act, 1970. 2ed. Green, 1977.

HAYTON, D.J.
Registered land. 3ed. Sweet & Maxwell, 1981.

HOLLAND, J.A. & LEWIS, J.R.
Principles of registered land conveyancing. Butterworths, 1967.

JONES, R.
Law and practice of conveyancing in South Africa. 2ed. Juta, 1976.

KELLY, J.H.
Draftsman. 14ed. Butterworths, 1978.

KENNY, P.H. & BEVAN, C.
Conveyancing law. 2ed. Macdonald & Evans, 1983.

KEY, T. & ELPHINSTONE, H.W.
Precedents in conveyancing. 15ed. Sweet & Maxwell, 1953–54 3 vols.

LANG, A.G. & EVERETT, D.
Land dealings and conveyancing casebook. Butterworths (Australia), 1979.

MELLOWS, A.R.
Conveyancing searches. Oyez, 1975.

MOERAN, E.
Introduction to conveyancing. Oyez, 1979.

MOERAN, E.
Practical conveyancing. 8ed. Oyez, 1981 (Practice notes no.44).

NEWMAN, P.E.
Conveyancing of leasehold property. Fourmat, 1982.

RUOFF, T.B.F. & ROPER, R.B.
Law and practice of registered conveyancing. 4ed. Sweet & Maxwell, 1979.

SCOTTISH HOME & HEALTH DEPARTMENT
Conveyancing legislation and practice. HMSO, 1966 (Cmnd. 3118).

SMITH, T.B.
Property problems in sale. Sweet & Maxwell, 1979.

SOARES, P.C.
Tax strategy for conveyancing and land transactions. Oyez Longman, 1984.

STEELE, R.T.
Do it yourself conveyancing. David & Charles, 1978.

STERK, J.
Alberta conveyancing law and practice. Carswell, 1981.

STUCKEY, G.
Conveyancing Acts 1919–1969 and regulations. 2ed. Law Book Co., 1970.

WILKINSON, H.W.
Standard conditions of sale of land. 2ed. Oyez, 1974.

WILLIAMS, W.J.
The law and practice relating to the contract for the sale of land and title to land. 4ed. Butterworths, 1975 supp. 1980.

WILSON, M.
Conveyancing fees and duties on sale of freehold and leasehold. 4ed. Fourmat, 1984.

WITCHELL, R.G.
Practice and procedure vol. 2. Conveyancing. 5ed. Oyez, 1974.

WOLSTENHOLME, E.P. & CHERRY, B.L.
Conveyancing statutes. 13ed. Butterworths, 1972. 6 vols.

WYLIE, J.C.W.
Irish conveyancing law. Professional Books, 1978.

COPYHOLD

See also Conveyancing; Gavelkind; Real Property

Encyclopaedias

Statutes in Force. Group: Property, England and Wales.
Halsbury's Laws of England. 4ed. vol. 9.
Halsbury's Statutes of England. 3ed. vol. 7.
The Digest. vol. 13

Encyclopaedia of Court Forms in Civil Proceedings (Atkin). 2ed. vol.13.
Encyclopaedia of Forms and Precedents. 4ed. see index vol.

Texts

ADKIN, B.W.
Copyholds and other land tenures. 3ed.
Estates Gazette, 1919 supp. 1924.

COOKE, G.W.
A treatise on the law and practice of copyhold enfranchisement...Stevens, 1853.

ELTON, C.I.
A treatise on the law of copyholds and customary tenures of land. 2ed. Wildy, 1893 supp. 1898.

GRAY, C.M.
Copyhold, equity and the common law. Harvard U.P., 1963 (USA).

HART, G.E.
The enfranchisment of copyholds and the extinguishment of manorial incidents (under the Property Acts, 1922 and 1924). Butterworths, 1926.

ROUSE, R.
Copyhold and court-keeping practice with precedents. Maxwell, 1837.

ROUSE, R.
Copyhold and enfranchisement manual. 3ed. Maxwell, 1866.

SCRIVEN, J.
Treatise on the law of copyholds. 7ed. Butterworths, 1896.

SHELFORD, L.
Law of copyholds. Sweet, 1853 supp. 1858.

WATKINS, C.
A treatise on copyholds. 4ed. Maxwell, 1825. 2 vols.

COPYRIGHT

See also Advertising; Patents; Press Law; Printers and Publishers; Trade Marks.

Encyclopaedias and periodicals

Statutes in Force. Group: Copyright.
Halsbury's Laws of England. 4ed. vool. 7.
Halsbury's Statutes of England. 3ed. vol.7.
The Digest. vol. 13
Encyclopaedia of Court Forms in Civil Proceedings (Atkin). 2ed. vol.12
Encyclopaedia of Forms and Precedents. 4ed. vol.7.

Annual of Industrial Property Law. The Author. 1889–
Bulletin of the Copyright Society of the USA. 1953–

Copyright. 1965–
Copyright Bulletin, UNESCO. 1948–
Copyright Law Journal (USA). 1983–
Copyright Law Symposium, ASCAP. 1952–
European Intellectual Property Review. 1978–
I.P. Newsletter. 1978–
Intellectual Property Decisions. 1978–
MacGillivray Copyright Cases. 1901–1949. 9 vols.

Texts

BARKER, R.E.
Photocopying practices in the UK. Faber, 1970.

BARNES, J.J.
Authors, publishers and politicians: the quest for an Anglo-American copyright agreement, 1815–54. Ohio State U.P., 1974.

BIRRELL, A.
Seven lectures on the law and history of copyright in books. 1889 repr. Rothman, 1971.

BOGSCH, A.
The law of copyright under the universal convention. 3ed. Sijthoff, 1972.

BRETT, H. (ed.)
Legal protection of computer software. E.S.C., 1981.

BUSH, G.P.
Technology and copyright: annotated bibliography and source materials. Lomond, 1972 (USA).

CABINET OFFICE
Intellectual property rights and innovation.
HMSO, 1983 (Cmnd. 9117).

CARTER-RUCK, P.F. & SKONE
JAMES, E.P.
Copyright modern law and practice. Faber,
1965.

CAVENDISH, J.M.
Handbook of copyright in British publishing
practice. Cassell, 1974.

CAWTHRA, B.I.
Industrial property rights in the EEC:
patents, trade marks and copyright. Gower,
1973.

COMMONWEALTH SECRETARIAT
Copyright in developing countries. 2ed.
1976.

CONNORS, J.A. (ed.)
Protecting intellectual property in the Asian
Pacific. Oyez Longman, 1984.

COPELING, A.J.C.
Copyright law in South Africa.
Butterworths (South Africa), 1969.

COPINGER, W.A. & SKONE JAMES,
E.P.
Copyright. 12ed. Sweet & Maxwell, 1980.

CORNISH, W.R.
Intellectual property: patents, copyright,
trade marks and allied rights. Sweet &
Maxwell, 1981.

CRABB, G.
Copyright and contract. Nat. Council for
Educ. Tech., 1976.

CRABB, G.
Copyright clearance: a practical guide. Nat.
Council for Educ. Tech., 1976.

DAVIES, G.
Challenges to copyright and related rights
in the European Community. ESC Pub.,
1983.

DRONE, E.S.
Treatise on the law of property in
intellectual productions in Great Briatain
and the US embracing copyright in works of
literature and art and playright in dramatic
and musical compositions. 1879 repr.
Rothman, 1972.

FLINT, M.F.
A user's guide to copyright. Butterworths,
1979.

FOX, H.G.
Canadian law of copyright and industrial
designs. 2ed. Carswell, 1967.

FYSH, M. & THOMAS, R.W.
Industrial property citator. ELC Pub., 1982.

GUY, D. & LEIGH, G.
The E.E.C. and intellectual property. Sweet
& Maxwell, 1981.

HUNNINGS, N.M.
Industrial property cases from Common
Market law reports. ELC, 1973.

JOHANNES, H.
Industrial property and copyright in
European community law. Sijthoff, 1975.

KASE, F.J.
Copyright thought in continental Europe.
Rothman, 1967 (USA).

KUPFERMAN, T.R. & FONER, M.
Universal copyright convention analysed.
Federal Legal P., 1955 (USA).

LADDIE, H., PRESCOTT, P &
VITORIA, M.
Modern law of copyright. Butterworths,
1980.

LAHORE, J.
Information technology: the challenge to
copyright. Sweet & Maxwell, 1984.

LAHORE, J.
Intellectual property in Australia: patents,
designs, trade marks, confidential
information and unfair competition.
Butterworths (Australia), 1981. Looseleaf.

LAW, S. & LIVES, E.
Keep music legal: from the manuscript to
mass production. Sea Dream Music, 1982.

McFARLANE, G.
Practical introduction to copyright.
McGraw-Hill, 1982.

MADDISON, R.
Copyright and related rights: principles,
problems and trends. Economist
Intelligence Unit, 1983.

MELVILLE, L.W.
Forms and agreements on intellectual
property and international licensing. 3ed.
Sweet & Maxwell, 1979. Looseleaf.

MELVILLE, L.W.
Precedents on intellectual property and
international licensing. 2ed. Clark
Boardman, 1972. Looseleaf.

NIBLETT, B.
Legal protection of computer programs.
Oyez, 1980.

NIMMER, M.
Cases on copyright. 2ed. West, 1979.

NIMMER, M.
Nimmer on copyright. Bender. 4 vols. and service.

PLOMAN, E.W. & HAMILTON, L.C.
Copyright: intellectual property in the information age. Routledge, 1980.

PUBLISHERS ASSOCIATION
Copyright concessions for developing countries. 1970.

REMER, D.
Legal care for your software: a step-by-step guide for computer software writers. Addison-Wesley, 1982.

ROTHENBERG, S.
Copyright and public performance of music. Nijhoff, 1954.

RUSSELL-CLARKE, A.D.
Copyright in industrial designs. 5ed. Sweet & Maxwell, 1974.

SMITH, A.D.
Microfilm: some legal implications. 2ed. Business Equip. Trade Assoc., 1978.

TRADE, BOARD OF
Copyright committee report (Gregory). HMSO, 1952 (Cmd. 8662).

TRADE, DEPARTMENT OF
Reform of the law relating to copyright, design and performers' protection: a consultative document. HMSO, 1981 (Cmnd. 8302).

TRADE, DEPARTMENT OF
Report of the committee to consider the law of copyright and designs (Whitford). HMSO, 1977 (Cmnd. 6732).

ULMER, E.
Law applicable to intellectual property rights. Kluwer, 1977.

WHALE, R.F.
Copyright. 3ed. ESC Pub., 1983.

WHITE, T.A.B.
Patents for inventions and the protection of industrial designs. 4ed. Stevens, 1974.

WHITE, T.A.B. & JACOB, R.
Patents, trade marks, copyright and industrial designs. Stevens, 1970 (Concise college texts).

ZWEIGERT, K. & KROPHOLLER, J.
Sources of international uniform law.. vol. 3; law of copyright, competition and industrial property. Sijthoff, 1973 supp. 1973.

CORONER

See also Forensic Science; Treasure Trove

Encyclopaedias and periodicals

Statutes in Force. Group: Coroners, England & Wales.
Halsbury's Laws of England. 4ed. vol. 9.
Halsbury's Statutes of England. 3ed. vol.7.
The Digest. vol.13.
Encyclopaedia of Court Forms in Civil Proceedings (Atkin). 2ed. vol.13.
Encyclopaedia of Forms and Precedents. 4ed. vol. 4.

British Journal of Criminology. 1960–
British Medical Journal. 1857–
Criminal Law Review. 1954–
Journal of Criminal law, Criminology and Police Science. 1910–
Lancet. 1823–
Medicine Science and the Law. 1960–
Medico Legal Journal. 1901–

Texts

CORONERS SOCIETY OF ENGLAND AND WALES
Reports and memoranda on the coroners' system.

GRINDON, J.B.
A compendium of the law of coroners. Crockford, 1850.

HILL, G.
Treasure trove in law and practice from the earliest time to the present day. Oxford U.P., 1935.

HOME OFFICE
Report of the Committee on Death Certification and Corners (Brodrick). HMSO, 1971 (Cmnd. 4810).

HOME OFFICE
Report of the Departmental Committee on Coroners (Wright). HMSO, 1936.

HUNNISETT, R.F.
Medieval coroners. Cambridge U.P., 1962.

JERVIS, J.
The office and duties of coroners. 9ed. Sweet & Maxwell, 1957.

KNEALE, S.J.
Manx coroners. Victoria P., 1963.

MARSHALL, T.
Canadian law of inquests: handbook for coroners. Carswell, 1980.

THURSTON, G.
Coronership. 2ed. B.Rose, 1980.

WALLER, K.M.
Coronial law and practice in New South Wales. Law Book Co., 1973.

WELLINGTON, R.H.
The King's coroner. Clowes, 1906. 2 vols.

CORPORAL PUNISHMENT

See also Punishment

Encyclopaedias

Halsbury's Laws of England. 4ed. vols.11 & 15.
Halsbury's Statutes of England. 3ed. vols. 8, 25.

Texts

KNEALE, A.
Against birching: judicial corporal punishment in the Isle of Man. N.C.C.L., 1974.

NATIONAL COUNCIL FOR CIVIL LIBERTIES
Case against corporal punishment and a model Bill 'Protection of Minors Bill'. 1974.

SCOTT, G.R.
The history of corporal punishment: a survey of flagellation in its historical, anthropological and sociological aspects. 1952 repr. Gale Research, 1974.

SCOTT, G.R.
Flogging: yes or no? Torchstream Books, 1953.

CORPORATION TAX

See also Revenue Law.

Encyclopaedias and periodicals

Statutes in Force, Group; Income, Corporation and Capital Gains Tax.
Halsbury's Laws of England. 4ed. vol.9.
Halsbury's Statutes of England. 3ed. vol.33, 34, 36.

The Digest. vol.13.
Encyclopaedia of Forms and Precedents. 4ed. see index vol.

British Tax Review. 1956–
Taxation. 1927–

Texts

AULT, H.J. & RADLER, A.J.
German corporation tax. 2ed. Kluwer, 1980.

BRAMWELL, R.
Taxation of companies. 2ed. Sweet & Maxwell, 1979.

CARMICHAEL, K.S.
Corporation tax. 3ed. HFL, 1978.

CAVITCH, Z.
The planning for corporations and shareholders. Bender, 1974 (USA). Looseleaf.

CHOWN, J.
Reform of corporation tax, Inst. of Fiscal Studies, 1971.

CHOWN, J.F.
Taxation and the multinational enterprise. Finan. Times, 1974.

CHOWN, J.F. & NORMAN, R.
Corporation tax under the imputation system. Finan. Times, 1974.

COPE, J.M.
Business taxation. Nelson, 1972.

KAHN, D.
Basic corporate taxation 3ed. Inst. Continuing Legal Educ., 1981 supp. 1983.

KAHN, D.
Corporation tax and tax of partnerships and partners. West, 1979 supp. 1981 (USA).

KELLY, F.N. & CARMICHAEL, K.S.
Irish income tax and corporation tax. 11ed. HFL, 1980.

MOULLIN, M. & SARGENT, J.
Guide to taxation of companies. McGraw-Hill, 1981.

MULRONEY, M.
Foreign corporations – US income taxation. Tax Management, 1974 (USA). Looseleaf.

OROJO, J.O.
Company tax law in Nigeria. Sweet & Maxwell, 1979.

PRITCHARD, W.E.
Corporation tax. Polytech Pub., 1974.

RICHARDSON, R.J.
The taxation of corporations and their shareholders. 3ed. CCH, 1980 (Australia).

SHRAND, D. & KEETON, A.A.F.
Company law and company taxation in South Africa. Legal & Finan., 1974.

STORZ, M.
Taxation of businesses and business transactions. Oyez, 1972.

TAITZ, A.
Corporations capital tax in Canada. CCH, 1981.

TOLLEY
Corporation tax. Annual.

TONKIN, A.S. & THOMPSON, M.I.
Law and taxation of private companies. 2ed. Butterworths (New Zealand)

TOPPLE, B.S.
Corporation tax. 5ed. Macdonald & Evans, 1981.

VAN HOORN, J. (ed.)
Taxation of companies in Europe. Int. Bureau Fiscal Document., 1972 (USA). Looseleaf.

WHEATCROFT, G.S.A. (ed.)
British tax encyclopaedia. Stevens. 5 vols. Looseleaf.

CORPORATIONS

See also Companies; Local Government; Public Authorities; Ultra Vires.

Encyclopaedias and periodicals

Halsbury's Laws of Englaned. 4ed. vol.9.
The Digest. vol.13.
Encyclopaedia of Forms and Precedents. 4ed. see index vol.

Journal of Business Law. 1937–
Journal of World Trade Law. 1967–

Texts

AFTERMAN, A.B. & BAXT, R.
Cases and materials on corporations and associations. 4ed. Butterworths (Australia), 1984.

BRICE, S.W.
Laws of corporations & companies: a treatise on the doctrine of ultra vires. 3ed. Stevens & Haynes, 1893.

COMMERCE CLEARING HOUSE
Ontario Business Corporations Act, with regulations. 3ed. 1973.

DAVIES, R.A.
Canadian corporation precedents. 2ed. Carswell, 1974. 3 vols.

HADDEN, T.
Control of corporate groups. Insitute of Advanced Legal Studies, 1983.

HAMILTON, R.
Cases on corporations, including partnerships. 2ed. West, 1981 (USA).

HAMILTON, R.
Law of corporations. West, 1980 (USA).

HENN, H.
Cases on corporations. West, 1974 supp.
1980 (USA).

HENN, H.
Hornbook on corporations. 2ed. West,
1970 (USA).

HILL, R.
Tax aspects of incorporation. Institute of
Chartered Accountants, 1983.

HOCHSTEDLER, E.
Corporations as criminals. Sage, 1984.

INTERNATIONAL BAR
ASSOCIATION
Codes of conduct for transnational
corporations. 1981.

JORDAN, S.A.
Corporation law of France, principal
features including taxes, costs of
incorporation, exchange control. Jordan,
1973.

KUUSI, J.
Host state and the transnational
corporations: analysis of legal relationships.
Saxon House, 1979.

LEIGH, L.H.
Criminal liability of corporations in Engish
law. Weidenfeld & N., 1969.

LINDGREN, K.E.
Corporation and Australian society. Sweet
& Maxwell, (Australia), 1974.

NELSON, R. (ed.)
Corporate development in the Middle East.
Oyez, 1978.

ORHNIAL, T. (ed.)
Limited liability and the corporation.
Croom Helm, 1982.

PAUL T.F.
The law and administration of incorporated
societies. Butterworths (New Zealand),
1972.

PURVIS, R.N.
Corporation crime. Butterworths
(Australia), 1979.

SIMMONDS, K.
Multinational corporations law. Oceana,
1978 (USA). 5 looseleaf vols.

SUNDSTROM, G.O.Z.
The public international utility corporation.
Sijthoff, 1972.

WALLACE, C.D.
Legal control of the multinational
enterprise: national regulatory techniques
and the prospects for international control.
Nijhoff, 1982.

WALLACE, W.L.C.
Corporation: its shareholders and Canadian
income taxes. 2ed. CCH, 1974.

COSTS

See also Practice and Procedure.

Encyclopaedias and periodicals

Halsbury's Laws of England. 3ed. & 4ed.
see index vols.
Halsbury's Statutes of England. 3ed. see
index vol.
Encyclopaedia of Court Forms in Civil
Procedings (Atkin). 2ed. vol.13.

Texts

AHERN, J.
The costs book (Victoria & Federal).
Butterworths (Australia), 1975 looseleaf.

AHERN, J.
Legal costs (NSW). Butterworths
(Australia). Looseleaf.

BIGGS, A.K.
Costs in matrimonial causes. Fourmat,
1979 (chart).

Law Society's Gazette. 1903–
New Law Journal. 1965–
Solicitors' Journal. 1857–
County County Practice. Annual.

BIGGS, A.K.
County court costs and fees. 9ed. Fourmat,
1984.

BIGGS, A.K.
Fees in matrimonial proceedings. Fourmat,
1980.

BUTTERWORTH'S COSTS
Butterworth's costs in civil litigation and non litigation work. 4ed. 1971. 2 vols. Looseleaf.

CHAVASSE, C.P.G.
Contentious costs: the discretionary items. Oyez, 1980 (Practice notes no. 69).

CHAVASSE, C.P.G.
Conveyancing and other non-contentious costs. 7ed. Oyez, 1980.

COLLINS, H.C.
Reminders on county court costs. 2ed. Oyez, 1981.

COUNCIL ON TRIBUNALS
Report on the award of costs as statutory inquiries. HMSO, 1964.

GRAHAM-GREEN, G.J.
Criminal costs and legal aid. 3ed. Butterworths, 1973 supp. 1978.

LORD CHANCELLOR'S OFFICE
Report of the Committee on the Enforcement of Judgement Debts (Payne). 1969 (Cmnd. 3909).

LUNN, R.M. & SIMPSON, D.D.
South Australian legal costs. Butterworths (Australia), 1981. Looseleaf.

O'RIORDAN, D.P.
Supreme court fees and fixed costs. 7ed. Fourmat, 1984.

RAKUSEN, M.L.
Costs in matrimonial causes. Butterworths, 1984.

SUPREME Court practice 1985. Sweet & Maxwell, 1984. 2 vols.

TEASDALE, J.P.
Guide to costs and legal aid in criminal cases. Oyez, 1979.

WILLIAMS, D.B.
Costs- a practical introduction. Jordan, 1978.

YORSTON, K.
Costing procedures. 5ed. Law Book Co., 1976.

COUNCIL OF EUROPE

Encyclopaedias

Halsbury' Statutes of England. 3ed. vol.6. & 42A.

Texts

COUNCIL OF EUROPE
Manual of the Council of Europe. Stevens, 1970.

CRAWFORD, O.
Done this day: the European idea in action. Taplinger Pub. Co., 1970 (USA).

HURD, V.D.
The Council of Europe: design for a United States of Europe.. Manhattan Pub. Co., 1958 (USA).

ROBERTSON, A.H.
The Council of Europe: its structure, functions and achievements. 2ed. Praeger, 1961.

ROBERTSON, A.H.
European institutions: co-operation, integration, unification. 3ed. Stevens, 1973.

ROBERTSON, A.H.
Relations between the Council of Europe and the United Nations. Unitar, 1973.

COUNTY COURT

Encyclopaedias

Statutes in Force. Group: County Courts, England & Wales.
Halsbury's Laws of England. 4ed. vol.10
Halsbury's Statutes of England. 3ed. vol.7
The Digest. vol.13.

Encyclopaedia of Court Forms in Civil Proceedings (Atkin). 2ed. vol.13.
Encyclopaedia of Forms and Precedents. 4ed. see index vol.

Texts

BIGGS, A.K.
County court costs and fees. 9ed. Fourmat, 1984.

BIRKS, M.
Small claims in the county court: how to sue and defend actions without a solicitor. rev. ed. Lord Chancellor's Dept., 1981.

COLLINS, H.C.
Notes on county court practice and procedure. 5ed. Oyez, 1978.

COLLINS, H.C.
Reminders on county court costs. 2ed. Oyez, 1981.

COUNTY Court practice. Butterworths. Annual.

DEIGHAN, M.
County court practice and procedure. 2ed. Fourmat Pub., 1982.

LORD CHANCELLOR'S DEPARTMENT
County court districts (England & Wales). Index of place names. 12ed. HMSO, 1983.

LORD CHANCELLOR'S DEPARTMENT
London county courts directory: containing the streest and places within the London postal area and their county court districts. 11ed. HMSO, 1983.

McCLEARY, R.
County court precedents. 4ed. Butterworths, 1973 supp. 1978.

RUDINGER, E. (ed.)
How to sue in the county court. Consumers' Association, 1974.

VALENTINE, B.
County court procedure in Northern Ireland. SLS Legal Pubns. (NI), 1984.

WHEELER, C.W.G. & TOPHAM, T.
County court practice Victoria. 3ed. Butterworths (Australia), 1980, looseleaf.

WILLIAMS, E.
A.B.C. guide to the practice of the county court. Sweet & Maxwell, 1984.

WITCHELL, R.G.
Practice and procedure. vol.1: County courts and magistrates courts. 7ed. Oyez, 1979.

YELL, N. & WEST, W.T.
County court practice and procedure: general. B. Rose, 1983.

COUNTY PALATINE

Encyclopaedias

Halsbury's Laws of England. 4ed. vol. 8.
Halsbury's Statutes of England. 3ed. vol.8.

Texts

BENNETT, J.
The Chancery of Lancashire practice. Sherratt & Hughes, 1914.

CHANCERY OF LANCASTER
Rules. Rev. to 1961. 1961.

LAPSLEY, G.T.
County Palatine of Durham: a study in constitutional history. Blackwell, 1900.

COURT HAND

Texts

BAKER, J.H.
Manual of law French. Avebury, 1979.

CORNWALL, J.
How to read old title deeds, 16th -19th centuries. Univ. of Birmingham, 1964.

JENKINSON, H.
English court hand, 1066–1500. Oxford U.P., 1915.

JENKINSON, H.
The later court hands in England from the 15th to 17th century. Cambridge U.P., 1927.

LATHAM, R.E.
Revised medieval latin word list. Oxford U.P., 1965.

THOYTS, E.E.
How to decipher and understand old documents. Elliott Stock, 1893.

COURT MARTIAL

See also Air Force; Army; Military Law; Navy.

Encyclopaedias

Statutes in Force. Group: Armed Forces.
Halsbury's Laws of England. 4ed. vol. 41.
Halsbury's Statutes of England. 3ed. vol. 29.
Encyclopaedia of Court Forms in Civil Proceedings (Atkin). 2ed. vols. 12, 25 & 34.

Texts

CLODE, C.M.
Military forces of the Crown, their administration and government. Murray, 1869. 2 vols.

FELD, B.
Manual of courts martial practice and appeal. Oceana, 1957 (USA).

GENEROUS, W.T.
Swords and scales: the development of the uniform code of military justice. Kennikat, 1973 (USA).

NAVY DEPARTMENT
Naval court martial manual. HMSO, 1969. Looseleaf.

COURT OF PROTECTION

See also Mental Health.

Encyclopaedias

Statutes in Force. Group: Mental Health.
Halsbury's Statutes of England. 3ed.. vol.16
Encyclopaedia of Court Forms in Civil Proceedings (Atkin). 2ed. vol. 26.
Encyclopadeia of Forms and Precedents. 4ed. see index vol.

Texts

COMPTON, H.F.& WHITEMAN,R
Receivership under the Mental Health Act 1959. 5ed. Oyez, 1976 (Practice notes no.39)

HEYWOOD,N.A.& MASSEY, A.S.
Court of Protection practice. 10ed. Stevens, 1978 supp. 1982..

COURTS

See also Individual Courts by Name; Administration of Justice; Appeals; History; Practice and Procedure

Encyclopaedias

Statutes in Force. Groups: County Courts, England & Wales; Courts, House of Lords and Privy Council; Courts, Scotland; Courts, Supreme Court, England; & Wales; Supreme Court, Northern Ireland.

Texts

ABEL-SMITH, B. & STEVENS, R.
Lawyer and the courts: a sociological study of the English legal system, 1750–1965. Heinemann, 1967.

ABRAHAM, H. J.
The judicial process; an introductory analysis of the courts of the United States, England, and France. 4ed. Oxford U.P., 1980.

ABRAHAM, H.J.
The judiciary: Supreme Court in the governmental process. 6ed. Allyn & B., 1983 (USA).

ASHTON, R.
City and the court, 1603–43. Cambridge U.P., 1979.

ATIYAH, P.S.
From principles to pragmatism: changes in the function of the judicial process and the law. Oxford U.P., 1978.

ATKINSON, J.M & DREW, P.
Order in court: the organisation of verbal interaction in judicial settings. Macmillan, 1979.

CARTER, A.T.
History of the English courts. Butterworths, various eds.

CRAWFORD, J.
Australian courts of law. Oxford U.P. (Australia), 1983.

EVERSHED, F.R. Lord
Court of Appeal in England. Univ. of London, 1950.

GOODMAN, A.
The court guide. Sweet & Maxwell, 1980.

HANBURY, H.G. & YARDLEY, D.C.M.
English courts of law. 5ed. Oxford U.P., 1979.

HARDING, A.
Laws courts of medieval England. Allen & Unwin, 1973.

JACKSON, R.M.
Machinery of justice in England. 7ed. Cambridge U.P., 1977.

JACOB, J.I.H.
Commencement of actions in the High Court: new forms and procedure. Butterworths, 1980.

LAW COMMISSION
Jurisdiction of certain ancient courts. HMSO, 1976 (Law Com. no. 72).

LORD CHANCELLOR'S DEPARTMENT
Report of the Review Body on the Chancery Division of the High Court (Oliver). HMSO, 1981 (Cmnd. 8205).

LORD CHANCELLOR'S OFFICE
Courts in Northern Ireland: the future pattern. HMSO, 1977 (Cmnd. 6892)

LORD CHANCELLOR'S OFFICE
Rules of the Supreme Court. HMSO, 1964. Looseleaf.

McBRYDE, W.W. & DOWIE, S.J.
Petition procedure in the Court of Session. Green, 1980.

MORRISON, F.L.
Courts and the political process in England. Sage, 1973 (USA).

OWENS, J.L.
The law courts. Dent, 1976.

SCOTT, I.R.
Court administration: case for a judicial council. Univ. of Birmingham, 1979.

SHAW's directory of courts in England and Wales. Annual.

SIMMONS, F.
High Court practice manual. Oyez, 1979 supp. 1980.

USHER, J.
European Court practice. Sweet & Maxwell, 1983.

CRIME PREVENTION

Periodicals

Security Gazette. 1958–

Texts

AKERS, R. & SAGARIN, G.
Crime prevention and social control.
Praeger, 1975.

COFFEN, A.
The prevention of crime and delinquency.
Prentice-Hall, 1975.

CRAMER, J.A. (ed.)
Preventing crime. Sage, 1979.

EUROPEAN COMMITTEE ON CRIME PROBLEMS
Police and the prevention of crime. Council of Europe, 1979.

HOME OFFICE
Co-ordinating crime prevention efforts. 1980 (Research studies).

HOME OFFICE
Crime prevention and the police. 1979 (Research studies).

HOME OFFICE
Crime prevention and the police. 1979 (Research studies).

HOME OFFICE
Crime prevention publicity: an assessment. 1980 (Research studies).

JEFFERY, C.R.
Crime prevention through environmental design. Sage, 1971 (USA).

LEWIN, S.
Crime and its prevention. H.W.Wilson, 1968.

SAUVEPLANNE, J.G.
Security over corporeal moveables. Sijthoff, 1974.

STEYN, N.H.
Crime and its control. Juta, 1972 (South Africa).

CRIMINAL APPEALS

See also Appeals

Encyclopaedias and periodicals

Statutes in Force. Group: Criminal Law.
Halsbury's Laws of England. 4ed. vol.11.
Halsbury's Statutes of England. 3ed. vol.8.
The Digest. vols. 14 & 15.
Encyclopaedia of Court Forms in Civil Procedings (Atkin). 2ed. vol. 5.

Criminal Appeal Reports. 190–8
Criminal Law Review. 1954–
Journal of Criminal Law. 1973–

Texts

BLOM-COOPER, L.J. & DREWRY, G.
Final appeal: a study of the House of Lords in its judicial capacity. Oxford U.P., 1972.

HOME OFFICE
Report of the Interdepartmental Committee on the Court of Criminal Appeal (Donovan). HMSO, 1965 (Cmnd. 2755).

HOUSE OF LORDS
Form of appeal directions as to procedure applicable to criminal appeals from England, Wales & Northern Ireland. HMSO, 1976.

JUSTICE
Criminal appeals. Stevens, 1964.

KNIGHT, M.
Criminal appeals: a study of the powers of the court of appeal criminal division. Stevens, 1970 supp. 1975.

McLEAN, I.
Criminal appeals: a practical guide to appeals to and from the Crown Court. Sweet & Maxwell, 1980.

MEADOR, D.J.
Criminal appeals: English practices and American reforms. Virginia U.P., 1973.

THOMAS, D.A.
Principles of sentencing: the sentencing policy of the Court of Appeal Criminal Division. 2ed. Heinemann, 1979.

THOMPSON, D.R.
Procedings in the Criminal Division of the Court of Appeal: an index of practice and procedure. B.Rose, 1979.

CRIMINAL INJURIES

Encyclopaedias
Halsbury's Laws of England. 4ed. vol.11.
Halsbury's Statutes of England. 3ed. vol. 43.
Encyclopaedia of Court Forms in Civil Proceedings (Atkin). 2ed. vol.40.

Texts
CRIMINAL LAW REVISION COMMITTEE
Fourteenth report: offences against the person. HMSO, 1980 (Cmnd. 7844).

EDELHERTZ, H. & GEIS, G.
Public compensation to victims of crime. Praeger, 1974.

EUROPEAN COMMITTEE ON CRIME PROBLEMS
Compensation of victims of crime. Council of Europe, 1978.

GREER, D.S. & MITCHELL, V.A.
Compensation for criminal injuries to persons in Northern Ireland. Northern Ireland Legal Q., 1978.

HOME OFFICE
Criminal injuries compensation scheme: Working Party Report. HMSO, 1978.

HOME OFFICE & SCOTTISH HOME AND HEALTH DEPARTMENT
Review of the criminal injuries compensation scheme: report (Moriarty). HMSO, 1978.

JUSTICE
Compensation for victims of crimes of violence. Stevens, 1962.

KENNEDY, A. & McWILLIAM, H.R.
The law on compensation for criminal injuries in Republic of Ireland. I.L.R.C. 1979.

MIERS, D.
Responses to victimisation, Professional Books, 1968.

WILLIAMS, D.B.
Criminal injustries compensation. Oyez, 1972.

CRIMINAL INVESTIGATION

See also Forensic Science; Police.

Texts
BROWNLIE, A.R. (ed.)
Crime investigation: art or science? Scot. Academic P., 1984.

CARR, R.A. & STERN, N.H.
Crime, the police and criminal statistics: an analysis of official statistics for England and Wales using econometric methods. Academic P., 1979.

GILLIES, P.
The law of criminal investigation. Law Book Co., 1983 (Australia).

GRAU, J.J.
Criminal and civil investigator handbook. McGraw-Hill, 1981.

GREENWOOD, P.W. and others
The criminal investigation process.
D.C.Heath, 1977 (USA).

GROSS, H.
Criminal investigation. 5ed. Lawyers' Co-operative, 1962 (USA).

HARRIS, B.
Warrants of search and entry: a handbook for magistrates, police officers and others. B.Rose, 1973.

HAVARD, J.D.J.
The dectection of secret homicide. Macmillan, 1960.

HORGAN, J.J.
Criminal investigation. 2ed. McGraw-Hill, 1979.

KIRK, P.L.
Crime investigation. 2ed. Wiley, 1974.

MORRIS, P. & HEAL, K.
Criminal control and the police: a review of research. HMSO, 1981 (Home Office research studies, no.67).

WALLS, H.J.
Forensic science: an introduction to scientific crime detection. Praeger, 1974(USA).

CRIMINAL JUSTICE

See also Administration of Justice.

Encyclopaedias

Halsbury's Laws of England. 4ed. vol.11.
The Digest. vols. 14 & 15.

Texts

ALLEN, F.A.
Borderland of criminal justice: essays in law and criminology. Univ. of Chicago P., 1974 (USA).

ANDREWS, J.A. (ed.)
Criminal justice. Univ. of Wales P., 1968.

BERAN, N.J. & TOOMEY, B.G.
Mentally ill offenders and the criminal justice system. Praeger, 1979.

BINGHAM, R.
Modern cases and statutes on Crown Court crime. B.Rose, 1980 supp. 1982..

BOTTOMLEY, A.K.
Criminal justice: selected readings. Martin Robertson, 1978.

BOTTOMLEY, A. K.
Decisions in the penal process. Martin Robertson, 1973.

BRANDON, R. & DAVIES, C.
Wrongful imprisonment: mistaken convictions and their consequences. Allen & Unwin, 1973.

CENTRAL OFFICE OF INFORMATION
Criminal justice in Britain. 2ed. HMSO, 1978 (C.O.I. reference pamphlet 129).

CHAPPEL, D. & WILSON, P.
Australian criminal justice system. 2ed. Butterworths (Australia). 1977.

CLARK, R.S.
Fundamentals of criminal justice research. Lexington Books, 1977 (USA).

COHN, A.E. & UDOLF, R.
Criminal justice system and its psychology. Van Nostrand Reinhold, 1979 (USA).

COMMONWEALTH SECRETARIAT
Delay in the administration of criminal justice: Commonwealth development and experience. 1980.

CONRAD, J.P. (ed.)
Evolution of criminal justice: a guide for practical criminologists. Sage, 1979.

CRITES, L.
Female offender: total look at women in the criminal justice system. Lexington Books, 1977(USA).

CROFT, J.
Research in criminal justice. HMSO, 1978 (Home Office research studies).

EDELSTEIN, C.S. & WICKS, R.J.
An introduction to criminal justice. McGraw-Hill, 1977 (USA).

EVANS, R.G.
Developing policies for pubic security and criminal justice. Information Canada, 1973 (Canada).

FITZGERALD, M. & MUNCIE, J.
System of justice: introduction to the criminal justice system in England and Wales. Blackwell, 1983.

GABBAY, E.
Discretion in criminal justice. Gabbay, 1973.

GABBAY, E.
Open justice: evaluation of criminal justice. Gabbay, 1978.

GERBER, R.J.
Contemporary issues in criminal justice. Kennikat: Bailey Bros., 1976.

GORDON, G.H.
Criminal Justice (Scotland) Act, 1980. Green, 1981.

GROSS, E.
Theory of criminal justice. Oxford U.P., 1979 (USA).

GRYGIER, T.
Social protection code: a new model of criminal justice. Sweet & Maxwell, 1978 (American series of foreign penal codes).

GUNN, J. & FARRINGTON, D.P.
Abnormal offenders, delinquency and the criminal justice system. Wiley, 1982.

HIEMSTRA, V.G.
Introduction to the law of criminal procedure. Butterworths (S.Africa), 1978.

HODGKIN, E.C. & HODGKIN, N.I.
Involvement of the community in criminal justice and the treatment of offenders. B.Rose, 1978.

HOME OFFICE
Review of criminal justice policy, 1976. HMSO, 1977.

JUSTICE
Pre-trial criminal procedure: police powers and the prosecution process: a report. Stevens, 1979.

JUSTICE
The truth and the courts: a report. Stevens, 1980.

KING, M.
Framework of criminal justice. Croom Helm, 1981.

KONECNI, V.J. & EBBESEN, E.E.
Criminal justice system: a socio-psychological analysis. W.H. Freeman, 1982.

LETMAN, S.T.
Criminal justice: the main issues. McFarland: Bailey Bros & Swinfen, 1983.

MATHER, L.M.
Plea bargaining or trial? the process of criminal-case disposition. Lexington Books, 1979 (USA).

McBARNET, D.J.
Conviction: the law, the state and the construction of justice. Macmillan, 1981.

McLEAN, J.D. & WOOD, J.C.
Criminal justice and the treatment of offenders. Sweet & Maxwell, 1969.

MORRIS, A. & GILLER, H.
Providing criminal justice for children. Arnold, 1983.

NAGEL, S.S. (ed.)
Modelling the criminal justice system. Sage, 1977 (USA).

PARIZEAU, A. & SZABO, D.
Canadian criminal justice system. Lexington Books, 1978 (USA).

PATTENDEN, R.
Judge, discretion and the criminal trial. Oxford U.P., 1982.

RADZINOWICZ, Sir L. & HOOD, R.
Criminology and the administration of criminal justice: a bibliography. Mansell, 1976.

RAYMOND, B.
Introduction to criminal and civil litigation. Oyez, 1981.

ROESCH, R. & CORRADO, R.R.
Evaluation and criminal justice policy. Sage Pubns., 1981.

ROYAL COMMISSION ON CRIMINAL PROCEDURE
Report. HMSO, 1981 (Cmnd. 8092).

WALKER, N.D.
Punishment, danger and stigma: morality of criminal justice. 2ed. Blackwell, 1982.

WALTERS, G.
Criminal proceedings against juveniles. Oyez Longman, 1984.

WEISSMAN, J.C. & DUPONT, R.L.
Criminal justice and drugs: the unresolved connection. Kennikat Press: Bailey Bros., 1982.

CRIMINAL LAW

See also Animals; Bribery and Corruption; Confessions; Conspiracy; Corporations; Criminology; Evidence; Homicide; Juries; Obscenity; Perjury; Prostitution; Rape; Theft; Treason.
For specific crimes, see under the specific heading, e.g. Theft.

Encyclopaedias and periodicals

Statutes in Force. Group: Criminal Law.
Halsbury's Laws of England. 4ed. vol.11.
The Digest. vols. 14 & 15.
Encyclopaedia of Court Forms in Civil Proceedings (Atkin). 2ed. vol.20.
Cox's Reports of Cases in Criminal Law. 1843–1948.

Criminal Appeal Reports. 1908–
Criminal Law Rview. 1954–
Journal of Criminal Law. 1937–
Justice of the Peace and Local Government Review. 1837–
Law Reports of the Commonwealth: Criminal.|1985–

General texts

ALDRIDGE, T.M.
Criminal Law Act, 1977. Butterworths, 1978.

BAKER, FE.R. & WILKIE, G.H.
Criminal law. Butterworths. 6ed. 1980 (Police promotion handbook. no. 1).

BAKER, E.R. & WILKIE, G.H.
Criminal evidence and procedure. 6ed. Butterworths, 1979 (Police promotion handbook no. 2).

BLACKSTONE, W.
Commentaries on the laws of England. Various editions. 1765–69. repr. Univ. of Chicago P., 1979.

CARR, R.A. & STERN, N.H.
Crime, the police and criminal statistics: an analysis of official statistics for England and Wales using econometric methods. Academic P., 1979.

CHAMBLISS, W.J.
Criminal law in action. 2ed. Wiley, 1984.

CLARKSON, C. & KEATING, H.
Criminal law: text and materials. Sweet & Maxwell, 1984.

COUNCIL OF EUROPE
Measures to be taken in cases of kidnapping followed by a ransom demand. HMSO 1983.

COUNCIL OF EUROPE
Rate of criminal law in consumer protection. HMSO. 1983.

CRACKNELL, D.G.
Criminal law. 3ed. Butterworths, 1977.

CROSS, R. & JONES, P.A.
Cases and statutes on criminal law. 6ed. Butterworths, 1977.

CROSS, R. & JONES, P.A.
Introduction to criminal law. 10ed. Butterworths, 1984.

CURZON, L.B.
Cases in criminal law. 2ed. Macdonald & Evans, 1978.

CURZON, L.B.
Criminal law. 4ed. Macdonald & Evans, 1984.

EAST, E.H.
A treatise of the pleas of the Crown. 1893. 2 vols. 1ed 1736 repr. Professional Books, 1975.

ELLIOT, D.W. & WOOD, J.C.
A casebook on criminal law. 4ed. Sweet & Maxwell, 1982.

GLAZEBROOK, P.R. (ed.)
Reshaping the criminal law. Stevens, 1978.

GRIEW, E.J. (ed.)
Criminal Law Act, 1977. Sweet & Maxwell, 1978.

HART, H.L.A.
The morality of the criminal law. Oxford U.P., 1965 (Lionel Cohen lecture).

HOWARD, C. & ELLIOTT, I.D.
Criminal law. 4ed. Law Book Co., 1982 (Australia).

KENNY, C.S.
Outlines of criminal law. 19ed. Cambridge U.P., 1966.

LAW COMMISSION
Codification of the criminal law: general principles. The field of enquiry. HMSO, 1968 repr. 1977 (Working paper no.17)

LAW COMMISSION
Codification of the criminal law: subject III; territorial and extra territorial extent of the criminal law. HMSO, 1970 repr. 1972 (Working paper no.29).

LAW COMMISSION
Criminal law: report on the territorial and extraterritorial extent of the criminal law. HMSO, 1978 (Law Com. no. 91).

MORRIS, N. & PERLMAN, M.
Law and crime: essays in honour Sir John Barry. Gordon & B., 1972.

RUSSELL, W.O.
Crime. 12ed. Sweet & Maxwell, 1964. 2 vols.

SEAGO, P.
Criminal law. Sweet & Maxwell, 1981.

SLATER, J.C.N. & DOBSON, A.P.
Cases and statutes on criminal law. 2ed. Sweet & Maxwell, 1981.

SMITH, J.C. & HOGAN, R.
Criminal law. 5ed. Butterworths, 1983.

SMITH, J.C. & HOGAN, B.
Criminal law: cases and materials. 2ed. Butterworths, 1980.

Practice and procedure

ARCHBOLD, J.F.
Pleading, evidence and practice in criminal cases. 41ed. Sweet & Maxwell, 1982.

ARGUILE, R.
Criminal procedure. Butterworths, 1969.

BALDWIN, J. & McCONVILLE, M.
Negotiated justice: pressures on defendants to plead guilty. Martin Robertson, 1977.

BARNARD, D.
Criminal court in action. 2ed. Butterworths, 1980.

CARVELL, I.G. & GREEN, E.S.
Criminal law and procedure. Sweet & Maxwell, 1970 (Concise college texts).

CRIMINAL LAW REVISION COMMITTEE
Fourth report: order of closing speeches. HMSO, 1963 (Cmnd. 2148).

DEVLIN, J.D.
Criminal courts and procedure. 2ed. Butterworths, 1967.

DEVLIN, P.A.
Trial by jury. Stevens, 1970 (Hamlyn lecture no.8).

STANNARD, J.E.
Northern Ireland supplement to Smith & Hogan on Criminal Law (5ed.). SLS Legal Pubns (NI), 1984.

STAUNFORD, W.
Les plees del coron: 1607; 1ed. 1557 repr. 1975.

STEPHEN, J.F.
Digest of criminal law (indictable offences). 9ed. Sweet & Maxwell, 1950.

STEPHEN, J.F.
General view of the criminal law of England. 2ed. Macmillan, 1890.

STEPHENSON, G.
Criminal law and consumer protection. B. Rose, 1983.

WILLIAMS, G.L.
Criminal law: the general part. 2ed. Sweet & Maxwell, 1961.

WILLIAMS, G.L.
Textbook of criminal law. 2ed. Sweet & Maxwell, 1983.

WOOTTON, B.
Crime and the criminal law: reflections of a magistrate and social scientist. 2ed. Stevens, 1981 (Hamlyn lecture no. 15).

FRIEDLAND, M.C.
Double jeopardy. Oxford U.P., 1969.

GRAHAM-GREEN, G.J.
Criminal costs and legal aid. 3ed. Butterworths, 1973 supp. 1978.

HAMPTON, C.
Criminal procedure and evidence. 3ed. Sweet & Maxwell, 1982.

JUSTICE
The prosecution process in England and Wales. Stevens, 1970.

McLEAN, I.G. & MORRISH, P.
The magistrates court: an index of common penalties and formalities before justices. 5ed. B.Rose, 1980.

MORRISH, P. & McLEAN, I.G.
The Crown Court: an index of common penalties and formalities in cases tried on indictment or committed for sentence and appeal in criminal courts. 11ed B.Rose, 1983.

ROYAL COMMISSION ON CRIMINAL PROCEDURE
Report. HMSO, 1981 (Cmnd. 8092).

SCOTT, J.R.
Criminal procedure: statement and trial of multiple offences. B.Rose, 1971.

STONE's Justices' manual. Butterworths. 3 vols. Annual.

WILLIAMS, G.L..
The proof of guilt: a study of the English criminal trial. 3ed. Sweet & Maxwell, 1963.

Liability

ADAMS, F.
Crminal onus and excurpations (New Zealand). Sweet & Maxwell, 1968.

BATY, T.
Vicarious liability. Oxford U.P., 1916.

BRETT, P.
An inquiry into criminal guilt. Sweet & Maxwell, 1963.

EDWARDS, J.L.J.
Mens rea in statutory offences. Macmillan, 1955.

FINGARETTE, H. & HASSE, A.F.
Mental disabilities and criminal responsibility. Univ. of California P., 1979 (USA).

HOWARD, C.
Strict responsibility. Sweet & Maxwell, 1963.

KENNY, A.J.
Freewill and responsibility. Routledge, 1979.

LAW COMMISSION
D.P.P. v. Smith (Imputed criminal intent). HMSO, 1967. (Law Com. no.10).

LAW COMMISSION
Codification of the criminal law: general principles, parties, complicity and laibility for the acts of another. HMSO, 1972 repr. 1977 (Working paper no.43).

LAW COMMISSION
Codification of the criminal law: general principles, criminal liability of corporations. HMSO, 1972 repr. 1977 (Working paper no.44).

LAW COMMISSION
Criminal law: report on the mental element in crime. HMSO, 1978 (Law Com. no. 89).

WILLIAMS, Glanville L.
The mental element in crime (Lionel Cohen lectures). Magnes P., 1965.

Defences

CLYNE, P.
Guilty but insane: Anglo-American attitudes to insanity and criminal guilt. Nelson, 1973.

COMMITTEE TO CONSIDER CHANGES IN THE LAW OF INSANITY & CRIME
Report (Atkin). HMSO, 1924 (Cmd. 2005).

CRIMINAL LAW REVISION COMMITTEE
Third report: criminal procedure (insanity). HMSO, 1969 (Cmnd. 2149).

GOLDSTEIN, A.S.
The insanity defence. Yale U.P., 1967.

KEETON, G.W.
Guilty but insane. Macdonald, 1961.

LAW COMMISSION
Codification of the criminal law: general practices: defences of general application. HMSO, 1974 repr. 1977 (Working paper no.55).

LAW COMMISSION
Criminal law: report on defences of general application. HMSO, 1977 (Law Com. no. 83).

NEW YORK CITY BAR ASSOCIATION
Mental illness, due process and the criminal defendant. Fordham U.P., 1980 (USA).

ROLLIN, H.R.
The mentally abnormal offender and the law. Pergamon, 1969.

WALKER, N.
Crime and insanity in England. vol. 1. Historical perspective. Edinburgh U.P., 1968.

WALKER, N. & McCABE, S.
Crime and insanity in England. vol.2. New solutions and new problems. Edinburgh U.P., 1973.

History

BELLAMY, J.G.
Crime and public order in England in the later middle ages. Routledge, 1973.

BELLAMY, J.G.
Criminal law and society in late mediaeval and Tudor England. A. Sutton, 1984.

COCKBURN, J.S. (ed.)
Crime in England, 1550–1800. Methuen, 1977.

CORNISH, W.R. and others
Crime and law in 19th century Britain. Irish U.P., 1977.

PIKE, L.
History of crime in England. 2 vols. Smith, Elder & Co., 1873–76 repr. 1968.

PLUCKNETT, T.F.
Edward I and criminal law. Cambridge U.P., 1960.

RADZINOWICZ, L.
A history of English criminal law and in administration from 1750. Sweet & Maxwell, 1948–1984. 5 vols.

STEPHEN, J.F.
History of criminal law of England. Macmillan, 1883 repr. 1977. 3 vols.

TOBIAS, J.J. (ed.)
Nineteenth century crime in England: prevention and punishment. David & Charles, 1972.

Scotland

ALISON, A.J.
Principles and practice of the criminal law of Scotland. Blackwood, 1832–33. 2 vols.

ANGUS, J.W.
A dictionary of crimes and offences according to the law of Scotland. 3ed. Green, 1936.

ARNOTT, A.J.E. & DUNCAN, J.A.
Scottish criminal. Edinburgh U.P., 1970.

GANE, C.H.W. & STODDART, C.N.
Casebook on Scottish criminal law. Green, 1980.

GORDON, G.H.
The criminal law of Scotland. 2ed. Green, 1978 supp. 1984.

GRAMPIAN POLICE
Scottish criminal law, police duties and procedure. Rev. ed. Aberdeen U.P., 1978. Looseleaf.

HUME, D.
Commentaries on the law of Scotland respecting the description and punishment of crimes. Bell & Bradfute, 1797. 2 vols.

HUME, D.
Commentaries on the law of Scotland respecting the trial for crimes. Bell & Bradfute, 1829. 2 vols. with Bells supp. 1844.

MACDONALD, J.H.A.
A practical treatise on the criminal law of Scotland. 5ed. Green, 1948.

MOORE, G. & WOOD, C.
Social work and criminal law in Scotland. Aberdeen U.P., 1981.

RENTON, R.W. & BROWN, R.H.
Criminal procedure according to the law of Scotland. 5ed. Green, 1983. Looseleaf.

SCOTTISH HOME & HEALTH DEPARTMENT
Identification procedure under Scottish criminal law: report by the working group (Bryden). HMSO, 1978 (Cmnd. 7096).

SCOTTISH LAW COMMISSION
Expenses in criminal cases. 1966. (Memorandum no.2).

SHEENAN, A.V.
Criminal procedure in Scotland and France. HMSO, 1975.

SHIELDS, J.V.M. & DUNCAN, J.A.
State of crime in Scotland. Tavistock, 1964.

Other jurisdictions

AGUDA, T.A.
The criminal law and procedure in the Southern States of Nigeria. 3ed. Sweet & Maxwell, 1982.

BASSIOUNI, M.C. & NANDA, V.P.
Treatise on international criminal law and punishment. Thomas, 1973 (USA).

BATES, A.P., BUDDIN, T.L. & MEURE, D.J.
The system of criminal law: cases and materials (New South Wales, Victoria, South Australia). Butterworths (Australia), 1979.

BRETT, P. & WALLER, L.
Criminal law text and cases. 5ed. Butterworths (Australia), 1983.

BROWN, D.
Criminal procedure in Uganda and Kenya. 2ed. Sweet & Maxwell, 1970.

BUCKLE, S.R.T. & BUCKLE, L.G.
Bargaining for justice: case disposition and reform in the criminal courts. Praeger, 1977 (USA).

BURBRIDGE, G.
Digest of the criminal law of Canada. Carswell, 1980.

CARTER, R.F.
Criminal law of Queensland. 6ed. Butterworths (Australia), 1982.

COLLINGWOOD, J.J.R.
Criminal law of East and Central Africa. Sweet & Maxwell, 1967.

DE SCHUTTER, D.
Bibliography of international criminal law. Sijthoff, 1972.

FRIEDLAND, M.L.
Cases and materials on criminal law and procedure. 5ed. Carswell, 1979 (Canada)

GILLIES, P.
The law of criminal complicity. Law Book Co., 1980 (Australia).

HATCHARD, J. & NDULO, M.
Casebook of criminal law. Govt. of Zambia: African Law Reports, 1983.

HERLIHY, J.M. & KENNY, R.G.
An introduction to the criminal law of Queensland and Western Australia. Butterworths (Australia), 1978.

HEUMANN, M.
Plea bargaining: experiences of prosecutors, judges and defence attorneys. Univ. of Chicago P., 1978 (USA).

HOWARD, C. & ELLIOTT, I.D.
Criminal law. 4ed. Law Book Co., 1982 (Australia).

KLEIN, J.F.
Let's make a deal: negotiating justice. Lexington, 1976 (USA).

LAFAVE, W.
Modern criminal law: cases, comments, etc. West, 1978 (USA).

LANSDOWN, A.
Outlines of South African criminal law and procedure. 2ed. Juta, 1961.

MEWETT, A.W. & MANNING, M.M.
Criminal law. 1977 (Canada).

MILNER, A.
The Nigerian penal system. Sweet & Maxwell, 1972.

NASH, G.
Bourke's criminal law Victoria. 3ed. Butterworths (Australia), 1981. Looseleaf.

OKONKWO, C.O. & McLEAN, I.
Cases on the criminal law: procedure and evidence on Nigeria, excluding the North. Sweet & Maxwell, 1966.

OKONKWO, C,O. & NAISH, M.E.
Criminal law in Nigeria. 2ed. Sweet & Maxwell, 1980.

PERKINS, R.M. & BOYCE, R.N.
Cases and materials on criminal law and procedure. 5ed. Foundation P., 1977 (USA).

RICHARDSON, S.S. & WILLIAMS, T.H.
The criminal procedure code of Northern Nigeria. Sweet & Maxwell, 1963.

ROULSTON, R.P. and others
Intorduction to criminal law in New South Wales. 2ed. Butterworths (Australia), 1980.

SALHANY, R.E. & CARTER, R.J.
Studies in Canadian criminal evidence. Canada Law Book Co., 1972.

SCHMEISER, D.A.
Criminal law: cases and comments. 3ed. Butterworths (Canada) 1977.

SEIDMAN, R.B.
A sourcebook of the criminal law of Africa: cases, statutes and materials. Sweet & Maxwell, 1966.

SONENBERG, D.S., BOURKE, J.P. & NEW, C.I.
Criminal law in Victoria. 2ed. Butterworths (Australia), 1969.

STUART, D.
Canadian criminal law – a treatise. Carswell, 1982.

STUART, D.
Criminal law casebook. Carswell, 1982.

TASCHEREAU, H.
The criminal code. Carswell, 1983.

WATSON, R.S. & PURNELL, H.
Criminal law and procedure in New South Wales. Law Book Co., 1971. 3 vols.

WATT, D.
Criminal law precedents. Carswell, 1978. 2 vols.

WISE, E.M. & MUELLER, G.O.W.
Studies in comparative criminal law. Thomas, 1975 (USA).

CRIMINOLOGY

See also Criminal Law; Punishment.

Periodicals

Australian and New Zealand Journal of Criminology.
British Journal of Criminology & Penology. 1960–
Canadian Journal of Crime and Corrections. 1958–
Contemporary Crisis. 1977.
Crime and Community Forum. 1976–
Crime and Delinquency (USA). 1955–
Criminal Law Review. 1954–

Criminology. 1953–
International Journal of Criminology.
International Journal of Offender Therapy and Comparative Criminology.
Journal of Criminal Justice.
Journal of Criminal Law Criminology and Police Science (USA). 1910–
Journal of Research in Crime and Delinquency.

Texts

ANDERTON, C.J.
Crime in perspective. Manchester Stat. Soc., 1979.

BALDWIN, J. & BOTTOMS, A.E.
The urban criminal: a study in Sheffield. Tavistock, 1976.

BELSON, W.A.
Juvenile theft: the casual factors. Harper & Row, 1975.

BORRELL, C. & CASHINELLA, B.
Crime in Britain today. Routledge, 1975.

BOTTOMLEY, A.K.
Criminology in focus. Martin Robertson, 1979.

BRANTINGHAM, P.J.
Environmental criminology. Sage Pubns., 1982.

BURROWS, J. & TARLING, R.
Clearing up crime. HMSO, 1982 (Home Office research studies, no.73).

CABINET OFFICE
Vandalism. HMSO, 1979.

CAMPS, F.E.
On crime. David & Charles, 1973.

CLARKE, R.V.G. & MAYHEW, P.
Designing out crime. HMSO, 1980 (Home Office research studies).

COHEN, S. & YOUNG, J. (eds.)
The manufacture of news: social problems and deviance and the mass media. 2ed. Constable, 1981.

COUNCIL OF EUROPE
Criminological aspects of economic crime. 1978.

COUTTS, J.A. (ed.)
The accused: a comparative study. Sweet & Maxwell, 1966.

CRESSEY, D.R.
Other people's money: a study on the social psychology of embezzlement. 1953 repr. Patterson Smith, 1973.

CRUFT, J.
Managing criminolgical research. HMSO, 1981 (Home Office research studies, no.69).

CROFT, J.
Concerning crime. HMSO, 1982 (Home Office research studies, no.75).

DOWNES, D.M. & ROCK, P.
Unstanding deviance: guide to the sociology of crime and rule-breaking. Oxford U.P., 1982.

EUROPEAN COMMITTEE ON CRIME PROBLEMS
Council of Europe activities in the field of crime problems, 1956–1976. Council of Europe, 1977.

EUROPEAN COMMITTEE ON CRIME PROBLEMS
International exchange of information on current criminological research projects in member states. Council of Europe, 1980.

EUROPEAN COMMITTEE ON CRIME PROBLEMS
Protection of users of legal data processing systems: symposium proceedings., 1979. Council of Europe, 1980.

EUROPEAN COMMITTEE ON CRIME PROBLEMS
Report on decriminalisation. Council of Europe, 1981.

EUROPEAN COMMITTEE ON CRIME PROBLEMS
Social change and juvenile delinquency. Council of Europe, 1979.

EUROPEAN COMMITTEE ON CRIME PROBLEMS
Standard terms in contracts: colloquy proceedings. Council of Europe, 1980.

FAIRHEAD, S.
Persistent petty offenders. HMSO, 1981 (Home Office research studies, no.66).

GATRELL, V.A.C.
Crime and the law: the social history of crime in Western Europe since 1500. Europa, 1980.

GIBBONS, D.C.
Society, crime and criminal behaviour. 4ed. Prentice-Hall, 1982.

GLAZEBROOK, P.R. (ed.)
Reshaping the criminal law. Stevens, 1978.

GOODERSON, R.
Alibi. Heinemann, 1977 (Cambridge studies in criminology).

GRYGIER, T. and others
Criminology in transition: essays in honour of Herbert Mannheim. Tavistock, 1965.

HENSHEL, R.L. & SILVERMAN, R.A.
Perception in criminology. Columbia U.P., 1975.

HOLYST, B.
Comparative criminology. Lexington Books, 1983 (USA).

HOME OFFICE
Crime and comparative research. HMSO, 1979 (Research studies).

HOME OFFICE
Crime and community. HMSO, 1979 (Research studies).

HOME OFFICE
Crime in public view. HMSO, 1979 (Research studies).

HOME OFFICE
Previous convictions, sentence and reconviction: a statistical study of a sample of 5000 offenders convicted in January 1971. HMSO, 1979 (Research studies).

HOME OFFICE
Race, crime and arrests. HMSO, 1979 (Research studies).

HOME OFFICE
Research and criminal policy. HMSO, 1980 (Research studies).

HOME OFFICE
Social inquiry reports: a survey. HMSO, 1979 (Research studies).

HOME OFFICE
Tackling vandalism. HMSO, 1979 (Research studies).

HOME OFFICE
Taking offenders out of circulation. HMSO, 1980 (Research studies).

HOME OFFICE
Youth custody and supervision: a new sentence. HMSO, 1978 (Cmnd. 7406).

HOOD, R. (ed.)
Crime, criminology and public policy – essays in honour of Sir Leon Radzinowitz. Heinemann, 1974.

HOOD, R. & SPARKS, R.F.
Key issues in criminology. Weidenfeld & N., 1970.

HOUGH, M. & MAYHEW, P.
The British crime survey. Report 1.
HMSO, 1982 (Home Office research studies, no.76).

HURWITZ, S. & CHRISTIANSEN, K.O.
Criminology. 2ed. Allen & Unwin, 1983.

JUSTICE
Breaking the rules: the problem of crimes and contraventions: a report. Stevens, 1980.

McCLINTOCK, F.H. & AVISON, N.H.
Crime in England and Wales. Heinemann, 1968.

MAGUIRE, M.
Burglary in a dwelling. Heinemann, 1982 (Cambridge studies in criminology).

MANNHEIM, H.
Copmparative criminology. Routledge & Kegan Paul, 1965. 2 vols.

MAYS, J.B.
Crime and its treatment. 2ed. Longman, 1975.

MEIER, R.F.
Theory of criminology. Sage, 1977 (USA).

PHILLIPSON, M.
Sociological aspects of crime and delinquency. Routledge & Kegan Paul, 1971.

PLATT, T. & TAKAGI, P. (ed.)
Crime and social justice. Macmillan, 1981.

PRINS, H.A.
Criminal behaviour: an introduction of its study and treatment. 2ed. Sweet & Maxwell, 1982.

RADZINOWICZ, Sir L.
Ideology and crime: a study of crime and its social and historical context. Heinemann, 1966.

RADZINOWICZ, Sir L.
In search of criminology. Heinemann, 1961.

RADZINOWICZ, Sir L. & HOOD, R.
Criminology and the administration of criminal justice: a bibliography. Mansell, 1976.

RADZINOWICZ, Sir L. & KING, J.
Growth of crime: the international experience. new ed. Penguin, 1979.

ROCK, P.
Deviant behaviour. Hutchinson, 1973.

ROSS, A.
On guilt, responsibility and punishment. Stevens, 1975.

RULE, J. (ed.)
Outside the law: studies in crime and order, 1650–1850. University of Exeter, 1983.

SAGARIN, E. (ed.)
Criminology: new concerns. Sage, 1979.

SAVITZ, L.D. & JOHNSTON, N.
Contemporary criminology. Wiley, 1982.

SCHAFER, S.
The political criminal: the problem of morality and crime. Collier-Macmillan, 1974 (USA).

SIMON, R.J.
Women and crime. Lexington Books, 1975.

SUMNER, C.
Crime, justice and underdevelopment. Heinemann, 1982 (Cambridge studies in criminology).

TAYLOR, I., WALTON, P. & YOUNG, J.
The new criminology: for a social theory of deviance. Routledge, 1973.

TUTT, N. (ed.)
Alternative strategies for coping with crime. Blackwell, 1978.

VERMES, M.
The fundamental questions of criminology. Sijthoff, 1978.

VOLD, G.B.
Theoretical criminology. 2ed. Oxford U.P., 1981 (USA).

WALKER, N. HAMMOND, W. & OTHERS
The violent offender – reality of illusion?. Blackwell, 1970.

WALSH, D. & POOLE, A. (eds.)
Dictionary of criminology. Routledge & Kegan Paul, 1983.

WEISSER, M.
Crime and criminality in early modern Europe. Harvester P., 1979.

WRIGHT, M.
Use of criminology literature. Butterworths, 1974.

CROWN

See also Administrative Law; Petition of Right.

Encyclopaedias

Statutes in Force, Groups: Crown Proceedings; Constitutional Law.
Halsbury's Laws of England. 4ed. vols. 8 & 11.
Halsbury's Statutes of England. 3ed. vols. 6 & 8.

The Digest. vol.16.
Encyclopaedia of Court Forms in Civil Proceedings (Atkin). 2ed. vol.14, see also index vol.
Encyclopaedia of Forms and Precedents. 4ed. see index vol.

Texts

BAILEY, A.
The succession to the English Crown. 1879.

BELL, R.M.
Law relating to actions by and against the Crown. 1948.

CHITTY, J.
Treatise on the law of the prerogatives of the Crown and the relative duties and rights of the subject. Butterworths, 1820 repr. 1969.

FOSTER, Sir M.
Crown law. 1762ed. Professional Books, 1982. (Classical English law texts).

HALL, W.E.
A treatise on the foreign powers and jurisdiction of the British Crown. Oxford U.P., 1894.

HOGG, P.W.
Liability of the Crown in Australia, New Zealand and the United Kingdom. Sweet & Maxwell, 1972.

KEITH, A.B.
The King and imperial crown: the powers and duties of His Majesty. Oxford U.P., 1936.

KEITH, A.B.
The privileges and rights of the crown. Oxford U.P., 1936.

LANG, A.G.
Crown land in New South Wales. Butterworths (Australia). 1973.

MOORE, W.H.
Acts of state in English Law. Murray, 1906.

MORGAN, J.H.
Public authorities and legal liability, with an introductory chapter on remedies against the Crown. Univ. of London P., 1925.

ROBERTSON, G.S.
The law and practice of civil proceedings by and against the Crown. Stevens, 1908.

WILLIAMS, G.L.
Crown proceedings. Stevens, 1948.

CROWN COURT

See also Assizes

Encyclopaedias

Statutes in Force. Group: Criminal Law, 1: General.
Halsbury's Laws of England. 4ed. vols. 11 and index vol.

Halsbury's Statutes of England. 3ed. vol.41.
Encyclopaedia of Court Forms in Civil Proceedings (Atkin). 2ed. see index vol.

Texts

BARNARD, D.
The criminal court in action. 2ed. Butterworths, 1980.

BINGHAM, R.
Modern cases and statutes on Crown Court crime. B.Rose, 1980 supp. 1982.

FALLON, P.
Crown court practice: sentence. Butterworths, 1975.

FALLON, P.
Crown court practice: trial. Butterworths, 1978 supp. 1979.

McLEAN, I.
Criminal appeals: a practical guide to appeals to and from the Crown Court. Sweet & Maxwell, 1980.

McLEAN, I.
Crown court – pattern of sentencing. B.Rose, 1981.

MORRISH, P. & McLEAN, I.
Crown Court: an index of common penalties and formalities in cases tried on indictment or committed for sentence, and appeals in criminal courts. 11ed. B.Rose, 1983.

ROYAL COMMISSION ON ASSIZES AND QUARTER SESSIONS
Report (Beeching). HMSO, 1969 (Cmnd. 4153).

SCOTT, I.R.
Crown court. Butterworths, 1972.

CROWN OFFICE

Encyclopaedias

Halsbury's Laws of England. 4ed. see index vol.
Halsbury's Statutes of England. 3ed. vol.41.
Encyclopaedia of Court Forms in Civil Proceedings (Atkin). 2ed. vols. 1, 14 & 18.

Texts

GRIFFITS, J.O.
Guide to the practice of the Crown Office and Associates Department. Sweet & Maxwell, 1947 supp. 1950.

SHORT, F.H.
Crown Office rules and forms. Stevens & Haynes, 1886.

SHORT, F.H. & MELLOR, F.H.
Crown Office practice. 2ed. Stevens & Haynes, 1908.

CUSTOMS AND EXCISE

See also Civil Service; Government Departments; Inland Revenue; Revenue Law; Value Added Tax.

Encyclopaedias and periodicals

Statutes in Force. Groups: Customs and Excise; Road Traffic, sub-group 2.
Halsbury's Laws of England. 4ed. vol. 12.
Halsbury's Statutes of England. 3ed. vol.9.
Encyclopaedia of Court Forms in Civil Proceedings (Atkin). 2ed. vol.34.
Encyclopaedia of Forms and Precedents. 4ed. vols. 7, 16 & 22.

Commissioners of Customs & Excise. Annual Report. 1857–

Texts

CROMBI, J.I.C.
Her Majesty's Customs and Excise. Allen & Unwin, 1962.

DE PAGTER, H. & VAN RAAN, R.
Valuation of goods for customs purposes. Kluwer, 1981.

GRAS, N.S.B.
The early English customs system. Harvard U.P., 1918.

HIGHMORE, N.J.
Customs laws. 4ed. Stevens, 1921.

HIGHMORE, N.J.
Excise laws. 3ed. HMSO, 1923. 2 vols & supp. 1931.

VINER, J.
The customs union issue. Carnegie Endowment for International Peace, 1950.

CY-PRES DOCTRINE
See also Charities.

Encyclopaedias

Halsbury's Laws of England. 4ed. vol. 5, 35.
Encyclopaedia of Court Forms in Civil Proceedings (Atkin). 2ed. vols. (& 14.
Encyclopaedia of Forms and Precedents. 4ed. vol.4.

Texts

SHERIDAN, L.A. & DELANY, V.T.H.
Cy-pres doctrine. Sweet & Maxwell, 1959.

'D' NOTICE
See also Censorship.

Encyclopaedias

Halsbury's Laws of England. 4ed. vol.8.

Texts

BUNYAN, T.
The history and practice of political police in Britain. Quartet, 1977.

HEDLEY, P. & AYNSLEY, C.
The 'D' Notice affair. M.Joseph, 1968.

PRIME MINSTER
The 'D' notice system. HMSO, 1967 (Cmnd. 3312).

PRIVY COUNCIL
Report of the Commitee of Privy Counsellors appointed to inquiry into 'D' notice matters (Radcliffe). HMSO, 1967 (Cmnd. 3309).

DAMAGES
See also Industrial Injuries; Negligence; Personal Injuries.

Encyclopaedias and periodicals

Statutes in Force. Group: Tort and Delict.
Halsbury's Laws of England. 4ed. vol.12.
Halsbury's Statutes of England. 3ed. see index vol.
The Digest. vol.17.
Encyclopaedia of Court Forms in Civil Proceedings (Atkin). 2ed. see index vol.
Encyclopaedia of Forms and Precedents. 4ed. see index vol.

Current Law. 1947–

Texts

CHARLES, W.
Assessment of damages in personal injury cases. Carswell, 1982 (Canada).

COOPER-STEPHENSON, K. & SAUNDERS, I.E.
Personal injury damages in Canada. Carswell, 1981.

CORBETT, M.M. & BUCHANAN, J.L.
Quantum of damages in bodily and fatal injury cases. 2ed. Sweet & Maxwell (S.Africa), 1965. Looseleaf.

FRUMER, L.R. and others
Personal injuries: actions, defenses and damages. Bender, 1957. 21 vols. looseleaf (USA).

GLASS, H.H. & McHUGH, M.H.
Liability of employers in damages for personal injury. 2ed. Law Book Co. (Australia), 1979.

GOLDSMITH, I.
Damages for personal injury and death in Canada. Carswell, 1935–81. 4 vols. looseleaf.

KEMP, D.A.McL.
Damages for personal injury and death. 2ed. Oyez, 1983.

KEMP, D.A.McL. & KEMP, M.S.
The quantum of damages. 4ed. Sweet & Maxwell, 1975. 2 vols. Looseleaf service.

LAW COMMISSION
Report on personal injury litigation: assessment of damages. HMSO, 1973 (Law Com. no. 56).

McCORMICK, C.
Hornbook on damages. West, 1935 (USA).

McEWAN, R.G. & PATON, A.
Casebook on damages in Scotland. Green, 1983.

McGREGOR, H.
McGregor on damages. 14ed. Sweet & Maxwell, 1980.

MANN, A.
Medical assessment of injuries for legal purposes. 3ed. Butterworths (Australia), 1979.

MUNKMAN, J.
Damages for personal injuries and death. 6ed. Butterworths, 1980.

OGUS, A.I.
On damages. Butterworths, 1973.

STEIN, J.
Damages and recovery: personal injuries and death actions. Lawyers' Co-operative, 1972 (USA).

STREET, H.
Principles of the law of damages. Sweet & Maxwell, 1962.

WHITEMAN, M.M.
Damages in international law. 1937 repr. Kraus Thompson, 1976. 2 vols.

WOOLF, A.D.
The time barrier in personal injury claims. Butterworths, 1969.

DEBTS AND DEBTORS

See also Attachment of Earnings; Bankruptcy; Liens; Receivers.

Encyclopaedias

Statutes in Force. Groups: Bankruptcy and Deeds of Arrangement; Enforcement.
Halsbury's Laws of England. 4ed. see index vol.
Halsbury's Statutes of England. 3ed. vol.40.

Texts

CHAMBERS, G.S.
Enforcement of money payments in magistrates' courts. 2ed Shaw, 1973.

COUNTY Court practice. Butterworths. Annual.

DUNLOP, C.
Creditor-debtor law in Canada. Carswell, 1981.

EPSTEIN, D.
Cases and materials on debtors and creditors. 2ed. West, 1982 (USA).

EPSTEIN, D.
Debtor-creditor relations. 2ed. West, 1980 (USA).

LAW COMMISSION
Charging orders. HMSO, 1976 (Law Com. no. 74).

LAW COMMISSION
Interest. HMSO, 1976 (Working paper no. 66).

LAW COMMISSION
Law of contract: report on interest. HMSO, 1978 (Law Com. no. 88).

PARK, W.D.
Collection of debts. 4ed. Oyez, 1976.

STONE's Justices' manual. Butterworths. 3 vols. Annual.

TREBILCOCK, M.J.
Debtor and creditor: cases, notes and materials. Univ. of Toronto P., 1980 (Canada).

WILLIAMS, R.V. & HUNTER, M.
Law and practice in bankruptcy. 19ed. Sweet & Maxwell, 1979.

WILSON, W.A.
Law of Scotland relating to debt. Green, 1982.

DECLARATORY JUDGMENT

See also Administrative Law.

Encyclopaedias

Halsbury's Laws of England. 4ed. see index vol.
Encyclopaedia of Court Forms in Civil Proceedings (Atkin). 2ed. vol.14.

Texts

BORCHARD, E.M.
Declaratory judgments. 2ed. Banks-Baldwin Pub. Co., 1942 (USA).

DE SMITH, S.A.
Judicial review of administrative action. 4ed. Sweet & Maxwell, 1980.

SARNA, L.
The law of declaratory judgments. Carswell, 1978 (Canada).

YOUNG, P.W.
Declaratory orders. Butterworths (Australia), 1975.

ZAMIR, I.
The declaratory judgment. Stevens, 1962.

DEEDS

See also Conveyancing; Mortgages; Real Property; Vendor and Purchaser.

Encyclopaedias

Halsbury's Laws of England. 4ed. vol.12.
The Digest. vol.17.
Encyclopaedia of Court Forms in Civil Proceedings (Atkin). 2ed. see index vol.

Texts

BEAL, E.
Cardinal rules of legal interpretation. 3ed. Carswell, 1924 (Canada).

BURROWS, R.
Interpretation of documents. 2ed. Butterworths, 1946.

FEARNLEY, A.L.
Guide to the inspection of deeds. Pitman, 1933.

NORTON, R.F.
Treatise on deeds. 2ed. Sweet & Maxwell, 1928 repr. Gaunt, 1981.

ODGERS, C.E.
The construction of deeds and statutes. 5ed. Sweet & Maxwell, 1967.

DEEDS OF ARRANGEMENT

See also Bankruptcy; Receivers.

Encyclopaedias

Statutes in Force. Group: Bankruptcy and Deeds of Arrangement.
Halsbury's Law of England. 4ed. vol.3.
Halsbury's Statutes of Englaand. 3ed. vol.3.

Encyclopaedia of Court Forms in Civil Proceedings (Atkin). 2ed. vol.7.
Encyclopaedia of Forms and Precedents. 4ed. vol.2.

Texts

BALL, W.V.
Bankruptcy, deeds of arrangement and bills of sale. 5ed. Pitman, 1934.

CHALMERS, M.D. & HOUGH, E.
The Bankruptcy Acts 1914 & 1926, and the Deeds of Arrangement Act 1914. 9ed. Waterlow, 1938.

GRIFFITHS, O. & HOLMES, W.D.
The law relating to bankruptcy, deeds of arrangement, receiverships and trusteeships. 8ed. Sweet & Maxwell, 1967.

LAWRANCE, G.W.
Precedents of deeds of arrangements. 10ed. Sweet & Maxwell, 1931.

POTTER, H., ADAMS, T. & DICKSON, A.W.
Principles of the law of bankruptcy and deeds of arrangements. 2ed. Butterworths, 1939.

DELEGATED LEGISLATION

See also Administrative Law; By-Laws; Local Government; Public Authorities.

Encyclopaedias and periodicals

Statutes in Force. Group: Statutes and Statutory Instruments.

Statute Law Review.

Texts

BRICE, S.W.
Law of corporations and companies: a treatise on the doctrine of ultra vires. 3ed. Stevens, 1893.

CARR, C.T.
Delegated legislation. Cambridge U.P., 1921.

FAIRLIE, J.A.
Administrative procedure in connection with statutory rules and orders in Great Britain. University of Illinois P., 1927.

HALSBURY's statutory instruments.
Butterworths. 24 vols. with replacement and looseleaf service.

KERSELL, J.K.
Parliamentary supervision of delegated legislation. Stevens, 1960.

PEARCE, D.C.
Delegated legislation in Australia and New Zealand. Butterworths (Australia), 1977.

SIEGHART, M.A.
Government by decree. Stevens, 1950.

STREET, H.A.
Ultra vires. Sweet & Maxwell, 1930 repr. Professional Books.

WILLIS, J.
Parliamentary powers of English government departments. Harvard U.P., 1933.

DELICT

See also Tort

Encyclopaedias and periodicals

Statutes in Force. Group: Tort & Delict.
Encyclopaedia of the Laws of Scotland. vols.10, 12.

Juridical Review. 1889–

Texts

GLEGG, A.T.
The law of reparation in Scotland. 4ed. Green, 1955.

MACINTOSH, J.C. & NORMAN-SCOBLE, C.
Negligence in delict. 5ed. Juta, 1970.

McKERRON, R.G.
The law of delict. 7ed. Juta, 1971 (S. Africa).

NEWMAN, E. & McQUOID-MASON, D.J.
Law of obligations. Butterworths (S.Africa), 1978.

SCOTTISH LAW COMMISSION
Reform of the laws relating to prescription and limitation of action. 1970.

WALKER, D.M.
The law of damages in Scotland. Green, 1955.

WALKER, D.M.
The law of delict in Scotland. 2ed. Green, 1981.

WALKER, D.M.
Principles of Scottish private law. 3ed. Oxford U.P., 1982–3. 4 vols.

DELINQUENCY

See also Criminology.

Periodicals

Halsbury's Laws of England. 4ed. vol. 29.

British Journal of Criminology. 1960–
Crime and Delinquency (USA). 1955–
Howard Journal of Penology and Crime Prevention. 1921–
Journal of Research in Crime and Delinquency (USA). 1964–
Juvenile Justice Digest (USA). 1973–

Texts

BERSANI, C.A. (ed.)
Crime and delinquency: a reader. Collier-Macmillan, 1970.

BOSS, P.
Social policy and the young delinquent. Routledge, 1967.

BOTTOMS, A.E. & McCLINTOCK, F.H.
Criminals coming of age. Heineman, 1973.

CAVAN, R.S. (ed.)
Readings in juvenile delinquency. 2ed. Lippincott, 1969 (USA).

CORNISH, D.B. & CLARKE, R.V.G.
Residential treatment and its effects on delinquency. HMSO, 1975 (Home Office research study no. 32).

CRESSEY, D.R. & WARD, D.A. (eds.)
Delinquency, crime and social process. Harper, 1969 (USA).

ELLIOTT, D.S. & VOSS, H.L.
Delinquency and the dropout. Lexington, 1974 (USA).

EUROPEAN COMMITTEE ON CRIME PROBLEMS
Prevention of juvenile delinquency: the role of institutions of socialisation in a changing society. Council of Europe, 1982.

EUROPEAN COMMITTEE ON CRIME PROBLEMS
Social change and juvnile delinquency. Council of Europe, 1979.

FRIDAY, P.C. & STEWART, V.L. (eds.)
Youth crime and juvenile justice: international perspectives. Praeger, 1977 (USA).

GLUECK, S. & GLUECK, E.T.
Delinquents and non-delinquents in perspective. C.C.Thomas, 1968 (USA).

GRIFFIN, B.S. & GRIFFIN, C.T.
Juvenile delinquency in perspective. Harper & Row, 1978 (USA).

GRUNHUT, M.
Juvenile offenders before the courts. Oxford U.P., 1956 repr. Greenwood P., 1978.

GUNN, J. & FARRINGTON, D.P.
Abnormal offenders, delinquency and the criminal justice system. Wiley, 1982.

HASKELL, M.R. & YABLONSKY, L.
Crime and delinquency. rev. ed. Houghton Mifflin, 1982 (USA).

HOGHUGHI, M.
The delinquent: directions for social control. Hutchinson, 1983.

HOME OFFICE
The child, the family and the young offender. HMSO, 1965.

HOME OFFICE
Children in trouble. HMSO, 1968 (Cmnd. 3601).

HOME OFFICE
Report of the Committee on Children and Young Persons (Ingleby). HMSO, 1960 (Cmnd. 1191).

JENSEN, G.F.
Sociology of delinquency: current issues. Sage Pubns., 1981.

KASSEBAUM, G.G.
Delinquency and social policy. Prentice, 1974 (USA).

KORNHAUSER, R.R.
Social sources of delinquency. Univ. of Chicago P., 1978 (USA).

MAYERS, M.O.
Hard-core delinquent: an experiment in control and care in a community home with children. Gower, 1980.

MAYS, J.B. (ed.)
Juvenile delinquency, the family and the social group: a reader. Longman, 1972.

MAYS, J.B.
Social treatment of young offenders. Longman, 1975.

MURRAY, C.A. & COX, L.A.
Beyond probation: juvenile corrections and the chronic delinquent. Sage, 1980.

PHILLIPSON, M.
Sociological aspects of crime and delinquency. Routledge, 1971.

ROCK, P.
Deviant behaviour. Hutchinson, 1973.

RUTTER, M. & GILLER, H.
Juvenile delinquency: trends and perspectives. Penguin, 1983.

SANDERS, W.B.
Juvenile delinquency. Praeger, 1976 (USA).

SCOTTISH HOME AND HEALTH DEPARTMENT
Report of the Committee on Children and Young Persons (Scotland) (Kilbrandon). HMSO, 1964 (Cmnd. 2306).

TROJANOWICZ, R.C.
Juvenile delinquency: concepts and control. 2ed. Prentice-Hall, 1978 (USA).

WARD, C. (ed.)
Vandalism. Architectural P., 1973.

WEST, D.J.
Delinquency: its roots, careers and prospects. Heinemann, 1982 (Cambridge studies in criminology).

WEST, D.J.
Present conduct and future delinquency. Heinemann, 1969.

WEST, D.J. & FARRINGTON, D.P.
The delinquent way of life. Heinemann, 1977.

WEST, D.J. & FARRINGTON, D.P.
Who becomes delinquent. Cambridge U.P., 1973.

DEMURRAGE

See also Shipping

Encyclopaedias and periodicals

Halsbury's Laws of England. 4ed. vols. 9, 37.

Encyclopaedia of Court Forms in Civil Proceedings (Atkin). 2ed. vol.8.

Encyclopaedia of Forms and Precedents. 4ed. vol.4.

Lloyd's Maritime and Commercial Law Quarterly.

Texts

STEPHENS, J.E.R.
The law relating to demurrage. Syren & Shipping Ltd, 1907.

TIBERG, H.
Law of demurrage. 3ed. Sweet & Maxwell, 1979.

DENTISTS

See also Anaesthetics; Doctors; Medical Jurisprudence; National Health.

Encyclopaedias and periodicals

Statutes in Force. Group: Medical and Related Professions.
Halsbury's Laws of England. 4ed. see index vol.
Halsbury's Statutes of England. 3ed. vol.21.
Encyclopaedia of Courts Forms in Civil Proceedings (Atkin). 2ed. vols. 5, 28.
Encyclopaedia of Forms and Precedents. 4ed. vol.9.

Anaesthesia. 1946–
British Dental Journal. 1880–
British Journal of Anaesthesia. 1923–
International Dental Journal. 1951–
Journal of Forensic Science. 1960–
Lancet. 1823–
Medicine, Science and the Law. 1960–
Medico-Legal Journal. 1901–

Texts

BULLOCK, F.
The law relating to medical, dental and veterinary practice. Bullock, 1929.

CAMERON, J.M. & SIMS, B.G.
Forensic dentistry. Churchill Livingstone, 1974.

DENTAL BOARD
Dental register of Ireland. Annual.

FORBES, G. & WATSON, A.A.
Legal aspects of dental practice. Wright, 1975.

GENERAL DENTAL COUNCIL
Dentists register. Annual.

GENERAL DENTAL COUNCIL
Notice for guidance of dentists. 1970.

GUSTAFSON, G.
Forensic odontology. Elsevier, 1966.

HOWARD, W.W. & PARKS, A.L.
Dentist and the law. 3ed. Mosby, 1974 (USA).

LUNTZ, L.L. & LUNTZ, P.
Handbook for dental identification: techniques in forensic dentistry. Lippincott, 1973 (USA).

MILLER, S.L.
Legal aspects of dentistry. Putnam, 1970.

ROYAL COMMISSION ON THE NATIONAL HEALTH SERVICE
Report (Merrison). HMSO, 1979. (Cmnd. 7615).

ROYAL COMMISSION ON THE NATIONAL HEALTH SERVICE
The working of the National Health Service. HMSO, 1978.

SAMSON, E.
Dentist and the state: a critical examination and interpretation of the general dental services regulations as they affect the dentist in surgery. Kimpton, 1973.

SEEAR, J.E.
Law and ethics in dentistry. Wright (Bristol), 1975.

SOPHER, I.M.
Forensic dentistry. C.C.Thomas, 1976 (USA).

SPELLER, S.R.
Law of doctor and patient. Lewis, 1973.

WILLIG, S.H.
Legal considerations in dentistry. Will & Wilk, 1971 (USA).

WOODALL, I.R.
Legal, ethical and management aspects of the dental care system. 2ed. Mosby, 1983.

DETENTION CENTRES

See also Borstal; Prisons.

Encyclopaedias and periodicals

Halsbury's Laws of England. 4ed. see index vol.

British Journal of Criminology. 1960– . (as British Journal of Delinquency. 1950–60).

Texts

BRODY, S.R.
The effectiveness of sentencing: a review of the literature. HMSO, 1976 (Home Office research study no. 35).

HOME OFFICE
Detention centres. HMSO, 1970.

HOME OFFICE
Hostels for offenders. HMSO, 1979 (Research studies).

HOME OFFICE
Junior attendance centres. HMSO, 1980 (Research studies).

HOME OFFICE
Youth custody and supervision: a new sentence. HMSO, 1978 (Cmnd. 7406).

KLARE, H.J.
The changing concept of crime and its treatment. Pergamon, 1966.

STANFIELD, R.A.
The detention centre. B.Rose, 1978.

DEVELOPMENT TAX

See also Revenue Law.

Texts

BAGNALL, K.R. & LEWISON, K.
Development land tax. Shaw, 1978. Looseleaf.

COLLEGE OF LAW
Capital transfer tax and development land tax. 2ed. Law Notes, 1977.

COLLEGE OF LAW
Development land tax and the Community Land Act, 1975. Law Notes, 1976.

DOBRY, G. (ed.)
Land development encyclopaedia. Butterworths, 1976. Looseleaf.

DOBRY, G., STEWART-SMITH, W.R. & BARNES, M.
Development gains tax. Butterworths, 1975.

HARDMAN, J.P. and others
Development land tax. Inst. of Chartered Accountants, 1977.

JOSEPH. C.
Development land tax: a practical guide. 2ed. Oyez, 1979 supp. 1980.

JOSEPH, C. & EDWARDS, R.G.
The R.I.C.S. handbook of community land and development. R.I.C.S., 1976.

DICTIONARIES

JOSEPH, C. & SKINNER, B.
Land: Development Land Tax and Community Land Act. 2ed. Oyez, 1975.

LAWTON, P. & GOY, D.
The 1974 developments tax. Sweet & Maxwell, 1974.

MAAS, R.W.
Tolley's development land tax. 4ed. Tolley, 1982.

MATTHEWS, J.P. & JOHNSON, T.A.
Development land tax. Estates Gazette, 1977.

TINGLEY, K.R. & HUGHES, P.F. (eds.)
Key to development gains and first lettings. Taxation Pub. Co. 1974.

DEVOLUTION

See also Constitutional Law.

Encyclopaedias

Halsbury's Laws of England. vol. 17.

Texts

CALVERT, H. (ed.)
Devolution. Professional Books, 1975.

DICEY, A.V. & RAIT, R.S.
Thoughts on the union between England and Scotland. 1920 repr. Greenwood.

GRANT, J.P.
Independence and devolution: the legal implcations for Scotland. Green, 1976.

LORD PRESIDENT OF THE COUNCIL
Devolution within the U.K: some alternatives for discussion. HMSO, 1974.

MANSERGH, P.N.S.
The government of Northern Ireland: a study in devolution. Oxford U.P., 1936.

ROYAL COMMISSION ON THE CONSTITUTION 1968–1973.
Report (Kilbrandon). HMSO, 1973 (Cmnd. 5460).

SMITH T.B.
British justice: the Scottish contribution. Stevens, 1961.

SMITH, T.B.
Studies critical and comparative. Green, 1962.

SMITH, T.B.
The United Kingdom. Stevens, 1955.

TURNER, A.C.
Scottish home rule. Blackwell, 1952.

DICTIONARIES

See also Legal Maxims.

Legal

ADLER, J.A.
Elsevier's dictionary of criminal science in eight languages. Elsevier, 1970.

ANDERSON, R.J.B. (ed.)
Anglo-Scandinavian law dictionary. Universitetsforlaget, 1977 (Norway).

ANGUS, J.
Dictionary of crimes and offences in Scotland. 3ed. Green, 1936.

ATTORNEY's pocket dictionary. Godwin, 1981.

BACKE, T.
Concise Swedish-English glossary of legal terms. Gleerup, 1973.

BAKER, J.H.
Manual of law French. Avebury Pub., 1979.

BALLENTINE, J.A.
Ballentine's law dictionary with pronunciations. 3ed. Lawyers' Co-operative, 1969.

DICTIONARIES

BEATON, J.A.
Scots law terms and expressions. Green, 1982.

BECK's English-German law dictionary. Bender, 1979.

BESELER, D. & JACOBS, B.
Law dictionary German-English. 3ed. De Gruyter, 1971.

BLACK, H.C.
Law dictionary. 4ed. West, 1968.

BROOM, H.
Selection of legal maxims classified and illustrated. 10ed. Sweet & Maxwell, 1939 repr. 1974.

BUTLER, W.E. & NATHANSON, A.J. (ed.)
Mongolian-English Russian dictionary of legal terms and concepts. Nijhoff, 1982.

CURZON, L.B.
Dictionary of law. 2ed. Macdonald & Evans, 1983.

DALRYMPLE, A.W.
French-English and English-French dictionary of legal words and phrases. 2ed. Stevens, 1951.

DALRYMPLE, A.W. & GIBB, A.D.
A dictionary of words and phrases judically defined and commented on by the Scottish Supreme Courts. Green, 1946.

DIETL, C.-E.
Dictionary of legal, commercial and political terms. Bender, 1979.

DODGSON, C. (ed.)
A to Z of legal terms. Star Books, 1983.

EGBERT, L.D. & MORALES-MACEDO, F.
Multilingual law dictionary: English-francais-espanol-Deutsch. Sijthoff:Oceana, 1978.

FARANI, M.
Law dictionary, English-Urdu. Pakistan Law, 1972.

GIBB, A.
Student's glossary of Scottish legal terms. 2ed. Green, 1982.

GILBERTSON, G.
Harrap's German and English glossary of terms in international law. Harrap, 1980.

GORDON, F.S. & HEMNES, F.S. (eds.)
Legal word book. Houghton Mifflin, 1978.

HIEMSTRA, V.G. & GONIN, H.L.
Trilingual legal dictionary: English/Latin/Afrikaans. Juta, 1981.

HINDE, G.W.
New Zealand law dictionary. 2ed. Butterworths (New Zealand), 1972.

HUDSON, A.H.
Dictionary of commercial law. Butterworths, 1983.

IVAMY, E.R.H.
Dictionary of company law. Butterworths, 1983.

JACOB, G.
Law dictionary. 16ed. Strahan, 1835 supp. 1838.

JOWITT, Earl (ed.)
The dictionary of English law. 2ed. Sweet & Maxwell, 1977. 2 vols. + supp. 1984.

KELHAM, R
A dictionary of the Norman or old French language. 1779 repr. Tabard, 1978.

KNIEPKAMP, H.P.
Legal dictionary: English-German and German-English. Oceana, 1954.

LE DOCTE, E.
Multilingual law dictionary. 3ed. Sweet & Maxwell, 1983.

LEWIS, R.
Welsh legal terms. Gomerian P., 1972.

MARAIS, C.C.
Judicial dictionary: Afrikaans/English, English/Afrikaans. Hennap, 1980.

MARANTELLI, S.E.
The Australian legal dictionary. Hargreen Pub. Co., 1980 (Australia).

MARTIN, E.A. (ed.)
A concise dictionary of law. Oxford U.P., 1983.

MASTELLONE, L.
Legal and commercial dictionary: English/Italian. Butterworths (Australia), 1980.

MITCHELL, E.
The businessman's legal lexicon. Business Books, 1970.

MOZLEY, H.N. & WHITELEY, G.C.
Law dictionary. 9ed. Butterworths, 1977.

MUKHERJEE, T.P.
Law lexicon. Tripathi, 1981 (India). 2 vols.

DICTIONARIES

OSBORN, P.G.
Concise law dictionary. 7ed. Sweet & Maxwell, 1983.

PRISCHEPENKO, N.P.
Russian-English law dictionary. Praeger, 1969.

QUEMNER, T.A.
Dictionnaire juridique francais-anglais and anglais-francais. 5ed. Navarre, 1974.

RADIN, M. & GRENE, L.G.
Law dictionary. 2ed. Oceana, 1970.

RAISTRICK, D.
Index to legal citations and abbreviations. Professional Books, 1981.

RICE, M.D. (ed.)
Prentice-Hall dictionary of business, finance and law. Prentice-Hall, 1983.

ROBB, L.A.
Dictionary of legal terms: Spanish-English and English-Spanish. Wiley, 1955.

ROMAIN, A.
Dictionary of legal and commercial terms. Vol. 1: English-German; vol.2: German-English. Butterworths, 1983. 2 vols.

SLOANE, S.B.
Legal speller with useful medical terms. Saunders, 1977.

STROUD, F.
A judicial dictionary. 4ed. Sweet & Maxwell. 5 vols.+ supp. 1982.

THOMAS, C.H.
Legal lexicon of taxation. Professional Books, 1980.

TOMLINS, T.E.
Law dictionary, explaining the rise, progress and present state of the British law. 4ed. Strahan, 1835 supp. 1849.

VASAN, R.S.
Canadian law dictionary. Law & Business Pubns. (Canada), 1981.

VASAN, R.S.
Latin words and phrases for lawyers. Law & Business Pubns. (Canada), 1981.

WAHAB, L.I.
Law dictionary, English-Arabic: civil, criminal, administrative, commercial, international. Baghdad,National Print & Pub., 1964.

WALKER, D.M.
The Oxford companion to law. Oxford U.P., 1980.

WHARTON, J.J.S.
Law lexicon. 14ed. Stevens, 1938.

WORDS & Phrases legally defined. 2ed. Butterworths, 1970. 5 vols. with annual supplement.

YOGIS, J.A.
Canadian law dictionary. Barron, 1983 (USA).

Medical

ENGLISH, H.B. & ENGLISH, A.L.
A comprehensive dictionary of psychological and psycho-analytical terms. Longman, 1958.

LEVITT, W.M.
Short encyclopaedia of medicine for lawyers. Butterworths, 1966.

RILEY, P.A. & CUNNINGHAM, P.J. (eds.)
The Faber pocket medical dictionary. Faber, 1974.

SCHMIDT, J.E.
Attorney's dictionary of modern medicine. Bender. 4 vols. looseleaf.

THOMSON, W.A.R. (ed.)
Black's medical dictionary. 30ed. Black, 1974.

THOMSON, W.A.R.
Concise medical dictionary. Churchill-Livingstone, 1973.

WAKELEY, E. (ed.)
Faber's medical dictionary. 2ed. Faber, 1975.

General and commercial

ABRAHAM, L.A. & HAWTREY, S.C.
Parliamentary dictionary. 3ed. Butterworths, 1970.

BRANCH, A.E. (ed.)
Dictionary of shipping: international trade terms and abbreviations. 2ed. Witherby, 1982.

BRODIE, P.R.
Dictionary of shipping and shipbroking terms (French-English/English-French). Lloyds, 1980.

BROWN, R.H.
Marine reinsurance terms and abbreviations. Witherby, 1981.

CLEGG, J.
Dictionary of the social services. Nat. Council of Social Service, 1972.

CONCISE Oxford dictionary. new ed. Oxford U.P., 1977.

FOWLER, H.W.
Dictionary of modern English usage. 2ed. Oxford U.P., 1965.

GILPIN, A.
Dictionary of economic terms. 3ed. Butterworths, 1973.

INTERNATIONAL CARGO HANDLING CO-ORDINATION ASSOCIATION
Multilingual glossary of cargo handling terms. 1952.

LEWIS, C.T. & SHORT, C.
Latin dictionary. Oxford U.P., 1879.

OSBORN, P.G. & GRANDAGE, S.
Concise commercial dictionary. Sweet & Maxwell, 1971.

OXFORD English dictionary. Oxford U.P., 1888–1928 supp. 1933, 1974, 1976. 12 vols.

PARTRIDGE, E.
Dictionary of slang. 7ed. Routledge, 1970. 2 vols.

PAXTON, J.
Dictionary of the European Community. 2ed. Macdonald & Evans, 1982.

SEIDE, K.
Dictionary of arbitration and its terms. Oceana, 1970 (USA).

WEBSTER's new international dictionary of the English language. 3ed. Webster, 1962.

YORSTON, K.
Australian commercial dictionary. 5ed. Law Book C., 1972.

DIGESTS

Periodicals

Annual Survey of Commonwealth Law. 1965–
Annual Survey of English Law. 1928–1940 & 1945.
Current Law. Monthly parts & annual volume. 1947– (also Scottish ed.).

Texts

The DIGEST. Butterworths. 69 vols. current ed.+ annual supplement.

ESTATES Gazette digest. Annual.

IRISH digest. Incorporated Council of Law Reporting for Ireland repr. Professional Books.
1867–1893: R.D. Murray & G.Y. Dixon (eds.).
1894–1918: T.H. Maxwell (ed.)
1919–1928: R.H. Ryland (ed.)
1929–1938: R.H. Ryland (ed.)
1939–1948: R.A. Herrison (ed.)
1949–1958: R.A. Harrison (ed.)
1959–1970: E.F. Ryan (ed.)

JENKS, E.
Digest of English civil law. Butterworths, 1905–1947.

LLOYDS law reports digest. Lloyds, 1919–

MEWS, J.
Digest of English case law. 2ed. Sweet & Maxwell, 1928; continued by annual vol. to 1969.

DILAPIDATIONS

See also Ecclesiastical Law; Fixtures; Landlord and Tenant.

Encyclopaedias

Statutes in Force. Group: Church of England.
Halsbury's Laws of England. 4ed. vol.14.
Encyclopaedia of Court Forms in Civil Proceedings (Atkin). 2ed. vols. 4, 18, 33.
Encyclopaedia of Forms and Precedents. 4ed. vols. 8, 11.

Texts

ADKIN, B.W.
Law of dilapidations. 4ed. Estates Gazette, 1954.

FRENCH, C.A.M.
Dilapidation practice. Estates Gazette, 947. 1947.

WEST, W.A.
The law of dilapidations: with some hints on practice. 8ed. Estates Gazette, 1979.

DIPLOMATIC LAW AND PRACTICE

Encyclopaedias and periodicals

Statutes in Force. Group: International Relations.
Halsbury's Laws of England. 4ed. see index vol.
Halsbury's Statutes of England. 3ed. vols. 6, 24.
Encyclopaedia of Court Forms in Civil Proceedings (Atkin). 2ed. vol.30.
Encyclopaedia of Forms and Precedents. 4ed. vols. 11, 21.

American Journal of International Law. 1907–
British Yearbook of International Law. 1920–
Foreign Service Journal. 1924–
International and Comparative Law Quarterly. 1952–
Diplomatic Service List. Annual.
London Diplomatic List. Monthly.

Texts

BARCLAYS, Sir T
Problems of international practice and diplomacy. Sweet & Maxwell, 1907.

BLOOMFIELD, L.M.
Crimes against internationally protected persons, prevention and punishment. Praeger, 1975.

BORCHARD, E.M.
The diplomatic protection of citizen's abroad. Banks Law Pub. Co., 1922 (USA).

BROWNLIE, I.
African boundaries: a legal and diplomatic encyclopedia. C.Hurst, 1979.

CLARK, E.
Diplomat: the world of international diplomacy. Taplinger, 1974 (USA).

CORBETT, P.E.
Law in diplomacy. Princeton U.P., 1959.

DENZA, E.
Diplomatic law: commentary on the Vienna Convention on diplomatic relations. B.I.I.C.L.: Oceana, 1976.

FOREIGN OFFICE
Report of the Committee on Representational Services Overseas (Plowden). HMSO, 1964 (Cmnd. 2276).

HARDY, M.
Modern diplomatic law. Manchester U.P., 1968.

HILL, M.
Immunities and privileges of international officials. Carnegie Endowment for International Peace, 1947 (USA).

JENKS, C.W.
International immunities. Stevens, 1961.

JOSEPH, C.
Nationality and diplomatic protection. Sijthoff, 1969.

LEWIS, C.S.
State and diplomatic immunity. Lloyd's, 1980.

MICHAELS, D.B.
International privileges and immunities: a case for a universal statute. Nijhoff, 1971.

PRZETACZNIK, F.
Protection of officials of foreign states according to international law. Nijhoff, 1983.

SATOW, E.
A guide to diplomatic practice. 5ed. Longman, 1978.

SEN, B.
A diplomat's handbook of international law and public administration. 2ed. Nijhoff, 1979.

TURACK, D.C.
The passport in international law. Heath, 1972 (USA).

WILSON, C.E.
Diplomatic privileges and immunities. Univ. of Arizona P., 1967.

DIRECTORIES

ADEFIDIYA, A.
Directory of law libraries in Nigeria. 2ed. Oceana, 1970.

ALDRIDGE, T.M.
Registers and records. 4ed. Oyez, 1984.

AMERICAN ASSOCIATION OF LAW LIBRARIES
Directory of law librarians. Annual.

ANDERSON, I.G.
Councils, committees and boards: a handbook of advisory, consultative, executive and similar bodies in British public life. 3ed. CBD Research, 1977.

ASSOCIATION OF LAW TEACHERS
Directory of members. Annual.

BIDWELL, R.
A guide to government ministers. Nijhoff, 1972. 4 vols.

FORD, M.E.
Directory of women attorneys in the United States. Ford Associates, 1974.

GRICE, S. (ed.)
Commonwealth organizations: handbook of official and unofficial organizations active in the Commonwealth. Commonwealth Secretariat, 1977.

HODGE, A.G. (ed.)
Scottish law directory. Hodge. Annual.

LAWYERS' law directory. Professional Books, 1985.

McCAFFRAY, C.
Index to Sheriff Court Districts in Scotland. Green, 1980.

MISKIN, C.M. (ed.)
Directory of law libraries. 2ed. Legal Publishing Services for BIALL, 1984.

OYEZ's directory of local authorities in England & Wales. Oyez Longman, 1983.

PARLIAMENT house book. Green. 3 vols. Annual.

PATON, A.
Map of Sheriffdoms and Sheriff Court districts. 2ed. Green, 1980.

RUOFF, T. (ed.)
Fourmat legal directory. Fourmat, 1981.

SOLICITOR's and barrister's diary and directory. Waterlow. Annual.

WORLD PEACE THROUGH LAW
World legal directory. 1973 (USA).

DISCOVERY

Encyclopaedias

Halsbury's Laws of England. 4ed. vol.13.
The Digest. vol.18.

Encyclopaedia of Court Forms in Civil Proceedings (Atkin). 2ed. vol.15.

DIVORCE

Texts

BARTHOLD, W.
Attorney's guide to effective discovery techniques. Prentice-Hall, 1974.

BRAY, E.
Digest of the law of discovery. 2ed. Sweet & Maxwell, 1910.

BRAY, E.
Principles and practice of discovery. Reeves & Turner, 1885.

CHOATE, C.E.
Discovery in Canada. Carswell, 1978.

COUNTY Court practice. Butterworths. Annual.

DANIELL, E.R.
Practice of the High Court of Chancery. 8ed. Stevens, 1914.

HARE, T.
A treatise on the discovery of evidence. 2ed. Stevens, 1877.

LEVINE, J.B.
Discovery: comparisons between English and American civil discovery law with reform proposals. Oxford U.P., 1982.

PARK, W.D.
Notes on the discovery and inspection of documents. 2ed. Oyez, 1975 (Practice notes no. 58).

ROSS, R.E.
Law of discovery. Butterworths, 1912.

SETON, H.W.
Forms of decrees, judgments and orders in equity. 7ed. Stevens, 1912. 3 vols.

SUPREME Court practice 1985. Sweet & Maxwell, 1984. 2 vols.

DIVORCE

See also Family Law; Marriage; Matrimonial Proceedings.

Encyclopaedias and periodicals

Statutes in Force. Group: Family Law, 3: Matrimonial Proceedings.
Halsbury's Laws of England. 4ed. vol. 13.
Halsbury's Statutes of England. 3ed. vol.43.
Encyclopaedia of Court Forms in Civil Proceedings (Atkin). 2ed. vol.16.

Encyclopaedia of Forms and Precedents. 4ed. see index vol.
Family Law. 1971–
Family Law Reports. 1980–

Texts

BARI, B.P.
Law of marriage and divorce. Eastern Book Co., 1981 (India).

BENNETT, S.A.
Short guide to divorce in the Sheriff Court. W. Green, 1984.

BIGGS, A.K.
Fees in matrimonial causes. 2ed. Fourmat, 1982.

BROWN, G.G.
Divorce. Shaw, 1974. Looseleaf.

BROWN, G.G.
Separation. Shaw, 1981.

BUTTERWORTH's family law service. Butterworths. Looseleaf.

CLIVE, E.
Divorce (Scotland) Act 1979. Green, 1980.

CONSUMERS' ASSOCIATION
On getting divorced. Hodder, 1983.

DESAI, K.
Indian law of marriage and divorce. 4ed. Tripathi, 1981.

DEWAN, P.
Family law: law of marriage and divorce in India. Sterling: Books from India, 1984.

FRIEDMAN, G.
How to conduct your own divorce in England and Wales, and a guide to the divorce laws. 3ed. Wildy, 1983.

GRANT, B.
Conciliation and divorce. B.Rose, 1981.

GRAY, K.J.
Reallocation of property on divorce. 2ed. Professional Books, 1984.

HAHLO, H.
Reform of the South African divorce law. Juta, 1980.

HUMPHREYS, T.S.
Humphrey's notes on matrimonial causes proceeding in County Courts and District Registries. 15ed. Oyez, 1981.

JACKSON, J.
Matrimonial finance and taxation. 3ed. Butterworths, 1980.

KRONBY, M.
Divorce practice manual. 2ed. Butterworths (Canada), 1977.

LATEY, W.
The law and practice in divorce and matrimonial causes. 15ed. Longman, 1973.

LAW COMMISSION
Family law: the financial consequences of divorce. The basic policy: a discussion document. HMSO, 1980 (Law Com. no. 103).

LAW COMMISSION
Family law: financial relief after foreign divorce. HMSO, 1980 (Working paper no 77).

LAW COMMISSION
Time restriction on presentation of divorce and nullity petitions. HMSO, 1980 (Working paper no. 76).

LORD CHANCELLOR'S DEPARTMENT
Report of the Interdepartmental Committee on Conciliation (Robinson). HMSO, 1983.

MACDONALD, J.C. & FERRIER, L.K.
Canadian divorce law and practice. Carswell. 2 vols. looseleaf.

MAIDMENT, S.
Child custody and divorce. Croom Helm, 1984.

MORTLOCK, B.
The inside of divorce. Constable, 1972.

MURCH, M.
Justice and welfare in divorce. Sweet & Maxwell, 1980.

PALSSON, L.
Marriage and divorce in comparative conflict of laws. Sijthoff, 1974.

PASSINGHAM, B. & HARMER, C.
Law and practice in matrimonial cases. 4ed. Butterworths, 1984.

PELLING, P.M. & PURDIE, R.A.J.
Matrimonial and domestic injunctions: practice and procedure. Butterworths, 1982.

PUGH, L.M.
Matrimonial proceedings before magistrates. 4ed. Butterworths, 1981.

RAKUSEN, M.L.
Costs in matrimonial causes. Butterworths, 1984.

RAKUSEN, M.L. & HUNT, D.P.
Distribution of matrimonial assets on divorce. Butterworths, 1979.

RAYDEN, W.
Law and practice in divorce and family matters. 14ed. Butterworths, 1982.

ROYAL COMMISSION ON MARRIAGE AND DIVORCE
Report (Morton). HMSO, 1956 (Cmd. 9678).

SANCTUARY, G. & WHITEHEAD, C.
Divorce and after. Oyez, 1976.

SIM, W.J.
Divorce law and practice in New Zealand. 8ed. Butterworths (New Zealand), 1971.

STANDING ADVISORY COMMISSION ON HUMAN RIGHTS
Report on the law in Northern Ireland relating to divorce and homosexuality. HMSO, 1977.

TOLSTOY, D.
The law and practice of divorce and matrimonial causes: including proceedings in magistrates' courts. 7ed. Sweet & Maxwell, 1971.

WALLERSTEIN, J.S. & KELLY, J.B.
Surviving the breakup: How children and parents cope with divorce. Grant McIntyre, 1980.

WHITE, P.
Tax planning on marriage breakdown. 3ed. Oyez, 1984.

WILKINSON, M.
Children and divorce. Blackwell, 1981.

WITCHELL, R.G.
Practice and procedure. vol.4: matrimonial proceedings. 6ed. Oyez, 1977.

DOCKS AND HARBOURS
See also Shipping; Waters and Watercourses

Encyclopaedias
Statutes in Force. Group: Harbours, Docks and Piers.
Halsbury's Laws of England. 4ed. see index vol.

Texts
COULSON, H.J.W. & FORBES, V.A.
Law of waters, sea, tidal and inland. 6ed. Sweet & Maxwell, 1952.

DOUGLAS, R.P.A.
An outline of the law relating to harbours in Great Britain managed under statutory powers. 2ed. Lloyds, 1983.

GEEN, G.K. & DOUGLAS, R.P.A.
Law and administration of pilotage. 2ed. Lloyds, 1983.

PARKS, A.
Law of tug, tow and pilotage. 2ed. Chapman & Hall, 1982.

ROSE, F.D.
Modern law of pilotage. Sweet & Maxwell, 1984.

TEMPERLEY, R.
The Merchant Shipping Act. 7ed. Sweet & Maxwell, 1976.

DOCTORS
See also Anaesthetics; Dentists; Hospitals; Medical Jurisprudence: National Health.

Encyclopaedias and periodicals
Statutes in Force. Group: Medical and Related Professions.
Halsbury's Laws of England. 4ed. see index vol.
Encyclopaedia of Court Forms in Civil Proceedings (Atkin). 2ed. vol.28.
Encyclopaedia of Forms and Precedents. 4ed. vol.16.

British Journal of Anaesthesia. 1923–
British Medical Journa. 1857–
Journal of the Irish Medical Association. 1937–
Lancet. 1823–
Medicine Science and the Law. 1960–
Scottish Medical Journal. 1956–

Texts
BULLOCK, F.
The law relating to medical, dental and veterinary practice. Bullock, 1929.

FOX, R.M.
The medico-legal report: theory and practice. Churchill-Livingstone, 1970.

FREEMAN, A.
Legal proceedings against doctors and health authorities: a special report on the conduct of medical negligence claims. Ravenswood, 1980.

KLEIN, R.
Complaints against doctors: a study in professional accountability. Knight, 1973.

KNIGHT, B.
Legal aspects of medical practice. 3ed. Churchill-Livingstone, 1982.

LEIGH-TAYLOR, N.
Doctors and the law. Oyez, 1976 (It's your law no. 8).

McLEAN, S.
Legal issues in medicine.. Gower, 1981.

McLEAN, S.
Medicine, morals and law. Gower, 1983.

MARTIN, C.
The law relating to medical practice. 2ed. Pitman, 1979.

MASON, J.
The law and medical ethics. Butterworths, 1983.

NATHAN, Lord
Medical negligence. Butterworths, 1957.

QUIMBY, C.
Law for the medical practitioner. Croom Helm, 1979.

SCHUTZ, B.M.
Legal liability in psychotherapy: a guide for risk management. Jossey-Bass, 1982.

SIDLEY, N.T. (ed.)
Law and ethics: a guide for the health professional. Human Science P.: Europa, 1984.

SIMPSON, C.K.
A doctor's guide to court: a handbook on medical evidence. 2ed. Butterworths, 1967.

SPELLER, S.R.
Law of doctor and patient. Lewis, 1973.

SPELLER, S.R.
Law relating to hospitals and kindred institutions. 6ed. Lewis, 1978.

TAYLOR, J.L.
Doctor and negligence. Pitman, 1971.

TAYLOR, J.L.
Doctor and the law. 3ed. Pitman, 1983.

TAYLOR, N.
Doctors and the law. Oyez, 1976.

WHINCUP, M.
Legal aspects of medical and nursing services. 3ed. Ravenswood, 1982.

DOMESTIC VIOLENCE

See also Child Abuse.

Encyclopaedias

Halsbury's Laws of England. 4ed. vol. 22.

Texts

BORKOWSKI, M.
Marital violence. Tavistock Pubns., 1983.

BORLAND, M.
Violence in the family. Manchester U.P., 1976.

COOTE, A. & GILL, T.
Battered women and the new law. 2ed. N.C.C.L., 1979.

EEKELAAR, J.
Family violence. Butterworths, 1978.

FOAKES, J.
Family violence. Hemstal P., 1984.

FREEMAN, M.
Violence in the home. Gower, 1978.

MILLER, N.
Battered spouses. G.Bell, 1975.

PADDINGTON LAW CENTRE
Injunctions for battered wives. 1975.

PAHL, J.
A refuge for battered women: a study of the role of a women's centre (DHSS). HMSO, 1978.

PETHICK, J.
Battered wives: a select bibliography. Univ. of Toronto P., 1979.

PIZZEY, E.
Scream quietly or the neighbours will hear. I.F. Books, 1974.

SCOTTISH LAW COMMISSION
Report on occupancy rights in the matrimonial home and domestic violence. HMSO, 1980 (Scot. Law Com. no. 60).

THORMAN, G.
Family violence. Nelson, 1980.

TRACEY, R.
Battered wives. Bow Pubns., 1974.

DOMICILE

See also Conflict of Laws; Divorce.

Encyclopaedias

Halsbury's Laws of England. 4ed. vol.8.
Halsbury's Statutes of England. 3ed. vol.43.
Encyclopaedia of Court Forms in Civil Proceedings (Atkin). 2ed. vol.2, 16, 18.
Encylopaedia of Forms and Precedents. 4ed. vol.20.

Texts

BENTWICH, N.
Law of domicile in its relation to succession and the doctrine of renvoi. Sweet & Maxwell, 1911.

FARNSWORTH, A.
The residence and domicil of corporations. Butterworths, 1939.

KAHN, E.
South African law of domicile of natural persons. Juta, 1972.

KENNAN, K.K.
A treatise on residence and domicile. Lawyers' Co-operative, 1934 (USA).

PHILLIMORE, R.
Law of domicil. Benning, 1847..

DOUBLE JEOPARDY

Encyclopaedias

Halsbury's Laws of England. 4ed. vol. 11.

Texts

FRIEDLAND, M.L.
Double jeopardy. Oxford U.P., 1969.

MILLER, L.G.
Double jeopardy and the federal system. Chicago U.P., 1968.

SIGLER, J.A.
Double jeopardy: the development of a legal and social policy. Cornell U.P., 1969 (USA).

DOUBLE TAXATION

See also Revenue Law

Encyclopaedias

Halsbury's Laws of England. 4ed. vol. 23.

Texts

ADAMS, J.D.R.
The international taxation of multinational enterprise in developed countries. Greenwood, 1977 (USA).

CARROLL, M.
U.S. tax treaties with the European Community member countries: corporate aspects. Tax Management, 1974 (USA). Looseleaf.

COHEN, J. & GREENFIELD, R.
US/UK double tax treaties guide. Oyez, 1980.

COLE, R.T. (ed.)
U.S.-U.K. double tax treaty with commentary by P.A. Lerner. Inst. for Internat. Research, 1976.

DELOITTE, & HASKINS,
Double taxation relief. Tolley, 1979.

DIBDEN, R.
Index to double taxation agreements. 5ed. Butterworths, 1973.

GOODMAN, W.D.
International double taxation of estates and inheritances. Butterworths, 1978.

HAMILTON, N.
United States/United Kingdom double taxation. Company Communications Centre, 1980.

INLAND REVENUE
Double taxation agreements of the U.K. HMSO, 1969. 2 vols.

KOCH, F.E.
The double taxation conventions. Stevens, 1947.

McGREGOR, H.
Double taxation. Sweet & Maxwell, 1978.

NEWMAN, J.
United Kingdom double taxation treaties. Butterworths, 1979.

ORGANISATION FOR ECONOMIC CO-OPERATION AND DEVELOPMENT
An analysis of bilateral double taxation conventions and protocols signed between 1st July 1963 and 1st January 1973 among OECD countries. 1975.

ORGANISATION FOR ECONOMIC CO-OPERATION AND DEVELOPMENT
Double taxation of income and capital. Revised texts of certain articles of the 1963 OECD Draft Convention and of the commentary thereon. 1974.

DRAFTING

See also Conveyancing; Forms and Precedents; Statutes.

Periodicals

Statute Law Review. 1980–

Texts

COMMITTEE ON THE PREPARATION OF LEGISLATION
Report (Renton). HMSO, 1975 (Cmnd 6053).

DALE, Sir W.
Legislative drafting: a new approach. Butterworths, 1977.

DICK, R.C.
Legal drafting. Carswell, 1973.

DICKERSON, F.R.
The fundamentals of legal drafting. Little, Brown & Co., 1965.

DICKERSON, F.R.
Legislative drafting. 2ed. Little, Brown & Co., 1977 (USA).

DICKERSON, F.R.
Materials on legal drafting. West. 1981 (USA).

HEBSON, R.
The lawyer's draftbook. CBD Research, 1978.

KELLY, J.H.
Draftsman. 14ed. Butterworths, 1979.

NAMASIVAYAM, S.
The drafting of legislation. Ghana U.P., 1967.

PIESSE, E.L.
The elements of drafting. 6ed. Law Book Co., 1981.

RENTON, D.
The preparation of legislation. Sweet & Maxwell, 1981.

ROBINSON, S.
Drafting. Butterworths, 1980.

ROBINSON, S.
Drafting: its application to conveyancing and commercial documents. Butterworths (Australia), 1973.

STATUTE LAW SOCIETY
Renton and the need for reform. Sweet & Maxwell, 1979.

THORNTON, G.C.
Legislative drafting. 2ed. Butterworths, 1978.

THRING, Lord
Practical legislation: the composition and language of Acts of Parliament and business documents. Murray, 1902.

YOGIS, J.A. & CHRISTIE, I.M.
Legal writing and research manual. 2ed. Butterworths (Canada), 1974.

DRAINS AND SEWERS

See also Local Government; Public Health.

Encyclopaedias and periodicals

Statutes in Force, Group: Land Drainage. Halsbury's Laws of England. 4ed. vol. 38.

Halsbury's Statutes of England. 3ed. vol. 18.

Encyclopaedia of Court Forms in Civil Proceedings (Atkin). 2ed. vol. 32.

Encyclopaedia of Forms and Precedents. 4ed. vols. 11, 16.

Effluent and Water Treatment Journal. 1961–

Journal of Planning and Environment Law. 1948–

Texts

CALLIS, R.
Callis on sewers. 4ed. Butterworths, 1824.

COULSON, H.J.W. & FORBES, U.A.
Law relating to waters (sea, tidal and inland) and to land drainage. 6ed. Sweet & Maxwell, 1952.

GARNER, J.F.
Law of sewers and drains. 6ed. Shaw, 1981.

MACMORRAN, A. & WILLIS, W.A.
Law relating to sewers and drains. Shaw, 1904.

WILKINSON, H.W.
Pipes, mains, cables and sewers. 4ed. Oyez, 1984 (Practice notes no. 57).

WISDOM, A.S.
Sewerage and sewage disposal. B.Rose, 1979.

WOOLRYCH, H.W.
A treatise on the law of sewers, including the Drainage Acts. 3ed. Butterworths, 1864.

DRINKING AND DRIVING

See also Blood Tests; Road Traffic.

Encyclopaedias

Statutes in Force. Group: Road Traffic, sub-group 1.

Halsbury's Laws of England. 4ed. vol. 40.
Halsbury's Statutes. 3ed. vol. 42.

Texts

AMERICAN MEDICAL ASSOCIATION
Alcohol and the impaired driver: a manual on the medico-legal aspects of chemical tests for intoxication. 2ed. 1973 (USA).

BRITISH MEDICAL ASSOCIATION
The drinking driver. 1965.

CARR, B.R. and others
Breathalizer legislation; and inferential evaluation. Ministry of Transport, 1974 (Canada).

ENVIRONMENT, DEPARTMENT OF THE
Drinking and driving: report of the Departmental Committee (Blennerhasset). HMSO, 1976.

ERWIN, R.E. & MINZER, M.K.
Defense of drink driving cases. 3ed. Bender, 1971 (USA). Looseleaf.

HALNAN, P.
Drinking/driving: the new law. Oyez Longman, 1984.

LATHAM, D. & HALNAN, P.
Drink/driving offences. Oyez, 1979.

McLEAN, I. & MORRISH, P.
Trial of breathalyser offences: a practitioner's index of practice and procedure. B.Rose, 1975 supp. 1979.

McLEOD, R.M. & TAKACH, J.D.
Breathalizer law in Canada: the prosecution and defence of drinking and driving offences. Sarich, 1973.

ROSS, H.L.
Deterring the drinking driver: legal policy and social control. Lexington Books, 1982 (USA).

STONE's Justices' manual. Butterworths. Annual.

STRACHAN, B.
The drinking driver and the law. 3ed. Shaw, 1982.

TURNER, A.J. & COOPER, M.
Points and the excess alcohol provisions of the Transport Act 1981. B.Rose, 1983.

WALLS, H.J. & BROWNLIE, A.D.
Drinks, drugs and driving. 2ed. Sweet & Maxwell, 1984.

DRUGS

See also Food and Drugs

Encyclopaedias and periodicals

Statutes in Force. Group: Medicines, Poisons and Drugs.
Halsbury's Laws of England. 4ed. vol. 30.
Halsbury's Statutes of England. 3ed. vol. 41.
Encyclopaedia of Court Forms in Civil Proceedings (Atkin). 2ed. vol. 21.

British Journal of Criminology. 1960–
British Journal of Addictions. 1947–
Criminal Law Review. 1954–
Criminologist. 1966–
Drug Dependence. Excerpta Medica (USA). 1972–
Drug Forum: the Journal of Human Issues (USA). 1972–
Journal of Drug Education (USA). 1971–

Texts

BAYLISS, F.P.C.
Law on poisons, medicines and related substances. Ravenswood Pubns., 1979.

BEAN, P.
The social control of drugs. Wiley, 1974.

BRADSHAW, S.
Drug misuse and the law. Macmillan, 1972.

CHATTERJEE, S.K.
Legal aspects of international drug control. Nijhoff, 1982.

CLOYD, J.W.
Drugs and information control: role of men and manipulation in the control of drug trafficking. Greenwood Press, 1982 (Contributions in legal studies).

DALE, J.R. & APPLELBE, G.E.
Pharmacy law and ethics. 2ed. Pharmaceutical P., 1979.

DANBY, G.
Drugs: law and practice. Hemstal P., 1984.

EUROPEAN COMMITTEE ON CRIME PROBLEMS
Penal aspects of drug abuse. Council of Europe, 1974.

FARRIER, D.
Drugs and intoxication. Sweet & Maxwell, 1980.

FERGUSON, R.W.
Drug abuse control. Holbrook P., 1975 (USA).

GLATT, M.M.
Drugs, society and man: a guide to addiction and its treatment. Medical & Technical P., 1974.

HEALTH AND SOCIAL SECURITY, DEPARTMENT OF
Treatment and rehabilitation: report of the Advisory Council on the Misuse of Drugs. HMSO, 1982.

HOME OFFICE
Rehabilitation of drug addicts: report of the Advisory Committee on Drug Dependence (Wayne). HMSO, 1968.

HOTCHEN, J.S.
Drug misuse and the law: the regulations. Macmillan, 1975.

INCIARDI, J.A. & CHAMBERS, C.D. (eds.)
Drugs and the criminal justice system. Sage Pubns., 1974 (USA).

LYDIATE, P.W.H.
The law relating to the misuse of drugs. Butterworths, 1977.

MOORE, J.J.
Investigating drug abuse. United Nations, 1976.

PETTIT, W.
Manual of pharmaceutical law. 3ed. Macmillan, 1962.

REED, T.
Drug offences in South Africa. Juta, 1978.

WALLS, H.J. & BROWNLIE, A.D.
Drinks, drugs and driving. 2ed. Sweet & Maxwell, 1984.

WEST, W.T.
Drugs law. B Rose, 1982.

EASEMENTS

See also Light and Air; Party Walls; Rights of Way.

Encyclopaedias and periodicals

Statutes in Force. Group: Property, England & Wales, sub-group 1.
Halsbury's Laws of England. 4ed. vol. 14.
Halsbury's Statutes of England. 3ed. see index vol.
The Digest. vol. 19.
Encyclopaedia of Court Forms in Civil Proceedings (Atkin). 2ed. vol. 17.
Encyclopaedia of Forms and Precedents. 4ed. vol. 7.
Conveyancer. 1915–1936.
Conveyancer and Property Lawyer. 1936–
Law Society's Gazette. 1903–
Journal of the Law Society of Scotland. 1956–

Texts

BRADBROOK, A.J. & NEAVE, M.A.
Easements and restrictive covenants in Australia. Butterworths (Australia), 1981.

GALE, C.J.
The law of easements. 14ed. Sweet & Maxwell, 1972.

ELPHINSTONE, L.H.
Covenants affecting land. Solicitors' Law Stat. Soc., 1946.

JACKSON, P.
Law of easements and profits. Butterworths, 1978.

PRESTON, C.H.S. & NEWSOM, G.H.
Restrictive covenants affecting freehold land. 7ed. Sweet & Maxwell, 1982.

WILKINSON, H.W.
Pipes, mains, cables and sewers. 4ed. Oyez, 1984 (Practice notes no. 57).

WOODLEY, D.G.
Coal mining law for the land practitioner. Oyez, 1972.

ECCLESIASTICAL LAW

See also Blasphemy; Burials and Cremation; Dilapidations; Parish Church.

Encyclopaedias and periodicals

Statutes in Force. Groups: Church of England; Church of Scotland; Church in Wales.
Halsbury's Laws of England. 4ed. vol. 14.
Halsbury's Statutes of England. 3ed. vol. 10.
The Digest. vol. 19.
Encyclopaedia of Court Forms in Civil Proceedings (Atkin). 2ed. vol. 18.
Encyclopaedia of Forms and Precedents. 4ed. vol. 8.
Catholic Directory. 1837– . Annual.
Catholic Directory for Scotland. 1829–
Church of England Year Book. Annual.
Church of Scotland Year Book. Annual.
Concilium. 1965–
Crockford's Clerical Directory. Annual.
Journal of Ecclesiastical History. 1953–
York Journal of Convocation. 1880–

Texts

ADAMS, N. & DONAHUE, C.
Select pleas in ecclesiastical courts: from MSS in Canterbury Cathedral. Tr. from Latin. Selden Society., 1981.

ARNOLD-BAKER, C.
The new law and practice of parish administration. 2ed. Longman, 1970.

BLUNT, J.H.
The book of church law. 11ed. Longman, 1921.

BOUSCAREN, T.
Canon law: a text and commentary. 4ed. Bruce, 1966 (USA).

BOX, H.S.
The principles of canon law. Oxford U.P., 1949.

BURN, R.
Ecclesiastical law. 9ed. Sweet, Stevens & Norton, 1842. 4 vols.

CANON LAW SOCIETY
The code of canon law. C.L.S., 1983.

CHURCH OF ENGLAND
The Canons of the Church of England. 2ed. 1975. Looseleaf.

CHURCH OF ENGLAND
Opinions of the Legal Board. 5ed. 1973 repr. with supps. 1976.

COX, J.T.
Practice and procedure of the Church of Scotland. 6ed. Church of Scotland Committee on General Admin., 1976.

CRIPPS, H.W.
A practical treatise on the law relating to the church and the clergy. 8ed. Sweet & Maxwell, 1937.

DALE, W.L.
The law of the parish church. 5ed. Butterworths, 1975.

DUGGAN, C.
Canon law in mediaeval England. Variorum Pubns., 1982.

EVANS, E.J.
Tithes and the Tithe Commutation Act 1836 – National statutes and the local community. Bedford Square P., 1978.

GIBSON, E.
Codex juris ecclesiastica anglicani. 2ed. Baskett, 1761. 2 vols.

GREEN, C.A.H.
The setting of the constitution of the Church in Wales. Sweet & Maxwell, 1937.

HOULBROOKE, R.A.
Church courts and the people during the English reformation, 1520–1570. Oxford U.P., 1979.

KEMP, E.W.
An introduction to Canon law in the Church of England. Hodder & Stoughton, 1957.

MACMORRAN, K.M.
A handbook for churchwardens and parochial church councillors. 3ed. Elphinstone, 1971.

MAITLAND, F.W.
Roman Canon law in the Church of England. 1898 repr. B.Franklin (USA), 1969.

MAKOWER, F.
Constitutional history and constitution of the Church of England. Sonnenschein, 1895.

MARCHANT, R.A.
The church under the law: justice, administration and discipline in the diocese of York, 1560–1640. Cambridge U.P., 1969.

MOORE, E.G.
An introduction to English Canon law. Oxford U.P., 1967.

NEW code of canon law. Collins, 1983.

NICKLEM, B.
Law and the laws: being the marginal comments of a theologian. Sweet & Maxwell, 1952.

OGLE, A.
Canon law in Mediaeval England: an examination of William Lyndwood's "Provinciale" in reply to the late Professor F.W. Maitland. 1912 repr. B.Franklin (USA), 1971.

PHILLIMORE, R.J.
The ecclesiastical law of the Church of England. 2ed. Sweet & Maxwell, 1895. 2 vols.

RITCHIE, C.I.A.
The ecclesiastical courts of York. Herald P., 1956.

RODES, R.E.
Ecclesiastical administration in medieval England. Univ. of Notre Dame P., 1976 (USA).

ROYAL COMMISSION ON THE CONSTITUTION AND WORKING OF THE ECCLESIASTICAL COURTS
Report (Stubbs). HMSO, 1883 (C.3760).

WHITE, E.J.
Law in the Scriptures. Thomas Law, 1935 (USA).

EDUCATION

See also Legal Education

Encyclopaedias

Statutes in Force, Group: Education.
Halsbury's Laws of England. 4ed. vol. 15.
Halsbury's Statutes of England. 3ed. vol. 11.
The Digest. vol. 19.

Encyclopaedia of Court Forms in Civil Proceedings (Atkin). 2ed. see index vol.
Encyclopaedia of Forms and Precedents. 4ed. vol. 8.

Texts

ADAMS, N.
Law and teachers today. Hutchinson, 1983.

ANDREWS, C.
The Education Act 1918. Routledge, 1976.

BARRELL, G.R.
Teachers and the law. 5ed. Methuen, 1979.

BIRCH, I.K.
Constitutional responsibility for education in Australia. Australian National Univ. P., 1975.

BIRCH, I.K.
The school and the law. Melbourne U.P., 1976.

BOER, B.W. & GLEESON, V.B.
The law of education. Butterworths (Australia), 1982.

BULLIVANT, B.
The governor's guide. 3ed. Home & School Council, 1982.

DENT, H.C.
The educational system of England and Wales. Hodder, 1982.

HARRISON, G. & BLOY, D.
Essential law for teachers. Oyez, 1980.

KAPLIN, W.A.
Law of higher education: legal implications of administrative decision-making. Jossey-Bass 1979.

KNOTT, A.E.
Australian schools and the law. Univ. of Queensland P., 1977.

NATIONAL COUNCIL FOR EDUCATION TECHNOLOGY
Copyright and education: a guide to the use of copyright material in educational institutions. 1972.

TAYLOR, G. & SAUNDERS, J.
The law of education. 9ed. Butterworths. Looseleaf.

ELECTIONS

See also Bribery and Corruption; Parliament.

Encyclopaedias and periodicals

Statutes in Force, Group: Elections.
Halsbury's Laws of England. 4ed. vol. 15.
Halsbury's Statutes of England. 3ed. vols. 11, 42.
The Digest. vol. 20.

Encyclopaedia of Court Forms in Civil Proceedings (Atkin). 2ed. vol. 18.
Encyclopaedia of Forms and Precedents. 4ed. see index vol.

Public Law. 1956–

Texts

BUTLER, D.E.
The electoral system in Britain since 1918. 2ed. Oxford U.P., 1963.

HAND, G., GEORGEL, J. & SASSE, C.
European electoral systems handbook. Butterworths, 1979.

HERMAN, V. & HAGGER, M.
Legislation of direct election to the European Parliament. Gower, 1980.

HOME OFFICE
Report of the working party on the electoral register (Hayzelden). HMSO, 1978.

HOME OFFICE & SCOTTISH HOME AND HEALTH DEPARTMENT
Draft regulations for the conduct of European Assembly elections in Great Britain. HMSO, 1978 (Cmnd. 7323).

LEVER, H.
South African voter. Juta, 1972.

O'LEARY, C.
The elimination of corrupt practices in British elections, 1868–1911. Oxford U.P., 1962.

O'LEARY, C.
Irish elections, 1918–77. St Martin's P., 1979.

O'MALLEY & HARDCASTLE's reports of election cases. repr. Wildy, 1978. 7 vols.

PARKER, F.R.
Conduct of parliamentary elections. Knight, 1970 supp. 1978.

PARKER, F.R.
The powers, duties and liabilities of an election agent and returning officer. 6ed. Knight, 1959.

QUALTER, T.H.
The election process in Canada. McGraw-Hill, 1970.

RIESS, L.
History of the English electoral law in the Middle Ages. Cambridge U.P., 1949 repr. Octagon, 1973.

ROGERS, F.N.
On elections and registration. Stevens, 1929–1935.

ROSE, R.
Electoral behavior: a comparative handbook. Free Press, 1974 (USA).

ROSS, J.F.S.
Elections and electors. Eyre & Spottiswoode, 1955.

SCHOFIELD, A.N.
Schofield's election law, ed. by P. Little. Shaw, 1984. Looseleaf.

SMITH, T.E.
Elections in developing countries. St Martin's P., 1960.

TERRY, G.P.W.
Representation of the Peoples Act. 3ed. Knight, 1939.

WARD, D.
Parliamentary elections. 4ed. Butterworths, 1935.

ELECTRICITY

See also Gas

Encyclopaedias

Statutes in Force. Group: Energy, 1: Electricity.
Halsbury's Laws of England. 4ed. vol. 16.
Halsbury's Statutes of England. 3ed. vol. 11.

The Digest. vol. 20.
Encyclopaedia of Court Forms in Civil Proceedings (Atkin). 2ed. see index vol.
Encyclopaedia of Forms and Precedents. 4ed. vol. 23.

Texts

DALTON, J.
Electricity Act 1947. Butterworths, 1948.

DALTON, J.
The Electricity (Supply) Act, 1926, annotated and explained. Butterworths, 1927.

REEVES, P.
Electricity and gas consumers' guide: a summary of the practice of supply authorities and the law applicable to domestic gas and electricity consumers. Lucian P., 1981.

WILL, J.S.
Law relating to electricity supply. 6ed. Butterworths, 1932.

EMPLOYER'S LIABILITY

See also Employment Law; Factories; Negligence; Occupational Diseases; Personal Injuries; Shops and Offices; Statutory Sick Pay; Strict Liability; Tort.

Encyclopaedias and periodicals

Statutes in Force. Group: Employment.
Halsbury's Laws of England. 4ed. vol. 16.
Halsbury's Statutes of England. 3ed. see index vol.
The Digest. vol. 24.
Encyclopaedia of Court Forms in Civil Proceedings (Atkin). 2ed. see index vol.

Encyclopaedia of Forms and Precedents. 4ed. vols. 13, 20.

Industrial Law Journal. 1972–
Journal of Business Law. 1957–
Legal Action (formerly L.A.G. Bulletin). 1973–

Texts

ARSCOTT, P.
Employer's guide to health and safety. 3ed. Kogan Page, 1980.

ATIYAH, P.S.
Vicarious liability in the law of torts. Butterworths, 1967.

BATT, F.R.
Law of master and servant. 5ed. Pitman, 1967.

BENEDICTUS, R.
Safety representatives. Sweet & Maxwell, 1980 (Law at work).

DEWIS, M.
Law of health and safety at work. Macdonald & Evans, 1978.

DRAKE, C.
Health and safety at work: a new approach. Sweet & Maxwell, 1983.

ENCYCLOPAEDIA of health and safety at work, law and practice. Sweet & Maxwell. 3 vols. looseleaf.

FIFE, I. & MACHIN, E.A.
Health and safety at work. Butterworths, 1980.

GLASS, H.H. & McHUGH, M.H.
The liability of employers in damages for personal injury. Law Book Co., 1966 (Australia).

INDEX and digest of decisions etc. under the National Insurance, National Insurance (Industrial Injuries) and the Family Allowances Acts. HMSO, 1964. 2 vols. looseleaf.

INTERNATIONAL LABOUR OFFICE
Encyclopaedia of occupational health and safety. 1972. 2 vols.

JANNER, G.
Compendium of health and safety law. 3ed. Business Books, 1982.

McKOWN, R.
Comprehensive guide to factory law. 6ed. Godwin, 1976.

MUNKMAN, J.H.
Damages for personal injuries and death. 6ed. Butterworths, 1980.

MUNKMAN, J.H.
Employer's liability at common law. 9ed. Butterworths, 1979.

REDGRAVE, A.
Health and safety in factories. 2ed. Butterworths, 1982.

ROWE, P.
Health and safety. Sweet & Maxwell, 1980 (Law at work).

SELWYN, N.
Law of health and safety at work. Butterworths, 1982.

UPEX, R.
Termination of employment. Sweet & Maxwell, 1983.

VANDYK, N.D.
Accidents and the law. Oyez, 1979 (It's your law no. 6).

EMPLOYMENT LAW

See also Children and Young Persons; Contract; Employer's Liability; Factories; Industrial Law; Redundancy; Shops and Offices; Statutory Sick Pay; Trade Unions; Workmen's Compensation.

Encyclopaedias and periodicals

Statutes in Force, Group: Employment.
Halsbury's Laws of England. 4ed. vol. 16.
Halsbury's Statutes of England. 3ed. see index vol.
The Digest. vol. 34.
Encyclopaedia of Court Forms in Civil Proceedings (Atkin). 2ed. see index vol.
Encyclopaedia of Forms and Precedents. 4ed. vol. 20.
British Journal of Industrial Relations. 1963–

Bulletin of the Industrial Law Society.
Department of Employment Gazette. 1893–
Industrial Cases Reports (formerly Industrial Court Reports). 1972–
Industrial Law Journal. 1972–
Industrial Relations Journal. 1972–
Industrial Relations Law Reports. 1972–
Industrial Tribunal Reports. 1966–
Managerial Law. 1975– .(Published as Knights Industrial Law Reports, 1966–1974)

Texts

ALDRIDGE, T.M.
Service agreements. 4ed. Oyez, 1982 (Practice notes no. 52).

ALLAN, R.G.
New deal for employment: or how to prepare for a genuine participation, or how to avoid unfair dismissal. Printhouse Ltd., 1978.

ANDERMAN, S.D.
Law of unfair dismissal. 2ed. Butterworths, 1984.

BATT, F.R.
The law of master and servant. 5ed. Pitman, 1967.

BERCUSSON, B.
The Employment Protection (Consolidation) Act 1978. Sweet & Maxwell, 1979.

BERCUSSON, B.
Fair wages resolution. Mansell, 1978.

BOURN, C.
Job security. Sweet & Maxwell, 1980 (Law at work).

BOWERS, J.
Practical approach to employment law. Financial Training Pubns., 1982.

CARBY-HALL, J.R.
Labour relations and the law. MCB Books, 1975.

CARBY-HALL, J.R.
Principles of industrial law. Knight, 1969.

CARBY-HALL, J.R.
Worker participation in Europe. Croom Helm, 1977.

CHANDLER, P.
A to Z of employment and safety law. Kogan Page, 1981.

CLEGG, H.
System of industrial relations in Great Britain. 3ed. Blackwell, 1979.

CONSUMERS' ASSOCIATION
Dismissal, redundancy and job hunting. C.A., 1977.

COOPER, W.M. & WOOD, J.C.
Outlines of industrial law. 6ed. Butterworths, 1972.

CREIGHTON, B.
Labour law: cases and materials. Law Book Co., 1983 (Australia).

CRONIN, J.B. & GRIME, R.P.
Introduction to industrial law. Butterworths, 1974.

CRONIN, J.B. & GRIME, R.P.
Labour Law. Butterworths, 1970.

CUNNINGHAM, M.
Non-wage benefits. Pluto P., 1981.

DAVIES, P. & FREEDLAND, M.R.
Labour law: text and materials. 2ed.
Weidenfeld & Nicholson, 1984.

DAVIES, P. & FREEDLAND, M.R.
Transfer of employment. Sweet & Maxwell, 1982.

DEADMAN, W.B. & HOCKEY, P.J.
Prices and pay codes. Farringdon, 1973.

DEWIS, M.
The law on health and safety at work.
Macdonald & Evans, 1978.

DIX, D.K.
Contracts of employment. 6ed.
Butterworths, 1980.

DRAKE, C.D.
Employment Acts 1974–80. Sweet & Maxwell, 1981.

DRAKE, C.D.
Labour Law. 3ed. Sweet & Maxwell, 1981.

ECCLES, G.
Employment Act, 1980: a practical guide.
Oyez, 1980.

EGAN, B.
Dismissals: the complete practical guide.
New Commercial Pub. Co., 1977.

ELIAS, P., NAPIER, B. & WALLINGTON, P.
Labour law: cases and materials.
Butterworths, 1981.

EMPLOYMENT, DEPARTMENT OF
Basic rules for safety and health at work.
2ed. HMSO, 1975.

ENCYCLOPAEDIA of health and safety at work, law and practice. Sweet & Maxwell. 3 vols. Looseleaf.

FIFE, I. & MACHIN, E.A.
Health and safety at work. Butterworths, 1980.

FINANCIAL TIMES
Employment and the law: a management guide to recent legislation. 1976.

FLEEMAN, R.K. & RHODES, R.J.
Employment law: a guide. Fleeman Consultants, 1976.

FOX, A.
Beyond contract: work, power and trust relations. Faber, 1974.

FOX, R.
Payments on termination of employment.
Oyez, 1981.

FREEDLAND, M.R.
Contract of employment. Oxford U.P., 1980.

GOLZEN, G.
Working abroad. 6ed. Kogan Page, 1983.

GREENHALGH, R.M.
Industrial tribunals. Inst. of Personnel Management, 1973.

GRIME, R.
Maritime and offshore employment law.
Sweet & Maxwell, 1984.

GRUNFELD, C.
Law of redundancy. 2ed. Sweet & Maxwell, 1980.

HARDING, J.
Employment and the probation and after care service handbook. B.Rose, 1979.

HARVEY, R.J.S.
Industrial relations and employment law.
Butterworths, 1971. 2 vols. Looseleaf.

HEPPLE, B.A.
Labour law in Great Britain and Ireland to 1978: a bibliography. Sweet & Maxwell, 1981.

HEPPLE, B.A. & O'HIGGINS, P.
Employment Law. 4ed. Sweet & Maxwell, 1981.

HEPPLE, B.A. & O'HIGGINS, P. (eds.)
Encyclopaedia of labour relations law.
Sweet & Maxwell, 1972. 3 vols. Looseleaf.

HEPPLE, B.A. & O'HIGGINS, P.
Sweet & Maxwell's labour relations statutes and materials. 2ed. Sweet & Maxwell, 1983.

HILLIER, A.
Contracts of employment: engagement, termination and redundancy. Training for Business, 1974 supp. 1976.

HILLIER, A.
Dismissal, fair or unfair? the new rules.
Training for Business, 1976.

HILLIER, A.
Employment Act 1982. Tolley, 1983.

HOWARD, G.
Guide to self certification. Industrial Soc., 1982.

HOWARD, G.
Guide to statutory sick pay. Industrial Soc., 1982.

HUMPHRIES, J.
Part-time work. Kogan Page, 1983.

INDUSTRIAL WELFARE SOCIETY
Legal problems of employment. 4ed. 1966.

INTERNATIONAL LABOUR OFFICE
Chronological index of legislation 1919–78. 1980.

INTERNATIONAL LABOUR ORGANIZATION
Maritime labour conventions and recommendations. I.L.O. 1983.

JANNER, G.
Consolidated compendium of employment law. Business Books, 1982.

JANNER, G.
Employment forms. 2ed. Business Books, 1982.

JANNER, G.
Guide to sick pay and absenteeism. Business Books, 1982.

JANNER, G.
Handbook of draft letters of employment law. 2ed. Business Books, 1981.

JANNER, G.
Practical guide to the Employment Act, 1980. Hutchinson, 1980.

KAHN-FREUND, O.
Labour and the law. 3ed. Sweet & Maxwell, 1983.

KEENAN, D.J.
Principles of employment law. Andersen Keenan Pub. Ltd., 1979.

KITCHEN, J.
Labour law and offshore oil. Croom Helm, 1977.

LARMAN ASSOCIATES
Concise guide to employment law. 1977.

LOCAL AUTHORITIES' CONDITIONS OF SERVICE ADVISORY BOARD
The LACSAB employee relations handbook. 1976.

McCARRY, G.J. & SAPPIDEEN, C.
Statutory conditions of employment. Butterworths (Australia), 1980.

McGLYNE, J.E.
Unfair dismissal cases. 2ed. Butterworths, 1979.

MACKEN, J.J.
Australian industrial law: the constitutional basis. 2ed. Law Book Co., 1980.

MACKEN, J.J.
The common law of employment. 2ed. Law Book Co., 1984 (Australia).

MARSH, G.B.
Employer and employee: a complete and practical guide to the modern law of employment. 2ed. Shaw, 1981.

MESHER, J.
Compensation for unemployment. Sweet & Maxwell, 1976.

MITCHELL, E.
Employer's guide to the law on health, safety and welfare at work. 2ed. Business Books, 1977.

MORSE, G. & WILLIAMS, D.
Profit sharing: legal aspects of employee share schemes. Sweet & Maxwell, 1979.

NAPIER, P. (ed.)
Comparative dismissal law. Croom Helm, 1982.

NAPIER, P.
Discipline. Sweet & Maxwell, 1980 (Law at work).

NEWELL, D.
Employer's guide to the Employment Act 1982. Kogan Page, 1982.

NEWELL, D.
New employment law legislation. Kogan Page, 1983.

PAYNE, D.
Employment law manual. Gower. Looseleaf.

PEARSON, R. & KENAGHAN, F.
Employment and the law: a management guide to recent legislation. Financial Times, 1976.

PERRITT, H.H.
Employee dismissal: law and practice. Wiley, 1984.

RIDEOUT, R.
Cases in labour law. Sweet & Maxwell, 1984.

RIDEOUT, R.
Principles of labour law. 4ed. Sweet & Maxwell, 1983.

RUBIN, G.
Wages and salaries. Sweet & Maxwell, 1980 (Law at work).

SCHOFIELD, P.G. & BURKE, C.
Cases and statutes on labour law. Sweet & Maxwell, 1978.

SELWYN, N.M.
Law of Employment. 4ed. Butterworths, 1982.

SLADE, E.A. (ed.)
Tolley's employment handbook. 3ed. Tolley, 1983.

SMITH, F. & BEECH, D.
Employee benefits. Waterlow, 1984.

SMITH, I.
Employment contracts. Sweet & Maxwell, 1980 (Law at work).

SYKES, E.I.
The employer, the employee and the law. 4ed. Law Book Co.,1980 (Australia).

SYKES, E.I. & YERBURY, D.
Labour law in Australia: individual aspects. 2ed. Butterworths (Australia), 1980.

TIERNEY, F.
Employee benefits in Canada. 1977. Looseleaf.

TILLYARD, F.
The worker and the State. 3ed. Routledge, 1948.

UNESCO
Immigrant workers in Europe – their legal status: a comparative study. HMSO, 1982.

UPEX, R.
Dismissal. Sweet & Maxwell, 1980 (Law at work).

VON PRODZYNSKI, F. & McCARTHY, C.
Employment law. Sweet & Maxwell, 1984 (Irish law texts).

WALLINGTON, P. (ed.)
Butterworth's employment law handbook. 2ed. Butterworths, 1981.

WEBB, J.
Industrial relations and the contract of employment. Law Book Co., 1974 (Australia).

WEDDERBURN OF CHARLTON, Lord
Cases and materials on labour law. Cambridge U.P., 1967.

WEDDERBURN OF CHARLTON, Lord (ed.)
Labour law and industrial relations: building on Kahn-Freund. Oxford U.P., 1983.

WEDDERBURN OF CHARLTON, Lord & MURPHY, W.T. (eds.)
Labour law and the community: perspectives for the 1980's – workshop papers. IALS, 1982.

WHINCUP, M.
Modern employment guide: job security and safety. 4ed. Heinemann, 1983.

WRIGHT, M.
Labour law. 3ed. Macdonald & Evans, 1981.

EMPLOYMENT PROTECTION

Encyclopaedias and periodicals

Halsbury's Laws of England. 4ed. vol.16.
Encyclopaedia of Court Forms in Civil Proceedings (Atkin). 2ed. see index vol.

Managerial Law. 1975–

Texts

ANDERMAN, S.D.
Employment of protection: a new legal framework. Butterworths, 1976.

BERCUSSON, B.
The Employment Protection Act, 1974–1980. Sweet & Maxwell, 1981.

CARBY-HALL, J.R.
Modern employment protection law: managerial implications. The Author, 1979.

CLEMITSON, I.
A worker's Guide to the Employment Protection Act. Spokesman Books, 1976.

HARRIES, J.
Employment protection: the 1975 Act explained. Oyez, 1975.

HARVEY, R.J. & THOMPSON, A.
Employment Protection (Consolidation) Act, 1978. Butterworths, 1979.

HENDERSON, J.
Guide to the Employment Protection Act.
Industrial Society, 1975.

HENDERSON, J.
Guide to the Employment Protection
(Consolidation) Act. Industrial Society,
1978.

LOWE, R. & MARSH, G.B.
Employment protection. Sweet & Maxwell,
1976.

MITCHELL, E.
The employer's guide to the law on
employment protection and sex and race
discrimination. Business Books, 1976.

PARSONS, G.T.E. & RATFORD, W.R.
Employees' rights in receiverships and
liquidations. Tolley, 1980.

RUBERSTEIN, M.
Practical guide to the Employment
Protection Act. Inst. of Personnel
Management, 1975.

UPEX, R.V.
Employment protection legislation. Oyez,
1978.

ENCYCLOPAEDIAS

The DIGEST (formerly English and
Empire Digest). Butterworths. 69 vols. +
supplement.

DUNEDIN, Viscount (ed.)
Encyclopaedia of the Laws of Scotland.
3ed. Green. 16 vols. 1926–1935 supp.
1949–1952. 5 vols.

ENCYCLOPAEDIA of Court Forms in
Civil Proceedings (Atkin). 2ed.
Butterworths. 41 vols.

ENCYCLOPAEDIA of European
Community Law. Sweet & Maxwell. 11
vols. Looseleaf.

ENCYCLOPAEDIA of Forms &
Precedents other than Court Forms. 4ed.
Butterworths. 24 vols. & annual supp.

FREEMANTLE, M.P. & MESKIN, P.M.
(eds.)
South African encyclopaedia of forms and
precedents.

HALSBURY's laws of England. 4ed.
Butterworths. 56 vols.

HALSBURY's statutes of England. 3ed.
Butterworths. 52 vols. (4ed. in preparation).

JOUBERT, W.A. (ed.)
Encyclopaedia of the Law of South Africa.
1976. 24 vols.

STATUTES in force. HMSO. 90 looseleaf
binders. Microfiche edition: Unifo
Publishers (USA).

WALKER, D.M.
The Oxford companion to law. Oxford
U.P., 1980.

For an encyclopaedia on a specific subject
see under that subject.

ENGLISH LEGAL SYSTEM

See also Constitutional Law; Courts; Jurisprudence and Legal Philosophy.

Texts

ARCHER, P.
The Queen's courts. 2ed. Penguin, 1964.

BERLINS, M. & DYER, C.
The law machine. Penguin, 1982.

BRANDON, S.
English legal system. Sweet & Maxwell,
1979 (Nutshell).

CENTRAL OFFICE OF
INFORMATION
Justice and the law in Britain. HMSO,
1982.

COUNTER, K.
Framework and functions of English Law:
an introduction to the English legal system.
Pergamon, 1968.

DENNING, Lord
Due process of law. Butterworths, 1980.

EDDEY, K.J.
English legal system. 3ed. Sweet & Maxwell, 1982 (Concise college texts).

GELDART, W.M.
Elements of English Law. 8ed. Oxford U.P., 1975.

HODGSON, J. (ed.)
English legal heritage. Oyez, 1979.

INGMAN, T.
The English legal process. Financial Training Pubns., 1983.

JACKSON, R.M.
Machinery of justice in England. 7ed. Cambridge U.P., 1977.

JAMES, P.S.
Introduction to English Law. 10ed. Butterworths, 1979.

JONES, G.
Sovereignty of the law: selections from Blackstone's commentaries on the laws of England. Macmillan, 1973.

JUSTICE
Lawyers and the legal system: critique of legal services in England and Wales. Stevens, 1978.

KIRALFY, A.K.R.
The English legal system. 7ed. Sweet & Maxwell, 1984.

LAWSON, F.
Remedies of English law. 2ed. Butterworths, 1980.

METCALFE, O.K.
General principles of English law. 11ed. Cassell, 1980.

NEWTON, C.R.
General principles of law. 3ed. Sweet & Maxwell, 1983 (Concise college texts).

NEWTON, C.R. & PARKER, R.S.
Cases and statutes on general principles of law. Sweet & Maxwell, 1980.

PHILLIPS, O.H.
A first book of English Law. 7ed. Sweet & Maxwell, 1977.

PRICE, J.
English legal system. Macdonald & Evans, 1979.

RADCLIFFE, G.R.Y. & CROSS, Lord
English legal system. 6ed. Butterworths, 1977.

REDMOND, P.
General principles of English law. 5ed. Macdonald & Evans, 1979.

ROSHIER, B. & TEFF, H.
Law and society in England. Sweet & Maxwell, 1980.

ROYAL COMMISSION ON LEGAL SERVICES
Final report (Benson). HMSO, 1979 (Cmnd. 7648).

SMITH, K. & KEENAN, D.J.
English law. 7ed. Pitman, 1982.

SMITH, P.F. & BAILEY, S.H.
The modern English legal system. Sweet & Maxwell, 1984.

WALKER, R.J. & WALKER, M.G.
English legal system. 5ed. Butterworths, 1980.

WILLIAMS, G.L.
Learning the law. 11ed. Sweet & Maxwell, 1982.

WILSON, G.P.
Cases and materials on the English legal system. Sweet & Maxwell, 1973.

ZANDER, M.
Cases and material on the English legal system. 4ed. Weidenfeld & Nicholson, 1984.

ENTERTAINMENT

See also Theatres

Encyclopaedias and periodicals

Statutes in Force. Group; Entertainment.
Halsbury's Laws of England. 4ed. see index vol.
Halsbury's Statutes of England. 3ed. vol.20.
Encyclopaedia of Court Forms in Civil Proceedings (Atkin). 2ed. vol.23.
Encyclopaedia of Forms and Precedents. 4ed. vols. 9, 20, 22.
Performing Right Yearbook. Annual.
Performing Right News. 1976–

Texts

COTTERELL, L.E.
Performance: study of the law and practice of entertainment and the performing arts. J.F.Offord, 1977.

GREATER LONDON COUNCIL
Technical regulations for places of public entertainment. 1966.

ISAACS, S.C.
Law relating to theatres, music halls and other public entertainments. Stevens, 1927.

IVAMY, E.R.H.
Show business and the law. Stevens, 1955.

LAW, S. & LIVES, E.
Keep music legal: from the manuscript to mass production. Sea Dream Music, 1982.

ROTHENBERG, S.
Copyright and public performance of music. Nijhoff, 1954.

ENVIRONMENT LAW

See also Pollution: Town and Country Planning.

Encyclopaedias and periodicals

Statutes in Force. Group: Environment. Halsbury's Laws of England. 4ed. see index vol.

Ecologist. 1970–
Journal of Planning & Environment Law. 1948–

Texts

BATES, G.M.
Environmental law in Australia. Butterworths (Australia), 1982.

BIGHAM, D.A.
Law and administration relating to protection of the environment. Oyez, 1973 supp. 1975.

BLUNDELL, L.A. & DOBRY, G
Planning appeals and enquiries. 3ed. Sweet & Maxwell, 1982.

CANADIAN INDUSTRIES
Digest of environmental pollution legislation in Canada. Canadian Indust. Ltd.,1973. 2 vols.

FISHER, D.E.
Environmental law in Australia. Queensland U.P., 1950.

FOX, F.
The countryside and the law. David & Charles, 1971.

FRANSON, R.T. & LUCAS, J.G.R.
Canadian environmental law. Butterworths (Canada), 1976. Looseleaf.

HAWKINS, K.
Environment and enforcement: regulation and the social definition of pollution. Oxford U.P. 1984.

KERSE, C.S.
Law relating to noise. Oyez, 1975.

McLOUGHLIN, J.
Law relating to pollution: an introduction. Manchester U.P., 1972.

MOORE, V.W.E. & CATCHPOLE, L.
Local Government Planning and Land Act, 1980. Sweet & Maxwell, 1981.

MYNORS, C. (ed.)
Urban conservation and historic buildings: a guide to legislation. Architect. Press, 1984.

O'KEEFE, P.J. & PROTT, L.
Law and the cultural heritage. Vol.1: Discovery and excavation. Professional Books, 1983.

SCHNEIDER, J.
World public order of the environment. Stevens, 1979.

SLOAN, I.J.
Environment and the law. Oceana, 1971 (USA).

TAYLOR, V.
Environmental law: cases and texts. Aztec, 1974 (USA).

TECLAFF, L.A. & UTTON, A.E.
International environmental law. Praeger, 1974.

WALKER, A.
Law of industrial pollution control.
Godwin, 1979.

WEBSTER, C.
Environmental health law. Sweet & Maxwell, 1981.

WHITTAKER, C.
The Architectural Journal handbook of environmental powers. Architect. P., 1976.

EQUAL OPPORTUNITIES/EQUAL PAY

Encyclopaedias and periodicals

Halsbury's Laws of England. 4ed. vol. 16.

Industrial Law Journal. 1972–

Industrial Relations Review and Reports. 1971–

Managerial Law. 1975–

Texts

ADAMS, S.
Sex discrimination. Sweet & Maxwell, 1980 (Law at work).

BELOFF, M.J.
Sex discrimination and the new law. Butterworths, 1976.

COMMISSION FOR RACIAL EQUALITY
Reports. 1977–

CREIGHTON, W.B.
Working women and the law. Mansell, 1979.

EMPLOYMENT, DEPARTMENT OF
Report on the implementation of Equal Pay Act 1970. HMSO, 1972.

EQUAL OPPORTUNITIES COMMISSION
Annual report. HMSO.

GILL, T. & WHITTY,
Women's rights in the workplace. Pelican,

HEPPLE, B.A.
Equal pay and the industrial tribunals. Sweet & Maxwell, 1984.

HOME OFFICE
Equality for women. HMSO, 1974 (Cmnd. 5724).

JACKSON, K.
Guide to sex discrimination and fair employment in Northern Ireland. Industrial Society, 1977.

LISTER, R. & LOWE, M.
Equal pay and how to get it. N.C.C.L., 1975.

LUSTGARTEN, L.
Legal control of racial discrimination. Macmillan, 1980.

McKEAN, W.A.
Equality and discrimination under international law. Oxford U.P., 1983.

McMULLEN, J.
Rights at work. 2ed. Pluto, 1983.

MALONE, M.
Practical guide to discrimination law. Ross Anderson Pubns., 1980 supp. 1982.

MEPHAN, G.J.
Equal opportunity and equal pay. Inst. of Personnel Management, 1974.

NASH, M.
Sex Discrimination Act: a guide for managers. Inst. of Personnel Management, 1975.

PETTMAN, B. (ed.)
Equal pay for women: progress and problems in seven countries. MCB Books, 1975.

RONALDS, C.
Anti-discrimination legislation in Australia. Butterworths (Australia). 1979.

SACHS, A. & WILSON, J.H.
Sexism and the law: a study of male beliefs and judicial bias in Britain and America. Martin Robertson, 1978.

SCHMIDT, F. (ed.)
Discrimination in employment: a study of six countries by the comparative labour law group. Almqvist, 1978.

TAUBENFELD, H.J.
Sex-based discrimination: international law and organization. Oceana, 1978 (USA). 5 looseleaf vols.

WALKER, D.J.
A simple guide to the complicated provision of the Sex Discrimination Act, 1975 Shaw, 1975.

EQUITY

See also Chancery Practice; Charities; Gifts; Injunctions.

Encyclopaedias

Halsbury's Laws of England. 4ed. vol.16.
The Digest. vol. 20.
Encyclopaedia of Court Forms in Civil Proceedings (Atkin). 2ed. vol.18.

Encyclopaedia of Forms and Precedents. 4ed. see index vol.

Texts

ASHBURNER, W.
Principles of equity. 2ed. Butterworths,1933.

BRYSON, W.H.
The equity side of the Exchequer. Cambridge U.P., 1975.

CHILDRES, R.
Equity, restitution and damages. 2ed. Foundation P., 1974 (USA).

CURZON, L.B.
Equity. 3ed. Macdonald & Evans, 1979.

EDWARDS, R.J. & LANGSTAFF, B.F.J.
Cases and statutes on equity and trusts. Sweet & Maxwell, 1974.

HANBURY, H.G. & MAUDSLEY, R.H.
Modern equity: the principles of equity. 11ed. Stevens, 1981.

HEWARD, E.
Chancery practice. Butterworths, 1983.

HEYDON, J.D., GUMMON, W.M.C. & AUSTIN, R.P.
Cases and materials on equity and trusts. 2ed. Butterworths (Australia), 1982.

JOLOWICZ, J.A. & JONES, G.
Judicial protection of fundamental rights under English Law: infiltration of equity into English commercial law. Kluwer, 1980.

KEETON, G.W. & SHERIDAN, L.A.
A casebook on equity and trusts. 2ed. Professional Books, 1974.

KEETON, G.W. & SHERIDAN, L.A.
Equity. 2ed. Professional Books, 1976 repr. 1982.

KODILINYE, G.
An introduction to equity in Nigeria. Sweet & Maxwell, 1975.

LEWIS, J.R.
Outlines of equity. Butterworths, 1968.

MAITLAND, F.W.
Equity. 2ed. 1936 repr. 1969.

MEAGHER, R.P., GUMMON, W.M.C. & LEHANE, J.R.F.
Equity: doctrines and remedies. 2ed. Butterworths (Australia), 1983.

NEVILL, A.G. & ASHE, A.W.
Equity proceedings with precedents (NSW). Butterworths (Australia), 1981.

NEWMAN, R.A.
Equity in the world's legal systems: a comparative study. Bruylant, 1974.

PETTIT, P.H.
Equity and the law of trusts. 5ed. Butterworths, 1984.

POTTER, H.
An introduction to the history of equity and its courts. Sweet & Maxwell, 1931.

RIDDALL, J.G.
Equity and trusts. 2ed. Butterworths, 1974 (Law students companion).

SAMUELS, R.
Equity and succession. Sweet & Maxwell, 1974 (Concise college texts).

SETON, H.W.
Forms of decrees, judgments and orders in equity. 7ed. Stevens, 1912. 3 vols.

SHERIDAN, L.A.
Fraud in equity: a study in English and Irish law. Pitman, 1957.

SHERIDAN, L.A. & KEETON, G.W.
Equity: chancery procedure and the nature of injunctions. B.Rose, 1983.

SNELL, E.H.T.
The principles of equity. 28ed. Sweet & Maxwell, 1982.

SPRY, I.C.F.
Equitable remedies, injunctions and specific performance. 2ed. Sweet & Maxwell, 1980.

STORY, J.
Commentaries on equity jurisprudence as administered in England and America. 14ed. Little, Brown, 1918.

STRAHAN, J.A.
Digest of equity. 6ed. Butterworths, 1939.

TILEY, J.
Casebook on equity and succession. Sweet & Maxwell, 1968.

TURNER, R.W.
The equity of redemption: its nature, history and connections with equitable estates generally. Cambridge U.P., 1931.

YALE, D.E.C. (ed.)
Lord Nottingham's manual of Chancery practice. Selden Society, 1965 (Cambridge studies in English legal history).

ESTATE AGENTS

See also Agency; Auctions and Auctioneers.

Encyclopaedias and periodicals

Halsbury's Statutes of England. 4ed. vols. 1, 42.
Encyclopaedia of Court Forms in Civil Proceedings (Atkin). 2ed. vol.4.
Encyclopaedia of Forms and Precedents. 4ed. vol.2.

Estates Gazette. 1858–
Estate Agents' Yearbook and Directory.
Property and Compensation Reports. 1950–
Property Journal. 1974–

Texts

CARD, R.
Estate Agents Act 1979. Butterworths, 1979.

DOUGLAS, C.M. & LEE, R.G.
Estate Agents Act 1979. Sweet & Maxwell, 1979.

GRATTAN-DOYLE, H.N.
Law of Auctioneers' and Estate Agents' Commission. 2ed. Estates Gazette, 1957.

LUXFORD, J.H.
Real estate agency in New Zealand. 5ed. Butterworths, 1975.

MACINTYRE, D.
Law relating to auctioneers and estate agents. Sweet & Maxwell, 1958.

MONOPOLIES COMMISSION
Report on estate agents. HMSO, 1969.

MURDOCH, J.R.
Estate Agents Act 1979. 2ed. Estates Gazette, 1982.

MURDOCH, J.R.
Law of estate agency and auctions. 2ed. Estates Gazette, 1984.

STAPLETON, T.B.
Estate management practice 2ed. Estates Gazette, 1984.

STEPHENS, N.
Practice of estate agency. Estates Gazette, 1981.

STOREY, H. & GOLDBERG, A.H.
Real estate agency in Victoria. 2ed. Butterworths (Australia), 1975.

ESTATE DUTY

See also Capital Transfer Tax; Probate; Revenue Law.

Encyclopaedias and periodicals

Halsbury's Laws of England. 4ed. see index vol.
Halsbury's Statutes of England. 3ed. see index vol.
The Digest. vol. 21.
Encyclopaedia of Court Forms in Civil Proceedings (Atkin). 2ed. vol.34.
Encyclopaedia of Forms and Precedents. 4ed. see index vol.
British Tax Review. 1956–
Taxation. 1927–
Money Which. 1957–

Texts

ADAMS, E.C. & RICHARDSON, I.L.M.
Law of estate and gift duties in New Zealand. 5ed. Butterworths (New Zealand), 1977.

ARGENT, H.D.
Death duty mitigation. 3ed. Business Books, 1971.

BEATTIE, C.N.
Elements of estate duty. 8ed. Butterworths, 1974.

DATTA, C.R.
Estate Duty. Eastern P., 1974 (India).

FORD, H.A.J.
Principles of the law of death duty. Law Book Co., 1971 (Australia).

GOODMAN, W.D.
International double taxation of estates and inheritances. Butterworths, 1978.

HAMBRO's capital taxes and estate planning guide. Oyez, 1982.

HARRIS, P.
Estate planning through life assurance. Sweet & Maxwell, 1977.

IND, R.C.
Estate duty. Macdonald & Evans, 1974.

JAMESON, M.B.
Canadian estate tax. Butterworths, 1960.

LOWNDES, C.L.B. and others
Federal estate and gift taxes. 3ed. West, 1974 (USA).

MOLLOY, A.P.
Estate planning. 2ed. Butterworths (New Zealand), 1975.

MORCOM, J.B.
Estate duty saving and capital gains tax. 5ed. Butterworths, 1972.

RAY, R.P.
Practical capital transfer tax planning. Butterworths, 1982.

SOARES, P.
Land and tax planning. Oyez, 1982.

STANLEY, O.
Taxation of farmers and landowners. Butterworths, 1981.

TOLHURST, A.F.
Australian gift and estate duty. Butterworths (Australia), 1970.

TRIMM, L.
Estate duty planning: the positive approach. Financial Techniques, 1974.

TRIMM, L.
Personal estate planning: a new system of capital taxation. Financial Techniques, 1975.

WHEATCROFT, G.S.A.
Guide to the estate duty statutes. 2ed. Sweet & Maxwell, 1972.

ESTOPPEL

See also Equity; Judgements; Res Judicata.

Encyclopaedias

Halsbury's Laws of England. 4ed. vol.16.
The Digest. vol.21.
Encyclopaedia of Court Forms in Civil Proceedings (Atkin). 2ed. see index vol.
Encyclopaedia of Forms and Precedents. 4ed. see index vol.

Texts

BIGELOW, M.M.
A treatise on the law of estoppel. 6ed. Little, Brown & Co., 1913 (USA).

BOWER, G.S. & TURNER, A.K.
Estoppel by representation. 3ed. Butterworths, 1977.

CABABE, M.
Principles of estoppel. Maxwell, 1888.

EVEREST, L.F. & STRODE, E.
Law of estoppel. 3ed. Stevens, 1923.

EWART, J.S.
An exposition of the principles of estoppel by misrepresentation. Carswell, 1900 (Canada).

FIELD, C.D.
Law relating to estoppel. Sardar Patel, 1974 (India).

HERMAN, H.M.
Commentaries on the law of estoppel and res judicata. F.D.Linn, 1886 (USA).

EUROPEAN COMMUNITIES

Encyclopaedias and periodicals

Statutes in Force. Group: Constitutional Law, 5: European Communities.
Halsbury's Laws of England. 4ed. see index vol.
Halsbury's Statutes of England. 3ed. vol.42A.
The Digest. see index.

Official Journal of the European Communities (special edition) 1952–1972.
Official Journal of the European Communities 'L' & 'C' series, vol.16, 1973– (English).

Bulletin of the European Communities. 1968–
Common Market Law Reports. 1961–
Common Market Law Review. 1963–
Compendium of Case Law Relating to the European Communities.
European Court Reports. 1962–
European Law Digest. 1973–
European Law Review. 1975–
Recueil de la Jurisprudence de la Cour, 1954– (for English edition see European Court Reports).

General topics

ALTING VON GEUSAU, F.A.M.
Beyond the European Communities. Sijthoff, 1969.

AUDRETSCH, H.A.H.
Supervision in European Community law: observance by the member states of their treaty obligations. North-Holland, 1978.

BALASA, B.A. (ed.)
European economic integration. North-Holland, 1975.

BALASA, B.A.
The theory of economic integration. Greenwood P., 1982.

BALFOUR, C.
Industrial relations in the Common Market. Routledge, 1972.

CAMPBELL, A.R.
Common Market Law. rev. ed. Longman, 1969–74. 3 vols. Looseleaf service and annual supp.

COLLINS, L.
European Community law in the United Kingdom. 3ed. Butterworths, 1984.

DAGTOGLOU, P.D. (ed.)
Basic problems of the European community. Blackwell, 1975.

DRUKER, I.E.
Financing the European communities. Sijthoff, 1975.

EASSON, A.J.
Tax law and policy in the E.E.C. Sweet & Maxwell, 1980.

ENCYCLOPAEDIA of European Community Law. Sweet & Maxwell. 11 vols. Looseleaf.

EUROPEAN COMMUNITIES
Comparative tables of the social security systems in the member states of the European Communities. 9ed. 1977.

EUROPEAN COMMUNITIES
Freedom of movement for workers within the Community. 1977.

EUROPEAN COMMUNITIES
Law of property in the European Community. 1977.

EUROPEAN COMMUNITIES COMMISSION
Thirty years of Community law. 1981 (European perspectives).

EVERTS, P. (ed.)
The European Community in the world: the external relations of the enlarged European community. Rotterdam U.P., 1972.

GIJLSTRA, D.J. & MURPHY, D.F.
Leading cases and materials on the law of the European Communities. 4ed. Kluwer, 1982.

HARTLEY, T.C.
European Economic Community immigration law. North-Holland, 1978.

KAPTEYN, P.J.G. & VAN THEMAAT, P.
Introduction to the law of the European Communities. Sweet & Maxwell, 1973.

KORAH, V.
Introductory guide to European Economic Community law and practice. E.S.C., 1978.

LASOK, D.
Law of the economy in the European Communities. Butterworths, 1980.

LASOK, D. & BRIDGE, J.W.D.
An introduction to the law and institutions of the European Communities. 3ed. Butterworths, 1982.

LASOK, D. & CAIRNS, W.J.
Harmonizatioin of law within the Common Market customs law. Kluwer, 1984.

LIPSTEIN, K.
Law of the European Economic Community. Butterworths, 1974.

MACKENZIE-STUART, A.J.
The European Communities and the rule of law. Stevens, 1977 (Hamlyn lecture).

MACKENZIE-STUART, A.J.
"Non-contractual" liability of the European Economic Community. Oxford U.P., 1975.

MATHIJSEN, P.S.R.F.
A guide to European Community law. 3ed. Sweet & Maxwell, 1980

MORGAN, A.
From summit to Council: evolution in the E.E.C. P.E.P., 1976.

MYLES, G.
E.E.C. brief: a handbook of E.E.C. law, practice and policy for the academic, business, professional and public sectors. Locksley P., 1979. 2 vols. looseleaf.

PAISLEY, S.E.
A guide to E.E.C. law in Northern Ireland. SLS Legal Pubns. (NI), 1984.

PARRY, A. & HARDY, S.
E.E.C. law. 2ed. Sweet & Maxwell, 1981.

PLENDER, R.M.A.
Practical introduction to European Community law. Sweet & Maxwell, 1980.

PLENDER, R.M.A. & USHER, J.
Cases and materials on the law of the European Communities. Macmillan, 1980.

RUDDEN, B. & WYATT, D.
Basic Community laws. Oxford U.P., 1980.

SANT, M.
Regional policy and planning for Europe. Saxon House, 1974.

SIMMONDS, K.R. (ed.)
Sweet and Maxwell's European Community Treaties. 4ed. 1980.

SMIT, H. & HERZOG, P.E. (eds.)
The law of the European economic community: a commentary on the E.E.C. Treaty. Bender, 1976. 5 vols. Looseleaf. (USA).

USHER, J.
European Community law and national law. Allen & Unwin, 1981.

WATSON, P.
Social security law of the European Communities. Mansell, 1980.

WHEATCROFT, G.S.A.
Value added tax in the enlarged Common Market. Cassell, 1973.

WORTLEY, B. (ed.)
Introduction to the law of the E.E.C. Manchester U.P., 1972.

WORTLEY, B.A. (ed.)
The law of the Common Market. Manchester U.P., 1974.

WYATT, D. & DASHWOOD, A.
Substantive law of the European Economic Community. Sweet & Maxwell, 1980.

EUROPEAN COMMUNITIES

Formation and accession

AXLINE, W.A.
European Community law and organizational development. Oceana, 1968 (USA).

BALASSA, B.A.
European economic integration. North-Holland, 1975.

BATHURST, M.E., SIMMONDS, K.R. and others
Legal problems of an enlarged European Community. Sweet & Maxwell, 1972.

FURMSTON, M.P.
Effect on English domestic law of membership of the European Communities and of ratification of the European Convention on Human Rights. Nijhoff, 1983.

GALTUNG, J.
The European community: a superpower in the making. Allen & Unwin, 1973.

GOVERNMENT OF IRELAND
The accession of Ireland to the European Communities. 1972.

KITSINGER, U.
Diplomacy and persuasion: how Britain joined the Common Market. Thames & Hudson, 1973.

LORD CHANCELLOR'S DEPARTMENT
Legal and constitutional implications of UK membership of the European Communities. HMSO, 1967(Cmnd. 3301).

PESCATORE, P.
The law of integration. Sijthoff, 1974.

PUISSOCHET, J.P.
The enlargement of the European Communities: a commentary on the accession of Denmark, Ireland and United Kingdom. Sijthoff, 1975.

SAVAGE, K.
History of the Common Market. 2ed. Kestrel, 1976.

SHEPHERD, R.J.
Public opinion and European integration. Saxon House, 1975.

SIEMERS, J.P. (ed.)
European integration: select international bibliography of theses and dissertations, 1957–1977. Sijthoff, 1979.

WALL, E.H.
Europe: unification and law. Penguin, 1969.

WALL. E.H.
The European Communities Act 1972. Butterworths, 1973.

WATSON, A.
Europe at risk. Harrap, 1972.

Agriculture and commerce

ALLEN, J.
The European Common Market and the G.A.T.T. Washington U.P., 1961 (USA).

ANDREWS, S.
Agriculture and the Common Market. Iowa State, 1973.

BEEVER, C.R.
European unity and the Trade Union movement. Sijthoff, 1960.

BLAKE, H.M. & RAHL, J.A. (eds.)
Business regulations in the Common Market nations. Shepard's, 1969 (USA). 4 vols.

BOHNING, W.R.
Migration of workers in the U.K. and the E.C. Oxford U.P., 1972.

BOLT, G.J.
Communicating with E.E.C. markets. Kogan Page, 1973.

BOLT, G.J.
Marketing in the E.E.C. Kogan Page, 1973.

BRITISH INSTITUTE OF INTERNATIONAL AND COMPARATIVE LAW
Legal provision relating to transport in the Common Market. 1963.

DE GARA, J.
Trade relations between the Common Market and the Eastern bloc. Bruges, De Dempel, 1964.

EUROPEAN COMMUNITIES COMMISSION
The development of a European capital market. 1967.

EUROPEAN COMMUNITIES COMMISSION
Legal status of rail, road and inland waterway transport in the member states of the E.E.C. 1962.

GOLDMAN, B.
European commercial law. Stevens, 1973.

GUY, D. & LEIGH, G.
The E.E.C. and intellectual property. Sweet & Maxwell, 1981.

HENIG, S.
External relations of the European community associations and trade agreements. Chatham, 1971.

ISAACS, S.A.
E.E.C. banking law. Lloyd's, 1984.

JOHANNES, H.
Industrial property and copyright in European Community Law. Sijthoff, 1976.

KNOX, F.
The Common Market and world agriculture. Praeger, 1972.

LAW COMMISSION
Law of contract: report on the proposed EEC Directive on the law relating to commercial agents. HMSO, 1977 (Law Com. no. 84).

LAWSON, R.G.
Advertising and labelling laws in the Common Market. 3ed. Jordan, 1982.

MAGNIFICO, G.
European monetary unification. Wiley, 1973 (USA).

MICALLEF, J.
The European company. Rotterdam U.P., 1975.

NORTH, P.M.
Contract conflicts: the E.E.C. convention on the Law Applicable to Contractual Obligations — a comparative study. North-Holland, 1982.

PENNINGTON, R.R.
Companies in the Common Market. 2ed. Oyez, 1970.

REICH, N. & MICKLITZ, H.W.
Consumer legislation in the European Community countries: a comparative analysis. Van Nostrand Reinhold, 1980.

SCHMITTHOFF, C. (ed.)
European company law texts. Stevens, 1974.

SCHMITTHOFF, C. (ed.)
The harmonisation of European company Law. Stevens, 1973.

SLOT, P.J.
Technical and administrative obstacles to trade in the E.E.C. Sijthoff, 1975.

SNOW, R.F.
The impact of EEC law on commercial dealings. College of Law, 1978.

STORM, P.M. and others
Branches and subsidiaries in the European Common Market; legal and tax aspects. Kluwer, 1973.

STRASSER, D.
The finances of Europe. E.C.Commission, 1980 (European perspectives).

VAN YPERSELE, J. & KOEUNE, J.-C.
The European monetary system. Woodhead-Faulkner, 1984.

VAULONT, N.
The customs union of the European Economic Community. E.C.Commission, 1981 (European perspectives).

ZAPHIRIOU, G.
European business law. Sweet & Maxwell, 1970.

Competition

ALEXANDER, W.
The E.E.C. rules of competition. Kluwer, 1973.

BAROUNOS, D., HALL, D.F. & JAMES, J.R.
E.E.C. anti-trust law: principles and practice. Butterworths, 1975.

BECKERLEY, B. (ed.)
European Economic Community competition law: an analysis of recent decisions and developments. E.S.C., 1978.

BELLAMY, C.W. & CHILD, G.D.
Common Market law of competition. 2ed. Sweet & Maxwell, 1978.

BRITISH INSTITUTE OF INTERNATIONAL AND COMPARATIVE LAW
Commercial agency and distribution agreements in Europe: law and practice in the Common Market countries and Switzerland. B.I.I.C.L., 1964.

CAWTHRA, B.
Restrictive agreements in the E.E.C.- the need to notify. Butterworths, 1972.

CUNNINGHAM, J.P.
Competition law of the E.E.C.: a practical guide. Kogan Page, 1973 supp. 1975.

DERINGER, A.
Competition law of the European Economic Community: a commentary on articles 85–90. CCH, 1968 (USA).

EUROPA INSTITUTE (LEYDEN)
European competition policy. 1973.

GEORGE, K.D. & JOLL. C. (eds.)
Competition policy in the U.K. and E.E.C. Cambridge U.P., 1975.

GERVEN, W. van & LUKOFF, F.L. (eds.)
Commercial agency and distribution agreements and related problems of licensing in the law of the E.E.C. countries. Univ. of Louvain Law School, 1970.

GIJLSTRA, D.J. & MURPHY, D.C.
Leading cases and materials on the competition law of the E.E.C. Kluwer, 1976.

GRAUPNER, R.
Rules of competition in the European Economic Community. Nijhoff, 1965.

KORAH, V.
Competition law of Britain and the Common Market. Elek, 1975.

MAAS, H.H.
European competition policy. Sijthoff, 1973.

McLACHLAN, D.L. & SWANN, D.
Competition policy in the European Community. Oxford U.P., 1967.

OBERDORFER, C.W. and others
Common Market cartel law. 2ed. CCH, 1971.

RAHL, J.A.
Common Market and American antitrust: overlap and conflict. McGraw-Hill, 1970.

TOEPKE, U.P.
European Economic Community competition law: business issues and legal principles in Common Market antitrust cases. Wiley, 1982.

WALSH, A.E. & PAXTON, J.
Competition policy: European and international trends and practices. Macmillan, 1975.

Institutions – Commission and general

COOMBES, D.
Politics and bureaucracy in the European Community: a portrait of the Commission of the E.E.C. 1970.

LANGROD, J.
The international civil service. Sijthoff, 1963.

MAYNE, R.J.
The institutions of the European Community. Research Pubns., 1968.

PALMER, M. and others
European unity: a survey of the European organisations. Allen & Unwin, 1968.

POLACH, J.G.
Euratom, its background, issues and economic implications. Oceana, 1964 (USA).

ROBERTSON, A.H.
European institutions: co-operation, integration, unification. 3ed. Stevens, 1973.

SCHERMERS, H.G.
International institutional law. Sijthoff, 1972–1974. 3 vols.

European Parliament

BIRKE, W.
European elections by direct suffrage: a comparative study. Sijthoff, 1971.

COCKS, B.
European Parliament: structure procedure and practice. Nijhoff, 1973.

FITZMAURICE, J.
Party groups in the European Parliament. Saxon House, 1975.

FORSYTH, M.
The Parliament of the European Communities. P.E.P., 1964.

HAND, G., GEORGEL, J. & SASSE, C.
European electoral systems handbook. Butterworths, 1979.

HERMAN, V. & HAGGER, M.
Legislation of direct elections to the European Parliament. Gower, 1980.

HOME OFFICE & SCOTTISH HOME
AND HEALTH DEPARTMENT
Draft regulations for the conduct of
European Assembly elections in Great
Britain. HMSO, 1978 (Cmnd. 7323).

European Court of Justice and legal matters

BERGSTEN, E.E.
Community law in the French courts: the
law of treaties in modern attire. Nijhoff,
1967.

BREDIMAS, A. (ed.)
Methods of interpretation and Community
law. North-Holland, 1978.

BRINKHORST, L.J. & SCHERMERS,
H.G.
Judicial remedies in the European
Communities. 2ed. Sweet &
Maxwell:Kluwer, 1979.

BRINKHORST, L.J. & WITTENBERG,
G.W.
The rules of procedure of the Court of
Justice of the European Communities.
Sijthoff, 1962.

BROWN, L.N. & JACOBS, F.G.
The Court of Justice of the European
Communities. 2ed. Sweet & Maxwell,
1983.

COURT OF JUSTICE OF THE
EUROPEAN COMMUNITIES
Digest of case-law relating to the European
Communities. A series. D series. Looseleaf.

DONNER, A.M.
Role of the lawyer in the European
communities. Edinburgh U.P., 1968.

ELLES, N.
Community law through the cases. Stevens,
1973.

EUROPEAN COMMUNITIES
Community legal order. 1981.

EUROPEAN COMMUNITIES
The Court of Justice of the European
Communities. 2ed. 1980.

FELD, W.J.
Court of the European Communities: new
dimensions in international adjudication.
Nijhoff, 1964.

PALMER, M.
The European Parliament. Pergamon,
1981.

GREEN, A.W.
Political integration by jurisprudence: the
work of the Court of Justice of the
European Communities in European
political integration. Sijthoff, 1969.

JACOBS, F.G. & DURAND, A.
References to the European Court: practice
and procedures. Butterworths, 1975.

LASOK, K.P.E.
The European Court of Justice: practice
and procedure. Butterworths, 1984.

LAUWAARS, R.H.
Lawfulness and legal force of Community
decisions. Sijthoff, 1973.

LOUIS, J.-V.
The Community legal order.
E.C.Commission, 1979.

MANN, C.J.
The function of judicial decision in
European economic integration. Nijhoff,
1972.

SCHERMERS, H.G.
Judicial protection in the European
Communities. 2ed. Kluwer, 1979.

TOTH, A.G.
Legal protection of individuals in the
European Communities. North-Holland,
1978. 2 vols.

USHER, J.
European Court practice. Sweet &
Maxwell, 1983.

VALENTINE, D.G.
Court of Justice of the European
Communities. Stevens, 1965. 2 vols.

VANDESANDEN, G.
Pleading before the Court of Justice of the
European Communities. Law Society,
1983.

WALL, E.H.
Court of Justice of the European
Communities: jurisdiction and procedure.
Butterworths, 1966.

EUROPEAN FREE TRADE ASSOCIATION

Encyclopaedias and periodicals
Halsbury's Laws of England. 4ed. vol. 12.
Halsbury's Statutes of England. 3ed. vols. 9, 37.
Encyclopaedia of Forms and Precedents. 4ed. vol.20.

Journal of World Trade Law. 1967–

Texts
GREEN, S.A. & GABRIEL, K.W.
Rules of origin. 4ed. EFTA, 1971.

LAMBRINIDIS, J.S.
Structure, function and law of a free trade area: the European Free Trade Association. Stevens, 1965.

MIDDLETON, R.
Negotiating on non-tariff distortion of trade: the EFTA precedents. St Martin's P., 1975.

SZOKOWCZY-SYLLABA, A.
European Free Trade Association: restrictive business practies. Stampfli, 1973.

WALSH, A.E. & PAXTON, J.
Trade and industrial resources of the Common Market and E.F.T.A. countries. Rothman, 1970.

EUTHANASIA

See also Homicide

Texts
ANDERSON, J.N.D.
Issues of life and death: abortion, birth control, capital punishment and euthanasia. Norfolk P., 1976.

BEHNKE, J.A. & BOK, S.
Dilemmas of euthanasia. Doubleday, 1975.

DOWNING, A.B. (ed.)
Euthanasia and the right to death: the case for voluntary euthanasia. P.Owen, 1969.

GOULD, J. & CRAIGMYLE, Lord
Implications of euthanasia: a medical, legal and ethical study. Arlington P., 1973.

HORAN, D.J. & MALL, D.
Death, dying and euthanasia. University P., 1977 (USA).

KOHL, M.
Morality of killing: sanctity of life, abortion and euthanasia. P.Owen, 1974.

RAMSAY, P.
Ethics at the edges of life: medical and legal intersections. Yale U.P., 1978 (USA).

RUSSELL, O.R.
Freedom to die: moral and legal aspects of euthanasia. Human Science P.:Eurospan, 1977 (USA).

TRICHE, C.W. & TRICHE, D.S.
Euthanasia controversy 1812–1974: a bibliography with select annotations. Whitston, 1975 USA).

VERE, D.
Voluntary euthanasia: is there an alternative? Christian Medical Fellowship, 1979.

WILLIAMS, G.L.
Voluntary euthanasia: the next step. Euthanasia Society, 1955.

EVIDENCE

See also Confessions; Criminal Law; Estoppel; Oaths and Affirmations; Witnesses.

Encyclopaedias and periodicals

Statutes in Force. Group: Evidence.
Halsbury's Laws of England. 4ed. vol. 17.
Halsbury's Statutes of England. 3ed. see index vol.
The Digest. vol. 22.

Encyclopaedia of Court Forms in Civil Proceedings (Atkin). 2ed. vol. 18.
Encyclopaedia of Forms and Precedents. 4ed. see index vol.

Criminal Law Review. 1954–

Texts

AGUDA, T.A.
Law of evidence in Nigeria. 2ed. Sweet & Maxwell, 1974.

ARCHBOLD, J.F.
Pleading, evidence and practice in criminal cases. 41ed. Sweet & Maxwell, 1982.

BAKER, E.R. & WILKIE, G.H.
Criminal evidence and procedure. 7ed. Butterworths, 1982 (Police promotion handbook no. 2).

BATES, F.
Principles of evidence. 2ed. Law Book Co., 1980 (Australia).

BOSE, S.K.
Law of evidence. 5ed. Eastern P., 1972 (India).

CAMPBELL, E. & WALLER, L. (ed.)
Well and truly bred: essays on evidence in honour of Sir Richard Eggleston. Law Book Co; Sweet & Maxwell, 1983.

CARTER, P.
Cases and statutes on evidence. Sweet & Maxwell, 1981.

CLAYTON, R.
Evidence. Sweet & Maxwell, 1970 (Nutshell series).

CLEGG, J. & COWSILL, E.
Evidence: law and practice. Oyez Longman, 1984.

COCKLE, E.
Cases and statutes on evidence. 11ed. Sweet & Maxwell, 1970.

COHEN, L.J.
Probable and the provable. Oxford U.P., 1977.

COLE, J.S.R.
Irish cases on evidence. 2ed. I.L.S.I., 1982.

CRAWFORD, T.
Proof in criminal cases. 3ed. Sweet & Maxwell, 1956 (Australia).

CRIMINAL LAW REVISION COMMITTEE
Ninth report: evidence (written statements, formal admissions and notices of alibi). HMSO, 1966 (Cmnd. 3145).

CRIMINAL LAW REVISION COMMITTEE
Eleventh report: evidence (general). HMSO, 1972 (Cmnd. 4991).

CROPPER, J.
Criminal evidence and preparation of cases for prosecution. Butterworths, 1965.

CROSS, R.
On evidence. 5ed. Butterworths, 1979.

CROSS, R.
The golden thread of the English criminal law. Cambridge U.P., 1976.

CROSS, R. & WILKINS, N.
Outline of the law of evidence. 5ed. Butterworths, 1980.

CURZON, L.B.
Law of evidence. Macdonald & Evans, 1978.

DICKSON, W.G.
A treatise on the law of evidence in Scotland. 3ed. Clark, 1887. 2 vols.

EDWARDS, E.J.
Cases on evidence in Australia. 3ed. Law Book Co., 1981.

EGGLESTON, R.
Evidence, proof and probability. 2ed. Weidenfeld & Nicholson, 1983.

FIELD, C.D.
Law of evidence in India and Pakistan. 10ed. Sardar Patel, 1970.

GARROW, J.M.E. & WILLIS, J.D.
The principles of the law of evidence in New Zealand. 6ed. Butterworths (New Zealand), 1973.

EVIDENCE

GLASBEEK, H.J.
Cases and materials on evidence.
Butterworths (Australia), 1974.

GOBBO, J.A. and others
Cross on evidence. 2ed. Australia.
Butterworths (Australia), 1978 supp. 1980.

HAMPTON, C.
Criminal procedure and evidence. 3ed.
Sweet & Maxwell, 1982.

HEYDON, J.D.
Cases and materials on evidence. 2ed.
Butterworths, 1984.

HOFFMAN, L.C.
South African law of evidence. 2ed.
Butterworths (S.A.), 1970.

HOME OFFICE
Report of the Departmental Committee on Evidence of Identification in Criminal Cases (Devlin). HMSO, 1976.

JACKSON, J.D.
Northern Ireland supplement to Cross on evidence. 5ed. SLS Legal Pubns (NI), 1984.

JONES, B.W. & GARD, S.A.
On evidence, civil and criminal. Lawyers Co-operative. 7 vols. (USA).

JUSTICE
False witness. Stevens, 1973.

KEAN, M.
Civil Evidence Act, 1968. Butterworths, 1969.

LANGAN, P.St.J.
Civil procedure. 3ed. Sweet & Maxwell, 1983.

LAW REFORM COMMITTEE
Thirteenth report: hearsay evidence in civil proceedings. HMSO, 1966 (Cmnd. 2964).

LAW REFORM COMMITTEE
Fifteenth report: the rule in Hollington v. Hewthorn. HMSO, 1967 (Cmnd. 3391).

LAW REFORM COMMITTEE
Sixteenth report: privilege in civil proceedings. HMSO, 1967 (Cmnd. 3472).

LAW REFORM COMMITTEE
Seventeenth report: evidence of opinion and expert evidence. HMSO, 1970 (Cmnd. 4489).

LEMPERT, R.O. & SALTZBURG, S.A.
Modern approach to evidence: text, problems, transcripts and cases. West, 1982 (USA).

McWILLIAMS, P.K.
Canadian criminal evidence. Canada Law Book Co., 1974.

MAY, H.J.
South African cases and statutes on evidence. 4ed. Juta, 1962.

MAY, R.
Modern law of criminal evidence. Sweet & Maxwell, 1984.

MILDRED, R.
The expert witness. Godwin, 1982.

MONIR, M.
Principles and digest of the law of evidence.
Univ. Book Co., 1976 (Canada). 2 vols.

MORTON, J.D.
Evidence in criminal cases: a basic guide.
Butterworths, 1961 (Canada).

MURPHY, P.W.
Practical approach to evidence. Financial Training Pubns., 1980.

MURPHY, P.W. & BARNARD, D.
Evidence and advocacy. Financial Training Pubns., 1984.

MURPHY, P.W. & BEAUMONT, J.
Evidence: cases and argument. Financial Training Pubns, 1982.

NOKES, G.D.
An introduction to evidence. 4ed. Sweet & Maxwell, 1967.

PEIRIS, G.L.
Law of evidence in Sri Lanka. Lake House Investments, 1974.

PHIPSON, S.L.
The law of evidence. 13ed. Sweet & Maxwell, 1982 supp. 1984.

PHIPSON, S.L.
Manual of the law of evidence. 11ed. Sweet & Maxwell, 1980.

POWELL, E.
Law of evidence. 10ed. 1921.

RAJU, V.B.
Commentaries on the Evidence Act. 3ed.
Eastern Book Co., 1976 (India). 2 vols.

RICHARDSON, W.P.
On evidence. 10ed. Brooklyn Law School, 1974 (USA).

ROSCOE, H.
Digest of the law of evidence and practice in criminal cases. 16ed. Stevens, 1952.

ROSCOE, H.
Digest of the law of evidence on the trial of civil actions. 20ed. Stevens, 1934.

ROWE, & KNAPP,
Evidence and procedure in the magistrates' courts. Oyez, 1982.

RUDD, G.R.
Nigerian law of evidence. Butterworths, 1964.

SAMET, (ed.)
Computer generated output as admissible evidence. Heydon, 1982.

SARATHI, V.P.
Elements of the law of evidence. 3ed. Eastern Book Co., 1977 (India).

SCHAFER, W.J.
Confessions and statements. C.C.Thomas, 1968 (USA).

SCHLESINGER, S.
Exclusionary injustice: the problem of illegally obtained evidence. Dekker, 1980 (Australia).

SCHWEITZER, S.C.
Proof of traumatic injuries. Lawyers' Co-operative, 1972 (USA). 4 vols.

SCOTTISH LAW COMMISSION
Draft evidence code – first part. 1968 (Memorandum no. 8).

SCOTTISH LAW COMMISSION
Proposals for reform of the law of evidence relating to corroboration. HMSO, 1967 (Scot. Law Com. no. 4).

SEABROOKE, S.
Evidence. Sweet & Maxwell, 1981 (Nutshell).

SIMPSON, K.
A doctor's guide to court: a handbook on medical evidence. 2ed. Butterworths, 1967.

SOPINKA, J. & LEDERMAN, S.N.
Law of evidence in civil cases. Butterworths (Canada), 1974.

STEPHEN, J.F.
Digest of the law of evidence. 12ed. Macmillan, 1936.

TAYLOR, J.P.
A treatise on the law of evidence. 12ed. Sweet & Maxwell, 1931. 2 vols.

WAIGHT, P.K. & WILLIAMS, S.C.R.
Cases and materials on evidence. Law Book Co., 1980 (Australia).

WAKELING, A.A.
Corroboration in Canadian law. Carswell, 1977.

WALKER, A.G. & WALKER, N.M.L.
The law of evidence in Scotland. new ed. W.Hodge, 1983.

WATT, D.
Corroboration. Butterworths (Canada), 1978.

WIGMORE, J.H.
Evidence. 3ed. Little, Brown & Co., 1940 (USA). 10 vols.

WILLS, W.
Principles of circumstantial evidence. 7ed. Butterworths, 1937.

WILLS, W.
Law of evidence. 3ed. Stevens, 1938.

EXECUTION

See also Sheriffs.

Encyclopaedias

Halsbury's Laws of England. 4ed. vol. 17.
Halsbury's Statutes of England. 3ed. vol. 18.

The Digest. vol. 21.
Encyclopaedia of Court Forms in Civil Proceedings (Atkin). 2ed. vol. 19.

Texts

BLACK, A.
Execution of a judgment, including other methods of enforcement. 6ed. Oyez, 1979.

MATHER, P.E.
Sheriff and execution law. 3ed. Sweet & Maxwell, 1936.

SUPREME Court practice 1985. Sweet & Maxwell, 1984.

EXECUTORS AND ADMINISTRATORS

See also Capital Transfer Tax; Probate; Succession; Trusts and Trustees; Wills.

Encyclopaedias

Statutes in Force. Group: Succession. Halsbury's Laws of England. 4ed. vol. 17, 48.
Halsbury's Statutes of England. 3ed. see index vol. under Personal Representative
The Digest. vols. 23, 24.
Encyclopaedia of Court Forms in Civil Proceedings (Atkin). 2ed. see index vol.

Texts

AMROLIA, H.A.
Probate and administration in Kenya. Sweet & Maxwell, 1968.

BARTON, H.D.
Executorship law and accounts. 6ed. Butterworths, 1971 (New Zealand).

CURRIE, J.
The confirmation of executors in Scotland. 7ed. Green, 1973.

FAIRBAIRN, W.J.
Handbook for executors and administrators. 3ed. Juta, 1974 (South Africa).

FORSYTH, T.A.
Brief outline of the law relating to trusts, wills, executors and administrators. Butterworths, 1973 (New Zealand).

GARROW, J.M. & WILLIS, J.D.
Law of wills and administration and succession on intestacy. 4ed. Butterworths (New Zealand), 1971.

HARVEY, B.W.
The law and practice of Nigerian wills, probate and succession. Sweet & Maxwell, 1968.

ING, N.D.
Bona vacantia. Butterworths, 1971.

JOSLING, J.F.
Apportionment for executors and trustees. 4ed. Oyez, 1976 (Practice notes no. 5).

MELLOWS, A.R.
Taxation for executors and trustees. 5ed. Butterworths, 1981.

MEYEROWITZ, D.
The law and practice of administration of estates. 5ed. Juta, 1976 supp. 1982 (South Africa).

RANKING, D.F.
Executorship law and accounts. 22ed. H.F.L., 1983.

SHERRING, T. & SLADEN, M.
Law and accounts for executors and trustees. Gee, 1981.

SHRAND, D.
Administration of deceased estates in South Africa. 3ed. Legal & Financial, 1973.

SMITH, P.W.
Distribution on intestacy. 2ed. Oyez, 1981.

TAYLOR, J.N.R.
Executorship law and accounts. 4ed. Macdonald & Evans, 1979.

VICKERY, B.G.
Law and accounts of executors, administrators and trustees. 20ed. Cassell, 1980.

WIDDIFIELD, C.H.
Executors' accounts: being a treatise on the administration of estates. 5ed. Carswell, 1967 (Canada).

WILLIAMS, E.V., MORTIMER, H.C. & SUNNUCKS, J.H.G.
Executors, administrators and probate. 16ed. Sweet & Maxwell, 1982.

WILSON, W.A. & DUNCAN, A.G.M.
Trust, trustees and executors. Green, 1975.

WOODMAN, R.A.
Administration of assets. 2ed. Law Book Co., 1978 (Australia).

WRIGHT, R.J.D.
Testator's family maintenance in Australia and New Zealand. 3ed. Law Book Co., 1974.

EXPLOSIVES

See also Firearms; Mines and Quarries.

Encyclopaedias

Statutes in Force. Group: Firearms and Explosives.
Halsbury's Laws of England. 4ed. vol. 18.
Halsbury's Statutes of England. 3ed. vols. 8, 13.

Encyclopaedia of Court Forms in Civil Proceedings (Atkin). 2ed. vol. 40.
Encyclopaedia of Forms and Precedents. 4ed. see index vol.

Texts

GAUR, A.N.
Law relating to arms, ammunition and explosives. 3ed. Eastern Book Co., 1978 (India).

THOMPSON, J.H.
Guide to the Explosives Act 1875 as amended by the Explosives Act 1923, with remarks on the Explosive Substances Act 1883. 4ed. 1941.

WATTS, H.E.
Law relating to explosives. Griffin, 1954.

EXPORT TRADE

See also Commercial Law

Encyclopaedias and periodicals

Halsbury's Laws of England. 4ed. see index vol.

Journal of Business Law. 1957–
Journal of World Trade Law. 1967–

Texts

BAXTER, I.G. & FLETHAM, I.R.
Export practice. Carswell, 1971 (Canada).

BRANCH, P.
Elements of export practice. Sweet & Maxwell, 1979.

DALE, R.
Anti-dumping law in a liberal trade order. Macmillan, 1980.

DAY, D.
Law of international trade. Butterworths, 1981.

DESCHAMPNEUFS, H.
Export for the small business. Kogan Page, 1984.

EDWARDS, H.
Export credit. Gower, 1980.

GLICK, L.A.
Trading with Saudi Arabia: a guide to the shipping, trade, investment and tax laws of Saudi Arabia. Croom Helm, 1980.

ORGANISATION FOR ECONOMIC CO-OPERATION AND DEVELOPMENT
Export cartels: report of the Committee of Experts on Restrictive Business Practices. 1974.

RYAN, K.W.
International trade law. Law Book Co., 1976 (Australia).

SCHMITTHOFF, C.M.
Export trade: law and practice of international trade. 7ed. Sweet & Maxwell, 1980.

STANBROOK, C.
Dumping: a manual on the E.E.C. anti-dumping law and procedure. European Business Pubns., 1980.

WHITEHEAD, G.
Elements of export law. Woodhead-Faulkner, 1984.

EXTRADITION

See also Aliens; Asylum; International Law.

Encyclopaedias

Statutes in Force. Group: Extradition.
Halsbury's Laws of England. 4ed. vol. 18.
Halsbury's Statutes of England. 3ed. vol. 13.
The Digest. vol. 24.
Encyclopaedia of Court Forms in Civil Proceedings (Atkin). 2ed. vols. 5, 19.

Texts

BASSIOUNI, M.C.
International extradition and world public order: the law and practice of the United States. Sijthoff, 1974.

BIRON, H.C. & CHALMERS, K.E.
Law and practice of extradition. 1903 repr. Rothman, 1981..

BOOTH, V.E.H.
British extradition law and procedure. Sijthoff, 1980.

CLARKE, E.
A treatise upon the law of extradition. 4ed. Stevens & Haynes, 1903.

EUROPEAN COMMITTEE ON CRIME PROBLEMS
Legal aspects of extradition among European states. Council of Europe, 1970.

KAVASS, I.I. & SPRUDZS, A. (eds.)
Extradition laws and treaties of the United States. Hein, 1979. 2 vols. looseleaf.

MOORE, J.B.
A treatise on extradition and interstate rendition. Boston Book Co., 1891. 2 vols.

RAFUSE, R.W.
The extradition of nationals. Univ. of Illinois P., 1939.

SHEARER, I.A.
Extradition in international law. Manchester U.P.:Oceana, 1971.

STANBROOK, I. & STANBROOK, C.
Extradition: the law and practice. B.Rose, 1980.

WIJNGAERT, C. van den
Political offence exception of extradition. Kluwer, 1980.

FACTORIES

See also Employer's Liability; Employment Law; Industrial Law; Shops and Offices; Trade Unions.

Encyclopaedias and periodicals

Statutes in Force. Group: Employment.
Halsbury's Laws of England. 4ed. vols. 16, 20.
Halsbury's Statutes of England. 3ed. vol. 13.
The Digest. vol. 24.
Encyclopaedia of Court Forms in Civil Proceedings (Atkin). 2ed. see index vol.

Encyclopaedia of Forms and Precedents. 4ed. vol. 9.
Health and Safety Bulletin. 1976–
Industrial Law Journal. 1972–
Journal of Business Law. 1957–

Texts

CRONIN, J.
Factories Act and accident prevention. Sweet & Maxwell, 1972.

CRONIN, J. & GRIME, R.P.
Introduction to industrial law. Butterworths, 1974.

CUSWORTH, G.R.N.
Health and Safety at Work etc Act 1974. Butterworths, 1975.

ENCYCLOPEDIA of factories, shops and offices law and practice. Sweet & Maxwell. 3 vols. looseleaf.

FIFE, I. & MACHIN, E.A.
Redgrave's health and safety in factories.
2ed. Butterworths, 1982.

HEALTH AND SAFETY EXECUTIVE
The Factories Act 1961: a short guide.
HMSO, 1971.

HUTCHINS, E.L. & HARRISON, A.
History of factory legislation. 3ed.
P.S.King, 1926 repr. Cass, 1966.

McKOWN, R.
Comprehensive guide to factory law. 6ed.
Godwin, 1976.

SAMUELS, H.
Factory law. 8ed. Knight, 1969 supp. 1973.

THOMAS, M.W.
Early factory legislation. 1948 repr.
Greenwood, 1970.

FAIR TRADING

See also Consumer Protection; Product Liability.

Encyclopaedias and periodicals

Statutes in Force. Group: Trade.
Halsbury's Laws of England. 4ed. see index vol.
Halsbury's Statutes of England. 3ed. vol. 43.
Encyclopaedia of Forms and Precedents. 4ed. supp vol.

Journal of Business Law. 1957–
Journal of World Trade Law. 1967–
Product Liability Bulletin. 1979–
Product Liability International. 1979–
Which? 1957–

Texts

BORRIE, G.J.
Development of consumer law and policy: bold spirits and timorous souls. Stevens, 1984 (Hamlyn lectures).

CRANSTON, R.
Consumers and the law. 2ed. Weidenfeld & Nicholson, 1984.

CRANSTON, R.
Regulating business: law and consumer agencies. Macmillan, 1979.

CUNNINGHAM, J.P.
The Fair Trading Act 1973: consumer protection and competition law. Sweet & Maxwell, 1974 supp. 1978.

FLEMING, M.C.
Fair Trading Act 1973. Sweet & Maxwell, 1974.

HARVEY, B.W.
The law of consumer protection and fair trading. Butterworths, 1978.

HERMANN, A.H. & JONES, C.
Fair trading in Europe. Kluwer, 1977.

NATIONAL FEDERATION OF CONSUMER GROUPS
Handbook of consumer law. Hodder, 1982.

OFFICE OF FAIR TRADING
Bargain offer claims. HMSO, 1975.

OFFICE OF FAIR TRADING
Fair deal: shopper's guide. HMSO.

WOODROFFE, G.
Goods and services: the new law. Sweet & Maxwell, 1982.

FAMILY LAW

See also Adoption; Children and Young Persons; Cohabitation; Divorce; Maintenance; Marriage; Matrimonial Proceedings.

Encyclopaedias and periodicals

Statutes in Force. Group: Family Law.
Halsbury's Laws of England. 4ed. see index vol. under Children & Young Persons,

Divorce, Husband & Wife, Infants.
Halsbury's Statutes of England. 3ed. mainly vols. 17, 40.

FAMILY LAW

The Digest. vol. 27.
Encyclopaedia of Court Forms in Civil Proceedings (Atkin). 2ed. vols. 16, 21.
Encyclopaedia of Forms and Precedents. 4ed. vol. 10 Husband & Wife.
Annual Survey of Commonwealth Law. 1965–
Canadian Journal of Family Law. 1978–
Current Law. 1947–
Family Law. 1971–

Family Law Quarterly (USA). 1967–
Family Law Reports. 1980–
Family Law Reports (Australia). 1976
Justice of the Peace. 1837–
The Magistrate. 1921–
Modern Law Review. 1937–
New Law Journal. 1965– (published as Law Journal 1866–1964)
Reports of Family Law (Canada). 1971–
Solicitors' Journal. 1857–

Texts – United Kingdom

ANTHONY, E.G. & BERRYMAN, J.D.
Legal guide to domestic proceedings, including affiliation and children's orders. Butterworths, 1968.

BARNARD, D.
The family court in action. Butterworths, 1983.

BERKIN, M. & YOUNG, M.
Domestic Proceedings and the Magistrates' Courts Act, 1978. B.Rose, 1979.

BROMLEY, P.M.
Family law. 6ed. Butterworths, 1981.

CLIVE, E.M. & WILSON, J.C.
Law of husband and wife in Scotland. 2ed. Green, 1982.

COLLEGE OF LAW
Emergency procedures in matrimonial cases (with precedents). 1977.

CRETNEY, S.M.
Principles of family law. 4ed. Sweet & Maxwell, 1984.

DAVIDSON, V.
Family law. Sweet & Maxwell, 1980 (New nutshell).

EEKELAAR, J.M.
Family law and social policy. 2ed. Weidenfeld & Nicholson, 1984 (Law in context).

EVERSLEY, W.P.
Law of domestic relations. 6ed. Sweet & Maxwell, 1951.

FRASER, P. Lord
Law of Scotland relative to parent and child and guardian and ward. 3ed. Green, 1906.

FREEMAN, M.D.A.
Family law. 2ed. Butterworths, 1976 (Cracknell's law students' companion).

GLENDON, M.A.
The new family and the new property. Butterworths, 1981.

GLENDON, M.A.
State, law and the family: family law in transition in the United States and Western Europe. North-Holland, 1977.

GRANT, B. & LEVIN, J.
Family law. 4ed. Sweet & Maxwell, 1982 (Concise college texts).

GRAVESON, R.H. & CRANE, F.R. (eds.)
Century of family law, 1857–1957. Sweet & Maxwell, 1957.

HALL, J.C.
Sources of family law. Cambridge U.P., 1966 & supp.

HARRIS, B.
Guide to the new law of family proceedings in magistrates' courts including adoption. 2ed. B.Rose, 1981.

HOGGETT, B.
The family, law and society: cases and materials. Butterworths, 1983.

HOGGETT, B.
Parents and children. 2ed. Sweet & Maxwell, 1981.

JUSTICE
Parental rights and duties and custody suits. Stevens, 1975.

LAW COMMISSION
Family law: declarations in family matters. HMSO, 1984 (Law Com. no. 132).

LAW COMMISSION
Family law: the financial consequences of divorce. The basic policy: a discussion document. HMSO, 1980 (Law Com. no. 103).

LAW COMMISSION
Family law: financial relief after foreign divorce. HMSO, 1980 (Working paper no. 77).

LAW COMMISSION
Family law: illegitimacy. HMSO, 1979 (Working paper no. 74).

LAW COMMISSION
Family law: orders for sale under the Matrimonial Causes Act, 1973. HMSO, 1980 (Law Com. no. 99).

LAW COMMISSION
Time restrictions on presentation of divorce and nullity petitions. HMSO, 1980 (Working paper no. 76).

LESLIE, G.R.
The family in a social context. 2ed. Oxford U.P., 1973.

LORD CHANCELLOR'S DEPARTMENT
Report of the Interdepartmental Committee on Conciliation (Robinson). HMSO, 1983.

MOSTYN, F.E.
Marriage and the law – the law of the family. Oyez, 1976 (It's your law no. 9).

PACE, P.J.
Family law. 2ed. Macdonald & Evans, 1984.

PINDER, J.S. & PAGE, P.J.
Cases and statutes on family law. Sweet & Maxwell, 1979.

RICHMAN, J. & DEALY, F.S.T.
Practical family law. Rose, 1980.

SCARMAN, Sir L.
Family law and law reform (Lecture delivered at University of Bristol, 14 March 1966).

Texts – Australia & New Zealand

BROMLEY, P.M. & WEBB, P.R.H.
Family law in New Zealand. Butterworths (N.Z.), 1974.

BROUN, M. & FOWLER, S.
Australian family law and practice. Law Book Co. 2 vols. looseleaf.

FINLAY, H.A.
Family courts – gimmick or panacea? Butterworths (Australia), 1969.

FINLAY, H.A. & BISSETT-JOHNSON, A.
Family law in Australia. 3ed. Butterworths (Australia), 1983.

HAMBLY, D. & TURNER, J.N.
Cases and materials on Australian family law. Law Book Co., 1971.

Texts – Canada

ALBERTA UNIVERSITY INSTITUTE OF LAW RESEARCH AND REFORM
Family court working paper. 1972.

SCOTTISH LAW COMMISSION
Report on occupancy rights in the matrimonial home and domestic violence. HMSO, 1980 (Scot. Law Com. no. 60).

SEAGO, P. & BISSETT-JOHNSON, A.
Cases and materials on family law. Sweet & Maxwell, 1976.

SMITH, R.M.
Matrimonial and Family Proceedings Act: a practical guide. Oyez Longman, 1984.

STONE, O.
Family law. Macmillan, 1977.

SWEET & MAXWELL
Family law statutes. 3ed. 1981.

WALTON, F.P.
A handbook of husband and wife according to the law of Scotland. 3ed. Green, 1951.

WEBB, P.R.H. & BEVAN, H.K.
Source book of family law. Butterworths, 1964.

WILKINSON, G.S.
Summary matrimonial and guardianship orders. 5ed. Oyez, 1977.

WYNN, M.
Family policy. Joseph, 1970.

INGLIS, B.D.
Family law. 2ed. vol. 1: 1968; vol. 2: 1970. Sweet & Maxwell (New Zealand).

INGLIS, B.D. & MERCER, A.G.
Family law centenary essays. Sweet & Maxwell, 1967 (New Zealand).

LUXFORD, J.H. & WEBB, P.R.H.
Domestic proceedings under the jurisdiction of the magistrates' court in New Zealand. 2ed. Butterworths, 1970.

NYGH, P.E. & TURNER, R.F.
Family law service. Butterworths (Australia), 1974. Looseleaf.

CANADA LAW REFORM COMMISSION
The family court. 1974 (Working paper no. 1).

FAMILY LAW

CANADA LAW REFORM COMMISSION
Family law study: an information memorandum. 1972.

CANADA LAW REFORM COMMISSION
Report on family law. 1976.

CARSWELL's family law digest. 6 vols. + 1982 cum. supp.

FODDEN, S.R.
Family law: cases and materials. Butterworths (Canada), 1977.

GUSHUE, R. & DAY, D. (eds.)
Family law in Newfoundland. Carswell, 1973.

HOVIUS, B.
Family law: cases, notes, materials. Carswell, 1982.

IRVING, H.
Family law: an interdisciplinary perspective. Carswell, 1981.

KEALEY, G.J. & HARRIS, H.A.
Separation agreements and marriage contracts. Butterworths (Canada), 1977.

MACDONALD, & FERRIER,
Law and practice under the Family Law Reform Act. Carswell. Looseleaf.

MANITOBA LAW REFORM COMMISSION
Working paper on family law. 1975.

MENDES DA COSTA, D.
Studies in Canadian family law. Butterworths, 1972. 2 vols.

NEWFOUNDLAND FAMILY LAW STUDY
Family law in Newfoundland. 1973.

ONTARIO LAW REFORM COMMISSION
Report on family law. 1969.

ONTARIO LAW REFORM COMMISSION
Report on family law. Part V: family courts. 1974.

ONTARIO LAW REFORM COMMISSION
Study of the family law project. 1968–9. 13 vols.

ONTARIO MINISTRY OF THE ATTORNEY GENERAL
Family law reform. 1976.

QUEBEC CIVIL CODE REVISION OFFICE
Report on the family. Part 1. 1974.

QUEBEC CIVIL CODE REVISION OFFICE
Report on the family court. 1975.

SANDERS, D.
Family law and native people; prepared for the Law Reform Commission of Canada. 1975.

STEINBERG, D.
Family law in the family court. Vol. 1. 2ed. Carswell, 1981.

Texts – Ireland

BINCHY, W.
A casebook on Irish family law. Professional Books, 1984.

SHATTER, A.J.
Family law in the Republic of Ireland. 2ed. Sweet & Maxwell, 1981.

Texts – U.S.A.

ALDOUS, J. & HILL, R.
International bibliography of research in marriage and the family, 1900–1964. Univ. of Minnesota P., 1967 (USA).

AREEN, J.
Family law, cases and materials. Foundation P., 1978 supp. 1981 (USA).

ASSOCIATION OF AMERICAN LAW SCHOOLS
Selected essays on family law. 1950.

BISKIND, E.L.
Boardman's New York family law. Clark Boardman, 1964. Looseleaf.

CLARK, H.H.
Cases on domestic relations. 3ed. West, 1980 (USA).

CLARK, H.H.
The law of domestic relations in the United States. West, 1968 (USA).

FOOTE, C., LEVY, R.J. & SANDER, F.E.A.
Cases and materials on family law. 2ed. Little, Brown, 1976 (USA).

GLENDON, M.A.
State, law and the family: family law in transition in the United States and Western Europe. North-Holland, 1977.

GOLDSTEIN, J. & KATZ, J.
The family and the law. Free Press, 1965 (USA).

Texts – other countries

BUXBAUM, D.C. (ed.)
Family law and customary law in Asia: a contemporary legal perspective. Nijhoff, 1968.

CHLOROS, A.G.
European family law. Kluwer, 1976.

COMMONWEALTH SECRETARIAT
Family law: the Commonwealth experience. 1984.

GLENDON, M.A.
State, law and the family: family law in transition in the United States and Western Europe. North-Holland, 1977.

HAHLO, H.R.
The South African law of husband and wife. 4ed. Juta, 1975.

KRAUSE, H.D.
Cases and materials on family law. West, 1976 (USA).

PLOSCOWE, M., FOSTER, H.H. & FREED, D.J.
Family law cases and materials. 2ed. Little, Brown, 1972 (USA).

WADLINGTON, W. & PAULSEN, M.G.
Cases and other materials on domestic relations. 3ed. Foundation P., 1978 (USA).

IBRAHIM, A.
Family law in Malaysia and Singapore. Malayan Law Journal, 1978.

NWOGUGU, E.I.
Family law in Nigeria. Heinemann, 1977.

OBI, S.N.C.
Modern family law in Southern Nigeria. Sweet & Maxwell, 1966.

PALSSON, L.
Marriage and divorce in comparative conflict of laws. Sijthoff, 1974.

ROBERTS, S.
Botswana-Tswana family law. Sweet & Maxwell, 1972.

FAMILY PROVISION

See also Wills.

Encyclopaedias and periodicals

Statutes in Force. Group: Family.
Halsbury's Laws of England. 4ed. vol. 17.
Halsbury's Statutes of England. 3ed. vol. 45.
Encyclopaedia of Court Forms in Civil Proceedings (Atkin). 2ed. vol. 22.
Encyclopaedia of Forms and Precedents. 4ed. vol. 23.

Family Law. 1971–
Family Law Reports. 1980–
Justice of the Peace. 1837–
Legal Action (formerly L.A.G. Bulletin). 1973–

Texts

BERKIN, M. & YOUNG, M.
Matrimonial suits and property proceedings. 2ed. B.Rose, 1984.

CANADA LAW REFORM COMMISSION
Family property. 1975 (Working paper no. 8).

DUCKWORTH, P.
Matrimonial property and finance. 2ed. Oyez, 1983.

FIELD, F.
Fair shares for families: need for a family impact statement. Study Commission on the Family, 1980.

FISHER, R.L.
Matrimonial Property Act 1976.
Butterworths (New Zealand), 1977.

GRAY, K.J.
Reallocation of property on divorce.
Professional Books, 1977.

HAMES, J.H.
Applications under s.17 Married Women's
Property Act 1882. 3ed. Oyez, 1971
(Practice notes no. 42).

JACKSON, J.
Matrimonial finance and taxation. 3ed.
Butterworths, 1980.

KIRALFY, A.K.R. (ed.)
Comparative law of matrimonial property.
Sijthoff, 1972.

LAW COMMISSION
Family law: first report on family property, a new approach. HMSO, 1973 (Law Com. no. 52).

LAW COMMISSION
Family law: third report on family property.
The matrimonial home (co-ownership and occupation rights) and household goods.
HMSO, 1978 (Law Com. no. 86).

LAW COMMISSION
Family provision on death: second report on family property. HMSO, 1974 (Law Com. no. 61).

MARTYN, J.G.R.
Modern law of family provision. Sweet & Maxwell, 1978.

MAURICE, S.G.
Family provision practice. 5ed. Oyez, 1983
(Practice notes no. 33).

MILLER, G.
Family property and financial provision.
2ed. Sweet & Maxwell, 1983.

TYLER, E.L.G.
Family provision. 2ed. Professional Books, 1984.

FILMS

See also Censorship; Obscenity.

Encyclopaedias and periodicals

Statutes in Force. Group: Entertainment.
Halsbury's Laws of England. 4ed. see index vol.
Halsbury's Statutes of England. 3ed. vol. 35.
Encyclopaedia of Court Forms in Civil Proceedings (Atkin). 2ed. vols. 12, 37.

Encyclopaedia of Forms and Precedents. 4ed. vol. 22.

Films and Filming. 1954–
Kinematograph Weekly. 1907–
Sight and Sound. 1932–

Texts

ALCHIN, G.
Manual of law for the cinema trade. Pitman, 1934.

BRODY, S.
Screen violence and film censorship: a review of research. HMSO, 1977 (Home Office research studies).

CHERNOFF, G. & SARTIN, H.
Photography and the law. 5ed. Amphoto, 1977.

CINEMATOGRAPH FILMS COUNCIL
Report: review of films legislation. HMSO, 1968 (Cmnd. 3584).

HOME OFFICE
Report of the Committee on Obscenity and Film Censorship (Williams). HMSO, 1979 (Cmnd. 7772).

HOME OFFICE
Report of the Departmental Committee on Children and the Cinema (Wheare). 1950 (Cmnd. 7945).

HUNNINGS, N.M.
Film censors and the law. Allen & Unwin, 1967.

TRADE, DEPARTMENT OF
Proposals for the setting up of a British Film Authority: report on the Interim Act Committee on the Film Industry (Wilson). HMSO, 1978 (Cmnd. 7071).

FIRE LAW

See also Insurance

Encyclopaedias and periodicals

Statutes in Force. Group: Fire Services.
Halsbury's Laws of England. 4ed. vol. 18.
Halsbury's Statutes of England. 3ed. vols. 13, 41.
Encyclopaedia of Court Forms in Civil Proceedings (Atkin). 2ed. see index vol.
Encyclopaedia of Forms and Precedents. 4ed. see index vol.

Fire. 1908–
Fire Prevention. 1971–
Fire Prevention Science and Technology. 1972–
Fire Protection Review. 1938–
National Fire Prevention Gazette. 1962–

Texts

EVERTON, A.
Fire and the law. Butterworths, 1972.

HOME OFFICE
Guide to the Fire Precautions Act 1971: hotels and boarding houses. HMSO, 1972.

INSTITUTION OF HEATING AND VENTILATION ENGINEERS
Survey of fire legislation. 1974.

JONES, P.E.
Fire Court. Clowes, 1966–1970. 2 vols.

TAYLOR, J. & COOKE, G. (eds.)
Fire Precautions Act in practice. Architectural P., 1978.

FIREARMS

See also Criminal Law

Encyclopaedias

Statutes in Force. Group: Firearms and Explosives.
Halsbury's Laws of England. 4ed. vol. 11, 36.

Halsbury's Statutes of England. 3ed. vol. 8.
The Digest. vols. 14, 15.

Texts

CLARKE, P.J. & ELLIS, J.
Law relating to firearms. Butterworths, 1980.

GREENWOOD, C.
Firearms control. Routledge, 1972.

GAUR, A.N.
Law relating to arms, ammunition and explosives. 3ed. Eastern Book Co., 1978 (India).

HARDING, R.
Firearms and violence in Australia. International Scholarly P., 1981.

HOME OFFICE
Control of firearms in Great Britain: a consultative document. HMSO, 1973 (Cmnd. 5297).

HOME OFFICE
Firearms – what you need to know about the law. Home Office, 1984.

SANDYS-WINSCH, G.
Gun law. 3ed. Shaw, 1979.

WEATHERHEAD, A.D. & ROBINSON, B.M.
Firearms in crime. HMSO, 1970 (Home Office Research Unit report no. 4).

WILBRAHAM, Sir R.B.
Letting and taking of shooting rights in England and Wales. rev. ed. R.I.C.S., 1980.

FISHING AND FISHERIES

See also Angling; Sea, Law of; Waters and Watercourses.

Encyclopaedias and periodicals

Statutes in Force. Group: Fisheries.
Halsbury's Law of England. 4ed. vol. 18.
Halsbury's Statutes of England. 3ed. see index vol.
The Digest. vol. 25.
Encyclopaedia of Court Forms in Civil Proceedings (Atkin). 2ed vols. 15, 22, 25.

American Journal of International Law. 1907–

Australian Yearbook of International Law. 1965–
British Yearbook of International Law. 1920–
Canadian Yearbook of International Law. 1963–
International and Comparative Law Quarterly. 1952–
International Court of Justice Reports. 1947–

Texts

AMIN, S.H.
Law of fisheries in the Persian-Arabian Gulf. Royston, 1984.

BAYITCH, S.A.
Inter-American law of fisheries: an introduction. Oceana, 1957 (USA).

CHRISTY, F.T.
Fisherman quotas: a tentative suggestion for domestic management. Univ. of Rhode Island, Law of the Sea Institute, 1973.

COULSON, H.J..W. & FORBES, U.A.
The law of waters (sea, tidal and inland) and to land drainage. 6ed. Sweet & Maxwell, 1952.

FENN, P.T.
Origin of the right of fishery in territorial waters. Harvard U.P., 1926.

HALL, R.G.
A history of the foreshore and the law relating thereto. Stevens & Haynes, 1888.

JOHNSTON, D.M.
The international law of fisheries. Yale U.P., 1965 (USA).

KNIGHT, H.G.
The future of international fisheries management. West, 1975 (USA).

KNIGHT, H.G.
Managing the sea's living resources: legal and political aspects of high seas fisheries. West, 1977 (USA).

KOERS, A.W.
International regulation of marine fisheries. Fishing News Ltd., 1973 (USA).

LEONARD, L.L.
International regulation of fisheries. Columbia U.P., 1944 (USA).

LITTLER, P.
Water rights including fishing rights. 2ed. Oyez, 1981.

ODA, S.
International control of sea resources. Sijthoff, 1963.

OKE, G.C.
Fishery laws. 4ed. Butterworths, 1924.

PONTECORVO, G. (ed.)
Fisheries conflicts in the North Atlantic: problems of management and jurisdiction. Ballinger, 1974.

REISENFELD, S.A.
Protection of coastal fisheries under international law. Carnegie Endowment for Internat. Peace, 1943 (USA).

WOOLRYCH, H.W.
Law of waters, including rights in the sea, rivers, canals, etc. 2ed. Butterworths, 1851.

WOOSNAM, C.R.
Letting of fishing rights in England and Wales. R.I.C.S., 1979.

FIXTURES

See also Dilapidations; Landlord and Tenant; Personal Property.

Encyclopaedias

Halsbury's Laws of England. 4ed. see index vol.
Encyclopaedia of Court Forms in Civil Proceedings (Atkin). 2ed. vols. 4, 18, 28.

Encyclopaedia of Forms and Precedents. 4ed. vols. 11, 14.

Texts

ADKIN, B.W. & BOWEN, D.
Law relating to fixtures. 3ed. Estates Gazette, 1947.

AMOS, A. & FERARD, J.
Law of fixtures and other property comprising the law relative to annexations to freeholds in general. 3ed. Stevens, 1883.

WRIGHT, S.
Fixtures: law and practice. 4ed. Estates Gazette, 1912.

FLATS

See also Landlord and Tenant; Rent.

Encyclopaedias

Halsbury's Laws of England. 4ed. see index vol.
Halsbury's Statutes of England. 3ed. vol.42.

Encyclopaedia of Forms and Precedents 4ed. vol.11.

Texts

ALDRIDGE, T.M.
Your home and the law. 2ed. Oyez, 1979 (It's your law series no. 7).

GEORGE, E.F. & GEORGE, A.
The sale of flats. 5ed. Sweet & Maxwell, 1978.

PAGE, R.G.
The law relating to flats. Butterworths, 1934.

FOOD AND DRUGS

See also Drugs; Public Health.

Encyclopaedias

Statutes in Force. Group: Food.
Halsbury's Laws of England. 4ed. vol.18.
Halsbury's Statutes of England. 3ed. vol.14, 39.

The Digest. vol.25.
Encyclopaedia of Court Forms in Civil Proceedings (Atkin). 2ed. vols. 32 & 40.

Texts

AGRICULTURE, FISHERIES & FOOD, MINISTRY OF
Food quality and safety: a century of progress. HMSO, 1976.

BELL, W.J. & O'KEEFE, J.A.
Sale of food and drugs. 14ed. Butterworths, 1968 with Looseleaf Service.

BIGWOOD, E.J. & GERARD, A.
Fundamental principles and objectives and a comparative food law. Karger, 1972. 4 vols.

DICKERSON, R.
Products liability and the food consumer. Greenwood, 1972 (USA).

EUROPEAN COMMUNITIES
Symposium on enforcement of food law. 1980.

FORDER, K.J.
Law and the meat trade. Meat Trades Journal, 1973.

INSTITUTE OF PRACTITIONERS IN ADVERTISING
Is it legal? A guide to the laws affecting the design and content of food labels and advertisements. 1979.

JUKES, D.J.
Food legislation in the United Kingdom: a concise guide. Butterworths, 1984.

KOTAS, R. & DAVIS, B.
Food and beverage control. 1980.

O'KEEFE, J.A.
Law of food and drugs. Butterworths, 1978.

PAINTER, A.A.
Law of food and drugs. Butterworths, 1980. 2 vols. looseleaf.

PAULUS, I.
The search for pure food: a sociology of legislation in Britain. Martin Robertson, 1974.

PEARSON, D.
Concise guide to food legislation. Univ. of Reading, National College of Food Technology, 1976.

TOULMIN, H.A.
Law of foods, drugs, cosmetics. 2ed. Anderson, 1963. 4 vols. supp.

WORLD HEALTH ORGANISATION
Toxicological evaluation of certain food additives, etc. 1976.

FOOTPATHS

See also Commons and Inclosures; Rights of Way.

Encyclopaedias and periodicals

Statutes in Force. Group: Commons, England and Wales.
Halsbury's Laws of England. 4ed. vol. 21, 40.
Halsbury's Statutes of England. 3ed. vol.15.
The Digest. vols. 11, 36(1).

Texts

CAMPBELL, I.
Practical guide to the law of footpaths and bridleways. Commons, Open Spaces & Footpaths Preservation Soc., 1974.

CHAPMAN, D.H.
Footpaths and bridleways in England and Wales. rev. ed. R.I.C.S., 1979.

Encyclopaedia of Court Forms in Civil Proceedings (Atkin). 2ed. vol.20.
Encyclopaedia of Forms and Precedents. 4ed. vols. 10, 11, 12.

Journal of Commons, Open Spaces & Footpaths Preservation Society. 1927–

GARNER, J.F.
Rights of way and access to the countryside. 3ed. Oyez, 1974 (Practice notes no.55).

RYAN, G. & CAMERON, S.
The law relating to open spaces, commons and footpaths. Commons, Open Spaces & Footpaths Preservation Soc., 1981.

FOREIGN JUDGMENTS

See also Judgments.

Encyclopaedias

Statutes in Force. Group: Enforcement, 3: External Judgments.

Halsbury's Laws of England. 4ed. see index vol.

Halsbury's Statutes of England. 3ed. see index vol.
The Digest. vols. 50, 51.
Encyclopaedia of Court Forms in Civil Proceedings (Atkin). 2ed. vols. 7, 22 & 29.
Encyclopaedia of Forms and Precedents. 4ed. vol.20.

Texts

COUNCIL OF EUROPE
The practical guide to the recognition and enforcement of foreign judicial decisions in Civil and Commercial Law. 1975.

SUPREME Court practice 1985. Sweet & Maxwell, 1984. 2 vols.

FORENSIC SCIENCE

See also Coroner; Criminal Investigation.

Periodicals

Australian Journal of Forensic Sciences.
The Crimiinologist. 1966–
Forensic Photography. 1972–
Journal of the Forensic Science Society. 1960–

Medicine Science & the Law. 1960–
Medico-Legal Journal. 1901–

Texts

BALLANTYNE, B. (ed.)
Forensic toxicology. Wright, Bristol, 1974.

BLASSINGAME, W.
Science catches the criminal. Dodd Mead, 1975 (USA).

CAMPS, F.
Practical forensic medicine. Hutchinson, 1971.

CAMPS, F.
Recent advances in forensic pathology. Churchill, 1969.

CAMERON, J.M. & SIMS, B.G.
Forensic dentistry. Churchill Livingstone, 1974.

COOKE, G.
The role of the forensic psychologist. Nelson, 1980.

CURRY, A.S. (ed.)
Advances in forensic and clinical toxicology. Chemical Rubber Co., 1973.

CURRY, A.S.
Methods of forensic science. Interscience, 1965.

ECKERT, W.G. (ed.)
Introduction to forensic science. Mosby, 1980.

GORDON, I. & SHAPIRO, H.A.
Forensic medicine: a guide to princples. Churchill Livingstone, 1975.

HARRISON, W.R.
Suspect documents: their scientific examination. Sweet & Maxwell, 1958.

HAVARD, J.D.J.
The detection of secret homicide: a study of the medico-legal system of investigation of sudden and unexplained deaths. Macmillan, 1960.

HOUTS, M.
Lawyer's guide to medical proof. Bender, 1967 (USA).

JAFFE, F.
Guide to pathological evidence. Carswell, 1976 (Canada).

LUDWIG, J. (ed.)
Current methods of autopsy practice. W.B.Saunders, 1972.

LUNTZ, L.L. & LUNTZ, P.
Handbook for dental identification: techniques in forensic dentistry. Lippincott, 1974.

MANN, A.
Medical assessment of injuries for legal purposes. 3ed. Butterworths (Australia), 1979.

MASON, J.K.
Forensic medicine for lawyers. 2ed. Butterworths, 1983.

POLSON, C.J. & GEE, D.J.
The essentials of forensic medicine. 3ed. Pergamon, 1973.

WALLS, H.J.
Forensic science: an introduction to scientific crime detection. 2ed. Sweet & Maxwell, 1974.

FORESTS

See also Agriculture.

Encyclopaedias

Statutes in Force. Group: Forestry.
Halsbury's Laws of England. 4ed. vol.19.
Halsbury's Statutes of England. 3ed. vol.14, see also index vol.
The Digest vol.2.

Encyclopaedia of Courts Forms in Civil Proceedings (Atkin). 2ed. vols. 25, 28.
Encyclopaedia of Forms and Precedents. 4ed. vol.9.

Texts

ADKIN, B.W.
Laws of forestry, trees, trespass and game. Estates Gazette, 1914.

HART, C.E.
The commoners of Dean forest. Bellows, 1951.

HART, C.E.
The verders and forest laws of Dean. David & Charles, 1971.

HART, C.E.
The verderers and Speech Court of the Forest of Dean. Bellows, 1950.

MANWOOD, J.
Treatise and discourse of the Lawes of the Forrest. 1ed. Societie of Stationers, 1615. 5ed. 1741.

POLLARD, R.S.W.
Trees and the law. 2ed. Arboricultural Assoc., 1976.

FORMS AND PRECEDENTS

See also Drafting; Pleading.

AMERICAN jurisprudence pleading and practice forms annotated. Lawyers' Co-op., 1966–1974. 25 vols.

AUSTRALIAN encyclopaedia of forms and precedents. Butterworths (Australia).

ATKIN's encyclopaedia of court forms in civil proceedings. 2ed. Butterworths. 41 vols. Annual supp.

BRITTS, M.G.
Pleading precedents. 2ed. Law Book Co., 1980 (Australia).

BULLEN, E., LEAKE, S.M. & JACOB, I.H.
Precedents of pleadings in the Queen's Bench Division of the High Court of Justice. 12ed. Sweet & Maxwell, 1975.

CHITTY, T. & JACOB, I.H.
Queen's Bench Forms. 20ed. Sweet & Maxwell, 1969.

CLARK, C.
Publishing agreements: a book of precedents. Allen & Unwin, 1980.

COLINVAUX, R., STEEL, D. & RICKS, V.E.
Forms and precedents. Stevens, 1973 (British shipping laws vol.6).

DANIELL, E.R.
Forms and precedents in Chancery. 7ed. Stevens, 1932.

ENCYCLOPAEDIA of Forms and Precedents 4ed. Butterworths. 24 vols. annual supp.

FARRAND, J.T. & SCAMMELL, E.H. (eds.)
Precedents for the conveyancers. Sweet & Maxwell. 2 vols. looseleaf.

McCLEARY, R.
County court precedents. 4ed. Butterworths, 1973 supp. 1978. 2 vols.

MELVILLE, L.W.
Forms and agreements on intellectual property and international licensing. 3ed. Sweet & Maxwell, 1979. 2 vols. looseleaf.

OKE, G.C.
Magisterial formulist. 19ed. Butterworths, 1978 supp. 1980.

PRIDEAUX, F.
Forms and precedents in conveyancing. 25ed. Stevens, 1958–9. 3 vols.

QUEEN'S Bench Masters practice forms. 1975.

SOUTH African encyclopaedia of forms and precedents. Butterworths (S.Africa), 1967– .15 vols.

WALLACE, I.N.D.
Building and engineering standard forms. Sweet & Maxwell, 1969 supps. 1970, 1973.

WALLACE, I.N.D.
Further building and engineering standard forms. Sweet & Maxwell, 1973.

WILLISTON, W.B. & ROLLS, R.J.
Canadian court forms. Butterworths (Canada), 1975. 3 vols.

FRANCE

See also European Communities.

Periodicals

Conseil d'Etat, Etudes et Documents. 1947–
Droit Social, 1938–
International and Comparative Law Quarterly, 1952–
Public Law. 1956–
Recuil Dalloz. 1845–
Recuil des Decisions du Conseil d'Etat. 1821–
Revue du Droit et de la Science Politique. 1894–
Revue Trimestrielle de Droit Civil, 1902–
Revue Trimestrielle de Droit Commercial, 1948–

Dalloz (Petit Codes)
Code Civil. Annual.

Code de Commerce. Annual.
Code Penal. Annual.
Code de Procedure Penale et Code de Justice Militaire. Annual.
Code de Procedure Civile. Annual.
Code Administratif. Irregular.
Code de Loyers et de la Copropriete. Irregular.
Code Rural et Code Forestier. Irregular.
Codes de la Securite Sociale et de la Mutualite. Irregular.
Codes de la Sate Publique, de la Famille et de l'Aide Sociale. Irregular.
Code du Travail. Irregular.
Code General des Impotes. Irregular.
Code des Societes. Irregular.

Texts

AMOS, M.S. & WALSON, F.P.
Introduction to French law. 3ed. Oxford U.P., 1967.

AUBRY, C. & RAU, C.
French civil law. English translation. West, 1965–1972. 5 vols (USA).

BRISSAUD, J.B.
A history of French private law, trans. by R Howell. 2ed. 1912 repr. Rothman, 1969.

BRISSAUD, J.B.
A history of French public law, trans. by J.W. Garner, 1915 repr. Rothman, 1969.

BROWN, L.N. & GARNER, J.F.
French administrative law. 3ed. Butterworths, 1983.

CALAIS-AULOY, J.
Consumer legislation in France. Van Nostrand Reinhold, 1982.

DAVID, R.
English law and French law. Stevens, 1980.

DAVID, R.
French law: its structure, sources and methodology. Louisiana State U.P., 1972 (USA).

DAVID, R. & DE VRIES, H.P.
French legal system: an introduction to civil law systems. Oceana, 1958 (USA).

DELAUME, G.R.
American-French private international law. 2ed. Oceana, 1961 (USA).

DELVOLVE, J.-L.
Arbitration in France. Kluwer, 1984.

HALPERN, L.
Taxes in France. 4ed. Butterworths, 1984.

KAHN-FREUND, O. and others.
A source-book on French law: systems, methods, outlines of contract. 2ed. Oxford U.P., 1979.

KOCK, G.L. (trans.)
French code of criminal procedure. Rothman, 1964 (American series of foreign penal codes, vol.7).

LE GALL, K.
French company law. Oyez, 1974.

MOUREAU, J.F. & MUELLER, G.O.W. (trans.)
French penal code. Rothman, 1960 (American series of foreign penal codes, vol.1).

NICHOLAS, B.
French law of contract. Butterworths, 1982.

PLANIOL, M.F. & RIPERT, G.
Treatise on the civil law: trans. by Louisiana State Law Insitute. 1959. 3 vols. in 6.

ROBLOT, R.
French business taxation. Oyez, 1974.

ROBLOT, R.
French company law. Oyez, 1974.

SPRUDZS, A.
Foreign law abbreviations: French. Oceana, 1968.

FRAUD

See also Conspiracy; Criminal Law; Mistake.

Encyclopaedias

Halsbury's Laws of England. 4ed. vol. 31.
Halsbury's Statutes of England. 3ed. see index vol.
The Digest vols. 25, 35.

Texts

AGNEW, W.F.
The statute of frauds. Butterworths, 1876.

BOWER, G.S. & TURNER, A.K.
The law of actionable misrepresentation. 3ed. Butterworths, 1974.

CAMPBELL, D.
Investigation of fraud. 2ed. Rose, 1979.

COMMONWEALTH SECRETARIAT
Commercial frauds: problems and remedies in the judicial process. 1982.

ELLEN, E.
International maritime fraud. Sweet & Maxwell, 1981.

Encyclopaedia of Court Forms in Civil Proceedings (Atkin). 2ed. see index vol.
Encyclopaedia of Forms and Precedents 4ed. see index vol.

HOVENDEN, J.E.
A general treatise on the principles and practices by which Courts of Equity are guided as to remedial correction of fraud. Sweet, 1825. 2 vols.

KERR, W.W.
Law of fraud and mistake. 7ed. Sweet & Maxwell, 1952.

KRAUSS, L.I.
Computer fraud and countermeasures. Prentice-Hall, 1979.

WILLIAMS, J.
The statute of frauds, s.4 in the light of its judicial interpretation. Cambridge U.P., 1932.

FRIENDLY SOCIETIES

See also Clubs.

Encyclopaedias

Statutes in Force. Group: Friendly and Other Societies.
Halsbury's Laws of England. 4ed. vol.19.
Halsbury's Statutes of England. 3ed. vol.44.
The Digest vol.25.

Encyclopaedia of Court Forms in Civil Proceedings (Atkin). 2ed. vol.20.
Encyclpaedia of Forms and Precedents. 4ed. vol. 9.

Texts

FULLER, F.B.
Law relating to Friendly Societies. 4ed. Stevens, 1926.

INSTITUTE OF CHARTERED ACCOUNTS
Auditors' reports under the Friendly and Industrial & Provident Societies Act 1968. 1969.

REGISTRY OF FRIENDLY SOCIEITES
Reports of the Chief Registrar. HMSO. Annual.

REGISTRY OF FRIENDLY SOCIETIES, NORTHERN IRELAND
Reports of the Registrar. HMSO. Annual.

GAME LAWS

See also Angling; Criminal Law.

Encyclopaedias and periodicals

Statutes in Force. Group: Animals.
Halsbury's Laws of England. 4ed. vol. 2.
Halsbury's Statutes of England. 3ed. vol. 14. The Digest vol. 25.
Encyclopaedia of Court Forms in Civil Proceedings (Atkin) 2ed, see index vol.

Encyclopaedia of Forms and Precedents 4ed. see index vol.

Gamekeeper and Countryside. 1897–
Stone's Justices Manual. Annual.

Texts

OKE, G.C.
Game laws. 5ed. Butterworths, 1912.

WIGRAM, W.K.
Justice's note-book. 15ed. Stevens, 1951.

WILBRAHAM, Sir R.B.
Letting and taking of shooting rights in England and Wales. rev. ed. R.I.C.S., 1980

'WOODMAN'
Game Laws in England and Wales. Jenkins, 1962.

GAS

See also Electricity; Oil; Public Health.

Encyclopaedias and periodicals

Statutes in Force. Group: Energy.
Halsbury's Laws of England. 4ed. vol.19.
Halsbury's Statutes of England. 3ed. vol.42.
The Digest. vol.25.
Encyclopaedia of Court Forms in Civil Proceedings (Atkin). 2ed. see index vol.
Encyclopaedia of Forms and Precedents. 4ed. mainly vol.23.

The Economist. 1843–
Gas & Oil Power. 1905–
Gas Marketing. 1971–
Gas World & Gas Journal. 1884–
Journal of Energy and Natural Resources Law. 1983–
Journal of World Trade Law. 1967–

Texts

ASKEW, H.R.
Law, procedure and practice relating to the Gas Undertaking Acts. Stevens, 1930.

BRITISH GAS CORPORATION
A guide to the gas safety regulations. 1973.

DAINTITH, T.
UK oil and gas law. Sweet & Maxwell, 1984. Looseleaf.

DAINTITH, T. & WILLOUGHBY, G.D.M.
Manual of United Kingdom oil and gas law. Sweet & Maxwell, 1984.

DUPUY, R.J. (ed.)
Settlement of disputes on the new natural resources: workshop proceedings. Nijhoff, 1983.

ENERGY, DEPARTMENT OF
United Kingdom offshore oil and gas policy. 1974 (Cmnd. 5696).

HAYLLAR, R.F. & ROUSE, R.M.
Taxation of offshore oil and gas. Butterworths, 1980 looseleaf.

McCLURE, J.G. & LAVIES, A.G.
United Kingdom oil and gas tax legislation. 1980.

MICHAEL, W.H. & WILL, J.S.
The law relating to gas and water. vol.1, Gas. 8ed. Butterworths, 1935.

UNITED Kingdom offshore legislation guide. Benn Technical, 1983. Looseleaf.

WHITEHEAD, H.
United Kingdom offshore legislation guide. Kogan Page, 1980.

GAVELKIND

See also Copyhold.

Encyclopaedias

Halsbury's Laws of England. 4ed. mainly vol. 39.
Halsbury's Statutes of England. 3ed. vol.13.
The Digest, mainly vol.24.

Texts

ELTON, C.I.
Tenures of Kent. Parker, 1867.

EMMET, L.E.
Notes on perusing titles and on practical conveyancing. 18ed. Oyez, 1983 supp. 1984.

SANDYS, C.
Consuetudines kanciae: a history of gavelkind. Smith, 1851.

TAYLOR, S.
The history of gavelkind, with the etymology thereof. repr. Sherwin & Freutel, 1970 (USA).

WHARTON, J.J.S.
Law Lexicon. 14ed. Stevens, 1946.

GAZUMPING

See also Conveyancing.

Periodicals

Conveyancer and Property Lawyer. 1936–
Journal of Planning and Environment Law. 1948–

Law Society's Gazette. 1903–
New Law Journal, 1965–
Solicitors' Journal, 1857–

Texts

LAW COMMISSION
Transfer of land: report on "subject to contract" agreements. HMSO, 1975 (Law Com. no.65).

LAW COMMISSION
Transfer of land: "subject to contract" agreements. HMSO, 1973 repr. 1977 (Working paper no.51).

GENERAL AGREEMENT ON TARIFFS AND TRADE

See also International Law.

Periodicals

The Economist. 1843–
Journal of World Trade Law. 1967–

Texts

DAM, K.W.
General agreement of tariffs and trade: the law and the International Economic Organization. Univ. of Chicago P., 1977 (USA).

GENERAL AGREEMENT ON TARIFFS AND TRADE
Effective tariff protection. 1971.

GOLT, S.
General agreement on tariffs and trade negotiations. 1973–1979: the closing stages. National Planning, 1979 (USA).

GRUBEL, H.G. & JOHNSON, H.G.
Effective tariff protection: proceedings of a conference. GATT, 1971.

HUDEC, R.E.
General agreement on tariffs and trade legal system and trade diplomacy. Praeger, 1975.

JACKSON, J.
World trade and the law of G.A.T.T. Bobbs-Merrill, 1969.

LORTIE, P.
Economic integration and the law of general agreement n tariffs and trade. Praeger, 1975.

GENOCIDE

See also War Crimes

Encyclopaedias

Halsbury's Laws of England. 4ed. see index vol.
Halsbury's Statutes of England. 3ed. vol.40.
Encyclopaedia of Court Forms in Civil Proceedings (Atkin). 2ed. vol.14.

Texts

BOWEN, M.
Passing by: the United States and genocide in Burundi. Carnegie Endowment for International Peace, 1972.

SARTRE, J.P.
On genocide: and a summary of the evidence and the judgments of the International War Crimes Tribunal. Beacon P., 1968 (USA).

GERMANY

See also European Communities

Texts

AULT, H.J. & RADLER, A.J.
German corporation tax. 2ed. Kluwer, 1980.

BRUCHER, H. & PULCH, D. (eds.)
The German law of foreign investment shares. Knapp:Macdonald & Evans, 1972.

COBLER, S.
Law, order and politics in West Germany. Penguin, 1978.

COHN, E.J.
Manual of German law. 2ed. B.I.I.C.L., 1968–71. 2 vols.

DROBNIG, U.
American-German private international law. rev. ed. Oceana, 1972.

ERCKLENTZ, E.W.
Modern German corporation law. Oceana, 1979–81. 3 vols.

GERMANY
The German civil code (as amended to January l, 1975). Trans. North-Holland, 1975.

GRES, J. & JUNG, H.
German employment law. Kluwer, 1981.

HORN, N.
German private and commercial law: an introduction. Oxford U‹P‹, 1982.

JUNG, H. & GRESS, J.
Statutory business operations in Germany. Kluwer, 1984.

KONIG, K.
Public administration in the Federal Republic of Germany. Kluwer, 1983.

MUELLER, R. (ed.)
GmbH – German Law concerning companies with limited liability. 3ed. Knapp:Macdonald & Evans, 1977.

MUELLER, R. & GALBRAITH, E.G.
The German stock corporation law. 2ed. Knapp:Macdonald & Evans, 1976.

MUELLER, R & SCHNEIDER, H.
The German law against restraints of competition Knapp:Macdonald & Evans, 1973.

MUELLER, R., STIEFEL, E. & BRUCHER, R.
Doing business n Germany. 7ed. Macdonald & Evans, 1972.

OLIVER, M.C.
The private company in Germany. Macdonald & Evans, 1976.

PELTZER, M. & BOER, R.
German labour management relations act. 2ed. Macdonald & Evans, 1976.

PELTZER, M. & NEBENDORF, K.
Banking in Germany. Macdonald & Evans, 1973.

SCHNEIDER, H. & HELLWIG, H.J. (eds.)
The German Banking Act. Macdonald & Evans, 1977.

SCHNEIDER, H. & HELLWIG, H.J. (eds.)
German labour law. Macdonald & Evans, 1977.

SCHNEIDER, H. & KINGSMAN, D.J.
German Co-Determination Act. Macdonald & Evans, 1976.

STAUBACH, F.
The German law of agency and distributorship agreements. Oyez, 1977.

SZLADITS, C.
Guide to foreign legal materials: French, German, Swiss. Oceana, 1959 (USA).

VOLHARD, R. & WEBER, D. (eds.)
Real property in Germany. Macdonald & Evans, 1975.

GHANA

See also Africa

Encyclopaedias and periodicals

Statutes in Force. Group: Commonwealth and Other Territories, Ghana.
Halsbury's Laws of England. 4ed. vol. 6.
Halsbury's Statutes of England. 3ed. vol. 4.
The Digest. see index vol.
University of Ghana Law Journal. 1964–

Texts

ACQUAH-DADZIE, K.
Ghana criminal court in action. Merlin Books, 1983.

ACQUAH-DADZIE, K.
Landlord and tenant in Ghana. Merlin Books, 1982.

ALLOTT, A.N.
Essays in African law, with special reference to the law of Ghana. Greenwood, 1976.

ASANTE, S.K.B.
Property law and social goals in Ghana, 1844–1966. Ghana U.P., 1975.

BENTSI-ENCHILL, K.
Choice of law in Ex-British Africa. Sweet & Maxwell, 1970.

BENTSI-ENCHILL, K.
Ghana land law. Sweet & Maxwell, 1964.

ELIAS, T.O.
Ghana and Sierra Leone: the development of their laws and constitution. Stevens, 1962.

KLUDZE, A.K.P.
Restatement of African law, vol. 6: Ghana I: the Ewe law of property. Sweet & Maxwell. 1973.

OLLENNU, N.A.
Basic principles of customary land law in Ghana. Sweet & Maxwell, 1962.

OLLENNU, N.A.
The law of testate and intestate succession in Ghana. Sweet & Maxwell, 1966.

RUBIN, L. & MURRAY, P.
The constitution and government of Ghana. 2ed. Sweet & Maxwell, 1964.

SARBAH, J.M.
Fanti customary laws. 3ed. Cass, 1969.

UCHE, U.U.
Contractual obligations in Ghana and Nigeria. Cass, 1971.

GIBRALTAR

Periodicals

Gibraltar Law Reports. 1812–1977, 1978–

Texts

TOLLEY's taxation in Gibraltar. Tolley, 1982.

GIFTS

See also Equity; Wills.

Encyclopaedias and periodicals

Halsbury's Laws of England. 4ed. vol. 20.
Halsbury's Statutes of England. 3ed. see index vol.
The Digest. vol. 25.
Encyclopaedia of Court Forms in Civil Proceedings (Atkin). 2ed. mainly vol. 9.
Encyclopaedia of Forms and Precedents. 4ed. mainly vol. 9.
New Law Journal. 1965–

Texts

DAWSON, J.P.
Gifts and promises: continental and American law compared. Yale U.P., 1980 (USA).

GULLIVER, A.G.
Cases and materials on gratuitous transfers. West, 1967 (USA).

KERR, W.W.
Law of fraud and mistake. 7ed. Sweet & Maxwell, 1952.

SHAH, S.M.
Principles of the law of transfer. 6ed. Tripathi, 1980 (India).

WHEATCROFT, G.S.A.
Taxation of gifts and settlements. 3ed. Pitman, 1958.

GIPSIES

See also Caravans and Camp Sites.

Encyclopaedias and periodicals

Halsbury's Statutes of England. 3ed. vol.24.

New Society. 1962–

Texts

ACTON, T.A.
Gypsy policies and social change. Routledge, 1974.

ADAMS, B.
Gypsies and government policy in England. Heinemann, 1975.

CRIPPS, J.
Accomodation for gypsies: a report on the working of the Caravan Sites Act 1968. HMSO (Department of the Environment), 1977.

HEAP, D. (ed.)
Encyclopaedia of planning law and practice. Sweet & Maxwell. 4 vols. Looseleaf.

GOLD CLAUSE

Encyclopaedias

Encyclopaedia of Court Forms in Civil Proceedings (Atkin). 2ed. vol.8.

Texts

PLESCH, A.
The gold clause: a collection of international cases and opinions. Stevens, 1935.

GOVERNMENT

See also Administrative Law; Cabinet; Constitutional Law; Legislation; Parliament; Privy Council; Sovereignty.

Encyclopaedias and periodicals

Halsbury's Laws of England. 4ed. see index vol.
The Digest, see index vol.
Encyclopaedia of Court Forms of Civil Proceedings (Atkin). 2ed. see index vol.

Parliamentary Affairs. 1947–
Public Administration. 1923–
Public Law. 1953–

Texts

BARKER, Sir E.
Essays on government. Oxford U.P., 1945.

BENTHAM, J.
Fragment on government by F.C. Montague. 1949 repr. Greenwood, 1980..

BIRCH, A.H.
The British system of government. 4ed. Allen & Unwin, 1980.

CARTER, G.M. & HERZ, J.H.
Government and politics in the twentieth century. 3ed. Praeger, 1973 (USA).

CHAPMAN, B.
The profession of government: public service in Europe. new ed. Greenwood, 1980.

CHESTER, D.N.
Organisation of British central government. 2ed. Allen & Unwin, 1968.

CLARKE, J.J.
Outlines of central government including judicial system of England. 12ed. Pitman, 1958.

ELTON, G.R.
Tudor revolution in government. Cambridge U.P., 1953.

FINER, H.
Future of government. 2ed. Methuen, 1949.

FINER, H.
Theory and practice of modern government. 2ed. Methuen, 1946.

FLEISHMAN, J.L.
Public duties: moral obligations of government officials. Harvard U.P., 1981 (USA).

FRIEDMANN, W.G.
The state and the rule of law in a mixed economy. Stevens, 1971.

FRIEDMANN, W.G. & GARNER, J.F.
Government enterprise: a comparative study. Stevens, 1970.

HARTLEY, T.C. & GRIFFITH, J.A.G.
Government and law. 2ed. Weidenfeld & N., 1981.

INFORMATION CANADA
Organization of the government of Canada. 9ed. 1974.

JENNINGS, Sir W.I.
Approach to the self-government. Cambridge U.P., 1956.

JENNINGS, Sir W.I.
Cabinet government. 3ed. Cambridge U.P., 1959.

JONES, B.
British government today. Butterworths, 1972 (Concise college texts).

LASKI, H.J.
Reflection on the constitution, the House of Commons, the Cabinet and the civil service. Manchester U.P., 1951.

LEEMANS, A.F.
Management of change in government. Nijhoff, 1975.

LUCAS, W.W.
Primordial functions of government and legal status of sovereignty. Bowes & Bowes 1938.

MARRIOTT, Sir J.A.R.
The mechanism of the modern state. Oxford U.P., 1927. 2 vols.

MUIR, R.
How Britain is governed. 4ed. Constable, 1940.

MURRAY, J.O.
Government and people. Harrap, 1973.

OGLIVIE, Sir C.
The King's government and the common law. 1471–1641. 1959 repr. Greenwood, 1978..

PRICE, J.H.
Comparative government: four modern constitutions. Hutchinson, 1975.

RANDALL, F.
British government and politics. 3ed. Macdonald & Evans, 1984.

RECONSTRUCTION, MINISTRY OF
Report of the Committee on the Machinery of Government. HMSO, 1918 (Cd. 9230).

RICHARDS, S.G.
Introduction to British government. Macmillan, 1978.

ROYAL INSTITUTE OF PUBLIC ADMINISTRATION
The organisation of British central government, 1914–56. 1957.

RUSH, M.
Parliamentary government in Britain. Holmes & Meier, 1981.

SAWER, G.
Australian government today. 11ed. Melbourne U.P., 1973.

SCHWARTZ, B.
Law and the executive in Britain. New York Univ. P., 1949.

SCHWARTZ, B. & WADE, H.W.R.
Legal control of government. Oxford U.P., 1972.

SIEGHART, M.A.
Government by decree. Stevens, 1950.

STACEY, F.
British government, 1966 to 1975: years of reform. 1975.

STACEY, F.
Government of modern Britain. 1968.

STREET, H.
Government liability. Cambridge U.P., 1953.

THORNHILL, W. (ed.)
The modernization of British government. 1975.

ULLMANN, W.
Principles of government and politics in the middle ages. Methuen, 1961 repr. 1974.

VERNEY, D.V.
British government and politics. 3ed. Harper & Row, 1976.

WHEARE, K.C.
Federal government. 4ed. Oxford U.P., 1963.

WHEARE, K.C.
Government by committee: essay on the British Constitution. Oxford U.P., 1955 repr. Greenwood, 1979.

WILSON, Sir H.
The governance of Britain. Weidenfeld & N., 1976.

WISEMAN, H.V.
The Cabinet in the Commonwealth. Stevens, 1958.

WRAITH, R.
Open government. Allen & Unwin, 1977.

GOVERNMENT DEPARTMENTS

See also Departments by Name; Civil Service.

Encyclopaedias

Statutes in Force. Group: Government Departments and Public Offices.
Halsbury's Laws of England. 4ed. see index vol.
Halsbury's Statutes of England. 3ed. see index vol.

The Digest see index vol.
Encyclopaedia of Court Forms in Civil Proceedings (Atkin). 2ed. see index vol.
Encyclopaedia of Forms and Precedents. 4ed. mainly vol.12.

Texts

GARNER, J.
Commonwealth Office, 1925–68. Heinemann, 1978.

MANAGEMENT AND PERSONNEL OFFICE
Civil service year book. HMSO. Annual

POTTINGER, G.
Secretaries of State for Scotland, 1926–76: fifty years of the Scottish Office. Scot. Academic P., 1979.

ROSEVEARE, H.G.
The Treasury: the evolution of a British institution. Penguin, 1969.

Whitehall series

BIGGE, Sir L.A.S.
The Board of Education. 2ed. Allen & Unwin, 1934.

FIDDES, Sir G.V.
The Dominion and Colonial offices. Allen & Unwin, 1926.

FLOUD, Sir F.L.C.
The Ministry of Agriculture and Fisheries. Allen & Unwin, 1927.

GORDON, H.C.
The War Office. Allen & Unwin, 1935.

HEATH, Sir T.L.
The Treasury. Allen & Unwin, 1927.

New Whitehall series

BRIDGES, E.E.
The Treasury. Allen & Unwin, 1964.

CROMBIE, Sir J.I.C.
Her Majesty's Customs and Excise. Allen & Unwin, 1962.

CLARK, Sir F.
The Central Office of Information. Allen & Unwin, 1970.

EMMERSON, Sir H.C.
The Ministry of Works. Allen & Unwin, 1956.

INCE, Sir G.H.
Ministry of Labour and National Service. Allen & Unwin, 1960.

JEFFRIES, Sir C.J.
The Colonial Office. Allen & Unwin, 1956.

JENKINS, Sir G.
The Ministry of Transport and Civil Aviation. Allen & Unwin, 1959.

JOHNSTON, Sir A.
The Inland Revenue. Allen & Unwin, 1965.

ROSEVEARE, H.G.
Treasury. 1660–1870: the foundations of control. 1973.

WILLIS, J.
Parliamentary powers of English government departments. 1933 repr. Harvard U.P., 1968.

MURRAY, Sir G.E.P.
The Post Office. Allen & Unwin, 1927.

NEWSHOLME, Sir A.
The Ministry of Health. Allen & Unwin, 1925.

SETON, Sir M.
The India Office. Allen & Unwin, 1926.

SMITH, Sir H.L.
The Board of Trade. Allen & Unwin, 1928.

TILLEY, Sir J.A.C. & GASELEE, Sir, S.
The Foreign Office. Allen & Unwin, 1933.

TROUP, Sir E.
The Home Office. Allen & Unwin, 1935.

KING, Sir G.S.
The Ministry of Pensions and National Insurance. Allen & Unwin, 1958.

MELVILLE, Sir H.W.
Department of Scientific and Industrial Research. Allen & Unwin, 1962.

MILNE, Sir D.
The Scottish Office and other Scottish Government departments. Allen & Unwin, 1956.

NEWSAM, Sir F.A.
The Home Office. Allen & Unwin, 1954.

SHARP, Lady
The Ministry of Housing and Local Government. Allen & Unwin, 1969.

STRANG, Lord
The Foreign Office. Allen & Unwin, 1955.

WINNIFRITH, Sir A.J.D.
Ministry of Agriculture, Fisheries and Food. Allen & Unwin, 1962.

GOVERNMENT LIABILITY
See also Crown.

Texts

HOGG, P.
Liability of the Crown in Australia, New Zealand and the United Kingdom. Sweet & Maxwell, 1972.

JAYSON, L.S.
Handling federal tort claims. Bender, 1964. 2 vols. Looseleaf.

STREET, H.
Government liability: a comparative study. Cambridge U.P., 1953.

GUARANTEES
See also Contract; Mortgages.

Encyclopaedias and periodicals

Statutes in Force. Group: Contract.
Halsbury's Laws of England. 4ed. vol 20.
Halsbury's Statutes of England. 3ed. see index vol.
The Digest. vol.25.

Encyclopaedia of Court Forms in Civil Proceedings (Atkin). 2ed. vol.20.
Encyclopaedia of Forms and Precedents. 4ed. mainly vol. 9.
Law Quarterly Review. 1885–

Texts

CHITTY, J.
Chitty on contract. 25ed. Sweet & Maxwell, 1983.

COLINVAUX, R.
The law of insurance. 5ed. Sweet & Maxwell, 1984.

HEWITSON, T.
Suretyship: its origin and history in outline. Law Book Co., 1928 (Australia).

HOLDEN, J.M.
The law and practice of banking. Vol. 2: securities for bankers' advances. 6ed. Pitman, 1980.

ROWLATT, Sir S.A.T.
The law of principal and surety. 4ed. Sweet & Maxwell, 1982.

SNELL, E.H.T.
Principles of equity. 28ed. Sweet & Maxwell, 1982.

HABEAS CORPUS
See also Certiorari; Constitutional Law; Prerogative Orders.

Encyclopaedias and periodicals

Statutes in Force. Group: Rights of the Subject.
Halsbury's Laws of England. 4ed. vols. 11, 37.
Halsbury's Statutes of England. 3ed. vol.8. The Digest mainly vol.16.
Encyclopaedia of Court Forms in Civil Proceedings (Atkin). 2ed. mainly vol.14.

Criminal Law Review. 1954–
Irish Jurist. 1935–
Law Quarterly Review. 1885–
Modern Law Review. 1937–
Stone's Justices Mannual. Annual.

Texts

ARCHBOLD, J.F.
Pleading, evidence and practice in criminal cases. 41ed. Sweet & Maxwell, 1982.

BENNETT, A.
Habeas corpus. Faber, 1973.

DUKER, W.F.
Constitutional history of habeas corpus. Greenwood, 1980.

HARVEY, D.A.C.
Law of habeas corpus in Canada. Butterworths, 1974.

HURD, R.C.
Treatise on the right of personal liberty and on the writ of habeas corpus. 2ed. 1876 repr. Da Capo P., 1972.

KUTNER, L.
World habeas corpus. Oceana, 1962 (USA).

SHARPE, R.J.
The law of habeas corpus. Oxford U.P., 1976.

SOKOL, R.P.
Federal habeas corpus. 2ed. Michie, 1969 (USA).

HALL MARKING

Encyclopaedias

Statutes in Force. Group: Sale of Goods.
Halsbury's Laws of England. 4ed. vol. 48.
Halsbury's Statutes of England. 3ed. vol.43.
The Digest. vol.46.

Texts

DE CASTRO, J.P.
The law and practice of hall marking gold and silver wares. 2ed. Crosby Lockwood, 1935.

RYLAND, A.
Assay of gold and silver wares: account of the laws relating to the standards and marks and of the assay offices. 1852.

WILKINSON, W.R.T.
History of hall marks. Queen Anne P., 1975.

HIGHWAYS AND BRIDGES

Encyclopaedias and periodicals

Statutes in Force, Group: Town and Country Planning, sub-group 1.
Halsbury's Laws of England. 4ed. vol. 21.
Halsbury's Statutes of England. 3ed. mainly vols. 15, 41.
The Digest, vol.26.
Encyclopaedia of Court Forms in Civil Proceedings (Atkin). 2ed mainly vol.10.

Encyclopaedia of Forms and Precedents. 4ed. vol.10.

Cambridge Law Journal. 1921–
Law Quarterly Review. 1885–
Local Government Review. 1971–
Stone's Justices Manual. Annual.

Texts

COMMITTEE ON CONSOLIDATION OF HIGHWAY LAW
Report (Reading). HMSO, 1958/59 (Cmnd. 630).

COULSON, H.J.W. & FORBES, U.A.
Law of water, sea, tidal and inland and land drainage. 6ed. Sweet & Maxwell, 1952.

HIJACKING

CROASDELL, W.C.
Law of private street works and law of highways in relation thereto. 2ed. Hamish Hamilton, 1947.

CROSS, C.A. (ed.)
Encyclopaedia of highway law and practice. Sweet & Maxwell, 1965. 3 vols. Looseleaf.

CROSS, C.A. & GARNER, J.F.
Highway law including the Highways Act 1959, annotated. Sweet & Maxwell, 1960.

CROSS, C.A. & SAUVAIN, S.
The Highways Act 1980. Sweet & Maxwell, 1981.

DAVIES, K.
The concise law of highways. Butterworths, 1969.

GARDINER, E.J.O.
Private street works. Solicitors' Law Stat. Soc., 1936.

GARNER, J.F.
Road charges. 4ed. Oyez, 1974 (Practice notes no.37).

HARRIS, R. & RYAN, G.
An outline of the law relating to common land and public access to the countryside. Sweet & Maxwell, 1967.

HEAP, D. (ed.)
Encyclopaedia of the law of town and country planning. Sweet & Maxwell. 4 vols. Looseleaf.

MAHAFFY, R.P. & DODSON, D.
Road traffic. 3ed. Butterworths, 1981. 2 vols.

MARNHAM, B.
Public Utilities and Street Works Act, 1950. Knight, 1952.

MAZENGARB, O.C.
Negligence on the highway. 4ed. Butterworths, 1962.

PARRISH, H.
The law relating to private street works. Butterworths, 1979.

PARRISH, H.
Public Utilities and Street Works Act 1950. Butterworths, 1950.

PRATT, J.T. & MACKENZIE, W.W.
Law of highways, main roads and bridges. 21ed. Butterworths, 1967 & supp.

TRANSPORT, DEPARTMENT OF
Review of highway inquiry procedures: report. HMSO, 1978 (Cmnd. 7133).

HIJACKING

See also Aviation; Piracy.

Encyclopaedias

Halsbury's Laws of England. 4ed. see index vol.
Halsbury's Statutes of England 3ed. vol.41.

Texts

AGRAWALA, S.K.
Aircraft hijacking and international law. Tripathi:Oceana, 1973.

BASSIOUNI, M.C. & NANDA, V.P.
A treatise on international criminal law. vol.1. C.C.Thomas, 1973 (USA).

CLYNE, P.
An anatomy of skyjacking. Transatlantic, 1974.

COMMONWEALTH SECRETARIAT
Three international conventions on hijacking and offences on board aircraft. 1982.

JOYNER, N.D.
Aerial hijacking as an international crime. Oceana, 1974 (USA).

McWHINNEY, E.
Aerial piracy and international law. Oceana, 1971 (USA).

McWHINNEY, E.
The illegal diversion of aircraft and international law. Oceana, 1975 (USA).

SHUBBER, S.
Jurisdiction over crimes on board aircraft. Nijhoff, 1973.

HINDU LAW

Texts

CHADHA, P.N.
Hindu law. 4ed. Eastern Book Co., 1978 (India).

DERRETT, J.D.M.
Introduction to modern Hindu law. Oxford U.P., 1963.

DERRETT, J.D.M. & DUNCAN, M.
Essays in classical and modern Hindu law. Brill, 1976–78. 4 vols.

GOUR, H.S.
Hindu code. 5ed. Sardar Patel, 1973 (India). 4 vols.

GOUR, H.S.
Hindu law of marriage and divorce. Sardar Patel, 1974 (India).

MAYNE, J.D.
Treatise on Hindu law and usage. 11ed. Higginbothams, 1950.

MULLA, Sir D.F.
Principles of Hindu law. 12e. Tripathi, 1959 (India).

SCHOLAR, A.
Hindu law. 10ed. Eastern Book Co., 1968 (India).

SEN, P.
The general principles of Hindu jurisprudence. Calcutta U.P., 1918.

SETHI, R.B. & GOPALA-KRISHNA, T.P.
Hindu Succession Act. 5ed. Law Book Co., 1974.

VIRDI, P.K.
Grounds for divorce in Hindu and English law. Verry, 1973 (India).

HISTORY

See also Primitive Law.

Periodicals

Cambridge Law Journal. 1921–
Irish Jurist. 1935–
The Journal of Legal History. 1980–
Juridical Review. 1889–

Law Quarterly Review. 1885–
Modern Law Review. 1937–
Northern Ireland Legal Quarterly. 1964–

General texts

ALLEN, Sir C.K.
Law in the making. 7ed. Cambridge U.P., 1964.

AMES, J.B.
Lectures on legal history and miscellaneous legal essays. Harvard U.P., 1913.

BABINGTON, A.
Rule of law in Britain from the Roman occupation to the present day. Rose, 1978.

BAKER, J.H.
Introduction to English legal history. 2ed. Butterworths, 1979.

BAKER, J.H. (ed.)
Legal records and the historian: conference papers. Royal Historical Society, 1979.

BONFIELD, L.
Marriage settlements, 1601–1740: the adoption of the strict settlement. Cambridge U.P., 1983 (Cambridge studies in legal history).

BRYCE, J.
Studies in history and jurisprudence. Oxford U.P., 1901. 2 vols.

CAMERON, J.R.
Frederick William Maitland and the history of English law. Greenwood, 1977.

CASTLES, A.C.
Introduction to Australian legal history. Sweet & Maxwell, 1971.

HISTORY

CURZON, L.B.
English legal history. 2ed. Macdonald & Evans, 1979.

FIFOOT, C.H.S.
English law and its background. Bell, 1932.

HARDING, A.
Law making and law makers in British history. Royal Historical Society, 1980.

HARDING, A. (ed.)
Shropshire Eyre Roll of 1256. Selden Society, 1981.

HARDING, A.
A social history of English law. Penguin, 1966.

HOLDSWORTH, Sir W.S.
Essays in law and history. Oxford U.P., 1946.

HOLDSWORTH, Sir W.S.
A history of English law. 7ed. Sweet & Maxwell, 1956–1972. 17 vols.

IVES, E.W.
Common lawyers of prereformation England: Thomas Kebell – a case study. Cambridge U.P., 1983.

IVES, E.W. & MANCHESTER, P.H.
Law, litigants and the legal profession. Conference papers. Royal Historical Society.

JACKSON, A.M.
Glasgow Dean of Guild Courts: a history. Glasgow Dean of Guild Laws & Trustees, 1983.

JENKS, E.
A short history of English law. 6ed. Methuen, 1949.

KIRALFY, A.K.R. & MACQUEEN, H.L. (eds.)
New perspectives in Scottish legal history. F. Cass., 1984.

McGREGOR, O.R.
Social history and law reform. Stevens, 1981.

MANCHESTER, A.M.
Sources of English legal history, 1750–1950. Butterworths, 1984.

MANCHESTER, A.M.
Modern legal history of England and Wales, 1750–1950. Butterworths, 1980.

MEEKINGS, C.A.F.
Studies in thirteenth-century justice and administration. Hambledon Press, 1982.

MILSOM, S.F.C.
Historical foundations of the common law. Butterworths, 1969.

MILSOM, S.F.C.
The nature of Blackstone;s achievement. Selden Study, 1981 (Lecture series).

PIKE, L.O.
A history of crime in England. Smith, Elder & Co., 1873–76. 2 vols.

PLUCKNETT, T.F.T.
Concise history of the common law. 5ed. Butterworths, 1956.

PLUCKNETT, T.F.T.
Early English legal literature. Cambridge U.P., 1958 repr. Seer.

PLUCKNETT, T.F.T.
Studies in English legal history. Hambledon P., 1983.

POLLOCK, F. & MAITLAND, F.W.
History of English law before the time of Edward I. Cambridge U.P., 1968. 2 vols.

POTTER, H. & KIRALFY, A.K.R.
Historical introduction to English law and its institutions. 4ed. Sweet & Maxwell, 1958.

POUND, R.
Interpretation of legal history. Cambridge U.P., 1946.

PUBLIC RECORD OFFICE
Records of the general eyre. HMSO, 1983.

RUBIN, G.R. & SUGERMAN, D.
Law, economy and society: essays in the history of English law, 1750–1914. Professional Books, 1983.

RULE, J. (ed.)
Outside the law: studies in crime and order, 1650–1850. University of Exeter, 1983.

STEPHEN, J.F.
History of criminal law in England. repr. Hein, 1977. 3 vols.

STUBBS, W.
Constitutional history of England in its origins and development. Selections. Cass, 1979.

TANNER, J.R.
English constitutional conflicts of the seventeenth century, 1603–89. Greenwood Press, 1983.

TIERNEY, B.
Religion, law and the growth of constitutional through, 1150–1650. Cambridge U.P., 1982.

VINOGRADOFF, Sir P.
Essays in legal history. Oxford U.P., 1913.

VINOGRADOFF, Sir P.
Oxford studies in social and legal history. Oxford U.P., 1921.

WHITELOCK, D.
English historical documents. Cambridge U.P., 1955.

WIENER, F.B.
Uses and abuses of legal history. Quaritch, 1961.

WINDEYER, W.J.V.
Lectures on legal history. 2ed. Law Book Co., 1949 (Australia).

WINFIELD, Sir P.H.
The chief sources of English legal history. Harvard U.P., 1925.

WINFIELD, Sir P.H.
Select legal essays. Sweet & Maxwell, 1952.

Early and medieval law

ADAMS, G.B.
Council and courts in Anglo-Norman England. 1926 repr. Russell & Russell, 1965.

ADAMS, G.B.
The origin of the English constitution. Yale U.P.

ASHTON, R.
City and the court, 1603-43. Cambridge U.P., 1979.

ATTENBOROUGH, F.L.
Laws of the earliest English Kings. 1922 repr. Russell & Russell, 1963.

BALDWIN, J.F.
King's Council in England during the middle ages. Oxford U.P., 1913.

BELL, H.E.
Introduction to the history and record of the Court of Wards and Liveries. Cambridge U.P., 1953.

BELLAMY, J.G.
Crime and public order in England in the later middle ages. Routledge, 1973.

BELLAMY, J.G.
The law of treason in England in the later middle ages. Cambridge U.P., 1970.

BLATCHER, M.
Court of King's Bench, 1450-1550: a study in self help. Athlone P., 1978.

BOLLAND, W.C.
Manual of year book studies. Cambridge U.P., 1925.

BRACTON, H.de
De legibus et consuetudinibus angliae ed. by G.E. Woodbine. Flesher & Young, 1640.

CAM, H.M.
The hundred and the hundred rolls. Merlin P., 1930.

CAM, H.M.
Law-finders and law-makers in medieval England: collected studies in legal and constitutional history. Merlin P., 1962.

CAM, H.M.
Liberties and communities in medieval England. Merlin P., 1944.

CHEW, H.M.
English ecclesiastical tenants in chief and knight service. Oxford U.P., 1932.

FORTESCUE, Sir J.
De laudibus legum angliae. Cambridge U.P., 1942.

GLANVILLE, R. de
Tractatus de legibus et consuetudinibus regni angliae. Wight, 1604.

HAND, G.J.
English law in Ireland, 1290-1324. Cambridge U.P., 1967.

HARDING, A.
The law courts of medieval England. Allen & Unwin, 1973.

HARMER, F.E.
Anglo-Saxon writs. Barnes & Noble, 1952.

HELMHOLZ, R.H.
Marriage litigation in medieval England. Cambridge U.P., 1974.

HENRY, R.L.
Contracts in local courts of medieval England. Longmans, Green, 1926.

HUNNISETT, R.F.
The medieval coroner. Cambridge U.P., 1961.

JOLLIFFE, J.E.A.
Constitutional history of medieval England from the English settlement to 1485. 3ed. Blackwell, 1954.

JONES, W.J.
The Elizabethan Court of Chancery.
Oxford U.P., 1967.

KEETON, G.W.
The Norman Conquest and the common law. Barnes & Noble, 1966.

LAPSLEY, G.F.
Crown, community and parliament in the middle ages. Blackwell, 1951.

LODGE, E.C. & THORNTON, G.A.
English constitutional documents. 1307–1485. Cambridge U.P., 1935.

MAITLAND, F.W.
Domesday book and beyond: three essays on the early history of England. Cambridge U.P., 1897 repr. Collins, 1960.

MORRIS, W.A.
The mediaeval English sheriff to 1300. Manchester U.P., 1927.

OGILVIE, Sir C.
King's government and the common law, 1471–1641. Greenwood, 1978.

REEVES, J.
History of the English law, from the time of the Saxons, to the end of the reign of Philip and Mary. 2ed. 1787 repr. Rothman, 1969. 4 vols.

RICHARDSON, W.C.
History of the court of augmentations, 1536–1554. Louisiana U.P., 1961.

STENTON, D.M.
English justice between the Norman Conquest and the Great Charter, 1066–1215. American Philos. Soc., 1965.

THOMAS, A.H.
Calendar of early Mayor's Court rolls, 1298–1412. Cambridge U.P., 1924–32. 4 vols.

ULLMANN, W.
Law and politics in the middle ages. Hodder, 1975.

ULLMANN, W.
The medieval idea of law. Harper, 1946.

VEALL, D.
The popular movement for law reform. 1640–1660. Oxford U.P., 1970.

WEST, F.J.
Justiciarship in England, 1066–1232. Cambridge U.P., 1966.

WILKINSON, B.
Studies in the constitutional history of the 14th & 15th centuries. Manchester U.P., 1937.

Miscellaneous

BELLAMY, J.G.
Tudor law of treason: an introduction. Routledge & Kegan Paul, 1978.

BERCHMAN, E.
Victims of piracy: Admiralty Court, 1575–1678. Hamilton, 1979.

BREWER, J. & STYLES, J.
Ungovernable people? English and their law in the seventeenth and eighteenth centuries. Hutchinson, 1979.

COCKBURN, J.S. (ed.)
Crime in England, 1550–1800. Methuen, 1977.

CORNISH, W.R. and others
Crime and law in 19th century Britain. Irish U.P., 1977.

DICEY, A.V.
Lectures on the relation between law and public opinion during the nineteenth century. 1914 repr. Macmillan, 1962.

DOWDELL, E.G.
A hundred years of quarter sessions: the government of Middlesex, 1660–1760. Cambridge U.P., 1932.

ENEVER, F.A.
History of the law of distress for rent and damge feasant. Routledge, 1931.

FIFOOT, C.H.S.
History of sources of the common law: tort and contract. Stevens, 1949.

GARDINER, S.R. (ed.)
Constitutional documents of the puritan revolution, 1625–60. 3ed. Oxford U.P., 1980.

GATRELL, V.A.C.
Crime and the law: the social history of crime in Western Europe since 1500. Europa, 1980.

GLASSEY, L.K.J.
Politics and the appointment of Justices of the Peace, 1675–1720. Oxford U.P., 1979.

GOEBEL, J.
Felony and misdemeanour: a study in the historyof English criminal procedure. Commonwealth Fund, 1937 (USA).

GUY, J.A.
The Cardinal's Court: the impact of Thomas Wolsey in Star Chamber. Harvester P., 1977.

HIBBERT, C.
Roots of evil: social history of crime and punishment. Greenwood, 1978.

JACKSON, R.M.
History of quasi-contract in English law. Cambridge U.P., 1936.

JONES, G.H.
History of the law of charity, 1532–1827. Cambridge U.P., 1969.

KNAFLA, L.A.
Law and politics in Jacobean England: tracts of Lord Chancellor Ellesmere. Cambridge U.P., 1977.

NENNER, H.
By colour of law: legal culture and constitutional politics in England, 1660–89. Univ. of Chicago P., 1977.

PHILIPS, D.
Crime and authority in Victorian England. Croom Helm, 1977.

PLUCKNETT, T.F.T.
Edward I and criminal law. Cambridge U.P., 1960.

PLUCKNETT, T.F.T.
Legislation of Edward I. Oxford U.P., 1949.

PREST, W.
Lawyers in early modern Europe and America. Croom Helm, 1981.

PUTNAM, B.
The place in legal history of Sir William Shareshull. Cambridge U.P., 1950.

RADZINOWICZ, L.
A history of the English criminal law and its administration from 1750. Stevens, 1948–68. 4 vols.

ROBSON, R.
The attorney in the 18th century. Cambridge U.P., 1959.

SMITH, J.H.
Cases and materials on the development of legal institutions. West, 1965 (USA).

STEPHEN, J.F.
A history of the criminal law of England. Macmillan, 1883. 3 vols.

WEISSER, M.
Crime and criminality in early modern Europe. Harvester P., 1979.

WHITELOCK, D.
Anglo-Saxon wills. Cambridge U.P., 1930

WINFIELD, P.H.
History of conspiracy and abuse of legal procedure. Cambridge U.P., 1921.

HOMICIDE

See also Criminal Law; Euthanasia.

Encyclopaedias and periodicals

Statutes in Force. Group: Criminal Law, 4: Offences Against the Person.
Halsbury's Laws of England. 4ed. vol.11.
Halsbury's Statutes of England. 3ed. vol.8.
The Digest. see index vol.

British Journal of Criminology. 1960–
Criminal Law Review. 1954–

The Criminologist. 1966–
International Journal of Criminology and Penology. 1973–
Journal of Criminal Law. 1936–
Modern Law Review. 1937–

Texts

BIGGS, J.
Guilty mind: psychiatry and the law of homicide. Johns Hopkins P., 1955.

BRESLER, F.S.
Scales of justice. Weidenfeld & N., 1973.

CRIMINAL LAW REVISION COMMITTEE
Second report: suicide. HMSO, 1960 (Cmnd. 1187).

CRIMINAL LAW REVISION COMMITTEE
Twelfth report: penalty for murder. HMSO, 1973 (Cmnd. 5184).

DELL, S.
Murder into manslaughter. Oxford U.P., 1984.

ELWYN-JONES, Lord
On trial: seven intriguing cases of capital crime. Macdonald & James, 1978.

GIBSON, E.
Homicide in England and Wales, 1967–1971. HMSO, 1975.

GIBSON, E. & KLEIN, S.
Murder 1957 to 1968: a Home Office statistical division report on murder in England and Wales. HMSO, 1969.

GOODMAN, J.
Posts-mortem: the correspondence of murder. 1971.

HAVARD, J.D.J.
The detention of secret homicide. Macmillan, 1960.

HOLLIS, C.
The Homicide Act. Gollancz, 1964.

KUTASH, I.L.
Violence: perspectives on murder and aggression. Jossey-Bass, 1979.

MORRIS, T. & BLOM-COOPER, L.J.
A calendar of murder: criminal homicide in England since 1957. Joseph, 1964.

NEUSTATTER, W.L.
The mind of the murderer. Johnson, 1957.

NEW ZEALAND PROPERTY LAW AND EQUITY REFORM COMMITTEE
The effect of culpable homicide on rights of succession: report. 1976.

WEST, D.J.
Murder followed by suicide. Heinemann, 1965.

WOLFGANG, M.E.
Studies in homicide. Wiley, 1968.

HOMOSEXUALITY

See also Sexual Offences.

Encyclopaedias and periodicals

Halsbury's Laws of England. 4ed. see index vol.
Halsbury's Statutes of England. 3ed. vol.8.

Bulletin of the Campaign for Homosexual Equality. 1976– (as CHE, 1971–76).

Texts

BAILEY, D.S.
Homosexuality and the Western Christian tradition. Longmans, Green, 1955.

BANCROFT, J.H.
Deviant sexual behaviour: modification and assessment. Oxford U.P., 1974.

BAUBY, C.
Between consenting adults: dialogue for intimate living. Macmillan, 1973.

BEER, C., JEFFFREY, R. & MUNYARD, T.
Gay workers: trade unions and the law. N.C.C.L., 1981.

CAMPAIGN FOR HOMOSEXUAL EQUALITY
The case for homosexual law reform. 1976.

CRANE, P.
Gays and the law. Pluto Press, 1982.

CURRY, H. & CLIFFORD, D.
Legal guide for lesbian and gay couples. Addison-Wesley, 1981.

FERRIS, D.
Homosexuality and the social services. N.C.C.L., 1977.

GALLOWAY, B. (ed.)
Discrimination against gay people in modern Britain. Routledge & Kegan Paul, 1983.

HOME OFFICE
Report of the Departmental Committee on Homosexual Offences and Prostitution (Wolfenden). HMSO, 1957 (Cmnd. 247).

HONORE, T.
Sex law. Duckworth, 1978.

PARKER, W. (ed.)
Homosexuality: a select bibliography of over 3000 items. 1972.

STANDING ADVISORY COMMISSION ON HUMAN RIGHTS
Report on the law in Northern Ireland relating to divorce and homosexuality. HMSO, 1977.

WEST, D.J.
Homosexuality. 2ed. Duckworth, 1977 (USA).

WILSON, P.
The sexual dilemma: abortion, homosexuality, prostitution and criminal threshold. Queensland U.P., 1971 (Australia).

HONG KONG

Encyclopaedias and periodicals

The Laws of Hongkong. 1966–

Hong Kong Law Journal. 1971–
Hong Kong Law Reports. 1905–

Justitia: Hong Kong University Law Review. 1972–

Texts

BRAMWELL, H.
Conveyancing in Hong Kong. Butterworths, 1981.

NORTON-KYSHE, J.W.
The history of the laws and courts of Hongkong. Unwin, 1898.

PEGG, L.
Family law in Hong Kong. Butterworths, 1981.

WESLEY-SMITH, P.
Legal literature in Hong Kong. Univ. of Hong Kong, 1979.

WILLOUGHBY, P.
Hong Kong revenue law. Bender, 1981. Looseleaf.

HOSPITALS

See also Doctors; Medical Jurisprudence; National Health; National Insurance; Nursing.

Encyclopaedias and periodicals

Statutes in Force. Groups: Public Health; Social Security and Health Services.
Halsbury's Laws of England. 4ed. see index vol.
Halsbury's Statutes of England. 3ed see index vol.
The Digest. see index vol. Encyclopaedia of Court Forms in Civil Proceedings (Atkin). 2ed. see index vol.

Encyclopaedia of Forms and Precedents. 4ed. see index vol.

British Medical Journal. 1957–
Community Health. 1969–
Medicine Science and the Law. 1960–
Public Health. 1888–

Texts

BRENNAN, J.L.
Medico-legal problems in hospital practice. Ravenswood, 1980.

BRIDGMAN, R.F. & ROEMER, M.I.
Hospital legislation and hospital systems. W.H.O., 1972.

FARNDALE, W.A.J.
Law on hospital consent forms. Ravenswood, 1979.

FARNDALE, W.A.J. & LARMAN, E.C.
Legal liability for claims arising from hospital treatment. Ravenswood, 1973.

FARNDALE, W.A.J. & RUSSELL, S.
Law on accidents to health service staff and volunteers. Ravenswood, 1977 (Case studies on health service management law and practice).

HEALTH AND SOCIAL SECURITY, DEPARTMENT OF
Guide to good practices in hospital administration. HMSO, 1971.

HOSPITALS Directory of England and Wales. Annual.

NICHOLS, J.E.
Guide to hospital security. Gower Pub. Co., 1983.

PAINE, L. (ed.)
Hospital liability. International Hospital Fedn., 1981.

ROYAL COMMISSION ON THE NATIONAL HEALTH SERVICE
Report (Morrison). HMSO, 1979 (Cmnd. 7615).

ROYAL COMMISSION ON THE NATIONAL HEALTH SERVICE
The working of the National Health Service. HMSO, 1978.

SCOTTISH HOME & HEALTH DEPARTMENT
Administrative practice of Hospital Boards in Scotland: report. HMSO, 1966.

SPELLER, S.R.
Law relating to hospitals and kindred institutions. 6ed. Lewis, 1978.

WARREN, D.G.
Problems in hospital law. 3ed. Aspen, 1979 (USA).

WILLIAMS, B.
Occupiers' Liability Act 1957 and the liability of hospitals. Ravenswood, 1977 (Case studies on health service management law and practice).

WORLD HEALTH ORGANISATION
Hospital legislation and hospital systems. 1973.

HOUSING

See also Building and Engineering Law: Flats; Landlord and Tenant; Rent; Town and Country Planning.

Encyclopaedias and periodicals

Statutes in Force. Group: Housing.
Halsbury's Laws of England. 4ed. vol. 22.
Halsbury's Statutes of England. 3ed. see index vol.
The Digest. see index vol.
Encyclopaedia of Court Forms in Civil Proceedings (Atkin). 2ed. vol.20.
Encyclopaedia of Forms and Precedents 4ed. vol.10.

Conveyancer and Property Lawyer. 1936–
Estates Gazette. 1858–
Housing Law Reports. 1982–
Legal Action (formerly L.A.G. Bulletin). 1973–
Local Government Review. 1971–

Texts

ALDRIDGE, T.M.
Housing Act, 1980: practical guide. Oyez, 1980.

ARDEN, A.
Housing Act, 1980. Oyez, 1980.

ARDEN, A.
Housing: security and rent control. Sweet & Maxwell, 1978.

ARDEN, A. & PARTINGTON, M.
Housing law. Sweet & Maxwell, 1981 supp. 1984.

AVGHERIONOS, G. & TELLING, A.E.
Housing Repairs and Rents Act, 1954. Estates Gazette, 1954.

CARNWATH, R.
Guide to the Housing (Homeless Persons) Act 1977. Knight, 1978.

CLARKE, J.J.
Law of housing and planning. 5ed. Pitman, 1949.

COCHRANE, R.G.A.
Law of housing in Scotland. Hodge, 1977.

CUTTING, M.
Housing rights handbook. Penguin, 1979.

ENCYCLOPAEDIA of housing law and practice. Sweet & Maxwell. 3 vols. Looseleaf.

GARNER, J.F.
Alteration or conversion of houses. 5ed. Oyez, 1981 (Practice notes no.47).

HADDEN, T.B.
Housing: repairs and improvements. Sweet & Maxwell, 1979.

HADDEN, T.B. & TRIMBLE, W.D.
Housing law in Northern Ireland. SLS Legal Pubns. (NI), 1984.

HAWKINS, N.
Housing grants: a guide to improvement and other grants. Kogan Page, 1982.

HILL, H.A.
Complete law of housing. 4ed. Butterworths, 1947.

HOATH, D.C.
Council housing. 2ed. Sweet & Maxwell, 1982.

HOUSING CORPORATION
Annual report.

HUTTMAN, E.D.
Housing and social services for the elderly: social policy trends. Praeger, 1977.

JACOBS, S.
Right to a decent house. Routledge, 1976.

LEGAL ACTION GROUP
Law in a housing crisis: a guide to the law and practice on security, rent, repairs, and rights to housing in marriage breakdowns. 1975.

LIELL, P.
Council houses and the Housing Act 1980. 1981.

LONDON HOUSING AID CENTRE
Shorthold tenancies. 1979.

MACEY, J.P.
Housing Act 1974. Butterworths, 1974.

MACEY, J.P.
Housing Finance Act 1972. Butterworths, 1972.

MACEY, J.P. & BAKER, C.V.
Housing management. 2ed. Butterworths, 1973.

MAGNUS, S.W.
Housing Repairs and Rents Act 1954. Butterworths, 1954.

MAGOR, D.L. & THROWER, C.K.
Housing benefits: law and practice. Rating & Valuation Assoc., 1984.

MARTEN, D. & LUFF, P.
Guarantees for new homes: guide to the National House Building Council scheme. 2ed. 1981.

NATIONAL CAMPAIGN FOR THE HOMELESS
Facts on council house sales. 1979.

RAYNSFORD, N. & McGURK, P.
Guide to housing benefits. London Housing Centre, 1982.

SMITH, M.E.H.
A guide to housing. 2ed. supp. Main changes in housing law, 1977–80. Housing Centre Trust, 1981.

SMITH, P.F.
Housing Act 1980. Butterworths, 1980.

SMYTHE, J.
Homelessness: a digest of court decisions. Shelter, 1982.

TIPLADY, D.
Housing welfare law. Oyez, 1975.

WEST, W.A.
The law of housing. 4ed. Estates Gazette, 1979.

HOUSING ASSOCIATIONS

Encyclopaedias and periodicals

Halsbury's Laws of England. 4ed. see index vol.

Halsbury's Statutes of England. 3ed. mainly vol.44.

Encyclopaedia of Court Forms in Civil Proceedings (Atkin). 2ed. vol.21.

Encyclopaedia of Forms and Precedents. 4ed. vol.10.

Conveyancer & Property Lawyer. 1936–
Estates Gazette. 1858–
Local Government Review. 1971–
Voluntary Housing.

Texts

BAKER, C.V.
Housing Associations. Estates Gazette, 1976.

CENTRAL HOUSING ADVISORY COMMITTEE
Housing Associations. 1971.

ENVIRONMENT, DEPARTMENT OF THE
Final report on the Working Party on Housing Co-operatives (Campbell). HMSO, 1976.

HANDS, J.
Housing co-operatives. 1975.

HOUSING CORPORATION
Practice notes for Housing Societies and Associations. 1972 & supp. Better housing. 1972.

NATIONAL BUILDING AGENCY
Housing Associations: a review of recent trends. 1974.

NATIONAL BUILDING AGENCY
Increasing conversion capability: management study for one housing association. 1974.

NATIONAL FEDERATION OF HOUSING ASSOCIATIONS
Co-ownership Housing Associations. 1975.

NATIONAL FEDERATION OF HOUSING ASSOCIATIONS
A guide to Housing Associations. 1975.

PAGE, D.
Co-operative housing handbook. 1975.

UNITED NATIONS
Nonprofit Housing Associations: organization, financing and structural integration. 1976.

WADDILOVE, L.E.
Housing Associations. 1962.

HOVERCRAFT

See also Aviation; Shipping.

Encyclopaedias

Halsbury's Laws of England. 4ed. vol. 43.
Halsbury's Statutes of England. 3ed. see index vol.
Encyclopaedia of Court Forms in Civil Proceedings (Atkin). 2ed. see index vol.

Texts

KOVATS, L.J.
The law of hovercraft. Lloyds, 1975.

MARGO, R.D.
Aviation insurance: the law and practice of aviation insurance including hovercraft and satellite insurance. Butterworths, 1980.

HUMAN RIGHTS

See also Bill of Rights; Civil Rights and Liberties.

Encyclopaedias and periodicals

Halsbury's Laws of England. 4ed. vol. 18.

European Human Rights Reports. 1979–
Human Rights Bulletin. 1969–
Human Rights Journal. 1968–
Human Rights Review. 1976–
Legal Action (formerly L.A.G. Bulletin). 1973–
Rights (formerly Civil Liberty). 1977–
Universal Human Rights. 1979–

Texts

AMNESTY INTERNATIONAL
Workshop on human rights: reports and recommendations. 1975.

BEDDARD, R.
Human rights and Europe. 2ed. Sweet & Maxwell, 1980.

BRIDGE, J.W. & LASOK, D.
Fundamental rights. Sweet & Maxwell, 1973.

BROWNLIE, I.
Basic documents on human rights. 2ed. Oxford U.P., 1981.

CAREY, J.
International protection of human rights. Oceana, 1968 (USA).

CAREY, J.
United Nations protection of civil and political rights. Syracuse, 1970 (USA).

CASTBERG, F.
European Convention on Human Rights. Sijthoff, 1974.

CLARK, R.S.
A United Nations High Commissioner for human rights. Humanities P., 1972.

CLAUDE, R.P. (ed.)
Comparative human rights. Johns Hopkins P., 1976 (USA).

COUNCIL FOR SCIENCE AND SOCIETY
Scholarly freedom and human rights: the problem of persecution and oppression of science and scientists. Rose, 1977.

COUNCIL OF EUROPE
Conditions of detention and the European Convention on Human Rights and Fundamental Freedoms. HMSO, 1982.

COUNCIL OF EUROPE
European Convention on Human Rights: collected texts. 11ed. 1976.

COUNCIL OF EUROPE
Stock-taking on the European Convention on Human Rights: a periodic note on the concrete results achieved under the Convention. HMSO, 1983.

CRANSTON, M.
What are human rights? Bodley, 1973.

DOWRICK, F.E.
Human rights: problems, perspectives, texts. Saxon House, 1979.

DUPUY, R.J. (ed.)
Right to health as a human right. Sijthoff, 1979.

DRZEMCZEWSKI, A.Z.
European Human Rights Convention in domestic law: a comparative study. Oxford U.P. 1983.

EIDE, A. & SCHOU, A. (eds.)
International protection of human rights. Almqvist & Wiksell, 1968 (Nobel symposium).

EUROPEAN CONVENTION ON HUMAN RIGHTS
Year Book. Annual.

EZEJIOFOR, G.
Protection of human rights under law. Butterworths, 1964.

FAWCETT, J.E.S.
The application of the European Convention on Human Rights. Oxford U.P., 1969.

FLATHMAN, R.E.
The practice of rights. Cambridge U.P., 1977.

GORMLEY, W.P.
Human rights and environment: the need for international co-operation. Sijthoff, 1976.

GOTLIEB, A.E.
Human rights, federalism and minorities. Canadian Inst. of Internat. Affairs, 1970.

HANNUM, H.
Guide to international human rights practice. Macmillan, 1984.

HASS, E.B.
Human rights and international action: the case of freedom of association. Stanford, 1970.

HAKSAR, U.
Minority protection and International Bill of Human Rights. Verry, 1975 (India).

HENKIN, A.H. (ed.)
Human dignity: the internationalisation of human rights. Sijthoff, 1979.

INTERNATIONAL human rights: instruments of the United Nations, 1948–82. Mansell, 1984.

JACOBS, F.G.
The European Convention on Human Rights. Oxford U.P., 1980.

JOYCE, J.A.
Human rights: international documents. Oceana, 1979. 3 vols.

LAUTERPACHT, Sir H.
An International Bill of the rights of man. Columbia U.P., 1945.

LAUTERPACHT, Sir H.
International law and human rights. Garland, 1973.

LILLICH,, R.B. & NEWMAN, F.C.
International human rights: problems of law and policy. Little, Brown, 1979.

LUARD, E. (ed.)
The international protection of human rights. Thames & Hudson, 1967.

McDOUGAL, M.S.
Human rights and world public order: the basic policies of an international law of human dignity. Yale U.P., 1980 (USA).

MERON, T.
Human rights in international law: legal and policy issues. Oxford U.P., 1984. 2 vols.

MIKAELSEN, L.
European protection of human rights: practice and procedure of the European Commission of Human Rights on the admissibility of applications from individuals and states. Sijthoff, 1980.

MOSKOWITZ, M.
International concern with human rights. Sijthoff, 1975.

NATIONAL COUNCIL FOR ONE PARENT FAMILIES
Human rights of those born out of wedlock: conference proceedings. 1968.

NEDJATI, Z.M.
Human rights under the European Convention. North-Holland, 1978.

RAMCHARAN, B.G.
Humanitarian good offices in international law: good offices of the United Nations Secretary General in the field of human rights. Nijhoff, 1983.

RAMCHARAN, B.G.
International law and fact finding in the field of human rights. Nijhoff, 1983.

ROBERTSON, A.H.
Human rights in Europe. 2ed. Manchester U.P., 1977.

ROBERTSON, A.H.
Human rights in national and international law. Manchester U.P., 1968.

ROBERTSON, A.H.
Human rights in the world: an introduction to the study of the international protection of human rights. 2ed. Manchester U.P., 1982.

ROBERTSON, A.H.
Privacy and human rights. Manchester U.P., 1975.

SIEGHART, P.
International law of human rights. Oxford U.P., 1983.

SOHN, L.B. & BUERGENTHAL, T.
Basic documents on international protection and human rights. Bobbs-Merrill, 1973.

STANDING ADVISORY COMMISSION ON HUMAN RIGHTS
The protection of human rights by law in Northern Ireland. Northern Ireland Office, 1977.

TARDU, M.
Human rights: the international petition system, a repertoire of practice. Oceana, 1978 (USA). 3 vols. looseleaf.

TRINDADE, A.A.C.
Application of the rule of exhaustion of local remedies in international law: its rationale in the international protection of individual rights. Cambridge U.P., 1983.

UNESCO
Human rights, comments and interpretations: a symposium. 1973.

UNIFO
International human rights instruments of the United Nations, 1948–1982. Unifo, 1983.

UNITED NATIONS
Human rights: a compilation of international instruments. HMSO, 1983.

UNITED NATIONS
Human rights: a compilation of international instruments of the United Nations. 1973.

UNITED NATIONS
United Nations action in the field of human rights. 1981.

UNITED NATIONS
United Nations and human rights. 1974.

UNITED NATIONS
Yearbook on human rights. Annual.

VALLAT, Sir F. (ed.)
Introduction to the study of human rights. Europa, 1972.

VEEHOVEN, W.A.
Case studies in human rights and fundamental freedoms: a world survey. Nijhoff, 1975. 2 vols.

ZUIJDWIJK, A.J.M.
Petitions to the United Nations about violations of human rights. Gower Pub.Co., 1982.

HUMAN TRANSPLANTS
See also Medical Jurisprudence.

Periodicals

British Medical Journal. 1857–
Medicine Science and the Law. 1960–
Medico-Legal Journal. 1901–

Texts

BARBER, B. and others
Research on human subjects. Russell Sage, 1973 (USA).

FARNDALE, W.A.J.
Law of human transplants and bequest of bodies. White's, 1970.

HERSHEY, N. & MILLER, R.D.
Human experimentation and the law. Aspen, 1979 (USA).

KATZ, J.
Experimentation with human beings. Russell Sage, 1972 (USA).

KATZ, J. & CAPRON, A.M.
Catastrophic disease: who decides what? A psychosocial and legal analysis of the problems posed by hemodialysis and organ transplantation. Russell Sage, 1975 (USA).

NIZSALOVSZKY, E.
Legal approach to organ transplantation and some other extraordinary medical actions. 1974 (USA).

OOSTHUIZEN, G.C.
Ethics of tissue transplantation: a South African approach. Struik, 1972.

RAPAPORT, F.T. & DAUSSET, J. (eds.)
Human transplantation. 1968.

SALIWANCHIK, R.
Legal protection for microbiological and genetic engineering inventions. Addison-Wesley, 1982.

WOLSTENHOLME, G.E.W. & O'CONNOR, M. (eds.)
Law and ethics of transplantation. 1968.

WORLD HEALTH ORGANISATION
Use of human tissues and organs for therapeutic purposes: a survey of existing legislation.

IDENTIFICATION
See also Evidence.

Encyclopaedias

Halsbury's Laws of England. 4ed. see index vol.
The Digest. mainly vol.22.

Texts

CLIFFORD, B.R. & BULL, R.
The psychology of personal identification. Routledge, 1978.

HAIN, P.
Mistaken identity: the wrong face of the law. 1976.

HOME OFFICE
Identification parades and the use of photographs for identification. HMSO, 1978 (Circular no. 109/1978).

HOME OFFICE
Report of the Departmental Committee on Evidence of Identification in Criminal Cases (Devlin). HMSO, 1976.

NATIONAL COUNCIL FOR CIVIL LIBERTIES
Identification parades and procedures: evidence to the Devlin Committee on identification procedures. N.C.C.L., 1974.

ROLPH, C.H.
Personal identify. Joseph, 1957.

SCOTTISH HOME & HEALTH DEPARTMENT
Identification procedures under Scottish criminal law: report by the working group (Bryden). HMSO, 1978 (Cmnd. 7096).

IMMIGRATION

See also Race Relations.

Encyclopaedias and periodicals

Statutes in Force. Group: Immigration.
Halsbury's Laws of England. 4ed. vol.1.
Halsbury's Statutes of England. 3ed. vol.41.
The Digest. see index vol.

Immigration Law: Bulletin of the Immigration Law Practitioners' Association. 1984–
Modern Law Review. 1937–
New Law Journal. 1965– (as Law Journal. 1882–1964).

Texts

BEVAN, V.
British immigration: a legal history. Croom Helm, 1984.

COMMON COUNCIL FOR AMERICAN UNITY
The alien and the immigration law. Greenwood P., 1973 (USA).

EVANS, J.
Immigration law. 2ed. Sweet & Maxwell, 1983.

GOLDSTEIN, R.S.
Immigration law of the United States. Butterworths, 1980.

GRANT, L. & MARTIN, I.
Immigration law and practice. Cobden Trust, 1982.

HARTLEY, T.C.
European Economic Community immigration law. North-Holland, 1978.

INTERNATIONAL BAR ASSOCIATION
Comparative immigration law: seminar. I.B.A., 1979.

MACDONALD, I.A.
Immigration law and practice in the United Kingdom. Butterworths, 1983.

MACDONALD, I.A.
The new immigration law. Butterworths, 1972.

MACDONALD, I.A.
Race relations and immigration law. Butterworths, 1969.

MACDONALD, I.A. & BLAKE, N.J.G.
The new nationality law. Butterworths, 1982.

MOORE, R. & WALLACE, T.
Slamming the door: the administration of immigration control. Martin Robertson, 1975.

SUPPERSTONE, M.
Immigration: law and practice. Oyez, 1983.

UNESCO
Immigrant workers in Europe – their legal status: a comparative study. HMSO, 1982.

IMPEACHMENT

See also Trials.

Texts

BERGER, R.
Impeachment: the constitutional problems.
Harvard U.P., 1973 (USA).

BLACK, C.L.
Impeachment: a handbook. Yale U.P., 1974 (USA).

HOFFER, P.C. & HULL, N.E.H.
Impeachment in America, 1635–1805. Yale U.P., 1984.

TITE, C.G.C.
Impeachment and parliamentary judicature in early Stuart England. Athlone P., 1974.

INCEST

See also Sexual Offences.

Encyclopaedias

Statutes in Force. Group: Criminal Law, 5: Sexual Offences and Obscenity.
Halsbury's Laws of England. 4ed. vol.11.
Halsbury's Statutes of England. 3ed. vol.8.
The Digest. see index vol.

Texts

CLARK, H.H.
Law of domestic relations in the United States. West, 1968.

FOOTE, C., LEVY, R.J. & SANDER, F.E.A.
Cases and materials on family law. 2ed. Little, Brown, 1976 (USA).

HAMBLY, D. & TURNER, J.N.
Cases and materials on Australian family law. Law Book Co., 1971.

HAWKES, D.
Truth about incest. Luxor P., 1972.

HERMAN, J.L.
Father/daughter incest. Havard Univ.P., 1982.

INGLIS, B.D.
Family law. 2ed. Sweet & Maxwell, 1968. vol.1 (New Zealand).

JOSKE, P.E.
Matrimonial causes and marriage law and practice of Australia and New Zealand. 5ed. Butterworths, 1969 & supp.

KULLINGER, J.L.
Incest: the secret passion. 1973 (USA).

MAISCH, H.
Incest. Trans. from German by C. Bearne. Deutsch, 1973.

RUSH, F.
Best kept secrets: sexual abuse of children. Prentice-Hall, 1980 (USA).

INCOME TAX

See also Revenue Law; Tax Havens; Tax Planning.

Encyclopaedias and periodicals

Statutes in Force. Group: Income, Corporation and Capital Gains Taxes.
Halsbury's Laws of England. 4ed. vol.23.
Halsbury's Statutes of England. 3ed. mainly vol.33.
The Digest. vol. 28.

Encyclopaedia of Court Forms in Civil Proceedings (Atkin). 2ed. mainly vol. 34.
Encyclopaedia of Forms and Precedents. 4ed. see index vol.

INCOME TAX

Australian and New Zealand income tax report (AITR). 1936–1968.
British Tax Review. 1956–
Simon's Tax Cases. 1973–
Simon's Tax Intelligence. 1973–
Tax Case Reports. 1875–
Tax Practitioner's Diary. Annual.

Taxation. 1927–
Taxation Reports. 1940–
Taxes. 1922–
Tolley's Income Tax. Annual.
Whillan's Tax Tables and Tax Reckoner. Annual.

Texts

BARRETT, R.I.
Principles of income taxation. 2ed. Butterworths (Australia), 1981.

BEATTIE, C.N.
Elements of the law of income and capital gains taxation. 9ed. Sweet & Maxwell, 1970.

BRITISH tax encyclopaedia. Sweet & Maxwell. 8 vols. (5 Looseleaf.)

BUTTERWORTHS Income Tax Assessment Act and related legislation. Butterworths (Australia), 1983.

BUTTERWORTHS income tax service. Looseleaf.

BUTTERWORTHS yellow tax handbook: income tax, corporation tax and capital gains tax. Annual.

COOPER, J.
Key to income tax. Taxation Pub., 1982.

DE VOIL, P.W.
Tax appeals. Butterworths, 1969.

FARNSWORTH, A.
Addington: author of the modern income tax. Stevens, 1951.

GRUNDY, M.
Tax and the family business. 4ed. Sweet & Maxwell, 1970.

HARRISON, E.R.
Index to tax cases. 6ed. HMSO, 1950. Looseleaf.

INLAND REVENUE
Income taxes outside the United Kingdom. HMSO. Looseleaf.

INLAND REVENUE
Taxes Acts. 4 vols. HMSO. Annual.

KELLY, F.N. & CARMICHAEL, K.S.
Irish income tax and corporation tax. 11ed. HFL, 1980.

MANNIX, E.F. & HARRIS, D.W.
Australian income tax law and practice. Butterworths (Australia). Looseleaf.

MANNIX, E.F. & MANNIX, J.E.
Australian income tax guide. 28ed. Butterworths (Australia), 1983.

MANNIX, E.F. & MANNIX, J.E.
Leading cases in Australian income tax. 4ed. Butterworths (Australia), 1981.

MUSTOE, N.E.
Income tax and landed property. 3ed. Estates Gazette, 1957 supp. 1963.

PAUL, T.F.
Land and income tax handbook. 5ed. Butterworths, 1975 (New Zealand).

PINSON, B.
Revenue law. 15ed. Sweet & Maxwell, 1982 supp. 1983.

POTTER, D.C. & MONROE, H.H.
Tax planning with precedents. 9ed. Sweet & Maxwell, 1982.

PRITCHARD, W.
Income tax. 12ed. Polytech., 1983.

RYAN, K.W.
Manual of the law of income tax in Australia. 5ed. Law Book Co., 1980 supp. 1983.

SABINE, B.E.V.
A history of income tax. Allen & Unwin, 1966.

SAPPIDEEN, R.
Australian income taxation of companies and company distributions. Butterworths (Australia), 1979.

SILKE, A.D., DIVARIS, C. & STEIN, M.L.
South African income tax. 9ed. Juta, 1978 (S.Africa).

SIMON, J.A.
Simon's taxes. 3ed. Butterworths. 9 vols. Looseleaf.

SOLLY, M.
Anatomy of a tax haven, vol. 2: Manx income tax. Tolley, 1979.

SPICER, E.E. & PEGLER, E.C.
Income tax. 30ed. HFL, 1981. Looseleaf.

SUMPTION, A.
Taxation of overseas income and gains. 4ed. Butterworths, 1982.

TOBY, R.A.
Theory and practice of income tax. Sweet & Maxwell, 1978.

TOCH, N.
Income tax. Macdonald & Evans. Annual.

VAN NIEKERIK, A.F.
Income tax in the South African law. Butterworths, 1977. Looseleaf.

WHITEMAN, P.G. & WHEATCROFT, G.S.A.
Income tax. 2ed. Sweet & Maxwell, 1976 supp. 1984.

WILLIAMS, R.G. & MENDES, B.
Comprehensive aspects of taxation. 32ed. Cassell, 1975.

WYLIE, O.P.
Taxation of the family. Butterworths, 1983.

INDIA

Encyclopaedias

Statutes in Force. Group: Commonwealth and Other Territories.
Halsbury's Laws of England. 4ed. mainly vol.6.
Halsbury's Statutes of England. 3ed. see index vol.
The Digest. vol.8.

Texts

AGGARWALA, B.R.
Supreme Court practice and procedure. 3ed. Tripathi, 1978.

AUSTIN, G.
The Indian constitution: cornerstone of a nationa. 2ed. Oxford U.P., 1973.

BHATIA, H.S.
Origin and development of legal and political system in India. Deep & Deep, 1976. 3 vols.

BULCHANDANI, K.R.
Labour law. Himalaya Pub. Co., 1980 (India).

BULCHANDANI, K.R.
Law of partnership, sale of goods and negotiable instruments. Himalaya Pub. Co., 1980 (India).

CHAR, S.V.D.
Readings in the constitutional history of India, 1757–1947. Oxford U.P. (India), 1983.

DATTA, R. (ed.)
Union catalogue of the Central Government of India publications held by libraries in London, Oxford and Cambridge. Mansell, 1970.

DERRETT, J.D.M.
Religion, law and the state in India. Faber, 1968.

DEWAN, P.
Family law: law of marriage and divorce in India. Sterling: Books from India, 1984.

GAJENDRAGADKAR, P.B.
The constitution of India: its philosophy and basic postulates. Univ. of Bombay, 1969.

GLEDHILL, A.
Fundamental rights in India. Stevens, 1955.

GLEDHILL, A.
The Republic of India: the development of its laws and constituion. 2ed. Stevens, 1964.

HASSUMANI, A.P.
Some problems of administrative law in India. Asia Pub. House, 1965.

JAIN, M.P.
Indian constitutional law. 2ed. Tripathi, 1970.

JAIN, H.C.
Indian legal materials. Tripathi, 1970.

JOSHI, R.
The Indian constitution and its working. Sangam Books, 1979 (India).

LINGAT, R.
Classical law of India. California U.P., 1973.

MUKHERJEA, A.J.
Parliamentary procedure in India. 3ed.
Oxford U.P. (India), 1983.

NIGAM, R.C.
Law of crimes in India. Asia Pub. House,
1965. vol.1.

NOORANI, A.G. (ed.)
Public law in India. Vikas, 1982.

PEARL, D.
Interpersonal conflict of laws in India,
Pakistan and Bangladesh. Sweet &
Maxwell, 1981.

PHADKE, Y.D. & SRINIVASAN, R.
Constitution of India; new ed. Amerind
Pub.Co., 1983 (India).

PILLAI, T.K.N.
Law of evidence. Sangam Books, 1979
(India).

PYLEE, M.V.
Constitutional government in India. 2ed.
Asia Pub. House, 1968.

RAJU, V.B.
Commentaries on the constitution of India.
Eastern Book Co., 1977.

SEERVAI, H.M.
Constitutional law of India. 3ed. Sweet &
Maxwell, 1983.

SENGUPTA, S.
Business law of India. Oxford U.P., 1979.

SHUKLA, V.N.
Commentaries on the constitution of India.
6ed. Eastern Book Co., 1981.

SINGH, M.
Constitution of India: studies in
perspecctive. Eastern Book Co., 1975.

SINHA, A.N.
Law of citizenship and aliens in India. Asia
Pub. House, 1962.

SUBRAMANIAN, N.A.
Case law on the Indian constitution.
Sangam Books, 1979 (India).

INDICTMENTS

See also Magistrates; Prosecutions.

Encyclopaedias

Statutes in Force. Group: Criminal Law.
Halsbury's Laws of England. 4ed. vol. 11.
Halsbury's Statutes of England. 3ed. vol.8.
The Digest. mainly vol.14.

Texts

ARCHBOLD, J.F.
Pleading, evidence and practice in criminal
cases. 41ed. Sweet & Maxwell, 1982.

ROSCOE, H.
Criminal evidence: the law, evidence and
practice in criminal cases. 16ed. Stevens,
1952.

ROWLANDS, E.B.B.
Criminal proceedings on indictment and
information. 2ed. Stevens, 1910.

INDUSTRIAL AND PROVIDENT SOCIETIES

See also Insurance

Encyclopaedias

Statutes in Force. Group: Friendly and
Other Societies.
Halsbury's Laws of England. 4ed. vol.24.
Halsbury's Statutes of England. 3ed. vol.14,
17.
The Digest. vol. 28(2).

Encyclopaedia of Court Forms in Civil
Proceedings (Atkin). 2ed. vol.21.
Encyclopaedia of Forms and Precedents.
4ed. vol. 10.

Texts

FULLER, F.B.
Laws relating to Friendly and Industrial Societies. 4ed. Stevens, 1926.

INDUSTRIAL ASSURANCE COMMISSIONER
Guide to the law relating to Friendly Societies and Office of the Industrial Assurance Commssioner. 2ed. 1976.

PRATT, F.T.
Friendly and Industrial Societies. 15ed. Stevens, 1931.

REGISTRY OF FRIENDLY SOCIETIES
Guide to the law relating to Industrial and Provident Societies. 1979.

INDUSTRIAL INJURIES

See also Damages; Employer's Liability; National Insurance; Workmen's Compensation.

Encyclopaedias

Statutes in Force. Groups: Employment; Social Security and Health Services.
Halsbury's Laws of England. 4ed. vol.33.
Halsbury's Statutes of England. 3ed. mainly vol.45 but see index vol.

The Digest. vol.34.
Encyclopaedia of Court Forms in Civil Proceedings (Atkin). 2ed. vol.28.

Texts

BROADHURST, V.A.
Health and Safety at Work Act in practice. Heyden, 1978.

CUSWORTH, G.R.N.
The Health and Safety at Work etc. Act 1974. Butterworths, 1975.

ENVIRONMENT, DEPARTMENT OF THE
Protecting people at work: an introduction to the Health and Safety at Work etc. Act 1974. HMSO, 1974.

FARMER, D.
Health and safety at work: an appraisal for management. Woodhead-Faulkner, 1975.

GRIME, R.P.
The law of noise–induced hearing loss and its compensation. Sweet & Maxwell, 1975.

JANNER, G.
Compendium of health and safety laws. 2ed. Business Books, 1982.

JONES, W.T.
The Health and Safety at Work Act, a practical handbook. Graham & Trotman, 1975 supp. 1977.

MITCHELL, E.
The employer's guide to the law on health, safety and welfare at work. 2ed. Business Books, 1977.

MUNKMAN, J.
Employers' liability at common law. 9ed. Butterworths, 1979.

REDGRAVE, A.
Health and safety in factories. 2ed. Butterworths, 1982.

RITSON, J.
Health and Safety at Work Act. Ravenswood, 1983.

ROWLAN, M.
Industrial injuries benefit scheme. Legal Action Group, 1983.

WRIGGLESWORTH, F.
A guide to the Health and Safety at Work Act. 3ed. Industrial Society, 1978.

YOUNG, A.F.
Industrial injuries insurance. Routledge & Kegan Paul, 1964.

INDUSTRIAL LAW

See also Employment Law; Factories; Trade Unions.

Encyclopaedias and periodicals

Statutes in Force. Group: Industrial Development.

Halsbury's Laws of England. 4ed. see index vol.

Encyclopaedia of Court Forms in Civil Proceedings (Atkin). 2ed, see index vol.

Industrial Cases Reports. 1975– (as Industrial Court Reports 1972–74, Restrictive Practices Cases. 1957–72).

Industrial Law Journal. 1972–
Industrial Law Review. 1946–1960.
Journal of Business Law. 1957–
Knight's Industrial Reports. 1966–75.
Managerial Law. 1975–
Modern Law Review. 1937–
New Law Journal, 1965– (as Law Journal, 1882–1964).
Solicitors' Journal. 1857–

Texts

CARBY-HALL, J.R.
Principles of industrial law. Knight, 1969.

COOPER, W.M.
Outlines of industrial law. 6ed. Butterworths, 1972.

CRABTREE, A. & KENNAN, D.J.
Essentials of industrial law. Pitman, 1970.

CRONIN, J.B. & GRIME, R.P.
Introduction to industrial law. Butterworths, 1974.

CRONIN, J.B. & GRIME, R.P.
Labour law. Butterworths, 1970.

DENYER, R.L.
Industrial law and its application in the factory. Macmillan, 1973.

FRANK, W.F.
Legal aspects of industry and commerce. 8ed. Harrap, 1978.

GAYLER, J.I. & PURVIS, R.L.
Industrial law. 2ed. Harrap, 1972.

GOW, J.J.
Mercantile and industrial law of Scotland. Green, 1964.

JESSUP, C.N.
Alley's industrial law Victoria. 2ed. Butterworths (Australia), 1981. Looseleaf.

McCALLUM, R.C. & TRACEY, R.R.S.
Cases and materials on industrial law in Australia. Butterworths (Australia), 1980

MILLER, I.
Industrial law in Scotland. Green, 1970.

MILLS, C.P.
New South Wales industrial laws service. 4ed. Butterworths (Australia), 1977. Looseleaf.

MILLS, C.P. & SORRELL, G.H.
Federal industrial laws service. 5ed. Butterworths (Australia), 1975. Looseleaf.

ROBERTS, G. & MAJOR, W.T.
Commercial and industrial law. 2ed. Macdonald & Evans, 1972 repr. 1975.

SALTER, J. & THOMAS, P.
Planning law for industry. Sweet & Maxwell, 1981. 2 vols.

SAMUELS, H.
Industrial law. 6ed. Pitman, 1961.

SELWYN, N.M.
Industrial law. Butterworths, 1970 (Notebook series).

SIM, R.S. & POWELL-SMITH, V.
Casebook on industrial law. Butterworths, 1969.

SMITH, I.T. & WOOD, J.C.
Industrial law. 2ed. Butterworths, 1983.

WHINCUP, M.H.
Industrial law. Pergamon, 1969.

INDUSTRIAL RELATIONS

See also Trade Unions.

Encyclopaedias and periodicals

Statutes in Force. Group: Employment.
Halsbury's Laws of England. 4ed. see index vol.
Halsbury's Statutes of England. 3ed. vol.44, 45.

British Journal of Industrial Relations. 1963–

Industrial Law Journal. 1972–
Industrial Law Review. 1946–1960.
Industrial Relations Digest. 1973–
Industrial Relations Journal. 1970–
Industrial Relations Law Reports. 1972–
Industrial Relations Review and Reports. 1971–

Texts

AARON, B.
Labor courts and grievance settlement in Western Europe. Univ. of California P., 1971.

AARON, B. & WEDDERBURN, K.W.
Industrial conflict: a comparative legal survey. Longman, 1972.

ADVISORY, CONCILIATION AND ARBITRATION SERVICE
Industrial relations handbook. HMSO, 1980.

ANDERMAN, S.D.
Law of unfair dismissal. 2ed. Butterworths, 1984.

ARNOT, R.P.
The general strike, May 1926: its origin and history. 1926 repr. Kelley, 1969 (USA).

BALFOUR, C.
Industrial relations in the Common Market. Routledge, 1972.

CAMPBELL, A.
The Industrial Relations Act. Longman, 1971.

CARBY-HALL, J.R.
Labour relations and the law. MCB Books, 1975.

CHRISTIE, I.M.
The liability of strikers in the law of tort: a comparative study of the law in England and Canada. Industrial Relations Centre, 1967 (Canada).

CLEGG, H.
System of industrial relations in Great Britain. 3ed. Blackwell, 1979.

EMPLOYMENT AND PRODUCTIVITY, DEPARTMENT OF
In place of strife: a policy for industrial relations. HMSO, 1969 (Cmnd. 3688).

ENCYCLOPAEDIA of labour relations law. Sweet & Maxwell. 3 vols. Looseleaf.

ENGLAND, J. & REAR, J.
Industrial relations and law in Hong Kong. 2ed. Oxford U.P., 1982.

FLANDERS, A. & GLEGG, H.A. (eds.)
The system of industrial relations in Great Britain. Blackwell, 1954.

GUNTER, H.
Transnational industrial relations. I.L.O., 1972.

HARVEY, R.J.S. (ed.)
Industrial relations. Butterworths. Looseleaf.

HEPPLE, B.A. (ed.)
Labour relations statutes and materials. 2ed. Sweet & Maxwell, 1983.

HEPPLE, B.A. & O'HIGGINS, P.
Employment law. 4ed. Sweet & Maxwell, 1981.

HOLBORN LAW SOCIETY
Advance manual on the Trade Union and Labour Relations Act 1974. 1974.

INTERNATIONAL encyclopaedia for labour law and industrial relations. Kluwer, 1977. Looseleaf.

JACKSON, J.
Labour relations: the new law. Butterworths, 1974.

JACKSON, M.P.
Industrial relations: a textbook. Croom Helm, 1977.

KAHN-FREUND, O.(ed.)
Labour relations and the law: a comparative study. Stevens, 1965.

LEVINE, M.J.
Comparative labour relations law. General Learning P., 1975.

MARSH, A.I. & EVANS, E.O.
The concise encyclopaedia of industrial relations. Gower, 1978.

MAZENGARB, O.C.
Industrial relations and industrial law. 4ed. Butterworths, 1975 (NewZealand).

PHILLIPS, G.E.
Labour relations and collective bargaining. Butterworths, 1977 (Canada).

PRIME MINISTER'S OFFICE
Industrial democracy. HMSO, 1978 (Cmnd. 7231).

REYNOLDS, F. (ed.)
A guide to industrial relations legislation in Northern Ireland. Industrial Soc., 1977. 2 vols.

RICHARDSON, J.H.
An introduction to the study of industrial relations. Allen & Unwin, 1954.

RIDEOUT, R.W.
Practice and procedure of the National Industrial Relations Court. Sweet & Maxwell, 1973.

RIDEOUT, R.W.
Principles of labour law. 4ed. Sweet & Maxwell, 1983.

ROBERTS, B.C. (ed.).
Industrial relations. rev. ed. Methuen, 1968.

ROYAL COMMISSION ON TRADE UNIONS AND EMPLOYERS' ASSOCIATIONS
Report (Donovan). HMSO, 1968 (Cmnd. 3623).

SELWYN, N.M.
Guide to the Industrial Relations Act 1971. Butterworths, 1971.

SIMPSON, R.C. & WOOD, J.
Industrial Relations and the 1971 Act. Pitman, 1973.

SPERO, S.
Labour relations in British nationalised industry. Allen & Unwin, 1971.

SWEET & MAXWELL
Labour relations statutes and materials. 1980–81. 1980.

WEEKES, B.E
Industrial relations and the limits of law: the industrial effects of the Industrial Relations Act 1971. Blackwell, 1975.

INDUSTRIAL TRIBUNALS

See also Tribunals and Inquiries.

Encyclopaedias and periodicals

Statutes in Force. Group: Tribunals and Inquiries.
Halsbury's Laws of England. 4ed. vol. 16.
Halsbury's Statutes of England. 3ed. mainly vol.45.

Encyclopaedia of Court Forms in Civil Proceedings (Atkin). 2ed. see index vol.

Industrial Tribunal Reports. 1966–

Texts

ANGEL, J.
How to prepare yourself for an industrial tribunal. Inst. of Personnel Management, 1980.

BATESON, P. & McKEE, J.
Industrial tribunals in Northern Ireland. SLS Legal Pubns. (NI) & supp.

EGAN, B.
The industrial tribunals handbook. New Commercial Pub. Co., 1978.

GOODMAN, M.J.
Industrial tribunals procedure. 2ed. Sweet & Maxwell, 1979.

GREENHALGH, R.
Industrial tribunals: a practical guide. Inst. of Personnel Management, 1973.

HEPPLE, B.A.
Equal pay and the industrial tribunals. Sweet & Maxwell, 1984.

HOWELL, A.
The industrial tribunal. Rose, 1981.

JACKSON, J.
Industrial tribunals handbook.
Butterworths, 1976.

LESLIE, W.
Industrial tribunal practice in Scotland.
Green, 1981.

MULHERN, J. & McLEAN, I.
Industrial tribunal: practical guide to
employment law and tribunal procedure.
B.Rose, 1982.

RIDEOUT, R.W.
Industrial tribunal law. McGraw-Hill,
1980.

ROBERTSON, D.
Employer's action guide to handling
industrial tribunal cases. Kogan Page, 1977.

WHITESIDES, K. & HAWKER, G.
Industrial tribunals. Sweet & Maxwell,
1975.

WILLIAMS, D.B. & WALKER, D.J.
Industrial tribunals: practice and procedure.
Butterworths, 1980 supp. 1981.

INFORMATIONS

See also Indictments; Magistrates; Prosecutions.

Encyclopaedias

Halsbury's Laws of England. 4ed. see index vol.
The Digest. see index vol.
Encyclopaedia of Court Forms in Civil Proceedings (Atkin). 2ed. see index vol.

Encyclopaedia of Forms and Precedents. 4ed. see index vol.

Texts

ARCHBOLD, J.F.
Pleading, evidence and practice in criminal cases. 41ed. Sweet & Maxwell, 1982.

ROBERTSON, G.S.
Civil proceedings by and against the Crown
Stevens, 1908.

ROSCOE, H.
Criminal evidence: the law, evidence and
practice in criminal cases. 16ed. Stevens,
1952.

ROWLANDS, E.B.B.
Criminal proceedings on indictment and
information. 2ed. Stevens, 1910.

SHORTT, J.
Information (criminal and quo warranto)
etc. mandamus and prohibitions. 1887.

INJUNCTIONS

See also Equity; Prerogative Orders; Ultra Vires.

Encyclopaedias

Halsbury's Laws of England. 4ed. vol.24.
Halsbury's Statutes of England. 3ed. see index vol.
The Digest. vol.28.
Encyclopaedia of Court Forms in Civil Proceedings (Atkin). 2ed. vol.22.

Encyclopaedia of Forms and Precedents. 4ed. see index vol.

Stone's Justices Manual. Annual
Supreme Court Practice.

Texts

BEAN, D.
Injunctions. 3ed. Oyez, 1984.

DREWRY, C.S.
Law and practice of injunctions.
Butterworths, 1841 supp. 1849.

EDEN, R.H.
Law of injunctions. Butterworths, 1821.

HETHERINGTON,
Mareva injunctions. Law Book Co., 1983 (Australia).

KERR, W.W.
A treatise on the law and practice of injunctions. 6ed. Sweet & Maxwell, 1927 repr. Gaunt, 1981.

McALLISTER, D.
Mareva injunctions. Carswell, 1983 (Canada).

ROW, C.M.
Law of injunctions. 4ed. Sardar Patel, 1976 (India). 2 vols.

SPELLING, T.C. & LEWIS, J.H.
A treatise on the law governing injunctions. Thomas, 1926 (USA).

SPRY, I.C.F.
Equitable remedies: injunctions and specific performance. Law Book Co., 1971 (Australia).

INLAND REVENUE

See also Civil Service; Customs and Excise; Revenue Law.

Periodicals

Taxes. 1922– (as Tax Clerk's Journal, 1912–1921).

Texts

JOHNSTON, Sir A
The Inland Revenue. Allen & Unwin, 1965.

INNS AND INNKEEPERS

See also Bailment.

Encyclopaedias

Statutes in Force. Group: Hotels and Refreshment Houses.
Halsbury's Laws of England. 4ed. vol.24.
Halsbury's Statutes of England. 3ed. vol.17.
The Digest. vol. 29.

Encyclopaedia of Court Forms in Civil Proceedings (Atkin). 2ed. mainly vol. 6.
Encyclopaedia of Forms and Precedents. 4ed. see index vol.

Texts

BULL, F.J. & HOOPER, J.D.G.
Hotel and catering law: an outline of the law relating to hotels, guest houses, restaurants and other catering businesses. 7ed. Barrie & Jenkins, 1979.

CHANDLER, P.
Hotel and catering managers' guide to the law. Case Law, 1981. Looseleaf.

DINSDALE, W.A.
Innkeepers and carriers by land. 3ed. Butterworths, 1952.

FIELD, D.
Cases and statutes on hotel and catering law. 2ed. Sweet & Maxwell, 1979 (Concise college casenotes).

FIELD, D.
Hotel and catering law. 4ed. Sweet & Maxwell, 1982 (Concise college texts).

LAW REFORM COMMITTEE
Second report: innkeepers' liability for property of travellers, guests and residents. HMSO, 1954 (Cmnd. 9161).

MITCHELL, E
The caterer's lawyer and hotelier's and restaurateur's legal guide. Business Books, 1977.

PANNETT, A.
Principles of hotel and catering law. Holt, R.& W., 1984.

POLLARD, R.S.W. & SULLIVAN, D.D.H.
Hotels and the law. Stevens, 1953.

RICHARDS, M.
Legal aspects of the hotel and catering industry. Bell, 1975.

SHERRY, J.H.
Laws of innkeepers. Cornell U.P., 1982 (USA).

INNS OF COURT

Encyclopaedias and periodicals

Halsbury's Laws of England. 4ed. vols. 3, 37.
Halsbury's Statutes of England. 3ed. see index vol.
The Digest. vol. 3.

Graya. 1927–

Texts

ABADY, J.
The Inns of Court and civilization. 1954.

BARTON, Sir D.P., BENHAM, C. & WATT, F.
The story of our Inns of Court. Foulis, 1924.

BLACKHAM, R.J.
Wig and gown: the story of the Temple, Gray's and Lincoln's Inn. Low, Marston, 1932.

BLAND, D.S.
A bibliography of the Inns of Court and Chancery. Selden Society, 1965.

DANIELL, T.
Inns of Court. Wildy, 1971.

LOFTIE, W.J.
The Inns of Court and Chancery. rev. ed. Seeley, 1908.

MEGARRY, R.E.
Inns ancient and modern: a topographical and historical introduction to the Inns of Court, Inns of Chancery and Serjeants' Inns. Selden Society, 1972.

PREST, W.R.
The Inns of Court under Elizabeth I and the early Stuarts, 1590–1640. Longman, 1972.

RINGROSE, H.
The Inns of Court, a historical description. 1909.

SCOTT, J.
The Inns of Court: their functions and privileges. 1869.

Gray's Inn

ATKIN, J.R.A., Baron
The moot book of Gray's Inn. Butterworths, 1924.

BELLOTT, H.H.L.
Gray's Inn and Lincoln's Inn. Methuen, 1925.

COWPER, F.H.
A prospect of Gray's Inn. Stevens, 1952.

DOUTHWAITE, W.R.
Gray's Inn, notes illustrative of its history and antiquities. Benson & Page, 1876.

INNS OF COURT

DUKE, H.E.
The story of Gray's Inn: an outline history from earliest times to the present day. 1950.

Inner & Middle Temple

BEDWELL, C.E.A.
Brief history of the Middle Temple. Butterworths, 1909.

BELLOTT, H.H.L.
The Inner and Middle Temple: legal, literary and historic associations. Methuen, 1902.

GODWIN, G.
The Middle Temple: the society and fellowship. Stales P., 1954.

HART, E.A.P.
The Hall of the Inner Temple. Sweet & Maxwell, 1952.

HUTCHINSON, J.
A catalogue of notable Middle Templars, with brief biographical notices. Hon. Soc. of the Middle Temple, 1902.

LAMB, C.
The Old Benchers of the Inner Temple. Oxford U.P., 1927.

MACASSEY, Sir, L.L.
Middle Temple's contribution to the national life. Sol. Law Stat. Soc., 1930.

MACKINNON, Sir F.D.
Inner Temple papers. Stevens, 1948.

Lincoln's Inn

BALLS, Sir W.V.
Lincoln's Inn: its history and traditions. Stevens, 1947.

BELLOTTT, H.H.L.
Gray's Inn and Lincoln's Inn. Methuen, 1925.

HURST, Sir G.
Lincoln's Inn essays. Constable, 1949.

HURST, Sir G.
Short history of Lincoln's Inn. Constable, 1946.

Temple Church

ADDISON, C.G.
The Temple Church. Longman, 1843.

BAYLIS, T.H.
The Temple Church and Chapel of St Ann. 3ed. G.Philip, 1900.

BURGE, W.
The Temple Church: an account of its restoration and repairs. 1843.

RANGER, C.
Gray's Inn Journal, 1752–1754. Oceana, 1977.

PITT-LEWIS, G.
The history of the Temple, with special reference to the Middle Temple. J.Long, 1898.

SISLOE, Lord
The peculiarities of the Temple. Estates Gazette, 1972.

THORPE, W.G.
Middle Temple table talk, with some talk about the table itself. Hutchinson, 1894.

THORPE, W.G.
The still life of the Middle Temple with some of its table talk, preceded by fifty years' reminiscences. 1892 repr. Hein, 1973.

WILLIAMSON, J.B.
Middel Temple Hall. Soc. of the Middle Temple, 1928.

WORSLEY, C.
Master Worsley's book on the history and constitution of the Honourable Society of the Middle Temple. Masters of the Bench, 1910.

ROXBURGH, Sir R.F.
The origins of Lincoln's Inn. Cambridge U.P., 1963.

SIMPSON, Sir J.W.
Some account of the Old Hall of Lincoln's Inn. Dolphin P., 1928.

SPILSBURY, W.H.
Lincoln's Inn, its ancient and modern buildings. 2ed. Reeves & Turner, 1873.

TURNER, G.J.
Lincoln's Inn. 1903.

HERD, C.O.
A note on the restoration of the Temple Church (1185–1240). 2ed. The author, 1959.

TEMPLE CHURCH
A full and complex guide to the Temple Church. 1843.

WORLEY, G.
The Church of the Knights Templar in London. 2ed. 1911.

INSANITY

See also Criminal Law; Mental Health.

Encyclopaedias

Statutes in Force. Group: Mental Health.
Halsbury's Laws of England. 4ed. vols. 11, 17.
Halsbury's Statutes England. 3ed. see index vol.
The Digest. vol.29.

Encyclopaedia of Court Forms in Civil Proceedings (Atkin). 2ed. vol.22.
Encyclopaedia of Forms and Precedents. 4ed. vol.13.

Texts

ABRAHAMS, G.
Lunatics and lawyers. Home & Van Thal, 1951.

BERAN, N.J. & TOOMEY, B.G.
Mentally ill offenders and the criminal justice system. Praeger, 1979.

CLYNE, P.
Guilty but insane: Anglo-American attitudes to insanity and criminal guilt. Nelson, 1973.

CRIMINAL LAW REVISION COMMITTEE
Third Report: criminal procedure (insanity). HMSO, 1963 (Cmnd. 2149).

FINGARETTE, H.
The meaning of criminal insanity. California U.P., 1974 (USA).

FINGARETTE, H. & HASSE, A.F.
Mental disabilities and criminal responsibility. California U.P., 1979 (USA).

GOLDSTEIN, A.S.
The insanity defense. Yale U.P., 1967.

GOSTIN, L.
Representing the mentally ill. Oyez, 1984.

HEYWOOD, N.A. & MASSEY, A.
Court of protection practice. 10ed. Stevens, 1978 supp. 1982..

HOME OFFICE
Report of the Committee on Mentally Abnormal Offenders (Butler). HMSO, 1975 (Cmnd. 6244).

LAW COMMISSION
Codification of the criminal law: general principles. The mental element in crime. HMSO, 1970 repr. 1977 (Working paper no.31).

LAW COMMISSION
Criminal law: report on the mental element in crime. HMSO, 1978 (Law Com. no.89).

PARTRIDGE, R.
Broadmoor: a history of criminal lunacy and its problems. Chatto & Windus, 1953 repr. 1975.

VENABLES, H.D.S
Guide to the law affecting mental patients. Butterworths, 1975.

WALKER, N.
Crime and insanity in England, vol. 1: the historical perspective. Edinburgh U.P., 1968.

WALKER, N. & McCABE, S.
Crime and insanity in England, vol. 2: new solutions and new problems. Edinburgh U.P., 1973.

WHITEHEAD, T.
Mental illness and the law. 2ed. Blackwell, 1982.

WHITEHORN, H.
Court of protection handbook. 6ed Oyez, 1983 (Practice notes, no. 39).

INSURANCE

See also Industrial and Provident Societies.

Encyclopaedias and periodicals

Statutes in Force, Group: Insurance.
Halsbury's Laws of England. 4ed. vol.25.
Halsbury's Statutes of England. 3ed. see index vol.

The Digest. vol. 29.
Encyclopaedia of Court Forms in Civil Proeedings (Atkin). 2ed. vol.22.
Encyclopaedia of Forms and Precedents. 4ed. vol.13.

INSURANCE

Insurance Directory & Yearbook. Annual.
Insurance Law Reports. 1982–
Law Quarterly Review. 1885–
Modern Law Review. 1937–

New Law Journal. 1965– (as Law Journal 1882–1964).
Solicitors' Journal. 1857–

Texts – general

ATHEARN, J.L.
Risk and insurance. 5ed. West Pub.Co., 1984 (USA).

BARR, W.C.
Elements of insurance in a nutshell. Sweet & Maxwell, 1968.

BIRDS, J.
Modern insurance law. Sweet & Maxwell, 1982.

BUTTERWORTHS insurance law handbook. 1983.

CANNAR, K.S.
Cases in insurance law. Woodhead-Faulkner, 1985.

CANNAR, K.S.
Liability insurance claims. Witherby, 1983.

CARTER, R.L. & DICKINSON, G.M.
Barriers to trade in insurance. Trade Policy Res. Centre, 1979.

COCKERELL, H.A.L. & SHAW, G.W.
Insurance broking and agency: the law and practice. Witherby, 1979.

COLINVAUX, R.
Law of insurance. 5ed. Sweet & Maxwell, 1984.

DINSDALE, W.A. & McMURDIE, D.C.
Elements of insurance. 5ed. Pitman, 1980.

ENCYCLOPAEDIA of insurance law. Sweet & Maxwell, 1984. Looseleaf.

GREENE, M.R.
Risk and insurance. 4ed. South-Western Pub. Co:Eurospan, 1977 (USA).

HANSELL, D.S.
Elements of insurance law. 3ed. Macdonald & Evans, 1978.

HICKMOTT, G.J.R.
Principles and practice of interruption insurance. Witherby, 1982.

HODGSON, G.
Lloyd's of London: a reputation at risk. A.Lane, 1984.

INSURANCE INSTITUTE OF LONDON
Advantages and disadvantages of the tort system and alternative methods of accident compensation. 1978.

INTERNATIONAL handbook: a legal guide for the insurer and reinsurer, 1983–85. City Financial Insurance Pubns., 1983.

IVAMY, E.R.H.
Casebook on insurance law. 4ed. Butterworths, 1984.

IVAMY, E.R.H.
Dictionary of insurance law. Butterworths, 1981.

IVAMY, E.R.H.
General principles of insurance law. 4ed. Butterworths, 1979 supp. 1982.

IVAMY, E.R.H.
Personal accident, life and other insurances. 2ed. Butterworths, 1980.

JOSKE, P.E. & BROOKING,
Insurance law on Australia and New Zealand. Butterworths (Australia), 1975.

KUNREUTHER, H.
Disaster insurance protection: public policy lessons. Wiley, 1978 (USA).

LATIMER, P.
Cases and text on insurance law: Australia and New Zealand. Butterwoths (Australia), 1977.

LAW COMMISSION
Insurance law: non-disclosure and breach of warranty. HMSO, 1980 (Law Com. no.104).

LAW COMMISSION & SCOTTISH LAW COMMISSION
Private international law: report on the choice of law rules in the draft non-life insurance services directive. Joint report with Scottish Law Commission. HMSO, 1979.

MacGILLIVRAY, E.J. & PARKINGTON, M.
Insurance law. 7ed. Sweet & Maxwell, 1981.

PICARD, M.P.
Elements of insurance law, relating to all risks other than marine. 2ed. Sweet & Maxwell, 1939.

RAYNES, H.E.
A history of British insurance. 2ed. Pitman, 1964.

RAYNES, H.E.
Principles of British insurance. Pitman, 1953.

REJDA, G.
Principles of insurance. Europa, 1982.

SCOTTISH LAW COMMISSION
Report on the Married Women's Policies of Assurance (Scotland) Act, 1880. HMSO, 1978 (Cmnd. 7245).

SRINIVASAN, M.N.
Principles of insurance law (life and non-life). Ramamiya, 1977 (India).

THOMAS, R.G.
Guidebook to insurance law in Australia and New Zealand. CCH, 1981.

WELSON, J.B. & TAYLOR, H.
Insurance administration. 8ed. Pitman, 1963.

WORLD insurance year book. Longman. 1984.

Accident

BANFIELD, G.E.
Principles and law of accident insurance. 5ed. Pitman, 1950.

DINSDALE, W.A.
History of accident insurance. Sweet & Maxwell, 1955.

DINSDALE, W.A.
Principles and practice of accident insurance. 8ed. Buckley, 1969.

WELFORD, A.W.B.
Law relating to accident insurance. 2ed. Butterworths, 1932.

WELSON, J.B.
Accident insurance claims. 2ed. Pitman, 1963.

Aircraft

MARGO, R.D.
Aviation insurance: the law and practice of aviation insurance including hovercraft and satellite insurance. Butterworths, 1980.

SHAWCROSS, C. & BEAUMONT, K.M.
Air law. 4ed. Shaw, 1977.

Employer's liability

WHITMORE, E.
Employers' liability insurance. Pitman, 1962.

Fire

EVERTON, A.
Fire and the law. Butterworths, 1972.

GODWIN, F.
The principles and practice of fire insurance in the United Kingdom. 7ed. Pitman, 1954.

IVAMY, E.R.H.
Fire and motor insurance. 4ed. Butterworths, 1984.

ROWLATT, J.
Law of fire insurance. Pitman, 1929.

SMITH, T.R. & FRANCIS, H.W.
Fire insurance theory and practice. 5ed. Stone & Cox, 1967.

TAYLOR, H.
Fire insurance law. 2ed. Pitman, 1959.

WELFORD, A.W.B. & OTTERBARRY, W.W.
Law relating to fire insurance. 4ed. Butterworths, 1948.

Life

BROWN, H.A.
Life assurance: its tax implications and practical uses. Witherby, 1977.

BUNYON, C.J.
Law of life assurance. 5ed. Layton, 1914.

INSURANCE

DENBOW, C.
Life insurance in the Commonwealth Caribbean. Butterworths, 1984.

DAVIS, B.
Tax planning for life assurance and pensions. 1980.

FRANKLIN, P.J. & WOODHEAD, C.
United Kingdom life assurance industry. Croom Helm, 1980.

HARRIS, P.
Estate planning through life assurance. Sweet & Maxwell, 1977.

HARRIS, P. & HEWSON, D.
Life assurance and tax planning. Sweet & Maxwell, 1970.

HOUSEMAN, D. & DAVIES, B.P.A.
Law of life assurance. 10ed. Butterworths, 1983.

NEW, L.J.
Life assurance: from proposal to policy. 8ed. Pitman, 1968.

Marine

ARNOULD, Sir J.
The law of marine insurance and average. 16ed. Stevens, 1981 (British shipping laws, 9–10).

BROWN, R.H.
Analysis of marine insurance clauses. Book 1: the Institute Cargo Clauses, 1982. 2ed. Witherby, 1983.

BROWN, R.H.
Dictionary of marine insurance terms. 4ed. Witherby, 1964.

BROWN, R.H.
Marine insurance. Vol.1: Principles. Witherby, 1981.

CHALMERS, D.
Marine Insurance Act 1906. 9ed. Butterworths, 1983.

GOODACRE, J.K.
Marine insurance claims. 2ed. Witherby, 1981.

HUDSON, N.G.
Marine claims handbook. 4ed. Lloyd's, 1984.

IVAMY, E.R.H.
Marine insurance. 3ed. Butterworths, 1979 supp. 1982.

REFERENCE book of marine insurance clauses. 55ed. Witherby, 1983.

SUMMERSKILL, M.B.
Oil rigs: law and insurance. Sweet & Maxwell, 1979.

TETLEY, W.
Marine cargo claims. 2ed. Butterworths, 1978.

Motor

BINGHAM, L.
Motor claims cases. 8ed. Butterworths, 1980.

CHATERED INSURANCE INSTITUTE
Motor insurance practice. Oyez Longman, 1984.

COCKERELL, H.
Motor insurance and the consumer. Woodhead-Faulkner, 1980.

DINSDALE, W.A.
Motor insurance. 3ed. Stone & Cox, 1956.

IVAMY, E.R.H.
Fire and motor insurance. 4ed. Butterworths, 1984.

WILLIAMS, D.B.
The Motor Insurers' Bureau. Oyez, 1975.

Professional indemnity

APPLEYARD, G.R.
Professional practice insurance, 2ed. Macdonald & Evans, 1973.

JESS, D.
Guide to the insurance of professional negligence risks. Butterworths, 1982.

MADGE, P.
Professional indemnity insurance. Butterworths, 1968.

Reinsurance

BELLEROSE, R.P.
Reinsurance for the beginner. 2ed.
Witherby, 1980.

CARTER, R.L.
Reinsurance. 2ed. Kluwer, 1983.

GOLDING, C.E.
The law and practice of reinsurance. 4ed.
Buckley, 1965.

IRUKWU, J.O.
Reinsurance in the Third World. Witherby, 1982.

KILN, R.
Reinsurance in practice. Witherby, 1981.

Miscellaneous

CHARTERED INSURANCE INSTITUTE
Insurances of liability. Oyez Longman, 1984.

EAGLE, M.G.
Special perils insurance. Pitman, 1963.

HEPPELL. E.A
Products liability insurance. Pitman, 1967.

HICKMOTT, G.J.R.
Principles and practice of interruption insurance. Witherby, 1982.

INTERNATIONAL ATOMIC ENERGY AGENCY
Insurance for nuclear installations: report. 1970.

LAW REFORM COMMITTEE
Fifth Report: conditions and exceptions in insurance policies. HMSO, 1956 (Cmnd. 62).

LAW REFORM COMMITTEE FOR SCOTLAND
Fourth Report: the effect on the liability of insurance companies of special conditions and exceptions in insurance policies and of non-disclosure of facts by persons effecting such policies. HMSO, 1957 (Cmnd. 330).

LLOYD'S OF LONDON
Product liability and insurance. Lloyd's, 1977.

MACKEN, A.G. & HICKMOTT, G.J.R.
The insurance of profits. 6ed. rev. Pitman, 1965.

PASSAMANECK, S.M.
Insurance in Rabbinic Law. Edinburgh U.P., 1974.

PROPERTY and pecuniary insurances.
Oyez Longman, 1984.

RILEY, D.
Consequential loss insurance and claims. 5ed. Sweet & Maxwell, 1981.

WHITEHEAD, G.
Elements of cargo insurance. Woodhead-Faulkner, 1983.

WILKINSON, H.W.
Personal property. Sweet & Maxwell, 1971.

INTERNATIONAL LAW

See also Act of State; Comparative Law; Conflict of Laws; Extraditin; General Agreement on Tariffs and Trade; Peace; Prize Law; Treaties; United Nations; War.

Encyclopaedias and periodicals

Halsbury's Laws of England. 4ed. vol. 18 and index.

American Journal of International Law. 1907–

British Yearbook of International Law. 1963–

Bulletin of Legal Developments. 1966–

Current Legal Problems. 1948–

International Affairs. 1922–
International and Comparative Law Quarterly. 1952–
Internatinal Law Quarterly. 1947–1951.
Internatinal Law Reports. 1950–
Journal of Comparative Legislation & International Law. 1896–1951.

Journal of World Trade Law. 1957–
Transactions of the Grotius Society. 1915–1959.
Yearbook of World Affairs. 1947–

General texts

ADAMS, J. (ed.)
Essays for Clive Schmitthoff. Professional Books, 1984.

AKEHURST, M.B.
A modern introduction to international law. 5ed. Allen & Unwin, 1984.

BOS, M.
Methodology of international law. North-Holland, 1984.

BRIERLY, J.L.
The law of nations. Oxford U.P., 1963.

BROWN, D.J.
Public international law. Sweet & Maxwell, 1970.

BROWNLIE, I. (ed.)
Basic documents in international law. 3ed. Oxford U.P., 1983.

BROWNLIE, I.
Principles of public international law. 3ed. Oxford U.P., 1979.

CASTEL, J.G.
International law. 3ed. Butterworths (Canada), 1975.

CHAMBERS, N.
International law. 3ed. Sweet & Maxwell, 1966 (Nutshell series).

ESSAYS in international and comparative law: in honour of Judge Erades. Nijhoff, 1983.

FENWICK, C.G.
International law. 4ed. Oceana, 1968.

GILBERTSON, G.
Harrap's German and English glossary of terms in international law. Harrap, 1980.

GLAHN, G. von
Law among nations: an introduction to public internatinal law. 4ed. Macmillan, 1981.

GREEN, N.A.M.
International law: law of peace. 2ed. Macdonald & Evans, 1982.

GREIG, D.W.
International law. 2ed. Butterworths, 1975.

GROSS, L.
Essays on international law and organization. Nijhoff, 1984. 2 vols.

HALL, W.E.
A treatise on international law. 8ed. Oxford U.P., 1924.

HIGGINS, A.P.
Studies in international law and relations. Cambridge U.P., 1928.

HOLLAND, Sir T.E.
Lectures on international law. Sweet & Maxwell, 1933.

HURST, Sir C.
International law: collected papers, Stevens, 1950.

HYDE, C.C.
International law, chiefly as interpreted and applied by the United States. 2ed. Little, Brown, 1947. 3 vols.

JACOBS, F.G.
Public international law. Butterworths, 1968 (Cracknell's law students' companion).

JANKOVIC, B.M.
Public international law. Transnational Pubns. (USA): Bowker, 1984.

KELSEN, H.
Principle of international law. 2ed. Holt, Rinehart & Winston, 1966.

KOROWICZ, M.S.
Introduction to international law. Nijhoff, 1959.

LAUTERPACHT, E.
International law. Cambridge U.P., 1970–78. 4 vols.

LAUTERPACHT, Sir H.
The function of law in the international community. 1933 repr. Shoestring, 1966.

LAWRENCE, T.J.
The principles of international law. 8ed. Macmillan, 1937.

LEVI, W.
Contemporary international law. Sage, 1979 (USA).

LORIMER, J.
Institutes of the law of nations. Blackwood, 1883–84. 2 vols.

MacDONALD, R.St.J. & JOHNSTON, D.M.
Structure and process of international law: essays in legal philosophy, doctrine and theory. Nijhoff, 1983.

MAINE, Sir H.J.S.
International law. 3ed. Murray, 1915.

MANN, F.A.
Studies in international law. 2ed. Oxford U.P., 1981.

MERRILLS, J.G.
Anatomy of international law. 2ed. Sweet & Maxwell, 1981.

O'CONNELL, D.P.
International law. 2ed. Stevens, 1970. 2 vols.

O'CONNELL, D.P.
International law for students. Sweet & Maxwell, 1971.

OPPENHEIM, L.F.L. & LAUTERPACHT, H.
International law: a treatise. Vol. 1: 8ed. 1955; Vol. 2: 7ed. 1952. Longmans.

PHILLIMORE, Sir R.J.
Commentaries upon international law. Butterworths, 1879–89. 4 vols.

SANDERS, A.J.G.M.
International law in an African context. Butterworths, 1978 (S.Africa).

SCHWARZENBERGER, G.
The dynamics of international law. Professional Books, 1976.

SCHWARZENBERGER, G.
The frontiers of international law. Stevens, 1962.

SCHWARZENBERGER, G.
The inductive approach to international law. Stevens, 1965.

Air
see under AVIATION

Arbitration

ANAND, R.P.
International courts and contemporary conflicts. Asia Pub. Co., 1974.

ANAND, R.P.
Studies in international adjudication. Oceana, 1970 (USA).

SCHWARZENBERGER, G.
International law as applied by international courts and tribunals. Vol.1: general principles. 3ed. Stevens, 1957; Vol. II: the law of armed conflict. Stevens, 1968; Vol. III: international constitutional law. Stevens, 1976.

SCHWARZENBERGER, G.
International law and order. Stevens, 1971.

SCHWARZENBERGER, G. & BROWN, E.D.
A manual of international law. 6ed. Professional Books, 1976.

SHAW, M.N.
International law. Hodder & Stoughton, 1977.

SORENSEN, M.(ed.)
Manual of public international law. Macmillan, 1968.

STARKE, J.G.
An introduction to internatinal law. 9ed. Butterworths, 1984.

SWIFT, R.N.
International law: current and classic. Wiley, 1969.

TUNKIN, G.I.
Theory of international law. Harvard U.P., 1974.

TWISS, Sir T.
The law of nations. Allen & Unwin, 1875.

VERZIJL, J.H.W.
International law in historical perspective. Sijthoff, 1968–1974. 7 vols.

WARD, R.P.
Enquiry into the foundations and history of the law of nations in Europe, from the time of the Greeks and Romans to the age of Grotius. 1795 repr. Garland, 1973.

WESTLAKE, J.
International law. 2ed Cambridge U.P., 1910–12. 2 vols.

BAR-YAACOV, N.
The handling of international disputes by means of inquiry. Oxford U.P., 1974.

CARLSTON, K.S.
Process of international arbitration. Greenwood, 1972.

INTERNATIONAL LAW

CURWURAH, A.O.
International arbitration: settlement of boundary disputes in international law. Manchester U.P., 1967.

DONELAN, M.D. & GRIEVE, M.J.
International disputes: case histories, 1945–1970. Europa, 1973.

DRUCKMAN, D.
Human factors in international negotiations: social psychological aspects of international conflict. Sage, 1973.

GRIEVES, F.L.
Supranationalism and international adjudication. Illinois U.P., 1969:

JENKS, C.W.
Prospects of international adjudication. Oceana, 1969 (USA).

KATZ, M.
Relevance of international adjudication. Harvard U.P., 1969.

MERRILLS, J.G.
International dispute settlement. Sweet & Maxwell, 1984.

NANTWI, E.K.
Enforcement of international judicial decisions and arbitral awards in public international law. 2ed. Sijthoff, 1967.

NORTHEDGE, F.S. & DONELAND, M.D.
International disputes: the political aspects. Europa, 1971.

RANDOLPH, L.L.
Third party settlement of disputes in theory and practice. Sijthoff: Europa, 1973.

SCHWEBEL, S.M.
Effectiveness of international decisions. Oceana, 1971 (USA).

SEIDE, K. (ed.)
A dictionary of arbitration and its terms. Oceana, 1970 (USA).

SIMPSON, J.L. & FOX, H.
International arbitration. Stevens, 1959.

STUYT, A.M.
Survey of international arbitrations, 1794–1970. Oceana, 1972 (USA).

UNITED NATIONS. OFFICE OF LEGAL AFFAIRS
Reports of international arbitral awards. Vols.1–11. 1948–1961 repr. Kraus, 1973.

VALLAT, F.
International disputes: the legal aspects. Europa, 1972.

Bibliography

COLLECTION of bibliographic and research sources: international law bibliography. Oceana, 1983–4. 2 vols. looseleaf.

DELUPIS, I. (ed.)
Bibliography of international law. Bowker, 1976.

HARVARD UNIVERSITY, LAW SCHOOL LIBRARY
Catalogue of international law and relations. 1965–67. 20 vols.

LEKNER, M.A. & STEINER, W.A.F.
University of Cambridge Squire Law Library. Catalogue of international law. Oceana, 1972. 4 vols.

MERRILLS, J.G. (ed.)
Current bibliography of international law. Butterworths, 1978.

SCHWARZENBERGER, G. & BROWN, E.D.
A manual of international law. 6ed. Professional Books, 1976. Study notes.

WIKTOR, C.L.
Canadian bibliography of international law. Univ. of Toronto P., 1983.

Cases

ANNUAL Digest and reports of public internationl law cases. 1919–1949 (continued by International Law Reports).

BENTWICH, N. de M.
Students' leading cases and statutes on international law. Sweet & Maxwell, 1913.

BISHOP, W.W.
International law: cases and materials. 3ed. Little, Brown, 1971 (USA).

COBBETT, P.
Leading cases and opinions on international law. Sweet & Maxwell.
Vol.1: peace. 6ed. 1947.
Vo.2: war and neutrality. 5ed. 1937.

GREEN, L.C.
International law through the cases. 3ed.
Oceana, 1970 (USA).

HARRIS, D.J.
Cases and materials on international law.
3ed. Sweet & Maxwell, 1983.

HOLDER, W.E. & BRENNAN, G.A.
International legal system: cases and
materials with emphasis on theAustralian
perspective. Butterworths (Australia), 1972.

Diplomatic practice
see under DIPLOMATIC LAW AND
PRACTICE

ORFIELD, L.B & RE, E.D.
Cases and materials on international law.
Bobbs-Merrill, 1965 (USA).

PARRY, C. (ed.)
British international law cases. Oceana,
1964–1971. 8 vols.

PARRY, C. & HOPKINS, J.A.
Commonwealth international law cases.
Oceana, 1974– . 10 vols.

Expropriation

FRIEDMAN, S.
Expropriation in international law. 1953
repr. Greenwood, 1981.

JACOBS, M.S.
Law of expropriation. Juta, 1981 (S.Africa).

JENNINGS, R.Y.
The acquisition of territory in international
law. Manchester U.P., 1963.

KATZAROV, K.
The theory of nationalisation. Sijthoff,
1964.

WHITEMAN, M.
Damages in international law. GPO (USA),
1937–43. 3 vols.

WORTLEY, B.A.
Expropriation in public international law.
Cambridge U.P., 1959 repr. Arno, 1977.

Extradition
see under EXTRADITION

Finance

ALEXANDROWICZ, C.H.
International economic organizations.
Stevens, 1952.

ALEXANDROWICZ, C.H.
World economic agencies: law and practice.
Stevens, 1962.

AUFRICHT, H.
The international monetary fund: legal
bases, structure and functions. Stevens,
1964.

DELUPIS, I.D.
Finance and protection of investments in
developing countries. Gower, 1973.

GOLD, J.
Membership and non-membership in the
International Monetary Fund: a study of
international law and organization. I.M.F.,
1974.

GOLD, J.
Voting and decisions in International
Monetary Fund. I.M.F., 1972.

HANSON, J.L.
Monetary theory and practice. 6ed.
Macdonald & Evans, 1978.

INTERNATIONAL MONETARY
FUND
Annual report.

INTERNATIONAL MONETARY
FUND
Proposals for increasing the resources of the
International Monetary Fund. HMSO,
1977 (Cmnd. 6704).

KNECHTLE, A.A.
Basic problems in international fiscal law.
HFL, 1979.

MEERHAEGHE, M.A.G. van
International economic institutions. 2ed.
Longman, 1971.

MERSKY, R.M.
Transnational economic boycotts and
coercion. Oceana, 1978 (USA). 2 vols.

ROBINSON, S.W.
Multinational banking. Sijthoff, 1972.

SCHWARZENBERGER, G.
Foreign investment and international law.
Stevens, 1969.

INTERNATIONAL LAW

SHUSTER, M.R.
Public international law of money. Oxford U.P., 1973.

Human rights
see under HUMAN RIGHTS

International Court of Justice

ANAND, R.P.
Compulsory jurisdiction of International Court of Justice. Asia Pub. House, 1961.

ANAND, R.P.
International courts and contemporary conflicts. Asia Pub. House, 1974.

ELIAN, G.
International Court of Justice. Sijthoff, 1971.

ELIAS, T.O.
International Court of Justice and some contemporary problems: essays on international law. Nijhoff, 1983.

GAMBLE, J.K. & FISCHER, D.D.
The International Court of Justice: an analysis of a failure. D.C.Heath, 1976 (USA).

GROSS, L.(ed.)
The future of the International Court of Justice. Oceana, 1976 (USA). 2 vols.

HAESLER, T.
Exhaustion of local remedies in the case law of international courts and tribunals. Sijthoff, 1968.

HUDSON, M.O.
Permanent Court of International Justice. 1920–1942: a treatise. 1943 repr. Arno, 1972.

HUSSAIN, I.
Dissenting and separate opinions at the World Court. Nijhoff, 1984.

KEITH, K.J.
Extent of the advisory jurisdiction of International Court of Justice. Sijthoff, 1971.

International Labour Organisation

ALCOCK, A.E.
History of the International Labour Organisation. 1971.

JENKINS, C.W.
International Labour Organisation in the U.N. Family. Unitar, 1971.

STEUBER, U.
International banking. Sijthoff, 1976.

LAUTERPACHT, Sir H.
The development of international law by the International Court. 2ed. Stevens, 1958; Gratius Pubns., 1983.

LISSITZYN, O.J.
International Court of Justice: its role in the maintenance of international peace and security. Carnegie Endowment for Internat. Peace, 1951 repr. Greenwood, 1978.

PRATAP, D.
The advisory jurisdiction of the International Court. Oxford U.P., 1972.

ROSENNE, S.
Documents on the International Court of Justice. Sijthoff, 1974.

ROSENNE, S.
The law and practice of the International Court of Justice. Sijthoff, 1965. 2 vols.

ROSENNE, S.
Procedure in the International Court: a commentary on the 1978 Rules of the International Court of Justice. Nijhoff, 1983.

ROSENNE, S.
The World Court: what it is and how it works. 3ed. rev. Sijthoff, 1973.

SCHWARZENBERGER, G.
International law as applied by International Courts and Tribunals.
Vol.1: general principles. 3ed. Sweet & Maxwell, 1957.
Vol.2: the law of armed conflict. Sweet & Maxwell, 1968.
Vol.3: international constitutional law – fundamentals, United Nations, related agencies. Sweet & Maxwell, 1976.

STARKE, J.G.
New rules of International Court of Justice. Australian Nat. Univ., 1973.

JOHNSTON, E.A.
International Labour Organisation. Europa, 1970.

LANDY, E.A.
Effectiveness of international supervision: three decades of I.L.O. experience. Stevens, 1966.

LOWE, B.E.
International protection of labour: International Labour Organisation, history and law. Macmillan, 1935.

International Law Association

INTERNATIONAL LAW ASSOCIATION
Index of the reports of conferences (1873–1972). 1975.

International Law Commission

BRIGGS, H.W.
The International Law Commission. Cornell U.P., 1965.

INTERNATIONAL LAW COMMISSION
Yearbook. 1956– Annual.

International organisations

AKEHURST, M.B.
Law governing employment in international organisations. Cambridge U.P., 1967.

BENNETT, A.L.
International organizations: principles and issues. Prentice-Hall, 1977.

BIBO, I.
The paralysis of international institutions and the remedies: a study of self-determination, concord among the major powers and political arbitration. Harvester P., 1976.

BOWETT, D.W.
The law of international institutions. 4ed. Stevens, 1982.

CLAUDE, I.L.
Swords into plowshares: the problems and progress of international organization. 3ed. Random House, 1965.

COX, R.W. & JACOBSON, H.K.
The anatomy of influence: decision making in international organization. Yale U.P., 1973.

DETTER, I.
Law making by international organizations. Norstedt & Soners, 1965.

JENKS, C.W.
The proper law of international organizations. Oceana, 1962 (USA).

League of Nations
see under LEAGUE OF NATIONS

MORSE, D.A.
Origin and evolution of the International Labour Office and its role in the world community. 1969.

INTERNATIONAL LAW ASSOCIATION
Reports on conferences. 1873–

RAMCHARAN, B.G.
International Law Commission. Nijhoff, 1977.

UNITED NATIONS
The work of the International Law Commission. 3ed. 1980.

LADOR-LEDERER, J.J.
International non-governmental organizations and economic entities. Sijthoff, 1963.

LUARD, D.E.T.
International agencies: the emerging framework of interdependence. Oceana, 1977 (USA).

PANHUYS, H.F., BRINKHORST, L.J. & MAAS, H.H.
International organization and integration. Sijthoff, 1968.

REUTER, P.
International institutions. Trans. Allen & Unwin, 1958.

ROBERTSON, A.H.
Law of international institutions in Europe. Manchester U.P., 1961.

ROCHESTER, J.M.
International institutions and world order. Sage, 1974.

RODGERS, R.S.
Facilitation problems of international associations. Columbia U.P., 1961.

SCHNEIDER, J.W.
Treaty-making power of international organisations. Droz, 1959.

INTERNATIONAL LAW

Mandates

BENTWICH, N.
The mandates system. Longmans, Green, 1930.

CHOWDHURI, R.N.
International mandates and trusteeship systems. 1955.

HALL, H.D.
Mandates, dependencies and trusteeship. Stevens, 1948.

TOUSSAINT, C.E.
Trusteeship system of the United Nations. 1956 repr. Greenwood, 1976.

Maritime
see under SEA, LAW OF; SHIPPING

Minorities

ALCOCK, A., TAYLOR, B.K. & WELTON, J.M. (eds.)
The future of cultural minorities. St Martins P., 1979 (USA).

GOTLIEB, A.E.
Human rights, federalism and minorities. Inst. of Internat. Affairs, 1970 (Canada).

HAKSAR, V.
Minority protection and international bill of human rights. Oxford U.P., 1975.

IMAM, M. (ed.)
Minorities and the law. Tripathi, 1972 (India).

McKEAN, W.A.
Equality and discrimination under international law. Oxford U.P., 1983.

SAID, A.A. & SIMMONS, L.R.
Ethnicity in an international context. Transaction P., 1976 (USA).

Nationality
see under NATIONALITY AND CITIZENSHIP

Neutrality
see under WAR

Pollution
see under POLLUTION

Private international law
see under CONFLICT OF LAWS

Recognition

CHEN, T.C.
The international law of recogniation. Stevens, 1951.

HERVEY, J.G.
Legal effects of recognition in international law as interpreted by the courts of the United States. 1928 repr. Hein, 1974.

LAUTERPACHT, H.
Recognition in international law. Cambridge U.P., 1947.

PATEL, S.R.
Recognition in the Law of Nations. Tripathi, 1958 (India).

Sanctions

BROWN-JOHNS, C.L.
Multilateral sanctions in international law: a comparative analysis. Praeger, 1975.

DOXEY, M.P.
Economic sanctions and international enforcement. 2ed. Macmillan, 1980.

HINDMARSH, A.E.
Force in peace: force short of war in international relations. 1933 repr. Kennikat, 1973.

HOGAN, A.E.
Pacific blockade. Oxford U.P., 1908.

MERSKY, R.M.
Transnational economic boycotts and coercion. Oceana, 1978 (USA). 2 vols.

Smuggling

MASTERSON, W.E.
Jurisdiction in marginal seas with special reference to smuggling. Macmillan, 1929.

Sovereignty

LARSON, A. & JENKKS, C.W.
Sovereignty within the law. Oceana, 1965 (USA).

O'CONNELL, D.P.
The law of state succession. Cambridge U.P., 1956.

STANKIEWICZ, W.J. (ed.)
In defence of sovereignty. Oxford U.P., 1969.

WYNDHAM PLACE TRUST
Man's wider loyalties: the limitation of national sovereignty. 1970.

Trade
see under COMMERCIAL LAW

Treaties
see under TREATIES

Tribunals

CHENG, B.
General principles of law as applied by international courts and tribunals. Stevens, 1953.

HUDSON, M.O.
International tribunals, past and future. Carnegie Endowment for Internat. Peace, 1944.

RALSTON, J.H.
The law and procedure of international tribunals. Stanford U.P., 1926 supp. 1936.

SCHECHTER, A.H.
Interpretation of ambiguous documents by international administrative tribunals. Stevens, 1964

WHITE, G.M.
Use of experts by international tribunals. Syracuse U.P., 1965.

United Nations
see under UNITED NATIONS

Miscellaneous

AMERICAN SOCIETY OF INTERNATIONAL LAW
Legal aspects of international terrorism. 1979.

BOS, M.
Present state of international law and other essays written in honour of the centenary celebration of the International Law Association, 1873–1973. Nijhoff, 1973.

BOWETT, D.W.
Legal regime of islands in international law. Kluwer, 1979.

BOWETT, D.W.
Self defence in international law. Manchester U.P., 1958.

BRIERLY, J.L.
The basis of obligations in international law. Oxford U.P., 1958.

BUCHHEIT, L.C.
Seccession: the legitimacy of self determination. Yale U.P., 1978 (USA).

CRAWFORD, J.
The creation of states in international law. Oxford U.P., 1979.

D'AMATO, A.A.
The concept of custom in international law. Cornell U.P., 1971 (USA).

DELUPIS, I.
International law and the independent state. Crane, 1974.

DHOKALIA, R.P.
The codification of public international law. Manchester U.P., 1970.

FRIEDMANN, W.G.
The changing structure of international law. Stevens, 1964.

FRIEDMANN, W.G.
Transnational law in a changing society: essays in honour of Philip C. Jessup. Columbia U.P., 1972.

GOODWIN-GILL, G.S.
International law and the movement of persons between states. Oxford U.P., 1978.

GRZYBOWSKI, K.
Soviet public international law. Sijthoff, 1970.

JENKS, C.W.
Law in the world community. Longmans, Green, 1967.

JENKS, C.W.
A new world of law? A study of the creative imagination in international law. Longmans, Green, 1969.

JORDAN, R.S. (ed.)
International administration: its evolution and contemporary applications. Oxford U.P., 1971.

KEETON, G.W. & SCHWARZENBERGER, G.
Making international law work. Stevens, 1946.

LEVI, W.
International law and international politics. Sage, 1977.

LIPSKY, G.A. (ed.)
Law and politics in the world community. Univ. of California P., 1953.

MACDONALD, R.S., MORRIS, G.L. & JOHNSTON, D.M.
Canadian perspectives on international law and organization. Toronto U.P., 1974.

McWHINNEY, E.
The international law of detente: arms control, European security, and East-West co-operation. Sijthoff, 1978.

MICHAELS, D.B.
International privileges and immunities: a case for a universal statute. Sijthoff, 1971.

OKOYE, F.C.
International law and the new African states. Sweet & Maxwell, 1972.

PARRY, C. (ed.)
Law officer's opinions to the Foreign Office, 1793–1860. repr. Oceana, 1975. 97 vols.

PARRY, C. (ed.)
Law officers' opinions to the Foreign Office, 1861–1939. repr. Oceana.

PLENDER, R.
International migration law. Sijthoff, 1972.

RIFAAT, A.M.
International aggression: a study of the legal concept – its development and definition in international law. Almqvist & Wiksell, 1979.

ROBINSON, J.
International law and organization. Sijthoff, 1967.

ROSENNE, S.
League of Nations Committee of Experts for the Progessive Codification of International Law. Oceana, 1972. 2 vols.

SHEIKH, A.
International law and national behaviour: a behavioural interpretation of contemporary international law and politics. Wiley, 1974.

SUMMERS, L.M.
The international law of peace. Oceana, 1972.

SYMMONS, C.R.
Maritime zones of islands in international law. Nijhoff, 1979.

THIRLWAY, H.W.A.
International customary law and codification. Sijthoff, 1972.

VISSCHER, Ch. de
Theory and reality in public international law. Tran. by P.E. Corbett. Princeton U.P., 1968.

INTERPRETATION

See also Drafting; Legislation; Statutes.

Encyclopaedias

Halsbury's Laws of England. 4ed. vol. 44 and index.
Halsbury's Statutes of England. 3ed. vol. 32.
The Digest. see index vol.
Encyclopaedia of Forms and Precedents. 4ed. see index vol.

Texts

ALLEN, Sir C.K.
Law in the making. 7ed. Oxford U.P., 1964.

BEAL, E.
Cardinal rules of legal interpretation. 3ed. Carswell, 1924.

BREDIMAS, A. (ed.)
Methods of interpretation and community law. North-Holland, 1978.

BROOM, H.
Legal maxims. 10ed. Sweet & Maxwell, 1939 repr. 1974.

BURROWS, R.
Interpretation of documents. 2ed. Butterworths, 1946.

CRAIES, W.F.
Statute law. 7ed. Sweet & Maxwell, 1971.

CROSS, Sir F.
Statutory interpretation. Butterworths, 1976.

LAW COMMISSION & SCOTTISH LAW COMMISSION
Interpretation of statutes. 1967 repr. 1977 (Working paper no. 14; Memorandum No.6).

LAW COMMISSION & SCOTTISH LAW COMMISSION
The interpretation of statutes. HMSO, 1969 (Law Com. no. 21; Scot. Law Com. no.11).

MAXWELL, Sir P.R.
The interpretation of statutes. 12ed. Sweet & Maxwell, 1969.

NORTON, R.F.
Treatise on deeds. 2ed. Sweet & Maxwell, 1928.

ODGERS, Sir C.E.
The construction of deeds and statutes. 5ed. Sweet & Maxwell, 1967.

ODGERS, W.B.
Principles of pleading and practice in civil actions. 22ed. Sweet & Maxwell, 1981.

PEARCE, D.C.
Statutory interpretation in Australia. Butterworths (Australia), 1974.

PLUCKNETT, T.F.T.
Statutes and their interpretation in the early 14th century. Cambridge U.P., 1922.

RUSSELL, Sir A.
Legislative drafting and forms. 4ed. Butterworths, 1938.

STROUD, F.
A judicial dictionary. 4ed. Sweet & Maxwell. 5 vols. + supp.

WORDS and phrases legally defined. 2ed. Butterworths, 1970. 5 vols & annual supp.

INVESTMENT

See also Banks and Banking.

Encyclopaedias and periodicals

Statutes in Force. Group: Investment.
Halsbury's Laws of England. 4ed. see index vol.
Halsbury's Statutes of England. 3ed. see index vol.
The Digest. see index vol.
Encyclopaedia of Courts Forms in Civil Proceedings (Atkin). 2ed. mainly vol.41.

Encyclopaedia of Forms and Precedents. 4ed. see index vol.

British Tax Review. 1956–
Economist. 1843–
Investors Chronicle and Stock Exchange Gazette. 1967–

Texts

BARRINGTON, T.J.
Irish administrative system. Inst. of Public Admin., 1980.

DAY, M.J. & HARRIS, P.I.
Unit Trusts. Oyez, 1974.

DIAMOND, W.H.
Capital formation and investment incentives. Bender, 1981 (USA). 2 vols looseleaf.

ELGIN, W.F.
Guide to sound investment. 4ed. Jordan, 1980.

FRIEDMANN, W.G. & PUGH, R.C.(eds.)
Legal aspects of foreign investment. Stevens, 1959.

GRAYSON, T.J.
Investment trusts. 1928 repr. Arno, 1975.

INTERNATIONAL CENTRE FOR SETTLEMENT OF INVESTMENT DISPUTES
Convention on the settlement of investment disputes between states and nationals of other states. 1970. 3 vols. in 4.

INTERNATIONAL CENTRE FOR SETTLEMENT OF INVESTMENT DISPUTES
Investment laws of the world: the developing nations. 1973–75. 6 vols. Looseleaf.

LILLICH, R.B.
The protection of foreign investments. Syracuse U.P., 1965.

McDANIELS, J.F.
International financing and investment. Oceana, 1964 (USA).

NURSAW, W.G.
The art and practice of investments. 3ed. 1974.

REUBER, G.L.
Private foreign investment in development. Oxford U.P., 1973.

SCHWARZENBERGER, G.
Foreign investments and international law. Stevens, 1969.

WALLACE, D.
International control of investment. Praeger, 1974.

IRELAND, REPUBLIC OF

Periodicals

Irish Current Law Statutes Annotated. 1984–
Irish Jurist. 1935–
Irish Law Times and Solicitor's Journal. 1867–
Irish Reports. 1838–

Texts

BARRINGTON, T.J.
Irish administrative system. 2ed. Institute of Public Admin., 1982.

BARTHOLOMEW, P.C.
The Irish judiciary. Inst. of Public Admin., 1971.

CHUBB, F.B.
Cabinet government in Ireland. Inst. of Public Admin., 1974.

CHUBB, F.B.
The constitution and constitutional change in Ireland. Inst. of Public Admin., 1978.

CHUBB, F.B.
Government and politics of Ireland. Inst. of Public Admin., 1974.

CHUBB, F.B.
A sourcebook of Irish government. Inst. of Public Admin., 1964.

DELANY, V.T.H.
The administration of justice in Ireland. 4ed. Inst. of Public Admin., 1975.

DONALDSON, A.G.
Comparative aspects of Irish law. Duke U.P., 1957.

DOOLAN, B.
Constitutional law and constitutional rights in Ireland. Gill & Macmillan, 1984.

DOOLAN, B.
Principles of Irish law. Gill & Macmillan, 1981.

GRIMES, R.H. & HORGAN, P.T.
Introduction to law in the Republic of Ireland. Sweet & Maxwell, 1980.

KELLY, J.M.
Fundamental rights in the Irish law and constitution. 2ed. Oceana, 1968.

KELLY, J.M.
The Irish constitution. Jurist Pub. Co., 1980.

KOHN, L.
The constitution of the Irish Free State. Allen & Unwin, 1932.

MEGHAN, P.J.
Local government in Ireland. 5ed. Inst. of Public Admin., 1975.

MEGHAN, P.J.
A short history of the public service in Ireland. Inst. of Public Admin., 1962.

O'CASEY, J.P.
Office of the Attorney General in Ireland. Inst. of Public Admin., 1980.

O'HIGGINS, P.
Bibliography of periodical literature relating to Irish law. Northern Ireland L.Q., 1966 supp. 1973.

SMYTH, J.M.
Houses of the Oireachtas. 4ed. Inst. of Public Admin., 1979.

IRON AND STEEL

See also European Communities.

Encyclopaedias

Halsbury's Laws of England. 4ed. see index vol.
Halsbury's Statutes of England. 3ed. vol.45.

Texts

GUMBEL, W. & POTTER, K.
Iron and Steel Act 1953. Butterworths, 1953.

ISLAMIC LAW

Texts

AMIN, S.H.
Wrongful appropriation of property in Islamic law and its remedies. Royston, 1983.

ANDERSON, J.N.D.
Islamic law in Africa. 1955 repr. Cass, 1970.

ANDERSON, J.N.D.
Islamic law in the modern world. Stevens, 1959 repr. 1975.

COULSON, N.J.
Conflicts and tensions in Islamic jurisprudence. Univ. of Chiacgo P., 1969.

COULSON, N.J.
History of Islamic law. Edinburgh U.P., 1979.

DJAMOUR, J.
Muslim Matrimonial Court in Singapore. Athlone P., 1966.

FYZEE, A.A.A.
Outlines of Muhammadan Law. 4ed. Oxford U.P., 1974.

GHANEM, I.
Islamic medical jurisprudence. Probsthain, 1982.

HASAN, A.
Early development of Islamic jurisprudence. Islamic Research Inst., 1970.

IBRAHIM, A.
Islamic law in Malaya. Malayan L. J., 1966.

IBRAHIM, A.
The legal status of the Muslims in Singapore. Malayan L.J., 1965.

IBRAHIM, A.
Sources and development of Muslim law. Malayan L.J., 1965.

KERR, M.H.
Islamic reform: political and legal theories of Muhammad Abdul and Rashid Rita. California U.P., 1967.

KHADDURI, M.
The Islamic law of nations. Johns Hopkins P., 1966 (USA).

KHADDURI, M.
War and peace in law of Islam. Johns Hopkins P., 1955.

KHADDURI, M. & LIEBESNY, H.J. (eds.)
Origin and development of Islamic law. Middle East Inst., 1955 (USA).

MULLA, Sir D.F.
Principles of Muhammadan law. 15ed. Luzak, 1963 (India).

PEARL, D.
A textbook of Muslim law. Croom Helm, 1979.

ROBERTS, R.
The social laws of the Qoran: considered and compared with those of the Hebrew and other ancient codes. Curzon P., 1971.

SCHACHT, J.
Introduction to Islamic law. new ed. Oxford U.P., 1982.

SCHACHT, J.
Origins of Muhammadan jurisprudence. Oxford U.P., 1979.

VAHIDI, M.
Islamic law of evidence and procedure. Royston, 1984.

ISLE OF MAN

See also Channel Islands.

Encyclopedias and periodicals

Acts of Tynwald. 1948–
Statutes in Force, Group: Constitutional Law.
Halsbury's Laws of England. 4ed. see index vol.

Halsbury's Statutes of England. 3ed. see index vol.
The Digest. see index vol.

Manx Law Bulletin. 1983–

Texts

BAWDEN, T.A. (ed.)
Standing orders of the Legislative Council. Isle of Man Court, 1982.

COMMISSION ON THE CONSTITUTION
Isle of Man: joint evidence of the Home Office and Tynwald. HMSO, 1970.

COMMISSION ON THE ISLE OF MAN CONSTITUTION
Report (MacDermott). HMSO, 1959. 2 vols.

FARRANT, R.D.
Mann, its land tenure, constituion, lord's rent and deemsters. Oxford U.P., 1937.

HOME OFFICE
Relationships between the United Kingdom and the Channel Islands and the Isle of Man. HMSO, 1973.

HOME OFFICE
Report of the Departmental Committee on the Constitution etc of the Isle of Man (MacDonnell). HMSO, 1911–13 (Cd. 5950, Cd. 6026) 2 vols.

HOME OFFICE
Report of the Joint Working Party on the Constitutional Relationship between the Isle of Man and the United Kingdom (Stonham). HMSO, 1969.

ISLE OF MAN, HIGH COURT OF JUSTICE
Rules of the High Court of Justice of the Isle of Man. 1952.

JOHNSON, J.
A view of the jurisprudence of the Isle of Man, with the history of its ancient constitution, legislative government and extra-ordinary privileges: together with the practice of the cours. Ramsey, 1811.

KEETON, G.W. & LLOYD, D. (eds.)
The United Kingdom: the development of its laws and constitutions. Stevens, 1955. Ch. 21.

KINVIG, R.H.
The Isle of Man: a social, cultural and political history. 2ed. Liverpool U.P., 1975.

KNEALE, S.J.
Manx coroners. Victoria P., 1963.

MILLS, M.A. (ed.)
The ancient ordinances and statute laws of the Isle of Man. Phoenix P., 1821.

MOORE, R.B.
The Isle of Man and international law. Brown, 1926.

PHILLIPS, O.H.
Constitutional and administrative law. 6ed. Sweet & Maxwell, 1978.

ROBERTS-WRAY, Sir K.
Commonwealth and colonial law. Stevens, 1966. Appendix 1.

SOLLY, M.
Anatomy of a tax haven. Vol. 1: Isle of Man; Vol.2: Manx income tax. Shearwater P., 1979.

WADE, E.C.S. & PHILLIPS, G.G.
Constitutional law. 9ed. Longman, 1977.

YOUNG, G.V.C. (ed.)
Subject guide and chronological table relating to the Acts of Tynwald, 1776–1975. Shearwater P., 1977.

YOUNG, G.V.C. (ed.)
Subject guide to and chronological table of the Acts of the Parliaments of England, Great Britain, United Kingdom and of Northern Ireland extending or relating to the Isle of Man, 1350–1975. Shearwater P., 1978.

ITALY

See also European Communities.

Periodicals

The Italian Practice in International Law. 1971.
The Italian Yearbook of International Law. 1975–

Texts

CALISSE, C.
History of Italian law. 1928 repr. Kelley (USA).

CAPPELLETTI, M., MERRYMAN, J.H. & PERILLO, J.M.
Italian legal system: an introduction. Stanford U.P., 1967.

DELANEY, J. (ed.)
Italian penal code. Sweet & Maxwell, 1978. (American series of foreign penal codes).

GRISOLI, A.
Guide to foreign legal materials Italian. Oceana, 1965 (USA).

KING, R.
Land reform: the Italian experience. Bell & Hyman, 1973.

LA VILLA, G.
The Italian law of agency and distributorship agreements. Oyez, 1977.

MERRYMAN, J.H.
Italian civil code. Oceana, 1970 (USA).

SPRUDZS, A.
Italian abbreviations and symbols: law and related subjects. Oceana, 1969 (USA).

VERRUCOLI, P.
Italian Company Law. Oyez, 1977.

JAMAICA

Encyclopaedias and periodicals

Statutes in Force. Group: Constitutional Law.
Halsbury's Laws of England. 4ed. mainly vol.6.
Halsbury's Statutes of England. 3ed. vol.4.
The Digest. see index vol.

Annual Survey of Commonwealth Law. 1965–
Caribbean Law Journal. 1952–53.
Jamaica Law Reports. 1953–1955, 1962–

Texts

BARNETT, L.G.
Constitutional law of Jamaica. Oxford U.P., 1977.

BAYITCH, S.A.
Latin America and the Caribbean: a bibliographical guide to works in English. Univ. of Miami P., 1967.

LEIBOWITZ, A.H.
Colonial emancipation in the Pacific and the Caribbean: a legal and political analysis. Praeger, 1976.

PHILLIPS, F.
Freedom in the Caribbean: a study in constitutional change. Oceana, 1976 (USA).

JEWISH LAW

Periodicals

Israel Law Review. 1966–
Jewish Yearbook of International Law. 1948–

Texts

ELON, M.
Principles of Jewish law: the Judaica compendium of the institutions of Jewish law. Nijhoff, 1975.

FALK, Z.W.
Introduction to Jewish law of the Second Commonwealth. Brill, 1972–8. 2 vols.

GERSHFIELD, E.M.
Studies in Jewish jurisprudence. Sepher-Hermon, 1972. 3 vols.

GOODHART, A.L.
Five Jewish lawyers of the common law. Oxford U.P., 1950.

HERZOG, I.
The main institution of Jewish Law. 2ed. Soncino P., 1965–7. 2 vols.

HERZOG, I.
Studies in Jewish jurisprudence. Sephor-Hermon, 1974.

ISRAEL, MINISTRY OF JUSTICE
Selected judgments of the Supreme Court of Israel. 1963–75. 4 vols (and special vol. 'What is a Jew?'

JACKSON, B.S.
Essays in Jewish and comparative legal history. Brill, 1975.

JACKSON, B.S.
Theft in early Jewish Law. Oxford U.P., 1972.

MAIMONIDES
The code of Maimonides. Yale U.P. various years.

QUINT, E.B. & HECHT, N.S.
Jewish jurisprudence: its sources and modern applications. Harwood Acad., 1980.

SCHREIBER, A.M.
Jewish law and decision making. Temple U.P., 1979.

JUDGES

See also Administration of Justice; Magistrates.

Encyclopaedias

Statutes in Force, Group: Judicial Remuneration and Pensions.
Halsbury's Laws of England. 4ed. see index vol.
Halsbury's Statutes of England. 3ed see index vol.
The Digest. see index vol.
Encyclopaedia of Court Forms in Civil Proceedings (Atkin). 2ed. see index vol.

Texts

ABRAHAM, H.J.
Judicial process: an introductory analysis of the Courts of the United States, England and France. 4ed. Oxford U.P., 1980.

ABRAHAM, H.J.
The judiciary: Supreme Court in the Governmental process. 6ed. Allyn & B., 1983 (USA).

ATIYAH, P.S.
From principles to pragmatism: changes in the function of the judicial process and the law. Oxford U.P., 1978.

BARTHOLOMEW, P.C.
The Irish judiciary. Notre Dame P., 1971.

BELL, J.
Policy arguments in judicial decisions. Oxford U.P., 1983.

BRINKHORST, L.J. & SCHERMERS, H.G.
Judicial remedies in the European Communities. 2ed. Sweet & Maxwell, 1979.

CAMPBELL, Lord
Lives of the Chief Justices of England. 3ed. Murray, 1874. 4 vols.

CAPPELLETTI, M. & JOLOWICZ, J.A.
Public interest parties and the active rule of the judge in civil litigation. Giuffre, 1975.

CARDOZO, B.B.
The nature of the judicial process. 1921 repr. Yale U.P., 1977 (USA).

CECIL, H.
The English judge. Stevens, 1970 (Hamlyn lecture).

COUNCIL OF EUROPE
Judicial organisation in Europe. 1975.

DAWSON, J.P.
History of lay judges. Harvard U.P., 1960.

DE SMITH, S.A.
Judicial review of administrative action. 4ed. Sweet & Maxwell, 1980.

DEVLIN, Lord
The judge. Oxford U.P., 1979.

DUMAN, D.
The judicial bench in England, 1727–1875: the reshaping of a professional elite. Royal Historical Society, 1982.

DWORKIN, R.G.
Political judges and the rule of law. British Academy, 1980.

FIFOOT, C.H.S.
Judge and jurist in the reign of Queen Victoria. Stevens, 1959.

FOSS, E.
Biographia juridica: a biographical dictionary of the judges of England, 1066–1870. Murray, 1870.

GALEOTTI, S.
Judicial control of public authorities in England and Wales. Stevens, 1954.

GIBB, A.D.
Judicial corruption in the United Kingdom. Green, 1957.

GRAY, W.F.
Some old Scots judges: anecdotes and impressions. Constable, 1914.

GREEN, E.
Judicial attitutes in sentencing. Macmillan, 1961.

GRIFFITH, J.A.G.
Politics of the judiciary. 2ed. Fontana, 1981.

HERMANN, A.H.
Judges, law and businessmen. Kluwer, 1983.

HOME OFFICE
Working party on judicial training and information: consultative working paper. HMSO, 1976.

JAFFE, L.L.
English and American judges as lawmakers.
Oxford U.P., 1969.

JUSTICE.
The judiciary: the report of a JUSTICE sub-committee. Stevens, 1972.

KEETON, G.W.
English law, the judicial contribution.
David & Charles, 1974.

LORD CHANCELLOR'S DEPARTMENT
Judicial studies and information: report of the working party (Bridge). HMSO, 1978.

MACMILLAN, A.R.G.
The evolution of the Scottish judiciary. 1942.

PATTENDEN, R.
Judge, discretion and the criminal trial.
Oxford U.P., 1982.

PROTT, L.V.
Latent power of culture and the international judge. Professional Books, 1977.

REYNOLDS, F.
The judge as lawmaker. McGibbon & Kee, 1967.

ROBSON, P. & WATCHMAN, P.
Politics, society and the judiciary. Gower, 1980.

SACHS, A. & WILSON, J.H.
Sexism and the law: a study of male beliefs and judicial bias in Britain and America.
Martin Robertson, 1978.

SHETREET, S.
Judges on trial: a study of the appointment and accountability of the English judiciary.
North-Holland, 1976.

SPARROW, G.
The great judges. Hutchinson, 1974.

JUDGMENTS

See also Estoppel; Foreign Judgements.

Encyclopaedias

Statutes in Force, Group: Enforcement.
Halsbury's Laws of England. 4ed. vol.26.
Hslbury's Statutes of England. 3ed. see index vol.
The Digest. vol.30.

Encyclopaedia of Court Forms in Civil Proceedings (Atkin). 2ed. vol.23 and see index vol.
Encyclopaedia of Forms and Precedents.
4ed. see index vol.

Texts

BLACK, A.
Execution of a judgement, including other methods of enforcement. 6ed. Oyez, 1979.

HUMPHREYS, T.S.
Notes on District Registry practice and procedure. 22ed. Oyez, 1980.

JOSLING, J.F.
Execution of a judgment. 5ed. Oyez, 1974 (Practice notes no.4).

JOSLING, J.F.
Summary of judgment in the High Court.
Oyez, 1974 (Practice notes no.16).

SCOTTISH LAW COMMISSION
Judgements Extension Acts. 1969 (Memorandum no. 12).

SETON, Sir H.W.
Forms of decrees, judgments and orders in equity. 7ed. Stevens, 1912. 3 vols.

SLESSER, Sir H.
The art of judgment and other studies.
Stevens, 1962.

ZAMIR, I.
The declaratory judgment. Stevens, 1962.

JUDICIAL PRECEDENT

Texts

BARWICK, Sir G.
Precedent in the southern hemisphere.
Oxford U.P., 1970.

CROSS, R.
Precedent in English law. 3ed. Oxford U.P., 1977.

GOODHART, A.L.
Precedent in English and continental law.
Cambridge U.P., 1934.

MONTROSE, J.L.
Precedent in English law, and other essays.
Irish U.P., 1968.

STONE, J.
Recent trends in English precedent. Assoc. General Pubns., 1946 (Australia).

JUDICIAL REVIEW

See also Declaratory Judgment

Encyclopaedias

Halsbury's Laws of England. 4ed. vol. 37.

Texts

BASU, D.D.
Limited government and judicial review.
Sarker, 1972 (India).

BETH, L.P.
The development of judicial review in Ireland, 1937–1966. Inst. of Public Admin., 1967.

CAPPELLETTI, M.
Judicial review in the contemporary world.
Bobbs-Merrill, 1971.

CORWIN, E.S.
Doctrine of judicial review and other essays.
1914 repr. P.Smith, 1963..

DE SMITH, S.A.
Judicial review of administrative action. 4ed.
Sweet & Maxwell, 1980.

DESHPANDE, V.S.
Judicial review of legislation. Eastern Book Co., 1975 (India).

ELY, J.H.
Democracy and distrust: theory of judicial review. Harvard U.P., 1980 (USA).

FAZAL, M.A.
Control of administrative action in India and Pakistan. Oxford U.P., 1969.

GABIN, S.B.
Judicial review and the reasonable doubt test. Kennikat, 1980 (USA).

GALEOTTI, S.
The judicial control of public authorities in England and Italy. Stevens, 1954.

JOHNSTON, R.E.
The effect of judicial review on federal-state relations in Australia, Canada and the United States. Louisiana U.P., 1970.

JOLOWICZ, J.A. & JONES, G.
Judicial protection of fundamental rights under English law: infiltration of equity into English commercial law. Kluwer, 1980.

KAVANAGH, J.
A guide to judicial review. Carswell, 1978 (Canada).

McWHINNEY, E.
Judicial review in the English-speaking world. 4ed. Univ. of Toronto P., 1969 (Canada).

MARKOSE, A.T.
Judicial control of administrative action in India. Madras L.J., 1956.

MAX-PLANCK-INSTITUT
Judicial protection against the executive.
Carl Heyman, 1970–72. 3 vols.

PANNICK, D.
Judicial review of the death penalty.
Duckworth, 1982.

ROSE-INNES, L.
Judicial review of administrative tribunals in South Africa. Juta, 1963.

STRAYER, B.L.
Judicial review of legislation in Canada. Univ. of Toronto P., 1968.

THIO, S.M.
Locus standi and judicial review. Singapore U.P., 1971.

ZAMIR, I.
The declaratory judgment. Stevens, 1962.

JURIES

See also Constitutional Law; Criminal Law.

Encyclopaedias

Statutes in Force, Group: Juries.
Halsbury's Laws of England. 4ed. vol.26.
Halsbury's Statutes of England. 3ed. vol.44.
The Digest. vol.30.

Encyclopaedia of Court Forms in Civil Proceedings (Atkin). 2ed. vol.23.
Supreme Court Practice.
County Court Practice.

Texts

ARCHBOLD, J.F.
Pleading, evidence and practice in criminal cases. 41ed. Sweet & Maxwell, 1982.

BALDWIN, J. & McCONVILLE, M.
Jury trials. Oxford U.P., 1979.

BARBER, D. & GORDON, G.
Members of the jury. Wildwood, 1976.

CORNISH, W.R.
The jury. rev.ed. Penguin, 1971.

CRIMINAL LAW REVISION COMMITTEE
Tenth report: secrecy of the jury room. HMSO, 1968 (Cmnd. 3750).

DEVLIN, Sir P.
Trial by jury. rev.ed. Stevens, 1966 (Hamlyn lectures).

DYKE, J.M. van
Jury selection procedure: our uncertain commitment to representative panels. Ballinger, 1977.

GRIEW, E.J.
Dishonesty and the jury. Leicester U.P., 1974.

JONES, A
Jury service. Hales, 1983.

KALVEN, H. & ZEISEL, H.
The American jury. Univ. of Chicago P., 1971.

McCABE, S.
The shadow jury at work. Blackwell, 1974.

McCABE, S. & PURVES, R.
Jury at work. Blackwell, 1972.

MATHER, P.E.
Sheriff and execution law. 3ed. Stevens, 1935.

SAKS, M.J.
Jury verdicts: the role of group size and social decision rules. Lexington, 1977 (USA).

SIMON, R.J.
Jury system in America: a critical overview. Sage, 1975.

WILLOCK, I.D.
Origins and developments of the jury in Scotland. Stair Society, 1966 (vol. 23).

JURISPRUDENCE AND LEGAL PHILOSOPHY

See also English Legal System.

Texts

ALLEN, Sir C.K.
Aspects of justice. Sweet & Maxwell, 1958.

ALLEN, Sir C.K.
Law in the making. 7ed. Oxford U.P., 1964.

ALLOTT, A.N.
Limits of law. Butterworths, 1980.

ANDERSON, Sir N.
Liberty, law and justice. Stevens, 1978 (Hamlyn lectures).

ATIYAH, P.S.
Law and modern society. Oxford U.P., 1983.

ATIYAH, P.S.
Promises, morals and law. New ed. Oxford U.P., 1983.

AUSTIN, J.
Province of jurisprudence determined. 2ed. B.Franklin, 1970 (USA). 3 vols.

BAKER, N.L.
Law and the individual. Macdonald & Evans, 1982.

BARRY, B.
The liberal theory of justice: a critical examination of the principal doctrines in "A theory of justice" by John Rawls. Oxford U.P., 1973.

BENDITT, T.M.
Law as rule and principle: problems of legal philosophy. Harvester P., 1978.

BENTHAM, J.
A fragment on government and an introduction to the principles of morals and legislation, ed. by W Harrison. Blackwell, 1948.

BENTHAM, J.
An introduction to the principles of morals and legislation, ed. by J.H. Burns and H.L.A. Hart. Athlone P., 1970.

BENTHAM, J.
Limits of jurisprudence defined, being part two of an introduction to the principles of morals and legislations. 1845 repr. Greenwood, 1971

BENTHAM, J.
Of laws in general, ed. by H.L.A. Hart. Athlone P., 1970.

BENTHAM, J.
The theory of legislation. 1864 repr. Routledge & Kegan Paul, 1976.

BENTHAM, J.
Works of Jeremy Bentham, reproduced from the edition of 1838–1843 ...by J. Bowring repr. Russell & Russell, 1962. 11 vols.

BLOM-COOPER, L. & DREWRY, G. (eds.)
Law and morality. Duckworth, 1976.

BODENHEIMER, E.
Jurisprudence the philosophy and method of the law. Harvard U.P., 1975.

BRETT, P.
An essay on a contemporary jurisprudence. Butterworths (Australia), 1975.

BRYCE, J.
Studies in history and jurisprudence. Oxford U.P., 1901. 2 vols.

BUCKLAND, W.W.
Some reflections on jurisprudence. Cambridge U.P., 1945 repr. Shoe String, 1973.

CAIN, M.
Marx and Engels on law. Academic P., 1980.

CAMPBELL, C. & WILES, P.
Law and society: readings in the sociology of law. Martin Robertson, 1979.

CARDOZO, B.N.
Growth of the law. 1924 repr. Greenwood, 1963.

CARDOZO, B.N.
Nature of the judicial process. 1921 repr. Yale U.P., 1977.

CARDOZO, B.N.
Paradoxes of legal science. 1928 repr. Greenwood.

CARLSTON, K.S.
Law and structures of social action. 1956 repr. Greenwood, 1980.

CASTBERG, F.
Problems of legal philosophy. 2ed. Universitetsforlaget, 1958.

COHEN, M.
Ronald Dworkin and contemporary jurisprudence. Duckworth, 1984.

COHEN, M.R. & COHEN, F.S.
Readings in jurisprudence and legal philosophy. Little, Brown, 1960.

CONWAY, C.
Jurisprudence with test questions. Sweet & Maxwell, 1971 (Nutshell series).

CROSS, Sir R.
Precedent in English law. 3ed. Oxford U.P., 1977.

CURZON, L.B.
Jurisprudence. Macdonald & Evans, 1979.

CUTLER, A. & NYE, D.
Justice and predictablity. Macmillan P., 1983.

DENNING, Lord
The discipline of law. Butterworths, 1979.

DENNING, Lord
Freedom under the law. Stevens, 1968 (Hamlyn lectures no.1).

DENNING, Lord
The road to justice. Sweet & Maxwell, 1955.

D'ENTREVES, A.P.
Natural Law. 1953 repr. Hutchinson, 1970.

DEVLIN, Lord
The enforcement of morals. Oxford U.P., 1968.

DHYANI, S.N.
Jurisprudence: a study of Indian legal theory. Metropolitan Book Co., 1972.

DIAS, R.W.M.
Bibliography of jurisprudence. 3ed. Butterworths, 1978.

DIAS, R.W.M.
Jurisprudence. 4ed. Butterworths, 1976.

DOWRICK, F.E.
Justice according to the English common lawyers. Butterworths, 1961.

DWORKIN, R.M. (ed.)
The philosophy of law. Oxford U.P., 1977.

DWORKIN, R.M.
Taking rights seriously. Duckworth, 1978.

EBENSTEIN, W.
Pure theory of law. 1945 repr. Kelley.

FEINBERG, J. & GROSS, H.
Philosophy of law. 2ed. Wadsworth Pub. Co., 1980 (USA).

FINCH, J.D.
Introduction to legal theory. 3ed. Sweet & Maxwell, 1979.

FINNIS, J.M.
Natural law and natural rights. Oxford U.P., 1980.

FLICK, G.A.
Natural justice: principles and practical application. Butterworths (Australia), 1979.

FRIEDMAN, L.M.
Law and society. Prentice-Hall, 1977.

FRIEDMANN, W.G.
Law in a changing society. 2ed. Butterworths, 1970.

FRIEDMANN, W.G.
Legal theory. 5ed. Stevens, 1967.

FRIEDMANN, W.G.
The state and the rule of law in a mixed economy. Stevens, 1971.

FRIEDRICH, C.J.
The philosophy of law in historical perspective. 2ed. Univ. of Chicago P., 1963.

GIERKE, O.
Natural law and the theory of society, 1500–1800. trans. Cambridge U.P., 1950.

GINSBERG, M. (ed.)
Law and opinion in England in the twentieth century. Stevens, 1959.

GOLDING, M.P.
Philosophy of law. Prentice-Hall, 1975.

GOODHART, A.
Essays in jurisprudence. Wiley, 1931.

GUEST, A.G. (ed.)
Oxford essays in jurisprudence. Oxford U.P., 1961.

GURVITCH, G.
Sociology of law. Routledge, 1947.

HACKER, P.M.S. & RAZ, J. (eds.)
Law, morality and society: essays in honour of H.L.A. Hart. Oxford U.P., 1979.

HAMBURGER, M.
Awakening of western legal thought; trans. 1942 repr. Greenwood, 1970.

HARRIS, J.W.
Law and legal science: inquiry into the concepts "Legal rule" and "Legal system". Oxford U.P., 1979.

HARRIS, J.W.
Legal philosophies. Butterworths, 1981.

HARRISON, J.
Hume's theory of justice. rev. ed. Oxford U.P., 1984.

HART, H.L.A.
The concept of law. Oxford U.P., 1961.

HART, H.L.A.
Definition and theory in jurisprudence. Oxford U.P., 1953.

HART, H.L.A.
Essays in jurisprudence and philosphy. Oxford U.P., 1983.

HART, H.L.A.
Essays on Bentham: jurisprudence and political theory. Oxford U.P., 1982.

HART, H.L.A.
Law, liberty and morality. Oxford U.P., 1963.

HART, H.L.A.
The morality of the criminal law. Oxford U.P., 1965.

HART, H.L.A.
Punishment and responsibility: essays in the philosophy of law. Oxford U.P., 1968.

HART, H.L.A., HACKER, P.M.S. & RAZ, J. (eds.)
Law, morality and society. Oxford U.P., 1977.

HARVEY, B.W. (ed.)
The lawyer and justice: a collection of addresses by judges and jurists to the Holdsworth Club of the University of Birmingham. Sweet & Maxwell, 1978.

HERBERT, Sir A.P.
More uncommon law. Methuen, 1982.

HERBERT, Sir A.P.
Uncommon law. 4ed. Methuen, 1978.

HIRST, P.H.
On law and ideology. Macmillan, 1979.

JACKSON, P.
Natural justice. 2ed. Sweet & Maxwell, 1980.

JAMES, M.H. (ed.)
Bentham and legal theory. Northern Ireland L.Q., 1973.

JOLOWICZ, H.F.
Lectures on jurisprudence. Athlone P., 1968.

JONES, J.W.
Historical introduction to the theory of law. 1940 repr. Kelley, 1956; Greenwood, 1972..

KAGAN, K.K.
Three great systems of jurisprudence. Stevens, 1955.

KAHN-FREUND, O.
Selected writings. Sweet & Maxwell, 1978.

KAMENKA, E. & others
Law and society. Arnold, 1978.

KANT, I.
Philosophy of law. Clark, 1887.

KAPLAN, M.A.
Justice: human nature and political obligation. Collier-Macmillan, 1977 (USA).

KEETON, G.W.
Elementary principles of jurisprudence. 2ed. Pitman, 1949.

KELSEN, H.
General theory of law and state, trans by A. Wedberg. 1945 repr. Russell & Russell, 1961.

KELSEN, H.
Pure theory of law trans. from German Univ. of California P., 1978 (USA).

KOHLER, J.
Philosophy of law, trans. from German. 1914 repr. Rothman, 1969.

LAMONT, W.D.
Law and the moral order: study in ethics and jurisprudence. Pergamon, 1981.

LASKI, H.J.
Studies in law and politics. Allen & Unwin, 1932.

LASOK, D. (ed.)
Fundamental duties. Pergamon, 1980.

LEVI, S.E.H.
Introduction to legal reasoning. rev.ed. Univ. of Chicago P., 1962.

LEVY, B.H.
Cardozo and frontiers of legal thinking. Oxford U.P., 1938.

LLOYD OF HAMPSTEAD, Lord
The idea of law. rev.ed. Penguin, 1981.

LLOYD OF HAMPSTEAD, Lord
Introduction to jurisprudence. 4ed. Sweet & Maxwell, 1979.

LUCAS, J.R.
On justice. Oxford U.P., 1980.

LYONS, D.
In the interest of the governed: a study in Bentham's philosophy of utility and law. Oxford U.P., 1973.

MacCORMICK, N.
Legal reasoning and legal theory. Oxford U.P., 1978.

MacCORMICK, N.
Legal right and social democracy: essays in legal and political philosphy. Oxford U.P., 1982.

MAINE, Sir H.J.S.
Ancient law, its connnection with the early history of society and its relation to modern ideas. Murray, 1930.

MARSHALL, H.H.
Natural justice. Sweet & Maxwell, 1959.

MENON, K.
Outlines of jurisprudence. 3ed. Asia Pub. House, 1961.

MICKLEM, B.
Law and the laws: being the marginal comments of a theologian. Green, 1952.

MITCHELL, B.
Law, morality and religion in a secular society. Oxford U.P., 1967.

MUNGHAM, G. & BANKOWSKI, Z.
Essays in law and society. Routledge, 1980.

OLIVECRONA, K.
Law as fact. 2ed. Sweet & Maxwell, 1971.

OSBORN, P.G.
Jurisprudence. Sweet & Maxwell, 1958 (Nutshall series).

PATON, Sir G.W.
A textbook of jurisprudence. 4ed. Oxford U.P., 1972.

PHILLIPS, P.
Marx and Engels on law and laws. Martin Robertson, 1980.

POLLOCK, Sir F.
Jurisprudence and legal essays. Macmillan, 1961 repr. Greenwood, 1978.

POTTER, H.
Quest of justice. Sweet & Maxwell, 1951.

POUND, R.
Contemporary justice theory. Claremont College, 1940 (USA).

POUND, R.
An introduction to the philosophy of law. Yale U.P., 1954.

POUND, R.
Jurisprudence. West, 1959. 5 vols.

POUND, R.
Justice according to law. Yale U.P., 1951 repr. Kennikat, 1973.

RAWLS, J.
A theory of justice. Oxford U.P., 1972.

RAZ, J.
Authority of law: essays on law and morality. new ed. Oxford U.P., 1983.

RAZ, J.
Concept of a legal system: an introduction to the theory of legal system. 2ed. Oxford U.P., 1980.

RAZ, J.
Practical reasoning. Oxford U.P., 1978.

REASONS, C.E. & RICH, R.M.
The sociology of law. Butterworths (Canada), 1978.

ROBERTS, S.
Order and dispute: introduction to legal anthropology. Penguin, 1979.

ROBSON, P. & WATCHMAN, P.
Justice, Lord Denning and the constitution. Gower, 1981.

ROSS, A.N.C.
On guilt, responsibility and punishment. Stevens, 1975.

ROSS, A.N.C.
On law and justice. Stevens, 1958.

ROSTOW, E.V.
Ideal in law. Univ. of Chicago P., 1978.

SALMOND, Sir J.W.
Jurisprudence. 12ed. Sweet & Maxwell, 1966.

SAWER, G.
Law in society. Oxford U.P., 1965.

SCHAEFER, D.L.
Justice or tyranny? A critique of John Rawl's "Theory of justice". Kennikat, 1979 (USA).

SIMPSON, A.W.B. (ed.)
Oxford essays in jurisprudence. 2nd series. Oxford U.P., 1973.

SMITH, A.
Lectures on jurisprudence. Oxford U.P., 1978.

SMITH, T.B.
British justice: the Scottish contribution. Stevens, 1961 (Hamlyn lecture).

STEIN, A.
Legal evolution: the story of an idea. Cambridge U.P., 1980.

STOLJAR, S.
Moral and legal reasoning. Macmillan, 1980.

STONE, J.
Human law and human justice. Stevens, 1965.

STONE, J.
Legal system and lawyers' reasoning. Stevens, 1964.

STONE, J.
Social dimensions of law and justice. Stevens, 1966.

STORME, P.M.
Effectiveness of judicial protection and constitutional order. Kluwer, 1983.

STRACHAN, B.
Natural justice. Shaw, 1976.

SUMMERS, R.S. (ed.)
Essays in legal philosphy. Blackwell, 1968.

SUMMERS, R.S. (ed.)
More essays in legal philosophy: general assessment of legal philosophies. Blackwell, 1971.

TENCH, D.
Towards a middle system of law. Hodder, 1981.

TORRANCE, T.F.
Juridical and physical law. Scottish Academic Press, 1982.

VAN EIKEMA HOMMES, H.J.
Major trends in the history of legal philosophy, trans. from Dutch. North-Holland, 1979.

VINOGRADOFF, Sir P.
Collected papers. Oxford U.P., 1928. 2 vols.

VINOGRADOFF, Sir. P.
Outlines of historical jurisprudence. Oxford U.P., 1920–2. 2 vols.

WATKIN, T.G.
The nature of law. North-Holland, 1980.

WATSON, A.
Nature of law. Edinburgh U.P., 1977.

WATSON, A.
Society and legal change. Scottish Academic P., 1977.

WORTLEY, B.A.
Jurisprudence. Manchester U.P., 1967.

JUVENILE COURTS

See also Children and Young Persons; Magistrates.

Encyclopaedias and periodicals

Halsbury's Laws of England. 4ed. vol. 24 and see index vol.
Halsbury's Statutes of England. 3ed. see index vol.
The Digest. vol.33.

Encyclopaedia of Court Forms in Civil Proceedings (Atkin). 2ed. see index vol.

Justice of the Peace. 1839–
The Magistrate. 1921–

Texts

ANDERSON, R.
Representation in the juvenile court. Routledge & Kegan Paul, 1978.

ASQUITH, S.
Children and justice: decision making in children's hearings and juvenile courts. Edinburgh U.P., 1983.

AUSTIN, P.M. (ed.)
Notes on juvenile court law. 10ed. Rose, 1978.

CAVENAGH, W.E.
Guide to procedure in the juvenile court. B.Rose, 1982.

CAVENAGH, W.E.
The juvenile court. Rose, 1976.

CENTRAL COUNCIL FOR EDUCATION AND TRAINING IN SOCIAL WORK
Social work, the social worker in the juvenile court: some suggestions for training. 1974.

CHATTERTON, C.E.M.
What, when and how in the juvenile court. Rose, 1981.

CICOUREL, A.V.
Social organisation of juvenile justice. Heinemann, 1976.

GRANT, D.W. & COOK, H.S.
Adoption proceedings in juvenile courts: a guide to the law and practice of adoption proceedings before magistrates. Rose, 1972.

GRAY, B.
Communication and chairmanship in the juvenile court. Rose, 1980.

HALL, J.G. & MITCHELL, B.H.
Child abuse: procedure and evidence in juvenile courts. Rose, 1978.

KLEIN, M.M. (ed.)
Western systems of juvenile justice. Sage Pubns., 1984.

MARTIN, F.M. & MURRAY, K.
Scottish juvenile justice system. Scottish Academic Press, 1983.

MOORE, T.G. & WILKINSON, T.P.
Juvenile court: a guide to the law and practice. Rose, 1984.

MORRIS, A. & McISAAC, M.
Juvenile justice? Heinemann, 1978.

MORRISON, A.C.L.
Notes on juvenile court law. 9ed. Butterworths, 1971.

MUMFORD, G.H.F.
Table of proceedings in juvenile courts. Shaw, 1977.

MUMFORD, G.H.F. & SELWOOD, J.T.
A guide to juvenile court law. 8ed. Jordan, 1974.

PAIN, K.W.
Practice and procedure in juvenile courts. Fourmat Pub., 1982.

PARSLOE, P.
Juvenile justice in Britain and the United States: the balance of needs and rights. Routledge & Kegan Paul, 1978.

RUSHFORTH, M.
Committal to residential care: a case study in juvenile justice. HMSO, 1978 (Scottish Office research studies).

WATSON, J.A.F. & AUSTIN, P.M.
The modern juvenile court for magistrates, social workers, police and others. Shaw, 1975.

KENYA

See also Africa.

Encyclopaedias and periodicals

Statutes in Force. Group: Constitutional Law.
Halsbury's Laws of England. 4ed. vol.6.
Halsbury's Statutes of England. 3ed. vol.4.

East African Law Journal. 1965–
Kenya Law Reports. 1897–1956.

Texts

AMROLIA, H.A.
Probate and administration in Kenya. Sweet & Maxwell, 1968.

BROWN, D.
Criminal procedure in Uganda and Kenya. 2ed. Sweet & Maxwell, 1970.

COTRAN, E.
Restatement of African law, vol.1: Kenya 1: Laws of marriage and divorce. Sweet & Maxwell, 1968.

COTRAN, E.
Restatement of African law. Vol.2: Kenya II: Succession. Sweet & Maxwell, 1969.

GERTZEL, C.
Government and politics in Kenya. Athlone P., 1972.

GHAI, Y.P. & McAUSLAN, J.P.W.B.
Public law and political change in Kenya: a study of the legal framework of government from colonial times in the present. Oxford U.P., 1970.

HYDEN, G.
Development administration: the Kenyan experience. Oxford U.P., 1970.

TREVELYAN, E.A.
A digest of the decisions of the Supreme Court of Kenya. Oceana, 1966.

KING'S REMEMBRANCER

BONNER, Sir G.A.
Office of the King's Remembrancer in England. Butterworths, 1930.

LABORATORIES
See also Hospitals

Texts

COOKE, A.J.D.
A guide to laboratory law. Butterworths, 1976.

UNIERSITIES FEDERATION FOR ANIMAL WELFARE
Welfare of laboratory animals: legal, scientific and humane requirements. 1977.

LAND
See also Conveyancing; Crown; Drains and Sewers; Real Property.

Encyclopaedias and periodicals

Statutes in Force. Groups: Agriculture; Compulsory Acquisition; Land Drainage; Property, England & Wales.
Halsbury's Laws of England. 4ed. see index vol.
Halsbury's Statutes of England. 3ed. see index vol.
The Digest. see index vol.

Encyclopaedia of Court Forms in Civil Proceedings (Atkin). 2ed. see index vol.
Conveyancer and Property Lawyer. 1936–
Estates Gazette. 1858–
Estates Gazette Digest of Land and Property Cases. Annual.
Property and Compensation Reports. 1950–
Rating and Valuation Reporter. 1961–

Texts

BARBER, P.
Land law notebook. Butterworths, 1969.

BARNSLEY, D.G.
Land options. Oyez, 1978.

BUTT, P.
Introduction to land law. Law Book Co., 1980 (Australia).

CURZON, L.B.
Land law. 4ed. Macdonald & Evans, 1982.

DALTON, P.J.
Land law. 3ed. Pitman, 1983.

DAVIES, K.
Law of property in land. Estates Gazette, 1979.

DAWSON, I.J. & PEARCE, R.A.
Licenses relating to the occupation or use of land. Butterworths, 1979.

DOUGLAS, R.
Land people and politics: a history of the land question in the United Kingdom. 1878–1952. Allison & B., 1976.

ELIAS, T.O.
Nigerian land law. 4ed. Sweet & Maxwell, 1971.

ENCYCLOPAEDIA of the law of town and country planning. Sweet & Maxwell. 4 vols. Looseleaf.

ENVIRONMENT, DEPARTMENT OF THE
Land. HMSO, 1974 (Cmnd. 5730).

FRANCIS, E.A.
The law and practice relating to Torrens title in Australia. 2 vols. Butterworths (Australia), 1972–73.

LAND

GARNER, J.F.
Public control of land. Sweet & Maxwell, 1956.

GREEN, E.S. & HENDERSON, N.
Land law. 4ed. Sweet & Maxwell, 1980 (Concise college texts).

HARGREAVES, A.D.
An introduction to the principles of land law. 4ed. Sweet & Maxwell, 1963.

HARGREAVES, A.D. & HELMORE, B.A.
Introduction to the principles of land law. Law Book Co., 1973 (Australia).

HARRIS, B. & RYAN, G.
Law relating to common land and access to the countryside. Sweet & Maxwell, 1967.

HARVEY, B.W.
Settlement of land. Sweet & Maxwell, 1973.

HARWOOD, M.
Cases and materials on English land law. 2ed. Sweet & Maxwell, 1982.

HARWOOD, M.
English land law. Sweet & Maxwell, 1975.

HAWKINS, A.J.
Law relating to owners and occupiers of land. Butterworths, 1971.

HEAP, Sir D.
The land and the development. Stevens, 1975 (Hamlyn lectures).

HEAP, Sir D.
Land and the law. I.B.A.: Sweet & Maxwell, 1984.

HELMORE, R.A.
Sale of land in Australia. Law Book Co., 1971.

HINDE, G.W. & SIM, P.B.A.
Land law of New Zealand. Butterworths (New Zealand), 1977–78. 2 vols.

HOLDSWORTH, Sir W.S.
An historical introduction to the land law. Oxford U.P., 1927.

KIRKWOOD, J.S.
Information technology and land administration. Estates Gazette, 1984.

KOLBERT, C.F. & MACKAY, N.A.M.
History of Scots and English land law. Geographical Pubns., 1977.

KOLBERT, C.F. & O'BRIEN, T.
Land reform in Ireland: a legal history of the Irish land problem and its settlement. Univ. of Cambridge, Dept. of Land Economy, 1975.

LANG, A.G. & EVERETT, D.
Land dealings and conveyancing casebook. Butterworths (Australia), 1979.

LAW COMMISSION
Rights of access to neighbouring land. HMSO, 1980 (Working paper no.78).

LAW COMMISSION
Transfer of land: appurtenent rights. HMSO, 1971 repr. 1977 (Working paper no.36).

LAW COMMISSION
Transfer of land: the law of positive and restrictive covenants. HMSO, 1984 (Law Com. no. 127).

LAW COMMISSION & SCOTTISH LAW COMMISSION
Taxation of income and gains derived from land. HMSO, 1971 (Law Com. no.43; Scot. Law Com. no.21).

LAW REFORM COMMITTEE FOR SCOTLAND
Second report: the procedural law relating to actions of removing and actions of ejection. HMSO, 1957 (Cmnd. 114).

McAUSLAN, P.
Land, law and planning. Weidenfeld & N., 1975.

MAUDSLEY, R.H. & BURN, E.H.
Land law: cases and materials. 4ed. Butterworths, 1980.

MEEK, C.K.
Land law and custom in the colonies. 2ed. Oxford U.P., 1949.

MELLOWS, A.R.
Taxation of land transactions. 3ed. Butterworths, 1983.

O'KEEFE, J.A.B.
Legal concept and principles of land value. Butterworths, 1974 (New Zealand).

PRESTON, C.H.S. & NEWSOM, G.H.
Restrictive covenants affecting freehold land. 7ed. Sweet & Maxwell, 1982.

PROPHET, J.
Fair rents: a practical guide to the statutory regulation of rents and residential tenancies etc. 2ed. Shaw, 1979.

RIDDALL, J.G.
Introduction to land law. 3ed. Butterworths, 1983.

SIMPSON, A.W.B.
An introduction to the history of land law. Oxford U.P., 1961.

SIMPSON, S.R.
Land law and registration. Book 1.
Cambridge U.P., 1978.

SOARES, P.C.
Tax strategy for conveyancing and land transactions. Oyez Longman, 1984.

SWINFEN-GREEN, E. & HENDERSON,
Land law. 4ed. Sweet & Maxwell, 1980.

TURNER, D.M.
An approach to land values. Geographical Pubns., 1977.

TYLER, E.L.G.
Cases and statutes on land law. Sweet & Maxwell, 1974 (Concise college texts).

WOODLEY, D.G.
Coal mining law for the land practitioner. Oyez, 1972.

WYLIE, J.C.W.
Irish land law. Professional Books, 1975 supp. 1981.

LAND CHARGES

Encyclopaedias and periodicals

Statutes in Force, Group: Property, England & Wales, Sub-group 2.
Halsbury's Laws of England. 4ed. vol.26.
Halsbury's Statutes of England. 3ed. see index vol.
The Digest. see index vol.

Encyclopaedia of Court Forms in Civil Proceedings (Atkin). 2ed. mainly vol.23.
Encyclopaedia of Forms and Precedents. 4ed. see index vol.
Conveyancer & Property Lawyer. 1936–

Texts

COMMITTEE ON LAND CHARGES
Report (Roxburgh). HMSO, 1956 (Cmnd. 9825).

COMMITTEE ON LOCAL LAND CHARGES
Report (Stainton). HMSO, 1951 (Cmnd. 8440).

COSWAY, A.H.
Practical guide to the Land Charges Act, 1925. 2ed. Pitman, 1933.

EATON, E.W. & PURCELL, J.P.
Land Charges Acts, 1888 and 1900. Stevens, 1901.

GARNER, J.F.
Local land charges. 9ed. Shaw, 1982.

HAMILTON, R.N.D.
Land charges (other than local land charges). Sol. Law Stat. Soc., 1951.

LAND REGISTRY
Computerised Land Charges Department: a practical guide for solicitors. HMSO, 1974.

LAW COMMISSION
Charging orders. HMSO, 1975 (Law Com. no.74).

LAW COMMISSION
Charging orders on land. HMSO, 1972 repr. 1977 (Working paper no.46).

LAW COMMISSION
Proposals for charges in the law relating to land charges affecting unregistered land and to local land charges. HMSO, 1967 repr. 1977 (Working paper no. 10).

LAW COMMISSION
Transfer of land: report on land charges affecting unregistered land. HMSO 1969 (Law Com. no. 18).

LAW COMMISSION
Transfer of land: report on local land charges. HMSO, 1975 (Law Com. no. 62).

RUOFF, T.B.F.
Searching without tears: the land charges computer. Oyez, 1974.

LAND REGISTRATION

See also Conveyancing; Real Property; Title.

Encyclopaedias and periodicals

Statutes in Force. Group: Property, England & Wales, Sub-group 2.
Halsbury's Laws of England. 4ed. vol.26.
Halsbury's Statutes of England. 3ed. vol.27.
The Digest. vol.38

Encyclopaedia of Court Forms in Civil Proceedings (Atkin). 2ed. vol.23.
Encyclopaedia of Forms and Precedents. 4ed. vol.17.

Conveyancer & Property Lawyer. 1936–

Texts

DOWSON, Sir E. & SHEPPARD, V.L.O.
Land registration. 2ed. HMSO, 1956.

FORTESCUE-BRICKDALE, Sir C. & STEWART-WALLACE, Sir J.S.
Land Registration Act, 1925. 4ed. Stevens, 1939.

HALLIDAY, J.M.
The Land Registration (Scotland) Act, 1979. Green, 1979.

HAYTON, D.J.
Registered land. 3ed. Sweet & Maxwell, 1981.

HOLLAND, J.A. & LEWIS, J.R.
Principles of registered land conveyancing. Butterworths, 1967.

KEY, T. & ELPHINSTONE, H.W.
Conveyancing precedents. 15ed. 1953 repr. Professional Books. vol.3.

LAND REGISTRY
Report to the Lord Chancellor. Annual.

LAW COMMISSION
Transfer of land: land registration (first paper). HMSO, 1970 repr. 1977 (Working paper no.32).

LAW COMMISSION
Transfer of land: land registration (second paper). HMSO, 1971 repr. 1977 (Working paper no.37).

LAW COMMISSION
Transfer of land: land registration (third paper). HMSO, 1972 repr. 1977 (Working paper no.45).

LAW COMMISSION
Transfer of land: land registration (fourth paper). HMSO, 1976 (Working paper no.67).

POTTER, H.
Principles of land law under the Land Registration Act 1925. 2ed. Sweet & Maxwell, 1948.

PRIDEAUX, F.
Conveyancing forms and precedents. 25ed. Stevens, 1959. 3 vols.

RUOFF, T.B.F.
Concise land registration practice. 3ed. Sweet & Maxwell, 1983.

RUOFF, T.B.F.
Land registration forms. 3ed. Sweet & Maxwell, 1983.

RUOFF, T.B.F. & ROPER, R.B.
The law and practice of registered conveyancing. 4ed. Sweet & Maxwell, 1979.

SIMPSON, S.R.
Land law and registration. Book 1. Cambridge U.P., 1978.

STEWART-WALLACE, Sir J.S.
Introduction to the principles of land registration. Stevens, 1937.

WALLACE, H.
Land registry practice in Northern Ireland, & supp. SLS Legal Pubns.

WOLSTENHOLME, E.F. & CHERRY, Sir B.L.
Conveyancing statutes. 13ed. Oyez, 1972. vol. 6.

WONTNER, J.J.
Wontner's guide to land registry practice. 14ed. Oyez, 1982.

LAND TENURE

See also Conveyancing; Copyhold; Landlord and Tenant; Leases; Mortmain; Real Property; Title.

Encyclopaedias

Statutes in Force. Group: Land Tenure, Scotland.
Halsbury's Laws of England. 4ed. vol.39.
The Digest. see index vol.

Texts

ADKIN, B.W.
Copyholds and other land tenures. 3ed. Estates Gazette, 1919 supp. 1924.

DAWSON, I.J. & PEARCE, R.A.
Licenses relating to the occupation or use of land. Butterworths, 1979.

DENMAN, D.R.
Origins of ownership: brief history of land ownership and tenure from earliest times to the modern era. Allen & Unwin, 1959.

ELTON, C.I.
A treatise on the law of copyholds and customary tenures of land. 2ed. Wildy, 1893 supp. 1898.

FINLASON, W.F.
The history of law and tenures of land in England and Wales. Stevens & Haynes, 1870.

HALLIDAY, J.M.
The Land Tenure Reform (Scotland) Act 1974. Green, 1974.

JOHN, E.
Land tenure in early England. Leicester U.P., 1960.

KOLBERT, C.F.
Land reform in Ireland: a legal history of the Irish land problem and its settlement. Cambridge Univ. Dept. of Land Economy, 1975.

LIVERSAGE, V.
Land tenure in the colonies. Cambridge U.P., 1945.

MEEK, C.K. (ed.)
Colonial law: a bibliography with special reference to native African systems of law and land tenure. repr. Greenwood, 1979.

LAND TRANSFER

See also Land Registration; Real Property; Stamp Duty.

Encyclopaedias

Statutes in Force. Group: Property, England & Wales, Sub-group 2.
Halsbury's Laws of England. 4ed. see index vol.
The Digest. see index vol.

Texts

FORTESCUE-BRICKDALE, Sir C. & SHELDON, W.H.
Land Transfer Acts. 2ed. Stevens, 1905.

LAND TRANSFER COMMITTEE
Report (Rushcliffe). HMSO, 1942–43 (Cmd. 6467).

LAND TRANSFER COMMITTEE
Report (Tomlin).HMSO, 1934–5 (Cmnd. 4776).

ROBBINS, L.G.G. & MAW, F.T.
Devolution of real estate. 4ed. Butterworths, 1908.

ROYAL COMMISSION ON THE LAND TRANSFER ACTS
Report (Viscount St Aldwyn). HMSO, 1909 (Cd. 4509); 1911 (Cd. 5494).

TYSSEN, A.D.
Real representative law: part I of the Land Transfer Act of 1897. Clowes, 1898.

LANDLORD AND TENANT

See also Dilapidations; Fixtures; Flats; Housing; Joint Tenancy; Land Tenure;
Leases; Light and Air; Party Walls; Real Property; Rent.

Encyclopaedias and periodicals

Statutes in Force. Group: Landlord and Tenant.
Halsbury's Laws of England. 4ed. vol.27.
Halsbury's Statutes of England. 3ed. mainly vol. 18.
The Digest. mainly vols. 30, 31.
Encyclopaedia of Court Forms in Civil Proceedings (Atkin). 2ed. vol.24.

Encyclopaedia of Forms and Precedents. 4ed. mainly vol.11.
Conveyancer & Property Lawyer. 1936–
Estates Gazette. 1858–
Legal Action (formerly L.A.G. Bulletin). 1973–

Texts

ADKIN, B.W.
Handbook of the law relating to landlord and tenant. 18ed. Estates Gazette, 1982.

ALDRIDGE,. T.M.
Housing Act, 1980: a practical guide. Oyez, 1980.

ALDRIDGE, T.M. & JOHNSON, T.A.
Managing business property: a legal handbook. Oyez, 1978.

ARDEN, A.
Housing: security and rent control. Sweet & Maxwell, 1978.

BARBER, M.P.(ed.)
Landlord and tenant in a nutshell. Sweet & Maxwell, 1966.

BROOKING, & CHERNON, A.
Tenancy law and practice Victoria. 2ed. Butterworths (Australia), 1980.

COLLEGE OF LAW
Residential tenancies (including the Rent (Agriculture) Act 1976 and the Rent Act 1977). 1977.

DAVIES, M.R.
Letting and managing residential or business premises: a legal and practical outline. R.I.C.S., 1978.

DONELL, R.A.
Landlord and tenant. Law Society, 1969.

DONNELLY, J.S.
Landlord and tenant in nineteenth century Ireland. Gill & Macmillan, 1974.

EVANS, D.L.
Law of landlord and tenant. 2ed. Butterworths, 1978.

FARRAND, J.T. & ARDEN, A.
The Rent Acts (amended and annotated). 2ed. Sweet & Maxwell, 1981.

FOA, E.
General law of landlord and tenant. 8ed. Thames Bank, 1957.

GREGORY, M. & PARRISH, M.
Essential law for landowners and farmers. Granada, 1980.

HADDEN, T.
Housing: repairs and improvements. Sweet & Maxwell, 1979.

HARPER, M.
Landlord v. Tenant. Wildwood House, 1977.

HARRISON, J.G.
Handbook on taxation of land. Institute of Chartered Accountants, 1982.

HILL, H.A. & REDMAN, J.H.
Law of landlord and tenant. 17ed. Butterworths, 1982.

LAW COMMISION
Codification of the law of landlord and tenant: report on obligations of landlords and tenants. HMSO, 1975 (Law Com. no. 67).

LAW COMMISSION
Landlord and tenant: report on the Landlord and Tenant Act 1954, Part II . HMSO, 1969 (Law Com. no. 17).

LAW COMMISSION
The law of landlord and tenant: provisional proposals relating to convenants restricting dispositions, parting with possession, change of user and alterations. HMSO, 1970 repr. 1977 (Working paper no.25).

LAW COMMISSION
Provisional proposals for amendments to the Landlord and Tenant Act 1954. Part II (business tenancies). HMSO, 1967 repr. 1977 (Working paper no.7).

LAW COMMISSION
Provisional proposals relating to obligations of landlords and tenants. HMSO, 1967 repr. 1977 (Working paper no.8).

LAW COMMISSION
Provisional proposals relating to termination of tenancies. HMSO, 1968 repr. 1977 (Working paper no.16).

LEWIS, J.R. & HOLLAND, J.A.
Landlord and tenant. 2ed. Felton P., 1978.

LONDON HOUSING AID CENTRE
Shorthold tenancies. 1979.

LOMNICKI, A.J.
A summary of landlord and tenant law. Batsford, 1975.

MALE, J.M.
Landlord and tenant. Macdonald & Evans, 1982.

NATIONAL CONSUMER COUNCIL
Tenancy agreements between councils and their tenants. HMSO, 1978.

NELKIN, D.
Limits of the legal process: study of landlords, law and crime. Academic Press, 1983.

ONWUAMAEGBU, M.O.
Nigerian law of landlord and tenant. Sweet & Maxwell, 1966.

PARTINGTON, M.
Landlord and tenant. 2ed. Weidenfeld & N., 1980.

PATON, G.C.H. & CAMERON, J.G.S.
The law of landlord and tenant in Scotland. Green, 1967.

PETTIT, P.H.
Landlord and tenant under the Rent Act, 1977. Butterworths, 1978.

PETTIT, P.H.
Private sector tenancies. 2ed. Butterworths, 1981.

ROBERTSON, P. & SEAWARD, M.
Security of tenure in the private rented sector. Association of Housing Aid, 1983.

STAPLETON, T.B.
Estate management practice. Estates Gazette, 1981.

TEH, G.L.
Residential tenancies handbook – Victoria. Butterworths (Australia), 1982.

WILLIAMS, E.K.
Canadian law of landlord and tenant. 4ed. Carswell, 1973.

WOODFALL, W.
The law of landlord and tenant. 28ed. Sweet & Maxwell, 1978. 3 vols. Looseleaf.

YATES, D. & HAWKINS, A.J.
Landlord and tenant law. Sweet & Maxwell, 1981.

LANDS TRIBUNAL

Encyclopaedias and periodicals

Statutes in Force. Groups: Property, England & Wales; Tribunals and Inquiries.
Halsbury's Laws of England. 4ed. vol.8.
Halsbury's Statutes of England. 3ed. mainly vol.6 but see index vol.
The Digest. see index vol.

Texts

ROACH, R.F.C.
Lands tribunal practice and procedure and guide to costs. Sweet & Maxwell, 1961.

ROBERTS, M. & EMENY, R.
Lands tribunal index, 1965–1972. RICS, 1974.

Encyclopaedia of Court Forms in Civil Proceedings (Atkin). 2ed. vol.25.
Encyclopaedia of Forms and Precedents. 4ed. see index vol.

Lands Tribunal Cases. 1974–

RODGERS, S.C.
The Lands Tribunal. Estates Gazette, 1952.

VANS OSS, M.D. & MACDERMOT, N.
Lands tribunal law and procedure. Butterworths, 1950.

LAW COMMISSION

See also Law Reform; Scottish Law Commission

Encyclopaedias and periodicals

Statutes in Force. Group: Government Departments and Public Offices.
Halsbury's Laws of England. 4ed. vol.8.
Halsbury's Statutes of England. 3ed. vol.32.

Conveyancer & Property Law. 1936–
Criminal Law Review. 1954–
Law Society's Gazette. 1903–
New Law Journal. 1965–
Solicitors' Journal. 1857–

Texts

FARRAR, J.
Law reform and the Law Commission. Sweet & Maxwell, 1974.

LAW COMMISSION
Annual reports. HMSO.

LAW COMMISSION
First programme of the Law Commission. HMSO, 1965 (Law Com. no.1).

LAW COMMISSION
Second programme of law reform. HMSO, 1968 (Law Com. no. 14).

LAW COMMISSION
Third programme of law reform. HMSO, 1973 (Law Com. no.54).

LAW COMMISSION
First programme on consolidation and statute law revision. HMSO, 1966 (Law Com. no.2).

LAW COMMISSION
Second programme on consolidation and statute law revision. HMSO, 1971 (Law Com. no.44).

LAW COMMISSION
Working papers nos. 1–64. 1966–1975 repr. Professional Books, 1977. 7 vols. (later vols. also reprinted).

RAISTRICK, D.
Law Commission digest. Professional Books, 1979.

LAW MERCHANT

See also Commercial Law.

Encyclopaedias

Halsbury's Laws of England. 4ed. see index vol.
Halsbury's Statutes of England. 3ed. see index vol.
The Digest. see index vol.

Texts

BEWES, W.A.
The romance of the law merchant. Sweet & Maxwell, 1923.

MALYNES, G. de
Consuetudo vel lex mercatoria, or the ancient law merchant. 1636.

MITCHELL, W.
An essay on the early history of the law merchant. Cambridge U.P., 1904.

SELDEN SOCIETY
Select cases concerning the law merchant.
Vol.1: Local courts. 1270–1638.
Vol.2: Central courts including assizes 1239–1633.
Vol.3: 1251–1779.

LAW OFFICERS

Encyclopaedias
Halsbury's Laws of England. 4ed. see index vol.
Halsbury's Statutes of England. 3ed. see index vol.
The Digest. see index vol.

Texts
CASEY, J.P.
Office of the Attorney General in Ireland. Inst. of Public Admin., 1980.

EDWARDS, J.Ll.J.
The Attorney General, politics and the public interest. Sweet & Maxwell, 1984.

EDWARDS, J.Ll.J.
The law officers of the Crown. Sweet & Maxwell, 1964 repr. 1977.

NORTON-KYSHE, J.W.
The law and privileges relating to colonial attorneys-general, and to the offices corresponding to the Attorney-General of England in the United States of America. Stevens & Haynes, 1900.

NORTON-KYSHE, J.W.
The law and privileges relating to the Attorney General and Solicitor General of England. Stevens & Haynes, 1897.

LAW REFORM

See also Law Commission; Scottish Law Commission.

Periodicals
Cambridge Law Journal. 1921–
Law Quarterly Review. 1885–
Law Society's Gazette, 1903–
Modern Law Review. 1937–

New Law Journal. 1965– (as Law Journal. 1882–1964).
Solicitor's Journal. 1857–

Texts
ARCHER, P. & MARTIN A. (eds.)
More law reform: new collection of essays on law reform. B.Rose, 1983.

BENNION, F.A.R.
Tangling with the law: reforms in legal process. Chatto & Windus, 1970.

BORRIE, G.
Law reform: a damp squib? An inaugural lecture delivered in the University of Birmingham. Birmingham Univ., 1970.

GARDINER, G.A. & MARTIN, A. (eds.)
Law reform now. Gollancz, 1963.

KEETON, R.E.
Venturing to do justice: reforming private law. Harvard U.P., 1969.

KIRBY, Sir, M.
Reform the law: essays on the renewal of the Australian legal system. Oxford U.P. (Australia), 1984.

LAW COMMISSION
Annual reports. HMSO.

LAW COMMISSION
First programme of the Law Commission. HMSO, 1965 (Law Com. no.1).

LAW COMMISSION
Second programme of law reform. HMSO, 1968 (Law Com. no.14).

LAW COMMISSION
Third programme of law reform. HMSO, 1973 (Law Com. no.54).

LAW COMMISSION
First programme on consolidation and statute law revision. HMSO, 1966 (Law Com. no. 2).

LAW COMMISSION
Second programme on consolidation and statute law revision. HMSO, 1971 (Law Com. no. 44).

LAW COMMISSION
Working papers 1–64. HMSO, 1966–75 repr. Professional Books, 1977. 7 vols. Later papers also available in reprint vols.

McGREGOR, O.R.
Social history and law reform. Stevens, 1981.

MARTIN, A,.
Methods of law reform. Southampton Univ., 1967 (Inaugural lecture).

NAGEL, S.S.
Improving the legal process: effects of alternatives. Lexington, 1975 (USA).

RAISTRICK, D.
Law Commision digest. Professional Books, 1979.

SANDERS, A.J.G.M.
Southern Africa in need of law reform. Butterworths (S.Africa), 1981.

SCARMAN, Sir L.
Law reform: the new pattern. Sweet & Maxwell, 1968.

SCOTTISH LAW COMMISSION
Annual reports. HMSO.

SCOTTISH LAW COMMISSION
First programme of law reform. HMSO, 1965 (Scot. Law Com. no.1).

SCOTTISH LAW COMMISSION
Second programme of law reform. HMSO, 1968 (Scot. Law Com. no.8).

SCOTTISH LAW COMMISSION
Third programme of law reform. HMSO, 1973 (Scot. Law Com. no.29).

SCOTTISH LAW COMMISSION
First programme of consolidation and statute law reform. HMSO, 1966 (Scot.Law Com. no.2).

SCOTTISH LAW COMMISSION
Second programme of consolidation and statute law revision. HMSO, 1973 (Scot. Law Com. no.27).

STATUTE LAW SOCIETY
Renton and the need for reform. Sweet & Maxwell, 1979.

STATUTE LAW SOCIETY
Statute law deficiences. Sweet & Maxwell, 1970.

STATUTE LAW SOCIETY
Statute law: the key to clarity. Sweet & Maxwell, 1972.

STATUTE LAW SOCIETY
Statute law: a radical simplification. Sweet & Maxwell, 1964.

VANDERBILT, A.T.
The challenge of law reform. Princeton U.P., 1955 repr. Greenwood, 1976.

VEALL, D.
The popular movement for law reform, 1640–1660. Oxford U.P., 1970.

WILLIAMS, G.L.
Reform of the law. Gollancz, 1951.

LAW REPORTERS AND REPORTING

Encyclopaedias

Halsbury's Laws of England. 4ed. see index vol.

Texts

ABBOTT, L.W.
Law reporting in England, 1485–1585. Athlone P., 1973.

AUSTRALIAN and New Zealand citator to UK reports 1558–1972. 1973 plus Cumulative Supplement 1973–1981. 1982. Butterworths (Australia).

DANIELS, W.T.S.
History of the law reports. 1884 repr.
Wildy, 1968.

HOLDSWORTH, Sir W.S.
Law reporting in the nineteenth and
twentieth centuries. N.Y.U.Law School,
1941.

MORAN, C.G.
Heralds of the law: a short history of law
reporting. Stevens, 1948.

SOULE, C.C.
Lawyers' reference manual of law reports
and citations. 2ed. Soule & Bugbee, 1884
(USA).

WALLACE, J.W.
The reporters. 4ed. 1882 repr. Professional
Books.

LAYTIME

See also C.I.F. & F.O.B. Contracts; Carriers/Carriage of Goods; Charterparties;
Demurrage; Shipping.

Encyclopaedias and periodicals

The Digest. vol.41.

Lloyd's Maritime and Commercial Law
Quarterly. 1974–

Texts

SUMMERSKILL, M.B.
Laytime. 3ed. Sweet & Maxwell, 1982.

LEAGUE OF NATIONS

See also International Law; United Nations.

Texts

AUFRICHT, H.
Guide to League of Nations publications: a
bibliographical survey of the work of the
League, 1920–1947. 1951 repr. AMS
Press, 1974.

BENDINER, E.
A time for angels: the tragicomic history of
the League of Nations. Weidenfeld & N.,
1975.

BIRCHFIELD, M.E.
Consolidated catalog of League of Nations
publications offered for sale. Oceana,
1976.

BURTON, M.E.
Assembly of the League of Nations. 1941
repr. Fertig, 1973.

GIBBONS, S.R. & MORICAN, P.
League of Nations and the U.N.O.
Longman, 1970.

HENIG, R.B.
League of Nations. Barnes & Noble, 1973.

RAFFO, P.
The League of Nations. Historical Assoc.,
1974.

SCHWARZENBERGER, G.
League of Nations and world order: a
treatise on the principles of universality in
the theory and practice of the League of
Nations. 1936 repr. Hyperion, 1979.

SCOTT, G.
Rise and fall of the League of Nations.
Macmillan, 1974.

WALTERS, F.P.
History of the League of Nations. Oxford
U.P., 1952.

ZIMMERN, A.E.
League of Nations and the rule of law,
1918–1935. 1939 repr. Russell & Russell,
1969.

LEASES

See also Conveyancing; Land Tenure; Landlord and Tenant; Real Property; Title.

Encyclopaedias and periodicals

Statutes in Force. Group: Property, England & Wales.
Halsbury's Laws of England. 4ed. vols. 27, 42 and see index vols.
Halsbury's Statutes of England. 3ed. mainly vol.18.
The Digest. see index vol.
Encyclopaedia of Court Forms in Civil Proceedings (Atkin). 2ed. see index vol.

Encyclopaedia of Forms and Precedents. 4ed. see index vol.
Conveyancer and Property Lawyer. 1936–
Estates Gazette. 1858–
Estates Gazette Digest of Land and Property Cases. Annual.

Texts

ALDRIDGE, T.M.
Leasehold law. Oyez, 1980. 3 vols. Looseleaf.

ALDRIDGE, T.M.
Letting business premises. 4ed. Oyez, 1981.

ALDRIDGE, T.M.
Rent control and leasehold enfranchisement. 8ed. Oyez, 1980.

ARNOLD, J.C.
Covenants relating to leasehold and tenancy agreements. Butterworths, 1930.

BISHOP, D.
Industrial leases: standard form and commentary. College of Estate Management, 1983.

ENVIRONMENT, DEPARTMENT OF THE
Houses held on ground lease: some rights under the Landlord and Tenant Act 1954 explained. HMSO, 1972.

GEORGE, E.F. & GEORGE, A.
Sale of flats. 5ed. Sweet & Maxwell, 1984.

HAGUE, N.
Leasehold enfranchisement in the public and private sectors. Oyez, 1981.

KERR, A.J.
Law of lease. Butterworths (S.Africa), 1969.

LEACH, W.A.
Practical points on leases. Estates Gazette, 1961.

LEASEHOLD COMMITTEE
Report (Jenkins). HMSO, 1950 (Cmd. 7982).

LEASEHOLD COMMITTEE
Report (Uthwatt). HMSO, 1949 (Cmd. 7706).

LEWISON, K.
Drafting business leases. Oyez, 1980.

LLOYD, D. & MONTGOMERY, J.
Business lettings. Butterworths, 1956.

MACMILLAN, S.K.
Law of leases. Estates Gazette, 1970.

NEWMAN, P.E.
Conveyancing of leasehold property. Fourmat, 1982.

ROSS, M.J.
Drafting and negotiating commercial leases. 2ed. Butterworths, 1984.

ROSS, M.J.
Practical guide to commercial leases. Butterworths, 1980.

SKEFFINGTON, A.
Leasehold enfranchisement. Fabian Society, 1956.

UNDERHILL, Sir A.
Leasehold enfranchisement. 2ed. Cassell, 1887.

WALFORD, E.O.
Practical hints on draft leases. 3ed. Butterworths, 1942.

WHITFIELD, A.H.
Introduction to the law of leases. Estates Gazette, 1961.

WILSON, M.
Conveyancing: fees and duties on sale of freehold and leasehold. 4ed. Fourmat, 1984.

YATES, D.
Leases of business premises. Sweet & Maxwell, 1979.

LEGAL AID AND ADVICE

See also Solicitors; Welfare Law.

Encyclopaedias and periodicals

Statutes in Force. Group: Legal Aid.
Halsbury's Laws of England. 4ed. vols. 11, 37 and see index vol.
Halsbury's Statutes of England. 3ed. vol.44.
The Digest. see index vol.
Encyclopaedia of Court Forms in Civil Proceedings (Atkin). 2ed. vol.25.

Encyclopaedia of Forms and Precedents. 4ed. vol.21.
Law Society's Gazette. 1903–
Legal Action (formerly L.A.G. Bulletin). 1973–

Texts

BAKER, J.
Neighbourhood advice centre: community project in Camden. Routledge, 1978.

BIGGS, A.K.
Legal aid financial conditions and resources. Fourmat, 1984.

BROWNELL, E.A.
Legal aid in the United States. Greenwood, 1951.

BYLES, A. & MORRIS, P.
Unmet need: case of the neighbourhood law centre. Routledge, 1977.

CASS, M.
The legal needs of the poor. Butterworths (Australia), 1975.

CHATTERTON, C.E.M.
Legal aid applications to magistrates' courts. Basset Pubns., 1984.

COMMITTEE ON LEGAL AID & ADVICE IN ENGLAND & WALES
Report (Rushcliffe). HMSO, 1948 (Cmd. 6641).

COMMITTEE ON LEGAL AID & ADVICE IN SCOTLAND
Report (Cameron). HMSO, 1945 (Cmd. 6925).

COMMITTEE ON LEGAL AID FOR THE POOR
Final report (Finlay). HMSO, 1928 (Cmd. 3016).

EUROPEAN COMMITTEE ON LEGAL CO-OPERATION
Explanatory report... (European Agreement on the transmission of applications for legal aid). Council of Europe, 1977.

FABIAN SOCIETY
Legal services for all. 1978.

FOGGO-PAYS, E.
Introductory guide to counselling. Ravenswood Pubns., 1982.

GRAHAM-GREEN, G.J.
Criminal costs and legal aid. 3ed. Butterworths, 1973 supp. 1978.

GROSS, P.
Legal aid and its management. Juta, 1976 (S.Africa).

HARRIS, B.
Legal aid and advice: a guide for magistrates and social workers. Rose, 1975.

HARRIS, B.
Legal aid and advice: a guide to the Legal Aid Act 1974 and regulations particularly for practitioners in the Magistrates' Courts. Rose, 1974.

INTERNATIONAL LEGAL AID ASSOCIATION
Dictory of legal aid and advice facilities available throughout the world. 1965–6. 2 vols. 2 supps. to 1972.

THE LAW SOCIETY
Legal aid solicitors' referral list. 1976. 26 booklets covering England and Wales.

LEGAL ACTION GROUP.
Legal aid – how to make the best use of it: a guide for solicitors to the law and practice of the legal aid and advice schemes. 1976.

LORD CHANCELLOR'S DEPARTMENT
Legal aid handbook 1984. HMSO, 1984.

MATTHEWS, E.J.T. & OULTON, A.D.M.
Legal aid and advice. Butterworths, 1971 supp. 1978.

MOERAN, E.
Legal aid summary. 2ed. Oyez, 1981.

MOERAN, E.
Practical legal aid. 3ed. Oyez, 1982.

POLLOCK, S.
Legal aid: the first 25 years. Oyez, 1975.

SACHS, E.
Legal aid. Eyre & Spottiswoode, 1951.

SACKVILLE, R.
Legal aid in Australia. Butterworths (Australia), 1975.

STODDART, C.N.
The law and practice of legal aid in Scotland. Green, 1979.

TEASDALE, J.P.
Guide to costs and legal aid in criminal cases. Oyez, 1979.

WILKINS, J.L.
Legal aid in criminal matters: a bibliography. Univ. of Toronto, 1971.

WILKINS, J.L.
Legal aid in the criminal courts. Univ. of Toronto, 1975.

ZANDER, M.
Legal services for the community. M.T.Smith, 1978.

ZEMANS, F.H. (ed.)
Perspectives on legal aid: an international survey. F.Pinter, 1979 (USA).

LEGAL DRESS

DUGDALE, Sir W.
Origines juridicales. 3ed. Wilkinson, Dring & Harper, 1680.

HARGREAVES-MAUDSLEY, W.M.
A history of legal dress in Europe until the end of the eighteenth century. Oxford U.P., 1963.

NORTON-KYSHE, J.W.
Law of gloves. Stevens & Haynes, 1904.

LEGAL EDUCATION

See also Education.

Periodicals

Law Teacher. 1967–
Legal Studies (formerly Journal of the Society of Public Teachers of Law). 1924–
Wig and Gavel: the official magazine of the London Law Students. 1980–

Texts

BATES, N.
Introduction to legal studies. 3ed. Butterworths (Australia), 1980.

BURRIS, R.W.
Teaching law with computers. Westview, 1980 (USA).

CAMPBELL, C. and others
Tomorrow's lawyers: computers and legal training. Soc. for Computers & Law, 1981.

CHALMERS, D.R.C.
Textbook for legal studies – Tasmania. Butterworths (Australia), 1983.

COMMITTEE ON LEGAL EDUCATION
Report (Ormrod). HMSO, 1971 (Cmnd. 4595).

COMMITTEE ON LEGAL EDUCATION FOR STUDENTS FROM AFRICA
Report (Denning). HMSO, 1961 (Cmnd. 1255).

GREEN, A.W.
Bibliography on British legal education. West Chester State College, 1973 (USA).

HARRIS, P. & LEWIS, R.
Teaching the law. Assoc. of Law Teachers, 1980.

KERSLEY, R.H. & GIBSON, A.
Gibson's 1876–1962: a chapter in legal education. Law Notes, 1973.

LAWSON, F.H.
Oxford law school, 1850–1965. Oxford U.P., 1968.

SHERIDAN, L.A.
Legal education in the seventies. Queen's Univ. Belfast, 1967 (Inaugural lecture).

SWORDS, P. de L. & WALWER, F.K.
Costs and resources of legal education. Columbia U.P., 1975.

WILLIAMS, G.L.
Learning the law. 11ed. Stevens, 1982.

LEGAL EXECUTIVES

See also Legal Profession.

Periodicals

The Legal Executive. 1963–

Texts

INSTITUTE OF LEGAL EXECUTIVES
Becoming a legal executive. 1971.

JONES, C.
Solicitor's clerk. Wilson, Pt.1, 14ed. 1951; Pt.2, 12ed. 1940.

LOCKWOOD, L.C.
Solicitor's clerk in court. Sweet & Maxwell, 1968.

LEGAL MAXIMS

See also Dictionaries.

BAXTER, J.H. & JOHNSON, C.
Medieval Latin word-list from British and Irish sources. Oxford U.P., 1934 repr. 1948.

BROOM, H.
Selection of legal maxims classified and illustrated. 10ed. Sweet & Maxwell, 1939 repr. 1974.

BYRNE, W.J.
Dictionary of English law and concise legal encyclopaedia. Sweet & Maxwell, 1923.

JONES, J.W.
Translation of all the Greek, Latin, Italian, and French quotations which occur in Blackstone's commentaries, etc. also in the notes of Christian, Archbold and Williams. Oxford U.P., 1823.

JOWITT, Lord
The dictionary of English law. 2ed. Sweet & Maxwell, 1977 supp. 1984.

LATIN for lawyers. 3ed. Sweet & Maxwell, 1960.

MOZLEY, H.N. & WHITELEY, G.C.
Law dictionary. 9ed. Butterworths, 1977.

OSBORN, P.G.
Concise law dictionary. 7ed. Sweet & Maxwell, 1983.

STROUD, F.
Judicial dictionary of words and phrases. 4ed. Sweet & Maxwell, 1971–5. 5 vols. supp. 1982.

TRAYNER, J.
Latin maxims. 4ed. Green, 1894.

WHARTON, G.F.
Legal maxims. 3ed. Stevens & Haynes, 1903.

WHARTON, J.J.S.
Law lexicon: an epitome of the law of England. 14ed. Stevens, 1938.

WORDS and phrases legally defined. Butterworths, 1969–75. 5 vols. & annual supp.

LEGAL PROFESSION

See also Advocates and Advocacy; Bar and Barristers; Legal Executives; Notaries; Solicitors.

Encyclopaedias and periodicals

Statutes in Force. Group: Lawyers and Notaries.
Halsbury's Laws of England. 4ed. see index vols. under Barristers, Solicitors and Notaries.
Halsbury's Statutes of England. 3ed. see index vol.
The Digest. see index vol.

Guardian Gazette (formerly Law Guardian). 1965–
Law Society's Gazette. 1903–
The Law Teacher. 1967–
The Legal Executive. 1963–
Legal Studies (formerly Journal of the Society of Public Teachers of Law). 1924–

Texts

ABEL-SMITH, B. & STEVENS, R.
Lawyers and the courts: a sociological study of the English legal system. 1750–1965. Heinemann, 1967.

BING, J. & HARVOLD, T.
Legal decision and information systems. Universitetsforlaget, 1977.

CAMPBELL, D.J.
Annotated bibliography on the legal profession and legal services, 1960–78. Univ. Coll. Cardiff P., 1980.

CARR-SAUNDERS, Sir A.M. & WILSON, P.A.
The professions. Cass, 1964.

CLAY, J.L.
The young lawyer. Butterworths, 1955.

DONNER, A.M.
The role of the lawyer in the European communities. Edinburgh U.P., 1968.

FORBES, J.
The divided legal profession. Law Book Co., 1979 (Australia).

GILBERT, M.
The law. David & Charles, 1977.

HOGAN, B.A.
A career in law. Sweet & Maxwell, 1981.

HOROWITZ, D.L.
The jurocracy. Lexington, 1977.

JUSTICE
Lawyers and the legal system: critique of legal services in England and Wales. Stevens, 1978.

LUND, Sir T.G.
The practice and etiquette of the Bar affecting solicitors. Law Society, 1953.

LUND, Sir T.G.
Professional ethics. Internat. Bar Assoc., 1970.

MacCORMICK, D.N. (ed.)
Lawyers in the social setting. Green, 1976 (Wilson memorial lectures).

MEGARRY, Sir R.
Lawyer and litigant in England. Stevens, 1962 (Hamlyn lectures).

PHILIPS, Sir F.
The evolving legal profession in the Commonwealth. Oceana, 1978 (USA).

PREST, W.
Lawyers in early modern Europe and America. Croom Helm, 1981.

ROYAL COMMISSION ON LEGAL SERVICES
Final report (Benson). HMSO, 1979 (Cmnd. 7648).

ROYAL COMMISSION ON LEGAL SERVICES IN SCOTLAND
Report (Hughes). HMSO, 1980 (Cmnd. 7846).

SOCIETY FOR COMPUTERS AND LAW
Tomorrow's lawyers: computers and legal training. 1981.

SQIBB, G.D.
Doctors' commons: a history of the College of Advocates and Doctors of Law. Oxford U.P., 1977.

THOMAS, P.A.
Law in the balance: legal services in the 1980's. Martin Robertson, 1982.

WEBSTER, R.M.
Professional ethics and practice for Scottish solicitors. The Author, 1976.

ZANDER, M.
Lawyers and the public interest: a study of restrictive practices. Weidenfeld & N., 1968.

LEGISLATION

See also Administrative Law; Delegated Legislation; Drafting; Government;
Interpretation; Parliament; Statutes.

Encyclopaedias and periodicals

Statutes in Force. Group: Statutes and
Statutory Instruments.
Halsbury's Laws of England. 4ed. see index
vols.

Public Administration. 1923–
Public Law. 1956–
Statute Law Review. 1980–

Texts

ALLEN, Sir C.K.
Law in the making. 7ed. Oxford U.P., 1964.

BENNION, F.
Statute law. 2ed. Oyez, 1983.

BENTHAM, J.
Introduction to principles of morals and
legislation. 3ed. 1876 repr. Athlone P.,
1970.

BENTHAM, J.
Theory of legislation. 1864 repr. Routledge
& Kegan Paul, 1976.

CARR, Sir C.T.
Delegated legislation. Cambridge U.P.,
1921.

COMMITTEE ON THE
PREPARATION OF LEGISLATION
Report (Renton). HMSO, 1975 (Cmnd.
6053).

DICKERSON, R.
The fundamentals of legal drafting. Little,
Brown, 1965.

FINER, H.
Theory and practice of modern
government. 2ed. Methuen, 1946. 2 vols.

GRUMM, J.G.
Paradigm for the comparative analysis of
legislative systems. Sage, 1973.

INTERNATIONAL LABOUR OFFICE
Chronological index of legislation, 1919–
78. 1980.

KELLY, J.H.
Draftsman. 14ed. Butterworths, 1978.

LAMBERT, S.
Bills and Acts: legislative procedure in
eighteenth century England. Cambridge
U.P., 1971.

MAY, Sir T. Erskine
Parliamentary practice. 20ed Butterworths,
1983.

PAGE, A.C. & MIERS, D.R.
Legislation. Sweet & Maxwell, 1982.

STATUTE LAW SOCIETY
Renton and the need for reform. Sweet &
Maxwell, 1979.

STATUTE LAW SOCIETY
Statute law deficiencies. Sweet & Maxwell,
1970.

STATUTE LAW SOCIETY
Statute law: the key to clarity. Sweet &
Maxwell, 1972.

STATUTE LAW SOCIETY
Statute law: a radical simplification. Sweet
& Maxwell, 1964.

THORNTON, G.C.
Legislative drafting. 2ed. Butterworths,
1979.

TOMASIC, R.
Legislation and society in Australia. Allen &
Unwin, 1980.

ZANDER, M.
Lawmaking process. Weidenfeld & N.,
1980.

LEGITIMACY AND ILLEGITIMACY

See also Children and Young Persons; Marriage.

Encyclopaedias and periodicals

Statutes in Force. Group: Family Law.
Halsbury's Laws of England. 4ed. mainly vols. 1 & 8.
Halsbury's Statutes of England. 3ed. see index vol.
The Digest. see index vol.

Encyclopaedia of Court Forms in Civil Proceedings (Atkin). 2ed. see index vol.
Encyclopaedia of Forms and Precedents. 4ed. see index vol.
Family Law. 1971–

Texts

BARBER, D. (ed.)
One parent families. Hodder, 1973.

BRAMALL, M.
Working paper on illegitimacy. NCUMC, 1968.

BRITISH MEDICAL ASSOCIATION & MAGISTRATES' ASSOCIATION
The law in relation to the illegitimate child: a report. 1952.

CHISLETT, A.J.
Affiliation proceedings. Butterworths, 1958.

CHURCH OF ENGLAND
Fatherless by law? The law and welfare of children designated illegitimate. Church Information Office, 1966.

CHURCH OF ENGLAND
Illegitimacy – present attitudes, social trends and case work, conference report, 22–26 June 1964. Church Information Office, 1964.

CLARKE HALL, W. & MORRISON, A.C.L.
Law relating to children and young persons. 9ed. Butterworths, 1977 supp. 1981.

COMMITTEE ON ONE-PARENT FAMILIES
Report (Finer). HMSO, 1974 (Cmnd. 5629).

COUNCIL FOR CHILDREN'S WELFARE
The plight of one-parent families. 1972.

COUNCIL OF EUROPE
Explanatory report on the Convention on the Legal Status of Children Born out of Wedlock. 1975.

GILL, D.
Illegitimacy: sexuality and the status of women. Blackwell, 1977.

HARRIS, B. (ed.)
The use of blood tests in determining paternity: a handbook for solicitors, doctors and court officials. Rose, 1973.

HARTLEY, S.F.
Illegitimacy as a social problem. Univ. of California P., 1975 (USA).

JEGER, L.M.
Illegitimate children and their parents: a summary of the relevant English law and social services. NCUMC, 1951.

JOSLING, J.F.
Affiliation law and practice. 4ed. Oyez, 1977.

KRAUSE, H.D.
Illegitimacy: law and social policy. Bobbs-Merrill, 1971 (USA).

LAW COMMISSION
Blood tests and proof of paternity in civil proceedings. HMSO, 1968 (Law Com. no.16).

LAW COMMISSION
Draft proposals on powers of the Court of Appeal to sit in private and restrictions upon publicity in legitmacy proceedings. HMSO, 1966 repr. 1977 (Working paper no.2).

LAW COMMISSION
Family law: illegitimacy. HMSO, 1979 (Working paper no.74).

LAW COMMISSION
Proof of paternity in civil proceedings. HMSO, 1967 repr. 1977 (Working paper no.12).

LORD CHANCELLOR'S OFFICE
Report on the law of succession in relation to illegitimate persons (Russell). HMSO, 1966 (Cmnd. 3051).

LUSHINGTON, G.
Law of affiliation and bastardy. 7ed.
Butterworths, 1951.

NATIONAL COUNCIL FOR ONE
PARENT FAMILIES
Accident of birth: response to the Law
Commission's working paper on
illegitimacy. 1980.

NATIONAL COUNCIL FOR THE
UNMARRIED MOTHER AND HER
CHILD
Illegitimacy and the community today.
1966.

PUXON, M.
Legitimacy and legitimation. Oyez, 1965.

SCHATKIN, S.B.
Disputed paternity proceedings. 4ed.
Bender, 1975 (USA). 2 vols. Looseleaf.

SCOTTISH LAW COMMISSION
Family law: report on illegitimacy. HMSO,
1984 (Scot. Law Com. no. 82).

SCOTTISH LAW COMMISSION
Reform of the law relating to legitimation
per subsequens matrimonium. HMSO,
1967 (Scot. Law Com. no.5).

SOCIETY OF PUBLIC TEACHERS OF
LAW
The illegitimate child in English law. 1969.

TEICHMAN, J.
The meaning of illegitimacy. Teichman,
New Hull, 1978.

TURNER, J.N.
Improving the lot of children born outside
marriage: a comparison of three recent
reforms: England, New Zealand and West
Germany. NCOPF, 1973.

WILKINSON, G.S.
Affiliation law and practice. 4ed. Oyez,
1977 (Practice notes no.41).

WILKINSON, G.S.
Legal aspects of illegitimacy. NCUMC,
1965.

LESOTHO

See also Africa

Encyclopaedias

Statutes in Force. Group: Commonwealth
and Other Territories.

Texts

HAMNETT, I.
Chieftainship and legitimacy: an
anthropological study of executive law in
Lesotho. Routledge, 1975.

PALMER, V.V. & PULTER, S.M.
The legal system of Lesotho. Michie, 1972.

PULTER, S.M.
Family law and litigation in Basotho society.
Oxford U.P., 1976.

LETTERS OF CREDIT

See also Banks and Banking; Commercial Credits; Negotiable Instruments.

Encyclopaedias

Statutes in Force. Group: Banking and
Currency.

Halsbury's Laws of England. 4ed. vols. 3, 41.
The Digest. see index vol.

Texts

DAVIS, A.G.
Law relating to commercial letters of credit.
3ed. Pitman, 1963.

PURVIS, R.N. & DARVAS, R.
The law and practice of commercial letters
of credit, shipping documents and
termination of disputes in international
trade. Butterworths (Australia), 1975.

SARNA, L.
Letters of credit. Carswell, 1984 (Canada).

LIBEL AND SLANDER

See also Criminal Law; Press Law; Printers and Publishers; Tort.

Encyclopaedias

Statutes in Force. Group: Criminal Law.
Halsbury's Laws of England. 4ed. vol.28.
Halsbury's Statutes of England. 3ed. vol.19.
The Digest. vol.32.

Encyclopaedia of Court Forms in Civil Proceedings (Atkin). 2ed. vol.25.
Encyclopaedia of Forms and Precedents. 4ed. see index vol.

Texts

BALL, Sir W.V.
The law of libel and slander. Stevens, 1936.

BOWER, G.S.
A code of the law of actionable defamation. 2ed. Sweet & Maxwell, 1923.

BUTTON, W.A.
Principles of the law of libel and slander. 2ed. Sweet & Maxwell, 1946.

CARTER-RUCK, P.F.
Libel and slander. Faber, 1972.

COMMITTEE ON THE LAW OF DEFAMATION
Report (Porter). HMSO, 1948 (Cmd. 7536).

DAILY EXPRESS
The Laski libel action: verbatim report. n.d. (1947).

DEAN, J.
Hatred, ridicule or contempt: a book of libel cases. Constable, 1953.

DUNCAN, C. & HOOLAHAN, A.
Guide to defamation practice. 2ed. Sweet & Maxwell, 1958.

DUNCAN, C. & NEILL, B.
Defamation. 2ed. Butterworths, 1983.

FRASER, H.
Libel and slander: law and practice. 7ed. Butterworths, 1936.

GATLEY, J.C.C.
Gatley on libel and slander. 8ed. Sweet & Maxwell, 1981.

HOOPER, D.
Public scandal, odium and contempt: an investigation of recent libel cases. Seckel & Warburg, 1984.

HYDE, H.M.
Privacy and the press. Butterworths, 1947.

KING, J.
The law of criminal libel. Carswell, 1912.

LLOYD, H.
The legal limits of journalism. Pergamon, 1968.

LORD CHANCELLOR'S OFFICE
Committee on defamation: report (Faulks). HMSO, 1975 (Cmnd. 5909).

ODGERS, W.B.
A digest of the law of libel and slander. Stevens, 1929.

O'SULLIVAN, R.
Law of defamation. Sweet & Maxwell, 1958.

PHELPS, R.H. & HAMILTON, E.D.
Libel: rights, risks, responsibilities. 2ed. Dover Pubns., 1978.

PRESS COUNCIL
Reforming the law of defamation: a memorandum. 1973.

SMITH, J.W.
Leading cases in various branches of the law. 13ed. Sweet & Maxwell, 1929 repr. Professional Books.

WILLIAMS, J.S.
Law of defamation in Canada. Butterworths (Canada), 1976.

LIBRARIES

See also Museums.

Encyclopaedias and periodicals

Statutes in Force. Group: Libraries, Museums and Galleries.
Halsbury's Laws of England. 4ed. vol.28.
Halsbury's Statutes of England. 3ed. see index vol.
The Digest. see index vol.
Encyclopaedia of Court Forms in Civil Proceedings (Atkin). 2ed. see index vol.
Encyclopaedia of Forms and Precedents. 4ed. see index vol.

Aslib Proceedings. 1957–
Assistant Librarian. 1953–
International Journal of Legal Information (formerly International Journal of Law Libraries). 1973–
Journal of Law and Information Science (Australia). 1982–
Journal of Librarianship. 1969–
Law Librarian. 1970–
Law Library Journal (USA). 1907–
Legal Information Management Index (USA). 1984–
Legal Reference Services Quarterly (USA). 1981–
Library and Information Science Abstracts. 1950–
Library Association Record. 1898–

Texts

ASHWORTH, W.
Handbook of special librarianship and information work. 5ed. Aslib, 1982.

BRITISH LIBRARY
Guide to government department and other libraries. 26ed. B.L., 1984.

HEWITT, A.R.
Public library law, and the law as to museums and art galleries in England and Wales, Scotland and Northern Ireland. 5ed. Assoc. of Assistant Libns., 1975.

LADENSON, A. (ed.)
American library laws. 4ed. American Library Assoc., 1974 supp. 1978.

MONTGOMERY, A.C.
Acronyms and abbreviations in library and information work: a reference handbook of British usage. Library Assoc., 1975.

MORRIS, R.J.B.
Parliament and the public libraries. Mansell, 1977.

PEMBERTON, J.E.
Politics and public libraries in England and Wales, 1850–1970. Library Assoc., 1977.

SMITH, A.D.
Microfilm: some legal implications. 2ed. Business Equipment Trade Assoc., 1978.

THOMPSON, A.H.
Censorship in public libraries in the United Kingdom during the twentieth century. Bowker, 1976.

UNESCO
Public library legislation: a comparative study. Unipub, 1972.

Law libraries

ADEFIDIYA, A.
Directory of law libraries in Nigeria. 2ed. Oceana, 1970.

AMERICAN ASSOCIATION OF LAW LIBRARIES
Directory of law libraries. Annual.

AUSTRALIAN LAW LIBRARIANS' GROUP
Directory of law libraries in Australia and Papua New Guinea. Butterworths (Australia), 1977.

BALLANTYNE, G.
The Signet Library Edinburgh and its librarians, 1722–1972. Scottish Library Assoc., 1979.

BANKS, M.A.
Using a law library. 3ed. Carswell, 1980 (Canada).

BLUNT, A.
Law librarianship. Bingley, 1980.

BRITISH LIBRARY
Report of the working party on provision for law. B.L., 1983.

BURTON, W.C. (ed.)
Legal thesaurus. Collier Macmillan, 1982.

DANE, J. & THOMAS, P.A.
How to use a law library. Sweet & Maxwell, 1979.

DAVIES, J.C.
Catalogue of manuscripts in the library of the Honourable Society of the Inner Temple. Oxford U.P., 1972. 3 vols.

ELLINGER, W.B.
Subject headings for the literature of law and international law. Rothman, 1969 (USA).

HOUDEK, F.G. (ed.)
Introducing the American Association of Law Libraries. AALL, 1983.

JAIN, H.C.
Law library administration and reference. Metropolitan Book Co., 1972 (India).

LEKNER, M.A. & STEINER, W.A.F.P.
University of Cambridge Squire law library law catalogue. Oceana, 1974. 14 vols.

LEKNER, M.A. & STEINER, W.A.F.P.
University of Cambridge Squire law library catalogue of international law. Oceana, 1972. 4 vols.

MARKE, J.J. & SLOANE, R.
Legal research and law library management. New York Law Journal Seminar Press, 1982.

MERSKY, R.M.
Collecting and managing rare law books. Glanville, 1982 (USA).

MISKIN, C.E. (ed.)
Directory of law libraries in the British Isles. 2ed. Legal Library Services, 1985.

MISKIN, C.E.
Library and information services for the legal profession. British Library, 1981 (BL R&DD report no. 5633).

MOYS, E.M.
Classification scheme for law books. 2ed. Butterworths, 1982.

MOYS, E.M. (ed.)
European law libraries guide. Morgan-Grampian, 1971.

MOYS, E.M. (ed.)
Manual of law librarianship: the use and organisation of legal literature. Deutsch, 1976.

MUELLER, H.P., KEHOE, P.E. & HURTADO, L. (eds.)
Law librarianship: a handbook. Rothman for AALL, 1983 (AALL pubn. no. 19). 2 vols.

REYNOLDS, T.H.
Rare books for law libraries. Glanville, 1983 (USA).

ROBERTS, S.A.
Survey of the use of law library collections at four British universities. Lib. Management Research Unit, Loughborough, 1977.

SAINSBURY, I.M.
Legal subject headings for law libraries. Butterworths, 1974.

SCHWERIN, K.
Classification for international law and relations. 3ed. Oceana, 1969.

STEINER, W.A.F.P.
Classification scheme and list of subject headings for the Squire law library of the University of Cambridge. Oceana, 1973.

ZAGAYKO, F.F.
International law: a classification for libraries. Oceana, 1965 (USA).

LICENSING

See also Magistrates

Encyclopaedias and periodicals

Statutes in Force. Group: Intoxicating Liquor.
Halsbury's Laws of England. 4ed. vol.26.
Halsbury's Statutes of England. 3ed. see index vol.
The Digest. see index vol.
Encyclopaedia of Court Forms in Civil Proceedings (Atkin). 2ed. see index vol.
Encyclopaedia of Forms and Precedents. 4ed. see index vol.

Justice of the Peace. 1837–
Local Government Review. 1971–
Magistrate. 1922–

Texts

ALLAN, J. & CHAPMAN, C.
The Licensing (Scotland) Act 1976. Green, 1977.

ANTHONY, E. & BERRYMAN, J.D.
A guide to licensing law: for betting shops, bookmakers, clubs and licensed premises. 3ed. Rose, 1976.

BELFAST & ULSTER LICENSED VINTNERS' ASSOCIATION
Guide to the licensing laws of Northern Ireland. 1970.

BOURKE, B.J. & CORRIDON, M.J.
Bourke's liquor laws Victoria. Butterworths (Australia), 1982. Looseleaf.

DEPARTMENTAL COMMITTEE ON LIQUOR LICENSING
Report (Erroll). HMSO, 1972 (Cmnd. 5154).

FIELD, D. & PINK, M.
Liquor licensing law. Sweet & Maxwell, 1983.

LINCOLN, A.
Liberty and licensing. C.P.C., 1973.

McDONALD, B.J.
Licensing laws of New South Wales. Butterworths (Australia), 1975. Looseleaf.

PAIN, K.W.
Licensing practice and procedure. Fourmat, 1984.

PATERSON, J.
Licensing Acts. Butterworths. Annual.

UNDERHILL, M.
The new licensing guide. 8ed. Oyez, 1982.

WHITESIDE, G.L.
Handbook for licensing justices. 3ed. B.Rose, 1982..

LIENS

See also Bailment; Debts and Debtors; Mortgages; Personal Property; Shipping.

Encyclopaedias

Statutes in Force. Group: Sale of Goods, Sub-group 1.
Halsbury's Laws of England. 4ed. vol.28.
Halsbury's Statutes of England. 3ed. mainly vol.19.

The Digest. vol.32.
Encyclopaedia of Court Forms in Civil Proceedings (Atkin). 2ed. see index vol.
Encyclopaedia of Forms and Precedents. 4ed. see index vol.

Texts

ASHBURNER, W.
Concise treatise on mortgages, pledges and liens. 2ed. Butterworths, 1911.

EAGLESON, J.G.
The law relating to bills of sales; contracts of sale, liens on crops and wool and stock mortgages. Sweet & Maxwell, 1911 (Australia).

Maritime

PRICE, G.
The law of maritime liens. 1940 repr. Professional Books.

THOMAS, D.R.
Maritime liens. Sweet & Maxwell, 1980.

Solicitors

CORDERY, A.
Cordery on solicitors. 7ed. Butterworths, 1981.

LIGHT AND AIR

See also Easements; Landlord and Tenant.

Encyclopaedias

Halsbury's Laws of England. 4ed. vol.14.
The Digest. vol.19.
Encyclopaedia of Court Forms in Civil Proceedings (Atkin). 2ed. vol.17.
Encyclopaedia of Forms and Precedents. 4ed. see index vol.

Texts

ANSTEY, B. & CHAVASSE, M.
The right to light. Estates Gazette, 1963.

COMBE, R.G.N.
A treatise upon the law of light. Butterworths, 1911.

COMMITTEE ON THE LAW RELATING TO RIGHTS OF LIGHT
Report (Harman). HMSO, 1957-8 (Cmnd. 473).

FLETCHER, B.
On light and air. 5ed. Batsford, 1908.

FOA, E.
General law of landlord and tenant. 8ed. Thames Bank Pub., 1957.

HUDSON, A.A. & INMAN, A.
Law of light and air. 2ed. Wilson, 1905.

KERR, R.
On ancient lights. Murray, 1865.

LATHAM, F.L.
A treatise on the law of window lights. Butterworths, 1867.

ROSCOE, E.S.
Digest of the law of light. 4ed. Clowes, 1904.

SWARBRICK, J.
Easements of light. Batsford, 1938. 2 vols.

WOODFALL, W.
The law of landlord and tenant. 28ed. Sweet & Maxwell, 1978. 3 vols. Looseleaf.

WOOLRYCH, H.W.
Law of window lights. 2ed. Butterworths, 1864.

LIMITATION OF ACTIONS

See also Prescription.

Encyclopaedias

Statutes in Force. Group: Limitation of Actions.
Halsbury's Laws of England. 4ed. vol.28.
Halsbury's Statutes of England. 3ed. mainly vol.19.

The Digest. vol.32.
Encyclopaedia of Court Forms in Civil Proceedings (Atkin). 2ed. see index vol.

Texts

BRUNYATE, A.
Limitation of actions in equity. Stevens, 1932.

COMMITTEE ON LIMITATION OF ACTIONS IN CASES OF PERSONAL INJURY
Report (Davies). HMSO, 1962 (Cmnd. 1829).

COMMITTEE ON THE LIMITATION OF ACTIONS
Report (Tucker). HMSO, 1949 (Cmd. 7740).

FRANKS, M.H.
Limitation of actions. Sweet & Maxwell, 1959.

JOSLING, J.F.
Periods of limitation: with some practical notes thereon. 5ed. Oyez, 1981.

LAW COMMISSION
Limitation Act 1963. HMSO, 1970 (Law Com. no.35).

LAW COMMISSION
Time restrictions on presentation of divorce and nullity petititions. HMSO, 1980 (Working paper no.76).

LAW REFORM COMMITTEE
Limitation of actions in personal injury claims: final report. HMSO, 1977 (Cmnd. 6923).

LAW REFORM COMMITTEE
Twentieth report: interim report on limitation of actions in personal injury claims. HMSO, 1974 (Cmnd. 5630).

LIGHTWOOD, J.M.
The limit of actions. Sweet & Maxwell, 1909.

LINDGREEN, K.E.
Time in the performance of contracts. 2ed. Butterworths (Australia), 1982.

PARTINGTON, M.
Claim in time: study of the time limit rules for claiming social security benefits. Pinter, 1978.

PINEUS, K. & ROHREKE, H.G.
Time-barred actions. Lloyds, 1984.

PRESTON, C.H.S. & NEWSOM, G.H.
Limitation of actions. 3ed. Sol. Law Stat. Soc., 1953 & supp.

ROSCOE, H.
Digest of the law of evidence on the trial of civil actions. 20ed. Stevens, 1934.

SCOTTISH LAW COMMISSION
Reform of the law relating to prescription and limitation of actions. HMSO, 1970 (Scot. Law Com. no.15).

WALKER, D.M.
The law of prescription and limitation of actions in Scotland. 3ed. Green, 1981.

WILLIAMS, J.S.
Limitation of actions. 2ed. Butterworths (Canada), 1978.

WOOLF, A.D.
The time barrier in personal injury claims. Butterworths, 1969.

LIQUIDATORS

See also Bankruptcy; Companies; Receivers.

Encyclopaedias

Statutes in Force. Groups: Bankruptcy and Deeds of Arrangement; Companies.
Halsbury's Laws of England. 4ed. vol.7 and index.
The Digest. mainly vol.10.

Encyclopaedia of Court Forms in Civil Proceedings (Atkin). 2ed. vol.11.
Encyclopaedia of Forms and Precedents. 4ed. mainly vol.6.

Texts

COLLEGE OF LAW
Bankruptcy and liquidation. 1976.

FAIRBAIRN, W.J.G.
Handbook for trustees and liquidators. 4ed. Juta, 1978 (S.Africa).

FARRAR, J.
Company insolvency. Sweet & Maxwell, 1979.

GORE-BROWN, Sir F
Handbook on the formation, management and winding up of joint stock companies. 43ed. Jordan, 1977. Looseleaf.

GOWER, L.C.R.
The principles of modern company law. 4ed. Sweet & Maxwell, 1978 supp. 1981.

GRIFFITHS, O. & TAYLOR, E.M.
Liquidators and receivers. 6ed. Textbooks, 1950.

HARDMAN, J.P. & BERTRAM, A.D.W.
Taxation consequences of liquidation. Butterworths, 1978.

HOLT, B.A.W.
Powers and duties of a liquidator in a voluntary winding-up. Jordan, 1953.

HOOPER, A.C.
Voluntary liquidation: a handbook on the voluntary winding-up of English Companies etc. 5ed. Gee, 1978.

LOOSE, P.
Liquidators: their legal powers and duties. Jordan, 1972.

MUSTOE, N.E.
Bankruptcy, liquidation and receivership. Butterworths, 1939.

PALMER, F.B.
Company law. 22ed. Sweet & Maxwell, 1976. 3 vols. (2 looseleaf) supp. to vol. 1 1979.

PARSONS, G.T.E. & RATFORD, W.R.
Employees' rights in receiverships and liquidations. Tolley, 1980.

RANKING, D.F. de l'H., SPICER, E.E. & PEGLER, E.C.
Rights and duties of liquidators, trustees and receivers. 22ed. Pitman, 1955.

SALES, C.A.
Law relating to bankruptcy, liquidations and receiverships. 6ed. Macdonald & Evans, 1977.

WILLIAMS, Sir R.V. & HUNTER, M.
The law and practice in bankruptcy. 19ed. Sweet & Maxwell, 1979.

LITIGANTS IN PERSON

Encyclopaedias

Halsbury's Laws of England. 4ed. see index vol.
Encyclopaedia of Court Forms in Civil Proceedings (Atkin). 2ed. see index vol.

Texts

JUSTICE
Litigants in person: a report. Stevens, 1971.

JUSTICE
The unrepresented defendants in magistrates' courts. Stevens, 1971.

LIVERPOOL COURT OF PASSAGE

See also Courts; History.

Encyclopaedias

Halsbury's Laws of England. 4ed. see index vol.
Halsbury's Statutes of England. 3ed. see index vol.
Encyclpaedia of Court Forms in Civil Pfoceedings (Atkin). 2ed. vol.25.

Texts

PEEL, W.
Jurisdiction and practice of Court of Passage, City of Liverpool. 2ed. Henry Young, 1934.

RUSSELL, C.
Practice of the Court of Passage of the Borough of Liverpool. 1862.

LOCAL GOVERNMENT

See also By-Laws; Delegated Legislation; Drains and Sewers; Public Health; Rating and Valuation.

Encyclopaedias and periodicals

Statutes in Force. Group: Local Government.
Halsbury's Laws of England. 4ed. vol.28.
Halsbury's Statutes of England. 3ed. see index vol.
The Digest. vol.33.
Encyclopaedia of Court Forms in Civil Proceedings(Atkin). 2ed. see index vol.
Encyclopaedia of Forms and Precedents. 4ed. vol.13.

Local Government Chronicle. 1855–
Local Government Review (formerly Justice of the Peace and Local Government Review). 1971–
Muncipal Review. 1930–
Public Administration. 1923–
Public Law. 1956–

Texts

ALEXANDER, A.
Local government in Britain since reorganization. Allen & Unwin, 1982.

ARNOLD, T.J.
A treatise on the law relating to municipal corporations. 7ed. Shaw, 1935.

ARNOLD-BARKER, C.
The Local Government Act, 1972. Butterworths, 1973.

ARNOLD-BAKER, C.
Local Government Planning and Land Act 1980. Butterworths, 1981.

BALLARD, A.
British borough charters, 1042–1216. Cambridge U.P., 1913.

BALLARD, A.
British borough charters, 1217–1307. Cambridge U.P., 1923.

BARBER, M.P.
Local government. 3ed. rev. Macdonald & Evans, 1974.

BARRINGTON, T.J.
From big government to local government: the road to decentralization. Inst. of Public Admin., 1975.

BEATTIE, D.J.
Ultra vires in its relation to local authorities. Sol. Law Stat. Soc., 1936.

BOWMAN, M. & HAMPTON, W.
Local democracies: study in comparative local government. Longman, 1984.

BRAND, J.
Local government reform in England, 1888–1974. Croom Helm, 1974.

CAIRNS, M.B.
Law of tort in local government. 2ed. Shaw, 1970.

CAM, H.M.
The hundred and the hundred rolls: an outline of local government in medieval England. Merlin P., 1930.

CHESTER, D.N.
Central and local government. Macmillan, 1951.

CLARKE, J.J.
Outlines of local government of the United Kingdom. 20ed. Pitman, 1969.

CROSS, C.A.
Local Government Act 1972. Sweet & Maxwell, 1973.

CROSS, C.A.
Principles of local government law. 6ed. Sweet & Maxwell, 1981

DAVIES, R.U.
Parish Council and Town Council accounts. Knight, 1977.

DOWSON, Sir O.F. & WIGHTWICK, H.W.
The law relating to local elections in England and Wales. 4ed. Knight, 1962.

EDDEY, K.J.
Outline of local government law. Butterworths, 1969.

EDDISON, T.
Local government: management and corporate planning. 2ed. L.Hills, 1975.

ENVIRONMENT, DEPARTMENT OF THE
Committee of inquiry into the system of remuneration of members of local authorities. HMSO, 1977.
Vol. 1: report (Cmnd. 7010).
Vol. 2: the surveys of councillors and local authorities.

ENVIRONMENT, DEPARTMENT OF THE
Local government finance: report of the committee of enquiry(Layfield). HMSO, 1976 (Cmnd. 6453).

ENVIRONMENT, DEPARTMENT OF THE
Local government in England and Wales: a guide to the new system. HMSO, 1974.

ENVIRONMENT, DEPARTMENT OF THE
Organic change in local government. HMSO, 1979 (Cmnd. 7457).

FOULKES, D.
Local Government Act 1974. Butterworths, 1974.

GARNER, J.F.
Administrative law. 5ed. Butterworths, 1979.

GARNER, J.F.
Civic ceremonial. 3ed. Shaw, 1979.

GARNER, J.F.
'Municipal Engineering' points of law. The Municipal Group, 1977.

GOLDING, L.
Dictionary of local government in England and Wales. English U.P., 1962.

GRIFFITHS, A.
Local government administration. Shaw, 1977.

HART, Sir W.O. & GARNER, J.F.
Introduction to the law of local government and administration. 9ed. Butterworths, 1973.

HAYNES, R.J.
Organization theory and local government. Allen & Unwin, 1980.

HEPWORTH, N.P.
Finance of local government. 7ed. Allen & Unwin, 1984.

HILL, D.M.
Democratic theory and local government. Allen & Unwin, 1974.

HOGWOOD, B.W.
Regional government in England. Oxford U.P., 1982.

JACKSON, P.W.
Local government. 3ed. Butterworths, 1976.

JENNINGS, Sir W.I.
Principles of local government law. 4ed. Univ. of London P., 1960.

KEITH-LUCAS, B. & RICHARDS, P.G.
History of local government in the twentieth century. Allen & Unwin, 1978.

KNOWLES, R.
Modern management in local government. Rose, 1977.

LASKI, H.J. and others (eds.)
Century of municipal progress, 1835–1935. Greenwood, 1978.

LEWIS, N. & GATESHILL, B.
Commission for local administration: a preliminary approval. RIPA, 1978.

LIELL, P.
Council houses and the Housing Act, 1980. Butterworths, 1981.

LOCAL Government forms and precedents in England and Wales. Butterworths, 1953–57. 5 vols.

LOCAL Government in Southern Ireland. Irish Academic P., 1978.

MACMILLAN, Lord
Local government law and administration in England and Wales. Butterworths, 1934–69. 47 vols. in 51.

MARSHALL, A.H.
Financial administration in local government. Univ. of London P., 1974.

MINOGUE, M. (ed.)
Consumer's guide to local government. Macmillan, 1978.

MUNICIPAL Year Book. Annual.

OYEZ Longman directory of local authorities in England and Wales. Annual.

PEARCE, C.
Machinery of change in local government, 1888–1974. Allen & Unwin, 1980.

PROPHET, J.
The councillor: a handy guide to the functions of a councillor. 9ed. Shaw, 1979.

PROPHET, J.
The law of local councils. 2ed. Shaw, 1979.

REDCLIFFE-MAUD, Lord & WOOD, B.
English local government reformed. Oxford U.P., 1974.

REDLICH, J.
History of local government in England. Macmillan, 1958.

RICHARDS, P.G.
Reformed local government system. 3ed. Allen & Unwin, 1978.

ROYAL COMMISSION ON LOCAL GOVERNMENT, 1924–25
Report (Onslow). HMSO, 1925 (Cmd. 2506).

ROYAL COMMISSION ON LOCAL GOVERNMENT IN ENGLAND & WALES, 1966–69
Vol. 1: report (Redcliffe-Maud). HMSO, 1969 (Cmnd. 4040).
Vol. 2: memorandum of dissent. HMSO, 1969 (Cmnd. 4040–1).
Vol 3: research appendices. HMSO, 1969 (Cmnd. 404–II)

ROYAL COMMISSION ON LOCAL GOVERNMENT IN GREATER LONDON
Report (Herbert). HMSO, 1960 (Cmnd. 1164).

ROYAL COMMISSION ON LOCAL GOVERNMENT IN SCOTLAND, 1966–69
Report (Wheatley). HMSO, 1969 (Cmnd. 4150).

SCHOFIELD, A.N.
Byelaws of local authorities. Shaw, 1939.

SCHOFIELD, A.N. & LITTLE, P.
Schofield's election law. Shaw, 1984. Looseleaf.

SCOTT, C.D.
Local and regional government in New Zealand. Allen & Unwin, 1979.

SCOTTISH OFFICE
Report of the Committee of Inquiry into Local Government in Scotland. HMSO, 1981. (Cmnd. 8115).

SMELLIE, K.B.
A history of local government. 4ed. Allen & Unwin, 1968.

WEBB, S. & WEBB, B.
History of English local government. Cass, 1963. 11 vols.

WISDOM, A.S.
Appropriation of land by local authorities. 3ed. Rose, 1978.

WISDOM, A.S.
Local authorities' byelaws. 5ed. Rose, 1978.

WISDOM, A.S.
Local authorities' powers of purchase: a summary. 7ed. Rose, 1978.

WOOD, B.
The process of local government reform, 1966–74. Allen & Unwin, 1976.

YARDLEY, D.C.M.
Source book of English administrative law. 2ed. Butterworths, 1970.

LOCUS STANDI

See also Courts; Practice and Procedure.

Encyclopaedias

Halsbury's Laws of England. 4ed. see index vol.

Texts

LOCUS standi reports, 1961–1983. Butterworths, 1984.

SMETHURST, J.M.
Treatise on the locus standi of petitioners against private Bills in Parliament. Stevens & Haynes, 1866.

STEIN, L. (ed.)
Locus standi. Law Book Co., 1979 (Australia).

THIO, S.M.
Locus standi and judicial review. Singapore U.P., 1971.

LONDON

See also Mayor's Court.

Encyclopaedias

Halsbury's Laws of England. 4ed. vol.29 and index vol.
Halsbury's Statutes of England. 3ed. see index vol.
The Digest. see index vol.

Encyclopaedia of Court Fomrs in Civil Proceedings (Atkin). 2ed. see index vol.
Encyclopaedia of Forms and Precedents. 4ed. see index vol.

Texts

DONNISON, D.V. & EVERSLEY, D.E.C. (eds.)
London urban pattern, problems and policies. Heinemann, 1973.

THOMAS, A.H. (ed.)
Calendar of plea and memoranda rolls of the City of London, 1325–1364. Cambridge U.P., 1929.

TOPOLSKI, F. & COWPER, F.H.
Legal London illustrated. Stevens, 1961.

UNWIN, G.
The guilds and companies of London. 4ed. Cass, 1963.

Building Acts

CHANTER, H.R.
London building law. Batsford, 1946.

DICKSEE, B.
London Building Acts. 6ed. Stanford, 1931.

GREATER LONDON COUNCIL
London Building Acts (Amendment) Act 1939: section 20– code of practice for buildings of excess height and/or additional cubic extent. 1974.

GREATER LONDON COUNCIL
London building constructional by-laws. 1973.

KNOWLES, C.C. & PITT, P.H.
History of building regulations in London, 1189–1972. Architectural P., 1973.

SOPHIAN, T.J.
London Building Act, 1930. Estates Gazette, 1930.

Courts

CHEW, H.M.
London possessory assizes: a calendar. London Record Soc., 1965.

CHEW, H.M. & KELLAWAY, W. (eds.)
London assize of nuisance, 1301–1431. London Record Soc., 1973.

LORD CHANCELLOR'S OFFICE
London county courts directory. HMSO.

Government

CORPORATION OF THE CITY OF LONDON
The Corporation of London: its origin, constitution, powers and duties. 1950.

GREATER LONDON COUNCIL
Index to statutes affecting local government in Greater London. 2ed. 1974. Looseleaf.

ROYAL COMMISSION ON LOCAL GOVERNMENT IN GREATER LONDON
Report (Herbert). HMSO, 1960 (Cmnd. 1164).

Parish registers

GREATER LONDON COUNCIL
Parish registers for the diocese of London. 1972.

GREATER LONDON COUNCIL
Parish registers for the diocese of Southwark. 1970.

PARISH registers of the Corporation of London. 2 vols.

Port of London

HARPER, R.W.
Port of London Act 1908. Stevens, 1910.

LE MESURIER, H.
Law relating to the port of London authority. Stevens, 1934.

Water

O'HAGAN, H.
Law of water in Greater London. 1920.

LORD CHANCELLOR

See also Biographies.

Encyclopaedias

Statutes in Force. Group: Government Departments and Public Offices.
Halsbury's Laws of England. 4ed. vol.8.
Halsbury's Statutes of England. 3ed. see index vol.

The Digest. see index vol.
Encyclopaedia of Court Forms in Civil Proceedings (Atkin). 2ed. see index vol.

Texts

ATLAY, J.B.
The Victorian Chancellors. Smith, Elder, 1906–08 repr. Wildy, 1972. 2 vols.

CAMPBELL, J.C.
Lives of the Lord Chancellors and Keepers of the Great Seal of England from the earliest times till the reign of King George IV. 5ed 1868 repr. Murray, 1973. 10 vols.

HEUSTON, R.F.V.
Lives of the Lord Chancellors, 1885–1940. Oxford U.P., 1964.

HOUSE OF LORDS
Lord Chancellor. HMSO, 1977.

MAXWELL-LYTE, H.C.
Historical notes on the use of the Great Seal of England. HMSO, 1926.

O'FLANAGAN, J.R.
Lives of the Lord Chancellors and Keepers of the Great Seal of Ireland. Longmans, Green, 1870 repr. 1971. 2 vols.

MAGISTRATES

See also Licensing; Remand.

Encyclopaedias and periodicals

Statutes in Force. Group: Magistrates, England & Wales.
Halsbury's Laws of England. 4ed. see index vol.
Halsbury's Statutes of England. 3ed. see index vol.
The Digest. vol.38.
Encyclopaedia of Court Forms in Civil Proceedings (Atkin). 2ed. vol.25 and see index vol.

Encyclopaedia of Forms and Precedents. 4ed. see index vol. under Justices of the Peace.

Court: the Journal of Legal Practice in Magistrates' Courts. 1976–
Justice of the Peace. 1837–
The Magistrate. 1922–

Texts

ANTHONY, E. & BERRYMAN, J.D.
Magistrates' court guide. Butterworths. Annual.

APPAVOO, S.M.
The magistrates' powers of sentencing. Shaw, 1975.

BERKIN, M. & YOUNG, M.
Domestic Proceedings and Magistrates' Courts Act, 1978. Rose, 1979.

BOEHRINGER, G.H. & McCABE, S.
Hospital order in London magistrates' courts. Blackwell, 1973.

BOTTOMLEY, A.K.
Prison before trial: a study of remand decisions in magistrates' courts. Bedford Sq. P., 1970.

BOWDEN, J.
Binding over in the magistrates' court. Rose, 1976.

BRADLEY, E.L. & SENIOR, J.J.
Bail in magistrates' courts. Rose, 1977.

BRETTEN, R.
"Special reasons". 4ed. Shaw, 1977.

BROOKE-TAYLOR, J.C. & BOOTH, D.M.
Magistrates' court handbook. 6ed. Rose, 1984.

BURNEY, E.
Justice of the Peace: magistrate, court and community. Hutchinson, 1979.

CARLEN, P.
Magistrates' justice. Martin Robertson, 1976.

CHAMBERS, G.S.
The enforcement of money payments in magistrates' courts. 2ed. Shaw, 1974.

CHAMBERS, G.S.
An outline of magisterial procedure: the law in the working of the magistrates' courts. Rose, 1973–6. 4 parts.

CHISLETT, A.J.
The justice at home. 2ed. Rose, 1976.

COMMITTEE ON APPEALS FROM DECISION OF COURTS OF SUMMARY JURISDICTION
Report (Taylor). HMSO, 1932–3 (Cmd. 4296).

DAVID, R.
Magistrate in the Crown Court. B.Rose, 1982.

DAVIES, D.M.
Appointment as a magistrates. 3ed. Rose, 1976.

DEVLIN, K.
Sentencing offenders in magistrates' courts. Sweet & Maxwell, 1970.

FITZHERBERT, A.
Boke of Justyces of Peas. 1506 repr. Professional Books, 1974.

FREEMAN, M.D.A.
Domestic Proceedings and Magistrates' Courts Act, 1978. Sweet & Maxwell, 1978.

FREEMAN, M.D.A. & LYON, C.M.
Matrimonial jurisdiction of magistrates' courts. Rose, 1981.

GERLIS, S.
Summary matrimonial and guardianship orders. 6ed. Oyez, 1981.

GILES, F.T.
The magistrates' courts. Stevens, 1963.

GLASSEY, L.K.J.
Politics and the appointment of Justices of the Peace, 1675–1720. Oxford U.P., 1970.

GLEASON, J.H.
Justices of the Peace in England, 1558–1640. Oxford U.P., 1969.

GRIERSON, E.
Confessions of a country magistrate. Gollancz, 1972.

HARRIS, B.
Criminal jurisdiction of magistrates. 9ed. Rose, 1984.

HARRIS, B.
Guide to the new law of family proceedings in magistrates' courts including adoption. Rose, 1979.

HARRIS, B.
Magistrates' A.B.C.: Justice of the Peace guide. Rose, 1981.

HARRIS, B.
Magistrates' companion: a guide for magistrates in announcing sentence and other orders of the court. Rose, 1981.

HARRIS, B.
Magistrates' meetings. B.Rose, 1984.

HARRIS, B.
Maintenance and custody orders in the magistrates' courts. 3ed. Rose, 1976.

HARRIS, B.
Warrants of search and entry: a handbook for magistrates, police officers and others. Rose, 1973.

HARRISON, .F. & MADDOX, A.J.
The work of a magistrate. 4ed. Shaw, 1980.

HARROLD, B. & WHITE, A.
Summary process and prosecution. Butterworths, 1974.

HAYARD, E.J. & WRIGHT, H.
Office of magistrates. 9ed. Butterworths, 1953.

HENHAM, J.A.
Magistrates' remand and sentencing powers. 6ed. (of Magistrates' summary jurisdiction). B.Rose, 1983.

HOME OFFICE
Bail procedures in magistrates' courts: report of the working party (Graham-Harrison). HMSO, 1974.

HOME OFFICE
Sentencing practice in magistrates' courts. HMSO, 1979 (Research studies).

HOWARD LEAGUE FOR PENAL REFORM
Granting bail in magistrates' courts: proposals for reform. 1972.

INTERDEPARTMENTAL COMMITTEE ON MAGISTRATES' COURTS IN LONDON
Report (Aarvold). HMSO, 1962 (Cmnd. 1606).

JAMES, D.A.G.
Reciprocal enforcement: a practical guide to magistrates' courts' jurisdiction and procedure in international domestic proceedings. Rose, 1984.

JONES, C.E.
An elementary introduction to the work of a magistrates' court. 3ed. Rose, 1982.

JONES, M.
Justice and journalism: a study of the influence of newspaper reporting upon the administration of justice by magistrates. Rose, 1974.

JUSTICE
The unrepresented defendants in magistrates' courts. Stevens, 1971.

LAW COMMISSION
Family law: matrimonial proceedings in magistrates' courts. HMSO, 1973 repr. 1977 (Working paper no.53).

LAW COMMISSION
Family law: report on matrimonial proceedings in magistrates' courts. HMSO, 1976 (Law Com. no.77).

McCOLL, M.
Court teasers: practical situations arising in magistrates' courts. Rose, 1979.

McGREGOR, O.R., BLOM-COOPER, L. & GIBSON, C.
Separated spouses: a study of the matrimonial jurisdiction of magistrates' courts. Duckworth, 1970.

McLEAN, I. & MORRISH, P.
The magistrates' court: an index of common penalties and formalities in cases before justices. 6ed. Rose, 1984.

MOISER, C.H.
Guide to notifications by magistrates' courts to outside agencies. Bassett Pubns., 1983.

MOISER, C.H.
Practice and procedure in magistrates' courts. Fourmat Pub., 1982.

NORTHERN IRELAND OFFICE
Report of the Committee on County Courts and Magistrates' Courts in Northern Ireland (Jones). HMSO, 1974 (Cmnd. 5824).

OKE, G.C.
Magisterial formulist. 19ed. Butterworths, 1979 supp. 1982.

OSBORNE, B.
Justices of the Peace, 1361–1848: a history of the Justices of the Peace for the counties of England. Sedgehill P., 1960.

PAGE, Sir L.
Justice of the Peace. 3ed. Faber, 1967.

PASSINGHAM, B.
Domestic Proceedings and Magistrates' Courts Act, 1978. Butterworths, 1978.

PLANE, R. & BURTON, J.
Penalities and orders in magistrates' courts. 3ed. Shaw, 1972.

ROYAL COMMISSION ON JUSTICES OF THE PEACE
Report (du Parcq). HMSO, 1947–8 (Cmd. 7463).

ROYAL COMMISSION ON SELECTION OF JUSTICES OF THE PEACE
Report (James). HMSO, 1910 (Cd. 5250).

RUSSELL, Sir A.
The magistrate. 2ed. Butterworths, 1958.

SHANNON, F.
A handbook of cautions, oaths and recognizances etc. for use in the magistrates' courts. 9ed. Shaw, 1979.

SKYRME, Sir T.
The changing image of the magistracy. 2ed. Macmillan, 1983.

SOFTLEY, P.
Compensation orders in magistrates' courts. HMSO, 1978 (Home Office research studies).

SOFTLEY, P.
Fines in magistrates' courts. HMSO, 1978 (Home Office research studies).

STEVENS, R.D.S.
Bias and impartiality in magistrates' courts. B.Rose, 1982.

STONE's Justices' manual. Butterworths. Annual. 3 vols.

VENNARD, J.
Contested trials in magistrates' courts. HMSO, 1982 (Home Office research studies, no.71).

WALTERS, G.
Sentencing handbook: a guide to sentencing in magistrates' courts. Oyez, 1980.

WITCHELL, R.G.
Practice and procedure. Vol.1: County courts and magistrates' courts. 7ed. Oyez, 1979.

YOUNG, A.F. & CLARKE, K.
Chairmanship in magistrates' courts. 3ed. Rose, 1981.

MAINTENANCE AND CHAMPERTY

Encyclopaedias

Halsbury's Laws of England. 4ed. vol.9.
Halsbury's Statutes of England. 3ed. vol.8.
The Digest. vol.1.

Encyclopaedia of Court Forms in Civil Proceedings (Atkin). 2ed. vol.25.

Texts

BODKIN, E.H.
Law of maintenance and champerty. Stevens, 1935.

LAW COMMISSION
Proposals for reform of the law relating to maintenance and champerty. HMSO, 1966 (Law Com. no. 7).

TAPP, W.J.
An enquiry into the present state of the law of maintenance and champerty. Stevens, 1861.

WINFIELD, P.H.
History of conspiracy and abuse of legal procedure. Cambridge U.P., 1921.

MAINTENANCE OF DEPENDANTS

See also Divorce; Family Law: Family Provision.

Encyclopaedias and periodicals

Statutes in Force. Group: Family Law.
Halsbury's Laws of England. 4ed. see index vols.
Halsbury's Statutes of England. 3ed. mainly vol.42.
The Digest. see index vol.
Encyclopaedia of Court Forms in Civil Proceedings (Atkin). 2ed. see index vol.

Encyclopaedia of Forms and Precedents. 4ed. see index vol.

Family Law. 1971–
Legal Action (formerly L.A.G. Bulletin). 1973–

Texts

BROMLEY, P.M.
Family Law. 6ed. Butterworths, 1982.

CONVENTION on the recovery abroad of maintenance. HMSO, 1975 (Cmnd. 6084).

HARRIS, B.
Maintenance and custody orders in the magistrates' courts and consents to marriage. 2ed. Rose, 1974.

LATHAM, C.T.
How much? Determining maintenance in magistrates' courts. Rose, 1976.

LAW REFORM COMMITTEE FOR SCOTLAND
Fifth report: the need for provision allowing the enforcement in Scotland of orders for maintenance made by the courts of other Commonwealth countries (except England & Wales) and reciprocally, the enforcement in those countries of orders for aliment made by Scottish courts. HMSO, 1958 (Cmnd. 449).

LAW REFORM COMMITTEE FOR SCOTLAND
Seventh report: the procedure in actions in the sheriff courts between spouses for payment of aliment. HMSO, 1959 (Cmnd. 907).

SCOTTISH LAW COMMISSION
Aliment and financial provision. 1976 (Memorandum no. 22) 2 vols.

WILLIAMS, D.B. & NEWMAN, J.
Tax on maintenance payments. 8ed. Oyez, 1984.

MALAWI

See also Africa

Encyclopaedias

Statutes in Force. Group: Commonwealth and Other Territories.

Halsbury's Laws of England. 4ed. vol.6.
Halsbury's Statutes of England. 3ed. vol.4.

Texts

IBIK, J.O.
Restatement of African law, vol.3: Malawi I law of marriage and divorce. Sweet & Maxwell, 1970.

IBIK, J.O.
Restatement of African law, vol.4: Malawi II: the law of land, succession, movable property, agreements and civil wrongs. Sweet & Maxwell, 1972.

MALAWI
Laws of Malawi. 1969. Government of Malawi. 10 vols. and annual supp.

MALAWI
Malawi treaty series. Government Printer, 1964–

MALAYA/MALAYSIA

Encyclopaedias amd periodicals

Statutes in Force. Group: Commonwealth and Other Territories.
Halsbury's Laws of England. 4ed. vol.6.
Halsbury's Statutes of England. 3ed. vol.4.

Malaya Law Review. 1959–
Malayan Law Journal. 1932–

Texts

DJAMOUR, J.
Malaya kinship and marriage in Singapore. Athlone P., 1965.

ESMAN, M.J.
Administration and development in Malaysia: institution building and reform in a plural society. Cornell U.P., 1972.

GROVES, H.E.
The constitution of Malaysia. Malaysia Pubns., 1964.

HOOKER, M.B.
Adat laws in modern Malaya: land tenure, traditional government and religion. Oxford U.P., 1972.

HOOKER, M.B.
The personal law of Malaysia: an introduction. Oxford U.P., 1976.

MYINT SOE, U.
Law of banking and negotiable instruments in Singapore and Malaysia. Oxford U.P., 1977.

SHERIDAN, L.A. (ed.)
Malaya and Singapore. The Borneo territories: development of their law and constitution. Stevens, 1961.

SHERIDAN, L.A. & GROVES, H.E.
The constitution of Malaysia. 3ed. Sweet & Maxwell, 1983.

SINNADURAI, V.
The law of contract in Malaysia and Singapore: cases and commentary. Oxford U.P., 1979.

SUFFIAN, M. etc. (ed.)
Constitution of Malaysia: its development, 1957–77. Oxford U.P., 1979.

WONG, D.S.
Tenure and land dealings in the Malay States. Singapore U.P., 1975.

MANDAMUS

See also Certiorari; Prerogative Orders; Prohibition.

Encyclopaedias and periodicals

Halsbury's Laws of England. 4ed. mainly vols.1 & 11.
Halsbury's Statutes of England. 3ed. see index vol.
The Digest. see index vol.

Encyclopaedia of Court Forms in Civil Proceedings (Atkin). 2ed. see index vol.

Law Quarterly Review. 1885–
Modern Law Review. 1937–

Texts

GRIFFITS, S.O.
Guide to the practice of the Crown Office and Associates Department. Sweet & Maxwell, 1947 supp. 1950.

HENDERSON, E.G.
Foundations of English administrative law: certiorari and mandamus in the seventeenth century. Kelley, 1978 (USA).

IMPEY, W.J.
Law and practice of the writ of madamus. Clarke, 1826.

SHORT, F.H. & MELLOR, F.H.
Crown Office practice 2ed. Stevens & Haynes, 1908.

SHORTT, J.
Informations (criminal and quo warranto), mandamus, prohibitions, etc. Clowes, 1887.

SUPREME court practice 1985. Sweet & Maxwell, 1984. 2 vols.

MARKETS AND FAIRS

Encyclopaedias

Statutes in Force, Group: Trade
Halsbury's Laws of England. 4ed. vol.29
see also index vol.
Halsbury's Statutes of England. 3ed. vol.21.
The Digest. vol.33.

Encyclopaedia of Court Forms in Civil
Proceedings (Atkin). 2ed. vol.25.
Encyclopaedia of Forms and Precedents.
4ed. vol.13.

Texts

GACHES, L.
Law relating to markets and fairs. Eyre &
Spottiswoode, 1898.

HOME OFFICE
Guide to safety at fairs. HMSO, 1976.

PEASE, J.G. & CHITTY, H.
Law of markets and fairs. 2ed. Knight,
1958.

MARRIAGE

See also Divorce; Ecclesiastical Law; Family Law; Legitimacy and Illegitimacy;
Matrimonial Proceedings; Women.

Encyclopaedias and periodicals

Statutes of Force. Group: Family Law.
Halsbury's Laws of England. 4ed. see index vol.
Halsbury's Statutes of England. 3ed. see index vol.
The Digest. see index vol.
Encyclopaedia of Court Forms in Civil
Proceedings (Atkin). 2ed. see index vol.

Encyclopaedia of Forms and Precedents.
4ed. see index vol.

Family Law. 1971–
Family Law Quarterly (USA). 1967–
Marriage Guidance. 1947–
New Law Journal. 1965– (see Law Journal 1882–1964).
Solicitors' Journal. 1857.

Texts – United Kingdom

ARNOLD, J.C.
Marriage law of England. Staples, 1951.

BLAKE, S.H.
Laws of marriage. B.Rose, 1983.

BONFIELD, L.
Marriage settlements, 1601–1740: the
adoption of the strict settlement. Cambridge
U.P. 1983 (Cambridge studies in legal
history).

BROMLEY, P.M.
Family law. 6ed. Butterworths, 1981.

CONSUMERS' ASSOCIATION
Formal aspects of marriage. 1971.

FRASER, Lord
Treatise on husband and wife according to
the law of Scotland. 2ed. Clark, 1876–8. 2
vols.

HALLETT, V.G.H. & WARREN, N.
Settlements, wills and capital transfer tax.
Sweet & Maxwell, 1979.

HAW, R.
The state of matrimony. SPCK, 1952.

HELMHOLZ, R.H.
Marriage litigation in medieval England.
Cambridge U.P., 1974.

HONORE, T.
Sex law. Duckworth, 1978.

HOPKINS, F.
Formation and annulment of marriage.
Oyez, 1976.

JACKSON, J.
Formation and annulment of marriage. 2ed.
Butterworths, 1969.

LAW COMMISSION
Breach of promise of marriage. HMSO, 1969 (Law Com. no.26).

LAW COMMISSION
Family law: declarations in family matters. HMSO, 1973 repr. 1977 (Working paper no.48).

LAW COMMISSION
Family law: jactitation of marriage. HMSO, 1971 repr. 1977 (Working paper no.34).

LAW COMMISSION
Family law: jurisdiction in suits for nullity of marriage. HMSO, 1971 repr. 1977 (Working paper no.38).

LAW COMMISSION
Family law: report on nullity of marriage. HMSO, 1970 (Law Com. no.33).

LAW COMMISSION
Family law: report on polygamous marriages. HMSO, 1971 (Law Com. no. 42).

LAW COMMISSION
Family law: report on solemnisation of marriage in England and Wales. HMSO, 1973 (Law Com. no.53).

LAW COMMISSION
Family law: solemnisation of marriage. HMSO, 1971 repr. 1977 (Working paper no.35).

LAW COMMISSION
Nullity of marriage. HMSO, 1968 repr. 1977 (Working paper no.20).

LAW COMMISSION
Polygamous marriages. HMSO, 1968 repr. 1977 (Working paper no.21).

LAW COMMISSION
Proposal for the abolition of the matrimonial remedy of restitution of conjugal rights. HMSO, 1969 (Law Com. no.23).

LAW COMMISSION
Restitution of conjugal rights. HMSO, 1969 repr. 1977 (Working paper no.22).

ROYAL COMMISSION ON MARRIAGE AND DIVORCE
Report (Morton). HMSO, 1955–6 (Cmd. 9678).

SCOTTISH LAW COMMISSION
Family law: report on jurisdiction in consistorial causes affecting matrimonial status. HMSO, 1972 (Scot. Law Com. no.25).

SCOTTISH LAW COMMISSION
Family law: report on liability for adultery and enticement of a spouse. HMSO, 1976 (Scot. Law Com. no.42).

SCOTTISH LAW COMMISSION
Liability of a paramour in damages for adultery and enticement of a spouse. 1974 (Memorandum no. 18).

TURNER-SAMUELS, M.
The law of married women. Thames Bank Pub. Co., 1957.

WALTON, F.P.
A handbook of husband and wife according to the law of Scotland. 3ed. Green, 1951.

Other countries

BARI, B.P.
Law of marriage and divorce. Eastern Book Co., 1981 (India).

CARTER, H. & GLICK, P.
Marriage and divorce: a social and economic study. 2ed. Harvard U.P., 1976 (USA).

COTRAN, E.
Restatement of African law, vol.1: Kenya 1: Laws of marriage and divorce. Sweet & Maxwell, 1968.

DESAI, K.
Indian law of marriage and divorce. 4ed. Tripathi, 1981.

EPSTEIN, L.M.
Jewish marriage contract: a study in the status of the woman in Jewish law. 1927 repr. Arno, 1973.

HAHLO, H.R. & KAHN, E.
South African law of husband and wife. 4ed. Juta, 1975.

IBIK, J.O.
Restatement of African Law: Vol.3: Malawi I: Law of marriage and divorce. Sweet & Maxwell, 1970.

KEALEY, G.J. & HARRIS, H.A.
Separation agreements and marriage contracts. Butterworths (Canada), 1977.

PALSSON, L.
Marriage and divorce in comparative conflict of laws. Sijthoff, 1974.

PHILLIPS, A. & MORRIS, H.F.
Marriage laws in Africa. Oxford U.P., 1971.

PRYLES, M.C.
Conflicts in matrimonial law: cases and text. Butterworths (Australia), 1975.

RHEINSTEIN, M.
Marriage stability, divorce and the law. Chicago U.P., 1972 (USA).

WAKIL, S.P.
Marriage, family and society: Canadian perspectives. Butterworths (Canada), 1975.

MATRIMONIAL PROCEEDINGS

See also Divorce; Family Law; Marriage.

Encyclopaedias and periodicals

Statutes in Force. Group: Family Law.
Halsbury's Laws of England. 4ed. see index vol.
Halsbury's Statutes of England. 3ed. see index vol.
The Digest. see index vol.
Encyclopaedia of Court Forms in Civil Proceedings (Atkin). 2ed. see index vol.

Encyclopaedia of Forms and Precedents. 4ed. see index vol.
Family Law. 1971–
Family Law Reports. 1976–
Justice of the Peace. 1837–
Magistrate. 1921–

Texts

ANTHONY, E. & BERRYMAN, J.D.
Legal guide to domestic proceedings. Butterworths, 1968.

BAKER, W.B.
Matrimonial jurisdiction of registrars. SSRC:Centre for Socio-legal Studies, 1978.

BERKIN, M. & YOUNG, M.
Matrimonial suits and property proceedings. 2ed. Rose, 1984.

BIGGS, A.K.
Costs in matrimonial causes. Fourmat, 1979.

BIGGS, A.K.
Fees in matrimonial proceedings. 3ed. Fourmat, 1983.

BIGGS, A.K.
Matrimonial proceedings. Fourmat, 1980.

COLLEGE OF LAW
Emergency procedure in matrimonial cases (with precedents). 1977.

FREEMAN, M.D.A.
Domestic Proceedings and Magistrates' Courts Act, 1978. Sweet & Maxwell, 1978.

FREEMAN, M.D.A. & LYON, C.M.
Matrimonial jurisdiction of magistrates' courts. Rose, 1981.

GERLIS, S.
Summary matrimonial and guardianship orders. 6ed. Oyez, 1981.

HARRIS, B.
Guide to the new law of family proceedings in magistrates' courts including adoption. 2ed. Rose, 1981.

HUMPHREYS, T.S.
Humphrey's notes on matrimonial causes proceeding in county courts and district registries. 15ed. Oyez, 1981.

JAMES, D.A.G.
Reciprocal enforcement: a practical guide to magistrates' courts' jurisdiction and procedure in international domestic proceedings. Rose, 1984.

JOSLING, J.F.
Summary matrimonial and guardianship orders. 4ed. Oyez, 1973 supp. 1974 (Practice notes no.30).

LAW COMMISSION
Family law: declarations in family matters. HMSO, 1973 repr. 1977 (Working paper no.48).

LAW COMMISSION
Family law: jurisdiction in matrimonial causes (other than nullity). HMSO, 1970 repr. 1977 (Working paper no.28).

LAW COMMISSION
Family law: matrimonial and related proceedings, financial relief. HMSO, 1967 repr. 1977 (Working paper no.9).

LAW COMMISSION
Family law: matrimonial proceedings in magistrates' courts. HMSO, 1973 repr. 1977 (Working paper no.53).

LAW COMMISSION
Family law: orders for sale under the Matrimonial Causes Act, 1973. HMSO, 1980 (Law Com. no.99).

LAW COMMISSION
Family law: report on financial provision in matrimonial procedings. HMSO, 1969 (Law Com. no.25).

LAW COMMISSION
Family law: report on jurisdiction in matrimonial causes. HMSO, 1972 (Law Com. no.48).

LAW COMMISSION
Family law: report on matrimonial proceedings in magistrates' courts. HMSO, 1976 (Law Com. no.77).

LAW COMMISSION
Family law: report on solemnisation of marriage in England and Wales. HMSO, 1973 (Law Com. no.53).

LAW COMMISSION
Report on the powers of Appeal Courts to sit in private and the restrictions upon publicity in domestic proceedings. HMSO, 1966 (Law Com. no.8).

NORTH, P.M.
The private international law of matrimonial causes in the British Isles and the Republic of Ireland. North-Holland, 1978.

PASSINGHAM, B.
The Divorce Reform Act, 1969. Butterworths, 1970.

PASSINGHAM, B.
Domestic Proceedings and Magistrates' Courts Act, 1978. Butterworths, 1978.

PASSINGHAM, B. & HARMER, C.
Law and practice in matrimonial causes. 4ed. Butterworths, 1984.

PUGH, L.M.
Matrimonial proceedings before magistrates. 4ed. Butterworths, 1981.

RAKUSEN, M.L.
Costs in matrimonial causes. Butterworths, 1984.

RAYDEN, W.
Law and practice in divorce and family matters. 13ed. Butterworths, 1979. 2 vols. & supp.

TOLSTOY, D.
The law and practice of divorce and matrimonial causes: including proceedings in magistrates' courts. 7ed. Sweet & Maxwell, 1971.

WILKINSON, G.S.
Summary matrimonial and guardianship orders. 5ed. Oyez, 1977.

MAYOR'S COURT

Encyclopaedias

Halsbury's Laws of England. 4ed. vol.10 and index.
Halsbury's Statutes of England. 3ed. see index vol.

The Digest. vol.33.
Encyclopaedia of Court Forms in Civil Proceedings (Atkin). 2ed. vol.26.

Texts

ASHLEY, H.
Doctrine and practice of attachment in the Mayor's Court. 2ed. Wilson, 1819.

CANDY, G.
The jurisdiction, process, practice and mode of pleading in ordinary actions in the Mayor's Court. Stevens, 1879.

GLYN, L.E. & JACKSON, F.S.
Mayor's Court practice. 3ed. Butterworths, 1910.

MEDICAL EVIDENCE
See also Evidence.

Periodicals
Medicine, Science and the Law. 1960–
Medico-Legal Journal. 1933–

Texts
CAMPS, F.E. & PURCHASE, W.B.
Practical forensic medicine. Hutchinson, 1956.

DIX, D.K. & TODD, A.H.
Medical evidence in personal injury cases. Lewis, 1961.

GORDON, I. & SHAPIRO, H.A.
Forensic medicine: a guide to principles. Churchill Livingstone, 1975.

HOUTS, M.
Courtroom medicine. Thomas, 1958 (USA).

KERR, D.J.A.
Forensic medicine: a textbook for students and a guide for the practitioner. 6ed. Black, 1957.

MANN, A.
Medical assessment of injuries for legal purposes. 3ed. Butterworths (Australia), 1979.

MASON, J.K.
Forensic medicine for lawyers. 2ed. Butterworths, 1983.

POLSON, C.J.
The essentials of forensic medicine. 3ed. Pergamon, 1973.

SIMPSON, C.K.
A doctor's guide to court: a handbook on medical evidence. Butterworths, 1962.

SIMPSON, C.K.
Forensic medicine. 7ed. Arnold, 1974.

SMITH, Sir S.A. & FIDDES, F.S.
Forensic medicine: a textbook for students and practitioners. 10ed. Churchill, 1955.

MEDICAL JURISPRUDENCE
See also Anaesthetics; Dentists; Doctors; Drugs; Forensic Science; Hospitals; Human Transplants; Nursing; Personal Injuries.

Encyclopaedias and periodicals
Statutes in Force. Group: Medical and Related Professions.
Halsbury's Laws of England. 4ed. see index vol.
Halsbury's Statutes of England. 3ed. vol.21.
The Digest. mainly vol.33 but see index vol.

British Medical Journal. 1857–
Medicine, Science and the Law. 1960–
Medico-Legal Journal. 1933–
Medical Directory. Annual.

Texts
BANDER, E.J. & WALLACE, J.J.
Medical legal dictionary. Oceana, 1970 (USA).

BAYLISS, F.P.C.
Law on poisons, medicines and related substances. Ravenswood, 1979.

BERESFORD, H.R.
Legal aspects of neurological practice. Davis, 1975 (USA).

BRENNAN, J.L.
Medico-legal problems in hospital practice. Ravenswood, 1980.

DALE, J.R. & APPELBE, G.E.
Pharmacy law and ethics. Pharmaceutical P., 1979.

DAUBE, D.
Legal problems in medical advance. Magnes P., 1971 (Israel).

FARNDALE, W.A.J.
Law on human transplants and bequests of bodies. Ravenswood, 1971.

GHANEM, I.
Islamic medical jurisprudence. Probsthain, 1982.

GLAISTER, J. & RENTOUL, E.
Medical jurisprudence and toxicology. 13ed. Livingstone, 1973.

GORDN, I, TURNER, R. & PRICE, T.W.
Medical jurisprudence. 3ed. Livingstone, 1953.

GRADWOHL, R.B.H.
Gradwohl's legal medicine. 3ed. Wright, 1976.

HADFIELD, S.J.
Law and ethics for doctors: with a section on general practice in the National Health Service. Eyre & Spottiswoode, 1958.

HASLAM, J.
Medical jurisprudence as it relates to insanity according to the law of England. 1817. repr. Garland, 1979.

HERSHEY, N. & MILLER, R.D.
Human experimentation and the law. Aspen, 1979 (USA).

HOLDER, A.R.
Legal issues in paediatrics and adolescent medicine. Wiley, 1977.

KNIGHT, B.
Legal aspects of medical practice. 3ed. Churchill Livingstone, 1982.

LEVITT, W.M.
Short encyclopaedia of medicine for lawyers. Butterworths, 1966.

McLEAN, S. & MAHER, G.
Medicine, morals and the law. Gower Pub.Co.1983.

MARTIN, C.R.A.
Law relating to medical practice. 2ed. Pitman, 1979.

MASON, J.K.
Forensic medicine for lawyers. Wright, 1978.

MEANEY, T.F., LALLI, A.F. & ALFIDI, R.J. (eds.)
Complications and legal implication of radiologic special procedures. Mosby, 1973 (USA).

MEDICAL DEFENCE UNION
Law and the doctor. rev. ed. 1975.

MEYERS, D.W.
The human body and the law: a medico-legal study. Edinburgh U.P., 1970.

MORITZ, A.R. & MORRIS, R.C.
Handbook of legal medicine. 4ed. Mosby, 1975 (USA).

MORRIS, R.C. & MORITZ, A.R.
Doctor and patient and the law. 5ed. Mosby, 1971 (USA).

SALIWANCHIK, R.
Legal protection for microbiological and genetic engineering inventions. Addison-Wesley, 1982.

SIDLEY, N.T. (ed.)
Law and ethics: a guide for the health professional. Human Science P.: Eurospan, 1984.

SPELLER, S.R.
Law of doctor and patient. Lewis, 1973.

TAYLOR, A.S.
Principles and practice of medical jurisprudence. 13ed. Churchill, 1984.

WHINCUP, M.H.
Legal aspects of medical and nursing services. 3ed. Ravenswood, 1982.

WOOD, C. (ed.)
The influence of litigation on medical practice: proceedings of a conference sponsored jointly by the Royal Society of Medicine and the Royal Society of Medicine Foundation Inc., 16–18 May 1977, London. Academic P., 1977.

MEDICAL NEGLIGENCE

See also Negligence; Tort.

Encyclopaedias and periodicals

Statutes in Force. Group: Medical and Related Professions.
Halsbury's Laws of England. 4ed. see index vol.
The Digest. vol.33.

Encyclopaedia of Court Forms in Civil Prceedings (Atkin). 2ed. vol.29.
Medico-Legal Journal. 1933–

Texts

CHAPMAN, C.B.
Malpractice: doctors, patients and the courts. 1976.

FARNDALE, W.A.J.
Medical negligence: legal case studies. Ravenswood, 1969.

FARNDALE, W.A.J. & LARMAN, E.C.
Legal liability for claims arising from hospital treatment. 2ed. Ravenswood, 1976.

FREEMAN, A.
Legal proceedings against doctors and health authorities: a special report on the conduct of medical negligence claims. Ravenswood, 1980.

HOLDER, A.R.
Medical malpractice law. 2ed. Wiley, 1978.

KRAMER, C.
Medical malpractice. 4ed. Practising Law Inst., 1976 (USA).

TAYLOR, J.L.
The doctor and negligence. Pitman, 1971.

TAYLOR, J.L.
The doctor and the law. 3ed. Pitman, 1983.

MEETINGS

See also Companies.

Encyclopaedias

Halsbury's Laws of England. 4ed. vols.7, 11 and index vol.
Halsbury's Statutes of England. 3ed. vol.8 but see index vol.
The Digest. see index vol.

Encyclopaedia of Court Forms in Civil Proceedings (Atkin). 2ed. see index vol.
Encyclopaedia of Forms and Precedents. 4ed. see index vol.

Texts

BLACKWELL, G.
Law of meetings. 9ed. Butterworths, 1967.

HEAD, F.D.
Meetings. 6ed. Pitman, 1957.

HORSLEY, M.G.
Meetings: procedure, law and practice. 2ed. Butterworths (Australia)., 1983.

MARTIN, E. & GRAHAM-HELWIG, H.
How to take minutes. Pitman, 8ed. 1975.

MAUDE, B.
Managing meetings. Business Books, 1975.

MOORE, M.
Law and procedure of meetings. Sweet & Maxwell, 1979.

RENTON, N.E.
Guide for meetings and organisations. 3ed. Law Book Co., 1980 (Australia).

SHACKLETON, F.
The law and practice of meetings. 7ed. Sweet & Maxwell, 1983.

SHAW, Sir S. & SMITH, E. D.
The law of meetings. 5ed. Macdonald & Evans, 1979.

SIM, R.S.
Questions and answers on the law of meetings. Butterworths, 1970.

MENTAL HEALTH

See also Court of Protection; Insanity.

Encyclopaedias

Statutes in Force. Group: Mental Health.
Halsbury's Laws of England. 4ed. mainly vol. 30.
Halsbury's Statutes of England. 3ed. mainly vol.25.

The Digest. vol.33.
Encyclopaedia of Court Forms in Civil Prceedings (Atkin). 2ed. vol.26.
Encyclopaedia of Forms and Precedents. 4ed. see index vol.

Texts

ABRAHAMS, G.
Lunatics and lawyers. Home & Van Thal, 1951.

BLUGLASS, R.
Guide to the Mental Health Act, 1983. Churchill Livingstone, 1983.

CRAFT, M. & CROFT, A. (eds.)
Mentally abnormal offenders Bailliere: Tindall, 1984.

COMMITTEE ON MENTALLY ABNORMAL OFFENDERS
Report (Atkin). HMSO, 1923 (Cmd. 2005).

COMPTON, H.F. & WHITEMAN, R.
Receivership under the Mental Health Act 1959. 5ed. Oyez, 1976.

EDWARDS, A.H.
Mental health services. 4ed. Shaw, 1975.

FORD, D.A. & HALSEY, M.D.
Mental health: the new law. Butterworths, 1984.

FRENCH, C.W.
Notes on the Mental Health Act 1959. 3ed. rev. Shaw, 1975.

GOSTIN, L.O.
A human condition. Mind, 1975–7. 2 vols.

GOSTIN, L.O., BUCHAN, A. & RASSABY, E.
Mental health: tribunal procedure. Oyez Longman, 1984.

HEALTH AND SOCIAL SECURITY, DEPARTMENT OF
A review of the Mental Health Act 1959. HMSO, 1976.

HOGGETT, B.M.
Mental health law. 2ed. Sweet & Maxwell, 1984.

JONES, K.
Lunacy, law and conscience, 1744–1845. Routledge & Kegan Paul, 1955.

KILBY, R.L.J.
Notes on the Mental Health Act, 1983. Shaw, 1983.

MILLS, G.E. & POYSER, A.H.R.W.
Lunacy practice. Butterworths, 1934.

MOORE, M.S.
Law and psychiatry: rethinking the relationship. Cambridge U.P., 1984.

MORRIS, N.
Madness and the criminal law. Univ. of Chicago P., 1982.

NEW YORK CITY BAR ASSOCIATION
Mental illness, due process and the criminal defendant. 1980 (USA).

O'SULLIVAN, J.
Mental health and the law. Law Book Co., 1981 (Australia).

ROYAL COMMISSION ON LUNACY AND MENTAL DISORDERS
Report (Macmillan). HMSO, 1925 (Cmd. 2700).

ROYAL COMMISSION RELATING TO MENTAL ILLNESS AND MENTAL DEFICIENCY
Report (Percy). HMSO, 1956–7 (Cmnd. 169).

SPELLER, S.R.
Mental Health Act, 1959. 2ed. Inst. of Hospital Administrators, 1964.

THEOBALD, H.S.
Law of lunacy. Stevens, 1924.

TIBBETT, J.E.
Social workers as mental health officers. HMSO, 1978 (Scottish Office social research studies).

VENABLES, H.D.S.
Guide to the law affecting mental patients. Butterworths, 1975.

WEISSTUB, B.D.N.
Law and mental health. Pergamon, 1984.

WHITEHEAD, T.
Mental illness and the law. 2ed. Blackwell, 1983.

WING, J.K. & OLSEN, R.
Community care for the mentally disabled. Oxford U.P., 1979.

WORLD HEALTH ORGANIZATION
Law and mental health. 1978.

MIDWIVES

See also Nursing; Public Health.

Encyclopaedias and periodicals

Statutes in Force. Group: Medical and Related Professions.
Halsbury's Laws of England. 4ed. vol.30.
Halsbury's Statutes of England. 3ed. mainly vol.21.
The Digest. see index vol.

Texts

STONE's Justices manual. Butterworths. Annual. 3 vols.

Encyclopaedia of Court Forms in Civil Proceedings (Atkin). 2ed. vol.28.

Midwife, Health Visitor & Community Nurse. 1965–

Midwives Chronicle & Nursing Notes. 1887–

WIGRAM, W.K.
Justice's notebook. 15ed. Stevens, 1951.

MILITARY LAW

See also Air Force; Army; Court Martial; Navy; Public Order; War.

Encyclopaedias and periodicals

Statutes in Force. Group: Armed Forces.
Halsbury's Laws of England. 4ed. see index vol.
Halsbury's Statutes of England. 3ed. see index vol.

The Digest. see index vol.
Army List. Annual.
Army Quarterly & Defence Journal. 1920–

Texts

BANNING, S.T.
Military law. Gale & P., 25ed. 1955.

BYRNE, E.M.
Military law. 3ed. Naval Inst. P., 1981 (USA).

DAHL, R.C. & WHELAN, J.F.
Military law dictionary. Oceana, 1960. (USA).

DEFENCE, MINISTRY OF. ARMY DEPARTMENT
Manual of military law. HMSO. Looseleaf.

DEFENCE, MINISTRY OF. ARMY DEPARTMENT
Queen's regulations for the army. HMSO. Looseleaf.

KARSTEN, P.
Law, soldiers and combat. Greenwood, 1978 (USA).

SHARMA, O.P.
Military law in India. Tripathi, 1973.

TOWNSHEND-STEVENS, R.
A practical digest of military law. Sifton Praed, 1933.

WINTHROP, W.W.
Military law and precedents. 2ed. 1920 repr. Arno, 1979.

MINERALS

See also Mines and Quarries; Oil.

Encyclopaedias and periodicals

Statutes in Force. Group: Mines and Minerals.
Halsbury's Laws of England. 4ed. vol.31.
Halsbury's Statutes of England. 3ed. see index vol.
The Digest. vol.33.

Encyclopaedia of Court Forms in Civil Proceedings (Atkin). 2ed. vol.27.
Encyclopaedia of Forms and Precedents. 4ed. vol.13.
Mineralogical Abstracts. 1959–
Mineralogical Magazine. 1876–

Texts

ENEVER, F.A.
Law of support in relation to minerals. Sol. Law Stat. Soc., 1947.

MACSWINNEY, R.F.
The law of mines, quarries and minerals. 5ed. Sweet & Maxwell, 1922.

STEVENS, Sir R.
Planning control over mineral working. 1976.

MINES AND QUARRIES

See also Explosives; Minerals; Stannaries.

Encyclopaedias and periodicals

Statutes in Force. Group: Mines and Minerals.
Halsbury's Laws of England. 4ed. vol.31.
Halsbury's Statutes of England. 3ed. mainly vol.22.
The Digest. vol.33.
Encyclopaedia of Court Forms in Civil Proceedings (Atkin). 2ed. vol.27.

Encyclopaedia of Forms and Precedents. 4ed. vol.13.
Bulletin of the Institution of Mining and Metallurgy. 1892–
Mining Journal. 1835–
Mining Year Book. Annual.

Texts

BAR COUNCIL
Planning and mineral working. Papers from a conference held at Oxford, Sept. 1978 organised by the Bar Council, Law Society and Royal Institution of Chartered Surveyors. Sweet & Maxwell, 1978 (Journal of Planning and Environment Law occasional papers).

BOWEN, D.
Coal Act 1938. Hamish Hamilton, 1938.

BRITISH QUARRYING AND SLAG FEDERATION
Quarry tips. 1972.

ENEVER, F.A.
The Coal Act, 1938, with the Coal (Registration of Ownership) Act, 1937. Sol. Law Stat. Soc., 1938.

HEALTH AND SAFETY EXECUTIVE
The law relating to safety and health in mines and quarries. HMSO, 1972. 4 vols. supp. 1977.

INSTITUTION OF MINING & METALLURGY
Legal aspects of prospecting in the United Kingdom: conference proceedings. 1983.

LANG, A.G. & CROMMELIN, M.
Australian mining and petroleum law. Butterworths (Australia), 1979.

MACSWINNEY, R.F.
The law of mines, quarries and minerals. 5ed. Sweet & Maxwell, 1922.

MINING JOURNAL
Legal and institutional arrangements in minerals development. 1982.

PENNINGTON, R.R.
Stannary law: a history of the mining law of Cornwall and Devon. David & Charles, 1973.

POST, A.M.
Deep sea mining and the law of the sea. Nijhoff, 1983.

SINCLAIR, J.
Coal mining law. Pitman, 1958.

TOWNSHEND-ROSE, F.H.E.
Introduction to mining law. Colliery Guardian 1958.

WOODLEY, D.G.
Coal mining law for the land practitioner. Oyez, 1972.

WRIGHT, R.J.
Canadian mining law. Butterworths (Canada), 1976. 6 vols. Looseleaf.

MISTAKE

See also Fraud.

Encyclopaedias

Halsbury's Laws of England. 4ed. vol.32.
Halsbury's Statutes of England. 3ed. see index vol.
The Digest. vol.35.

Encyclopaedia of Court Forms in Civil Proceedings (Atkin). 2ed. see index vol.
Encyclopaedia of Court Forms and Precedents. 4ed. see index vol.

Texts

CHAMPNESS, R.
Mistake in the law of contract. Stevens, 1933.

KERR, W.W.
Kerr on the law of fraud and mistake. 7ed. Sweet & Maxwell, 1952.

STOLJAR, S.J.
Mistake and misrepresentations: a study in contractual principles. Sweet & Maxwell, 1968.

MONEY

See also Banks and Banking; Bills of Exchange; Criminal Law.

Encyclopaedias and periodicals

Statutes in Force. Groups: Banking and Currency; Public Finance and Economic Controls.
Halsbury's Laws of England. 4ed. vol.32.
Halsbury's Statutes of England. 3ed. see index vol.
The Digest. vol.35.
Encyclopaedia of Court Forms in Civil Proceedings (Atkin). 2ed. vol.27.

Encyclopaedia of Forms and Precedents. 4ed. see index vol.

Bank of England Quarterly Bulletin. 1960–
The Banker. 1926–
Economist. 1843–
International Currency Review. 1969–

Texts

ARGY, V.
Post war international money crisis: an analysis. Allen & Unwin, 1981.

COUNCIL OF EUROPE
The European Monetary System. HMSO, 1978 (Cmnd. 7419).

HANSON, J.L.
Monetary theory and practice. 6ed. Macdonald & Evans, 1978.

HECLO, H. & WILDAVSKY, A.
The private government of public money. 2ed. Macmillan, 1981.

LAZAR, L.
Transnational economic and monetary law: transactions and contracts. Oceana, 1979. 7 looseleaf vols.

MANN, F.A.
The legal aspect of money. 4ed. Oxford U.P., 1982.

PARKER, A.
Exchange control. Jordan, 1975. Looseleaf.

SARPKAYA, S.
The money market in Canada. 2ed. Butterworths (Canada), 1980.

SHUSTER, M.R.
The public international law of money. Oxford U.P., 1973.

TREASURY
The European Monetary System. HMSO, 1978 (Cmnd. 7405).

WOOD, P.
Law and practice of international finance. Sweet & Maxwell, 1980.

MONEYLENDERS

See also Pawnbrokers.

Encyclopaedias

Halsbury's Laws of England. 4ed. vol.32.
Halsbury's Statutes of England. 3ed. see index vol.
The Digest. vol.35.

Encyclopaedia of Court Forms in Civil Proceedings (Atkin). 2ed. vol.27
Encyclopaedia of Forms and Precedents. 4ed. vol.15.

Texts

MESTON, Lord
Law relating to moneylenders. 5ed. Oyez, 1968.

STRATTON, I.G.C. & BLACKSHAW, I.S.
Law relating to moneylenders. Butterworths, 1971.

THORP, L.T. & WATSON, A.A.
The law of moneylending. Wilson, 1928.

MONOPOLIES AND RESTRICTIVE TRADE PRACTICES

See also Companies; Competition.

Encyclopaedias and periodicals

Statutes in Force. Group: Trade.
Halsbury's Laws of England. 4ed. vol.47.
Halsbury's Statutes of England. 3ed. vol.37, 43.
The Digest. mainly vol.43.
Encyclopaedia of Forms and Precedents. 4ed. vol.22.

Industrial Cases Reports (as Industrial Court Reports. 1972–74). 1975–
Journal of Business Law. 1957–
Journal of World Trade Law. 1967–
Lloyd's Maritime and Commercial Law Quarterly. 1974–
Restrictive Practices Cases. 1957–1972.

Texts

ALBERY, M. & FLETCHER-COOKE, C.F.
Monopolies and restrictive trade practices. Stevens, 1956.

ALLEN, G.C.
Monopoly and restrictive practices. Allen & Unwin, 1968.

BARKER, R.E. & DAVIES, G.R. (eds.)
Books are different: an account of the defence of the net book agreement before the Restrictive Practices Court in 1962. Macmillan, 1966.

COMMISSION ON MONOPOLIES AND RESTRICTIVE PRACTICES
Report (Cairns). HMSO, 1955-6 (Cmd. 9504).

CUNNINGHAM, J.P.
The Fair Trading Act, 1973: consumer protection and competition law. Sweet & Maxwell, 1974 supp. 1978.

CUNNINGHAM, J.P.
Restrictive practices and monopolies in E.E.C. Law. Kogan Page, 1973.

GUENAULT, P.H. & JACKSON, J.M.
The control of monopoly in the United Kingdom. 2ed. Longman, 1974.

HAILSHAM, Lord & McEWEN, R.
Law relating to monopolies, restrictive trade practices and resale price maintenance. Butterworths, 1956.

HEATHCOTE-WILLIAMS, H., ROBERTS, E. & BERNSTEIN, R.
Law of restrictive trade practices and monopolies. Eyre & Spottiswoode, 1956.

HEYDON, J.D.
On the restraint of trade doctrine. Butterworths, 1971.

HUNNINGS, N.M.
Monopolies and mergers. European Law Centre 1980. 2 vols.

HUNNINGS, N.M.
Restrictive agreements. Common Law Reports, 1976.

HUNTER, A. (ed.)
Monopoly and competition: selected readings. Penguin, 1969.

KORAH, V.L.
Competition law of Britain and the Common Market. Elek, 1975.

KORAH, V.L.
Monopolies and restrictive practices. Penguin, 1968.

LEVER, J.F.
The law of restrictive practices and resale price maintenance. Sweet & Maxwell, 1964.

MARTIN, A.
Restrictive trade practices and monopolies. Routledge, 1957.

MEINHARDT, P.
Inventions, patents and monopoly. Gower P., 1971.

MONOPOLIES COMMISSION
Reports. HMSO.

ORGANIZATION FOR ECONOMIC CO-OPERATION AND DEVELOPMENT
Comparative summary of legislations on restrictive business practice. 1979.

PRICES AND CONSUMER PROTECTION, DEPARTMENT OF
A review of monopolies and mergers policy: a consultative document. HMSO, 1978 (Cmnd. 7198).

ROWLEY, C.K.
The British Monopolies Commission. Allen & Unwin, 1966.

STEVENS, R. & YAMEY, B.S.
The Restrictive Practices Court: a study of the judicial process and economic policy. Weidenfeld & Nicolson, 1965.

SUTHERLAND, A.
The Monopolies Commission in action. Cambridge U.P., 1969.

TRADE AND INDUSTRY, DEPARTMENT OF
Monopolies, mergers and restrictive practices: international conference proceedings, Cambridge, 1969. 1971.

WIDMER, G.K.
Restrictive trade practices and mergers. Law Book Co., 1977 (Australia).

WILBERFORCE, Lord, CAMPBELL, A. & ELLES, N.P.M.
The law of restrictive trade practices and monopolies. 2ed. Sweet & Maxwell, 1966 supp. 1973.

MORTGAGES

See also Building Societies; Contract; Conveyancing; Deeds; Guarantees; Liens; Title

Encyclopaedias and periodicals

Statutes in Force. Group: Property, England & Wales, Sub-Group 1.
Halsbury's Laws of England. 4ed. vol.32.
Halsbury's Statutes of England. 3ed. see index vol.
The Digest. vol.35.
Encyclopaedia of Court Forms in Civil Proceedings (Atkin). 2ed. vol.28.

Encyclopaedia of Forms and Precedents. 4ed. vol.14.
Building Societies Gazette. 1869–
Building Societies Institute Quarterly. 1947–
Building Societies Year Book. Annual.
Conveyancer and Property Lawyer. 1936–

Texts

COOTE, R.H.
A treatise on the law of mortgage. 9ed. Stevens, 1927.

CROFT, C.E. & TAMP, W.M.
The mortgagee's power of sale. Butterworths (Australia), 1980.

FAIREST, P.B.
Mortgages. 2ed. Sweet & Maxwell, 1980.

FISHER, W.R. & LIGHTWOOD, J.M.
Law of mortgage. 9ed. Butterworths, 1977.

FRANCIS, E.A.
Law and practice in all States of Australia relating to mortgages and securities for the payment of money. 2ed. Butterworths (Australia), 1975.

KRATOVIL, R.
Modern mortgage law and practice. 2ed. Prentice-Hall, 1981 (USA).

McKEE, W.S.
Real estate mortgages. Tax Management, 1975 (USA). Looseleaf.

MARRIOTT, A.S. & DUNN, G.W.
Practice in mortgage actions in Ontario. 3ed. Carswell, 1971.

MAUDSLEY, R.H. & BURN, E.H.
Land law: cases and materials. 3ed. Butterworths, 1975.

NOKES, G.D.
An outline of the law relating to mortgages and receiverships. 3ed. Estates Gazette, 1951. 2 vols.

RUDDEN, B. & MOSELEY, H.
An outline of the law of mortgages. Estates Gazette, 1967.

SNELL, E.H.T.
The principles of equity. 28ed. Sweet & Maxwell, 1982.

TURNER, R.W.
The equity of redemption: its nature, history and connection with equitable estates generally. Cambridge U.P., 1931.

WALDOCK, C.H.M.
The law of mortgages. 2ed. Stevens, 1950.

MORTMAIN

See also Charities; Land Tenure.

Encyclopaedias

Halsbury's Laws of England. 4ed. vol. 5 and see index vol.
The Digest. see index vol.

Texts

BOUCHIER-CHILCOTT, T.
Law of mortmain. Stevens & Haynes, 1905.

BRISTOWE, L.S.
Treatise on the Mortmain and Charitable Uses Act. Reeves & Turner, 1891.

FINLASON, W.F.
History of the laws of mortmain and the laws against testamentary dispositions for pious purposes, etc. Stevens & Haynes, 1853.

RABAN, S.
Mortmain legislation and the English Church, 1279–1500. Cambridge U.P., 1982.

RAWLINSON, J.
Notes on the Mortmain Act. Stevens, 1877.

SHELFORD, L.
Law of mortmain and charitable uses and trusts. Sweet, 1836.

TUDOR, O.D.
Law of charities. 7ed. Sweet & Maxwell, 1984.

MOTOR VEHICLES

See also Road Traffic.

Encyclopaedias

Statutes in Force. Group: Road Traffic.
Halsbury's Laws of England. 4ed. mainly vol.40 but see index vol.
Halsbury's Statutes of England. 3ed. see index vol.
The Digest. see index vol.
Encyclopaedia of Court Forms in Civil Proceedings (Atkin). 2ed. see index vol.
Encyclopaedia of Forms and Precedents. 4ed. see index vol.

Texts

ADVISORY COMMITTEE FOR THE CONTROL OF MOTOR RALLIES
Control of motor rallies: a report. 1976.

BINGHAM, L.
Motor claims cases. 8ed. Butterworths, 1980.

BRANDRETH, C.
Parking law. David & Charles, 1977.

CONSUMERS' ASSOCIATION
A.B.C. of motoring law. 1978.

CONSUMERS' ASSOCIATION
The law for motorists. 1971.

GIBB, A.D.
Law of collisions on land. 5ed. Sweet & Maxwell, 1947.

HORSLEY, D.B.
Manual of motor vehicle law. 2ed. Carswell, 1974 (Canada).

KITCHIN, L.D. & DUCKWORTH, J.
Road transport law. 24ed. Butterworths, 1983.

LAMBERT, J.
Motor vehicle safety standards and product liability. Economist Intelligence Unit, 1983. 3 vols. (In Japan; In the USA; In West Germany, France and the U.K.).

NEWSOME, E.L.
The Trade Descriptions Act and the motor vehicle. Rose, 1977.

NIEKIRK, P.H.
Motor driving offences. Butterworths, 1967.

SHEPHERD, W.
A to Z of motor trade law. R.Sewell, 1981.

SOCIETY OF MOTOR MANUFACTURERS AND TRADERS
Summary of international vehicle legislation. 1975 . 8 vols. Looseleaf.

STEAD, R.
The Motor Vehicles (Construction and Use) Regulations: a digest of decided cases. 2ed. Rose, 1975.

TERRELL, E.
Law of running down cases. 3ed. Butterworths, 1964.

TOYNE, C.C.
Motor vehicle technical regulations: a guide to the Motor Vehicles (Construction and Use) Regulations and the Road Vehicles Lighting Regulations. Rose, 1975.

VICERY, N.A.
Motor and traffic law – Victoria. 4ed. Butterworths (Australia). Looseleaf.

WICKERSON, J.
The motorist and the law. Oyez, 1974.

MUSEUMS

See also Libraries.

Encyclopaedias and periodicals

Statutes in Force. Group: Libraries, Museums and Galleries.

Halsbury's Laws of England. 4ed. vol.28 and see index vol.

Halsbury's Statutes of England. 3ed. see index vol.

Museums Bulletin. 1961–

Museums Journal. 1901–

Texts

CHAMBERS, G.F.
Law relating to public libraries and museums. 4ed. 1899.

EDGE, N.C.W.
General law for librarians, curators and those in charge of institutions to which the public have access. 1934.

HEWITT, A.R.
Consolidation of the law relating to public libraries and museums. 1931.

HEWITT, A.R.
Public library law and the law as to museums and art galleries in England and Wales, Scotland and Northern Ireland. 5ed. Assoc. of Assistant Libns., 1975.

NAMES

See also Business Names; Trade Marks

Encyclopaedias

Halsbury's Laws of England. 4ed. see index vol.

Halsbury's Statutes of England. 3ed. see index vol.

The Digest. vol.35 but see index vol.

Encyclopaedia of Court Forms in Civil Proceedings (Atkin). 2ed. see index vol.

Encyclopaedia of Forms and Precedents. 4ed. vol.15 but see index vol.

Texts

BANDER, E.J.
Change of name and law of names. Oceana, 1973 (USA).

EWEN, C.L.E.
History of the surnames of the British Isles: their origin, evolution, etymology and legal status. 1931.

FALCONER, T.
On surnames and the rules of law affecting their change. 2ed. Reynell, 1862.

FOX-DAVIES, A.C. & CARLYON BRITTON, P.W.P.
Law of names and changes of names. 1906.

JOSLING, J.F.
Change of name. 12ed. Oyez, 1980.

JOSLING, J.F.
Registration of business names. 3ed. Oyez, 1955.

LINELL, A.
The law of names, public, private and corporate. Butterworths, 1938.

NATIONAL HEALTH

See also Dentists; Doctors; Hospitals; Nursing.

Encyclopaedias and periodicals

Statutes in Force. Group: Social Security and Health Services.
Halsbury's Laws of England. 4ed. vol.33.
Halsbury's Statutes of England. 3ed. mainly vols. 23 & 43.
The Digest. vol.35.

Encyclopaedia of Court Forms in Civil Proceedings (Atkin). 2ed. vol.28.

British Medical Journal. 1857–
Community Health. 1969–
Health Services Journal. 1946–
Public Health. 1888–

Texts

BLACK, Sir D. & THOMAS, G.
Providing for the health service. Croom Helm, 1978.

BROWN, R.G.S.
Changing National Health Service. 2ed. Routledge, 1978.

BROWN, R.G.S.
Reorganizing the National Health Service: case study of administrative change. Routledge, 1979.

BUTLER, J.R. & VAILE, M.S.B.
Health and health services: an introduction to health care in Britain. Routledge, 1984.

FARNDALE, W.A.J. & RUSSELL, S.
Law of accidents to Health Service staff and volunteers: case studies on law and practice for health service management. Ravenswood, 1977.

FELDSTEIN, P.J.
Health Association and the demand for legislation: the political economy of health. Wiley, 1977 (USA).

FINCH, J.
Health services law. Sweet & Maxwell, 1981.

FREEMAN, A.
Legal proceedings against doctors and health authorities: a special report on the conduct of medical negligence claims. 1980.

GILES, G.H.
Ophthalmic services under the National Health Service Acts. Butterworths, 1953.

GODBER, Sir G.
Health service: past, present and future. Athlone P., 1975.

HEALTH AND SOCIAL SECURITY, DEPARTMENT OF
Future structure of the National Health Service. HMSO, 1970.

HEALTH AND SOCIAL SECURITY, DEPARTMENT OF
Reorganization of the National Health Service and local government in England and Wales. HMSO, 1974.

HEALTH SERVICE COMMISSIONER
Annual Reports. HMSO.

LEVITT, R.
The reorganised National Health Service. Croom Helm, 1976.

LUMLEY, W.G.
Lumley's public health. 12ed. Butterworths. 12 vols. & supps.

NATIONAL CONSUMER COUNCIL
Patients' rights: a guide for NHS patients and doctors. HMSO, 1983.

ORGANISATION FOR ECONOMIC CO-OPERATION AND DEVELOPMENT
British National Health Service: policy trends and their implication for eduction. 1975.

ROYAL COMMISSION ON THE NATIONAL HEALTH SERVICE
Report (Merrison). HMSO, 1979 (Cmnd. 7615).

ROYAL COMMISSION ON THE NATIONAL HEALTH SERVICE
The task of the Commission: a guide for those who wish to submit evidence. HMSO, 1976.

ROYAL COMMISSION ON THE
NATIONAL HEALTH SERVICE
The working of the National Health
Service. HMSO, 1978.

SPELLER, S.R.
National Health Service Act, 1946.
Annotated. Lewis, 1948 supp. 1951.

WORLD HEALTH ORGANISATION
Approaches to national health planning.
1972.

WORLD HEALTH ORGANISATION
Training in national health planning. 1970.

NATIONAL INSURANCE

See also Hospitals; Industrial Injuries; Insurance; Pensions; Social Security.

Encyclopaedias and periodicals

Statutes in Force. Group: Social Security
and Health Services.
Halsbury's Laws of England. 4ed. see index
vol.
Halsbury's Statutes of England. 3ed. mainly
vol.45.
The Digest. vol.35.
Encyclopaedia of Court Forms in Civil
Proceedings (Atkin). 2ed. vol. 28.

Encyclopaedia of Forms and Precedents.
4ed. see index vol.

Journal of Social Welfare Law. 1978–
Legal Action (formerly L.A.G. Bulletin).
1973–
New Law Journal, 1965– . (as Law Journal
1882–1964).
Social Services Quarterly. 1947–
Solicitors' Journal. 1857–

Texts

COMMITTEE ON PROCEDURE FOR
DETERMINATION OF
UNEMPLOYMENT INSURANCE
CLAIMS
Report (Morris). HMSO, 1929–38 (Cmd.
3475).

DEPARTMENTAL COMMITTEE ON
NATIONAL INSURANCE
Report (Davies). HMSO, 1913 (Cd. 6853–
4).

HEALTH AND SOCIAL SECURITY,
DEPARTMENT OF
The law relating to family allowances and
national insurance: the statutes, regulations
and orders as now in force. Annotated and
indexed. HMSO. 2 vols. Looseleaf.

KEAST, H.
Case law on national insurance and
industrial injuries. 1952.

KOHLER, P.A. & ZACHER, H.F. (ed.)
Evolution of social insurance, 1881–1981:
studies of Great Britain, France,
Switzerland, Austria and Germany.
F.Pinter, 1982.

MICKLETHWAIT, Sir R.
The National Insurance Commissioners.
Stevens, 1976.

POTTER, D. (ed.)
The National Insurance Act, 1946.
Butterworths, 1946.

POTTER, D. & STANSFIELD, D.H.
National insurance. 2ed. Butterworths,
1949.

POTTER, D. & STANSFIELD, D.H.
National insurance industrial injuries. 2ed.
Butterworths, 1950.

REPORT on social insurance (Beveridge).
HMSO, 1942–43. (Cmd. 6604).

NATIONAL PARKS

See also Commons and Inclosures.

Encyclopaedias

Statutes in Force. Group: Environment.
Halsbury's Laws of England. 4ed. vol.34.
Halsbury's Statutes of England. 3ed mainly vol.24.
Encyclopaedia of Forms and Precedents. 4ed. vol.23.

Texts

BROWNING, N.
National parks and access to countryside. Thames Bank Pub. Co., 1950.

ENVIRONMENT, DEPARTMENT OF THE
National park policies: review committee report. HMSO, 1974.

RODDIS, R.J.
Law of parks and recreation grounds. 4ed. 1974.

NATIONALITY AND CITIZENSHIP

See also Aliens; Conflict of Laws.

Encyclopaedias and periodicals

Statutes in Force. Group: Nationality.
Halsbury's Laws of England. 4ed. vol.4.
Halsbury's Statutes of England. 3ed. vol.1.
The Digest. mainly vol.2.
Encyclopaedia of Forms and Precedents. 4ed. vol.15.

International & Comparative Law Quarterly. 1952–
Public Law. 1956–

Texts

BAR-YAACOV, N.
Dual nationality. Stevens, 1961.

COCKBURN, A.E.
Nationality, or the law relating to subjects and aliens, considered with a view to future legislation. Ridgway, 1869.

DUMMETT, A.
Citizenship and nationality. Runnymede Trust, 1976.

FLOURNOY, R.W. & HUDSON, M.O.
Nationality laws of various countries. Oxford U.P., 1929.

HANCOCK, W.K. & LATHAM, R.T.E.
Survey of British Commonwealth affairs. Vol. 1: problems of nationality, 1918–36. Oxford U.P., 1937.

HOME OFFICE
British nationality law: discussion of possible changes. HMSO, 1977 (Cmnd. 6795).

JONES, J.M.
British nationality law and practice. 2ed. Oxford U.P., 1956.

JOSEPH, C.
Nationality and diplomatic protection. Sijthoff, 1969.

PANHUYS, H.F. van
The role of nationality in international law. Sijthoff, 1959.

PARRY, C.
British nationality, including citizenship of the United Kingdom and colonies and the status of aliens. Stevens, 1951.

PARRY, C.
Nationality and citizenship laws of the Commonwealth and Republic of Ireland. Stevens, 1957–60. 2 vols.

PIGGOTT, Sir F.
Nationality including naturalization and English law on the high seas and beyond the realm. Clowes, 1907.

ROSANTHAL, D.
Nationality laws and international commerce: problem of extraterritoriality. Routledge, 1982.

VERZIJL, J.H.W.
International law in historical perspective. Vol. V: nationality and other matters relating to individuals. Sijthoff, 1972.

WEIS, P.
Nationality and statelessness in international law. 2ed. Sijthoff, 1979.

NAVY

See also Admiralty; Court Martial; Military Law; Prize Law; Shipping; War.

Encyclopaedias

Statutes in Force. Group: Armed Forces. Halsbury's Laws of England. 4ed. mainly vol.41.

Halsbury's Statutes of England. 3ed. mainly vol.29

The Digest. mainly vol.39.

Texts

CABLE, J.
Gunboat diplomacy: political applications of limited naval force. 2ed. Macmillan, 1981.

COMMITTEE TO CONSIDER THE ADMINISTRATION OF JUSTICE UNDER THE NAVAL DISCIPLINE ACT
Report (Pilcher). HMSO, 1950–51 (Cmd. 8094, Cmd. 8119).

DEFENCE, MINISTRY OF. NAVY DEPARTMENT
Admiralty manual of navigation. HMSO, 1971–4. 2 vols.

DEFENCE, MINISTRY OF. NAVY DEPARTMENT
Manual of naval law. HMSO. Looseleaf.

DEFENCE, MINISTRY OF. NAVY DEPARTMENT
Naval court-martial manual. HMSO. Looseleaf.

DEFENCE, MINISTRY OF. NAVY DEPARTMENT
Navy list. HMSO. Annual.

DEFENCE, MINISTRY OF. NAVY DEPARTMENT
Queen's regulations for the Royal Navy. HMSO. Looseleaf.

HALL, J.A.
Law of naval warefare. 2ed. Chapman & Hall, 1921.

PRITCHARD, W.T.
Digest of law and practice of the Court of Admiralty. 3ed. Butterworths, 1887. 2 vols.

ROSCOE, E.S.
Studies in the history of the Admiralty Court and Prize Court. 2ed. Stevens, 1932.

ROSCOE, E.S.
Jurisdiction and practice of the Court of Admiralty. 5ed. Stevens, 1931 repr. Professional Books.

SENIOR, W.
Naval history of law courts. Longmans, Green, 1927.

SMITH, H.A.
Law and the custom of the sea. 3ed. Stevens, 1959.

STEPHENS, J.E.R., GIFFORD, C.E. & SMITH, F.H.
Manual of naval law and court martial procedure, in which is embodied Thring's criminal law of the navy. 2ed. Stevens, 1912.

NEGLIGENCE

See also Accidents; Damages; Employer's Liability; Medical Negligence; Roman Law; Tort.

Encyclopaedias and periodicals

Halsbury's Laws of England. 4ed. vol.34.
Halsbury's Statutes of England. 3ed. see index vol.
The Digest. vol.36.
Encyclopaedia of Court Forms in Civil Proceedings (Atkin). 2ed. vol.2

Encyclopaedia of Forms and Precedents. 4ed. see index vol.
Law Quarterly Review. 1885–
Modern Law Review. 1937–

Texts

BINGHAM, R.
All the modern cases of negligence. 3ed. Sweet & Maxwell, 1978 supp. 1984.

CHARLESWORTH, J.
The law of negligence. 7ed. Sweet & Maxwell, 1983 supp. 1984 (Common law library).

DUGDALE, A.M. & STANTON, K.M.
Professional negligence. Butterworths, 1982.

HART, H.L.A.
Negligence, mens rea and criminal responsibility (in Oxford Essays in Jurisprudence. Oxford U.P., 1961).

JACKSON, R. & POWELL, J.
Professional negligence. Sweet & Maxwell, 1982.

LAWSON, F.H.
Negligence in civil law. Oxford U.P., 1951.

MANNIX, E.F. & MANNIX, J.E.
Professional negligence. 3ed. Butterworths (Australia), 1976.

MILLNER, M.A.
Negligence in modern law. Butterworths, 1967.

UNDERWOOD, A. & WOOD, S.C.
Professional negligence. Fourmat, 1981.

WELSON, J.B.
Law of negligence: legal liabilities as covered by liability policies. Pitman, 1930.

WILLIAMS, G.L.
Joint torts and contributory negligence. Sweet & Maxwell, 1951 repr. 1977.

NEGOTIABLE INSTRUMENTS

See also Banks and Banking; Bills of Exchange; Letters of Credit.

Encyclopaedias and periodicals

Statutes in Force. Group: Bills of Exchange and Promissory Notes.
Halsbury's Laws of England. 4ed. vol. 4.
Halsbury's Statutes of England. 3ed vol.3. Bills of Exchange.
The Digest. see index vol.

Encyclopaedia of Court Forms in Civil Proceedings (Atkin). 2ed. vol.8.
The Banker. 1926–
Journal of Business Law. 1957–

Texts

BYLES, Sir J.B.
Bills of exchange: the law of bills of exchange, promissory notes, bank notes and cheques. 23ed. Sweet & Maxwell, 1972.

CHALMERS, Sir M.D.
Chalmers on bills of exchange. 13ed. Sweet & Maxwell, 1964.

COWAN, D.V. & GERING, L.C.
The law of negotiable instruments in South Africa. 4ed. Juta, 1966.

HOLDEN, J.M.
The history of negotiable instruments in English law. Univ. of London P., 1955.

JACOBS, B.
A short treatise on the law of bills of exchange, cheques, promissory notes and negotiable instruments generally. 4ed. Sweet & Maxwell, 1944.

KOBRIN, D.L. & STOTT, V.
Negotiable instruments. Anderson Keenan, 1980.

McLOUGHLIN, J.
Introduction to negotiable instruments. Butterworths, 1975.

MYINT SOE, U.
Law of banking and negotiable instruments in Singapore and Malaysia. 1977.

RAJANAYAGAM, M.J.L.
The law relating to negotiable instruments in Australia. Butterworths (Australia), 1980.

RICHARDSON, D.
Guide to negotiable instruments and the Bills of Exchange Act. 7ed. Butterworths, 1983.

RYDER, F.R.
Negotiable instruments. Penguin, 1970.

SINGH, A.
Negotiable Instruments Act. Eastern Book Co., 1980 (India).

WHALEY, D.
Problems and materials on negotiable instruments. Little, Brown, 1981 (USA).

WILLIS, W.
Law of negotiable securities. 5ed. Sweet & Maxwell, 1930.

NEW ZEALAND

Encyclopaedias and periodicals

Statutes in Force. Group: Commonwealth and Other Territories.
Halsbury's Laws of England. 3ed. see New Zealand Pilot; 4ed. vol. 6.
The Digest. vol.8.
Encyclopaedia of Court Forms in Civil Proceedings (Atkin). 2ed. see index vol.
New Zealand Encyclopaedia of Forms and Precedents.

New Zealand Journal of Public Administration. 1938–
New Zealand Law Journal. 1925–
New Zealand Law Society Newsletter. 1965–
New Zealand Universities Law Review. 1963–
Otago Law Review. 1965–
Victoria University of Wellington Law Review. 1953–

Texts

ADAM, M. (ed.)
Australian and New Zealand citator of UK reports 1558–1972. Butterworths, 1973.

ADAMS, Sir F.B.
Criminal law and practice in New Zealand. 2ed. Sweet & Maxwell, 1972.

DERHAM, D.P., MAHER, F.K.H. & WALLER, P.L.
Introduction to law. 2ed. Sweet & Maxwell (NZ), 1972.

MAHER, F.K.H., WALLER, P.L. & DERHAM, D.P.
Cases and materials on the legal process, New Zealand ed. Law Book Co., 1972.

MULHOLLAND, R.D.
Introduction to the New Zealand legal system. 2ed. Wellington U.P., 1976.

O'KEEFE, J.A.B. & FARRANDS, W.L.
Introduction to New Zealand law. 3ed. Butterworths (NZ), 1976.

PATERSON, D.A.
An introduction to administrative law in New Zealand. Butterworths (NZ), 1968.

PEARCE, D.C.
Delegated legislation in Australia and New Zealand. Butterworths (Australia), 1977.

ROBSON, J.L.
New Zealand: the development of its laws and constitution. 2ed. Stevens, 1967.

SCOTT, C.D.
Local and regional government in New Zealand. Allen & Unwin, 1979.

SCOTT, K.J.
The New Zealand constitution. Oxford U.P., 1962.

SIM, W.J.
Practice of the Supreme Court and Court of Appeal of New Zealand. 11ed. Butterworths (NZ), 1972. 2 vols.

NIGERIA

Encyclopaedias and periodicals

Statutes in Force. Group: Commonwealth and Other Territories.
Halbury's Laws of England. 4ed. vol.6.
Halsbury's Statutes of England. 3ed. vol.4.
The Digest. vol.8.

Journal of the Centre of Islamic Studies, Ahmadu Bello Universities, Zaria. 1966–
Law in Society: Journal of the Law Society Ahmadu Bello University, Zaria. 1964/65–

Nigerian Bar Journal. 1958–
Nigerian Commercial Law Reports. 1964–
Nigerian Constitutional Law Reports. 1980–
Nigerian Criminal Law Reports. 1980–
Nigerian Journal of International Affairs. 1975–
Nigerian Law Journal. 1964–
Nigerian Law Reports. 1881–

Texts

ADAMOLEKUN, L.
Public administration: a Nigerian and comparative perspective. Longman, 1983.

ADEBAYO, A.
Principles and practice of public administration in Nigeria. Wiley, 1981.

ADEFIDIVA, A.
Directory of law libraries in Nigeria. 2ed. Oceana, 1970.

ADESANYA, M.O. & OLOYEDE, E.O.
Business law in Nigeria. rev. ed. Evans Bros., 1980.

ADEWOYE, O.
Judicial system in Southern Nigeria, 1854–1954. Longman, 1977.

AGUDA, T.A.
A guide to practice and procedure in the High Courts of Nigeria. Sweet & Maxwell, 1968.

AGUDA, T.A.
Law and practice relating to evidence in Nigeria. Sweet & Maxwell, 1980.

AGUDA, T.A.
Law of evidence in Nigeria. 2ed. Sweet & Maxwell, 1974.

AGUDA, T.A.
Practice and procedure of the Supreme Court, Court of Appeal and High Courts in Nigeria. Sweet & Maxwell, 1980.

AGUDA, T.A.
Principles of practice and procedure in civil actions in the High Courts of Nigeria. new ed. Sweet & Maxwell, 1980.

AGUDA, T.A., BRETT, Sir L. & McLEAN, I.
The criminal law and procedure in the southern States of Nigeria. 3ed. Sweet & Maxwell, 1982.

AGYEI, A.K.
Capital gains tax in Nigeria. G.Burn, 1984.

AIHE, D.O. & OLUYEDE, P.A.
Cases and materials on constitutional law in Nigeria. Oxford U.P., 1979.

AKANDE, J.
Introduction to the Nigerian constitution. Sweet & Maxwell, 1982.

AYUA, I.
Nigerian company law: a clear and concise comprehensive appraisal of company law and practice in Nigeria. G.Burn, 1983.

BALOGON, M.J.
Public administration in Nigeria. Macmillan, 1983.

CAMPBELL, M.J.
Law and practice of local government in Northern Nigeria. African Univ. P., 1963.

COKER, G.B.A.
Family property among the Yorubas. 2ed. Sweet & Maxwell, 1966.

ELIAS, T.O.
Law and social change in Nigeria. Univ. of Lagos, 1972.

ELIAS, T.O.
Nigeria: the development of its laws and constitution. Stevens, 1967.

ELIAS, T.O.
Nigerian land law. 4ed. Sweet & Maxwell, 1971.

ELIAS, T.O. (ed.)
Nigerian press law. Univ. of Lagos, 1969.

HARVEY, B.W.
A guide to the law and practice of costs in Nigeria. Sweet & Maxwell, 1968.

HARVEY, B.W.
The law and practice of Nigerian wills, probate and succession. Sweet & Maxwell, 1968.

HICKS, A.
Nigerian law of hire-purchase. Ahmada Bello Univ.Press: Books on Africa, 1983.

KASUNMU, A.B. (ed.)
Supreme Court of Nigeria, 1956–70. Heinemann, 1977.

KASUNMU, A.B. & SALACUSE, J.W.
Nigerian family law. Butterworths, 1966.

KEAY, E.A. & RICHARDSON, S.S.
The native and customary courts of Nigeria. Sweet & Maxwell, 1966.

KODILINYE, G.
An introduction to equity in Nigeria. Sweet & Maxwell, 1975.

McNEIL, J.L. & RAINS, R.
Nigerian cases and statutes on contract and tort. Sweet & Maxwell, 1965.

MBANEFO, L.N.
Nigerian shipping laws. Professional Books, 1983.

MILNER, A.
The Nigerian penal system. Sweet & Maxwell, 1972.

MURRAY, D.J. (ed.)
Studies in Nigerian administration. 2ed. Hutchinson, 1978.

NWABUEZE, B.O.
Constitutional history of Nigeria. Longman, 1982.

NWABUEZE, B.O.
Constitutional law of the Nigerian Republic. Butterworths, 1964.

NWABUEZE, B.O.
The machinery of justice in Nigeria. Butterworths, 1963.

NYLANDER, A.V.J.
The nationality and citizenship laws of Nigeria. Sweet & Maxwell, 1974.

OBI, S.N.C.
Modern family law in Southern Nigeria. Sweet & Maxwell, 1966.

OBILADE, A.O.
The Nigerian legal system. Sweet & Maxwell, 1979.

ODUMOSU, O.I.
The Nigerian Constitution: history and development. Sweet & Maxwell, 1964

OKONKWO, C.O.
Introduction to Nigerian law. Sweet & Maxwell, 1980.

OKONKWO, C.O. & McLEAN, I.
Cases on the criminal law: procedure and evidence of Nigeria, excluding the North. Sweet & Maxwell, 1966.

OKONKWO, C.O. & NAISH, M.E.
Criminal law in Nigeria. 2ed. Sweet & Maxwell, 1980.

OKORO, D.R.N.
The customary laws of succession in Eastern Nigeria and the statutory and judicial rules governing the application. Sweet & Maxwell, 1966.

OLA, C.S.
Nigerian taxation. 3ed. G.Burn, 1984.

OLA, C.S.
Town and country planning law in Nigeria. Oxford U.P., 1977.

OLA, R.O.F.
Local administration in Nigeria. K. Paul International, 1983.

OLAWOYE, C.O.
Title to land in Nigeria. Lagos U.P., 1974.

OLAWOYIN, G.A. & OLAFARE, A.
Commercial law of Nigeria. Woodhead-Faulkner, 1985.

ONOKERHORAYE, A.G.
Social services in Nigeria: an introduction. K. Paul International, 1983.

ONWUAMAEGBU, M.O.
Nigerian law of landlord and tenant. Sweet & Maxwell, 1966.

OROJO, J.O.
Company law and practice in Nigeria. 2ed. Sweet & Maxwell, 1984. 2 vols.

OROJO, J.O.
Company tax law in Nigeria. Sweet & Maxwell, 1979.

OROJO, J.O.
A guide to business contracts in Nigeria. Sweet & Maxwell, 1968.

OROJO, J.O.
A guide to the conduct and etiquette of legal practitioners in Nigeria. Sweet & Maxwell, 1979.

OROJO, J.O.
Introduction to Nigerian company law. Sweet & Maxwell, 1984.

OROJO, J.O.
Nigerian commercial law and practice.
Sweet & Maxwell, 1983. 2 vols.

PARK, A.E.W.
The sources of Nigerian law. Sweet &
Maxwell, 1972.

RICHARDSON, S.S. & WILLIAMS,
T.H.
The criminal procedure code of Northern
Nigeria. Sweet & Maxwell, 1963.

ROGERS, M. & EDGE, I.
Business laws of Nigeria. 1980.

SAGAY, I.E.
Casebook on the Nigerian law of contract.
Professional Books, 1983.

SAGAY, I.E.
Nigerian law of contract. Sweet & Maxwell,
1984.

UCHE, U.U.
Contractual obligations in Ghana and
Nigeria. Cass, 1972.

UMEH, J.A.
Compulsory acquisition of land and
compensation in Nigeria. Sweet & Maxwell,
1973.

WILLOUGHBY, P.G.
A guide to the form and drafting of
conveyances in Nigeria. Sweet & Maxwell,
1968.

NISI PRIUS

See also Juries.

Texts

ARCHBOLD, J.F.
Law of nisi prius. 2ed. Sweet, 1845. 2 vols.

ARCHBOLD, J.F.
Pleading, evidence and practice in criminal
cases. 41ed. Sweet & Maxwell, 1982.

BULLER, Sir F.
Law of trials at nisi prius. 7ed. Pheney &
Sweet, 1817.

CARRINGTON, F.A. & KIRWIN, A.V.
Reports at nisi prius, 1843–53. Sweet. 3
vols.

CARRINGTON, F.A. & MARSHMAN,
J.R.
Reports at nisi prius, 1840–42. Sweet.

CARRINGTON, F.A. & PAYNE, J.
Reports at nisi prius, 1823–41. Sweet. 9
vols.

COUNTY Court practice. Butterworths.
Annual.

ESPINASSE, I.
Digest of the law of actions at nisi prius.
4ed. Butterworths, 1812.

ESPINASSE, I.
Reports of cases argued and ruled at nisi
prius, 1793–1807. Butterworths, 1793–
1819.

PEAKE, T.
Additional cases; being a continuation of
cases at nius prius...1795–1812. Clarke,
1829.

PEAKE, T.
Cases determined at nisi prius, 1790–1794.
2ed. Hunter, 1820.

ROSCOE, H.
Digest of the law of evidence on the trial of
civil actions (nisi prius). 20ed. Stevens,
1934.

SELWYN, W.
Abridgment of the law of nisi prius. 13ed.
Stevens, 1869. 2 vols.

SUPREME Court practice 1985. Sweet &
Maxwell, 1984. 2 vols.

NOISE

See also Nuisance; Public Health.

Encyclopaedias and periodicals

Halsbury's Laws of England. 4ed. see index vols.
Halsbury's Statutes of England. 3ed. mainly vol.44.
The Digest. vol.36.

Encyclopaedia of Court Forms in Civil Proceedings (Atkin). 2ed. see index vol.
Legal Action (formerly L.A.G. Bulletin). 1973–
Noise News Digest. 1970–

Texts

ANTHROP, D.F.
Noise pollution. D.C. Heath, 1973.

BRAGDON, C.R.
Noise pollution: a guide to information sources. Gale Research, 1979 (USA).

COMMITTEE ON THE PROBLEM OF NOISE
Report (Wilson). HMSO, 1963 (Cmnd. 2056).

CONFEDERATION OF BRITISH INDUSTRY
Industrial noise and the public: guidance for companies of all sizes on environmental noise legislation. 1979.

DUERDEN, C.
Noise abatement. Butterworths, 1970.

EMPLOYMENT, DEPARTMENT OF
Code of practice for reducing the exposure of employed persons to noise. HMSO, 1974.

EMPLOYMENT, DEPARTMENT OF
Noise and the worker. 3ed. HMSO, 1971.

ENVIRONMENT, DEPARTMENT OF THE
Insulation against traffic noise. HMSO, 1973.

ENVIRONMENT, DEPARTMENT OF THE
Neighbourhood noise: report of the Working Group on the Noise Abatement Act. HMSO, 1971.

GRIME, R.P.
The law of noise-induced hearing loss and its compensation. Univ. of Southampton, 1975.

HILDEBRAND, J.L.
Noise pollution and the law. Hein, 1970 (USA).

KERSE, C.S.
The law relating to noise. Oyez, 1975.

MILNE, A.
Noise pollution: impact and countermeasures. David & Charles, 1979.

NOISE ABATEMENT SOCIETY
Law on noise. 1969.

NOISE ADVISORY COUNCIL
A study of Government noise insulation policies: report of the working group on law and administration. HMSO, 1981.

NOISE ADVISORY COUNCIL
Noise in public places: report by a working group. HMSO, 1974.

NOISE ADVISORY COUNCIL
Noise in the next ten years: report by the Panel on Noise in the seventies. HMSO, 1974.

NOISE ADVISORY COUNCIL
Noise units: reports by a Working Party for the Research Sub-Committee. HMSO, 1975.

PENN, C.N.
Noise control. Shaw, 1979.

PUBLIC HEALTH ADVISORY SERVICE
Noise and noise abatement. 1975.

NORTH ATLANTIC TREATY ORGANISATION

See also International Law; Treaties.

Periodicals

NATO Review. 1952–

Texts

ALTING VON GEUSAU, F.A.M.
NATO and security in the seventies.
Sijthoff, 1971.

BATHURST, M. & SIMPSON, J.L.
Germany and the North Atlantic
Community. Stevens, 1956.

BECKETT, Sir E.
The North Atlantic Treaty, the Brussels
Treaty and the Charter of the United
Nations. Stevens, 1950.

GORDON, C.
Atlantic alliance: a bibliography. Nichols,
1978 (USA).

IRELAND, T.P.
Creating the entangling alliance: the origins
of the North Atlantic Treaty Organization.
Greenwood, 1981 (USA).

McCLOSKEY, M.
North Atlantic Treaty Organization:
guardian of peace and security. Rosen, 1966
(USA).

NORTH ATLANTIC TREATY
ORGANIZATION
NATO – facts and figures. 1971.

ROBERTSON, A.H.
European institutions: co-operation,
integration, unification. 3ed. Stevens, 1973.

SCHWARZENBERGER, G.
A manual of international law. 6ed.
Professional Books, 1976.

NORTHERN IRELAND

See also Constitutional Law.

Encyclopaedias and periodicals

Halsbury's Laws of England. 4ed. see index
vol.
Halsbury's Statutes of England. 3ed. see
index vol.
The Digest. see index vol.

Bulletin of Northern Ireland Law. 1981–
Gazette of the Incorporated Law Society of
Northern Ireland. 1964–

Irish Jurist, vols. 1–31, 1935–65. New
Series. 1966–
Irish Law Times and Solicitors' Journal.
1868–
Northern Ireland Legal Quarterly. 1936–
Northern Ireland Law Reports. 1925–

Texts

ARTHUR, P.
Government and politics of Northern
Ireland. 2ed. Longman, 1984.

BOYLE, K.
Law and state: case of Northern Ireland.
Martin Robertson, 1975.

CALVERT, H.
Constitutional law in Northern Ireland: a
study in regional government. Sweet &
Maxwell, 1968.

DEUTSCH, R. (ed.)
Northern Ireland 1921–74: a select
bibliography. Garland, 1975 (USA).

DICKSON, B.
The legal system of Northern Ireland. SLS
Legal Pubns. (NI), 1984.

HAND, G.J.
English law in Ireland, 1290–1324.
Cambridge U.P., 1967.

KEETON, G.W.
The United Kingdom: the development of its laws and constitution. Stevens, 1955. 2 vols.

LAWRENCE, R.J.
The government of Northern Ireland: public finance and public services, 1921–64. Oxford U.P., 1965.

MANSERGH, P.N.S.
The Government of Northern Ireland: a study in devolution. Allen & Unwin, 1936.

NARAIN, B.J.
Public law in Northern Ireland. Shanway, 1975.

NORTHERN IRELAND OFFICE
Northern Ireland and the E.E.C. 1972.

NORTHERN IRELAND OFFICE
Violence and civil disturbances in Northern Ireland in 1969: report of the Tribunal of Inquiry (Scarman). HMSO, 1972 (Cmd. 566). 2 vols.

O'HIGGINS, P.
A bibliography of periodical literature relating to Irish law. N.I.L.Q., 1966.

QUEKETT, Sir A.S.
The constitution of Northern Ireland, 1928–47. HMSO. 3 vols.

SWEET & MAXWELL
A legal bibliography of the British Commonwealth of Nations. 2ed. 1955–64. Vol.4: Irish law to 1956.

NOTARIES

See also Legal Profession; Solicitors.

Encyclopaedias

Statutes in Force. Group: Lawyers and Notaries.
Halsbury's Laws of England. 4ed. vol.34.
Halsbury's Statutes of England. 3ed. vol.23.
The Digest. vol.36.

Texts

BROOKE, R.
Treatise on the office and practice of a notary of England with a collection of precedents. 9ed. Stevens, 1939.

CHENEY, C.R.
Notaries public in England in the thirteenth and fourteenth centuries. Oxford U.P., 1972.

ELLIOTT, R.C. & BANWELL, E.
The South African notary. 5ed. Juta, 1977.

LIEBERS, A.
Notary public: the complete study guide. 5ed. Arco, 1976 (USA).

MONTGOMERY, E.J.
Manual on the practice of notaries public in Ireland. Matheson, Ormsby & Prentice, 1976.

NUCLEAR ENERGY

Encyclopaedias and periodicals

Statutes in Force. Groups: Atomic Energy and Radioactive Substances; Energy.
Halsbury's Laws of England. 4ed. mainly vol.16.

Halsbury's Statutes of England. 3ed. see index vol.

Nuclear Law Bulletin. 1968–

Texts

BLOUSTEIN, E.J.
Nuclear energy: public policy and the law. Oceana, 1964 (USA).

COMMERCE CLEARING HOUSE
Nuclear regulation reporter. 1975 (USA). 2 vols.

GREENHALGH, G.
The necessity for nuclear power. Graham & Trotman, 1980.

GUHIN, M.A.
Nuclear paradox: security risks of the peaceful atom. American Enterprise Inst., 1976.

HYDEMAN, L.M. & BERMAN, W.H.
International control of nuclear maritime activities. Univ. of Michigan, 1960.

INTERNATIONAL ATOMIC ENERGY AGENCY
Agreements registered with the International Atomic Energy Agency (up to Dec. 31 1973). 6ed. 1976.

INTERNATIONAL ATOMIC ENERGY AGENCY
Convention on the Physical Protection of Nuclear Material. IAEA:HMSO, 1983.

INTERNATIONAL ATOMIC ENERGY AGENCY
Experience and trends in nucelar law. 1972.

INTERNATIONAL ATOMIC ENERGY AGENCY
Insurance for nuclear installations. 1970.

INTERNATIONAL ATOMIC ENERGY AGENCY
International conventions on civil liability for nuclear damage. 1976.

INTERNATIONAL ATOMIC ENERGY AGENCY
The law and practices of the I.A.E.A. 1970.

INTERNATIONAL ATOMIC ENERGY AGENCY
Licensing and regulatory control of nuclear installations. 1975.

INTERNATIONAL ATOMIC ENERGY AGENCY
Maritime carriage of nuclear fuels. 1973.

INTERNATIONAL ATOMIC ENERGY AGENCY
Nuclear law for a developing world. 1969.

INTERNATIONAL ATOMIC ENERGY AGENCY
Nuclear techniques in environmental pollution. 1971.

JUSTICE
Plutonium and liberty: some possible consequences of nuclear reprocessing for an open society. Stevens, 1978.

LEACHMAN, R.B. & ALTHOFF, P. (eds.)
Preventing nuclear theft: guidelines for industry and government. Praeger, 1972 (USA).

LIPSCHUTZ, R.D.
Radioactive waste: politics, technology, and risk. Ballinger, 1975 (USA).

NUCLEAR ENERGY AGENCY
Nuclear legislation: nuclear third party liability, 1976: an analytical study. 1977.

ORGANISATION FOR ECONOMIC CO-OPERATION AND DEVELOP[MENT
Regulations governing nuclear installations and radiation protection. 1972.

SETHNA, J.M.
International legal controls and sanctions concerning the production and use of nuclear energy. Rothman, 1966 (USA).

STREET, H. & FRAME, F.R.
Law relating to nuclear energy. Butterworths, 1966.

UNITED NATIONS ASSOCIATION
Nuclear energy: its nature, control and use. 1959.

WEINSTEIN, J.L.
Nuclear liability. Pergamon, 1962.

WILLRICH, M. (ed.)
International safeguards and nuclear industry. Johns Hopkins U.P., 1973 (USA).

WILLRICH, M. & TAYLOR, T.B.
Nuclear theft: risks and safeguards. Ballinger, 1974 (USA).

YOUNG, J.van
Judges and science: the case law on atomic energy. 1964 repr. Arno, 1979 (USA).

NUCLEAR WARFARE AND WEAPONS

Texts

FISCHER, G.
The non-proliferation of nuclear weapons: translated from the French by D. Willey. Saxon House, 1971.

GREENWOOD, T., FEIVESON, H.A. & TAYLOR, T.
Nuclear proliferation: motivations, capabilities, and strategies for control. McGraw-Hill, 1977.

HOME OFFICE
Nuclear weapons. 3ed. HMSO, 1974.

JASANI, B.
Nuclear proliferation problems. MIT Press, 1975 (USA).

McKNIGHT, A.
Atomic safeguards: a study in international verification. Unitar, 1971.

MARWAH, O. & SCHULZ, A.
Nuclear proliferation and the near-nuclear countries. Ballinger, 1975 (USA).

MINISTRY OF FOREIGN AFFAIRS (N.Z.)
French nuclear testing in the Pacific International Court of Justice nuclear test case: New Zealand and France. Government Printer, 1973 (New Zealand).

NASH, H.T.
Nuclear weapons and international behaviour. Sijthoff, 1975.

QUESTER, G.H.
The politics of nuclear proliferation. Johns Hopkins U.P., 1973 (USA).

SCHWARZENBERGER, G.
The legality of nuclear weapons. Stevens, 1958.

SHAKER, M.I.
Nuclear non-proliferation treaty: origin and implementation, 1959–1979. Oceana, 1980 (USA). 3 vols.

SINGH, N.
Nuclear weapons and international law. Stevens, 1959.

STOCKHOLM INTERNATIONAL PEACE RESEARCH INSTITUTE
The near-nuclear countries and the non-proliferation treaty. 1972.

STOCKHOLM INTERNATIONAL PEACE RESEARCH INSTITUTE
Prospects for arms control in the ocean. 1972.

STOCKHOLM, INTERNATIONAL PEACE RESEARCH INSTITUTE
Safeguards against nuclear proliferation. 1975.

STOCKHOLM INTERNATIONAL PEACE RESEARCH INSTITUTE
The test ban. 1971.

WILLRICH, M.
Non-proliferation treaty. Michie, 1969 (USA).

WILLRICH, M.
Strategic arms limitation talks. Ballinger, 1974 (USA).

NUISANCE

See also Noise; Public Health; Tort.

Encyclopaedias and periodicals

Halsbury's Laws of England. 4ed. vol.34.
Halsbury's Statutes of England. 3ed. see index vol.
The Digest. vol.36.
Encyclopaedia of Court Forms in Civil Proceedings (Atkin). 2ed. vol.29.
Encyclopaedia of Forms and Precedents. 4ed. see index vol.

Law Quarterly Review. 1885–
Legal Action (formerly L.A.G. Bulletin). 1973–
Modern Law Review. 1937–

Texts

CLERK, J.F. & LINDSELL, W.H.B.
The law of torts. 15ed. Sweet & Maxwell, 1982.

GARRETT, F.E.W.
Law of nuisance. 3ed. Butterworths, 1908.

GIBBONS, D.
A treatise on the law of dilapidations and nuisance. 2ed. J.Weale, 1849.

KEANE, D.D.
Nuisances Removal Act. 6ed. Stevens, 1870.

MACKENZIE, W. & HANDFORD, P.
Model by-laws as to nuisances, new streets and buildings.Butterworths, 1904.

PEARCE, E.H. & MESTON, D.
Law relating to nuisances. Sweet & Maxwell, 1926.

SALMOND, Sir J.W.
The law of torts. 18ed. Sweet & Maxwell, 1981.

STEER, W.R.
Law of smoke nuisance. 2ed. National Smoke Abatement Society, 1948.

WINFIELD, Sir P.H. & JOLOWICZ, J.A.
Law of tort. 12ed. Sweet & Maxwell, 1984.

NURSING

See also Hospitals; Medical Jurisprudence; National Health.

Encyclopaedias and periodicals

Statutes in Force. Group: Medical and Related Professions.
Halsbury's Laws of England. 4ed. vol.30.
Halsbury's Statutes of England. 3ed. vol.21.
The Digest. see index vol.

Nursing Mirror. 188–
Nursing Standard. 1969–
Nursing Times. 1905–

Texts

CAPE. B.F. & DOBSON, P.
Bailliere's nurses' dictionary. 18ed. Bailliere, 1974.

CREIGHTON, H.
Law every nurse should know. 4ed. W.B.Saunders, 1981 (USA).

FENNER, K.M.
Ethics and law in nursing: professional perspectives. Van Nostrand, 1980.

HARGREAVES, M.
Practical law for nurses. Pitman, 1979.

INTERNATIONAL COUNCIL OF NURSES
Nursing legislation: report. 1972.

LESNIK, M.J. & ANDERSON, B.E.
Nursing practice and the law. 2ed. 1962 repr. Greenwood, 1975 (USA).

MURCHISON, I. and others
Legal accountability in the nursing process. 2ed. Mosby, 1982 (USA).

O'SULLIVAN, J.
Law for nurses. 3ed. Law Book Co., 1983 (Australia).

ROYAL COMMISSION ON THE NATIONAL HEALTH SERVICE
Report (Merrison). HMSO, 1979 (Cmnd. 7615).

ROYAL COMMISSION ON THE NATIONAL HEALTH SERVICE
The working of the National Health Service. HMSO, 1978.

SPELLER, S.R.
Law for nurses and nurse-administrators. Lewis, 1940.

SPELLER, S.R.
Law notes for nurses. 8ed with supplement for Scotland. Royal Coll. of Nursing, 1976.

WAKEFORD, R.E.
The law and the nurse. English U.P., 1973.

WHINCUP, M.H.
Legal aspects of medical and nursing services. 3ed. Ravenswood, 1982.

WHINCUP, M.H.
Legal rights and duties in medical and nursing service. 8ed. Ravenswood, 1982.

OATHS AND AFFIRMATIONS

See also Evidence; Perjury.

Encyclopaedias

Halsbury's Laws of England. 4ed. see index vol.
Halsbury's Statutes of England. 3ed. see index vol.
The Digest. see index vol.

Encyclopaedia of Court Forms in Civil Proceedings (Atkin). 2ed. see index vol.
Encyclopaedia of Forms and Precedents. 4ed. see index vol.

Texts

BENTHAM, J.
Swear not at all: an exposure of the needlessness and mischievousness as well as the anti-Christianity of the ceremony of an oath. 1817.

BOLAND, D. & SAYER, B.H.
Oaths and affirmations. 2ed. Sweet & Maxwell, 1961.

COUNTY Court practice. Butterworths. Annual.

DANIELL, E.R.
Forms and precedents in Chancery. 7ed. Stevens, 1932.

DANIELL, E.R.
Practice of the High Court and Chancery. 8ed. Stevens, 1914.

FORD, C.
Handbook on oaths. 8ed. Law Times, 1910.

STRINGER, F.A.
Oaths and affirmations. 4ed. Stevens, 1929.

SUPREME Court practice 1985. Sweet & Maxwell, 1984. 2 vols.

OBSCENITY

See also Censorship; Criminal Law; Films; Press Law; Printers and Publishers; Theatres.

Encyclopaedias and periodicals

Halsbury's Laws of England. 4ed. vol.11.
Halsbury's Statutes of England. 3ed. vol.8.
The Digest. vol.15.

Criminal Law Review. 1954–
Journal of Criminal Law. 1936–

Texts

ARTS COUNCIL OF GREAT BRITAIN
Obscenity laws: report of the working party. Deutsch, 1969.

BARBER, D.F.
Pornography and society: a new survey. Skilton, 1972.

BURNS, A.
To deprave and corrupt: pornography, its causes, its forms, its effects. Davis-Poynter, 1972.

CHURCH OF ENGLAND BOARD FOR SOCIAL RESPONSIBILITY
Obscene publications: law and practice. 1970.

CRAIG, A.
The banned books of England and other countries. 1962 repr. Greenwood, 1977..

DHAVAN, R. & DAVIES, C.
Censorship and obscenity. Martin Robertson, 1978.

FOX, R.G.
Concept of obscenity. Law Book Co., 1967 (Australia).

HOME OFFICE
Report of the Committee on Obscenity and Film Censorship (Williams). HMSO, 1979. (Cmnd. 7772).

KILPATRICK, J.J.
The smut peddlers. 1961 repr. Greenwood, 1973.

NATIONAL COUNCIL FOR CIVIL LIBERTIES
Against censorship. 1972.

ROBERTSON, G.
Obscenity: an account of censorship laws and their enforcement in England and Wales. Weidenfeld & Nicolson, 1979.

ROLPH, C.H.
Does pornography matter? Routledge & Kegan Paul, 1962.

RUSHDOONY, R.J.
The politics of pornography. Arlington, 1974 (USA).

ST. JOHN-STEVAS, N.
Obscenity and the law. Secker & Warburg, 1956 repr. Da Capo, 1974.

SCHAUER, F.F.
Law of obscenity. Bureau of Nat. Affairs, 1976 (USA).

SHARP, D.B. (ed.)
Commentaries on obscenity. Scarecrow, 1971 (USA).

SIMONS, G.L.
Pornography without prejudice: a reply to objectors. Abelard, 1972.

SIMPSON, A.W.B.
Pornography and politics: look back to the Williams Committee. Waterlow, 1983.

SOBEL, L.A.
Pornography, obscenity and the law. Clio, 1979 (USA).

OCCUPATIONAL DISEASES

See also Employer's Liability; Industrial Injuries; Workmen's Compensation.

Encyclopaedias and periodicals

Halsbury's Laws of England. 4ed. see index vol.
Halsbury's Statutes of England. 3ed. mainly vol.45.
The Digest. vol.34.

Industrial Law Journal. 1972–
Medicine Science and the Law. 1960–
Medico-Legal Journal. 1901–

Texts

ASHFORD, N.A.
Crisis in the workplace: occupational disease and injury: a report to the Ford Foundation. MIT Press, 1976 (USA).

COMMITTEE ON SAFETY AND HEALTH AT WORK
Report. HMSO, 1975 (Cmnd. 5034).

EMPLOYMENT, DEPARTMENT OF
Basic rules for safety and health at work. 2ed. HMSO, 1975.

EMPLOYMENT, DEPARTMENT OF
Safety and health at work. HMSO, 1972.

FRENCH, G.
Occupation health. Med. & Tech., 1973.

HUNTER, D.
Diseases of occupation. 5ed. English Universities P., 1975.

JACKSON, J.
Health and safety: the new law. 2ed. Butterworths, 1974.

MAYERS, M.R.
Occupational health. 1969.

REDGRAVE, A.
Health and safety in factories. 2ed. Butterworths, 1982.

WORLD HEALTH ORGANISATION
Environmental and health monitoring in occupational health. 1974.

OCCUPIERS' LIABILITY
See also Tort.

Encyclopaedias and periodicals

Statutes in Force. Group: Tort and Delict.
Halsbury's Laws of England. 4ed. see index vols.
Halsbury's Statutes of England. 3ed. vol.23.
The Digest. see index vol.

Encyclopaedia of Forms and Precedents. 4ed. vol.20.
Conveyancer and Property Lawyer. 1936–
Estates Gazette. 1858–

Texts

DiCASTRI, V.
Occupiers' liability in Canada. Carswell, 1981.

FINDLAY, W.
Law on the liability of property owners and occupiers for accidents. Sweet & Maxwell, 1928.

HILL, H.A. & REDMAN, J.H.
Law of landlord and tenant. 17ed. Butterworths, 1982.

LAW COMMISSION
Liability for damage or injury to tresspassers and related questions of occupiers' liability. HMSO, 1973 repr. 1977 (Working paper no. 52).

LAW COMMISSION
Report on liability for damage or injury to trespassers and related questions of occupiers' liability. HMSO, 1976 (Law Com. no. 75).

LAW REFORM COMMITTEE
Third Report: occupiers' liability to invitees, licensees and trespassers. HMSO, 1954 (Cmd. 9305).

LAW REFORM COMMITTEE FOR SCOTLAND
First report: the law relating to (a) the liability of an occupier of land or other property to persons suffering injury while on the property, and (b) the obligations of the lessor towards third parties invited, or allowed, by the lessee to be on the subjects let. HMSO, 1957 (Cmnd. 88).

NORTH, P.M.
Occupiers' liability. Butterworths, 1971.

OFFICIAL SECRETS
See also 'D' Notice; Press Law.

Encyclopaedias

Statutes in Force. Group: Criminal Law.
Halsbury's Laws of England. 4ed. vol.11.
Halsbury's Statutes of England. 3ed. vol.8.
The Digest. vols.11, 15.

Texts

AITKEN, J.
Officially secret. Weidenfeld & N., 1971.

CIVIL SERVICE DEPARTMENT
Disclosures of official information: report on overseas practice. HMSO, 1979.

HOME OFFICE
Reform of Section 2 of the Official Secrets Act 1911. HMSO, 1978 (Cmnd. 7285).

HOME OFFICE
Report of the Departmental Committee on Section 2 of the Official Secrets Act, 1911 (Franks). HMSO, 1972 (Cmnd. 5104).

MICHAEL, J.
Politics of secrecy: case for a freedom of information law. NCCL, 1979.

OIL

See also Gas; Pollution.

Encyclopaedias and periodicals

Halsbury's Laws of England. 4ed. see index vol.
Halsbury's Statutes of England. 3ed. see index vol.
The Digest. see index vol.
Encyclopaedia of Forms and Precedents. 4ed. vol. 21.
Gas and Oil Power. 1905–
Journal of Energy and Natural Resources. 1983–

Offshore Oil. 1974–
Oil and Gas International Yearbook. Annual.
Petroleum Economist. 1934–
Petroleum Times. 1899–
U.K. Offshore Oil and Gas Yearbook.

Texts

ABECASSIS, D.W.
Law and practice relating to oil pollution from ships. Butterworths, 1978.

BROWN, E.A.
The law of oil and gas leases. 2ed. Bender, 1958 (USA).

CATTAN, H.
The law of oil concessions in the Middle East and North Africa. Oceana, 1967 (USA).

CROOK, L. (ed.)
Oil terms: a dictionary of terms used in oil exploration and development. Wilton House Pubns., 1975.

CUMMINGS, G.B.
Oil pollution of beaches. Inst. Munic. Engineers, 1974.

DAINTITH, T. & WILLOUGHBY, G.D.M.
A manual of oil and gas law. Sweet & Maxwell, 1984.

DAINTITH, T. & WILLOUGHBY, G.D.M.
United Kingdom oil and gas law. Sweet & Maxwell. Looseleaf.

DUPUY, R.J. (ed.)
Settlement of disputes on the new natural resources: workshop proceedings. Nijhoff, 1983.

ENERGY, DEPARTMENT OF
Development of the oil and gas resources of the United Kingdom. HMSO, 1975.

ENERGY, DEPARTMENT OF
United Kingdom offshore oil and gas policy. HMSO, 1974 (Cmnd. 5696).

GOLD, E.
Oil pollution: a survey of worldwide legislation. Garland, 1972. Looseleaf.

HAYLLAR, R.F. & ROUSE, R.M.
Taxation of offshore oil and gas. Butterworths, 1980. Looseleaf.

HENDERSON, H.
Oil and gas law: the North Sea exploitation. Oceana, 1979. Looseleaf.

INTERNATIONAL MARITIME CONSULTATIVE ORGANISATION
Oil pollution: charts of prohibited zones. 1972.

KITCHEN, J.
Labour law and off-shore oil. Croom Helm, 1977.

LANG, A.G. & CROMMELIN, M.
Australian mining and petroleum law. Butterworths (Australia), 1979.

LEVINE, E.
Legal aspects of North Sea oil. Wilton House Pubns., 1978.

McCLURE, J.G. & LAVIES, A.G.
United Kingdom oil and gas tax legislation. Tax & Finan. Planning, 1980.

MEURS, A.P.H. van.
Petroleum economics and offshore mining legislation: a geological evaluation. Elsevier, 1971.

SAETER, M. & SMART, I.
Political implications of North Sea oil and gas. Sijthoff, 1975.

SIBTHROP, M.M.
The North Sea: challenge and opportunity. Europa, 1975.

SIBTHORP, M.M.
Oceanic management. Europa, 1977.

SUMMERSKILL, M.
Oil rigs – their law and insurance. Stevens, 1979.

SWAN, P.N.
Ocean oil and gas drilling and the law. Oceana, 1979 (USA).

UNITED Kingdom offshore legislation guide. Benn Technical, 1983. Looseleaf.

WARDLEY-SMITH, J.
Control of oil pollution on the sea and inland waters. Graham & Trotman, 1976.

WHITEHEAD, H.
United Kingdom offshore legislation guide. Kogan Page, 1980.

OMBUDSMAN

See also Adminstrative Law; Parliament.

Encyclopaedias and periodicals

Statutes in Force. Group: Parliament.
Halsbury's Laws of England. 4ed. vol.1 and index.
Halsbury's Statutes of England. 3ed. vol.6.
Encyclopaedia of Court Forms in Civil Proceedings (Atkin). 2ed. vol.40.

Law Quarterly Review. 1885–
Modern Law Review. 1937–
Public Administration. 1923–
Public Law. 1956–
Scandinavian Studies in Law. Annual.

Texts

AARON, T.J.
The control of police discretion: the Danish experience. 1966 (USA).

ANDERSON, S.V.
Ombudsman papers. Inst. of Govt. Studies, 1969 (USA).

CLOTHIER, C.M.
Ombudsman: jurisdiction, powers and practice. Manchester Stat. Soc., 1981.

COMMONWEALTH SECRETARIAT
Ombudsman in the Commonwealth: a survey. 1983.

GELLHORN, W.
Ombudsmen and others: citizen protectors in nine countries. 1966.

GREGORY, R. & HUTCHESSON, P.
The parliamentary ombudsman: a study in the control of administrative action. Allen & Unwin, 1975.

HEALTH SERVICE COMMISSIONER
Annual report.

HIDEN, M.
Ombudsman in Finland: the first fifty years. Trans. by A. Bell. Inst. of Govt. Studies, 1973 (USA).

HILL, L.B.
The model ombudsman: institutionalizing New Zealand's democratic experiment. Princeton U.P., 1976 (USA).

HILL, L.B.
Parliament and the ombudsman in New Zealand. 1974.

JUSTICE
The citizen and his council: ombudsman for local government. Stevens, 1969.

JUSTICE
The citizen and the administration: the redress of grievances. Stevens, 1961.

JUSTICE
The citizen and the public agencies. Stevens, 1976.

JUSTICE
Our fettered ombudsman. Stevens, 1977.

KEITH-LUCAS, B. & ARNOLD-BAKER, C.
An ombudsman for local government. Allen & Unwin, 1969.

LERHARD, M. & SPINK, R.
Danish ombudsman, 1955–1969. Schultz, 1972 (USA).

LEWIS, N. & GATESHILL, B.
Commission for local administration: a preliminary appraisal. RIPA, 1978.

NATIONAL COUNCIL FOR CIVIL LIBERTIES
The children's ombudsman. 1975.

NORTHERN IRELAND
COMMISSIONER FOR COMPLAINTS
Annual report.

PARLIAMENTARY COMMISSIONER
FOR ADMINSTRATION
Reports.

ROWAT, D.C.
Ombudsman: citizens defender. 2ed. Allen & Unwin, 1968.

ROWAT, D.C.
The ombudsman plan. McClelland, 1973 (Canada).

SAWER, G.
Ombudsmen. 2ed. 1968.

STACEY, F.
The British ombudsman. Oxford U.P., 1971.

STACEY, F.
Ombudsmen compared. Oxford U.P., 1978.

WEEKS, K.M.
Ombudsmen around the world: a comparative chart. Inst. of Govt. Studies, 1973 (USA).

WHEARE, K.C.
Maladministration and its remedies. Stevens, 1973 (Hamlyn lectures).

WILLIAMS, D.W.
Maladministration: remedies for injustice: a guide to the powers of practice of the British ombudsmen and similar bodies. Oyez, 1977.

WYNER, A.J.
Executive ombudsmen in the United States. Inst. of Govt. Studies, 1973 (USA).

WYNER, A.J.
The Nebraska ombudsman: innovation in State Government. Inst. of Govt. Studies, 1974 (USA).

OXFORD UNIVERSITY

Encyclopaedias and periodicals

Halsbury's Laws of England. 4ed. see index vols.
Halsbury's Statutes of England. 3ed. vol.11.
The Digest. vols.16, 19.
Encyclopaedia of Court Forms in Civil Proceedings (Atkin). 2ed. vol.41.

Lawyer (as Oxford Lawyer). 1959–1965.
Oxford University Calendar. Annual.
Oxford University Gazette. 1970–
Oxford Vade Mecum.

Texts

CORDEAUX, E.H. & MERRY, D.H.
Bibliography of printed works relating to the University of Oxford. Bodleian Library, 1968.

LAWSON, F.H.
The Oxford Law School, 1850–1965. Oxford U.P., 1968.

OXFORD UNIVERSITY
Statutes, decrees and regulations. Annual.

SEWELL, R.C.
Inquiry into the constitution and practice of Chancellor's Court in the University of Oxford. Butterworths, 1839.

SHADWELL, L.L.
Enactments in parliament concerning Universities of Oxford and Cambridge, and the Colleges of Winchester, Eton and Westminster. Oxford U.P., 1911–12. 4 vol.s

SKENE, W.B.
Acts relating to the Universities of Oxford and Cambridge. 2ed. Oxford U.P.,1898.

WILLIAMS, J.
The law of the universities. Butterworths, 1910.

PACKAGING

Encyclopaedias and periodicals
Halsbury's Laws of England. 4ed. see index vols.
The Digest. see index vol.

Canning and Packing. 1931–
Packaging Abstracts. 1943–
Packaging News. 1954–
Packaging Review. 1897–

Texts
FAHY, E.R.
Guide to the packaging of hazardous materials and the legal requirements of the regulatory system. McGraw-Hill, 1973.

LAWSON, R.G.
Advertising and labelling laws in the Common Market. Jordan, 1975. Looseleaf.

ORGANISATION FOR ECONOMIC CO-OPERATION AND DEVELOPMENT
Package standardization. 1976.

PACKAGING REVIEW
Directory and buyers' guide. Annual.

PAINE, F.A. (ed.)
Packaging and the law. Butterworths, 1973.

WONG, J.
Law of packing in modern export trade. Singapore U.P., 1976.

PAKISTAN

Encyclopaedias and periodicals
Statutes in Force. Group: Commonwealth and Other Territories.
Halsbury's Laws of England. 4ed. see index vol.
Halsbury's Statutes of England. 3ed. vol.4, 43.

Karachi Law Journal. 1964–
Kashmir Law Journal. 1962–
Pakistan Bar Journal. 1951–1960.
Pakistan Law Review. 1952–

Texts
BURKE, S.M.
Mainspring of Indian and Pakistani foreign policies. Univ. of Minnesota P., 1974.

CHAUDHURI, G.W.
Constitutional development in Pakistan. 2ed. 1969.

DATTA, R. (ed.)
Union catalogue of the Government of Pakistan publications held by libraries in London, Oxford and Cambridge. Mansell, 1967.

GLEDHILL, A.
Pakistan: the development of its laws and constitution. 1957 repr. Greenwood, 1980.

JENNINGS, Sir W.I.
Constitutional problems in Pakistan. new ed. Cambridge U.P., 1973.

PEARL, D.
Interpersonal conflict of laws in India, Pakistan and Bangladesh. Sweet & Maxwell, 1981.

REHMAN, T.
Islamization of Pakistan law. Hamdard Foundation, 1978.

PAPUA NEW GUINEA

Encyclopaedias

Statutes in Force. Group: Commonwealth and Other Territories.

Texts

ANDREW,
Criminal law and practice of Papua New Guinea. Law Book Co., 1979 (Australia).

CHALMERS, & PALIWALA, A.
Introduction to the law of Papua New Guinea. Law Book Co., 1977 (Australia).

FITZPATRICK, P.
Law and state in Papua New Guinea. Academic Press, 1980.

GOLDRING, J.
Constitution of Papua New Guinea. Law Book Co., 1979 (Australia).

GRIFFIN, J.A.
Criminal procedure in Papua New Guinea. Law Book Co., 1977 (Australia).

O'REGAN, R.S.
The common law in Papua New Guinea. Law Book Co., 1971 (Australia).

POTTER, M.
Traditional law in Papua New Guinea: an annotated and selected bibliography. Aust.Nat.Univ.P., 1973.

WEISBROT, D., PALIWALA, A. & SAWYERR, A.
Law and social change in Papua New Guinea. Butterworths (Australia), 1982.

YOUNG, L.K., GRIFFIN, J.A. & GOLDRING, J.L.
Constitutional development in Papua and New Guinea. Int.Comm. of Jurists, Australian Section, 1971.

ZORN, J.G. & BAYNE, P.
Law and development in Melanesia. Butterworths (Australia), 1975.

PARISH CHURCH

See also Ecclesiastical Law.

Encyclopaedias and periodicals

Statutes in Force. Group: Church of England.
Halsbury's Laws of England. 4ed. see index vol.
Halsbury's Statutes of England. 3ed. vol.10.
The Digest. vol.19.

Church News. 1947–
Church Observer. 1948–
Church Times. 1863–

Texts

BEVERIDGE, W.E.
Managing the church. S.C.M. Press, 1971.

BILLING, S.
Law relating to pews. 1845.

CHURCH OF ENGLAND
Year book. Annual.

CRIPPS, H.W.
Law relating to church and clergy. 8ed. 1937.

CROCKFORD'S clerical directory. Oxford U.P. Annual.

DALE, Sir W.
Law of the parish church. 5ed. Butterworths, 1975.

MACMORRAN, K.
Handbook for church wardens and parochial church councillors. 3ed. Mowbrays, 1971.

SOCIETY OF FRIENDS
Church government. 1968.

PARISH COUNCILS

See also Local Government.

Encyclopaedias and periodicals

Halsbury's Laws of England. 4ed. mainly vol.28.
Halsbury's Statutes of England. 3ed. vol. 19, 42.
The Digest. vol. 33.
Encyclopaedia of Court Forms in Civil Proceedings (Atkin). 2ed. see index vol.
Encyclopaedia of Forms and Precedents. 4ed. see index vol.

Local Government Chronicle. 1855–
Local Government Review. 1971– (as Justice of the Peace & Local Government Review. 1837–1970).
Public Administration. 1923–

Texts

ARNOLD-BAKER, C.
The new law and practice of parish administration. 2ed. Longcross, 1979.

ARNOLD-BAKER, C.
Powers and constitution of parish councils: handbook. 6ed. Nat.Assoc. of Local Councils, 1968.

DAVIS, R.U.
Parish council and town council accounts. Knight, 1977.

WEBB, B. & WEBB, S.
Parish and county. Longmans, Green, 1929.

PARKS AND GARDENS

See also National Parks.

Encyclopaedias and periodicals

Statutes in Force. Group: Environment.
Halsbury's Laws of England. 4ed. see index vol.
Halsbury's Statutes of England. 3ed. see index vol.
The Digest. see index vol.
Encyclopaedia of Forms and Precedents. 4ed. see index vol.

The Garden. 1804–
Garden News. 1958–
Parks and Recreation (as Journal of Park Administration, Horticulture and Recreation. 1936–57). 1958–
Parks and Sports Grounds. 1935–

Texts

EVANS, W.
The law for gardens and small estates. David & Charles, 1975.

HARRIS, B. & RYAN, G.
The law relating to common land and public access to the countryside. Sweet & Maxwell, 1967.

PURTON, R.W.
Parks and open spaces. Blandford, 1975.

RODDIS, R.J.
The law of parks and recreation grounds. 4ed. Shaw, 1974.

PARLIAMENT

See also Administrative Law; Cabinet; Constitutional Law: Elections: Government; Legislation; Privilege.

Encyclopaedias and periodicals

Statutes in Force. Group: Parliament.
Halsbury's Laws of England. 4ed. vol.34.
Halsbury's Statutes of England. 3ed. mainly vol.24.
The Digest. vol.36.
Encyclopaedia of Forms and Precedents. 4ed. see index vol.

Dod's Parliamentary Companion. 1832–
House of Commons Journal. 1547–1761. 1972–

House of Lords Journal. 1510–1829. 1830–
The Parliamentarian. 1966–
Parliamentary Affairs. 1947–
Parliamentary Debates (Hansard). 5th series. 1909–
Public Law. 1956–
Vacher's Parliamentary Companion. 1831–

Texts

ABRAHAM, L.A. & HAWTREY, S.C.
Parliamentary dictionary. 3ed. Butterworths, 1970.

ANSON, Sir W.
Law and custom of the constitution, vol.1: Parliament. 5ed. Oxford U.P., 1935.

CAMPION, Lord
Parliament: a survey. Allen & Unwin, 1952.

CROMWELL, H.
Compact guide to parliamentary procedures. 1966 repr. Crowell, 1973.

ELYSYNGE, H.
Manner of holding parliaments in England. 1768 repr. Rothman, 1972.

HANSON, A.H. & WISEMAN, H.V.
Parliament at work: a case book of parliamentary procedure. new ed. Greenwood, 1976.

JENNINGS, Sir W.I.
Parliament. Cambridge U.P., 1969.

MAY, Sir T.E.
Parliamentary practice. 20ed. Butterworths, 1983.

ROBERT, H.M.
Parliamentary practice: introduction to parliamentary law. 1923 repr. Irvington, 1975.

WILDING, N.W. & LAUNDY, P.
Encyclopaedia of parliament. 4ed. Cassell, 1972.

House of Lords

BAILEY, S.D. (ed.)
The future of the House of Lords: symposium. Hansard Soc., 1954.

BLOM-COOPER, L. & DREWRY, G.
Final appeal: a study of the House of Lords in its judicial capacity. Oxford U.P., 1972.

MORGAN, J.H.
The House of Lords and the constitution. Methuen, 1910.

PIKE, L.O.
Constitutional history of the House of Lords. Macmillan, 1894.

STEVENS, R.
Law and politics: the House of Lords as a judicial body, 1880–1976. Weidenfeld & N., 1979.

House of Commons

BERRINGTON, H.
Backbench opinion in the House of Commons, 1945–1955. Pergamon, 1973.

BLAKE, Lord
The office of Prime Minister. British Academy, 1975.

BATSELL, J.
Precedents of the proceedings in the House of Commons, with observations. 1818 repr. Irish U.P., 1971. 5 vols.

PARLIAMENT

HOUSE OF COMMONS LIBRARY
Journal of the House of Commons: bibliographical and historical guide. 1971.

HOUSE OF COMMONS LIBRARY
Official dress worn in the House of Commons. 1961.

HOUSE OF COMMONS LIBRARY
Votes and standing orders of the House of Commons: the beginning. 1971.

NEALE, J.E.
Elizabethan House of Commons. Cape, 1949.

PANQUET, D.
An essay on the origins of the House of Commons. Cambridge U.P., 1925.

RICHARDS, P.G.
The backbenchers. Allen & Unwin, 1974.

TIMES, The
Guide to the House of Commons (published after each election).

WALKLAND, S.A. & RYLE, M. (eds.)
Commons in the seventies. Martin Robertson, 1977.

Historical

BOND, M.
Guide to the records of parliament. HMSO, 1971.

CANNON, J.
Parliamentary reform, 1640-1832. Cambridge U.P., 1973.

GRAHAM, H.
The Mother of Parliaments: a history. Methuen, 1910.

ILBERT, C.
Parliament: its history, constitution and practice. 3ed. Oxford U.P., 1948.

LAPSLEY, G.F.
Crown, community and parliament in the later Middle Ages. Blackwell, 1951.

LUTTRELL, N.
Parliamentary diary, 1691-93. Oxford U.P., 1972.

NEALE, J.E.
Elizabeth I and her parliaments, 1559-1581. Cape, 1953. 2 vols.

POLLARD, A.F.
Evolution of parliament. 2ed. Longmans, Green, 1926.

RICHARDSON, H.G.
Parliament in the Middle Ages. Blackwell, 1972.

SMITH, H.S.
Parliaments of England from 1715 to 1847. 2ed. Political Reference Pubns., 1973.

WILKINSON, B.
Creation of medieval parliaments. Wiley, 1972.

WORDEN, B.
Rump parliament, 1648-1653. Cambridge U.P., 1974.

Miscellaneous

ABSE, L.
Private member. Macdonald, 1973.

ALLEN, Sir C.K.
Law and orders: an inquiry into the nature and scope of delegated legislation and executive powers in England. 3ed. Sweet & Maxwell, 1965.

BAILEY, S.D.
British parliamentary democracy. 1959 repr. Greenwood, 1978.

BOURINOT, J.G.
Parliamentary procedure and practice in the Dominion of Canada. 1884 repr. Irish U.P., 1972.

CHESTER, D.N. & BOWRING, N.
Questions in parliament. 1962 repr. Greenwood.

GRIFFITH, J.A.G
Parliamentary scrutiny of government bills. Allen & Unwin, 1974.

HERBERT, Sir A.P.
The ayes have it. Methuen, 1937.

HERBERT, Sir A.P.
The point of parliament. 2ed. Methuen, 1947.

HOLLIS, C.
Parliament and its sovereignty. Bodley, 1973.

HUOPANUINI, J.
Parliaments and European rapprochement. Sijthoff, 1973.

KEETON, G.W.
The passing of parliament. 2ed. Benn, 1954.

KILMUIR, Lord
Law of parliamentary privilege. Univ. of London, 1959.

LAUNDY, P.
Office of Speaker in the Parliaments of the Commonwealth. Quiller P., 1984.

LEES, J.D. & SHAW, M.
Committees in legislatures. Martin Robertson, 1979.

MARGACH, J.
How parliament works. Stacey, 1972.

MARKESINIS, B.S.
Theory and practice of dissolution of parliament: a comparative study with special reference to the United Kingdom and Greek experience. Cambridge U.P., 1972.

MARSHALL, G.
Parliamentary sovereignty and the Commonwealth. Oxford U.P., 1957.

ORNSTEIN, N.J.
Role of the legislative in western democracies. American Enterprise Institution, 1981.

PACHAURI, P.S.
Law of parliamentary privileges in U.K. and in India. Oceana, 1971.

PALMER, M.
The European Parliament. Pergamon, 1981.

PATERSON, A.
The law lords. new ed. Macmillan, 1983.

PAXTON, J.
World legislatures. Macmillan, 1974.

RICHARDS, P.G.
Parliament and conscience. Allen & Unwin, 1971.

SMYTH, J.M.
Houses of the Oireachtas. 4ed. Inst. of Public Admin., 1979.

STUDY OF PARLIAMENT GROUP
Specialist committees in the British parliament: the experience of a decade. 1976.

STURGIS, A.F.
Standard code of parliamentary procedure. 2ed. McGraw-Hill, 1966.

WHEARE, K.C.
Legislatures. Oxford U.P., 1968.

WILLIAMS, O.C.
Historical development of private bill procedure. HMSO, 1948–9. 2 vols.

WILSON, Sir H.
The governance of Britain. Weidenfeld & N., 1976.

PAROLE

See also Probation; Rehabilitation of Offenders.

Encyclopaedias and periodicals

Halsbury's Laws of England. 4ed. vol. 37.
Halsbury's Statutes of England. 3ed. vol.25.

British Journal of Criminology. 1960–
Criminal Law Review. 1954–
Journal of Criminal Law. 1936–

Texts

AMOS, W.E. & NEWMAN, C.I.
Parole: legal issues – decision-making– research. Federal Legal P., 1975 (USA).

CARTER, R.M. & WILKINS, L.T.
Probation, parole and community corrections. 2ed. Wiley, 1976 (USA).

CAVANDINO, P.
Parole: the case for change. Rose, 1973.

CITIZENS INQUIRY ON PAROLE AND CRIMINAL JUSTICE INC
Prison without walls: report on New York parole. Praeger, 1975 (USA).

HALL WILLIAMS, J.E.
Ten years of parole. Inst. for Study of Treatment of Delinquency, 1978.

HAWKINS, K. (ed.)
Parole: a select bibliography with speech reference to American experience. 2ed. Univ. of Cambridge, Inst. of Criminology, 1971.

HOME OFFICE
Parole: your questions answered. HMSO, 1976.

HOWARD LEAGUE FOR PENAL REFORM
Parole decision: a guide compiled from official sources. Rose, 1977.

MORRIS, P. & BEVERLY, F.
On licence: a study of parole. Wiley, 1975.

NUTTALL, C.P.
Parole in England and Wales. HMSO, 1977 (Home Office research studies).

PARKER, W.C.
Parole: origins, development, current practices and statutes. rev. ed. Amer.Correc.Assoc., 1975 (USA).

PAROLE BOARD
Annual reports. HMSO.

SCOTTISH HOME AND HEALTH DEPARTMENT
Parole Board for Scotland. Annual reports. HMSO.

STANLEY, D.T.
Prisoners among us: the problem of parole. Brookings Inst., 1976 (USA).

WEST, D.J. (ed.)
The future of parole. Duckworth, 1972.

PARTNERSHIP

See also Agency; Companies.

Encyclopaedias

Statutes in Force. Group: Partnership and Business Names.
Halsbury's Laws of England. 4ed. vol.35.
Halsbury's Statutes of England. 3ed. vol.24.
The Digest. vol.36.

Encyclopaedia of Court Forms in Civil Proceedings (Atkin). 2ed. vol.30.
Encyclopaedia of Forms and Precedents. 4ed. vol.16.

Texts

BAMFORD, B.R.
Law of partnership and voluntary associations in South Africa. 3ed. Juta, 1982.

BAXT, R., BIALKOWER, L. & MORGAN, R.J.
Guidebook to partnership law. CCH, 1980 (Australia).

BULCHANDANI, K.R.
Law of partnership, sale of goods and negotiable instruments. Himalaya Pub. House, 1980 (India).

BURGESS, R. & MORSE, G.
Partnership law and practice in England and Wales. Sweet & Maxwell, 1980.

DRAKE, C.D.
Partnership law. 3ed. Sweet & Maxwell, 1983.

FLANAGAN, T. & MILMAN, D.
Modern partnership law. Croom Helm, 1983.

HARMER, C. & CAMP, P.
Practical partnerships. Oyez, 1982.

HARROWES, D.H.S.
Managing the partnership office. Butterworths, 1978.

HIGGINS, P.F.P. & FLETCHER, K.L.
The law of partnership in Australia and New Zealand. 4ed. Law Book Co., 1981.

IVAMY, E.R.H.
Casebook on partnership. 2ed. Professional Books, 1982.

KITCHEN, S.
Important aspects of professional partnerships. Macdonald & Evans, 1974.

LAWTON, J.P., GOLDBERG, D. & FRASER, R.
The law of partnership taxation. 2ed. Oyez, 1979.

LINDLEY, N.
Law of partnership. 15ed. Sweet & Maxwell, 1984.

MARSHALL, E.A.
Scottish cases on partnership and companies (excluding winding up and reconstruction). Green, 1980.

MILLER, J.B.
Law of partnership in Scotland. Green, 1972.

MOBERLY, W.
Partnership management. Financial Training Pubns., 1983.

PENNINGTON, R.R.
Partnership and company law. Butterworths, 1962.

POLLOCK, Sir F.
Digest of the law of partnership. 15ed. Stevens, 1952.

RANKING, D.F. & SPICER, E.E.
Mercantile law. 14ed. HFL, 1975.

RAY, E.E.
Partnership taxation. 2ed. HFL, 1978.

REDMOND, P.W.D.
Partnership law. 11ed. Macdonald & Evans, 1977.

SMITH, P.
Family business: company or partnership? Sweet & Maxwell, 1980.

STRAHAN, J.A. & OLDHAM, N.H.
Law of partnership. 6ed. Sweet & Maxwell, 1944.

STRATTON, I.G.C. & BLACKSHAW, L.S.
Partnership. 2ed. Oyez, 1972.

TAYLOR, E.M.
Partnership law. 11ed. Macdonald & Evans, 1977.

UNDERHILL, Sir A.
Principles of the law of partnership. 11ed. Butterworths, 1981.

UNDERHILL, Sir A.
Principles of the law of partnership, being a New Zealand ed. of the 8th English ed. by P.R.H. Webb. Butterworths (NZ), 1972.

WESTWOOD, J.
Partnership law. 8ed. Cassell, 1971.

WHITE, P.
Law and tax for professional partnerships. Oyez Longman, 1984.

WRIGHT, E.K. & HARDMAN, J.P.
Professional goodwill and partnership annuities. 2ed. Macdonald & Evans, 1972.

PARTY WALLS

See also Boundaries and Fences; Easements; Landlord and Tenant

Encyclopaedias and periodicals

Statutes in Force. Group: Property, England & Wales, Sub-group 1.
Halsbury's Laws of England. 4ed. vols. 4, 38.
Halsbury's Statutes of England. 3ed. vols. 20, 27.
The Digest. vol.7.
Encyclopaedia of Forms and Precedents. 4ed. vol.16.

Chartered Surveyor. 1921–
Conveyancer and Property Lawyer. 1936–
Journal of Planning and Environment Law. 1948–
Estates Gazette. 1858–

Texts

ALDRIDGE, T.M.
Boundaries, walls and fences. 5ed. Oyez, 1982.

LEACH, W.A.
Party structures and rights in London. 2ed. Estates Gazette, 1974.

RUDALL, A.R.
Party walls. 3ed. Jordan, 1972.

WOOLRYCH, H.W.
Law of party walls and fences. Butterworths, 1845.

PASSING OFF
See also Copyright; Tort; Trade Marks.

Encyclopaedias

Halsbury's Laws of England. 4ed. vol.48 and index vol.
The Digest. vol.46.
Encyclopaedia of Court Forms in Civil Proceedings (Atkin). 2ed. vol.38.
Encyclopaedia of Forms and Precedents. 4ed. see index vol.

Texts

CUTLER, J.
'Passing off", or illegal substitution of the goods of one trader for the goods of another trader. Gay & Bird, 1904.

DIX, D.K.
Law relating to competitive trading. Sweet & Maxwell, 1938.

KERLY, Sir D.M.
The law of trade marks and trade names. 11ed. Sweet & Maxwell, 1983.

PEARCE, E.H.
Passing off: the law as to limitation and deception in trade. Sol.Law Stat.Soc., 1928.

PASSPORTS

Encyclopaedias

Statutes in Force. Group: Nationality.
Halsbury's Laws of England. 4ed. vols. 4, 18 and index vol.
Halsbury's Statutes of England. 3ed see index vol.
The Digest. see index vol.

Texts

JUSTICE
Going abroad: a report on passports. Rose, 1974.

TURACK, D.C.
The passport in international law. Heath, 1972 (USA).

PATENTS
See also Copyright; Trade Marks.

Encyclopaedias and periodicals

Statutes in Force. Group: Patents, Designs and Trade Marks.
Halsbury's Laws of England. 4ed. vol.35.
Halsbury's Statutes of England. 3ed. vol.24.
The Digest. vol.36.
Encyclopaedia of Court Forms in Civil Proceedings (Atkin). 2ed. vol.30.
Encyclopaedia of Forms and Precedents. 4ed. vol.16.

Annual of Industrial Property Law.
British Patents Abstracts. 1951–
Designs and Trade Marks.
European Intellectual Property Review. 1978–
Fleet Street Patent Law Reports. 1963–
Official Journal (Patents). 1884–
Patent law Review. 1969–
Reports on Patent, Design, Trade Mark and Other Cases. 1884–

Texts

BAKER, R.
New and improved. British Library, 1976.

BAXTER, J.W.
World patent law and practice. 2ed. Sweet & Maxwell, 1974 & supp. 1976.

BLOXAM, G.A.
Licensing rights in technology: a legal guide for managers in negotiation. Gower, 1972.

BOEHM, K.
The British patent system. Cambridge U.P., 1967.

BOWMAN, W.S.
Patent and antitrust law: a legal and economic appraisal. Univ. of Chicago P., 1973 (USA).

BRETT, H.
Patents Act, 1977: an introductory guide. 2ed. ESC Pub., 1978.

BURGE, D.A.
Patent and trade mark tactics and practice. 2ed. Wiley, 1984.

CALVERT, R.
Encyclopaedia of patent practice and invention management. Kreiger, 1974.

CAWTHRA, B.I.
Industrial property rights in the E.E.C.: patents, trademarks and copyright. ESC Pub., 1973.

CAWTHRA, B.I.
Patent licensing in Europe. Butterworths, 1978.

CHARTERED INSTITUTE OF PATENT AGENTS
European patents handbook. Oyez, 1978. 2 vols. Looseleaf.

CHARTERED INSTITUTE OF PATENT AGENTS
Guide to the Patents Act, 1977. 2ed. Sweet & Maxwell, 1984.

CHARTERED INSTITUTE OF PATENT AGENTS
Register of patent agents. Annual.

COMMITTEE TO CONSIDER THE LAW ON COPYRIGHT AND DESIGNS
Copyright and designs law: report of the committee (Whitford). HMSO, 1977 (Cmnd. 6732).

COMMITTEE TO EXAMINE THE PATENT SYSTEM AND PATENT LAW
The British patent system: report of the committee (Banks). HMSO, 1970 (Cmnd. 4407).

CONFEDERATION OF BRITISH INDUSTRY
The new European patent system and its implications for industry: conference papers. 1974.

CONFEDERATION OF BRITISH INDUSTRY
Patents and trade marks in the European Community. 1976.

CONVENTION on the grant of European patents (European Patent Convention) with related documents, Munich, 1973. HMSO, 1974 (Cmnd. 5656).

CORNISH, W.R.
Intellectual property: patents, copyright, trade marks and allied rights. Sweet & Maxwell, 1981.

DAVENPORT, N.
United Kingdom patent systems: a brief history. Mason, 1979.

DEPARTMENTAL COMMITTEE ON PATENTS AND DESIGNS
Report (Swan). HMSO, 1944–5 (Cmd. 6618); 1945–6 (Cmd. 6789); 1946–7 (Cmd. 7206).

DEPARTMENTAL COMMITTEE ON PATENTS AND DESIGN ACTS
Report (Sargant). HMSO, 1930–1 (Cmd. 3829).

DOL, T. & SHATTUCK, W.L. (eds.)
Patent and know-how licensing in Japan and the United States. Univ. of Washington P., 1977 (USA).

FINLAY, I.F.
Guide to foreign-language printed patents and applications. Aslib, 1969.

FOX, H.G.
Canadian law and practice relating to letters patent for inventions. 4ed. Carswell, 1969.

FOX, H.G.
Monopolies and patents: a study of the history and future of the patent monopoly. Univ. of Toronto P., 1947.

GALL, G.
European patent applications: questions and answers. Oyez Longman, 1984.

GEVERS, J.
Patent law and practice of the major European countries. BNA, 1976 (USA). 3 vols.

HEARN, P.
The business of industrial licensing: a practical guide to patents, know-how, trademarks and industrial designs. Gower, 1981.

JEHORAM, H.C. (ed.)
Design protection. Sijthoff, 1975.

JOHNSTON, D.
Design protection. Design Council, 1978.

KASE, F.J.
Designs: a guide to official literature on design protection. Sijthoff, 1975.

LADAS, S.P.
Patents, trade marks and related rights: national and international protection. Harvard U.P., 1975 (USA). 3 vols.

LAHORE, J.
Intellectual property in Australia; patents, designs trade marks, confidential information and unfair competition. Butterworths (Australia), 1981. Looseleaf.

LIEBERMAN, A.
Glossary of United States patent practice: English-French-German. Sweet & Maxwell, 1970.

MEINHARDT, P.
Inventions, patents and monopoly. Gower P., 1971.

MELVILLE, I.W.
Precedents on intellectual property and international licensing. 2ed. Sweet & Maxwell, 1972.

NATIONAL ASSOCIATION OF CREDIT MANAGEMENT
Patent law and practice. rev. ed. 1975–77 (USA). 2 vols. Looseleaf.

PATENT law of the United Kingdom: texts, commentary and notes on practice. 3ed. Sweet & Maxwell, 1975 & supp. 1978.

PATENT OFFICE
Applying for a patent. rev. ed. 1978.

PATENT OFFICE
Patents, designs and trademarks: report of the Comptroller General. Annual.

PENNINGTON, R.R.
European patents at the cross-roads. Oyez, 1976.

REPORT on the Patent Acts (Fry). HMSO, 1901 (Cd. 506). Appendix (Cd. 530).

ROSENBERG, P.D.
Patent law fundamentals. Boardman, 1978 (USA).

RUSSELL-CLARKE, A.D.
Copyright in industrial designs. 5ed. Sweet & Maxwell, 1974.

SINNOTT, J.P.
World patent law: patent statutes, treaties and regulations. Bender, 1974. 2 vols. Looseleaf.

TAYLOR, C.T. & SILBERSTON, Z.A.
The economic impact of the patent system: a study of the British experience. Cambridge U.P., 1973.

TERRELL, T.
The law of patents. 13ed. Sweet & Maxwell, 1982.

TRADE, DEPARTMENT OF
Patent law reform: consultative document. HMSO, 1975 (Cmnd. 6000).

TRADE, DEPARTMENT OF
Reform of the law relating to copyright, design and performers' protection: a consultative document. HMSO, 1981 (Cmnd. 8302).

VAUGHAN, F.L.
The United States patent system: legal and economic conflicts in American patent history. Greenwood, 1973 (USA).

VITORIA, M. (ed.)
Patents Act, 1977: Queen Mary College Patent Conference papers. 1978.

WALTON, A.M. & LADDIE, H.I.L.
Patent law of Europe and the United Kingdom. Butterworths, 1978. Looseleaf.

WHITE, T.A.B.
Patents for inventions and the protection of industrial designs. 4ed. Stevens, 1974.

WHITE, T.A.B. & JACOB, R.
Patents, trade marks, copyright and industrial designs. 3ed. Sweet & Maxwell, 1983.

WILDS, T.
Glossary of Japanese patent law terms (In English and Japanese). Marlin, 1980 (USA).

WITTMAN, A.
Patent documentation. Sweet & Maxwell, 1979.

PAWNBROKERS

See also Bailment; Moneylenders.

Encyclopaedias
Halsbury's Laws of England. 4ed. vol. 36 and index vol.
Halsbury's Statutes of England. 3ed. vol.24.
The Digest. see index vol.

Encyclopaedia of Court Forms in Civil Proceedings (Atkin). 2ed. vol.30.
Encyclopaedia of Forms and Precedents. 4ed. vol.16.

Texts
ATTENBOROUGH, C.L.
Law relating to pawnbroking. 3ed. 1926.

COBBETT, J.P.
Law of pawns or pledges and the rights and liabilities of pawnbrokers. 2ed. 1849.

FOLKARD, H.C.
The law of loans and pledges. 2ed. Butterworths, 1876.

MESTON, Lord
Law relating to moneylenders. 5ed. Oyez, 1968.

STUBBS, L.P.
Guide to pawnbrokers. 2ed. 1870.

TURNER, F.
The contract of pawn as it exists at common law. 2ed. 1883.

PAY/PRICE CONTROL

Encyclopaedias
Halsbury's Laws of England. 4ed. see index vol.
Halsbury's Statutes of England. 3ed. see index under Wages & Salaries and Prices.

Texts
BRACEWELL-MILNES, B.
Pay and price control guide. Butterworths, 1973.

EUROPEAN COMMUNITIES
Effects of national price controls in the European Economic Community. 1971.

FELS, A.
The British Prices and Incomes Board. Cambridge U.P., 1972.

PRICE COMMISSION
Annual reports. HMSO.

PRICES AND CONSUMER PROTECTION, DEPARTMENT OF
Price and pay code: a consultative document. HMSO, 1973 (Cmnd. 5247).

PRICES AND CONSUMER PROTECTION, DEPARTMENT OF
Review of the price code: a consultative document. HMSO, 1974 (Cmnd. 5779).

PEACE

See also International Law; War.

Encyclopaedias and periodicals

The Digest. see index vol.

Herald of Peace. 1819–
Newspeace. 1971–
Peace and Freedom. 1952–
Peace News. 1936–
Peace Press. 1965–

Texts

BRIERLY, J.O.
Law of nations: an introduction to the international law of peace. 6ed. Oxford U.P., 1963.

CLARK, G. & SOHN, L.B.
World peace through world law: two alternative plans. World Without War, 1973.

GROB, F.
The relativity of war and peace. Yale U.P., 1949.

HIGGINS, R.
United Nations peacekeeping. vol. 2: Asia. Oxford U.P., 1970.

HIGGINS, R.
United Nations peacekeeping. vol. 3: Africa. Oxford U.P., 1979.

HIGGINS, R.
United Nations peacekeeping. vol. 4: Europe 1946–1979. Oxford U.P., 1981.

KELSEN, H.
Peace through law. 1944 repr. Garland, 1973.

LAUTERPACHT, Sir H.
International law: collected papers Vol.4: Law of peace, pts. VII-VIII. Cambridge U.P., 1978.

LISSITZYN, O.J.
The International Court of Justice: its role in the maintenance of international peace and security. Carnegie Endowment for Internat. Peace, 1951 repr. Octagon, 1971.

SUMMERS, L.M.
The international law of peace. Oceana, 1972.

PEERAGE LAW

See also Law Officers; Parliament.

Encyclopaedias

Statutes in Force. Group: Peerages and Honours.
Halsbury's Laws of England. 4ed. vol. 35.
Halsbury's Statutes of England. 3ed. vol.24.

The Digest. vol.37.
Encyclopaedia of Court Forms in Civil Proceedings (Atkin). 2ed. vol.31.

Texts

BURKE's peerage, and baronetage and knightage. 105ed. 1970.

DEBRETT's peerage and baronetage. Debrett, 1979.

KELLY'S handbook. Annual.

PALMER, F.B.
Peerage law in England: a practical treatise for lawyers and laymen. Stevens, 1907.

PALMER, J.
Practice in the House of Lords on appeals, writs and error, and claims of peerage. Stevens, 1830.

RIDDELL, J.
Inquiry into the law and practice in Scottish peerages before and after the union. Clarke, 1842. 7 vols.

ROUND, J.H.
Peerage and pedigree: studies of peerage law and family history. 1910 repr. Tabard Press, 1970. 2 vols.

SUGDEN, E.B.
Life peerages. Sweet, 1856.

PENSIONS

See also Employment Law; National Insurance; Social Security.

Encyclopaedias and periodicals

Statutes in Force. Groups: Judicial Remuneration and Pensions; Public Service Pensions; Social Security and Health Services.
Halsbury's Laws of England. 4ed. see index vols.
Halsbury's Statutes of England. 3ed. see index vol.

The Digest. see index vol.
Encyclopaedia of Court Forms in Civil Proceedings (Atkin). 2ed. vol.34.
Encyclopaedia of Forms and Precedents. 4ed. see index vol.
Legal Action (formerly L.A.G. Bulletin). 1973–
Pennant. 1946–

Texts

CALLUND, D.
Employee benefits in Europe: international survey of State and private schemes in 16 countries. 3ed. Callund, 1979.

CREEDY, J.
State pensions in Britain. Cambridge U.P., 1982.

DAVIS, B.
Tax planning for life assurance and pensions. Butterworths, 1980.

DEPARTMENTAL COMMITTEE ON OLD AGE PENSIONS
Report (Adkins). HMSO, 1919 (Cmd. 410).

HOSKING, G.A.
Pension schemes and retirement benefits. 5ed. Sweet & Maxwell, 1984.

HYMANS, C.A. (ed.)
Handbook on pensions and employee benefits. Harrap, 1976.

JACKSON, J.
Occupational pensions: the new law. New Commercial Pub. Co., 1977.

OLDFIELD, M.
Understanding pension schemes. Fourmat Pub., 1983.

ORGANISATION FOR ECONOMIC CO-OPERATION & DEVELOPMENT
Old age pension schemes. 1977.

ROBB, A.C.
Shaw's guide to superannuation for local authorities. 6ed. Shaw, 1974.

WALFORD, J. (ed.)
Self-employed pensions. 5ed. Financial Times Business Pub., 1982.

PERJURY

See also Criminal Law; Oaths and Affirmations.

Encyclopaedias and periodicals

Statutes in Force. Group: Criminal Law.
Halsbury's Laws of England. 4ed. vol.11 and index vol.
Halsbury's Statutes of England. 3ed. mainly vol.8.

The Digest. see index vol.
Criminal Law Review. 1954–
Journal of Criminal Law. 1936–

Texts

ARCHBOLD, J.F.
Pleading, evidence and practice in criminal cases. 41ed. Sweet & Maxwell, 1982.

CRIMINAL LAW REVISION COMMITTEE
Sixth report: perjury and attendance of witnesses. HMSO, 1964 (Cmnd. 2465).

GIBB, A.D.
Perjury unlimited: a monograph on Nuremburg. Green, 1954.

JUSTICE
False witness: the problem of perjury: a report. Stevens, 1973.

JUSTICE
The truth and the courts: a report. Stevens, 1980.

LAW COMMISSION
Criminal law: perjury and kindred offences. HMSO, 1970 repr. 1977 (Working paper no.33).

RUSSELL, Sir W.O.
Crime: a treatise on felonies and misdemeanours. 12ed. Stevens, 1964. 2 vols.

WILLIAMS, G.L.
Criminal law: the general part. 2ed. Stevens, 1961.

PERPETUITIES

See also Cy-Pres Doctrine; Real Property; Trusts and Trustees.

Encyclopaedias

Halsbury's Laws of England. 4ed. vol.35.
The Digest. vol.37.
Encyclopaedia of Forms and Precedents. 4ed. see index vol.

Texts

BURGESS, R.
Perpetuities in Scots law. Green, 1979.

DEPARTMENTAL COMMITTEE ON .. RULE AGAINST PERPETUITIES
Report (Schuster). HMSO, 1927 (Cmd. 2918).

FRATCHER, W.F.
Perpetuities and other restraints. Univ. of Michigan Law School, 1954.

GRAY, J.C.
The rule against perpetuities. 4ed. Little, Brown, 1942 (USA).

HOOPES, T.W.
The rules against perpetuities. The Author, 1961.

LAW REFORM COMMITTEE
Fourth report: the rule against perpetuities. HMSO, 1956 (Cmnd. 18).

MAUDSLEY, R.H.
Modern law of perpetuities. Butterworths, 1979.

MORRIS, J.C.H. & LEACH, W.B.
The rule against perpetuities. 2ed. Stevens, 1962.

PERSONAL INJURIES

See also Accidents; Criminal Injuries; Damages; Employer's Liability; Tort; Workmen's Compensation.

Encyclopaedias and periodicals

Halsbury's Laws of England. 4ed. vol. 37 and see index vol.
Halsbury's Statutes of England. 3ed. see index vol.
The Digest. see index vol.

Encyclopaedia of Court Forms in Civil Proceedings (Atkin). 2ed. see index vol.
Current Law. 1947–
Medicine Science and the Law. 1960–
Medico-Legal Journal. 1901–

Texts

ALLEN, D.K., BOURN, C.J. & HOLYOAK, J.H.
Accident compensation after Pearson. Sweet & Maxwell, 1979.

AMADOR, F.V.G.
Recent codification of the law of state reponsibility for injuries to aliens. Oceana, 1974 (USA).

BRITTS, M.G.
Comparable verdicts in personal injury claims. Law Book Co., 1973 (Australia).

COMMITTEE ON PERSONAL INJURIES LITIGATION
Report (Winn). HMSO, 1968 (Cmnd. 3691).

CORBET, M.M. & BUCHANAN, J.L.
Quantum of damages in bodily and fatal injury cases. 3ed. Sweet & Maxwell, 1976. 2 vols. Looseleaf (S. Africa).

DIX, D.K. & TODD, A.H.
Medical evidence in personal injury cases. Lewis, 1961.

FRUMER, L.R., BENOIT, R.L. & FRIEDMAN, M.I.
Personal injury – actions, defenses, damages. Bender, 1957. 21 vols. Looseleaf (USA).,

GHOSH, D.
Economics of personal injury. Saxon House, 1976.

GLASS, H.H. & McHUGH, M.H.
Liability of employers in damages for personal injury. Sweet & Maxwell, 1966 (Australia).

GOLDSMITH, I.
Damages for personal injury and death in Canada, 1958–1972. Carswell, 1974.

GRAY, H.R.
Law of civil injuries. Hutchinson, 1955.

ISON, T.G.
The forensic lottery: a critique on tort liability as a system of personal injury compensation. Staples P., 1967.

JUSTICE
No fault on the roads: a report. Stevens, 1974.

KEMP, D.A.McI.
Damages for personal injury and death. Oyez, 1980.

KEMP, D.A. McI. & KEMP, M.S.
The quantum of damages. 4ed. Sweet & Maxwell, 1975. 3 vols.

LAW COMMISSION
Personal injury litigation: assessment of damages. HMSO, 1971 repr. 1977 (Working paper no.41).

LAW COMMISSION
Personal injury litigation: assessment of damages, itemization of pecuniary loss and the use of actuarial tables as an aid to assessment. HMSO, 1970 repr. 1977 (Working paper no.27).

LAW COMMISSION
Report on personal injury litigation: assessment of damages. HMSO, 1973 (Law Com. no.56).

LAW REFORM COMMITTEE
Twentieth report: interim report on limitations of actions in personal injury claims. HMSO, 1974 (Cmnd. 5630).

LORD CHANCELLOR'S DEPARTMENT
Report of the personal injuries litigation procedure working party (Cantley). HMSO, 1979 (Cmnd. 7476).

LUNTZ, H.
Assessment of damages in personal injury and death. 2ed. Butterworths (Australia), 1983.

MANN, A.
Medical assessment of injuries for legal purposes. 3ed. Butterworths (Australia), 1979.

MUNKMAN, J.H.
Damages for personal injuries and death. 6ed. Butterworths, 1980.

PALMER, G.
Compensation for incapacity: study of law and social change in New Zealand and Australia. Oxford U.P.(NZ), 1980.

PRITCHARD, J.M.
Personal injury litigation. 3ed. Oyez, 1980.

ROYAL COMMISSION ON CIVIL LIABILITY AND COMPENSATION FOR PERSONAL INJURY
Report (Pearson). HMSO, 1978 (Cmnd. 7054–I, II & III). 3 vols.

SCOTTISH LAW COMMISSION
Damages for injuries causing death. 1967. (Memorandum no.5).

SCOTTISH LAW COMMISSION
Damages for injuries causing death. 1972 (Memorandum no.17).

SCOTTISH LAW COMMISSION
Damages for personal injuries: deductions and heads of claim. 1975 (Memorandum no.21).

SCOTTISH LAW COMMISSION
Report on the law relating to damage for injuries causing death. HMSO, 1973 (Scot. Law Com. no.31).

STATSKY, W.P.
Torts: personal injury litigation. West, 1982 (USA).

TEFF, H. & MUNRO, C.R.
Thalidomide: the legal aftermath. Saxon House, 1976.

WILLIAMS, D.B.
Hit and run and uninsured driver personal injury claims: role of the Motor Insurers' Bureau. 6ed. B.Rose, 1983.

WOOLF, A.D.
The time barrier in personal injury claims. Butterworths, 1969.

WUNDER, M.H.
The conduct of a personal injury act: the case for the plaintiff. 2ed. Carswell, 1980 (Canada).

PERSONAL PROPERTY

See also Bailment; Fixtures; Liens; Possession; Real Property.

Encyclopaedias

Halsbury's Laws of England. 4ed. vol.35.
Halsbury's Statutes of England. 3ed mainly vol.25.
The Digest. vol.37.

Texts

GARROW, J.M.E. & GRAY, H.R.
Law of personal property in New Zealand. 5ed. Butterworths, 1968.

GOODEVE, L.A.
The modern law of personal property. 9ed. Sweet & Maxwell, 1949.

LAW REFORM COMMITTEE
Twelfth report: transfer of title to chattels. HMSO, 1966 (Cmnd. 2958).

LAW REFORM COMMITTEE
Eighteenth report: conversion and detinue. HMSO, 1971 (Cmnd. 4774).

MARRIOTT, E.G.
Outline of personal property. Estates Gazette, 1965.

SCOTTISH LAW COMMISSION
Corporation moveables – general introduction and summary of provisional proposals. 1961 (Memorandum no.24.)

SCOTTISH LAW COMMISSION
Corporeal moveables – lost and abandoned property. 1976 (Memorandum no. 29).

SCOTTISH LAW COMMISSION
Corporeal moveables – mixing union and creation. 1976 (Memorandum no.28).

SCOTTISH LAW COMMISSION
Corporeal moveables – passing of risk and ownership. 1976 (Memorandum no.25).

SCOTTISH LAW COMMISSION
Corporeal moveables – protection of the onerous bona fide acquirer of another's property. 1976 (Memorandum no.27).

SCOTTISH LAW COMMISSION
Corporeal moveables – remedies. 1976 (Memorandum no.31).

SCOTTISH LAW COMMISSION
Corporeal moveables – some problems of classification. 1976 (Memorandum no.26).

SCOTTISH LAW COMMISSION
Corporeal moveables – usucapion or acquisitive prescription. 1976. (Memorandum no.30).

SCOTTISH LAW COMMISSION
Report on lost and abandoned property. HMSO, 1980 (Scot. Law Com. no.59).

VAINES, J.C.
Personal property. 5ed. Butterworths, 1973.

WILKINSON, H.W.
Personal property. Sweet & Maxwell, 1971.

WILLIAMS, J.
Principles of the law of personal property. 18ed. Sweet & Maxwell, 1926.

PETITION OF RIGHT
See also Crown.

Encyclopaedias
Halsbury's Laws of England. 4ed. vol.11.
Halsbury's Statutes of England. 3ed. see index vol.

The Digest. see index vol.
Encyclopaedia of Court Forms in Civil Proceedings (Atkin). 2ed. vol.14.

Texts
CLODE, W.
Petition of right. Clowes, 1887.

ROBERTSON, G.S.
Civil proceedings by and against the Crown. Stevens, 1908.

SCOTT, Sir L. & HILDERSLEY, A.
Case of requisition: in re a petition of right of De Keyser's Royal Hotel Ltd. v. The King. Oxford U.P., 1920.

PIRACY
See also Criminal Law; Hijacking; Prize Law; Shipping.

Encyclopaedias
Statutes in Force. Group: Criminal Law.
Halsbury's Laws of England. 4ed. vol.11.
Halsbury's Statutes of England. 3ed. vol.8.
The Digest. see index vol.

Texts
BERCHMAN, E.
Victims of piracy: Admiralty Court, 1575–1678. Hamilton, 1979.

COLOMBOS, C.J.
The international law of the sea. 6ed. Longmans, 1967.

DUBNER, B.H.
Law of international sea piracy. Nijhoff, 1979.

McDOUGAL, M.S. & BURKE, W.T.
The public order of the oceans. Yale U.P., 1962 (USA).

McWHINNEY, E.
Aerial piracy and international law. Sijthoff, 1971.

MARSDEN, R.G.
Documents relating to law and custom of the sea. Navy Records Society, 1916.

OPPENHEIM, L.
International law. vol. 1: peace. 8ed. Longmans, 1955.

WHITEMAN, M.M.
Digest of international law. Govt. Printing Office, 1963–5 (USA). Vol.4.

PLEA-BARGAINING
See also Criminal Law.

Texts
BALDWIN, J. & McCONVILLE, M.
Negotiated justice: pressures on defendants to plead guilty. Martin Robertson, 1977.

BOND, J.E.
Plea bargaining and guilty pleas. Clark Boardman, 1975 (USA). Looseleaf.

BUCKLE, S.R.T. & BUCKLE, L.G.
Bargaining for justice: case disposition and reform in the criminal courts. Praeger, 1977 (USA).

EDWARDS, M.F. & MEYER, K.L.
Settlement and plea bargaining. Assn. of Trial Lawyers, 1981 (USA).

HEUMANN, M.
Plea bargaining: experiences of prosecutors, judges and defence attorneys. Univ. of Chicago P., 1978.

KLEIN, J.F.
Let's make a deal: negotiating justice. Lexington, 1976 (USA).

MARKOWITZ, J.C.
Plea bargaining: an annotated bibliography. American Judicature Society, 1978.

PLEADING

See also Criminal Law; Forms and Precedents; Practice and Procedure.

Encyclopaedias

Halsbury's Laws of England. 4ed. vol.36.
The Digest. see index vol.
Encyclopaedia of Court Forms in Civil Proceedings (Atkin). 2ed. vol.32.

Texts

ARCHBOLD, J.F.
Pleading, evidence and practice in criminal cases. 41ed. Sweet & Maxwell, 1982.

BALDWIN, J. & McCONVILLE, M.
Negotiated justice: pressures on defendants to plead guilty. Martin Robertson, 1977.

BUCKLE, S.R.T. & BUCKLE, L.G.
Bargaining for justice: case disposition and reform in the criminal courts. Praeger, 1977 (USA).

BULLEN, E. & LEAKE, S.M.
Precedents of pleadings in the Queen's Bench Division for the High Court of Justice. 12ed. Sweet & Maxwell, 1975.

CAIRNS, A.
The county court pleader. Sweet & Maxwell, 1949.

DU CANN, R.
The art of the advocate. Penguin, 1964.

HEUMANN, M.
Plea bargaining: experiences of prosecutors, judges and defence attorneys. Univ. of Chicago P., 1978 (USA).

KLEIN, J.F.
Let's make a deal: negotiating justice. Lexington, 1976 (USA).

McEWAN, R.G.
Pleading in court. Green, 1980.

ODGERS, W.B.
The principles of pleading and practice. 22ed. Sweet & Maxwell, 1981.

SUPREME Court practice 1985. Sweet & Maxwell, 1984. 2 vols.

VANDESANDEN, G.
Pleading before the Court of Justice of the European Communities. Law Society, 1983.

POLICE

See also Arrest; Bail; Civil Rights and Liberties; Forensic Science; Public Order.

Encyclopaedias and periodicals

Statutes in Force. Group: Police.
Halsbury's Laws of England. 4ed. vol. 36.
Halsbury's Statutes of England. 3ed. mainly vol.25.
The Digest. vol.37.
Encyclopaedia of Court Forms in Civil Proceedings (Atkin). 2ed see index vol.

Criminal Law Review. 1954–
Police Journal. 1928–
Police Review. 1893–

Texts

ABRAHAMS, G.
Police questioning and judges' rules. Oyez, 1964.

ALDERSON, J.C. & STEAD, P.J. (eds.)
The police we deserve. Wolfe, 1973.

ALLEN, Sir C.K.
The Queen's peace. Stevens, 1953.

ALLEN, R.J.
Effective supervision in the police service. McGraw-Hill, 1978.

AVERY, J.
Police – force or service? Butterworths (Australia), 1981.

BAKER, E.R. & WILKIE, G.H. (eds.)
Police promotion handbooks. Butterworths.
1. Criminal law. 6ed. 1980.
2. Criminal evidence and procedure. 7ed. 1981.
3. General police duties. 7ed. 1983.
4. Road traffic. 7ed. 1980.

BECKER, H.K.
Issues in police administration. Scarecrow, 1971.

BELSON, W.A.
The public and the police. Harper & Row, 1975.

BOUZA, A.V.
Police administration: organization and performance. Pergamon, 1978.

BROWN, J. & HOWES, G. (eds.)
The police and the community. Saxon House, 1975.

BROWNE, D.
The rise of Scotland Yard. Greenwood, 1956.

BUNYAN, T.
The history and practice of the political police in Britain. Quartet, 1977.

BUNYARD, R.S.
Police: organization and command. Macdonald & Evans, 1978.

CAIN, M.E.
Society and the policeman's role. Routledge, 1973.

CALVERT, F.
Constable's pocket guide to powers of arrest and charges. 6ed. Butterworths, 1978.

CAMPBELL, D.
Police: the exercise of power. Macdonald & Evans, 1978.

CARR, R.A. & STERN, N.H.
Crime, the police and criminal statistics: an analysis of official statistics for England and Wales using econometric methods. Academic P., 1979.

COASE, B.G.
Precedents for police use. Rose, 1980.

CRITCHLEY, T.A.
History of the police in England and Wales. rev. ed. Constable, 1978.

DITCHFIELD, J.A.
Police cautioning in England and Wales. HMSO, 1976.

EUROPEAN COMMITTEE ON CRIME PROBLEMS
Police and the prevention of crime. 1979.

FIRMIN, S.
Scotland Yard. Hutchinson, 1951.

GRAMPIAN POLICE
Scottish criminal law, police duties and procedures. rev. ed. Aberdeen U.P., 1978. Looseleaf.

HALL, S. and others.
Policing the crisis: mugging, the state and law and order. Macmillan, 1978.

HAHN, H.
The police in urban society. Sage, 1971.

HARRISON, R.
The C.I.D. and the F.B.I. Muller, 1956.

HART, J.M.M.
The British police. Allen & Unwin, 1951.

HOME OFFICEC
Crime prevention and the police. HMSO, 1979 (Research studies).

HOME OFFICE
The establishment of an independent element in the investigation of complaints against the police: report of a working party (Plowden). HMSO, 1981. (Cmnd. 8193).

HOME OFFICE
The feasibility of an experiment in the tape recording of police interrogation: report of a committe (Hyde). HMSO, 1976 (Cmnd. 6630).

HOME OFFICE
Handling of complaints against the police: report of the working group for England and Wales (Gordon-Brown). HMSO, 1974 (Cmnd. 5582). Scotland. HMSO, 1974 (Cmnd. 5583).

HOME OFFICE
Police complaints and discipline
procedures. HMSO, 1983 (Cmnd. 9072).

HOME OFFICE
Police interrogation: an observational study
in four police stations. HMSO, 1980
(Research studies).

HOME OFFICE
Report of the Departmental Committee on
Metropolitan Police Court Districts
(Jurisdiction) (Belper). HMSO, 1900
(Cd.374). 1904 (Cd. 2215–6).

HOME OFFICE
Report on police conditions of service
(Oaksey). HMSO, 1949 (Cmd. 7674, 7707,
7831).

HOUGHTON, R.
Police charges. 4ed. Police Review, 1972.

JUDGE, A.
The first fifty years: the story of the Police
Federation. Police Federation, 1968.

JUSTICE
Pre-trial criminal procedure, police powers
and the prosecution process: a report.
Stevens, 1979.

KELLY, W. & KELLY, N.
Policing in Canada. Macmillan, 1976.

LAURIE, P.
Scotland Yard. Bodley Head, 1970.

LEIGH, L.H.
Police powers in England and Wales. 2ed.
Butterworths, 1984.

LUXFORD, J.H.
Police law in New Zealand. 3ed.
Butterworths, 1967.

MARK, Sir R.
Policing a perplexed society. Allen &
Unwin, 1976.

MARSHALL, G.
Police and government. Methuen, 1967.

MAWBY, R.L.
Policing the city: case study of crime and
law enforcement in Sheffield. Gower, 1979.

MILTE, K.L. & WEBER, T.A.
Police in Australia: developments, functions
and procedures. Butterworths (Australia),
1977.

MORIARTY, C.C.H.
Police law. 24ed. Butterworths, 1981.

MORIARTY, C.C.H.
Police procedure and administration. 6ed.
Butterworths, 1955.

MORRIS, P. & HEAL, K.
Crime control and the police: a review of
research. HMSO, 1981 (Home Office
research studies, no. 67).

MOSSE, G.L. (ed.)
Police forces in history. Sage, 1975.

MOYLAN, Sir J.F.
Scotland Yard and the metropolitan police.
2ed. Putnam, 1934.

NORTHERN IRELAND OFFICE
Handling of complaints against the police:
report of the Working Party for Northern
Ireland. HMSO, 1976 (Cmnd. 6475).

POWELL, C.M.
Police officers' manual. 6ed. Carswell, 1976
(Canada).

PUNCH, M.E..
Policing the inner city. Macmillan, 1979.

REITH, C.
New study of police history. Oxford U.P.,
1956.

ROYAL COMMISSION ON DUTIES
OF THE METROPOLITAN POLICE
Report (Lyttleton). HMSO, 1908 (Cd.
4156).

ROYAL COMMISSION ON POLICE
POWERS
Report (Hamilton). HMSO, 1928–9
(Cmd.3297).

ROYAL COMMISSION ON THE
POLICE
Final Report (Willink). HMSO, 1962.
(Cmnd. 1728).

SCOTT, Sir H.
Scotland Yard. Penguin, 1957.

SLOAN, K.
Cases for the police. Butterworths, 1977.

SLOAN, K.
Police law primer. 2ed. Butterworths, 1980.

SMITH, C.R.
Examination of the procedure for dealing
with complaints against the police. Police
Federation, 1972.

WEGG-PROSSER, C.
The police and the law. 2ed. Oyez, 1979.

WHITTAKER, B.
The police. Penguin, 1964.

POLLUTION

See also Environment Law; Oil; Public Health; Waters and Watercourses.

Encyclopaedias and periodicals

Statutes in Force. Group: Environment.
Halsbury's Laws of England. 4ed. mainly vols. 38 & 43.
Halsbury's Statutes of England. 3ed. vol. 44.
The Digest. mainly vol. 47.
Encyclopaedia of Court Forms in Civil Proceedings (Atkin). 2ed. see index vol.
Encyclopaedia of Forms and Precedents. 4ed. see index vol.

Environmental Pollution. 1970–
Environmental Pollution Management. 1971–
Journal of Planning and Environment Law. 1948–
P.M. Newsletter (formerly Pollution Monitor. 1971–1982). 1983–

Texts

AMIN, S.H.
Pollution control in the Arab Gulf. Royston, 1984.

BARROS, J. & JOHNSTON, D.M.
The international law of pollution. Free P., 1974 (USA).

BRITISH INSTITUTE OF INTERNATIONAL AND COMPARATIVE LAW
International environmental law: proceedings. 1976.

BRITISH SULPHUR CORPORATION LTD
World guide to pollution control in the fertilizer industry. 1975.

CANADIAN INDUSTRIES
Digest of environmental pollution legislation in Canada. 1973.

CENTRAL UNIT ON ENVIRONMENTAL POLLUTION
Pollution control in Great Britain: how it works: review of legislative and administrative procedures. 2ed. HMSO, 1979.

COLLARD, C.A.
The law and practice relating to pollution control in France. Graham & Trotman, 1976.

DELL'ANNO, P.
The law and practice relating to pollution control in Italy. Graham & Trotman, 1976.

DIDIER, J.M. & Others
The law and practice relating to pollution control in Belgium and Luxembourg. Graham & Trotman, 1976.

ENVIRONMENT, DEPARTMENT OF THE
Pollution control in Great Britain: how it works. 2ed. HMSO, 1979.

ERCMAN, S.
European environmental law: legal and economic appraisal. Bubenberg, 1976 (Switzerland).

FRANSON, R.T. & LUCAS, A.R.
Canadian environmental law. Butterworths (Canada), 1976. 6 vols. Looseleaf.

GARNER, J.F.
Control of Pollution Act, 1974. Butterworths, 1975.

GARNER, J.F. & HARRIS, D.J.
Control of pollution encyclopaedia. Butterworths, 1978. Looseleaf.

GORMLEY, W.P.
Human rights and environment: the need for international co-operation. Sijthoff, 1976.

GRAEFF, J.J.de & POLACK, J.H.
The law and practice relating to pollution control in the Netherlands. Graham & Trotman, 1976.

GREATER LONDON COUNCIL
Pollution: a report. 1971.

GUNNINGHAM, N.
Pollution, social interest and the law. Robertson, 1974.

HARGROVE, J.L. (ed.)
Law, institutions and the global environment. Oceana:Sijthoff, 1972.

HAWKINS, K.
Environmenta and enforcement: regulation and the social definition of pollution. Oxford U.P., 1984.

INTERNATIONAL ATOMIC ENERGY AGENCY
Nuclear techniques in environmental pollution. 1971.

JENSEN, C.H.
The law and practice relating to pollution control in Denmark. Graham & Trotman, 1976.

JOHNSON, B.
The United Nations system and the human environment. Inst. for Study of Internat.Organ., 1972.

LAW and practice relating to pollution control in the member states of the European Communities. 2ed. Graham & Trotman, 1982. 10 vols.

McKNIGHT, A.D.
Environmental pollution control: technical, economic and legal aspects. Allen & Unwin, 1974.

McLOUGHLIN, J.
The law and practice relating to pollution control in the United Kingdom. Graham & Trotman, 1976.

McLOUGHLIN, J.
The law relating to pollution: an introduction. Manchester U.P., 1972.

ORGANISATION FOR ECONOMIC CO-OPERATION & DEVELOPMENT
Legal aspects of transfrontier pollution. 1978.

RABIE, A.
South African environmental legislation. Univ. of S.Africa, 1976.

ROYAL COMMISSION ON ENVIRONMENTAL POLLUTION
1st Report. HMSO, 1971 (Cmnd. 4585).
2nd Report: three issues in industrial pollution. HMSO, 1972 (Cmnd. 4894).
3rd Report: pollution in some British and coastal waters. HMSO, 1972 (Cmnd. 5054).
4th Report: pollution control: progress and problems. HMSO, 1974 (Cmnd. 5780).
5th Report: air pollution control: an integrated approach. HMSO, 1976 (Cmnd. 6371).
6th Report: nuclear power and the environment. HMSO, 1976 (Cmnd. 6618).

RUBIN, E.H. & SCHWARTZ, M.D. (eds.)
The pollution crisis: official documents. Oceana, 1972 (USA), 2 vols.

RUSTER, B. & SIMMA, B.
International protection of the environment: treaties and related documents. Oceana, 1976. 10 vols.

SCANNELL, Y.
The law and practice relating to pollution control in Ireland. Graham & Trotman, 1976.

SERWER, D.
International co-operation for pollution control. Interbook, 1972.

SHAW, B.
Environmental law: people, pollution and land use. West, 1976 (USA).

SIV, M.R.
Environmental legislation: a source book. Praeger, 1976 (USA).

SLOAN, I.J.
Environment and the law. Oceana, 1971 (USA).

SPRINGER, A.L.
International law of pollution: protecting the global environment in a world of sovereign states. Quorum Books; Greenwood Press, 1983 (USA).

STEIGER, H. & KIMMINCH, O.
The law and practice relating to pollution control in the Federal Republic of Germany. Graham & Trotman, 1976.

TECLAFF, L.A. & UTTON, A.E. (eds.)
International environmental law. Praeger, 1974.

WALKER, A.
Law of industrial pollution control. Godwin, 1979.

WHITTAKER, C.A.J.
Handbook of environmental powers. Architectural P., 1976.

Air

COUNCIL OF EUROPE
Legal aspects of air pollution control. 1972.

DEPARTMENTAL COMMITTEE ON AIR POLLUTION
Report (Beaver). HMSO, 1954 (Cmd. 9011, 9322).

EDELMAN, S,
Law of air pollution control. Environmental Res.& Applications, 1970 (USA).

ENVIRONMENT, DEPARTMENT OF THE
Air pollution information: your rights and obligations. HMSO, 1977.

GARNER, J.F.
Clean air: law and practice. 4ed. Shaw, 1977.

HAVIGHURST, C.C. (ed.)
Air pollution control. Oceana, 1969 (USA).

HEALTH AND SAFETY EXECUTIVE
Industrial air pollution, 1975. HMSO, 1977.

JACOBY, H.D. & STEINBRUNER, J.
Clearing the air: federal policy on automotive emissions control. Ballinger, 1973 (USA).

SCHACHTER, E.R.
Enforcing air pollution controls: case study of New York City. Praeger, 1974.

TOMANY, J.P.
Air pollution: the emissions, the regulations and the controls. Elsevier, 1974 (USA).

Water

ABECASSIS, D.W.
Law and practice relating to oil pollution from ships. Butterworths, 1978.

ADVISORY COMMITTEE ON POLLUTION OF THE SEA
Law relating to compensable damage caused by marine pollution with special reference to environmental damage. Graham & Trotman, 1983.

AMERICAN SOCIETY OF INTERNATIONAL LAW
The question of an Ocean Dumping Convention. 1972.

BATES, J.H.
U.K. marine pollution law. Lloyd's, 1984.

CUMMING, G.B.
Oil pollution of beaches. Inst. of Munic.Engineers, 1974.

DAVID DAVIES MEMORIAL INSTITUTE OF INTERNATIONAL STUDIES
Water pollution as a world problem: the legal scientific and political aspects. 1971.

ENVIRONMENT, DEPARTMENT OF THE
Report of the Director of Water Pollution Research. HMSO. Annual.

ENVIRONMENT, DEPARTMENT OF THE
River pollution survey of England and Wales updated, 1973. HMSO, 1975.

GOLD, E.
Oil pollution: a survey of worldwide legislation. Gard, 1972 (USA). Looseleaf.

INTERNATIONAL CONFERENCE ON MARINE POLLUTION, London, 1973.
Final Act. HMSO, 1974 (Cmnd. 5748).

INTERNATIONAL convention relating to intervention on the High Seas in cases of oil pollution casualties, Brussels, 1969–70. HMSO, 1975 (Cmnd. 6056).

INTERNATIONAL MARITIME CONSULTATIVE ORGANISATION
Oil pollution: charts of prohibited zones. 1972.

M'GONIGLE, R.M. & ZACHER, M.
Pollution, politics and international law: tankers at sea. California U.P., 1980 (USA).

NEWSOM, G. & SHERRATT, J.G.
Water pollution. Sherratt, 1972.

ODIDI OKIDI, C.
Regional control of ocean pollution: legal and institutional problems and prospects. Sijthoff, 1978.

PLANO, J.C.
International approaches to the problems of marine pollution. Sussex Univ.,Inst.for Study of Internat.Organ., 1972.

ROSS, W.M.
Oil pollution as an international problem: a study of Puget Sound and the Strait of Georgia. Victoria Univ., 1973.

SCHACHTER, O. & SERWER, D.
Marine pollution problems and remedies. Interbook, 1970 (USA).

SHINN, R.A.
The international politics of marine pollution control. Praeger, 1974.

TRADE, DEPARTMENT OF
Manual on the avoidance of pollution of the sea by oil. 4ed. HMSO, 1974.

WISDOM, A.S.
Freshwater pollution. Rose, 1979.

WISDOM, A.S.
Law of pollution of waters. 2ed. Shaw, 1966.

POOR LAW

See also Social Security; Welfare Law.

Encyclopaedias

Halsbury's Laws of England. 4ed. see index vol.
Halsbury's Statutes of England. 3ed. see index vol.
The Digest. see index vol.

Texts

BURN, R.
History of the poor laws. 1764 repr. Kelley.

CHECKLAND, S.G. & CHECKLAND, O.A. (eds.)
The poor law report of 1834. 1974.

FRASER, D. (ed.)
The new poor law in the nineteenth century. Macmillan, 1976.

LINDSAY, J.
The Scottish poor law. Stockwell, 1975.

MARSHALL, J.D.
The old poor law, 1795–1834. St Martin's P., 1969.

NICHOLLS, Sir G.
History of the English poor law. repr. 1958. 3 vols.

NICHOLLS, Sir G.
History of the Irish poor law. 1856 repr. 1968.

NICHOLLS, Sir G.
History of the Scotch poor law. 1856. repr. 1968.

OXLEY, G.W.
Poor relief in England and Wales, 1601–1834. David & Charles, 1974.

ROSE, M.E.
The English poor law, 1730–1930. David & Charles, 1971.

TOWNSEND, J.
A dissertation on the poor laws, by a well-wisher to mankind, Joseph Townsend. 1786 rep. 1971.

TRATTNER, W.
From poor law to welfare state. 2ed. Free Press:Collier Macmillan, 1979.

WEBB, S. & WEBB, B.
English poor law history: Part I. The old poor law. Longmans, Green, 1927. Part II. The last hundred years. Longmans, Green, 1929. 2 vols.

Reports

COMMITTEE ON POOR LAW AND THE RELIEF OF DISTRESS
Report (Hamilton). 1909 (Cd. 4499, 4945).

COMMITTEE ON THE TRANSFER OF FUNCTIONS OF POOR LAW AUTHORITIES
Report (Maclean). HMSO, 1917–18 (Cd. 8917).

DEPARTMENTAL COMMITTEE ON POOR LAW ORDERS
Report (Provis). HMSO, 1913 (Cd. 6968).

POOR PERSONS

See also Legal Aid and Advice.

Encyclopaedias and periodicals

Halsbury's Laws of England. 4ed. see index vol.

The Digest. see index vol.

Justice of the Peace. 1837–

Legal Action (formerly L.A.G. Bulletin). 1973–

Modern Law Review. 1937–

New Law Journal (as Law Journal. 1882–1964). 1965–

Solicitors' Journal. 1857–

Texts

ABEL-SMITH, B. & TOWNSEND, P.
The poor and the poorest. Bedford Square P., 1965.

ABEL-SMITH, B., ZANDER, M. & BROOKE, R.
Legal problems and the citizen. Heinemann, 1973.

ATKINSON, A.B.
Poverty in Britain and the reform of social security. Cambridge U.P., 1969.

BERNEY, A.L. and others
Legal problems of the poor: cases and materials. Little, Brown, 1975 (USA).

BOYSON, R. (ed.)
Down with the poor. Churchill, 1971.

BRUNDAGE, A.
Making of the new poor law: the politics of inquiry, enactment and implementation. Hutchinson, 1978.

BRYANT, R. & BRADSHAW, J.
Welfare rights and social action: the York experiment. CPAG, 1970.

BULL, D.
Action for welfare rights. Fabian, 1970.

CARLIN, J.E., HOWARD, J. & MESSINGER, S.I.
Civil justice and the poor. Sage, 1967 (USA).

CASS, M. & SACKVILLE, R.
Legal needs of the poor. Butterworths (Australia), 1975.

COMMITTEE ON LEGAL SERVICES TO THE POOR IN THE DEVELOPING COUNTRIES
Legal aid and world poverty. Praeger, 1974 (USA).

COMMITTEE ON POOR PERSONS RULES
Report (Lawrence). HMSO, 1924–25 (Cmd. 2358).

COOPER, G.
Cases and materials on law and poverty. 2ed. West, 1973 (USA).

GEORGE, V. & LAWSON, R. (eds.)
Poverty and inequality in Common Market countries. Routledge, 1980.

JORDAN, W.
Paupers: the making of the new claiming class. Routledge, 1973.

LA FRANCE, A.B. and others
Handbook on the law of the poor. West, 1973 (USA).

LEGAL ACTION GROUP
Legal advice centres – an explosion? 1972.

LEGAL ACTION GROUP
Legal services for the future. 1974.

MORRIS, P., WHITE, R & LEWIS, P.
Social needs and legal action. Martin Robertson, 1973.

PARTINGTON, M.
Recent developments in legal services for the poor: some reflections on experience in Coventry. Weidenfeld & N., 1975.

PARTINGTON, M., HULL, J. & KNIGHT, S.
Welfare rights: a bibliography on law and the poor, 1970–1975. Pinter, 1976.

POLLARD, D.W.
Social welfare law. Oyez Longman, 1978. Looseleaf.

PROSSER, T.
Test cases for the poor: legal techniques in the politics of social welfare. Child Poverty Action Group, 1983.

ROACH, J.L. & ROACH, J.K. (eds.)
Poverty: selected readings. Penguin, 1972.

RODGERS, B.
The battle against poverty. Routledge, 1969. 2 vols.

SACKVILLE, R.
Law and poverty in Australia.
Aust.Govt.Pub.Service, 1976.

SANGER, M.B.
Welfare of the poor. Academic P., 1980.

SMITH, C. & HOATH, D.C.
Law and the under privileged. Routledge, 1975.

SMITH, R.H.
Justice of the poor. Patterson Smith, 1919 repr. Carnegie Foundn., 1972 (USA).

TOWNSEND, P. (ed.)
The concept of poverty. Heinemann, 1970.

POSSESSION

See also Bailment; Personal Property; Real Property.

Encyclopaedias and periodicals

Statutes in Force. Group: Property, England & Wales, Sub-group 1.
Halsbury's Laws of England. 4ed. see index vols.
Halsbury's Statutes of England. 3ed. see index vol.
The Digest. see index vol.

Encyclopaedia of Court Forms in Civil Proceedings (Atkin). 2ed. see index vol.
Encyclopaedia of Forms and Precedents. 4ed. see index vol.

Conveyancer and Property Lawyer. 1936–
Estates Gazette. 1858–

Texts

CHESHIRE, G.C. & BURN, E.H.
Modern law of real property. 13ed. Butterworths, 1982.

GOODHART, A.L.
Essays in jurisprudence and the common law. Cambridge U.P., 1932. Ch.6.

HILL, H.A. & REDMAN, J.H.
Law of landlord and tenant. 17ed. Butterworths, 1982.

HOLDSWORTH, Sir W.S.
An historical introduction in the land law. Oxford U.P., 1972.

HOLMES, O.W.
The common law. Macmillan, 1887 repr. 1968.

LIGHTWOOD, J.M.
A treatise on possession of land. Stevens, 1894.

MAITLAND, F.W.
Collected papers. 1911. repr. Professional Books. 3 vols.

MEGARRY, R.E. & WADE, H.W.R.
The law of real property. 5ed. Sweet & Maxwell, 1984.

POLLOCK, Sir F. & WRIGHT, Sir R.S.
An eassy on possession in the common law. Oxford U.P., 1888.

POSTAL SERVICES

See also Telecommunications.

Encyclopaedias and periodicals

Statutes in Force. Group: Post and Telecommunications.
Halsbury's Laws of England. 4ed. vol.36.
Halsbury's Statutes of England. 3ed. mainly vol.25.
The Digest. see index vol.
Encyclopaedia of Court Forms in Civil Proceedings (Atkin). 2ed. see index vol.
Encyclopaedia of Forms and Precedents. 4ed. see index vol.

Post Office Guide. Annual.
Post Office Telecommunications Journal. 1948–

Texts

CODDING, G.A.
The Universal Postal Union. NYU Press, 1964 (USA).

ELLIS, K.
The Post Office in the 18th century. Oxford U.P., 1958.

HOME OFFICE
The interception of communications in Great Britain. HMSO, 1980 (Cmnd. 7873).

INDUSTRY, DEPARTMENT OF
Report of the Post Office Review Committee (Carter). 1977(Cmnd. 6850).

MURRAY, Sir G.E.P.
The Post Office. Allen & Unwin, 1927.

PLOMAN, E.W. (ed.)
International law governing communications and information: a collection of documents. Greenwood Press, 1982.

PRIME MINSTER'S OFFICE
The interception of communications in Great Britain: Report (Diplock). HMSO, 1981 (Cmnd. 8191).

POWERS

See also Personal Property; Real Property; Trusts and Trustees; Ultra Vires.

Encyclopaedias

Halsbury's Laws of England. 4ed. vol.36.
Halsbury's Statutes of England. 3ed. see index vol.
The Digest. vol.37.

Texts

CHANCE, H.
Treatise of powers. Butterworths, 1841. 2 vols.

FARWELL, Sir G.
Powers. 3ed. Stevens, 1916.

ST LEONARDS, E.B. Baron
Treatise on powers. 8ed. Sweet, 1861.

SUPREME Court practice 1985. Sweet & Maxwell, 1984. 2 vols.

POWERS OF ATTORNEY

See also Agency; Solicitors.

Encyclopaedias

Statutes in Force. Group: Agency.
Halsbury's Laws of England. 4ed. see index vols.
Halsbury's Statutes of England. 3ed. see index vol.

The Digest. see index vol.
Encyclopaedia of Court Forms in Civil Proceedings (Atkin). 2ed. see index vol.
Encyclopaedia of Forms and Precedents. 4ed. see index vol.

Texts

ALCOCK, F.B.
Powers of attorney. Pitman, 1935.

ALDRIDGE, T.M.
Powers of attorney. 5ed. Oyez, 1981.

BOULTON, A.H.
Powers of attorney and other instruments conferring authority. 9ed. Inst. of Chartered Secretaries, 1973.

BROOKE, R.
Treatise on the office and practice of notary of England. 9ed. Stevens, 1939.

CAPLIN, C.
Powers of attorney. 5ed. Oyez, 1981 (Practice notes).

HEYWOOD, N.A. & MASSEY, A.S.
Court of protection practice. 10ed. Sweet & Maxwell, 1978 supp. 1982.

LAW COMMISSION
The incapacitated principal. HMSO, 1976 (Working paper no.69).

LAW COMMISSION
Powers of attorney. HMSO, 1967 repr. 1977 (Working paper no.11).

LAW COMMISSION
Powers of attorney. HMSO, 1970 (Law Com. no.30).

MILLS, G.E. & POYSER, A.H.
Management and administration of estates in lunacy. 2ed. Butterworths, 1927.

VENABLES, H.D.S.
Guide to the law affecting mental patients. Butterworths, 1975.

PRACTICE AND PROCEDURE
See also Pleading.

Encyclopaedias and periodicals
Halsbury's Laws of England. 4ed. vol.37.
The Digest. see index vol.
Encyclopaedia of Court Forms in Civil Proceedings (Atkin). 2ed. see index vol.
County Court Practice. Annual.
Parliament House Book. Annual.
Stone's Justices Manual. 2 vols. Annual.
Supreme Court Practice.

Texts
ARCHBOLD, J.F.
Pleading evidence and practice in criminal cases. 41ed. Sweet & Maxwell, 1982.

ARONSON, M.I., REABURN, N.S. & WEINBERG, M.S.
Litigation – evidence and procedure. 3ed. Butterworths (Australia), 1982.

BISHOP, J.
Criminal procedure. Butterworths (Australia), 1983.

BULLEN, E. & LEAK, S.M.
Precedents of pleadings in the Queen's Bench Division of the High Court of Justices. 12ed. Sweet & Maxwell, 1975.

CAMILLERI, B.J.
Practice and procedure of the High Court and Federal Court of Australia. Butterworths (Australia), 1978. Looseleaf.

CARRINGTON, P.D. & BABCOCK, B.A.
Civil procedure: cases and comments on the process of adjudication. 2ed. Little, Brown, 1977 (USA).

CHITTY, T. & JACOB, I.H.
Queen's Bench forms. 20ed. Sweet & Maxwell, 1969.

COLMAN, A.
The practice and procedure of the commercial court. Lloyd's, 1983.

COLLINS, H.C.
Notes on County Court practice and procedure. 5ed. Oyez, 1978.

COUNCIL OF EUROPE
The practical guide to the recognition and enforcement of foreign judicial decisions in civil and commercial law. 1975.

DEIGHAN, M.
County court practice and procedure. 2ed. Fourmat Pub., 1982.

DENNING, Lord
Due process of law. Butterworths, 1980.

EMMINS, C.J.
Practical approach to criminal procedure. 2ed. Financial Training Pubns., 1983.

FAGE, J.
Supreme court practice and procedure. 3ed. Fourmat, 1984.

FALLON, P.
Crown Court practice: sentence. Butterworths, 1975 & supp.

FALLON, P.
Crown Court practice: trial. Butterworths, 1978 supp. 1979.

GANE, C.H.W. & STODDART, C.N.
Criminal procedure in Scotland: cases and materials. Green, 1983.

GANZ, G.
Administrative procedures. Sweet & Maxwell, 1974.

HAMPTON, C.
Criminal law and procedure. 3ed. Sweet & Maxwell, 1982.

HAMPTON, C.
Criminal procedure and evidence. 3ed. Sweet & Maxwell, 1983.

HARROLD, B. & WHITE, A.
Summary process and prosecution. Butterworths, 1974.

JACOB, J.I.H.
Commencement of actions in the High Court: new forms and procedures. Butterworths, 1980.

LANGAN, P. St.J.
Civil procedure. 3ed. Sweet & Maxwell, 1983.

LEWIS, J.R.
Civil and criminal procedure. Sweet & Maxwell, 1968.

McBRYDE, W.W. & DOWIE, N.J.
Petition procedure in the Court of Session. Green, 1980.

MAHER, F.W.K.
Cases and materials on the legal process. 3ed. Law Book Co., 1979 (Australia).

MOORE, T.G. & WILKINSON, T.P.
Juvenile court: a guide to the law and practice. Rose, 1984.

MUGHAL, A.K.
Cases and statutes on criminal procedure. Butterworths, 1973.

ODGERS, W.B.
The principles of pleading and practice in civil action. 22ed. Sweet & Maxwell, 1981.

O'HARE, J. & HILL, R.N.
Civil litigation. 2ed. Oyez, 1982.

O'LEARY, K.F. & HOGAN, A.E.
Principles of practice and procedure, illustrated by reference to the Supreme Court Act 1970 (NSW). Butterworths (Australia), 1976.

RAYMOND, B.
Introduction to criminal and civil litigation. Oyez, 1981.

RENTON, R.W. & BROWN, R.H.
Criminal procedure according to the law of Scotland. 4ed. Green, 1972.

RITCHIE, A.V.
Supreme Court procedure NSW. Butterworths (Australia), 1972. Looseleaf.

ROYAL COMMISSION ON CRIMINAL PROCEDURE
Report. HMSO, 1981. (Cmnd. 8092).

RYAN, K., WELD, H. & LEE, W.C.
Queensland and Supreme Court proactice. Butterworths (Australia). Looseleaf.

SCOTT, I.R.
The Crown Court. Butterworths, 1972.

SCOTTISH COURTS ADMINISTRATION
Report of the Scottish Committee on Jurisdiction and Enforcement. HMSO, 1980.

SIMMONS, F.
High Court practice manual. Oyez, 1979 supp. 1980.

THOMPSON, D.R.
Proceedings in the Criminal Division of the Court of Appeal: an index of practice and procedure. Rose, 1979.

USHER, J.
European Court practice. Sweet & Maxwell, 1983.

WILLIAMS, E.
ABC guide to the practice of the County Court. 2ed. Sweet & Maxwell, 1982.

WILLIAMS, E.
ABC guide to the practice of the Supreme Court 1984-85. 42ed. Sweet & Maxwell, 1984.

WILLIAMS, N.J.
Supreme Court Practice Victoria. 2ed. Butterworths (Australia), 1973. Looseleaf.

WITCHELL, R.G.
Practice and procedure. Vol. 1: County Courts and Magistrates Courts. 7ed. Oyez, 1979. Vol.3: High Court. 7ed. Oyez, 1979. Vol.4. Matrimonial Proceedings. 6ed. Oyez, 1977. Vol.5: Non-contentious probate and private limited companies. 6ed. Oyez, 1977.

WYLIE, I.M.
The law and practice of the District Courts of Queensland. 2ed. Butterworths (Australia), 1983.

YELL, N. & WEST, W.T.
County court practice and procedure: general. B.Rose, 1983.

PRENATAL INJURIES

LAW COMMISSION
Injuries to urborn children. HMSO, 1973 repr. 1977 (Working paper no.47).

LAW COMMISSION
Report on injuries to unborn children. HMSO, 1975 (Cmnd. 5709) (Law Com. no.60).

SCOTTISH LAW COMMISSION
Report on liability for antenatal injury. HMSO, 1973 (Scot. Law Com. no.30).

SUNDAY TIMES
Thalidomide children and the law: a report. Deutsch, 1973.

TEFF, H. & MUNRO, C.R.
Thalidomide: the legal aftermath. Saxon House, 1976.

PREROGATIVE

See also Constitutional Law; Crown.

Encyclopaedias

Halsbury's Laws of England. 4ed. vol.8.
The Digest. vol.11.
Encyclopaedia of Court Forms in Civil Proceedings (Atkin). 2ed. vol.14.

Texts

CHITTY, J.
A treatise on the law of the prerogatives of the Crown. Butterworths, 1820.

DICEY, A.V.
Introduction to the study of the law of the Constitution. 10ed. Macmillan, 1961.

FIGGIS, J.N.
The theory of the Divine Right of Kings. 2ed. Cambridge U.P., 1914.

JENNINGS, Sir W.I.
Cabinet government. 3ed. Cambridge U.P., 1959.

MACKINTOSH, J.P.
The British cabinet. 3ed. Sweet & Maxwell, 1977.

PREROGATIVE ORDERS

See also Ceritorari; Habeas Corpus; Mandamus; Prohibition.

Encyclopaedias

Halsbury's Laws of England. 4ed. see index vol.
Halsbury's Statutes of England. 3ed. vol.8.
The Digest. see index vol.
Encyclopaedia of Court Forms in Civil Proceedings (Atkin). 2ed. vol.14.

Texts

GRIFFITS, J.O.
Practice of the Crown Office and Associates Department. Sweet & Maxwell, 1947 supp. 1950.

SHORT, F.H. & MELLOR, F.H.
The practice on the Crown side of the King's Bench Division. Stevens & Haynes, 1908.

PRESCRIPTION

See also Limitation of Actions; Title.

Encyclopaedias

Statutes in Force. Groups: Prescription and Limitations, Scotland; Property, England and Wales.
Halsbury's Laws of England. 4ed. vol.14.
Halsbury's Statutes of England. 3ed. vol.9.

The Digest. vols. 11, 19, but see index vol.
Encyclopaedia of Court Forms in Civil Proceedings (Atkin). 2ed. see index vol.
Encyclopaedia of Forms and Precedents. 4ed. see index vol.

Texts

CARSON, T.H.
Prescription and custom. Sweet & Maxwell, 1907.

CARSON, T.H. & BOMPAS, H.B.
Real property and conveyancing statutes. 13ed. Sweet & Maxwell, 1927 repr. Professional Books.

HERBERT, T.A.
History of the law of prescription in England. Clay, 1891.

SCOTTISH LAW COMMISSION
Prescription and limitation of actions. 1969 (Memorandum no.9).

SCOTTISH LAW COMMISSION
Reform of the law relating to prescription and limitation of actions. HMSO, 1970 (Scot. Law Com. no.15).

WALKER, D.M.
The law of prescription and limitation of actions in Scotland. 3ed. Green, 1981.

PRESS LAW

See also Advertising; Censorship; Copyright; 'D' Notice; Libel and Slander; Obscenity; Offical Secrets; Printers and Publishers; Privacy.

Encyclopaedias and periodicals

Halsbury's Laws of England. 4ed. vol.37.
Halsbury's Statutes of England. 3ed. vols. 19, 43.
The Digest. vol.37.
Encyclopaedia of Court Forms in Civil Proceedings (Atkin). 2ed. see index under Newspaper.

Encyclopaedia of Forms and Precedents. 4ed. see index vol. under Newspaper.

Journal of Media Law and Practice. 1980–
Journalist. 1908–
U.K. Press Gazette. 1965–

Texts

ABRAHAMS, G.
Law for writers and journalists. Jenkins, 1958.

ADAM, G.S.
Journalism, communication and the law. Prentice-Hall (Canada), 1976.

ARMSTRONG, M.
Media law in Australia: a manual. Oxford U.P. (Australia), 1984.

BELOFF, N.
Freedom under foot. M.T.Smith, 1976.

BLACKWELL, L. & BAMFORD, B.R.
Newspaper law of South Africa. Sweet & Maxwell, 1963.

BRADLEY, D.
The newspaper: its place in a democracy. Van Nostrand Reinhold, 1966 (USA).

BRUCKER, H.
Communication is power: unchanging values in a changing journalism. Oxford U.P., 1973 (USA).

BURROWS, J.F.
News media law in New Zealand. Sweet & Maxwell, 1974.

CHENERY, W.L.
Freedom of the press. 2ed. Greenwood, 1978 (USA).

CLIVE, E.M. & WATT, G.A.
Scots law for journalists. 2ed. Green, 1983.

CLOUTMAN, B.M. & LUCK, F.W.
Law of printers and publishers. 2ed. Bale & Danielsson, 1949.

DAWSON, T.
Law of the press. 2ed. Staples, 1947.

HYDE, H.M.
Privacy and the press. Butterworths, 1947.

INGLISS, B.
Freedom of the press in Ireland, 1784–1841. 1954 repr. Greenwood, 1974.

JAMES, A.
Media and the law. Brennan Pubns., 1977.

JONES, M.
Justice and journalism: a study of the influence of newspaper reporting upon the administration of justice by magistrates. Rose, 1974.

JUSTICE & INTERNATIONAL PRESS INSITUTE
The law and the press: the report of a joint working party. Stevens, 1965.

LEVY, H.P.
The Press Council: history, procedure and cases. Macmillan, 1967.

LLOYD, H.
The legal limits of journalism. Pergamon, 1968.

McNAE, L.C.J.
Essential law for journalism. 8ed. Butterworths, 1982.

OVERBECK, W.
Major principles of media law. Holt, R.& W., 1982.

PEMBER, D.R.
Privacy and the press: the law, the mass media and the first amendment. Washington U.P., 1972 (USA).

PRESS COUNCIL
Outline of the Council's practice and principles. 1973.

PRESS COUNCIL
Press and people. Annual report.

RICHARDS, A.
Law for journalists. Macdonald & Evans, 1977.

ROBERTSON, G. & NICOL, A.
Media law: thr rights of journalists and broadcasters. Oxford U.P., 1984.

ROYAL COMMISSION ON THE PRESS
Report (Ross). HMSO, 1948–49. (Cmd. 7690, 7700).

ROYAL COMMISSION ON THE PRESS, 1974–77
Final report (McGregor). HMSO, 1977 (Cmnd. 6810).
Appendices (Cmnd. 6180–1).

Analysis of newspaper content (McQuail). HMSO, 1977 (Cmnd. 6810–4).

Industrial relations in the national newspaper industry: a report by the Advisory Conciliation and Arbitration Service. HMSO, 1976 (Cmnd. 6680).

Industrial relations in the provincial newspaper and periodical industries: a report by the Advisory Conciliation and Arbitration Service. HMSO, 1977 (Cmnd. 6810–2).

Interim Report: The national newspaper industry. HMSO, 1976.

Working Paper No. 1: new technology and the press: study of experience in the United States. HMSO, 1975.

Working Paper No.2: review of sociological writing on the press. HMSO, 1976.

SAWER, G.
Guide to Australian law for journalists, printers and publishers. 2ed. Melbourne U.P., 1968.

SIMONS, H.
The media and the law. Praeger, 1975 (USA).

SMITH, R.C.
Press law. Sweet & Maxwell, 1978 (Concise college texts).

SOBRABJEE, S.J.
The law of press censorship in India. Tripathi, 1976.

SPIERS, J. (ed.)
Underground and alternative press in Britain: a bibliographical guide. Harvester P., 1977.

SWINDLER, W.F.
Problems of law in journalism. 1955 repr. Greenwood, 1973 (USA).

UNESCO
Legislation for press, film and radio. 1951.

VAN GERPEN, M.
Privileged communication and the press: the citizens right to know versus the law's right to confidential news source evidence. Greenwood, 1979 (USA).

WASHINGTON CONFERENCE ON THE MEDIA AND THE LAW, Virginia, 1975.
The media and the law. 1976.

WHALE, J.
Journalism and government: a British view. S.Carolina U.P., 1972.

PRIMITIVE LAW

Texts

BARKUN, M.
Law without sanctions: order in primitive societies and the world community. Yale U.P., 1968.

DIAMOND, A.S.
The comparative study of primitive law. Athlone U.P., 1965.

DIAMOND, A.S.
Primitive law, past and present. Methuen, 1971.

GOITEIN, H.
Primitive ordeal and modern law. Allen & Unwin, 1923.

HARTLAND, E.S.
Primitive law. Methuen, 1924.

HOEBEL, E.A.
The law of primitive man: a study in comparative dynamics. Harvard U.P., 1954.

MAINE, Sir H.J.S.
Ancient law, its connection with the early history of society and its relation to modern ideas. Murray, 1930.

PRINTERS AND PUBLISHERS

See also Advertising; Copyright; Libel and Slander; Press Law.

Encyclopaedias

Halsbury's Laws of England. 4ed. see index vol.
Halsbury's Statutes of England. 3ed. mainly vol.19..

The Digest. vol.37 but see index vol.
Encyclopaedia of Court Forms in Civil Proceedings (Atkin). 2ed. see index vol.

Texts

CLARK, C.
Publishing agreements: a book of precedents. Allen & Unwin, 1980.

CLOUTMAN, B.M. & LUCK, F.W.
Law of printers and publishers. 2ed. Bale & Danielsson, 1949.

JONES, H.K.
Butterworths: history of a publishing house. Butterworths, 1980.

LINDEY, A.
Entertainment, publishing and the arts: agreements and the law. 2ed. Clark Boardman, 1980 (USA). 2 vols. looseleaf.

MUMBY, F. & NORRIE, I.
Publishing and bookselling. 5ed. Bowker, 1974 (USA).

SARNA, L.
Authors and publishers: agreements and legal aspects of publishing. Carswell, 1980 (Canada).

SAWER, G.
Guide to Australian law for journalists, printers and publishers. 2ed. Melbourne U.P., 1968.

TAYLOR, B.W. & MUNRO, R.J.
American law publishing 1860–1900: readings and bibliography. Glanville, 1982. 3 vols.

PRISONS

See also Detention Centres.

Encyclopaedias and periodicals

Statutes in Force. Group: Criminal Law.
Halsbury's Laws of England. 4ed. mainly vol.37.
Halsbury's Statutes of England. 3ed. mainly vol.25.
The Digest. vol.37 but see index vol.
Encyclopaedia of Court Forms in Civil Proceedings (Atkin). 2ed. see index vol.

British Journal of Criminology. 1960–
Criminal Law Review. 1954–
The Criminologist. 1966–
Howard Journal of Penology and Crime Prevention. 1921.
International Journal of Criminology and Penology. 1973–
Journal of Criminal Justice. 1973–
Journal of Criminal Law. 1936–

Texts

ADVISORY COUNCIL ON THE PENAL SYSTEM
The length of prison sentences: interim report. HMSO, 1977.

ADVISORY COUNCIL ON THE PENAL SYSTEM
Powers of the courts dependent on imprisonment: report. HMSO, 1977.

ADVISORY COUNCIL ON THE PENAL SYSTEM
Sentences of imprisonment: a review of maximum penalties (Younger & Serota). HMSO, 1978.

BERK, R.A. & ROSSI, P.H
Prison reform and states elites. Ballinger, 1977 (USA).

BOTTOMLEY, A.K.
Decisions in the penal process. Martin Robertson, 1973.

BOTTOMLEY, A.K.
Prison before trial. Bedford Square P., 1970.

BRIGGS, D.
In place of prison. M.T.Smith, 1975.

CROSS, R.
Punishment, prison and the public. Stevens, 1971 (Hamlyn lectures).

DAVIES, M.
Prisoners of society: attitudes and aftercare. Routledge, 1974.

DUFFEE, D.
Correctional policy and prison organization. Prentice-Hall, 1975 (USA).

FITGERALD, M.
Prisoners in revolt. Penguin, 1977.

FITZGERALD, M. & SIM, J.
British prisons. 2ed. Blackwell, 1982.

FOWLES, A.J.
Prison welfare: an account of an experiment at Liverpool. HMSO, 1978 (Home Office research studies).

FOX, Sir L.W.
The English prison and borstal systems. Routledge & Kegan Paul, 1952.

FOX, Sir L.W.
The modern English prison. Routledge & Kegan Paul, 1934.

FREEMAN, J. (ed.)
Prisons past and future. Heinemann, 1978.

HAWKINS, G.
The prison: policy and practice. Univ. Chicago P., 1976 (USA).

HOME OFFICE
Adjudication procedures in prisons: working party report. HMSO, 1975.

HOME OFFICE
Life sentence prisoners. HMSO, 1979 (Research studies).

HOME OFFICE
Prisons and the prisoner: the work of the prison service in England and Wales. HMSO, 1977.

HOME OFFICE
Report of the Committee of Inquiry into the United Kingdom Prison Services (May). HMSO, 1979 (Cmnd. 7673).

HOME OFFICE
Report on prison escapes and security (Mountbatten). HMSO, 1966 (Cmnd. 3175).

HOME OFFICE
Report on the work of the Prison Department. HMSO. Annual.

HOME OFFICE
Youth custody and supervision: a new sentence. HMSO, 1978 (Cmnd. 7406).

HOWARD, D.L.
The English prisons: their past and their future. Methuen, 1960.

HOWARD, D.L.
John Howard: prison reformer. Johnson, 1958.

HOWARD, J.
The state of prisons. 1ed. Dent, 1929 repr. with modern introduction by M Wright. Professional Books, 1977.

JARVIS, D.C.
Institutional treatment of the offender. McGraw-Hill, 1978 (USA).

JONES, H. and others
Open prisons. Routledge, 1977.

KERPER, H.B.
Legal rights of the convicted. West, 1974 (USA).

KING, R.D.
Albany: birth of a prison – end of an era. Routledge, 1977.

KLARE, H.J.
Anatomy of prison. Hutchinson, 1960.

McCONVILLE, S.
Use of imprisonment: essays on the changing state of English penal policy. Routledge, 1975.

NORTHERN IRELAND OFFICE
Report on the administration of the prison service, 1972–1976. HMSO, 1977.

PATERSON, Sir A.
Paterson on prisons: collected papers. F.Muller, 1951.

RUGGLES-BRISE, Sir E.
The English prison system. Macmillan, 1921.

SHORT, R.
Care of long term prisoners. Macmillan, 1979.

SINGER, R.G. & STATSKY, W.P.
Rights of the imprisoned. Bobbs-Merrill, 1974 (USA).

SMITH, A.D.
Women in prison: a study in penal methods. Stevens, 1962.

SPARKS, R.F.
Local prisons: the crisis in the English penal system. Heinemann, 1971.

WEBB, S.J. & WEBB, B.
English prisons under local government. Longmans, Green, 1922 repr. 1963.

WHITING, J.R.S.
Prison reform in Gloucestershire. Phillimore, 1975.

WOLFF, M.
Prison – the penal institutions of Britain. Eyre & Spottiswoode, 1967.

PRIVACY

See also Computers; Press Law.

Encyclopaedias and periodicals

Halsbury's Laws of England. 4ed. see index vols.

Law Quarterly Review. 1885–
Modern Law Review. 1937–

Texts

ASSOCIATION OF THE BAR OF THE CITY OF NEW YORK
Government databanks and rights of individuals. 1974.

BRECKENRIDGE, A.C.
Right of privacy. Nebraska U.P., 1970 (USA).

BUNYAN, T.
The history and practice of the political police in Britain. Quartet, 1977.

CLARKE, C.F.O.
Private rights and freedom of the individual. Ditchley Foundation, 1972.

COMMITTEE ON DATA PROTECTION
Report (Lindop). HMSO, 1978 (Cmnd. 7341).

COMMITTEE ON PRIVACY
Report (Younger). HMSO, 1972 (Cmnd. 5012).

DIAL, O.E. & GOLDBERG, E.M.
Privacy, security and computers: guidelines for municipal and other public information systems. Praeger, 1975 (USA).

DIONISOPOULOS, P.A. & DUCAT, C.R.
Right to privacy: essays and cases. West, 1976 (USDA).

ERNST, M.L. & SCHWARTZ, A.U.
Privacy: the right to be let alone. Greenwood, 1977 (USA).

FLAHERTY, D.H.
Privacy and government data banks: an international perspective. Mansell, 1979.

HEWITT, P.
Computers, records and the right to privacy. Input Two-nine, 1979.

HEWITT, P.
Privacy: the information gatherers. Input Two-nine, 1978.

HOME OFFICE
Computers: safeguards for privacy. HMSO, 1975 (Cmnd 6354).

HOME OFFICE
Computers and privacy. HMSO, 1975 (Cmnd. 6353).

HONDIUS, F.W.
Emerging data protection in Europe. North-Holland, 1975.

HYDE, H.M.
Privacy and the press. Butterworths, 1947.

JONES, M. (ed.)
Privacy. David & Charles, 1974.

LATIN, H.A.
Privacy: a selected bibliography and topical index of social science materials. Rothman, 1976 (USA).

McCLELLAN, G.S.
Right to privacy. Wilson, 1976.

MADGWICK, D. & SMYTHE, T.
The invasion of privacy. Pitman, 1974.

MANNING, M.
The Protection of Privacy Act: an analysis and commentary. Butterworths (Canada), 1974. supp. 1978.

ORGANISATION FOR ECONOMIC CO-OPERATION AND DEVELOPMENT
Digital information and privacy problem. 1971.

PEMBER, D.R.
Privacy and the press: the law, the mass media and the first amendment. Washington U.P., 1972 (USA).

PRIVY COUNCIL
Report of the Committee of Privy Councillors appointed to enquire into the interception of communications (Birkett). HMSO, 1957 (Cmnd. 283).

ROBERTSON, A.H.
Privacy and human rights. Manchester U.P., 1973.

ROWE, B.C. (ed.)
Privacy, computers and you. Nat. Computer Centre, 1972.

RULE, J.
Private lives and public surveillance. Allen Lane, 1973.

SHATTUCK, J.H.F.
Rights of privacy. Sweet & Maxwell, 1979.

SLOUGH, M.C.
Privacy, freedom and responsibility. C.C.Thomas, 1969 (USA).

SMITH, R.E.
Compilation of State and Federal laws on privacy. Privacy Journal, 1976 (USA).

VAN GERPEN, M.
Privileged communication and the press: the citizens right to know versus the law's right to confidential news source evidence. Greenwood, 1979 (USA).

WACKS, R.
Protection of privacy. Sweet & Maxwell, 1980.

PRIVATE ACTS
See also Statutes

Encyclopaedias

Halsbury's Laws of England. 4ed. see index vol.
The Digest. see index vol.

Texts

HUGHES, C.
The British statute book. Hutchinson, 1937.

ILBERT, Sir .P.
Legislative methods and forms. Oxford U.P., 1901.

INDEX to Local and Personal Acts, 1901–1947. HMSO, 1949 (Supplementary Index 1948–66).

LANDERS, T.
Procedure and practice relating to private bills in parliament. 1919.

WILLIAMS, O.C.
Historical development of private bill procedure and Standing Orders in the House of Commons. HMSO, 1948–9. 2 vols.

PRIVILEGE
See also Libel and Slander; Parliament.

Encyclopaedias and periodicals

Halsbury's Laws of England. 4ed. see index vols.
The Digest. see index vol.

Encyclopaedia of Court Forms in Civil Proceedings (Atkin). 2ed. see index vol.

Public Law. 1956–

Texts

ALLEN, Sir C.K.
Law and orders. 3ed. Sweet & Maxwell, 1965.

DE SMITH, S.A.
Judicial review of administrative action. 4ed. Sweet & Maxwell, 1980.

HEUSTON, R.F.V.
Essays on constitutional law. Sweet & Maxwell, 1964.

KEAN, M.
The Civil Evidence Act, 1968. Butterworths, 1969.

KEITH, A.B.
The privileges and rights of the Crown. Oxford U.P., 1935.

MAY, Sir T.E.
Parliamentary practice. 20ed. Butterworths, 1983.

PACHAURI, P.S.
Law of parliamentary privileges in U.K. and India. Tripathi, 1971.

WADE, E.C.S. & PHILLIPS, G.G.
Constitutional and administrative law. 9ed. Longman, 1977.

PRIVY CONCIL
See also Constitutional Law; Government.

Encyclopaedias

Statutes in Force. Group: Courts, House of Lords and Privy Council.
Halsbury's Laws of England. 4ed. vols.8, 30.
Halsbury's Statutes of England. 3ed. mainly vol.21.

The Digest. see index vol.
Encyclopaedia of Court Forms in Civil Proceedings (Atkin). 2ed. see index vol.

Texts

BENTWICH, N.
Practice of the Privy Council in judicial matters. 3ed. Sweet & Maxwell, 1937.

FITZROY, A.
The history of the Privy Council. Murray, 1928.

HOWELL, P.A.
The judicial committee of the Privy Council, 1833–1876: its origins, structure and development. Cambridge U.P., 1979.

LEADAM, I.S. & BALDWIN, J.F.
Great Britain, Privy Council. 1918 repr. Greenwood, 1968.

PRESTON, T.
Privy Council appeals. Eyre & Spottiswoode, 1900.

SAFFORD, F. & WHEELER, G.
Practice of the Privy Council in judical matters in appeals. Sweet & Maxwell, 1901.

WALLACE, W.R.
Cost in Privy Council appeals. Green, 1911.

PRIZE LAW

See also International Law; Navy; Sea, Law of; Shipping; War.

Encyclopaedias

Halsbury's Laws of England. 4ed. vol.37.
Halsbury's Statutes of England. 3ed. vols. 25, 29.
The Digest. vol.37.

Texts

BATY, T.
Prize law and continuous voyage. Stevens & Haynes, 1915.

COLOMBOS, C.J.
A treatise on the law of prize. 3ed. Longman, 1949.

HOLLAND, T.E.
Manual of naval prize law. Oxford U.P., 1888.

LLOYD's reports of prize cases. 1915–24. 10 vols. 2ed. series, 1940–57. 1 vol.

LUSHINGTON, G.
A manual of naval prize law. Butterworths, 1866.

ROSCOE, E.S.
Lord Stowell, his life and the development of English prize law. Constable, 1916.

ROSCOE, E.S. (ed.)
Reports of prize cases, 1745 to 1859. 1905 repr. Professional Books. 2 vols.

ROSCOE, E.S.
Studies in the history of the Admiralty Court and Prize Court. 2ed. Stevens, 1932 repr. Professional Books.

TREHERN, E.C.M. & GRANT, A.W. (eds.)
British and colonial prize cases, 1914–22. Stevens, 1916–22. 3 vols.

TWISS, Sir T.
Doctrine of continuous voyages as applied to contraband. Butterworths, 1877.

WILDMAN, R.
Law of search, and capture and prize. Benning, 1854.

PROBATE

See also Capital Transfer Tax; Death Duties; Estate Duty; Executors and Administrators; Revenue Law; Succession; Wills.

Encyclopaedias and periodicals

Statutes in Force. Group: Succession.
Halsbury's Laws of England. 4ed. vol.17.
Halsbury's Statutes of England. 3ed. see index vol.
The Digest. see index vol.
Encyclopaedia of Court Forms in Civil Proceedings (Atkin). 2ed. vol.32.
Encyclopaedia of Forms and Precedents. 4ed. see index vol.

Real Property, Probate and Trust Journal (USA). 1966–

Texts

AMROLIA, H.A.
Probate and administration in Kenya. Sweet & Maxwell, 1968.

BIGGS, A.K.
Probate: probate fees, intestacy tables, capital transfer tax scales. 7ed. Fourmat, 1984.

BIGGS, A.K. & ROGERS, A.P.
Probate practice and procedure. Fourmat, 1980.

FEENEY, T.G.
Canadian law of wills: construction. Butterworths (Canada), 1978.

FEENEY, T.G.
Canadian law of wills: probate. Butterworths (Canada), 1976.

GIBSON, A.
Gibson's probate: an explanatory treatise on the law and practice of probate. 18ed. Law Notes, 1975.

GRIFFITH, R.G.B.
Probate law and practice in Victoria. Sweet & Maxwell, 1965.

HEWITT, E.E. & BONGIORNO, B.D.
Administration and probate (Victoria). 2ed. Butterworths (Australia), 1971.

HOLLOWAY, D.R.Le B.
A probate handbook. 7ed. Oyez Longman, 1984.

HULL, R. and others
Probate practice, including common form and contentious proceedings. 3ed. Carswell, 1972 (Canada).

McCREDIE, L.
Administration of the estates of deceased persons in Victoria. Butterworths (Australia), 1979.

MAPLE, G.J.
The practitioners' probate manual. 21ed. Waterlow, 1979.

MASON, K. & HANDLER, L.G.
Wills, probate and administration service. Butterworths (Australia), 1975. Looseleaf.

MELLOWS, A.R.
Law of succession. 4ed. Butterworths, 1983.

SUPREME Court practice 1985. Sweet & Maxwell, 1984. 2 vols.

TRISTRAM, T.H. & COOTE, H.
Probate practice. 26ed. Butterworths, 1983.

WHICH?
Guide to wills and probate. new ed. Hodder, 1983.

WILCOCK, J.
Aspects of practical trust administration. 2ed. Insitute of Bankers, 1982.

WILLIAMS, Sir E.V., MORTIMER, H.C. & SUNNUCKS, J.H.G.
Executors, administrators and probate (16ed of Williams on executors, 4ed. of Mortimer on probate). Sweet & Maxwell, 1982.

WITCHELL, R.G.
Practice and procedure, vol.5. Non-contentious probate and private limited companies. 6ed. Oyez, 1977.

WRIGHT, R.R.
Uniform probate code practice manual. ALI-ABA, 1972 (USA).

PROBATION

See also Delinquency; Magistrates; Parole; Rehabilitation of Offenders.

Encyclopaedias and periodicals

Halsbury's Laws of England. 4ed. mainly vol.29.
Halsbury's Statutes of England. 3ed. vol.43.

The Digest. vol.14.
Encyclopaedia of Court Forms in Civil Proceedings (Atkin). 2ed. vol.21.
Encyclopaedia of Forms and Precedents. 4ed. vol.10.

British Journal of Criminology. 1960–
The Criminologist. 1966–
International Journal of Criminology. 1973–
Justice of the Peace. 1837–
Probation Journal. 1912–

Texts

BOCHEL, D.
Probation and after-care: its development in England and Wales. Scottish Academic P., 1976.

CARTER, R.M. & WILKINS, L.T.
Probation, parole and community corrections. 2ed. Wiley, 1976 (USA).

CARTLEDGE, G.C.
Probation in Europe. European Assembly for Probation & After Care: Nat. Assn. of Probation Officers, 1982.

COOKS, R.A.F.
Home Office approved probation hostels. Justice of the Peace, 1956.

DAVIES, M.
Financial penalties and probation. HMSO, 1971 (Home Office research studies).

DRESSLER, D.
Practice and theory of probation and parole. 2ed. Columbia U.P., 1970 (USA).

FIELDING, N.
Probation practice. Gower Pub. Co., 1984.

HARDING, J.
Employment and probation and after care service handbook. Rose, 1979.

HAXBY, D.
Probation: a changing service. Constable, 1978.

GRUNHUT, M.
Probation and mental treatment. Tavistock, 1963.

HOME OFFICE
Hostels for probationers. HMSO, 1970.

HOME OFFICE
Probation and after-care service in England and Wales. 5ed. HMSO, 1973.

HOME OFFICE
Probation research a preliminary report. HMSO, 1966.

HOME OFFICE
Probationers in their social environment. HMSO, 1975.

HOME OFFICE
Report on the probation service (Morison). HMSO, 1962 (Cmnd. 1650).

HOME OFFICE
Report on the work of the probation and after-care department. HMSO. Annual.

HOME OFFICE
Social enquiry reports and the probation service. HMSO, 1973.

HOME OFFICE
Social work in the environment: a study of one aspect of the probation service. HMSO, 1975.

HOME OFFICE
A survey of group work in the probation service. HMSO, 1966.

HOME OFFICE
Trends and regional comparisons in probation (England and Wales). HMSO, 1966.

HOWARD LEAGUE FOR PENAL REFORM
Between probation and custody: young adult offenders. 1975.

JARVIS, F.V.
Probation officers' manual. 3ed. Butterworths, 1980.

KILLINGER, G.G., KERPER, H.B. & CROMWELL, P.F.
Probation and parole in the criminal justice system. West, 1976 (USA).

KING, J.F.S. (ed.)
The probation and after-care service. 3ed.
Butterworths, 1969.

NEWMAN, C.L.
Sourcebook on probation, parole and
pardons. 3ed. C.C.Thomas, 1975 (USA).

ST. JOHN, J.
Probation: the second chance. Vista, 1961.

SMITH, A.B. & BERLIN, L.
Introduction to probation and parole. West,
1976 (USA).

PRODUCT LIABILITY

See also Contract; Fair Trading; Sale of Goods; Tort.

Periodicals

Common Market Law Review. 1963–
Consumer Affairs Bulletin. 1962–
Journal of Business Law. 1957–
Journal of Products Liability (USA). 1977–
Journal of World Trade Law. 1967–
Product Liability Bulletin. 1979–
Product Liability International. 1979–
Which? 1957–

Texts

ABBOTT, H.
Safe enough to sell? Design and product
liability. Design Council, 1980.

BORRIE, G. & DIAMOND, A.L.
The consumer, society and the law. 4ed.
Penguin, 1981.

BRAUN, J. & ALLEN, P.
Trading standards legislation: a
comparative directory of European
Community legislation. Inst. of Trading
Standards Admin., 1979.

CAVANAGH, S.W. & PHEGAN, C.S.
Product liability in Australia. Butterworths
(Australia), 1983.

CONSUMER COUNCIL
Justice out of reach. 1970.

DICKERSON, R.
Products liability and the food consumer.
Greenwood, 1972 (USA).

EPSTEIN, R.A.
Modern products liability law. Quorum,
1981 (USA).

EUROPEAN ASSOCIATION FOR
LEGAL AND FISCAL STUDIES
Product liability in Europe: businessmen's
guide to European company law. Kluwer,
1975.

FRUMER, L.R. & FRIEDMAN, M.I.
Products liability. Bender, 1960 (USA). 4
vols. Looseleaf.

HEPPELL, E.A.
Products liability insurance. 1967.

HURSH, R.D. & BAILEY, H.J.
American law of products liability. 2ed.
Lawyers Co-op., 1974. 6 vols.

INTERNATIONAL INSTITUTE FOR
THE UNIFICATION OF PRIVATE
LAW
Products liability. 1972. 3 vols.

IRVING, R.
Outline of the law of product liability and
consumer protection. Rose, 1980.

JANNER, G.
Product liability. Business Books, 1979.

LAMBERT, J.
Motor vehicle safety standards and product
liability. Economist Intelligence Unit, 1983.
3 vols. (In Japan; In the USA; In West
Germany, France and the UK).

LAW COMMISSION & SCOTTISH
LAW COMMISSION
Liability for defective products. HMSO,
1975 (Working paper no.64; Memorandum
no.20).

LAW COMMISSION & SCOTTISH
LAW COMMISSION
Liability for defective products. HMSO,
1977 (Law Com. no.82; Scot. Law Com.
no.45).

LLOYD'S OF LONDON
Product liability and insurance. Lloyd's,
1977.

MILLER, C.J.
Product liability and safety encyclopaedia.
Butterworths, 1978.

WADDAMS, S.M.
Products liability. 2ed. Carswell, 1980 (Canada).

WHINCUP, M.H.
Defective goods. Sweet & Maxwell, 1979.

PROHIBITION

See also Prerogative Orders.

Encyclopaedias

Halsbury's Laws of England. 4ed. vol.1, 11 and index.
Halsbury's Statutes of England. 3ed. see index vol.

The Digest. see index vol.
Encyclopaedia of Court Forms in Civil Proceedings (Atkin). 2ed. vol.14.

Texts

CURLEWIS, H.R. & EDWARD, D.S.
Law of prohibition, founded on the decision of the courts of England, Ireland, Australia, and New Zealand. 1911.

LLOYD, M.
Law of prohibition and practice of the same. 1849.

SHORTT, J.
Informations (Criminal and Quo Qarranto), mandamus, prohibitions, etc. Clowes, 1887.

PROSECUTIONS

See also Administration of Justice; Double Jeopardy; Indictments; Informations; Law Officers; Police.

Encyclopaedias and periodicals

Statutes in Force. Group: Criminal Law.
Halsbury's Laws of England. 4ed. see index vols.
Halsbury's Statutes of England. 3ed. see index vol.
The Digest. see index vol.

Criminal Law Review. 1954–
Journal of Criminal Justice. 1973–
Journal of Criminal Law. 1936–
Justice of the Peace. 1837–
The Magistrate. 1922–

Texts

ARCHBOLD, J.F.
Pleading, evidence and practice in criminal cases. 41ed. Sweet & Maxwell, 1982.

BROME, V.
Reverse your verdict: a collection of private prosecutions. Hamilton, 1971.

DEVLIN, Lord
The criminal prosecution in England. Oxford U.P., 1960.

EDWARDS, J.Ll.J.
The Law Officers of the Crown. Sweet & Maxwell, 1964 repr. 1977.

GROSMAN, B.A.
The prosecutor: an enquiry into the exercise of discretion. Univ. of Toronto P., 1970.

HARROLD, B. & WHITE, A.
Summary process and prosecution. Butterworths, 1974.

HOME OFFICE & LAW OFFICERS' DEPARTMENT
An independent prosecution service for England and Wales. HMSO, 1983 (Cmnd. 9074).

JUSTICE
Pre-trial criminal procedure: police powers and the prosecution process: a report. Stevens, 1979.

JUSTICE
The prosecution process in England and Wales. Stevens

LAW OFFICERS' DEPARTMENT
Proposed Crown prosecution service: the distribution of functions between the headquarters and local offices of the service. HMSO, 1984 (Cmnd. 9411).

MATHEW, Sir T.
The office and duties of the Director of Public Prosecutions. Athlone P., 1950.

MOODY, S.R. & TOMBS, J.
Prosecution in the public interest. Scottish Academic Press, 1982.

WILCOX, A.F.
The decision to prosecute. Butterworths, 1972.

PROSTITUTION

See also Criminal Law; Sexual Offences.

Encyclopaedias

Statutes in Force. Group: Criminal Law.
Halsbury's Laws of England. 4ed. vol.11.
Halsbury's Statutes of England. 3ed. vol.8.
The Digest. see index vol.

Texts

ACTON, W.
Prostitution, considered in its moral, social and sanitary aspects in London and other large cities and garrison towns. 1879 repr. Cass, 1972.

BRITISH SOCIAL BIOLOGY COUNCIL COMMITTEE ON PROSTITUTION
Women of the streets: sociological study. 1955.

CRIMINAL LAW REVISION COMMITTEE
Sixteenth report: prostitution in the street. HMSO, 1984 (Cmnd. 9329).

DEPARTMENTAL COMMITTEE ON HOMOSEXUAL OFFENCES AND PROSTITUTION
Report (Wolfenden). HMSO, 1956–57 (Cmnd. 247).

FLEXNER, A.
Prostitution in Europe. 1914 repr. Patterson Smith, 1969.

HONORE, T.
Sex law. Duckworth, 1978.

GLOVER, E.G.
The psychopathology of prostitution. 3ed. Inst. for Study & Treat. of Delinquency, 1969.

HOME OFFICE
Report of the Working Party on Vagrancy and Street Offences. HMSO, 1976.

JAMES, T.E.
Prostitution and the law. Heinemann, 1951.

NATIONAL COUNCIL FOR CIVIL LIBERTIES
Vagrancy, an archaic law: a memorandum of evidence to the Home Office Working Party on Vagrancy and Street Offences. 1975.

SANDFORD, J.
Prostitutes: portraits of people in the sexploitation business. Secker & Warburg, 1975.

SERENY, G.
Invisible children: child prostitution in America, Britain and Germany. Deutsch, 1984.

SION, A.
Prostitution and the law. Faber, 1977.

WILSON, P.
The sexual dilemma: abortion, homosexuality, prostitution and the criminal threshold. Queensland U.P., 1971.

WINN, D.
Prostitutes. Hutchinson, 1974.

PUBLIC ADMINISTRATION

See also Administrative Law; Civil Service.

Encyclopaedias and periodicals

Statutes in Force. Group: Local Government.
Halsbury's Laws of England. 4ed. see index vol.
The Digest. vol.38.

Local Government Review (as Justice of the Peace and Local Government Review, 1837–1970). 1971–
Public Administration. 1923–
Public Law. 1956–

Texts

APPLEBY, P.H.
Public administration for the welfare state. 1971.

BARBER, M.P.
Public administration. 3ed. Macdonald & Evans, 1982.

BARRINGTON, T.J.
Irish administrative system. 2ed. Institute of Public Administration, 1982.

BROWN, R.G.S. & STEEL, D.R.
The administrative process in Britain. 2ed. Methuen, 1979.

FESLER, J.W.
Public administration: theory and practice. Prentice-Hall, 1980.

FRASER, D.
Power and authority in the Victorian City. Blackwell, 1979.

FREEDMAN, J.
Crisis and legitimacy: understanding the American administrative process. Cambridge U.P., 1979.

GLADDEN, E.N.
The essentials of public administration. Cass, 1972. 2 vols.

GLADDEN, E.N.
An introduction to public administration. 2ed. Staples, 1952.

GOLEMBIEWSKI, R.T.
Public administration: readings in institution, processes, behaviour. 3ed. Rand McNally, 1976 (USA).

GRAVES, W.B.
Public administration in a democratic society. Greenwood, 1972 (USA).

GREENWOOD, J.R. & WILSON, D.J.
Public administration in Britain. Allen & Unwin, 1984

HAYNES, R.J.
Organization theory and local government. Allen & Unwin, 1980.

HENRY, N.
Public administration and public affairs. 2ed. Prentice-Hall, 1980.

ILCHMAN, W.F.
Comparative public administration and conventional wisdom. Sage, 1971.

NIGRO, F.A. & NIGRO, L.G.
Modern public administration. 4ed. Harper & Row, 1977.

SEN, B.
Diplomat's handbook of international law and public administration. Nijhoff, 1978.

SHARNASKY, I.
Public administration. Rand McNally, 1975 (USA).

UNITED NATIONS
Directory of national agencies and institutions for the improvement of public administration. 1973.

ZANDER, M.
Lawmaking process. Weidenfeld & N., 1980.

PUBLIC AUTHORITIES

See also By-Laws; Delegated Legislation.

Encyclopaedias

Halsbury's Laws of England. 4ed. see index vol.

Halsbury's Statutes of England. 3ed. see index vol.
The Digest. vol.38.

Texts

CHESTER, Sir D.N.
Nationalization of British industry, 1945–51. HMSO, 1976.

GALEOTTI, S.
Judicial control of public authorities in England and Wales. Stevens, 1954.

HAMSON, C.J. & PLUCKNETT, T.F.T.
Executive discretion and judicial control. Stevens, 1954 (Hamlyn lecture).

JUSTICE
The citizen and the public agencies. Stevens, 1976.

MITCHELL, J.D.B.
Contracts of public authorities. 1954 (L.S.E. thesis).

NATIONAL CONSUMER COUNCIL
Report No.1. Consumers and the nationalized industries. 1976.

PEIRSON, D.
Major public corporations: a statutory analysis. RIPA, 1974.

PREST, A.R. (ed.)
Public sector economics. Weidenfeld & N., 1968.

REES, M.
The public sector in the mixed economy. 1973.

ROBINSON, G.E.
Public authorities and legal liability. Univ.of London P., 1925.

SPERO, S.
Labour relations in British nationalized industry. New York U.P., 1971.

WEIDENBAUM, M.L.
The modern public sector: new ways of doing the government's business. 1970.

PUBLIC HEALTH

See also Burials and Cremation; Drains and Sewers; Food and Drugs; Gas; Housing; Local Government: Midwives; Nuisance; Pollution: Waters and Watercourses.

Encyclopaedias and periodicals

Statutes in Force. Group: Public Health.
Halsbury's Laws of England. 4ed. vol.38.
Halsbury's Statutes of England. 3ed. see index vol.
The Digest. vol.38
Encyclopaedia of Court Forms & Civil Proceedings (Atkin). 2ed. vol.32.
Encyclopaedia of Forms and Precedents. 4ed. vol.16.

Community Health. 1969–
Health Services Journal. 1946–
International Digest of Health Legislation.
Journal of Planning and Environmental Law. 1948–
Public Health. 1888–
Royal Society of Health Journal. 1955–

Texts

BELL, N.K.
Who decides? Conflicts of rights in health care. Humane Press, 1982 (USA).

BLACK, Sir D & THOMAS, G.
Providing for the health services. Croom Helm, 1978.

BLAMPAIN, J.
National health and insurance and health resources: the European experience. Harvard U.P., 1978 (USA).

BRAND, J.L.
Doctors and the state: British medical professional and government action in public health, 1870–1912. Johns Hopkins U.P., 1966.

BROWN, R.G.S.
Reorganizing the National Health Service: case study of administrative change. Methuen, 1979.

BURR, M.
Law and health visitors. B. Edsall, 1982.

BUTLER, J.R. & VAILE, M.S.B.
Health and health services: an introduction to health care in Britain. Routledge, 1984.

CATER, A.J.E.
Synopsis of public and health and social medicine. 3ed. Wright, 1979.

CIBA FOUNDATION
Human rights in health. 1974 (USA).

ECKSTEIN, H.
English health service. Harvard U.P., 1959.

ENCYCLOPAEDIA of public health law and practice. 2 vols. Sweet & Maxwell. Looseleaf.

FINCH, J.
Health services law. Sweet & Maxwell, 1981.

GARNER, J.F. & CROW, R.K.
Clear air – law and practice. 4ed. Shaw, 1976.

HANLON, J.J. & PICKETT, G.E.
Public health: administration and practice. 8ed. Mosby, 1983 (USA).

HEALTH AND SOCIAL SECURITY, DEPARTMENT OF
Prevention and health, everybody's business: a reassessment of public and personal health. HMSO, 1976.

HEALTH AND SOCIAL SECURITY, DEPARTMENT OF
State of the public health: report of the Chief Medical Officer. HMSO. Annual.

HEALTH SERVICE COMMISSIONER
Annual report. HMSO.

HENSEY, B.J.
Health services of Ireland. 3ed. Inst.of Public Admin., 1979.

LUMLEY, W.G.
Public health. 12ed. Butterworths. 12 vols. & supps.

McKINLAY, J.B.
Law and ethics in health care. M.I.T.P., 1982.

SCAMMELLS, B.
Administration of health and welfare services. Manchester U.P., 1971.

SCOTTISH HOME AND HEALTH DEPARTMENT
Community medicine in Scotland. HMSO, 1973.

SMOLENSKY, J.
Principles of community health. 4ed. Saunders, 1977.

WADE, Lord
Europe and the British health service. NCSS, 1974.

WEBSTER, C.
Environmental health law. Sweet & Maxwell, 1981.

WILSON, J.G.
Public health law in questions and answers. Lewis, 1972.

WISDOM, A.S.
Sewerage and sewage disposal. Rose, 1979.

WORLD HEALTH ORGANISATION
Evaluation of community health centres. 1972.

WORLD HEALTH ORGANISATION
International health regulations: a practical guide. 1975.

WORLD HEALTH ORGANISATION
Legislative action to combat smoking around the world: survey of existing legislation. 1977.

WORLD HEALTH ORGANISATION
Protection against ionizing radiations: a survey of current world legislation. 1972.

PUBLIC LENDING RIGHT

See also Libraries.

Periodicals

Author. 1881–
The Bookseller. 1933–
Library Association Record. 1899–

Texts

BROPHY, B.
Guide to public lending right. Gower Pub.Co., 1983.

EDUCATION AND SCIENCE, DEPARTMENT OF
Public lending right: an account of an investigation of technical and cost appeals. HMSO, 1975.

EDUCATION AND SCIENCE, DEPARTMENT OF
Public lending right: working party report. HMSO, 1972.

FINDALTER, R. (ed.)
Public lending right: a matter of justice. Deutsch, 1971.

MORRIS, R.J.B.
The public lending right handbook. Rose, 1980.

PUBLIC ORDER

See also Civil Rights and Liberties; Constitutional Law; Police.

Encyclopaedias and periodicals

Statutes in Force. Group: Criminal Law.
Halsbury's Laws of England. 4ed. vol.11.
Halsbury's Statutes of England. 3ed. vol.8.
The Digest. vol.14.

Criminal Law Review. 1954–
Journal of Criminal Justice. 1973–
Journal of Criminal Law. 1936–

Texts

BAUMANN, C.E.
Diplomatic kidnapping: a revolutionary tactic of urban terrorism. Nijhoff, 1973.

BROWNLIE, I.
Law of public order and national security. 2ed. Butterworths, 1981.

CALVERT, P.
A study of revolution. Oxford U.P., 1970.

CARTER, A.
The political theory of anarchism. Routledge, 1971.

CHAMBLISS, W.J. & SEIDMAN, R.
Law, order and power. 2ed. Addison-Wesley, 1982.

COBDEN TRUST
Incitement to disaffection. 1976.

DASH, S.
Justice denied: a challenge to Lord Widgery's report on "Bloody Sunday". NCCL, 1972.

DEAN-DRUMMOND, A.
Riot control. Royal United Services Inst., 1975.

FIELD, S. & SOUTHGATE, P.
Public disorder: a review of research and a study in one inner city area. HMSO, 1982 (Home Office research studies, no.72).

FRIEDLANDER, R.A.
Terrorism: documents of international and local control. Oceana, 1978 (USA).2 vols.

GURR, T.
Rogues, rebels and reformers: toward a theory of public order. Sage, 1976 (USA).

HALL, S. and others
Policing the crisis: mugging, the state and law and order. Macmillan, 1978.

HAMILTON, P.
Espionage and subversion in an industrial society. Hutchinson, 1967.

HAMILTON, P.
Espionage, terrorism and subversion: an examination and a philosophy of defence for management. Heims, 1979.

HOME OFFICE
The Brixton disorders, April 10–12, 1981: report of an inquiry (Scarman). HMSO, 1981 (Cmnd. 8427).

HOME OFFICE
Public disorder: a review of research and a study in one inner city area. HMSO, 1982 (Research studies).

HOME OFFICE
Red Lion Square disorders of June 15, 1974. Report of Inquiry by the Rt. Hon. Lord Justice Scarman. HMSO, 1975 (Cmnd. 5919).

HOME OFFICE
Report of the Committee appointed to consider authorised procedures for the interrogation of persons suspected of terrorism (Parker). HMSO, 1972 (Cmnd. 4901).

HOME OFFICE & SCOTTISH OFFICE
Review of the Public Order Act 1936 and related legislation. HMSO, 1980 (Cmnd. 7891).

LEACH, E.R.
Custom, law and terrorist violence. Edinburgh U.P., 1977.

McDOUGAL, M.S.
Studies in world public order. Yale U.P., 1960 (USA).

MATHER, T.C.
Public order in the age of the Chartists. Manchester U.P., 1959.

MATHEWS, A.S.
Law, order and liberty in South Africa. Juta, 1972.

MURPHY, J.G.
Civil disobedience and violence. Wadsworth, 1972.

MURTY, B.S.
Propaganda and world public order: the legal regulation of the ideological instrument of coercion. Yale U.P., 1968.

NORTHERN IRELAND GOVERNMENT
Disturbances in Northern Ireland: report of the Commission appointed by the Governor of Northern Ireland. HMSO, 1969 (Cmd. 532).

NORTHERN IRELAND GOVERNMENT
Report of the Advisory Committee on the Police in Northern Ireland (Hunt). HMSO, 1969 (Cmd. 535).

NORTHERN IRELAND GOVERNMENT
Violence and civil disturbances in Northern Ireland in 1969: report of the Tribunal of Inquiry (Scarman). HMSO, 1971 (Cmd. 566).

NORTHERN IRELAND OFFICE
Report of the enquiry into allegations against the security forces of physical brutality in Northern Ireland arising out of events on the 9th August 1971 (Compton). HMSO, 1971 (Cmnd. 4823).

NORTHERN IRELAND OFFICE
Report of the Law Enforcement Commission. HMSO, 1974 (Cmnd. 5627).

REPORT of the Tribunal appointed to enquire into the events on Sunday, Jan. 30, 1972 ... in Londonderry (Widgery). HMSO, 1972 (HC 220).

WILLIAMS, D.G.T.
Keeping the peace. Hutchinson, 1967.

WILLIAMS, W.L.
Intergovernmental military forces and world public order. Sijthoff, 1971.

WOODCOCK, G.
Anarchism. Penguin, 1962.

ZWIEBACH, B.
Civility and disobedience. Cambridge U.P., 1975.

PUBLIC RECORDS

Encyclopaedias

Halsbury's Laws of England. 4ed. see index vol.
Halsbury's Statutes of England. 3ed. see index vol.

Texts

LORD CHANCELLOR'S DEPARTMENT
Modern public records, selection and access: report of a committee (Wilson). HMSO, 1981 (Cmnd. 8204).

LORD CHANCELLOR'S OFFICE
Modern public records: government response to the report of the Wilson Committee. HMSO, 1982 (Cmnd. 8531).

PUNISHMENT

See also Capital Punishment; Corporal Punishment; Criminal Law; Parole; Prisons; Probation.

Encyclopaedias

Statutes in Force. Group: Criminal Law.

Periodicals

British Journal of Criminology. 1960–
The Criminologist. 1966–
Howard Journal of Penology and Crime Prevention. 1921–
International Journal of Criminology and Penology. 1973–
Prison Service Journal. 1960–

Texts

ADVISORY COUNCIL ON THE PENAL SYSTEM
Powers of the courts dependent on imprisonment: report. HMSO, 1977.

ADVISORY COUNCIL ON THE PENAL SYSTEM
Sentences of imprisonment: a review of maximum penalties (Younger & Serota). HMSO, 1978.

ANDENAS, J.
Punishment and deterrence. Michigan U.P., 1974 (USA).

BLOM-COOPER, L. (ed.)
Progress in penal reform. Oxford U.P., 1974.

BRIGGS, D.
In place of prison. M.T.Smith, 1975.

CAIRD, R.
A good and useful life: imprisonment in Britain today. Granada, 1974.

CEDERBLOM, J.B. & BLIZEK, W.L.
Justice and punishment. Ballinger:Wiley, 1977 (USA).

CROSS, R.
Punishment, prison and public. Stevens, 1972 (Hamlyn lectures).

ELLIOT, M.A.
Conflicting penal theories in statutory law. Univ. Chicago P., 1931.

EUROPEAN COMMITTEE ON CRIME PROBLEMS
Treatment of long-term prisoners. Council of Europe, 1977.

EWING, A.C.
Morality of punishment with some suggestions for a general theory of ethics. 1929 repr. Patterson Smith, 1970 (USA).

EZORSKY, G.
Philosophical perspectives of punishment. NYU Press, 1973 (USA).

FITZGERALD, P.J.
Criminal law and punishment. Oxford U.P., 1962.

GERBER, R.J. & McNANY, P.D. (eds.)
Contemporary punishment: views, explanations and justifications. Notre Dame, 1972.

GRUPP, S.E.
Theories of punishment. Indiana U.P., 1972 (USA).

HALL WILLIAMS, J.E.
English penal system in transition. Butterworths, 1970.

HART, H.L.A.
Punishment and responsibility: essays in the philosphy of law. Oxford U.P., 1968.

HAWKINS, K.
Deprivation of liberty for young offenders. Cambridge Univ. Inst.of Criminol., 1967.

HEATH, J.
Eighteenth century penal theory. Oxford U.P., 1963.

HIBBERT, C.
Roots of evil: social history of crime and punishment. Greenwood, 1978.

HINDE, R.S.E.
The British penal system, 1773–1950. Duckworth, 1951.

HODGKIN, E.C. & HODGKIN, N.I.
Involvement of the community in criminal justice and the treatment of offenders. Rose, 1978.

HOME OFFICE
Hostels for offenders. HMSO, 1979 (Research studies).

HOME OFFICE
Penal practice in a changing society: aspects of future development (England and Wales). HMSO, 1959 (Cmnd. 645).

HOME OFFICE
The sentence of the court: a handbook for courts on the treatment of offenders. 3ed. HMSO, 1978.

HOME OFFICE
Taking offenders out of circulation. HMSO, 1980 (Research studies).

HONDERICH, T.
Punishment: the supposed justifications. Penguin, 1976.

HOWARD LEAGUE FOR PENAL REFORM
Between probation and custody. 1975.

JOHNSTON, N.
Sociology of punishment and correction. 2ed. Wiley, 1970.

KLEINIG, J.
Punishment and desert. Nijhoff, 1973.

McCONVILLE, S.
The use of imprisonment: essays in the changing state of English penal policy. Routledge, 1975.

MASESTRO, M.T.
Cesare Beccaria and the origins of penal reform. Temple U.P., 1972.

MANNHEIM, H.
The dilemma of penal reform. Allen & Unwin, 1939.

MURPHY, J.G.
Punishment and rehabilitation. Wadsworth, 1974.

ROLPH, C.H.
Common sense and about crime and punishment. Gollancz, 1961.

ROSS, A.
On guilt, responsibility and punishment. Stevens, 1975.

STEYN, J.H.
Role of punishment in the maintenance of law and order. S.African Inst.Race Rel., 1972.

THOMAS, D.A.
The penal equation: derivations of the penalty structure of English criminal law. Cambridge Univ. Inst.of Criminol., 1978.

VEDDER, C.B. & KAY, B.A.
Penology: a realistic approach,. 4ed. C.C.Thomas, 1973 (USA).

WALKER, N.
Crime and punishment in Britain. 2ed. Edinburgh U.P., 1968.

WALKER, N.
Punishment, danger and stigma: morality of criminal justice. 2ed. Blackwell, 1982.

WOOTTON, Barbara, Baroness
Crime and penal policy. Allen & Unwin, 1978.

QUEEN'S BENCH

See also Courts.

Encyclopaedias

Halsbury's Laws of England. 4ed. see index vol.
Halsbury's Statutes of England. 3ed. see index vol.
The Digest. see index vol.
Encyclopaedia of Court Forms in Civil Proceedings (Atkin). 2ed. see index vol.

Texts

ARCHBOLD, J.F.
Practice of the Court of King's Bench, Common Pleas and Exchequer. 14ed. Sweet, 1885.

BLATCHER, M.
Court of King's Bench, 1450–1550; a study in self help. Athlone P., 1978.

BLAND, J.
The conduct of an action in the King's Bench Division. 2ed. Field & Queen, 1913.

CHITTY, T. & JACOB, I.H.
Queen's Bench Forms. 20ed. Sweet & Maxwell, 1969.

WILSHERE, A.N.M.
Outlines of procedure in the King's Bench Division. 4ed. Sweet & Maxwell, 1930 supp. 1934.

WONTNER, J.J.
Guide to High Court practice in the King's Bench and Chancery Divisions. Pitman, 1935.

RACE RELATIONS

See also Immigration.

Encyclopaedias and periodicals

Statutes in Force. Group: Rights of the Subject.
Halsbury's Laws of England. 4ed. vol.4.
Halsbury's Statutes of England. 3ed. vol.40.

Equals. 1975–
New Community. 1971–

Texts

ABBOTT, S. (ed.)
Prevention of racial discrimination in Britain. Oxford U.P., 1971.

BANTON, M.
Race relations. Tavistock, 1967.

BISKUP, P.
Not slaves, not citizens: the aboriginal problem in Western Australia, 1898–1954. Crane, 1973.

BURNEY, E. & WAINWRIGHT, D.
After four years: practical guide to the Race Relations Act: what it says and what it means. Runnymede Trust, 1972.

CLAIBORNE, L.
Race and law in Britain and the United States. Minority Rights Group, 1979.

COMMISSION FOR RACIAL EQUALITY
Reports. HMSO. 1977–

COMMUNITY RELATIONS COMMISSION
Digest of views on review of race relations legislation. HMSO, 1975.

DANIEL, W.W.
Racial discrimination in England: a P.E.P. Report. PEP, 1969.

EMPLOYMENT, DEPARTMENT OF
Take seven: race relations at work – the report on a survey into immigrant labour relations at seven English firms. HMSO, 1972.

FIELD, S.
Ethnic minorities in Britain: a study of trends in their position since 1961. HMSO, 1981 (Home Office research studies, no.68).

GORDON, P.
White law: racism in the police, court and prisons. Pluto, 1983.

HEINEMAN, B.W.
Politics of the powerless: a study of the campaign against racial discrimination. Oxford U.P., 1972.

HEPPLE, B.
Race, jobs and the law in Britain. Allen Lane, 1968.

HOME OFFICE
Police/immigrant relations in England and Wales. HMSO, 1973 (Cmnd. 5438).

HOME OFFICE
Race, crime and arrests. HMSO, 1979 (Research studies).

HOME OFFICE
Race relations research. HMSO, 1975.

HOME OFFICE
Racial discrimination. HMSO, 1975 (Cmnd. 6234).

HORRELL, M. and others
Survey of race relations in South Africa, 1972. Inst.of Race Rel., 1973.

HUMPHRY, D.
Police power and black people. Panther, 1972.

LAWRENCE, D.
Black migrants, white natives: a study of race relations in Nottingham. Oxford U.P., 1974.

LESTER, A. & BINDMAN, G.
Race and law. Longman, 1973.

LITTLE, K.
Negroes in Britain: a study of racial relations in English society. Routledge, 1972.

LUSTGARTEN, L.
Legal control of racial discrimination. Macmillan, 1980.

MACDONALD, I.A.
Race relations – the new law. Butterworths, 1977.

McKEAN, W.A.
Essays on race relations and the law in New Zealand. Sweet & Maxwell, 1971.

MASON, P.
Race relations. Oxford U.P., 1970.

PALLEY, C.
Constitutional law and minorities. Minority Rights Group, 1980.

REX, J.
Race, community and conflict: study of Sparkbrook. Oxford U.P., 1969.

REX, J.
Race relations in sociological theory. Oxford U.P., 1970.

RICHMOND, A.H.
Migration and race relations in an English city: a study in Bristol. Oxford U.P., 1973.

RIMMER, M.
Race and industrial conflict. Heinemann, 1972.

TUCK, M. & SOUTHGATE, P.
Ethnic minorities, crime and policing: a survey of the experiences of West Indians and whites. HMSO, 1981 (Home Office research studies, no.10).

TUSSMAN, J.
Supreme Court on racial discrimination. Oxford U.P., 1963 (USA).

UNESCO
Apartheid, its effects on education, science, culture and information. 2ed. 1972.

UNITED NATIONS
Elimination of Racial Discrimination Committee report. 1975.

UNITED NATIONS
Racial discrimination. 1971.

VIERDAG, E.W.
The concept of discrimination in international law. Nijhoff, 1973.

WALKER, D.J. & REDMAN, M.J.
Racial discrimination: a simple guide to the provisions of the Race Relations Act 1976. Shaw, 1978.

RADIO AND TELEVISION

See also Telecommunications

Encyclopaedias and periodicals

Halsbury's Laws of England. 4ed. see index vols.
Halsbury's Statutes of England. 3ed. see index vol.
Encyclopaedia of Forms and Precedents. 4ed. vol.22.

BBC Handbook.
Broadcast. 1959–
Commercial Televison and Radio Year Book. Annual.
Independent Broadcasting. 1974–
Journal of Media Law and Practice. 1980–
The Listener. 1929–

Texts

ARMSTRONG, M.
Broadcasting law and policy in Australia. Butterworths (Australia), 1981.

BRIGGS, A.
History of broadcasting in the United Kingdom. Oxford U.P., 1961–70. 3 vols.

ELLMORE, R.T.
Broadcasting law and regulation. TAB Books, US.: Foulsham, 1982.

HOME OFFICE
Report of the Committee on Broadcasting. HMSO, 1962 (Cmnd. 1753).

HOME OFFICE
Report of the Committee on Broadcasting Coverage. HMSO, 1974 (Cmnd. 5774).

HOME OFFICE
Report of the Committee on the Future of Broadcasting (Annan). HMSO, 1977 (Cmnd. 6735).

JAMES, A.
Media and the law. Brennan Pubns., 1977.

MOSTESHAR, S. & BATE, S.de B.
Satellite and cable television: international protection. Oyez Longman, 1984.

MUNRO, C.R.
Television censorship and the law. Saxon House, 1979.

OLSSON, H.R.
Legal and business problems of television and radio. Practising Law Inst., 1976 (USA).

POST OFFICE
Television Advisory Committee Report. 1967.

ROBERTSON, G. & NICOL, A.
Media law: the rights of journalists and broadcasters. Oxford U.P., 1984.

ROSS, L. & ETZIONI, A.
Economic and legal foundation of cable television. Sage, 1974 (USA).

SOCOLOW, W.A.
The law of radio broadcasting. 1939 repr. Hein, 1978. 2 vols.

UNESCO
Legislation for press, film and radio. 1951.

WASHINGTON CONFERENCE ON THE MEDIA AND THE LAW, Virginia. 1975.
The media and the law. 1976.

RAILWAYS

See also Carriers/Carriage of Goods; Transport.

Encyclopaedias

Statutes in Force. Groups: Railways, Canals and Pipelines; Transport.
Halsbury's Laws of England. 4ed. vol.38.
Halsbury's Statutes of England. 3ed. mainly vol.26.

The Digest. vol.38.
Encyclopaedia of Court Forms in Civil Proceedings (Atkin). 2ed. see index vol.
Encyclopaedia of Forms and Precedents. 4ed. see index vol.

Texts

BONNER, G.A.
British transport law by road and rail. David & Charles, 1973.

JAMES, L.
Law of the railway. Rose, 1980.

KAHN-FREUND, O.
The law of carriage by inland transport. 4ed. Stevens, 1965.

LESLIE, A.
The law of transport by railway. 2ed. Sweet & Maxwell, 1928.

LIPSETT, L.R. & ATKINSON, T.J.D.
The law of carriage by railway in Great Britain and Ireland. Pitman, 1928.

RIDLEY, J.G.
The law of the carriage and goods by land, sea and air. 4ed. Shaw, 1975.

TRANSPORT, DEPARTMENT OF
International regulations concerning the carriage of dangerous goods by rail (RID). 7ed. HMSO, 1978.

WILLIAMS, E.E.G.
Modern railway law. Stevens, 1928.

RAPE

See also Criminal Law; Sexual Offences.

Encyclopaedias and periodicals

Statutes in Force. Group: Criminal Law.
Halsbury's Laws of England. 4ed. vol.11.
Halsbury's Statutes of England. 3ed. vol.8.
The Digest.
Encyclopaedia of Court Forms in Civil Proceedings (Atkin). 2ed. vol.16.

Criminal Law Review. 1954–
Journal of Criminal Justice. 1973–
Journal of Criminal Law. 1936–

Texts

AMIR, M.
Patterns in forcible rape. Univ.Chicago P., 1971 (USA).

BAILEY, F.L. & ROTHBLATT, H.B.
Crimes of violence: rape and other sex crimes. Lawyers Co-op., 1973 (USA).

BROWNMILLER, S.
Against our will: men, women and rape. Secker & Warburg, 1975.

CHAPPELL, D., GEIS, R. & GEIS, G.
Forcible rape: the crime, the victim and the criminal. Columbia U.P., 1977 (USA).

COOTE, A. & GILL, T.
The rape controversy: the law, the myth, the facts, changes that are needed, and what to do if it happens to you. NCCL, 1975.

CRICK, B.
Crime, rape and gin. Elek:Pemberton, 1974.

HOME OFFICE
Report of the Advisory Group on the law of rape (Heilbron). HMSO, 1975 (Cmnd. 6352).

KEMMER, E.J.
Rape and rape-related issues: an annotated bibliography. Garland, 1977 (USA).

MACDONALD, J.M.
Rape: offenders and their victims. Nelson, 1971 (USA).

RATING AND VALUATION

See also Local Government.

Encyclopaedias and periodicals

Statutes in Force. Group: Rating.
Halsbury's Laws of England. 4ed. mainly vol.39.
Halsbury's Statutes of England. 3ed mainly vol.27.
The Digest. vol.38.
Encyclopaedia of Court Forms in Civil Proceedings (Atkin). 2ed. vol.33.
Encyclopaedia of Forms and Precedents. 4ed. vol.16.

Conveyancer and Property Lawyer. 1936–
Estates Gazette. 1858–
Journal of Planning and Environment Law. 1948–
Rating and Valuation Reporter (as Rating and Income Tax, 1924). 1961–
Rating Appeals (as De Rating and Rating Appeals, 1930–1961). 1962–
Ryde's Rating Cases, 1956–
The Valuer. 1932–

Texts

ADAMSON, A.V.
The valuation of company shares and businesses. 6ed. Law Book Co., 1980 (Australia).

AMIES, F.A.
Law of rating. Rating Pub., 1965.

AMIES. F.A. & BOOTH, E.R.
The law and practice of valuations for rating. 4ed. Butterworths, 1947.

ARMOUR, S.B.
Valuation for rating. 4ed. Green, 1971.

BEAN, P.R. & LOCKWOOD, A.
Rating valuation practice. 6ed. Stevens, 1969.

CARTER, R.
Valuation of land for estate duty. 2ed. Estates Gazette, 1961.

COLE, V.L.
Valuation of business, shares and property. Butterworths (Australia), 1980.

EMERY, R. & WILKES, H.M.
Principles and practice of rating valuation. 4ed. Estates Gazette, 1984.

ENVIRONMENT, DEPARTMENT OF
Report of the Committee on the Rating of Plant and Machinery (McNairn). HMSO, 1972.

FARADAY, P.M.
Rating. 5ed. Estates Gazette, 1951.

FORDHAM, C.M.
Valuation of agricultural holdings for rent.
6ed. RICS, 1974.

GIBSON, H. & JACKSON, E.
Valuation of plant and machinery for rating.
Estates Gazette, 1972.

GLADWIN, F.H.
Practical guide to valuation for rating. 3ed.
Shaw, 1973.

GUEST, C.W.G.
Law of valuation in Scotland. 2ed. Hodge,
1954.

HEPWORTH, N.P.
Finance of local government. 6ed. Allen &
Unwin, 1981.

HOUSING AND LOCAL
GOVERNMENT, MINISTRY OF
Distribution of rateable values between
different classes of property in England and
Wales. HMSO, 1963.

HOUSING AND LOCAL
GOVERNMENT, MINISTRY OF
Rating of site values: report of the
Committee of Enquiry (Simes). HMSO,
1952.

INSTITUTE OF MUNICIPAL
TREASURERS AND ACCOUNTANTS
Rating Act. 1966.

JOHNSON, T.A. (ed.)
Current aspects of law and valuation.
Coll.of Estate Management, 1969.

KARSLAKE, H.H.
Your new rates. Oyez, 1972.

KARSLAKE, H.H. & NICHOLLS, A.D.
Industrial valuations. Estates Gazette, 1974.

LAMB, P.
Guide to rating practice and procedure.
3ed. Estates Gazette, 1963.

LAWRENCE, D.M.
Valuation of land, houses and buildings.
6ed. Estates Gazette, 1972.

LEACH, W.A.
Rating valuation and appeals. 3ed. Estates
Gazette, 1967.

McVEAGH, J.P.
Land valuation law in New Zealand. 7ed.
Butterworths (NZ), 1978.

MEACHER, M.
Rate rebates: a study of the effectiveness of
means tests. CPAG, 1973.

MUSTOE, N.E.
Complete valuation practice. 5ed. Estates
Gazette, 1960.

POOLE, R. & POOLE, P.M.
Valuation of pipeline basements and
wayleaves. Estates Gazette, 1963.

RYDE, W.C.
Rating: law and practice. 13ed.
Butterworths, 1976 supp. 1984.

WESTBROOK, R.W.
Valuation of licensed premises. 2ed. Estates
Gazette, 1983.

WESTBROOK, R.W.
Valuer's casebook of approved valuation.
vol. 1. Estates Gazette, 1968; vol.2. Estates
Gazette, 1974.

WRIGHT, H.J.
Rating law and practice. Rating & Valuation
Assoc., 1975.

REAL PROPERTY

See also Conveyancing; Copyhold: Deeds; Land; Land Registration; Land Tenure; Landlord and Tenant; Leases; Mortgages; Personal Property; Possession; Powers; Restrictive Covenants; Succession; Title; Vendor and Purchaser

Encyclopaedias and periodicals

Statutes in Force. Group: Property,
England & Wales.
Halsbury's Laws of England. 4ed. vol.39.
Halsbury's Statutes of England. 3ed. see
index vol.
The Digest. vol.38.

Conveyancer and Property Lawyer. 1936–

Estates Gazette. 1858–
Estates Gazette Digest of Land and
Property Cases. Annual.
Journal of Planning and Environment Law.
1948–
Property and Compensation Reports.
1950–
Property and Investment Review. 1970–
Property Law Bulletin. 1980–

REAL PROPERTY

Texts

BURGESS, R.
Perpetuities in Scots Law. Green, 1979.

CAMPBELL, D.
Legal aspects of alien acquisitions of real property. 1980.

CHALLIS, H.W.
Law of real property. 3ed. Butterworths, 1911 repr. 1963.

CHERMATZ, J.P. & DAGGETT, H.S. (eds.)
Comparative studies in community property law. Greenwood, 1977.

CHESHIRE, G.C.
The modern law of real property. 13ed. Butterworths, 1982.

CRACKNELL, D.G.
Basic property Acts and cases. B.Rose, 1982.

CREAN, M.J.
Principles of real estate analysis: law, finance appraisal and investment. Van Nostrand Reinhold, 1979.

CRIBBET, J.E.
Principles of the law of property. 2ed. Foundation, 1974 (USA).

CROFT, C.E.
The mortgagee's power of sale. Butterworths (Australia), 1980.

DAVIES, K.
Law of property in land. Estates Gazette, 1979.

DENMAN, D.R.
Place of property: new recognition of the function and form of property rights in land. Geographical Pubns., 1978.

DOBRY, G. (ed.)
Land development encyclopaedia. Butterworths, 1976. Looseleaf.

EASTWOOD, R.A.
Principles of the law of real property; founded upon the 24th edition of Williams. Sweet & Maxwell, 1933.

EUROPEAN COMMUNITIES
Law of property in the European community. 1977.

FORBES, Sir H.H.V.
Real property law. 2ed. Estates Gazette, 1974.

GREER, D.S. & MITCHELL, V.A.
Compensation for criminal damage to property. SLS Legal Pubns. (NI), 1984.

HARGREAVES, A.D.
An introduction to the principles of land law. 4ed. Sweet & Maxwell, 1963.

HARLAND, D.J.
The law of minors in relation to contracts and property. Butterworths (Australia), 1974.

HARVEY, B.W.
Settlements of land. Sweet & Maxwell, 1973.

HARWOOD, M.
English land law. 2ed. Sweet & Maxwell, 1982.

JACKSON, D.C.
Principles of property law. Sweet & Maxwell, 1967 (Australia).

LAWSON, F.H. & RUDDEN, B.
Introduction to the law of property. 2ed. Oxford U.P., 1982.

LINDGREN, K.E.
Time in the performance of contracts especially contracts for the sale of property. Butterworths (Australia), 1976.

MACPHERSON, C.B. (ed.)
Property: mainstream and critical positions. Blackwell, 1978.

MEGARRY, R.E.
A manual of the law of real property. 6ed. Sweet & Maxwell, 1982.

MEGARRY, R.E. & WADE, H.W.R.
The law of real property. 5ed. Sweet & Maxwell, 1984.

MORRIS, J.H.C. (ed.)
Sweet & Maxwell's property statutes. 4ed. Sweet & Maxwell, 1982.

RABIN, E.H.
Fundamentals of modern real property law. Foundation, 1974 (USA).

RADCLIFFE, G.R.Y.
Real property law. 2ed. Oxford U.P., 1938.

RIDDALL, J.G.
Introduction to land law. 3ed. Butterworths, 1983.

RIVINGTON, H.G.
Law of property in land. 5ed. Law Notes, 1959.

ROYAL INSTITUTION OF CHARTERED SURVEYORS
Current problems in property law: Blundell Memorial Lectures. RICS, 1977.

SACKVILLE, R. & NEAVE, M.A.
Property law: cases and materials. 3ed. Butterworths (Australia), 1981.

SINCLAIR, A.M.
Introduction to real property law. Butterworths (Canada), 1969.

SMITH, T.B.
Property problems in sale. Sweet & Maxwell, 1979.

TOPHAM, A.F.
Real property. 11ed. Butterworths, 1969.

WALDRON, J.K.
Guidelines on real property: current Irish law. Waldron, 1972.

WALKER, D.M.
Principles of Scottish private law. Vol.3, book 5: law of property. Oxford U.P., 1983.

WILLIAMS, J.
Principles of the law of real property. 24ed. Sweet & Maxwell, 1926.

WYLIE, J.C.W.
Irish land law. Professional Books, 1975 supp. 1981.

ZIADEH, F.
Property law in the Arab World. Graham & Trotman, 1978.

RECEIVERS

See also Bankruptcy; Banks and Banking; Debts and Debtors; Liquidators.

Encyclopaedias

Statutes in Force. Group: Bankruptcy and Deeds of Arrangement.
Halsbury's Laws of England. 4ed. vol.39.
Halsbury's Statutes of England. 3ed. vol.27.
The Digest. vol.39.

Encyclopaedia of Court Forms in Civil Proceedings (Atkin). 2ed. vol.33.
Encyclopaedia of Forms and Precedents 4ed. see index vol.

Texts

BLANCHARD, P.
The law of company receiverships in Australia and New Zealand. Butterworths (Australia), 1982.

COMPTON, H.F. & WHITEMAN, R.
Receivership under the Mental Health Act, 1959. 5ed. Oyez, 1976 (Practice notes).

GRIFFITHS, O.
The law relating to bankruptcy, deeds of arrangement, receiverships and trusteeships. 8ed. Macdonald & Evans, 1967.

INSTITUTE OF CHARTERED ACCOUNTANTS
Receivership: a practitioner's guide. 1975.

KERR, W.W.
The law and practice as to receivers appointed by the High Court of Justice or out of court. 15ed. Sweet & Maxwell, 1978.

PARSONS, G.T.E. & RATFORD, W.R.
Employee's rights in receiverships and liquidations. Tolley, 1980.

RANKING, D.F. and others
The rights and duties of liquidators, trustees and receivers. 22ed. Pitman, 1955.

REDUNDANCY

See also Employment Law

Encyclopaedias and periodicals

Statutes in Force. Group: Employment.
Halsbury's Laws of England. 4ed. vol. 16.
Halsbury's Statutes of England. 3ed. vol. 12.
Encyclopaedia of Court Forms in Civil Proceedings (Atkin). 2ed. see index vol.

Encyclopaedia of Forms and Precedents. 4ed. vol. 20.

Knight's Industrial Reports. 1966–1974.
Managerial Law. 1975–

Texts

ARMSTRONG, M.
Employer's action guide to handling redundancy procedures. Kogan Page, 1977.

EGAN, B.
Dismissals: the complete practical guide. New Commercial Pub. Co., 1977.

FARNDALE, W.A.J. & COOPER, A.J.
Law on redundancy payments: with special reference to the National Health Service. Ravenswood, 1971.

FOX, R.
Payments on termination of employment. 2ed. Oyez Longman, 1984.

FULBROOK, J.
Admininstrative justice and the unemployed. Mansell, 1978.

GRUNFELD, C.
The law of redundancy. 2ed. Sweet & Maxwell, 1980.

HILL, M
Policies for the unemployed: help or coercion? CPAG, 1974.

MESHER, J.
Compensation for unemployment. Sweet & Maxwell, 1976.

OFFICE OF POPULATION CENSUSES AND SURVEYS
Effects of the Redundancy Payments Act. HMSO, 1971.

PERRITT, H.H.
Employee dismissal: law and practice. Wiley, 1984.

RIDEOUT, R.W.
Reforming the Redundancy Payments Act. Inst. of Personnel Management, 1969.

RUDINGER, E.
Dismissal, redundancy and job hunting. Consumers' Assoc., 1976.

SAMUELS, H. & STEWART-PEARSON, N.
Redundancy payments. 2ed. Knight, 1970.

WHINCUP, M.H.
Redundancy and the law. Pergamon, 1967.

REFUGEES

See also International Law.

Encyclopaedias and periodicals

Halsbury's Laws of England. 4ed. vol. 18 and index vol.

British Yearbook of International Law. 1920–

International and Comparative Law Quarterly. 1952–

Yearbook of World Affairs. 1947–

Texts

AIBONI, S.A.
Protection of refugees in Africa. Almquist & Wiksell, 1979.

D'SOUZA, F.
Refugee dilemma: international recognition and acceptance. 2ed. Minority Rights Group, 1983.

GOODWIN-GILL, G.S.
Refugee in international law. Oxford U.P., 1983.

GRAHL-MADSEN, A.
The status of refugees in international law. Vol.1: Refugee character. Sijthoff, 1966.
Vol.2 Asylum, entry and sojourn. Sijthoff, 1972.

HOLBORN, L.W.
The international refugee organisation. Oxford U.P., 1956.

HOLBORN, L.W.
Refugees – a problem of our time: the work of the United Nations High Commissioner for Refugees, 1951–72. Scarecrow P., 1975. 2 vols.

PICTET, J.S.
Humanitarian law and the protection of war victims. Sijthoff, 1975.

SCHECTMAN, J.B.
The refugee in the world: displacement and integration. Barnes, 1962 (USA).

SIMPSON, J.H.
The refugee problem. Oxford U.P., 1939.

THOMASHEFSKY, J.M.
The development of international protection of refugees. New York U.P., 1949 (USA).

REHABILITATION OF OFFENDERS

See also Parole; Probation.

Encyclopaedias and periodicals

Halsbury's Laws of England. 4ed. vol. 11 and index.
Halsbury's Statutes of England. 3ed. vol.44.
British Journal of Criminology. 1960–
Criminal Law Review. 1954–
International Journal of Criminology and Penology. 1973–
Journal of Criminal Justice. 1973–
Journal of Criminal Law. 1936–

Texts

BARR, H.
Role of the volunteer: a reappraisal. NACRO, 1972.

BARR, H.
Volunteers in prison after-care. NACRO, 1971.

BEAN, P.
Rehabilitation and deviance. Routledge, 1976.

BOCHEL, D.
Probation and after-care: its development in England and Wales. Scottish Academic P., 1976.

DAVIES, M.
Prisoners of society: attitudes and after-care. Routledge, 1974.

GLICKMAN, M.J.A.
From crime to rehabilitation. Gower, 1983.

HARRIS, B.
A guide to the Rehabilitation of Offenders Act, 1974. Rose, 1976.

HOME OFFICE
A guide to the Rehabilitation of Offenders Act 1974. HMSO, 1975.

HOME OFFICE
Social work in prison: an experiment in the use of extended contact with offenders. HMSO, 1975.

HOME OFFICE
Wiping the slate clean. HMSO, 1975.

HOWARD, D.L.
Education of offenders. Cambridge Inst.of Criminol., 1972.

JUSTICE
Living it down: the problem of old convictions. Stevens, 1972.

KING, J.F.S. (ed.)
The probation and after-care service. 3ed. Butterworths, 1969.

MURPHY, J.G.
Punishment and rehabilitation. Wadsworth, 1974.

NATIONAL ASSOCIATION FOR THE CARE AND RESETTLEMENT OF OFFENDERS
Manual and directory. 1967.

NEW Careers: a handbook of training and employment opportunities for prisoners and ex-prisoners. Pillory P., 1972.

WALLER, I.
Men released from prison. Toronto U.P., 1974.

WRIGHT, M.
Making good: prisons, punishment and beyond. Hutchinson, 1982.

RELIGION

See also Ecclesiastical Law.

Texts

BURSTEIN, A.
Religion, cults and the law. 2ed. Oceana, 1980 (USA).

HARDING, A.L.
Religion, morality and law. Southern Methodist, 1956 (USA).

ROBILLIARD, St.J.A.
Religion and the law. Manchester U.P., 1984.

REMAND

See also Magistrates

Encyclopaedias and periodicals

Halsbury's Laws of England. 4ed. see index vol.
Halsbury's Statutes of England. 3ed. vol.21.
The Digest. vol.14.

Justice of the Peace. 1837–
The Magistrate. 1922–

Texts

BOTTOMLEY, A.K.
Prison before trial: a study of remand decisions in Magistrates' Courts. Bedford Square P., 1970.

GIBBENS, T.C.N. and others
Medical remands in the criminal court. Oxford U.P., 1977.

GIBSON, E.
Time spent awaiting trial. HMSO, 1960 (Home Office Research Unit report).

KING, M.
Bail or custody. 2ed. Cobden Trust, 1973.

HOWARD LEAGUE FOR PENAL REFORM
No brief for the dock: report on custody during trial. 1977.

SOOTHILL, K.
Medical remands in Magistrates' Courts. 1974.

REMEDIES

See also Prerogative Orders

Encyclopaedias

Halsbury's Laws of England. 4ed. vol.9.

Texts

LAW COMMISSION
Remedies in administrative law. HMSO, 1971 repr. 1977 (Working paper no.40).

LAW COMMISSION
Report on remedies in administrative law. HMSO, 1976 (Law Com. no.73).

LAWSON, F.H.
Remedies of English Law. 2ed. Butterworths, 1980.

WALKER, D.M.
The law of civil remedies in Scotland. Green, 1975.

REMINISCENCES

COMYN, J.
Irish at law: selection of famous and unusual cases. Sphere, 1983.

DENNING, Lord
Family story. Butterworths, 1982.

DENNING, Lord
Landmarks in the law. Butterworths, 1984.

HAWKES, C.P.
Bench and Bar in the saddle. Methuen, 1928.

HAWKES, C.P.
Chambers in the Temple, comments and conceits "in camera". Methuen, 1930.

HAWKES, C.P.
Heyday, a salad of memories and impressions. Methuen, 1933.

HEALY, M.
The old Munster circuit. 1939 repr. Wildy, 1977.

HINE, R.L.
Confessions of an un-common attorney. Dent, 1945.

HINE, R.L.
Relics of an un-common attorney. Dent, 1951.

MEGARRY, Sir R.E.
Miscellany-at-law: a diversion for lawyers and others. Sweet & Maxwell, 1955.

MEGARRY, Sir R.E.
A second miscellany-at-law. Sweet & Maxwell, 1973.

RENT

See also Landlord and Tenant.

Encyclopaedias and periodicals

Statutes in Force. Group: Landlord and Tenant.
Halsbury's Laws of England. 4ed. see index vol.
Halsbury's Statutes of England. 3ed. vol.18.
The Digest. vol.31.
Encyclopaedia of Court Forms in Civil Proceedings (Atkin). 2ed. vol.24.
Encyclopaedia of Forms and Precedents. 4ed. see index vol.

Conveyancer and Property Lawyer. 1936–
Estates Gazette. 1858–
Estates Gazette Digest of Land and Property Cases. Annual.
Legal Action (formerly L.A.G. Bulletin). 1973–

Texts

ADAMS, B.
The study of rent tribunal cases in London. Centre for Environmental Studies, 1971.

ALDRIDGE, T.M.
Housing Act, 1980: a practical guide. 8ed. Oyez, 1980.

ALDRIDGE, T.M.
Rent control and leasehold enfranchisement. 7ed. Oyez, 1977.

ARDEN, A.
Housing security and rent control. Sweet & Maxwell, 1978.

BEIRNE, P.
Fair rent and legal fiction: housing rent legislation in a capitalist society. Macmillan, 1977.

BERNSTEIN, R. & REYNOLDS, K.
Handbook of rent review. Sweet & Maxwell, 1981. Looseleaf.

CLARKE, D.N. & ADAMS, J.E.
Rent reviews and variable rents. Oyez, 1981.

ENVIRONMENT, DEPARTMENT OF THE
Preventing rent arrears. HMSO, 1983.

ENVIRONMENT, DEPARTMENT OF THE
The review of the Rent Acts: a consultative paper. HMSO, 1977.

FARRAND, J.T. & ARDEN, A.
The Rent Acts and regulations (amended and annotated). 2ed. Sweet & Maxwell, 1981.

FIELD-FISHER, T.G., IBBOTSON, S. & ROYDHOUSE, E.
Rent regulation and control. Butterworths, 1967.

HARVEY, A.
Remedies for rent arrears: case studies in the London Borough of Camden. Shelter, 1979.

HAYEK, F.A.
Verdict on rent control: essays on the economic consequences of political action to restrict rents in five countries. Inst.of Economic Affairs, 1972.

MADDOCKS, B.C. & MALONE, M.
Renting business premises. Ross Anderson Pubns., 1984.

MAGNUS, S.W.
The Rent Act, 1968. Butterworths, 1969.

MAGNUS, S.W.
Rent Act, 1977. Butterworths, 1978.

MEGARRY, R.E.
Rents Act 1967–1970. 10ed. Sweet & Maxwell. 3 vols.

NEVITT, A.A.
The nature of rent controlling legislation in the United Kingdom. Centre for Environmental Studies, 1970.

NORTHERN IRELAND DEPARTMENT OF HOUSING, LOCAL GOVERNMENT AND PLANNING
Rent restriction law of Northern Ireland: report of the Committee on Rent Restriction Law (Porter). HMSO, 1975.

PROPHET, J.
Fair Rents: a practical guide to the statutory regulation of rents of residential tenancies etc. 2ed. Shaw, 1979.

ROSSI, H.
Guide to the Rent (Agriculture) Act, 1976. Shaw, 1977.

ROSSI, H.
Guide to the Rent Act, 1974. Shaw, 1974.

SCOTTISH DEVELOPMENT DEPARTMENT
Rent rebates for council tenants: report. HMSO, 1970.

STAPLETON, T.B.
Estate management practice. Estates Gazette, 1981.

RENTCHARGES

See also Conveyancing.

Encyclopaedias

Statutes in Force. Group: Property, England & Wales. Sub-Group 1.
Halsbury's Laws of England. 4ed. vol.39.
Halsbury's Statutes of England. 3ed. see index vol.

The Digest. vol.39.
Encyclopaedia of Court Forms in Civil Proceedings (Atkin). 2ed. vol.33.
Encyclopaedia of Forms and Precedents. 4ed. vol.17.

Texts

EASTON, H.C.
Rentcharge conveyancing. Sweet & Maxwell, 1960.

EASTON, J.M.
Law of rentcharges. 2ed. Sweet & Maxwell, 1971.

ENVIRONMENT, DEPARTMENT OF THE
Apportionment of rents. HMSO, 1978.

ENVIRONMENT, DEPARTMENT OF THE
Redemption of rentcharges. HMSO, 1978.

LAW COMMISSION
Transfer of land: rentcharges. HMSO, 1973 repr. 1977 (Working paper no.49).

LAW COMMISSION
Transfer of land: report on rentcharges. HMSO, 1975 (Law Com. no.68).

LUMLEY, W.G.
Law of annuities of rent charges. Shaw, 1833.

MILLARD, P.W.
Law relating to tithe rent charge and other payments in lieu of tithe. 3ed. Butterworths, 1937.

RUOFF, T.B.F.
Rent charges in registered conveyancing. Sweet & Maxwell, 1961.

RES JUDICATA

See also Estoppel; Judgments.

Encyclopaedias

Halsbury's Laws of England. 4ed. vol.16.

Texts

BOWER, G.S. & TURNER, A.K.
The doctrine of res judicata. 2ed. Sweet & Maxwell, 1969.

CANEY, L.R.
Treatise on the law relating to novation, including delegation compromise and res judicata. 2ed. Juta, 1973 (South Africa).

CHAND, H.
The law of res judicata. 1894.

RESTITUTION

See also Criminal Injuries.

Encyclopaedias

Halsbury's Laws of England. 4ed. see index vol.
The Digest. vol.14.
Encyclopaedia of Court Forms in Civil Proceedings (Atkin). 2ed. see index vol.

Texts

EUROPEAN COMMITTEE ON CRIME PROBLEMS
Compensation of victims of crime. Council of Europe, 1978.

GOFF, R. & JONES, G.
Law of restitution. 2ed. Sweet & Maxwell, 1978.

HOME OFFICE
Reparation by the offender. HMSO, 1970.

HOWARD LEAGUE FOR PENAL REFORM
Making amends: criminals, victims and society. Rose, 1977.

HUDSON, J. & GALAWAY, B.
Restitution in criminal justice: critical assessment of sanctions. Lexington, 1977 (USA).

MIERS, D.
Responses to victimisation: a comparative study of compensation for criminal violence in Great Britain and Ontario. Professional Books, 1978.

JUSTICE
Compensation for victims of crimes of violence. Stevens, 1962.

SCHAFER, S.
Restitution to victims of crime. Stevens, 1960.

SCOTTISH HOME AND HEALTH DEPARTMENT
Reparation by the offender to the victim in Scotland: report by the committee (Lord Dunpark). HMSO, 1977. (Cmnd. 6802).

SOFTLEY, P.
Compensation orders in Magistrates' Courts. HMSO, 1978 (Home Office research studies).

VASARHELYL, I.
Restitution in international law. Akad.Kiado, 1964.

RESTRICTIVE COVENANTS

See also Land Charges; Landlord and Tenant; Real Property.

Encyclopaedias and periodicals

Statutes in Force. Group: Property, England & Wales. Sub-Group 1.
Halsbury's Laws of England. 4ed. vol.16 and index vol.
Halsbury's Statutes of England. 3ed. see index vol.
The Digest. see index vol.

Encyclopaedia of Court Forms in Civil Proceedings (Atkin). 2ed. vol.34.
Encyclopaedia of Forms and Precedents. 4ed. see index vol.

Conveyancer and Property Lawyer. 1936–
Estates Gazette. 1858–

Texts

BRADBROOK, A.J. & NEAVE, M.A.
Easements and restrictive covenants in Australia. Butterworths (Australia), 1981.

ELPHINSTONE, Sir L.H.
Covenants affecting land. Sol.Law Stat.Soc., 1946 supp. 1951.

NEWSOM, G.H.
Discharge and modificaton of restrictive covenants. Sweet & Maxwell, 1957.

PRESTON, C.H.S. & NEWSOM, G.H.
Restrictive covenants affecting freehold land. 7ed. Sweet & Maxwell, 1982.

REVENUE LAW

See also Capital Gains Tax; Capital Transfer Tax; Corporation Tax; Customs and Excise; Double Taxation; Estate Duty; Income Tax; Inland Revenue; Probate; Stamp Duties; Tax Planning; Value Added Tax.

Encyclopaedias and periodicals

Statutes in Force. Groups: Customs and Excise; Income, Corporation & Capital Gains Taxes.
Halsbury's Laws of England. 4ed. see index vol.
Halsbury's Statutes of England. 3ed. see index vol.
The Digest. vol.39.
Encyclopaedia of Court Forms in Civil Proceedings (Atkin). 2ed. vol.34.

Annotated Tax Cases, 1922–1975.
Australasian Tax Reports. 1969–
British Tax Review. 1956–
Income Tax Digest and Accountants Review. 1940–
Simon's Tax Cases. 1973–
Simon's Tax Intelligence. 1973–
Tax Case Leaflets.
Tax Cases. 1875–
Taxation. 1927–
Taxation Reports. 1940–

Texts

BAGNALL, K.R. & LEWISON, K.
Development land tax. Shaw, 1978. Looseleaf.

BAXT, R. & Others
Cases and materials on taxation. 2ed. Butterworths (Australia), 1984.

BINGHAM, T.
Tax evasion: the law and the practice. Howden Finan. Service, 1980.

BOUUAERT, I.C.
Tax problems of cultural foundations and of patronage in the European community. Kluwer, 1977.

BRAMWELL, R. & DICK, J.
Taxation of companies. 2ed. Sweet & Maxwell, 1979 supp. 1983.

BRITISH tax encyclopaedia. Sweet & Maxwell, 1962. 5 looseleaf vols. 3 bound vols.

BUTTERWORTH'S budget tax tables. Annual.

BUTTERWORTH's orange tax handbook. Capital transfer tax. Annual.

BUTTERWORTH's tax practitioner's diary. Annual. (Sept.).

BUTTERWORTH's yellow tax handbook, income tax, corporation tax and capital gainst tax. Annual.

CENTRAL OFFICE OF INFORMATION
British system of taxation. HMSO, 1975.

CERTIFIED ACCOUNTANTS EDUCATIONAL TRUST
Residence of individuals: liability to tax in the U.K. 2ed. 1975.

CHOWN, .F.
Taxation and the multi-national enterprise. Longman, 1974.

CLARKE, K. & READING, B.
International employment tax handbook. Woodhead-Faulkner, 1982. Looseleaf.

CONFEDERATION OF BRITISH INDUSTRY
Taxation in Western Europe: a guide for industrialists. 11ed. CBI, 1974.

COOMBES, J.
Capital transfer tax. Professional Books, 1977.

CORRIGAN, K.
Tax law. Sweet & Maxwell, 1984 (Irish law texts).

CRAIGMYLE & Co.
Charitable giving and taxation. 6ed. Craigmyle, 1973.

CUMYN, A.P.F.
Non-resident's guide to Canadian taxation. De Boo, 1977.

DAILY MAIL
Income tax guide. Annual.

DAVIES, F.R.
Introduction to revenue law. Sweet & Maxwell, 1980.

DE VOIL, P.W.
Tax appeals. Butterworths, 1969.

DEADMAN, W.B. & FRANKLIN, H.W.
Unified personal tax. Farringdon, 1973.

DIBDEN, R.
Index to double taxation agreements. 5ed. Butterworths, 1973.

DOBRY, G., STEWARD-SMITH, W.R. & BARNES, M.
Development gains tax. Butterworths, 1975.

DOSSER, D. (ed.)
British taxation and the Common Market. Knight, 1973.

DOWELL, S.
History of taxation and taxes in England. 3ed. 1888 repr. Cass, 1965.

EASSON, A.J.
Tax law and policy in the E.E.C. Sweet & Maxwell, 1980.

EASTAWAY, N. (ed.)
Guide to the Taxes Acts and capital transfer tax. Butterworths, 1978.

EUROPEAN COMMUNITIES
Inventory of taxes levied by the state and the local authorities in the member states of the European Communities. 1976.

GEORGE, E.F.
Taxation and property taxation. Taxation Pub.Co., 1970.

GROUT, V. (ed.)
Tax cases. 3ed. Tolley, 1979.

HALPERN, L.
Taxes in France. 4ed. Butterworths, 1984.

HARDMAN, J.P.
Development land tax. Inst.Chartered Accountants, 1977.

HARRISON, E.R.
Index to tax cases. 6ed. HMSO, 1950 and supps.

HARVEY, E.L. (ed.)
Tolley's income tax. Tolley. Annual.

HARVEY, E.L. (ed.)
Tolley's taxation in the Republic of Ireland. Tolley. Annual.

HAYLLAR, R.F. & ROUSE, R.M.
Taxation of offshore oil and gas. Butterworths, 1980. Looseleaf.

REVENUE LAW

HEPKER, M.Z.
Modern approach to tax law. Heinemann, 1973.

HILL, R.
Tax aspects of incorporation. Inst. Chartered Accountants, 1983.

HUGHES, P.F.
Taxation manual. 12ed. Taxation Pub.Co., 1972 supp. 1973.

INLAND REVENUE
Income taxes outside the UK. HMSO, 1973. 9 vols. Looseleaf.

INLAND REVENUE
Taxes Acts. 4 vols. HMSO. Annual.

IRONSIDE, D.J.
Personal taxation: new united system. Inst.Chartered Accountants, 1972.

KARAM, N.H.,
The tax laws of Kuwait. Tr. Butterworths, 1979.

KAY, J.A.
British tax system. 3ed. Oxford U.P., 1983.

KELLY, F.N. & CARMICHAEL, K.S.
Irish income tax and corporation profits tax. 8ed. HFL, 1975. Looseleaf.

KNECHTLE, A.A.
Basic problems in international fiscal law. HFL, 1979.

LAWTON, J.P.
The taxation of property. Institute for Fiscal Studies, 1975 (Lecture series).

LAWTON, J.P., GOLDBERG, D. & FRASER, R.
Law of partnership taxation. 2ed. Oyez, 1979.

LEWIS, M.
British tax law. Macdonald & Evans, supp. 1979.

LIVENS, L.J. (ed.)
Taxation in the Channel Islands and Isle of Man. Tolley, 1976.

LIVENS, L.J. (ed.)
Taxation in Gibraltar. Tolley, 1975.

MAYSON, S.W.
Practical approach to revenue law. 4ed. Financial Training Pubns., 1983.

MELLOWS, A.R.
Taxation for executors and trustees. 5ed. Butterworths, 1981.

MELLOWS, A.R.
Taxation of land transactions. 3ed. Butterworths, 1983.

MONROE, M.H.
Intolerable inquisition? Stevens, 1981 (Hamlyn lecture).

MORCOM, J.B. & PARRY, D.J.T.
Capital transfer tax. 2ed. Woodhead-Faulkner, 1978.

MOULLIN, M. & SARGENT, J.
Guide to the taxation of companies. McGraw-Hill, 1982.

MUSTOE, N.E.
Income tax on landed property. 3ed. Estates Gazette, 1957 supp. 1963.

NATIONAL COUNCIL FOR ONE PARENT FAMILIES
Tax law and child care: the case for reform. 1980.

NORTON, M.
Covenants: a guide to the tax advantages of giving for charities. Directory of Social Change, 1980.

OROJO, J.O.
Company tax law in Nigeria. Sweet & Maxwell, 1979.

PICKERILL, R.J.
Capital allowance in law and practice. Inst.Chartered Accountants, 1977.

PICKERELL, R.J.
Corporate tax strategy. Inst.Chartered Accountants, 1980.

PINSON, B.
Revenue law. 15ed. Sweet & Maxwell, 1982 supp. 1983.

PLUNKETT, H.G.S. & CHAPMAN, P.F.A.
Taxation appeals. Oyez, 1975.

PRITCHARD, W.E.
Essentials of income tax. 2ed. Polytech Pubs., 1974.

PRITCHARD, W.E. & JONES, I.J.
Back duty. Butterworths, 1976.

RAY, E.E.
Partnership taxation. Bodley, 1972.

SABINE, B.E.V.
Short history of taxation. Butterworths, 1980.

SABINE, B.E.V.
Time limits for tax claims, elections and reliefs. Butterworths, 1984.

SAPPIDEEN, R.
Australian income taxation of companies and company distributions. Butterworths (Australia), 1979.

SHOCK, J.
Capital allowances. Sweet & Maxwell, 1984.

SILKE, A.S. and others (eds.)
Hambro's tax guide. Annual.

SIMON, J.A.
Simon's taxes. 3ed. Butterworths. 9 vols. Looseleaf.

SKOTTOWE, P.F. (ed.)
Butterworth's digest of tax cases. Butterworths, 1971 supp. 1971–73. 1974.

SOARES, P.C.
Tax strategy for conveyancing and land transactions. Oyez Longman, 1984.

SPICER, E.E. & PEGLER, E.C.
Income tax. 29ed. HFL, 1975.

STANLEY, O.
Taxation of farmers and landowners. 2ed. Butterworths, 1984.

STEINAECKER, M.F.
Domestic taxation and foreign trade. Praeger, 1973.

STORZ, M.
Personal tax records. Oyez, 1971.

STORZ, M.
Taxation of business and business transactions. Oyez, 1972.

SUMPTION, A.
Taxation of overseas income and gains. 4ed. Butterworths, 1982.

SUMPTION, A. & LAWTON, J.P.
Tax and tax planning. 10ed. Oyez, 1982.

SWEENEY, C.A. & TEFLER, J.H.
Revenue law in Australia. Butterworths (Australia), 1976.

SWEET & MAXWELL
Tax statutes. 1981.

THOMAS, C.H.
Legal lexicon of taxation. Professional Books, 1980.

THOMAS, G.W.
Taxation and trusts. Sweet & Maxwell, 1981.

TILEY, J.
Capital transfer tax. 2ed. Butterworths, 1978.

TILEY, J.
Revenue law. 2ed. Butterworths, 1978 supp. 1979.

TOLHURST, A.F., WALLACE, E.W. & ZIPFINGER, F.P.
Australian revenue duties, stamp duties. Butterworths (Australia), 1979. Looseleaf.

WALKER, M.
Concise tax service. Butterworths (Australia), 1980. Looseleaf.

WHITE, P.
Law and tax for professional partnerships. Oyez Longman, 1984.

WHITEHOUSE, C. & BUTTLE, E.S.
Revenue law: principles and practice. 2ed. Butterworths, 1984.

WHITEMAN, P.G. & WHEATCROFT, G.S.A.
Income tax and surtax. 2ed. Sweet Maxwell, 1976 supp. 1984.

WILLIAMS, D.B.
A guide to tax on maintenance payments. 2ed. Oyez, 1978.

WILLIAMS, R.G.
Elements of taxation. 14ed. Cassell, 1975.

REVERSIONS

See also Conveyancing.

Encyclopaedias

Halsbury's Laws of England. 4ed. see index vol.
Halsbury's Statutes of England. 3ed. vol.27.
The Digest. see index vol.
Encyclopaedia of Forms and Precedents. 4ed. mainly vol.4.

Texts

BENZ, N. & TAPPENDEN, H.J.
Valuations of reversions and life interest.
Cambridge U.P., 1951.

PETERS, J.P.E.F.
Reversionary practices. Sol. Law Stat. Soc., 1959.

WITHERS, A.H.
Legal risks incident to investments in reversionary interests in personality. Butterworths, 1915.

WITHERS, A.H.
Reminders on reversions. Butterworths, 1929.

WITHERS, A.H.
Withers on reversions. 2ed. Butterworths, 1933.

REVOLUTION

See also Public Order

Encyclopaedias

Halsbury's Laws of England. see index vol.
The Digest. see index vol.

Texts

FOSTER, Sir M.
A report of some proceedings on...the trial of the rebels in the year 1746...and other Crown cases (and) a discourse on Crown law. 3ed. Brooke, 1792.

HOOK, S.
Revolution, reform, and social justice: studies in the theory and practice of Marxism. New York Univ. P., 1975.

JUVILER, P.H.
Revolutionary law and order. Collier-Macmillan, 1977 (USA).

KENT, E. (ed.)
Revolution and the rule of law. Prentice Hall, 1972 (USA).

MARCUSE, H.
Counter revolution and revolt. Allen Lane, 1972.

MILLER, N. & AYA, R.
National liberation: revolution in the third world. Free Press, 1971 (USA).

RUSSELL, D.E.H.
Rebellion, revolution and armed force: a comparative study of fifteen countries with special emphasis on Cuba and South Africa. Academic Press, 1975.

RIGHTS OF WAY

See also Boundaries and Fences; Commons and Inclosures; Footpaths.

Encyclopaedias and periodicals

Halsbury's Laws of England. 4ed. vol.14.
Halsbury's Statutes of England. 3ed. vol.15.
The Digest. vol.19 but see index vol.
Encyclopaedia of Court Forms in Civil Proceedings (Atkin). 2ed. mainly vol.17.
Encyclopaedia of Forms and Precedents. 4ed. mainly vol.7.

Journal of the Commons, Open Spaces and Footpaths Preservation Society. 1927–

Texts

FREEMAN, W.M.
Rights of way. 4ed. Sol.Law Stat.Soc., 1958.

GARNER, J.F.
Rights of way and access to the countryside. 4ed. Oyez, 1981.

RYAN, G. & CAMERON, S.
The law relating to open spaces, commons and footpaths. Commons, Open Spaces & Footpaths Preserv.Soc., 1981.

SCOTTISH RIGHTS OF WAY SOCIETY
Walker's guide to the law of right of way in Scotland. 3ed. 1977.

WOOLRYCH, H.W.
Law of ways, including highways, turnpike roads and tolls, private rights of way, bridges and ferries. 2ed. Saunders & Benning, 1847.

ROAD TRAFFIC

See also Drinking and Driving; Police; Transport.

Encyclopaedias and periodicals

Statutes in Force. Group: Road Traffic.
Halsbury's Laws of England. 4ed. vol. 40.
Halsbury's Statutes of England. 3ed. see index vol.
Road Traffic Law Bulletin. 1984–
Road Traffic Reports. 1970–
Traffic Cases. vols. 1–33.

Texts

BAKER, E.R. & WILKIE, G.H.
Police promotion handbooks. No.5: road traffic. 7ed. Butterworths, 1980.

BINGHAM, L.
Motor claims cases. 8ed. Butterworths, 1980.

BRETTON, R.
"Special reasons". 4ed. Shaw, 1977.

BROWN, D.
Traffic offences. Butterworths (Australia), 1983.

BURTON, J. & HUBBER, D.C.
Penalities and orders for road traffic offences. 2ed. Shaw, 1980.

CANAGARAYAR, J.K.
Diverson of traffic offenders. Sweet & Maxwell, 1981.

COHEN, J. & PRESTON, B.
Causes and prevention of road accidents. Faber, 1968.

CONSUMERS' ASSOCIATION
ABC of motoring law. 1978.

DAVIES, M.R.R.
Law of road traffic. 5ed. Shaw, 1973. Looseleaf.

ENCYCLOPAEDIA of road traffic law and practices. Sweet & Maxwell. 4 vols. Looseleaf.

ENVIRONMENT, DEPARTMENT OF
Highway code. HMSO, 1976.

EUROPEAN CONFERENCE OF MINISTERS OF TRANSPORT
European rules concerning road traffic, signs and signals. HMSO, 1974.

GRAMPIAN POLICE
Road traffic law. 8ed. Aberdeen U.P., 1979. Looseleaf.

HOME OFFICE
Offences relating to motor vehicles: statistics. HMSO. Annual.

HOME OFFICE & DEPARTMENT OF TRANSPORT
Report of the Inter-Departmental Working Party on Road Traffic Law (Bohan). HMSO, 1981.

HOOD, R.
Sentencing the motoring offender. Heinemann, 1972.

KITCHIN, L.D. & DUCKWORTH, J.
Road transport law. 24ed. Butterworths, 1983.

KRIEFMAN, S.
Driving while disqualified. HMSO, 1975
(Home Office Research Unit report no.27).

MAHAFFY, R.P. & DODSON, D.
Road traffic. 3ed. Butterworths, 1977. 2 vols. Looseleaf.

MOISER, C.H.
Endorsements and disqualifications under the Road Traffic Acts. 7ed. Rose, 1979.

MOISER, C.H.
Guide to disqualifications and endorsements for traffic offences. 2ed. Bassett Pubns., 1984.

PLANE, R. & BURTON, J.
Penalties and orders for road traffic offences. Police Review, 1974. Looseleaf.

PUGH, J.
Law relating to heavy goods vehicles. Rose, 1980.

ROYDHOUSE, E.
Road traffic legislation. Butterworths, 1973.

SOCIETY OF MOTOR MANUFACTURERS AND TRADERS
Summary of international vehicle legislation. 1975. 8 vols. Looseleaf.

STEAD, R.
The Motor Vehicles (Construction and Use) Regulations: a digest of decided cases. 2ed. Rose, 1975.

TRANSPORT, DEPARTMENT OF
European Agreement Concerning the International Carriage of Dangerous Goods by Road (ADR). 4ed. HMSO, 1978.

VICKERY, N.A.
Motor and traffic law Victoria. 4ed. Butterworths (Australia). Looseleaf.

WALLS, H.J. & BROWNLIE, A.B.
Drinks, drugs and driving. 2ed. Sweet & Maxwell, 1984.

WHITELOCK, F.A.
Death on the road: a study in social violence. Butterworths, 1971.

WICKERSON, J.
The motorist and the law. Sweet & Maxwell, 1974 (It's your law series no.4).

WILKINSON, G.S.
Road traffic offences. 11ed. Oyez, 1982 supp. 1983.

WILLETT, T.C.
The criminal on the road. Tavistock, 1964.

WILLETT, T.C.
Drivers after sentence. Heinemann, 1973.

WILLIAMS, D.B.
Hit and run and uninsured driver personal injury claims: role of the Motor Insurers' Bureau. 4ed. B.Rose, 1983.

ROMAN DUTCH LAW

See also Roman Law.

Texts

FEENSTRA, R. & WAAL, C.J.D.
Seventeenth century Leyden Law professors and their influence on the development of the civil law: a study of Bronchorst, Vinnius and Voet. North-Holland, 1975.

FORSYTH, C.F. & BENNETT, T.W.
Private international law: the modern Roman-Dutch law, including the jurisdiction of the Supreme Court. Juta, 1981 (S.Africa).

GROTIUS, H.
The jurisprudence of Holland. Oxford U.P., 1926–36. 2 vols.

LEE, R.W.
An introduction to Roman Dutch law. 5ed. Oxford U.P., 1953.

NATHAN, M.
The common law and South Africa: a treatise based on Voet's commentaries on the Pandects. African Book Co., 1904–7. 4 vols.

PALMER, V.V.
The Roman-Dutch and Lesotho law of delict. Sijthoff, 1969.

ROBERTS, A.A.
A South African legal bibliography. Dept.of Justice, 1942.

WESSELS, J.W.
History of the Roman Dutch Law. African Book Co., 1908.

ROMAN LAW
See also Civil Law

Texts

BONNER, S.F.
Roman declamation in the late Republic and early Empire. Liverpool U.P., 1949.

BUCKLAND, W.W.
Elementary principles of the Roman private law. Cambridge U.P., 1972.

BUCKLAND, W.W.
Equity in Roman law. Hodder & Stoughton, 1911.

BUCKLAND, W.W.
The main institution of Roman private law. Cambridge U.P., 1931.

BUCKLAND, W.W.
A manual of Roman private law. Cambridge U.P., 1939.

BUCKLAND, W.W.
Roman law of slavery: from Augustus to Justinian. Cambridge U.P., 1908 repr. 1970.

BUCKLAND, W.W.
A textbook of Roman law from Augustus to Justinian. 3ed. Cambridge U.P., 1963.

BUCKLAND, W.W. & McNAIR, A.D.
Roman law and common law. 2ed. Cambridge U.P., 1965 repr. 1974.

CROOK, J.A.
Law and life of Rome. new ed. Thames & Hudson, 1984.

CURZON, L.B.
Roman law. Macdonald & Evans, 1966.

DAUBE, D.
Roman law: linguistic, social and philosophical aspects. Edinburgh U.P., 1969.

DAUBE, D. (ed.)
Studies in the Roman law of sale dedicated to the memory of Francis de Zulueta. Oxford U.P., 1959.

DUFF, P.W.
Personality in Roman private law. 1938 repr. Kelley, 1971.

FINLEY, M.I.
Studies in Roman property. Cambridge U.P., 1976.

GREENIDGE, A.H.J.
Roman public life. Macmillan, 1901.

GREENIDGE, A.H.J.
The legal procedure of Cicero's time. Macmillan, 1901.

JOLOWICZ, H.F.
Roman foundation of modern law. Oxford U.P., 1957.

JOLOWICZ, H.F. & NICHOLAS, B.
Historical introduction to the study of Roman law. 3ed. Cambridge U.P., 1972.

KELLY, J.M.
Roman litigation. Oxford U.P., 1966.

KELLY, J.M.
Studies in the civil judicature of the Roman Republic. Oxford U.P., 1976.

KUNKEL, W.
An introduction to Roman legal and constitutional history. 2ed. Oxford U.P., 1973.

LEAGE, R.W.
Roman private law founded on the institutes of Gaius and Justinian. 3ed. Macmillan, 1961.

LEE, R.W.
The elements of Roman law. 4ed. Sweet & Maxwell, 1936.

MACKINTOSH, J.
Roman law in modern practice. Green, 1934.

MACKINTOSH, J.
The Roman law of sale. 2ed. T.& T.Clarke, 1907.

MACKINTOSH, J.
Some aspects of Roman law. Patna Univ., 1934.

MOYLE, J.B.
Institutes of Justinian. 5ed. Oxford U.P., 1913.

NICHOLAS, B.
An introduction of Roman law. Oxford U.P., 1962.

ROBY, H.J.
Roman private law in the times of Cicero and of the Antonines. 1902 repr. Nijhoff, 1973. 2 vols.

SCHULZ, F.
Classical Roman law. Oxford U.P., 1951.

SCHULZ, F.
History of Roman legal science. Oxford U.P., 1946 repr. 1953.

SCHULZ, F.
Principles of Roman law. Oxford U.P., 1936.

SCRUTTON, T.E.
The influence of the Roman on the law of England. Cambridge U.P., 1885.

SHERWIN-WHITE, A.N.
The Roman citizenship. 2ed. Oxford U.P., 1973.

SOHM, R.
The Institutes: a textbook of the history and system of Roman private law. 1907 repr. Rothman, 1970.

THOMAS, J.A.C. (ed.)
The Institutes of Justinian: text, translation and commentary. North-Holland, 1975.

VAN WARMELO, P.
Introduction to the principles of Roman civil law. Juta, 1976 (S.Africa).

VINOGRADOFF, P.
Roman law in medieval Europe. 2ed. 1929 repr. Speculum Historiale, 1968.

WATSON, A.
Contract of mandate in Roman law. Oxford U.P., 1961.

WATSON, A.
Law making in the later Roman Republic. Oxford U.P., 1974.

WATSON, A.
The law of obligations in the later Roman Republic. Oxford U.P., 1965.

WATSON, A.
The law of persons in the later Roman Republic. Oxford U.P., 1967.

WATSON, A.
The law of property in the later Roman Republic. Oxford U.P., 1968.

WATSON, A.
The law of succession in the later Roman Republic. Oxford U.P., 1970.

WATSON, A.
Roman private law around 200 B.C. Oxford U.P., 1971.

WATSON, A.
Rome of the XII tables: persons and property. Oxford U.P., 1976.

WENGER, L.
Institutes of the Roman law of civil procedure. Liberal Arts P., 1940 (USA).

WESTRUP, C.W.
Introduction to early Roman law. Levin & Munksgaard, 1944–1950. 4 vols.

ZULUETA, F.de
The Institutes of Gaius. Oxford U.P., 1946–1953. 2 vols.

ZULUETA, F.de
The Roman law of sales. Oxford U.P., 1945.

SALE OF GOODS

See also Auctions and Auctioneers; Commercial Law; Consumer Protection; Trade Descriptions.

Encyclopaedias and encyclopaedias

Statutes in Force. Group: Sale of Goods.
Halsbury's Laws of England. 4ed. vol.41.
Halsbury's Statutes of England. 3ed. vols. 30, 43.
The Digest. vol.39.
Encyclopaedia of Court Forms in Civil Proceedings (Atkin). 2ed. vol.34.

Encyclopaedia of Forms and Precedents. 4ed. vol.17.

Product Liability Bulletin. 1979–
Product Liability International. 1979–

Texts

ADAMS, J.
Material and cases on sale of goods. Croom Helm, 1982.

ATIYAH, P.S.
Sale of goods. 6ed. Pitman, 1980.

AUSTIN, C.G.
The law of the sale of goods. Pitman, 1932.

BENJAMIN, J.P.
Sale of goods. 2ed. Sweet & Maxwell, 1981.

BENJAMIN, J.P.
Treatise on the law of sale of personal property. 9ed. Sweet & Maxwell, 1964.

BISCOE, P.M.
Law and practice of credit factoring. Butterworths, 1975.

BLACKBURN, C.
A treatise on the effect of the contract of sale. 3ed. Stevens, 1910.

BLAIR, M.C.
Sale of Goods Act 1979. Butterworths, 1980.

BRITISH INSTITUTE OF INTERNATIONAL AND COMPARATIVE LAW
Symposium on some comparative aspect of the law relating to sale of goods. 1964.

BULCHANDANI, K.R.
Law of partnership, sale of goods, negotiable instruments. Tripathi, 1980 (India).

CHALMERS, M.D.
Sale of Goods Act, 1893. 18ed. Butterworths, 1981.

DOBSON, A.P.
Sale of goods and consumer credit. 2ed. Sweet & Maxwell, 1984.

EASTWOOD, R.A.
The contract of the sale of goods. 2ed. Butterworths, 1946.

FRIDMAN, G.H.L.
Sale of goods in Canada. Carswell, 1973.

GRAVESON, R.H. & GRAVESON, D.
The Uniform Laws of International Sales Act 1967. Butterworths, 1968.

GREIG, D.
Sale of goods. Butterworths, 1974.

IVAMY, E.R.H.
Casebook on sale of goods. 4ed. Lloyd's, 1980.

LAWSON, R.G.
Law of sale and hire purchase in New Zealand. Reed, 1973.

LEWIS, J.R.
Law for the retailer and distributor. 3ed. Jordan, 1979.

MACKEURTAN, H.G.
Law of sale of goods in South Africa. 4ed. Sweet & Maxwell, 1972.

MACLEOD, J.H.
Sale and hire-purchase. Butterworths, 1971.

MAJOR, W.T.
Sale of goods. 3ed. Macdonald & Evans, 1975.

NORMAN, R.
Purchase and sale in South Africa. 4ed. Butterworths (S.Africa), 1972.

PARRIS, J.
Retention of title on the sale of goods. Granada, 1982.

PHILLIPS, J.D.
Sale of goods, hire purchase and agency. Sweet & Maxwell, 1969.

POTHIER, R.J.
Treatise on the contract of sale. Butterworths, 1839.

SAMUEL, G.
Case in consumer law. Macdonald & Evans, 1979.

SCHMITTHOFF, C.M.
Sale of goods. 2ed. Sweet & Maxwell, 1966.

SUTTON, K.C.T.
Law of sale of goods in Australia and New Zealand. 2ed. Law Book Co., 1974.

SZASZ, I.
A uniform law on international sale of goods: the CMEA general conditions. Akademiai Kiado, Budapest:Sijthoff, 1976.

SALVAGE

See also Collisions at Sea; Shipping.

Encyclopaedias and periodicals

Halsbury's Laws of England. 4ed. vols.1, 25.

Halsbury's Statutes of England. 3ed. vols. 1, 31.

Lloyd's Weekly Casualty Reports. 1920–

Texts

KENNEDY, W.R.
Civil salvage. 4ed. Stevens, 1958.

NEWSOM, H.
Law of salvage, towage, pilotage. 1886.

NORRIS, M.J.
The law of salvage. Baker, Voorhis, 1958 supp. 1966.

ROYAL YACHTING ASSOCIATION
Salvage and salvage claims. nd.

SUTTON, C.T.
Assessing of salvage awards. Stevens, 1949.

SAUDI ARABIA

Texts

COULSON, N.J.
Contract law in Saudi Arabia and the Gulf States. Graham & Trotman, 1980.

EL-SHEIKH, F.El.R.A.
Legal regime of foreign private investment in the Sudan and Saudi Arabia: a case study of developing countries. Cambridge U.P., 1984.

KAY, E.
Legal aspects of business in Saudi Arabia. Graham & Trotman, 1979.

NASR, K.
Business laws and taxation of Saudi Arabia. 2ed. Inter Crescent, 1981 (USA).

SCOTLAND

See also Devolution.

Encyclopaedias and periodicals

Encyclopaedia of the Laws of Scotland.
Halsbury's Laws of England. 4ed. see index vol.
Halsbury's Statutes of England. 3ed. see index vol.
The Digest. see index vol.
Encyclopaedia of Forms and Precedents. 4ed. vols. 2, 3, 6.

Juridical Review. 1889–
Scots Laws Times. 1893–
Scottish Law Review. 1885–
Session Cases. 1821–

Texts

ANTON, A.E.
Private international law: a treatise from the standpoint of Scots law. Green, 1967.

ANTONIO, D.G.
Scots law. Macdonald & Evans, 1975.

BALFOUR, J.
Practicks; ed. by P.G.B. McNeill. 1754 repr. Stair Society (vols. 21 & 22).

BEATON, J.A.
Scots law terms and expressions. Green, 1982.

BELL, G.J.
Commentaries on the law of Scotland and on the principles of mercantile jurisprudence. 7ed. T.& T.Clark, 1870. 2 vols.

BELL, G.J.
Principles of the law of Scotland. 10ed. T.& T.Clark, 1899.

BELL, W.
A dictionary and digest of the laws of Scotland. 7ed. Bell & Bradfute, 1890.

BRODIE-INNES, J.W.
Comparative principles of the laws of England and Scotland. Green, 1903.

BURN-MURDOCK, H.
Notes on English law as differing from Scots law. Green, 1924.

CAMPBELL, A.H.
The structure of Stair's Institutions. 21st David Murray Lecture, Glasgow, 1954.

COULL, J.W. & MERRY, E.W.
Principles and practice of Scots law.
Butterworths, 1971.

CRAIG, T.
Jus feudale. 1608.

ERSKINE, J.
An institute of the law of Scotland. 8ed. Bell & Bradfute, 1871. 2 vols.

ERSKINE, J.
Principles of the law of Scotland. 21ed. Bell & Bradfute, 1911.

GIBB, A.D.
Law from over the border. Green, 1950.

GIBB, A.D.
A preface to Scots law. 3ed. Green, 1961.

GIBB, A.D.
Select cases in the law of Scotland. 2ed Green, 1951.

GIBB, A.D.
Students' glossary of Scottish legal terms. 2ed. Green, 1982.

GIBB, A.D. & DALRYMPLE, A.W. (eds.)
A dictionary of words and phrases judicially defined and commented on by the Scottish Supreme Courts. Green, 1946.

GLOAG, W.M. & HENDERSON, R.C.
Introduction to the law of Scotland. 8ed. Green, 1980.

GRANT, J.P.
Independence and devolution: the legal implications for Scotland. Green, 1976.

HODGE, A.G. (ed.)
Scottish law directory. Hodge. Annual.

HOPE, T.
Major practicks; ed. by J.A.Clyde. Stair Society, 1937-8 (vols.3 & 4).

HOPE, T.
Minor practicks. 2ed. 1734.

HUME, D. Baron
Commentaries. 4ed. 1844.

HUME, D. Baron
Lectures. Stair Society. 6 vols.

KEITH, R. & CLARKE, G.
A guide to Scots law. Cassell, 1978.

KELLAS, J.G.
Scottish political system. Cambridge U.P., 1973.

KIRALFY, A.K.R. & MacQUEEN, H.L. (eds.)
New perspectives in Scottish legal history. F.Cass., 1984.

LORIMER, J.
A handboook of the law of Scotland. 2ed. T.& T.Clark, 1862.

McBRYDE, W.W. & DOWIE, N.J.
Petition and procedure in the Court of Session. Green, 1980.

McDOUALL, A. (Lord Bankton)
Institute. 1751-3. 3 vols.

MACKENZIE, G.
Institutes of the law of Scotland. 1684.

MARSHALL, E.A.
General principles of Scots law. 4ed. Green, 1982.

PARLIAMENT House Book. Green. Annual. 2 vols.

PATERSON, A.A. & BATES, T.St.J.N.
Legal system of Scotland: cases and materials. Green, 1983.

POTTINGER, G.
Secretaries of State for Scotland, 1926-76: fifty years of the Scottish Office. Scot.Academic P., 1979.

ROYAL COMMISSION ON LEGAL SERVICES IN SCOTLAND
Report (Hughes). HMSO, 1980 (Cmnd. 7846).

SCOTTISH OFFICE
Legal system of Scotland. 3ed. HMSO, 1981.

SCOTTISH OFFICE
Report of the Committee of Inquiry into Local Government in Scotland. HMSO, 1981 (Cmnd. 8115).

SMITH, T.B.
British justice: the Scottish contribution. Stevens, 1961.

SMITH, T.B.
The doctrines of judicial precedent in Scots law. Green, 1952.

SMITH, T.B.
Scotland: the development of its laws and constitution. Stevens, 1962.

SMITH, T.B.
A short commentary on the law of Scotland. Stevens, 1962.

SPOTTISWOODE, R.
Practicks. 1706.

STAIR, Viscount
Institutions of the law of Scotland. 6ed. by D.M.Walker. Stair Society, 1981 (repr. of 1ed. 1684).

STAIR SOCIETY
Introduction to Scottish legal history, 1958 (Stair Society, vol.20).

SUTHERLAND, R.
Lord Stair and the law of Scotland. Glasgow University, 1981.

WALKER, D.M.
The law of civil remedies in Scotland. Green, 1975.

WALKER, D.M.
Principles of Scottish private law. 3ed. Oxford U.P., 1982-3. 4 vols.

WALKER, D.M.
Scottish courts and tribunals. 3ed. Green, 1975.

WALKER, D.M.
Scottish legal system: an introduction to the study of Scots law. 5ed. Green, 1982.

WALKER, D.M.
Stair tercentenary studies. Stair Society, 1981 (vol.33).

WEBSTER, B.
Acts of David II, 1329-71. Edinburgh U.P. 1982.

WILSON, W.A.
Introductory essays on Scots law. 2ed. Green, 1984.

SCOTTISH LAW COMMISSION

See also Law Commission; Law Reform.

Encyclopaedias

Halsbury's Statutes of England. 3ed. vol.32.

Texts

SCOTTISH LAW COMMISSION
Annual Report.

SCOTTISH LAW COMMISSION
First programme of consolidation and statute law revision. HMSO, 1966 (Scot.Law Com. no.2).

SCOTTISH LAW COMMISSION
Second programme of consolidation and statute law revision. HMSO, 1973 (Scot.Law Com. no.27).

SCOTTISH LAW COMMISSION
Third programme of consolidation and statute law revision. HMSO, 1978 (Scot.Law Com. no.46).

SCOTTISH LAW COMMISSION
First programme of law reform. HMSO, 1965 (Scot.Law Com. no.1).

SCOTTISH LAW COMMISSION
Second programme of law reform. HMSO, 1968 (Scot.Law Com. no.8).

SCOTTISH LAW COMMISSION
Third programme of law reform. HMSO, 1973 (Scot.Law Com. no.29).

SEA, LAW OF

See also Fishing and Fisheries; International Law; Shipping; Territorial Waters.

Encyclopaedias

Halsbury's Laws of England. 4ed. see index vol.
Halsbury's Statutes of England. 3ed. see index vol.
Encyclopaedia of Court Forms in Civil Proceedings (Atkin). 2ed. vol.27.

Texts

ALEXANDER, L.M. (ed.)
The law of the sea: the future of the sea's resources. Law of Sea Inst., 1968.

ALEXANDER, L.M. (ed.)
The law of the sea: international rules and organisations for the sea. Law of Sea Inst., 1969.

ALEXANDER, L. M.(ed.)
The law of the sea: national policy recommendations. Law of Sea Inst., 1970.

ALEXANDER, L.M. (ed.)
The law of the sea: the needs and interests of developing countries. Law of Sea Inst., 1973.

ALEXANDER, L.M. (ed.)
The law of the sea: a new Geneva Conference. Law of Sea Inst., 1972.

ALEXANDER, L.M. (ed.)
The law of the sea: offshore boundaries and zones. Ohio State U.P., 1967.

ALEXANDER, L.M. (ed.)
The law of the sea: the United Nations and Ocean Management. Law of Sea Inst., 1971.

ANAND, R.P.
Law of the sea: Caracas and beyond. Nijhoff, 1980.

ANAND, R.P.
Legal regime of the sea-bed and the developing countries. Sijthoff, 1976.

ANAND, R.P.
Origin and development of the law of the sea: history of international law revisited. Nijhoff, 1982.

ANDRASSY, J.
International law and the resources of the sea. Columbia U.P., 1970.

BARSTON, R.P. & BIRNIE, P.W.
Maritime dimension. Allen & Unwin, 1980.

BOUCHEZ, L.J.
The regime of bays in international law. Sijthoff, 1964.

BOUCHEZ, L.J. & KAIJEN, L.
Future of the law of the sea. Nijhoff, 1973.

BOWETT, D.W.
The law of the sea. Manchester U.P., 1967.

BRITISH INSTITUTE OF INTERNATIONAL AND COMPARATIVE LAW
Developments in the law of the sea, 1958–1964. BIICL, 1965.

BROWN, E.D.
The legal regime of hydrospace. Stevens, 1971.

BROWN, E.D.
Offshore energy and mineral resources and the law of the sea. Graham & Trotman, 1980.

BROWN, E.D.
Passage through the territorial sea, straits used for international navigation and archipelagos. David Davies Memorial Institute of International Studies, 1974.

BURKE, W.T. and others
National and international law enforcement in the ocean. Univ.of Washington P., 1976 (USA).

BUTLER, W.E.
The law of Soviet territorial waters. Praeger, 1967.

BUTLER, W.F.
The Soviet Union and the law of the sea. Hopkins U.P., 1971.

CHURCHILL, R. & LOWE, A.V.
Law of the sea. Manchester U.P., 1983.

CHURCHILL, R. and others (eds.)
International conference on new directions in the law of the sea. BIICL, 1973–1975. 4 vols.

COLOMBOS, C.J.
International law of the sea. 6ed. Longman, 1967.

COUPER, A.D.
The law of the sea. Macmillan, 1978.

DUBNER, B.H.
Law of international sea piracy. Nijhoff, 1979.

DUPUY, R.J.
Law of the sea: current problems. Sijthoff, 1974.

DUPUY, R.J.
Management of humanity's resources: law of the sea. Nijhoff, 1983.

EL-HAKIM, A.A.
Middle Eastern States and the law of the sea. Manchester U.P., 1980.

FRANKOWSKA, M. (ed.)
Scientific and technological revolution and the law of the sea. Earlscourt Pubns., 1974.

FRIEDMANN, W.
The future of the oceans. Braziller, 1971 (USA).

FULTON, T.W.
Sovereignty of the sea: an historical account of the claims of England to the Dominion of the British seas. 1911 repr. Kraus, 1973.

GAMBLE, J.K. & PONTECORVO, G.
Law of the sea: the emerging regime of the oceans. Ballinger, 1973 (USA).

GAMBLE, J.K. & QUINN, C.
Law of the sea: a bibliography of the periodical literature of the 1970's. Ballinger, 1975.

GANDHI, D.S.
Shipowners, mariners and the new law of the sea: the effects of technical, legal and political constraints upon the traditional users of the world's oceans. Fairplay Pubns., 1978.

HILDRETH, R.G. & JOHNSON, R.W.
Ocean and coastal law. Prentice-Hall, 1983.

HJERTONSSON, K.
The new law of the sea: influence of the Latin American States. Sijthoff, 1973.

HOLLICK, A.I. & OSGOOD, R.E.
New era of ocean politics. Johns Hopkins U.P., 1974 (USA).

LAY, S.H., CHURCHILL, R. & NORDQUIST, M.
New directions in the law of the sea documents. Oceana, 1973. 2 vols.

LUARD, E.
Control of the sea-bed: who owns the resources of the ocean. Heinemann, 1977.

McDOUGAL, M.S. & BURKE, W.T.
The public order of the ocean. Yale U.P., 1962.

McFEE, W.
The law of the sea. Faber, 1951.

MANGONE, G.J.
Law for the world ocean. Sweet & Maxwell, 1981.

MARSDEN, R.G. (ed.)
Law and custom of the sea documents. Navy Records Office, 1915–16. 2 vols.

MARSTON, G.
Marginal seabed: United Kingdom legal practices. Oxford U.P., 1981.

MASTERSON, W.E.
Jurisdiction in marginal seas with special reference to smuggling. Macmillan, 1929.

O'CONNELL, D.P.
The influence of law on sea power. Manchester U.P., 1975.

O'CONNELL, D.P.
International law of the sea. Oxford U.P. vol. 1: 1983; vol. 2: 1984.

ODA, S.
The international law of the ocean development: basic documents. Sijthoff, 1972–1977. 3 vols.

ODA, S.
The law of the sea in our time: I – new developments, 1966–1975. Sijthoff, 1977.

ODA, S.
The law of the sea in our time: II – the United Nations Seabed Committee, 1968–1977. Sijthoff, 1977.

OUDENJIK, J.K.
Status and extent of adjacent waters. Sijthoff, 1970.

PAPADAKIS, N.
International law of the sea: a bibliography. Sijthoff, 1979.

PAPADAKIS, N.
The international legal regime of artificial islands. Sijthoff, 1977.

POST, A.M.
Deep sea mining and the law of the sea. Nijhoff, 1983.

RAO, P.S.
The public order of ocean resources: a critique of the contemporary law of the sea. MIT Press, 1975 (USA).

RAPSALOS. C.L. & STEPHANOU, C.A. (eds.)
New law of the sea: selected colloquium papers. Elsevier, 1983.

REMBE, N.S.
Africa and the international law of the sea. Sijthoff, 1980.

SEBEK, V.
Eastern European states and the development of the law of the sea: regional documents, national legislation. Oceana, 1977. 2 vols. looseleaf.

SEBENIUS, J.K.
Negotiating the law of the sea. Harvard U.P., 1984.

SIBTHORP, M.M. & UNWIN, M.
Oceanic management: conflicting uses of the Celtic Sea and other western U.K. waters. Europa, 1977.

SIMMONDS, K.R.
Cases on the law of the sea. Oceana, 1976. 3 vols.

SMITH, H.A.
The law and custom of the sea. 3ed.
Stevens, 1959.

STROHL, M.P.
The international law of bays. Nijhoff, 1963.

SULLIVAN, J.J.
Pacific Basin enterprise and the changing law of the sea. Lexington, 1977 (USA).

SYMMONS, C.R.
Maritime zones of islands in international law. Nijhoff, 1979.

UNITED NATIONS
List of terms relating to the law of the sea. 1977.

UNITED NATIONS
National legislation and treaties relating to the law of the sea. 1974.

UNITED NATIONS
The sea: a select bibliography on the legal, political, economic and technological aspects, 1976–7. 1978.

YATES, G.T. & YOUNG, J.H.
Limits to national jurisdiction over the sea. Virginia U.P., 1974.

ZACKLIN, R.
The changing law of the sea: western hemisphere perspectives. Nijhoff, 1974.

SEASHORE

See also Waters and Watercourses.

Encyclopaedias and periodicals

Statutes in Force. Group: Coast Protection and Flooding.
Halsbury's Laws of England. 4ed. see index vol.
Halsbury's Statutes of England. 3ed. vols. 35, 39 and see index vol. under Foreshore.
Encyclopaedia of Forms and Precedents. 4ed. vol.9.

Texts

HALL, R.G.
Rights of the Crown and privileges of the subject in the sea-shores of the realm. 2ed. Stevens & Haynes, 1875.

HILDRETH, R.G. & JOHNSON, R.W.
Ocean and coastal law. Prentice-Hall, 1983.

MOORE, S.A.
A history of the foreshore and the law relating thereto. Stevens & Haynes, 1888.

PHEAR, J.B.
A treatise on rights of water, including public and private rights to the sea and seashore. Stevens & Norton, 1859.

ROUND, O.S.
Riparian rights: being the law relating to running streams, angling, and the seashore. Draper, 1859.

SEDITION

See also Criminal Law.

Encyclopaedias

Statutes in Force. Group: Criminal Law.
Halsbury's Laws of England. 4ed. vol. 11.
Halsbury's Statutes of England. 3ed. vol.1.
The Digest. vols. 14, 15.

Texts

BROWNLIE, I.
Law of public order and national security. 2ed. Butterworths, 1981.

LAW COMMISSION
Codification of the criminal law: treason, sedition and allied offences. HMSO, 1977 (Working paper no.72).

YOUNG, T. & KETTLE, M.
Incitement to disaffection. Cobden Trust, 1976.

SENTENCING

See also Punishment.

Encyclopaedias and periodicals

Halsbury's Laws of England. 4ed. vols.11, 37 & 41.
Halsbury's Statutes of England. 3ed. vols. 7 & 42.
The Digest. vols.14, 15.

Criminal Law Review. 1954–
Howard Journal of Penology and Crime Prevention. 1921–.

Texts

ANCEL, M.
Suspended sentence. Heinemann, 1971.

ANDENAES, J.
Punishment and deterrence. Michigan Univ. P., 1974 (USA).

APPAVOO, S.M.
Magistrate's power of sentencing. Shaw, 1975.

ASHWORTH, A.
Sentencing and penal policy. Weidenfeld & N., 1983.

BOOTH, D.M. & PIRIE, N.F.
New powers of sentencing. Butterworths (Canada), 1973.

BOTTOMLEY, A.K.
Decisions in the penal process. Martin Robertson, 1973.

BOYLE, C.K. & ALLEN, M.J.
Sentencing law and practice in Northern Ireland. SLS Legal Publications, 1984.

BRODY, S.R.
The effectiveness of sentencing – a review of the literature. HMSO, 1976 (Home Office research study no.35).

CORNISH, D.B. & CLARKE, R.V.G.
Residential treatment and its effects on delinquency. HMSO, 1975 (Home Office research study no.32).

COUNCIL OF EUROPE
The effectiveness of punishment and other measures of treatment. 1967.

COUNCIL OF EUROPE
Sentencing report by the sub-committee on crime problems. 1974.

CROSS, R.
The English sentencing system. 3ed. Butterworths, 1981.

DAUNTON-FEAR, M.
Sentencing in South Australia. Law Book Co., 1980.

DAVIES, M.
Financial penalties and probation. HMSO, 1970 (Home Office research study no.5).

DAWSON, R.O.
Sentencing: the decision as to type, length and condition of sentence. Little, Brown, 1969 (USA).

DEVLIN, K.
Sentencing offenders in magistrates' courts. Sweet & Maxwell, 1970.

DURANT, M., THOMAS, M. & WILLOCK, H.D.
Crime, criminals and the law: a study of public attitudes and knowledge carried out for the Home Office. HMSO, 1972.

EUROPEAN COMMITTEE ON CRIME PROBLEMS
Sentencing. Council of Europe, 1975.

FALLON, P.
Crown Court practice: sentence. Butterworths, 1975 supp. 1976.

FITZGERALD, P.J.
Criminal law and punishment. Oxford U.P., 1962.

FRANKEL, M.E.
Criminal sentences: law without order. Hill & Wang, 1973 (USA).

GREEN, E.
Judicial attitudes in sentencing. Macmillan, 1961.

GROSS, H. & HIRCH, A. von
Sentencing. Oxford U.P., 1981 (USA).

HARRIS, B.
Magistrates' companion: a guide for magistrates in announcing sentence and other orders of the court. Rose, 1981.

HENHAM, J.A.
Magistrates' remand and sentencing powers. 6ed. (of Magistrates' summary jurisdiction). B. Rose, 1983.

HINES, V.G.
Judicial discretion in sentencing of judges and magistrates. B.Rose, 1982.

HOGARTH, J.
Sentencing as a human process. Univ.of Toronto P., 1971 (Canada).

HOME OFFICE
Sentence of the court: a handbook for courts on the treatment of offenders. 3ed. HMSO, 1978.
Supp. Children & Young Persons Act, 1969. 1971.
Supp. Detention centres. 1971.

HOME OFFICE
Sentencing practice in Magistrates' Courts. HMSO, 1979 (Research studies).

HOME OFFICE
Sexual offences, consent and sentencing. HMSO, 1979 (Research studies).

HOOD, R.G.
Sentencing the motoring offender. Heinemann, 1972.

HOOD, R.G.
Tolerence and the tariff: some reflections on fixing the time prisoners serve in custody. NACRO, 1974.

LAW REFORM COMMISSION OF CANADA
Studies in sentencing. 1974.

McLEAN, I.
Crown Court – pattern of sentencing. Rose, 1981.

McLEAN, I. & MORRISH, P.
The Magistrates' Court – an index of common penalties and formalities of cases before justices. 5ed. Rose, 1980.

McCLEAN, J.D. & WOOD, J.C.
Criminal justice and the treatment of offenders. Sweet & Maxwell, 1969.

McCONVILLE, S. (ed.)
The uses of imprisonment. Routledge, 1975.

MORRISH, P. & McLEAN, I.
Crown Court: an index of common penalties and formalities in cases tried on indictment or committed for sentence and appeal in criminal courts. 11ed. Rose, 1983.

MULLINS, C.
Sentence on the guilty. Justice of the Peace, 1957.

NOTT, D. & CORDEN, J.
Deferring sentence. Univ. of York, 1984.

PAGE, L.
The sentence of the court. Faber, 1949.

RUBIN, S.
Law of criminal correction. 2ed. West, 1973 (USA).

SCARMAN, Sir L.G.
Control of sentencing. Howard League for Penal Reform, 1974.

SOFTLEY, B.
A survey of fine enforcement. HMSO, 1973 (Home Office research study no.16).

THOMAS, D.A.
Current sentencing practice. Sweet & Maxwell. Looseleaf.

THOMAS, D.A.
Principles of sentencing: the sentencing policy of the Court of Appeal, Criminal Division. 2ed. Heinemann, 1979.

WALKER, N.D.
Crime and punishment in Britain. Heinemann, 1965.

WALKER, N.D.
Sentencing in a rational society. new ed. Penguin, 1972.

WALTERS, G.
Sentencing handbook: a guide to sentencing in magistrates' courts. Oyez, 1980.

YOUNGER, Sir K.G.
Sentencing. Howard League for Penal Reform, 1974.

SEXUAL OFFENCES

See also Homosexuality; Incest; Prostitution; Rape.

Encyclopaedias

Statutes in Force. Group: Criminal Law.
Halsbury's Laws of England. 4ed. vol.11.
Halsbury's Statutes of England. 3ed. vol.8.
The Digest. vols. 14, 15.

Texts

CRIMINAL LAW REVISION COMMITTEE
Working Party on Sexual Offences: report. HMSO, 1980.

GEBHARD, P.H.
Sex offenders: an analysis of types. Harper, 1965 (USA).

HOME OFFICE
Age of consent in relation to sexual offences: working paper. HMSO, 1979.

HOME OFFICE
Report of the Policy Advisory Committee on sexual offences and the age of consent in relation to sexual offences. HMSO, 1981 (Cmnd. 8216).

HOME OFFICE
Sexual offences, consent and sentencing. HMSO, 1979 (Research studies).

HONORE, T.
Sex law. Duckworth, 1978.

MACNAMARA, D.E.J.
Sex, crime and the law. Collier-Macmillan, 1978 (USA).

MAISCH, H.
Incest trans. from German by M.Bearne. Deutsch, 1973.

RADZINOWICZ, L. (ed.)
Sexual offences. Macmillan, 1957.

RODABAUGH, B.J. & AUSTIN, M.
Sexual assault: a guide for community action. Garland Pub., 1981 (USA).

SCOTTISH OFFICE
Investigating sexual assault. HMSO, 1983.

WALKER, M.J. & BRODSKY, S.L. (eds.)
Special animals: the victim and the rapist. D.C. Heath, 1976.

WALTERS, D.R.
Physical and sexual abuse of children: causes and treatment. Indiana U.P., 1976.

WEST, D.J. and others
Understanding sexual attacks. Heinemann, 1978 (Cambridge studies in criminology).

SHERIFFS

See also Execution

Encyclopaedias

Halsbury's Laws of England. 4ed. vol.42.
Halsbury's Statutes of England. 3ed. vol.30.
The Digest. vol.41.
Encyclopaedia of Court Forms in Civil Proceedings (Atkin). 2ed. vol.36 but see index vol.
Encyclopaedia of Forms and Precedents. 4ed. vol.10.

Texts

ATKINSON, G.
Sheriff law: a treatise on the office and duty of sheriff and under-sheriff. 6ed. Sweet, 1879.

BEAUMONT, C.H.
The law relating to sheriffs and their offices. Oyez, 1968 (Practice notes no.59).

CHURCHILL, C. & BRUCE, A.C.
The law of the office and duties of the sheriff. 2ed. Stevens, 1882.

DALTON, M.
Officium vicecomitum: the office and authority of sheriffs. 1670 repr. Professional Books, 1973.

GLADWIN, I.
The sheriff: the man and his office. Gollancz, 1974.

IMPEY, J.
The practice of the office of sheriff and under sheriff. 6ed. Clarke, 1835.

MATHER, P.E.
Sheriff and execution law. 3ed. Stevens, 1935.

MORRIS, W.A.
The medieval English sheriff to 1300. 1927 repr. Manchester U.P., 1969.

SEWELL, R.C.
A treatise on the law of sheriff. Butterworths, 1842.

WATSON, W.H.
A practical treatise on the office and duty of sheriff. 2ed. Sweet, 1848.

SHIPPING

See also Admiralty; Bottomry; Carriers/Carriage of Goods; Charterparties; Collisions at Sea; Demurrage; Laytime; Prize Law; Sea, Law of; Transport.

Encyclopaedias and periodicals

Statutes in Force. Group: Shipping.
Halsbury's Laws of England. 4ed. vol.43.
Halsbury's Statutes of England. 3ed. vol.31 but see index vol.
The Digest. vols. 41, 42.
Encyclopaedia of Court Forms in Civil Proceedings (Atkin). 2ed. see index vol.
Encyclopaedia of Forms and Precedents. 4ed. vols. 15, 21.

Lloyds's Law Reports. 1919–
Lloyd's List. 1734–
Lloyd's Maritime and Commercial Law Quarterly. 1974–
Lloyd's Register of Shipping. Annual.
Lloyd's Register of Yachts. Annual.

Texts

ABACASSIS, D.W.
Law and practice relating to oil pollution from ships. Butterworths, 1978.

ABBOTT, C.
Law relating to merchant ships and seamen. 14ed. 1901 repr. Professional Books.

ALEXANDER, L.M. & CLINGAN, T.A. (eds.)
Hazards of maritime transit. Ballinger, 1974 (USA).

AMOS, H.
Shipping conferences. Kluwer: Lloyd's, 1983.

ARNOULD, J.
Marine insurance. 16ed. Stevens, 1981. 2 vols.

ASTLE, W.E.
International cargo carriers liabilities. Fairplay Pubns., 1983.

ASTLE, W.E.
Legal developments in marine commerce. Fairplay Pubns., 1983.

ASTLE, W.R.
Shipowners' cargo liabilities and immunities. 3ed. Witherby, 1967.

ASTLE, W.E.
Shipping and the law. Fairplay Pubns., 1980.

BAMFORD, B.R.
Law of shipping and carriage of goods in South Africa. 2ed. Juta, 1973.

SHIPPING

BOCZEK, B.A.
Flags of convenience: an international legal study. Harvard U.P., 1962.

BRANCH, A.
Economics of shipping practice and management. Chapman & Hall, 1982.

BRICE, G.
Maritime law of salvage. Sweet & Maxwell, 1983.

BRODIE, P.R.
Dictionary of shipping and shipbroking terms (French-English/English-French). Lloyd's, 1980.

BROWN, R.H.
Analysis of marine insurance clauses. Bk.1: The Institute Cargo Clauses, 1982. Witherby, 1982.

BROWN, R.H.
Dictionary of marine insurance terms. 4ed. Witherby, 1964.

BROWN, R.H.
Marine insurance. Vol.1: principles. 4ed. Witherby, 1978.

BROWN, R.H.
Marine insurance. Vol. 3: hull practice. Witherby, 1975.

BROWN, R.H.
Marine insurance abbreviations. Witherby, 1968.

BROWN, R.H.
Marine reinsurance. Witherby, 1981.

BUCKNILL, A.
Law relating to tug and tow. 2ed. Stevens, 1927.

CARVER, T.G.
Carriage by sea. 13ed. Stevens, 1982.

CHALMERS, M.D.
Marine Insurance Act, 1906. 9ed. Butterworths, 1983.

CHORLEY, R.S.T. & GILES, O.C.
Shipping law. 8ed. Pitman, 1980

CLARKE, M.A. (ed.)
Shipbuilding contracts. Lloyd's, 1982.

CLARKE, M.A.
Aspects of The Hague rules: a comparative study in English and French law. Nijhoff, 1976.

COLINVAUX, R.P. & STEEL, D.
Forms and precedents. Stevens, 1973 (British shipping laws, vol.6).

DOVER, V.
A handbook to marine insurance. 8ed. Witherby, 1975.

ELLEN, E.
International maritime fraud. Sweet & Maxwell, 1981.

GEEN, G.K. & DOUGLAS, R.P.A.
Law and administration of pilotage. 2ed. Lloyd's, 1983.

GOODACRE, J.
Collected papers on marine claims. Witherby, 1980.

GOODACRE, J.
Marine insurance claims. 2ed. Witherby, 1981.

GORTON, L. & IHRE, R.
Contracts of affreightment. Lloyd's, 1985.

GORTON, L. and others
Shipbroking and chartering practice. Lloyd's, 1984.

GRIME, R.P.
Shipping law. Sweet & Maxwell, 1979 (Concise college texts).

HAGBERG, L. (ed.)
Enforced sale of vessels. Kluwer, 1977.

HEALTH & SAFETY EXECUTIVE
Guide to tanker marking regulations. HMSO, 1979.

HERMAN, A.
Shipping conferences. Lloyd's, 1983.

HILL, C.
Maritime law. Pitman, 1981.

HILL, D.J.
Freight forwarders. Sweet & Maxwell, 1972.

HODGSON, G.
Lloyd's of London: a reputation at risk. A.Lane, 1984.

HOPKINS, F.N.
Business and law for the shipmaster. 6ed. Brown Son & F., 1982.

HUDSON, N.G. & ALLEN, J.C.
Marine claims handbook. 4ed. Lloyd's, 1984.

IHRE, R., GORTON, L. & SANDEVARN, A.
Shipbroking and chartering practice. 2ed. Lloyd's, 1984.

INSTITUTE OF CHARTERED SHIPBROKERS
Shipbrokers manual. Vol.1. Lloyd's, 1983.

INTERNATIONAL ATOMIC ENERGY AGENCY
Martime carriage of nuclear fuels. 1973.

INTERNATIONAL CARGO HANDLING CO-ORDINATION ASSOCIATION
Multilingual glossary of cargo handling terms. 1982.

INTERNATIONAL LABOUR ORGANIZATION
Maritime labour conventions and recommendations. I.L.O. 1983.

IVAMY, E.R.H.
Casebook on shipping law. 3ed. Lloyd's, 1983.

IVAMY, E.R.H.
Marine insurance. 3ed. Butterworths, 1979 supp. 1982.

IVAMY, E.R.H.
Shipping law consolidated. Lloyd's, 1984. Looseleaf.

JACKSON, D.
Enforcement of maritime claims. Lloyd's, 1984.

KENNEDY, W.R.
Law of civil salvage. 4ed. Stevens, 1958 (British shipping laws, vol.12).

KITCHEN, J.
The employment of merchant seamen. Croom Helm, 1979.

LLOYD'S
Marine cargo surveys, seminar proceedings. Lloyd's, 1978.

LLOYD'S REGISTER
Rules for the construction and classification of steel ships. 1974.

LOWNDES, R. & RUDOLF, G.R.
Law of general average and the York-Antwerp rules. 10ed. Stevens, 1975 (British shipping laws, vol.7).

McGUFFIE, K.C., FUGEMAN, P.A. & GRAY, P.V.
Admiralty practice. 11ed. Stevens, 1964 supp. 1975 (British shipping laws, vol.1).

MACLACHLAN, D.
The treatise on the law of merchant shipping. 7ed. 1932 repr. Professional Books.

MANGONE, G.
Law for the world ocean. Sweet & Maxwell, 1981.

MANKABADY, S.
Hamburg Rules on the carriage of goods by sea. Kluwer, 1978.

MARSDEN, R.G.
Collision at sea. 11ed. Stevens, 1961 supp. 1973 (British shipping laws, vol.4).

MBANEFO, L.N.
Nigerian shipping laws. Professional Books, 1983.

MITCHELHILL, A.
Bills of lading law and practice. Chapman & Hall, 1982.

NORRIS, M.J.
Law of seamen. 3ed. Lawyers Co-op, 1970 (USA). 3 vols. and supp.

O'CONNELL, D.
International law of the sea. Vol. 1. Oxford U.P., 1982.

PARKS, A.L.
Law of tug, tow and pilotage. 2ed. Chapman & Hall, 1982.

PAYNE, W. & IVAMY, E.R.H.
Carriage of goods by sea. 11ed. Butterworths, 1979.

PINEUS, K. & ROHREKE, H.G.
Time-barred actions. Lloyd's, 1984.

PURVIS, R.N. & DARVAS, R.
The law and practice of commercial letters of credit, shipping documents and termination of disputes in international trade. Butterworths (Australia), 1975.

ROSE, F.D.
Modern law of pilotage. Sweet & Maxwell, 1984.

SASSOON, D.
C.I.F. and F.O.B. contracts. 3ed. Stevens, 1984.

SCRUTTON, T.E.
Charterparties and bills of lading. 19ed. Sweet & Maxwell, 1984.

SELMER, K.S.
The survival of general average. Oslo U.P., 1958.

SINGH, N.
International maritime law conventions. Stevens, 1983. 4 vols.

SINGH, N.
The maritime flag and international law. Kluwer, 1978.

SINGH, N. & COLINVAUX, R.P.
Ship-owners. Stevens, 1968 (British shipping laws, vol. 13).

STANTON, L.F.H.
A guide to the Merchant Shipping Acts. Brown Son & F., 1980. 2 vols.

STANTON, L.F.H.
The law and practice of sea transport. Brown Son & Ferguson, 1964.

STEVENS, E.F.
Shipping practice. 9ed. Pitman, 1971.

SUMMERSKILL, M.B.
Laytime. 3ed. Sweet & Maxwell, 1982.

TANGSUBKUL, P.
ASEAN and the law of the sea. Gower, 1982.

TEMPERLEY, R.
Merchant Shipping Acts. 7ed. Stevens, 1976 (British shipping laws, vol. 11).

TETLEY, W.
Marine cargo claims. 2ed. Butterworths, 1978.

THOMAS, D.R.
Maritime liens. Sweet & Maxwell, 1980.

TIBERG, H.
The law of demurrage. 3ed. Sweet & Maxwell, 1979.

TRADE, DEPARTMENT OF
Action on safety and pollution at sea: new Merchant Shipping Bill. HMSO, 1978 (Cmnd. 7217).

TRADE, DEPARTMENT OF
Carriage of dangerous goods in ships. HMSO, 1978. Looseleaf.

TRADE, DEPARTMENT OF
Merchant shipping: a guide to government publications. HMSO, 1975.

ULLMAN, G.H.
Ocean freight forwarder, the exporter and the law. Cornell Maritime, 1967 (USA).

VILLAR, G.R.
The merchant fleet in the Falklands War. Lloyd's, 1984.

WILFORD, M., COGHLIN, T. & HEALY, N.J.
Time charters. 2ed. Lloyd's, 1982.

YIANNOPOULOS, A.N.
Negigence clause in ocean bills of lading, conflict of laws and the Brussels Convention 1924. Louisiana U.P., 1962 (USA).

SHOPS AND OFFICES

See also Employer's Liability; Employment Law; Factories; Trade Unions.

Encyclopaedias and periodicals

Statutes in Force. Group: Trade.
Halsbury's Laws of England. 4ed. vols. 16, 20, 47.
Halsbury's Statutes of England. 3ed. vol.13.
Encyclopaedia of Court Forms in Civil Proceedings (Atkin). 2ed. see index vol.

Encyclopaedia of Forms and Precedents. 4ed. vol.21.

British Journal of Industrial Relations. 1963–

Journal of Business Law. 1957–

Texts

DAVIES, R.
The Offices, Shops and Railway Premises Act 1963. Oyez, 1965.

ENCYCLOPAEDIA of health and safety at work, law and practice. Sweet & Maxwell. 3 vols. Looseleaf.

FIFE, I. & MACHIN, E.
Health and safety at work. Butterworths, 1980.

HOME OFFICE
Shoplifting and thefts by shop staff. HMSO, 1983.

LEWIS, J.R.
Law for the retailer and distributor. 3ed. Jordan, 1979.

REDGRAVE, A. & FIFE, I.
Health and safety in factories. 2ed. Butterworths, 1982.

SAMUELS, H.
Law relating to shops. 4ed. Knight, 1975.

SAMUELS, H. & STEWART-PEARSON, N.
Offices, Shops and Railway Premises Act, 1963. 2ed. Knight, 1971.

SKOTTOWE, P.F.
Law relating to Sunday. Butterworths, 1936.

TOLLEY's health and safety at work handbook. Tolley, 1983.

SINGAPORE

See also Malaya/Malaysia.

Encyclopaedias

Statutes in Force. Group: Commonwealth and Other Territories.
Halsbury's Laws of England. 4ed. vol.6.
Halbury's Statutes of England. 3ed. vols. 1, 4, 6.

Encyclopaedia of Court Forms in Civil Proceedings (Atkin). 2ed. vol. 5.

Texts

BOYCE, P.
Malaysia and Singapore in international diplomacy: documents and commentaries. Sydney U.P.: Methuen, 1968.

DIAMOUR, J.
Malay kinship and marriage in Singapore. Athlone P., 1965.

DIAMOUR, J.
Muslim matrimonial court in Singapore. Athlone P., 1966.

IBRAHIM, A.
Family law in Malaysia and Singapore. Malayan Law Journal, 1978.

JAIN, M.P.
Administrative law of Malaysia and Singapore. Malayan Law Journal, 1980.

LIAN, K.K.
Credit and security in Singapore: legal problems of development finance. Crane, 1973.

MYINT SOE, U.
Law of banking and negotiable instruments in Singapore and Malaysia. 1977.

SHERIDAN, L.A. (ed.)
Malaya and Singapore: the Borneo territories. Stevens, 1961 (British Commonwealth series).

SINNADURAI, V.
The law of contract in Malaysia and Singapore: cases and commentary. Oxford U.P., 1979.

SOIN, B.S.
Singapore master tax guide. 4ed. CCH, 1980 (Australia).

SRINIVASAGAM, E. and others (eds.)
Tables of the written laws of the Republic of Singapore, 1819–1971. Malayan Law Rev., 1972.

SOCIAL SECURITY

See also National Insurance; Pensions; Poor Law; Welfare Law.

Encyclopaedias and periodicals

Statutes in Force. Group: Social Security and Health Services.
Halsbury's Laws of England. 4ed. vol. 33.
Halsbury's Statutes of England. 3ed. mainly vol.45, but see index vol.
Encyclopaedia of Court Forms in Civil Proceedings (Atkin). 2ed. vol.14.

Journal of Social Welfare Law. 1978–

Reported Decisions of the Commissioner: National Insurance and Family Allowances Act, 1948–1972.
National Insurance (Industrial Injuries) Acts, 1948–1972.

SOCIAL SECURITY

Selected Decisions of the Commissioner on Claims under the National Insurance, National Insurance (Industrial Injuries) and Family Allowances Acts.
Series G: Claims for Maternity Benefit, Widow's Benefit, Guardian's Allowance and Death Grant.
Series P: Claims for Retirement Pensions.
Series S: Claims for Sickness Benefit.
Series U: Claims for Unemployment Benefit.
Series I: Claims under the National Insurance (Industrial Injuries) Acts.
Series F: Claims under the Family Allowances Acts.

Texts

ADLER, M. & BRADLEY, A. (eds.)
Justice, discretion and poverty: Supplementary Benefit Appeal Tribunals in Britain. Professional Books, 1975.

ATKINSON, A.B.
Poverty in Britain and the reform of social security. Cambridge U.P., 1970.

BAUGH, W.E.
Introduction to the social services. Macmillan, 1973.

BELL, J.S.
How to get industrial injuries benefit. Sweet & Maxwell, 1966.

BOULTON, A.H.
Law and practice of social security. Jordan, 1972.

BRIGGS, E. & REES, A.M.
Supplementary benefits and the consumer. Bedford Square P., 1980.

CALVERT, H. (ed.)
Encyclopaedia of social security law. Sweet & Maxwell. Looseleaf.

CALVERT, H.
Social security law. 2ed. Sweet & Maxwell, 1978.

CALVERT, H.
Welfare legal system. Univ.Newcastle P., 1973.

CONFEDERATION OF BRITISH INDUSTRY
Social Security Pensions Act, 1975: guidance for employers. CBI, 1976.

EUROPEAN COMMUNITIES
Comparative tables of the social security systems in the member states of the European Communities. 9ed. 1977.

EUROPEAN COMMUNITIES
Employment jurisdiction and social security jurisdiction in the countries of the European Communities. 1973.

EUROPEAN COMMUNITIES
Practical handbook of social security for employed persons and their families moving within the Community. 1975. Looseleaf.

EUROPEAN COMMUNITIES
Supplementary social security schemes in the E.E.C. 1973.

FAMILY WELFARE ASSOCIATION
A guide to the social services. Annual.

FULBROOK, J.
Social security. Sweet & Maxwell, 1980.

GEORGE, V.
Social security: Beveridge and after. Routledge, 1968.

GEORGE, V.
Social security and society. Routledge, 1973.

HEALTH AND SOCIAL SECURITY, DEPARTMENT OF
Handbook for industrial medical boards. HMSO. Looseleaf.

HEALTH AND SOCIAL SECURITY, DEPARTMENT OF
The law relating to social security and family allowances: the statutes, regulations and orders as now in force annotated and indexed. HMSO, 1976. 3 vols. Looseleaf.

HEALTH AND SOCIAL SECURITY, DEPARTMENT OF
The law relating to supplementary benefits and family income supplements. HMSO, 1972. Looseleaf.

HEALTH AND SOCIAL SECURITY, DEPARTMENT OF
Pensions appeal tribunals entitlement appeals: notes for the guidance of applicants. HMSO, 1976.

HEALTH AND SOCIAL SECURITY, DEPARTMENT OF
Report of the Committee on Abuse of Social Security Benefits (Fisher). HMSO, 1973. (Cmnd. 5228).

HEALTH AND SOCIAL SECURITY, DEPARTMENT OF
Social security and law: digest of Commissioners' decisions. HMSO. Looseleaf.

KEWLEY, T.H.
Australian social security today: major developments from 1900 to 1978. Sydney U.P., 1980.

KEWLEY, T.H.
Social security in Australia, 1960–1972. 2ed. Sydney U.P., 1973.

LEGAL ACTION GROUP
A lawyer's guide to supplementary benefit. 2ed. LAG, 1978.

LAWSON, R. & REED, R.
Social security in the European Community. PEP, 1975.

LISTER, R.
As man and wife? A study of the cohabitation rule. CPAG, 1973.

LISTER, R.
Welfare benefits. Sweet & Maxwell, 1981.

LYNES, T.
Penguin guide to supplementary benefits. 2ed. Penguin, 1974.

McCLEAN, J.D.
The legal context of social work. Butterworths, 1975.

MATTHEWMAN, J. & LAMBERT, N.
Social security and state benefits. Tolley, 1981.

MICKLETHWAIT, R.
The National Insurance Commissioners. Stevens, 1976.

NELIGAN, D.
Social security case law: digest of commissioners' decisions. HMSO, 1979.

OGUS, A.J. & BARENDT, E.M.
Law of social security. 2ed. Butterworths, 1982.

PARTINGTON, M.
Claim in time: study of the time limit rules for claiming social security benefits. Pinter, 1978.

POLLARD, D.W.
Social welfare law. Oyez, 1976. Looseleaf.

RAYNES, H.E.
Social security in Britain: a history. 2ed. 1960 repr. Greenwood, 1976.

SAMUELS, A.
Social security and family law. BIICL, 1979.

SHORE, W.
Social security, the fraud in your future. Macmillan, 1975.

STREET, D.
Welfare industry: functionaries and recipients in public aid. Sage, 1979.

SUPPLEMENTARY BENEFITS COMMISSION
Cohabitation. 2ed. HMSO, 1976.

SUPPLEMENTARY BENEFITS COMMISSION
Exceptional needs payments. HMSO, 1973.

SUPPLEMENTARY BENEFITS COMMISSION
Handbook. 4ed. HMSO, 1974.

WALLEY, Sir J.
Social security: another British failure. Knight, 1972.

WATSON, P.
Social security law of the European Communities. Mansell, 1980.

SOCIAL WORKERS

Periodicals

Journal of Social Welfare Law. 1978–

Texts

ALVES, J.T.
Confidentiality in social work. Greenwood, 1984.

BATES, F.
Australian social worker and the law. Law Book Co., 1979.

BRITISH ASSOCIATION OF SOCIAL WORKERS
Law and the social worker. 1974.

DAVIES, M.
Support systems in social work. Routledge, 1977.

HEALTH, MINISTRY OF
Report of the Working Party on Social Workers in the Local Authority Health and Welfare Services. HMSO, 1959.

HUTTMAN, E.D.
Housing and social services for the elderly: social policy trends. Praeger, 1977.

JAMISON, R., THWAITES, D.J. & GAMBLE, H.E.C.
Social work and the law. Butterworths (Australia), 1979.

JONES, H.
Residential community: a setting for social work. Routledge, 1979.

JONES, R.M.
Social work statutes. Sweet & Maxwell, 1980.

LEEDING, A.E.
Child care manual for social workers. 4ed. Butterworths, 1982.

McLEAN, J.D.
Legal context of social work. 2ed. Butterworths, 1980.

MACMORLAND, B.
ABC of services and information for disabled peopled. 3ed. Disablement Income Group Charitable Trust, 1977.

MATHIESON, D. & WALKER, A.
Social enquiry reports. 1972.

MOORE, G. & WOOD, C.
Social work and criminal law in Scotland. Aberdeen U.P., 1981.

PARKER, H.J.
Social work and the courts. Arnold, 1979.

PERRY, F.G.
A guide to the preparation of social inquiry reports. Rose, 1975.

PRITCHARD, C. & TAYLOR, R.
Social work: reform or revolution. Routledge, 1978.

RAISBECK, B.L.
Law and the social worker. Macmillan, 1977.

ROBERTS, G.
Essential law for social workers. 2ed. Oyez, 1981.

SIMPSON, T.
Advocacy and social change: study of welfare rights workers. Nat.Inst.Social Change, 1978.

SKIDMORE, R.A. & THACKERAY, M.G.
Introduction to social work. 3ed. Prentice-Hall, 1982.

STEVENSON, O.
Claimant or client? Social worker's view of the Supplementary Benefits Commission. 1974.

THOMAS, D.N.
Organizing for social change: study in the theory and practice of community work. Allen & Unwin, 1977.

TIBBETT, J.E.
Social workers as mental health officers. HMSO, 1978 (Scottish Office social research studies).

WARHAM, J.
An introduction to administration for social workers. Routledge & K.P., 1967.

WRIGHT, D.
The social worker and the courts. Heinemann, 1979.

YOUNGHUSBAND, E.L.
Social work in Britain, 1950–75. Allen & Unwin, 1978. 2 vols.

ZANDER, M.
Social workers, their clients and the law. 3ed. Sweet & Maxwell, 1981.

SOLICITORS

See also Advocates and Advocacy; Bar and Barristers; Legal Aid and Advice; Legal Executives; Legal Profession; Notaries.

Encyclopaedias and periodicals

Statutes in Force. Group: Lawyers and Notaries.
Halsbury's Laws of England. 4ed. vol.44.
Halbury's Statutes of England. 3ed. vol.44.
The Digest. vol.43.

Encyclopaedia of Court Forms in Civil Proceedings (Atkin). 2ed. vol. 36 but see index vol.
Encyclopaedia of Forms and Precedents. 4ed. vol.21.

Solicitors' Journal. 1856–
Law Society Annual Report.
Law Society's Gazette. 1903–

Lay Observer. Annual Report.
Scottish Lay Observer. Annual Report.

Texts

ADAMSON, H.C.
The Solicitors Act 1974. Butterworths, 1975.

BARCLAY, J.B.
Society of Solicitors in the Supreme Courts of Scotland, 1784–1984. Soc. of Solicitors, 1984.

BIRKS, M.
Gentlemen of the law. Stevens, 1960.

CORDERY, A.
The law relating to solicitors. 7ed. Butterworths, 1981.

HALBERSTADT, R.
Basic bookkeeping for solicitors. 2ed. Sweet & Maxwell, 1982.

HARROWES, D.H.S.
Managing the partnership office. Butterworths, 1978.

HERBERT, D.
The law as to solicitors: based on the Solicitors' Act 1932. Eyre & Spottiswoode, 1932.

JUSTICE
Complaints against lawyers. Stevens, 1970.

KING, A. & BARLOW, J.
Solicitors and their business clients. Financial Training Pubns., 1982.

KING, M.
The effects of a duty solicitor scheme: an assessment of the impact upon a Magistrates Court. Cobden Trust, 1976.

KIRK, H.
Portrait of a profession: a history of solicitors' profession, 1100 to the present day. Oyez, 1976.

LAW SOCIETY
Compensation fund: instructions for the guidance of persons who intend to apply for a grant. The Society, 1975.

LAW SOCIETY
Dealing with complaints about solicitors. The Society, 1973.

LAW SOCIETY
Digest, vol.1. Conveyancing: practice and costs. The Society, 1954 and supp.

LAW SOCIETY
A guide to the professional conduct of solicitors. The Society, 1974.

LAW SOCIETY
The Solicitors: Accounts Rules. 1975; The Solicitors' Trust Account Rules.1975; The Accountant's Report Rules.1975; The Solicitors' Accounts (Deposit Interest) Rules, 1975. The Society, 1975.

LAW SOCIETY
Solicitors' indemnity rules, 1975. The Society, 1975.

LAW SOCIETY.
Solicitors' practice rules, 1975. The Society, 1975.

LEVENSON, H.
Price of justice. Cobden Trust, 1981.

LUND, T.G.
A guide to the professional conduct and etiquette of solicitors. The Law Society, 1960.

LUND, T.G.
The Solicitors' Act 1941. Butterworths, 1943.

MONOPOLIES AND MERGERS COMMISSION
Services of solicitors in England and Wales: a report on the supply of services of solicitors in England and Wales in relation to restrictions on advertising. HMSO, 1976 (1975–76 H.C.557).

MONOPOLIES AND MERGERS COMMISSION
Services of solicitors in Scotland: a report on the supply of services of solicitors in Scotland in relation to restrictions on advertising. HMSO, 1976. (1975–76. H.C. 558).

PODMORE, D.
Solicitors and the wider community. Heinemann, 1980.

ROYAL COMMISSION ON LEGAL SERVICES
Final Report (Benson). HMSO, 1979 (Cmnd. 7648).

ROYAL COMMISSION ON LEGAL SERVICES IN SCOTLAND
Report (Hughes). HMSO, 1980 (Cmnd. 7846).

RUOFF, T.
The solicitor and the silicon chip. Oyez, 1981.

SANCTUARY, G.
Before you see a solicitor. Oyez, 1973.

SCOTT, J.
Legibus: a history of Clifford Turner, 1900–1980. Clifford Turner & King Thorne & Stace Ltd., 1980.

SLINN, J.
A history of Freshfields. Freshfields, 1984.

SOLICITOR's and barrister's directory and diary. Waterlow. Annual 2 vols.

SHUTTLEWORTH, C.W.
Checklists for solicitors. 3ed. Oyez, 1979.

SOAR, P.H.M.
The solicitor's practice. Butterworths, 1980. Looseleaf.

STEWART, J.B.
The partners: inside America's most powerful law firms. Simon & Schuster, 1983 (USA).

WEBSTER, R.M.
Professional ethics and practice for Scottish solicitors. The author, 1976.

WILLIAMS, P.H.
A gentleman's calling: the Liverpool attorney-at-law. Liverpool Law Society, 1980.

SOUTH AFRICA

Encyclopaedias and periodicals

Law of South Africa. 24 vols.
Statutes in Force. Group: Commonwealth and Other Territories.
Halsbury's Laws of England. 4ed. see index vol.

Halsbury's Statutes of England. 3ed. vol.4.
The Digest. vol. 8 (2).
Encyclopaedia of Court Forms in Civil Proceedings (Atkin). 2ed. vol. 35.

Annual Survey of South Africa Law. 1947–

Texts

BAMFORD, B.R.
The law of partnership and voluntary associations in South Africa. 3ed. Juta, 1982.

BAMFORD, B.R.
The law of shipping and carriage in South Africa. 2ed. Juta, 1973.

BEKKER, J.J. & COERTZER, J.J.J.
Seymour's customary law of South Africa. 4ed. Juta, 1981.

BURRELL, T.D.
South African patent law and practice. Butterworths (S.Africa), 1973.

CILLIERS, A.C.
Law of costs. Butterworths (S.Africa), 1972.

CILLIERS, H.S. & BENADE, M.L , & DE VILLIERS, S.W.L..
Company law. 3ed. Butterworths (S.Africa), 1977.

CONRADIE, A.M.
The law of carriage of goods by railway in South Africa. Butterworths (S.Africa), 1964.

COWEN, D.V. & GERING, L.
The law of negotiable instruments in South Africa. 4ed. Sweet & Maxwell, 1966.

DE VILLIERS, J.E. & MACINTOSH, .C.
The law of agency in South Africa. 2ed. Juta, 1956.

DU PLESSIS, J.R.
Elementary introduction to the study of South African law. Juta, 1981.

FORSYTH, C.F. & BENNETT, T.W.
Private international law: the modern Roman-Dutch law, including the jurisdiction of the Supreme Court. Juta, 1981.

HAHLO, H.R.
The South African law of husband and wife. 4ed. Juta, 1975.

HAHLO, H.R. & KAHN, E.
The South African legal system and its background. Juta, 1968.

HALL, C.G.
Water rights in South Africa. 4ed. Juta, 1974.

HIEMSTRA, V.G.
Introduction to the law of criminal procedure. Butterworths (S.Africa), 1978.

HIEMSTRA, V.G. & GONIN, H.L.
Trilingual legal dictionary (English/Latin/Afrikaans). Juta, 1981.

HOSTEN, W.J. and others
Introduction to South African law and legal theory. Butterworths (S.Africa), 1977.

KAHN, E. & ZEFFERTT, D.
Select South African legal problems: essays in memory of R.G. McKerron. Juta, 1974.

KERR, A.J.
The law of agency. 6ed. Butterworths (S.Africa), 1972.

KERR, A.J.
Native law of succession in South Africa. Butterworths (S.Africa), 1961.

LANSDOWN, A.V. & CAMPBELL, J.
South African criminal law and procedure. vol.5: criminal procedure and evidence. Juta, 1981.

MAASDORP. A.F.S.
Institutes of South African law. Juta, 1968–1972. 4 vols.

MATTHEWS, A.S.
Law order and liberty in South Africa. Juta, 1971.

MEYER, J.
Local government law. Butterworths (S.Africa), 1977–78. 2 vols.

MILTON, J.R.L.
South African criminal law and procedure. vol.2: common law crimes. 2ed. Juta, 1981.

NATHAN, C.J.M., BARNETT, M. & BRINK, A.
Uniform rules of court/Eenvormige Hofreels (bilingual). 2ed. Juta, 1977.

NATHAN, M.
The common law of South Africa. 2ed. Central News Agency, 1913.

OOSTHUIZEN, A.J.
Law of property. Juta, 1981.

ROBERTS, A.A.
A South African legal bibliography. Dept.of Justice, 1942 (S.Africa).

SCHOEMAN, T.
Guide to the Companies Act and regulations. Juta, 1973.

SMITH, C.
The law of insolvency. Butterworths (S.Africa), 1974.

SPIRO, E.
Conflict of laws. Juta, 1973.

STORRY, J.G.
Customary law and practice. Juta, 1979.

VAN DE VYVER, J.D.
The South African law of censorship. Butterworths (S.Africa), 1978.

VAN NIEKERK, A.F.
Income tax in the South African law. Butterworths (S.Africa), 1977. Looseleaf.

WILLE, G. & GIBSON, H.T.R.
Principles of South African law. 7ed Juta, 1977.

WILLE, G. & MILLIN, P.
Mercantile law of South Africa. 17ed. Hartors, 1975.

WILLIS, N.
Banking in South African law. Juta, 1981.

SOVEREIGNTY

See also Crown; Jurisprudence and Legal Philosophy.

Encyclopaedias

Halsbury's Laws of England. 4ed. see index vols.
Halbury's Statutes of England. 3ed. vol.8.
Encyclopaedia of Court Forms in Civil Proceedings (Atkin). 2ed. vols. 14, 30, 35.

Texts

BLIX, H.
Sovereignty, aggression and neutrality. Hammarskjold Foundation, 1970.

CRAWFORD, J.
Creation of states in international law. Oxford U.P., 1979.

DELUPIS, I.
International law and the independent state. Crane Rusak, 1974 (USA).

JACOBS, C.E.
Eleventh amendment and sovereign immunity. Greenwood, 1973 (USA).

KLEIN, R.A.
Sovereign equality among states. Toronto U.P., 1974.

LARSON, A. & JENKS, C.W.
Sovereignty within the law. Oceana, 1965.

LUCAS, W.W.
The primordial functions of government and legal status of sovereignty. Bowes & Bowes, 1938.

MARSHALL, G.
Parliamentary sovereignty and the Commonwealth. Oxford U.P., 1957.

MERRIAM, C.E.
History of the theory of sovereignty since Rousseau. 1900 repr. Garland, 1972 (USA).

ROSTOW, E.V.
The sovereign prerogative: the Supreme Court and the quest for law. Yale U.P., 1962 (USA).

WILKS, M.
The problem of sovereignty in the later Middle Ages. Cambridge U.P., 1963.

SOVIET LAW

Encyclopaedias and periodicals

Soviet statutes and decisions.

Review of socialist law.
Soviet law and government.

Texts

ARMSTRONG, G.M.
Soviet law of property. Nijhoff, 1984.

BAADE, H.W.
The Soviet impact on international law. Oceana, 1965.

BARRY, D.D.
Soviet law after Stalin. vol.1: the citizen and the state in contemporary Soviet law. Sijthoff, 1977.

BARRY, D.D. and others (eds.)
Contemporary Soviet law: essays in honour of John N. Hazard. Nijhoff, 1975.

BASSIOUNI, M.C. & SAVITSKI, V.M.
The criminal justice system of the USSR. Nelson, 1979.

BUTLER, W.E.
Basic documents on the Soviet legal system. Oceana, 1983.

BUTLER, W.E.
Collected legislation of the USSR and the constituent union republics. Oceana, 1979. 6 vols. Looseleaf.

BUTLER, W.E.
Russian law: historical and political perspectives. Sijthoff, 1977.

BUTLER, W.E.
Soviet commercial and maritime arbitration. Oceana, 1980. Looseleaf.

BUTLER, W.E.
Soviet law. Butterworths, 1983.

FELDBRUGGE, F.J.M.
Codification in the communist world. Sijthoff, 1975.

FELDBRUGGE, F.J.M.
Encyclopaedia of Soviet law. Nijhoff, 1973. 2 vols.

HAZARD, J.N.
Soviet system of government. 5ed. Chicago U.P., 1980.

HAZARD, J.N. & HOYA, T.W.
Soviet law and western legal systems: a manual for comparison. 2ed. Columbia U.P., 1970.

HAZARD, J.N. & WEISBERG, M.C.
Cases and readings in Soviet law. Columbia U.P., 1950 (USA).

HAZARD, J.N. and others
The Soviet legal system. 4ed Oceana, 1982.

JOHNSON, E.L.
An introduction to the Soviet legal system. Methuen, 1969.

KOLDAYEV, V.
Soviet citizens: their rights and their duties. Novosti P., 1977.

RUDDEN, B.
Soviet insurance law. Sijthoff, 1966.

SIMONS, W.B.
Soviet codes of law. Sijthoff, 1980.

WALKER, G.
Official publications of the Soviet Union and Eastern Europe, 1945–1980: a selected annotated bibliography. Mansell, 1982.

SPACE LAW

See also Aviation; International Law.

Encyclopaedias and periodicals

Halsbury's Laws of England. 4ed. vol.2.

Annals of Air and Space Law (Canada). 1976–

Journal of Space Law (USA). 1973–

Journal of Air Law and Commerce (as Journal of Air Law 1930–1938). 1939–

Yearbook of Air and Space Law.

Texts

BHATT, S.
Legal control of outer space law, freedom and responsibility. Chandra, 1973 (India).

BRITISH INSTITUTE OF INTERNATIONAL AND COMPARATIVE LAW
Space law: some current problems. BIICL, 1966.

CHRISTOL, C.Q.
Modern international law of outer space. Pergamon, 1982.

COHEN, M. (ed.)
Law and politics in space. Leicester U.P., 1964.

COOPER, J.C.
Explorations in aerospace law. McGill U.P., 1968 (Canada).

CSABAFI, I.A.
The concept of state jurisdiction in international space law. Nijhoff, 1971.

FAWCETT, J.E.S.
International law and the use of outer space. Manchester U.P., 1969.

FORKOSCH, M.
Outer space and legal liability. Nijhoff, 1982.

GAL, G.
Space law. Sijthoff, 1969.

GROOVE, S.
Studies in space law: its challenges and prospects. Sijthoff, 1977.

HALEY, A.G.
Satellite communications. Inst.of Air & Space Law, McGill Univ., 1964.

HALEY, A.G.
Space law and government. Appleton-Century-Crofts, 1963 (USA).

HALEY, A.G.
Space torts: liability for damages. Inst.of Air & Space Law, McGill Univ., 1964.

HIRSCH, R. & TRENTO, J.
National Aeronautics and Space Administration. Praeger, 1973.

INSTITUTE OF ADVANCED LEGAL STUDIES
Union list of air and space law literature. 2ed. IALS, 1975.

JENKS, C.W.
Space law. Stevens, 1965.

KISH, J.
The law of international spaces. Sijthoff, 1973.

LACHS, M.
Law of outer space: an experience in contemporary lawmaking. Sijthoff, 1972.

LAY, S.H. & TAUBENFELD, H.J.
The law relating to activites of man in space.
Chicago U.P., 1970.

LEE, R.S. & JASENTULIYANA, N.
Manual on space law. Oceana, 1978 (USA).
4 vols.

McDOUGLAS, M.S. and others
Law and public order in space. Yale U.P.,
1963 (USA).

McWHINNEY, E. & BRADLEY, M.
New frontiers in space law. Sijthoff, 1969.

MARKOV, M.G.
Public international law of outer space.
Fribourg, 1973 (Switzerland).

MATTE, N.M.
Aerospace law. Carswell, 1969 (Canada).

MATTE, N.M.
Treatise on air-aeronautical law. 3ed. Sweet
& Maxwell, 1982.

MATTE, N.M. & DESAUSSURE, H.
The legal implications of remote sensing
from outer space. Sijthoff, 1976.

MOSTESHAR, S. & BATE, S.de B.
Satellite and cable television – international
protection. Oyez Longman, 1984.

NOZARI, F.
Law of outer space. Norstedt, 1973.

OGUNBANWO, O.O.
International law and outer space activities.
Nijhoff, 1975.

REIJNEN, G.C.M.
Utilization of outer space and international
law. Elsevier, 1981.

TAUBENFELD, H.J.
Space and society. Oceana, 1964.

WADEGAGONKAR, D.
Orbit of space law. Stevens, 1984.

WILSON, I.L.
Law and politics in outer space: a
bibliography. Arizona U.P., 1972.

ZHUKOV, G.P. & KOLOSOV, Y.M.
International space law. trans. from
Russian. Praeger, 1984.

SPECIFIC PERFORMANCE

See also Contract; Equity.

Encyclopaedias

Halsbury's Laws of England. 4ed. vol.44.
Halsbury's Statutes of England. 3ed. vol.32.
The Digest. vol.43.

Encyclopaedia of Court Forms in Civil
Proceedings (Atkin). 2ed. vol.37.
Encyclopaedia of Forms and Precedents.
4ed. see index vol.

Texts

BOWEN, H.S.
Outlines of specific performance. 1886.

FRY, E.
A treatise on the specific performance of
contracts. 6ed. Stevens, 1921.

SPRY, J.C.F.
Equitable remedies, injunctions and
specific performance. 3ed. Sweet &
Maxwell, 1984.

WONTNER, J.J.
Specific performance practice: being a
guide to practice in actions for specific
performance. Pitman, 1933.

SQUATTING

See also Trespass

Encyclopaedias

Halsbury's Laws of England. 4ed. see index
vol.

Halsbury's Statutes of England. 3ed. see
index vol. under Trespass.

Texts

BAILEY, R.
The squatters. Penguin, 1973.

CANT, D.H.
Squatting and private property rights. UCL, School of Environmental Studies, 1978.

LAW COMMISSION
Criminal law: report on conspiracy and criminal law reform. HMSO, 1976 (Law Com. no.76).

LAW COMMISSION
Entering and remaining on property. HMSO, 1974 (Working paper no.54).

PRICHARD, A.
Squatting. Sweet & Maxwell, 1981.

WATKINSON, D.
Squatting: trespass and civil liberties. N.C.C.L., 1976.

SRI LANKA

Encyclopaedias and periodicals

Statutes in Force. Group: Commonwealth and Other Territories.
Halsbury's Laws of England. 4ed. vol.6.

Ceylon Law Journal. 1936–
Ceylon Law Recorder. 1919–
Ceylon Law Society Journal. 1954–
Ceylon Law Weekly. 1931–
University of Ceylon Law Review. 1958–

Texts

COORAY, L.J.M.
Constitutional and administrative law of Sri Lanka. Hansa, 1973 (Sri Lanka).

COORAY, L.J.M.
An introduction to the legal system of Ceylon. Lake House Invest., 1972.

JENNINGS, Sir W.I.
The constitution of Ceylon. 2ed. Oxford U.P., 1951.

NADARAJA, T.
The legal system of Ceylon in its historical setting. Brill, 1973.

PEIRIS, G.L.
General principles of criminal liability in Ceylon. Lake House Invest., 1972.

TAMBIAH, H.W.
Principles of Ceylon law. Cave, 1972.

WICKREMESINGHE, K.D.P.
Civil procedure in Ceylon. 1971.

WICKREMESINGHE, K.D.P.
The law of partition in Ceylon. 1971.

STAMP DUTIES

See also Revenue Law.

Encyclopaedias

Statutes in Force. Group: Stamp Duty.
Halsbury's Laws of England. 4ed. vol.44.
Halsbury's Statutes of England. 3ed. vol.32 but see index vol.

Encyclopaedia of Court Forms in Civil Proceedings (Atkin). 2ed. vol.34.
Encyclopaedia of Forms and Precedents. 4ed. vol.21.

Texts

ALPE, N.
The law of stamp duties. 24ed. Jordan, 1960.

HARPER, A.C.
Stamp duty and capital duty. Inst. Chartered Accountants, 1979.

HILL, D.G.
Stamp duties. Law Book Co., 1979 (Australia). Looseleaf.

MASTERS, S.V. (ed.)
Tolley's stamp duties: a comprehensive, concise exposition of stamp duty law and practice. 2ed. Tolley, 1981.

MONROE, J.G. & NOCK, R.S.
The law of stamp duties. 5ed. Sweet & Maxwell, 1976.

SERGEANT, E.G. & SIMS, B.J.
Stamp duties and capital duty. 8ed. Butterworths, 1982 supp. 1983.

SIMS, B.J.
Capital duty. Butterworths, 1975.

STANNARIES

See also Mines and Quarries

Encyclopaedias

Statutes in Force. Group: Mines and Minerals.
Halsbury's Laws of England. 4ed. vol. 7.
Halsbury's Statutes of England. 3ed. vol.22.
Encyclopaedia of Court Forms in Civil Proceedings (Atkin). 2ed. vol.10, 11,27.

Texts

BATTEN, J.
Stannaries Act, 1869. Butterworths, 1873.

HARRISON, Sir G.
Report on the laws and jurisdiction of stannaries in Cornwall. 1835.

PEARCE, T.
The law and customs of the stannaries in the counties of Cornwall and Devon. D.Browne, 1725.

PENNINGTON, R.P.
Stannary law: a history of the mining law of Cornwall and Devon. David & Charles, 1973.

TREGONING, J.
The laws of the stannaries of Cornwall. 2ed. 1824.

STATISTICS

BETTING, Gaming and Lotteries Act 1963 .Permits and licences, England, Wales and Scotland. HMSO. Annual.

CARR, R.A. & STERN, N.H.
Crime, the police and criminal statistics: an analysis of official statistics for England and Wales using econometric methods. Academic P., 1979.

CENTRAL STATISTICAL OFFICE
Annual abstract of statistics. HMSO.

CENTRAL STATISTICAL OFFICE
Monthly digest of statistics. HMSO.

HOME OFFICE
Criminal statistics: England and Wales. HMSO. Annual.

JUDICIAL Statistics England and Wales. HMSO. Annual.

JUDICIAL Statistics Scotland. HMSO. Annual Cmnd. Paper.

LEGAL Aid and advice Annual Reports.
HMSO. Annual H.C. Paper.

OFFENCES of drunkeness: England and Wales. HMSO. Annual.

OFFENCES relating to motor vehicles: England and Wales. HMSO. Annual.

PRISONS DEPARTMENT
Report on the work of the Prisons Department of the Home Office: statistical tables. HMSO. Annual.

SCOTTISH HOME AND HEALTH DEPARTMENT
Criminal statistics: Scotland. HMSO. Annual.

STATUTE OF WESTMINSTER

See also Commonwealth Law; Constitutional Law.

Encyclopaedias

Halsbury's Laws of England. 4ed. vol.6.
Halsbury's Statutes of England. 3ed. vol.4.
The Digest. vol. 8(2).

Texts

MAHAFFY, R.P.
The statute of Westminster, 1931. Butterworths, 1932.

WHEARE, Sir K.C.
The statute of Westminster and dominion status. 5ed. Oxford U.P., 1953.

STATUTES

See also Drafting; Interpretation; Legislation.

Encyclopaedias and periodicals

Statutes in Force. Group: Statutes and Statutory Instruments.
Halsbury's Laws of England. 4ed. vol.44.
Halsbury's Statutes of England. 3ed. vol.32.
The Digest. vol.44.

Encyclopaedia of Court Forms in Civil Proceedings (Atkin). 2ed. see index vol.

Statute Law Review. 1980–

Texts

BENNION, F.
Statute law. 2ed. Oyez, 1983.

CRAIES, W.F.
Statute law. 7ed. Sweet & Maxwell, 1971.

DALE, Sir W.
Legislative drafting: a new approach. Butterworths, 1977.

DICKERSON, F.R.
Interpretation and application of statutes. Little, Brown, 1975 (USA).

DRIEDGER, E.A.
Construction of statutes. Butterworths (Canada), 1974.

EVERSHED, Sir R.
Impact of the statute on the law of England. British Academy (Proceedings, vol.XLII), 1956.

HUGHES, C.
British statute book. Hutchinson, 1957.

ILBERT, Sir C.P.
Legislative methods and forms. Oxford U.P., 1901

ILBERT, Sir C.P.
The mechanics of law making. Columbia U.P., 1914 (USA).

JOWITT, Earl
Statute law revision and consolidation. Univ.of Birmingham, Holdsworth Club, 1951.

PEARCE, D.C.
Statutory interpretation in Australia. Butterworths (Australia), 1974.

STATUTE LAW SOCIETY
Renton and the need for reform. Sweet & Maxwell, 1979.

STATUTE LAW SOCIETY
Statute law deficiencies. Sweet & Maxwell, 1970.

STATUTE LAW SOCIETY
Statute law: the key to clarity. Sweet & Maxwell, 1972.

STATUTE LAW SOCIETY
Statute law: a radical simplication. Sweet & Maxwell, 1974.

STATUTORY PUBLICATIONS OFFICE
Chronological table of the statutes covering the period 1235 to date. HMSO. Annual.

STATUTORY PUBLICATIONS OFFICE
Index to the statutes covering the legislation in force on December 31. HMSO. Annual. 2 vols.

STATUTORY PUBLICATIONS OFFICE
Statutes in force: official revised edition. HMSO. Looseleaf. Microfiche ed. pub. by Unifo. 700+ fiches.

STATUTORY INSTRUMENTS

See also Delegated Legislation

Encyclopaedias

Statutes in Force. Group: Statutes and Statutory Instruments.
Halsbury's Laws of England. 4ed. vols. 1,17,34.

Halsbury's Statutes of England. 3ed. vol.32. but see index vol.
The Digest. vol.44.
Halsbury's Statutory Instruments.

Texts

STATUTORY PUBLICATIONS OFFICE
Index to government orders in force December 31. HMSO. Biennial.

STATUTORY PUBLICATIONS OFFICE
List of statutory instruments. HMSO. Monthly. Annual cumulation.

STATUTORY PUBLICATIONS OFFICE
Table of government orders, 1671 to date. HMSO. Annual.

STATUTORY SICK PAY

See also Employment Law

Texts

HOWARD, G.
Guide to self certification. Industrial Society, 1982.

HOWARD, G.
Guide to statutory sick pay. Industrial Society, 1982.

HOWARD, G.
Statutory sick pay: a practical guide. Oyez, 1983.

JANNER, G.
Guide to sick pay and absenteeism. Business Books, 1982.

TOLLEY's guide to statutory sick pay. Tolley, 1983.

STOCK EXCHANGE

Encyclopaedias

Halsbury's Laws of England. 4ed. vol.7 and see index.
Halsbury's Statutes of England. 3ed. see index vol.
The Digest. vol.44.

Encyclopaedia of Court Forms in Civil Proceedings (Atkin). 2ed. vol.37.
Encyclopaedia of Forms and Precedents. 4ed. vol.21.

Texts

AMERICAN STOCK EXCHANGE, INC.
Constitution and rules, revised to June 1, 1981. CCH, 1981.

COOPER, G. & CRIDLAND, R.J.
Law and procedure of the Stock Exchange. Butterworths, 1971.

FORBES, R.F. & JOHNSTON, D.L.
Canadian companies and the stock exchanges. CCH (Canada), 1981.

NEW YORK STOCK EXCHANGE, INC.
Constitution and rules, as of August 1, 1981. CCH, 1981.

POLEY, A.P.
Law and practice of the Stock Exchange. 5ed. Pitman, 1932.

STOCK EXCHANGE
Rules and regulations of the Stock Exchange. Stock Exchange. Looseleaf.

STRICT LIABILITY

See also Tort

Texts

EDWARDS, J.Ll.J.
Mens rea in statutory offences. Macmillan, 1955.

HOWARD, C.
Strict responsibility. Sweet & Maxwell, 1963.

POTTER, H.
Principles of liability in tort. Sweet & Maxwell, 1948.

SUCCESSION

See also Executors and Administrators; Probate; Real Property; Wills.

Encyclopaedias

Statutes in Force. Group: Succession.
Halsbury's Laws of England. 4ed. see index vol.

Halsbury's Statutes of England. 3ed. vol.45 and see index.

Texts

BARBER, P.
Succession notebook. Butterworths, 1970.

CORBETT, M.M.
The law of succession. Juta, 1980 (S.Africa).

COTRAN, E.
Law of succession in Kenya. Sweet & Maxwell, 1969.

COULSON, N.J.
Succession in the Muslim family. Cambridge U.P., 1971.

CURZON, L.B.
Law of succession. 2ed. Macdonald & Evans, 1981.

HARDINGHAM, I.J.
Law of intestate succession in Australia and New Zealand. Law Book Co., 1978.

HARVEY, B.W.
The law and practice of Nigerian wills, probate and succession. Sweet & Maxwell, 1968.

HUTLEY, F.C., WOODMAN, R.A. & WOOD, O.
Cases and materials on succession. Law Book Co., 1975 (Australia).

MELLOWS, A.R.
Law of succession. 4ed. Butterworths, 1983.

MESTON, M.C.
Succession (Scotland) Act, 1964. Green, 1969.

MILLER, G.
The machinery of succession. Professional Books, 1977.

OKORO, D.R.N.
The customary laws of succession in Eastern Nigeria and the statutory and judicial rules governing the application. Sweet & Maxwell, 1966.

OLLENNU, N.A.
The law of testate and intestate succession in Ghana. Sweet & Maxwell, 1966.

OOSTERHOFF, A.H.
Cases and materials on wills and succession. Carswell, 1980 (Canada).

PARRY, D.H. & CLARKE, J.B.
The law of succession. 8ed. Sweet & Maxwell, 1983.

TYLER, E.L.G.
Family provision. 2ed. Professional Books, 1984.

TAKEOVERS AND MERGERS

See also Companies

Encyclopaedias and periodicals

Halsbury's Laws of England. 4ed. see index vol.
Encyclopaedia of Forms and Precedents. 4ed. vol.6.

Journal of Business Law. 1957–

Texts

COOKE, P. & VAN DER BECK, J.M.
Tax aspects of acquisitions and mergers. Kluwer, 1980.

COWLING, K.
Mergers and economic performance. Cambridge U.P., 1980.

DAVIES, P.L.
The regulation of takeovers and mergers.. Sweet & Maxwell, 1976.

ECONOMISTS ADVISORY GROUP
Acquisitions and mergers: government policy in Europe. Palace Pub., 1976.

FIRTH, M.
Share prices and mergers: a study of stock market effeciency. Saxon House, 1976.

HARVEY, J.L. & NEWGARDEN, A. (eds.)
Management guides to mergers and acquisitions. Wiley, 1969.

HUNNINGS, N.M.
Monopolies and mergers. European Law Centre, 1980. 2 vols.

ISSUING HOUSES ASSOCIATION
City code on takeovers and mergers. 5ed. 1976.

JOHNSTON, A.
City take-over code. Oxford U.P., 1980.

KNIGHT, W.J.L.
The acquisition of private companies. 2ed. Oyez, 1979.

MORIN, D. & CHIPPINDALE, W.
Acquisitions and mergers in Canada. Carswell, 1977.

MORSE, G.
Company finance, takeovers and mergers. Sweet & Maxwell, 1979.

OFFICE OF FAIR TRADING
Mergers: a guide to the procedures under the Fair Trading Act, 1973. HMSO, 1978.

ORGANISATION FOR ECONOMIC CO-OPERATION AND DEVELOPMENT
Mergers and competition policy. 1975.

PRICES AND CONSUMER PROTECTION, DEPARTMENT OF
A review of monopolies and mergers policy: a consultative document. HMSO, 1978 (Cmnd. 7198).

ROBERTS, R.J.
Anticombines and antitrust: the competition law of Canada and the antitrust law of the United States. Butterworths (Canada), 1980.

SCHMITTHOFF, C.M. (ed.)
European company law texts. Stevens, 1974.

WEINBERG, M.A., BLANK, M.V. & GREYSTOKE, A.L.
Take-overs and mergers. 4ed. Sweet & Maxwell, 1979.

WIDMER, G.K.
Restrictive trade practices and mergers. Law Book Co., 1977 (Australia).

TANZANIA

See also Africa.

Encyclopaedias and periodicals

Statutes in Force. Group: Commonwealth and Other Territories.
Halsbury's Laws of England. 4ed. vol.6.
Halsbury's Statutes of England. 3ed. vol.4.

Annual Survey of African Law.
Annual Survey of Commonwealth Law. 1965–
Journal of the Denning Law Society. 1963–

Texts

AYANY, S.G.
History of Zanzibar: a study in constitutional development, 1934–64. H.Zell, 1977.

JAMES, R.W. & FIMBO, G.M.
Customary land law of Tanzania: a source book. H.Zell, 1977.

LEE, E.C.
Local taxation in Tanzania. Oxford U.P., 1966.

LIEBENOW, J.G.
Colonial rule and political development in Tanzania. 1954 repr. Greenwood, 1971.

MARTIN, R.
Personal freedom and the law in Tanzania. Oxford U.P., 1975.

NANJIRA, D.D.
Status of aliens in East Africa: Asians and Europeans in Tanzaniia, Uganda and Kenya. Praeger, 1975.

SEATON, E.E. & MALITI, S.J.
Tanzania treaty practice. Oxford U.P., 1974.

TAX HAVENS

See also Income Tax; Revenue Law; Tax Planning.

Periodicals

British Tax Review. 1956–
Taxation. 1927–

Texts

AVERY JONES, J.F. (ed.)
Tax havens and measures against tax evasion and avoidance in the E.E.C. Rothman, 1974.

DIAMOND, W.H. & DIAMOND, D.B.
Tax havens of the world. Bender, 1974 (USA). Looseleaf.

GRUNDY, M.
Grundy's tax havens: a world survey. 4ed.
Sweet & Maxwell, 1983.

SOLLY, M.
Anatomy of a tax haven. Vol.2: Manx
income tax. Shearwater P., 1979.

SPITZ, B. (ed.)
Tax havens encyclopaedia. Butterworths,
1975. Looseleaf.

TAX PLANNING

See also Income Tax; Revenue Law; Tax Havens.

Periodicals

British Tax Review. 1956–
Tax Planning Review. 1979–

Texts

ADAMS, P.R.
Australian tax planning. 3ed. Butterworths
(Australia), 1973.

BRIGGS, J.
Planning your personal finances. Oyez,
1979.

CAULFIELD, B.I. & NORRIS, W.V.W.
Wills and tax planning. The Law Society,
1979.

DAVIS, R.
Tax planning for life assurance and
pensions. Butterworths, 1980.

EASTAWAY, N.
Tax planning for medical practitioners.
Butterworths, 1984.

EASTAWAY, N.
Tax and financial planning for professional
partnerships. Butterworths, 1981.

GRUNDY, M.
World of international tax planning.
Cambridge U.P., 1984.

HALLETT, V.G.H. & WARREN, N.
Trust planning for capital transfer tax.
Sweet & Maxwell, 1978.

HARRIS, P.
Estate planning through life assurance.
Sweet & Maxwell, 1977.

HARRIS, P. & HEWSON, D.
Life assurance and tax planning. Sweet &
Maxwell, 1970.

HEPKER, M.Z.
Tax strategy for companies. 2ed. Oyez,
1980.

LIVENS, L.J.P. & THOMAS, N.
Tax planning review, 1979. Butterworths,
1979.

NELSON-JONES, J.A. & SMITH, B.
Practical tax saving. 4ed. Butterworths,
1984.

PEAT, MARWICK & MITCHELL
Practical tax planning. Butterworths, 1983.

POTTER, D.C. & MONROE, H.H.
Tax planning with precedents. 9ed. Sweet
& Maxwell, 1982.

RAY, R.P., RAY, M.W. & EASTWAY,
N.A.
Ray's practical capital transfer tax planning.
2ed. Butterworths, 1982.

RICE, R.S.
Family tax planning. Bender, 1960 (USA).
2 vols. Looseleaf.

SAUNDERS, M.R.
Principles of tax planning. 2ed. Tax
Management, 1978.

SAUNDERS, M.R.
Tax planning for businesses in Europe. 2ed.
Butterworths, 1984.

SOARES, P.C.
Land and tax planning. 2ed. Oyez
Longman, 1984.

SOARES, P.C.
Trusts and tax planning. rev.repr. Oyez,
1983.

SPITZ, B.
International tax planning. 2ed.
Butterworths, 1983.

SPRY, I.C.F.
Arrangements for the avoidance of taxation.
Law Book Co., 1972 (Australia).

SUMPTION, A. & CLARKE, G.
Tax planning. 11ed. Oyez Longman, 1984.

TOLLEY's tax planning for new businesses.
Tolley, 1983.

VENABLES, R.C.
Tax planning through wills (with precedents). 2ed. Butterworths, 1984.

WARD, D.A.
Current tax planning. Carswell, 1972 (Canada). 2 vols. Looseleaf.

WHITE, P.
Children in tax planning. Oyez, 1980.

WHITE, P.
Tax planning for the family. 2ed. Oyez, 1982.

WHITE, P.
Tax planning on marriage breakdown. 3ed. Oyez, 1984.

TAXICABS

Encyclopaedias and periodicals

Halsbury's Laws of England. 4ed. vol. 40.
Halsbury's Statutes of England. 3ed. vol.28.

Encyclopaedia of Court Forms in Civil Procedings (Atkin). 2ed. vol.8.

Taxi Drivers Compendium. Annual.

Texts

COMMITTEE ON THE TAXICAB SERVICE
Report (Runciman). HMSO, 1953 (Cmd. 8804).

INTERDEPARTMENTAL COMMITTEE ON CABS AND PRIVATE HIRE VEHICLES
Report (Hindley). HMSO, 1939 (Cmd. 5938).

HOME OFFICE
Report of the Departmental Committee on the London Taxicab Trade (Stamp). HMSO, 1970 (Cmnd. 4483).

STONE's Justices manual. Butterworths. 3 vols. annual.

TELECOMMUNICATIONS

See also Postal Services; Radio and Television.

Encyclopaedias and periodicals

Statutes in Force. Group: Post and Telecommunications.
Halsbury's Laws of England. 4ed. see index vol.

Halsbury's Statutes of England. 3ed. vol.25, 26.
The Digest. vol.45.
Telecommunications Policy. 1976–

Texts

ALEXANDROWICZ, C.H.
The law of global communications.
Columbia U.P., 1971 (USA).

CHAYES, A., FAWCETT, J. & ITO, M.
Satellite broadcasting. Oxford U.P., 1973.

CODDING, G.A.
The International Telecommunications Union. 1952 repr. Arno, 1972..

HOME OFFICE
The interception of communications in Great Britain. HMSO, 1980 (Cmnd. 7873).

INTERNATIONAL Telecommunication Convention and related documents. Malaga -Torremolinos. 25 Oct. 1974. HMSO, 1974 (Cmnd. 5678).

JONES, E.B.
Earth satellite telecommunications systems and international law. Univ.of Texas, 1970 (USA).

LEIVE, D.M.
International telecommunications and international law: the regulation of the radio spectrum. Sijthoff, 1970.

McWHINNEY, E. (ed.)
The international law of communications. Sijthoff, 1971.

MATTE, N.M.
Legal implications of remote sensing from outer space. Sijthoff, 1976.

PRIME MINSTER'S OFFICE
The interception of communications in Great Britain: report (Diplock). HMSO, 1981 (Cmnd. 8191).

SMITH, D.D.
Communications via satellite: a vision in retrospect. Sijthoff, 1976.

WALLENSTEIN, G.D.
International telecommunications agreements. Oceana, 1977 (USA). Looseleaf.

TERRITORIAL WATERS

See also Continental Shelf; International Law; Sea, Law of.

Encyclopaedias and periodicals

Halsbury's Laws of England. 4ed. see index vol.
Halsbury's Statutes of England. 3ed. see index vol.
Encyclopaedia of Court Forms in Civil Proceedings (Atkin). 2ed. vol.9, 27.

American Journal of International Law. 1907–
British Yearbook of International Law. 1920–
International and Comparative Law Quarterly. 1952–
International Law Reports. 1950–

Texts

BUTLER, W.E.
The law of Soviet territorial waters. Praeger, 1967 (USA).

DUBNER, B.H.
Law of territorial waters of mid-ocean archipelagos. Nijhoff, 1976.

FULTON, T.W.
Sovereignty of the sea, an historical account of the claims of England to the dominion of the British seas and the evolution of the territorial waters etc. 1911 repr. Kraus Thompson, 1973.

HALL, R.G.
Rights of the Crown and privileges of the subject in the sea-shores of the realm. 2ed. Stevens & Haynes, 1875.

HILDRETH, R.G. & JOHNSON, R.W. Ocean and coastal law. Prentice-Hall, 1983.

JESSUPP, P.C.
Law of territorial waters and maritime jurisdiction. Jennings, 1927 repr.

MARSTON, G.
Marginal seabed: United Kingdom legal practice. Oxford U.P., 1981.

MOORE, S.A.
History of the foreshore and the law relating thereto. Stevens & Haynes, 1888.

OUDENDIJK, J.K.
Status and extent of adjacent waters. Sijthoff, 1970.

SWARZTRAUBER, S.A.
Three mile limit of territorial seas. Naval Inst.P., 1972 (USA).

WHITEHEAD, H.
United Kingdom offshore legislation guide. Kogan Page, 1981.

THEATRES

See also Censorship; Entertainment.

Encyclopaedias and periodicals

Statutes in Force. Group: Entertainment.
Halsbury's Laws of England. 4ed. see index vol.
Halsbury's Statutes of England. 3ed. vol.35.
The Digest. vol.45.
Encyclopaedia of Court Forms in Civil Proceedings (Atkin). 2ed. vol.37.
Performing Right News. 1976–
Performing Right Yearbook.

Texts

COTTERELL, L.E.
Performance: study of the law and practice of entertainment and the performing arts. J.Offord, 1977.

ISAACS, S.C.
Law relating to theatres, music halls and other public entertainments. 1927.

IVAMY, E.R.H.
Show business and the law. Stevens, 1955.

JACOBS, M.C.
Outline of theatre law. 1949 repr. Greenwood, 1973(USA).

ROTHENBERG, S.
Copyright and public performance of music. Nijhoff, 1954.

STRONG, A.A.
Dramatic and musical law. 3ed. 1910.

THEFT

See also Criminal Law.

Encyclopaedias and periodicals

Statutes in Force. Group: Criminal Law.
Halsbury's Laws of England. 4ed. vol.11.
Halsbury's Statutes of England. 3ed. vol.8.
The Digest. mainly vols. 14, 15.
Encyclopaedia of Court Forms in Civil Proceedings (Atkin). 2ed. see index vol.
Encyclopaedia of Forms and Precedents. 4ed. vols. 4, 10.
Criminal Law Review. 1954–
Journal of Criminal Law. 1937–
Justice of the Peace. 1837–

Texts

BAUMER, T.L. & ROSENBAUM, D.P.
Combating retail theft: programmes and strategies. Butterworths, 1984.

CRIMINAL LAW REVISION COMMITTEE
Eighth report: theft and related offences. HMSO, 1966 (Cmnd. 2977).

GRIEW, E.
The Theft Acts, 1968 and 1978. 4ed. Sweet & Maxwell, 1982.

JACKSON, B.S.
Theft in early Jewish law. Oxford U.P., 1972.

MAGUIRE, M.
Burglary in a dwelling. Heinemann, 1982 (Cambridge studies in criminology).

SMITH, J.C.
Law of theft. 5ed. Butterworths, 1984.

TYSKA, L.A. & FENNELLY, L.J.
Controlling cargo theft: a handbook of transportation security. Butterworths, U.S., 1983.

WHITESIDE, J.
Theft Act precedents. Butterworths, 1968.

WINCHESTER, S. & JACKSON, H.
Residential burglary: the limits of prevention. HMSO, 1982 (Home Office research studies, no.74).

TITLE

See also Conveyancing; Land Registration; Land Tenure; Leases; Mortgages; Prescription; Real Property; Vendor and Purchaser.

Encyclopaedias and periodicals

Statutes in Force. Groups: Property, England & Wales; Conveyancing and Registration of Writs, Scotland.
Halsbury's Laws of England. 4ed. see index vols.
Halsbury's Statutes of England. 3ed. vol.30.
Encyclopaedia of Court Forms in Civil Proceedings (Atkin). 2ed. see index vol.

Encyclopadia of Forms and Precedents. 4ed. see index vol.
Conveyancer. 1915–1936.
Conveyancer and Property Lawyer. 1936–
Estates Gazette. 1858–
Property and Compensation Reports. 1950–

Texts

BAALMAN, J. & WELLS, T.de M.
Land titles office practice. 4ed. Law Book Co., 1980 (Australia).

BASYE, P.E.
Clearing land titles. 2ed. West, 1970 (USA).

COLLINS, D.
Strata title units in New South Wales. Butterworths (Australia), 1974.

EMMET, L.E.
Notes on perusing titles and on practical conveyancing. 18ed. Oyez, 1983 supp. 1984.

FLICK, C.P.
Abstract and title practice with forms. 2ed. West, 1958 (USA). 3 vols. & supp.

JACKSON, W.H. & GOSSET, T.
Investigation of title. 6ed. Stevens, 1950.

LAW COMMISSION
Transfer of land: root of title to freehold land. HMSO, 1966 repr. 1977 (Working paper no.1)

LAW COMMISSION
Transfer of land: interim report on root of title to freehold land. HMSO, 1967 (Law Com. no.9).

McALLISTER, D.L.
Registration of title in Ireland. Incorp.Council of Law Rep.for Ireland, 1974.

MOORE, H.
Abstracts of title. 6ed. Butterworths, 1925.

OLAWOYE, C.O.
Title to land in Nigeria. Evans, 1974.

PRESTON, R.
Essays on abstracts of title. 2ed. Clarke, 1823–24. 2 vols.

SCOTTISH LAW COMMISSION
Probate or letters of administration as links in title to heritable property under the Succession (Scotland) Act, 1964. 1966 (Memorandum no. 1).

WILLIAMS, W.J.
Law and practice relating to the contract for the sale of land and title to land. 4ed. Butterworths, 1975 supp. 1983.

TORRENS TITLE

See also Land Registration.

Periodicals

Australian Lawyer (formerly Australian Conveyancer and Solicitors Journal. 1948–1959). 1960–
Australian Law Journal. 1927–

Texts

BAALMAN, J.
The Torrens system in New South Wales. 2ed. Law Book Co., 1974.

FRANCIS, E.A.
Law and practice relating to Torrens title in Australasia. Butterworths (Australia), 1972. 2 vols.

HINDE, G.W.
New Zealand Torrens system centenary essays. Butterworths (New Zealand), 1970.

PONCE, F.D.
The Philippines Torrens system. Manila, Central Books, 1964.

RUOFF, T.B.F.
An Englishman looks at the Torrens system. Law Book Co., 1957 (Australia).

THOM, D.J.
Canadian Torrens systems. 2ed. Carswell, 1962.

WHALAN, D.
Torrens system in Australia. Law Book Co., 1982.

TORT

See also Accidents; Delict; Employer's Liability; Libel and Slander; Negligence; Nuisance; Occupiers' Liability; Passing Off; Personal Injuries: Prenatal Injuries; Strict Liability; Trespass; Vicarious Liability.

Encyclopaedias and periodicals

Statutes in Force. Group: Tort and Delict.
Halsbury's Laws of England. 4ed. see index vol.
Halsbury's Statutes of England. 3ed. see index vol.
The Digest. vol.45.
Encyclopaedia of Court Forms in Civil Proceedings (Atkin). 2ed. see index vol.

Cambridge Law Journal. 1921–
Law Quarterly Review. 1885–
Modern Law Review. 1937–
New Law Journal. 1965–
Solicitors' Journal. 1857–

Texts

ADDISON, C.G.
Wrongs and their remedies, being the law of torts. 8ed. 1906 repr. Professional Books.

ARMOUR, L.A.J.
Cases in tort. Macdonald & Evans, 1977.

ATIYAH, P.S.
Accidents, compensation and the law. 3ed. Weidenfeld & N., 1980.

ATIYAH, P.S.
Vicarious liability in the law of torts. Butterworths, 1967.

BAKER, C.D.
Tort. 3ed. Sweet & Maxwell, 1981.

BOWDEN, G.F. & MORRIS, A.S.
Introduction to the law of contract and tort. Estates Gazette, 1978.

BRADBURY, P.L. & BARRETT, B.
Cases and statutes on tort. 3ed. Sweet & Maxwell, 1984.

CAIRNS, M.B.
Law of tort in local government. 2ed. Shaw, 1970.

CHARLESWORTH, J.
Negligence. 7ed. Sweet & Maxwell, 1983.

CLERK, J.F. & LINDSELL, W.H.
The law of torts. 15ed. Sweet & Maxwell, 1982 supp. 1984.

CRACKNELL, D.G.
Torts. 6ed. Butterworths, 1983.

DAVIS, A.G.
The law of torts in New Zealand. 2ed. Butterworths (NZ), 1959.

DIAS, R.W.M. & MARKESINIS, B.S.
English law of torts: a comparative introduction. Bruylant, 1976.

DIAS, R.W.M. & MARKESINIS, B.S.
Tort law. Oxford U.P., 1984.

TORT

FIFOOT, C.H.S.
History and sources of the common law: tort and contract. 1949 repr. Greenwood, 1970.

FLEMING, J.G.
Introduction to the law of torts. 2ed. Oxford U.P., 1978.

FLEMING, J.G.
The law of torts. 6ed. Law Book Co., 1983.

FRIDMAN, G.H.L.
Introduction to the law of torts. Carswell, 1978 (Canada).

GATLEY, J.C.
Libel and slander. 8ed. Sweet & Maxwell, 1981.

GERBER, P.
Torts and related problems in the English and Australian conflict of laws. Muller, 1974.

HARARI, A.
The place of negligence in the law of torts. Law Book Co., 1962 (Australia).

HART, H.L.A. & HONORE, A.M.
Causation in the law. Oxford U.P., 1958.

HAWKINS, A.J.
Law relating to owners and occupiers of land. Butterworths, 1971.

HEPPLE, B.A. & MATTHEWS, M.H.
Sourcebook on tort. Butterworths, 1974.

HEPPLE, B.A. & MATTHEWS, M.H.
Tort: cases and materials. 2ed. Butterworths, 1980.

HEYDON, J.D.
Economic torts. 2ed. Sweet & Maxwell, 1978.

HIGGINS, P.F.P.
Elements of torts in Australia. Butterworths (Australia), 1970.

HOGG, P.W.
Liability of the Crown in Australia, New Zealand and the United Kingdom. Sweet & Maxwell, 1972.

INSURANCE INSTITUTE OF LONDON
Advantages and disadvantages of the tort system and alternative methods of accident compensation. The Institute, 1978.

ISON, T.G.
The forensic lottery: a critique on tort liability as a system of personal injury compensation. Staples P., 1967.

JAMES, P.S.
General principles of the law of torts. 4ed. Butterworths, 1978.

KLAR, L.N.
Studies in Canadian tort law. 1977.

KODILINYE, G.
The Nigerian law of torts. Sweet & Maxwell, 1982.

LAW COMMISSION
Breach of confidence. HMSO, 1974 repr. 1977 (Working paper no.58).

LAW COMMISSION
Civil liability for dangerous things and activities. HMSO, 1970 (Law Com. no.32).

LAW COMMISSION & SCOTTISH LAW COMMISSION
Liability for defective products. HMSO, 1975 repr. 1977 (Working paper no.64, Memorandum no.20).

LAW REFORM COMMITTEE
Ninth report: liability in tort between husband and wife. HMSO, 1961 (Cmnd. 1268).

LAWSON, F.H.
Negligence in the civil law. Oxford U.P., 1950.

LAWSON, F.H. & MARKESINIS, B.S.
Tortious liability for unintentional harm in the common law and the civil law. Cambridge U.P., 1982. 2 vols.

LINDEN, A.M.
Canadian tort law. 2ed. Butterworths (Canada), 1977.

LLOYD, M.G.
Torts. 5ed. Butterworths, 1978.

LUNTZ, H., HAMBLY, A.D. & HAYES, R.
Torts: cases and commentary. Butterworths (Australia), 1980.

McMAHON, B.M.E. & BINCHY, W.
Irish law of torts. Professional Books, 1981. Books, 1982.

McMAHON, B.M.E. & BINCHY, W.
Casebook on the Irish law of torts. Professional Books. 1983.

MILLER, C.J. & LOVELL, P.A.
Product liability. Butterworths, 1977.

MORSE, C.G.J.
Torts in private international law. North-Holland, 1979.

NATHAN, Lord
Medical negligence. Butterworths, 1957.

NORTH, P.M.
The modern law of animals. Butterworths, 1972.

NORTH, P.M.
Occupiers liability. Butterworths, 1971.

POLLOCK, F.
The law of torts. 15ed. Stevens, 1951.

POTTER, H.
Principles of liability in tort. Sweet & Maxwell, 1948.

PRICHARD, M.J.
Scott v Shepherd 1773 and the emergence of the tort of negligence. 1976 (Selden Society lecture 1973).

PROSSER, W.L.
Handbook of the law of torts. 4ed. West, 1971 (USA).

SALMOND, J.W.
The law of torts. 18ed. Sweet & Maxwell, 1981.

SPRY, I.C.F.
Equitable remedies, injunctions and specific performance. 3ed. Sweet & Maxwell, 1984.

STREET, H.
Torts. 7ed. Butterworths, 1983.

TYAS, J.G.M.
Law of torts. 4ed. Macdonald & Evans, 1982.

VEITCH, E.
East African cases on the law of tort. Sweet & Maxwell, 1972.

WEIR, J.A.
Casebook on tort. 5ed. Sweet & Maxwell, 1983.

WHITE, G.E.
Tort law in America: an intellectual history. Oxford U.P., 1980.

WILLIAMS, G.L.
Liability for animals. Cambridge U.P., 1939.

WILLIAMS, G.L.
Joint torts and contributory negligence. Sweet & Maxwell, 1951 repr. 1977.

WILLIAMS, G.L. & HEPPLE, B.A.
Foundations of the law of torts. 2ed. Butterworths, 1984.

WINFIELD, P.H.
Province of the law of tort. Cambridge U.P., 1931.

WINFIELD, Sir P.H. & JOLOWICZ, J.A.
Textbook of the law of tort. 12ed. Sweet & Maxwell, 1984.

TOWN AND COUNTRY PLANNING

See also Environment Law; Housing.

Encyclopaedias and periodicals

Statutes in Force. Group: Town and Country Planning
Halsbury's Laws of England. 4ed. vol.46.
Halsbury's Statutes of England. 3ed. see index vol.
The Digest. vol.45.
Encyclopaedia of Court Forms in Civil Proceedings (Atkin). 2ed. vol.38.

Texts

ALDER, J.
Development control. Sweet & Maxwell, 1979.

ARNOLD-BAKER, C.
Local Government Planning and Land Act, 1980. Butterworths, 1981.

Estates Gazette. 1858–
Journal of Planning and Environment Law. 1948–
The Planner (as Journal of Royal Town Planning Institute). 1941–
Planning. 1972–
Property and Compensation Reports. 1950–

BAR COUNCIL
Planning and mineral working, papers from a conference held at Oxford, Sept. 1978, organised by the Bar Council, Law Society and Royal Institution of Chartered Surveyors. Sweet & Maxwell, 1978(Journal of Planning and Environment Law occasional papers).

BEAUMONT, C.H.
The Town and Country Planning Acts, 1971 and 1972. Butterworths, 1973.

BLUNDELL, J.A. & DOBRY, G.
Planning appeals and enquiries. 3ed. Sweet & Maxwell, 1982.

BOWHILL, A.
Planning application fees. Oyez, 1981.

BROADY, M.
Planning for people: essays on the social context of planning. Bedford Square P., 1969.

BURKE, G.
Town planning and the surveyor. Estates Gazette, 1980.

CHADWICK, G.F.
Systems view of planning. 2ed. Pergamon, 1978.

CULLINGWORTH, J.B.
Town and country planning in Britain. 7ed. Allen & Unwin, 1982.

DAVIES, M.R.
Principles and practice of planning. Butterworths, 1956.

DENYER-GREEN, B.
Development and planning law. Estates Gazette, 1982.

DOBRY, G.
Control of demolition. HMSO, 1974.

ELKIN, S.L.
Politics and land use planning. Cambridge U.P., 1974.

FOGG, A.S.
Australian town planning law: uniformity and change. University of Queensland P., 1982.

GARNER, J.F. (ed.)
Planning law in Western Europe. North-Holland, 1975.

GARNER, J.F.
Practical planning law. Croom Helm, 1981.

GARNER, J.F.
Slum clearance and compensation. 4ed. Oyez, 1975 (Practice notes no.45).

GRANT, M.
Planning law handbook. Sweet & Maxwell, 1981.

GRANT, M.
Urban planning law. Sweet & Maxwell, 1982.

HAMILTON, R.N.D.
A guide to development and planning. 7ed. Oyez, 1981.

HAMILTON, R.N.D.
Planning procedure tables. 4ed. Oyez, 1981.

HEAP, D. (ed.)
Encyclopaedia of the law of town and country planning. Sweet & Maxwell. 4 vols. Looseleaf.

HEAP, Sir D.
An outline of planning law. 8ed. Sweet & Maxwell, 1982.

HEAP, D.
The land and the development, or the turmoil and torment. Stevens, 1975 (Hamlyn lecture).

HEAP, Sir D.
Town and country planning: or how to control land development. 2ed. Rose, 1981.

HOUSING & LOCAL GOVERNMENT, MINISTRY OF
Town and country planning. HMSO, 1967 (Cmnd. 3333).

JAMES, D.E.H.
Notes on the need for planning permission. 3ed. Oyez, 1984.

JOURNAL OF PLANNING AND ENVIRONMENT LAW
A future for old buildings? Listed buildings, the law and practice. Sweet & Maxwell, 1977 (Occasional papers no.3).

JOYCE, F.
Local government and environmental planning and control. Gower Pub.Co., 1982.

LITTLE, A.J.
Planning controls and their enforcement. 5ed. Shaw, 1983.

LOMNICKI, A.J.
Summary of town and country planning law and the law of compulsory purchase. Batsford, 1973.

McAUSLAN, P.
The ideologies of planning law. Pergamon, 1980.

McAUSLAN, P.
Land, law and planning. Weidenfeld & N., 1975.

McKOWN, R.
Comprehensive guide to town planning law and procedure. 2ed. Godwin, 1973.

McLEOD, T.L.
Guide to planning law in the magistrates' court. B.Rose, 1982.

MOBBS, M.
Local government planning and environment service NSW. Butterworths (Australia). Looseleaf.

MOORE, V.W.E. & CATCHPOLE, L.
Local Government Planning and Land Act, 1980. Sweet & Maxwell, 1981.

MORRIS, G., HOOPER, A. & BARKER, M.
Planning and environment law (Victoria). Butterworths (Australia). Looseleaf.

NEWMAN, P.E.
Town and country planning casebook. Estates Gazette, 1975.

NUTLEY, W.G. (ed.)
Contemporary planning policies. Sweet & Maxwell, 1984.

O'SULLIVAN, P.
Irish planning and acquisition law. Inst.of Public Admin., 1978.

PARRISH, H.
Law relating to private street works. Rose, 1979.

RATCLIFFE, J.
Introduction to urban land administration. Estates Gazette, 1978.

ROBERTS, N.A.
The reform of planning law: a study of the legal, political and administrative reform of the British land use planning system. Macmillan, 1976.

ROWAN-ROBINSON, J. and others
The enforcement of planning control in Scotland. Scottish Development Office, 1984.

SCOTTISH LAW COMMISSION
Applications for planning permission. 1967 (Memorandum no.4).

SHEPHERD, K.M. & O'SULLIVAN, P.
Sourcebook on planning law in Ireland. Professional Books, 1983.

STURGE, L.F.
Town and Country Planning Act, 1968 and the Civic Amenities Act, 1967. Estates Gazette, 1969.

TELLING, A.E.
Planning law and procedure. 6ed. Butterworths, 1982.

WILLIAMS, A.
Town and country planning law. Macdonald & Evans, 1981.

YOUNG, E.
Developments in planning law in Scotland, 1973–6. Planning Exchange, 1977.

YOUNG, E.
Law of planning in Scotland. Hodge, 1978.

TRADE DESCRIPTIONS

See also Passing Off; Sale of Goods.

Encyclopaedias

Statutes in Force. Group: Sale of Goods.
Halsbury's Laws of England. 4ed. vol. 48 and see index.

Halsbury's Statutes of England. 3ed. vol.37.

Texts

EGAN, B.
Trade descriptions: prosecutions enforcement and complaints. LRS Pubns., 1970.

INSTITUTE OF PRACTITIONERS IN ADVERTISING
Is it legal? A guide to the laws affecting the design and content of food labels and advertisments. The Institute, 1979.

LEAPER, W.J.
Implications for business of the new Trades Descriptions Act. Business Pubns., 1969.

NEWSOME, E.L.
The Trade Descriptions Act and the motor vehicle. Rose, 1977.

O'KEEFE, J.A.
Law relating to trade descriptions. Butterworths, 1971. Looseleaf.

O'KEEFE, J.A.
The Trade Descriptions Act, 1968. Butterworths, 1968.

PEARCE, E.H.
Passing off, the law as to imitation and description in trade. Sol.Law Stat.Soc., 1928.

TRADE MARKS

See also Business Names; Copyright; Passing Off; Patents.

Encyclopaedias and periodicals

Statutes in Force. Group: Patents, Designs and Trade Marks.
Halsbury's Laws of England. 4ed. vol. 48.
Halsbury's Statutes of England. 3ed. vol. 37.
The Digest. vol. 46.
Encyclopaedia of Court Forms in Civil Proceedings (Atkin). 2ed. vol. 38.

Encyclopaedia of Forms and Precedents. 4ed. vol. 22.
Fleet Street Patent Law Reports. 1963–
Reports of Patent Cases. 1884–
Trade Marks Journal. 1876–

Texts

BURGE, D.A.
Patent and trademark tactics and practice. 2ed. Wiley, 1984.

CHARTERED INSTITUTE OF PATENT AGENTS
European patents handbook. Oyez, 1978. 2 vols. Looseleaf.

CHOWLES, V.G. & WEBSTER, G.C.
South African law of trade marks and trade names. 2ed. Butterworths (S.Africa), 1973.

CORNISH, W.R.
Intellectual property: patents, copyright, trade marks and allied rights. Sweet & Maxwell, 1981.

FOX, H.G.
Canadian law of trademarks and unfair competition. 3ed. Carswell, 1972.

GILSON, J.
Trademark protection and practice. Bender, 1974 (USA).

GUIDEBOOK to Australian trademarks law. CCH Australia, 1979.

HEARN, P.
The business of industrial licensing: a practical guide to patents, know-how, trademarks and industrial designs. Gower 1980.

KASE, F.J.
Trademarks: a guide to official trademark literature. Sijthoff, 1974.

KERLY, Sir D.M.
Law of trademarks and tradenames. 11ed. Sweet & Maxwell, 1972.

LAWSON, R.G.
Advertising and labelling laws in the Common Market. 3ed. Jordan, 1982. Looseleaf.

MAK, W. & MOLYN, H.
Introduction to trade-mark law. Kluwer, 1981.

MEINHARDT, P.
Inventions, patents and trade marks. Gower, 1971.

MEINHARDT, P. & HAVELOCK, K.R.
Concise trade mark law and practice. Gower, 1983.

MICHAELS, A.
Practical guide to trade marks. E.S.C.Pub., 1982.

MOULTON, H.F.
The present law and practice relating to letters patent for inventions. Butterworths, 1913.

MOULTON, H.F. & EVANS-JACKSON, J.H.
Patents, designs and trade marks Acts. 2ed. Butterworths, 1930.

MOULTON, H.F. & LANGDON-DAVIES, P.G.
The law of merchandise marks. Butterworths, 1954.

NATIONAL ASSOCIATION OF CREDIT MANAGEMENT
Digest of commercial laws of the world: patents and trademarks. Oceana, 1968. 2 vols. Looseleaf.

PAINTER, A.A.
Is it legal? Guide to labelling and packaging. Pt 1: laws affecting the design and content of food, medicines and pet food labels and advertising. Institute of Practitioners in Advertising, 1983.

PATENT OFFICE
Applying for a trade mark. HMSO, 1975.

PATTISHALL, B.W. & HILLIARD, D.C.
Trademarks, trade identity and unfair trade practices. Bender, 1974 (USA) Looseleaf.

REID, B.C.
Practical introduction to trademarks. Waterlow, 1984.

RUSSELL, R.W.
Patents and trademarks in Japan. 3ed. Russell, 1974.

SAFFORD, F.
The law of merchandise marks. Waterlow, 1983.

SEBASTIAN, L.B.
Digest of cases of trade marks. Stevens, 1879.

SEBASTIAN, L.B.
Law of trade marks. 5ed. Stevens, 1911.

SEBASTIAN, L.B.
Trade Marks Registration Acts. 2ed. Stevens, 1922.

TRADE AND INDUSTRY, DEPARTMENT OF
Report of the Committee on British Trade Mark Law and Practice (Mathys). HMSO, 1974 (Cmnd. 5601).

WEBSTER, G.C.
Patents, trademarks and designs in Africa. 2ed. Patlaw, 1973. Looseleaf.

WHITE, T.A.B. & JACOB, R.
Patents, trade marks, copyrights and industrial designs. 3ed. Sweet & Maxwell, 1983.

TRADE SECRETS

See also Competition; Patents.

Encyclopaedias

Halsbury's Laws of England. 4ed. see index vol.
Halsbury's Statutes of England. 3ed. vol. 37.

Encyclopaedia of Forms and Precedents. 4ed. vol. 22.

Texts

CHOATE, R.A. & FRANCIS, W.H.
Cases on patent law: also including trade secrets. West, 1973 (USA).

MILGRIM, R.M.
Trade secrets. Bender, 1967 (USA). 2 vols. Looseleaf.

TURNER, A.E.
The law of trade secrets. Sweet & Maxwell, 1962.

WISE, A.N.
Trade secrets and know-how throughout the world. Clark Boardman, 1974 (USA). 5 vols. Looseleaf.

TRADE UNIONS

See also Arbitration; Employment Law; Factories; Industrial Law; Industrial Relations; Shops and Offices.

Encyclopaedias and periodicals

Statutes in Force. Group: Employment.
Halsbury's Laws of England. 4ed. mainly vol. 47 but see index.
Halsbury's Statutes of England. 3ed. see index vol.
Encyclopaedia of Court Forms in Civil Proceedings (Atkin). 2ed. vol. 38.
Encyclopaedia of Forms and Precedents. 4ed. vol. 22.

British Journal of Industrial Relations. 1963–

Bulletin of the Industrial Law Society.
Bulletin of the Society for the Study of Labour History. 1960–
Employment Gazette (under other names 1893–1970). 1970–
Industrial Cases Reports. 1975–
Industrial Court Reports. 1972–74.
Industrial Law Journal. 1972–
Industrial Relations Journal. 1970–
Industrial Relations Law Reports. 1972–

Texts

ALLEN, V.L.
International bibliography of trade unionism. Merlin P., 1969.

ASSINDER, G.F.
The legal position of trade unions. 2ed. Stevens, 1912.

BALFOUR, C.
Unions and the law. Saxon House, 1973.

CAMPBELL, A.
Trade unions and the individual. ESC Pub., 1980.

COMMISSION ON INDUSTRIAL RELATIONS
Trade union recognition. HMSO, 1974.

EWING, K.D.
Trade unions, the Labour Party and the law. Edinburgh U.P., 1983.

GRUNFELD, C.
Modern trade union law. Sweet & Maxwell, 1970.

HEDGES, R.Y. & WINTERBOTTOM, A.
The legal history of trade unionism. Longmans, Green, 1930.

HENDERSON, J.
Guide to the Trade Union and Labour Relations Act, 1974. Butterworths, 1974.

HOME, J.
Trade unionists and the law. Shaw, 1983.

HUGHES, J. & POLLINS, H.
Trade unions in Great Britain. David & Charles, 1973.

INTERNATIONAL LABOUR ORGANISATION
Report on trade union rights and their relation to civil liberties. ILO, 1970.

JENKS, C.W.
International protection of trade union freedom. Stevens, 1957.

KERR, A. & WHYTE, G.
Trade union law in the Republic of Ireland. Professional Books, 1985.

KIDNER, R.
Trade union law. 2ed. Sweet & Maxwell, 1983.

LOCKYER, J.
Industrial arbitration in Great Britain. Inst.of Personnel Management, 1980.

McCARTHY, W.E. J.
The closed shop in Britain. Blackwell, 1964.

PELLING, H.M.
A history of British trade unionism. Macmillan, 1963.

RIDEOUT, R.W.
The right to membership of a trade union. Athlone P., 1963.

RIDEOUT, R.W.
Trade unions: some social and legal problems. Tavistock, 1964.

RIDEOUT, R.W.
Trade unions and the law. Allen & Unwin, 1973.

ROBERTSON, N. & SAMS, K.I. (eds.)
Select documents on British trade unionism. Rowman, 1972. 2 vols.

ROYAL COMMISSION ON TRADE UNIONS AND EMPLOYERS' ASSOCIATIONS
Report (Donovan). HMSO, 1968 (Cmnd. 3623).

SMITH, D.W.
The legal status of Australian trade unions. Butterworths (Australia), 1975.

SWEENEY, S.
Closed shop agreements: a practical guide. Inst.of Personnel Management, 1976.

TRANSPORT

See also Aviation; Carriers/Carriage of Goods; Railways; Shipping.

Encyclopaedias and periodicals

Statutes in Force. Group: Transport.
Halsbury's Laws of England. 4ed. see index vol.
Halsbury's Statutes of England. 3ed. see index vol.

Encyclopaedia of Court Forms in Civil Proceedings (Atkin). 2ed. vol. 39.
Encyclopaedia of Forms and Precedents. 4ed. vols. 3, 10.

Commercial Transport. 1972–
Journal of Business Law. 1957–
Journal of World Trade Law. 1967–
Journal of Transport Economics and Policy. 1967–
Lloyd's Maritime and Commercial Law Quarterly. 1974–
Railway and Canal Traffic Cases. 1855–1934.
Road Traffic Reports. 1970–
Traffic Cases. 1935–1976.

Texts

BONNER, G.A.
British transport law by road and rail. David & Charles, 1973.

CLARKE, M.
International carriage of goods by road: C.M.R. Sweet & Maxwell, 1982.

DONALD, A.E.
C.M.R. Convention on the Contract for the International Carriage of Goods by Road. Beattie, 1981.

ENVIRONMENT, DEPARTMENT OF
Your lorry abroad: guide for British goods vehicles operators making journeys overseas. HMSO, 1974.

HAANAPPEL, P.C.
Ratemaking in international air transport. Kluwer, 1977.

HILL, D., EVANS, M. & SIMMONDS, K.R.
Transport laws of the world. Oceana, 1977 (USA). Looseleaf.

JAMES, L.
The law of the railway. Rose, 1980.

KAHN-FREUND, O.
The law of carriage by inland transport. 4ed. Stevens, 1965.

KITCHIN, L.D. & DUCKWORTH, J.
Road transport law. 24ed. Butterworths, 1983.

LESLIE, A.
The law of transport by railway. 2ed. Sweet & Maxwell, 1928.

LOWE, D.
The transport manager's handbook 1978. Kogan Page, 1977.

MESSENT, A.
C.M.R. Lloyd's, 1984.

POWELL-SMITH, V.
The Transport Act, 1968. Butterworths, 1969.

PUGH, J.
Law relating to heavy goods vehicles. Rose, 1980.

RIDLEY, J.G.
Law of the carriage of goods by land, sea and air. 6ed. Shaw, 1982.

SHAW, S.
Air transport: a marketing perspective. Pitman, 1982.

SUMMERS, D.
H.G.V. law guide. Butterworths, 1981.

TRANSPORT, DEPARTMENT OF
European Agreement concerning the International Carriage of Dangerous Goods by Road (ADR). 4ed. HMSO, 1978.

WALLIS, P.
Transport Act 1982. Fourmat, 1982.

ZWEIGERT, K. & KROPHOLLER, J.
Sources of international uniform law. Vol. 2: transport law. Sijthoff, 1972 supp. 1973.

TREASON

See also Criminal Law; Revolution.

Encyclopaedias

Statutes in Force. Group: Criminal Law.
Halsbury's Laws of England. 4ed. vol. 11.
Halsbury's Statutes of England. 3ed. vol. 8.
The Digest. vols. 14, 15.

State Trials (ed. Howell). 1163–1828. 34 vols.
State Trials. new series (ed. Macdonnell). 1820–1858. 8 vols.

Texts

BELLAMY, J.G.
Law of treason in England in the later middle ages. Cambridge U.P., 1970.

BELLAMY, J.G.
Tudor law of treason: an introduction. Routledge, 1978.

BOVERI, M.
Treason in the twentieth century. 1956.

FOSTER, Sir M.
Report of some proceedings on...the trial of the rebels in 1746 to which are added discourses on crown law, treason, etc. 3ed. Brooke, 1792.

LAW COMMISSION
Codification of the criminal law: treason, sedition and allied offences. HMSO, 1977 (Working paper no.72).

THOMAS, D.
State trials. Vol.1: public conscience; vol. 2: treason. Routledge, 1972.

WEST, R.
New meaning of treason. Viking, 1964.

TREASURE TROVE

See also Coroner

Encyclopaedias

Halsbury's Laws of England. 4ed. vols. 8, 9.
Halsbury's Statutes of England. 3ed. vol.7.
The Digest. vol.13.

Encyclopaedia of Court Forms in Civil Proceedings (Atkin). 2ed. vols. 13, 14, 25.

Texts

BLANCHET, A. & GRUEBER, H.
Treasure trove. 1902.

HILL, G.F.
Treasure trove: the law and practice of antiquity. Milford, 1933.

HILL, G.F.
Treasure trove in law and practice from the earliest times to the present day. Oxford U.P., 1936 repr. Scientia Verlag, 1979.

RHIND, A.H.
Law of treasure trove. 1858.

TREATIES

See also International Law.

Encyclopaedias and periodicals

Halsbury's Laws of England. 4ed. vol. 18.
Halsbury's Statutes of England. 3ed. vols. 6, 37.
Encyclopaedia of Court Forms in Civil Proceedings (Atkin). 2ed. vols. 5, 18.
Encyclopaedia of Forms and Precedents. 4ed. vols. 18, 22.

American Journal of International Law. 1907–
British Yearbook of International Law. 1920–
International and Comparative Law Quarterly. 1952–
International Law Reports. 1950–

Texts

ADAMS, L.J.
Theory, law and policy of contemporary Japanese treaties. Sijthoff, 1974.

AGRAWALA, S.K. (ed.)
Essays on the law of treaties. Tripathi, 1979 (India).

ARMSTRONG, J.W.S.
War and treaty legislation, 1914–1921. Hutchinson, 1922.

BLIX, H.
Treaty maker's handbook. Almqvist, 1974.

BOWMAN, M. & HARRIS, D.
Multilateral treaties: index and current status. Butterworths, 1983.

DRAPER, G.I.A.D.
Red Cross Conventions. Stevens, 1958.

ELIAS, T.O.
The modern law of treaties. Sijthoff, 1974.

GRENVILLE, J.A.S.
The major international treaties, 1914–1973: a history and guide with texts. Methuen, 1974.

McNAIR, Sir A.D.
The law of treaties. Oxford U.P., 1961.

OAKES, Sir A. & MOWAT, R.B. (eds.)
The great European treaties of the nineteenth century. Oxford U.P., 1970.

PARRY, C. (ed.)
The consolidated treaty series. Oceana, 1969–1981. 231 vols. and 4 index vols.

PARRY, C. & HOPKINS, C.A.
An index of British treaties, 1101–1968. HMSO, 1970. 3 vols.

ROHN, P.H.
World treaty index. 2ed. ABC-Clio Press, 1983. 5 vols.

ROSENNE, S.
Law of treaties: a guide to the legislative history of the Vienna Convention. Sijthoff, 1971.

ROZAKIS, C.L.
The concept of jus cogens in the law of treaties. North-Holland, 1976.

SCHNEIDER, J.W.
Treaty making power of international organisations. Droz, 1959.

SCOTT, G.L.
Chinese treaties. Oceana, 1975.

SINCLAIR, I.M.
The Vienna Convention on the Law of Treaties. Manchester U.P., 1973.

SPRUDZS, A.
Treaty sources in legal and political research. Univ.of Arizona P., 1971.

TREATIES and alliances of the world: a survey of international treaties in force and communities of states. 2ed. Scribner, 1974.

WIKTOR, C.L.
Canadian treaty calendar, 1928–1978. Oceana, 1982. 2 vols.

TRESPASS

See also Boundaries and Fences; Criminal Law; Rights of Way; Squatting; Tort.

Encyclopaedias and periodicals

Halsbury's Laws of England. 4ed. see index vol.
Halsbury's Statutes of England. 3ed. see index vol.
The Digest. vol.46.
Encyclopaedia of Court Forms in Civil Proceedings (Atkin). 2ed. see index vol.
Encyclopaedia of Forms and Precedents. 4ed. see index vol.
Criminal Law Review. 1954–
Law Quarterly Review. 1885–

Texts

BEVEN, T.
The House of Lords on the law of trespass to realty and children as trespassers. Stevens & Haynes, 1909.

LAW COMMISSION
Criminal law: offences of entering and remaining on property. HMSO, 1974 repr. 1977 (Working paper no.54).

LAW COMMISSION
Liability for damage or injury to trespassers and related questions of occupiers liability. HMSO, 1973 repr. 1977 (Working paper no.52)

LAW COMMISSION
Report on liability for damage or injury to trespassers and related questions of occupiers liability. HMSO, 1976 (Law Com. no.75).

TRIALS

See also Court Martial; Impeachment.

Encyclopaedias

Halsbury's Laws of England. 4ed. see index vol.
Halsbury's Statutes of England. 3ed. vol.8.
Encyclopaedia of Court Forms in Civil Proceedings (Atkin). see index vol.

Texts

BALDWIN, J. & McCONVILLE, M.
Jury trials. Oxford U.P., 1979.

BARNARD, D.
Civil court in action. 2ed. Butterworths, 1984.

BARNARD, D.
The criminal court in action. 2ed. Butterworths, 1980.

DEVLIN, J.D.
Criminal courts and procedure. 2ed. Butterworths, 1967.

DEVLIN, P.A.
Trial by jury. Stevens, 1970 (Hamlyn lecture no.8).

FALLON, P.
Crown Court practice: trial. Butterworths, 1978 supp. 1979.

STONE, M.
Proof of fact in criminal trials. Green, 1984.

WILLIAMS, G.L.
The proof of guilt: a study of the English criminal trial. 3ed. Sweet & Maxwell, 1963.

TRIBUNALS AND INQUIRIES

See also Industrial Tribunals.

Encyclopaedias and periodicals

Statutes in Force. Group: Tribunals and Inquiries.
Halsbury's Laws of England. 4ed. see index vols.
Halsbury's Statutes of England. 3ed. see index vol. under Tribunals and under Names of Appropriate Tribunals.
Encyclopaedia of Court Forms in Civil Proceedings (Atkin). 2ed. vol.40.
Encyclopaedia of Forms and Precedents. 4ed. vol.20.

Cambridge Law Journal. 1921–
Law Quarterly Review. 1885–
Modern Law Review. 1937–
Public Administration. 1923–
Public Law. 1956–

Annual Report of the Council on Tribunals. 1959–

Texts

BELL, K.
Tribunals in the social services. Routledge & K.P., 1969.

COMMITTEE ON ADMINISTRATIVE TRIBUNALS AND ENQUIRIES
Report (Franks). HMSO, 1957 (Cmnd. 218).

FARMER, J.A.
Tribunals and government. Weidenfeld & N., 1974.

FROST, A. & HOWARD, C.
Representation and administrative tribunals. Routledge, 1977.

INSTITUTE OF JUDICIAL ADMINISTRATION
The future of administrative tribunals. 1971.

KEETON, G.W.
Trial by tribunal. Museum P., 1960.

LISTER, R.
Justice for the claimant: a study of supplementary benefit appeal tribunals. C.P.A.G., 1974.

LORD CHANCELLOR'S DEPARTMENT
The functions of the Council on Tribunals: special report. HMSO, 1980 (Cmnd. 7805).

POLLARD, R.S.W. (ed.)
Administrative tribunals at work. Stevens, 1950.

VANDYK, N.D.
Tribunals and inquiries. Oyez, 1965.

WRAITH, R.E. & HUTCHESSON, P.G.
Administrative tribunals. Allen & Unwin, 1973.

TRUSTS AND TRUSTEES

See also Charities; Executors and Administrators; Perpetuities; Powers.

Encyclopaedias

Statutes in Force. Groups: Property, England and Wales, Sub-Group 4; Trusts and Liferents, Scotland.
Halsbury's Laws of England. 4ed. vol.48.
Halsbury's Statutes of England. 3ed. mainly vol.38.

The Digest. vol.47.
Encyclopaedia of Court Forms in Civil Procedings (Atkin). 2ed. vol.41.
Encyclopaedia of Forms and Precedents. 4ed. vol.22.

Texts

BOGERT, G.G.
Law of trusts and trustees. West, 1935. 15 vols. supp. (USA).

BRADSHAW, F.M.
The law of charitable trusts. Butterworths (Australia), 1982.

CHESTERMAN, M.R.
Charities, trusts and social welfare. Weidenfeld & N., 1979 (Law in context).

CHICK, A.F.
Outline of the law of trusts. Heinemann, 1968.

CURZON, L.B.
Law of trusts. 2ed. Macdonald & Evans, 1980.

FAIRBURN, W.J.G.
Handbook for trustees and liquidators. 3ed. Juta, 1973 (S.Africa).

FORD, H.
Cases on trusts. 5ed. Law Book Co., 1984 (Australia).

FORD, H.
Principles of the law of trusts. Law Book Co., 1983 (Australia).

FORSYTH, T.A.
Brief outline of the law relating to trusts, wills, executors and administrators. Butterworths (NZ), 1973.

GARROW, J.M.
Law of trusts and trustees in New Zealand. 4ed. Butterworths (NZ), 1972.

HALLETT, V.G.H. & WARREN, N.
Trust planning for capital transfer tax. Sweet & Maxwell, 1978.

HARDINGHAM, I.J. & BAXT, R.
Discretionary trusts. Butterworths (Australia), 1975 supp. 1978.

HARRIS, J.W.
Variation of trusts. Sweet & Maxwell, 1974.

HEYDON, J.D., GUMMON, W.M.C. & AUSTIN, R.P.
Cases and materials on equity and trusts. 2ed. Butterworths (Australia), 1982.

TRUSTS AND TRUSTEES

HONORE, A.M.
South African law of trusts. 2ed. Sweet & Maxwell, 1976.

JACOBS, K.S.
Law of trusts in Australia. 4ed. Butterworths (Australia), 1977.

JACOBS, K.S.
Law of trusts in New South Wales. 3ed. Butterworths (Australia), 1971.

JOSLING, J.F.
Apportionments for executors and trustees. 4ed. Oyez, 1976.

KEETON, G.W.
Modern developments in the law of trusts. Northern Ireland L.Q., 1971

KEETON, G.W. & SHERIDAN, L.A.
Comparative law of trusts in the Commonwealth and the Irish Republic. Rose, 1976 supp. 1981.

KEETON, G.W. & SHERIDAN, L.A.
Digest of the English law of trusts. Rose, 1979.

KEETON, G.W. & SHERIDAN, L.A.
The law of trusts. 11ed. Rose, 1983.

LAW REFORM COMMITTEE
The powers and duties of trustees: consultative document. HMSO, 1978.

LAW REFORM COMMITTEE
Report no.23: the powers and duties of trustees. HMSO, 1982 (Cmnd. 8733).

LEWIN, T.
Law of trusts. 16ed. Sweet & Maxwell, 1964.

LONGLEY, A.R.
Charity trustee's guide. 2ed. Bedford Square P., 1982.

MAUDSLEY, R.H. & BURN, E.H.
Trusts and trustees: cases and materials. 2ed. Butterworths, 1978.

MEAGHER, R.P. & GUMMON, W.M.C.
Jacob's law of trusts in Australia. 4ed. Butterworths (Australia), 1977.

MELLOWS, A.R.
Taxation for executors and trustees. 5ed. Butterworths, 1981.

MELLOWS, A.R.
Trustees handbook. 3ed. Butterworths, 1975.

NATHAN, J.A. & MARSHALL, O.R.
Cases and commentary on the law of trusts. 7ed. Sweet & Maxwell, 1980.

NEWMAN, R.A.
Trusts. 2ed. Foundation P., 1955 (USA).

NOSSAMAN, W.L. & WYATT, J.L.
Trust administration and taxation. 2ed. Bender, 1957 (USA). 3 vols. Looseleaf.

OAKLEY, A.J.
Constructive trusts. Sweet & Maxwell, 1978.

PARKER, D. & MELLOWS, A.R.
Modern law of trusts. 4ed. Sweet & Maxwell, 1979.

PETTIT, P.H.
Equity and the law of trusts. 5ed. Butterworths, 1984.

RIDDALL, J.G.
The law of trusts. 2ed. Butterworths, 1982.

SHERRING, T.
Capital transfer tax: discretionary trusts after the Finance Act, 1982. Tolley, 1982.

SHERRING, T. & SALDEN, M.
Law and accounts for executors and trustees. Gee, 1981.

SHRAND, D.
Trusts in South Africa. Juta, 1976.

SLADEN, M.
Practical trust administration. 2ed. Europa, 1983.

SOARES, P.C.
Trusts and tax planning. Oyez, 1979 supp. 1980.

THOMAS, G.W.
Taxation and trusts. Sweet & Maxwell, 1981.

UNDERHILL, Sir A.
Law relating to trusts and trustees. 13ed. Butterworths, 1979 supp. 1982.

VICKERY, B.G.
Law and accounts of executors, administrators and trustees. 20ed. Cassell, 1980.

VINTER, E.
A treatise on the history and law of fiduciary relationship and resulting trusts. 3ed. Stevens, 1955.

WALKER, N.M.L.
Judicial factors. Green, 1984.

WATERS, D.W.M.
The constructive trust. Athlone P., 1964.

WATERS, D.W.M.
Law of trusts in Canada. Carswell, 1974.

WATERS, D.W.M.
The law of trusts in the 80's. Carswell, 1980.

WILSON, W.A. & DUNCAN, A.G.M.
Trusts, trustees and executors. Green, 1975.

TUG AND TOW

See also Shipping

Encyclopaedias and periodicals

Halsbury's Laws of England. 4ed. vol.43.
Halsbury's Statutes of England. 3ed. vol.31.
Encyclopaedia of Forms and Precedents. 4ed. vol.21.

Lloyds Law Reports. 1919–

Texts

BUCKNILL, A.
Law relating to tug and tow. 2ed. Stevens, 1927.

DOUGLAS, R.
Harbour law. 2ed. Lloyd's, 1983.

KOVATS, L.J.
The law of tugs and towage. Rose, 1980.

NEWSON, H.
Law of salvage, towage, pilotage. 1886.

PARKS, A.L.
Law of tugs, tow and pilotage. 2ed. Chapman & Hall, 1982.

ULTRA VIRES

See also Companies; Injunctions; Judicial Review.

Encyclopaedias and periodicals

Halsbury's Laws of England. 4ed. vol.7 and see index vol.
Encyclopaedia of Court Forms in Civil Proceedings (Atkin). 2ed. vols. 12, 20, 32.
Encyclopaedia of Forms and Precedents. 4ed. vols. 2, 5, 6.

Public Administration. 1923–
Public Law. 1956–

Texts

BEATTIE, D.J.
Ultra vires in relation to local authorities. Sol.Law Stat.Soc., 1936.

BRICE, S.W.
Law of corporations and companies, a treatise on the doctrine of ultra vires. 3ed. Stevens & Haynes, 1893.

DE SMITH, S.A.
Judicial review of administrative action. 4ed. Sweet & Maxwell, 1980.

STREET, H.A.
Ultra vires: being an investigation of the principles which limit the powers and liabilities of corporations etc. Sweet & Maxwell, 1930 repr. Professional Books.

UNFAIR DISMISSAL

See also Employment Law; Employment Protection; Industrial Law; Industrial Relations.

Encyclopaedias and periodicals

Halsbury's Laws of England. 4ed. vol.16.
Halsbury's Statutes of England 3ed. see index vol.
The Digest. vol.34.
Encyclopaedia of Court Forms in Civil Proceedings (Atkin). 2ed. see index vol.
British Journal of Industrial Relations. 1963–

Industrial Law Journal. 1972–
Industrial Relations Journal. 1970–
Industrial Relations Law Reports. 1972–
Industrial Relations Review and Report. 1971–
Managerial Law (as Knights Industrial Law Reports, 1966–1974). 1975–

Texts

ALLAN, R.G.
New deal for employment: or how to prepare for a genuine participation or how to avoid unfair dismissal. Printhouse, 1978.

ANDERMAN, S.D.
Law of unfair dismissal. 2ed. Butterworths, 1984.

COCKERILL, A. & HODKINSON, C.
A guide to unfair dismissal. Christopher James & Co., 1974.

CONSUMERS' ASSOCIATION
Dismissal, redundancy and job hunting. CA, 1977.

EGAN, B.
Dismissals: the complete practical guide. New Commercial Pub.Co., 1977.

FOX, R.
Payments on termination of employment. 2ed. Oyez Longman, 1984.

FULBROOK, J.
Administrative justice and the unemployed. Mansell, 1978.

HARVEY, R.J.S. (ed.)
Industrial relations and employment law. Butterworths. Looseleaf.

INDUSTRIAL SOCIETY
Unfair dismissal. 1973.

JACKSON, D.
Unfair dismissal: how and why the law works. Cambridge U.P., 1975.

McGLYNE, J.E.
Unfair dismissal cases. 2ed. Butterworths, 1978.

MEAD, M.W.T.
Unfair dismissal handbook. Oyez, 1981.

UNITED NATIONS

See also International Law.

Encyclopaedias and periodicals

Halsbury's Laws of England. 4ed. vol. 18 and see index.
Halsbury's Statutes of England. 3ed. see index vol.
American Journal of International Law. 1907–
British Yearbook of International Law. 1920–

International and Comparative Law Quarterly. 1952–
International Review of Criminal Policy. 1952–
United Nations Juridical Yearbook. 1963–
United Nations Law Reports. 1966–
United Nations Yearbook on Human Rights. 1946–

Texts

ALEXANDROWICZ, C.H.
Law making functions of the specialised agencies of the United Nations. Angus, 1973.

ASAMOAH, O.Y.
The legal significance of the declaration of the General Assembly of the United Nations. Sijthoff, 1966.

BAILEY, S.D.
The General Assembly of the United Nations: a study of procedure and practice. 1964 repr. Greenwood, 1978 (USA).

BAILEY, S.D.
The procedure of the U.N. Security Council. Oxford U.P., 1975.

BENTWICH, N. & MARTIN, A.
A commentary on the Charter of the United Nations. Routledge, 1950.

BHUTTO, Z.A.
Peace-keeping by the United Nations. Pakistan Pub.House, 1967.

BOKOR-SZEGO, H.
Role of the United Nations in international legislation. Trans from Hungarian. Sijthoff, 1978.

BOWETT, D.W. (ed.)
United Nations forces: a legal study of United Nations practice. Stevens, 1964.

BRIERLY, J.L.
The Covenant and the Charter. Cambridge U.P., 1947.

CASSESE, A.
United Nations peace-keeping: legal essays. Sijthoff, 1978.

CASTANDENA, J.
Legal effects of United Nations resolutions. Columbia U.P., 1969 (USA).

CHAMBERLIN, W. and others
Chronology and fact book of the United Nations, 1941-1976. 4ed. Oceana, 1976.

CLARK, R.S.
United Nations High Commissioner for Human Rights. Humanities P., 1972.

COHEN, B.V.
The United Nations: constitutional developments, growth and possibilities. Harvard U.P., 1961 (USA).

DJONOVICH, D.J. (ed.)
United Nations resolutions. Oceana, 1972-78. 14 vols.

EICHELBERGER, C.M.
Organizing for peace: a personal history of the founding of the United Nations. Harper & Row, 1977.

ELMANDIJRA, M.
The United Nations system: an analysis. Faber, 1973.

FORSYTHE, D.P.
United Nations peacemaking: the Conciliation Commission for Palestine. Johns Hopkins U.P., 1972 (USA).

GOODRICH, L.M.
The United Nations in a changing world. Columbia U.P., 1974.

GOODRICH, L.M., HAMBRO, E. & SIMONS, A.P.
Charter of the United Nations: commentary and documents. 3ed. Columbia U.P., 1969.

GUTTERIDGE, J.A.C.
The United Nations in a changing world. Manchester U.P., 1969.

HALDERMAN, J.W.
The United Nations and the rule of the law: Charter development through the handling of international disputes and situations. Oceana, 1967 (USA).

HAZZARD, S.
Defeat of an ideal: a study of the self destruction of the United Nations. Little, Brown, 1973 (USA).

HIGGINS, R.
The development of international law through the political organs of the United Nations. Oxford U.P., 1963.

HIGGINS, R.
United Nations peacekeeping. 2: Asia. Oxford U.P., 1970.

HIGGINS, R.
United Nations peacekeeping 1946-1967. 3: Africa. Oxford U.P., 1979.

HIGGINS, R.
United Nations peacekeeping . 4: Europe 1946-1979. Oxford U.P., 1981.

INDRA, N.T.
Peace-keeping power of the United Nations General Assembly. Chandra, 1974 (India).

JONES, G.J.
The United Nations and the domestic jurisdiction of States. Univ.Wales P., 1979.

KAPUNGU, L.T.
United Nations and economic sanctions against Rhodesia. Lexington, 1973.

KAUFMAN, J.
United Nations decision making. Sijthoff, 1980.

KELSEN, H.
The law of the United Nations. Stevens, 1950.

KOH, B.C.
United Nations Administrative Tribunal. Louisiana U.P., 1970 (USA).

KOUL, A.K.
Legal framework of UNCTAD in world trade. Sijthoff, 1977.

LAUTERPACHT, E.
The U.N emergency force: basic documents. Stevens, 1960.

LERNER, N.
U.N. Convention on the Elimination of All Forms of Racial Discrimination. Sijthoff, 1970.

LUARD, E.
The United Nations. Macmillan, 1978.

MERON, T.
United Nations secretariat: the rule and the practice. Lexington, 1977 (USA).

MOSKOWITZ, M.
Roots and reaches of United Nations actions. Sijthoff, 1980.

NICHOLAS, H.G.
The United Nations as a political institution. 5ed. Oxford U.P., 1975.

RAJAN, M.S.
Expanding jurisdiction of the United Nations. Oceana, 1981 (USA).

RAJAN, M.S.
United Nations and domestic jurisdiction. 2ed. Asia Pub.Co., 1961.

RAMAN, K.V.
Dispute settlement through the United Nations. Oceana, 1977 (USA).

ROBERTSON, A.H.
Relations between the Council of Europe and the United Nations. Unitar, 1973.

ROSS, A.
Constitution of the United Nations: analysis of structure and function. Munksgaard, 1950.

ROWE, E.T.
Strengthening the United Nations: a study of the evolution of member state commitments. Sage, 1974.

SCHWARZENBERGER, G.
International law as applied by international courts and tribunals. Vol.3: international constitutional law, fundamentals, United Nations, related agencies. Stevens, 1976.

SHARP, W.R.
United Nations Economic and Social Council. Columbia U.P., 1969.

SINGER, J.D.
Financing international organization: the United Nations budget process. Nijhoff, 1961.

SOHN, L.B.
Cases on United Nations law. 2ed. Foundation P., 1967 (USA).

TWITCHETT, K.J. (ed.)
The evolving United Nations: a prospect for peace? Europa, 1971.

UNITED NATIONS
Basic facts about the United Nations: a summary of its purposes, structure, activities. UN, 1970.

UNITED NATIONS
United Nations action in the field of human rights. UN, 1981.

UNITED NATIONS COMMISSION ON INTERNATIONAL TRADE LAW
UNCITRAL arbitration rules. 1977.

VANDENBOSCH, A. & HOGAN, W.N.
The United Nations: background, organisation, functions, activities. 1952 repr. Greenwood.

WEISSBERG, G.
The international status of the United Nations. Oceana, 1961 (USA).

WIGHTMAN, D.
Economic co-operation in Europe: a study of the United Nations Economic Commission for Europe. Stevens, 1956.

WIGHTMAN, D.
Toward economic co-operation in Asia: the United Nations Economic Commission for Asia and the Far East. Stevens, 1963.

WORTLEY, B.A.
United Nations: the first ten years. 1957 repr. Greenwood, 1974.

WRIGHT, Q.
International law and the United Nations. Asia Pub. House, 1960.

YEMIN, E.
Legislative powers in the United Nations and specialised agencies. Humanities P., 1969.

UNITED STATES OF AMERICA

Encyclopaedias and periodicals

Halsbury's Laws of England. 4ed. see index vols.
Halsbury's Statutes of England. 3ed. vols. 6, 24, 29.
Encyclopaedia of Court Forms in Civil Proceedings (Atkin). 2ed. vol.35.
Encyclopaedia of Forms and Precedents. 4ed. vols. 1, 20, 23.

Administrative Law Review. 1949–
American Bar Association Journal. 1915–
American Journal of Legal History. 1957–
Annual Survey of American Law. 1942–
Harvard Law Review. 1887–
International Organisation. 1947–
Public Administration Review. 1940–

Texts

ANTIEAU, C.J.
Modern constitutional law. Lawyers Co-op., 1969. 2 vols. & supp.

BALDWIN, H.
General view of the origin and nature of the constitution and government of the United States. 1837 repr. Da Capo, 1970.

BETH, L.P.
Politics, the constitution and the Supreme Court: an introduction to the study of the constitution. Harper & Row, 1962 (USA).

BRECKENRIDGE, A.C.
Congress against the court. Nebraska U.P., 1970.

CAMPBELL, D. & HEPPERLE, W.
United States legal system: a practice handbook. Nijhoff, 1983.

CHASE, H.W. & DUCAT, C.R.
Constitutional interpretation: cases, essays and materials. West, 1974.

COLUMBIA UNIVERSITY
Constitutions of the United States: national and state. 2ed. Oceana, 1974. 5 vols.

CORWIN, E.S.
Constitution and what it means today. 13ed. Princeton U.P., 1973.

COX, A.
Rule of the Supreme Court in American government. Oxford U.P., 1975.

DAVIES, J.
Institutions and methods of the law. West, 1982 (USA).

FERGUSON, J.H. & McHENRY, D.E.
American federal government. 13ed. McGraw-Hill, 1977.

FRIEDELBAUM, S.H.
Contemporary constitutional law: case studies in the judicial process. Houghton Mifflin, 1972.

GRILLIOT, H.J.
Introduction to the law and legal system. 2ed. Houghton Mifflin, 1979.

GROSSMAN, J.B.
Constitutional law and judicial policy making. Wiley, 1972 supp. 1982.

GUIDE to American law. West, 1983. 12 vols.

HASKINS, G.D.
History of the United States Supreme Court. 2 vols. Collier Macmillan, 1982.

HAY, P.
An introduction to United States law. North-Holland, 1976.

JAFFE, L.L.
English and American judges as law makers. Oxford U.P., 1969.

KARLEN, D.
Judicial administration: the American experience. Butterworths, 1970.

KEMPIN, F.G.
Historical introduction to Anglo-American law in a nutshell. 2ed. West, 1973.

KIMBALL, S.
Historical introduction to the legal system. West, 1966 (USA).

MELLINKOFF, D.
Lawyers and the system of justice. West, 1976 (USA).

MILLER, A.
Presidential power. West, 1977 (USA).

MORRIS, A.
The constitution and American education. 2ed. West, 1980 (USA).

NICHOLAS, H.
The nature of American politics. Oxford U.P., 1980.

RAWLE, W.
View of the constitution of the United States of America. 1829 repr. Da Capo, 1970.

REYNOLDS, W.
The judicial process. West, 1980 (USA).

SAYE, A.B.
Principles of American government. 9ed. Prentice-Hall, 1982.

SCHWARTZ, R.L.
Commentary on the constitution of the United States. Macmillan, 1969. 5 vols.

SMITH, E.C.
Constitution of the United States with case summaries. 10ed. Barnes & Noble, 1975.

STORY, J.
Commentaries on the constitution of the United States. 1833. 3 vols. repr. Da Capo, 1971.

TUGWELL, R.G.
Emerging constitution. Harper & Row, 1974.

VANDERBILT, A.T.
Doctrine of the separation of powers and its present day significance. Nebraska U.P., 1963.

WILLIAMS, J.
Constitutional analysis. West, 1979 (USA).

VAGRANCY

See also Poor Law.

Encyclopaedias

Statutes in Force. Group: Criminal Law.
Halsbury's Laws of England. 4ed. vol.11.
Halsbury's Statutes of England. 3ed. vol.8.

Texts

COOK, T.
Vagrant alcoholics. Routledge, 1975.

DEPARTMENTAL COMMITTEE ON VAGRANCY
Report (Wharton). HMSO, 1906 (Cd. 2852, 2891, 2892).

HOME OFFICE
Report of the Working Party on Vagrancy and Street Offences (Brennan). HMSO, 1976.

STEWART, J.
Of no fixed abode: vagrancy and the welfare state. Manchester U.P., 1975.

STONE's Justices' manual. Butterworths. 3 vols. annual.

VALUE ADDED TAX

See also Customs and Excise; Revenue Law.

Encyclopaedias and periodicals

Statutes in Force. Group: Customs and Excise.
Halsbury's Laws of England. 4ed. vol. 12.
Halsbury's Statutes of England. 3ed. vol.42, vol.42A for EEC Regulations.
Encyclopaedia of Court Forms in Civil Proceedings (Atkin). 2ed. vol.40 and annual supplement.

Encyclopaedia of Forms and Precedents. 4ed. annual supplement.

British Tax Review. 1956–
Simon's Tax Cases. 1973–
Simon's Tax Intelligence. 1973–
Taxation. 1927–
Value Added Tax Tribunal Reports. 1973–

Texts

ASSOCIATION OF CERTIFIED AND CORPORATE ACCOUNTANTS
Value added tax: law and practice. 1972.

BRITISH tax encyclopaedia. Sweet & Maxwell, 1962. 5 vols. Looseleaf.

BUTTERWORTHS' handbook on value added tax. Butterworths, 1983.

BUTTERWORTHS' orange tax handbook (development land tax, capital transfer tax, value added tax). Butterworths. Annual.

DE VOIL, P.
Value added tax. Butterworths, 1972. Looseleaf.

GROUT, V.
Grout's value added tax cases. Tolley, 1982.

HUGHES, P.F. & TINGLEY, K.R.
Key to value added tax. 2ed. Taxation Pub.Co., 1973.

JOSEPH, C.
Value added tax: the British system explained. Financial Techniques, 1972.

MAINPRICE, H.H.
Value added tax. Butterworths, 1978.

PARKINSON, D.
Value added tax in the E.E.C. Graham & Trotman, 1980.

RELF, D.G. & PRESTON, C.A.L.
Value added tax casebook. Oyez, 1980.

RELF, D.G. & PRESTON, C.A.L.
Value added tax guide. Oyez, 1981.

RYBCZYNSKI, T.M.
Value added tax: European experience and the British outlook. Blackwell, 1972.

SIMMONDS, B.
Practical guide to value added tax. Gee, 1972.

SIMON, J.A.
Simon's taxes. 3ed. Butterworths. 9 vols. Looseleaf.

TOLLEY's practical guide to VAT planning. Tolley, 1983.

WARREN, P.B.
Businessman's guide to valued added tax. Gower, 1972.

WHEATCROFT, G.S.A.
Value added tax: a guide to the V.A.T. provisions of the Finance Bill 1972. Cassell, 1972.

WHEATCROFT, G.S.A.
Value added tax in Great Britain. Sweet & Maxwell, 1973.

WHEATCROFT, G.S.A.
Value added tax in the enlarged Common Market. Cassell, 1973.

WHEATCROFT, G.S.A. & AVERY-JONES, J.F.
Encyclopaedia of value added tax. Sweet & Maxwell, 1973. Looseleaf.

VENDOR AND PURCHASER

See also Contract; Conveyancing; Deeds; Real Property; Sale of Goods; Title.

Encyclopaedias and periodicals

Statutes in Force. Groups: Property, England and Wales; Conveyancing and Registration of Writs, Scotland; Sale of Goods.
Halsbury's Laws of England. 4ed. vol. 42.
Encyclopaedia of Court Forms in Civil Proceedings (Atkin). 2ed. see index vol.
Encyclopaedia of Forms and Precedents. 4ed. see index vol.

Conveyancer and Property Lawyer. 1936–
Journal of Business Law. 1957–
Law Quarterly Review. 1885–
Modern Law Review. 1937–
New Law Journal. 1965–
Property Law Bulletin. 1980–

Texts

DART, J.H.
Law relating to vendors and purchasers of real estate. 8ed. Stevens, 1929. 2 vols.

DiCASTRI, V.
Law of vendor and purchaser: the law and practice relating to contracts for sale of land in the common law provinces of Canada. 2ed. Carswell, 1978 (Canada).

NORMAN, R.
Purchase and sale in South Africa. 4ed. Butterworths (SA), 1972.

STONHAM, R.M.
Law of vendor and purchaser. Sweet & Maxwell, 1964 (Australia).

SUGDEN, E.B.
Law of vendors and purchasers. 14ed. Sweet, 1862.

WILLIAMS, T.C.
Law relating to vendors and purchasers of real estate and chattels real. 4ed. Sweet & Maxwell, 1936. 2 vols.

VETERINARY LAW

Encyclopaedias and periodicals

Statutes in Force. Group: Medical and Related Professions.
Halsbury's Laws of England. 4ed. vol. 30.
Halsbury's Statutes England. 3ed. vol.21.
Encyclopaedia of Court Forms in Civil Proceedings (Atkin). 2ed. vols. 5, 28.
Encyclopaedia of Forms and Precedents. 4ed. vol.1.

British Veterinary Journal. 1949–
Registers and Directory of Veterinary Surgeons. 1881. Annual.
Veterinary Annual. 1949–
Veterinary Bulletin. 1931–
Veterinary Record. 1888–

Texts

BLACK's veterinary dictionary. Black, 1975.

BULLOCK, F.
Law relating to medical, dental and veterinary practice. Bullock, 1929.

EDUCATION AND SCIENCE, DEPARTMENT OF
Report of the Committee of Inquiry into the Veterinary Profession (Swann). HMSO, 1975. (Cmnd. 6143, 6143–1).

HANNAH, H.W. & STURM, D.F.
Law for the veterinarian and livestock owner. 3ed. Interstate, 1974 (USA).

SOAVE, O. & CRAWFORD, L.M.
Veterinary medicine and the law. Williams & Wilkins, 1980 (USA).

WORLD HEALTH ORGANISATION
Veterinary contribution to public health practice. 1975.

VICARIOUS LIABILITY

See also Criminal Law; Employment Law; Tort.

Encyclopaedias

Halsbury's Laws of England. 4ed. see index vol.

Texts

ATIYAH, P.S.
Vicarious liability in the law of torts. Butterworths, 1967.

BATT, F.R.
Law of master and servant. 5ed. Pitman, 1967.

BATY, T.
Vicarious liability: history of the liability of employers, partners, associations and trade union members. Oxford U.P., 1916.

VILLAGE HALLS

Texts

NATIONAL COUNCIL FOR SOCIAL SERVICE
Model documents for village halls. Model A: freehold. Model B: leasehold. NCSS, 1968.

NATIONAL COUNCIL FOR SOCIAL SERVICE
Village hall: licensing and statutory requirements. NCSS, 1970.

VIOLENCE

See also Child Abuse; Criminal Law; Criminology; Domestic Violence; Public Order.

Encyclopaedias and periodicals

Halsbury's Laws of England. 4ed. vol.11, see also index vol.
Halsbury's Statutes of England. 3ed. vol.8.

British Journal of Criminology. 1960–
Criminal Law Review. 1954–

Texts

ALEXANDER, Y.
International terrorism: national, regional and global perspectives. Praeger, 1976.

BAILEY, F.L. & ROTHBLATT, H.B.
Crimes of violence: homicide and assault. Lawyers Co-op., 1973 (USA). Looseleaf.

CLUTTERBUCK, R.
Britain in agony: the growth of political violence. Faber, 1978.

COUNCIL OF EUROPE
International co-operation in the prosecution and punishment of acts of terrorism. HMSO, 1983.

EUROPEAN COMMITTEE ON CRIME PROBLEMS
Violence in society. Council of Europe, 1975.

FRIEDLANDER, R.A.
Terrorism: documents of international and local control. Oceana, 1979–81 (USA). 3 vols.

GIBSON, B.
Birmingham bombs. Rose, 1976.

GUNN, J.
Violence in human society. Praeger, 1973.

HOME OFFICE
Review of the operation of the Prevention of Terrorism (Temporary Provisions) Acts, 1974 and 1976 (Shackleton). HMSO, 1978 (Cmnd. 7324).

HOUSING AND LOCAL GOVERNMENT, MINISTRY OF
Report of the Working Party on Crowd Behaviour at Football Matches (Lang). HMSO, 1969.

KUTASH, I.L.
Violence perspectives on murder and aggression. Jossey-Bass, 1979.

LEONARD, L.L.
Global terrorism confronts the nations. Unifo, 1984. 37 microfiche and index.

McCLINTOCK, F.H.
Crimes of violence. Macmillan, 1963.

RIFAAT, A.M.
International aggression: a study of the legal concept – its development and definition in international law. Almqvist, 1979.

WALKER, N.D. and others
Violent offender: reality or illusion. Blackwell, 1970.

WEST, D.J. & WILES, P.
Research on violence. Cambridge Inst.of Criminol., 1974.

WOLFGANG, M.E. & FERRACUTI, F.
The subculture of violence. Tavistock, 1967.

VIVISECTION

Encyclopaedias and periodicals

Statutes in Force. Group: Animals.
Halsbury's Laws of England. 4ed. vol.2.
Halsbury's Statutes of England. 3ed. vol.2.

Animals' Defender and Anti-Vivisection News. 1881–

Annual Report of the Scottish Society for Prevention of Vivisection. 1912–

A.V. Times (as Abolitionist, 1899, and as Anti-Vivisectionist, 1949). 1969–

United Against Cruelty to Animals. 1965–

Texts

GAY, W.I. (ed.)
Methods of animal experimentations. Academic P., 1965–1981. 6 vols.

HOME OFFICEC
Experiments on living animals: return of experiments performed under the Cruelty to Animals Act, 1876. HMSO. Annual.

HOME OFFICE
Report of the Departmental Committee on Experiments on Animals (Littlewood). HMSO, 1965 (Cmnd. 2641).

UNIVERSITIES FEDERATION FOR ANIMAL WELFARE
Humane killing of animals. UFAW, 1967.

UNIVERSITIES FEDERATION FOR ANIMAL WELFARE
Welfare of laboratory animals: legal, scientific and humane requirements. UFAW, 1977.

WALES

See also Devolution.

Encyclopaedias

Statutes in Force. Group: Constitutional Law.
Halsbury's Laws of England. 4ed. see index vols.
Halsbury's Statutes of England. 3ed. vol.42, see also index vol.

Encyclopaedia of Court Forms in Civil Proceedings (Atkin). 2ed. see index vol. under Welsh.
Encyclopaedia of Forms and Precedents. 4ed. see index vol.

Texts

ANDREWS, J.A. (ed.)
Welsh studies in public law. Univ.of Wales P., 1970.

BOWEN, I.
The statutes of Wales. Unwin, 1908.

ELLIS, T.P.
Welsh tribal law and custom in the middle ages. Oxford U.P., 1926. 2 vols.

EMANUEL, H.D.
The Latin texts of the Welsh laws. Univ.of Wales P., 1967.

FOWLER, J.
Some account of the ancient laws and institutes of Wales. 1887.

GREEN, C.A.H.
Setting of the constitution of the Church in Wales. Sweet & Maxwell, 1937.

HOWEL, the Good, King of Wales
Ancient laws and institutes of Wales. Commissioners on the Public Records, 1841.

JENKINS, D.
Celtic law papers: introduction to Welsh mediaeval law and government. Librairie Encyclopedique, 1973.

JENKINS, D. & OWEN, M.
The Welsh law of women. Univ.of Wales P., 1980.

JONES, T.I.J.
Acts of Parliament concerning Wales, 1714–1901. Univ.of Wales P., 1959.

JONES, W.
Practice of the Court of Great Sessions in Wales. Butterworths, 1829.

LEWIS, T.
Glossary of mediaeval Welsh law. 1912.

OLDNALL, W.R.
The Welsh jursidiction. 1816.

OWEN, H.
Administration of English law in Wales and the Marches. Owen, 1900.

PALMER. A.N. & OWEN, E.
History of ancient land tenures in the Marches of North Wales. 2ed. Palmer & Owen, 1910.

PROBERT, W.
Ancient laws of Cambria. E.Williamson, 1823.

RUSSELL, W.O.
Practice of the Court of Great Sessions on the Carmarthen Circuit. Butterworths, 1814.

SKEEL, C.A.J.
The Council in the Marches of Wales: a study in local government during the 16th and 17th centuries. Rees, 1904.

WADE-EVANS, A.W.
Welsh mediaeval law: the text of the laws of Howel the Good. Oxford U.P., 1909 repr. Scientia Verlag, 1979.

WILLIAMS, W.L.
Account of the King's Court of Great Sessions in Wales. 1916.

WILLIAMS, W.R.
History of the Great Sessions in Wales, 1542–1830. Edwin Davies, 1899.

WAR

See also Air Force; Army; International Law; Military Law; Navy; Peace; Prize Law; United Nations.

Encyclopaedias and periodicals

Statutes in Force. Group: War and Emergency.
Halsbury's Laws of England. 4ed. vol.49.
Encyclopaedia of Forms and Precedents. 4ed. see index vol.

American Journal of International Law. 1907–
British Yearbook of International Law. 1920–

Grotius Society Transactions. 1915–1959.
Harvard International Law Journal. 1959–
International and Comparative Law Quarterly. 1952–
International Law Reports. 1950–
Law Quarterly Review. 1885–

Texts

ARON, R.
Peace and war: a theory of international relations. Weidenfeld & N., 1966.

BAILEY, S.D.
Prohibition and restraints in war. Oxford U.P., 1972.

BALLIS, W.B.
Legal position of war: changes in its practice and theory from Plato to Vattel. 1937 repr. Garland, 1973.

BATY, T. & MORGAN, S.H.
War – its conduct and legal results. Murray, 1915.

BEST, G.
Humanity in warfare: the modern history of the international law of armed conflicts. Methuen, 1983.

BLAINEY, G.
Causes of war. 2ed. Macmillan, 1977.

BOND, J.E.
Rules of riot: international conflict and the law of war. Princeton U.P., 1973 (USA).

CASTREN, E.
The present law of war and neutrality. Helsinki U.P., 1954 (Finland).

DRAPER, G.I.A.D.
The implementation of the modern law of armed conflicts. Jerusalem, Magnes P., 1973.

FALK, R.A. (ed.)
The international law of civil war. Johns Hopkins U.P., 1971 (USA).

FALK, R.A. (ed.)
The Vietnam war and international law.
Princeton U.P., 1972. 3 vols.

FISCHER, G.
The non-proliferation of nuclear weapons.
trans. D.Willey. Europa, 1971.

FRIEDMAN, L. (ed.)
Law of war, documentary history.
Greenwood, 1977 (USA).

GRABER, D.A.
The development of the law of belligerent occupation, 1863–1914: an historical survey. Columbia U.P., 1949 (USA).

GREENSPAN, M.
The modern law of land warfare. Univ.of California P., 1959 (USA).

GROB, F.
The relativity of war and peace. Yale U.P., 1949 (USA).

HALL, J.A.
Law of naval warfare. 2ed. Chapman & Hall, 1921.

HALL, W.E.
The rights and duties of neutrals.
Longmans, Green, 1874.

HIGGINS, A.P.
Hague Peace Conference and other international conferences concerning the laws and usages of war. 2ed. Cambridge U.P., 1909.

HIGGINS, A.P.
War and the private citizen: studies in international law. P.S.King, 1912.

HOLLAND, T.E.
The laws of war on land (written and unwritten). Oxford U.P., 1908 repr. Scientia Verlag, 1977.

HOWARD, M. (ed.)
Restraints on war: studies in the limitation of armed conflict. Oxford U.P., 1979.

HULL, R.H. & NOVOGROD, J.C.
Law and Vietnam. Oceana, 1968 (USA).

JESSUP, P.
Neutrality: its history, economics and law.
Columbia U.P., 1933–36. 4 vols. repr. 1972.

KALSHOVEN, F.
Belligerent reprisals. Sijthoff, 1971.

KALSHOVEN, F.
The law of warfare: a summary of the recent history and development. Sijthoff, 1973.

KARSTEN, P.
Law, soldiers and combat. Greenwood, 1978 (USA).

KHADDURI, M.
War and peace in the law of Islam. Johns Hopkins U.P., 1955 (USA).

LUARD, E.
The international regulation of civil wars.
Thames & Hudson, 1972.

McMAHON, M.M.
Conquest and modern international law: the legal limitations on the acquisition of territory by conquest. 1940 (USA) repr. Kraus, 1973.

McNAIR, A.D. & WATTS, A.D.
The legal effects of war. 4ed. Cambridge U.P., 1966.

MILLER, R.I.
The law of war. D.C. Heath, 1975.

MOORE, J.N.
Law and civil war in the modern world.
Johns Hopkins U.P., 1974 (USA).

NORTHEDGE, F.S.
Use of force in international relations. Free P., 1974.

PAGE, A.
War and alien enemies. 2ed. Stevens, 1915.

PHILLIPSON, C.
Termination of war and treaties of peace.
Dutton, 1916 (USA).

ROBERTS, A. & GUELFF, R.
Documents on the laws of war. Oxford U.P., 1982.

SCHINDLER, D. & TOMAN, J.
Laws of armed conflicts. 2ed. Sijthoff, 1980.

SCHWARZENBERGER, G.
International law as applied by international courts and tribunals. Vol.2. The law of armed conflict. Stevens, 1968.

SCHWARZENBERGER, G.
The legality of nuclear weapons. Stevens, 1958.

SINGH, B. & KO-WANG, M.
Theory and practice of modern guerilla warfare. Asia Pub. House, 1971.

SPAIGHT, J.M.
Air power and war rights. 3ed. Longmans, Green, 1947.

SPAIGHT, J.M.
War rights on land. Macmillan, 1911.

STONE, J.
Legal controls of international conflict; a treatise on the dynamics of disputes and war law. 1954 repr. Garland, 1973.

SUTTER, K.
International law of guerilla warfare: politics of law making. F.Pinter, 1983.

THOMAS, A.V.W. & THOMAS, A.J.
Legal limits on the use of chemical and biological weapons. Southern Methodist U.P., 1970 (USA).

TOMAN, J.
Index to the Geneva Conventions for the Protection of War Victims, 12th August. 1949. Sijthoff, 1973.

VERWEY, W.D.
Riot control agents and herbicides in war. Sijthoff, 1971.

WILLRICH, M.
Non-proliferation treaty: framework for nuclear arms control. Johns Hopkins U.P., 1969 (USA).

WAR AND CONTRACT

Encyclopaedias and periodicals

Halsbury's Laws of England. 4ed. see index vol.
Halsbury's Statues of England. 3ed. see index vol.
Encyclopaedia of Forms and Precedents. 4ed. see index vol.

International and Comparative Law Quarterly. 1952–
Law Quarterly Review. 1885–

Texts

CAMPBELL, H.
Law of war and contract. 2ed. Oxford U.P., 1917.

McNAIR, A.D. & WATTS, A.D.
The legal effects of war. 4ed. Cambridge U.P., 1966.

PHILLIPSON, C.
Effect of war on contracts. Stevens & Haynes, 1909.

SCOTT, Sir L.F.
Trading with the enemy: the effect of war on contracts. 2ed. Stevens, 1914.

TROTTER, W.F.
Law of contract during war. 4ed. Hodge, 1960.

WEBBER, G.J.
Effect of war on contracts. 2ed. Sol.Law Stat.Soc., 1946.

WAR COMPENSATION

Encyclopaedias and periodicals

Halsbury's Laws of England. 4ed. see index vol.
Halsbury's Statutes of England. 3ed. vol.38.
Encyclopaedia of Forms and Precedents. 4ed. see index vol.

War Compensation Court Reports. 1920–1929.

Texts

ELPHINSTONE, L.H.
Concise guide and summary to the War Damages Acts, 1941–1942. Sol.Law Stat.Soc., 1942.

BURKE, J. (ed.)
Encyclopaedia of war damage and compensation. Hamilton, 1941–1952.

BURKE, J.
War damage guide. Sweet & Maxwell, 1943.

JONES, T.M.
The Requisition Land and War Works Act, 1945. Butterworths, 1945.

SLACK, G.G.
The War Damage Acts and the War Risks Insurance Act, 1939. Butterworths, 1944 supp. 1950.

WAR CRIMES

Encyclopaedias and reports

Halsbury's Laws of England. 4ed. see index vol.

Law Reports of Trials of War Criminals. 1947–1949. 15 vols.

Trial of German Major War Criminals. 1946–1949. 23 vols.

Trial of Major War Criminals. 1947–1949. 42 vols.

Texts

ALEXANDROV, G.N. & KHLESTOV, O.N. (eds.)
Responsibility for war crimes and crimes against humanity: documents. Progress, 1970 (USSR).

APPLEMEN, J.A.
Military tribunals and international crimes. Bobbs-Merrill, 1954 repr. Greenwood (USA).

BROWNING, F. & FOREMAN, D.
Wasted nations: report of the International Commission of Enquiry into United States Crimes in Indo-China. Harper & Row, 1972.

DAVIDSON, E.
Nuremberg fallacy: wars and war crimes since World War II. Why the U.N. and Nuremberg doctrines do not keep the peace. Macmillan, 1973.

DULL, P.S. & UNEMURA, M.T.
The Tokyo trials: a functional index to the proceedings of the International Military Tribunal for the Far East. Michigan U.P., 1957 (USA).

JUDGMENT of the International Military Tribunal for the trial of German major war criminals. HMSO, 1946 (Cmd. 6964).

KAHN, L.
Nuremberg trials. Ballentine, 1972.

KURTHA, A.N.
Prisoners of war and war crimes, containing texts of the 1949 Geneva Convention and the Nuremberg judgment with full commentary. Pakistan Herald, 1973 (Pakistan).

MAUGHAM, F.
U.N.O. and war crimes. 1951 repr. Greenwood, 1974 (USA).

NEUMANN, I.S. & ROSENBAUM, R.A. (eds.)
European war crimes trials: bibliography. Greenwood, 1978.

PAPADATOS, P.A.
The Eichmann trial. Stevens, 1964.

SARTRE, J.P.
On genocide: and a summary of the evidence and the judgments of the international war crimes tribunal. Beacon P., 1968.

WOETZEL, R.K.
The Nuremberg trials in international law. Stevens, 1960.

WATERS AND WATERCOURES

See also Angling; Canals; Pollution; Public Health.

Encyclopaedias

Statutes in Force. Group: Water
Halsbury's Laws of England. 4ed. vol.49.
Halsbury's Statutes of England. 3ed. vols. 26, 39, 43.
The Digest. vol.47.

Encyclopaedia of Court Forms in Civil Proceedings (Atkin). 2ed. vol.41.
Encyclopaedia of Forms and Precedents. 4ed. see index vol.

Texts

ASHFORD, F.B.
The Water Act, 1945. Sweet & Maxwell, 1946.

COULSON, H.J.W. & FORBES, U.A.
The law of waters, sea, tidal and inland and land drainage. 6ed. Sweet & Maxwell, 1952.

ENVIRONMENT, DEPARTMENT OF THE
The water industry in England and Wales: the next steps. HMSO, 1977.

GEEN, G.K. & DOUGLAS, R.P.A.
Law and administration of pilotage. 2ed. Lloyd's, 1983.

HALL, C.G.
Water rights in South Africa. 3ed. Oxford U.P., 1957.

HER MAJESTY'S STATIONERY OFFICE
Water laws in selected European countries. HMSO, 1975.

HOME OFFICE
Report of the Working Party on Water Safety (McIntyre). HMSO, 1977.

JACOBSTEIN, J.M. & MERSKY, R.M.
Water law bibliography, 1847–1965: source book on U.S. water and irrigation studies, legal, economic and political. Jefferson Law Book Co., 1966.

LA FOREST, G.V.
Water law in Canada: the Atlantic Provinces. Dept.of Regional Economic Expansion, 1973.

LITTLER, P.
Water rights including fishing rights. 2ed. Oyez, 1981.

McLOUGHLIN, J.
Water Act, 1973. Sweet & Maxwell, 1973.

MICHAL, W.H. & WILL, J.S.
The law relating to gas and water. Vol. 2: water. 8ed. Butterworths, 1935.

NATIONAL WATER COUNCIL
A guide to the model water byelaws. 1977.

PHEAR, J.B.
Rights of water, including public and private rights to the sea and seashore. Stevens & Norton, 1859.

TECLAFF, L.A.
The river basin in history and law. Nijhoff, 1967.

TELLING, A.E.
Water authorities. Butterworths, 1974.

TRELEASE, F.J.
Cases and materials on water law. 3ed. West, 1979 (USA).

WELSH WATER AUTHORITY
Water byelaws. 1978.

WISDOM, A.S.
Aspects of water law. Rose, 1982.

WISDOM, A.S.
Freshwater pollution. Rose, 1979.

WISDOM, A.S.
Law of rivers and watercourses. 4ed. Shaw, 1979.

WISDOM, A.S. & SKEET, J.L.G.
Law and management of water resources and supply. Shaw, 1981.

WOOLRYCH, H.W.
Law of waters, including rights in the sea, rivers, canals, etc. 2ed. 1851.

WEIGHTS AND MEASURES

See also Food and Drugs

Encyclopaedias

Statutes in Force. Group: Weights and Measures.
Halsbury's Laws of England. 4ed. vol.50.
Halsbury's Statutes of England. 3ed. vol.39.
The Digest. vol.47.

Texts

INSTITUTE OF TRADING STANDARDS
Weights and measures inspectors handbook. 1969.

O'KEEFE, J.A.
Law of weights and measures. 2ed. Butterworths, 1977. Looseleaf.

OWEN, G.A.
Law relating to weights and measures. 2ed. Butterworths, 1947.

ROSE, P.B.
Guide to the Weights and Measures Act, 1963. Butterworths, 1965.

WELFARE LAW

See also Legal Aid and Advice; Social Security.

Encyclopaedias and periodicals

Statutes in Force. Group: Social Security and Health Services.
Halsbury's Laws of England. 4ed. see index vols.
Halsbury's Statutes of England. 3ed. vol.45.
Encyclopaedia of Court Forms in Civil Proceedings (Atkin). 2ed. vols. 9, 28.

Encyclopaedia of Forms and Precedents. 4ed. vols. 13, 17.
Journal of Social Welfare Law. 1978–
Legal Action (formerly L.A.G. Bulletin). 1973–
Law and State. 1977–

Texts

ARDEN, A.
Housing: security and rent control. Sweet & Maxwell, 1978.

BAKER, J.
Neigbourhood Advice Centre: community project in Camden. Routledge, 1978.

BROWN, M.
Introduction to social administration in Britain. 5ed. Hutchinson, 1982.

BYLES, A. & MORRIS, P.
Unmet need: case of the Neighbourhood Law Centre. Routledge & Kegan Paul, 1977.

CALVERT, H.
Welfare legal system. Univ.Newcastle P., 1973.

CARNWATH, R.
A guide to the Housing (Homeless Persons) Act 1977. Knight, 1978.

CHESTERMAN, M.R.
Charities, trusts and social welfare. Weidenfeld & N., 1979 (Law in context).

CITIZENS ADVICE BUREAUX
Citizens advice notes. Looseleaf. Annual supp.

COHEN, R. & RUSHTON, A.
Welfare rights. Heinemann, 1982.

DINGWALL, R. & EEKELAAR, J.
Care proceedings: practical guide for social workers, health visitors and others. Blackwell, 1982.

ENCYCLOPAEDIA of social services law. Sweet & Maxwell. Looseleaf.

FABIAN SOCIETY
Legal services for all. 1978.

FAMILY WELFARE ASSOCIATION
Guide to the social services 1978. Macdonald & Evans, 1978.

FELDMAN, A.M.
Welfare economics and social choice theory. Nijhoff, 1980.

FOGGO-PAYS, E.
Introductory guide to counselling. Ravenswood. Pubns., 1982.

FRIEDLANDER, W.A.
Introduction to social welfare. 5ed. Prentice-Hall, 1980.

GRACE, C. & WILKINSON, P.
Negotiating the law: social work and legal services. Routledge & Kegan Paul, 1978.

GRIMOND, J.
Common welfare. M.T.Smith, 1978.

HEALTH AND SOCIAL SECURITY, DEPARTMENT OF
Social workers and solicitors in child care cases. HMSO, 1981.

HOATH, D.
Council housing. 2ed. Sweet & Maxwell, 1982.

HUNT, A.
The sociological movement in law. Macmillan, 1978.

JORDON, B.
Freedom and the welfare state. Routledge & Kegan Paul, 1978.

LISTER, R.
Welfare benefits. Sweet & Maxwell, 1981.

MACMORLAND, B.
ABC of services and information for disabled peopled. 3ed. Disablement Income Group Charitable Trust, 1977.

PARTINGTON, M.
The Housing (Homeless Persons) Act 1977 and the code of guidance (annotated). Sweet & Maxwell, 1978.

PARTINGTON, M. & JOWELL, J.L.
Welfare law and policy: studies in teaching, practice and research. Pinfold, 1979.

PEARL, D. & GRAY, K.
Social welfare law. Croom Helm, 1981.

POLLARD, D.
Social welfare law. Oyez. Looseleaf.

SANGER, M.B.
Welfare of the poor. Academic P., 1980.

SIMPSON, T.
Advocacy and social change: study of welfare rights workers. Nat.Inst.for Social Work, 1978.

SMITH, C. & HOATH, D.C.
Law and the underprivileged. Routledge, 1975.

STREET, D.
Welfare industry: functionaries and recipients in public aid. Sage, 1979.

STREET, H.
Justice in the welfare state. 2ed. Stevens, 1975.

SWEET & MAXWELL
Social work statutes. 1980.

THOMAS, D.N.
Organizing for social change: study in the theory and practice of social work. Allen & Unwin, 1977.

TIPLADY, D.
Housing welfare law. Oyez, 1975.

TRATNER, W.
From poor law to welfare state. 2ed. Free Press:Collier Macmillan, 1979.

WING, J.K. & OLSEN, R.
Community care for the mentally disabled. Oxford U.P., 1979.

WOLFENDEN, Sir J
Future of voluntary organizations: report of the Wolfenden Committee. Croom Helm, 1977.

YOUNGHUSBAND, E.L.
Social work in Britain, 1950–75. Allen & Unwin, 1978. 2 vols.

ZANDER, M.
Legal services for the community. M.T.Smith, 1978.

WILLS

See also Executors and Administrators; Perpetuities; Probate; Succession.

Encyclopaedias

Statutes in Force. Group: Succession.
Halsbury's Laws of England. 4ed. vol.50.
Halsbury's Statutes of England. 3ed. vol.39.
The Digest. vol.47.

Encyclopaedia of Court Form in Civil Proceedings (Atkin). 2ed. vols.29, 32.
Encyclopaedia of Forms and Precedents. 4ed. vol.23.

WILLS

Texts

BAILEY, S.J.
Law of wills, including intestacy and administration of estates. 7ed. Pitman, 1973.

BRIGHOUSE, H.
Short forms of wills. 10ed. Sweet & Maxwell, 1978.

CAULFIELD, B.I. & NORRIS, W.V.W.
Wills and tax planning. Oyez, 1979.

CONSUMERS' ASSOCIATION
Wills and probate. Hodder & Stoughton, 1978.

DAVIES, D.T.
Will precedents and capital transfer tax. 2ed. Butterworths, 1984.

FEENEY, T.G.
Canadian law of wills: probate and construction. Butterworths (Canada), 1982.

GARROW, J.M. & WILLIS, J.D.
Law of wills and administration and succession on intestacy. 4ed. Butterworths (New Zealand), 1971.

HALLETT, V.G.H. & WARREN, N.
Settlements, wills and capital transfer tax. Sweet & Maxwell, 1979.

HARDINGHAM, I.J., NEAVE, M.A. & FORD, H.A.J.
Law of wills and intestacy in Australia and New Zealand. Law Book Co., 1983 (Australia).

HAWKINS, F.V.
On the construction of wills. 3ed. Sweet & Maxwell, 1925.

HOLLOWAY, D.R.
A probate handbook. 6ed. Oyez, 1982.

HUTLEY, F.C. & INGLIS, M.W.
Australian wills precedents. 3ed. Butterworths (Australia), 1980. Italian translation by L Masbellore. 1983.

JARMAN, T.
Treatise on wills. 8ed. Sweet & Maxwell, 1951. 3 vols.

LAW REFORM COMMITTEE
The making and revocation of wills: consultative document. HMSO, 1977.

LAW REFORM COMMITTEE
The making and revocation of wills: twenty-second report. HMSO, 1980 (Cmnd. 7902).

OOSTERHOFF, A.H.
Cases and materials on wills and succession. Carswell, 1980 (Canada).

PAGE, W.H.
Law of wills, including probate, will contents, etc. Anderson, 1960 (USA). 9 vols. & suppl.

PARKER, A. (ed.)
Modern wills precedents. Butterworths, 1969.

PETTIT, D.M.
The will draftsmans handbook. Oyez, 1978.

RUTTER, W.A.
Wills. 7ed. Gilbert Law, 1973 (USA).

SHEARD, T.
Drafting of wills. Carswell, 1963 (Canada).

SHEEHAN, M.M.
Will in medieval England. Pontifical, 1963.

SPARKS, B.M.
Contracts to make wills: legal relations arising out of contracts to devise or bequeath. New York Univ.P., 1967 (USA).

THEOBALD, H.S.
The law of wills. 14ed. Stevens, 1982 supp. 1984.

VENABLES, R.C.
Tax planning through wills (with precedents). 2ed. Butterworths, 1984.

WHITE, P.
Post death rearrangements to wills and intestacies. Oyez Longman, 1984.

WILLIAMS, W.J.
Law relating to wills. 5ed. Butterworths, 1980 supp. 1983.

WITNESSES
See also Evidence; Perjury.

Encyclopaedias and periodicals
Statutes in Force. Groups: Criminal Law; Evidence.
Halsbury's Laws of England. 4ed. see index vols.
Halsbury's Statutes of England. 3ed. see index vol.

Encyclopaedia of Court Forms in Civil Proceedings (Atkin). 2ed. see index vol.
Encyclopaedia of Forms and Precedents. 4ed. vols. 2, 18.
Criminal Law Review. 1954–

Texts
COHEN, H.
Spouse witnesses in criminal cases. 1913.

LOFTUS, E.F.
Eyewitness testimony. Harvard U.P., 1979.

STEPHEN, H.
Prisoners on oath, present and future. Butterworths, 1898.

TIERNEY, K.
How to be a witness. Oceana, 1971 (USA).

WROTTESLEY, F.J.
Examination of witnesses in court. 2ed. Sweet & Maxwell, 1926.

WOMEN
See also Domestic Violence; Equal Opportunities; Marriage.

Encyclopaedias
Halsbury's Laws of England. 4ed. see index vols.
Halsbury's Statutes of England. 3ed. see index vol.

Texts
BULLOUGH, V.L.
Subordinate sex: a history of attitudes towards women. Univ.Illinois P., 1973 (USA).

BURKHART, K.W.
Women in prison. Doubleday, 1973 (USA).

CARMICHAEL, C.M.
Women, law and the genesis traditions. Edinburgh U.P., 1979.

CLEVERDON, C.L.
Woman suffrage movement in Canada. 2ed. Univ.Toronto P., 1974.

COOTE, A. & GILL, T.
Battered women and the new law. 2ed. Interaction Print, 1979.

COOTE, A. & GILL,, T.
Women's rights: a practical guide. 3ed. Penguin, 1981.

CREIGHTON, W.B.
Working women and the law. Mansell, 1979.

EDWARDS, S.
Women on trial. Manchester U.P., 1984.

FLEXNER, E.
Century of struggle: the woman's rights movement in the United States. Harvard U.P., 1973.

GOODMAN, N. & PRICE, J.
Studies of female offenders. HMSO, 1967 (Home Office research studies).

HEMER, J. & STANYER, A.
Handbook for widows. Virago, 1978.

HEVENER, N.K.
International law and the status of women. Westview: Bowker, 1982 (USA).

HEWITT, P.
Rights for women: a guide to the Sex Discrimination Act, the Equal Pay Act, paid maternity leave, pension schemes and unfair dismissal. NCCL, 1975.

HONORE, T.
Sex law. Duckworth, 1978.

JENKINS, D. & OWEN, M.
Welsh law of women. Univ.Wales P., 1980.

LING-MALLISON,E.
Law relating to women. Sol.Law Stat.Soc., 1930.

McCAUGHAN, M.M.
Legal status of married women in Canada. Carswell, 1977.

NORTON, C.S.
English laws for women in the nineteenth century. 1854 repr. Hyperion, 1980.

PAHL, J.
A refuge for battered women: a study of the role of a women's centre (DHSS). HMSO, 1978.

PERATIS, K.W. & CARY, E.
Woman and the law. Sweet & Maxwell, 1979.

ROBERTS, S., COOTE, A. & BALL, E.
Positive action for women: the next step. NCCL, 1981.

ROOKE, P.J.
Women's rights. Wayland, 1972.

SMART, C.
Women, crime and criminology: a feminist critique. Routledge, 1979.

ZUKER, M.A. & CALLWOOD, J.
Law is not for women: a legal handbook for women. Pitman, 1976 (Canada).

WORKMEN'S COMPENSATION

See also Accidents; Employer's Liability; Industrial Injuries; Occupational Diseases; Personal Injuries.

Encyclopaedias and reports

Halsbury's Laws of England. 4ed. vol.33.
Halsbury's Statutes of England. 3ed. vol.45.
Encyclopaedia of Court Forms in Civil Proceedings (Atkin). 2ed. vols. 28, 31.

Butterworth's Workmen's Compensation Cases. 1909–1950. 41 vols.
Workmen's Compensation and Insurance Reports. 1912–1933. 22 vols.

Texts

ANDERSON, & RENDIT,
Workers compensation Victoria. 3ed. Butterworths (Australia), 1980. Looseleaf.

BLAIR, E.H.
Reference guide to workmen's compensation law. Thomas Law, 1974 (USA). Looseleaf.

BOULTER, M.
Workers' compensation practice in New South Wales. Sweet & Maxwell, 1966 (Australia).

BUTTERWORTH's digest of workmen's compensation cases. 1933. supp. 1942.

DEPARTMENTAL COMMITTEE ON ALTERNATIVE REMEDIES
Workmen's compensation (contributory negligence) (Monckton). HMSO, 1945 (Cmd. 6580, 6642). Final report. HMSO, 1946 (Cmd. 6860).

HEALTH AND SOCIAL SECURITY, DEPARTMENT OF
Memorandum on the Workmen's Compensation Act, 1925–1945. HMSO, 1946 repr. 1962.

HOME OFFICE
Report of the Departmental Committee on Workmen's Compensation (Digby). HMSO, 1904 (Cd.2208), 1905 (Cd. 2334).

MACDONALD, I.A.
Law relating to worker's compensation. 4ed. Butterworths (New Zealand), 1968 supp. 1970.

MILLS, C.P.
Workers compensation New South Wales. 2ed. Butterworths (Australia), 1979. Looseleaf.

ROYAL COMMISSION ON
WORKMEN'S COMPENSATION
Report (Hetherington). HMSO, 1945
(Cmd. 6588).

WILLIS, W.A.
Workmen's Compensation Acts. 37ed.
Butterworths, 1945 supp. 1946.

WORLD BANK

Texts

CHERIAN, J.
Investment contracts and arbitration: the World Bank Convention on the settlement of investment disputes. Sijthoff, 1975.

MASON, E.S. & ASHER, R.E.
World Bank since Bretton Woods. Brookings, 1973 (USA).

X-RAY

See also Medical Jurisprudence

Encyclopaedias and periodicals

Halsbury's Statutes of England. 3ed. see index vol. under Radio Active Substances.

Radiography. 1935–

Texts

BUCKLEY, C.L.
X-Ray report. H.K.Lewis, 1957.

DONALDSON, S.
The roentgenologist in court. C.C.Thomas, 1937 (USA).

HADLEY, A.
101 lessons in x-ray terminology for the medical transcriber. Lippincott, 1972.

HOSPITAL PHYSICISTS ASSOCIATION
Diagnostic x-ray protection: the role of the radological protection adviser. 1973.

MEANEY, T.F., LALLI, A.F. & ALFIDI, R.J. (eds.)
Complications and legal implications of radiologic special procedures. Mosby, 1973 (USA).

YEAR BOOKS

See also History.

Texts

BOLLAND, W.J.
A manual of yearbook studies. Cambridge U.P., 1925.

BOLLAND, W.J.
The year books. Cambridge U.P., 1921.

SELDEN SOCIETY
Year book series, various eds. 1887– repr. 1973–

YORK-ANTWERP RULES

See also Shipping

Encyclopaedias and periodicals

Halsbury's Laws of England. 4ed. vol.25.
Halsbury's Statutes of England. 3ed. vol.7.
Encyclopaedia of Court Forms in Civil Proceedings (Atkin). 2ed. vol.8.

Lloyd's Law Reports. 1919–

Texts

BUGLASS, L.J.
General average and the York-Antwerp rules, 1974: American law and practice. Cornell Maritime P., 1974.

DOVER, V.
General average and the York-Antwerp rules. Stone & Cox, 1950.

LOWNDES, R. & RUDOLF, G.R.
The law of general average and the York-Antwerp rules. 10ed. Stevens, 1975 (British shipping laws).

ZAMBIA

See also Africa.

Encyclopaedias

Statutes in Force. Group: Commonwealth and Other Territories.
Halsbury's Laws of England. 4ed. vol.6.
Halsbury's Statutes of England. 3ed. vol.4.

Texts

HATCHARD, J. & NDULO, M.
Casebook of criminal law. Govt. of Zambia: African Law Reports, 1983.

MULFORD, D.C.
Zambia: the politics on independence, 1957–1964. Oxford U.P., 1967.

PETTMAN, J.
Zambia: security and conflict. St Martin's P., 1974 (USA).

TORDOFF, W. (ed.)
Administration in Zambia. Manchester U.P., 1980.

TORDOFF, W. (ed.)
Politics in Zambia. Univ.of California P., 1974.

REGNAL YEARS
OF ENGLISH SOVEREIGNS

Regnal Years
of English Sovereigns

	FROM	TO	YEARS
William I	Oct. 14, 1066	Sept. 9, 1087	21
William II	Sept. 26, 1087	Aug. 2, 1100	13
Henry I	Aug. 5, 1100	Dec. 1, 1135	36
Stephen	Dec. 26, 1135	Oct. 25, 1154	19
Henry II	Dec. 19, 1154	July 6, 1189	35
Richard I	Sept. 3, 1189	Apr. 6, 1199	10
John	May 27, 1199	Oct. 19, 1216	18
Henry III	Oct. 28, 1216	Nov. 16, 1272	57
Edward I	Nov. 20, 1272	July 7, 1307	35
Edward II	July 8, 1307	Jan. 20, 1327	20
Edward III	Jan. 25, 1327	June 21, 1377	51
Richard II	June 22, 1377	Sept. 29, 1399	23
Henry IV	Sept. 30, 1399	Mar. 20, 1413	14
Henry V	Mar. 21, 1413	Aug. 31, 1422	10
Henry VI	Sept. 1, 1422	Mar. 4, 1461	39
Edward IV	Mar. 4, 1461	Apr. 9, 1483	23
Edward V	Apr. 9, 1483	June 25, 1483	1
Richard III	June 26, 1483	Aug. 22, 1485	3
Henry VII	Aug. 22, 1485	Apr. 21, 1509	24
Henry VIII	Apr. 22, 1509	Jan. 28, 1547	38
Edward VI	Jan. 28, 1547	July 6, 1553	7
Mary	July 6, 1553	Nov. 17, 1558	6
Elizabeth I	Nov. 17, 1558	Mar. 24, 1603	45
James I	Mar. 24, 1603	Mar. 27, 1625	23
Charles I	Mar. 27, 1625	Jan. 30, 1649	24
Charles II	Jan. 30, 1649	Feb. 6, 1685	37
James II	Feb. 6, 1685	Dec. 11, 1688	4
William and Mary	Feb. 13, 1689	Mar. 8, 1702	14
Anne	Mar. 8, 1702	Aug. 1, 1714	13
George I	Aug. 1, 1714	June 11, 1727	13
George II	June 11, 1727	Oct. 25, 1760	34
George III	Oct. 25, 1760	Jan. 29, 1820	60
George IV	Jan. 29, 1820	June 26, 1830	11
William IV	June 26, 1830	June 20, 1837	7
Victoria	June 20, 1837	Jan. 22, 1901	64
Edward VII	Jan. 22, 1901	May 6, 1910	10
George V	May 6, 1910	Jan. 20, 1936	26
Edward VIII	Jan. 20, 1936	Dec. 11, 1936	1
George VI	Dec. 11, 1936	Feb. 6, 1952	17
Elizabeth II	Feb. 6, 1952		

LAW REPORTS
UNITED KINGDOM AND IRELAND

Law Reports
United Kingdom and Ireland

Abbreviations used

Adm. Admiralty	Elect. Election	P. & D. Probate & Divorce
Agric. Agriculture	Eq. Equity	P.C. Privy Council
App. Appeal	Exch. Exchequer	Parl. Parliamentary
Bail Bail Court	H.L. House of Lords	Pat. Patent
Bky. Bankruptcy	Just. Justiciary	Poor Poor Law Cases
C.B. Crown Cases	K.B. King's Bench	Q.B. Queen's Bench
C.P. Common Pleas	L.S. Locus Standi	R.C. Rolls Court
C.S. Court of Session	Landl. Landlord	Rail. Railway Cases
Ch. Chancery	Mag. Magistrate	Ref. Court of Referees
Co.Ct. County Court	Marr. Marriage	Reg. Registration
Crim. Criminal	Merc. Mercantile	Sett. Settlement
Div. Divorce	Min. Mining	Trade M. Trade Marks
Ecc. Ecclesiastical	N.P. Nisi Prius	V.C. Vice Chancellor

Reports	Series	No. of Vols.	*Period*
Acton	Prize	2	1809–11
Adam (Scotland)	Just.	7	1893–1916
Addams	Ecc.	3	1822–26
Adolphus & Ellis	Q.B.	12	1834–40
Adolphus & Ellis (New Series)	Q.B.	18	1841–52
Alcock (Ireland)	Reg.	3	1832–41
Alcock & Napier (Ireland)	K.B.	1	1831–33
Aleyn	K.B.	1	1646–48
All England Law Reports			1936–
All England Law Reports Reprint		30	1843–1935
Ambler	Ch.	2	1737–84
Anderson	C.B.	2	1534–1603
Anderson's Agricultural Decisions (Scotland)	C.S.	1	1800-83
Andrews	K.B.	1	1737–1738
Annaly	K.B.	1	1733–1738
Annotated Tax Cases		52	1922–
Anstruther	Exch.	3	1792–97
Archbold	Poor		1842–58
Appeals from Munitions Tribunals		2	1916–17
Architects Law Reports		4	1904–09
Arkley (Scotland)	Just.	1	1846–48
Armstrong, Macartney & Ogle (Ireland)	N.P.	1	1840-42
Arnold	C.P.	1	1838–39
Arnold & Hodges	K.B.	1	1840–41
Arnot Criminal Trials (Scotland)		1	1536–1784
Aspinall Maritime Cases	Adm.	22	1870–1940

Atkyn	Ch.	3	1736–55
Austin	Co.Ct	1	1867–69
Bacon			1617–21
Ball & Beatty (Ireland)	Ch.	2	1807–14
Bamber	Min.		1923–14
Bankruptcy & Companies		20	1915–42
Bankruptcy & Insolvency		2	1853–55
Bar Reports		12	1865–71
Barnardiston	Ch.	2	1740–41
Barnardiston	K.B.	2	1726–34
Barnes	C.P.		1732–60
Barnewall & Adolphus	K.B.	5	1830–34
Barnewall & Alderson	K.B.	5	1817–22
Barnewall & Cresswell	K.B.	10	1822–30
Barron & Arnold	Elect.	1	1843–46
Barron & Austin	Elect.	1	1842
Bartholoman	Assize	1	1841
Batty (Ireland)	K.B.	1	1825–26
Beatty (Ireland)	Ch.	1	1814–30
Beavan	R.C.	36	1836–66
Beavan & Walford	Rail.	2	1846
Bell, Crown	C.C.	1	1858–60
Bell, Folio (Scotland)	C.S.	1	1793–95
Bell, Octavo (Scotland)	C.S.	1	1790–92
Bell, House of Lords (Scotland)	H.L.	7	1842–50
Bellewe	K.B.	1	1378–1400
Belt, Supp. to Vesey	Ch.	1	1746–56
Bendloe	K.B.	1	1531–1628
Benloe & Dallison	C.B.	1	1486–1579
Bernard (Irish)	Church	1	1870–75
Best & Smith	Q.B.	10	1861-69
Bidder	L.S.	7	1920–36
Bigelow		1	1066–1195
Bingham	C.B.	10	1822–34
Bingham, New Cases	C.B.	6	1834–40
Birkenhead	H.L.	1	1919–22
Bittleston	K.B.	2	1875–84
Bittleston, Wise & Parnell	Mag.	5	1844–52
Blackerby	Mag.	1	1505–1734
Blackham, Dundas & Osborne (Ireland)	N.P.	1	1846-48
Blackmore, Speakers' Decisions		2	1857–95
Blackstone (H.)	C.B.	2	1788–96
Blackstone (W.)	K.B.	2	1746–79
Bligh	H.L.	4	1819–21
Bligh, New Series	H.L.	11	1827–37
Bohun	Elect.	1	1628–99
Bosanquet & Puller	C.B.	1	1796–1804
Bosanquet & Puller, New Reports		2	1804–7
Bott	Poor	3	1560–1833
Bourke	Parl.	1	1842–56
Bracton		3	1218–40
Bridgman (J.)	C.B.	1	1613–21

LAW REPORTS: UNITED KINGDOM AND IRELAND

Bridgman (O.)	C.B.	1	1660–67
British & Colonial	Prize	3	1914–22
British Tax Cases (CCH)			1982–
Broderick & Fremantle		1	1840–64
Broderip & Bingham	C.B.	3	1819–22
Brooke	Ecc.	1	1850–72
Brooke, New Cases	K.B.	1	1515–58
Brown (Scotland)	Just.	2	1842–45
Brown	Ch.	4	1778–94
Brown	H.L.	8	1701–1800
Brown, Judicial Proceedings (Scotland)	C.S.	1	1816
Brown, Supp. to Morison		5	1622–1760
Browning & Lushington	Adm.	1	1863–65
Brownlow & Goldesborough	C.B.	1	1569–1624
Bruce (Scotland)	C.S.	1	1714–15
Brunskill (Ireland)	Landl.	6	1891–94
Buchanan (Scotland)	C.S.	1	1800–13
Buck	Bky.	1	1816–20
Building Law Reports			1976–
Bulstrode	K.B.	1	1609–26
Bunbury	Exch.	1	1712–41
Burrell & Marsden	Adm.	1	1584–1839
Burrow	K.B.	5	1756–71
Burrow	Sett.	1	1732–76
Burton (Scotland)	Crim.	2	1700–95
Butterworth, Company Law Cases			1983–
Butterworth, Rating Appeals		4	1913–31
Butterworth, Workmen's Compensation		41	1908–47
Butterworth. Workmen's Compensation (Ireland & Scotland)		18	1931–47
Cababe & Ellis	Q.B.	1	1882–85
Caldecott	K.B.	1	1776–85
Calendars of Proceedings	Ch.	3	1377-1600
Calthrop	K.B.	1	1609–18
Campbell	N.P.	4	1807–16
Cantwell (Ireland)		8	1596–1829
Carpmael	Pat.	2	1604–1842
Carrington & Kirwan	N.P.	2	1843–50
Carrington & Marshman	N.P.	1	1840–43
Carrington & Payne	N.P.	9	1823–41
Carrow, Hamilton & Allen (Scotland)	C.S.	3	1844–51
Carter	C.B.	1	1664–76
Carthew	K.B.	1	1687–1700
Cartmel	Trade M.	1	1876–92
Cary	Ch.		1557–1604
Cases in Chancery	Ch.		1660–88
Cases in Equity (Gilbert)		1	1706–26
Cases in K.B. temp. Hardwick		1	1733–38
Cases in Law & Equity		1	1720–73
Cases of Practice in C.P.	C.P.	1	1702–27
Cases of Practice in K.B.	K.B.	1	1584–1775
Cases of Settlement in K.B.	K.B.	1	1685-1733

Cases on Appeals (Scotland)	Land	1	1858–79
Cases on Appeals, New Series (Scotland)	Land	1	1880–1921
Cases on the Six Circuits (Ireland)		1	1841-43
Cases respecting assessed Taxes		Nos. 1 –2867	1823–72
Cases with Opinions		2	1700–75
Central Criminal Court Sessions Papers		158	1834–1913
Charley		3	1875–81
Chitty	Bail Ct.	2	1770–1822
Choyce	Ch.	1	1557–1606
Clark	H.L.	12	1847–66
Clark & Finnelly	H.L.	12	1831–46
Clayton	Crim.	1	1631–50
Clifford	Elect.	1	1796–97
Clifford & Rickard	L.S.	3	1873–84
Clifford & Stephen	L.S.	2	1867–72
Cockburn & Rowe	Elect.	1	1833
Coke	K.B.	7	1572–1616
Colles	H.L.	1	1697–1714
Collyer	Ch.	2	1844–46
Coltman	Reg.	1	1879–85
Comberbach	K.B.	1	1685–99
Commercial Cases		46	1895–1941
Commercial Law Reports			1981–83
Commissioners Decisions (N.I.)			1957–
Common Bench	C.P.	19	1845–56
Common Bench, New Series	C.P.	20	1856–65
Common Law & Equity	K.B.	6	1853–55
Common Market Law Reports			1962–
Comyns	K.B.	2	1695–1741
Connell (Scotland)	Agric.	1	1908–15
Connor & Lawson (Ireland)	Ch.	2	1841–43
Conroy	Exch.	1	1652–1788
Cooke	C.P.	1	1706–47
Cooke & Alcock (Ireland)	K.B.	1	1833–34
Cooper (C.P.)	Ch.	1	1837–39
Cooper (C.P.), (temp. Brougham)	Ch.	1	1832–34
Cooper (C.P.) (temp. Cottenham)	Ch.	2	1846–48
Cooper (G), temp. Eldon	Ch.	1	1815
Cooper (Lord) (Scotland)		1	1203–94
Corbett & Daniell	Elect.	1	1819
County Council Cases (Scotland)		64	1890–1962
County Court Reports (Cox)	Co.Ct.	34	1860–1919
County Courts Cases	Co.Ct.	3	1847–58
County Courts Chronicle	Co.Ct.	47	1847–1920
Couper (Scotland)	Just.	5	1868–85
Court of Session Cases (Scotland)	C.S.		
First Series (Shaw)		16	1821–38
Second Series (Dunlop)		24	1838–62
Third Series (Macpherson)		11	1862–73
Fourth Series (Rettie)		25	1873–98
Fifth Series (Fraser)		8	1898–1906
New Series			1907–

Cowper	K.B.	2	1774–78
Cox, Chancery	Ch.	2	1783–96
Cox, Company Cases		1	1848–49
Cox, Criminal Cases	Crim.	31	1843–1948
Cox, Magistrates Cases	Mag.	27	1859–1920
Cox & Atkinson	Reg.	1	1843–46
Cox, Macrae & Hertslet	Co.Ct.	3	1847–58
Craig & Phillips	Ch.	1	1840–41
Craigie, Stewart & Paton (Scotland)	H.L.	6	1726–1821
Crawford & Dix, Abridged (Ireland)		1	1837–38
Crawford & Dix, Circuit (Ireland)		3	1839–46
Cresswell	Bky.	1	1827–29
Criminal Appeal Reports	Crim.		1908–
Criminal Appeal Reports (Sentencing)	Crim.		1979–
Cripps	Ecc	1	1847–50
Crockford	Adm.	3	1860–71
Croke	K.B.	4	1582–1641
Crompton & Jervis	Exch.	2	1830–32
Crompton & Meeson	Exch.	2	1832–34
Crompton, Meeson & Roscoe	Exch.	2	1834–36
Cunningham	K.B.	1	1734–36
Curteis	Ecc.	3	1834–44
Dale	Ecc.	1	1868–71
Dalrymple	C.S.	1	1698-1720
Daniell	Exch.	1	1817–20
Danson & Lloyd	Merc.	1	1828–29
Dasent	Bky.	2	1853–55
Davies	Pat.	1	1785–1816
Davies (Ireland)	K.B.	1	1604–12
Davison & Merivale	K.B.	1	1843–44
Day	Elect.	1	1892–93
Deacon	Bky.	4	1835–40
Deacon & Chitty	Bky.	4	1832–35
Deane & Swabey	Ecc.	1	1855–57
Dearsly	C.C.	1	1852–56
Dearsley & Bell	C.C.	1	1856–58
Deas & Anderson (Scotland)	C.S.	5	1829–33
Decisions of English Judges (Scotland)	C.S.	1	1655–61
De Colyar	Co.Ct.	1	1867–82
De Gex	Bky.	1	1844–50
De Gex & Jones	Ch.	4	1857–59
De Gex & Smale	Ch.	5	1846–52
De Gex, Fisher & Jones	Ch.	4	1859–62
De Gex, Jones & Smith	Ch.	4	1862–66
De Gex Macnaghten & Gordon	Ch.	8	1851–57
Delane		1	1832–35
Denison	C.C.	2	1844–52
De-Rating & Rating Appeals (Rowe)			1930–
Dickens	Ch.	2	1559–1798
Dirleton (Scotland)	C.S.	1	1665–77
Dodson	Adm.	2	1811–22
Donnell	Land	1	1871–76
Donnelly	Ch.	2	1836–37

Douglas	Elect.	4	1774–76
Douglas	K.B.	4	1778–85
Dow	H.L.	6	1812–18
Dow & Clark	H.L.	2	1827–32
Dowlins	Bail	9	1830–41
Dowlins, New Series	Bail	2	1841–43
Dowlins & Lowndes	Bail	7	1843–49
Dowlins & Ryland	K.B.	9	1822–27
Dowlins & Ryland	Mag.	4	1822–27
Dowlins & Ryland	N.P.	1	1822–23
Drewery	Ch.	4	1852–59
Drewry & Smale	Ch.	2	1860–65
Drinkwater	C.P.	pts 1–5	1840–41
Drury, temp. Napier (Ireland)	Ch.	1	1858–59
Drury, temp. Sugden (Ireland)	Ch.	1	1843–44
Drury & Walsh (Ireland)	Ch.	2	1837–40
Drury & Warren (Ireland)	Ch.	4	1841–43
Duncan	Merc.	1	1855–86
Dunlop (Scotland)	C.S.	24	1838–62
Dunning	K.B.	1	1753–54
Durie (Scotland)	C.S.	1	1621–42
Durnford & East	K.B.	8	1785–1800
Dyer	K.B.	3	1513–82
Eagle & Younge	Tithe	4	1204–1825
East	K.B.	16	1800–12
Eden	Ch.	2	1757–66
Edgar (Scotland)	C.S.	1	1724–25
Edwards	Adm.	1	1808–12
Elchies (Lord) (Scotland)	C.S.	2	1733–54
Election Cases (Scotland)	Elect.	1	1784–96
Ellis & Blackburn	K.B.	8	1852–58
Ellis, Blackburn & Ellis	K.B.	1	1858
Ellis & Ellis	K.B.	3	1858–61
English Reports		178	1220–1865
Equity Cases Abridged	Ch.	2	1677–1744
Equity Reports	K.B.	3	1853–55
Erck (Ireland)	Ecc.	1	1608–1825
Espinasse	N.P.	6	1793–1807
Estates Gazette			1858–
European Court Reports			1954–
European Human Rights Reports			1979–
Exchequer Reports	Exch.	11	1847–56
Faculty of Advocates (Scotland)	C.S.	14	1752–1808
Faculty of Advocates, New Series (Scotland)	C.S.	7	1808–25
Faculty of Advocates, Third Series	C.S.	16	1825–41
Falconer	Co.Ct.	1	1856–72
Falconer (Sir D.) Decisions (Scotland)	C.S.	2	1746–53
Falconer & Fitzherbert	Elect.	1	1835–39
Family Law Reports			1980–
Fawcett	Ref.	1	1865
Fergusson (Scotland)	Div.	1	1811–17
Finch (Sir H.)	Ch.	1	1673–81

LAW REPORTS: UNITED KINGDOM AND IRELAND

Finch (T.)	Ch.	1	1689–1723
Finlay, Digest (Ireland)		1	1769–71
Fisheries Commissioner		1	1863–65
Fisheries Commission Appeals (Ireland)		1	1861–93
Fitzgibbon	K.B.	1	1727–32
Fitzgibbon (Ireland)	Land	25	1895–1920
Fitzgibbon (Ireland)	Local	17	
	Govt.	17	1889–1919
Fitzgibbon (Ireland)	Reg.	1	1894
Flanagan & Kelly (Ireland)	Ch.	1	1840–42
Fleet Street Reports			1967–
Foley	Poor	1	1556–1730
Fonblanque	Bky.	3 pts	1849–52
Forbes (Scotland)	C.S.	1	1705–13
Forrest	Exch.	1	1801
Fortescue	K.B.	1	1695–1738
Foster	C.C.	1	1743–61
Foster & Finlason	N.P.	4	1856–67
Fountainhall (Scotland)	C.S.	2	1678–1712
Fox & Smith (Ireland)	K.B.	2	1822–24
Fox & Smith	Reg.	1	1886–95
Francillon	Co.Ct.	2 pts	1847–52
Fraser (Scotland)	C.S.	8	1898–1906
Fraser	Elect.	2	1790–92
Freeman	Ch.	1	1660–1706
Freeman	K.B.	1	1670–1704
Gale	Exch.	2	1835–36
Gale & Davison	K.B.	3	1841–43
Gazette of Bankruptcy	Bky.	4	1862–63
Gifford	Ch.	5	1857–65
Gilbert	K.B.	1	1713–15
Gilbert	Exch.		1705–27
Gilmour & Falconer (Scotland)	C.S.	2 pts	1661–81
			1681–86
Glanville	Elect		1624
Glascock (Ireland)		1	1831–32
Glyn & Jameson	Bky.	2	1821–28
Godbolt	K.B.	1	1575–1638
Goodeve	Pat.	1	1785–1883
Gouldsborough	K.B.	1	1586–1602
Gow	N.P.	1	1818–20
Green (Ireland)	Land	1	1898–99
Greer (Ireland)	Land	6	1872–1903
Griffin	Pat.	2	1866–87
Griffith	Poor	1	1821–31
Gwillim	Tithe	4	1224–1824
Haggard, Admiralty	Adm.	3	1822–38
Haggard, Consistory	Ecc.	2	1788–1821
Haggard, Ecclesiastical	Ecc.	3	1827–33
Hailes (Lord) (Scotland)	C.S.	2	1776–91
Hale, Ecclesiastical Criminal	Ecc.	1	1475–1640

Hale, Ecclesiastical Precedents	Ecc.	1	1583–1736
Hall & Twells	Ch.	2	1849–50
Handbook for Magistrates		1	1853–54
Hansell	Bky.	3	1915–17
Harcarse (Scotland)	C.S.	1	1681–91
Hardres	Exch.	1	1655–60
Hare	Ch.	11	1841–53
Harrington (Ireland)	Crim.	1	1887–89
Harrison & Rutherfurd	C.P.	1	1865–66
Harrison & Wollaston	K.B. & Bail	2	1835–36
Hatsell	Parl.	4	1290–1818
Hawarde		1	1593–1609
Hay	Poor	1	1711–1859
Hay & Marriott	Adm.	1	1776–79
Hayes (Ireland)	Exch.	1	1830–32
Hayes & Jones (Ireland)	Exch.	1	1832–34
Hemming & Miller	V.C.	2	1862–65
Hetley	C.B.	1	1627–32
Hobart	K.B.	1	1603–25
Hodge	C.P.	3	1835–37
Hogan (Ireland)	Ch.	2	1816–34
Holt	Adm.	1	1863–67
Holt	K.B.	1	1688–1710
Holt	N.P.	1	1815–17
Holt	V.C.	2	1845
Home (Clerk)	C.S.	1	1735–44
Hopwood & Coltman	Reg.	2	1868–78
Hopwood & Philbrick	Reg.	1	1863–67
Horn & Hurlstone	Exch.	2	1838–39
House of Lords Cases	H.L.	12	1847–66
Housing Law Reports			1982–
Hovenden, Supplement	Ch.	2	1789–1817
Howard (Ireland)	Eq.	2	1775
Howard, Popery (Ireland)		1	1720–73
Howell, State Trials		34	1163–1820
Hudson & Brook (Ireland)	K.B.	2	1827–31
Hughes (Ireland)	Reg.		1893–1915
Hume (Scotland)	C.S.	1	1781–1822
Hunt, Annuity	Q.B.	1	1776–96
Hurlstone & Coltman	Exch.	4	1862–65
Hurlstone & Norman	Exch.	7	1856–62
Hurstone & Walmsley	Exch.	5 pts	1840–41
Hutton	C.B.	1	1612–39
Immigration Appeal Reports			1972–
Industrial Cases Reports			1972–
Industrial Relations Law Reports			1972–
Industrial Tribunal Reports		13	1966–78
Insurance Law Reports			1982–
Irish Common Law & Chancery		34	1850–66
Irish Jurist		18	1849–66
Irish Jurist		27	1935–

LAW REPORTS: UNITED KINGDOM AND IRELAND

Irish Law & Equity		26	1838–50
Irish Law Recorder, First Series		4	1827–31
Irish Law Recorder, Second Series		6	1833–38
Irish Law Times			1867–
Irish Reports, Common Law		11	1866–78
Irish Reports, Equity		11	1866–78
Irish Reports, Registration Appeals	Reg.	1	1868–76
Irish Law Reports		32	1878–93
Irish Reports			1894–
Irish Weekly Law Reports		8	1895–1902
Irvine (Scotland)	Just.	5	1852–67
Jacob	Ch.	1	1821–22
Jacob & Walker	Ch.	2	1819–21
Jebb (Ireland)	C.C.	1	1822–40
Jebb & Bourke (Ireland)	K.B.	1	1841–42
Jebb & Symes (Ireland)	K.B.	2	1838–41
Jenkins	Exch.	1	1220–1623
Johnson	V.C.	1	1858–60
Johnson & Hemming	V.C.	2	1859–62
Jones (T.)	K.B. & C.B.	1	1667–85
Jones (W.)	K.B. & C.B.	1	1620–41
Jones (Ireland)	Exch.	2	1834–38
Jones & Carey (Ireland)	Exch.	2 pts	1838–39
Jones & La Touche (Ireland)	Ch.	3	1844–46
Journal of Planning & Environment Law			1948–
Joyce	Ecc.	1	1865–81
Judgments under Criminal Law & Procedure (Ireland)	Crim.	1	1882–1902
Jurist, in all Courts		18	1837–54
Jurist, in all Courts, New Series		12 – 24	1855–66
Justice of the Peace			1837–
Justiciary Cases (Scotland)			1916–
Kames, Remarkable Decisions (Scotland)	C.S.	2	1716–52
Kames, Select Decisions (Scotland)	C.S.	1	1752–68
Kames & Woodhouselee (Scotland)	C.S.	5	1540–1796
Kay	V.C.	1	1853–54
Kay & Johnson	V.C.	1	1854–58
Keane & Grant	Reg.	1	1854-62
Keble	K.B.	3	1616–79
Keen	R.C.	2	1836–38
Keilwey	K.B.	1	1496–1531
Kelyng	C.C.	1	1662–69
Kelynge	Ch.	1	1730-34
Kenyon	K.B.	2	1753–59
Kilkerran (Scotland)	S.C.	1	1738–52
Knapp	P.C.	3	1829–36
Knapp & Ombler	Elect.	1	1834–35
Knight, Industrial Reports		17	1966–74
Knight, Local Government	Mag.		1903–
Konstam, Rating Appeals		2	1904–08

Konstam & Ward, Rating Appeals		1	1909–12
Lailey	Co.Ct.	1	1917–20
Lands Tribunal Cases		6	1974–79
Lands Tribunal Rating Appeals		12	1950–62
Lane	Exch.	1	1605–12
Latch	K.B.	1	1625–28
Law Journal		9	1823–31
Law Journal, New Series		118	1832–1949
Law Journal Cases on Assessed Taxes			1824–26
Law Journal County Courts Appeals	Co.Ct.	1	1935
Law Journal County Courts Reporter	Co.Ct.	20	1912–33
Law Journal County Courts Reports	Co.Ct.	14	1934–47
Law Reporters		2	1821–22
Law Reports			
First Series			
Admiralty & Ecclesiastical		4	1865–75
Chancery Appeal		10	1865–75
Common Pleas		10	1865–75
Crown Cases Reserved		2	1865–75
English & Irish Appeals		7	1866–75
Equity		20	1866–75
Exchequer		10	1865–75
Privy Council Appeals		6	1865–75
Probate & Divorce		3	1865–75
Queen's Bench		10	1865–75
Scotch & Divorce Appeals		2	1866–75
Second Series			
Appeal Cases		15	1875–90
Chancery Division		45	1875–90
Common Pleas Division		5	1875–90
Exchequer Division		5	1875–90
Probate Division		15	1875–90
Queen's Bench Division		25	1875–90
Third Series			
Appeal Cases			1891–
Chancery			1891–
Family			1972–
Probate			1891–1971
Queen's (King's) Bench			1891–
Law Reports Indian Appeals		77	1872–1950
Law Reports Industrial Cases			1972–
Law Reports, Ireland		32	1878–93
Law Reports, Registration Cases		3 pts	1868–71
Law Reports Restrictive Practice Cases			1958–72
Law Times Old Series		34	1843–59
Law Times Reports		177	1859–1947
Lawson (Ireland)	Reg.	4	1885–1914
Lawyer & Magistrate (Ireland)		6 pts	1898–99
Leach	C.C.	2	1730–1815
Leading Ecclesiastical Cases (Scotland)	C.S.	1	1849–74
Lee	Ecc.	2	1752–58
Lee, temp. Hardwicke	K.B.	1	1733–38

LAW REPORTS: UNITED KINGDOM AND IRELAND

Legal Reporter (Ireland)		3	1840–43
Leigh & Cave	C.C.	1	1861–65
Leonard	K.B.	4	1553–1615
Levinz	K.B.	3	1600–97
Lewin	C.C.	2	1822–38
Ley	K.B.	1	1608–29
Lilly, Assize		1	1688–93
Littleton	C.B.	1	1626–32
Lizar (Scotland)		1	1840–50
Lloyd & Goold, temp. Plunkett (Ireland)	Ch.	1	1834–39
Lloyd & Goold, temp. Sugden (Ireland)	Ch.	1	1835
Lloyd & Welsby		3	1829–30
Lloyd, Prize	Adm.	10	1914–22
Lloyd, Prize, New Series	Adm.	1	1940–53
Lloyd's List Law Reports		84	1919–50
Lloyd's List Law Reports, New Series			1951–
Loft	K.B.	1	1772–74
Longfield & Townsend (Ireland)	Exch.	1	1841–42
Lowndes & Maxwell	Bail	1	1852–54
Lowndes, Maxwell & Pollock	Bail	2	1850–51
Luder	Elect.	3	1785–90
Lumley	Poor	2	1834–42
Lushington	Adm.	1	1859–62
Lutwyche	C.B.	2	1682–1703
Lutwyche	Reg.	2	1843–53
MacCarthy, Land Cases (Ireland)		1	1887–92
M'Cleland	Exch.	1	1824
M'Cleland & Younge	Exch.	1	1824–25
MacDevitt, Land Cases (Ireland)		1	1882–84
McFarlane, Jury Court	C.S.	1	1838–39
Macgillivray, Copyright		9	1901–49
MacLaurin (Scotland)		1	1670–1773
Maclean & Robinson (Scotland)	H.L.	1	1839
Magnaghten & Gordon	Ch.	3	1848–52
Macpherson (Scotland)	C.S.	11	1862–73
Macqueen, Divorce		1	1842
McQueen, Scotch Appeal		4	1851–65
Macrae & Hertslet	Bky.	2	1847–54
Macrory	Pat.	1	1852–55
Maddock	V.C.	6	1815–22
Magisterial Cases		51	1896–1946
Magistrates' Cases		18	1892–1910
Manning, Digest	N.P.	1	1790–1820
Manning, Revision Cases		1	1832–35
Manning & Granger	C.P.	7	1840–44
Manning & Ryland	K.B.	5	1827–30
Manning & Ryland	Mag.	3	1827–30
Manson	Bky.	21	1894–1914
March, New Cases	K.B.	1	1640–42
March, Translation of Brooke	K.B.	1	1515–58
Maritime Law Cases, Old Series		3	1860–71
Maritime Law Cases, New Series		19	1870–1943

Marshall	C.P.	2	1813–16
Maule & Selwyn	K.B.	6	1813–17
Maxwell, Land Cases (Ireland)		1	1904–11
Meeson & Welsby	Exch.	17	1836–47
Megone, Company Cases		2	1888–91
Merivale	Ch.	3	1815–17
Millin, Petty Sessions (Ireland)		1	1875–98
Milward	Ecc.	1	1819–42
Minton Senhouse		9	1898–1907
Modern Reports	K.B.	12	1669–1755
Molloy (Ireland)	Ch.	3	1827–31
Monro, Acta Cancellariae		1	1545–1625
Montagu	Bky.	1	1829–32
Montagu & Ayrton	Bky.	3	1833–38
Montagu & Bligh	Bky.	1	1832–33
Montagu & Chitty	Bky.	1	1838–40
Montagu & McArthur	Bky.	2	1828–29
Montagu, Deacon & De Gex	Bky.	3	1840–44
Moody	C.C.	2	1824–44
Moody & Malkin	N.P.	1	1826–30
Moody & Robinson	N.P.	2	1830–44
Moore (A.)	C.P.	1	1796–1797
Moore (E.F.)	P.C.	15	1836–62
Moore (E.F.) New Series	N.S.	9	1862–73
Moore (E.F.) India Appeals	P.C.	14	1836–71
Moore (Sir F.)	K.B.	1	1485–1621
Moore (J.B.)	C.P.	12	1817–27
Moore & Payne	C.P.	5	1827–31
Moore & Scott	C.P.	4	1831–34
Morison, Dictionary (Scotland)	C.S.	21	1540–1808
Morrell	Bky.	10	1884–93
Mosely	Ch.	1	1726–31
Municipal Law Reports (Scotland)		3	1903–13
Murphy & Hurlstone	Exch.	1	1836–37
Murray (Scotland)	Jury	5	1815–30
Mylne & Craig	Ch.	5	1835–41
Mylne & Keen	Ch.	3	1832–35
Nelson	Ch.	1	1625–93
Nevile & Manning	K.B.	6	1832–36
Nevile & Manning	Mag.	3	1832–36
Nevile & Perry	K.B.	3	1836–38
Nevile & Perry	Mag.	2	1836–37
Neville & Macnamara	Rail.	19	1835–1928
New Irish Jurist		5	1900–05
New Magistrates' Cases	Mag.	5	1844–51
New Practice Cases	Bail	3	1844–48
New Reports in all the Courts		6	1862–65
New Sessions Cases	Mag.	4	1844–51
New Term Reports			
Arnold	C.P.	2	1838–39
Arnold & Hodges	K.B.	1	1840–41
Drinkwater	C.P.	1	1840–41

Gale	Exch.	2	1835–36
Harrison & Woolaston	K.B.	2	1835–36
Hodges	C.P.	3	1835–37
Horn & Hurlstone	Exch.	2	1838–39
Hurlstone & Walmsley	Exch.	1	1840–41
Murphy & Hurlstone	Exch.	1	1836–37
Willmore, Wollaston & Davison	K.B.	1	1837
Willmore, Wollaston & Hodges	K.B.	2	1838–39
Woolaston	Bail	1	1840–41
Newbon, Private Bills		5	1895–99
Nicholl, Hare & Carrow	Rail.	7	1835–55
Nolan	Mag.	1	1791–92
Northern Ireland Law Reports			1925–
Notes of Cases in the Ecclesiastical & Maritime Courts	Ecc.	7	1841–50
Noy	K.B.	1	1559–1649
Old Bailey Sessions Papers		1	1715–1834
O'Malley & Hardcastle	Elect.	7	1869–1929
Owen	C.P.	1	1556–1615
Oxley	Rail.	2	1897–1903
Palgrave, Rotuli Curiae Regis	K.B.	2	1194–99
Palmer	K.B.	1	1619–29
Parker	Exch.	1	1743–67
Paterson	Poor	1	1857–63
Paterson (Scotland)	H.L.	2	1851–73
Paton	H.L.	6	1726–1821
Peake	N.P.	2	1790–1812
Peckwell	Elect.	2	1802–06
Peere Williams	Ch.	3	1695–1736
Perry	Bky.	1	1831
Perry & Davison	K.B.	4	1838–41
Perry & Knapp	Elect.	1	1833
Philipps	Elect.	1	1780–81
Phillimore	Ecc.	3	1809–21
Phillimore, Judgements	Ecc.	1	1867–75
Phillips	Ch.	2	1841–49
Pigott & Rodwell	Reg.	1	1843–45
Pleading & Practice Cases		1	1837–38
Plowden	K.B.	2	1550–80
Pollexfen	K.B.	1	1669–85
Popham	K.B.		1592–1627
Power, Rodwell & Dew	Elect.	2	1847–56
Practical Register	Bail	1	
Practical Register	C.P.	1	1705–42
Practical Register	Ch.	1	
Pratt, Contraband		1	1740–50
Precedents in Chancery	Ch.	1	1689–1722
Price	Exch.	13	1814–24
Price, Notes	Exch.	1	1830–31
Property & Compensation			1949–
Queen's Bench Reports	Q.B.	18	1841–52
Railway & Canal Cases		7	1835–54

Railway & Canal Traffic Cases		29	1855–1950
Rating Appeals			1965–
Raymond (Lord)	K.B.	3	1694–1782
Raymond (Sir T.)	K.B.	1	1660–84
Rayner	Tithe	3	1575–1782
Real Property & Conveyancing Cases		2	1843–48
Register of the Privy Council of Scotland:			
First Series		14	1545–1625
Second Series		8	1625–60
Third Series		14	1661–89
Reported Cases on Costs (Ireland)		1	1867–91
Reports (The)		15	1893–95
Reports in Chancery	Ch.	1	1615–1712
Reports of Cases	C.P.	1	1706–47
Reports of Commercial Cases		46	1895–1941
Reports of Patents, Designs & Trade Marks Cases			1884–
Reserved Cases (Ireland)		1	1860–64
Rettie (Scotland)	C.S.	25	1873–98
Revised Reports		152	1785–1866
Rickards & Michael	L.S.	1	1885–89
Rickards & Saunders	L.S.	1	1890–94
Ridgeway, temp. Hardwicke	Ch.	1	1733–45
Ridgeway (Ireland)	App.	3	1784–96
Ridgeway, Lapp & Schoales (Ireland)	K.B.	1	1793–95
Ritchie's Reports	K.B.	1	1617–1721
Road Traffic			1970–
Roberts, Divorce (Ireland)		1	1816–1905
Roberts, Leeming & Wallis	Co.Ct.	1	1849–51
Robertson	Ecc.	2	1844–53
Robertson (Scotland)	H.L.	1	1707–27
Robinson C.	Adm.	6	1798–1808
Robinson W.	Adm.	3	1838–50
Robinson (Scotland)	H.L.	2	1840–41
Roche, Dillon & Kehoe (Ireland)	Land	1	1881–82
Rolle	K.B.	2	1614–25
Romilly		1	1767–87
Roscoe	Adm.	2	1745–1859
Rose	Bky.	2	1810–16
Ross, Leading Cases (Scotland)		3	1638–1849
Rothery, Wreck Commissioner's Judgements		1	1876–80
Rotuli Curiae Regis	K.B.	2	1194–1199
Rotuli Parliamentorum		6	1278–1553
Rowe, De-Rating Appeals		28	1930–57
Rowe, Interesting Cases	K.B.	1	1798–1823
Russell	Ch.	4	1823–29
Russell & Mylne	Ch.	2	1829–31
Russell & Ryan	C.C.	1	1790–1824
Ryan & Moody	N.P.	1	1823–26
Ryde, Rating Appeals		3	1871–93
Ryde, Rating Cases			1956–
Ryde & Komstam		1	1894–1904

Name	Court	Vols	Years
Ryley, Placita Parliamentaria		1	1290–1327
Salkeld	K.B.	3	1689–1712
Saunders	K.B.	3	1666–73
Saunders & Austin	L.S.	2	1894–1904
Saunders & Bidder	L.S.	2	1905–19
Saunders & Cole	Bail	2	1846–48
Sausse & Scully (Ireland)	Ch.	1	1837–40
Savile	C.P.	1	1580–94
Sayer	K.B.	1	1751–56
Schoales & Lefroy (Ireland)	Ch.	2	1802–06
Scots Law Times			1893–
Scots Revised Reports		45	1707–1873
Scott	C.P.	8	1834–40
Scott, New Reports	C.P.	8	1840–45
Scottish Jurist		45	1829–73
Scottish Land Courts Reports			1913–
Scottish Law Reporter		61	1865–1925
Scottish Law Review & reports of Cases in the Sherriff Courts		79	1885–1963
Searle & Smith, Divorce		1	1859–60
Select Cases in Chancery, temp. King	Ch.	1	1724–33
Select Cases relating to Evidence		1	1698–1732
Sessions Cases	K.B.	2	1710–48
Session Cases (Scotland)	C.S.		1907–
Session Notes (Scotland)		24	1925–48
Sessions Papers, Old Bailey	Crim.	1	1715–1834
Sessions Papers, Central Criminal Court	Crim.	158	1834–1913
Shaw (J.) (Scotland)	Just.	1	1848–52
Shaw (P.) (Scotland)	Just.	1	1819–31
Shaw (P.) Appeal (Scotland)	H.L.	2	1821–24
Shaw (P.) Dunlop & Bell	C.S.	16	1821–38
Shaw & Maclean (Scotland)	H.L.	3	1835–38
Shillman, Irish Workmen's Compensation Cases		1	1934–38
Shower	H.L.	1	1694–99
Shower, ed. Butt	K.B.	2	1678–95
Siderfin	K.B.	2	1657–70
Simon, Tax Cases			1973–
Simons	V.C.	17	1826–50
Simons, New Series	V.C.	2	1850–52
Simons & Stuart	V.C.	2	1822–26
Skinner	K.B.	1	1681–98
Smale & Giffard	Ch.	3	1852–57
Smethurst	L.S.	1	1867
Smith	K.B.	1	1803–06
Smith	Reg.	3	1896–1915
Smith & Batty (Ireland)	K.B.	1	1824–25
Smythe (Ireland)	C.P.	1	1839–40
Smythe & Bourke (Ireland)	Marr.	1	1842
Solicitors' Journal			1857–
Spinks	Ecc.	2	1853–55
Spinks, Prize Cases	Adm.	1	1854–56

Stair (Scotland)	C.S.	2	1661–81
Star Chamber Cases			1455–1547
Star Sessions Cases (Scotland)	C.S.	1	1824–25
Starkie	N.P.	3	1815–22
State Trials, ed. Howell		34	1163–1820
State Trials, N.S., ex Macdonnell		8	1820–58
Stillingfleet	Ecc.	2	1698–1704
Stone & Graham		1	1865
Strange	K.B.	2	1716–49
Stuart, Milne & Peddle (Scotland)	C.S.	2	1851–53
Stubbing, Munitions Tribunals Appeals		2	1916–17
Style	K.B.	1	1646–55
Swabey	Adm.		1855–59
Swabey & Tristram	P.&D.	4	1858–65
Swanston	Ch.	3	1818–19
Swinton (Scotland)	Just.	2	1835–41
Syme (Scotland)	Just.	1	1826–29
Talbot, ed. Williams	Ch.	1	1730–37
Tamlyn	R.C.	1	1829–30
Taunton	C.B.	8	1807–19
Tax Cases			1875–
Taxation Reports			1939–
Temple & Mew	Crim.	1	1848–51
Times Law Reports		71	1884–1952
Tomlins	Elect.	1	1689–1795
Tothill	Ch.	1	1559–1646
Traffic Cases			1949–
Tristram, Consistory Judgements	Ecc.	1	1872–90
Turner & Russell	Ch.	1	1822–24
Tyrwhitt	Exch.	5	1830–35
Tyrwhitt & Granger	Exch.	1	1835–36
VAT Tribunal			1973–
Vaughan	C.P.	1	1665–74
Ventris	K.B.	1	1668–91
Vernon	Ch.	2	1681–1720
Vernon & Scrivan (Ireland)	K.B.	1	1786–88
Vesey (with Belt's Supplement)	Ch.	3	1746–55
Vesey (with Hovenden's Supplement)	Ch.	22	1789–1817
Vesey & Beames	Ch.	3	1812–14
Walker, De-Rating Appeals (Scotland)		1	1929–30
Wallis (Ireland)	Ch.	1	1766–91
Webster	Pat.	2	1602–1855
War Compensation Court Judgements		8	1920–29
Weekly Law Reports			1953–
Weekly Notes		83	1866–1952
Weekly Reporter		54	1853–1906
Welsby, Hurlstone & Gordon	Exch.	11	1847–56
Welsh (Ireland)	Reg.	1	1830–40
West	Ch.	1	1736–39
West	H.L.	1	1839–41
Western	Tithe	1	1592–1822
White (Scotland)	Just.	3	1886–93

Wight (Scotland)	Elec.	2	1687–1803
Wightwick	Exch.	1	1810–11
Willes	C.P.	1	1737–60
Williams (Peere)	Ch.	3	1695–1736
Willmore, Wollaston & Davison	K.B.	1	1837
Willmore, Wollaston & Hodges	K.B.	2	1838–39
Wilmot, Opinions & Judgements	K.B.	1	1757–70
Wilson	Ch.	1	1818–19
Wilson	Exch.	1	1805-17
Wilson	K.B.	3	1742–74
Wilson & Shaw (Scotland)	H.L.	7	1825–34
Winch	C.P.	1	1621–25
Wolferstan & Bristow	Elect.	1	1859–65
Wolferstan & Dew	Elect.	1	1857–58
Wollaston	Bail	1	1840–41
Wood	Tithe	4	1650–1798
Workmen's Compensation & Insurance Reports		22	1912–33
Year Books (ed. Horwood)		5	1292–1307
Year Books (ed. Horwood & Pike)		15	1337–46
Year Books (ed. Maynard)		11	1307–1537
Year Books (Selden Society)			
Yelverton	K.B.	1	1603–13
Younge	Exch.	1	1830–32
Younge & Collyer	Ch.	2	1841–44
Younge & Collyer	Exch.	4	1834–42
Younge & Jervis	Exch.	3	1826–30

AUTHOR AND SHORT-TITLE INDEX

AUTHOR AND SHORT TITLE INDEX

Aaron, B. Labour courts. 238
Aaron, B. & Wedderburn, K.W. Industrial conflict. 238
Aaron, T.J. Police discretion. 345
Aarvold, C.D. Magistrates' courts committee. 306
Abady, J. Inns of court. 242
Abbott, C. Merchant ships. 430
Abbott, H. Safe enough to sell. 388
Abbott, L.W. Law reporting. 283
Abbott, S. Racial discrimination. 398
Abecassis, D.W. Oil pollution. 344, 370, 430
Abel-Smith, B. & Stevens, R. Lawyer & the courts. 126, 289
Abel-Smith, B. & Townsend, P. Poor. 372
Abel-Smith, B., Zander, M. & Brook, R. Legal problems. 372
Abernathy, M.G. Civil liberties. 75
Abortion Law Reform Assoc. Abortion Act. 3
Abraham, H.J. Freedom. 75
Abraham, H.J. Judicial process. 92, 126, 264
Abraham, H.J. Judiciary. 126, 264
Abraham, L.A. & Hawtrey, S.C. Parliamentary dictionary. 151, 350
Abrahams, G. Lunatics & lawyers. 244, 317
Abrahams, G. Police questioning. 366
Abrahams, G. Writers & journalists. 378
Abrahamson, M.W. Engineering law. 54
Abramson, H.J. Adoption in Ireland. 11
Abse, L. Private member. 351
Achike, O. Nigerian contract. 110
Ackland, J.W. Girls in care. 72
Acquah-Dadzie, K. Ghana criminal court. 210
Acquah-Dadzie, K. Landlord & tenant Ghana. 210
Acton, T.A. Gypsy policies. 211
Acton, W. Prostitution. 390
Adam, G.S. Journalism. 378
Adam, M. Australian & New Zealand citator. 331
Adamiak, R. Law book price guide. 42
Adamolekun, L. Nigerian public administration. 332
Adams, B. Gypsies. 211
Adams, B. Rent tribunals. 408
Adams, E.C. Land transfer. 115
Adams, E.C. & Richardson, I.L.M. Estate duties. 178
Adams, F. Criminal onus. 133
Adams, Sir F.B. New Zealand criminal law. 331
Adams, G.B. Constitutional history. 104, 220
Adams, G.B. Council & courts. 220
Adams, J. Clive Schmitthoff essays. 249
Adams, J.D.R. International taxation. 159
Adams, J.E. Precedents for conveyancer. 115
Adams, L.J. Japanese treaties. 466
Adams, M. Censorship. 67
Adams, N. Law and teachers. 165

Adams, N. & Donahue, C. Select pleas. 164
Adams, P.R. Australian tax planning. 451
Adams, S. Sex discrimination. 175
Adamson, A.V. Valuation. 401
Adamson, A.V. & Adamson, M.S. Company shares. 88
Adamson, H.C. Solicitors. 438
Addison, C.G. Contracts. 110
Addison, C.G. Temple Church. 243
Adebayo, A. Nigerian public administration. 332
Adefidiya, A. Nigerian law libraries. 294, 332
Adesanya, M.O. & Oloyede, E.O. Business law in Nigeria. 80, 332
Adewoye, O. Southern Nigeria judicial system. 332
Addison, C.G. Wrongs. 456
Adefidiya, A. Law libraries in Nigeria. 154, 294, 332
Adkin, B.W. Copyholds. 117, 278
Adkin, B.W. Dilapidations. 154
Adkin, B.W. Forestry, trees, trespass. 203
Adkin, B.W. Landlord & tenant. 279
Adkin, B.W. & Bowen, D. Fixtures. 200
Adler, J.A. Dictionary of criminal science. 149
Adler, M. & Bradley, A. Justice. 8, 435
Advisory Committee for the Control of Motor Rallies. Report. 324
Advisory Committee on Drug Dependence. Powers of arrest. 27
Advisory Committee on Pollution of the Sea. Compensable damage. 370
Advisory, Conciliation & Arbitration Service. Industrial relations handbook. 238
Advisory Council on the Penal System. Powers of the courts. 381, 396
Advisory Council on the Penal System. Sentences. 381, 396
Affley, G. Business law. 80
Afterman, A.B. & Baxt, R. Corporations and associations. 29, 121
Agarwala, O. Compulsory acquisition. 96
Aggarwala, B.R. Supreme Court (India). 234
Agnew, W.F. Frauds. 205
Agrawala, S.K. Hijacking. 217
Agrawala, S.K. Treaties. 466
Agriculture, Fisheries & Food, Ministry of. Animal disease. 20
Agriculture, Fisheries & Food, Ministry of. Food quality. 200
Aguda, T.A. Evidence in Nigeria. 186, 332
Aguda, T.A. Nigerian civil actions. 332
Aguda, T.A. Nigerian criminal law. 135, 332
Aguda, T.A. Nigerian Supreme Court Practice. 332
Agyei, A.K. Nigerian capital gains tax. 62, 332
Ahern, J. Costs book. 172
Ahern, J. Victorian conveyancing costs. 115
Ahern, J. & Siebel, K. Legal costs. 122

Aiboni, S.A. Protection of refugees. 405
Aihe, D.O. & Oluyede, P.A. Nigeria constitutional law. 332
Air Force Dept. Civilian industrial employees regulations. 17
Air Navigation. Orders. 33
Aitken, J. Officially secret. 343
Akande, J. Nigerian constitution. 332
Akehurst, M.B. International law. 249
Akehurst, M.B. International organizations. 254
Akers, R. & Sagarin, G. Crime prevention. 127
Akintan, S.A. International economic institutions. 14
Alberta Univ. Institute of Law Research & Reform. Family court. 194
Albery, M. & Fletcher-Cooke, C.F. Monopolies. 322
Alchin, G. Cinema trade. 197
Alcock, A., Taylor, B.K. & Welton, J.M. Cultural minorities. 255
Alcock, A.E. International labour organisation. 253
Alcock, F.B. Powers of attorney. 374
Alder, J. Development control. 458
Alderson, J.C. & Stead, P.J. Police we deserve. 366
Aldous, J. & Hill, R. Marriage & the family. 195
Aldridge, T.M. Boundaries. 53, 354
Aldridge, T.M. Business premises. 58, 285
Aldridge, T.M. Conveyancing precedents. 115
Aldridge, T.M. Criminal Law Act. 131
Aldridge, T.M. Enquiries before contract. 115
Aldridge, T.M. Enquiries of local authorities. 115
Aldridge, T.M. Housing Act. 225, 279, 408
Aldridge, T.M. Law Society's conditions of sale. 115
Aldridge, T.M. Leasehold law. 285
Aldridge, T.M. Letting business premises. 58, 285
Aldridge, T.M. National conditions of sale. 115
Aldridge, T.M. Powers of attorney. 374
Aldridge, T.M. Registers & records. 154
Aldridge, T.M. Rent control. 285, 408
Aldridge, T.M. Service agreements. 168
Aldridge, T.M. Your home. 200
Aldridge, T.M. & Johnson, T.A. Business property. 58, 279
Alexander, A. Local government. 300
Alexander, L.M. Law of the sea. 424
Alexander, L.M. & Clingan, T.A Maritime transit. 430
Alexander, W. EEC rules of competition. 94, 182
Alexander, Y. International terrorism. 478

Alexandrov, G.N. & Khelstov, O.N. War crimes. 483
Alexandrowicz, C.H. Communications. 452
Alexandrowicz, C.H. International economic organizations. 252
Alexandrowicz, C.H. United Nations. 472
Alexandrowicz, C.H. World economic agencies. 252
Alhadeff, D.A. Competition. 94
Alison, A.J. Criminal law. 134
Allan, D.E. Asian contract. 110
Allan, D.E. Credit & security. 38
Allan, J. & Chapman, C. Licensing (Scotland) Act. 296
Allan, R.G. Employment. 168, 471
Allen, Sir C.K. Administrative jurisprudence. 8
Allen, Sir C.K. Aspects of justice. 8, 268
Allen, Sir C.K. Law & orders. 8, 351, 384
Allen, Sir C.K. Law in the making. 8, 218, 258, 268, 290
Allen, Sir C.K. Queen's peace. 366
Allen, D.K. Bourn, C.J. & Holyoak, J.H. Accident compensation. 5, 362
Allen, F.A. Criminal justice. 129
Allen, G.C. Monopoly. 322
Allen, J. Common Market. 181
Allen, R.J. Police supervision. 366
Allen, V.L. Trade unions. 463
Allison, C.E. Care proceedings. 72
Allot, A.N. African law. 14, 210
Allott, A.N. Limits of law. 268
Alpe, N. Stamp duties. 445
Alting Von Geusau, F.A.M. European Communities. 179
Alting Von Geusau, F.A.M. NATO. 336
Alves, J.T. Confidentiality in social work. 436
Amador, F.V.G. Injuries to aliens. 362
American Association of Law Libraries. Directory. 154, 294
American Jurisprudence. Pleading & practice. 203
American Law Institute. Restatement:conflicts. 100
American Law Institute. Restatement:contract. 110
American Medical Association. Alcohol & the driver. 161
American Society of International Law. International terrorism. 256
American Society of International Law. Ocean dumping. 370
American Stock Exchange Inc. Constitution. 448
Amery, L.C.M.S. Constitution. 102
Ames, J.B. Legal history. 218
Amies, F.A. Rating. 401
Amin, S.H. Continental shelf. 109
Amin, S.H. Fisheries. 199

AUTHOR AND SHORT TITLE INDEX

Amin, S.H. Pollution control. 368
Amin, S.H. Wrongful appropriation. 260
Amir, M. Rape. 401
Amnesty International. Death penalty. 63
Amnesty International. Human rights. 228
Amos, A. & Ferard, J. Fixtures. 200
Amos, H. Shipping conferences. 430
Amos, M.S. English constitution. 102
Amos, M.S. & Walton, F.P. French law. 204
Amos, S. English code. 78
Amos, W.E. & Newman, C.L. Private legal issues. 352
Amrolia, H.A. Kenya probate. 189, 273, 386
Anand, R.P. International adjudication. 250
Anand, R.P. International courts. 250, 253
Anand, R.P. Law of the sea. 424
Anand, R.P. Sea-bed. 424
Ancel, M. Suspended sentence. 427
Andenaes, J. Punishment & deterrence. 396, 427
Anderman, S.D. Employment protection. 171
Anderman, S.D. Unfair dismissal. 168, 238, 471
Andersen, A. Companies Act. 88
Anderson, A.J. Intellectual freedom. 67
Anderson, F.W. Hanging. 63
Anderson, I.G. Councils, committees and boards. 154
Anderson, J.N.D. Changing law in developing countries. 92
Anderson, J.N.D. Islamic law. 260
Anderson, N. Life & death. 3, 185
Anderson, Sir N. Liberty, law & justice. 76, 268
Anderson, R. Juvenile court. 272
Anderson, R. & Simon, M. Contract glossary. 110
Anderson, R.J.B. Anglo-Scandinavian law dictionary. 149
Anderson, S.V. Ombudsman. 345
Anderson, T.K. Execution. 36
Anderton, C.J. Crime in perspective. 136
Andrassy, J. Resources of the sea. 109, 424
Andrews, C. Education Act. 165
Andrews, J.A. Criminal justice. 129
Andrews, J.A. Welsh studies. 8, 479
Andrews, S. Agriculture & Common Market. 181
Angel, J. Industrial Tribunal. 239
Anger, W.H., Anger, H.D. & Hume, F.R. Commercial law. 80
Angus, J.W. Dictionary of crimes. 134, 149
Annam, Lord. Broadcasting coverage report. 399
Annand, R. & Cain, B. Modern conveyancing. 115
Anson, Sir, W.R. Constitution. 102, 350
Anson, Sir W.R. Contract. 110
Anstey, B. & Chavasse, M. Light. 297

Anthony, E. & Berryman, J.D. Domestic proceedings. 193, 312
Anthony, E. & Berryman, J.D. Licensing law. 296
Anthony, E. & Berryman, J.D. Magistrates' court guide. 35, 305
Anthony, H.S. Depression. 52
Anthrop, D.F. Noise. 335
Antieau, C.J. Constitutionl law. 474
Anton, A.E. Private international law. 100, 421
Antonio, D.G. Scots law. 421
Appavoo, S.M. Magistrates' powers. 305, 427
Appleby, P.H. Public administration. 391
Applemen, J.F. Military tribunals. 483
Appleyard, G.R. Professional practice insurance. 247
Archbold, J.F. Criminal pleading. 22, 35, 99, 132, 186, 216, 235, 240, 267, 334, 361, 365, 375, 389
Archbold, J.F. King's Bench. 397
Archbold, J.F. Nisi prius. 334
Archer, J.A. Annuity tables. 21
Archer, P. Queen's Courts. 172
Archer, P. & Martin, A. More law reform now. 282
Architects' Journal. Legal handbook. 25, 55
Arden, A. Housing. 225, 279, 408, 485
Arden, A. & Partington, M. Housing law. 225
Arden, M.& Eccles, G. Companies Act. 88
Ardra, A. Business law. 80
Areen, J. Family law. 195
Argent, H.D. Death duty mitigation. 178
Arguile, R. Criminal procedure. 132
Argy, V. International money crisis. 320
Armitage, Sir A.L. Political activities of civil servants. 78
Armour, L.A.J. Tort. 456
Armour, S.B. Rating valuation. 401
Armstrong, G.M. Soviet property law. 441
Armstrong, J.W.S. War & treaty. 466
Armstrong, K.F. Anatomy. 19
Armstrong, M. Broadcasting law. 399
Armstrong, M. Media law. 378
Armstrong, M. Redundancy procedures. 405
Armstrong, W.E.I. I.C.E. Contractual claims. 54
Army Department. Cadet force regulations. 26
Army Department. Queen's regulations. 26
Army Department. TAVR. 26
Arnold, J.C. Leasehold & tenancy agreements. 285
Arnold, J.C. Marriage. 310
Arnold, M.S. Laws and customs. 84
Arnold, T.J. Municipal corporations. 300
Arnold-Baker, C. Art administrators' law. 28
Arnold-Baker, C. Local government. 300, 458
Arnold-Baker, C. Parish administration. 164, 349
Arnold-Baker, C. Parish councils. 349

Arnot, R.P. General strike. 238
Arnott, A.J.E. & Duncan, J.A. Scottish criminal. 134
Arnould, Sir J. Marine insurance. 52, 247, 430
Aron, R. Peace & war. 480
Aronson, M.I., Reaburn, N.S. & Weinberg, M.S. Litigation. 375
Aronstam, P. Consumer protection. 107
Arscott, P. Health & safety. 167
Arthur, P. Northern Ireland government & politics. 336
Arts Council. Obscenity. 341
Asamoah, O.Y. UN General Assembly. 472
Asante, S.K.B. Ghana property law. 210
Ashburner, W. Equity. 176
Ashburner, W. Mortgages, pledges & liens. 296
Ashe, T.M. Insider trading. 88
Ashford, F.B. Water. 484
Ashford, N.A. Crisis in the work-place. 342
Ashley, H. Mayor's Court. 313
Ashton, TR. City and the court. 126, 220
Ashworth, A. Sentencing. 427
Ashworth, W. Special librarianship. 294
Askew, H.R. Gas undertakings. 207
Aspland, L.M. Blasphemy. 49
Asquith, S. Children & justice. 72, 272
Assinder, G.F. Trade unions. 463
Association of American Law Schools. Family law. 195
Association of British Adoption Agencies. Guardian ad litem. 11
Association of Certified & Corporate Accountants. V.A.T. 476
Association of Law Teachers. Directory. 154
Astle, W.E. Bills of lading. 47
Astle, W.E. Cargo carriers. 66, 430
Astle, W.E. Marine commerce. 430
Astle, W.E. Shipowners' liabilites. 430
Athearn, J.L. Risk & insurance. 245
Atiyah, P.S. Accidents, compensation. 5, 456
Atiyah, P.S. Consideration. 113
Atiyah, P.S. Contract. 110
Atiyah, P.S. From principles to pragmatism. 126, 264
Atiyah, P.S. Law & modern society. 268
Atiyah, P.S. Promises, morals & law. 268
Atiyah, P.S. Rise & fall of freedom of contract. 110
Atiyah, P.S. Sale of goods. 106, 419
Atiyah, P.S. Vicarious liability. 167, 456, 477
Atkin, Lord. Moot book. 292
Atkins, R. & Graycar, A. Governing Australia. 31
Atkinson, A.B. Poverty in Britain. 372, 435
Atkinson, G. Sheriffs. 430
Atkinson, J.M. & Drew, P. Order in court. 7, 13, 126
Atlay, J.B. Victorian Chancellors. 47, 304

Attenborough, C.L. Pawnbroking. 358
Attenborough, F.L. Laws of earliest kings. 220
Attorney's pocket dictionery. 149
Aubry, C. & Rau, C. French civil law. 204
Auburn, F.M. Antarctic law. 26
Auburn, F.M. Ross dependency. 26
Audretsch, H.A.H. Supervision. 179
Aufricht, H. International Monetary Fund. 252
Aufricht, H. League of Nations publications. 284
Auguste, B.L. Continental shelf. 109
Ault, H.J. & Radler, A.J. German corporation tax. 120, 209
Ault, W.O. Open-field farming. 59
Austin, C.G. Sale of goods. 419
Austin, G. Indian constitution. 234
Austin, J. Jurisprudence. 268
Austin, P.M. Juvenile court. 272
Australian encyclopaedia of forms and precedents. 203
Australian Law Librarians' Group. Directory of law libraries. 294
Avery, J. Police. 366
Avery Jones, J.F. Tax havens. 450
Avgherionos, G & Telling, A.E. Housing repairs. 225
Axinn, S.M. Acquisition. 94
Axline, W.A. European Community. 181
Ayany, S.G. Zanzibar. 450
Aylmer, G.E. State's servants. 77
Baade, H.W. Soviet impact on international law. 441
Baade, H.W. & Everett, R.O. African law. 14
Baalman, J. Australia. 31
Baalman, J. Torrens system. 456
Baalman, J. & Wells, T. le M. Land titles. 455
Babington, A. Rule of law. 218
Backe, T. Swedish-English legal terms. 149
Bagehot, W. English constitution. 102
Bagnall, K.R. & Lewison, K. Development land tax. 148, 411
Bailey, A. English Crown. 139
Bailey, D.F. Unfair dismissal. 471
Bailey, D.S. Homosexuality. 223
Bailey, F. Company accounts. 5
Bailey, F.L. & Rothblatt, H.B. Crimes of violence. 401, 478
Bailey, H.J. Commercial law. 80
Bailey, I. Construction law. 55
Bailey, R. Squatters. 444
Bailey, S.D. Parliamentary democracy. 351
Bailey, S.D. Prohibition & restraints. 480
Bailey, S.D. House of Lords. 350
Bailey, S.D. Security Council. 472
Bailey, S.D. UN General Assembly. 472
Bailey, S.H. Administrative law. 8
Bailey, S.H., Harris, D. & Jones, B. Civil liberties. 76

AUTHOR AND SHORT TITLE INDEX

Bailey, S.J. Wills. 487
Bain, A. & Inglis, R.M.G. Apportioning tables. 23
Bainbridge, J.S. Law in Africa. 14
Baker, C.D. Tort. 456
Baker, C.V. Housing associations. 227
Baker, E.R. & Wilkie, G.H. Criminal evidence. 186
Baker, E.R. & Wilkie, G.H. Criminal law. 131
Baker, E.R. & Wilkie, G.H. Police promotion handbooks. 131, 186, 366
Baker, E.R. & Wilkie, G.H. Road traffic. 416
Baker, J. Neighbourhood advice centre. 286, 485
Baker, J.H. Law French. 124, 149
Baker, J.H. Legal history. 218
Baker, J.H. Legal records. 218
Baker, N.L. Law & the individual. 268
Baker, R. New & improved. 356
Baker, T. Burials. 57
Baker, W.B. Registrars' matrimonial jurisdiction. 312
Bakker, P. Inflation accounting. 5
Balagon, M.J. Northern Nigeria local government. 332
Balassa, B.A. European economic integration. 179, 181
Baldwin, E.T. Bankruptcy. 47
Baldwin, H. US constitution. 474
Baldwin, J. & Bottoms, A.E. Urban criminal. 136
Baldwin, J. & McConville, M. Jury trials. 267, 467
Baldwin, J. & McConville, M. Negotiated justice. 132, 364, 365
Baldwin, J.F. King's Council. 220
Balfour, C. Industrial relations. 179, 238
Balfour, C. Unions. 463
Balfour, J. Practicks. 421
Ball, B. & Rose, F. Business law. 80
Ball, Sir W.V. Bankruptcy. 37, 47, 144
Ball, Sir W.V. Libel & slander. 293
Ball, Sir W.V. Lincoln's Inn. 243
Ballantyne, B. Forensic toxicology. 202
Ballantyne, G. Signet library. 294
Ballard, A. British borough charters. 300
Ballentine, J.A. Law dictionary. 149
Ballis, W.B. War. 480
Bamford, B.R. Partnership in S.Africa. 353, 439
Bamford, B.R. Shipping in S.Africa. 66, 430, 439
Bancroft, J.H. Deviant sexual behaviour. 223
Bander, E.J. Change of name. 325
Bander, E.J. & Wallach, J.J. Medical legal dictionary. 314
Banfield, G.E. Accident insurance. 246
Banks, M.A. Law library. 294
Banks, M.A.L. Patent committee. 356

Banning, S.T. Military law. 318
Banton, M. Race relations. 398
Bar Council. Planning and mineral working. 319, 458
Barber, B. & others. Research on human subjects. 230
Barber, D. One parent families. 291
Barber, D. & Gordon, G. Jury. 267
Barber, D.F. Pornography. 341
Barber, M.P. Building contracts. 54
Barber, M.P. Landlord and tenant. 279
Barber, M.P. Local government. 300
Barber, M.P. Public administration. 391
Barber, P. Land law. 274
Barber, P. Succession. 448
Barclay, J.B. Society of Solicitors Scotland. 438
Barclay, Sir T. International practice & diplomacy. 153
Bari, B.P. Marriage & divorce. 155, 311
Barker, Sir E. Government. 212
Barker, R.E. Photocopying. 117
Barker, R.E. & Davies, G.R. Books are different. 322, 336
Barkun, M. Law without sanctions. 380
Barnard, D. Civil court. 467
Barnard, D. Criminal court. 132, 139, 467
Barnard, D. Family court. 193
Barnes, J.J. Authors, publishers, politicians. 33, 117
Barnett, A.J. Sark constitution. 69
Barnett, L. Jamaica. 263
Barnsley, D.G. Conveyancing. 115
Barnsley, D.G. Land options. 274
Barounos, D., Hall, D.F. & James, J.R. Anti-trust law. 94, 182
Barr, H. Volunteer. 406
Barr, W.C. Insurance. 245
Barrell, G.R. Teachers. 165
Barrett, R.I. Income taxation. 233
Barrington, T.J. From big government. 300
Barrington, T.J. Irish administrative system. 259, 391
Barros, J. & Johnston, D.M. Pollution. 368
Barry, B, Liberal theory of justice. 268
Barry, D.D. Soviet law. 441
Barston, R.P. & Birnie, P.W. Maritime dimension. 424
Barthold, W. Discovery techniques. 155
Bartholomew, P.C. Irish judiciary. 259, 264
Barton, Sir D.P., Benham, C. & Watt, F. Inns of Court. 242
Barton, H.D. Executorship. 187
Barwick, G. Precedent. 31, 266
Bar-Yaacov, N. Dual nationality. 328
Bar-Yaacov, N. International disputes. 250
Bassiouni, M.C. International extradition. 191
Bassiouni, M.C. & Nanda, V.P. International criminal law. 135, 217

Bassiouni, M.C. & Savitski, V.M. Criminal justice USSR. 441
Basu, D.D. Limited government. 266
Basye, P.E. Land titles. 455
Bateman, J. Auctions. 30
Bates, A.P., Buddin, T.L. & Meure, D.J. System of criminal law. 135
Bates, F. Australian social worker. 436
Bates, F. Evidence. 186
Bates, G.M. Environmental law. 174
Bates, J. & Hally, D. Financing of small business. 80
Bates, J.H. Marine pollution. 370
Bates, N. Legal studies. 287
Bateson, P. & McKee, J. Industrial tribunals. 239
Bathurst, M. & Simpson, J.L. Germany & NATO. 336
Bathurst, M.E., & others. Legal problems. 181
Bator, P.M. International trade in art. 28
Batsell, J. House of Commons proceedings. 350
Batt, F.R. Master & servant. 167, 168, 477
Batten, J. Stannaries. 445
Baty, T. Prize law. 385
Baty, T. Vicarious liability. 133, 477
Baty, T. & Morgan, J.H. War. 480
Bauby, C. Between consenting adults. 223
Baugh, W.E. Social services. 435
Baumann, O.E. Diplomatic kidnapping. 394
Baumer, T.L. & Rosenbaum, D.P. Retail theft. 454
Bauw, F.de & Wit, B.de. China trade law. 74, 81
Bawden, T.A. Legislative Council standing orders. 261
Baxt, R. Company law. 88
Baxt, R. Securities industry codes. 81
Baxt, R., Bialkower, L. & Morgan, R.J. Partnership. 353
Baxt, R. & others. Taxation cases. 411
Baxter, I. Banking. 38
Baxter, I.F.G. & Eberts, M.A. Child and the courts. 72
Baxter, I.G.& Fletham, I.R. Export practice. 190
Baxter, J.H. & Johnson, C. Medieval latin. 288
Baxter, J.W. Patent law. 356
Baxter, R.R. International waterways. 62
Baxter, R.R., Carroll, D. & Tondel, L.M. Panama Canal. 62
Bayitch, S.A. Inter-American fisheries. 199
Bayitch, S.A. Latin America. 263
Bayliss, F.P.C. Poisons. 162, 314
Baylist, T.H. Temple Church. 243
Beale, E. Bailments. 36
Beal, E. Interpretation. 143, 258
Beale, H. Breach of contract. 114
Beale, J.H. Bibliography. 42

Beale, J.H. Conflict of laws. 100
Bean, D. Injunctions. 241
Bean, P. Rehabilitation. 406
Bean, P. Social control of drugs. 162
Bean, P.R. & Lockwood, A. Rating valuation. 401
Beaton, J.A. Scots law terms. 150, 421
Beaton, R. Architect. 25
Beatson, J. & Matthews, M.H. Administrative law. 8
Beattie, C.N. Estate duty. 178
Beattie, C.N. Income tax. 62, 233
Beattie, D.J. Ultra vires. 300, 470
Beaumont, C.H. Sheriffs. 430
Beaumont, C.H. Town & country planning. 459
Becker, H.K. Police administration. 366
Beckerley, B. EEC competition law. 94, 182
Beckett, Sir W.E. North Atlantic Treaty. 336
Bedau, A. Death penalty. 63
Beddard, R. Human rights. 228
Bedwell, C.E.A. Middle Temple. 243
Beer, C., Jeffrey, R. & Munyard, T. Gay workers. 223
Beever, C.R. European unity. 181
Behnke, J.A. & Bok, S. Euthanasia. 185
Beirne, P. Fair rent. 408
Bekker, J.J. & Coertzer, J.J.J. South African customary law. 439
Belfast & Ulster Licensed Vintners' Assoc. Licensing laws. 296
Bell, G.J. Scotland. 421
Bell, H.E. Court of Wards history. 220
Bell, J. Policy arguments in judicial decisions. 264
Bell, J.S. Industrial injuries benefits. 435
Bell, K. Tribunals. 467
Bell, N.K. Who decides. 392
Bell, R.M. Crown actions. 139
Bell, W. Scottish law dictionary. 421
Bell, W.J. & O'Keefe, J.A. Food & drugs. 200
Bellamy, C. & Child, G.D. Common Market competition. 94, 182
Bellamy, J.G. Crime & public order. 134, 220
Bellamy, J.G. Criminal law & society. 134
Bellamy, J.G. Treason. 220, 221, 465
Bellerose, R.P. Reinsurance. 248
Bellord, N. Computers for lawyers. 97
Bellott, H.H.L. Gray's Inn & Lincoln's Inn. 242, 243
Bellott, H.H.L. Inner & Middle Temple. 243
Beloff, M.J. Sex discrimination. 175
Beloff, N. Freedom under foot. 378
Belson, W.A. Juvenile theft. 136
Belson, W.A. Public & the police. 366
Bendiner, E. Time for angels. 284
Benditt, T.M. Law as rule and principle. 268
Benedict, E. & Knauth, A.D. American admiralty. 10

Benedictus, R. Safety representatives. 167
Benjamin, J.P. Personal property. 419
Benjamin, J.P. Sale of goods. 419
Bennett, A. Habeas corpus. 216
Bennett, A.L. International organizations. 254
Bennett, D.M. Building contracts. 54
Bennett, G.F. & Bennett, J.C. Environmental literature. 42
Bennett, J. Palatine of Lancaster. 124
Bennett, J.M. New South Wales Bar. 31
Bennett, J.M. New South Wales Supreme Court. 31
Bennion, F.A.R. Consumer Credit Act. 106
Bennion, F.A.R. Consumer credit control. 106
Bennion, F.A.R. Statute law. 290, 446
Bennion, F.A.R. Tangling with the law. 282
Benson, Sir H. Royal Commission on legal services. 289
Bentham, J. Constitutional code. 78
Bentham, J. Fragment on government. 212, 268
Bentham, J. Laws in general. 268
Bentham, J. Jurisprudence. 268
Bentham, J. Morals & legislation. 268, 290
Bentham, J. Theory of legislation. 268, 290
Bentham, J. Swear not at all. 341
Bentham, J. Works. 268
Bentsi-Enchill, K. Ghana land law. 210
Bentsi-Enchill, K. Ex-British Africa. 14, 210
Bentwich, N. Domicil. 159
Bentwich, N. International law. 251
Bentwich, N. Mandates system. 255
Bentwich, N. Privy Council. 385
Bentwich, N. & Martin, A. UN Charter. 472
Benz, N. & Tappenden, H.J. Reversions. 415
Bequai, A. Computer crime. 97
Beran, N.J. & Tommey, B.G. Mentally ill offenders. 129, 244
Berchman, E. Victims of piracy. 221, 364
Bercusson, B. Employment protection. 168, 171
Bercusson, B. Fair wages. 168
Berelson, P.P. & Swanson, L.G. Law book guide. 42
Beresford, H.R. Neurological practice. 314
Berger, R. Impeachment. 232
Bergsten, E.E. Community law in French courts. 184
Berk, R.A. & Rossi, P.H. Prison reform. 381
Berkin, M. & Young, M. Domestic proceedings. 193, 305
Berkin, M. & Young, M. Matrimonial suits. 196, 312
Berkowitz, L. & Cockain, G.D.M. Companies. 88
Berlins, M. & Dyer, C. Law machine. 172
Berlins, M. & Wansell, G. Caught in the act. 72
Bernacchi, R.L. & Larsen, G.H. Data processing contracts. 97
Bernard, H. Death. 57
Berney, A.L. Legal problems. 372
Bernstein, R. & Reynolds, K. Rent review. 408
Berrington, H. Backbench opinion. 350
Berry, S. & Olsen, T. Liquidation. 37
Bersoni, C.A. Crime & delinquency. 145
Bertram, D. Receivership tax consequences. 37
Bes, J. Bulk carriers. 66
Beseler, D. & Jacobs, B. Law dictionary. 150
Best, G. Humanity in warfare. 480
Besterman, T. Law & international law. 42
Beth, L.P. Judicial review. 266
Beth, L.P. Politics. 474
Betting, Gaming & Lotteries Act 1963. Permits & licences. 445
Bevan, H.K. Child protection. 72
Bevan, H.K. Children. 11, 72
Bevan, H.K. & Perry, M.L. Children Act. 11
Beven, T. Negligence. 330
Beven, T. Trespass. 466
Beveridge, Sir W. Social insurance report. 327
Beveridge, W.E. Church. 348
Bewes, W.A. Law merchant. 281
Bhatia, H.S. Indian legal & political system. 234
Bhatt, S. Outer space. 442
Bhutto, Z.A. UN peacekeeping. 472
Bibo, I. International institutions. 254
Bicknell, B.A. Cases on the constitution. 105
Biddle, L.A. & Mew, R.L. Capital gains tax. 62
Bidwell, R. Guide to government ministers. 154
Bieber, D.M. Legal abbreviations. 3
Bigelow, M.M. Estoppel. 179
Bigge, Sir L.A.S. Board of Education. 214
Biggs, A.K. Costs in matrimonial causes. 122, 312
Biggs, A.K. County court costs. 122, 124
Biggs, A.K. Fees in matrimonial proceedings. 122, 155, 312
Biggs, A.K. Legal and financial conditions. 286
Biggs, A.K. Probate fees. 386
Biggs, A.K. & Rogers, A.P. Probate. 386
Biggs, J. Guilty mind. 222
Bigham, D.A. Protection of the environment. 174
Bigwood, E.J. & Gerard, A. Food. 201
Billing, S. Pews. 348
Binchy, W. Irish family law. 195
Bing, J. & Harold, T. Legal decisions. 97, 289
Bing, J. & Selner, K.S. Decade of computers. 97
Bingham, L. Motor claims. 247, 324, 416
Bingham, R. Crown court crime. 129, 139
Bingham, R. Negligence. 330

Bingham, T. Tax evasion. 411
Binns, G.D. Building regulations. 55
Birch, A.H. Government. 212
Birch, I.K. Australian constitutional responsibility for education. 165
Birch, I.K. School and law. 165.
Birchfield, M.E. League of Nations catalogue. 184
Birds, J. Modern insurance. 245
Birke, W. European elections. 183
Birkett, Sir N. Interception of communications. 383
Birks, M. Gentlemen of the law. 438
Birks, M. Small claims. 124
Biron, H.C. & Chalmers, K.E. Extradition. 191
Birrell, A. Copyright. 117
Biscoe, P.M. Credit factoring. 28, 81, 420
Bishop, D. Industrial leases. 285
Bishop, J. Criminal procedure. 375
Bishop, W.W. International law. 251
Biskind, E.L. New York family law. 195
Biskup, P. Not slaves, not citizens. 398
Black, A.. Execution. 36, 188, 265
Black, C.L. Impeachment. 232
Black, Sir D & Thomas, G. Health service. 826, 392
Black, H.C. Law dictionary. 150
Blackburn, C. Contract of sale. 112, 420
Blackford, R. & Jaque, C.. Chancery practice. 68
Blackham, R.J. Wig & gown. 242
Blackshaw, I. Doing business in Spain. 81
Blackstone, Sir W. Commentaries. 84, 131
Blackwell, G. Meetings. 316
Blackwell, L. & Bamford, B.R. Newspaper law of S.Africa. 378
Blainey, G. War. 480
Blair, E.H. Workmen's compensation. 489
Blair, M.C. Sale of Goods Act. 420
Blake, H.M. & Rahl, J.A. Business regulation in Common Market. 181
Blake, Lord. Prime Minster. 350
Blake, S.H. Marriage. 310
Blampain, J. National health. 392
Blanchard, P. Company receiverships. 404
Blanchet, A. & Grueber, H. Treasure trove. 465
Bland, D.S. Inns of Court. 242
Bland, J. King's Bench. 397
Blassingame, W. Science catches the criminal. 202
Blatcher, M. Court of King's Bench. 220, 397
Blaustein, A.P. Legal documents of China. 74
Blaustein, A.P. & Flanz, G.H. Constitutions. 102
Blegvad, B.M. & Others. Arbitration. 24
Blennerhasset, F. Drinking & driving. 161
Blix, H. Sovereignty. 441

Blix, H. Treaty making. 446
Blom-Cooper, L.J. Penal reform. 396
Blom-Cooper, L.J. & Drewry, G. Final appeal. 22, 127, 350
Blom-Cooper, L.J. & Drewry, G. Law & morality. 268
Bloomfield, L.M. Internationally protected persons. 153
Bloomfield, L.M. & Fitzgerald, G.F. Boundary waters problems. 53
Bloustein, E.J. Nuclear energy. 337
Bloxam, G.A. Licensing rights in technology. 356
Blundell, L.A. & Dobry, G. Planning appeals. 174, 459
Blunt, A. Law librarianship. 294
Blunt, J.H. Church law. 164
Bochel, D. Probation. 387, 406
Boczek, B.A. Flags of convenience. 431
Boddy, M. Building societies. 57
Bodenheimer, E. Jurisprudence. 268
Bodkin, E.H. Maintenance & champerty. 307
Boehm, K. British patent system. 356
Boehringer, G.H. & McCabe, S. Hospital order. 305
Boer, B.W. & Gleeson, V.B. Law of education. 165
Bogert, G.G. Trust & trustees. 468
Bogsch, A. Copyright. 117
Bohning, W.R. Migration of workers. 18, 181
Bokor-Szego, H. Role of United Nations. 472
Boland, D. & Sayer, B.H. Oaths & affirmations. 341
Bolland, W.J. Yearbooks. 220, 490
Bolt, G.J. Communicating with EEC Markets. 181
Bolt, G.J. Marketing in the EEC. 181
Bolton, H. Apportionment tables. 23
Bolton, P.M. Civil rights. 76
Bond, J.E. Plea bargaining. 364
Bond, J.E. Riot. 480
Bond, M. Records of parliament. 351
Bonfield, L. Marriage settlements. 218, 310
Bonner, Sir G.A. King's Remembrancer. 274
Bonner, G.A. Transport. 400, 464
Bonner, S.F. Roman declamation. 418
Boote, R. Solicitor's practice. 68
Booth, D.M. & Pirie, N.F. Sentencing. 427
Booth, V.E.H. Extradition. 191
Borchard, E.M. Declaratory judgments. 143
Borchard, E.M. Diplomatic protection. 153
Borkowski, M. Marital violence. 158
Borland, M. Violence. 71, 158
Borrell, C. & Cashinella, B. Crime in Britain. 136
Borrie, G.J. Commercial law. 81
Borrie, G.J. Consumer law. 107, 192
Borrie, G.J. Law reform. 282
Borrie, G.J. Public law. 8

AUTHOR AND SHORT TITLE INDEX

Borrie, G.J. & Diamond, A.L. Consumer. 107, 388
Borrie, G.J. & Greig, D.W. Commercial law. 81
Borrie, G.J. & Lowe, N.V. Contempt. 108
Bos, M. International law. 249, 256
Bose, S.K. Evidence. 186
Bosmajian, H.A. Obscenity.
Boss, P. Social policy & delinquent. 145
Bottomley, A. Cohabitator handbook. 79
Bottomley, A.K. Criminal justice. 129
Bottomley, A.K. Crimonology. 136
Bottomley, A.K. Penal process. 129, 381, 427
Bottomley, A.K. Prison before trial. 305, 381, 407
Bottoms, A.E. & McClintock, F.H. Criminals coming of age. 52, 145
Bouchez, L.J. Regime of bays. 424
Boucher-Chilcott, T. Mortmain. 323
Boucheze, L.J. & Kaijen, L. Sea. 424
Boult, R. Canadian law bibliography. 42, 61
Boulter, M. Workers' compensation. 489
Boulton, A.H. Business contracts. 81
Boulton, A.H. Company administration. 88
Boulton, A.H. Powers of attorney. 374
Boulton, A.H. Social security. 435
Boulton, W.W. Conduct & etiquette. 13, 40
Bourinot, J.G. Federal government. 61, 351
Bourke, B.J. & Corridon, M.J. Victoria liquor laws. 296
Bourinot, J.G. Parliamentary procedure. 61, 351
Bourke, J.P. & Fogarty, J.F. Maintenance, custody & adoption. 11
Bourn, C. Job security. 168
Bourne, R. & Newberger, E.H. Child abuse 71
Bouscaren, T. Canon law. 164
Bouuaert, I.C. Tax problems. 412
Boveri, M. Treason. 465
Bowden, G.F. & Morris, A.S. Contract & tort. 110, 456
Bowden, J. Binding over. 35, 305
Bowen, D. Coal Act. 319
Bowen, H.S. Specific performance. 443
Bowen, I. Wales. 479
Bower, M. Passing by. 208
Bower, G.S. Actionable defamation. 293
Bower, G.S. & Turner, A.K. Estoppel. 179
Bower, G.S. & Turner, A.K. Misrepresentation. 205
Bower, G.S. & Turner, A.K. Res Judicata. 410
Bowers, J. Employment law. 168
Bowett, D.W. International institutions. 254
Bowett, D.W. Law of the sea. 424
Bowett, D.W. Legal regime of islands. 256
Bowett, D.W. Self defence. 256
Bowett, D.W. UN forces. 472

Bowhill, A. Planning application fees. 459
Bowles, M. Annuities. 21
Bowman, M. & Hampton, W. Local democracies. 300
Bowman, M. & Harris, D. Multilateral treaties. 466
Bowman, W.S. Patent & Antitrust. 356
Bowstead, W. Agency. 15
Bowyer, G. Civil law. 75
Box, H.S. Canon law. 164
Boyce, P. Malaysia & Singapore. 434
Boyle, A. & Birds, J. Company law. 88.
Boyle, C.K. & Allen, M.J. Sentencing. 427
Boyle, C.L.M. & Percy, D.R. Contracts. 110.
Boyle, K., & Hadden, T. Law & state. 8, 336
Boynton, J.K. Compulsory purchase. 96
Boyson, R. Down with the poor. 372
Bracewell-Milnes, B. Pay & price control. 358
Bracton, H. de. De legibus. 220
Bradbrook, A.J. & Neave, M.A. Easements. 163, 411
Bradbury, P.L. Business law. 81
Bradbury, P.L. & Barrett, B. Tort cases. 456
Bradbury, P.L. & Dobson, A.P. Commercial law cases. 81.
Bradley, D. Newspaper law. 378.
Bradley, E.L. & Senior, J.J. Bail. 35, 305
Bradshaw, F.M. Charitable trusts. 69, 468.
Bradshaw, S. Drug misues. 162.
Bragdon, C.R. Noise pollution. 335.
Bramall, M. Illegitimacy. 291
Bramwell, H. Conveyancing in Hong Kong. 224
Bramwell, R. & Dick, J. Taxation of companies. 88, 120, 412
Branch, A. Shipping practice. 431
Branch, A.E. Dictionary of shipping, 3. 151
Branch, P. Export practice. 190
Brancker, J.W.S. I.A.T.A. 33
Brand, J. Local government reform. 300
Brand, J.L. Doctors & the state. 392
Brandon, R. & Davies, C. Wrongful imprisonment. 129
Brandon, S. English legal system. 172
Brandreth, C. Parking law. 65, 314
Brantingham, P.J. Environmental criminology. 136
Braun, J. Advertisments. 12
Braun, J. & Allen, P. Trading standards legislation. 388
Bray, E. Discovery. 155
Brazier, R. Contract cases. 110
Breckenridge, A.C. Congress. 474
Breckenridge, A.C. Privacy. 382
Bredinas, A. Methods of interpretation. 184, 258
Breit, W. & Elzinga, K.G. Antitrust cases. 94
Brennan, A.J.E. Vagrancy. 475
Brennan, J.C. Medico legal problems. 224,

314
Brennan, J.P. Compensation. 96
Bresler, F.S. Scales of justices. 222
Brett, E.A. East African colonialism. 14
Brett, H. Computer software protection. 117
Brett, H. Patents Act. 356
Brett, P. Contemporary jurisprudence. 268
Brett, P. Criminal guilt. 133
Brett, P. & Hogg, P.W. Administrative law. 8
Brett, P. & Waller, L. Criminal law. 135
Brewer, J. & Styles, J. Ungovernable people. 221
Brice, A.M. Architects. 25
Brice, G. Salvage. 431
Brice, S.W. Corporations. 121, 144, 470
Bridge, J.W. Fundamental rights. 76, 228
Bridman, R.W. Legal bibliography. 42
Bridges, E.E. The Treasury. 214
Bridgman, R.F. & Roemer, M.I. Hospital legislation. 224
Brierley, J.L. The covenant and charter. 472
Brierly, J.L. Law of nations. 249, 359
Brierly, J.L. Obligations in international law. 256
Briggs, A. Broadcasting. 399
Briggs, D. In place of prison. 381, 396
Briggs, E. & Rees, A.M. Suplementary benefits. 435
Briggs, H.W. International Law Commission. 254
Briggs, J. Personal finances. 451
Brighouse, H. Wills. 487
Brinkhorst, L.J. & Schermers, H.G. Judicial remedies. 184, 264
Brinkhorst, L.J. & Wittenberg, G.W. European Court. 184
Brissaud, J.B. French private law. 204
Brissaud, J.B. French public law. 204
Bristowe, L.S. Mortmain. 323
British & Irish Association of Law Librarians. Community law. 42
British & Irish Association of Law Librarians. Recommended holdings. 42
British Association of Social Workers. Social workers. 436
British Copyright Council. Photocopying. 33
British Gas Corporation. Gas safety regulations. 207
British Institute of Human Rights. Human rights. 76
British Institute of International & Comparative Law. Agency agreements. 182
British Institute of International & Comparative Law. Community law. 42
British Institute of International & Comparative Law. Environmental law. 368
British Institute of International & Comparative Law. Law of the sea. 424
British Institute of International &
Comparative Law. Sale of goods. 420
British Institute of International & Comparative Law. Space law. 443
British Institute of International & Comparative Law. Transport in Common Market. 181
British Institute of International & Comparative Law. Unfair competition. 94
British Library. Guide to government department libraries. 294
British Library. Provision for law. 295
British Medical Association. Alcohol. 17
British Medical Association. Drinking driver. 161
British Medical Association & Magistrates' Association. Illegitimate child. 291
British Quarrying & Slag Federation. Quarry tips. 319
British Social Biology Council. Women of the streets. 390
British Sulphur Corporation Ltd. Pollution control. 368
British Tax Encyclopaedia. 62, 64, 233, 412, 476
British Veterinary Association. Animal boarding. 20
British Veterinary Association. Pet Animals Act. 20
British Veterinary Association. Riding establishments. 20
British Waterways Board. Canal byelaws. 62
Britts, M.G. Personal injury. 362
Britts, M.G. Pleading precedents. 203
Broadhurst, V.A. Health and safety at work. 236
Broady, M. Planning for people. 459
Brockwell, C.J. Aborgines. 42
Brodie, P.R. Dictionary of shipping. 151, 431
Brodie-Innes, J.W. Comparative principles. 421
Brodrick, N. Death certification. 120
Brody, S.R. Effectiveness of sentencing. 148, 417
Brody, S.R. Screen violence. 67, 199
Brome, V. Reverse your verdict. 389
Bromley, P.M. Family law. 193, 308, 310
Bromley, P.M. & Webb, P.R.H. New Zealand family law. 194.
Brook, R. Notary. 337, 374
Brookes, E.A. & MacCaulay, J.B. Civil liberty. 76
Brooke-Taylor, J.C. & Booth, D.M. Magistrates' court handbook. 305
Brooking, R. Building contracts. 54
Brooking, R. & Chermnon, A. Tenancy law. 279.
Broom, H. Constitutional law. 102
Broom, H. Legal maxims. 150, 258, 288
Brophy, B. Public lending right. 393

Broun, M. & Fowler, S. Family law. 194
Brown, C.M. Boundary control. 53
Brown, D. Criminal procedure. 135, 273
Brown, D. Land acquisition. 96
Brown, D. Traffic offences. 416
Brown, D.J. Public international law. 249
Brown, E.A. Oil and gas leases. 344
Brown, E.D. Hydrospace. 424
Brown, E.D. Offshore energy. 424
Brown, E.D. Territorial sea. 424
Brown, G.G. Divorce. 155
Brown, G.G. Separation. 155
Brown, H.A. Life assurance. 246
Brown, H.J.J. Compulsory purchase. 96
Brown, H.J.J. Land Compensation Act. 96
Brown, J. & Howes, G. Police & the community. 366
Brown, L.N. & Garner, J.F. French administrative law. 9, 204
Brown, L.N. & Jacobs, F.G. European Court of Justice. 184
Brown, M. Social administration. 485
Brown, R.G.S. National Health Service. 326, 392
Brown, R.G.S. & Steel, D.R. Administrative process. 391
Brown, R.H. Marine insurance. 247, 431
Brown, R.H. Marine reinsurance terms. 3, 151, 431
Brown, S. Company resolutions. 88
Brown, W. Company law cases. 88
Browne, A. Admiralty. 10
Browne, D. Scotland Yard. 366
Browne, R.G.M. Admiralty procedure. 10
Brownell, E.A. Legal aid. 286
Browning, F. & Foreman, D. Wasted nations. 483
Browning, N. National parks. 328
Brown-Johns, C.L. Multilateral sanctions. 255
Brownlie, A.R. Crime investigation. 128
Brownlie, I. African boundaries. 14, 53, 153
Brownlie, I. Human rights. 228
Brownlie, I. Public international law. 249
Brownlie, I. Public order. 394, 427
Brownlie, I. International law. 249
Brownmiller, S. Against our will. 401
Bruce, R. McKem, B & Pollard, I. Australian corporate finance. 88
Brucher, H. & Puleh, D. German foreign investment shares. 209.
Brucker, H. Communication is power. 378
Brundage, A. Poor law. 372
Brunton, J.D. Law & the individual. 8
Brunyate, A. Limitation of actions. 297
Bryan, J.W. Conspiracy. 102
Bryant, R. & Bradshaw, J. Welfare rights. 372
Bryce, J. History & jurisprudence. 218, 268
Bryden, W.J. Scottish identification procedure report.

Bryson, W.H. Equity side of the Exchequer. 176
Buchheit, L.C. Secession. 256
Buckland, W.W. Jurisprudence. 268
Buckland, W.W. Roman law. 418
Buckland, W.W.& McNair, A.D. Roman law & common law. 84, 418
Buckle, S.R.T. & Buckle, L.G. Bargaining for justice. 135, 364, 365
Buckley, C.L. X-ray. 490
Buckley, H.B. Companies Acts. 88
Bucknil, A. Tug and tow. 431, 470
Buergenthal, T. International Civil Aviation Organisation. 33
Buglass, L.J. General average. 491
Building Societies Gazette. Judicial decisions. 57
Bulchandani, K.R. Labour law. 234
Bulchandani, K.R. Partnership. 234, 353, 420
Bull, D. Welfare rights. 372
Bull, F.J. & Hooper, J.D.G. Catering law. 241
Bull, R.J. Accounting. 6
Bullen, E., & Leake, S.M. Precedents of pleading. 203, 365, 375
Buller, Sir, F. Nisi prius. 334
Bullivant, B. Governor's guide. 165
Bullock, F. Medical, dental & veterinary practice. 147, 157, 477
Bullough, V.L. Subordinate sex. 488
Bunyan, T. Political police. 141, 366, 382
Bunyard, R.S. Police. 366
Bunyon, C.J. Life assurance. 246
Burbridge, G. Canadian criminal law digest. 135
Bureau European des Unions de Consommateurs. Advertising. 12
Burge, D.A. Patent and trademark. 356, 461
Burge, W. Temple Church. 243
Burgess, R. Perpetuities. 361
Burgess, R. & Morse, G. Partnership. 361, 403
Burke, D.B. American conveyancing. 353
Burke, G. Town planning. 459
Burke, H.T. Claims. 54
Burke, J. War damage. 482, 483
Burke, S.M. India & Pakistan foreign policy. 347
Burke, W.T. Ocean. 424
Burke's Peerage. 359
Burkhart, K.W. Women in prison. 488
Burn, C.R. & Quar, J.N. Commercial law of Scotland. 81.
Burn, J.S. Marriage registration. 49
Burn, R. Ecclesiastical law. 164
Burn, R. Poor laws. 371
Burnett, J.F.R. Conveyancing. 115
Burnett, M. Delinquent's challenge. 52
Burney, E. Justice of the Peace. 305
Burney, E. & Wainwright, D. After four years.

398
Burney, E., Wainwright, D. & Claiborne, L. Race. 398
Burn-Murdoch, H. English law & Scots law. 421
Burns, A. To deprave & corrupt. 341
Burns, C.B. Banking in Scotland. 38
Burr, M. Health visitors. 392
Burrell, T.D. S.African patents. 439
Burris, R.W. Teaching law with computers. 97, 287
Burrows, J. & Tarling, R. Clearing up crime. 136
Burrows, J.F. News media. 378
Burrows, R. Interpretation of documents. 143, 258
Burstein, A. Religion. 407
Burton, J. & Hubber, D.C. Road traffic offences. 416
Burton, M.E. League of Nations. 284
Burton, W.C. Legal thesauris. 295
Bush, G.P. Copyright. 117
Butcher, D. Official publications. 45
Butler, D.E. Electoral system. 166
Butler, J.R. & Vaile, M.S.B. Health services. 326, 392
Butler, Lord. Mentally Abnormal Offenders Committee. 244
Butler, W.E. Chinese soviet republic. 74
Butler, W.E. International comparative law. 92
Butler, W.E. Legislation of USSR. 441
Butler, W.E. Russian law. 441
Butler, W.E. Sea. 424
Butler, W.E. Soviet legal system. 441
Butler, W.E. Soviet territorial waters. 424, 453
Butler, W.E. & Nathanson, A.J. Mongolian-English-Russian dictionary. 150.
Butt, P. Land law. 274
Butterworth's Budget Tax Tables. 412
Butterworth's Capital Gains Tax Act. 62
Butterworth's Capital transfer tax tables. 64
Butterworth's Company Law. 89
Butterworth's Conveyancing Costs. 115
Butterworth's Costs. 123
Butterworth's Estate Duty Statutes.
Butterworth's Family Law Service. 155
Butterworth's Income Tax Service. 233
Butterworth's Insurance Law Handbook. 245
Butterworth's Orange Tax Handbook. 64, 412
Butterworth's Tax Practitioner's Diary. 412
Butterworth's Workmen's Compensation. 489
Butterworth's Yellow Tax Handbook. 62, 233, 412, 476
Button, W.A. Libel & slander. 293
Buttress, F.A. Abbreviations. 3
Buxbaum, D.C. Family law in Asia. 196
Buzek, F.J. Collision cases. 79.
Byamugisha, J.B. East African Insurance. 14
Byles, A. & Morris, P. Unmet need. 286, 485

Byles, J.B. Bills of exchange. 46, 330
Byrne, E.M. Military law. 318
Byrne, W.J. Law dictionary. 288
Byrom, R. Building society valuer. 57
Cababe, M. Estoppel. 179
Cabinet Office. Intellectual property rights. 118
Cabinet Office. Vandalism. 136
Cable, J. Gunboat diplomacy. 329
Butts, G.M. County court procedure. 268
Cain, M. Marx & Engels. 366
Cain, M.E. Society & the policeman. 396
Caird, R. Good & useful life. 365
Cairns, M.B. Tort in local government. 300, 456
Calabresi, G. Common law. 84
Calabresi, G. Costs of accidents. 5
Calais-Auloy, J. Consumer legislation in France. 204
Calisse, C. Italian law. 262
Callahan, D. Contraception. 48
Callis, R. Sewers. 161
Callund, D. Employee benefits. 92, 360
Calvert, F. Constable's pocket guide. 27, 366
Calvert, H.G. Constitutional law. 102, 336
Calvert, H. Devolution. 149
Calvert, H. Social Security.435
Calvert, H. Welfare legal system. 435, 485
Calvert, P. Revolution. 149
Calvert, R. Patent practice. 356
Cam.H.M. Hundred rolls. 220, 300
Cam, H.M. Law finders. 220
Cam, H.M. Liberties & communities. 220
Cambridge University. Statutes & ordinance. 60
Cameron, J.R. Frederick William Maitland. 218
Cameron, J.M. & Sims, B.G. Forensic dentistry. 147, 202
Camilleri, B.J. High Court of Australia. 31, 375
Campaign for Homosexual Equality. Homosexual law reform. 223
Campbell, A. Industrial relations. 238
Campbell, A. Trade Unions. 463
Campbell, A.H. Structure of Stair's institutions. 421
Campbell, A.R. Common Market. 179
Campbell, C. Data processing. 98
Campbell, C. & Wiles, P. Law & society. 268
Campbell, C. & others. Tomorrow's lawyers. 287
Campbell C.M. Bill of rights. 45, 76
Campbell, D. Fraud. 205
Campbell, D. Police. 366
Campbell, D. Real property. 403
Campbell, D.& Hepperle, W. U.S. legal system. 474
Campbell, D.J. Legal profession bibliography.

42. 289
Campbell, E. & Waller, L. Well and truly tried. 186
Campbell, G.A. Civil Service. 77
Campbell, H. War & contract. 482
Campbell, I. Footpaths. 201
Campbell, I. Commons. 85
Campbell, Lord. Chief Justices. 48, 264
Campbell, Lord. Lord Chancellors.47, 304
Campbell, M.J. Local government in Northern Nigeria. 332
Campion, Lord. Parliament. 350
Camps, F.E. Forensic medicine. 202, 314
Camps, F.E. Forensic pathology. 202
Camps, F.E. Crime. 136
Canada Law Reform Commission. Family law. 194, 195
Canada Law Reform Commission. Family property. 196
Canadian Commerce Clearing House. Corporations Act. 121
Canadian Government Publishing Office. Constitution. 61
Canadian Industries. Environmental pollution. 174, 368
Canagarayar, J.K. Traffic offenders. 416
Candy, G. Mayor's Court. 313
Caney, L.R. Novation. 110, 410
Cannar, K.S. Insurance law cases. 245
Cannar, K.S. Liability insurance. 245
Cannon, J. Parliamentary reform. 351
Canon Law Society. Code of canon law. 164
Cant, D.H. Squatting. 444
Cape, B.F. & Dobson, P. Nurses' dictionary. 340
Caplin, C. Powers of Attorney. 374
Caplovitz, D. Consumers. 107
Cappelletti, M. Judicial review. 266
Cappelletti, M. & Jolowicz, J.A. Public interest parties. 264
Cappelletti, M., Merryman, J.H. & Perillo, J.M. Italian legal system. 262
Carby-Hall, J.R. Employment protection. 171
Carby-Hall, J.R. Industrial law. 168, 237
Carby-Hall, J.R. Industrial relations. 168, 237
Carby-Hall, J.R. Labour relations. 168, 237
Carby-Hall, J.R. Worker participation. 168
Card, R. Estate Agents Act. 177
Cardozo, B.N. Growth of the law. 268
Cardozo, B.N. Juridical process. 264, 268
Cardozo, B.N. Paradoxes. 268
Care of Children Committee. Report. 72
Carey, J. Court & political rights. 228
Carey, J. Human rights. 228
Carlebach, J. Children in trouble. 23, 72
Carlen, P. Magistrates' justice. 72, 305
Carlin, J.E., Howard, J & Messinger, S.L. Poor. 372
Carlston, K.S. International arbitration. 250

Carlston, K.S. Social action. 268
Carmen, I.H. Movies. 67
Carmichael, C.M. Women. 488
Carmichael, K.S. Capital gains tax. 62
Carmichael, K.S. Corporation tax. 120
Carnwath, R. Housing (Homeless Persons) Act. 225, 485
Carr, B.R. Breathalizer legislation. 161
Carr, C.T. Administrative law. 8
Carr, C.T. Delegated legislation.144, 290
Carr, J.G. Accountancy. 6
Carr, R.A. & Stern, N.H. Crime. 128, 131, 266, 445
Carrington, F.A. & Kirwin, A.V. Nisi prius. 334
Carrington, F.A. & Marshman, J.R. Nisi prius. 224
Carrington, F.A. & Payne, J. Nisi prius. 334
Carrington, P.D. & Babcock, B.A. Civil procedure. 375
Carroll, M. U.S. tax treaties. 159
Carr-Saunders, Sir A.M. & Wilson, P.A. Professions. 289
Carson, T.H. Prescription. 378
Carson, T.H. & Bompas, H.B. Real property. 378
Carswell, J. Civil servant. 77
Caswell's family law digest. 195
Carter, A. Anarchism. 394
Carter, A.T. English courts. 126
Carter, G.M. & Hertz, J.H. Government & politics. 212
Carter, H. & Glick, P. Marriage & divorce. 311
Carter, J. Breach of contract. 114
Carter, P Cases on evidence. 186
Carter, R. Valuation. 401
Carter, R.F. Queensland criminal law. 135
Carter, R.L. Reinsurance. 248
Carter, R.L. & Dickinson, G.M. Insurance trade barriers. 245
Carter, R.M. & Wilkins, L.T. Probation parole. 352, 387
Carter-Ruck, P.F. & Skone James, E.P. Copyright. 118
Cartledge, G.C. Probation in Europe. 387
Cartwright, D.P. Canals. 62
Cartwright, T.. Royal Commissions. 8
Caruana, S. Alcoholism. 17
Carvell, I.G. & Green, E.S. Criminal law. 132
Carver, T.G. Carriage by sea. 47, 66, 431
Casey, J. Constitutional law. 102
Casey, J.P. Irish Attorney General. 282
Cass, M. & Sackville, R. Legal needs of the poor. 286, 372
Cassese, A. UN peace-keeping. 472
Castandena, J. UN resolutions. 472
Castberg, F. Human rights. 228
Castberg, F. Legal philosophy. 268

Castel, J.G. Canadian conflicts. 100
Castel, J.G. Civil law system. 61
Castel, J.G. Conflict of laws. 100
Castell, J.G. International law. 249
Castles, A.C. Australian legal history. 31, 218
Castren, E. War. 480
Cater, A.J.E. Public health. 392
Catholic Body in England & Wales. Artificial insemination. 28
Cattan, H. Oil concessions. 344
Caulfield, B.I. & Norris, W.V.W. Wills. 451, 487
Cavandino, P. Parole. 352
Cavan, R.S. Juvenile delinquency. 145
Cavenagh, S.W & Phegan, C.S. Australian product liability. 388
Cavenagh, W.E. Juvenile court. 272
Cavendish, J.M. Copyright. 33, 118
Cavitch, Z. Tax planning. 120
Cawthra, B.I. Industrial property rights. 118, 356
Cawthra, B.I. Patent licensing. 356
Cawthra, B. Restrictive agreements. 15, 94, 182
Cecil, H. English judge. 264
Cecil, H. Brief to counsel. 40
Cederblom, J.B. & Blizek, W.L. Justice & punishment. 396
Central Council for Education & Training in Social Work. Social work. 272
Central Housing Advisory Committee. Housing associations. 227
Central Office of Information. Justice. 172
Central Office of Information. Taxation. 412
Central Unit of Environmental Pollution. Pollution control. 368
Certified Accountants Educational Trust. Residence. 412
Chadha, P.N. Hindu law. 281
Chadwick, G.F. Planning. 459
Challis, H.W. Real property. 403
Chalmers, D. Marine insurance. 247
Chalmers, D.R.C. Textbook for legal studies. 287
Chalmers, M.D. Bills of exchange. 46, 330
Chalmers, M.D. Marine insurance. 431
Chalmers, M.D. Sale of goods. 420
Chalmers, M.D. & Hough, E. Bankruptcy Acts. 144
Chamberlin, W. Chronology of United Nations. 472
Chambers, G.F. Public libraries & museums. 325
Chambers, G.S. Enforcement of money payment. 142, 305
Chambers, G.S. Magisterial procedure. 305
Chambers, N. International law. 249
Chambliss, W.J. Criminal law. 131
Chambliss, W.J. & Seidman, R. Law, order & power. 394
Champness, R. Mistake. 113, 320
Chance, E.W. Mercantile law. 81
Chance, H. Powers. 374
Chancery Masters' practice forms. 68
Chancery of Lancaster Rules. 68, 124
Chand, H. Res judicata. 410
Chandler, D.B. Capital punishment. 63
Chandler, P. Employment. 168
Chandler, P. Hotel & catering manager's guide. 241
Chanter, H.R. London building. 303
Chapman, A.L. Capital transfer tax. 64
Chapman, B. Profession of government. 212
Chapman, C.B. Malpractice. 316
Chapman, D.H. Footpaths. 201
Chapman, F.A.R. Canadian law. 61
Chapman, R.A. Higher civil service. 77
Chappel, D. & Wilson, P. Australian criminal justice. 31, 129
Char, S.V.D. Indian constitutional history. 234
Charlebois, L.H. Francis, E.A. & Young, P.W. Conveyancing services. 115
Charles, W. Assessment of damages. 142
Charlesworth, J. Mercantile law. 81, 106
Charlesworth, J. Negligence. 330, 456
Charlesworth, J. Company law. 89
Chartered Institute of Patent Agents. European patents. 356, 461
Chartered Institute of Patent Agents. Patents Act. 356
Chartered Institute of Patent Agents. Register. 356
Chartered Insurance Institute. Insurances of liability. 248
Chartered Insurance Institute. Motor insurance. 247
Chase, H.W. & Ducat, C.R. Constitution. 474
Chatterjee, S.K. International drug control. 162
Chatterton, C.E.M. Juvenile Court. 272
Chatterton, C.E.M. Legal aid applications. 286
Chaudhuri, G.W. Constitutional development in Pakistan. 347
Chavasse, C.P.G. Contentious costs. 123
Chavasse, C.P.G. Conveyancing costs. 115, 123
Chayes, A., Fawcett, J. & Ito, M. Satellite broadcasting. 452
Checkland, S.G. & Checkland, C.A. Poor law. 371
Chen, T.C. Recognition. 255
Chenery, T.T. Bookmaking. 41
Chenery, W.L. Press. 378
Cheney, C.R. Notaries public. 337
Cheng, B. Air transport. 33
Cheng, B. International courts. 256
Cherian, J. Investment contracts. 24, 490

AUTHOR AND SHORT TITLE INDEX

Chermatz, J.P. & Daggett, H.S. Community property. 403
Chernoff, G. & Sartin, H. Photography. 197
Cheshire, G.C. International contracts. 110
Cheshire, G.C. Real property. 373, 403
Cheshire, G.C. & Fifoot, C.H.S. Contract. 110
Cheshire, G.C. & North, P.M. Private international law. 100
Chester, D.N. British central government. 212
Chester, D.N. Central & local government. 300
Chester, D.N. Nationalization. 392
Chester, D.N. & Bowring, N. Questions in parliament. 351
Chester, M.G. & Vogelaar, F.O.W. Dutch company law. 89
Chesterman, M. Small businesses. 81
Chesterman, M.R. Charities. 69, 468, 485
Chew, H.M. English ecclesiastical tenants. 220
Chew, H.M. London possessory assizes. 303
Chew, H.M. & Kellaway, W. London assize of nuisance. 303
Chick, A.F. Trusts. 468
Childress, R. Equity. 176
Chislett, A.J. Affiliation proceedings. 291
Chislett, A.J. Justice at home. 305
Chisholm, R. Australia's legal system. 41
Chitty, J. Contracts. 110, 215
Chitty, J. Crown prerogative. 139, 377
Chitty, T. & Jacob, I.H. Queen's Bench Forms. 203, 375, 397
Chloros, A.G. Bibliographical guide. 42
Chloros, A.G.. European family law. 196
Chloros, A.G. Codification. 78
Choate, C.E. Discovery. 155
Choate, R.A. & Francis, W.H. Patent law. 462
Chorley, R.S.T. Banking. 38
Chorley, R.S.T. & Giles, O.C. Shipping law. 431
Chorley, R.S.T. & Smart, P.E. Banking. 39
Chowdhuri, R.N. International mandates. 255
Chowdhurry, S.R. Bangladesh. 37
Chowles, V.G. & Webster, G.C. South African trade marks. 58, 461
Chown, J. Capital transfer tax. 64
Chown, J. Corporation tax. 121
Chown, J. Taxation. 121, 412
Chown, J. & Edwards-Ker, M. Acquisition of assets. 89
Chown, J. & Norman, R. Corporation tax. 121
Chrimes, S.B. Administrative history. 104
Chrimes, S.B. English constitutional idea. 104
Christie, I.M. Liability of strikers. 238
Christie, R. Rhodesian commercial law. 81
Christol, C. Q. Outer space. 442
Christoph, J.B. Capital punishment. 63
Christy, F.T. Fisherman quotas. 199

Chuang, R.Y. International Air Transport Association. 34
Chubb, F.B. Cabinet government. 59, 259
Chubb, F.B. Constitution of Ireland. 259
Chubb, B. Irish constitution. 103, 259
Chubb, F.B. Irish government & politics. 259
Church of England. Canons. 164
Church of England. Fatherless by law. 291
Church of England. Illegitimacy. 291
Church of England. Legal Board opinions. 164
Church of England. Obscene publications. 341
Church of England. Yearbook. 348
Churchill, C. & Bruce, A.C. Sheriffs. 430
Churchill, R. Law of the sea. 424
CIBA Foundation. Human rights in health. 392
Cicourel, A.V. Juvenile justice. 272
Cilliers, A.C. Law of costs. 439
Cilliers, H.S., Benade, M.L. & De Villiers, S.W.L. Company law. 89, 439
Cinematograph Films Council. Film legislation. 197
Citizens Advice Bureaux. Citizens' Advice Notes. 485
Citizen's Inquiry on Parole & Criminal Justice Inc. Prison without Walls. 352
Civil Aviation Authority. Aviation law. 34
Civil Service Department. Official information. 77, 343
Claiborne, G.R. Building regulations. 55
Claiborne, L. Race and law. 398
Clark, C. Publishing agreements. 203, 380
Clark, E. Diplomat. 153
Clark, F. Central Office of Information. 214
Clark, G. & Sohn, L.B. World peace. 359
Clark, H.H. Domestic relations. 195, 232
Clark, R.S. Criminal justice. 129
Clark, R.S. Human rights. 228, 472
Clarke, C.F.O. Private rights. 382
Clarke, D.N. & Adams, J.E. Rent reviews. 408
Clarke, E. Extradition. 191
Clarke, H.W. Constitutional law. 8
Clarke, J.J. Central government. 212
Clarke, J.J. Housing & planning. 225
Clarke, J.J. Local government. 300
Clarke, K. & Reading, B. International employment tax. 412
Clarke, M. Carriage of goods. 66, 464
Clarke, M. Shipbuilding contracts. 112
Clarke, M.A. Hague rules. 47, 431
Clarke, M.A. Shipbuilding contracts. 431
Clarke, P.J. & Ellis, J. Firearms. 198
Clarke, R.V.G. & Mayhew, P. Designing out crime. 136
Clarke, R.V.G. & Martin, D.N. Approved schools. 23
Clarke Hall, W. & Morrison, A.C.L. Children

& young persons. 72, 291
Clarkson, C. & Keating, H. Criminal law. 131
Clarkson, K.W. Business law. 81
Claude, I.L. Swords into plowshares. 254
Claude, R.P. Comparative human rights. 228
Clay, J.L. Young lawyer. 289
Clayton, P. Cohabitation guide. 79
Clayton, P. Small business. 81, 107
Clayton, R. Evidence. 186
Clegg, H. Industrial relations. 168, 238
Clegg, J. Social services dictionary. 152
Clegg, J. & Cowsill, E. Evidence. 186
Clemens, J.H. Balance sheets. 39
Clemitson, I. Employment protection. 171
Clerk, J.F. & Lindsell, W.H.B. Torts. 340, 456
Cleverdon, C.L. Woman suffrage. 488
Clifford, B.R. & Bull, R. Identification. 230
Clift, R.C. Accounting. 6
Clitheroe, J. Criminal defence. 13, 40
Clive, E.M. Divorce (Scotland) Act. 155
Clive, E.M. & Watt, G.A. Journalists. 379
Clive, E.M. & Wilson, J.F. Husband and wife. 193
Clode, C.M. Military forces. 125
Clode, W. Petition of right. 364
Clor, H.M. Censorship & freedom. 67
Clothier, C.M. Ombudsman. 345
Cloutman, B.M. Authors & publishers. 33
Cloutman, B.M. & Luck, F.W. Printers & publishers. 379, 380
Cloyd, J.W. Drugs. 162
Clutterbuck, R. Britain in agony. 478
Clyne, P. Guilty but insane. 133, 244
Clyne, P. Skyjacking. 217
Coase, B.G. Police precedents. 366.
Cobbett, J.P. Pawns or pledges. 358
Cobbett, P. Leading cases on international law. 251
Cobden Trust. Incitment to disaffection. 394
Cobler, S. Law, order & politics. 209
Cochrane, R.G.A. Housing in Scotland. 225
Cockburn, A.E. Nationality. 328
Cockburn, J.S. Assizes. 29
Cockburn, J.S. Crime. 134, 221
Cockerill, A. & Hodkinson, C. Unfair dismissal. 471
Cockerell, H.A.L. Motor insurance. 247
Cockerill, H.A.L. & Shaw, G.W. Insurance broking. 245
Cockle, E. Evidence. 186
Cocks, B. European parliament. 183
Cocks, R. Modern bar. 40
Codding, G.A. International telecommunications union. 452
Codding, G.A. Universal postal union. 374
Coddington, F.J.O. Advocacy. 13
Code of Advertising Practice Committee. Advertising. 12

Coffen, A. Prevention of crime. 127
Cohen, B.V. U.N. 472
Cohen, E. British civil service. 77
Cohen, H. Spouse witnesses. 488
Cohen, H.J. English Bar. 40
Cohen, J. & Greenfield, R. U.S/U.K. double tax treaties. 159
Cohen, J. & Preston, B. Road accidents. 416
Cohen, L.J. Probable and provable. 186
Cohen, M. Space law. 442
Cohen, M.L. Law & science. 43
Cohen, M.R. Ronald Dworkin. 269
Cohen, M.R. & Cohen, F.S. Jurisprudence. 269
Cohen, R. & Rushton, A. Welfare rights. 485
Cohen, S. Due process. 61
Cohen, S. & Young, J. Manufacture of news. 136
Cohn, A.E. & Udolf, R. Criminal justice system. 129
Cohn, E.J. German law. 209
Cohn, E.J., Domke, M & Eiseman, F. Arbitration. 24
Coke, E. Fourth institutes. 10
Coker, G.B.A. Family property among the Yorubas. 332
Colby, E. Builders. 55
Cole, J.S.R. Irish cases on evidence. 186
Cole, R.T. Double taxation. 159
Cole, S.D. Charters. 70
Cole, V.L. Valuation of business. 401
Colinvaux, R. Insurance. 215, 245
Colinvaux R & Steel, D. Forms & precedents. 203, 431
Collard, C.A. Pollution control in France. 368
Collection of bibliographic & research sources. 251
College of Law. Bankruptcy. 298
College of Law. Capital transfer tax. 64, 148
College of Law. Development land tax. 87, 148
College of Law. Emergency procedures. 193, 312
College of Law. Farmer, landowner & the law. 16
College of Law. Residential tenancies. 16, 279
Collingwood, J.J.R. Criminal law. 135
Collins, D. Strata title. 455
Collins, H.C. County court costs. 123, 124
Collins, H.C. County court practice. 124, 375
Collins, L. European community. 179
Colman, A. Commercial court. 81, 375
Colombos, C.J. Law of the sea. 10, 364, 424
Colombos, C.J. Prize. 385
Colton, M. State of the Bar. 40
Columbia University. US constitution. 474
Combe, R.G.N. Light. 297
Commerce Clearing House. Ontario Business Corporations Act. 121

AUTHOR AND SHORT TITLE INDEX

Commerce Clearing House. Nuclear regulation reporter. 337
Commercial Court Committee. Arbitration. 24
Commission for Racial Equality. Reports. 175, 398
Commission of the European Communities. Fundamental rights. 76
Commission on Industrial Relations. Trade union recognition. 463
Commission on Monopolies & Restrictive Practices. Report. 322
Commission on the Constitution. Isle of Man. 261
Committee on Administrative Tribunals & Enquiries. Report. 467
Committee on Appeals from Decisions of Courts of Summary Jurisdiction. Report. 305
Committee on Consolidation of Highway Law. Report. 216
Committee on Data Protection. Report. 98, 383
Committee on Land Charge. Report. 276
Committee on Legal Aid & Advice in England & Wales. Report. 286
Committee on Legal Aid & Advice in Scotland. Report. 286
Committee on Legal Aid & Advice for the Poor. Final Report. 286
Committee on Legal Education. 287
Committee on Legal Education for Students from Africa. Report. 287
Committee on Legal Services to the Poor in the Developing Countries. Legal aid. 372
Committee on Limitation of Actions & Bills of Exchange. Report. 46
Committee on Limitation of Actions in Cases of Personal Injury. Report. 297
Committee on Local Land Charges. Report. 276
Committee on Mentally Abnormal Offenders. Report. 317
Committee on Minister's Powers. Report. 8
Committee on One-Parent Families. Report. 291
Committee on Personal Injuries Litigation. Report. 362
Committee on Political Activities of Civil Servants. Report. 78
Committee on Poor Law and the Relief of Distress. Report. 371
Committee on Poor Persons Rules. Report. 372
Committee on Privacy. Report. 383
Committee on Procedure for Determination of Unemployment Insurance Claims. Report. 327
Committee on Safety & Health at Work. Report. 342

Committee on the Law of Defamation. Report. 293
Committee on the Law Relation to Rights of Light. Report. 297
Committee on the Limitation of Actions. Report. 297
Committee on the Preparation of Legislation. Report. 160, 290
Committee on the Problem of Noise. Report. 335
Committee on the Taxicab Service. Report. 452
Committee on the Transfer of Functions of Poor Law Authorities. Report. 371
Committee to Consider Changes in the Law of Insanity & Crime. Report. 133
Committee to Consider the Administration of Justice under the Naval Discipline Act. Report. 329
Committee to Consider the Law on Copyright & Designs. Report. 119, 356
Committee to Examine the Patent System & Patent Law. Report. 356
Common Council for American Unity. Immigration. 231
Commonwealth Secretariat. Abortion. 3
Commonwealth Secretariat. Child abduction. 72
Commonwealth Secretariat. Commercial frauds. 205
Commonwealth Secretariat. Copyright. 118
Commonwealth Secretariat. Criminal justice delay. 86, 129
Commonwealth Secretariat. Family law. 196
Commonwealth Secretariat. International hijacking conventions. 34, 217
Commonwealth Secretariat. Ombudsman. 345
Commonwealth Secretariat. Prosecution appeals. 22
Commonwealth Secretariat. Small jurisdictions' legal literature. 43
Community Relations Commission. Race relations. 43
Compton, H.F. & Whiteman, R. Receivership. 125, 317, 404
Comyn, J. Irish at law. 408
Confederation of British Industry. Capital transfer tax. 64
Confederation of British Industry. European patent system. 356
Confederation of British Industry. Government contracts. 113
Confederation of British Industry. Industrial noise. 335
Confederation of British Industry. Patents & trade marks. 356
Confederation of British Industry. Social Security Pensions Act. 435
Confederation of British Industry. Taxation in

W.Europe. 412
Conking, A. Admiralty jurisdiction. 10
Connors, J.A. Protecting intellectual property. 118
Conrad, J.P. Criminal justice. 129
Conradie, A.M. Carriage of goods. 66, 439
Conrick, V.M. & Thompson, D.C. Sale of real property. 16
Consumer Council. Justice out of reach. 388
Consumer Protection Advisory Committee. Disguised business sales. 107
Consumer Protection Advisory Committee. Rights of consumers. 107
Consumers' Association. Buying a house. 115
Consumers' Association. Dismissal. 168, 471
Consumers' Association. Marrriage. 310
Consumers' Association. Getting divorced. 155
Consumers' Association. Motorists. 324, 416
Consumers' Assocation. Wills & probate. 487
Convention on the grant of European patents. 356
Convention of the Recovery Abroad of Maintenance. 308
Conway, C. Jurisprudence. 269
Cook, R.J. & Senanayake, P. Human problem of abortion. 3
Cook, T. Alcoholics. 18, 475
Cooke, A.J.D. Laboratory law. 274
Cooke, G. Forensic psychologist. 202
Cooke, G.W. Copyhold enfranchisement. 117
Cooke, G.W. Enclosure Acts. 86
Cooke, P. & Van Der Beck, J.M. Tax aspects of acquisitions. 449
Cooks, R.A.F. Probation hostels. 387
Coombes, D. Politics & bureaucracy. 183
Coombes, J. Capital transfer tax. 64, 412
Cooper. D.D. The scaffold. 63
Cooper, G. Law and poverty cases. 372
Cooper, G. & Cridlan, R.J. Stock Exchange. 448
Cooper, J. Income tax. 233
Cooper, J. Public legal services. 40
Cooper, J.C. Aerospace law. 442
Cooper, W.M. & Wood, J.C. Industrial law. 168, 237
Cooper-Stephenson, K. & Saunders, I.E. Personal injury damages. 142
Cooray, L.J.M. Ceylon. 444
Cooray, L.J.M. Sri Lanka. 444
Coote, A. & Gill, T. Battered women. 158, 488
Coote, A. & Gill, T. Rape controversy. 401
Coote, A. & Gill, T. Women's rights. 488
Coote, A. & Grant, L. Civil liberty. 76
Coote, B. Exception clauses. 113
Coote, H.C. Admiralty practice. 11
Coote, R.H. Mortgage. 28, 323
Cope, J.M. Business taxation. 121

Copeling, A.J.C. Copyright. 118
Coper, M. Interstate trade. 81
Copinger, W.A. & Skone James, E.P. Copyright. 118
Corbett, M.M. Succession. 448
Corbett, M.M. & Buchanan, J.L. Quantum of damages. 142, 362
Corbett, P.E. Diplomacy. 153
Corbin, A. Contracts. 110
Cordeaux, E.H. & Merry, D.H. Oxford. 346
Cordery, A. Solicitors. 296, 438
Corfield, F. Community Land Act. 87
Corfield, Sir F. & Carnwath, R.J.A. Compulsory acquisition. 96
Cork, K. European insolvency practitioners. 37
Corley, R.N. & Holmes, E.M. Business law. 81
Cornish, D.B. Gambling. 41
Cornish, D.B. & Clarke, R.V.G. Residential treatment. 52, 145, 427
Cornish, W.R. Crime and law. 134, 221
Cornish, W.R. Intellectual property. 118, 356, 461
Cornish, W.R. Jury. 267
Cornwall, J. Title deeds. 124
Coroners Society. Reports. 119
Corporation of the City of London. Corporation of London. 303
Corrigan, K. Tax law. 412
Corwin, E.S. Constitution. 474
Corwin, E.S. Judicial review. 266
Costin, W.C. & Watson, J.S. Working of the constitution. 105
Cosway, A.H. Land Charges Act. 276
Cotran, E. Kenya marriage & divorce. 273, 311
Cotran, E. Succession in Kenya. 273, 448
Cotran, E. & Rubin, N.N. African law. 14
Cotterell, L.E. Performance. 174, 454
Coull, J.W. & Merry, E.W. Scots law. 422
Coulson, H.J.W. &Forbes, U.A. Waters. 20, 157, 161, 199, 216, 484
Coulson, N.J. Islamic law. 260
Coulson, N.J. Islamic jurisprudence. 260
Coulson, N.J. Muslim family succession. 448
Coulson, N.J. Saudi contract law. 111, 421
Council for Children's Welfare. One-parent families. 291
Council for Science & Society. Scholarly freedom. 228
Council of Europe. Air pollution control. 369
Council of Europe. Child abuse. 71
Council of Europe. Common standards for retrieval systems. 98
Council of Europe. Conditions of detention. 228
Council of Europe. Criminal law in consumer protection. 107, 131

… AUTHOR AND SHORT TITLE INDEX

Council of Europe. Economic crime. 136
Council of Europe. Effectiveness of punishment. 427
Council of Europe. European monetary system. 320
Council of Europe. Foreign judicial decisions. 81, 202, 375
Council of Europe. Human rights. 228
Council of Europe. International co-operation. 478
Council of Europe. Judicial organisation. 264
Council of Europe. Kidnapping followed by ransom. 131
Council of Europe. Legal status of children. 291
Council of Europe. Manual. 123
Council of Europe. Sentencing. 427
Council of Europe. Unfair contract terms. 107
Council of Europe. Unmarried couples. 79
Council of Europe. Young offenders. 24
Council on Tribunals. Costs. 123
Counter, K. Framework & functions. 172
Couper, A.D. Sea. 424
Court of Justice of the European Communities. Digest of case law. 184
Coutts, J.A. The accused. 136
Cowan, T.K. Cost accounting. 6
Cowen, D.V. & Gering, L. Negotiable instruments. 330, 439
Cowen, Z. Private international law. 100
Cowen, Z. & Zines, L. Australian federal jurisdiction. 31
Cowley, J.D. Abridgments bibliography. 43
Cowling, K. Mergers. 449
Cowper, F.H. Gray's Inn. 242
Cox, A. Supreme Court. 474
Cox, B. Civil liberties. 76
Cox, C. & Ross, H.J. Capital gains tax. 63
Cox, J.T. Church of Scotland. 164
Cox, R.W. & Jacobson, H.K. Anatomy of influence. 254
Crabb, G. Copyright. 118
Crabb, G. Copyright clearance. 118
Crabtree, A. & Kennan, D.J. Industrial law. 237
Cracknell, D.G. Charities. 69
Cracknell, D.G. Criminal law. 131
Cracknell, D.G. Property Acts. 403
Cracknell, D.G. Torts. 456
Craft, M. & Craft, A. Mentally abnormal offenders. 317
Craies, W.F. Statute law. 258, 446
Craig, A. Banned books. 341
Craig, T. Jus feudale. 422
Craigmyle & Co. Charitable giving. 412
Cramer, J.A. Preventing crime. 127
Crane, P. Gays. 223
Cranston, M. Human rights. 228
Cranston, R. Consumers. 107, 192

Cranston, R. Regulating business. 107, 192
Crawford, J. Australian courts of law. 31, 126
Crawford, J. Creation of states. 256, 441
Crawford, O. Done this day. 123
Crawford, T. Proof in criminal cases. 186
Crean, M.J. Real estate. 403
Creasy, E.S. Constitution. 103
Creedy, J. State pensions. 360
Creighton, B. Labour law. 168
Creighton, H. Nurses. 340
Creighton, S. Child abuse. 71
Creighton, W.B. Working women. 175, 488
Cressey, D.R. Other people's money. 136
Cressey, D.R. & Ward, D.A. Delinquency. 145
Cresswell, P. Banking law. 39
Cretney, S.M. Adoption. 12
Cretney, S.M. Family law. 193
Cretton, C. Capital gains tax. 63
Crew, A. Secret commissions. 54
Cribbett, J.E. Property. 403
Crick, B. Crime, rape & gin. 401
Criminal Law Revision Committee. Closing speeches. 132
Criminal Law Revision Committee. Criminal procedure (insanity). 133, 244
Criminal Law Revision Committee. Evidence (general). 186
Criminal Law Revision Committee. Evidence (written statements). 186
Criminal Law Revision Committee. Offences against the person. 128
Criminal Law Revision Committee. Penalty for murder. 222
Criminal Law Revision Committee. Perjury. 361
Criminal Law Revision Committee. Prostitution. 390
Criminal Law Revision Committee. Secrecy of jury room. 267
Criminal Law Revision Committee. Sexual offences. 429
Criminal Law Revision Committee. Suicide. 222
Criminal Law Revision Committee. Theft. 454
Cripps, C.A. Compulsory acquisition. 96
Cripps, H.W. Church & clergy. 164, 348
Cripps, J. Gypsies. 211
Critchley, T.A. History of police. 366
Crites, L. Female offender. 129
Croasdell, W.C. Private street works. 217
Crockford's clerical directory. 348
Croft, C.E. Mortgagees' power of sale. 323, 403
Croft, J. Concerning crime. 137
Croft, J. Criminal justice. 129
Croft, J. Criminological research. 137
Crombie, J.L.C. Customs & Excise. 140, 214

Cromwell, H. Parliamentary procedure. 350
Cronin, J.B. Factories Act. 191
Cronin, J.B. & Grime, R.P. Industrial law. 168, 191, 237
Cronin, J.B. & Grime, R.P. Labour law. 169, 237
Crook, J.A. Law & life of Rome. 418
Crook, L. Oil terms. 344
Cropper, J. Criminal evidence. 186
Cross, C. Community Land Act. 87
Cross, C.A. Highway law. 217
Cross, C.A. Local government. 300
Cross, C.A.& Garner, J.F. Highway law. 217
Cross, C.A. & Sauvain, S. Highways Act. 217
Cross, Sir R. Evidence. 99, 186
Cross, Sir R. Golden thread. 186
Cross, Sir R. Precedent. 266, 269
Cross, Sir R. Punishment. 381, 396
Cross, Sir R. Sentencing. 427
Cross, Sir R. Statutory interpretation. 258
Cross, R. & Wilkins, N. Evidence 186
Cross, Sir R. & Jones, P.A.Criminal law. 131
Crossman, R.H.S. Cabinet government. 59
Crossman, R.H.S. Diaries. 59
Crotti, A.F. Antitrust. 94
Crowther, Lord. Consumer credit. 106
Cruchley, I. Bankruptcy. 37
Crystal, M. & Nicholson, B. Bankruptcy. 37
Csabafi, I.A. Space law.442
Cufley, C.F.H. Ocean freights. 70
Cukwurah, I.O. Boundary disputes. 53
Cullingworth, J.B. Town & country planning. 459
Cumming, G.B. Oil pollution. 344, 370
Cumyn, A.P.F. Canadian taxation. 412
Cunningham, J.P. Competition law. 94, 182
Cunningham, J.P. Competition policy. 94
Cunningham, J.P. Fair Trading Act. 107, 192, 322
Cunningham, J.P. Restrictive practices. 94, 322
Cunningham, J.P. & Tinnion, J. Competition Act. 94
Cunningham, M. Non-wage benefits. 169
Curlewis, H.R. & Edwards, D.S. Prohibition. 389
Currie, J. Executors in Scotland. 189
Curry, A.S. Forensic Science. 202
Curry, A.S. Toxicology. 202
Curry, H. & Clifford, D. Lesbian and gay couples. 223
Curwurah, A.O. International arbitration. 251
Curzon, L.B. Criminal cases. 131
Curzon, L.B. Criminal law. 131
Curzon, L.B. Equity. 176
Curzon, L.B. Evidence. 136
Curzon, L.B. Jurisprudence. 269
Curzon, L.B. Land law. 274
Curzon, L.B. Law dictionary. 150

Cruzon, L.B. Legal history. 219
Curzon, L.B. Roman law. 418
Curzon, L.B. Succession. 449
Curzon, L.B. Trusts. 468
Cusworth, G.R.N. Health & safety at work. 191, 236
Cutler, A. & Nye, D. Justice and predictability. 269
Cutler, J. Passing off. 355
Cutmore, W.H. Building regulations. 55
Cutting, M. Housing rights. 226
Dagtoglou, P.D. European Community. 179
Dahl, R.C. & Whelan, J.F. Military law dictionary. 318
Daily Express. Laski libel. 293
Daily Mail. Income tax. 412
Daily Telegraph. Capital transfer tax. 64
Daintith, T. & Willoughby, G.D.M. Oil & gas. 207, 344
Dale.H.E. Civil service. 78
Dale, J.R. Pharmacy law. 314
Dale, J.R. & Appelbe, G.E. Pharmacy. 162
Dale, R. Anti-dumping law. 81, 190
Dale, Sir W. Drafting. 160, 446
Dale, W.L. Parish Church. 164, 348
Dalglish, D.J. Company law. 89
Dalhuisen, J. International insolvency. 37
Dalloz. Petit codes. 204
Dalrymple, A.W. French-English legal dictionary. 150
Dalrymple, A.W. & Gibb, A.D. Words & phrases. 150
Dalton, J. Electricity Act. 146
Dalton, M. Sheriffs. 430
Dalton, P.J. Land law. 274
Dalton, P.J. & Dexter, R.S. Constitutional law. 103
Daly D. Club law. 78
Dam, K.W. GATT. 208
D'Amato, A.A. Custom.257
Danby, G. Drugs. 162
Dane, J. & Thomas, P.A. How to use a law library. 295
Daniel, W.W. Racial discrimination. 398
Daniell, E.R. Chancery practice. 68, 155, 341
Daniell, E.R. Forms & precedents. 68, 203, 341
Daniell, T. Inns of Court. 242
Daniels, W.C.E. West African common law. 14, 85
Daniels, W.T.S. Law reports. 284
Dart, J.H. Vendors & purchasers. 477
Dash, S. Justice denied. 394
Datta, C.R. Estate duty. 178
Datta, R. Government of India publications. 234, 347
Dau, H. Festschriften bibliography. 43
Daube, D. Biblical law. 42
Daube, D. Medical advance. 34

AUTHOR AND SHORT TITLE INDEX

Daube, D. Roman law. 418
Daunton-Fear, M. South Australia sentencing. 427
Davenport, N. Patent system. 356
Davey, H. Registration of births. 49
David, R. English & French law. 92, 204
David, R. French law. 204
David, R. Magistrate in the Crown Court. 305
David, R. & Brierley, J.E.C. Major legal systems. 92
David, R. & De Vries, H.P. French legal system. 205
David Davies Memorial Institute. Water pollution. 370
Davidson, E. Nuremberg fallacy. 483
Davidson, V. Family law. 193
Davies, D.M. Magistrate. 305
Davies, D.T. Will precedents. 64, 487
Davies, Sir E. Limitations Committee. 297
Davies, F.R. Contract. 111
Davies, F.R. Revenue law. 412
Davies, G. Challenges to copyright. 118
Davies, J. Institutions & methods. 474
Davies, J.C. Inner Temple manuscripts. 295
Davies, K. Compulsory purchase. 96
Davies, K. Highways. 217
Davies, K. Property in land. 274, 403
Davies, M. Financial penalties. 387, 427
Davies, M. Prisoners of society. 381, 406
Davies, M. Support systems. 436
Davies, M.R. Letting & managing. 279
Davies, M.R.R. Planning. 459
Davies, P. & Freedland, M.R. Labour law. 169
Davies, P. & Freedland, M.R. Transfer of employment. 169
Davies, P.L. Takeovers & mergers. 89, 469
Davies, R. Offices & shops. 433
Davies, R.A. Canadian corporation precedents. 121
Davies, R.U. Council accounts. 300
Davies, R.V. Nationalization of land. 87
Davies, W.A. Aliens. 18
Davis, A.G. Letters of Credit. 80, 292
Davis, A.G. Torts. 456
Davis, B. Tax planning. 247, 360
Davis, J.L.R. Conflicts casebook. 100
Davis, K.C. Administrative law. 8
Davis, R. Tax planning. 451
Davis, R.P. Wild bird protection. 21
Davis, R.U. Parish council. 349
Dawson, F.G. & Head, I.L. Aliens. 18
Dawson, I.J. & Pearce, R.A. Licences relating to land. 274, 278
Dawson, J.P. Gifts & promises. 93, 211
Dawson, J.P. Lay judges. 264
Dawson, R.O. Sentencing. 427
Dawson, T. Press. 379
Day, D. International trade. 190

Day, M.J. & Harris, P.I. Unit trusts. 259
Deadman, W.H. & Franklin, H.W. Unified tax. 412
Deadman, W.B. & Hockey, P.J. Prices & pay codes. 169
Dean, J. Hatred, ridicule or contempt. 293
Dean-Drummond, A. Riot control. 394
Deane, H.B. Blockade. 50
Debrett's Peerage. 359
De Castro, J.P. Hall marking. 216
Defence, Ministry of. Manual of military law. 318
Defence, Ministry of. Queen's regulations. 318
De Gara, J. Trade relations. 181
Dehoghton, C. Company law. 89
Deighan, M. County court practice. 124, 375
Deighton, S. New criminals. 43, 98
Delaney, J. Italian penal code. 262
Delany, V.T.H. Administration of justice. 7, 259
Delany, V.T.H. Charities in Ireland. 69
De Laume, G.R. Private international law. 205
Dell, S. Murder into manslaughter. 222
Dell'Anno, P. Pollution control. 368
Delupis, I. Adoptions. 12
Delupis, I. Bibliography of international law. 43, 251
Delupis, I. International law. 257, 441
Delupis, I.D. Finance & investments. 252
Delvolve, J.L. Arbitration in France. 205
Demarco, C.T. Pharmacy.
Denison, C.M. & Scott, C.H. Appeals. 247
Denman, D.R. Land ownership. 22
Denmman, D.R. Place of property. 403
Denning, Lord. The changing law. 8
Denning, Lord. Discipline of law. 269
Denning, Lord. Due process of law. 273, 375
Denning, Lord. Family story. 408
Denning, Lord. Freedom. 7, 8, 76, 269
Denning, Lord. Landmarks. 408
Denning, Lord. Legal education committee. 287
Denning, Lord. Road to justice. 7, 279
Dent, H.C. Education system. 165
Dental Board. Dental register of Ireland. 147
D'Entreves, A.P. Natural law. 269
Denyer, R.L. Industrial law. 237
Denyer-Green, B. Compulsory purchase. 96
Denyer-Green, B. Development & planning. 459
Denza, E. Diplomatic law. 153
De Pagler, H. & Van Raan, R. Valuation of goods. 140
Departmental Committee on Air Pollution. Report. 369
Departmental Committee on Alternative Remedies. 489
Departmental Committee on Homosexual

Offences & Prostitution Report. 390
Departmental Committee on Liquor Licensing. Report. 296
Departmental Committee on National Insurance. Report. 327
Departmental Committee on Old Age Pensions. Report. 360
Departmental Committee on Patents & Designs. Report. 356
Departmental Committee on Poor Law Orders. Report. 371
Departmental Committee on Rule Against Perpetuities. Report. 361
Departmental Committee on Vagrancy. Report. 475
Derham, D.P. Introduction to law. 31, 331
Deringer, A. EEC competition law. 95, 183
Derrett, J.D.M. Religion in India. 234
Derrett, J.D.M. Modern Hindu law. 218
Desai, K. Indian marriage & divorce. 155, 311
Deschampneufs, H. Export. 190.
De Schutter, D. International criminal law bibliography. 135
Deshpande, V.S. Judicial Review. 266
De Smith, S.A. Constitutional law. 8, 103
De Smith, S.A. Judicial Review. 8, 143, 264, 384, 470
De Smith, S.A. New Commonwealth. 86, 103
Detter, I. International organizations. 254
Deutch, S. Unfair contracts. 111
Deutsch, R. Northern Ireland.336
De Villiers, J.E. & Macintosh, J.C. Agency in S.Africa. 439
Devlin, J.D. Criminal courts. 132, 467
Devlin, K. Sentencing. 305, 427
Devlin, Lord. Criminal prosecution. 389
Devlin, Lord. Enforcement of morals. 269
Devlin, Lord. Judge. 264
Devlin, Lord. Trial by jury. 132, 267, 467
De Voil, P.W. Tax appeals. 233, 412
De Voil, P.W. VAT. 476
Devan, P. Family law. 155, 234
Dewar, G.D.H. VAT.
Dewis, M. Health & safety. 167, 169
Dhavan, R. & Davies, C. Censorship. 67, 341
Dhokalia, R.P. Codification. 78, 257
Dhyani, S.N. Jurisprudence. 269
Dial, O.E. & Goldberg, E.M. Privacy. 383
Diamond, A.L. Commercial & consumer credit. 106
Diamond, A.L. Instalment credit. 106
Diamond, A.S. Primitive law. 380
Diamond, W.H. Capital formation. 259
Diamond, W.H. & Diamond, D.B. Tax havens. 450
Dias, R.W.M. Bibliography of jurisprudence. 43
Dias, R.W.M. Jurisprudence. 269
Dias, R.W.M. & Markesinis, B.S. Torts. 456

Dibden, R. Double taxation. 159, 412
Dicastri, V. Occupiers' liability. 343
Dicastri, V. Vendor & purchaser. 477
Dicey, A.V. Constitution. 103, 377
Dicey, A.V. Relations between law & public opinion. 211
Dicey, A.V. & Morris, J.H.C. Conflict of laws. 100
Dicey, A.V. & Rait, R.S. Scottish Union. 149
Dick, R.C. Drafting. 160
Dickerson, F.R. Drafting. 160, 290
Dickerson, F.R. Statute interpretation. 446
Dickerson, R. Products liability. 201, 388
Dickerson, R.W.V. Accountants. 6
Dicksee, B. London building. 303
Dickson, B. Northern Ireland legal system. 336
Dickson, W.G., Evidence in Scotland. 186
Didier, J.M. Pollution control. 368
Dienes, C.T. Birth control. 48
Dietl, C.E. Legal dictionary. 150
Digby, K.E. Workmen. 489
Dingwall, R. Protection of children. 72
Dingwall, R. & Eekelaar, J. Care proceedings. 72, 485
Dinsdale, W.A. Accident insurance. 246
Dinsdale, W.A. Innkeepers. 241
Dinsdale, W.A. Motor insurance. 247
Dinsdale, W.A. & McMurdie, D.C. Insurance. 245
Dionisopoulos, P.A. & Duscat, C.R. Privacy. 383
Di Palma, V. Capital gains tax. 63
Ditchfield, J.A. Police cautioning. 366
Diwan, P. Private international law. 100
Dix, D.K. Competitive trading. 355
Dix, D.K. & Crump, D.W. Contract of employment. 113, 169
Dix, D.K. & Todd, A.H. Medical evidence. 314, 362
Dixon, A. Mercantile & commercial law. 81
Djamour, J. Malay kinship. 309, 434
Djamour, J. Muslim matrimonial court. 260, 434
Djonovich, D.J. UN resolutions. 472
Dobbs, D. Remedies. 114
Dobry, G. Control of demolition. 459
Dobry, G. Land development. 148, 403
Dobry,G., Stewart-Smith, W.R. & Barnes, M. Development gains tax. 148, 412
Dobson, A.P. Sale of goods. 106, 420
Dodgson, C. A to Z of legal terms. 150
Dol, T. & Shattuck, W.L. Patent. 356
Domke, M. Arbitration. 24
Donald, A.E. C.M.R. 66, 464
Donald, D.W.A. Annuities. 21
Donaldson, A.G. Irish law. 259
Donaldson, Mr.Justice. Arbitration report. 24
Donaldson, S. Roentgenologist in court. 590

AUTHOR AND SHORT TITLE INDEX

Donelan, M.D. & Grieve, M.J. International disputes. 251
Dnnell, R.A. Landlord & tenant. 279
Donnelly, J.S. Landlord & tenant. 279
Donner, A.M. Role of the lawyer. 184, 289
Donnison, D.V. & Eversley, D.E.C. London. 303
Donovan, J.W. Tact in court. 13
Donoughmore, Lord. Minister's powers. 8
Doolan, B. Irish constitutional law. 103, 260
Doolan, B. Irish law. 260
Dornette, W.H.L. Anaesthesia. 19
Dosser, D. Taxation. 412
Douglas, C.M. & Lee, R.G. Estate Agents Act. 177
Douglas, R. Harbour law. 470
Douglas, R. Land. 274
Douglas, R.N. Social aspects. 31
Douglas, R.P.A. Harbours. 157
Douthwaite, W.R. Gray's Inn. 242
Dover, V. General average. 491
Dover, V. Marine insurance. 431
Dowdell, E.G. Quarter sessions. 221
Dowell, S. Taxation. 412
Downes, D.M. & Rock, P. Understanding deviance. 137
Downing, A.B. Euthanasia. 185
Dowrick, F.E. English common lawyers. 7, 269
Dowrick, F.E. Human rights. 228
Dowson, Sir E. & Sheppard, V.L.O. Land registration. 277
Dowson, Sir O.F. & Wightwick, H.W. Local elections. 300
Doxey, M.P. Economic sanctions. 255
Doyle, E.P. Banking. 39
Drake, C. Health & safety. 167
Drake, C.D. Employment Acts. 169
Drake, C.D. Labour law. 169
Drake, C.D. Partnership. 353
Draper, G.S.A.D. Armed conflicts. 480
Draper, G.S.A.D. Red Cross Conventions. 466
Dressler, D. Probation. 387
Drewry, C.S. Injunctions. 241
Drewry, G. Law, justice & politics. 8
Driedger, E.A. Statute construction. 446
Drion, H. Air law. 34
Drobnig, U. Private international law. 100, 209
Drone, E.S. Property in intellectual productions. 118
Drover, C.B. & Bosley, R.W.B. Banking. 39
Druckman, D. International negotiations. 251
Druker, I.E. Financing the European Communities. 179
Drzemczewski, A.Z. Human rights. 228
D'Souza, F. Refugee dilemma. 405
Duboff, L.D. Art law. 28

Dubner, B.H. Piracy. 364, 424
Dubner, B.H. Territorial waters. 452
Du Cann, R. Art of the advocate. 13, 365
Duckworth, P. Matrimonial property. 196
Duerden, C. Noise abatement. 335
Duff, P.W. Roman private law. 418
Duffee, D. Correctional policy. 381
Duffy, R.E. Art law. 28
Dugdale, D.F. New Zealand hire purchase. 106
Dugdale, Sir W. Origines juridiciales. 287
Duggan, A.J. & Darvall, L.W. Consumer protection. 107
Duggan, C. Canon law. 164
Duggan, M. Law and the computer. 98
Duke, H.E. Gray's Inn. 243
Duker, W.F. Habeas corpus. 216
Dull, P.S. & Unemura, M.T. Tokyo trials. 483
Duman, D. English and colonial bars. 40
Duman, D. Judicial bench. 264
Dummett, A. Citizenship. 328
Duncan, C. & Hoolahan, A. Defamation. 293
Duncan, C. & Neill, B. Defamation. 293
Duncan, J. Guernsey history. 69
Dunedin, Viscount. Laws of Scotland. 172
Dunlop, A.B. Approved school. 24
Dunlop, C. Creditor-debtor law. 142
Du Plessis, J.R. South African law. 439
Dupuy, R.J. Humanity's resources. 424
Dupuy, R.J. Law of the sea. 424
Dupuy, R.J. Natural resources dispute settlement. 207, 344
Duputy, R.J. Right to health. 228
Durant, M., Thomas, M. & Willock, H.D. Crime & criminals. 427
Dworkin, R.G. Polticial judges. 264
Dworkin, R.M. Philosophy. 169
Dworkin, R.M. Taking rights seriously. 76, 269
Dyke, J.M. van Jury selection. 267
Dykstra, G. Canadian legal bibliography. 43, 61
Dymond, R. Capital transfer tax. 64
Eagle, M.G. Special perils insurance. 248
Eagleson, J.G. Bills of sale. 47, 296
Eales, P.G. & De Vos, P.A.F. Bankruptcy. 37
Easson, A.J. EEC tax law. 179, 412
East, E.H. Pleas of the Crown. 131
Eastaway, N. Capital transfer tax. 64
Eastaway, N. Tax planning. 451
Eastaway, N. Taxes Acts. 64, 412
Easton, H.C. Rentcharge conveyancing. 409
Easton, J.M. Rent charges. 409
Eastwood, R.A. Real property. 403
Eastwood, R.A. Sale of goods. 420
Eaton, E.W. & Purcell, J.P. Land charges. 276
Ebeling, N.B. & Hill, D.A. Child abuse. 71
Ebenstein, W. Pure theory. 269
Eccles, G. Employment Act. 169

Eccles, G. & Cox, J. Companies Act. 89
Eckert, W.G. Forensic science. 202
Eckstein, H. Health service. 393
Economic Commission for Europe. Building regulations. 55
Economists Advisory Group. Acquisitions & mergers. 449
Eddey, K.J. English legal system. 173
Eddey, K.J. Local government. 300
Eddison, T. Local government. 300
Eddy, J.P. Professional negligence. 330
Eddy, J.P. & Loewe, L.L. Gaming. 41
Edelhertz, H. & Geis, G. Compensation. 128
Edelman, S. Air pollution. 370
Edelstein, C.S. & Wicks, R.J. Criminal justice. 129
Eden, R.H. Injunctions. 241
Edge, C.T. Small computer systems. 98
Edge, N.C.W. Law for librarians. 325
Education & Science, Dept. of Public lending right. 393
Education & Science, Dept. of. Veterinary profession. 477
Edwards, A.H. Mental health. 317
Edwards, E.J. Evidence in Australia. 186
Edwards, G. Alcohol dependence. 18
Edwards, H. Export credit. 190
Edwards, J.Ll.J. Attorney General. 282
Edwards, J.Ll.J. Law officers. 282, 389
Edwards, J.Ll.J. Mens rea. 133, 447
Edwards, M. Computer contracts. 98
Edwards, M.F. & Meyer, K.L. Settlement & plea bargaining. 365
Edwards, R.J. & Langstaff, B.F.J. Equity cases. 176
Edwards, S. Women on trial. 488
Eekelaar, J.M. Family law. 193
Eekelaar, J.M. Family violence. 158
Eekelaar, J.M. Marriage & cohabitation. 79
Effros, R.c. Financial centres. 39
Egan, B. Dismissals. 169, 405, 471
Egan, B. Industrial tribunals. 239
Egan, B. Trade descriptions. 13, 460
Egbert, L.D. & Morales-Macedo, F. Multilingual law dictionary. 150
Eggleston, R. Evidence. 186
Ehmann, D. & Marshall, M. Constitution of Guernsey. 69
Ehrenzweig, A.A. Private international law. 100
Ehrlich, J.W. Holy Bible. 42
Ehrmann, H.W. Comparative legal cultures. 93
Eichelberger, C.M. Peace. 472
Eid, A. & Schou, A. Human rights. 228
Elcock, H.J. Administrative justice. 8
Elder, A.J. Building regulations. 26, 56
Elgin, W.F. Sound investment. 159
El-Hakim, A.A. Middle East & sea law. 424

Elian, G. International Court. 253
Elias, P., Napier, B. & Wallington, P. Labour law. 169
Elias, T.O. African law. 14
Elias, T.O. African customary law. 14
Elias, T.O. Ghana & Sierra Leone. 210
Elias, T.O. International court. 253
Elias, T.O. International law. 14
Elias, T.O. Nigeria. 332
Elias, T.O. Nigerian land law. 274, 332
Elias, T.O. Nigerian press law. 332
Elias, T.O. Treaties. 466
Elkin, S.L. Politics & land use. 459
Ellen, E. Maritime fraud. 205, 431
Elles, N. Community law. 184
Ellinger, E.P. Letters of credit. 80
Ellinger, W.B. Subject of headings. 293
Elliot, D.W. & Street, H. Road accidents. 5
Elliot, D.W. & Wood, J.C. Criminal law. 131
Elliot, M.A. Penal theories. 396
Elliott, D.S. & Voss, H.L. Delinquency. 146
Elliott, R.C. & Boswell, E. South African notary. 337
Elliott, R.F. Building contract litigation. 54
Ellis, K. Post office. 374
Ellis, T.P. Welsh tribal law. 479
Ellmore, R.T. Broadcasting. 399
Elmandijra, M. UN system. 472
Elon, M. Jewish law. 263
Elphinstone, L.H. Land covenants. 163, 411
Elphinstone, L.H. War damage. 482
Else-Mitchell, R. Australian constitution. 31
El-Sheikh, F.El.R.A. Foreign private investment. 421
Elsynge, H. Parliaments. 350
Elton, C.I. Common lands. 86
Elton, C.I. Copyholds. 117, 278
Elton, C.I. Tenures of Kent. 207
Elton, G.R. Tudor constitution. 105
Elton, G.R. Tudor revolution. 212
Elwyn-Jones, Lord. On trial. 222
Ely, J.H. Democracy & distrust. 266
Elysnge, H. Parliaments. 350
Elzaki, A. Papua New Guinea legal materials. 43
Elzinga, K.G. Antitrust penalties. 95
Emanuel, H.D. Welsh laws. 479
Emanuel, M.R. Dogs. 21
Emden, A. Building contracts. 54
Emden, A. & Gill, W.H. Building contracts. 54
Emden, C.S. Civil servant. 78
Emden, C.S. Constitutional law. 103
Emden, C.A. People.
Emery, G.F. Barristers & solicitors.
Emery, R. & Wilkes, H.M. Rating valuation. 401
Emmerson, H.C. Ministry of Works. 214
Emmet, L.E. Titles. 115, 207, 455

AUTHOR AND SHORT TITLE INDEX

Emmins, C.J. Criminal procedure. 375
Employment, Dept. of. Equal pay. 175
Employment, Dept of. Noise. 335
Employment, Dept of. Safety and health at work. 169, 342
Employment, Dept of. Take seven. 398
Employment & Productivity, Dept. of. In place of strife. 238
Encel, S. Cabinet government. 31, 59
Encyclopaedia of British Oil & Gas Law. 344
Encyclopaedia of Consumer law. 107
Encyclopaedia of European Community. 179
Encyclopaedia of Factories, Shops & Offices. 191
Encyclopaedia of Health & Safety. 167, 169, 433
Encyclopaedia of Housing Law. 226
Encyclopaedia of insurance law. 245
Encycloapedia of Labour Relations Law. 238
Encyclopaedia of Public Health Law. 393
Encyclopaedia of Road Traffic. 416
Encyclopaedia of social services law. 485
Encyclopaedia of town and country planning. 274.
Encyclopaedia of the Laws of Scotland. 172
Energy, Dept. of. Oil & gas resources. 344
Energy, Dept.of Offshore oil & gas policy. 207, 344
Enever, F.A. Bona vacantia. 51
Enever, F.A. Coal Act. 319
Enever, F.A. Distress for tent. 221
Enever, F.A. Minerals. 319
England, J. & Rear, J. Hong Kong industrial relations. 238
English, H.B. & English, A.L. Dictionary of psychological terms. 151
Enright, C. Constitutional law. 31
Environment, Dept. of. Air pollution. 370
Environment, Dept. of. Apportionment of rents. 409
Environment, Dept. of. Drinking & driving. 161
Environment, Dept. of. Ground lease. 285
Environment, Dept. of. Highway code. 416
Environment, Dept. of Housing co-operatives. 227
Environment, Dept. of. Land. 274
Environment, Dept. of. Land registration. 335
Environment, Dept. of. Local authority remuneration. 301
Environment, Dept. of. Local government. 301
Environment, Dept. of. Local government finance. 301
Environment, Dept. of. Mobile home residents. 66
Environment, Dept. of. Mobile homes review. 66
Environment, Dept. of. National park 328.
Environment, Dept. of. Neighbourhood noise. 335
Environment, Dept. of. Organic change. 301
Environment, Dept. of. Planning appeals. 22
Environment, Dept. of. Pollution control.368
Environment, Dept. of. Protecting people at work. 236
Environment, Dept. of. Rating of plant. 401
Environment, Dept. of. Rent Acts. 408
Environment, Dept. of Rent Arrers. 408
Environment, Dept. of Rentcharges. 409
Environment, Dept. of. River pollution. 370
Environment, Dept. of. Road accidents.
Environment, Dept. of. Security of tenure. 58
Environment, Dept. of. Traffic noise. 335
Environment, Dept. of. Water industry. 484
Environment, Dept. of. Water pollution. 370
Environment, Dept. of. Your lorry abroad. 464
Epstein, D. Debtor-creditor cases. 143
Epstein, D. Debtor-creditor relations. 143
Epstein, L.M. Jewish marraige contract. 311
Epstein, R.A. Products liability. 388
Epstein, W. Last chance.
Equal Opportunities Commission. Annual report. 175
Ercklentz, E.W. German corporation law. 209
Ercman, S. Environmental law. 268
Erckson, M.L. Antitrust. 95
Ernst, M.L. & Schwartz, A.U. Privacy. 383
Erroll, Lord. Liquor licensing committee. 296
Erskine, J. Institute. 422
Erskine, J. Scotland. 422
Erwin, R.E. & Minzer, M.K. Defense of drink driving cases. 161
Esman, M.J. Malaysia. 309
Espinasse, I. Nisi prius. 334
Essays in international & comparative law. 249
Estates Gazette Digest. 152
Europa Institute (Leyden). Competition policy. 95, 183
European Association for Legal & Fiscal Studies. Product liability. 388
European Association of Advertising Agencies. Advertising. 13
European Committee on Crime Problems. Compensation. 128, 410
European Committee on Crime Problems. Crime Problems. 137
European Committee on Crime Problems. Criminological Research. 137
European Committee on Crime Problems. Decriminalisation. 137
European Committee on Crime Problems. Drug abuse. 162
European Committee on Crime Problems. Extradition. 191
European Committee on Crime Problems. Juvenile delinquency. 137, 146
European Committee on Crime Problems. Legal data user protection. 137

European Committee on Crime Problems. Long-term prisoners. 396
European Committee on Crime Problems. Police & crime prevention. 127, 366
European Committee on Crime Problems. Protection of users of data processing. 98
European Committee on Crime Problems. Sentencing. 428
European Committee on Crime Problems. Standard terms in contracts. 111, 137
European Committee on Crime Problems. Violence. 478
European Committee on Legal Co-operation. Legal aid. 286
European Committee on Legal Co-operation. Protection of users of computerised information. 98
European Communities. Community legal order. 184
European Communities. Court of Justice. 184
European Communities. European capital market. 181
European Communities. Food law. 201
European Communities. Freedom of movement. 180
European Communities. Glossary of abbreviations. 3
European Communities. Inventory of taxes. 412
European Communities. National price controls. 358
European Communities. Property. 180, 403
European Communities. Rail and road transport. 181
European Communities. Social security. 179, 435
European Communities Commission. Thirty years. 180
European Conference of Minsters of Transport. Road traffic. 416
European Convention on Human Rights. Yearbook. 228
Evans, D.L. Landlord & tenant. 279
Evans, E.J. Tithes. 164
Evans, J. Immigration. 231
Evans, K. Advocacy. 13
Evans, R.G. Criminal justice. 129
Evans, W. Gardens. 19, 349
Everest, L.F. & Strode, E. Estoppel. 179
Everling, D.U. Right of establishment. 182
Eversen, H.J. European Communities case law.
Evershed, Sir F.R. Court of Appeal. 22, 126
Evershed, Sir F.R. Statute. 446
Eversley, W.P. Domestic relations. 193
Everton, A. Fire. 198, 246
Everton, A.R. Trade winds. 95
Everts, P. European Community. 180
Ewart, J.S. Estoppel. 179

Ewen, C.L.E. Surnames. 825
Ewing, A.C. Punishment. 396
Ewing, K.D. Trade unions. 463
Ewing, K.D. & Finnie, W. Civil liberties in Scotland. 76
Ezejiofor, G. Human rights. 228
Ezorsky, G. Punishment. 396
Faber's anatomical atlas. 19
Fabian Society. Legal services for all. 286, 485
Fage, J. Supreme court practice. 375
Fahy, E.R. Packaging of hazardous materials. 347
Fairbairn, W.J.G. Executors & administrators. 189
Fairbairn, W.J.G. Trustees & liquidators. 37, 298, 468
Fairest, P.B. Mortgages. 57, 323
Fairhead, S. Persistent petty offenders. 137
Fairlie, J.A. Administrative procedure. 144
Fajgenbaum, J.L. & Hanks, P. Constitutional law. 31
Falconbridge, J.D. Conflict of laws. 100
Falconer, T. Surnames. 325
Falk, R.A. Civil war. 480
Falk, R.A. Vietnam war. 481
Falk, Z.W. Jewish law. 263
Faller, K. Social work. 71
Fallon, P. Crown Court. 139, 375, 428, 467
Family Welfare Association. Social services. 435, 485
Faraday, P.M. Rating. 401
Farani, M. Law dictionary. 150
Farmer, D. Health & safety at work. 236
Farmer, J.A. Tribunals. 468
Farndale, W.A.J. Hospital consent forms. 224
Farndale, W.A.J. Human transplants. 230, 315
Farndale, W.A.J. Medical negligence. 316
Farndale, W.A.J. & Cooper, A.J. Redundancy payments. 405
Farndale, W.A.J. & Laman, E.C. Hospital treatment. 224, 316
Farndale, W.A.J. & Russell, S. Health service accidents. 225, 326
Farnsworth, A. Addington. 233
Farnsworth, A. Residence & domicil. 159
Farrand, J.T. Contract & conveyance. 113, 115
Farrand, J.T. & Arden, A. Rent Acts. 279, 409
Farrand, J.T. & Scammell, E.H. Precedents. 204
Farrands, W.L. Company law. 89
Farrant, R.D. Isle of Man. 261
Farrar, H. Company insolvency. 37
Farrar, J. Company insolvency. 89, 298
Farrar, J. Law Commission. 281
Farrar, J.H. Legal method. 43, 85
Farrier, D. Drugs & intoxication. 18, 162
Farwell, Sir G. Powers. 374
Fattah, E.A. Capital punishment. 63

Faulks, Sir N. Defamation committee. 293
Favre, D.S. Animal law. 21
Fawcett, J.E.S. British Commonwealth. 86
Fawcett, J.E.S. Human rights. 228
Fawcett, J.E.S. Outer space. 442
Fay, E. Official Referee's business. 24
Fazal, M.A. Control of administrative action. 266
Fearnley, A.L. Inspection of deeds. 144
Feeney, T.G. Canadian wills. 386, 487
Feenstra, R. & Waal, C.J.D. Seventeenth century Leyden law professors. 75, 417
Feinberg, J. & Gross, H. Philosophy. 269
Feld, B. Courts martial. 125
Feld, W.J. Court of European Communities. 184
Feldbrugge, F.J.M. Communist codification. 441
Feldbrugge, F.J.M. Soviet law. 441
Feldman, A.M. Welfare economics. 486
Feldman, D.M. Birth control. 4, 48
Feldman, L. Care proceedings. 72
Feldman, L.P. Consumer protection. 107
Feldstein, P.J. Health association. 326
Fellows, A. Burial. 57
Fellow, R.F.   J.C.T. contract. 54
Fels, A. Prices & Incomes Board. 358
Fenn, P.T. Right of fishery. 199
Fenner, K.M. Nursing. 340
Fenwick, C.G. International law. 249
Ferguson, J.H. & McHenry, D.E. American government. 474
Ferguson, R.W. Drug abuse control. 162
Ferris, d. Homosexuality. 223
Fesler, J.W. Public administration. 391
Fessler, D. Contracts cases. 111
Fiddes, G.V. Colonial Office. 214
Field, C.D. Estoppel. 179
Field, C.D. Evidence in India & Pakistan. 186
Field, D. Hotel & catering law. 241
Field, D. Practical club law. 78
Field, D. & Pink, M. Liquor licensing. 296
Field, E. Hammond, W.H. & Tizard, J. Approved school boys. 24
Field, F. Fair shares. 196
Field, S. Ethnic minorities. 398
Field, S. & Southgate, P. Public disorder. 394
Field-Fisher, T.G. Ibbotson, S & Roydhouse, E. Rent regulation. 409
Field, N. Probation practice. 387
Fife, I. & Machin, E.A. Health & safety. 167, 169, 192, 433
Fifoot, C.H.S. Common law history. 85, 111, 221, 456
Fifoot, C.H.S. English law. 219
Fifoot, C.H.S. Judge & jury. 264
Figgis, J.N. Divine right. 377
Financial Times. Employment. 169
Finch, J. Health service. 326, 393

Finch, J.D. Legal theory. 269
Findlater, R. Public lending right. 393
Findlay, W. Property owners. 343, 457
Finegold, W.J. Artificial insemination. 28
Finer, H. Future of government. 212
Finer, H. Modern government. 212, 290
Finer, S.E. Five constitutions. 93, 103
Fingarette, H. Criminal insanity. 244
Fingarette, H. & Hasse, A.F. Mental disabilities. 133, 244
Finlason, W.F. Mortmain. 324
Finlason, W.F. Tenures of land. 278
Finlay, H.A. Family courts. 194
Finlay, H.A. & Bissett-Johnson, A. Family law in Australia. 194
Finlay, I.F. Foreign language patents. 396
Finley, M.I. Roman property. 418
Finney, J. Gaming, lotteries, fund raising. 41
Finnis, J.M. Natural law. 76, 269
Firnin, S. Scotland Yard. 366
Firth, M. Share prices & mergers. 449
Fisch, E.L., Freed, D.J. & Schachter, E.R. Charities. 69
Fischer, G. Non-proliferation. 339, 481
Fisher, D.E. Australian environment law. 174.
Foisher, R.L. Matrimonial property. 197
Fisher, W.R. & Lightwood, J.M. Mortgage. 57, 323
Fitzgerald, J. Building new families. 12
Fitzgerald, M. Prisoners in revolt. 381
Fitzgerald, M. & Sim, J. British prisons. 381
Fitzgerald, M. & Maurice, J. System of justice. 130
Fitgerald, P.J. Criminal law. 396, 428
Fitzherbert, A. Justyces of Peas. 305
Fitzmaurice, J. European Parliament. 183
Fitzpatrick, P. Papua New Guinea. 348
Fitzroy, A. Privy Council. 385
Flaherty, D.H. History of Canadian law. 61
Flaherty, D.H. Privacy & government data banks. 98, 383
Flanders, A. & Glegg, H.A. Industrial relations. 238
Flanager, T. & Milman, D. Partnership. 353
Flathman, R.C. Practice of rights. 228
Fleeman, R.K. & Rhodes, R.J. Employment. 169
Fleishman, J.L. Public duties. 212
Fleming, J.G. Torts. 457
Fleming, M.C. Fair trading. 192
Fletcher, B. Light & air. 297
Fletcher, I.F. Bankruptcy. 36
Fletcher, I.F. Conflict of laws. 100
Fletcher, L. Construction contract dictionary. 54
Flexner, A. Prostitution in Europe. 390
Flexner, E. Century of struggle. 488
Flick, C.P. Abstract & title. 455
Flick, G. Curl liberties in Australia. 76

Flick, G.A. Natural justice. 269
Flint, M.F. Copyright. 118
Flood, J.A. Barristers' clerks. 40
Flood, f.L.C. Ministry of Agriculture. 214
Flournoy, R.W. & Hudson, M.O. Nationality laws. 328
Foa, E. Landlord & tenant. 279, 297
Foakes, J. Family violence. 158
Fodden, S.R. Family law. 195
Fogg, A.S. Australian town planning. 459
Foggo-Poys, E. Counselling. 286, 486
Foighel, I. Nationalisation. 18
Folkard, H.C. Loans & pledges. 358
Folsom, R.H. Competition. 95
Fontaine, M. & Bourgoine, T. Belgian consumer legislation. 107
Foote, C., Levy, R.J. & Sander, F.E.A. Family law. 196, 232
Forbes, G. & Watson, A.A. Dental practice. 19, 147
Forbes, Sir H.H.V. Real property. 403
Forbes, J. Divided legal profession. 289
Forbes, R.F. & Johnston, D.L. Canadian companies. 448
Ford, C. Oaths. 341
Ford, D.A. & Holsey, M.D. Mental health. 317
Ford, H. Trusts. 468
Ford, H.A.J. Associations. 29
Ford, H.A.J. Companylaw. 89
Ford, H.A.J. Death duty. 178
Ford, M.E. US women attorneys. 154
Ford, P. & Ford, G. Parliamentary papers. 45
Forder, K.J. Meat trade. 201
Fordham, C.M. Agricultural holdings. 16, 402
Foreign Office. Representative service overseas. 153
Forkosch, M. Outer space. 442
Formoy, R.R. Company law. 89
Forsyth, C.F. & Bennett, T.W. Private international law. 417, 439
Forsyth, M. European parliament. 183
Forsyth, T.A. Trusts. 189, 468
Forsyth, W. Hortensius. 13
Forsythe, D.P. Conciliation Commission for Palestine. 472
Fortescue, Sir J. De laudibus. 220
Fortescue-Brickdale, Sir C. Land Registration Act. 277
Fortescue-Brickdale, Sir C. Land Transfer Acts. 278
Foskett, D. Compromise. 24
Foss, E. Biographia juridica. 48, 264
Foss, E. Judges. 48
Fox, H.G. Canadian trademarks. 461
Foster, Sir J., Sims, Capital taxes. 63, 64
Foster, Sir M. Crown law. 139
Foster, Sir M. Rebels. 415, 465
Foulkes, D. Administrative law. 8

Foulkes, D. Local government. 301
Fowler, H.W. Modern English usage. 152
Fowler, J. Wales. 479
Fowles, A.J. Prison welfare. 381
Fowlston, B. Commercial & industrial licencing. 81
Fox, A. Beyond contract. 169
Fox, F. Countryside. 174
Fox, H.G. Canadian Copyright. 118
Fox, H.G. Canadian letters patent. 356
Fox, H.G. Monopolies & patents. 357
Fox, J.C. Contempt of court. 108
Fox, Sir L.W. English prison. 381
Fox, R. Termination of employment payments. 169, 405, 471
Fox, R.M. Medico-legal report. 157
Fox, R.G. Concept of obscenity. 341
Fox-Andrews, J. Business tenancies. 58
Fox-Davies, A.C. & Carlyon Britton, P.W.P. Names. 425.
Frader, C.F. Aliens. 18
Francis, E.A. Mortgages and securities. 323
Francis, E.A. Torrens title. 274, 456
Frank, W.F. Industry & commerce. 81, 237
Frankel, M.E. Criminal sentence. 428
Franklin, A.W. Child abuse. 71
Franklin, M. Quebec law. 61
Franklin P.J. & Woodhead, C. Life assurance. 247
Frankowska, M. Scientific & technological revolution. 424
Franks, J.A. Company director. 89
Franks, M.H. Limitation of actions. 297
Franks, Sir O. Administrative tribunals. 467
Franson, R.T. & Lucas, J.G.R. Canadian environmental law. 174, 368
Fraser, D. Poor law. 371
Fraser, D. Power & authority. 391
Fraser, H. Libel & slander. 293
Fraser, Lord. Husband & wife. 310
Fraser, Lord. Parent & child. 72, 193
Fraser, Lord. Scottish constitution and law. 103
Fratcher, W.F. Perpetuities. 361
Freedland, M.R. Attachment of earnings. 30
Freedland, M.R. Contract of employment. 113, 169
Freedman, J. Crisis & legitimacy. 8, 391
Freedman, M. Contacts cases. 111
Freeman, A. Proceedings against doctors. 157, 316, 316
Freeman, J. Prisons. 381
Freeman, M.D.A. Children Act. 12, 72
Freeman, M.D.A. Child care. 12, 72
Freeman, M.D.A. Domestic proceedings. 305, 312
Freeman, M.D.A. Family law. 193
Freeman, M.D.A. Rights of children. 73, 76
Freeman, M.D.A. Violence in the home. 158

AUTHOR AND SHORT TITLE INDEX

Freeman, M.D.A. & Lyon, C.M. Cohabitation. 79
Freeman, M.D.A. & Lyon, C.M. Matrimonial jurisdiction. 305, 312
Freeman, W.M. Air and aviation law. 34
Freeman, W.M. Rights of way. 416
Freemantle, M.P. & Meskin, P.M. South African forms & precedents. 172
French, C.A.M. Dilapadations. 153
French, C.W. Mental health. 317
French, G. Occupational health. 342
Fricke, G. Compulsory acquisition of land. 96
Friday, P.C. & Stewart, V.L. Juvenile justice. 146
Fridman, G.H.L. Agency. 16
Fridman, G.H.L. Bankruptcy. 37
Fridman, G.H.L. Canadian business law. 81
Fridman, G.H.L. Contracts. 111
Fridman, G.H.L. Restitution. 114
Fridman, G.H.L. Sale of goods. 420
Fridman, G.H.L. Torts. 457
Friedelbaum, S.H. Judicial process. 474
Friedland, M.L. Criminal law cases. 135
Friedland, M.L. Double jeopardy. 132, 159
Friedlander, R.A. Terrorism. 394, 478
Friedlander, W.A. Social welfare. 486
Friedman, G. Divorce. 155
Friedman, J. Contract remedies. 114
Friedman, L. War. 481
Friedman, L.M. Law and society. 269
Friedman, S. Expropriation. 252
Friedmann, W.G. International law. 257
Friedmann, W.G. Law in a changing society. 269
Friedmann, W.G. Legal theory. 269
Friedmann, W.G. Oceans. 424
Friedmann, W.G. Public & private enterprise. 81
Friedmann, W.G. State & rule of law. 212, 269
Friedmann, W.G. Transnational law. 9, 257
Friedmann, W.G. & Garner, J.F. Government enterprise. 212
Friedmann, W.G. & Pugh, R.C. Foreign investment. 259
Friedrich, C.J. Philosophy. 269
Friend, W.L. Legal bibliographies. 43
Frohock, F.M. Abortion. 4
Frommel, S.N. & Thompson, J.H. Company law. 89
Frost, A. & Howard, C. Tribunals. 468
Frumer, L.R. & Friedman, M.I. Products liability. 388
Frumer, L.R., Benoit, R.L. & Friedman, M.I. Personal injuries. 142, 362
Fry, E. Specific performance. 114, 443
Fugate, W.L. Foreign commerce. 95
Fulbrook, J. Social security. 435
Fulbrook, J. Unemployed. 405, 471

Fuller, F.B. Building Societies. 57
Fuller, F.B. Friendly Societies. 206, 236
Fulton, T.W. Sovereignty of the sea. 425, 453
Furmston, M.P. Effect of EEC membership. 181
Future for Old Buildings. 56
Future of voluntary organizations. 70
Fysh, M. & Thomas, R.W. Industrial property. 118
Fyzee, A.A.A. Muhammandan law. 260
Gabbay, E. Criminal Justice. 130
Gabbay, E. Open justice. 130
Gabin, S.B. Judicial review. 266
Gaches, I. Markets & fairs. 310
Gajendragadkar, P.B. Constitution of India. 234
Gal, G. Space law. 442
Galbraith, V.H. Domesday book. 9
Gale, C.J. Easements. 115, 163
Galeotti, S. Judicial control. 264, 266, 392
BGall, G. European patent applications. 357
Gall, G.L. Canadian legal system. 61
Galloway, B. Discrimination against gay people. 223
Galtung, J. European Community. 181
Gamble, J.K. & Fischer, D.D. International Court. 253
Gamble, J.K. & Pontecorvo, G. Law of the sea. 425
Gamble, J.K. & Quinn, C. Law of the sea. 425
Gandhi, A.B. Carriage of goods. 47
Gandhi, D.S. Shipowners. 425
Gane, C.H.W. & Stoddart, C.N. Scottish criminal law. 134
Gane, C.H.W. & Stoddart, C.N. Scottish criminal procedure. 375
Ganz, G. Administrative procedures. 9, 376
Gardiner, E.J.O. Private street works. 217
Gardiner, G.A. & Martin, A. Law reform now. 282
Gardiner, S.R. Puritan constitutional documents. 105, 221
Gardner, R.F.R. Abortion. 4
Gardner, T.J. & Manian, V. Arrest. 27
Garner, J. Commonwealth Office. 213
Garner, J.F. Administrative law. 9, 301
Garner, J.F. Allotments. 19
Garner, J.F. Alteration of houses. 226
Garner, J.F. Civil ceremonial. 301
Garner, J.F. Clean air. 370
Garner, J.F. Compulsory purchase. 96
Garner, J.F. Control of pollution. 368
Garner, J.F. Local land charges. 276
Garner, J.F. Municipal engineering points. 301
Garner, J.F. Planning. 459
Garner, J.F. Public control of land. 275
Garner, J.F. Rights of way. 201, 416
Garner, J.F. Road charges. 217

Garner, J.F. Sewers & drains. 161
Garner, J.F. Slum clearance. 97, 459
Garner, J.F. & Crow, R.K. Clean air. 393
Garner, J.F. & Harris, D.J. Control of pollution. 368
Garrett, F.E.W. Nuisance. 340
Garrow, J.M. Trusts & trustees. 468
Garrow, J.M. & Gray, H.R. Personal property, New Zealand. 363
Garrow, J.M. & Willis, J.D. Evidence in New Zealand. 186
Garrow, J.M. & Willis, J.D. Wills. 189, 487
Gartside, L. Commerce. 81
Gatley, J.C.C. Libel & slander. 293, 457
Gattrell, V.A.C. Crime & law. 137, 221
Gaur, A.N. Arms, ammunition & explosives. 190, 198
Gay, W.I. Animal experimentations. 479
Gayler, J.I.& Purvis, R.L. Industrial law. 237
Gebhard, P.H. Sex offenders. 429
Geen, G.K.& Douglas, R.P.A. Pilotage. 157, 431, 484
Geldart, W.M. Elements. 173
Gelhorn, W. Ombudsmen. 345
Gellhorn, E. Antitrust. 95
General Agreement on Tariffs & Trade. Tariff protection. 208
General Dental Council. Dentists register. 147
Generous, W.T. Swords and scales. 125
George, E.F. Taxation. 412
George, E.F.& George, A. Flats. 115, 200, 285
George, K.D. & Joll, C. Competition policy. 95, 183
George, V. Social security. 435
George, V. & Lawson, R. Poverty & inequality. 372
George, P. Torts. 457
Gerber, R.J. Criminal justice. 130
Gerber, R.J. & McNany, P.D. Punishment. 396
Gerlis, S. Matrimonial & guardianship orders. 73, 305, 312
Germany. Civil code. 209
Gerhfield, E.M. Jewish jurisprudence. 263
Gertzel, C. Kenya. 273
Gerven, W.Van & Lukoff, F.L. Agency agreements. 183
Gevers, J. Patents. 357
Ghai, Y.P. & McAuslan, J.P.W.B. Public law in Kenya. 273
Ghanem, I. Islamic medical jurisprudence. 260, 315
Gheerbrant, P.A. & Palfreman, D. Banking cases. 39
Ghosh, D. Personal injury. 362
Ghosh, S.K. Bribery and corruption. 54
Giannastonio, E. Italian legal information retrival. 98.
Gibb, A.D. Collisions on land. 324
Gibb, A.D. Judicial corruption. 264
Gibb, A.D. Law from over the border. 422
Gibb, A.D. Preface to Scots law. 422
Gibb, A.D. Perjury unlimited. 361
Gibb, A.D. Scottish legal terms. 150, 422
Gibb, A.D. & Dalrymple, A.W. Dictionary. 422
Gibbens, T.C.N. Medical remands. 407
Gibbens, T.C.N. Psychiatric studies. 52
Gibbons D. Dilapidations & nuisance. 340
Gibbons, D.C. Society, crime & criminal behaviour. 137
Gibbons, S.R. & Morican, P. League of Nations. 284
Gibbs-Smith, C.H. Copyright. 28
Gibson, A. Conveyancing. 116
Gibson, A. Probate. 386
Gibson, B. Birmingham bombs. 478
Gibson, E. Codex juris ecclesiastica. 164
Gibson, E. Homicide. 223
Gibson, E. Time awaiting trial. 407
Gibson, E. & Klein, S. Murder 1957 to 1968. 223
Gibson, H. & Jackson, E. Valuation. 402
Gierke, O. Natural law. 269
Gijstra, D.J. & Murphy, D.F. Competition. 95, 183
Gijstra, D.J. & Murphy, D.F. European communities. 180
Gilbert, G.W. Motor insurance. 247
Gilbert, M. The law. 289
Gilbertson, G. German & English glossary. 150, 249
Giles, F.T. Magistrates' courts. 305
Giles, G.H. Ophthalmic services. 326
Giles, O.C. Commercial law. 81
Gill, D. Illegitimacy. 291
Gill, O. Whitegate. 24
Gill, R. Agricultural holdings. 16
Gill, T. & Whitty. Women's rights. 175
Gill, W.H. Arbitration. 24
Gillies, P. Criminal complicity. 135
Gillies, P. Criminal conspiracy. 102
Gillies, P. Criminal investigation. 128
Gilmore, G. Death of contracts. 111
Gilmore, G. & Black, C.L. Admiralty. 11
Gilpin, A. Dictionary of economic terms. 152
Gilson, J. Trademarks. 461
Ginnings, A.T. Arbitration. 24
Ginsberg, M. Law & opinion. 269
Giovannono, J.M. Child abuse. 71
Gladden, E.N. Public administration. 391
Gladwin, F.H. Valuation. 402
Gladwin, I. Sheriff. 430
Glahn, G. von. Law among nations. 249
Glaister, J. & Rentoul, E. Medical jurisprudence. 315

AUTHOR AND SHORT TITLE INDEX 549

Glanville, R. de. Tractatus. 220
Glasbeek, H.J. Evidence. 187
Glass, H.H. & McHugh, M.H.L. Liability of employers. 142, 167, 362
Glassey, L.K.J. Justices of the Peace. 221, 305
Glatt, M.M. Drugs, society & man. 162
Glazebrook, P.R. Reshaping criminal law. 131, 137
Gleason, J.H. Justice of the Peace. 305
Gledhill, A. India. 234
Gledhill, A. Pakistan. 347
Glegg, A.T. Reparation. 145
Glen, W.C. Burial. 57
Glen, W.C. & Glen, A. Registration of births. 49
Glendon, M.A. Family. 193
Glendon, M.A. State, law & family. 193, 196
Glick, L.A. Trading with Saudi Arabia. 81, 190
Glickman, M.J.A. From crime to rehabilitation. 406
Gloag, W.M. & Henderson, R.C. Law of Scotland. 422
Glover, E.G. Prostitution. 390
Gluckman, M. African custom and conflict. 15
Gluckman, M. African ideas and procedures. 15
Gluckman, M. African traditional laws. 15
Glueck, S. & Glueck, E.T. Delinquents. 146
Glyn, L.E. & Jackson, F.S. Mayor's court. 313
Gobbo, J.A and others. Cross on evidence (Australia). 187
Godber, Sir G. Health service. 326
Godwin, F. Fire insurance. 246
Godwin, G. Middle Temple. 243
Goebel, J. Felony & misdemeanour. 221
Goedhuis, D. National air legislation. 34
Goff, R. & Jones, G. Restitution. 114, 410
Goietein, H. Primitive ordeal. 380
Gold, E. Oil pollution. 344, 370
Gold, J. IMF. 252
Goldfarb, R.L. The contempt power. 108
Golding, C.E. Reinsurance. 248
Golding, L. Local government dictionary. 301
Golding, M.P. Philosophy. 269
Goldman, B. European commercial law. 81, 182
Goldring, J. Papua New Guinea constitution. 348
Goldring, J. & Maher, L.W. Australian consumer protection. 107
Goldring, J., Goldworthy, P.G. & Levine, J.R. Commercial transactions. 82
Goldsmith, I. Building contracts. 54
Goldsmith, I. Personal injury damages. 142, 362
Goldstein, A.S. The insanity defense. 133, 244
Goldstein, J. & Katz, J. Family & the law. 196

Goldstein, R.S. US immigration law. 231
Golembiewski, R.T. Public administration. 391
Golt, S. GATT. 208
Golzen, G. Working abroad. 169
Goodacre, J.K. Marine insurance. 247, 431
Goode, M.R. Criminal conspiracy. 102
Goode, R.M. Commercial law. 82
Goode, R.M. Commercial law statutes. 82
Goode, R.M. Consumer credit. 106
Goode, R.M. Consumer Credit Act. 106
Goode, R.M. Consumer Credit legislation. 106
Goode, R.M. Hire purchase. 106
Goode, R.M. Legal problems of credit. 106
Goode, R.M. & Grabiner, A.S. Exemption clauses. 113
Goode, R.M. & Ziegel, J.S. Hire purchase. 106
Gooderson, R. Alibi. 137
Goodeve, L.A. Personal property. 36, 363
Goodhart, A.L. Jewish lawyers. 263
Goodhart, A.L. Jurisprudence. 269, 373
Goodhart, A.L. Precedent. 266
Goodman, A. Court guide. 126
Goodman, J. Posts-mortem. 223
Goodman, Lord. Charity law. 70
Goodman, M.J. Industrial tribunals. 239
Goodman, N. & Price, J. Female offenders. 488
Goodman, W.D. Double taxation. 64, 159, 178
Goodrich, L.M. U.N. 472
Goodwin-Gill, G.S. International law. 257
Goodwin-Gill, G.S. Refugee. 405
Gordon, C. Atlantic alliance. 336
Gordon, F.S. & Hemnes, F.S. Legal word book. 150
Gordon, G.H. Criminal justice. 130
Gordon, G.H. Criminal law. 35, 134
Gordon, H.C. War Office. 214
Gordon, I. & Shapiro, H.A. Forensic medicine. 202, 324
Gordon, I., Turner, R.& Price, T.W. Medical jurisprudence. 315
Gordon, J.W. House of Lords. 22
Gordon, P. Whitelaw. 398
Gordon, P. Your rights. 76
Gordon, R.A. Compulsory acquisition. 97
Gordon, R.J.F. Caravans. 66
Gore-Brown, F. Companies. 89, 298
Gormley, W.P. Human rights. 228, 368
Gorton, L. Hybrid charter. 70
Gorton, L. & Ihre, R. Affreightment contracts. 113, 431
Gorton, L. & others. Shipbroking. 431
Gosse, R. Competition in Canada. 95
Gostin, L.O. Human condition. 317
Gostin, L.O. Mentally ill. 244

Gostin, L.O., Buchan, a. & Rossaby, E. Mental health. 317
Gotlieb, A.E. Human rights. 228, 255
Gotlieb, A.E. Treaty making. 61
Goudy, H. Bankruptcy. 37
Gough, J.W. Fundamental Law. 104
Gough, W.J. Company charges. 89
Gould, J. & Craigmyle, Lord. Euthanasia. 185
Gour, H.S. Hindu law. 218
Government of Ireland. Accession of Ireland. 181
Gow, J.J. Hire purchase in Scotland. 106
Gow, J.J. Mercantile law. 82, 237
Gower, L.C.B. Company law. 89, 298
Gower, L.C.B. Independent Africa. 15
Graber, D.A. Belligerent occupation. 481
Grace, C. & Wilkinson, P. Negotiating the law. 486
Gradwohl, R.B.H. Legal medicine. 315
Graeff, J.J.de & Polack, J.H. Pollution control. 368
Grahl-Madsen, A. Refugees. 30, 405
Graham, H. Mother of parliaments. 351
Graham-Green, G.J. Criminal costs. 123, 132, 286
Gram, P. Chartering documents. 70
Grampian Police. Road traffic 416
Grampian Police. Scottish criminal law. 134, 366
Grant, B. Conciliation & divorce. 155
Grand, B. & Levin, J. Family law. 193
Grand, D.W. & Cook, H.S. Adoption proceedings. 12, 273
Grandt, J. Bankers. 39
Grant, J.P. Independence & devolution. 149, 422
Grand, L. & Martin, I. Immigration law. 231
Grant, M. Planning law. 459
Gras, N.S.B. Customs system. 140
Grattan-Doyle, H.N. Auctioneers & estate agents. 30, 177
Grau, J.J. Criminal & civil investigator. 128
Graulich, P. Legal materials. 43
Graupner, R. Rules of competition. 95, 183
Graves, W.B. Public administration. 391
Graveson, R.H. Conflict of laws. 100
Graveson, R.H. Status in the common law. 85
Graveson, R.H. Uniform laws. 82, 420
Graveson, R.H. & Crane, F.R. Family law. 193
Gray, B. Juvenile court. 173
Gray, C.M. Copyhold. 117
Gray, H. Anatomy. 19
Gray, H.R. Civil injuries. 362
Gray, J.C. Perpetuities. 361
Gray, K.J. Reallocation of property. 155, 197
Gray, K.J. & Symes, P.D. Real property. 403
Gray, T.C. & Nunn, J.F. Anaesthesia. 19
Gray, W.F. Old Scots judges. 264

Grayson, T.J. Investment trusts. 259
Greater London Council.Index to statutes. 303
Greater London Council. London building. 303
Greater London Council. Parish registers. 303
Greater London Council. Pollution. 368
Greater London Council. Public entertainment. 174
Green, A.W. Legal education bbliography. 43, 287
Green, A.W. Political integration. 184
Green, C.A.H. Church in Wales. 164, 479
Green, E. Judicial attitudes. 264, 428
Green, E.S. & Henderson, N. Land law. 275
Green, L.C. International Law. 252
Green, N.A.M. International law. 249
Green, S.A. & Gabriel, K.W. Rules of origin. 185
Greene, M.R. Risk and insurance. 245
Greenhalgh, G. Nuclear power. 338
Greenhalgh, R.M. Industrial tribunals. 169, 239
Greenidge, A.H.L. Cicero's time. 418
Greenidge, A.H.J. Roman public life. 418
Greenspan, M. Warfare. 481
Greenstreet, B. Architects 26, 54, 113.
Greenwood, C. Firearms control. 198
Greenwood, J.R. & Wilson, D.J. Public administration. 391
Greenwood, P.W. Criminal investigation. 128
Greenwood, V. & Young, J. Abortion. 4
Greenwood, T., Feiveson, H.A. & Taylor, T. Nuclear proliferation. 339
Greer, D.S. & Mitchell, V.A. Criminal damage compensaion. 403
Greer, D.S. & Mitchell, V.A. Criminal injuries compensation. 128
Gregory, M. Angling. 20
Gregory, M. & Hutcheson, P. Parliamentary ombudsman. 345
Gregory, M. & Parrish, M. Landowners & farmers. 16, 279
Gregory, T. Banking. 39
Greig, D. Sale of goods. 420
Greig, D.W. International law. 249
Grenville, J.A.S. Treaties. 466
Gres, J. & Jung, H. German employment law. 209
Grice, S. Commonwealth organizations. 86, 154
Grierson, E. Confessions of a country magistrate. 305
Grieves, F.L. Supranationalism. 251
Griew, E.J. Criminal Law Act. 131
Griew, E.J. Dishonesty & jury. 267
Griew, E.J. Theft Acts. 454
Griffin, B.S. & Griffin, C.T. Juvenile delinquency. 146

Griffith, J.A.G. Central departments. 9
Griffin, J.A. Papua New Guinea criminal procedure. 348
Griffith, J.A.G. Local authorities. 9
Griffith, J.A.G. Parliamentary scrutiny. 351
Griffith, J.A.G. Policy to administration. 9
Griffith, J.A.G. Politics of the judiciary. 265
Griffith, J.A.G. & Street, H. Administrative law. 9
Griffith, O. Bankruptcy. 144, 404
Griffith, O. & Taylor, E.M. Liquidators & receivers. 298
Griffith, R.G.B. Probate. 386
Griffiths, A. Local government administration. 301
Griffiths, R. Censorship. 67
Griffits, S.O. Crown Office. 309, 377
Grilliot, H.J. Introduction in law. 7, 474
Grime, R. Maritime & offshore employment. 169
Grime, R. Shipping law. 431
Grime, R.P. Noise-induced hearing loss. 236, 335
Grimes, R.H. & Horgan, P.T. Ireland. 260
Grimond, J. Common welfare. 486
Grindon, J.B. Coroners. 119
Grisoli, A. Italian legal materials. 43, 262
Grob, F. War & peace. 359, 481
Groove, S. Space law. 442
Grosman, B.A. Prosecutor. 389
Gross, E. Criminal justice. 130
Gross, H. Criminal investigation. 129
Gross, H. & Hirch, A.von. Sentencing. 428
Gross, L. International court. 253
Gross, L. International law. 249
Gross, P. Legal aid. 286
Grossman, J.B. Constitutional law. 474
Grotius, H. Jurisprudence of Holland. 471
Grout, V. Tolley's tax cases. 412
Grout, V. VAT cases. 476
Grover, L.C.E. Apportionment. 23
Groves, H.E. Constitutional law. 93
Groves, H.E. Malaysia constitution. 309
Grubel, H. & Johnson, H. Tariff protection. 208
Grumm, J.G. Paradigm. 290
Grundy, M. Tax. 233
Grundy, M. Tax havens. 451
Grundy, M. Tax planning. 451
Grunfeld, C. Redundancy. 169, 405
Grunfeld, C. Trade union law. 463
Grunhut, M. Juvenile offenders. 146
Grunhut, M. Probation. 387
Grupp, S.E. Punishment. 396
Grygier, T. Criminology in transition. 137
Grygier, T. Social protection code. 130
Grzybowski, K. Soviet international law. 257
Guenault, P.H. & Jackson, J.M. Monopoly. 322

Guest, A.G. Consumer credit. 106
Guest, A.G. Hire purchase. 106
Guest, A.G. Jurisprudence. 269
Guest, A.g. & Lomnicka, E. Credit. 106
Guest, C.W.G. Valuation. 402
Guhin, M.A. Nuclear paradox. 338
Guidebook to Australian trademarks law. 461
Gulliver, A.G. Gratuitious transfers. 211
Gumbel, W. & Potter, K. Iron & Steel Act. 260
Gunn, J. Violence. 478
Gunn, J. & Farrington, D.P. Abnormal offenders. 130, 146
Gunningham, N. Pollution. 368
Gunter, H. Industrial relations. 238
Gupta, B.B. Comparative study of constitutions. 93, 103
Gurr, T. Rogues. 394
Gurvitch, G. Sociology of law. 269
Gushue, R. & Day, D. Family law in Newfoundland. 195
Gustafson, G. Forensic odontology. 147
Gutteridge, H.C. Codification. 100
Gutteridge, H.C. Comparative law. 93, 100
Gutteridge, H.C.& Megrah, M. Commercial credit. 39, 80
Gutteridge, J.A.C. U.N. 472
Guy, D. & Leigh, G. EEC & intellectual property. 118, 182
Guy, J.A. Cardinal's court. 221
Guyenot, J. French agency agreements. 16
Gwynne, d. & Brown, J. Children under supervision. 73
Haanappel, P.P.C. Air transport pricing. 34
Haanappel, P.P.C. Air transport ratemaking. 34, 464
Hacker, P.M.S. & Raz, J. Law, morality & society. 269
Hackett, M.G. Cambridge University. 60
Hadden, T. Company law. 89
Hadden, T. Control of corporate groups. 121
Hadden, T. Housing. 226, 279
Hadfield, S.J. Law for doctors. 315
Hadley, A. X-ray terminology. 490
Haesler, T. International Courts. 253
Hagberg, L. Enforced sale of vessels. 431
Hagberg, L. Maritime law. 27
Hagen, W.W. & Johnson, G.H. Business law.
Hague, N. Leasehold enfranchisement. 285
Hahlog, H.R. Husband & wife. 196, 311, 439
Hahlo, H.R. South African divorce. 155
Hahlo, H.R. & Kahn, E. South African legal system. 439
Hahlo, H.R. & Trebilcock, M.J. Company law. 89
Hahn, H. Police in urban society. 366
Hailsham, Lord & McEwen, R. Monopolies. 322
Hain, P. Mistaken identity. 230

Haksar, U. Minority protection. 228, 255
Halberstadt, R. Book-keeping. 6, 438
Halderman, J.W. U.N. and the rule of law. 472
Hale, M. History of common law. 85
Haley, A.G. Space law. 442
Haley, A.G. Space torts. 442
Hall, C.G. Water rights in South Africa. 439, 484
Hall, H.D. Mandates. 255
Hall, J. Comparative law. 93
Hall, J.A. Naval warfare. 329, 481
Hall, J.C. Family law. 193
Hall, J.G. & Mitchell, B.H. Child abuse. 71, 273
Hall, L.E. Liens. 36
Hall, M.J. United Arab Emirates companies law. 89
Hall, R.E. Abortion. 4
Hall, R.G. Foreshore law. 199
Hall, R.G. Rights of the Crown. 416, 453
Hall, S. Policing. 366, 394
Hall, W.E. Foreign jurisdiction. 139
Hall, W.E. International law. 249
Hall, W.E. Neutrals. 481
Hall Williams, J.E. Parole. 352
Hall Williams, J.E. Penal system. 396
Hallam, H. Constitutional history. 104
Hallett, C. & Stevenson, O. Child abuse. 71
Hallett, V.G.H. & Warren, N. Settlements. 64, 310, 487
Hallett, V.G.H. & Warren, N. Trust planning. 451, 468
Halliday, J.M. Conveyancing. 116
Halliday, J.M. Land registration. 277
Halliday, J.M. Land tenure. 278
Halnan, P. Drinking/driving. 161
Halpern, L. Taxes in France. 205, 412
Halpern, S. Future of our liberties. 45
Hambly, D. & Turner, J.N. Australian family law. 194, 232
Hambro's capital taxes. 178
Hambro's Tax Guide. 63, 64
Hamburger, M. Western legal thought. 269
Hames, J.H. Married Women's Property Act. 197
Hamilton, N. Double taxation. 159
Hamilton, P. Espionage & subversion. 394
Hamilton, R. Corporations. 121, 122
Hamilton, R.N.D. Compensation for compulsory acquisition. 116, 97
Hamilton, R.N.D. Development & planning. 459
Hamilton, R.N.D. Land charges. 276
Hamilton, R.N.D. Planning procedure tables. 459
Hammond, A. Criminal code. 78
Hammett, I. Chieftanship. 292
Hampton, C. Criminal procedure. 132, 187, 376

Hamson, C.J. Executive discretion. 392
Hanbury, H.G. Agency. 16
Hanbury, H.G. & Maudsley, R.H. Modern equity. 176
Hanbury, H.G. & Yardley, D.C.M. English courts. 126
Hancock, W.K. & Latham, R.T.E. Nationality. 328
Hand, G., Georgel, J. & Sasse, C. European electoral systems. 166, 183
Hand, G.J. English law in Ireland. 220, 336
Hands, J. Housing corporations. 227
Hanham, H.J. Nineteenth century constitution. 105
Hanlon, J.J. & Pickett, G.E. Public Health. 393
Hannah, H.W. & Sturm, D.F. Veterinarian. 477
Hannen, J.R. Borstal policy. 52
Hannum, H. Human rights. 278
Hansell, D.S. Insurance. 245
Hanson, A.H. & Wiseman, H.V. Parliament at work. 350
Hanson, J.L. Monetary theory. 252, 320
Harari, A. Negligence. 457
Harding, A. Law courts. 126, 220
Harding, A. Law making. 219
Harding, A. Shropshire Eyre Roll. 219
Harding, A. Social history of law. 219
Harding, A.L. Religion. 407
Harding, J. Employment, probation & after care. 169, 387
Harding, R. Firearms and violence. 198
Hardingham, I.J. & Bayt, R. Discretionary trials. 468
Hardingham, I.J., Neave, M.A. & Ford, H.A.J. Wills. 487
Hardingham, I.J. Intestate succession. 449
Hardman, J.P. Development land tax. 148, 412
Hardman, J.P. & Bertram, A.D.W. Liquidation. 298
Hardy, M. Diplomatic law. 153
Harfield, H. Bank letters of credit. 80
Hargreaves, A.D. Land law. 275, 403
Hargreaves, M. Nurses. 340
Hargreaves-Maudsley, W.M. Legal dress. 287
Hargrove, J.L. Global environment. 368
Haring, B. Medical ethics. 28
Harland, D.J. Law of minors. 73, 111, 403
Harlow, C. & Rawlings, R. Law and administration. 9
Harlow, P.A. Contractual claims bibliography. 43, 111
Harmer, C. & Camp, P. Partnership. 353
Harmer, F.E. Anglo-Saxon Writs. 220
Harper, A.C. Stamp duty. 63, 445
Harper, M. Landlord v Tenant. 279
Harper, R.W. Port of London. 304

Harper, W. Divorce. 155
Harries, J. Employment protection. 171
Harries, J.V. Consumers. 107
Harris, B. Bail. 35
Harris, B. Blood test. 50, 291
Harris, B. Criminal jurisdiction of magistrates. 305
Harris, B. Family proceedings. 12, 193, 305, 312
Harris, B. Legal aid. 286
Harris, B. Magistrates' ABC. 305
Harris, B. Magistrates' companion. 305, 428
Harris, B. Magistrates' meetings. 305
Harris, B. Maintenance & custody. 305, 308
Harris, B. Rehabilitation. 406
Harris, B. Search warrants. 129, 306
Harris, B. & Ryan, G. Common land. 86, 275, 349
Harris, D.J. Cases on international law. 252
Harris, G.E. Certiorari. 68
Harris, J. Your business. 82
Harris, J.W. Law & legal science. 269
Harris, J.W. Legal philosophies. 269
Harris, J.W. Variation of trusts. 468
Harris, P. Estate planning. 178, 247, 451
Harris, P. & Hewson, D. Life assurance. 247, 451
Harris, P. & Lewis, R. Teaching law. 288
Harris, R. Advocacy. 13
Harris, R. & Ryan, G. Common land. 217
Harrison, E.R. Index to tax cases. 233, 412
Harrison, F. & Maddox, A.J. Work of a magistrate. 306
Harrison, Sir G. Stannaries. 445
Harrison, G. & Bloy, D. Law for teachers. 165
Harrison, J.G. Taxation of land. 279
Harrison, J. Hume's theory. 270
Harrison, R. C.I.D. & F.B.I. 366
Harrison, W.N. Land law. 275
Harrison, W.R. Suspect documents. 292
Harrold, B. & White A. Summary process. 306, 376, 389
Harrowes, D.H.S. Partnership office. 353, 438
Hart, C.E. Commoners of Dean Forest. 203
Hart, C.E. Forest of Dean. 203
Hart, C.E. Venderers of Dean. 203
Hart, E.A.P. Inner Temple. 243
Hart, G.E. Copyhold. 117
Hart, H.L. Banking. 39
Hart, H.L.A. Concept of law. 270
Hart, H.L.A. Definition and theory. 270
Hart, H.L.A. Law, liberty & morality. 270
Hart, H.L.A. Jurisprudence. 270
Hart, H.L.A. Morality of criminal law. 131, 270
Hart, H.L.A. Negligence. 330
Hart, H.L.A. Punishment. 270, 396
Hart, H.L.A., Hacker, P.M.S. & Raz, J. Law,
morality & society. 270
Hart, H.L.A. & Honore, A.M. Causation. 457
Hart, J.M.M. British police. 366
Hart, Sir W.O. & Garner, J.F. Local government. 301
Hartland, E.S. Primitive law. 380
Hartley, S.F. Illegitimacy. 291
Hartley, T.C. EEC immigration law. 180, 231
Hartley, T.C. & Griffith, J.A.G. Government & law. 212
Harvard University, Law School Library. Catalogue of international law. 151
Harvey, A. Remedies for rent arrears. 409
Harvey, B.W. Consumer protection. 107, 192
Harvey, B.W. Costs in Nigeria. 332
Harvey, B.W. Lawyer and justice. 270
Harvey, B.W. Nigerian wills. 189, 333, 449
Harvey, B.W. Settlement of land. 275, 403
Harvey, C.P. Advocate's devil. 13
Harvey, E.L. Tolley's income tax. 412
Harvey, E.L. Tolley's Irish taxation. 412
Harvey, J.L. & Newgarden, A. Mergers & acquisitions. 449
Harvey, R.J. & Thompson, A. Employment protection. 171
Harvey, R.J.S. Industrial relations. 169, 238, 471
Harvey, W.B. East African legal system. 15
Harwood, M. Land. 275, 403
Hasan, A. Islamic jurisprudence. 261
Haskell, M.R. & Yablonsky, L. Crime & delinquency. 146
Haskins, G.D. U.S. Supreme Court. 474
Haslam, J. Medical jurisprudence. 315
Hassumani, A.P. Administrative law, India. 234
Hatchard, J. & Ndulo, M. Criminal law casebook. 135, 491
Havard, J.D. Secret homicide. 129, 202, 223
Havenga, J.D. Retailing. 95
Havighurst, C.C. Air pollution. 370
Haw, R. State of matrimony. 310
Hawke, N. Administrative law. 9
Hawkes, C.P. Bench & Bar. 408
Hawkes, C.P. Chambers in the Temple. 408
Hawkes, C.P. Heyday. 408
Hawkes, D. Incest. 232
Hawkins, A.J. Land. 275, 457
Hawkins, F.V. Wills. 487
Hawkins, G. Prison. 381
Hawkins, K. Deprivation of liberty. 396
Hawkins, K. Environment of enforcement. 174, 368
Hawkins, K. Parole. 353
Hawkins, N. Housing grants. 226
Haxby, D. Probation. 387
Hay, P. US law. 474
Hayard, E.J. & Wright, H. Office of a magistrate. 306

Hayek, F.A. Law, legislation & liberty. 9
Hayek, F.A. Rent control. 409
Hayllar, R.f. & Rouse, R.M. Oil & gas taxation. 207, 344, 412
Haynes, R.J. Local government. 301, 391
Hayton, D.J. Registrered land. 116, 277
Hayton, D.J. & Tiley, J. Capital transfer tax. 64
Hazard, J.N. Soviet Government. 441
Hazard, J.N. & Hoya, T.W. Soviet law 93, 441
Hazard, J.N. & Weisberg, M.C. Soviet law readings. 441
Hazard, J.N. & others. Soviet legal system. 441.
Hazell, R. Bar on trial. 40
Hazell, R. Conspiracy. 102
Hazzard, S. Defeat of an ideal. 472
Head, F.D. Meetings. 316
Headley, B.W. Cabinet ministers. 59
Healey, B. Arbitration. 25
Health, Ministry of, Social Workers.437
Health & Safety Executive. Agricultural legislation. 16
Health & Safety Executive. Air pollution. 370
Health & Safety Executive. Factories Act. 192
Health & Safety Executive Mines & quarries. 319
Health & Safety Executive. Tanker marking regulations. 421
Health & Social Security, Dept. of. Abortion Act. 4
Health & Social Security, Dept. of. Access to children. 73
Health & Social Security, Dept.of. Child abuse reports. 71
Health & Social Security, Dept.of. Children in care. 73
Health & Social Security, Dept.of. Family allowances. 327, 435
Health & Social Security, Dept.of. Hospital administration. 225
Health & Social Security, Dept.of. Industrial inquiries medical boards. 435
Health & Social Security, Dept. of. Maria Colwell. 71
Health & Social Security, Dept.of. Mental Health Act. 317
Health & Social Security, Dept.of. Mine, yours or ours? 12
Health & Social Security, Dept.of. National Health Service. 326
Health & Social Security, Dept.of. Pensions Appeal Tribunals. 435
Health & Social Security, Dept.of. Prevention & health. 393
Health & Social Security, Dept.of. Public health. 393
Health & Social Security, Dept.of. Social workers. 73, 486

Health & Social Security, Dept.of. Supplementary benefits. 435
Health & Social Security, Dept.of. Treatment & rehabilitation. 162
Health & Social Security, Dept.of. Workmen's compensation. 489
Health & Social Security for Northern Ireland, Dept.of. Legislation of services for children. 73
Health Service Commissioner. Report. 326, 345, 393
Healy, M. Munster circuit. 408.
Heap, D. Community Land Act. 87
Heap, Sir D. Land. 275
Heap, D. Planning encyclopaedia. 211
Heap, D. Town & Country Planning. 217
Hearn, P. Industrial licensing. 357
Heath, J. Penal theory. 396
Heath, T.L. The Treasury. 214
Heathcote-Williams, H., Roberts, E. & Berstein, R. Restrictive Trade Practices. 322
Hebson, R. Lawyer's draftbook. 160
Heclo, H. & Wildavsky, A. Public money. 320
Hedges, R.Y. & Winterbottom, A. Trade Unionism. 463
Hedley, P. & Aynsley, C. 'D' Notices. 141
Heere, W.P. Air law. 34
Heibron, R. Rape report. 401
Heim, A.W. Thicker than water. 12
Heineman, B.W. Politics of the powerless. 398
Helfer, R.E. & Kempe, C. Battered child. 71
Helmholz, R.H. Marriage litigation. 220, 310
Helmore, B.A. Sale of land. 275
Hemer, J. & Stanyer, A. Widows. 488.
Henderson, E.G. Administrative law. 9, 68, 309
Henderson, H. Oil and gas. 344
Henderson, J. Employment protection. 172
Henderson, J. Trade Unions. 463
Henham, J.A. Magistrates' powers. 306, 428
Henig, R.B. League of Nations. 284
Henig, S. European Community association. 182
Henkin, A.H. Human dignity. 228
Henn, H. Corporations. 122
Hennessy, J.M. TSB legislation. 39
Henry, N. Public administration. 391
Henry, R.L. Medieval contracts. 220
Hensey, B.J. Irish healt services. 393
Henshel, R.L. & Silverman, R.A. Perception. 137
Hepker, M.Z. Tax. 413
Hepker, M.Z. Tax strategy. 451
Hepker, M.Z. & Whitehouse, C.J. Capital transfer tax. 65
Heppell, E.A. Products liability insurance. 248, 388
Hepple, B.A. Equal pay. 175, 239

AUTHOR AND SHORT TITLE INDEX

Hepple, B.A. Labour relations. 238
Hepple, B.A. Race, jobs & law. 398
Hepple, B.A. & Matthews, M.H. Tort. 457
Hepple, B.A. & O'Higgins, P. Employment. 169, 238
Hepple, B.A. & O'Higgins, P. Labour law bibliography. 43, 169
Hepple, B.A.& O'Higgins, P. Labour relations. 169
Hepworth, N.P. Local government. 301, 402
Her Majesty's Stationery Office. Water laws. 484
Herbert, Sir A.P. The ayes have it. 351
Herbert, Sir A.P. More uncommon law. 270
Herbert, Sir A.P. Point of parliament. 351
Hebert, Sir A.P. Uncommon law. 270
Herbert, D. Solicitors. 438
Herbert, Sir E.S. London local government commission. 303
Herbert, T.A. Prescription. 378
Herd, C.O. Temple Church. 243
Herlihy, J.M. & Kenny, R.G. Criminal law. 135
Herman, A. Shipping. 431
Herman, H.M. Estoppel. 179
Herman, J.L. Father/daughter incest. 232
Hermann, A.H. Judges, law & businessmen. 82, 264
Hermann, A.H. & Jones, C. Fair trading. 192
Hershey, N. & Miller, R.D. Human experimentation. 230, 315
Hertz, M. Conflict of laws. 100
Hervey, J.G. Recognition in international law. 255
Herzog, I. Jewish law. 263
Hetherington, H.J.W. Mareva injunctions. 241
Heumann, M. Plea bargaining. 135, 265
Heuston, R.F.V. Constitutional law. 103, 384
Heuston, R.F.V. Lord Chancellors. 48, 304
Hevener, N.K. Status of women. 488
Heward, E. Chancery practice. 68, 176
Hewitt, A.R. Public library law. 294, 325
Hewitt, E.E. Administration & probate. 386
Hewitt, P. Abuse of power. 76
Hewitt, P. Computers, records & privacy. 98, 383
Hewitt, P. Privacy. 383
Hewitt, P. Rights for women. 488
Hewitson, T. Suretyship. 215
Heydon, J.D. Economic torts. 457
Heydon, J.D. Evidence. 187
Heydon, J.D. Restraint of trade. 113, 322
Heydon, J.D. Gummon, W.M.C. & Austin, R.P. Equity & trusts. 176, 468
Hewyood, J.S. Children in care. 73
Heywood, N.A. & Massey, A.S. Court of protection. 125, 244, 475
Hibbert, C. Roots of evil. 111, 396
Hickmott, G.J.R. Interuption insurance. 245, 248

Hicks, A. Nigerian hire-purchase. 333
Hiden, M. Ombudsman in Finland. 345
Hiemstra, V.G. Criminal procedure. 130, 440
Hiemstra, V.G. & Gonin, H.L. Trilingual legal dictionary. 150, 440
Higgins, A.P. Hague Peace Conference. 481
Higgins, A.P. International law. 249
Higgins, A.P. Law & order. 9
Higgins, A.P. War. 481
Higgins, P.F.P. Partnership in Australia & New Zealand. 353
Higgins, P.F.P. Torts in Australia. 457
Higgins, R. Development of international law. 472
Higgins, R. U.N. peacekeeping. 15, 359, 472
Highmore, N.J. Customs laws. 140
Highmore, N.J. Excise laws. 141
Hilbery, M. Advocacy. 13
Hildebrand, J.L. Noise pollution. 335
Hildreth, R.G. & Johnson, R.W. Ocean & coastal law. 425, 426, 453
Hill, C. Maritime law. 431
Hill, C.P.A. Charity trustees. 70
Hill, D.G. Stamp duties. 445
Hill, D.J. Freight forwarders. 66, 431
Hill, D.M. Democratic theory. 301
Hill, G. Treasure trove. 119, 465
Hill, H.A. Housing. 226
Hill, H.A. & Redman, J.H. Landlord & tenant. 229, 343, 373
Hill, L.B. Ombudsman. 345
Hill, M. Immunities & privileges. 153
Hill, M. Unemployed. 405
Hill, R. Tax aspects of incorporation. 122, 413
Hillier, A. Contracts of employment. 169
Hillier, A. Dismissal. 169
Hillier, A. Employment Act. 169
Hinde, G.W. Law dictionary. 150
Hinde, G.W. Torrens system. 456
Hinde, G.W. & Sim, P.B.A. New Zealand land law. 275
Hinde, R.S.E. Penal system. 396
Hindell, K. & Simms, M. Abortion. 4
Hindley, Sir C. Cabs. 452
Hindmarsh, A.E. Force in peace. 255
Hine, R.L. Uncommon attorney. 408
Hines, V.G. Judicial discretion. 428
Hirsch, R. & Trento, J. N.A.S.A. 441
Hirst, P.H. Law & ideology. 270
Hjertonsson, K. Law of the sea. 425
Hoath, D.C. Council housing. 226, 486
Hochstedler, E. Corporations as criminals. 122
Hodes, A. Art & antiques. 28
Hodge, A.G. Scottish law directory. 154, 422
Hodgin, R.W. Contract in East Africa. 15
Hodgin, R.W. Mercantile law. 82
Hodgkin, E.C. & Hodgkin, N.I. Involvement

of community. 130, 396
Hodgson, G. Lloyd's. 245, 431
Hodgson, J. English legal heritage. 173
Hoebel, E.A. Primitive man. 380
Hoffer, P.C. & Hull, N.E.H. Impeachment. 232
Hoffman, L.C. South African evidence. 187
Hoffman, D. & Schaub, S. German competiton law. 95
Hogan, A.E. Blockade. 255
Hogan, B.A. Career in law. 289
Hogarth, J. Sentencing. 428
Hogg, P.W. Canada Act. 61
Hogg, P.W. Canadian constitution. 61
Hogg, P.W. Crown liability. 139, 215, 457
Hoggett, B.M. Family, law & society. 193
Hoggett, B.M. Mental health. 317
Hoggett, B.M. Parents & children. 73, 193
Hoghughi, M. Delinquent. 146
Hogue, A. Common law. 85
Hogwood, B.W. Regional government. 301
Holborn, L.W. Refugees. 405
Holborn Law Society. Trade Union & Labour Relations Act. 238
Holden, D.A. Child legislation. 73
Holden, J.M. Bankers' advances. 215
Holden, J.M. Negotiable instruments. 330
Holden, J.M. Securities. 39, 215
Holder, A.R. Legal issues in paediatrics. 315
Holder, A.. Medical malpractice. 316
Holder, W.E. & Brennan, G.A. International legal system. 31, 252
Holdert, H.M.C. & Buzek, F.J. Collision cases. 79
Holdsworth, Sir W.S. History. 104, 219
Holdsworth, Sir W.S. Land law. 275, 373
Holdsworth, Sir W.S. Law reporting. 284
Holdsworth, Sir, W.S. Sources & literature. 43
Holland, J.A. & Lewis, J.R. Conveyancing. 116, 277
Holland, R.H.C. & Schwarzenburger, G. Law & justice. 9
Holland, Sir T.E. International law. 249
Holland, T.E. Prize. 385
Holland, T.E. War. 481
Holland, W. Unmarried couples. 79
Hollander, B. Art. 28
Holleman, J.F. Issues in African law. 15
Hollick, A.I. & Osgood, R.E. Ocean politics. 425
Hollis, C. Homicide Act. 223
Hollis, C. Parliament & its sovereign. 351
Holloway, D.R.Le B. Probate. 386, 487
Holmes, O.W. Common law. 85, 373
Holt, B.A.W. Liquidator. 298
Holyst, B. Comparative criminology. 137
Home, J. Trade unionists. 463
Home Office. Abnormal offenders. 244

Home Office. Adoption. 12
Home Office. Adjudication procedures in prisons. 381
Home Office. Age of consent. 429
Home Office. Animal experiments. 479
Home Office. Attachment of earnings. 30
Home Office. Bail. 35, 306
Home Office. British nationality. 328
Home Office. Brixton disorders. 394
Home Office. Broadcasting. 399
Home Office. Channel Islands. 103, 261
Home Office. Child, family and Young offender. 146
Home Office. Children and the cinema. 197
Home Office. Children and young persons. 73, 146
Home Office. Children in trouble. 146
Home Office. Comparative research. 137
Home Office. Complaints against the police. 366
Home Office. Computers. 383
Home Office. Coroners. 120
Home Office. Court of Criminal Appeal. 22, 127
Home Office. Crime and community. 137
Home Office. Crime in public view. 137
Home Office. Crime prevention. 127, 366
Home Office. Criminal injuries. 128
Home Office. Criminal justice policy. 130
Home Office. Criminal statistics. 445
Home Office. Data protection. 98
Home Office. Death certification. 120
Home Office. Detention centres. 148
Home Office. Electoral register. 166
Home Office. Equality for women. 175
Home Office. Evidence of identification. 187
Home Office. Fire Precautions Act. 198
Home Office. Firearms. 198
Home Office. Habitual drunken offender. 18
Home Office. Homosexual offences. 223
Home Office. Hostels for offenders. 148, 396
Home Office. Hostels for probationers. 387
Home Office. Human rights. 76
Home Office. Identification. 231
Home Office Interception of communications. 374, 452
Home Office. Interrogation. 394
Home Office. Isle of Man. 69, 103, 261
Home Office. Judicial training. 264
Home Office. Junior attendance centres. 148
Home Office. Life sentence prisoners. 381
Home Office. Lotteries. 41
Home Office. Magistrates' sentencing practice. 306, 417
Home Office Metropolitan police court districts. 367
Home Office. Motor vehicle offences. 416
Home Office. New trials. 22
Home Office. Nuclear weapons. 339

AUTHOR AND SHORT TITLE INDEX 557

Home Office. Obscenity. 67, 197, 341
Home Office. Official Secrets Act. 343
Home Office. Parole. 353
Home Office. Penal practice. 396
Home Office. Police cautioning.
Home Office. Police conditions of service. 367
Home Office. Police/immigrant relations. 398
Home Office. Police interrogation. 367
Home Office. Prevention of Terrorism Acts. 478
Home Office. Previous convictions. 137
Home Office. Prison department. 381
Home Office. Prison escapes. 381
Home Office. Prisons and the prisoner. 381
Home Office. Probation. 387
Home Office. Probation research. 387
Home Office. Probationers. 387
Home Office. Public disorder. 394
Home Office. Race, crime & arrests. 27, 137, 398
Home Office. Race relations research. 398
Home Office. Racial discrimination. 398
Home Office. Rape. 401
Home Office. Red Lion Square disorders. 394
Home Office. Rehabilitation. 406
Home Office. Rehabilitation of drug addicts. 162
Home Office. Reparation by the offender. 410
Home Office. Research & criminal policy. 137
Home Office. Safety at fairs. 310
Home Office. Sentence of the court. 396, 428
Home Office. Sexual offences. 428, 429
Home Office. Shoplifting. 433
Home Office. Social inquiry reports. 137, 387
Home Office. Social work. 387
Home Office. Social work in prison. 406
Home Office. Tackling vandalism. 137
Home Office. Taking offenders out of circulation. 137, 396
Home Office. Taperecording of police interrogation. 366
Home Office. Taxicab trade. 452
Home Office. United Kingdom & Isle of Man. 69, 103, 261
Home Office. Vagrancy & street offences. 390, 475
Home Office. Water safety. 484
Home Office. Wiping the slate clean. 406
Home Office. Workmen's compensation. 489
Home Office. Young adult offenders. 52
Home Office. Youth custody. 52, 137, 148, 382
Home Office & Law Officers Dept. Independent prosecution service. 389
Home Office & Scottish Home Dept. Artificial insemination. 28
Home Office & Scottish Home Dept. Criminal injuries. 128
Home Office & Scottish Home & Health Dept. European Assembly elections. 166, 174
Home Office & Scottish Office. Public Order Act. 394
Home Office & Transport, Dept.of. Road traffic. 416
Honderich, T. Punishment. 397
Hondius, E.H. Netherlands consumer legislation. 107
Hondius, F.W. Computer & international law. 98
Hondius, F.W. Data protection. 98, 383
Honig, J.P. Aircraft. 34
Honore, A.M. South African trusts. 469
Honore, T. Sex law. 223, 310, 390, 429, 489
Hood, R. Borstal. 52
Hood, R. Crime, criminology. 137
Hood, R. Motoring offender. 416, 428
Hood, R. Sentencing. 416, 428
Hood, R. Tolerence & the tariff. 428
Hood, R. & Sparks, R.F. Key issues. 137
Hook, S. Revolution. 415
Hooker, M.B. Adat laws. 309
Hooker, M.B. Malaysia. 309
Hooper, A.C. Voluntary liquidation. 299
Hooper, D. Public scandal. 293
Hooper, G. International trade. 82
Hoopes, T.W. Perpetuities. 361
Hooson, E. Bill of Rights. 45
Hope, T. Major practicks. 422
Hope, T. Minor practicks. 422
Hopkins, B.R. Charitable giving. 70
Hopkins, F. Formation & Annulment. 310
Hopkins, F.N. Business for shipmaster, 82, 431
Hopkins, L. & others. Accountancy. 6
Horan, D.J. & Mall, D. Death, dying & euthanasia. 185
Hordern, A. Legal abortion. 4
Horgan, M.O. & Roulston, F.R. Engineering contracts. 54
Horn, N. & Schmitthoff, C.M. Transnational law. 82
Horn, N. German private & commercial law. 209
Hornby, J.A. Company law. 89
Horowitz, D.L. Jurocracy. 289
Horrell, M. Race relations. 324
Horsley, D.B. Motor vehicle. 324
Horsley, M.G. Associations. 29
Horsley, M.G. Meetings. 316
Hosking, G.A. Pension schemes. 360
Hospital Physicists Association. Radiological protection. 490
Hosten, W.J. South African law. 440
Hotchen, J.S. Drug Misuse. 162
Houdek, F.G. Introducing A.A.L.L. 295
Hough, M. & Mayhew, P. British crime survey. 138

Houghton, A.R. & Cooper, N.H. European insolvency. 37
Houghton, R. Police charges. 367
Houlbrooke, R.A. Church courts. 164
Houlden, L.W. & Morawetz, C.H. Bankruptcy. 37
House of Lords. Form of appeal. 22, 127
House of Lords. Lord Chancellor. 304
Houseman, D. Life assurance. 247
Housing & Local Government, Ministry of. Crowd behaviour. 478
Housing & Local Government, Ministry of. Rateable values. 402
Housing & Local Government, Ministry of. Rating. 402
Housing & Local Government, Ministry of. Town & Country Planning. 459
Housing Corporation. Annual report. 226
Housing Corporation. Practice notes. 227
Houts, M. Courtroom medicine. 314
Houts, M. Medical proof. 202
Hovenden, J.E. Fraud. 205
Howard, C. Australian Constitution. 31
Howard, C. Australian criminal law. 131, 135
Howard, C. Self certification. 447
Howard, C. Statutory sick pay 447
Howard, C. Strict responsibility. 113, 448
Howard, D.L. Education of offenders. 406
Howard, D.L. English prisons. 382
Howard, D.L. John Howard. 382
Howard, G. Self certification. 169
Howard, G. Statutory sick pay. 169
Howard, J. State of prisons. 382
Howard, M. Restraints on war. 481
Howard, W.W. & Parks, A.L. Dentist. 147
Howard League for Penal Reform. Granting bail. 35, 306
Howard League for Penal Reform. Making awards. 410
Howard League for Penal Reform. No brief for the dock. 407
Howard League for Penal Reform. Parole decisions. 353
Howard League for Penal Reform. Probation & custody. 73, 387, 397
Howel, The Good. Ancient laws. 479
Howell, A. Industrial tribunal. 240
Howell, P.A. Privy Council. 385
Hoyle, M. Private international law. 100
Hoyle, M.S.W. International trade. 82
Hoyt, R.S. Royal demesne. 104
Hribar, Z. Company law. 89
Hudec, R.E. G.A.T.T. 208
Hudson, A. Commercial law dictionary. 82
Hudson, A.A. Building & engineering. 26, 54, 113
Hudson, A.A. & Inman, A. Light & air. 297
Hudson, A.H. Commercial law dictionary. 150
Hudson, J. & Galaway, B. Restitution. 410

Hudson, M.O. Court of international justice. 253
Hudson, M.O. International tribunals. 256
Hudson, N.G. Marine claims. 247, 431
Hughes, C. British statute book. 384, 446
Hughes, J. & Pollins, H. Trade unions. 463
Hughes, P.F. Taxation manual. 416
Hughes, P.F. & Tingley, K.R. Value added tax. 476
Hull, R. & others. Probate practice. 386
Hull, R.H. & Novogrod, J.C. Vietnam. 481
Hume, D. Commentaries. 134, 422
Hume, D. Lectures. 422
Humphreys, T.S. District registry. 265
Humphreys, T.S. Matrimonial causes. 156, 312
Humphries, J. Part-time work. 170
Humphry, D. Police power. 398
Hunnings, N.M. Film censors. 67, 197
Hunnings, N.M. Industrial property cases. 118
Hunnings, N.M. Monopolies. 322, 449
Hunnings, N.M. Restrictive agreements. 322
Hunnisett, R.F. Medieval coroner. 120, 220
Hunt, A. Sociological movement. 486
Hunt, A.J. Boundaries. 53
Hunter, A. Competition. 95
Hunter, A. Monopoly. 322
Hunter, D. Diseases of occupation. 342
Hunter, J.M. Northern Ireland bankruptcy. 37
Huopanuini, J. Parliaments & European rapprochement. 351
Hurd, R.C. Habeas corpus. 216
Hurd, V.D. Council of Europe. 123
Hursh, R.D. & Bailey, H.J. Products liability. 388
Hurst, Sir C. Internaitonal law. 249
Hurst, G. Lincoln's Inn. 243
Hurstfield, J. Freedom, corruption & government. 54
Hurwitz, S. & Christiansen, K.O. Criminology. 138
Hussain, I. Dissenting & separate opinions. 253
Hutchins, E.L. & Harrison, A. Factory legislation. 192
Hutchinson, J. Middle Templars. 243
Hutley, F.C. & Inglis, M.W. Wills. 487
Hutley, F.C., Woodman, R.A. & Wood, O. Succession. 449
Huttman, E.D. Housing & social services. 226, 437
Hyde, C.C. International law. 249
Hyde, H.M. Privacy. 293, 379, 383
Hydeman, L.M. & Berman, W.H. Nuclear maritime activities. 338
Hyden, G. Development administration. 273
Hymans, C. Pensions & employee benefits. 360

AUTHOR AND SHORT TITLE INDEX

Ibik, J.O. Malawi law of land. 308
Ibik, J.O. Malawi marriage & divorce. 308, 311
Ibrahim, A. Islamic law. 261
Ibrahim, A. Malaysia family law. 196, 434
Ihre, R., Gorton, L. & Sandevarn, A. Shipbroking. 70, 431
Ilbert, Sir C.P. Legislative methods. 384, 446
Ilbert, Sir C.P. Mechanics of law making. 446
Ilbert, Sir C.P. Parliament. 351
Ilchman, W.F. Public administration. 391
Imam, M. Minorities. 255
Impey, W.J. Mandamus. 309
Impey, W.J. Sheriff. 430
Inbau, F.E. Lie detector. 129
Ince, G.H. Ministry of Labour. 214
Inciardi, J.A. & Chambers, C.D. Drugs. 162
Ind, R.C. Estate duty. 178
Independent Broadcasting Authority. Advertising standards. 13
Index to Canadian literature. 43
Index to Local & Personal Acts. 384
Indra, N.T. Peacekeeping power. 472
Industrial Assurance Commissioner. Friendly societies. 236
Industrial Society. Unfair dismissal. 471
Industrial Welfare Society. Employment. 170
Industry, Dept.of. Post Office Review Committee. 374
Information Canada. Government of Canada. 212
Ing, N.D. Bona vacantia. 51, 189
Ingham, J.H. Animals. 21
Inglis, B.D. Family law. 194, 232
Inglis, B.D. & Mercer, A.G. Family law. 194
Ingliss, B. Freedom of press. 379
Ingman, T. English legal process. 173
Ingraham, B. Political crime. 93
Inland Revenue. Double taxation. 159
Inland Revenue Income tax. 233, 413
Inland Revenue. Taxes Acts. 63, 65, 233, 413
Inner London Probation and After-Care Service. Community service. 88
Insolvency Law Review Committee. Report. 37
Institute for Study & Treatment of Delinquency. Children still in trouble. 73
Institute of Advanced Legal Studies. Legal citations. 3
Institute of Advanced Legal Studies. Air & space law. 34, 43, 442
Institute of Advanced Legal Studies. Commonwealth union list. 43.
Institute of Advanced Legal Studies. Legal periodicals. 43
Institute of Advanced Legal Studies. United States literature. 43
Institute of Advanced Legal Studies. West European literature. 43

Institute of Chartered Accountants. Auditors' reports. 206
Institute of Chartered Accountants. Receivership. 404
Institute of Chartered Shipbrokers. Shipbrokers manual. 70, 432
Institute of Judicial Administration. Administrative tribunals. 468
Institute of Legal Executives. Becoming a legal executive. 288
Institute of Municipal Treasurers & Accountants. Rating Act. 402
Institute of Practitioners in Advertising. Advertising. 13
Institute of Practioners in Advertising. Is it legal. 13, 201, 460
Institute of Trading Standards. Handbook. 485
Institution of Heating & Ventilating Engineers. Fire legislation. 198
Institution of Mining & Metallurgy. Legal aspects of prospecting. 319
Insurance Institute of London. Annuity contracts. 21
Insurance Institute of London. Tort system. 5, 245, 457
Interdepartmental Committees on Cabs & Private Hire Vehicles. Report. 452
Interdepartmental Committee on Magistrates' Courts in London. Report. 306
International Atomic Energy Agency. Agreements. 338
International Atomic Energy Agency. Environmental pollution. 338, 369
International Atomic Energy Agency. Insurance for nuclear installations. 248, 338
International Atomic Energy Agency. International coventions. 338
International Atomic Energy Agency. Law & practices. 338
International Atomic Energy Agency. Licensing. 338
International Atomic Energy Agency. Maritime carriage. 66, 338, 432
International Atomic Energy Agency. Nuclear law. 338
International Atomic Energy Agency. Physical protection. 338
International Bar Association. Codes of conduct. 89, 122.
International Bar Association. Comparative immigration. 231
International Bar Association. Responsibilities of lawyers. 40
International Cargo Handling Co-ordination Association. Multilingual glossary. 82, 152, 432
International Centre for Settlement of Investment Disputes. Convention. 259

International Centre for Settlement of Investment Disputes. Investment laws. 259
International Conference of Marine Pollution. 370
International Convention for the Prevention of Pollution of the Sea by Oil. 370
International Council of Nurses. Nursing legislation. 340
International Council on Alcohol & Addiction. Drunkeness. 18
International Institute for the Unification of Private Law. Products liability. 388
International Labour Office. Conciliation & arbitration. 25
International Labour Office. Index of legislation. 170, 290
International Labour Office. Occupational health & safety. 167
International Labour Organisation. Maritime labour conventions. 170, 432
International Labour Organisation. Trade Union rights. 463
International Law Association. Reports of conferences. 254
International Law Commission. Yearbook. 254
International Legal Aid Association. Directory of legal aid. 286
International Maritime Consultative Organisation. Oil pollution. 344, 370
International Monetary Fund. Annual report. 252
International Monetary Fund. Increasing resources. 252
International Telecommunication Convention. 453
Ireland, T.P. Entangling alliance. 336
Irish digest. 152
Ironside, D.J. Personal taxation. 413
Irukwu, J.O. Reinsurance. 248
Irving, H. Family law. 195
Irving, R. Product liabilty. 107, 388
Isaacs, S.A. EEC banking law. 39, 182
Isaacs, S.C. Theatres. 174, 454
Isle of Man. Rules of High Court. 262
Ison, T.G. Forensic lottery. 5, 362, 457
Israel, Ministry of Justice. Selected judgments. 263
Issuing Houses Association. City code. 89, 449
Ivamy, E.R.H. Agency. 16
Ivamy, E.R.H. Carriage by sea. 66
Ivamy, E.R.H. Commercial law. 82
Ivamy, E.R.H. Company law dictionary. 89, 150
Ivamy, E.R.H. Fire & motor insurance. 246, 247
Ivamy.E.R.H. Insurance. 245
Ivamy., E.R.H. Marine insurance. 247, 432

Ivamy, E.R.H. Partnership. 353
Ivamy, E.R.H. Sale of goods. 420
Ivamy, E.R.H. Shipping. 432
Ivamy, E.R.H. Show business. 174, 454
Ives, E.W. Common lawyers. 219
Ives, E.W. & Manchester, P.H. Law, litigants & legal profession. 219
Jacka, A.A. Adoption. 12
Jackson, B.S. Jewish history. 263
Jackson, B.S. Theft. 263, 454
Jackson, D. Maritime claims. 432
Jackson, D. Unfair dismissal. 471
Jackson, D.C. Conflicts process. 100
Jackson, D.C. Property. 403
Jackson, J. Formation & annulment. 310
Jackson, J. G.A.T.T. 208
Jackson, J. Health & safety. 342
Jackson, J. Industrial tribunals. 240
Jackson, J. Labour relations. 238
Jackson, J. Matrimonial finance. 156, 197
Jackson, J. Occupational persons. 360
Jackson, K. Sex discrimination. 175
Jackson, M.P. Industrial relations. 238
Jackson, P. Easements. 163
Jackson, P. Natural justice. 9, 270
Jackson, P.W. Local government. 301
Jackson, R.M. Machinery of justice. 7, 9, 126, 173
Jackson, R.M. Quasi contract. 111, 222
Jackson, T. Legal profession. 15.
Jackson, W.H. & Gosset, T. Title. 455
Jacob, G. Law dictionary. 150
Jacob, J.I.H. Commencement of action. 126, 376
Jacobs, B. Bills of Exchange. 46, 331
Jacobs, C.E. Sovereign immunity. 441
Jacobs, F.G. Human Rights Convention. 228
Jacobs, F.G. International law. 249
Jacobs, F.G. & Durand, A. European Court. 184
Jacobs, K.S. Trusts. 469
Jacobs, M.C. Theatre law. 454
Jacobs, M.S. Arbitration. 25.
Jacobs, M.S. Expropriation. 252
Jacobstein, J.M. & Mersky, R.M. Water law bibliography. 484
Jacoby, H.D. & Steinburner, J. Clearing the air. 370
Jaconelli, J. Bill of Rights. 45
Jaffe, F. Pathological evidence. 202
Jaffe, L.L. Judges. 93, 165, 474
Jager, M.O., Taylor, R.B. & Craig, R.J. Company financial statements. 89
Jain, H.C. Indian legal materials. 234
Jain, H.C. Law library administration. 295
Jain, M.P. Indian constitution. 234
Jain, M.P. Malaysia administrative law. 434
Jain, J.D. & Jain, S.K. Mining legislation.XX
James, A. Media & law. 379, 399

AUTHOR AND SHORT TITLE INDEX

James, D.A.G. Reciprocal enforcement. 306, 312
James, D.E.H. Planning permission. 459
James, L. Railway. 400, 464
James, M.H. Bentham. 270
James, P.S. English law. 173
James, P.S. Torts. 457
James, R.W. Fimbo, G.M. Tanzania customary land law. 450
James, T.E. Prostitution. 390
Jameson, m.B. Canadian estate tax. 178
Jamison, R., Thwailes, D.J. & Gamble, H.E.C. Social work. 437
Jankovic, B.M. Public international law. 249
Janner, G. Employment forms. 170
Janner, G. Employment law. 170
Janner, G. Health & safety. 167, 236
Janner, G. Sick pay. 170, 447
Janner, G. Product liability. 388
Jarman, T. Wills. 487
Jarvis, D.C. Institutional treatment. 382
Jarvis, F.V. Probation officers. 387
Jasani, B. Nuclear proliferation. 339
Jauncey, Lord. Fishing in Scotland. 20
Jayewardene, C.H.S. Penalty of death. 63
Jayson, L.S. Tort claims. 215
Jeffery, C.R. Crime prevention. 127
Jeffries, Sir C.J. Colonial office. 214
Jeffries, J. Official publications of EEC. 45
Jegede, O. Nigerian legal bibliography. 43
Jeger, L.M. Illegitimate children. 291
Jehoram, H.C. Design protection. 357
Jenkins, C.W. International Labour Organisation. 253
Jenkins, D. Celtic law. 479
Jenkins, D. Co-oeratives.XX
Jenkins, D. & Owen, M. Welsh law of women. 479, 489
Jenkins, Sir G. Ministry of Transport. 214
Jenkins, Lord. Leasehold committee. 285
Jenkins, P.H.D. Agricultural holdings. 16
Jenkinson, H. Court hand. 125
Jenks, C.W. International adjudication. 251
Jenks, C.W. International immunities. 153
Jenks, C.W. International organizations. 254
Jenks, C.W. World community. 257
Jenks, C.W. New world of law. 257
Jenks, C.W. Space law. 442
Jenks, C.W. Trade Union. 463
Jenks, E. Civil law. 75
Jenks, E. Consideration. 113
Jenks, E. Digest. 152
Jenks, E. History. 219
Jenks, E. Parliamentary England. 59
Jennings, Sir I. British Commonwealth. 86
Jennings, Sir I. British constitution. 103
Jennings, Sir I. Cabinet Government. 59, 212, 377
Jennings, Sir I. Constitution of Ceylon. 44

Jennings, Sir I. Constitutional law. 86
Jennings, Sir I. Constitutional problems in Pakistan. 347
Jennings, Sir I. Local government. 301
Jennings, Sir I. Parliament. 350
Jennings, Sir I. Self-government. 212
Jennings, R.Y. Acquisition of territory. 252
Jennings, W.H. & Zuber, T.G. Canadian law. 61
Jensen, C.H. Pollution control. 369
Jensen, G.F. Delinquency. 146
Jeremie, P. Real property. 69
Jeremy, D. Business biography. 82
Jervis, J. Coroners. 120
Jesse, D. Professional negligence insurance. 247
Jessup, C.N. Industrial law. 237
Jessup, P. Neutrality. 481
Jessup, P.C. Territorial waters. 453
Jobling, M. Abused child. 43, 71
Joffe, V. Companies Act. 90
Johannes, H. Industrial property. 118, 182
Johansson, E. Official publications of Western Europe. 45
John, E. Land tenure. 278
Johnson, B. U.N. and human enironment. 369
Johnson, D. Air space. 34
Johnson, E.L. Soviet legal system. 442
Johnson, J. Isle of Man. 262
Johnson, J.C. Trucking mergers. 66
Johnson, K.W. & Williams, M.W. Illegal aliens. 18
Johnson, N. Constitution. 103
Johnson, T.A. Valuation. 402
Johnston, A. City take-over code. 449
Johnston, Sir A. Inland Revenue. 214, 241
Johnston, D. Design protection. 357
Johnston, D.L. Canadian securities. 39
Johnston, D.M. Fisheries. 199
Johnston, E.A. International Labour Organisation. 253
Johnston, K.F.A. Electrical engineering. 54
Johnston, N. Punishment. 397
Johnston, R.E. Judicial review. 266
Johnston, T.R. & Edgar, G.C. Company accounting. 6
Johnston, T.R., Jagar, M.O. & Taylor, R. Company accounting. 6
Joliet, R. Antitrust. 95
Joliffe, J.A. Constitutional history. 104, 220
Jolowicz, H.F. Jurisprudence. 270
Jolowicz, H.F. Roman foundations. 418
Jolowicz, H.F. & Nicholas, B. Roman law. 418
Jolowicz, J.A. & Jones, G. Judicial protection. 82, 176, 266
Jones, A. Jury services. 267
Jones, B. British government. 212
Jones, B.W. & Gard, S.A. Evidence. 187
Jones, C. Solicitor's clerk. 288

Jones, C.E. Magistrates' courts. 306
Jones, E.B. Satellite telecommunications. 453
Jones, F.H. Accounting. 6
Jones, F.H. Balance sheets. 6
Jones, G. Charity. 70, 222
Jones, G. Sovereignty of law. 173
Jones, G. U.N. & domestic jurisdiction. 472
Jones, G.P. Building contract. 55
Jones, G.P. I.C.E. Contract. 54
Jones, H. Open prisons. 382
Jones, H. Residential community. 437
Jones, H.K. Butterworths. 380
Jones, J.M. British nationality. 328
Jones, J.W. Greek, Latin, Italian & French quotations. 288
Jones, J.W. Theory of law. 270
Jones, K. Lunacy law. 317
Jones, M. Justice & journalism. 33, 306, 76379
Jones, M. Privacy. 383
Jones, P.E. Fire court. 198
Jones, R. South African conveyancing. 116
Jones, R.M. Social work statutes. 437
Jones, S.B. Boundary making. 53
Jones, T.I.J. Acts concerning Wales. 479
Jones, T.M. Requisitioned land. 483
Jones, W. Bailments. 36
Jones, W. Court of Great Sessions. 479
Jones, W.J. Elizabethan Court of Chancery. 221
Jones, W.T. Health & safety at work. 236
Jordan, B. Freedom & welfare state. 486
Jordan, R.S. International administration. 257
Jordan, S.A. Corporation law. 122
Jordan, W. Paupers. 372
Joseph, C. Development land law. 148
Joseph, C. Nationality & diplomatic protection. 154, 328
Joseph, C. VAT. 476
Joseph, C. & Edwards, R.G. Community land. 87, 148
Joseph, C. & Skinner, B. Development land. 87, 149
Joshi, R. Indian constitution. 234
Joske, P.E. Agency. 16
Joske, P.E. Australian federal government. 31
Josek, P.E. Australian insurance law. 245
Joske, P.E. Marriage. 232
Josling, J.F. Adoption. 12
Josling, J.F. Affiliation. 291
Josling, J.F. Apportionment. 23, 189, 469
Josling, J.F. Business names. 58, 315
Josling, J.F. Change of name. 325
Josling, J.F. Execution. 265
Josling, J.F. Matrimonial & guardianship orders. 312
Josling, J.F. Periods of limitation. 298
Josling, J.F. Summary of judgment. 265
Josling, J.F. & Alexander, L. Clubs. 29, 78
Joubert, W.A. South Africa. 172

Journal of Planning & Environmental Law. Compulsory purchase. 97
Journal of Planning & Environmental Law. Old buildings. 459
Jowitt, Earl. Dictionary. 150, 288
Jowitt, Earl. Statute law revision. 447
Joyce, F. Local government & planning. 459
Joyce, J.A. Human rights. 229
Joyce, J.A. Right to life. 63
Joyner, N.D. Hijacking. 34, 217
Juda, L. Ocean space rights. 109
Judge, A. First fifty years. 367
Judicial Statistics. 445
Jung, H. & Gress, J. Business in Germany. 82, 209
Just, A. Private company. 90
Justice. Administration. 9
Justice. Bankruptcy. 37
Justice. Breaking the rules. 138
Justice. Citizen & his council. 345
Justice. Citizen & the administration. 7, 9, 345
Justice. Citzen & public agencies. 345, 392
Justice. Compensation for victims. 128
Justice. Complaints against lawyers. 438
Justice. Compulsory acquistion. 97
Justice. Contempt of court. 108
Justice. Criminal appeals. 22, 127
Justice. False witness. 187, 361
Justice. Going abroad. 354
Justice. Judiciary. 265
Justice. Lawyers of legal system. 173, 289
Justice. Litigants in person. 406
Justice, Living it down. 406
Justice. Motor accident cases. 5
Justice. No fault. 5, 352
Justice. Our fettered ombudsman. 345
Justice. Parental rights & duties. 193
Justice. Plutonium & libert. 338
Justice. Preliminary investigations. 389
Justice. Pre-trial criminal procedure. 130, 367, 389
Justice. Prosecution process. 132, 389
Justice. Truth and courts. 130, 361
Justice. Unrepresented defendants. 299, 306
Justice.& Internatioal Press Institute. Law & the press. 379
Juta, H. Conduct of trials. 13
Juviler, P.H. Revolutionary law & order. 415
Kadish, M.R. & Kadish, S.R. Discretion to disobey. 76
Kagan, K.K. Jurisprudence. 270
Kahn, D.A. Corporation taxation. 121
Kahn, E. South African domicile. 159
Kahn, E. & Zeffert, D. South African legal problems. 440
Kahn, L. Nuremberg. 483
Kahn-Freund, O. Inland transport. 400, 464
Kahn-Freund, O. Labour. 170
Kahn-Freund, O. Labour relations. 238

AUTHOR AND SHORT TITLE INDEX

Kahn-Freund, O. Private international laws. 100
Kahn-Freund, O. Selected writings. 270
Kahn-Freund, O. Source book on French law. 205
Kalinowski, J. World competition. 95
Kalshoven, F. Belligerent reprisals. 481
Kalshoven, f. Warfare. 481
Katzarov, K. Nationalisation. 252
Kamenka, E. Law & society. 270
Kaven, H. & Zeisel, H. American jury. 267
Kant, I. Philosophy. 270
Kaplin, M.A. Justice. 270
Kaplin, W.A. Higher education. 165
Kapteyn, P.J.G. & Van Themaat, P. European Communities. 180
Kapungu, L.T. Sanctions against Rhodesia. 473
Karam, N.H. Kuwait banking laws. 39
Karam, N.H. Kuwait tax laws. 413
Karlen, D. Appellate courts. 22
Karlen, D. Judicial administration. 474
Karlake, H.H. Rates. 402
Karslake, H.H. & Nicholls, A.D. Industrial valuations. 402
Karsten, P. Law, soldiers & combat. 26, 318, 481
Kase, F.J. Copyright thought. 118
Kase, F.J. Designs. 357
Kase, F.J. Trademarks. 461
Kassebaum, G.G. Delinquency. 146
Kasunmu, A.B. Nigerian Supreme Court. 333
Kasummu, A.B. & Salacuse, J.W. Nigerian family law. 333
Katende, J.W. & others. Business organisations. 15
Katz, J. Human experimentation. 230
Katz, J. & Capron, A.M. Catastrophic disease. 230
Katz, M. International adjudication. 251
Kaufman, F. Confessions. 99
Kaufman, J. U.N. decision making. 473
Kavanagh, J. Judicial review. 266
Kavass, I.I. & Sprudzs, A. Extradition. 191
Kay, E. Business in Saudi Arabia. 421
Kay, J.A. Tax system. 413
Kay, M. Companies Acts. 90
Kealey, G.J. & Harris, H.A. Separation agreements. 195, 311
Kean, M. Civil Evidence Act. 187, 384
Keane, D.D. Nuisances Removal Act. 340
Keast, H. National insurance. 327
Keating, D. Building contracts. 26, 55, 113
Keay, E.A. & Richardson, S.S. Native & customary courts. 333
Keenan, D.J. Employment law. 170
Keener, W.A. Quasi-contracts. 111
Keeton, G.W. British Commonwealth. 86
Keeton, G.W. English law. 265

Keeton, G.W. Guilty but insane. 144
Keeton, G.W. Jurisprudence. 270
Keeton, G.W. Norman conquest. 85, 221
Keeton, G.W. Passing of Parliament. 351
Keeton, G.W. Trial by tribunal. 468
Keeton, G.W. Trusts. 469
Keeton, G.W.& Lloyd, D. United Kingdom. 69, 262, 337
Keeton, G.W. & Schwarzenberger, G. Making international law work. 257
Keeton, G.W. & Sheridan, L.A. Charities. 70
Keeton, G.W. & Sheridan, L.A. Comparative trust. 93, 469
Keeton, G.W. & Sheridan, L.A. Equity. 176
Keeton, G.W. & Sheridan, L.A. Trusts. 469
Keeton, R.E. Venturing to do justice. 282
Keir, D.L. Constitutional history. 104
Keir, D.L. & Lawson, F.H. Constitutional cases. 105
Keith, A.B. British Cabinet. 59
Keith, A.B. Constitutional law. 86
Keith, A.B. The Dominions. 86, 87
Keith, A.B. The King. 139
Keith, A.B. Privileges & rights. 139, 384
Keith, A.B. Responsible government. 87
Keith, A.B. Speeches & documents. 87
Keith, A.B. State succession. 103
Keith, K.J. International Court. 253
Keith, R. & Clarke, G. Scots law. 422
Keith-Lucas, B. & Arnold-Baker, C. Ombudsman. 345
Keith-Lucas, B. & Richard, P.G. Local government history. 301
Kelham, R. Norman dictionary. 150
Kellas, J.G. Scottish political system. 422
Kelly, F.N. & Carmichael, K.S. Irish income tax. 121, 233, 413
Kelly, J.E., & Perry, F.E. Banking points. 39
Kelly, J.H. Draftsman. 116, 160, 290
Kelly, J.M. Irish law & constitution. 76, 103, 260
Kelly, J.M. Roman civil judicature. 418
Kelly, J.M. Roman litigation. 418
Kelly, W. & Kelly, N. Policing in Canada. 367
Kelly's Handbook. 359
Kelman, a. & Sizer, R. Computer in court. 98
Kelsen, H. International law. 249
Kelsen, H. Law of the U.N. 473
Kelsen, H. Peace through law. 359
Kelsen, H. Theory of law. 270
Kemelfield, R.L. Architects, builders & engineers. 26, 56
Kemmer, E.J. Rape. 401
Kemmer, E.J. Rape bibliography. 43.
Kemp, D. Damages for personal injury. 142, 362
Kemp, D. & Kemp, M. Quantum of damages. 5, 142, 342
Kemp, E.W. Canon law. 164

Kempin, F.G. Anglo-American law. 474
Kennan, K.K. Residence and domicile. 159
Kennedy, A. & McWilliam, H.R. Compensation &/or criminal injuries. 128
Kennedy, W.P.M. Constitutional law. 103
Kennedy, W.R. Civil salvage. 421, 432
Kenny, A.J. Freewill and responsibility. 133
Kenny, C.S. Criminal law. 131
Kenny, P. Cohabitation. 79
Kenny, P.H. & Bevan, C. Conveyancing. 116
Kent, E. Revolution. 415
Kerly, Sir D.M. Trademarks. 58, 355, 461
Kerper, H.B. Legal rights. 382
Kerr, A. & Whyte, G. Trade union law. 463
Kerr, A.J. Agency. 16, 440
Kerr, A.J. Contract. 111
Kerr, A.J. Law of lease. 285
Kerr, A.J. Native law of succession. 440
Kerr, D.J.A. Forensic medicine. 314
Kerr, M.H. Islamic reform. 261
Kerr, R. Ancient lights. 297
Kerr, W.W. Fraud & mistake. 113, 205, 211, 320
Kerr, W.W. Injunctions. 241
Kerr, W.W. Receivers. 404
Kerse, C.S. EEC antitrust. 95
Kerse, C.S. Noise. 174, 335
Kersell, J.K. Parliamentary supervision. 144
Kersley, K.H. & Gibson, A. Gibson's. 288
Kewley, T.H. Social security. 436
Key, T. & Elphinstone, H.W. Conveyancing precedents. 116, 277
Keyes, W. Government contracts. 113
Khadduri, M. Islamic law. 261
Khadduri, M. War and peace. 481
Kiapi, A. Civil service laws. 15, 78
Kidner, R. Trade union law. 463
Kilbrandon, Lord. Royal Commission on the Constitution. 104
Kilby, R.L.J. Mental Health Act. 317
Killinger, G.G., Kerper, H.B. & Cromwell, P.F. Prbation & parole. 387
Kilmuir, Lord, Parliamentary privilege. 352
Kiln, R. Reinsurance. 248
Kilpatrick, J.J. Smut peddlers. 342
Kimball, S. legal system. 474
King, A. & Barlow, J. Solicitors. 438
King, D. & Thomas, P. Traveller's cheques. 39
King, Sir G.S. Ministry of Pensions. 214
King, J. Criminal libel. 293
King, J.F.S. Probation. 388, 406
King, L. Wilson, J. Children. 73
King, M. Bail. 35, 407
King, M. Criminal justice. 130
King, M. Duty solicitor. 438
King, R. Land reform. 262
King, R.D. Albany. 382
Kinvig, R.H. Isle of Man. 262

Kiralfy, A.K.R. English legal system. 173
Kiralfy, A.K.R. Matrimonial property. 93, 197
Kiralfy, A.K.R. & MacQueen, H.L. New perspectives. 219, 422
Kirby, Sir M. Reform the law. 31, 282
Kirk, H. Portrait of a profession. 438
Kirk, P.L. Crime investigation. 129
Kirkwood, J.S. Information technology. 98, 275
Kish, J. International spaces. 442
Kitagawa, Z. Business in Japan. 82
Kitchen, J. Labour law & offshre oil. 170, 344
Kitchen, J. Merchant seamen. 432
Kitchen, S. Professional partnerships. 353
Kitchin, L.D. & Duckworth, J. Road transport. 324, 416, 464
Kittrie, N.N. Comparative law. 93
Kitzinger, U. Diplomacy. 181
Klar, L.N. Canadian tort. 457
Klare, H.J. Anatomy of prison. 382
Klare, H.J. Changing concept of crime. 148
Klein, J.F. Let's make a deal. 135, 365
Klein, M.M. Juvenile justice. 273
Klein, R. & Howlett, A. Complaints against doctors. 157
Klein, R.A. Sovereign equality. 441
Kleinig, J. Punishment. 397
Kludze, A.K.T. Ewe property law. 210
Knafla, L.A. Law of politics. 222
Kneale, A. Birching. 120
Kneal, S.J. Manx Coroners. 120, 262
Knechtle, A.A. International fiscal law. 252, 413
Knickerbocker, D.C. & Silverstein, L.L. Annuities. 22
Kniepkamp, H.P. Legal dictonary: English-German. 150
Knight, B. Medical practice. 19, 157, 315
Knight, C. Byelaws. 59
Knight, H.G. International fisheries. 199
Knight, H.G. Sea's living resources. 199
Knight, M. Criminal appeals. 22, 127
Knight, W.J.L. Private companies. 90, 449
Knipe, J.C. Contract. 111
Knott, A.E. Australian schools. 165
Knowles, C.C. & Pitt, P.H. Building regulations. 56, 303
Knowles, R. Local government. 301
Knox, F. Common Market. 182
Kobrin, D.L. & Stott, V. Negotiable instruments. 331
Koch, F.E. Double taxation. 159
Kock, G.L. French code of criminal procedure. 205
Kodilinye, G. Equity in Nigeria. 176, 333
Kodilinye, G. Nigerian torts. 457
Koers, A.W. Marine fisheries. 199
Koestler, A. Reflections on hanging. 64
Koh, B.C. U.N. Administrative Tribunal. 473

AUTHOR AND SHORT TITLE INDEX

Kohl, M. Morality of killing. 4, 185
Kohler, J. Philosophy. 270
Kohler, P.A. & Zacher, H.F. Social insurance. 327
Kohlik, G. Commercial laws. 82
Kohn, L. Irish Constitution. 260
Kolbert, C.F. & Mackay, N.A.M. Scots & English land law. 275
Kolbert, C.F. & O'Brien, T. Land reform in Ireland. 275, 278
Koldayev, V. Soviet citizens. 442
Kollewijn, R.D. Private international law. 100
Konecni, V.J. & Ebbesen, E.E. Criminal justice system. 130
Konig, K. Germany public administration. 209
Korah, V. Competition. 95, 183, 322
Korah, V. EEC law. 180
Korah, V. Monopolies. 322
Korbin, J.E. Child abuse. 71
Kornberg, A. Influence in Parliament. 60
Kornhauser, R.R. Delinquency. 146
Kornitzer, M. Adoption. 12
Korowicz, M.S. International law. 249
Kos-Rabcewicz-Zubkowski, L. Arbitration. 25
Kotas, R. & Davis, B. Food control. 201
Koul, A.K. UNCTAD. 82, 463
Kovats, L.J. Hovercraft. 227
Kovats, L.J. Tugs & towage. 470
Kozak, E. Applications of computer technology. 98
Kramer, C. Medical malpractice. 316
Kramer, D.C. Civil rights. 76
Kratovil, R. Mortgage. 323
Krause, H.D. Family law. 196
Krause, H.D. Illegitimacy. 291
Krauss, L.I. Computer fraud. 98, 205
Kriefman, S. Driving while disqualified. 417
Kronby, M.C. Divorce. 156
Kuhn, A.K. Comparative commentaries. 100
Kullinger, J.L. Incest. 232
Kunkel, W. Roman legal history. 418
Kunreuther, H. Disaster insurance. 245
Kuo Lee Li. Space law bibliography. 43
Kupferman, T.R. & Foner, M. Copyright convention. 118
Kurtha, A.N. Prisoners of war. 483
Kutash, I.L. Violence. 223, 478
Kutner, L. Habeas corpus. 216
Kuusi, J. Host state. 90, 172
Lachs, M. Outer space. 442
Ladas, S.P. Patents. 357
Laddie, H. Prescott, P. & Vitoria, M. Copyright. 118
Ladenson, A. American library laws. 294
Lader, L. Abortion. 4
Lador-Lederer, J.J. International organizations. 254
Lafave, W. Criminal law. 135
La Forest, G.V. Water law. 484

Lafrance, A.S. Poor. 373
Lahore, J. Information technology. 98, 118
Lahore, J. Intellectual property. 118, 357
Lamb, C. Inner Temple. 243
Lamb, P. Rating. 402
Lambert, J. Motor vehicle safety. 324, 388
Lambert, S. Bills & Acts. 190
Lambrinidis, J.S. Free trade.185
Lamont, W.D. Law & moral order. 270
Land Registry. Land charges. 276
Land Registry. Reports. 277
Land Transfer Committee Report. 278
Landers, T. Private Bills. 374
Landy, E.A. International supervision. 253
Lane, E. Abortion Act. 4
Lane, P.H. Australian Constitution. 32
Lane, P.H. Australian Federal system. 32
Lang, A.G. Crown land. 139
Lang, A.G. & Crommelin, M. Australian moving. 319, 344
Lang, A.G. & Everett, D. Land dealings. 116, 275
Lang, J. Crowd behaviour. 478
Langan, P.St.J. Civil procedure. 187, 376
Langdon-Davies, P.G. Commons registration. 86
Langen, E. Commercial law. 87
Langrod, J. International civil service. 183
Lansdown, A. South African criminal law. 135, 440
Lansky, R. Books in English on Germany law. 43
Lansky, R. Developing countries bibliography. 43
Lapsley, G.F. Crowns, community & parliament. 104, 221, 351
Lapsley, G.T. County palatine. 124
Larman Associates. Employment law. 170
Larson, A. & Jenks, C.W. Sovereignty. 256, 441
Laski, H.J. Constitution. 103, 212
Laski, H.J. Law & politics. 270
Laski, H.J. Municipal progress. 301
Laski, H.J. State. 103
Laskin, B. British tradition in Canadian law. 61
Lasok, D. Fundamental duties. 270
Lasok, D. Law of the economy. 180
Lasok, D. & Bridge, J.W. European communities. 180
Lasok, D. & Cairns, W.J. Harmonization. 180
Lasok, K.P.E. European Court of Justice. 184
Latey, W. Divorce. 156
Latham, C.T. How much? 306, 308
Latham, D. & Halnan, P. Drink/driving offences. 161
Latham, F.L. Window lights. 297
Latham, R.E. Latin word list. 125
Latimer, P. Insurance law cases. 245

Latin, H.A. Privacy. 383
Latin for Lawyers. 288
Laundy, P. Office of Speaker. 352
Laurie, P. Scotland Yard. 367
Lauterpacht, E. Suez Canal settlement. 62
Lauterpacht, E. UN emerging force. 473
Lauterpacht, Sir H. Human rights. 229
Lauterpacht, Sir H. International Bill of Rights. 229
Lauterpacht, Sir H. International Court. 253
Lauterpacht, Sir H. International law. 249, 359
Lauterpacht, Sir H. Recognition. 255
Lauwaars, R.H. Community decisions. 9, 184
La Villa, G. & Cartella, M. Italian agency. 16, 262
Law S. & Lives, E. Keep music legal. 118, 174
Law Commission. Administration of justice. 7, 108
Law Commission. Administrative law. 9, 407
Law Commission. Ancient courts. 126
Law Commission. Animals.21
Law Commission. Annual report. 281, 282
Law Commission. Appeal Courts. 22
Law Commission. Appurtenant rights. 275
Law Commission. Assessment of damages. 362
Law Commission. Attempt. 102
Law Commission. Blood tests. 50, 291
Law Commission. Breach of confidence. 457
Law Commission. Breach of promise. 311
Law Commission. Charging orders. 143, 276
Law Commission. Classification of limitation. 100
Law Commission. Codification of criminal law. 131
Law Commission. Commercial agents. 16, 111, 182
Law Commission. Conspiracy. 102, 444
Law Commission. Contribution. 111
Law Commission Convenants restricting dispositions. 279
Law Commission. D.P.P. v. Smith. 133
Law Commission. Dangerous things. 457
Law Commission. Declarations in family matters. 193, 311, 312
Law Commission. Defences. 133
Law Commission. Divorce. 156, 194
Law Commission. Entering and remaining on property. 444, 466
Law Commission. Family property. 197
Law Commission. Financial consequences of divorce. 156, 193
Law Commission. Financial provision. 313
Law Commission. Financial relief. 156, 193
Law Commission. Firm offers. 113
Law Commission. Illegitimacy. 193, 391
Law Commission. Implied terms. 113, 114
Law Commission. Incapacitated principal. 375

Law Commission. Inchoate offences. 102
Law Commission. Injuries to unborn children. 377
Law Commission Insurance. 245
Law Commission. Interest. 111, 143
Law Commission. Interference with course of justice. 7
Law Commission. Jacititation of marriage. 311
Law Commission. Jurisdiction in matrimonial causes. 312, 313
Law Commission Jurisdiction in nullity suits. 311
Law Commission. Land charges. 276
Law Commission. Land registration. 277
Law Commission. Landlord & tenant. 279
Law Commission. Legitimacy proceedings. 291
Law Commission. Liability for injury to trespasses. 343, 3 467
Law Commission. Liability of corporations. 133
Law Commission. Limitation Act. 248
Law Commission. Local land charges. 276
Law Commission. Loss of services. 113
Law Commission. Maintenance & champerty. 307
Law Commission. Matrimonial proceedings. 306, 313
Law Commission. Mental element in crime. 133, 244
Law Commission Nullity of marriage. 311
Law Commission Obligations of landlords. 270, 280
Law Commission. Occupiers' liability. 343, 467
Law Commission Offences against religion. 49
Law Commission. Orders for sale. 194, 313
Law Commission. Parol evidence rule. 111
Law Commission. Parties. 133
Law Commission. Pecuniary restitution. 114
Law Commission. Penalty clauses. 114
Law Commission. Perjury & kindred offences. 361
Law Commission. Personal injury litigation. 142, 362
Law Commission. Polygamous marriages. 311
Law Commission. Positive & restrictive covenants. 275
Law Commission. Powers of Attorney. 375
Law Commission. Programme. 79, 281, 282
Law Commission. Programme on consolidation. 281, 282
Law Commission Proof of paternity. 291
Law Commission. Remedies. 9, 407
Law Commission. Rentcharges. 409
Law Commission. Restitution of conjugal rights. 311
Law Commission Restrictions on publicity. 313

AUTHOR AND SHORT TITLE INDEX

Law Commission. Rights of access. 275
Law Commission. Root of title. 455
Law Commission. Solemnisation of marriage. 311, 313
Law Commission. "Subject to contract" agreements. 208
Law Commission. Termination of tenancies. 280
Law Commission. Time restrictions. 194, 298
Law Commission. Treason & sedition. 427, 465
Law Commission & Scottish Law Commission. Choice of law rules. 245
Law Commission & Scottish Law Commission. Custody. 73
Law Commission & Scottish Law Commission. Defective products. 368, 457
Law Commission & Scottish Law Commission. Exemption clauses. 114
Law Commission & Scottish Law Commission. Interpretation. 258
Law Commission & Scottish Law Commission. Private international law. 100
Law Commission & Scottish Law Commission. Sale of goods. 111
Law Commission & Scottish Law Commission. Taxation of income. 275
Law Reform Commission of Canada. Studies in sentencing. 428
Law Reform Committee. Conditions & exceptions in insurance. 248
Law Reform Committee. Conversion & detinue. 363
Law Reform Committee. Hearsay evidence. 187
Law Reform Committee. Innkeepers liability. 242
Law Reform Committee. Innocent misrepresentation. 114
Law Reform Committee. Limitation of actions. 298, 362
Law Reform Committee. Making & revocation of wills. 487
Law Reform Committee. Occupiers' liability. 343
Law Reform Committee. Opinion and expert evidence. 187
Law Reform Committee. Perpetuities. 361
Law Reform Committee. Privilege in civil proceedings. 187
Law Reform Committee. Rule in Hollington v. Hewthorn. 187
Law Reform Committee. Sealing of contracts. 111
Law Reform Committee. Tort between husband & wife. 457
Law Reform Committee. Transfer of title to Chattels.
Law Reform Committee. Trustees. 469

Law Reform Committee for Scotland. Actions of removing. 275
Law Reform Committee for Scotland. Civil liability for animals. 21
Law Reform Committee for Scotland. Enforcement of orders for maintenance. 308
Law Reform Committee for Scotland. Exceptions in insurance policies. 248
Law Reform Committee for Scotland. Occupier's liability. 343
Law Reform Committee for Scotland. Payment aliment. 308
Law Revision Committee. Statute of frauds. 113
Law Society. Compensation fund. 438
Law Society. Complaints about solicitors. 438
Law Society. Digest. 438
Law Society. Legal aid. 286
Law Society. Professional conduct of solicitors. 438
Law Society. Solicitors' accounts rules. 438
Law Society. Solicitors' indemnity rules. 438
Law Society. Solicitors' practice rules. 438
Lawrance, D.M. Compulsory purchase. 97
Lawrance, D.M. Valuation. 402
Lawrance, G.W. Deeds of arrangements. 144
Lawrence, D. Black migrants. 398
Lawrence, R.J. Government of Northern Ireland. 337
Lawrence, T.J. International law. 249
Lawson, E. Accountancy. 6
Lawson, F.H. Negligence. 330, 457
Lawson, F.H. Oxford law school. 288, 345
Lawson, F.H. Property. 403
Lawson, F.H. Remedies. 173, 407
Lawson, F.H. & Bentley, D.J. Constitutional law. 103
Lawson, F.H. & Markesinis, B.S. Tortious liability. 93, 457
Lawson, R. Exclusion clauses. 114
Lawson, R. & Reed, R. Social security in the EEC. 436
Lawson, R.G. Advertising & labelling. 13, 182, 347, 461
Lawson, R.G. Sale & hire purchase. 420
Lawton, J.P. Taxation of property. 413
Lawton, J.P. & Goy, D. Development tax. 149
Lawton, J.P., Goldberg, D. & Fraser, R. Partnership taxation. 353, 413
Lawyers Committee on Blockades. UN & Egyptian blockade of Suez. 50
Lawyers' Law Directory. 154
Lay, S.H. & Taubenfeld, H.J. Man in space. 443
Lay, S.H., Churchill, R. & Nordquist, M. Law of the sea. 425
Laycock, G.K. Absconding from borstals. 52
Lazar, L. Transnational economic law. 321

Leach, E.R. Custom, law & terrorist violence. 394
Leach, R.H. Canada's new constitution. 61
Leach, W.A. Compulsory purchase. 97
Leach, W.A. Leases. 285
Leach, W.A. Party structures. 354
Leach, W.A. Rating. 402
Leachman, R.B. & Althoff, P. Nuclear theft. 378
Leadam, I.S. & Baldwin, J.F. Privy Council. 385
Leage, R.W. Roman private law. 418
Leake, S.M. Contracts. 111
Leaper, W.J. Advertising. 13
Leaper, W.J. Trades description. 460
Leasehold Committee. Report. 285
Leder, M. Consumer law. 107
Le Docte, E. Multilingual law dictionary. 150
Lee, E.C. Taxation in Tanzania. 450
Lee, L.T. & Paxman, J.M. Menstrual regulation. 48
Lee, R.S. & Jasentuliyana, N. Space law. 443
Lee, R.W. Roman Dutch law. 417
Lee, R.W. Roman law. 418
Leeding, A.E. Child care manual. 73, 437
Leemans, A.F. Management of change. 212
Lees, F. International banking. 39
Lees, J.D. & Shaw, M. Committees. 352
Legal Action Group Housing crisis. 226
Legal Action Group. Legal advice centres. 372
Legal Action Group. Legal aid. 286
Legal Action Group. Legal services. 372
Legal Action Group. Supplementary benefit. 436
Le Gall, K. French company law. 205
Le Geyt, P. Jersey. 69
Le Gras, A.J. Jersey. 69
Le Gros, C.S. Jersey. 69
Le Herissier, R.G. Jersey. 69
Leibowitz, A.H. Colonial emancipation. 263
Leigh, L.H. Liability of corporations. 122
Leigh, L.H. Police powers. 27, 367
Leigh-Taylor, N. Doctors & the law. 157
Leive, D.M. International telecommunications. 453
Lekner, M.A. & Steiner, W.A.F.P. Squire law catalogue. 251, 295
Le Mesurier, H. Port of London. 304
Lemmon, H.G. Seashore.Lempert, R.O. & Saltzburg, S.A. Evidence. 187
Leng, S.C. & Chiu, H. Justice in China. 74
Leonard, E.M. Poor relief. 371
Leonard, L.L. Fisheries. 199
Leonard, L.L. Global terrorism. 478
Le Patourel, J.H. Channel Islands. 69
Le Quesne, C. Jersey constitutional history. 60
Lerhard, M. & Spink, R. Danish ombudsman. 345
Lerner, N. UN Convention on racial discrimination. 473
Leslie, A. Railway. 400, 464
Leslie, G.R. Family. 194
Leslie, W. Industrial tribunal. 240
Lesnik, M.J. & Anderson, B.E. Nursing. 340
Lester, A. & Bindman, G. Race & law. 398
Letman, S.T. Criminal justice. 130
Leverson, H. Price of justice. 438
Lever, H. South African voter. 166
Lever, J.F. Restrictive practices. 372
Levi, S.E.H. Legal reasoning. 270
Levi, W. International law. 249, 257
Levine, E. North sea oil. 344
Levine, M.J. Labour relations. 238
Levitt, R. National Health Service. 326
Levitt, W.M. Medicine for lawyers. 151, 315
Levontin, A.V. Choice of law. 100
Levy, A. Custody. 73
Levy, B.H. Cardozo. 270
Levy, H.P. Press Council. 279
Levy, L. Treason against God. 49
Lewin, T. Trusts. 469
Lewis, A.N. Bankruptcy. 37
Lewis, C.S. Immunity. 154
Lewis, C.T. & Short, C. Latin dictionary. 152
Lewis, D. Just how just? 7
Lewis, J.R. Administrative law. 56
Lewis, J.R. Civil & criminal procedure. 376
Lewis, J.R. Equity. 176
Lewis, J.R. Retailer & distributor. 82, 420, 433
Lewis, J.R. & Holland, J.A. Landlord & tenant. 280
Lewis, M. Tax law. 413
Lewis, N. & Gateshill, B. Commission for local administration. 301, 345
Lewis, R. Welsh legal terms. 150
Lewis, T. Glossary of Welsh law. 480
Lewison, K. Drafting business leases. 82, 285
Leys, W.C.S. & Northey, J. Commercial law. 82
Lian, K.K. Credit & security in Singapore. 434
Liebenow, J.G. Colonial rule. 450
Lieberman, A. US patent practice. 357
Liebers, A. Notary public. 337
Lieck, A. Betting. 41
Liell, P. Council houses. 226, 301
Lightwood, J.M. Possession of land. 373
Lightwood, J.M. Time limit of actions. 298
Lillich, R.B. Foreign investments. 259
Lillich, R.B. & Newman, F.C. Human rights. 229
Lillie, J.A. Mercantile Law. 82
Lincoln, A. Liberty & licensing. 296
Linden, A.M. Canadian tort. 457
Lindey, A. Entertainment. 380
Lindgren, K.E. Time. 111, 114, 298, 403
Lindgren, K.E. Mason, H.H. & Gordon, B.L.J. Corporation. 122

AUTHOR AND SHORT TITLE INDEX

Lindley, N. Partnership. 353
Lindman, F.T. & Macintyre, D.M. Mentally disabled. 317
Lindsay, J. Scottish poor law. 371
Linell, A. Names. 325
Ling-Mallison, E. Women. 489
Lingat, R. Classical law, India. 234
Lipschutz, R.D. Radioactive waste. 338
Lipsett, L.R. & Atkinson, T.J.D. Carriage by railway. 400
Lipsky, G.A. Law & politics. 257
Lipstein, K. Conflict of laws. 101
Lipstein, K. EEC law. 180
Lipstein, K. Harmonisation of private international law. 101, 180
Lissitzyn, O.J. International court. 253, 359
Lister, R. As man & wife. 79, 436
Lister, R. Justice for the claimant. 468
Lister, R. Welfare benefits. 436, 486
Lister, R.& Lowe, M. Equal pay. 175
Litchfield, M. & Kentish, S. Babies for burning. 4
Little, A.J. Planning control. 459
Little, J.B. Burials. 57
Little, K. Negroes in Britain. 398
Littler, P. Water rights. 20, 199, 484
Livens, L.J. Taxation in Gibraltar. 413
Livens, L.J. Taxation in the Channel Islands. 413
Livens, L.J. & Thomas, N. Tax planning reivew. 451
Liversage, V. Land tenure. 278
Lividas, C. Winding up. 38
Llewellyn, K.N. Common Law. 85
Lloyd, D. Associations. 29
Lloyd, D. & Montgomery, J. Business lettings. 285
Lloyd, H. Journalism. 293, 379
Lloyd, Lord. Idea of law. 270
Lloyd, Lord. Jurisprudence. 270
Lloyd, M. Prohibition. 389
Lloyd, M.G. Torts. 457
Lloyds. Product liability. 248, 388
Lloyds Law Reports. Digest. 152
Lloyds Marine cargo survey. 432
Lloyds Register. Construction of steel ships. 432
Lloyds Register. Inland waterways. 62
Lloyds Reports of Prize Cases. 385
Local Authorities Conditions of Service Advisory Board. Employee relations handbook. 170
Lockwood, L.C. Solicitor's clerk. 288
Lockyer, J. Industrial arbitration. 25, 463
Lodge, E.C. & Thornton, G.A. Constitutional documents. 105, 221
Loewenstein, K. British Cabinet. 60
Loftie, W.J. Inns of Court. 242
Loftus, E.F. Eyewitness testimony. 488

Lolme, J.L.de. Constitution. 103
Lomnicki, A.J. Landlord & tenant. 280
Lomnicki, A.J. Town & country planning. 97, 459
London Housing Aid Centre. Shorthold tenancies. 226, 280
London Record Society. Assize of nuisance. 29
Long, M.J. & Sparrow, D.T. Family business. 82
Longley, A.R. Charity trustee's guide. 70, 469
Longley, H.L. Carriage of cargo. 66
Loose, P. Company director. 90
Loose, P. Liquidators. 299
Lord Chancellor's Dept. Chancery Division review. 68, 126
Lord Chancellor's Dept. Conciliation. 156, 194
Lord Chancellor's Dept. Council on Tribunals. 468
Lord Chancellor's Dept. County court districts. 124
Lord Chancellor's Dept. Judicial studies. 265
Lord Chancellor's Dept. Legal aid.
Lord Chancellor's Dept. London country courts. 124, 303
Lord Chancellor's Dept. Modern public records.
Lord Chancellor's Dept. Implications of UK membership. 181
Lord Chancellor's Dept. Personal injuries litigation. 362
Lord Chancellor's Office. Age of majority. 73
Lord Chancellor's Office. Committee on defamation. 293
Lord Chancellor's Office. Contempt of court. 109
Lord Chancerller's Office. Illegitimate succession. 291
Lord Chancellor's Office. Judgment debts. 123
Lord Chancellor's Office. Modern public records. 395
Lord Chancellor's Office. Northern Ireland courts. 126
Lord President of the Council. Devolution. 149
Lord-Smith, P. Arbitration for builders. 56
Lorimer, J. Law of Nations. 249
Lorimer, J. Law of Scotland. 422
Lortie, P. G.A.T.T. 208
Louis, J.V. Community legal order. 184
Lovell, C.R. Constitutional history. 104
Loveridge, Sir J. Guernsey constitution. 69
Lowe, D. Transport. 464
Lowe, N.V. & White, R.A.H. Wards of court. 73
Lowe, R. Commercial law. 82
Lowe, R. & Marsh, G.B. Employment

protection. 172
Lowe, R. & Woodroffe, G. Consumer law. 106, 107
Lowenfeld, A. Aviation law. 34
Lowndes, C.L.B. Federal estate & gift taxes. 178
Lowndes, R. & Rudolf, G.R. General average. 432, 491
Lowry, D.R. Blind rights. 50
Lowson, D.M. City lads. 52
Luard, E. Civil wars. 481
Luard, E. Human rights. 229
Luard, E. International agencies. 254
Luard, E. Sea-bed. 425
Luard, E. United Nations. 473
Lucas, J.R. On justice. 7, 270
Lucas, W.W. Primordial functions of government. 212, 441
Ludwig, J. Autopsy practice. 202
Lumb, R.D. Australian constitution. 32
Lumb, R.D. & Ryan, K.W. Australian constitution. 32
Lumley, W.G. Public health. 326, 393
Lumley, W.G. Rent charges. 409
Lund, T.A. Wild life law. 21
Lund, Sir T.G. Practice & etiquette. 289
Lund, Sir T.G. Professional ethics. 289, 438
Lund, Sir T.G. The Solicitors' Act 1941. 438
Lunn, R.M. & Simpson, D.D. South Australian legal costs. 123
Luntz, H. Damages. 362.
Luntz, L.L. & Luntz, P. Dental identification 147, 202
Lumpton, G.W. Civl aviation law. 34
Lushington, G. Prize. 385
Lustgarten, L. Racial discrimination. 175, 398
Luttrell, N. Parliamentary diary. 351
Luxford, J.H. Police. 367
Luxford, J.H. Estate agency. 177
Luxford J.H. & Webb, P.R.H. Domestic proceedings. 194
Lydiate, P.W.H. Misuse of drugs. 163
Lynes, T. Supplementary benefits. 436
Lyons, D. Interest of the governed. 270
Maas, H.H. European competition policy. 183
Maas, R.W. Development land tax. 149
Maasdorp, A.F.S. Institute of South African law. 440
McAllister, D.L. Mareva injunctions. 241
McAllister, D.L. Title in Ireland. 455
Macassey, Sir L.L. Middle Temple. 243
McAuslan, P. Land. 275, 459
McBarnet, D.J. Conviction. 130
McBride, T. Civil liberties. 76
McBryde, W.W. & Dowie, S.J. Petition procedure. 126, 376, 422
McCabe, S. Shadow jury. 267
McCabe, S. & Purves, R. Jury at work. 267
McCaffray, C. Sheriff Court Districts. 154

McCall, J. Consumer protection. 108
McCallum, R.C. & Tracey, R.R.S. Australian industrial law. 237
McCarry, G.J. & Sappideen, C. Conditions of employment. 170
McCarthy, W.E.J. Closed shop. 463
McCaughan, M.M. legal status of maried women. 489
McCleary, R. County court. 124, 204
McClellan, G.S. Privacy. 383
McClintock, F.H. Crimes of violence. 478
McClintock, F.H. & Avison, N.H. Crime. 138
McCloskey, M. N.A.T.O. 336
McClure, J.G. & Lavies, A.G. Oil gas tax. 207, 344
McColl, M. Court teasers. 306
McConville, S. Uses of imprisonment. 382, 397
McCormic, C. Damages. 142
McCormick, D.N. Lawyers. 289
MacCormick, N. Civil liberties. 76
MacCormick, N. Legal reasoning. 271
MacCormick, N. Legal right. 76, 271
McCredie, L. Administration of estates. 386
McCutcheon, B. Capital transfer tax. 65
McDaniels, J.F. International financing. 259
MacDermott, J.C. Protection from power. 76
McDonald, B.J. Clubs. 78
McDonald, B.J. Licensing laws. 296
McDonald, E.F. & Darvall, C. & Fernon, N.T.F. Bankruptcy. 38
Macdonald, I.A. Immigration. 231
Macdonald, I.A. Race relations. 231, 398
Macdonald, I.A. Worker's compensation. 489
Macdonald, I.A. & Blake, N.J.G. Nationality law. 231
Macdonald, J. Bill of Rights. 45
Macdonald, J.H.A. Criminal law. 134
Macdonald, J.M. Rape. 401
Macdonald, R.S. Morris, G.L. & Johnston, D.M. International law. 257
Macdonald, R.St.J. Arctic frontier. 26
Macdonald, R.St.J. & Johnson, D.M. Structure & process. 250
Mcdonall, A. Institute. 422
McDougal, M.S. Human rights. 229
McDougal, M.S. World public order.
McDougal, M.S. & Burke, W.T. Public order of oceans. 364, 425
McDouglas, M.S. Space. 443
McElroy, R.G. Impossibility. 114
McEwan, R.G. Pleading. 365
McEwan, R.G. & Paton, A. Damages. 142
McEwan, A.C. International boundaries. 53
Macey, J.P. Housing Act. 226
Macey, J.P. Housing Finance Act. 226
Macey, J.P. & Baker, C.V. Housing management. 226
McFarlane, G. Copyright. 118

AUTHOR AND SHORT TITLE INDEX

McFee, W. Law of the sea. 425
MacGillivray, E.J. & Parkington, M. Insurance. 245
McGlyne, J.E. Unfair dismissal. 170, 471
McGonigle, R.M. & Zacher, M. Pllution. 370
McGregor, H. Damages. 142
McGregor, H. Double taxation. 159
McGregor, H. Social history. 219, 283
McGregor, O.R., Blom-Cooper, L. & Gibson, C. Separated spouses. 306
McGuffie, K.C. Admiralty letter books. 11
McGuffie, K.C., Admiralty practice. 11, 432
MacIntosh, J.C. & Normanscoble, C. Negligence in delict. 145
MacIntyre, D. Auctioneers. 30, 177
McKean, W.A. Equality & discrimination. 175, 255
McKean, W.A. Race relations. 398
McKee, W.S. Mortgages. 323
Macken, A.G. & Hickmott, G.J.R. Insurance of profits. 248
Macken, J.J. Employment. 170
Macken, J.J. Industrial law. 32, 170
Mackenzie, G. Insitutes. 422
McKenzie, H.S. Building contracts. 215
Mackenzie, N.A.M. Legal status of aliens. 18
Mackenzie, W. & Handford, P. Nuisances. 340
Mackenzie-Stuart, A.J. European communities. 180
Mackenzie-Stuart, A.J. "Non-contractual" liability of EEC. 180
McKerron, R.G. Delict. 145
Mackeurtan, H.G. Sale of goods. 420
McKinlay, J.B. Law & ethics in health care. 393
Mackinnon, Sir F.D. Inner Temple. 243
Mackintosh, J. Roman law. 418
Mackintosh, J.P. British Cabinet. 60, 377
McKnight, A. Atomic safeguards. 339
McKnight, A.D. Environmental pollution. 369
McKnight, G. Computer crime. 98
McKown, R. Factory law. 167, 192
McKown, R. Town planning. 459
MacLachlan, D. Merchant shipping. 432
McLachan, D.L. & Swann, D. Competition policy. 95, 183
McLean, I.G. Criminal appeals. 22, 127, 140
McLean, I.G. Crown court. 140, 428
McLean, I.G. & Morrish, P. Breathalyser offences. 161
McLean, I. & Morrish, P. Magistrates' court. 132, 306, 428
McLean, J.D. Legal context of social work. 436, 437
McLean, J.D. & Wood, J.C. Criminal justice. 130, 428
McLean, S. Legal issues in medicine. 157
McLean, S. Medicine, morals & law. 157, 315

Macleod, J.H. Sale & hire purchase. 106, 420
McLeod, R.M. & Takach, J.D. Breathalizer law in Canada. 161
McLeod, T.L. Planning. 460
McLoughlin, J. Negotiable instruments. 331
McLoughlin, J. Pollution. 174, 369
McLoughlin, J. Pollution control. 369
McLoughlin, J. Water Act. 484
McMahon, M.M. Conquest. 481
McMahon, B.M.C. & Binchy, W. Irish torts. 457
Macmillan, A.R.G. Bona vacantia. 51
Macmillan, A.R.G. Scottish judiciary. 265
Macmillan, Lord. Local government. 301
Macmillan, P.R. Censorship. 67
Macmillan, S.K. Leases. 285
McMinn, W.G. Australian constitutional history. 32
McMonnies, P. Companies Act. 90
Macmorland, B. Services for disabled. 437, 486
MacMorran, A. & Willis, W.A. Sewers. 161
MacMorran, K. Church wardens. 164, 348
McMullen, J. Rights at work. 175
McNae, L.C.J. Journalists. 379
McNair, Sir A.D. Air law. 34
McNair, Sir A.D. Treaties. 466
McNair, A.D. & Watts, A.D. War. 481, 482
Macnamara, D.E.J. Sex, crime and the law. 429
MacNeil, I.R. Bankruptcy. 38
McNeil, J.L. & Rains R. Nigerian contract & tort. 333
McNeill, P.G.B. Adoption in Scotland. 12
Macpherson, C.B. Property. 403
Macpherson, J. Faculty of advocates. 14
MacQueen, J.F. War. 50
Macswinney, R.F. Mines. 319
McVeagh, J.P. Valuation. 402
McWhinney, E. Aerial piracy. 217, 364
McWhinney, E. Canadian jurisprudence. 61
McWhinney, E. Comunications. 453
McWhinney, E. Detente. 257
McWhinney, E. Illegal diversion of aircraft. 217
McWhinney.E. Judicial review. 266
McWhinney, E. & Bradley, M.A. Freedom of the air. 34
McWhinney, E. & Bradley, M. Space law. 443
McWilliams, P.K. Canadian criminal evidence. 187
Maddison, R. Copyright. 118
Maddocks, B.C. & Malone, M. Renting business premises. 409
Madge, P. Professional indemnity insurance. 247
Madgwick, D. & Smythe, T. Privacy. 383
Maestro, M.T. Cesare Beccaria. 3976
Magnet, J. Canadian constitutional law cases.

61
Magnifico, G. European monetary unification. 182
Magnus, S.W. Business tenancies. 58
Magnus, S.W. Housing Repairs & Rents Act. 226
Magnus, S.W. Rent Act. 409
Magnus, S.W. & Estrin, M. Companies. 90
Magore, D.L. & Thrower, C.K. Housing benefits. 226
Maguire, M. Burglary. 138, 454
Magwood, J. Canadian competition law. 95
Mahaffy, R.P. & Dodson, D. Road traffic. 217, 417
Maher, F.K.H., Waller, P.L. & Derham, D.P. Legal process. 32, 331
Maidment, S. Child custody. 156
Maimonides Code of Maimonides. 263
Maine, Sir H.J.S. Ancient law. 271, 380
Maine, Sir H.J.S. International law. 250
Mainprice, H.H. VAT. 476
Maisch, H. Incest. 232, 429
Maitland, F.W. Constitutional history. 104
Maitland, F.W. Domesday book. 221
Maitland, F.W. Equity. 176
Maitland, F.W. Forms of action. 85, 457
Maitland, F.W. Roman canon law. 164
Major, W.T. Contract. 111
Major, W.T. Sale of goods. 420
Mak, W. & Molyn, H. Trade-mark law. 461
Makower, F. Church of England. 164
Malawi. Laws. 308
Male, J.M. landlord & tenant. 280
Malby, A. & McKenna, B. Irish official publications. 45
Malone, M. Discrimination. 175
Malynes, G.de. Law merchant. 281
Management & Personal Office. Civil service yearbook. 213
Mance, H.O. International air transport. 34
Manchester, A.M. Legal history. 219
Mangone, B.J. World ocean. 425, 432
Manitoba Law Reform Commission. Family law. 195
Mankabady, S. Collision at sea. 79
Mann, A. Medical assessment of injuries. 142, 203, 314, 362
Mann, C.J. Judicial decision. 184
Mann, F.A. International law. 250
Mann, F.A. Money. 39, 321
Mannheim, H. Comparative criminology. 138
Mannheim, H. Penal reform. 397
Mannheim, H. & Wilkins, L.T. Prediction methods. 52
Manning, M. Privacy. 383
Mannino, M.J. Nursing anaesthetist. 19
Mannix, E.F. Professional negligence. 330
Mannix, E.F. & Harris, D.W. Australian income tax. 233

Mannix, E.f. & Mannix, J.E. Australian income tax. 233
Mansergh, P.N.S. Northern Ireland. 149, 337
Manson, K. Building law. 56
Manual of Air Force law. 17
Manual of military law. 27
Manwaring, G.E.. Naval history. 203
Manwood, J. Forest laws. 203
Maple, G.J. Probate. 386
Marantelli, S.E. Australian legal dictionary. 150
Marcham, F.G. Constitutional history. 104
Marchant, R.A. Church under the law. 164
Marcus, R. Law in Apocrypha. 42
Marcuse, H. Counter revolution. 415
Margach, J. How parliament works. 352
Margo, R.D. Aviation insurance. 34, 227, 246
Mark, Sir R. Minority verdict. 7
Mark, Sir R. Perplexed society. 367
Marke, J.J. & Sloane, R. Legal research. 295
Markesinis, B.S. Dissolution of parliament. 93, 352
Markesinis, B.S. & Munday, R.J.C. Agency. 16
Markose, A.T. Judicial review. 266
Markov, M.G. Outer space. 443
Markowitz, J.C. Plea bargaining. 365
Marnham, B. Public Utilities etc. Act. 217
Marriott, A.S. & Dunn, G.W. Mortgage. 323
Marriott, E.G. Personal property. 363
Marriott, Sir J.A.R. Mechanism of the modern state. 212
Marsden, R.G. Collisions at sea. 79, 432
Marsden, R.G. Law & custom of the sea. 364, 425
Marsh, A.I. & Evans, E.O. Industrial relations. 239
Marsh, G.B. Employer & employee. 170
Marsh, P. Contract negotiation. 111
Marsh, P. Contracting for engineers. 55
Marsh, S.B. & Soulsby, J.R. Business law. 82
Marshall, A.H. Financial administration. 301
Marshall, E. Rights in security. 38
Marshall, E.A. Partnership cases. 90, 354
Marshall, E.A. Scots law. 422
Marshall, E.A. Scots mercantile law. 82
Marshall, E.A. Scottish cases on agency. 16
Marshall, E.A. Scottish cases on contract. 111
Marshall, G. Constitutional conventions. 103
Marshall, G. Constitutional theory. 103
Marshall, G. Parliamentary sovereignty. 322, 441
Marshall, G. Police. 367
Marshall, G. & Moodie, G.C. The Constitution. 103
Marshall, H.H. Natural justice. 271
Marshall, J.D. Poor law. 371
Marshall, O.R. Assignment. 28, 111
Marshall, T. Inquests. 120

AUTHOR AND SHORT TITLE INDEX

Marston, G. Marginal seabed. 109, 415, 453
Marten, D. & Luff, P. Guarantees for homes. 226
Martin, A. Law reform. 283
Martin, A.W. Australian federation. 32
Martin, A. Restrictive trade practices. 322
Martin, C.R.A. Medical practice. 157, 315
Martin, E. & Graham-Helwig, H. Minutes. 316
Martin, E.A. Concise dictionary. 150
Martin, F.M. Children out of court. 73
Martin, F.M. & Murray, K. Scottish juvenile justice. 273
Martin, R. Personal freedom. 76, 450
Martyn, J.G.R. Family provision. 197
Marwah, O. & Schulz, A. Nuclear proliferation. 339
Mason, E.S. & Asher, R.E. World Bank. 490
Mason, H.H. Company law. 90
Mason, H.H. Priddle, L.G. & Fletcher, K.L. Commercial caes. 82
Mason, J. Medical ethics. 157
Mason, J.K. Aviation accident pathology. 34
Mason, J.K. Forensic medicine. 203, 324, 315
Mason, K. & Handler, L.G. Wills, probate. 386
Mason, P. Race relations. 398
Mastellone, L. Legal & commercial dictionary. 150
Masters, S.V. Stamp duties. 445
Masterson, W.E. Marginal seas. 256, 425
Mather, L.C. Securities. 39
Mather, L.M. Plea bargaining. 130
Mather, P.E. Sheriffs. 27, 36, 188, 267, 430
Mather, T.C. Public order. 394
Mathew, Sir T. Director of Public Prosecutions. 390
Mathews, A.S. Law order & liberty. 76, 395, 440
Mathieson, D. & Walker, A. Social enquiry reports. 437
Mathijsen, P.S.R.F. European community law. 180
Mattee, N.M. Aerospace law. 443
Matte, N.M. & Desaussure, H. Remote sensing from outer space. 443, 453
Mattern, T. Civil aviation law. 34
Matthewman, J. & Lambert, N. Social security. 436
Matthews, E.J.T. & Oulton, A.D.M. Legal aid. 286
Maude, B. Meetings. 316
Maudsley, R.H. Perpetuities. 361
Maudsley, R.H. & Burn, E.H. Land law. 275, 323
Maudsley, R.H. & Bure, E.H. Trusts. 469
Maugham, E. U.N.O. 483
Maurice, S.G. Family provision. 197
Mawby, R.I. Policing the city. 367

May, H.J. South African evidence. 187
May, R. Criminal evidence. 187
May, T.E. Constitutional history. 104
May, Sir, T.E. Parliamentary practice. 290, 350, 384
Mayers, M.O. Hard-core delinquent. 146
Mayers, M.R. Occupational health. 342
Mayne, J.D. Hindu law. 218
Mayne, R.J. European community institutions. 183
Mayo, J.W. Companies. 90
Mays, J.B. Crime & treatment. 138
Mays, J.B. Juvenile delinquency. 73, 146
Mays, J.B. Young offenders. 73, 146
Mayson, S.W. Revenue law. 413
Mayson, S.W. & French, D. Company law. 90
Max-Planck-Institut. Judicial protection. 266
Maxwell, Sir P.R. Interpretation. 258
Maxwell-Lyte, H.C. Great Seal. 304
Mazengarb, O.C. Industrial relations. 239
Mazengarb, O.C. Negligence. 217
Mbanefo, L.N. Nigerian shipping laws. 333, 432
Meacher, N. Rate rebates. 402
Mead, M.W.T. Unfair dismissal. 471
Meador, D.J. Criminal appeals. 22m 93=, 128
Meagher, R.P. & Gummon, W.M.C. Trusts. 469
Meagher, R.P., Gummon, W.M.C. & Lehane, J.R.F. Equity. 176
Meaney, T.F., Lalli, A.F. & Alfidi, R.J. Radiologic protection. 315, 490
Medical Defence Union. Law & the doctor. 315
Medical Practitioners Society & Royal College of General Practitioners. Abortion Act. 4
Medley, D.J. Original illustrations. 104
Meek, C.K. Colonial law. 15, 44, 298
Meek, C.K. Land law. 275
Meekings, C.A.F. Thirteenth century justice. 219
Meerhaeghe, M.A.G. Van. International economic institutions. 252
Megarry, Sir R.E. Inns ancient & modern. 242
Megarry, Sir R.E. Lawyer & litigant. 40, 289
Megarry, Sir R.E. Miscellany. 408
Megarry, Sir R.E. Real property. 403
Megarry, Sir R.E. Rent Acts. 23, 409
Megarry, Sir R.E. & Wade, H.W.R. Real property. 373, 403
Meghan, P.J. Local government. 260
Meghan, P.J. Public service. 260
Megrah, M.H. Bills of exchange. 46
Mehta, R.S. Minority rights. 76
Meier, R.F. Criminology. 138
Meiners, R.E. Legal environment. 83
Meinhardt, P. Company Law. 90
Meinhardt, P. Inventions. 322, 357, 461
Meinhardt, P. & Havelock, K.R. Trademark

law. 461
Mellinkoff, D. Lawyers & system of justice. 474
Mellows, A.R. Conveyancing searches. 116
Mellows, A.R. Executors. 413
Mellows, A.R. Succession. 386, 449
Mellows, A.R. Taxation for executors. 65, 189, 413, 469
Mellows, A.R. Taxation of land. 275, 413
Mellows, A.R. Trustees' handbook. 469
Meltsner, M. Cruel & unusual. 64
Melville, Sir H.W. D.S.I.R. 214
Melville, L.W. Forms & agreements. 118, 204
Melville, L.W. Industrial property. 118, 357
Mendelsohn, M. Franchising. 83
Mendes, Da Costa, D. Canadian family law. 195
Menon, K. Jurisprudence. 271
Mepham, G.J. Equal opportunity. 175
Merkin, R. & Williams, K. Competiton. 95
Meron, T. Human rights. 229
Meron, T. U.N. Secretariat. 473
Merriam, C.E. Sovereignty. 441
Merrills, J.G. Dispute settlement. 251
Merrills, J.G. International law bibliography. 44, 251
Merrills, J.G. International law anatomy. 250
Merryman, J.H. Civil law tradition. 75, 93
Merryman, J.H. Italian civil code. 262
Mersky, R.M. Boycotts & coercion. 252, 255
Mersky, R.M. Collecting & managing rare law books. 295
Mersky, R.M. & others. Medical literature. 44
Mesher, J. Compensation for unemployment. 170, 405
Messent, A. C.M.R. 66, 464
Meston, Lord. Betting & lotteries. 41
Meston, Lord. Consumer Credit Act. 106
Meston, Lord. Moneylenders. 28, 321, 358
Meston, M.C. Succession (Scotland) Act. 449
Metcalfe, O.K. English law. 123
Meurs, A.P.H. van. Petroleum economics. 344
Mewett, A.W & Manning, M.M. Criminal law. 135
Mews, J. Digest. 152
Meyer, J. Local government. 440
Meyer, M.L. Counselling. 18
Meyerowitz, D. Administration of estates. 189
Meyers, D.W. Human body & the law. 315
Meznerics, I. Banking. 39
Mian, Q.J. & Lerrick, A. Saudi business. 83
Micallef, J. European company. 182
Michael, J. Secrecy. 343
Michael, W.H. & Will, J.S. Gas & water. 207, 484
Michaels, A. Trademarks. 461
Michaels, D.B. International privileges. 154, 257
Mickleburgh, J. Consumer protection. 108

Micklem, B. Law and the laws. 271
Micklethwait, Sir R. National Insurance Commissioners. 327, 436
Middleton, R. Negotiating on non-tariff distrotion. 185
Miers, D. Victimisation. 128, 410
Mikaelsen, L. Human rights. 229
Mildred, R. Expert witness. 187
Milgrim, R.M. Trade secrets. 452
Millard, P.W. Tithe rentcharge. 410
Miller, A. Presidential power. 474
Miller, C.J. Contempt. 109
Miller, C.J. Product liability. 368, 457
Miller, G. Family property. 197
Miller, G. Machinery of succession. 449
Miller, I. Industrial law. 237
Miller, J.B. Partnership in Scotland. 354
Miller, N. Battered spouses. 158
Miller, N. & Aya, R. National liberation. 415
Miller, R.I. War. 481
Miller, S.L. Dentistry. 147
Millham, S. After grace, teeth. 24
Millner, M.A. Negligence. 330
Mills, C.P. NSW industrial laws. 237
Mills, C.P. NSW Workers' compensation. 489
Mills, C.P. & Sorrell, G.H. Federal industrial laws. 237
Mills, G.E. & Poyser, A.H. Lunacy practices. 317, 375
Mils, J. Building Societies. 57
Mills, M.A. Isle of Man. 262
Milne, A. Noise pollution. 335
Milne, Sir D. Scottish Office. 214
Milner, A. Nigerian penal system. 135, 333
Milner, A. & Abrahams, S. African banking. 3
Milner, J.B. Contracts. 111
Milson, S.F.C. Historical foundations. 85, 219
Milson, S.F.C. Nature of Blackstone. 219
Milte, K.L. & Weber, T.A. Police in Australia. 367
Milton, J.R.L. South African criminal law. 440
Mind. Act on trial. 73
Mining Journal. Mineral development. 319
Ministry of Foreign Affairs (N.Z.) French nuclear testing. 339
Minogue, M. Local government. 301
Miskin, G.E. Directory of law libraries. 295
Miskin, C.e. Library and information services. 295
Mitchelhill, A. Bills of lading. 432
Mitchell, B. Law, morality & religion. 271
Mitchell, E. Businessman's legal lexicon. 150
Mitchell, E. Caterers lawyer. 242
Mitchell, E. Director's lawyer. 90
Mitchell, E. Employment protection. 172
Mitchell.E. Health, safety and welfare. 170, 236
Mitchell, J. Constitutional law. 103
Mitchell, J.D.B. Public authorities. 392

AUTHOR AND SHORT TITLE INDEX

Mitchell, W. Law merchant. 281
Mobbs, M. Local government planning. 460
Moberly, W. Partnership management. 354
Moeran, E. Conveyancing. 116
Moeran, E. Legal aid. 286, 287
Moiser, C.H. Endorsements. 417
Moiser, C.H. Notifications by magistrates' courts. 306
Moiser, C.H. Practice & procedure magistrates' courts. 306
Moller, N.H. Civil aviation. 34
Moller, N.H. Farm law. 16
Molloy, A.P. Estate planning. 178
Monir, M. Evidence. 187
Monopolies & Mergers Commission. Advocates' services. 14
Monopolies & Mergers Commission. Barristers' services. 41
Monopolies & Mergers Commission. Services of solicitors. 438
Monopolies Commission. Estate agents. 177
Monopolies Commission. Reports. 322
Monroe, J.G. & Nock, R.S. Stamp duties. 445
Monroe, M.H. Intolerable inquisition. 413
Montgomery, A.C. Acronyms & abbreviations. 294
Montgomery, E.J. Notaries Public. 337
Montrose, J.L. Precedent. 266
Moody, S.R. & Tombs, J. Prosecution. 390
Moon, R.W. Business mergers. 83
Moore, E.G. Canon law. 164
Moore, G. & Wood, C. Social work & criminal law. 134, 437
Moore, H. Abstracts of title. 455
Moore, J.B. Extradition. 191
Moore, J.J. Drug abuse. 163
Moore, J.N. War. 481
Moore, M. Meetings. 316
Moore, M.S. Law & psychiatry. 317
Moore, R. & Wallace, T. Immigration. 231
Moore, R.B. Isle of Man. 262
Moore, S.A. Foreshore. 426, 453
Moore, T.G. & Wilkinson, T.P. Juvenile court. 273, 376
Moore, V.W.E. Community land. 87
Moore, V.W.E. & Catchpole, L. Local government planning. 174, 460
Moore, W.H. Acts of state. 6, 139
Moran, C.G. Heralds of the law. 284
Morcom, J.B. Estate duty. 63, 178
Morcom, J.B. & Party, D.J.T. Capital transfer tax. 65, 413
More, H.W. Administration of justice. 7
Morgan, A. From summit to council. 180
Morgan, A.M. Government publications. 45
Morgan, E.D. Animals. 21
Morgan, J.H. House of Lords. 350
Morgan, J.H. Public authorites. 139
Morgan, R. Computer contracts. 98, 113

Moriarty, C.C.H. Police law. 367
Moriarty, C.C.H. Police procedure. 367
Morin, D. & Chippindale, W. Acquisitions and mergers. 449
Morison, I.C., Tillett, J.P.K. & Welch, M.J.C. Banking Act. 39
Moritz, A.R. & Morris, R.C. Legal medicine. 315
Morris, A. Children. 73
Morris, A. Constitution of American education. 474
Morris, A. Parliamentary scrutiny.
Morland, N. Criminologist.
Morris, a. & Giller, H. Criminal justice for children. 130
Morris, A. & McIsaac, M. Juvenile justice. 273
Morris, G., Hooper, a. & Baker, M. Planning. 460
Morris, H.F. & Read, J.S. African legal system. 15
Morris, J.H.C. Conflict of laws. 101
Morris, J.H.C. Private international law. 101
Morris, J.H.C. Property statutes. 403
Morris, J.H.C. & Leach, W.B. Perpetuities. 361
Morris, L.C. Air & space law bibliography. 44
Morris, N. Madness.. 317
Morris, P. & Beverly, f. On licence. 353
Morris, N. & Perilan, N. Law & crime. 132
Morris, P. & Heal, K. Crime control. 129, 367
Morris, P., White, R. & Lewis P. Social needs. 372
Morris, R.C. & Moritz, A.R. Doctor & patient. 315
Morris, R.J.B. Parliament & public libraries. 294
Morris, R.J.B. Public lending right. 394
Morris, t. & Blom-Cooper, L.J. Calendar of murder. 223
Morris, W.A. Sheriff. 221, 430
Morrish, P. & McLean, I. Appeals in criminal courts. 22
Morrish, P. & McLean, I. Crown Court. 132, 140, 428
Morrison, A.C.L. Juvenile court law. 273
Morrison, F.L. Courts. 126
Morse, C.J.G. Torts. 101, 457
Morse, D.A. International Labour Office. 254
Morse, G. Company finance. 449
Mors, g. Companies Act. 90
Morse, g. Company structure. 90
Morse, G. & Williams, D. Profit sharing. 170
Mortlock, B. Inside of divorce. 156
Morton, J. Defending. 14
Morton, J.D. Evidence in criminal cases. 187
Moskowitz, M. Human rights. 229
Moskowitz, M. Roots & reaches. 473
Mosley, R.K. Cabinet Office. 60
Mosse, G.L. Police forces. 367

Mosteshar, S. & Bale, S.de B. Satellite & cable television. 399, 443
Mostyn, F.E. Marriage. 194
Moullin, M. & Sargent, J. Taxation of companies. 90, 121, 413
Moulton, H.F. & Evans-Jackson, J.H. Patents. 461
Moulton, H.F. & Langdon-Davies, P.G. Merchandise marks. 461
Moureau, J.F. & Mueller, G.O.W. French penal code. 205
Mouton, M.W. Continental shelf. 109
Moye, J.E. Business organisation. 83
Moylan, Sir J.F. Scotland Yard. 367
Moyle, J.B. Justinian. 418
Moys, E.M. Classification scheme. 295
Moys, E.M. European law librarie. 295
Moys, E.M. Manual of law librarianship. 295
Mozley, H.N. & Whiteley, G.C. Law dictionary. 150. 288
Mueller, H.P., Kehoe, P.e. & Hurtado, L. Law librarianship. 295
Mueller, R. Business in Germany. 82, 209
Mueller, R. GmbH. 209
Mueller, R. & Galbraith, E.G. German stock corporation. 209
Mueller, R. & Schneider, H. Competition. 95, 209
Mughal, A.K. Criminal procedure. 376
Muir, R. How Britain is governed. 212
Mukherjee, A.J. Parliamentary procedure. 235
Mukherjee, T.P. Law lexicon. 150
Mulford, D.C. Zambia. 491
Mulhern, J. & McLean, I. Industrial tribunal. 240
Mulholland, R.D. New Zealand legal system. 331
Mulla, Sir D.F. Hindu law. 218
Mulla, Sir D.F. Muhammadan law. 261
Mulla, Sir D.f. & Choppa, D.S. Insolvency. 38
Mullins, C. Sentence of the guilty. 428
Mulroney, M. Foreign corporations. 273
Mumford, G.H.F. Juvenile courts. 273
Mumford, G.H.F. & Selwood, J.T. Juvenile court law. 273
Municipal yearbook. 301
Mungham, G. & Bankowski, Z. Law & society. 271
Munkman, J.H. Advocacy. 14
Munkman, J.H. Capital transfer tax. 65
Munkman, J.H. Damages. 142, 167, 362
Munkman, J.H. Employer's liability. 167, 236
Munro, C.R. Television censorship. 67, 399
Murch, M. Divorce. 156
Murchison, I. Legal accountability. 340
Murdoch, J.R. Estate agency. 30, 177
Murdoch, J.R. Estate agents. 177
Murphy, J.G. Punishment. 397, 406
Murphy, P.W. Evidence. 187

Murphy, P.W. & Barnard, D. Evidence & advocacy. 187
Murphy, P.w. & Beaumont, J. Evidence. 187.
Murphy, W.F. Constitutional law. 93, 105
Murray, C.A. & Cox, L.A. Beyond probation. 146
Murray, D.J. Nigerian administration. 333
Murray, Sir G.E.P. Post Office. 214, 374
Murray, J. Commercial law. 83
Murray, J.O. Government & people. 212
Murty, B.S. Propaganda. 395
Mustill, Sir M.J. & Boyd, s. Commercial arbitration. 25
Mustoe, N.E. Agricultural law. 16
Mustoe, N.E. Bankruptcy. 299
Mustoe, N.E. British Civil Service. 78
Mustoe, N.E. Income tax. 233, 413
Mustoe, N.E. Valuation. 402
Mutharika, A.P. Alien. 18
Mutharika, A.p. Statelessness. 18
Myint Soe, U. Banking. 309, 331, 434
Myles, G. EEC brief. 180
Mynors, c. Urban conservation. 174
Nadaraja, T. Legal systems of Ceylon. 444
Nagel, S.S. Criminal justice. 130
Nagel, S.S. Improving the legal process. 283
Namasivayam, S. Drafting. 160
Nanjira, D.D. Aliens in East Africa. 450
Nantwi, E.K. International judicial decisions. 251
Napier, P. Discipline. 170
Napier, P. Dismissal. 170
Napley, D. Technique of persuasion. 14
Narain, B.J. Northern Ireland. 337
Narain, B.J. Public law. 337
Nardecchia, N. Citizens rights. 76
Nash, G. Criminal law Victoria. 135
Nash, G. Civil procedure. 32
Nash, H.T. Nuclear weapons. 339.
Nash, M. Sex Discrimination Act. 175
Nasr, K. Saudi business laws. 421
Nathan, C.J.M., Barnett, M. & Brink, A. Uniform rules of court. 440
Nathan, J.A. & Marshall, O.R. Trusts. 469
Nathan, Lord. Medical negligence. 157, 458
Nathan, M. Common law & S.Africa. 417, 440
National Association for Freedom. Charter of rights. 45
National Association for the Care & Resettlement of Offenders. Children in custody. 73
National Association for the Care & Resettlement of Children. Manual. 406
National Association of Credit Management. Commercial laws. 461
National Association of Credit Management. Patent law. 357
National Building Agency. Housing Associations. 227

National Campaign for the Abolition of Capital Punishment. Murder & capital punishment. 64
National Campaign for the Homeless. Council house sales. 226
National Consumer Council. Consumers & credit. 106
National Consumer Council. Consumers & nationalized industries. 392
National Consumer Council. Patients' rights. 76, 326
National Consumer Council. Tenancy agreements. 280
National Council for Civil Liberties. Against censorship. 342
National Council for Civil Liberties. Children's ombudsman. 73, 345
National Council for Civil Liberties. Corporal punishment. 120
National Council for Civil Liberties. Identification parades. 231
National Council for Civil Liberties. Rights of children. 73
National Council for Civil Liberties. Vagrancy. 390
National Council for Education Technology. Copyright & education. 165
National Council for One Parent Families. Accident of birth. 292
National Council for One Parent Families. Human rights. 229
National Council for One Parent Families. Tax & child care. 74, 413
National Council of Social Service. Lotteries. 41
National Council of Social Services. Village halls. 478
National Council for the Unmarried Mother & Her Child Illegitimacy. 292
National Federation of Consumer Groups. Handbook. 108, 192
National Federation of Housing Associations. Co-ownership Housing Associations. 277
National Federation of Housing Associations. Guide. 277
National Water Council. Byelaws. 59, 484
Naunton, B. Law & order. 7
Navy Dept. Court martial manual. 125
Navy Dept. Navigation. 329
Navy Dept. Navy list. 329
Navy Dept. Queen's regulations. 329
Neale, A.D. Antitrust. 95
Neale, J.E. Elizabeth I & parliaments. 351
Neale, J.E. House of Commons. 351
Nedjati, Z.M. Human rights. 229
Nedjati, Z.M. & Trice, J.E. Administrative law. 9, 93
Neligan, D. Social security. 436
Nelkin, D. legal process. 280

Nelson-Jones, J.A. & Smith, B. Practical tax saving. 451
Nenner, H. By colour of law. 222
Neumann, I.S. & Rosenbaum, R.A. War crimes. 44, 483
Neustatter & W.L. Mind of the murderer. 223
Nevill, A.G. & Ashe, A.w. Equity proceedings. 176
Nevitt, A.A. Rent. 409
New, L.J. Life assurance. 247
New York City Bar Association. Mental illness. 133, 317
New York Stock Exchange. Constituion & rules. 448
New Zealand Property law & Equity Reform Committee. Effect of culpable homicide. 223
Newell, D. Employment Act. 170
Newell, D. Employment law. 170
Newfoundland, Family Law Study. Family law in Newfoundland. 195
Newman, C.L. Probation. 388
Newman, E. & McQuoid-Mason, D.J. Obligations. 145
Newman, E.S. Law of philanthropy.
Newell, P. Last resort?
Newman, G. & Godfrey, R. Capital transfer tax. 65
Newman, J. Double tax. 160
Newman, P.E. Conveyancing. 116, 285
Newman, P.E. Town & country planning. 460
Newman, R.A. Equity. 93, 176
Newman, R.A. Trusts. 469
Newsam, Sir F.A. Home Office. 214
Newsholme, Sir FA. Ministry of Health. 214
Newsom, G. & Sherratt, J.G. Water pollution. 370
Newsom, G.H. Restrictive convenants. 411
Newsom, H. Salvage. 421, 470
Newsome, E.L. Trade Descriptions Act. 324, 460
Newton, C.r. General principles. 173
Newton, C.R. & Parker, R.S. General principles. 173
Niblett, B. Computer programs. 98, 119
Niblett, B. Computer science. 98
Nicholas, B. French contract. 111, 205
Nicholas, B. Roman law. 418
Nicholas, H. American politics. 474
Nicholas, H.G. U.N. 473
Nicholls, Sir G. Irish poor law. 371
Nicholls, Sir G. Poor law. 371
Nicholls, H.G. Scotch poor law. 371
Nicholls, W.J. & Carr, J.G. Company law. 90
Nichols, J.E. Hospital security. 225
Nicholson, H.M. Copyright. 33
Nicklem, B. Law & laws. 164
Nicol, A. & Rogers, H. Contempt. 109
Niekirk, P.H. Driving offences. 324

Nield, B. Assizes. 29
Nigam, R.C. Crimes in India. 235
Nightingale, B. Charities. 70
Nigro, F.A. & Nigro, L.G. Public administration. 391
Nimmer, M. Copyright. 119
Nishimura, S. Bills of exchange. 46
Nizsalovsky, E. Organ transplantation. 230
Nock, R.S. & Sherrins, T. Capital transfer tax. 65
Noise Abatement Society. Noise. 335
Noise Advisory Council. Noise insulation. 335
Nokes, G.D. Auction. 30
Nokes, G.D. Blasphemy. 49
Nokes, G.D. Evidence. 187
Nokes, G.D. Mortgages. 323
Nokes, G.D. & Bridges, H.P. Aviation. 34
Noonan, J.T. Abortion. 4
Noorani, A.G. Public law in India. 235
NormanA. Computer insecurity. 98
Norman, R. Purchase & sale. 420, 477
Norris, M.J. Salvage. 421
Norris, M.J. Seamen. 432
North, P.M. Animals, 21, 458
North, P.M. Contract conflicts. 101, 112, 180
North, P.M. International law of matrimonial causes. 101, 313
North, P.M. Occupiers' liability. 343, 458
North Atlantic Treaty Organisation. Facts & figures. 336
Northedge, F.S. Use of force. 481
Northedge, F.S. & Donelan, M.M. International disputes. 251
Northern Ireland Civil Rights Association. Bill of Rights. 46
Northern Ireland Commissioner for Companies. Annual report. 346
Northern Ireland Government. Disturbances. 395
Northern Ireland Government. Police. 395
Northern Ireland Office. Allegations of brutality. 395
Northern Ireland Office. County courts & magistrates courts. 306
Northern Ireland Office. Complaints. 367
Northern Ireland Office. Law enforcement commission. 395
Northern Ireland Office. Northern Ireland & the EEC. 337
Northern Ireland Office. Prison service. 382
Northern Ireland Office. Violence & civil distrubances. 337, 395
Northey, J.F. Company law. 90
Northey, J.F. New Zealand legal writing. 44
Northey, J.F. & Leigh, L.V. Company. 90
Norton, C.S. Women. 489
Norton, M. Covenants. 70, 413
Norton, R.F. Deeds. 258
Norton-Kyshe, J.W. Attorney-General. 282

Norton-Kyshe, J.W. Hong Kong laws & courts. 224
Norton-Kyshe, J.W. Law of gloves. 287
Nossaman, W.L. & Wyatt, J.L. Trust administration. 469
Nott, D. & Corden, J. Deferring sentence. 428
Nozari, F. Outer space. 443
Nuclear Energy Agency. Nuclear third party liability. 338
Nunn, E.W. Secretarial handbook. 90
Nursaw, W.G. Investment. 259
Nussbaum, A. Private international law. 101
Nutley, W.G. Planning policies. 460
Nutley, W.G. & Beaumont, C.H. Community Land Act. 87
Nutley, W.G. & Beaumont, C.H. Land Compensation Act. 97
Nuttall, C.P. Parole. 353
Nwabueze, B.O. Constitutional history. Nigeria. 333
Nwabueze, B.O. Constitutional law, Nigeria. 103, 333
Nwabueze, B.O. Constitutionalism. 15
Nwabueze, B.O. Judicialism. 15
Nwabueze, B.O. Nigerian machinery of justice. 333
Nwabueze, B.O. Presidentialism. 15
Nwogugu, E.I. Nigerian family law. 196
Nygh, P.E. Conflict of laws. 101
Nugh, P.E. & Turner, R.F. Family law. 194
Nylander, A.V.J. Nationality. 333
Oakley, A.J. Trusts. 469
Oakes, Sir A. & Mowat, R.B. European treaties. 466
Oates, R.K. Child abuse. 71
O'Barr, W.M. Linguistic evidence. 14
Obi, S.N.C. Family law in Southern Nigeria. 196, 333
Obieta, J.A. Suez Canal. 62
Obilade, A.O. Nigerian legal system. 333
O'Casey, J.P. Irish Attorney General. 260, 282
O'Connell, D.P. International law. 250, 425, 432
O'Connell, D.P. Sea power. 425
O'Connell, D.P. State succession. 256
O'Connell, J. Remedies. 114
Oda, S. Law of the sea. 425
Oda, S. Ocean development. 425
Oda, S. Sea resources. 199
Odgers, C.E. Construction of deeds. 144, 258
Odgers, W.B. Libel. 293
Odgers, W.B. Pleading. 258, 365, 376
Odidi Okidi, C. Ocean pollution. 370
Odumosu, O.I. Nigerian constitution. 333
Office of Fair Trading. Bargain offer claims. 192
Office of Fair Trading. Fair deal. 108, 192
Office of Fair Trading. Mergers. 450
Office of Fair Trading. Trade Descriptions

Act. 108
Office of Population Censuses & Surveys. Redundancy payments. 405
O'Flanagan, J.R. Lord Chancellors. 48, 304
Ogilvie, Sir C. King's government & common law. 85, 213, 221
Ogle, A. Canon law. 164
Ogunbanwo, O.O. Outer space. 443
Ogus, A.I. Damages. 5, 142
Ogus, A.I. & Barendt, E.M. Social security. 436
O'Hagan, H. Water. 304
O'Hare, J. & Hill, R.N. Civil litigation. 376
O'Higgins, P. Bibliography of Irish trials. 44
O'Higgins, P. Censorship. 67
O'Higgins, P. Civil liberties. 76
O'Higgins, P. Irish literature. 44, 260, 337
Oke, G.C. Fishery laws. 20, 199
Oke, G.C. Game. 206
Oke, G.C. Magisterial formulist. 204, 306
O'Keefe, J.A. Food and drugs. 201
O'Keefe, J.A. Trade descriptions. 460
O'Keefe, J.A. Weights & measures. 485
O'Keefe, J.A.B. Land values. 275
O'Keefe, J.A.B. & Farrands, W.L. New Zealand Law. 331
O'Keefe, P. & Parlett, D.S. Building regulations. 56
O'Keefe, P. & Tedeschi, M.A.G. International business. 32
O'Keefe, P.J. Law & cultural heritage. 174
Okonkwo, C.O. Nigerian law. 333
Okonkwo, C.O. & McLean, I. Criminal law. 135, 333
Okonkwo, C.O. & Naish, M.E. Nigerian criminal law. 135, 333
Okoro, D.R.N. Succession in Eastern Nigeria. 333, 449
Okoye, F.C. International law. 15, 257
Ola, C.S. Nigerian taxation. 333
Ola, C.S. Town & country planning. 333
Ola, R.O.F. Local administration. 333
Olawoye, C.O. Title to land in Nigeria. 333, 455
Olawoyin, G.A. & Olafare, A. Nigerian commercial law. 83, 333
Oldfield, M. Understanding pensions. 360
Oldnall, W.R. Welsh jurisdiction. 480
O'Leary, C. Corrupt practices. 166
O'Leary, KC. Irish elections. 166
O'Leary, K.F. & Hogan, A.E. Practice & procedure. 376
Oliphant, G.H.H. Horses. 21
Olivecrona, K. Law as fact. 271
Oliver, M.C. Company law. 90
Oliver, M.C. Private company in Germany. 90, 209
Oliver, Sir P. Chancery Division report. 8
Olle, J.G. Government publications. 65

Ollennu, N.A. Land law in Ghana. 210
Ollenu, N.A. Succession in Ghana. 210, 449
Olsson, H.R. Television & radio. 399
Oluyede, P.A. Administrative law. 15
O'Malley, L. Business law. 83
O'Malley, L. Commercial law. 83
O'Neill, J. Fetus-in-law. 4
Online Information Centre. Law data base. 98
Onokerchoraye, A.G. Nigerian social services. 333
Ontario Attorney General. Family law reform. 195
Ontario Law Reform Commission. Family courts. 195
Ontario Law Reform Commission. Family law. 195
Onwuamaegbu, M.O. Nigerian landlord & tenant. 280m 333
Oosterhoff, A.H. Wills & succession. 449, 487
Oosthuizen, A.J. Property. 440
Oosthuizen, G.C. Tissue transplantation. 230
Oppenheim, L.F.L. International law. 250, 364
O'Regan, R.S. Papua & New Guinea. 348
Orfield, L.B. & Re, E.D. International law. 252
Organisation for Economic Co-operation & Development. Double tax. 160
Organisation for Economic Co-operation & Development. Export cartels. 190
Organisation for Economic Co-operation & Development. Legal issues in information. 98
Organisation for Economic Co-operation & Development. Mergers. 450
Organisation for Economic Co-operation & Development. National health. 326
Organisation for Economic Co-operation & Development. Nuclear installations. 338
Organisation for Economic Co-operation & Development. Old age pension schemes. 360
Organisation for Economic Co-operation & Development. Package standardization. 347
Organisation for Economic Co-operation & Development. Privacy. 383
Organisation for Economic Co-operation & Development. Restrictive business practices. 322
Organisation for Economic Co-operation and Development. Transfrontier pollution. 369
Orhnial, T. Limited liability. 122
O'Riordan, D.P. Supreme Court fees. 123
Ornstein, N.J. Role of legislature. 352
Orojo, J.O. Business contracts. 353
Orojo, J.O. Conduct & etiquette. 333
Orojo, J.O. Legal practitioners in Nigeria. 333
Orojo, J.O. Nigerian commercial law. 333
Orojo, J.O. Nigerian company law. 90, 333

Orojo, J.O. Nigerian company tax. 121, 413
Osborn, P.G. Concise law dictionary. 3, 151, 288
Osborn, P.G. Jurisprudence. 271
Osborn, P.G. & Grandage, S. Commercial dictionary. 152
Osborne, B. Justices. 306
Osborough, N. Borstal. 52
O'Sullivan, J. Mental health. 317
O'Sullivan, J. Law for nurses. 340
O'Sullivan, P. Irish planning. 97, 460
O'Sullivan, R. Common law. 85
O'Sullivan, R. Defamation. 293
Oswald, J.F. Contempt. 109
Oudenijk, J.J. Adjacent waters. 425, 453
Overbeck, W. Media law. 379
Owen, G.A. Weights & measures. 485
Owen, H. Wales. 480
Owens, J.L. Law courts. 126
Oxford English Dictionary. 152
Oxford University Statutes. 346
Oxley, G.W. Poor relief. 371
Oyez. Directory of local authorities. 154, 301
Pace, P.J. Family law. 194
Pachauri, P.S. Parliamentary privileges. 352, 384
Packaging Review. Directory. 347
Paddington Law Centre. Battered wives. 158
Page, A. War. 481
Page, A.C. & Miers, D.R. Legislation. 290
Page, D. Co-operative housing. 227
Page, L. Advocacy. 14
Page, L. Sentence of the court. 428
Page, Sir L. Justices. 306
Page, R.G. Flats. 200
Page, W.H. Wills. 487
Paget, J. Banking. 39 158, 489
Pahl, J. Battered women. 158, 489
Pain, K.W. Juvenile courts. 273
Pain, K.W. Licensing. 296
Paine, F.A. Packaging. 347
Paine, L. Hospital liability. 225
Painter, A.A. Consumer protection. 108
Painter, A.A. Consumer protection for boat users. 51, 108
Painter, A.A. Food & drugs. 201
Painter, A.A. Is it legal. 461
Paisley, S.E. EEC law. 180
Palley, C. Minorities. 103, 399,
Pallister, A. Magna carta. 46, 77
Palmer, A.N. & Owen, E. Land tenures. 480
Palmer, D.M. Sources of information. 44
Palmer, E.E. Arbitration. 25
Palmer, F.B. Company law. 90, 299
Palmer, F.B. Company precedents. 90
Palmer, F.B. Peerage law. 359
Palmer, G. Compensation for incapacity. 362
Palmer, J. House of Lords Appeals. 184, 352
Palmer, M. European parliament. 184, 352

Palmer, M. European unity. 183
Palmer, N.E. Bailment. 36
Palmer, V.V. & Poulter, S.M. Lesotho legal system. 292
Palmer, V.V. Roman-Dutch. 417
Palsson, L. Marriage. 93, 156, 196, 312
Panhuys, H.F.Van. Nationality. 328
Panhuys, H.F. Brinkhorst, L.J. & Maas, H.H. International organization. 254
Pannam, C. Contract. 112
Pannam, C. Horse. 21
Pannett, A. Hotel & catering. 242
Pannick, D. Death penalty. 64, 266
Panquet, D. House of Commons. 351
Papadakis, N. Artificial islands. 425
Papadakis, N. Law of the sea. 425
Papadatos, P.A. Eichmann. 483
Papadatos, P.A. Eichmann. 483
Parizeau, A. & Szabo, D. Canadian criminal justice. 130
Park, A.E.W. Nigerian law. 334
Park, C. Continental shelf. 109
Park, W.D. Collection of debts. 143
Park, W.D. Discovery. 155
Park, W.D. Hire purchase. 106
Parker, A. Exchange control. 321
Parker, A. Wills. 487
Parker, D. & Mellows, A. Trusts. 469
Parker, F.R. Election agent. 166
Parker, F.R. Parliamentary elections. 166
Parker, H.J. Social work. 437
Parker, Lord. Arbitration. 25
Parker, S. Cohabitees. 79
Parker, W. Homosexuality. 223
Parker, W.C. Parole. 353
Parkinson, D. V.A.T. in E.E.C. 476
Parks, A.L. Tug, tow & pilotage. 157, 432, 470
Parliament house book. 154, 422
Parliamentary Commissioner for Administration Reports. 346
Parole Board. Annual report. 353
Parris, J. Arbitration. 25
Paris, J. Building contract. 55
Parris, J. Retention of title. 420
Parrish, H. Private street works. 217, 460
Parrish, H. Public Utilities etc. Act. 217
Parry, A. & Hardy, S. EEC law. 180
Parry, C. British international law. 252
Parry, C. Consolidated treaty series. 466
Parry, C. Law officers' opinions. 257
Parry, C. Nationality. 18, 328
Parry, C. & Hopkins, C.A. British treaties. 466
Parry, C. & Hopkins, J.A. Commonwealth international law. 252
Parry, D.H. & Clarke, J.B. Succession. 449
Parry, M. Cohabitation. 79
Parscoe, P. Juvenile justice. 74, 263
Parsons, G.T.E. & Ratford, W.R. Employees' rights in receiverships. 172, 299, 404

AUTHOR AND SHORT TITLE INDEX

Parsons, T. Admiralty practice. 11
Partington, M. Claim in time. 298, 436
Partington, M. Housing (Homeless Persons) Act. 486
Partington, M. Landlord & tenant. 280
Partington, M. Legal services. 372
Partington, M. & Jowell, J.L. Welfare law. 486
Partington, M., Hull, J. & Knight, S. Welfare rights. 372
Partridge, E. Slang. 152
Partridge, R. Broadmoor. 244
Passamaneck, S.M. Insurance in Rabbinic law. 248
Passingham, B. Divorce Reform Act. 313
Passingham, B. Domestic proceedings. 306, 313
Passingham, B. & Harmer, C. Matrimonial causes. 156, 313
Patel, S.R. Recognition. 255
Patent Office. Applying for a patent. 357
Patent Office. Report. 357
Patent Office. Trademarks. 461
Paterson, A. Law lords. 22, 352
Paterson, Sir A. Prisons. 382
Paterson, A.A. & Bates, T.St.J.N. Legal system of Scotland. 422
Paterson, D.A. New Zealand administrative law. 331
Paterson, W.E. Ednie, H.H. & Ford, H.A.J. Australian company. 90
Paton, A. Sheriffdoms. 154
Paton, G.C.H. & Cameron, J.G.S. Landlord & tenant. 280
Paton, G.W. Bailment. 36
Paton, Sir G.W. Jurisprudence. 271
Pattenden, R. Judge, discretion & criminal trial. 130, 265
Pattishall, B.W. & Hillard, D.C. Trademarks. 462.
Paul, T.F. Incorporated societies. 122
Paul, T.F. Land & income tax. 233
Paulus, I. Search for pure food. 201
Payne, D. Employment law. 170
Payne, W. & Ivamy, E.R.H. Carriage by sea. 66, 432
Paxman, J.M. Planned parenthood. 48
Paxton, J. European Community dictionary. 152
Paxton, J. World legislatures. 352
Peake, T. Nisi prius. 354
Pearce, C. Local government. 301
Pearcem, D. Australian administrative laws. 9
Pearce, D.C. Delegated legislation. 32, 144, 331
Pearce, D.C. Statutory interpretation. 258, 447
Pearce, E.H. Passing off. 355, 460
Pearce, E.H. & Meston, D. Nuisance. 340
Pearce, T. Stannaries. 445

Pearl, D. Interpersonal conflicts. 37, 101, 235, 347
Pearl, D. Muslim law. 361
Pearl, D. & Gray, K. Social Welfare. 486
Pearson, D. Food legislation. 201
Pearson, R. & Kenaghan, F. Employment. 170
Pease, J.G. & Chitty, H. Markets & fairs. 310
Pease, K. & others. Community service. 88
Peat, Marwick & Mitchell. Tax planning. 451
Peden, J.R. Unjust contracts. 112
Peel, W. Court of Passage. 299
Pegg, L. Hong Kong family law. 24
Peiris, G.L. Criminal liability in Ceylon. 444
Peiris, G.L. Evidence in Sri Lanka. 187
Peirson, D. Public corporation. 392
Pelling, H.M. British trade unionism. 463
Pelling, P.M. & Purdie, R.A.J. Injunctions. 156
Peltzer, M. & Boer, R. German labour management relations. 209
Peltzer, M. & Nebendorf, K. Banking in Germany. 209
Pember, D.R. Privacy. 379, 383
Pemberton, J.E. Official publications. 45
Pemberton, J.E. Politics & public libraries. 294
Penn, C.N. Noise control. 335
Pennington, R.R. Companies Acts. 90
Pennington, R.R. Company law. 91, 182
Pennington, R.R. Patents. 357
Pennington, R.R. Partnership. 354
Pennington, R.R. Stannary law. 445
Pennington, R.R. Hudson, A.H. & Mann, J.E. Banking. 39
Pension Appeal Tribunal. Assessment appeal. 22
Peratis, K.W. & Cary, E. Woman. 489
Perkins, R.M. & Boyce, R.N. Criminal law. 135
Perritt, H.H. Employee dismissal. 170, 405
Perry, F.E. Banking. 39
Perry, F.G. Social inquiry reports. 437
Pescatore, P. Law of integration. 181
Peters, J.P.E.F. Reversionary practice. 415
Pettrick, J. Battered wives. 158
Pettit, D.M. Will draftsman. 487
Pettit, P.H. Equity. 176, 469
Pettit, P.H. Landlord and tenant. 280
Pettit, P.H. Private sector tenances. 280
Pettit, W. Pharmaceutical law. 163
Pettman, B. Equal pay. 175
Pettman, J. Zambia. 491
Phadke, Y.D. & Srinivasan, R. India constitution. 235
Pharand, D. Arctic. 26
Phear, J.B. Rights of water. 426, 484
Phelan, A. Small boats. 51
Phelps, R.H. & Hamilton, E.D. Libel. 293
Philips, D. Crime and authority. 222
Philips, Sir F. Evolving legal profession. 87,

289
Phillimore, R. Domicil. 159
Phillimore, Sir R. International law. 250
Phillimore, R.J. Ecclesiastical law. 164
Phillip, A. American-Danish private international law. 101
Phillips, A. & Morris, H.F. Marriage laws. 15, 312
Phillips, A. & Smith, K. Charitable status. 70
Phillips, F. Caribbean. 263
Phillips, G.E. Labour relations. 239
Phillips, J.D. Sale of goods. 106, 420
Phillips, O.H. Constitutional and administrative. 9, 103, 262
Phillips, O.H. English law. 173
Phillips, O.H. & Jackson, P. Leading cases. 9, 105
Phillips, P. Marx & Engels. 271
Phillipson, C. Contracts. 482
Phillipson, C. War. 481
Phillipson, M. Crime & delinquency. 138, 146
Phipson, S.L. Evidence. 187
Picard, M.P. Insurance. 245
Picarda, H. Charities. 70
Pickerill, R.J. Capital allowance. 413
Pickerill, R.J. Corporate tax. 413
Pickthorn, K. Historical principles. 104
Pictet, J.S. Humanitarian law. 406
Piesse, E.L. Drafting. 160
Piggott, Sir F. Nationality. 329
Pike, A. Engineering tenders. 55
Pike, A. I.Mech.E/I.E.E. conditions. 55
Pike, L. History of crime. 134, 219
Pike, L.O. House of Lords. 350
Pillai, T.K.N. Evidence. 235
Pimsleur, M.G. Checklist. 44
Pinder, J.S. & Pace, P.J. Family law. 194
Pineus, K. & Rohreke, H.G. Limited liability. 79
Pineus, K. & Rohreke, H.G. Time-barred actions. 298, 432
Pinheironeto, J. Business in Brazil. 83
Pinner, H.L. Unfair competition. 95
Pinson, B. Revenue law. 63, 65, 253, 413
Pitt, P.H. & Dufton, J. Building law. 56
Pitt-Lewis, G. Temple. 243
Pizzey, E. Scream quietly. 158
Plane, R. & Burton, J. Penalties & orders. 306
Plane, R. & Burton, J. Road traffic offences. 417
Planiol, M.F. & Ripert, G. Civil law. 205
Plano, J.C. Marine pollution. 30
Platt, T. & Takagi, P. Crime & social justice. 138
Plender, R.M.A. European community law. 180
Plender, R.M.A. & Usher, J. European community cases. 180
Plender, R.O. Migration law. 18, 257

Plesch, A. Gold clause. 211
Ploman, E.W. Communications & information. 374
Ploman, E.W. & Hamilton, L.C. Copyright. 119
Ploscowe, M., Foster, H.H. & Freed, D.J. Family law. 196
Plucknett, T.F.T. Concise history. 85, 219
Plucknett, T.F.T. Edward I. 134, 222
Plucknett, T.F.T. Legal history. 219
Plucknett, T.F.T. Legal literature. 44, 219
Plucknett, T.F.T. Statutes. 258
Plunkett, H.G.S. & Chapman, P.F.A. Taxation appeals. 23, 413
Padmore, D. Solicitors. 438
Packson, J.R.H.H. Accountants' negligence. 6
Poingdestre, J. Jersey. 69
Polach, J.G. Euratom. 183
Poley, A.P. Stock Exchange. 448
Pollard, A.F. Evolution of parliament. 351
Pollard, D. Social welfare. 372, 436, 486
Pollard, D.E. Producers' associations. 83
Pollard, R.S.W. Administrative tribunals. 468
Pollard, R.S.W. Abolish blasphemy. 49
Pollard, R.S.W. Trees. 17, 203
Pollard, R.S.W. & Sullivan, D.D.H. Hotels. 242
Pollock, F. Common law. 85
Pollock, F. Contract. 112
Pollock, Sir F. Jurisprudence. 271
Pollice, Sir F. Partnership. 394
Pollock, Sir F. Torts. 458
Pollock, Sir F. & Maitland, F.W. History of law. 219
Pollock, Sir F. & Wright, Sir R.S. Possession. 373
Pollock, S. Legal aid. 287
Polson, C.J. & Gee, D.L. Forensic medicicine. 203, 314
Polson, C.J., Brittain, R.P. & Marshall, T.K. Disposal of the dead. 57
Polyviou, P. Equal protection. 77
Polyviou, P. Search and seizure. 77
Ponce, F.D. Philippines Torrens. 456
Pontecorvo, G. Fisheries conflicts. 199
Poole, R. & Poole, P.M. Valuation. 402
Poor, W. Charterparties. 47, 70
Porter, R. Building contract. 55
Post, A.M. Deep sea mining. 320, 425
Post Office. Television advisory committee. 400
Pothier, R.J. Contract of sale. 420
Potter, D. National insurance. 327
Potter, D. & Stanfield, D.H. National insurance. 327
Potter, D.C. & Monroe, H.W. Tax planning. 233, 451
Potter, D.C.L. Garages. 65
Potter, H. History of equity. 176

Potter, H. Land law. 277
Potter, H. Quest of justice. 271
Potter, H. Tort. 448, 458
Potter, H. & Kiralfy, A.K.R. Historical introduction. 219
Potter, H. Adams, T. & Dickson, A.W. Bankruptcy. 144
Potter, M. Papua New Guinea traditional law. 348
Pottinger, G. Secretaries of State. 214, 422
Potts, M. Abortion. 4
Pound, R. Common law. 85
Pound, R. Jurisprudence. 271
Pound, R. Justice. 9, 271
Pound, R. Legal history. 219
Pound, R. Philosophy. 271
Powell, C.M. Arrest. 27, 35
Powell, C.M. Police manual. 367
Powell, E. Evidence. 187
Powell, R. Agency. 16
Powell-Smith, V. Boundaries. 53
Powell-Smith, V. Company directors. 91
Powell-Smith, V. Contract. 112
Powell-Smith, V. Transport Act. 464
Powell-Smith, V. & Furmston, M. Building contract. 55
Power, B.J. Irish company law. 91
Powers, C.F. Bills of lading. 47
Pratap, D. International Court. 253
Pratt, F.T. Friendly societies. 86
Pratt, J.T. Enclosures. 86
Pratt, J.T. & Mackenzie, W.W. Highways. 217
Prentice, D. Companies Act. 91
Prescott, D.J. Charities. 70
Prescott, J.R.V. Boundaries. 53
Press Council. Defamation. 293
Press Council. Practice & principles. 379
Press Council. Press and people. 379
Prest, A.R. Public sector economics. 392
Prest, W. Lawyers. 222, 289
Prest, W.R. Inns of Court. 242
Preston, C.H.S. & Newsom, G.H. Limitation of actions. 298
Preston, C.H.S. & Newsom, G.H. Restrictive convenants. 163, 275, 411
Preston, R. Abstracts of title. 455
Preston, T. Privy Council. 385
Price, D. Appeals. 23
Price, G. Maritime liens. 11, 296
Price, J. Legal system. 173
Price, J.H. Comparative government. 213
Price, M.O. Legal citations. 3
Price, N. Pilots. 34
Price Commission. Annual report. 358
Prices & Consumer Protection, Dept.of. Consumer credit. 106
Prices and Consumer Protection, Department of. Monopolies. 322, 450
Prices & Consumer Protection, Dept. of. Price & pay code. 358
Prices & Consumer Protection, Dept.of. Review of the price code. 358
Prichard, A. Squatting. 444
Prichard, M.J. Scott v Shepherd. 458
Prideaux, F. Conveyancing forms. 204, 277
Priestley, P. Justice for juveniles. 74
Prime Minister. 'D' Notice system. 141
Prime Minster's Office. Industrial democracy. 239
Prime Minister's Office. Interception of communications. 374, 453
Prins, H.A. Criminal behaviour. 138
Prischepenko, N.P. Russian-English law dictionary. 151
Prison Dept. Report. 446
Pritchard, C. & Taylor, R. Social work. 437
Pritchard, F.E. Common calendar. 29
Pritchard, J.M Personal injury litigation. 352
Pritchard, W.E. Capital gains tax. 63
Pritchard, W.E. Corporation tax. 121
Pritchard, W.E. Income tax. 233, 413
Pritchard, W.E. & Jones, I.J. Back duty. 35, 413
Pritchard, W.T. & Hannen, J.C. Court of Admiralty. 11, 329
Privy Council. 'D' Notice. 141
Privy Council. Interception of communications. 383
Probert, W. Ancient laws. 480
Prophet, J. Councillor. 301
Prophet, J. Fair rents. 275, 409
Prophet, J. Local councils. 301
Prosser, T. Test cases for the poor. 372
Prothero, G.W. Statutes. 105
Prott, L.V. Latent power. 265
Pryles, M.C. Conflicts in matrimonial law. 312
Pryles, M.C. & Hanks, P. Conflict of law. 101
Przetacznik, F. Protection of officials. 154
Public Health Advisory Service. Noise. 335
Public Record Office. General eyre. 219
Publishers Association. Copyright concessions. 119
Publishers Association. Publishers practice. 33
Publishers Association. Royalty agreements. 33
Pugh, J. Heavy goods vehicles. 66, 417, 464
Pugh, L.M. Matrimonial proceedings. 156, 313
Puissochet, J.P. Enlargement of European Communities. 181
Puller, S.M. Family law. 292
Punch, M.E. Policing. 367
Purton, R.W. Parks. 349
Purver, J. Business law. 83
Purrvis, R.N. Corporate crime. 122
Purvis, R.N. Proprietary companies. 91
Purvis, R.N. & Darvas, R. Commercial letters of credit. 292, 432

Putnam, B. B. Sir William Shareshull. 222
Puxon, M. Legitimacy. 292
Pylee, M.V. Constitutional government. 235
Qualter, T.H. Election process. 166
Quebec Civil Code Revision Office. Family court. 195
Quebec Civil Code Revision Office. Family report. 195
Queen's Bench Masters. Practice forms. 204
Queen's regulations for the RAF. 17
Quekett, Sir A.S. Northern Ireland. 03, 337
Quemner, T.A. Dictionnaire juridique. 151
Quester, G.H. Nuclear proliferation. 339
Quick, J. & Garran, R.R. Australian Commonwealth. 32
Quimby, C. Medical practioner. 158
Quint, E.B. & Hecht, N.S. Jewish jurisprudence. 263
Rabin, S. Montmain. 324
Rabie, A. Environmental legislation. 369
Rabin, E.H. Property. 403
Radcliffe, G.R.Y. Real property. 403
Radcliffe, G.R.Y. & Cross, Lord. English legal system. 173
Radin, M. & Green, L.G. Law dictionary. 151
Radzinowicz, L. History of criminal law. 134, 222
Radzinowicz, L. Ideology & crime. 138
Radzinowicz, Sir L. In search of criminology. 138
Radzinowicz, L. Sexual offences. 429
Radzinowicz, Sir L. & Hood, R. Criminology. 44, 130, 138
Rae, M. First rights. 74, 77
Raffo, P. League of Nations. 284
Rafuse, R.W. Extradition. 191
Rahl, J.A. Common Market & American antitrust. 183
Raisbeck, B.L. Social worker. 437
Raistrick, D. Law Commission digest. 281, 283
Raistrick, D. Legal citations. 3, 151
Rajan, M.S. U.N. 473
Rajanayagam, M.J.L. Negotiable instruments. 331
Raju, V.B. Constitution of India. 235
Raju, V.B. Evidence Act, 187
Rakusen, M.L. Costs in matrimonial causes. 123, 156, 313
Rakusen, M.L. & Hunt, D.P. Matrimonial assets. 156
Ralston, J.H. International tribunals. 256
Raman, K.V. Dispute settlement. 473
Ramcharan, B.G. Humanitarian good offices. 229
Ramcharan, B.G. International law. 229
Ramcharan, B.G. International Law Commission. 254
Ramsay, P. Ethics. 185

Rand, H.B. Divine law. 42
Randall, F. British government. 213
Randolph, L.L. Settlement of disputes. 25, 251
Rankin, D.F. Executorship. 189
Ranking, D.F. Mercantile law. 25, 83, 354
Rankin, D.F. & Spicer, E.E. Company law. 91
Ranking, D.F., Spicer, E.E. & Pegler, E.C. Liquidators. 299, 404
Rao, P.S. Ocean resources. 425
Rapaport, F.T., & Dausset, J. Human transplantation. 230
Ratcliffe, J. Urban land. 460
Rapsalos, C.L. & Stephanou, C.A. Law of the sea. 425
Rawle, W. U.S. Constitution. 475
Rawlinson, J. Mortmain. 324
Rawls, J. Theory of justice. 271
Ray, E.E. Partnership taxation. 354, 413
Ray, P.K. Agricultural insurance. 17
Ray, R.P. Capital transfer tax. 65, 178, 451
Rayden, W. Divorce. 156, 313
Raymond, B. Bail. 35
Raymond, B. Litigation. 130, 376
Raynes, H.E. Insurance. 245
Raynes, H.E. Social security. 436
Raynor, L. Adoption. 12
Raynsford, N. & McGurk, P. Housing benefits. 226
Raz, J. Authority of law. 271
Raz, J. Conception of a legal system. 271
Raz, J. Practical reasoning. 271
Reams, B.D. & Ferguson, J.R. Consumer protection. 108
Reasons, C.E. & Rich, R.M. Sociology. 271
Reconstruction, Ministry of, Machinery of government. 213
Redcliffe-Maud, Lord & Wood, B. Local government reformed. 302
Redgrave, A. Health & safety in factories. 167, 236, 342, 433
Redlich, J. Local government. 302
Redmond, P. General principles. 173
Redmond, P.W.D. Mercantile law. 83
Redmond, P.W.D. Partnership law. 354
Reed, H.P. Bills of sale. 47
Reed, W. & Myddleton, D.R. Company accounts. 6
Reeday, T.G. Banking. 39
Rees, M. Public sector. 392
Reeves, J. History. 221
Reeves, P. Electricity & gas consumer. 167
Registry of Friendly Societies. Industrial & Provident Societies. 235
Rehman, T. Islamization. 347
Reich, N. & Micklitz, H.W. Consumer legislation. 93, 108, 182
Reid, B.C. Trademarks. 462
Reijnen, G.C.M. Outer space. 443

AUTHOR AND SHORT TITLE INDEX

Reik, T. Compulsion to confess. 99
Reisenfeld, S.A. Coastal fisheries. 199
Reith, G. Police history. 367
Relf, D.J. & Preston, c.A.L. Value added tax. 476
Rejda, G. Insurance. 246
Rembe, N.S. Africa & law of sea. 425
Remer, D. Software care. 98, 119
Rendel, M. Conseil d'Etat. 7
Rennie, M.T.M. Computer contracts. 98, 113
Renton, Sir D. Preparation of legislation. 160, 290
Renton, N.E. Meetings. 316
Renton, R.W. & Brown, R.H. Criminal procedure. 35, 376
Renvoise, J. Children in danger. 71
Reuber, G.L. Foreign investment. 259
Reuter, P. International institutions. 254
Rex, J. Race relations. 399
Reynolds, F. Industrial relations. 239
Reynolds, T.H. Race law books. 44, 295
Reynolds, W. Judicial process. 475
Rheinstein, M. Marriage stability. 312
Rice, M.D. Business dictionary. 15
Rice, R.S. Tax planning. 451
Richards, A. Journalists. 379
Richards, M. Hotels. 242
Richards, P.G. Backbenchers. 351
Richards, P.G. Local government. 302
Richards, P.G. Local Government Act.
Richards, P.G. Parliament & conscience. 352
Richards, S. British official publications. 45
Richards, S.G. British government. 213
Richardson, D. Negotiable instruments. 46, 331
Richardson, H.G. Parliament in the middle ages. 351
Richardson, H.J. Approved schools. 24
Richardson, J.E. Australian federalism. 32
Richardson, J.H. Industrial relations. 239
Richardson, R.J. Taxation of corporations. 121
Richardson, S.S. & Williams, T.H. Criminal procedure. 135, 334
Richardson, W.C. Court of augmentations. 221
Richardson, W.P. Evidence. 187
Richman, J. & Dealy, F.S.T. Family law. 194
Richmond, A.H. Migration. 399
Riddall, J.G. Equity & trusts. 176
Riddall, J.G. Land law. 275, 403
Riddall, J.G. Trusts. 469
Riddell, J. Scottish peerages. 359
Rideout, R.W. Industrial tribunal law. 240
Rideout, R.w. Labour law. 170, 239
Rideout, R.W. National industrial relations court. 239
Rideout, R.W. Redundancy payments. 405
Rideout, R.W. Trade unions. 463
Rider, B.A.K. Insider trading. 91

Ridley, J.G. Carriage of goods. 67, 400, 464
Riess, L. Electoral law. 166
Rifaat, A.M. International aggression. 257, 478
Rigge.M. & Young, M. Building Societies. 57
Riley, D. Insurance. 248
Riley, P.A. & Cunningham, P.J. Medical dictionary. 151
Rimmer, E.J. Architect. 26
Rimmer, M. Race. 399
Ringrose, H. Inns of Court. 242
Ritchie, A.V. NSW Supreme Court. 376
Ritchie, C.I.A. Ecclesiastical courts. 164
Ritson, J. Health & safety. 236
Rivington, H.G. Property. 403
Roach, J.L. & Roach, J.K. Poverty. 372
Roach, R.F.C. Lands tribunal. 280
Robb, A.C. Superannuation. 360
Robb, L.A. Legal terms: Spanish-English. 151
Robbins, L.C.G. & Maw, F.T. Devolution of real estate. 278
Robert, H.M. Parliamentary practice. 350
Roberts, A. & Guelff, R. War. 481
Roberts, A.A. S.African legal bibliography. 417, 440
Roberts, B.C. Industrial relations. 239
Roberts, D. Admiralty & prize. 11
Roberts, G. Social workers. 437
Roberts, G. & Major, W.T. Commercial & industrial. 237
Roberts, L.M. Bibliography of Festschriften. 44
Roberts, M. & Emeny, R. Lands tribunal index. 280
Roberts, N.A. Planning. 460
Roberts, R. Social laws of Qoran. 261
Roberts, R.J. Anticombines. 95, 450
Roberts, R.J. Antitrust. 95
Roberts, S. Botswana-Tswana family law. 196
Roberts, S. Order & dispute. 272
Roberts, S., Coote, A. & Ball, E. Women. 489
Roberts, S.A. Law library collections. 295
Roberts-Wray, Sir K. Commonwealth law. 87, 272
Robertson, A.H. Council of Europe. 123, 473
Robertson, A.H. European institutions. 123, 183, 336
Robertson, A.H. Human rights in Europe. 229
Robertson, A.H. International institutions. 254
Robertson, A.H. Privacy. 229, 383
Robertson, D. Industrial Tribunal. 240
Robertson, G. Obscenity. 67, 342
Robertson, G. Whose conspiracy? 102
Robertson, G. & Nicol, A. Media. 379, 400
Robertson, G.S. Civil proceedings. 139, 240, 364
Robertson, N. & Sams, K.I. Trade unionism. 463

Robertson, P. & Seaward, M. Security of tenure. 280
Robilliard, St.J.A. Religion. 407
Robinson, G.E. Public authorites. 392
Robinson, J. International law. 257
Robinson, J.M. Securities. 39, 83, 93
Robinson, S. Drafting. 160
Robinson, S.W. Multinational banking. 252
Roblot, R. French business taxation. 205
Roblot, R. French company law. 205
Robson, J.L. New Zealand. 331
Robson, P. & Watchman, P. Justice. 103, 271
Robson, P. & Watchman, P. Politics society & judiciary. 265
Robson, W.A. Civil service. 78
Robson, W.A. Justice. 9, 103
Robson, W.N. Trespasses by animals. 21
Roby, H.J. Roman private law. 418
Rochester, J.M. International institutions. 254
Rock, P. Deviant behaviour. 138, 146
Rockley, L.E. Accounts. 6
Rodabaugh, B.J. 7 Austin, M. Sexual assault. 429
Roddis, R.J. Caravans. 66
Roddis, R.J. Parks. 328, 349
Rodes, R.E. Ecclesiastical administration. 165
Rodgers, B. Poverty. 372
Rodger, F. British government publications. 45
Roesch, R. & Corrado, R.r. Evaluation & criminal justice. 130
Rogers, R.S. International associations. 254
Rodgers, S.C. The Land Tribunal. 280
Roebuck, D. Contract. 112
Rogers, F.N. Elections. 166
Rogers, W.V.H. & Clarke, M.G. Unfair Contract Terms Act. 112
Rogge, O.J. Why men confess. 99
Rohn, P.H. World treaty index. 466
Rollin, H.R. Mentally abnormal offender. 133
Rolph, C.H. Crime & punishment. 397
Rolph, C.H. Does pornography matter? 342
Rolph, C.H. Personal identity. 231
Romain, A. Legal dictionary. 151
Ronalds, C. Anti-discrimination. 175
Ronning, C.N. Diplomatic asylum. 30
Rooke, P.J. Women's rights. 489
Rooy, F.p.de. Documentary credits. 80
Rosanthal, D. Nationality. 329
Roscoe, E.S. Admiralty court. 11, 329, 385
Roscoe, E.S. Admiralty jurisdiction. 11, 329
Roscoe, E.S. Light. 297
Rosecoe, E.S. Lord Stowell. 385
Roscoe, E.S. Prize. 385
Roscoe, H. Civil evidence. 188, 298, 334
Roscoe, H. Criminal evidence. 187, 235, 240
Rose, F.D. Pilotage. 157, 432
Rose, G. Schools for young offenders. 24
Rose, M.E. English poor law. 371

Rose, P.B. Weights & measures. 485
Rose, R. Electoral behaviour. 166
Rose-Innes, L.A. Judicial review. 267
Rosen, F. Jeremy Benthan. 103
Rosenberg, P.D. Patent. 357
Rosenburg, J.W.L. Information retrieval. 99
Rosenne, S. Codification of international law. 257
Rosenne, S. International court. 263
Rosenne, S. Treaties. 466
Roseveare, H.G. Treasury. 214
Roshier, B. & Teff, H. Law & society. 173
Ross, A. U.N. Constitution. 473
Ross, A.E. On guilt. 138, 271, 397
Ross, A.N.C. On law & justice. 271
Ross, H.L. Drinking driver. 162
Ross, I.A. European bankruptcy. 38
Ross, J. Commercial leases. 83
Ross, J.F.S. Elections & electors. 166
Ross, L. & Etzioni, A. Cable televison. 400
Ross, M.J. Commercial leases. 285
Ross, R.E. Discovery. 155
Ross, W.M. Oil pollution. 370
Rossi, H. Community Land Act. 87
Rossi, H. Rent Act. 409
Rossi, H. Rent (Agriculture) Act. 17, 409
Rossi, M.G. Contempt. 109
Rostow, E.V. Ideal in law. 271
Rostow, E.V. Sovereign prerogative. 441
Roth, A.H. Aliens. 18
Rothenberg, S. Copyright. 119, 174, 454
Rotondi, M. Comparative law. 93
Roulston, R.P. & others. NSW criminal law. 135
Round, J.H. Peerage. 360
Round, O.S. Riparian rights. 426
Rouse, R. Copyhold. 117
Row, C.M. Injunctions. 241
Rowan-Robinson, J. Planning control, . 460
Rowat, D.C. Government. 61
Rowat, D.C. Ombudsman. 346
Rowe, B.C. Privacy. 383
Rowe, E.T. Strengthening the U.N. 473
Rowe, P. Health & safety. 167
Rowlands, E.B.B. Indictment & information. 235, 240
Rowlatt, Sir A.T. Principal & surey. 112, 215
Rowlatt, J. Fire insurance. 246
Rowley, C.K. Monopolies Commission. 322
Roxburgh, Sir R.F. Lincoln's Inn. 243
Royal Commission on Assizes & Quarter Sessions. Report. 29, 140
Royal Commission on Capital Punishment. Report. 64
Royal Commission on Civil Liability and Compensation for Personal Injury. Report. 261
Royal Commission on Criminal Procedure. Report. 130, 132, 376

AUTHOR AND SHORT TITLE INDEX

Royal Commission on Duties of the Metropolitan Police. Report. 367
Royal Commission on Environmental Pollution. Reports. 369
Royal Commission on Gambling. Report. 41
Royal Commission on Justices of the Peace. Report. 306
Royal Commission on Legal Services. Final report. 41, 173, 289, 438
Royal Commission on Legal Services in Scotland. Report. 41, 289, 422, 438
Royal Commission on Local Government. Report. 302
Royal Commission on Local Government in England & Wales, 1966-69. 302
Royal Commission on Local Government in Greater London. Report. 302, 303
Royal Commission on Local Government in Scotland. Report. 302
Royal Commission on Lunacy & Mental Disorders. Report. 317
Royal Commission on Marriage & Divorce. Report. 157, 311
Royal Commission on the National Health Service. Report. 147, 225
Royal Commission on the National Health Service. Working of NHS. 147, 225
Royal Commission on Police Powers. Report. 367
Royal Commission on Selection of Justices of the Peace. Report. 206
Royal Commission on the Constitution. Report. 104, 149
Royal Commission on the Constitution & Working of the Ecclesiastical Courts. 165
Royal Commission on the Land Transfer Acts. 278
Royal Commission on the National Health Service. 326, 340
Royal Commission on the Police. Final report. 367
Royal Commission on the Press. Report. 379
Royal Commission on Trade Unions & Employers' Association. Report. 239, 463
Royal Commission on Workmen's Compensation. 490
Royal Commission relating to Mental Illness & Mental Deficiency. Report. 317
Royal Institute of Public Administration. Organisation of British central government. 213
Royal Institution of Chartered Syurveyors. Agricultural holdings. 17
Royal Institution of Chartered Surveyors. Community land. 87
Royal Institution of Chartered Surveyors. Compulsory purchase valuation. 97
Royal Institution of Chartered Surveyors. Property. 403

Royal Yachting Association. Salvage. 421
Roydhouse, E. Road traffic legislation. 471
Rozakis, C.L. Jus cogens. 466
Rubenstein, M. Employment protection. 172
Rubin, E. & Schwartz, M.D. Pollution crisis. 369
Rubin, G. Wages & salaries. 170
Rubin, G.R. & Sugerman, D. Law, economy & society. 219
Rubin, L. & Murray, P. Constitution of Ghana. 210
Rubin, S. Criminal correction. 428
Rudall, A.R. Party walls. 354
Rudd, G.R. Nigerian evidence. 188
Rudden, B. Soviet insurance law. 442
Rudden, B. & Moseley, H. Mortgages. 323
Rudden, B. & Wyatt, D. Community laws. 180
Rudinger, E. How to adopt. 12
Rudinger, E. How to sue. 124
Rudinger, E. Dismissal. 495
Ruggles-Brise, Sir E. English prison system. 382
Rule, J. Outside the law. 138, 219
Rule, J. Private lives. 383
Ruoff, T.B.F. Land registration. 277
Ruoff, T.B.F. Land registration. 277
Ruoff, T.B.F. Rent charges. 410
Ruoff, T.B.F. Searching without tears. 276
Ruoff, T.B.F. Solicitor & automated office. 99
Ruoff, T.B.F. Solicitor & silicon chip. 99, 438
Ruoff, T.B.F. Torrens system. 456
Ruoff, T.B.F. & Roper, R.B. Registered conveyancing. 116, 277
Rush, F. Best kept secrets. 232
Rush, M. Parliamentary government. 212
Rushdoony, R.J. Pornography. 342
Rushforth, M. Residential care. 74, 273
Russell, Sir A. Legislative drafting. 258
Russell, Sir A. Magistrate. 306
Russell, C. Court of Passage. 299
Russell, D.E.H. Rebellion. 415
Russell, F. Arbitration. 25
Russell, O.R. Freedom to die. 185
Russell, R.W. Patents in Japan. 462
Russell, Sir W.O. Court of Great Sessions. 480
Russell, Sir W.O. Crime. 35, 132. 361
Russell-Clarke, A.D. Copyright in industrial designs. 119, 357
Russell-Davies, M. Burials. 57
Russell-Davies, M. Letting & managing. 58
Ruster, B. & Simma, B. Environment. 369
Ruster, G. Business transactions. 83
Rutland, R.A. Bill of Rights. 46
Rutter, M. & Giller, H. Juvenile delinquency. 146.
Rutter, W.A. Wills. 489
Ryan, F.J.O. & Cooke, J.C. Australian company practice. 91

Ryan, G. & Cameron, S. Open spaces. 86, 201, 416
Ryan, K., Weld, H. & Lee, W.C. Queensland Supreme Court. 376
Ryan, K.W. Civil law. 32, 75
Ryan, K.W. Income tax. 233
Ryan, K.W. International trade. 190
Rybczynski, T.M. VAT. 476
Ryde, W.C. Rating. 402
Ryder, F.R. Banking Act. 39
Ryder, F.R. Negotiable instruments. 331
Sabine, B.E.V. Income tax. 233
Sabine, B.E.V. Taxation. 413
Sabine, B.E.V. Time limits. 413
Sachs, A.H. & Wilson, J.H. Sexism. 175, 265
Sachs, E. Legal aid. 287
Sackville, R. Legal aid. 287
Sackville, R. Poverty in Australia. 373
Sackville, R. & Neave, M.A. Property law 404
Saeter, M. & Smart, I. North Sea oil & gas. 344
Safford, F. Merchandise marks. 462
Safford, F & Wheeler, G. Privy Council. 385
Sagarin, E. Criminology. 138
Sagay, I.E. Nigerian contract, 112, 334
Said, A.A. & Simmons, L.R. Ethnicity. 255
Sainsbury, I.M. Legal subject headings. 295
St.John, J. Probation. 388
St.John-Stevas, N. Agonizing choice. 48
St John-Stevas, N. Obscenity. 342
St Leonards, E.B. Powers. 374
Sainty, J.C. Admiralty officials. 11
Saks, M.J. Jury verdicts. 267
Sales, C.A. Bankruptcy. 38, 299
Salhany, R.E. & Carter, R.J. Canadian criminal evidence. 135
Saliwanchik, R. Microbilogical inventions. 230, 315
Salmond, Sir J.W. Jurisprudence. 271
Salmond, Sir J.W. Torts. 340, 458
Salter, J. & Thomas, P. Planning law. 237
Samet, Computer output as evidence. 188
Sampat-Mehta, R. Aliens. 18
Sampson, A. Changing anatomy of Britain. 9, 78
Samson, E. Dentist & State. 147
Samuel, G. Consumer law. 106, 108, 420
Samuels, A. Insolvency. 38
Samuela, A. Social security & family law. 436
Samuels, H. Appeals from local authority decisions. 23
Samuels, H. Factory law. 192
Samuels, H. Industrial law. 237
Samuels, H. Shops. 434
Samuels, H. & Stewart-Pearson, N. Offices, shops & railway premises. 434
Samuels, H. & Stewart-Pearson, N. Redundancy payments. 405
Samuels, R. Equity & succession. 177
Sanctuary, G. Before you see a solicitor. 439

Sanctuary, G. & Whitehead, C. Divorce & after. 156
Sanders, A.J.G.M. International law. 15, 250
Sanders, A.J.G.M. Southern Africa. 283
Sanders, D. Family law & native people. 195
Sanders, W.B. Juvenile delinquency. 146
Sandford, J. Prostitutes. 390
Sandison, F.G. Profit sharing. 91
Sandys, C. Gavelkind. 207
Sandys-Winsch, G. Animal law. 21
Sandys-Winsch, G. Gun law. 198
Sanger, M.B. Welfare. 373, 486
Sant, M. Regional policy and planning. 180
Sappideen, R. Australian income taxation. 233, 414
Sarathi, V.P. Evidence. 188
Sarbah, J.M. Fanti customary law. 210
Sarna, L. Authors & publishers. 33, 380
Sarna, L. Declaratory judgments. 143
Sarna, L. Letters of credit. 292
Sarpkaya, S. Money market. 321
Sarte, J.P. Ongernocide. 208, 483
Sarvis, B. & Rodman, H. Abortion. 4
Sassoon, D. CIF & FOB contracts. 59, 432
Satow, E. Diplomatic practice. 154
Saunders, M.R. Tax planning. 83, 451
Sauveplanne, J.G. Corporeal movables. 37, 127
Savage, K. Common Market. 181
Savage, N. Companies Act. 91
Savelle, M. Diplomatic history. 53, 61
Savitz, L.D. & Johnston, N. Contemporary criminolgy. 138
Sawer, G. Australian & law. 32
Sawer, G. Australian government today. 213
Sawer, G. Australian federalism. 32
Sawer, G. Constitution of Australia. 32
Sawer, G. Law for journalists. 379, 380
Sawer, G. Law in society. 10, 271
Sawer, G. Ombudsmen. 346
Saye, A.B. American government. 475
Scammell, W.S. & Densham, H.A.C. Agricultural holdings. 17
Scammels, B. Health & welfare services. 393
Scannell, Y. Pollution control. 369
Scarman, Lord. Brixton disorders. 394
Scarman, L. Control of sentencing. 428
Scarman, L. English law. 46, 77
Scarman, Sir L. Family law & law reform. 194
Scarman, Sir L. Law reform. 283
Scarman, Sir L. Northern Ireland tribunal. 395
Scarman, Sir L. Red Lion Square disorders. 394
Schacht, J. Islamic law. 261
Schacht, J. Muhammadan jurisprudence.261
Schachter, E.R. Air pollution. 370
Schachter, O. & Serwer, D. Marine pollution. 370
Schachter, R.D. & Sheppard, P.R. Legal aid

AUTHOR AND SHORT TITLE INDEX

handbook.
Schaefer, D.l. Justice or tyranny. 271
Schafer, S. Political criminal. 138
Schafer, S. Restitution to victims. 410
Schafer, W.J. Confessions. 99, 188
Schatkin, S.B. Disputed paternity. 292
Schauer, F.F. Obscenity. 342
Schechter, A.H. Interpretation of ambiguous documents. 256
Schectman, J.B. Refugee. 406
Schellen, A.M.C.M. Artificial insemination. 28
Schermers, H.G. International institutional law. 183
Schermers, J.G. Judical protection. 184
Schindler, D. & Toman, J. Armed conflicts. 481
Schlesinger, R.B. Comparative law. 93
Schlesinger, R.B. Formation of contracts. 112
Schlesinger, S. Exclusionary injustice. 188
Schmeiser, D.A. Civil liberties. 77
Schmeiser, D.A. Criminal law. 135
Schmidt, F. Discrimination. 93, 176
Schmitthoff, C.M. Arbitration. 25
Schmitthoff, C.M. Commercial law. 83
Schmitthoff, C.M. European company law. 91, 182, 450
Schmitthoff, C.M. Export trade. 83, 190
Schmitthoff, C.M. International trade. 83
Schmittoff, C.M. Sale of goods. 420
Schneider, H. & Hellwig, H.J. German Banking Act. 209
Schneider, H. & Hellwig, H.J. German labour law. 209
Schneider, H. & Kingsman, D.J. German Co-determination Act. 209
Schneider, J. Environment. 174
Schneider, J.W. Treaty making power. 254, 466
Schnepper, J.A. Bankruptcy. 38
Schoeman, T. Companies Act. 440
Schofield, A.N. Elections. 302
Schofield, A.N. Bylaws. 59
Schofield, A.N. Elections. 166
Schofield, P.G. & Burke, C. Labour law. 170
Scholar, A. Hindu law. 218
Schreiber, A.M. Jewish law. 263
Schubert, G. & Danelski, D.J. Judical behaviour. 94
Schuit, S.R. Dutch business law. 83
Schultz, J.S. Statutory sources. 94
Schulz, F. Roman law. 418, 4194
Schulz, F. Roman legal science. 419
Schutz, B.M. Psychotherapy. 158
Schwartz, B. Bill of Rights. 46
Schwartz, B. Law & the executive. 213
Schwartz, B. Roots of freedom. 104
Schwartz, B. & Wade, H.W.R. Legal Control. 10, 212
Schwartz, R.L. US constitution. 475
Schwarzenberger, G. Foreign investment. 252, 259
Schwarzenberger, G. International constitutional law. 104, 473
Schwarzenberger, G. International law. 250, 253
Schwarzenberger, G. Law of armed conflict. 481
Schwarzenberger, G. League of Nations. 284
Schwarzenberger, G. Nuclear weapons. 339, 481
Schwarzenberger, G. & Brown, E.D. Manual of international law. 250, 251, 336
Schwebel, S.M. International decisions. 251
Schweitzer, S.C. Traumatic injuries. 188
Schwerin, K. Classification for international law. 295
Scott, A.W. Private international law. 101
Scott, C.D. New Zealand Government. 302, 331
Scott, F.R. Essays on the constitution. 61
Scott, G. League of Nations. 284
Scott, G.L. Chinese treaties. 466
Scott, G.R. Capital punishment. 64
Scott, G.R. Corporal punishment. 120
Scott, G.R. Flogging. 120
Scott, Sir H. Scotland Yard. 367
Scott, I.R. Court administration. 126
Scotti, I.R. Crown Court. 140, 376
Scott, J. Inns of Court. 242
Scott, J. Logibus. 439
Scott, J.R. Criminal procedure. 133
Scott, K.J. New Zealand constitution. 331
Scott, Sir L. & Hildersley, A. Case of requisition. 364
Scott, L.F. Trading with the enemy. 482
Scottish Courts Administration. Jurisdiction & enforcement. 376
Scottish Development Dept. Rent rebates. 409
Scottish Home & Health Dept. Children & young persons. 146
Scottish Home & Health Dept. Community medicine. 393
Scottish Home & Health Dept. Conveyancing. 116
Scottish Home & Health Dept. Criminal statistics. 446
Scottish Home & Health Dept. Hospital Boards. 225
Scottish Home & Health Department. Identification procedure. 134, 231
Scottish Home & Health Dept. Parole Board. 353
Scottish Home & Health Department. Reparation. 410
Scottish Law Commission. Administrative law. 10
Scottish Law Commission. Adultery & enticement. 311
Scottish Law Commission. Annual report.

283, 423
Scottish Law Commission. Antenatal injury. 377
Scottish Law Commission. Consistorial causes affecting matrimonial status. 311
Scottish Law Commission. Corporeal moveables. 363
Scottish Law Commission. Corroboration. 188
Scottish Law Commission. Damages for injuries causing death. 362
Scottish Law Commission. Damages for personal injuries. 363
Scottish Law Commission. Evidence code. 188
Scottish Law Commission Expenses. 134
Scottish Law Commission. Floating charges. 91
Scottish Law Commission. Illegitimacy. 292
Scottish Law Commission. Judgments Extension Acts. 265
Scottish Law Commission. Legitimation. 292
Scottish Law Commission. Liability of a paramour. 311
Scottish Law Commission. Lost & abandoned property. 363
Scottish Law Commission. Married women's policies of assurance. 246
Scottish Law Commission. Occupancy rights. 158, , 194
Scottish Law Commission. Planning permission. 460
Scottish Law Commission. Prescription. 145, 298, 378
Scottish Law Commission. Probates. 455
Scottish Law Commission. Programme. 283, 423
Scottish Law Commission. Programme of consolidation. 283, 423
Scottish Law Commission. Rights in security. 91
Scottish Office. Legal system of Scotland. 422
Scottish Office. Local government. 302, 422
Scottish Office. Sexual assault. 429
Scottish Rights of Way Society. Right of way. 416
Scriven, J. Copyholds. 117
Scrutton, T.E. Charterparties. 47, 71, 432
Scrutton, T.E. Commons. 86
Scrutton, T.E. Roman influence. 419
Seabrook, G.A. Air law. 34
Seabrooke, S. Evidence. 188
Seago, P. & Bissett-Johnson, A. Family law. 194
Seago, P. Criminal law. 132
Sealy, L.S. Company law. 91
Seaton, E.E. & Maliti, S.T. Tanzania treaty practice. 450
Sebastian, L.B. Trade marks. 462
Sebek, V. Eastern European states. 425

Sebenius, J.K. Negotiating law of the sea. 425
Seear, J.E. Law & ethics in dentistry. 148
Seervai, H.M. Constitutional law of India. 235
Seide, K. Arbitration. 25, 152, 251
Seidman, R.B. Criminal law of Africa. 136
Selden Society. Law merchant. 281
Selden Society. Year Books. 490
Selmer, K.S. General average. 432
Selmer, K.S. Swansea debriefing. 99
Selwyn, N.M. Employment. 171
Selwyn, N.M. Health & safety. 167
Selwyn, N.M. Industrial relations. 239
Selwyn, N.M. Industrial law. 237
Selwyn, W. Nisi prius. 334
Sen, B. Diplomat's handbook. 154
Sen, P. Hindu jurisprudence. 218
Sengupta, S. Business law of India. 235
Senior, W. Doctors' commons. 11
Senior, W. Naval history. 329
Sereny, G. Invisible children. 390
Sergeant, E.G. & Sims, B.J. Stamp duties. 445
Sewer, D. Pollution control. 369
Sethi, R.B. & Gopala-Krishna, T.P. Hindu Succession Act. 218
Sethna, J.M. Nuclear energy. 338
Seton, Sir H.W. Forms of decrees. 68, 155, 177, 265
Seton, Sir M. India Office. 214
Sewell, R.C. Chancellor's court. 346
Sewell, R.C. Sheriff. 430
Shackleton, F. Meetings. 316
Shadwell, L.L. Universities of Oxford & Cambridge. 60, 346
Shah, S.M. Transfer. 211
Shaker, M.J. Nuclear non-proliferation. 339
Shannon, F. Cautions. 307
Sharma, S.R. Indian constitution. 318
Sharp, D.B. Obscenity. 342
Sharp, Lady. Ministry of Housing. 214
Sharp, W.R. United Nations. 473
Sharpe, R.J. Habeas corpus. 216
Shatter, A.J. Family law in Ireland. 195
Shattuck, J.H.F. Privacy. 383
Shaw, B. Environmental law. 369
Shaw, L. & Sichel, H. Accident proneness. 5
Shaw, M.N. International law. 250
Shaw, S. Air transport. 464
Shaw, Sir S. & Smith, E.D. Meetings. 316
Shaw's Directory of Courts. 126
Shawcross, C.N. & Beaumont, K.M. Air law. 34, 246
Shears, P. Nigerian business law. 83
Sheard, T. Wills. 487
Shearer, I.A. Extradition. 191
Sheehan, M.M. Wills. 487
Sheenan, A.V. Criminal procedure. 134
Sheikh, A. International law & national behaviour. 257
Sheldon, H.P. Banking. 40
Shelford, L. Copyholds. 117

AUTHOR AND SHORT TITLE INDEX

Shelford, L. Mortmain. 324
Shepherd, K.M. & O'Sullivan, P. Planning law in Ireland. 460
Shepherd, R.J. Public opinion. 181
Shepherd, W. Motor trade. 324
Sheppard, C.A. Languages in Canada. 61
Sheridan, L.A. Fraud in equity. 177
Sheridn, L.A. Legal education. 288
Sheridan, L.A. Malaya & Singapore. 309, 434
Sheridan, L.A. Rights in security. 38, 40, 83
Sheridan, L.A. & Delany, V.T.H. Cy-pres doctrine. 141
Sheridan, L.A. & Groves, H.E. Malaysia. 309
Sheridan, L.A. & Keeton, G.W. Equity. 177
Sherring, T. Capital transfer tax. 65
Sherring, T. & Sladen, M. Executors. 189, 469
Sherry, J.H. Innkeepers. 242
Sherwin-White, A.N. Roman society. 419
Shetreet, S. Judges on trial. 265
Shields, J.V.M. & Duncan, J.A. Crime in Scotland. 134
Shock, J. Capital allowances. 414
Shoolbred, C.F. Gaming & betting. 41
Shore, W. Social security. 436
Short, F.H. Crown Office. 140
Short, F.H. & Mellor, F.H. Crown Office. 140, 309, 377
Short, R. Long term prisoners. 382
Shortt, J. Informations. 240, 309, 389
Shrand, D. Administration of estates. 189
Shrand, D. Trusts in S. Africa. 469
Shrand, D. & Keeton, A.A.F. Company law. 121
Shubber, S. Crimes on aircraft. 34, 217
Shuklar, V.N. Constitution of India. 235
Shuster, M.R. International law of money. 253, 321
Shuttleworth, C.W. Solicitors. 439
Sibthorp, M.H. North sea. 344
Sibthorp, M.M. & Unwin, M. Oceanic management. 345, 425
Sidley, N.T. Law and ethics. 158, 315
Siegel, D. Conflicts. 101
Sieghart, M.A. Government by decree. 144, 213
Sieghart, P. Human rights. 229
Sieghart, P. Privacy. 99
Siemens, J.P. European integration. 181
Siffin, W.J. Public administration. 94
Sigler, J.A. Double jeopardy. 159
Silke, A.D., Divaris, C. & Stein, M.L. South African income tax. 233
Silke, A.S. Hambros tax guide. 4148
Sim, R.S. Meetings. 316
Sim, R.S. & Powell-Smith, V. Industrial law. 237
Sim, W.J. Divorce. 156
Sim, W.J. Supreme Court, New Zealand. 331
Simmonds, B. VAT. 476

Simmonds, K. Multinational corporations. 122
Simmonds, K.R. European community law. 172
Simmonds, K.R. European community treaties. 180
Simmonds, K.R. Law of the sea. 425
Simmons, F. High Court practice. 126, 376
Simon, F. & Wilson, S. Field Wing Bail Hostel. 35
Simon, J.A. Simon's taxes. 63, 65, 233, 414, 476
Simon, R.J. Jury system in America. 267
Simon, R.J. Women & crime. 138
Simon, S.I. Backduty. 35
Simons, G.L. Pornography. 342
Simons, H. Media & law. 379
Simons, W.B. Soviet codes. 442
Simpson, A.W.B. Biographical dictionary. 48
Simpson, A.W.B. Cannibalism in common law. 85
Simpson, A.W.B. History of contract. 112
Simpson, A.W.B. Jurisprudence. 271
Simpson, A.W.B. Land law. 275
Simpson, A.W.B. Pornography. 342
Simpson, C.K. Doctor's guide. 158, 314
Simpson, C.K. Forensic medicine. 314
Simpson, J.H. Refugee. 406
Simpson, J.L. & Fox, H. International arbitration. 251
Simpson, J.W. Lincoln's Inn. 243
Simpson, K. Doctor's guide to court. 188
Simpson, L. Contracts. 112
Simpson, R.C. Industrial relations. 239
Simpson, S.R. Land registration. 277
Simpson, S.R. Land law. 276
Simpson, T. Advocacy. 437, 486
Sims, B.J. Capital duty. 445
Sinclair, A.M. Real property. 404
Sinclair, I.M. Vienna Convention. 466
Sinclair, J. Coal mining. 320
Singer, J.D. Financing international organisation. 473
Singer, R.G. & Statsky, W.P. Rights of imprisoned. 382
Singh, A. Negotiable instruments. 331
Singh, B. & Ko-Wang, M. Warfare. 481
Singh, .M.M. Constitution of India. 235
Singh, N. Commercial law of India. 83
Singh, N. Maritime flag. 433
Singh, N. Maritime law conventions. 432
Singh, N. Nuclear weapons. 339
Singh, N. & Colinvaux, R.P. Shipowners. 433
Singleton, J.E. Conduct at the Bar. 14
Sinha, A.N. Citizenship in India. 235
Sinha, S.P. Asylum. 30
Sinnadurai, V. Contract in Malaysia. 112, 309, 434
Sinnott, J.P. Patent law. 357
Sion, A. Prostitution. 390

Sisloe, Lord. Temple. 243
Sit, J.F. Commercial law. 74, 83
Siv, M.R. Environmental legislation. 369
Skeel, C.A.S. Marches of Wales. 480
Skene, W.B. Universities of Oxford & Cambridge. 60, 346
Skeffington, A. Leasehold enfranchisement. 285
Skidmore, R.A. & Thackeray, M.G. Social work. 437
Skottowe, P.F. Blind. 50
Skottowe, P.F. Sunday. 434
Skottowe, P.F. Tax cases. 414
Skyrme, Sir T. Magistracy. 307
Slabotzky, A. Grain contracts. 25, 113
Slack, G.G. War damage. 483
Slade, E. Employment. 171
Sladen, M. Trust administration. 469
Slater, J.A. Mercantile law. 83
Slater, J.C.N. & Dobson, A.P. Criminal law. 132
Slesser, Sir H. Art of judgment. 265
Slinn, J. Freshfields. 439
Sloan, I.J. Environment. 174, 369
Sloan, K. Police law. 367
Sloane, S.B. Legal speller. 151
Slomnicka, B.I. Child care. 74
Slot, P.J. Obstacles to trade in EEC. 182
Smart, C. Women. 489
Smart, P.E. Banking. 40
Smellie, K.B. Local government. 302
Smethurst, J.M. Locus standi. 302
Smit, H. & Herzog, P.E. European Economic Community. 180
Smith, A. Jurisprudence. 271
Smith, A.B.& Berlin, L. Probation. 388
Smith, A.D. Microfilm. 119, 294
Smith, A.D. Women in prison. 382
Smith, C. Insolvency. 38, 440
Smith, C. & Hoath, D.C. Underprivileged. 373, 486
Smith, C.R. Adoption & fostering. 12
Smith, C.R. Complaints against police. 367
Smith, D.D. Communications via satellite. 453
Smith, D.T. Abortion. 4
Smith, D.W. Legal status. 463
Smith, E.C. US constitution. 475
Smith, F. & Beech, D. Employee benefits. 171
Smith, H.A. Associations. 29
Smith, H.A. Sea. 329, 426
Smith, Sir H.L. Board of Trade. 214
Smith, H.S. Parliaments of England. 351
Smith, I. Employment contracts. 171
Smith, I.T. & Wood, J.C. Industrial law. 237
Smith, J.C. Theft. 454
Smith, J.C. & Hogan, B. Criminal law. 132
Smith, J.C. & Thomas, J.A.C. Contract. 112
Smith, J.H. Legal institutions. 222
Smith, J.W. Leading cases. 293

Smith, K. & Keenan, D.J. Company law. 91
Smith, K. & Keenan, D.J. English law. 173
Smith, K. & Keenan, D.J. Mercantile law. 83
Smith, L.Y. Business law. 83
Smith, M.E.H. Housing. 226
Smith, P. Family business. 91, 354
Smith, P & Swann, D. Consumer. 108
Smith, P.F. Housing Act. 226
Smith, P.f. & Bailey, S.H. Legal system. 173
Smith, P.W. Intestacy. 189
Smith, R.C. Press. 379
Smith, R.E. Privacy. 383
Smith, R.H. Poor. 373
Smith, R.J. Children. 74
Smith, R.M. Matrimonial & Family Proceedings Act. 194
Smith, Sir S.A. & Fiddes, F.S. Forensic medicine. 314
Smith, S.M. Battered child. 71
Smith, T.B. British justice. 7, 149, 271, 422
Smith, T.B. Judicial precedent. 422
Smith, T.B. Property problems. 116, 404
Smith, t.B. Scotland. 422
Smith, T.B. Short commentary. 422
Smith, T.B. Studies critical & comparative. 149
Smith, T.B. United Kingdom. 149
Smith, T.E. Admiralty practice. 11
Smith, T.E. Elections. 166
Smith, T.R. & Francis, H.W. Fire insurance. 246
Smolensky, J. Community health. 393
Smyth, J.M. Oierachtas. 260, 352
Smythe, J. Homelessness. 226
Snell, E.H.T. Equity. 177, 215, 313
Snow, R.F. Commercial dealings. 83, 182
Soar, P.H.M. Solicitor's practice. 439
Soares, P.C. Land & tax planning. 178, 451
Soares, P.C. Tax strategy. 116, 276, 414
Soares, P.C. Trusts. 451, 469
Soave, O. & Crawford, L.M. Veterinary medicine. 477
Sobel, L.A. Pornography. 342
Sobrabjee, S.J. Press censorship. 379
Society for Computers & Law. Communications. 99
Society for Computers & Law. Computer technology. 44, 99
Society for Computers & Law. Lawyers in the Eighties. 99
Society for Computers & Law. Tomorrow's lawyers. 99, 289
Society for the Protection of Unborn Children. Comments on the Lane Committee. 4
Society of Authors. Publishing contracts. 33
Society of Conservative Lawyers. Bill of Rights. 46
Society of Friends. Church Government. 348
Society of Motor Manufacturers & Traders. International vehicle legislation. 324

AUTHOR AND SHORT TITLE INDEX

Society of Public Teachers of Law. Illegitimate child. 292
Socolow, W.A. Radio broadcasting. 400
Softley, P. Compensation orders. 307
Softley, P. Fines. 307, 428
Sohm, R. Institutes. 419
Sohn, L.B. U.N. law. 473
Sohn, L.B. & Buergenthal, T. International protection. 229
Soin, B.S. Singapore tax. 434
Sokol, R.P. Habeas corpus. 216
Solicitors' & barristers' diary & directory. 154, 439
Solly, M. Jersey. 69
Solly, M. Tax haven. 233, 262, 451
Solomons, D. Cost analysis. 6
Sonenberg, D.S., Bourke, J.P. & New, C.I. Criminal law. 136
Soothill, K. Medical remands. 407
Sopher, I.M. Forensic dentistry. 148
Sophian, T.J. Capital gains. 63
Sophian, T.J. Horses. 21
Sophian, T.J. London building. 303
Sopinka, J. & Lederman, S.N. Evidence. 188
Sorensen, M. International law. 250
Soule, C.C. Law reports & cititations. 284
South African Forms & Precedents. 204
Spaight, J.M. Air power. 481
Spaight, J.M. War rights. 481
Sparks, B.M. Contracts to make wills. 487
Sparks, R.F. Local prisons. 382
Sparrow, G. Great judges. 265
Speiser, S.M. Aviation handbook. 34
Speller, S.R. Doctor & patient. 148, 158, 315
Speller, S.R. Hospitals. 158, 225
Speller, S.R. Mental Health Act. 217
Speller, S.R. National Health Service. 327
Speller, S.R. Nurses. 340
Spelling, T.C. & Lewis, J.H. Injunctions. 241
Spencer, A.J. Small holdings. 19
Spencer Bower, G. & Turner, A.K. Actionable misrepresentation. 114
Spencer Bower, G. & Turner, A.K. Estoppel. 112
Spero, S. Labour relations. 239, 392
Spetz, S.N. Legal jams. 61, 75
Spicer, E.E. & Pegler, E.C. Bookkeeping. 6
Spicer, E.E. & Pegler, E.C. Income tax. 233, 414
Spiers, J. Underground & alternative press. 3796
Spigelman, J.J. Secrecy. 67
Spilsbury, W.H. Lincoln's Inn. 243
Spires, J.J. Doing business. 83
Spiro, E. Conflict of laws. 101, 440
Spitz, B. Tax planning. 451
Spitz, B. Tax havens. 451
Spotisswoode, R. Practicks. 422
Spratt, F.C. & McKenzie, P.D. Insolvency. 388

Springer, A.L. Pollution. 369
Springfield, D. Company executive. 91
Sprudzs, A. Benelux abbreviations. 3
Sprudzs, A. French abbreviations. 3, 205
Sprudzs, A. Italian abbreviations. 3, 262
Sprudzs, A. Treaty sources. 466
Spry, I.C.F. Avoidance of taxation. 452
Spry, I.C.F. Equitable remedies. 114, 177, 241, 443, 458
Squibb, G.D. Court of Chivalry. 75
Squibb, G.D. Doctor's commons. 289
Squire law library. Catalogue. 44
Srinivasagam, E. Republic of Singapore. 434
Srinivasan, M.N. Insurance law. 246
Stacey, F. Bill of Rights. 46, 77
Stacey, F. British government. 213
Stacey, F. British ombudsman. 346
Stacey, F. Government of modern Britain. 213
Stafford, J. Companies legislation. 91
Stair, Viscount. Institutions. 422
Stair Society. Scottish legal history. 423
Stair Society. Sources & literature of Scots law. 44
Stamp, E. & Marley, C. Accounting principles. 6
Stanbrook, C. Dumping. 83, 190
Stanbrook, I. & Stanbrook, C. Extradition. 191
Standing Advisory Commission on Human Rights. Divorce & homosexuality. 156, 224
Standing Advisory Commission on Human Rights. Protection of human rights. 229
Stanfield, R.A. Detention centre. 148
Stankiewicz, W.J. Sovereignty. 256
Stanley, D.T. Prisoners among us. 353
Stanley, O. Taxation of farmers. 17, 178, 414
Stannard, J.E. Criminal law. 132
Stanton, L.F.H. Merchant shipping. 433
Stanton, L.F.H. Sea transport. 433
Stapleton, T.B. Estate management. 177, 280, 409
Starke, J.G. Assignments. 28
Starke, J.G. International court. 253
Starke, J.G. International law. 250
Starke, J.G., Higgins, P.F.P. & Swanton, J. Contract. 112
Starkie, T. Slander. 109
Starr, R. Business transactions. 84
Statsky, W.P. Torts. 303
Statute Law Society. Radical simplification. 283, 290, 447
Statute Law Society. Renton. 160, 283, 290, 447
Statute Law Society. Statute law. 283, 290, 447
Statute Law Society. Statute law deficiencies. 283, 290, 447
Statutory Publications Office. Chronological table of the statutes. 447
Statutory Publications Office. Index to

government orders. 447
Statutory Publications Office. Index to the statutes. 447
StatutoryPublications Office. List of statutory instruments. 447
Statutory Publications Office. Statutes in force. 447
Statutory Publications Office. Table of government orders. 447
Staubach, F. German agency. 16, 209
Staunford, W. Plees del coron. 132
Stead, R. Construction & use regulations. 324
Steed, A.N. & Daly, E.J. Building standards. 56
Steele, R.T. Conveyancing. 116
Steer, W.R. Smoke nuisance. 340
Steiger, H. & Kimminch, O. Pollution control in Germany. 369
Stein, A. Legal evolution. 271
Stein, J. Damages & recovery. 142
Stein, L. Locus standi. 302
Stein, P. Fault in contract. 114
Steinaecker, M.F. Domestic taxation. 414
Steinberg, D. Family court. 195
Steiner, W.A.F.P. Classification scheme. 295
Stenton, D.M. English justice. 221
Stepan, J. & Kellogg, E.H. Contraceptives. 48
Stephen, H. Prisoners on oath. 488
Stephen, H.J. Commentaries. 35, 85, 104
Stephen, J.F. Criminal law. 132
Stephen, J.F. Digest. 132
Stephen, J.F. Evidence. 188
Stephen, J.F. History of criminal law. 134, 219, 222
Stephens, J.E.R. Demurrage. 147
Stephens, J.E.R., Gifford, C.E. & Smith, F.H. Naval law. 329
Stephens, N. Estate agency. 177
Stephens, O.H. Supreme Court. 99
Stephenson, C. & Marcham, P.G. Constitutional history. 105
Stephenson, D.A. Arbitration for contractors. 25, 56
Stephenson, I.S. Agriculture. 17
Stephenson, J. Building regulations. 56
Sterk, J. Alberta conveyancing. 116
Steuber, U. Banking. 253
Stevens, E.F. Shipping practice. 433
Stevens, I. Constitutional & adminstrative law. 104
Stevens, I.N. & Yardley, D.C.M. Protection of liberty. 77
Stevens, P.J. Aircraft. 34
Stevens, R. Law & politics. 23, 350
Stevens, Sir R. Mineral working. 319
Stevens, R. & Yamey, B.S. Restrictive practices court. 322
Stevens, R.D.S. Bias. 307
Stevens, T.M. & Borrie, G.J. Mercantile law. 84

Stevenson, O. Claimant or client. 437
Stewart, J. Of no fixed abode. 475
Stewart, J.B. Canadian House of Commons. 61
Stewart, J.B. Partners. 439
Stewart-Brown, R.D. Compulsory purchase. 97
Stewart-Wallace, Sir J.S. Land registration. 277
Steyn, J.H. Punishment. 397
Steyn, N.H. Crime. 127
Stirrat, G.M. Abortion. 4
Stock Exchange Rules & Regulations. 448
Stockholm International Peace Research Institute. Near-nuclear countries. 339
Stockholm International Peace Research Institute. Prospects for arms control. 339
Stockholm International Peace Research Institute. Nuclear proliferation. 339
Stockholm International Peace Research Institute. Test ban. 339
Stoddart, C.N. Legal aid. 287
Stokes, M. Construction law. 56
Stoljar, S. Moral & legal reasoning. 271
Stoljar, S.J. Agency. 16
Stoljar, S.J. History of contract. 112
Stoljar, S.J. Mistake. 114, 320
Stoljar, S.J. Quasi-contract. 112
Steon, C.D. Trees. 77
Stone, J. Human law. 272
Stone, J. International conflict. 482
Stone, J. Legal system. 272
Stone, J. Precedent. 266
Stone, J. Social dimensions. 272
Stone, M. Proof of fact. 467
Stone, O. Child's voice. 74
Stone, O. Family law. 194
Stone, R. Entry, search & seizure. 77
Stone, V.J. Civil liberties. 77
Stonham, R.M. Vendor & purchaser. 477
Storey, H. & Goldberg, A.H. Real estate agency. 177
Storm, P.M. Branches & subsidiaries in Common market. 182
Storm, P.M. Judicial protection. 272
Storry, J.G. Customary law. 440
Story, J. Bailments. 36
Story, J. U.S. Constitution. 475
Story, Judge. Equity jurisprudence. 177
Storz, M. Capital gains. 63
Storz, M. Personal tax records. 414
Storz, M. Taxation. 121
Storz, M. Taxation of business. 414
Strachan, B. Drinking driver. 162
Strachan, B. Natural justice. 77, 272
Strahan, J.A. Equity. 177
Strahan, J.A. & Oldman, N.H. Partnership. 354
Strang, Lord. Foreign Office. 214
Strasser, D. Finance of Europe. 182

AUTHOR AND SHORT TITLE INDEX

Stratta, E. Borstal boys. 52
Stratton, I.G.C. & Blackshaw, I.S. Moneylenders. 321
Stratton, I.G.C. & Blackshaw, I.S. Partnership. 354
Strayer, B.L. Judicial review. 267
Street, D. Welfare industry. 436, 486
Street, H. Damages. 142
Street, H. Fredom. 10, 77
Street, H. Government liability. 213. 215
Street, H. Torts. 458
Street, H. Welfare state. 7, 486
Street, H. & Frame, F.R. Nuclear energy. 338
Street, H.A. Gaming. 41
Street, H.A. Ultra vires. 145, 470
Stringer, F.A. Oaths & affirmations. 341
Strohl, M.P. Bays. 426
Strong, A. Dramatic & musical law. 454
Stroud, F. Judicial dictionary. 151, 258, 288
Strutt, Sir A. Cremation. 57
Stuart, D. Canadian criminal law. 136
Stubbs, L.P. Pawnbrokers. 358
Stubbs, W. Constitutional history. 104, 105, 219
Stuckey, G. Conveyancing Acts. 116
Study of Parliament Group. Specialist committees. 352
Sturge, L.F. Town & Country Planning. 460
Sturgis, A.F. Parliamentary procedure. 352
Sturt, R.F.B. Collision regulations. 79
Stuyt, A.M. International arbitrations. 25, 251
Subramanian, N.A. Indian constitution. 235
Suddards, R.W. Listed buildings. 56
Suffian, M. Malaysian constitution. 309
Sugden, E.B. Life peerages. 360
Sullivan, J.J. Pacific Basin enterprise. 426
Sullivan, L. Antitrust. 95
Summers, D. H.G.V. law guide. 464
Summers, L.M. Peace. 257, 359
Summers, R.S. Legal philosophy. 272
Summers, R.S. More essays. 272
Summerskill, M. Oil rigs. 247, 345
Summerskill, M.B. Laytime. 67, 433
Sumner, C. Crime, justice & underdevelopment. 138
Sumption, A. Capital gains tax. 63
Sumption, A. Overseas incomes. 234
Sumption, A. & Clarke, G. Tax planning. 414, 452
Sunday Times. Thalidomide. 74, 377
Sundstrom, G.O.Z. Community competition law. 95
Sundstrom, G.O.Z. Public international utility corporation. 122
Supperstone, M. Immigration. 231
Supplementary Benefits Commission. Cohabitation. 79, 436
Supplementary Benefits Commission. Exceptional needs payments. 436
Supplementary Benefits Commission.

Handbook. 436
Sussex, J. Community service. 88
Sussman, A. & Cohen, S.J. Child abuse. 71
Sussman, L.N. Paternity testing. 50
Sutherland.A. Monopolies Commission. 322
Sutherland, D.W. Novel disseisin. 29
Sutherland, R. Lord Stair. 423
Sutter, K. Guerilla warfare. 482
Sutton, C.T. Salvage. 421
Sutton, K.C.T. Consideration. 113
Sutton, K.C.T. Sale of goods. 420
Sutton, R. & Shannon, N.P. Contracts. 112
Swan, P.N. Ocean oil. 345
Swann, D. Competition. 96
Swann, D. & Lees, D. Antitrust policy. 96
Swarbrick, J. Easements. 297
Swarztrauber, S.A. Three mile limit. 453
Sweeney, C.A. & Tefler, J.H. Revenue law. 414
Sweeney, S. Closed shop. 463
Sweet & Maxwell. Commercial law. 94
Sweet & Maxwell. Companies Acts. 91
Sweet & Maxwell. Family law statutes. 194
Sweet & Maxwell. Labour relations statutes. 239
Sweet & Maxwell. Law reports. 3
Sweet & Maxwell. Legal bibliography. 44, 337
Sweet & Maxwell's Social work statutes. 486
Sweet & Maxwell. Tax statutes. 414
Swift, R.N. International law. 250
Swinfen-Green, E. & Henderson, N. Land law. 276
Swindlerd, W.F. Journalism. 379
Swords, P. de L. & Walwer, F.K. Legal education. 288
Sykes, E.I. Employer & employee. 171
Sykes, E.I. & Pryles, M.C. Private international law. 101
Sykes, E.I. & Tracey, R.R.S. Administrative law. 10
Sykes, E.I. & Yerbury, D. Australian labour law. 171
Sykes, E.I., Lanham, D.J. & Tracey, R.R.S. Administrative law. 10
Symmons, C.R. Maritime zones. 257, 426
Syz, J. Development banks. 40
Szabo, I. & Peteri, Z. Socialist approach. 94
Szaszy, I. Conflict of laws. 101
Szaszy, I. Private international law. 101
Szaszy, I. Sale of goods. 420
Szladits, C.A. Foreign & comparative bibliography. 44
Szladits, C.A. Foreign legal materials. 44, 209
Szokowczy-Syllaba, A. EFTA. 185
Taitz, a. Corporations capital tax. 121
Tambiah, H.W. Ceylon law. 444
Tangsubkul, P. ASEAN 433
Tanner, J.R. Constitutional documents. 105, 219
Taperell, G.g., Vermeesch, R.B. & Harland,

D.J. Trade practices. 84, 108
Tapp, W.J. Maintenance & champerty. 307
Tapper, C. Computers. 99
Tardu, M. Human rights. 229
Tarnopolosky, W.S. Bill of Rights. 46
Taschereau, H. Criminial code. 136
Tatalovich, R. & Daynes, B.W. politics of abortion. 4
Taubenfeld, H.J. Sex-based discrimination. 176
Taubenfeld, H.J. Space & society. 443
Tay, A.E.S. & Kamenka, E. Law making. 32
Taylor, A.S. Medical jurisprudence. 315
Taylor, B.W. & Munro, R.J. American law publishing. 44, 380
Taylor, C.T. & Silberston, Z.A. Patent system. 357
Taylor, E.M. Partnership. 354
Taylor, G. & Saunders, J. Education. 165
Taylor, G.D.s & Brenner, P.J. Australian legal process. 32
Taylor, H. Fire insurance. 246
Taylor, I., Walton, P. & Young, J. New criminololgy. 138
Taylor, J. & Cooke, G. Fire Precautions Act. 198
Taylor, J.L. Doctor & negligence. 158, 316
Taylor, J.L. Doctor & the law. 158, 316
Taylor, J.N.R. Executorship. 189
Taylor, J.P. Evidence. 188
Taylor, L. In whose best interests. 74
Taylor, N. Doctors & law. 158
TaylorS, . Gavelkind. 207
Taylor, S.E. & Parmar, H.A. Aviation law. 34
Taylor, V. Environmental law. 174
Tearle, B. legal essays. 44
Teasedale, J.P. Costs & legal aid. 123, 287
Teclaff, L.A. River basin. 484
Teclaff, L.A. & Utton, A.E. Environmental law. 174, 369
Teece, R.C. Legal profession. 32
Teff, H. & Munro, C.R. Thalidomide. 379
Teh, G.L. Residential tenancies. 280
Teichman, J. Illegitimacy. 292
Telling, A.E. Planning. 460
Telling, A.E. Water. 484
Temperley, R. Merchant shipping. 157, 433
Temple Church. Guide. 243
Tench, D. Middle system. 272
Terrell, E. Running down cases. 324
Terrell, T. Patents. 357
Terry, G.P.W. Representation. 166
Terry, J. Children Act. 12, 74
Tesch, C. Construction law. 56
Tetley, W. Marine cargo claims. 67, 247, 433
Theobald, H.S. Wills. 487
Theutenberg, B.J. Evolution of law of the sea. 26
Thio, S.M. Locus standi. 267, 302
Thirlway, H.W.A. International customary law. 257
Thom, D.J. Torrens system. 456
Thomas, A.H. Mayor'sCourt rolls. 221
Thomas, A.V.W. & Thomas, A.J. Biological weapons. 482
Thomas, C.H. Legal lexicon of taxation. 151, 414
Thomas, D. State trials. 465
Thomas, D.A. Penal equation. 397
Thomas, D.A. Sentencing. 128, 428
Thomas, D.N. Organizing for social change. 437, 486
Thomas, D.R. Maritime liens. 296, 433
Thomas, G.W. Taxation & trusts. 414, 469
Thomas, H. The civil service. 78
Thomas, J.A.C. Institutes of Justinian. 419
Thomas, J.L. Disease of animals. 21
Thomas, M.W. Factory legislation. 192
Thomas, P.A. Law in the balance. 289
Thomas, R.G. Insurance. 246
Thomashefsky, J.M. Refugees. 406
Thompson, A.H. Censorship in libraries. 294
Thompson, D.R. Criminal division proceedings. 128
Thompson, D.R. & Wollaston, H.W. Court of Appeal. 23
Thompson, G.H.M. Admiralty registrars. 11
Thompson, J.H. Bankruptcy. 38
Thompson, P.K.J. Unfair Contract Terms Act. 112
Thomson, W. Banking dictionary. 40
Thomson, W.A.R.Medical dicctionary. 151
Thorman, G. Family violence. 158
Thornhill, W. British government. 213
Thornton, C.E.I. & McBrien, J.P. Building society law. 57
Thornton, G.C. Legislative drafting. 160
Thorp, L.T. & Watson, A.A. Moneylending. 321
Thorpe, W.G. Middle Temple. 243
Thoyts, E.E. Old documents. 125
Thring, Lord. Practical legislation. 160
Thurston, G. Coronership. 120
Tibbett, J.E. Social workers. 317, 437
Tiberg, H. Demurrage. 67, 147, 433
Tierney, B. Religion, law & constitution. 219
Tierney, K. Witness. 488
Tiley, J. Capital transfer tax. 414
Tiley, J. Equity & succession. 177
Tiley, J. Revenue law. 414
Tillyard, F. Worker & state. 171
The Times. House of Commons. 351
Tingley, K.R. & Hughes, P.F. Capital transfer tax. 65
Tingley, K.R. & Hughes, P.F. Development gains. 149
Tiplady, D. Housing welfare. 226, 486
Tite, C.G.C. Impeachment. 232
Tobias, J.J. 19th century crime. 134
Toby, R.A. Income tax. 234

Toch, N. Income tax. 234
Toepke, U.P. EEC competition law. 96, 183
Tolhurst, A.F. Gift & estate duty. 178
Tolhurst, A.F. Wallace, E.W. & Zipfinger, F.P. Revenue duties. 414
Tolley's capital gains tax. 63
Tolley's capital transfer tax. 65
Tolley's company law. 91
Tolley's corporation tax. 121
Tolley's expansion list. 84
Tolley's health & safety. 434
Tolley's statutory sick pay. 447
Tolley's survival kit. 84
Tolley's tax planning. 452
Tolley's VAT planning. 476
Tolstoy, D. Divorce. 156, 313
Toman, J. Geneva Convention. 482
Tomany, J.P. Air pollution. 370
Tomasic, R. Australian legislation. 32, 290
Tomlin, T.E. Law dictionary. 151
Tomson, B. & Coplan, N. Engineering law. 26
Tonkin, A.S. & Thompson, M.I. Taxation of private companies. 121
Topham, A.F. Real property. 404
Topham, A.F. & Ivamy, E.R.H. Company law. 91
Topolski, F. & Cowper, F.H. Legal London. 303
Topp, A.G., Talbot, A.E. & Robson, R.McK. Company law. 91
Topple, B.S. Corporation tax. 121
Tordoff, W. Zambia. 491
Torrance, T.F. Juridical & physical law. 272
Toth, A.G. Legal protection of individuals. 184
Touche, A.G. Accounting requirements. 6
Toulmin, H.A. Foods, drugs, cosmetics. 201
Touggaint, C.E. Trusteeship. 255
Townsend, J.B. Extraterritorial antitrust. 96
Townsend, P. Poverty. 373
Townshend-Rose, F.E.H. Mining. 320
Townshend-Stevens, R. Military law. 318
Toyne, C.C. Motor vehicle regulations. 324
Tracey, R. Battered wives. 158
Trade, Board of. Bankruptcy committee. 38
Trade, Board of. Company law committee. 91
Trade, Board of. Consumer credit. 106
Trade, Board of. Copyright committee. 119
Trade, Dept.of. Carriage of dangerous goods. 67, 433
Trade, Dept.of. Changes in company law. 91
Trade, Dept.of. Companies inspection system. 91
Trade, Dept.of. Conduct of company directors. 91
Trade, Dept.of. Copyright & designs. 119
Trade, Dept.of. Copyright reform. 119
Trade, Dept.of. Film authority. 197
Trade, Dept.of. Industrial democracy. 92
Trade, Dept.of. Merchant shipping. 433

Trade, Dept.of. New form of incorporation. 91
Trade, Dept.of. Patent law reform. 357
Trade, Dept.of Pollution of the sea. 370
Trade, Dept.of. Purchase by a company of its own shares. 91
Trade, Dept.of. Safety and pollution at sea. 433
Trade & Industry, Dept.of. Consumer credit. 106
Trade Industry, Dept. of. Insolvency. 38
Trade & Industry, Dept.of. Monopolies. 322
Trade & Industry, Dept.of. Trade mark law. 462
Transport, Dept.of. Dangerous goods by rail. 400, 417
Transport, Dept.of. Dangerous goods by road. 464
Transport, Dept.of. Highway inquiry procedures. 217
Tratner, W. Poor law to welfare state. 486
Trayner, J. Latin maxims. 288
Treasury. Civil service. 78
Treasury, European Monetary System. 321
Trebilcock, M.J. Debtor & creditor. 143
Tregoning, J. Stannaries. 445
Trehern, E.C.M. & Grant, A.W. Prize. 385
Treitel, G.H. Contract. 112, 113
Trelease, F.J. Water law. 484
Trenerry, C. Contract of bottomry. 52
Trevelyan, E.A. Supreme Court of Kenya. 273
Tribe, D.H. Censorship. 67
Triche, C.W. & Triche, D.S. Euthanasia. 185
Trimm, L. Estate duty planning. 178
Trimm, L. Personal estate planning. 178
Trindade, A.A.C. Rule of exhaustion. 229
Tripathi, P.K. Fundamental rights. 77
Tristram, T.H. & Coote, H.C. Probate. 386
Tritten, K. European banks. 40
Trojanowics, R.C. Juvenile delinquency. 146
Trotter, W.F. Contract. 482
Tuck, M. Alcoholism. 18
Tuck, M. & Southgate, P. Ethnic minorities. 399
Tudor, O.D. Charities. 324
Tugwell, R.G. Emerging constitution. 475
Tunkin, G.L. International law. 250
Turack, D.C. Passport. 154
Turner, A.E. Trade secrets. 462
Turner, A.J. & Cooper, M. Points & excess alcohol provisions. 18, 162
Turner, D.F. Building contracts. 55
Turner, F. Contract of pawn. 358
Turner, G.J. Lincoln's Inn. 243
Turner, J.N. Improving the lot. 292
Turner, R.W. Equity of redemption. 177, 323
Turner-Samuels, M. Married women. 311
Turpin, C. Government contracts. 113
Tussman, J. Racial discrimination. 399
Tutt, N. Alternative strategies. 138

Twining, W. & Miers, D. Rules. 10
Twiss, Sir T. Black book. 11
Twiss, Sir T. Continuous voyages. 385
Twiss, Sir T. Law of Nations. 250
Twitchett, K.J. The evolving UN. 473
Tyas, J.G.M. Torts. 458
Tyler, E.L.G. Family provision. 197, 449
Tyler, E.L.G. Land law. 276
Tyska, L.A. & Fennelly, L.J. Cargo theft. 454
Tyssen, A.D. Charitable bequests. 70
Tyssen, A.D. Real representative law. 278
UNESCO. Human rights. 229
UNESCO. Immigrant workers. 171, 231
UNESCO. Press, film & radio. 379, 400
UNESCO. Public library legislation. 294
Uche, U.U. Contractual obligations. 210, 334
Uff, J. Construction law. 56
Ullman, G.H. Ocean freight. 433
Ullman, W. Law & politics in the middle ages. 221
Ullman, W. Medieval idea of law. 221
Ullman, W. Principles of government & politics. 213
Ulmer, E. Intellectual property. 119
Ulster Defence Regiment. Regulations. 27
Umeh, J.A. Acquisition of land. 97, 334
Underhill, Sir A. Leasehold enfranchisment. 285
Underhill, Sir A. Partnership. 354
Underhill, Sir A. Trusts & trustees. 469
Underhill, M. Gaming machines. 41
Underhill, M. Licensing guide. 296
Underwood, A. & Wood, S.C. Professional negligence. 330
Unifo. International human rights. 229
United Nations. Basic facts. 473
United Nations. Housing Associations. 227
United Nations. Human rights. 229, 473
United Nations. International arbitral awards. 251
United Nations. International Law Commission. 254
United Nations. Public administration. 391
United Nations. Racial discrimination. 399
United Nations. Sea. 44, 426
United Nations Association. Nuclear energy. 338
United Nations Commission on International Trade Law. Arbitration. 84, 473
Universities Federation of Animal Welfare. Humane killing. 479
Universities Federation for Animal Welfare. Laboratory animals. 21, 274, 479
Universities Federation of Animal Welfare Symposium. Animals. 21
University of Cambridge. Statutes. 60
Upex, R. Dismissal. 171
Upex, R. Employment protection. 172
Upex, R. Termination of employment. 168
Usher, J. European community law. 180

Usher, J. European Court practice. 184
Ussher, P. Company law. 92
Vahidi, M. Islamic evidence. 261
Vaines, J.C. Personal property. 36, 363
Valentine, B. County court procedure. 124
Valentine, D.G. Court of Justice. 184
Vallat, F. Human rights. 229
Vallat, F. International disputes. 251
Van Caenegem, R.C. Common law. 85
Vandenbosch, A. & Hogan, W.N. The UN. 473
Vanderbilt, A.T. Law reform. 283
Vanderbilt, A.T. Separation of powers. 475
Vanderlinden, J. Droit Africain. 15
Vandesanden, G. Pleading before the ECJ. 184, 365.
Van der Vyver, J.D. South African censorship. 67, 440
Vandyk, N.D. Accidents. 5, 168
Vandyk, N.D. Tribunals & inquiries. 468
Van Eikema Hommes, H.J. Legal philosophy. 272
Van Gerpen, M. Privileged communication. 380, 383
Van Hecke, G. Private international law. 101
Van Hoorn, J. Taxation of companies. 92, 121
Van Niekerk, A.F. Income tax. 234, 440
Van Oss, M.D. & Macdermot, N. Lands tribunal. 280
Van Stolk, M. Battered child. 72
Van Warmelo, P. Roman civil law. 419
Van Ypersele, J. & Koeune, J.-C. European monetary system. 182
Varma, B.R. Contempt. 109
Vasan, R.S. Canadian law dictionary. 61, 151
Vasan, R.S. Latin words & phrases. 151
Vasarhelyi, I. Restitution. 411
Vaughan, F.L. United States patent system. 357
Vaulont, N. Customs union. 182
Veall, D. Law reform. 221, 283
Vedder, C.B. & Kay, B.A. Penology. 397
Veehoven, W.A. Human rights. 230
Veitch, E. Tort. 458
Venables, H.D.S. Mental patients. 244, 317, 375
Venables, R.C. Tax planning. 452, 487
Vennard, J. Contested trials. 307
Ventris, F.M. Documentary credits. 40, 80
Verchere, B. Business operations. 84
Vere, D. Euthanasia. 185
Vermeesch, R.B. & Lindgreen, K.E. Business law. 84
Vermes, M. Criminology. 138
Verney, D.V. British government. 213
Vernon, D.H. Conflict of laws. 101
Verrucoli, P. Italian company law. 92, 262
Verwey, W.D. Riot control agents. 482
Verzijl, J.H.W. International law. 250, 329
Verzul, I.H.W. Nationality. 18

AUTHOR AND SHORT TITLE INDEX

Vick, R.W. & Schoolbred, C.F. Administration. 7
Vickery, B.G. Accounts of executors. 6
Vickery, B.G. Executors. 189, 469
Vickery, N.A. Motor & traffic law. 324, 417
Vieira, N. Civil rights. 77
Vierdag, E.W. Discrimination. 399
Villar, G.R. Merchant fleet. 433
Viner, J. Customs union. 141
Vinogradoff, Sir P. Collected papers. 272
Vinogradoff, Sir P. Historical jurisprudence. 272
Vinogradoff, Sir P. Legal history. 220
Vinogradoff, Sir P. Roman law. 419
Vinter, E. Fiduciary relationship. 469
Virdi, P.K. Hindu & English divorce. 218
Visscher, Ch. de. International law. 257
Vitoria, M. Patents Act. 357
Vogelarr, F.O.W. & Chester, M.G. Dutch company law. 92
Vold, G.B. Theoretical criminology. 138
Volhard, R. & Weber, D. Real property. 209
Von Prodzynski, F. & McCarthy, C. Employment. 171
Voskuil, C.C.A. & Wade, J.A. International trade. 84
Wacks, R. Privacy. 383
Waddams, S.M. Product liability. 389
Waddams, S.M. Study of law. 61
Waddilove, L.E. Housing associations. 227
Waddington, L.C. Arrest. 27
Wade, E.C.S. & Phillips, G.G. Constitutional and administrative. 10, 104, 262, 384
Wade, H.W.R. Administrative law. 10
Wade, H.W.R. Constitutional fundamentals. 104
Wade, Lord. Health services. 393
Wadegagonkar, D. Space law. 443
Wade-Evans, A.W. Howel the Good. 480
Wadlington, W. & Paulsen, M.G. Domestic relations. 196
Wadsworth, F.E. Banks. 40
Wagner, W.J. Air transport. 34
Wahab, L.I. Law dictionary, English-Arabic. 151
Waight, P.K. & Williams, C.R. Evidence. 188
Wakeford, R.E. Nurse. 340
Wakeley, E. Medical dictionary. 151
Wakeling, A.A. Corroboration. 188
Wakil, S.P. Marriage, family & society. 312
Walbert, D.F. & Butler, J.D. Abortion. 4
Waldock, C.H.M. Mortgages. 323
Waldron, J.K. Contract & agency. 112
Waldron, J.K. Equity. 177
Walford, E.O. Draft leases. 285
Walford, J. Self-employed pensions. 360
Walker, A. Industrial pollution. 175, 369
Walker, A.G. & Walker, N.M.L. Evidence in Scotland. 188
Walker, D.J. Sex discrimination. 176
Walker, D.J. & Redman, M.J. Racial discrimination. 399
Walker, D.M. Civil remedies Scotland. 407, 423
Walker, D.M. Contracts. 112
Walker, D.M. Damages in Scotland. 145
Walker, D.M. Delict. 145
Walker, D.M. Oxford companion. 151, 172
Walker, D.M. Prescription. 298, 378
Walker, D.M. Scottish courts. 423
Walker, D.M. Scottish legal system. 423
Walker, D.M. Scottish private law. 145, 404, 423
Walker, D.M. Stair tercentenary. 423
Walker, G. Soviet official publications. 442
Walker, M. Tax service. 414
Walker, M.J. & Brodsky, S.L. Special animals. 429
Walker, N. Crime & insanity. 133, 244
Walker, N. Crime & punishment. 397, 428
Walker, N. Legal pitfalls. 26, 56
Walker, N. Punishment. 130, 397
Walker, N. Sentencing. 428
Walker, N. & McCabe, S. Crime & insanity. 133, 244
Walker, N. & Others. Violent offenders. 138
Walker, N.M.L. Judicial factors. 469
Walker, P.G. The Cabinet. 60
Walker, R.E. New South Wales. 32
Walker, R.J. & Walker, M.G. English legal system. 173
Walkland, S.A. & Ryle, M. Commons in the seventies. 351
Wall, E.H. Europe. 181
Wall, E.H. European Communities Act. 181
Wallace, C.D. Multinational enterprise. 84, 122
Wallace, D. Investment. 259
Wallace, H. Land registry. 277
Wallace, I.N.D. Building & engineering. 55, 204
Wallace, I.N.D. I.C.E. Conditions. 55
Wallace, I.N.D. International civil engineering. 55, 113
Wallace, I.N.D. International form. 113
Wallace, J.W. The Reporters. 284
Wallace, W.L.C. Corporation. 122
Wallace, W.R. Privy Council. 385
Wallach, F. Commercial law. 84
Wallenstein, G. International telecommunications. 453
Waller, I. Men released from prison. 406
Waller, K.M. Coronial law. 120
Wallerstein, J.S. & Kelly, J.B. Surviving the breakup. 156
Walley, Sir J. Social security. 436
Wallington, P. Employment. 171
Wallis, P. Transport Act. 464
Walls, H.J. Forensic science. 129, 203
Walls, H.J. & Brownlie, A.D. Drinks, drugs &

driving. 162, 417
Walmsley, R.C. Agricultural arbitration. 17, 25
Walmsley, K. Company administration. 92
Walsh, A.E. & Paxton, J. Competition policy. 96, 183
Walsh, A.E. & Paxton, J. Trade. 185
Walsh, D. & Poole, A. Criminology dictionary. 138
Walter, J.A. Sent away. 52, 74
Walter, N. Blasphemy. 49
Walters, D.R. Sexual attacks. 429
Walters, F.P. League of Nations. 284
Walters, G. Proceedings against juveniles. 130
Walters, G. Sentencing. 307, 428
Walters, R Capital transfer tax. 65
Walton, A.M. & Laddie, H.I.L. Patent law. 357
Walton, F.P. Husband & wife. 194, 311
Ward, C. Vandalism. 146
Ward, D. Parliamentary elections. 166
Ward, D.A. Tax planning. 452
Ward, R.P. Law of nations. 250
Wardle, L.D. & Wood, M.A. Abortion. 4
Warham, J. Administration for social workers. 437
Warren, D.G. Hospitals. 225
Warren, P.B. VAT. 476
Washington Conference on the Media & the Law. 380, 400
Wassenbergh, H.A. Air law. 34
Wassenbergh, H.A. Air transport. 34
Wasserstein, B. Corporate finance. 92
Wasz-Hockert, O. Children. 72
Waters, D.F. Insolvency. 38
Waters, D.W.M. Constructive trust. 469
Waters, D.W.M. Trusts. 469
Watkin, T.G. Nature of law. 272
Watkins, C. Copyholds. 117
Watkins, E.S. Burials. 57
Watkinson, D. Squatting. 444
Watson, A. Europe at risk. 181
Watson, A. Law of persons. 419
Watson, A. Legal transplants. 75, 94
Watson, A. Making of civil law. 75
Watson, A. Mandate in Roman law. 419
Watson, A. Nature of law. 272
Watson, A. Roman law. 419
Watson, A. Roman obligations. 419
Watson, A. Roman private law. 419
Watson, A. Roman property. 419
Watson, A. Roman succession. 419
Watson, A. Rome of the XII tables. 419
Watson, A. Society and legal change. 272
Watson, G.D. Canadian civil procedure. 61
Watson, J.A.F. The child. 74
Watson, J.A.F. & Austin, P.M. Juvenile court. 273
Watson, P. Social security. 436
Watson, R.S. & Parnell, H. Criminal law. 136

Watson, W.H. Sheriff. 430
Watt, D. Corroboration. 188
Watt, D. Precedents. 136
Watt, J.M. Agricultural holdings. 17
Watt, J.Y. Savings banks. 22
Watts, H.E. Explosives. 190
Weatherhead, A.D. & Robinson, B.M. Firearms in crime. 198
Weatherill, J. Horses. 21
Weaving, J.F. Bankruptcy. 38
Webb, B. & Webb, S. Parish & county. 349
Webb, J. Industrial relations. 171
Webb, P.R.H. & Bevan, H.K. Family law. 194
Webb, S. & Webb, B. Local government. 302
Webb, S. & Webb, B. English poor law. 371
Webb, S. & Webb, B. English prisons. 382
Webber, G.J. Contracts. 482
Webster, B. Acts of David. 423
Webster, C. Environmental health. 175, 393
Webster, G.C. Patents. 462
Webster, R.M. Professional ethics. 289, 439
Webster's Dictionary. 152
Wedderburn of Charlton, Lord. Labour law. 171
Wedderburn of Charlton, Lord & Murphy, W.T. Labour law. 171
Weekes, B. Industrial relations. 129
Weeks, K.M. Ombudsmen. 346
Weerasooria, W.S. & Coops, F.C. Banking. 40
Wegenast, F. Canadian companies. 92
Wegg-Prosser, C. Police. 367
Weidenbaum, M.L. Public sector. 392
Weinberg, M.A., Blank, M.V. & Greystoke, A.L. Take-overs. 92, 450
Weinstein, J.L. Nuclear liability. 338
Weir, J.A. Torts. 458
Weis, P. Nationality. 329
Weisbrot, D., Paliwala, A. & Sawyer, A. Law & social change in PNG. 348
Weissberg, G. International status of the UN. 473
Weisser, M. Crime & criminality. 138, 222
Weissman, J.C. & Dupont, R.L. Criminal justice & drugs. 130
Weisstub, D.N. Mental health. 318
Welford, A.W.B. Accident insurance. 246
Welford, A.W.B. & Otterbarry, W.W. Fire insurance. 246
Wellington, R.H. The King's Coroner. 120
Wells, D.P. Child abuse. 72
Welsh Water Authority. Byelaws. 484
Welson, J.B. Accident insurance. 246
Welson, J.B. Negligence. 330
Welson, J.B. & Taylor, H. Insurance. 417
Wenger, L. Roman civil procedure. 419
Wesley-Smith, P. Hong Kong legal literature. 224
Wessels, J.W. Roman Dutch. 417
West, D.J. Delinquency. 146
West, D.J. Future of parole. 353

West, D.J. Murder & suicide. 223
West, D.J. Present conduct & future delinquency. 146
West, D.J. Understanding sexual attacks. 429
West, D.J. Young offender. 52
West, D.J. & Farrington, D.P. Delinquent. 146
West, F.J. Justiciarship. 221
West, R. Treason. 465
West, W.A. Dilapidations. 153
West, W.A. Housing. 226
West, W.T. Drugs. 163
Westbrook, R.W. Valuation. 402
Westbrook, R.W. Valuer's casebook. 402
Westlake, J. International law. 250
Westrup, C.W. Roman law. 419
Westwood, J. Partnership. 354
Whalan, D. Torrens system. 456
Whale, J. Journalism. 380
Whale, R.F. Copyright. 119
Whaley, D. Negotiable instruments. 331
Wharton, G.F. Legal maxims. 288
Wharton, J.J.S. Law lexicon. 151, 207, 288
Wheare, K.C. Constitutional structure. 87
Wheare, K.C. Federal government. 213
Wheare, K.C. Government by committee. 60, 104, 213
Wheare, K.C. Legislatures. 352
Wheare, K.C. Maladministration. 10, 346
Wheatcroft, G.S.A. Estate duty. 178
Wheatcroft, G.S.A. Tax encyclopaedia. 121
Wheatcroft, G.S.A. Taxation of gifts. 211
Wheatcroft, G.S.A. VAT. 476
Wheatcroft, G.S.A. & Avery-Jones, J.F. VAT. 476
Wheatcroft, G.S.A. & Hewson, G.D. Capital taxation. 63, 65
Wheatcroft, S. European air transport. 34
Wheeler, C.W.G. & Topham, T. Country court practice, Victoria. 124
Wheeler, G. Privy Council. 23
Which. Wills & probate. 386
Whincup, M.H. Consumer legislation. 108
Whincup, M.H. Consumer protection. 108
Whincup, M.H. Defective goods. 389
Whincup, M.H. Employment law. 171
Whincup, M.H. Medical and nursing. 158, 315, 340
Whincup, M.H. Redundancy. 405
White, E.J. Scriptures. 42, 165
White, G.E. Tort. 458
White, G.M. International tribunals. 256
White, P. Post death rearrangement to wills. 487
White, P. Tax for professional partnerships. 354, 414
White, P. Tax planning. 74, 452
White, P. Tax planning on marriage breakdown. 156, 452
White, T.A.B. Patents. 119, 357

White, T.A.B. & Jacob, R. Patents. 119, 387, 462
Whitehead, G. Cargo insurance. 248
Whitehead, G. Export law. 190
Whitehead, H. Offshore legislation. 207, 345, 462
Whitehead, T. Mental illness. 244, 318
Whitehorn, H. Court of Protection. 244
Whitehouse, C. & Buttle, E.S. Revenue law. 414
Whitelock, D. Anglo-Saxon wills. 222
Whitelock, D. English historical documents. 220
Whitelock F.A. Death on the road. 417
Whiteman, M.M. Damages in international law. 252
Whiteman, M.M. Digest of international law. 364
Whiteman, P.G. & Wheatcroft, G.S. Capital gains tax. 63
Whiteman, P.G. & Wheatcroft, G.S.A. Income tax. 234, 414
Whiteside, G.L. Licensing justices. 296
Whiteside, J. Theft Act. 454
Whitesides, K. & Hawker, G. Industrial tribunals. 240
Whitfield, A.H. Leases. 285
Whitfield, L.A. Australia. 32
Whiting, J.R.S. Prison reform. 382
Whittaker, B. Police. 367
Whittaker, C.A.J. Environmental powers. 175, 369
Whyte, J.D. & Lederman, W.R. Canadian constitution. 61
Whyte, W.S. & Powell-Smith, V. Building regulations. 56
Wickerson, J. Motorist & the law. 324, 417
Wickremesinghe, K.D.P. Civil procedure in Ceylon. 444
Wickremesinghe, K.D.P. Partition in Ceylon. 444
Widdifield, C.H. Executors' accounts. 189
Widmer, G.K. Restrictive trade practices. 322
Wiener, F.B. Uses & abuses of legal history. 220
Wightman, D. Economic co-operation in Europe. 473
Wigmore, J.H. Evidence. 188
Wigram, W.K. Justice's notebook. 318
Wijngaert, C. van den. Extradition. 191
Wiktor, C.L. Canadian bibliography. 44, 251
Wiktor, C.L. Canadian treaty calendar. 466
Wiktor, C.L. & Tanguay, G. Canada constitutions. 61
Wilberforce, Lord, Campbell, A. & Elles, N.P.M. Restrictive trade practices. 322
Wilbraham, Sir R.B. Shooting rights. 198, 206
Wilcock, J. Trust administration. 386
Wilcox, A.F. Decision to prosecute. 390
Wilding, N.W. & Laundy, P. Parliament. 350

Wildman, R. Search. 385
Wilford, M. Coghlin, T. & Healy, N.J. Time charters. 71, 113, 433
Wilkins, J.L. Legal aid. 287
Wilkinson, B.. Constitutional history. 221
Wilkinson, B. Medieval parliament. 351
Wilkinson, G.S. Affiliation. 292
Wilkinson, G.S. Illegitimacy. 292
Wilkinson, G.S. Road traffic. 417
Wilkinson, G.S. Summary matrimonial. 74, 194, 313
Wilklinson, G.S. Personal property. 36, 248
Wilkinson, H.W. Pipes. 161, 163
Wilkinson, H.W. Sale of land. 116
Wilkinson, M. Children & divorce. 74, 156
Wilkinson, W.R.T. Hall marks. 216
Wilks, M. Sovereignty. 441
Will, J.S. Electricity supply. 167
Willie, G. & Gibson, H.T.R. South African law. 440
Wille, G. & Millin, P. Mercantile law. 440
Willett, T.C. Criminal on the road. 417
Willett, T.C. Drivers after sentence. 417
Williams, A. Town & country planning. 460
Williams, B. Occupiers' Liability Act. 225
Williams, D.B. Costs. 123
Williams, D.B. Criminal injuries. 128
Williams, D.B. Hit and run. 363, 417
Williams, D.B. Industrial tribunals. 240
Williams, D.B. Motor Insurers' Bureau. 247
Williams, D.B. Tax on maintenance. 414
Williams, D.G.T. Keeping the peace. 395
Williams, D.W. Maladministration. 10, 346
Williams, E. County Court. 124, 376
Williams, E. Supreme Court. 376
Williams, E.E.G. Railway law. 400
Williams, E.K. Canadian landlord & tenant. 280
Williams, E.V., Mortimer, H.C. & Sunnucks, J.H.G. Executors. 189, 386
Williams, G.L. Animals. 21, 458
Williams, G.L. Criminal law. 132, 361
Williams, G.L. Crown proceedings. 139
Williams, G.L. Joint obligations. 112
Williams, G.L. Joint torts. 330, 458
Williams, G.L. Learning the law. 173, 288
Williams, G.L. The mental element. 133
Williams, G.L. Proof of guilt. 467
Williams, G.L. Reform of the law. 283
Williams, G.L. Sanctity of life. 4
Williams, G.L. Voluntary euthanasia. 185
Williams, G.L. Textbook of criminal law. 132, 361
Williams, G.L. & Hepple, B.A. Torts. 458
Williams, J. Constitutional analysis. 475
Williams, J. Rights of common. 86
Williams, J. Statute of frauds. 205
Williams, J. Personal property. 363
Williams, J. Real property. 404
Williams, J. Universities. 60, 346

Williams, J.S. Defamation in Canada. 293
Williams, J.S. Limitations. 298
Williams, N.J. Supreme Court, Victoria. 376
Williams, O.C. Private Bill procedure. 352, 384
Williams, P.H. Gentleman's calling. 439
Williams, R.G. Taxation. 414
Williams, R.G. & Bruce, G. Admiralty actions. 11
Williams, R.G. & Mendes, B. Taxation. 234
Williams, Sir R.V. Bankruptcy. 38
Williams, Sir R.V. & Hunter, M. Bankruptcy. 143, 299
Williams, T.C. Vendors & purchasers. 477
Williams, W.J. Sale of land. 116, 455
Williams, W.J. Wills. 487
Williams, W.L. King's Court of Great Sessions. 480
Williams, W.L. Military forces. 27, 395
Williams, W.R. Great Sessions. 480
Williams, W.W. Coastal changes. 109
Williamson, J.B. Temple. 243
Willig, S. Dentistry. 148
Willis, J. Parliamentary powers. 145, 214
Willis, N. Banking. 440
Willis, W. Negotiable securities. 331
Willis, W.A. Workmen's compensation. 490
Williston, W.B. & Rolls, R.J. Canadian court forms. 204
Willock, I.D. Jury in Scotland. 267
Willoughby, P. Hong Kong revenue law. 224
Willoughby, P.G. conveyances in Nigeria. 334
Willrich, M. International safeguards. 338
Willrich, M. Non-proliferation treaty. 339, 482
Willrich, M. Strategic arms limitation. 339
Willrich, M. & Taylor, T.B. Nuclear theft. 338
Wills, W. Evidence. 188
Wilshere, A.M. King's Bench. 397
Wilson, C.E. Diplomatic privileges. 154
Wilson, G. Cases & materials. 173
Wilson, G.P. Constitutional and administrative law. 10, 105
Wilson, H. Capital transfer tax. 65
Wilson, Sir H. Governance of Britain. 60, 212, 352
Wilson, I.L. Outer space. 443
Wilson, J.G. Public health. 393
Wilson, M. Conveyancing fees. 116, 285
Wilson, P. Sexual dilemma. 4, 224
Wilson, W.A. Debt. 143
Wilson, W.A. Scots law. 423
Windeyer, W.J.V. legal history. 220
Winchester, S. & Jackson, H. Residential burglary. 454
Wine, H.M. Private limited companies. 92
Winfield, P.H. Chief sources. 44, 220
Winfield, P.H. Conspiracy. 102, 222, 307
Winfield, P.H. Legal essays. 220
Winfield, P.H. Quasi-contracts. 112

AUTHOR AND SHORT TITLE INDEX

Winfield, P.H. Torts. 458
Winfield, Sir P.H. & Jolowicz, J.A. Tort. 340, 458
Wing, D. Short title catalogue. 44
Wing, J.K. & Olsen, R. Community care. 318, 486
Winnifrith, Sir A.J.D. Ministry of Agriculture. 214
Winthrop, W.W. Military law. 318
Wisdom, A.S. Appropriation of land. 302
Wisdom, A.S. Byelaws. 59, 302
Wisdom, A.S. Freshwater pollution. 370, 484
Wisdom, A.S. Local authorities' byelaws. 59, 302
Wisdom, A.S. Pollution of waters. 371
Wisdom, A.S. Powers of purchase. 97, 302
Wisdom, A.S. Rivers & watercourses. 484
Wisdom, A., S. Sewerage. 161, 393
Wisdom, A.S. Waterlaw. 20, 484
Wisdom, A.S. Water rights. 20
Wisdom, A.S. & Skeet, J.L.G. Water resources. 484
Wise, A.N. Trade secrets. 462
Wise, E.M. & Mueller, G.O.W. Comparative criminal law. 136
Wiseman, H.V. Cabinet. 213
Wisewall, F.L. Admiralty jurisdiction. 11
Witchell, R.G. Practice & procedure. 116, 124, 156, 307, 376, 386
Withers, A.H. Mixed charities. 70
Withers, A.H. Reversionary interest. 415
Withers, A.H. Reversions. 415
Woetzel, R.K. Nuremberg. 483
Wojcichowsky, S. Bibliography on abortion. 4
Wolfenden, Sir J. Voluntary organizations. 486
Wolff, M. Prison. 382
Wolff, M. Private international law. 101
Wolfgang, M.E. Homicide. 223
Wolstenholme, E.F. & Cherry, Sir B.L. Conveyancing statutes. 116, 277
Wolstenholme, G.E.W. & O'Connor, M. Transplantation. 230
Wong, D.S. Tenure in Malay States. 309
Wolfgang, M.E. & Ferracuit, F. Violence.
Wong, J. Packing. 347
Wontner, J.J. High Court practice. 397
Wontner, J.J. Land registry. 277
Wontner, J.J. Specific performance. 443
Wood, B. Local government reform. 302
Wood, C. Influence of litigation. 315
Wolfenden, Sir J. Homosexual offences committee.
Wood, P. International banking set-off. 40
Wood, P. International finance. 321
Wood, R.D. Building and civil engineering claims. 26, 56
Wood, R.D. Estimating. 56
Wood, R.D. J.C.T. agreement. 56
Woodall, I.R. Dental care. 148
Woodcock, C. Small business. 84

Woodcock, G. Anarchism. 395
Woodfall, W. Landlord and tenant. 23, 280, 297
Woodley, D.G. Coal mining. 163
'Woodman' Game. 206
Woodman, R.A. Administration of assets. 189
Woodman, R.A. Real property.
Wohlfarth, E. EEC.
Woodroffe, G. Consumer law. 108
Woodroffe, G. Goods of services. 192
Woodward, F.C. Quasi-contracts. 112
Wooldridge, F. Groups of companies. 92
Woolf, A.D. Time barrier. 142, 298, 363
Woolley, D. Advertising. 13
Woolrych, H.W. Party walls. 53, 354
Woolrych, H.W. Rights of common. 86
Woolrych, H.W. Sewers. 161
Woolrych, H.W. Waters. 20, 62, 199, 484
Woolrych, H.W. Ways. 416
Woolrych, H.W. Window lights. 297
Woosnam, C.R. Fishing rights. 199
Wootton, B. Crime and penal policy. 397
Wootton, Lady. Crime. 132
Wootton, Lady. Crime and penal policy. 397
Worden, B. Rump parliament. 351
Words & phrases legally defined. 151, 258, 288
Wordsall, A. Consumer law. 108
World Health Organisation. Abortion. 4
World Health Organisation. Community health centres. 393
World Health Organisation. Environmental & health monitoring. 342
World Health Organisation. Family planning. 48
World Health Organisation, Hospital legislation. 225
World Health Organisation. International health regulations. 393
World Health Organisation. Mental health. 318
World Health Organisation. National health planning. 327
World Health Organisation. Public health. 477
World Health Organisation. Radiation. 393
World Health Organisation. Smoking. 393
World Health Organisation. Toxicological evaluation. 201
World Health Organisation. Use of human tissues. 230
World Peace Through Law. World legal directory. 154
Worley, G. Temple Church. 243
Worsley, C. Middle Temple. 243
Wortley, B.A. Expropriation. 252
Wortley, B.A. Jurisprudence. 272
Wortley, B.A. U.N. 473
Wraith, R.E. Open government. 213
Wraith, R.E. West Africa. 14
Wraith, R.E. & Hutcheson, P.G.

Adminstrative tribunals. 10, 468
Wrigglesworth, F. Health & safety at work. 236
Wright, D. Social worker. 437
Wright, E.K. & Hardman, J.P. Professional goodwill. 354
Wright, E.K. & Penney, M.O. Tax planning. 65
Wright, H.J. Rating. 402
Wright, J.H.G. Building control. 56
Wright, M. Criminology literature. 44, 138
Wright, M. Labour law. 171
Wright, M. Making good. 406
Wright, Q. International law & the U.N. 473
Wright, R.J.D. Family maintenance. 189
Wright, R.R. Probate. 386
Wright, R.S. Criminal conspiracies. 102
Wright, S. Fixtures. 200.
Wrottesley, F.J. Witnesses. 14, 488
Wurdinger, H. Company law. 92
Wunder, M.H. Personal injury act. 363
Wurtzburg, E.A. & Mills, J. Building society law. 57
Wyatt, M.C. Company acquisition of own shares. 92
Wylie, I.M. District Courts, Queensland. 376
Wylie, J.C.W. Irish conveyancing law. 116
Wylie, J.C.W. Irish land law. 276, 404
Wylie, O. Taxation of the family. 234
Wyndham Place Trust. Man's wider loyalties. 256
Wyner, A.J. Executive ombudsmen. 346
Wyner, A.J. Nebraska ombudsmen. 346
Wynes, W.A. Legislative, executive & judicial powers. 10, 32
Yale, D.E.C. Lord Nottingham's manual. 177
Yardley, D.C.M. Administrative law. 10, 302
Yardley, D.C.M. Constitutional law. 104
Yates, D. Exclusion clauses. 114
Yates, D. Leases. 285
Yates, D. & Hawkins, A.J. Landlord & tenant. 280
Yates, G.T. & Young, J.H. National jurisdiction over the sea. 426
Ybema, S.B. Constitutionalism. 77
Yell, N. & West, W.T. County court practice. 124, 376
Yemin, E. Legislative powers in U.N. 473
Yiannopoulos, A.N. Bills of lading. 433
Yiannopoulos, A.N. Civil law. 75
Yogis, J.A. Canadian law dictionary. 151
Yogis, J.A. & Christie, I.M. Legal writing. 160
Yorston, K. Australian commercial dictionary. 84, 152
Yorston, K. Costing procedures. 123
Yorston, K. & Fortescue, E.E. Australian mercantile law. 84
Young, A.F. Industrial injuries. 236
Young, A.F. & Clarke, K. Chairmanship in magistrates' courts. 307

Young, E. Planning law. 460
Young, G.V.C. Subject guide to Acts relating to Isle of Man. 262
Young, J.van Judges of science. 338
Young, L.K., Griffin, J.A. & Goldring, J.L. Constitutional development in PNG. 348
Young, P.W. Declaratory orders. 143
Yount, T. & Kettle, M. Incitement to disaffection. 27m, 427
Young, W. Community service orders. 88
Younger, Sir K. Sentencing. 429
Younghusband, E.L. Social work. 437, 486
Zacklin, R. Law of the sea. 426
Zagayko, F.F. International law classification. 295
Zamir, I. Declaratory judgment. 143, 265, 267
Zander, M. Bill of Rights. 46
Zander, M. English legal system. 77, 173
Zander, M. Lawmaking process. 10, 290, 391
Zander, M. Lawyers. 41, 289
Zander, M. Legal services. 287, 486
Zander, M. Social workers. 437
Zander, M. State of knowledge. 41
Zaphiriou, G. European business law. 84, 182
Zellick, G. Liberty. 46
Zemans, F.H. Legal aid. 287
Zhukov, G.P. & Kolosov, Y.M. Space law. 443
Ziadeh, F. Property. 404
Ziegel, J.S. & Foster, W.F. Commercial law. 84
Ziman, L.D. Commercial contract. 112
Zimmerli, W. Law and the prophets. 42
Zimmern, A.E. League of Nations. 284
Zines, L. Australian constitution. 32
Zines, L.R. High Court. 32
Zorn, J.G. & Bayne, P. Melanesia. 348
Zouche, R. Admiralty jurisdiction. 11
Zuijdwijk, A.J.M. Petitions to the UN. 230
Zuker, M. & Callwood, J. Law is not for women. 489
Zulueta, F.de. Institutes of Gaius. 419
Zulueta, F.de. Roman law of sale. 419
Zweibach, B. Civility & disobedience. 395
Zweigert, K. & Kotz, H. Comparative law. 94
Zweigert, K. & Kropholler, J. Copyright. 96
Zweigert, K. & Kropholler, J. International uniform law. 84, 119, 464